HEALTHCARE DATA ANALYTICS

Chapman & Hall/CRC
Data Mining and Knowledge Discovery Series

SERIES EDITOR
Vipin Kumar
University of Minnesota
Department of Computer Science and Engineering
Minneapolis, Minnesota, U.S.A.

AIMS AND SCOPE

This series aims to capture new developments and applications in data mining and knowledge discovery, while summarizing the computational tools and techniques useful in data analysis. This series encourages the integration of mathematical, statistical, and computational methods and techniques through the publication of a broad range of textbooks, reference works, and handbooks. The inclusion of concrete examples and applications is highly encouraged. The scope of the series includes, but is not limited to, titles in the areas of data mining and knowledge discovery methods and applications, modeling, algorithms, theory and foundations, data and knowledge visualization, data mining systems and tools, and privacy and security issues.

PUBLISHED TITLES

ADVANCES IN MACHINE LEARNING AND DATA MINING FOR ASTRONOMY
Michael J. Way, Jeffrey D. Scargle, Kamal M. Ali, and Ashok N. Srivastava

BIOLOGICAL DATA MINING
Jake Y. Chen and Stefano Lonardi

COMPUTATIONAL BUSINESS ANALYTICS
Subrata Das

COMPUTATIONAL INTELLIGENT DATA ANALYSIS FOR SUSTAINABLE DEVELOPMENT
Ting Yu, Nitesh V. Chawla, and Simeon Simoff

COMPUTATIONAL METHODS OF FEATURE SELECTION
Huan Liu and Hiroshi Motoda

CONSTRAINED CLUSTERING: ADVANCES IN ALGORITHMS, THEORY, AND APPLICATIONS
Sugato Basu, Ian Davidson, and Kiri L. Wagstaff

CONTRAST DATA MINING: CONCEPTS, ALGORITHMS, AND APPLICATIONS
Guozhu Dong and James Bailey

DATA CLASSIFICATION: ALGORITHMS AND APPLICATIONS
Charu C. Aggarawal

DATA CLUSTERING: ALGORITHMS AND APPLICATIONS
Charu C. Aggarawal and Chandan K. Reddy

DATA CLUSTERING IN C++: AN OBJECT-ORIENTED APPROACH
Guojun Gan

DATA MINING FOR DESIGN AND MARKETING
Yukio Ohsawa and Katsutoshi Yada

DATA MINING WITH R: LEARNING WITH CASE STUDIES
Luís Torgo

FOUNDATIONS OF PREDICTIVE ANALYTICS
James Wu and Stephen Coggeshall

GEOGRAPHIC DATA MINING AND KNOWLEDGE DISCOVERY, SECOND EDITION
Harvey J. Miller and Jiawei Han

HANDBOOK OF EDUCATIONAL DATA MINING
Cristóbal Romero, Sebastian Ventura, Mykola Pechenizkiy, and Ryan S.J.d. Baker

HEALTHCARE DATA ANALYTICS
Chandan K. Reddy and Charu C. Aggarwal

INFORMATION DISCOVERY ON ELECTRONIC HEALTH RECORDS
Vagelis Hristidis

INTELLIGENT TECHNOLOGIES FOR WEB APPLICATIONS
Priti Srinivas Sajja and Rajendra Akerkar

INTRODUCTION TO PRIVACY-PRESERVING DATA PUBLISHING: CONCEPTS AND TECHNIQUES
Benjamin C. M. Fung, Ke Wang, Ada Wai-Chee Fu, and Philip S. Yu

KNOWLEDGE DISCOVERY FOR COUNTERTERRORISM AND LAW ENFORCEMENT
David Skillicorn

KNOWLEDGE DISCOVERY FROM DATA STREAMS
João Gama

MACHINE LEARNING AND KNOWLEDGE DISCOVERY FOR ENGINEERING SYSTEMS HEALTH MANAGEMENT
Ashok N. Srivastava and Jiawei Han

MINING SOFTWARE SPECIFICATIONS: METHODOLOGIES AND APPLICATIONS
David Lo, Siau-Cheng Khoo, Jiawei Han, and Chao Liu

MULTIMEDIA DATA MINING: A SYSTEMATIC INTRODUCTION TO CONCEPTS AND THEORY
Zhongfei Zhang and Ruofei Zhang

MUSIC DATA MINING
Tao Li, Mitsunori Ogihara, and George Tzanetakis

NEXT GENERATION OF DATA MINING
Hillol Kargupta, Jiawei Han, Philip S. Yu, Rajeev Motwani, and Vipin Kumar

RAPIDMINER: DATA MINING USE CASES AND BUSINESS ANALYTICS APPLICATIONS
Markus Hofmann and Ralf Klinkenberg

RELATIONAL DATA CLUSTERING: MODELS, ALGORITHMS, AND APPLICATIONS
Bo Long, Zhongfei Zhang, and Philip S. Yu

SERVICE-ORIENTED DISTRIBUTED KNOWLEDGE DISCOVERY
Domenico Talia and Paolo Trunfio

SPECTRAL FEATURE SELECTION FOR DATA MINING
Zheng Alan Zhao and Huan Liu

STATISTICAL DATA MINING USING SAS APPLICATIONS, SECOND EDITION
George Fernandez

SUPPORT VECTOR MACHINES: OPTIMIZATION BASED THEORY, ALGORITHMS, AND EXTENSIONS
Naiyang Deng, Yingjie Tian, and Chunhua Zhang

TEMPORAL DATA MINING
Theophano Mitsa

TEXT MINING: CLASSIFICATION, CLUSTERING, AND APPLICATIONS
Ashok N. Srivastava and Mehran Sahami

THE TOP TEN ALGORITHMS IN DATA MINING
Xindong Wu and Vipin Kumar

UNDERSTANDING COMPLEX DATASETS: DATA MINING WITH MATRIX DECOMPOSITIONS
David Skillicorn

Healthcare Data Analytics

Edited by

Chandan K. Reddy

Wayne State University

Detroit, Michigan, USA

Charu C. Aggarwal

IBM T. J. Watson Research Center

Yorktown Heights, New York, USA

CRC Press
Taylor & Francis Group
Boca Raton London New York

CRC Press is an imprint of the
Taylor & Francis Group, an **informa** business
A CHAPMAN & HALL BOOK

CRC Press
Taylor & Francis Group
6000 Broken Sound Parkway NW, Suite 300
Boca Raton, FL 33487-2742

First issued in paperback 2020

ISBN 13: 978-0-367-57568-7 (pbk)
ISBN 13: 978-1-4822-3211-0 (hbk)

Library of Congress Cataloging-in-Publication Data

Healthcare data analytics / editors, Chandan K. Reddy and Charu C. Aggarwal.
p. ; cm. -- (Chapman & Hall/CRC data mining and knowledge discovery series)
Includes bibliographical references and index.
ISBN 978-1-4822-3211-0
I. Reddy, Chandan K., 1980- , editor. II. Aggarwal, Charu C., editor. III. Series:
Chapman & Hall/CRC data mining and knowledge discovery series.
[DNLM: 1. Data Mining. 2. Statistics as Topic. W 26.55.I4]

RA409
610.2'1--dc23 2015000574

Visit the Taylor & Francis Web site at
http://www.taylorandfrancis.com

and the CRC Press Web site at
http://www.crcpress.com

Contents

Editor Biographies

Chandan K. Reddy is an Associate Professor in the Department of Computer Science at Wayne State University. He received his PhD from Cornell University and MS from Michigan State University. His primary research interests are in the areas of data mining and machine learning with applications to healthcare, bioinformatics, and social network analysis. His research is funded by the National Science Foundation, the National Institutes of Health, Department of Transportation, and the Susan G. Komen for the Cure Foundation. He has published over 50 peer-reviewed articles in leading conferences and journals. He received the Best Application Paper Award at the ACM SIGKDD conference in 2010 and was a finalist of the INFORMS Franz Edelman Award Competition in 2011. He is a senior member of IEEE and a life member of the ACM.

Charu C. Aggarwal is a Distinguished Research Staff Member (DRSM) at the IBM T. J. Watson Research Center in Yorktown Heights, New York. He completed his BS from IIT Kanpur in 1993 and his PhD from the Massachusetts Institute of Technology in 1996. He has published more than 250 papers in refereed conferences and journals, and has applied for or been granted more than 80 patents. He is an author or editor of 13 books, including the first comprehensive book on outlier analysis. Because of the commercial value of his patents, he has thrice been designated a Master Inventor at IBM. He is a recipient of an IBM Corporate Award (2003) for his work on bioterrorist threat detection in data streams, a recipient of the IBM Outstanding Innovation Award (2008) for his scientific contributions to privacy technology, a recipient of the IBM Outstanding Technical Achievement Award (2009) for his work on data streams, and a recipient of an IBM Research Division Award (2008) for his contributions to System S. He also received the EDBT 2014 Test of Time Award for his work on condensation-based privacy-preserving data mining. He has served as conference chair and associate editor at many reputed conferences and journals in data mining, general co-chair of the IEEE Big Data Conference (2014), and is editor-in-chief of the ACM SIGKDD Explorations. He is a fellow of the ACM, SIAM and the IEEE, for "contributions to knowledge discovery and data mining algorithms."

Contributors

Giovanni Acampora
Nottingham Trent University
Nottingham, UK

Charu C. Aggarwal
IBM T. J. Watson Research Center
Yorktown Heights, New York

Noha Alnazzawi
University of Manchester
Manchester, UK

Martin Alther
Wayne State University
Detroit, MI

Sophia Ananiadou
University of Manchester
Manchester, UK

Iyad Batal
General Electric Global Research
San Ramon, CA

Riza Batista-Navarro
University of Manchester
Manchester, UK

Luca Bogoni
Siemens Medical Solutions
Malvern, PA

Jesus Caban
Walter Reed National Military Medical Center
Bethesda, MD

Varun Chandola
State University of New York at Buffalo
Buffalo, NY

Annie T. Chen
University of North Carolina at Chapel Hill
Chapel Hill, NC

Diane J. Cook
Washington State University
Pullman, WA

Juan Cui
University of Nebraska-Lincoln
Lincoln, NE

Thomas M. Deserno
RWTH Aachen University
Aachen, Germany

Sanjoy Dey
University of Minnesota
Minneapolis, MN

Shobeir Fakhraei
University of Maryland
College Park, MD

Sahika Genc
GE Global Research
Niskayuna, NY

Lise Getoor
University of California
Santa Cruz, CA

Joydeep Ghosh
The University of Texas at Austin
Austin, TX

David Gotz
University of North Carolina at Chapel Hill
Chapel Hill, NC

Rohit Gupta
University of Minnesota
Minneapolis, MN

Sandeep Gupta
GE Global Research
Niskayuna, NY

Gerardo Hermosillo
Siemens Medical Solutions
Malvern, PA

William R. Hersh
Oregon Health & Science University
Portland, OR

Suresh Joel
GE Global Research
Bangalore, India

Stephan M. Jonas
RWTH Aachen University
Aachen, Germany

Siddhartha R. Jonnalagadda
Northwestern University
Chicago, IL

Georgios Kontonatsios
University of Manchester
Manchester, UK

Ioannis Korkontzelos
University of Manchester
Manchester, UK

Alexander Kotov
Wayne State University
Detroit, MI

Vipin Kumar
University of Minnesota
Minneapolis, MN

Rajesh Langoju
GE Global Research
Bangalore, India

Yan Li
Wayne State University
Detroit, MI

Shu Liao
Siemens Medical Solutions
Malvern, PA

Paulo Mendonca
GE Global Research
Niskayuna, NY

Claudiu Mihăilă
University of Manchester
Manchester, UK

Eberechukwu Onukwugha
University of Maryland
Baltimore, MD

Dirk Padfield
GE Global Research
Niskayuna, NY

Yubin Park
The University of Texas at Austin
Austin, TX

Abhijit Patil
GE Global Research
Bangalore, India

Bhushan D. Patil
GE Global Research
Bangalore, India

Zhigang Peng
Siemens Medical Solutions
Malvern, PA

Rajiur Rahman
Wayne State University
Detroit, MI

Kalpana Raja
Northwestern University
Chicago, IL

Rafal Rak
University of Manchester
Manchester, UK

Parisa Rashidi
University of Florida
Gainesville, FL

Chandan K. Reddy
Wayne State University
Detroit, MI

Marcos Salganicoff
Siemens Medical Solutions
Malvern, PA

Michael Schmidt
Columbia University Medical Center
New York, NY

Jack Schryver
Oak Ridge National Laboratory
Oakridge, TN

Xiang Sean Zhou
Siemens Medical Solutions
Malvern, PA

Yoshihisa Shinagawa
Siemens Medical Solutions
Malvern, PA

Daby Sow
IBM T. J. Watson Research Center
Yorktown Heights, NY

Michael Steinbach
University of Minnesota
Minneapolis, MN

Sreenivas Sukumar
Oak Ridge National Laboratory
Oakridge, TN

Paul Thompson
University of Manchester
Manchester, UK

Deepak S. Turaga
IBM T. J. Watson Research Center
Yorktown Heights, NY

Kiran K. Turaga
Medical College of Wisconsin
Milwaukee, WI

Athanasios V. Vasilakos
University of Western Macedonia
Kozani, Greece

Matthias Wolf
Siemens Medical Solutions
Malvern, PA

Shipeng Yu
Siemens Medical Solutions
Malvern, PA

Yiqiang Zhan
Siemens Medical Solutions
Malvern, PA

Preface

Innovations in computing technologies have revolutionized healthcare in recent years. The analytical style of reasoning has not only changed the way in which information is collected and stored but has also played an increasingly important role in the management and delivery of healthcare. In particular, data analytics has emerged as a promising tool for solving problems in various healthcare-related disciplines. This book will present a comprehensive review of data analytics in the field of healthcare. The goal is to provide a platform for interdisciplinary researchers to learn about the fundamental principles, algorithms, and applications of intelligent data acquisition, processing, and analysis of healthcare data. This book will provide readers with an understanding of the vast number of analytical techniques for healthcare problems and their relationships with one another. This understanding includes details of specific techniques and required combinations of tools to design effective ways of handling, retrieving, analyzing, and making use of healthcare data. This book will provide a unique perspective of healthcare related opportunities for developing new computing technologies.

From a researcher and practitioner perspective, a major challenge in healthcare is its interdisciplinary nature. The field of healthcare has often seen advances coming from diverse disciplines such as databases, data mining, information retrieval, image processing, medical researchers, and healthcare practitioners. While this interdisciplinary nature adds to the richness of the field, it also adds to the challenges in making significant advances. Computer scientists are usually not trained in domain-specific medical concepts, whereas medical practitioners and researchers also have limited exposure to the data analytics area. This has added to the difficulty in creating a coherent body of work in this field. The result has often been independent lines of work from completely different perspectives. This book is an attempt to bring together these diverse communities by carefully and comprehensively discussing the most relevant contributions from each domain.

The book provides a comprehensive overview of the healthcare data analytics field as it stands today, and to educate the community about future research challenges and opportunities. Even though the book is structured as an edited collection of chapters, special care was taken during the creation of the book to cover healthcare topics exhaustively by coordinating the contributions from various authors. Focus was also placed on reviews and surveys rather than individual research results in order to emphasize comprehensiveness in coverage. Each book chapter is written by prominent researchers and experts working in the healthcare domain. The chapters in the book are divided into three major categories:

- **Healthcare Data Sources and Basic Analytics:** These chapters discuss the details about the various healthcare data sources and the analytical techniques that are widely used in the processing and analysis of such data. The various forms of patient data include electronic health records, biomedical images, sensor data, biomedical signals, genomic data, clinical text, biomedical literature, and data gathered from social media.

- **Advanced Data Analytics for Healthcare:** These chapters deal with the advanced data analytical methods focused on healthcare. These include the clinical prediction models, temporal pattern mining methods, and visual analytics. In addition, other advanced methods such as data integration, information retrieval, and privacy-preserving data publishing will also be discussed.

- **Applications and Practical Systems for Healthcare:** These chapters focus on the applications of data analytics and the relevant practical systems. It will cover the applications of data analytics to pervasive healthcare, fraud detection, and drug discovery. In terms of the practical systems, it covers clinical decision support systems, computer assisted medical imaging systems, and mobile imaging systems.

It is hoped that this comprehensive book will serve as a compendium to students, researchers, and practitioners. Each chapter is structured as a "survey-style" article discussing the prominent research issues and the advances made on that research topic. Special effort was taken in ensuring that each chapter is self-contained and the background required from other chapters is minimal. Finally, we hope that the topics discussed in this book will lead to further developments in the field of healthcare data analytics that can help in improving the health and well-being of people. We believe that research in the field of healthcare data analytics will continue to grow in the years to come.

Acknowledgment: This work was supported in part by National Science Foundation grant No. 1231742.

Chapter 1

An Introduction to Healthcare Data Analytics

Chandan K. Reddy
Department of Computer Science
Wayne State University
Detroit, MI
reddy@cs.wayne.edu

Charu C. Aggarwal
IBM T. J. Watson Research Center
Yorktown Heights, NY
charu@us.ibm.com

1.1 Introduction

While the healthcare costs have been constantly rising, the quality of care provided to the patients in the United States have not seen considerable improvements. Recently, several researchers have conducted studies which showed that by incorporating the current healthcare technologies, they are able to reduce mortality rates, healthcare costs, and medical complications at various hospitals. In 2009, the US government enacted the Health Information Technology for Economic and Clinical Health Act (HITECH) that includes an incentive program (around $27 billion) for the adoption and meaningful use of Electronic Health Records (EHRs).

The recent advances in information technology have led to an increasing ease in the ability to collect various forms of healthcare data. In this digital world, data becomes an integral part of healthcare. A recent report on Big Data suggests that the overall potential of healthcare data will be around $300 billion [12]. Due to the rapid advancements in the data sensing and acquisition technologies, hospitals and healthcare institutions have started collecting vast amounts of healthcare data about their patients. Effectively understanding and building knowledge from healthcare data requires developing advanced analytical techniques that can effectively transform data into meaningful and actionable information. General computing technologies have started revolutionizing the manner in which medical care is available to the patients. Data analytics, in particular, forms a critical component of these computing technologies. The analytical solutions when applied to healthcare data have an immense potential to transform healthcare delivery from being reactive to more proactive. The impact of analytics in the healthcare domain is only going to grow more in the next several years. Typically, analyzing health data will allow us to understand the patterns that are hidden in the data. Also, it will help the clinicians to build an individualized patient profile and can accurately compute the likelihood of an individual patient to suffer from a medical complication in the near future.

Healthcare data is particularly rich and it is derived from a wide variety of sources such as sensors, images, text in the form of biomedical literature/clinical notes, and traditional electronic records. This heterogeneity in the data collection and representation process leads to numerous challenges in both the processing and analysis of the underlying data. There is a wide diversity in the techniques that are required to analyze these different forms of data. In addition, the heterogeneity of the data naturally creates various data integration and data analysis challenges. In many cases, insights can be obtained from diverse data types, which are otherwise not possible from a single source of the data. It is only recently that the vast potential of such integrated data analysis methods is being realized.

From a researcher and practitioner perspective, a major challenge in healthcare is its interdisciplinary nature. The field of healthcare has often seen advances coming from diverse disciplines such as databases, data mining, information retrieval, medical researchers, and healthcare practitioners. While this interdisciplinary nature adds to the richness of the field, it also adds to the challenges in making significant advances. Computer scientists are usually not trained in domain-specific medical concepts, whereas medical practitioners and researchers also have limited exposure to the mathematical and statistical background required in the data analytics area. This has added to the difficulty in creating a coherent body of work in this field even though it is evident that much of the available data can benefit from such advanced analysis techniques. The result of such a diversity has often led to independent lines of work from completely different perspectives. Researchers in the field of data analytics are particularly susceptible to becoming isolated from real domain-specific problems, and may often propose problem formulations with excellent technique but with no practical use. This book is an attempt to bring together these diverse communities by carefully and comprehensively discussing the most relevant contributions from each domain. It is only by bringing together these diverse communities that the vast potential of data analysis methods can be harnessed.

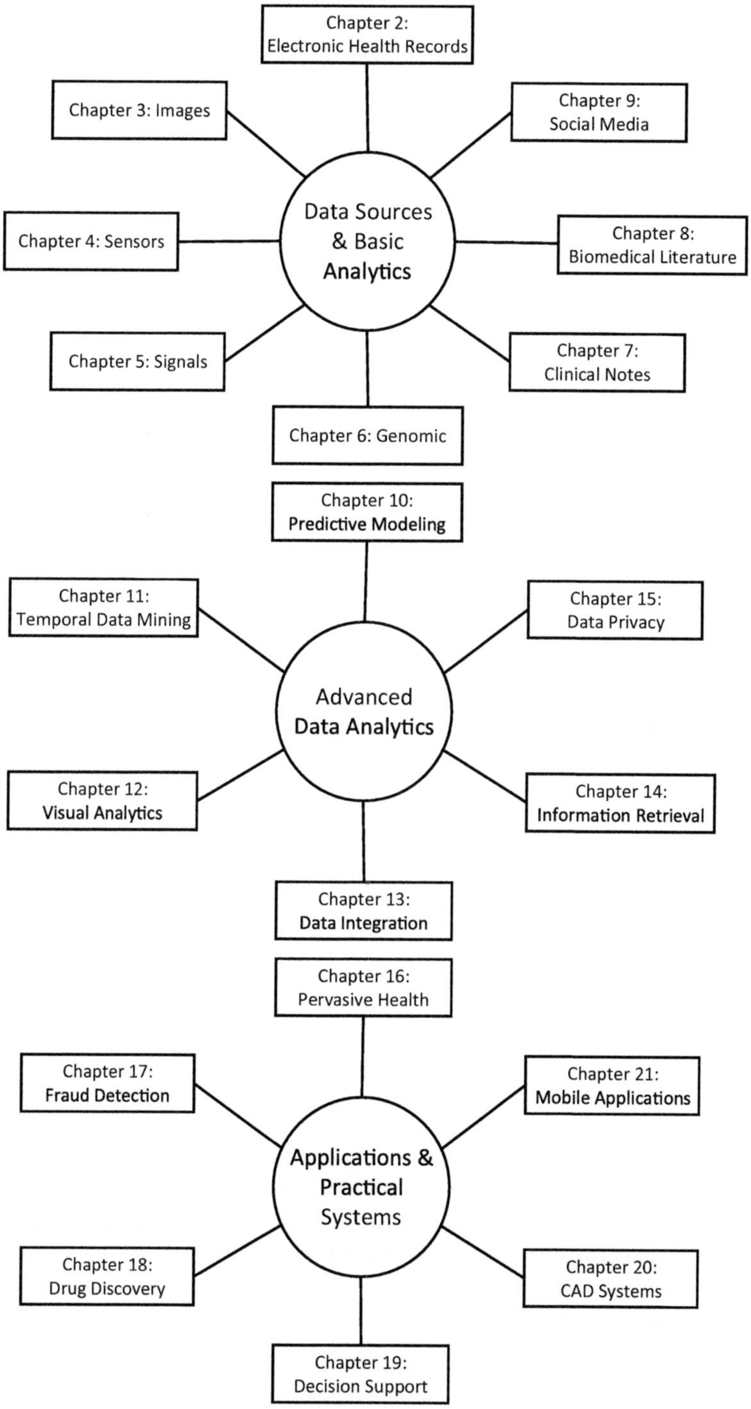

FIGURE 1.1: The overall organization of the book's contents.

Another major challenge that exists in the healthcare domain is the "data privacy gap" between medical researchers and computer scientists. Healthcare data is obviously very sensitive because it can reveal compromising information about individuals. Several laws in various countries, such as the Health Insurance Portability and Accountability Act (HIPAA) in the United States, explicitly forbid the release of medical information about individuals for any purpose, unless safeguards are used to preserve privacy. Medical researchers have natural access to healthcare data because their research is often paired with an actual medical practice. Furthermore, various mechanisms exist in the medical domain to conduct research studies with voluntary participants. Such data collection is almost always paired with anonymity and confidentiality agreements.

On the other hand, acquiring data is not quite as simple for computer scientists without a proper collaboration with a medical practitioner. Even then, there are barriers in the acquisition of data. Clearly, many of these challenges can be avoided if accepted protocols, privacy technologies, and safeguards are in place. Therefore, this book will also address these issues. Figure 1.1 provides an overview of the organization of the book's contents. This book is organized into three parts:

1. *Healthcare Data Sources and Basic Analytics:* This part discusses the details of various healthcare data sources and the basic analytical methods that are widely used in the processing and analysis of such data. The various forms of patient data that is currently being collected in both clinical and non-clinical environments will be studied. The clinical data will have the structured electronic health records and biomedical images. Sensor data has been receiving a lot attention recently. Techniques for mining sensor data and biomedical signal analysis will be presented. Personalized medicine has gained a lot of importance due to the advancements in genomic data. Genomic data analysis involves several statistical techniques. These will also be elaborated. Patients' in-hospital clinical data will also include a lot of unstructured data in the form of clinical notes. In addition, the domain knowledge that can be extracted by mining the biomedical literature, will also be discussed. The fundamental data mining, machine learning, information retrieval, and natural language processing techniques for processing these data types will be extensively discussed. Finally, behavioral data captured through social media will also be discussed.

2. *Advanced Data Analytics for Healthcare:* This part deals with the advanced analytical methods focused on healthcare. This includes the clinical prediction models, temporal data mining methods, and visual analytics. Integrating heterogeneous data such as clinical and genomic data is essential for improving the predictive power of the data that will also be discussed. Information retrieval techniques that can enhance the quality of biomedical search will be presented. Data privacy is an extremely important concern in healthcare. Privacy-preserving data publishing techniques will therefore be presented.

3. *Applications and Practical Systems for Healthcare:* This part focuses on the practical applications of data analytics and the systems developed using data analytics for healthcare and clinical practice. Examples include applications of data analytics to pervasive healthcare, fraud detection, and drug discovery. In terms of the practical systems, we will discuss the details about the clinical decision support systems, computer assisted medical imaging systems, and mobile imaging systems.

These different aspects of healthcare are related to one another. Therefore, the chapters in each of the aforementioned topics are interconnected. Where necessary, pointers are provided across different chapters, depending on the underlying relevance. This chapter is organized as follows. Section 1.2 discusses the main data sources that are commonly used and the basic techniques for processing them. Section 1.3 discusses advanced techniques in the field of healthcare data analytics. Section 1.4 discusses a number of applications of healthcare analysis techniques. An overview of resources in the field of healthcare data analytics is presented in Section 1.5. Section 1.6 presents the conclusions.

1.2 Healthcare Data Sources and Basic Analytics

In this section, the various data sources and their impact on analytical algorithms will be discussed. The heterogeneity of the sources for medical data mining is rather broad, and this creates the need for a wide variety of techniques drawn from different domains of data analytics.

1.2.1 Electronic Health Records

Electronic health records (EHRs) contain a digitized version of a patient's medical history. It encompasses a full range of data relevant to a patient's care such as demographics, problems, medications, physician's observations, vital signs, medical history, laboratory data, radiology reports, progress notes, and billing data. Many EHRs go beyond a patient's medical or treatment history and may contain additional broader perspectives of a patient's care. An important property of EHRs is that they provide an effective and efficient way for healthcare providers and organizations to share with one another. In this context, EHRs are inherently designed to be in real time and they can instantly be accessed and edited by authorized users. This can be very useful in practical settings. For example, a hospital or specialist may wish to access the medical records of the primary provider. An electronic health record streamlines the workflow by allowing direct access to the updated records in real time [30]. It can generate a complete record of a patient's clinical encounter, and support other care-related activities such as evidence-based decision support, quality management, and outcomes reporting. The storage and retrieval of health-related data is more efficient using EHRs. It helps to improve quality and convenience of patient care, increase patient participation in the healthcare process, improve accuracy of diagnoses and health outcomes, and improve care coordination [29]. Various components of EHRs along with the advantages, barriers, and challenges of using EHRs are discussed in Chapter 2.

1.2.2 Biomedical Image Analysis

Medical imaging plays an important role in modern-day healthcare due to its immense capability in providing high-quality images of anatomical structures in human beings. Effectively analyzing such images can be useful for clinicians and medical researchers since it can aid disease monitoring, treatment planning, and prognosis [31]. The most popular imaging modalities used to acquire a biomedical image are magnetic resonance imaging (MRI), computed tomography (CT), positron emission tomography (PET), and ultrasound (U/S). Being able to look inside of the body without hurting the patient and being able to view the human organs has tremendous implications on human health. Such capabilities allow the physicians to better understand the cause of an illness or other adverse conditions without cutting open the patient.

However, merely viewing such organs with the help of images is just the first step of the process. The final goal of biomedical image analysis is to be able to generate quantitative information and make inferences from the images that can provide far more insights into a medical condition. Such analysis has major societal significance since it is the key to understanding biological systems and solving health problems. However, it includes many challenges since the images are varied, complex, and can contain irregular shapes with noisy values. A number of general categories of research problems that arise in analyzing images are object detection, image segmentation, image registration, and feature extraction. All these challenges when resolved will enable the generation of meaningful analytic measurements that can serve as inputs to other areas of healthcare data analytics. Chapter 3 discusses a broad overview of the main medical imaging modalities along with a wide range of image analysis approaches.

1.2.3 Sensor Data Analysis

Sensor data [2] is ubiquitous in the medical domain both for real time and for retrospective analysis. Several forms of medical data collection instruments such as electrocardiogram (ECG), and electroencaphalogram (EEG) are essentially sensors that collect signals from various parts of the human body [32]. These collected data instruments are sometimes used for retrospective analysis, but more often for real-time analysis. Perhaps, the most important use-case of real-time analysis is in the context of intensive care units (ICUs) and real-time remote monitoring of patients with specific medical conditions. In all these cases, the volume of the data to the processed can be rather large. For example, in an ICU, it is not uncommon for the sensor to receive input from hundreds of data sources, and alarms need to be triggered in real time. Such applications necessitate the use of big-data frameworks and specialized hardware platforms. In remote-monitoring applications, both the real-time events and a long-term analysis of various trends and treatment alternatives is of great interest.

While rapid growth in sensor data offers significant promise to impact healthcare, it also introduces a data overload challenge. Hence, it becomes extremely important to develop novel data analytical tools that can process such large volumes of collected data into meaningful and interpretable knowledge. Such analytical methods will not only allow for better observing patients' physiological signals and help provide situational awareness to the bedside, but also provide better insights into the inefficiencies in the healthcare system that may be the root cause of surging costs. The research challenges associated with the mining of sensor data in healthcare settings and the sensor mining applications and systems in both clinical and non-clinical settings is discussed in Chapter 4.

1.2.4 Biomedical Signal Analysis

Biomedical Signal Analysis consists of measuring signals from biological sources, the origin of which lies in various physiological processes. Examples of such signals include the electroneurogram (ENG), electromyogram (EMG), electrocardiogram (ECG), electroencephalogram (EEG), electrogastrogram (EGG), phonocardiogram (PCG), and so on. The analysis of these signals is vital in diagnosing the pathological conditions and in deciding an appropriate care pathway. The measurement of physiological signals gives some form of quantitative or relative assessment of the state of the human body. These signals are acquired from various kinds of sensors and transducers either invasively or non-invasively.

These signals can be either discrete or continuous depending on the kind of care or severity of a particular pathological condition. The processing and interpretation of physiological signals is challenging due to the low signal-to-noise ratio (SNR) and the interdependency of the physiological systems. The signal data obtained from the corresponding medical instruments can be copiously noisy, and may sometimes require a significant amount of preprocessing. Several signal processing algorithms have been developed that have significantly enhanced the understanding of the physiological processes. A wide variety of methods are used for filtering, noise removal, and compact methods [36]. More sophisticated analysis methods including dimensionality reduction techniques such as Principal Component Analysis (PCA), Singular Value Decomposition (SVD), and wavelet transformation have also been widely investigated in the literature. A broader overview of many of these techniques may also be found in [1, 2]. Time-series analysis methods are discussed in [37, 40]. Chapter 5 presents an overview of various signal processing techniques used for processing biomedical signals.

1.2.5 Genomic Data Analysis

A significant number of diseases are genetic in nature, but the nature of the causality between the genetic markers and the diseases has not been fully established. For example, diabetes is well known to be a genetic disease; however, the full set of genetic markers that make an individual prone to diabetes are unknown. In some other cases, such as the blindness caused by Stargardt disease, the relevant genes are known but all the possible mutations have not been exhaustively isolated. Clearly, a broader understanding of the relationships between various genetic markers, mutations, and disease conditions has significant potential in assisting the development of various gene therapies to cure these conditions. One will be mostly interested in understanding what kind of health-related questions can be addressed through in-silico analysis of the genomic data through typical data-driven studies. Moreover, translating genetic discoveries into personalized medicine practice is a highly non-trivial task with a lot of unresolved challenges. For example, the genomic landscapes in complex diseases such as cancers are overwhelmingly complicated, revealing a high order of heterogeneity among different individuals. Solving these issues will be fitting a major piece of the puzzle and it will bring the concept of personalized medicine much more closer to reality.

Recent advancements made in the biotechnologies have led to the rapid generation of large volumes of biological and medical information and advanced genomic research. This has also led to unprecedented opportunities and hopes for genome scale study of challenging problems in life science. For example, advances in genomic technology made it possible to study the complete genomic landscape of healthy individuals for complex diseases [16]. Many of these research directions have already shown promising results in terms of generating new insights into the biology of human disease and to predict the personalized response of the individual to a particular treatment. Also, genetic data are often modeled either as sequences or as networks. Therefore, the work in this field requires a good understanding of sequence and network mining techniques. Various data analytics-based solutions are being developed for tackling key research problems in medicine such as identification of disease biomarkers and therapeutic targets and prediction of clinical outcome. More details about the fundamental computational algorithms and bioinformatics tools for genomic data analysis along with genomic data resources are discussed in Chapter 6.

1.2.6 Clinical Text Mining

Most of the information about patients is encoded in the form of *clinical notes*. These notes are typically stored in an unstructured data format and is the backbone of much of healthcare data. These contain the clinical information from the transcription of dictations, direct entry by providers, or use of speech recognition applications. These are perhaps the richest source of unexploited information. It is needless to say that the manual encoding of this free-text form on a broad range of clinical information is too costly and time consuming, though it is limited to primary and secondary diagnoses, and procedures for billing purposes. Such notes are notoriously challenging to analyze automatically due to the complexity involved in converting clinical text that is available in free-text to a structured format. It becomes hard mainly because of their unstructured nature, heterogeneity, diverse formats, and varying context across different patients and practitioners.

Natural language processing (NLP) and entity extraction play an important part in inferring useful knowledge from large volumes of clinical text to automatically encoding clinical information in a timely manner [22]. In general, data preprocessing methods are more important in these contexts as compared to the actual mining techniques. The processing of clinical text using NLP methods is more challenging when compared to the processing of other texts due to the ungrammatical nature of short and telegraphic phrases, dictations, shorthand lexicons such as abbreviations and acronyms, and often misspelled clinical terms. All these problems will have a direct impact on the various standard NLP tasks such as shallow or full parsing, sentence segmentation, text categorization, etc., thus making the clinical text processing highly challenging. A wide range of NLP methods and data mining techniques for extracting information from the clinical text are discussed in Chapter 7.

1.2.7 Mining Biomedical Literature

A significant number of applications rely on evidence from the biomedical literature. The latter is copious and has grown significantly over time. The use of text mining methods for the long-term preservation, accessibility, and usability of digitally available resources is important in biomedical applications relying on evidence from scientific literature. Text mining methods and tools offer novel ways of applying new knowledge discovery methods in the biomedical field [21][20]. Such tools offer efficient ways to search, extract, combine, analyze and summarize textual data, thus supporting researchers in knowledge discovery and generation. One of the major challenges in biomedical text mining is the multidisciplinary nature of the field. For example, biologists describe chemical compounds using brand names, while chemists often use less ambiguous IUPAC-compliant names or unambiguous descriptors such as International Chemical Identifiers. While the latter can be handled with cheminformatics tools, text mining techniques are required to extract less precisely defined entities and their relations from the literature. In this context, entity and event extraction methods play a key role in discovering useful knowledge from unstructured databases. Because the cost of curating such databases is too high, text mining methods offer new opportunities for their effective population, update, and integration. Text mining brings about other benefits to biomedical research by linking textual evidence to biomedical pathways, reducing the cost of expert knowledge validation, and generating hypotheses. The approach provides a general methodology to discover previously unknown links and enhance the way in which biomedical knowledge is organized. More details about the challenges and algorithms for biomedical text mining are discussed in Chapter 8.

1.2.8 Social Media Analysis

The rapid emergence of various social media resources such as social networking sites, blogs/microblogs, forums, question answering services, and online communities provides a wealth of information about public opinion on various aspects of healthcare. Social media data can be mined for patterns and knowledge that can be leveraged to make useful inferences about population health and public health monitoring. A significant amount of public health information can be gleaned from the inputs of various participants at social media sites. Although most individual social media posts and messages contain little informational value, aggregation of millions of such messages can generate important knowledge [4, 19]. Effectively analyzing these vast pieces of knowledge can significantly reduce the latency in collecting such complex information.

Previous research on social media analytics for healthcare has focused on capturing aggregate health trends such as outbreaks of infectious diseases, detecting reports of adverse drug interactions, and improving interventional capabilities for health-related activities. Disease outbreak detection is often strongly reflected in the content of social media and an analysis of the history of the content provides valuable insights about disease outbreaks. Topic models are frequently used for high-level analysis of such health-related content. An additional source of information in social media sites is obtained from online doctor and patient communities. Since medical conditions recur across different individuals, the online communities provide a valuable source of knowledge about various medical conditions. A major challenge in social media analysis is that the data is often unreliable, and therefore the results must be interpreted with caution. More discussion about the impact of social media analytics in improving healthcare is given in Chapter 9.

1.3 Advanced Data Analytics for Healthcare

This section will discuss a number of advanced data analytics methods for healthcare. These techniques include various data mining and machine learning models that need to be adapted to the healthcare domain.

1.3.1 Clinical Prediction Models

Clinical prediction forms a critical component of modern-day healthcare. Several prediction models have been extensively investigated and have been successfully deployed in clinical practice [26]. Such models have made a tremendous impact in terms of diagnosis and treatment of diseases. Most successful supervised learning methods that have been employed for clinical prediction tasks fall into three categories: (i) Statistical methods such as linear regression, logistic regression, and Bayesian models; (ii) Sophisticated methods in machine learning and data mining such as decision trees and artificial neural networks; and (iii) Survival models that aim to predict survival outcomes. All of these techniques focus on discovering the underlying relationship between covariate variables, which are also known as attributes and features, and a dependent outcome variable.

The choice of the model to be used for a particular healthcare problem primarily depends on the outcomes to be predicted. There are various kinds of prediction models that are proposed in the literature for handling such a diverse variety of outcomes. Some of the most common outcomes include binary and continuous forms. Other less common forms are categorical and ordinal outcomes. In addition, there are also different models proposed to handle survival outcomes where the goal is to predict the time of occurrence of a particular event of interest. These survival models are also widely studied in the context of clinical data analysis in terms of predicting the patient's survival time. There are different ways of evaluating and validating the performance of these prediction models. Different prediction models along with various kinds of evaluation mechanisms in the context of healthcare data analytics will be discussed in Chapter 10.

1.3.2 Temporal Data Mining

Healthcare data almost always contain time information and it is inconceivable to reason and mine these data without incorporating the temporal dimension. There are two major sources of temporal data generated in the healthcare domain. The first is the electronic health records (EHR) data and the second is the *sensor* data. Mining the temporal dimension of EHR data is extremely promising as it may reveal patterns that enable a more precise understanding of disease manifestation, progression and response to therapy. Some of the unique characteristics of EHR data (such as of heterogeneous, sparse, high-dimensional, irregular time intervals) makes conventional methods inadequate to handle them. Unlike EHR data, sensor data are usually represented as numeric time series that are regularly measured in time at a high frequency. Examples of these data are physiological data obtained by monitoring the patients on a regular basis and other electrical activity recordings such as electrocardiogram (ECG), electroencephalogram (EEG), etc. Sensor data for a specific subject are measured over a much shorter period of time (usually several minutes to several days) compared to the longitudinal EHR data (usually collected across the entire lifespan of the patient).

Given the different natures of EHR data and sensor data, the choice of appropriate temporal data mining methods for these types of data are often different. EHR data are usually mined using temporal pattern mining methods, which represent data instances (e.g., patients' records) as sequences of discrete events (e.g., diagnosis codes, procedures, etc.) and then try to find and enumerate statistically relevant patterns that are embedded in the data. On the other hand, sensor data are often analyzed using signal processing and time-series analysis techniques (e.g., wavelet transform, independent component analysis, etc.) [37, 40]. Chapter 11 presents a detailed survey and summarizes the literature on temporal data mining for healthcare data.

1.3.3 Visual Analytics

The ability to analyze and identify meaningful patterns in multimodal clinical data must be addressed in order to provide a better understanding of diseases and to identify patterns that could be affecting the clinical workflow. Visual analytics provides a way to combine the strengths of human cognition with interactive interfaces and data analytics that can facilitate the exploration of complex datasets. Visual analytics is a science that involves the integration of interactive visual interfaces with analytical techniques to develop systems that facilitate reasoning over, and interpretation of, complex data [23]. Visual analytics is popular in many aspects of healthcare data analysis because of the wide variety of insights that such an analysis provides. Due to the rapid increase of health-related information, it becomes critical to build effective ways of analyzing large amounts of data by leveraging human–computer interaction and graphical interfaces. In general, providing easily understandable summaries of complex healthcare data is useful for a human in gaining novel insights.

In the evaluation of many diseases, clinicians are presented with datasets that often contain hundreds of clinical variables. The multimodal, noisy, heterogeneous, and temporal characteristics of the clinical data pose significant challenges to the users while synthesizing the information and obtaining insights from the data [24]. The amount of information being produced by healthcare organizations opens up opportunities to design new interactive interfaces to explore large-scale databases, to validate clinical data and coding techniques, and to increase transparency within different departments, hospitals, and organizations. While many of the visual methods can be directly adopted from the data mining literature [11], a number of methods, which are specific to the healthcare domain, have also been designed. A detailed discussion on the popular data visualization techniques used in clinical settings and the areas in healthcare that benefit from visual analytics are discussed in Chapter 12.

1.3.4 Clinico–Genomic Data Integration

Human diseases are inherently complex in nature and are usually governed by a complicated interplay of several diverse underlying factors, including different genomic, clinical, behavioral, and environmental factors. Clinico–pathological and genomic datasets capture the different effects of these diverse factors in a complementary manner. It is essential to build integrative models considering both genomic and clinical variables simultaneously so that they can combine the vital information that is present in both clinical and genomic data [27]. Such models can help in the design of effective diagnostics, new therapeutics, and novel drugs, which will lead us one step closer to personalized medicine [17].

This opportunity has led to an emerging area of integrative predictive models that can be built by combining clinical and genomic data, which is called clinico–genomic data integration. Clinical data refers to a broad category of a patient's pathological, behavioral, demographic, familial, environmental and medication history, while genomic data refers to a patient's genomic information including SNPs, gene expression, protein and metabolite profiles. In most of the cases, the goal of the integrative study is biomarker discovery which is to find the clinical and genomic factors related to a particular disease phenotype such as cancer vs. no cancer, tumor vs. normal tissue samples, or continuous variables such as the survival time after a particular treatment. Chapter 13 provides a comprehensive survey of different challenges with clinico–genomic data integration along with the different approaches that aim to address these challenges with an emphasis on biomarker discovery.

1.3.5 Information Retrieval

Although most work in healthcare data analytics focuses on mining and analyzing patient-related data, additional information for use in this process includes scientific data and literature. The techniques most commonly used to access this data include those from the field of information retrieval (IR). IR is the field concerned with the acquisition, organization, and searching of knowledge-based information, which is usually defined as information derived and organized from observational or experimental research [14]. The use of IR systems has become essentially ubiquitous. It is estimated that among individuals who use the Internet in the United States, over 80 percent have used it to search for personal health information and virtually all physicians use the Internet.

Information retrieval models are closely related to the problems of clinical and biomedical text mining. The basic objective of using information retrieval is to find the *content* that a user wanted based on his requirements. This typically begins with the posing of a *query* to the IR system. A *search engine* matches the query to content items through metadata. The two key components of IR are: *Indexing*, which is the process of assigning metadata to the content, and *retrieval*, which is the process of the user entering the query and retrieving relevant content. The most well-known data structure used for efficient information retrieval is the inverted index where each document is associated with an identifier. Each word then points to a list of document identifiers. This kind of representation is particularly useful for a keyword search. Furthermore, once a search has been conducted, mechanisms are required to rank the possibly large number of results, which might have been retrieved. A number of user-oriented evaluations have been performed over the years looking at users of biomedical information and measuring the search performance in clinical settings [15]. Chapter 14 discusses a number of information retrieval models for healthcare along with evaluation of such retrieval models.

1.3.6 Privacy-Preserving Data Publishing

In the healthcare domain, the definition of privacy is commonly accepted as "a person's right and desire to control the disclosure of their personal health information" [25]. Patients' health-related data is highly sensitive because of the potentially compromising information about individual participants. Various forms of data such as disease information or genomic information may be sensitive for different reasons. To enable research in the field of medicine, it is often important for medical organizations to be able to share their data with statistical experts. Sharing personal health information can bring enormous economical benefits. This naturally leads to concerns about the privacy of individuals being compromised. The data privacy problem is one of the most important challenges in the field of healthcare data analytics. Most privacy preservation methods reduce the representation accuracy of the data so that the identification of sensitive attributes of an individual is compromised. This can be achieved by either perturbing the sensitive attribute, perturbing attributes that serve as identification mechanisms, or a combination of the two. Clearly, this process required the reduction in the accuracy of data representation. Therefore, privacy preservation almost always incurs the cost of losing some data utility. Therefore, the goal of privacy preservation methods is to optimize the trade-off between utility and privacy. This ensures that the amount of utility loss at a given level of privacy is as little as possible.

The major steps in privacy-preserving data publication algorithms [5][18] are the identification of an appropriate privacy metric and level for a given access setting and data characteristics, application of one or multiple privacy-preserving algorithm(s) to achieve the desired privacy level, and postanalyzing the utility of the processed data. These three steps are repeated until the desired utility and privacy levels are jointly met. Chapter 15 focuses on applying privacy-preserving algorithms to healthcare data for secondary-use data publishing and interpretation of the usefulness and implications of the processed data.

1.4 Applications and Practical Systems for Healthcare

In the final set of chapters in this book, we will discuss the practical healthcare applications and systems that heavily utilize data analytics. These topics have evolved significantly in the past few years and are continuing to gain a lot of momentum and interest. Some of these methods, such as fraud detection, are not directly related to medical diagnosis, but are nevertheless important in this domain.

1.4.1 Data Analytics for Pervasive Health

Pervasive health refers to the process of tracking medical well-being and providing long-term medical care with the use of advanced technologies such as wearable sensors. For example, wearable monitors are often used for measuring the long-term effectiveness of various treatment mechanisms. These methods, however, face a number of challenges, such as knowledge extraction from the large volumes of data collected and real-time processing. However, recent advances in both hardware and software technologies (data analytics in particular) have made such systems a reality. These advances have made low cost intelligent health systems embedded within the home and living environments a reality [33].

A wide variety of sensor modalities can be used when developing intelligent health systems, including wearable and ambient sensors [28]. In the case of wearable sensors, sensors are attached to the body or woven into garments. For example, 3-axis accelerometers distributed over an individual's body can provide information about the orientation and movement of the corresponding body part. In addition to these advancements in sensing modalities, there has been an increasing interest in applying analytics techniques to data collected from such equipment. Several practical healthcare systems have started using analytical solutions. Some examples include cognitive health monitoring systems based on activity recognition, persuasive systems for motivating users to change their health and wellness habits, and abnormal health condition detection systems. A detailed discussion on how various analytics can be used for supporting the development of intelligent health systems along with supporting infrastructure and applications in different healthcare domains is presented in Chapter 16.

1.4.2 Healthcare Fraud Detection

Healthcare fraud has been one of the biggest problems faced by the United States and costs several billions of dollars every year. With growing healthcare costs, the threat of healthcare fraud is increasing at an alarming pace. Given the recent scrutiny of the inefficiencies in the US healthcare system, identifying fraud has been on the forefront of the efforts towards reducing the healthcare costs. One could analyze the healthcare claims data along different dimensions to identify fraud. The complexity of the healthcare domain, which includes multiple sets of participants, including healthcare providers, beneficiaries (patients), and insurance companies, makes the problem of detecting healthcare fraud equally challenging and makes it different from other domains such as credit card fraud detection and auto insurance fraud detection. In these other domains, the methods rely on constructing profiles for the users based on the historical data and they typically monitor deviations in the behavior of the user from the profile [7]. However, in healthcare fraud, such approaches are not usually applicable, because the users in the healthcare setting are the beneficiaries, who typically are not the fraud perpetrators. Hence, more sophisticated analysis is required in the healthcare sector to identify fraud.

Several solutions based on data analytics have been investigated for solving the problem of healthcare fraud. The primary advantages of data-driven fraud detection are automatic extraction of fraud patterns and prioritization of suspicious cases [3]. Most of such analysis is performed with respect to an episode of care, which is essentially a collection of healthcare provided to a patient under the same health issue. Data-driven methods for healthcare fraud detection can be employed to answer the following questions: Is a given episode of care fraudulent or unnecessary? Is a given claim within an episode fraudulent or unnecessary? Is a provider or a network of providers fraudulent? We discuss the problem of fraud in healthcare and existing data-driven methods for fraud detection in Chapter 17.

1.4.3 Data Analytics for Pharmaceutical Discoveries

The cost of successful novel chemistry-based drug development often reaches millions of dollars, and the time to introduce the drug to market often comes close to a decade [34]. The high failure rate of drugs during this process, make the trial phases known as the "valley of death." Most new compounds fail during the FDA approval process in clinical trials or cause adverse side effects. Interdisciplinary computational approaches that combine statistics, computer science, medicine, chemoinformatics, and biology are becoming highly valuable for drug discovery and development. In the context of pharmaceutical discoveries, data analytics can potentially limit the search space and provide recommendations to the domain experts for hypothesis generation and further analysis and experiments.

Data analytics can be used in several stages of drug discovery and development to achieve different goals. In this domain, one way to categorize data analytical approaches is based on their application to pre-marketing and post-marketing stages of the drug discovery and development process. In the pre-marketing stage, data analytics focus on discovery activities such as finding signals that indicate relations between drugs and targets, drugs and drugs, genes and diseases, protein and diseases, and finding biomarkers. In the post-marketing stage an important application of data analytics is to find indications of adverse side effects for approved drugs. These methods provide a list of potential drug side effect associations that can be used for further studies. Chapter 18 provides more discussion of the applications of data analytics for pharmaceutical discoveries including drug-target interaction prediction and pharmacovigilance.

1.4.4 Clinical Decision Support Systems

Clinical Decision Support Systems (CDSS) are computer systems designed to assist clinicians with patient-related decision making, such as diagnosis and treatment [6]. CDSS have become a crucial component in the evaluation and improvement of patient treatment since they have shown to improve both patient outcomes and cost of care [35]. They can help in minimizing analytical errors by notifying the physician of potentially harmful drug interactions, and their diagnostic procedures have been shown to enable more accurate diagnoses. Some of the main advantages of CDSS are their ability in decision making and determining optimal treatment strategies, aiding general health policies by estimating the clinical and economic outcomes of different treatment methods and even estimating treatment outcomes under certain conditions. The main reason for the success of CDSS are their electronic nature, seemless integration with clinical workflows, providing decision support at the appropriate time/location. Two particular fields of healthcare where CDSS have been extremely influential are pharmacy and billing. CDSS can help pharmacies to look for negative drug interactions and then report them to the corresponding patient's ordering professional. In the billing departments, CDSS have been used to devise treatment plans that provide an optimal balance of patient care and financial expense [9]. A detailed survey of different aspects of CDSS along with various challenges associated with their usage in clinical practice is discussed in Chapter 19.

1.4.5 Computer-Aided Diagnosis

Computer-aided diagnosis/detection (CAD) is a procedure in radiology that supports radiologists in reading medical images [13]. CAD tools in general refer to fully automated second reader tools designed to assist the radiologist in the detection of lesions. There is a growing consensus among clinical experts that the use of CAD tools can improve the performance of the radiologist. The radiologist first performs an interpretation of the images as usual, while the CAD algorithms is running in the background or has already been precomputed. Structures identified by the CAD algorithm are then highlighted as regions of interest to the radiologist. The principal value of CAD tools is determined not by its stand-alone performance, but rather by carefully measuring the incremental value of CAD in normal clinical practice, such as the number of additional lesions detected using CAD. Secondly, CAD systems must not have a negative impact on patient management (for instance, false positives that cause the radiologist to recommend unnecessary biopsies and follow-ups).

From the data analytics perspective, new CAD algorithms aim at extracting key quantitative features, summarizing vast volumes of data, and/or enhancing the visualization of potentially malignant nodules, tumors, or lesions in medical images. The three important stages in the CAD data processing are candidate generation (identifying suspicious regions of interest), feature extraction (computing descriptive morphological or texture features), and classification (differentiating candidates that are true lesions from the rest of the candidates based on candidate feature vectors). A detailed overview of some CAD approaches to different diseases emphasizing the specific challenges in diagnosis and detection, and a series of case studies that apply advanced data analytics in medical imaging applications is presented in Chapter 20.

1.4.6 Mobile Imaging for Biomedical Applications

Mobile imaging refers to the application of portable computers such as smartphones or tablet computers to store, visualize, and process images with and without connections to servers, the Internet, or the cloud. Today, portable devices provide sufficient computational power for biomedical image processing and smart devices have been introduced in the operation theater. While many techniques for biomedical image acquisition will always require special equipment, the regular camera is one of the most widely used imaging modality in hospitals. Mobile technology and smart devices, especially smartphones, allows new ways of easier imaging at the patient's bedside and possess the possibility to be made into a diagnostic tool that can be used by medical professionals. Smartphones usually contain at least one high-resolution camera that can be used for image formation. Several challenges arise during the acquisition, visualization, analysis, and management of images in mobile environments. A more detailed discussion about mobile imaging and its challenges is given in Chapter 21.

1.5 Resources for Healthcare Data Analytics

There are several resources available in this field. We will now discuss the various books, journals, and organizations that provide further information on this exciting area of healthcare informatics. A classical book in the field of healthcare informatics is [39]. There are several other books that target a specific topic of work (in the context of healthcare) such as information retrieval [10], statistical methods [38], evaluation methods [8], and clinical decision support systems [6, 9].

There are a few popular organizations that are primarily involved with medical informatics research. They are American Medical Informatics Association (AMIA) [49], International Medical Informatics Association (IMIA) [50], and the European Federation for Medical Informatics (EFMI)

[51]. These organizations usually conduct annual conferences and meetings that are well attended by researchers working in healthcare informatics. The meetings typically discuss new technologies for capturing, processing, and analyzing medical data. It is a good meeting place for new researchers who would like to start research in this area.

The following are some of the well-reputed journals that publish top-quality research works in healthcare data analytics: *Journal of the American Medical Informatics Association (JAMIA)* [41], *Journal of Biomedical Informatics (JBI)* [42], *Journal of Medical Internet Research* [43], *IEEE Journal of Biomedical and Health Informatics* [44], *Medical Decision Making* [45], *International Journal of Medical Informatics (IJMI)* [46], and *Artificial Intelligence in Medicine* [47]. A more comprehensive list of journals in the field of healthcare and biomedical informatics along with details is available here [48].

Due to the privacy of the medical data that typically contains highly sensitive patient information, the research work in the healthcare data analytics has been fragmented into various places. Many researchers work with a specific hospital or a healthcare facility that are usually not willing to share their data due to obvious privacy concerns. However, there are a wide variety of public repositories available for researchers to design and apply their own models and algorithms. Due to the diversity in healthcare research, it will be a cumbersome task to compile all the healthcare repositories at a single location. Specific health data repositories dealing with a particular healthcare problem and data sources are listed in the corresponding chapters where the data is discussed. We hope that these repositories will be useful for both existing and upcoming researchers who do not have access to the health data from hospitals and healthcare facilities.

1.6 Conclusions

The field of healthcare data analytics has seen significant strides in recent years because of hardware and software technologies, which have increased the ease of the data collection process. The advancement of the field has, however, faced a number of challenges because of its interdisciplinary nature, privacy constraints in data collection and dissemination mechanisms, and the inherently unstructured nature of the data. In some cases, the data may have very high volume, which requires real-time analysis and insights. In some cases, the data may be complex, which may require specialized retrieval and analytical techniques. The advances in data collection technologies, which have enabled the field of analytics, also pose new challenges because of their efficiency in collecting large amounts of data. The techniques used in the healthcare domain are also very diverse because of the inherent variations in the underlying data type. This book provides a comprehensive overview of these different aspects of healthcare data analytics, and the various research challenges that still need to be addressed.

Bibliography

[1] Charu C. *Aggarwal. Data Streams: Models and Algorithms*. Springer. 2007.

[2] Charu C. Aggarwal. *Managing and Mining Sensor Data*. Springer. 2013.

[3] Charu C. *Aggarwal. Outlier Analysis*. Springer. 2013.

[4] Charu C. Aggarwal. *Social Network Data Analytics*. Springer, 2011.

[5] Charu C. Aggarwal and Philip S. Yu. *Privacy-Preserving Data Mining: Models and Algorithms*. Springer. 2008.

[6] Eta S Berner. *Clinical Decision Support Systems*. Springer, 2007.

[7] Richard J. Bolton, and David J. Hand. Statistical fraud detection: A review. *Statistical Science*, 17(3):235–249, 2002.

[8] Charles P. Friedman. *Evaluation Methods in Biomedical Informatics*. Springer, 2006.

[9] Robert A. Greenes. *Clinical Decision Support: The Road Ahead*. Academic Press, 2011.

[10] William Hersh. *Information Retrieval: A Health and Biomedical Perspective*. Springer, 2008.

[11] Daniel A. Keim. Information visualization and visual data mining. *IEEE Transactions on Visualization and Computer Graphics*, 8(1):1–8, 2002.

[12] J. Manyika, M. Chui, B. Brown, J. Bughin, R. Dobbs, C. Roxburgh, and A. H. Byers. Big data: The next frontier for innovation, competition, and productivity. McKinsey Global Institute Report, May 2011.

[13] Kunio Doi. Computer-aided diagnosis in medical imaging: Historical review, current status and future potential. *Computerized Medical Imaging and Graphics*, 31:2007.

[14] W. Hersh. *Information Retrieval: A Health and Biomedical Perspective*. Springer, 2009.

[15] R. B. Haynes, K. A. McKibbon, C. J. Walker, N. Ryan, D. Fitzgerald, and M. F. Ramsden. Online access to MEDLINE in clinical settings: A study of use and usefulness. *Annals of Internal Medicine*, 112(1):78–84, 1990.

[16] B. Vogelstein, N. Papadopoulos, V. E. Velculescu, S. Zhou, J. Diaz, L. A., and K. W. Kinzler. Cancer genome landscapes. *Science*, 339(6127):1546–1558, 2013.

[17] P. Edn, C. Ritz, C. Rose, M. Fern, and C. Peterson. Good old clinical markers have similar power in breast cancer prognosis as microarray gene expression profilers. *European Journal of Cancer*, 40(12):1837–1841, 2004.

[18] Rashid Hussain Khokhar, Rui Chen, Benjamin C.M. Fung, and Siu Man Lui. Quantifying the costs and benefits of privacy-preserving health data publishing. *Journal of Biomedical Informatics*, 50:107–121, 2014.

[19] Adam Sadilek, Henry Kautz, and Vincent Silenzio. Modeling spread of disease from social interactions. In *Proceedings of the 6th International AAAI Conference on Weblogs and Social Media (ICWSM'12)*, pages 322–329, 2012.

[20] L. Jensen, J. Saric, and P. Bork. Literature mining for the biologist: From information retrieval to biological discovery. *Nature Reviews Genetics*, 7(2):119–129, 2006.

[21] P. Zweigenbaum, D. Demner-Fushman, H. Yu, and K. Cohen. Frontiers of biomedical text mining: Current progress. *Briefings in Bioinformatics*, 8(5):358–375, 2007.

[22] S. M. Meystre, G. K. Savova, K. C. Kipper-Schuler, and J. F. Hurdle. Extracting information from textual documents in the electronic health record: A review of recent research. *Yearbook of Medical Informatics*, pages 128–144, 2008.

[23] Daniel Keim et al. *Visual Analytics: Definition, Process, and Challenges*. Springer Berlin Heidelberg, 2008.

[24] K. Wongsuphasawat, J. A. Guerra Gmez, C. Plaisant, T. D. Wang, M. Taieb-Maimon, and B. Shneiderman. LifeFlow: Visualizing an overview of event sequences. In *Proceedings of the SIGCHI Conference on Human Factors in Computing Systems*, 1747-1756. ACM, 2011.

[25] Thomas C. Rindfieisch. Privacy, information technology, and health care. *Communications of the ACM*, 40(8):92–100, 1997.

[26] E. W. Steyerberg. *Clinical Prediction Models*. Springer, 2009.

[27] E. E. Schadt. Molecular networks as sensors and drivers of common human diseases. *Nature*, 461(7261):218–223, 2009.

[28] Min Chen, Sergio Gonzalez, Athanasios Vasilakos, Huasong Cao, and Victor C. Leung. Body area networks: A survey. *Mobile Networks and Applications*, 16(2):171–193, April 2011.

[29] Catherine M. DesRoches et al. Electronic health records in ambulatory carea national survey of physicians. *New England Journal of Medicine* 359(1):50–60, 2008.

[30] Richard Hillestad et al. Can electronic medical record systems transform health care? Potential health benefits, savings, and costs. *Health Affairs* 24(5):1103–1117, 2005.

[31] Stanley R. Sternberg, Biomedical image processing. *Computer* 16(1):22–34, 1983.

[32] G. Acampora, D. J. Cook, P. Rashidi, A. V. Vasilakos. A survey on ambient intelligence in healthcare,*Proceedings of the IEEE*, 101(12):2470–2494, Dec. 2013.

[33] U. Varshney. Pervasive healthcare and wireless health monitoring. *Mobile Networks and Applications* 12(2–3):113–127, 2007.

[34] Steven M. Paul, Daniel S. Mytelka, Christopher T. Dunwiddie, Charles C. Persinger, Bernard H. Munos, Stacy R. Lindborg, and Aaron L. Schacht. How to improve R&D productivity: The pharmaceutical industry's grand challenge. *Nature Reviews Drug Discovery* 9 (3):203–214, 2010.

[35] R. Amarasingham, L. Plantinga, M. Diener-West, D. Gaskin, and N. Powe. Clinical information technologies and inpatient outcomes: A multiple hospital study. *Archives of Internal Medicine* 169(2):108–114, 2009.

[36] Athanasios Papoulis. *Signal Analysis*. McGraw-Hill: New York, 1978.

[37] Robert H. Shumway and David S. Stoffer. *Time-Series Analysis and Its Applications: With R Examples*. Springer: New York, 2011.

[38] Robert F. Woolson and William R. Clarke. *Statistical Methods for the Analysis of Biomedical Data*, Volume 371. John Wiley & Sons, 2011.

[39] Edward H. Shortliffe and James J. Cimino. *Biomedical Informatics*. Springer, 2006.

[40] Mitsa Thephano. *Temporal Data Mining*. Chapman and Hall/CRC Press, 2010.

[41] `http://jamia.bmj.com/`

[42] `http://www.journals.elsevier.com/journal-of-biomedical-informatics/`

[43] `http://www.jmir.org/`

[44] `http://jbhi.embs.org/`

[45] http://mdm.sagepub.com/

[46] http://www.ijmijournal.com/

[47] http://www.journals.elsevier.com/artificial-intelligence-in-medicine/

[48] http://clinfowiki.org/wiki/index.php/Leading_Health_Informatics_and_Medical_Informatics_Journals

[49] http://www.amia.org/

[50] www.imia-medinfo.org/

[51] http://www.efmi.org/

Part I

Healthcare Data Sources and Basic Analytics

Chapter 2

Electronic Health Records: A Survey

Rajiur Rahman
Department of Computer Science
Wayne State University
Detroit, MI
rajiurrahman@wayne.edu

Chandan K. Reddy
Department of Computer Science
Wayne State University
Detroit, MI
reddy@cs.wayne.edu

2.1 Introduction

An Electronic Health Record (EHR) is a digital version of a patient's medical history. It is a longitudinal record of patient health information generated by one or several encounters in any healthcare providing setting. The term is often used interchangeably with EMR (Electronic Medical Record) and CPR (Computer-based Patient Record). It encompasses a full range of data relevant to a patient's care such as demographics, problems, medications, physician's observations, vital signs, medical history, immunizations, laboratory data, radiology reports, personal statistics, progress notes, and billing data. The EHR system automates the data management process of complex clinical environments and has the potential to streamline the clinician's workflow. It can generate a complete record of a patient's clinical encounter, and support other care-related activities such as evidence-based decision support, quality management, and outcomes reporting. An EHR system integrates data for different purposes. It enables the administrator to utilize the data for billing purposes, the physician to analyze patient diagnostics information and treatment effectiveness, the nurse to report adverse conditions, and the researcher to discover new knowledge.

EHR has several advantages over paper-based systems. Storage and retrieval of data is obviously more efficient using EHRs. It helps to improve quality and convenience of patient care, increase patient participation in the healthcare process, improve accuracy of diagnoses and health outcomes, and improve care coordination. It also reduces cost by eliminating the need for paper and other storage media. It provides the opportunity for research in different disciplines. In 2011, 54% of physicians had adopted an EHR system, and about three-quarters of adopters reported that using an EHR system resulted in enhanced patient care [1].

Usually, EHR is maintained within an institution, such as a hospital, clinic, or physician's office. An institution will contain the longitudinal records of a particular patient that have been collected at their end. The institution will not contain the records of all the care provided to the patient at other venues. Information regarding the general population may be kept in a nationwide or regional health information system. Depending on the goal, service, venue, and role of the user, EHR can have different data formats, presentations, and level of detail.

The remainder of this chapter is organized as follows. Section 2.2 discusses a brief history of EHR development and Section 2.3 provides the components of EHRs. Section 2.4 presents a comprehensive review of existing coding systems in EHR. The benefits of using EHRs are explained in more detail in Section 2.5, while the barriers for the widespread adoption of EHRs are discussed in Section 2.6. Section 2.7 briefly explains some of the challenges of using EHR data. The prominent phenotyping algorithms are described in Section 2.8 and our discussion is concluded in Section 2.9.

2.2 History of EHR

The first known medical record can be traced back to the fifth century B.C. when Hippocrates prescribed two goals for medical records [2]:

- A medical record should accurately reflect the course of disease.
- A medical record should indicate the probable cause of disease.

Although these two goals are still appropriate, EHR has a lot more to offer. Modern EHR can provide additional functionalities that could not be performed using paper-based systems.

Modern-day EHR first began to appear in the 1960s. Early EHRs were developed due to physicians' concerns about the increasing complexity and size of medical data. Data retrieval was much faster using digital format. In 1967, Latter Day Saints Hospitals in Utah started using Health Evaluation through Logical Programming (HELP) software. HELP is notable for its pioneering logical decision support features. In 1969, Harvard Medical School developed its own software Computer Stored Ambulatory Record (COASTER) and Duke University began to develop The Medical Record (TMR).

In 1970, Lockheed unveiled the Technicon Medical Information Management System/ Technicon Data System (TDS). It was implemented at El Camion Hospital in California. It came with a groundbreaking Computer Provided Order Entry (CPOE) system. In 1979, Judith Faulkner, a computer programmer established Human Services Computing Inc., which developed the Chronicles data repository. The company later became Epic Systems. It was initially based on a single longitudinal patient record and designed to handle enterprise-wide data from inpatient, ambulatory, and payer environments.

In 1985, The Department of Veterans Affairs launched the automated data processing system, Decentralized Hospital Computer Program (DHCP), which includes extensive clinical and administrative capabilities within its medical facilities. It received the Smithsonian Award for best use of Information Technology in Medicine in 1995. The current variant of DHCP is VistA (Veterans Health Information Systems and Technology Architecture). By providing care to over 8 million veterans operating in 163 hospitals, 800 clinics, and 135 nursing homes, VistA manages one of the largest medical system in the United States [4]. In 1983, Epic Systems launched a patient scheduling software program called Cadence. This application helped clients to improve resource utilization and manage patient access. In 1988, Science Application International Corporation (SAIC) secured a $1.02 billion dollar contract from the U.S. Government to develop a composite healthcare system. In 1992, Epic Systems introduced the first Windows-based EHR software named EpicCare. Allscripts released the first software with an electronic prescribing solution for physicians in 1998.

From 2000 and beyond, EHR software has been increasingly trying to incorporate other functionalities to become an interactive companion for physicians and professionals. In January 2004, President George W. Bush launched an initiative for the widespread adaptation of EHRs within the next 10 years. He said in his State of the Union Address, "By computerizing health records, we can avoid dangerous medical mistakes, reduce costs, and improve care" [5]. In January 2009, in a speech at George Mason University, President Barack Obama said "[EHRs] will cut waste, eliminate red tape, and reduce the need to repeat expensive medical tests. It just won't save billions of dollars and thousands of jobs – it will save lives by reducing the deadly but preventable medical errors that pervade our health care system" [6]. The data from a National Ambulatory Medical Care Survey (NAMCS) and Physicians Workflow mail survey shows that in the year 2011, 54% of the physicians had adopted an EHR system. About three-quarters of the adopters reported that their system meets the federal "meaningful use" criteria. Almost half (47%) of the physicians said they were somewhat satisfied, and 38% reported being very satisfied with their system. About three-quarters of the adopters reported that EHR has resulted in enhanced patient care. Nearly one-half of physicians without an EHR system at the time of the survey said they had plans for purchasing one within the next year [1].

2.3 Components of EHR

The main purpose of EHR is to support clinical care and billing. This also includes other functionalities, such as improving the quality and convenience of patient care, improving the accuracy of diagnoses and health outcomes, improving care coordination and patient participation, improving cost savings, and finally, improving the general health of the population. Most modern EHR systems are designed to integrate data from different components such as administrative, nursing, pharmacy, laboratory, radiology, and physician' entries, etc. Electronic records may be generated from any department. Hospitals and clinics may have a number of different ancillary system providers; in that case, these systems are not necessarily integrated to the main EHR system. It is possible that these systems are stand-alone, and different standards of vocabularies have been used. If appropriate interfaces are provided, data from these systems can be incorporated in a consolidated fashion; otherwise a clinician has to open and log into a series of applications to get the complete patient record. The number of components present may also vary depending on the service provided. Figure 2.1 shows different components of an EHR system.

2.3.1 Administrative System Components

Administrative data such as patient registration, admission, discharge, and transfer data are key components of the EHR. It also includes name, demographics, employer history, chief compliant, patient disposition, etc., along with the patient billing information. Social history data such as marital status, home environment, daily routine, dietary patterns, sleep patterns, exercise patterns, tobacco use, alcohol use, drug use and family history data such as personal health history, hereditary diseases, father, mother and sibling(s) health status, age, and cause of death can also be a part of it. Apart from the fields like "comments" or "description," these data generally contain <name-value> pairs. This information is used to identify and assess a patient, and for all other administrative purposes. During the registration process, a patient is generally assigned a unique identification key comprising of a numeric or alphanumeric sequence. This key helps to link all the components across different platforms. For example, lab test data can create an electronic record; and another record is created from radiology results. Both records will have the same identifier key to represent a single patient. Records of a previous encounter are also pulled up using this key. It is often referred to as the medical record number or master patient index (MPI). Administrative data allows the aggregation of a person's health information for clinical analysis and research.

2.3.2 Laboratory System Components & Vital Signs

Generally, laboratory systems are stand-alone systems that are interfaced to the central EHR system. It is a structured data that can be expressed using standard terminology and stored in the form of a name-value pair. Lab data plays an extremely important part in the clinical care process, providing professionals the information needed for prevention, diagnosis, treatment, and health management. About 60% to 70% of medical decisions are based on laboratory test results [7]. Electronic lab data has several benefits including improved presentation and reduction of error due to manual data entry. A physician can easily compare the results from previous tests. If the options are provided, he can also analyze automatically whether data results fall within normal range or not.

The most common coding system used to represent the laboratory test data is Logical Observation Identifiers Names and Codes (LOINC). Many hospitals use their local dictionaries as well to encode variables. A 2009–2010 Vanderbilt University Medical Center data standardization study found that for simple concepts such as "weight" and "height," there were more than five internal representations. In different places there are different field names for the same feature and the values

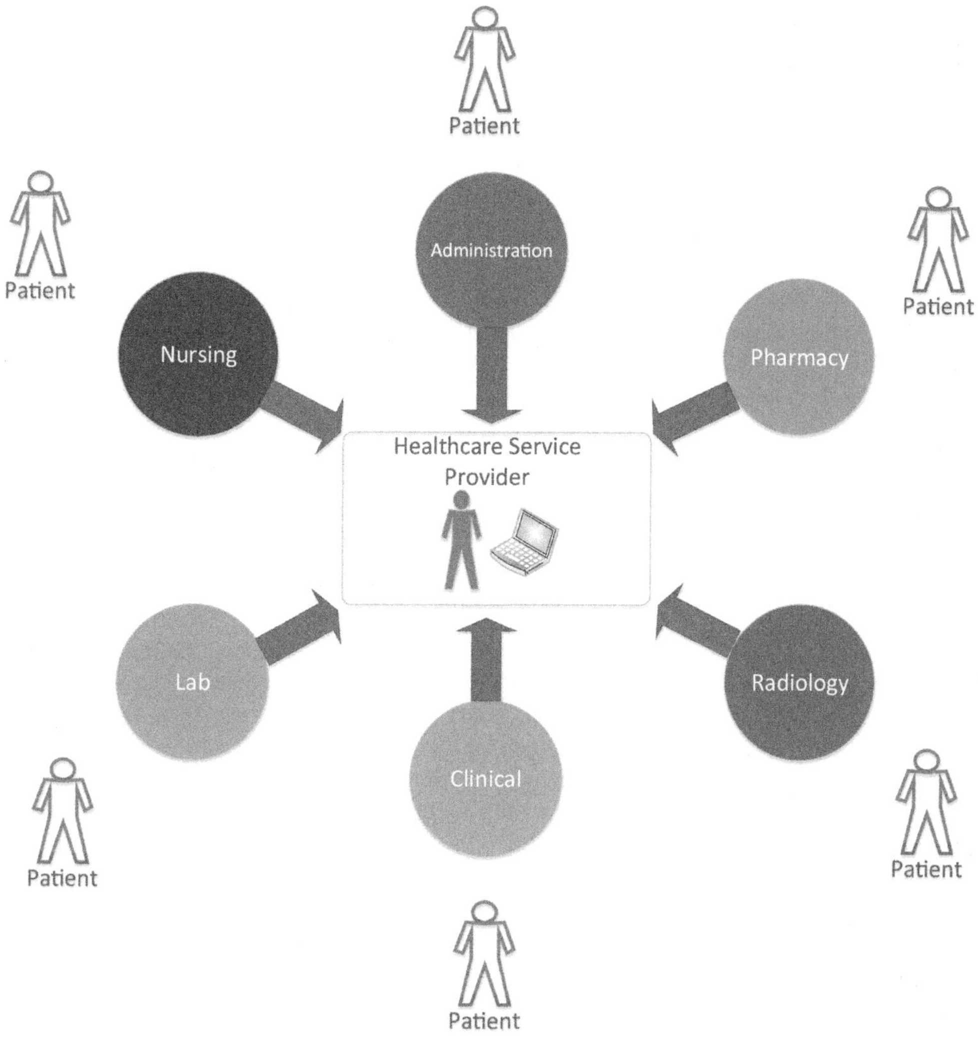

FIGURE 2.1: Various components of EHR.

are stored with different units (e.g., kilograms, grams, and pounds for weight; centimeters, meters, inches, and feet for height).

Vital signs are the indicators of a patient's general physical condition. It includes pulse, respiratory rate, blood pressure, body temperature, body mass index (BMI), etc. A typical EHR system must provide the option to accommodate these kinds of variables.

2.3.3 Radiology System Components

In hospital radiology departments, radiology information systems (RIS) are used for managing medical imagery and associated data. RIS is the core database to store, manipulate, and distribute patient radiological data. It uses Current Procedural Terminology (CPT) or International Classification of Diseases (ICD) coding systems to identify procedures and resources. Generally, an RIS consists of patient tracking, scheduling, result reporting, and image tracking capabilities. RIS is usually used along with a picture archiving communications system (PACS), which is a medical technology for providing economical storage and convenient access to the digital images. An RIS can generate an entire patient's imagery history and statistical reports for patients or procedures. Although many hospitals are using RIS, it may or may not be integrated with the central EHR system.

2.3.4 Pharmacy System Components

In hospitals and clinics, the pharmacy department's responsibility is to maintain the inventory, prescription management, billing, and dispensing medications. The pharmacy component in EHR will hold the complete medication history of a patient such as drug name, dosage, route, quantity, frequency, start and stop date, prescribed by, allergic reaction to medications, source of medication, etc. Pharmacists serve an important public health role by administering immunizations and must have the capabilities to document these services and share this information with other healthcare providers and public health organizations. They assure safe and effective medication and supporting patient-centered care. Pharmacies are highly automated in large hospitals. Again, it may be independent of central EHRs. The Food and Drug Administration (FDA) requires all the drugs to be registered and reported using a National Drug Code (NDC). Coding systems used are NDC, SNOMED, and RxNorm.

2.3.5 Computerized Physician Order Entry (CPOE)

Computerized Physician Order Entry (CPOE) is a very important part of EHRs. It is a system that allows a medical practitioner to enter medical orders and instructions for the treatment of a patient. For example, a doctor can electronically order services to laboratory, pharmacy, and radiology services through CPOE. Then it gets propagated over a network to the person responsible for carrying out these orders. As a digital system, CPOE has the potential to reduce medication-related errors. It is possible to add intelligent rules for checking allergies, contradictions, and other alerts. The primary advantages of CPOE are the following: overcomes the issue of illegibility, fewer errors associated with ordering drugs with similar names, more easily integrated with decision support systems, easily linked to drug-drug interaction warning, more likely to identify the prescribing physician, able to link the adverse drug event (ADE) reporting systems, able to avoid medication errors like trailing zeros, create data that is available for analysis, point out treatment and drug of choice, reduce under- and overprescribing, and finally, the prescriptions can reach the pharmacy quicker. While ordering, a professional can view the medical history, current status report from a different module, and evidence-based clinical guidelines. Thus, CPOE can help in patient-centered clinical decision support.

If used properly, CPOE decreases delay in order completion, reduces errors related to handwriting or transcriptions, allows order entry at point-of-care or off-site, provides error checking for duplicate or incorrect doses or tests, and simplifies inventory and positing of charges. Studies have shown that CPOE can contribute to shortened length of stay and reduction of cost [8]. There are some risks involved in adopting CPOE as well. It may slow down interpersonal communication in an emergency situation. If each group of professionals (e.g., physicians and nurses) works alone in their workstations, it may create ambiguity about the instructions. These factors led an increase in mortality rate by 2.8%–6.5% in the Children's Hospital of Pittsburgh's Pediatric ICU when a CPOE system was introduced [8]. Frequent alerts and warnings may also interrupt workflow. The adaptation rate of CPOE is slow. It may be partly due to physicians' doubt about the value of CPOE and clinical decision support.

2.3.6 Clinical Documentation

A clinical document contains the information related to the care and services provided to the patient. It increases the value of EHR by allowing electronic capture of clinical reports, patient assessments, and progress reports. A clinical document may include [9]

- Physician, nurse, and other clinician notes
- Relevant dates and times associated with the document
- The performers of the care described
- Flow sheets (vital signs, input and output, and problems lists)
- Perioperative notes
- Discharge summaries
- Transcription document management
- Medical records abstracts
- Advance directives or living wills
- Durable powers or attorney for healthcare decisions
- Consents (procedural)
- Medical record/chart tracking
- Release of information (including authorizations)
- Staff credentialing/staff qualification and appointments documentations
- Chart deficiency tracking
- Utilization management
- The intended recipient of the information and the time the document was written
- The sources of information contained within the document

Clinical documents are important because documentation is critical for patient care, serves as a legal document, quality reviews, and validates the patient care provided. Well-documented medical records reduce the re-work of claims processing, compliance with CMS (Centers for Medicare and Medicaid Services), Tricare and other payer's regulations and guidelines, and finally impacts coding, billing, and reimbursement. A clinical document is intended for better communication with the providers. It helps physicians to demonstrate accountability and may ensure quality care provided to the patient. A clinical document needs to be patient centered, accurate, complete, concise, and timely to serve these purposes.

The clinical document architecture (CDA) [10] is an XML-based electronic standard developed by the Health Level 7 International (HL7) to define the structure. It can be both read by human eyes and processed by automatic software.

2.4 Coding Systems

Standards play an important role in enhancing the interoperability of health information systems and the purposeful use of EHR systems. Collecting and storing information following standard coding systems provide better and accurate analysis of the data, seamless exchange of information, improved workflow, and reduced ambiguity. A complete healthcare system is complex and requires various EHR products. Different vendors have implemented standards in their own way. This practice has resulted in a significant variation in the coding practices and implemented methods for which systems cannot interoperate. To create an interoperable EHR, standardization is critical in the following four major areas:

- Applications interaction with the users
- System communication with each other
- Information processing and management
- Consumer device integration with other systems and application

Interoperability between the different EHR systems is a crucial requirement in the "meaningful use of certified EHR technology" to receive incentives. That is why conforming to a standard coding system is very important. In a practical EHR, we need standards for

- Clinical vocabularies
- Healthcare message exchanges
- EHR ontologies

There are three organizations mainly responsible for developing the related standards: Health Level Seven (HL7), Comité Europeen de Normalisation-Technical Committee (CEN-TC), and the American Society of Testing and Materials (ASTM). HL7 develops healthcare-related standards that are widely used in North America. CEN-TC is a prominent standard developing organization working in 19 member states in Europe. Both HL7 and CEN-TC collaborate with ASTM. Along with the standards developed by these organizations, EHR systems must comply with the Health Insurance Portability and Accountability (HIPAA) Act [11] to conserve the security and privacy of patient information.

2.4.1 International Classification of Diseases (ICD)

ICD stands for International Classification of Diseases, which is the United Nations-sponsored World Health Organization's (WHO) official coding standard for diseases, diagnoses, health management, and clinical purposes [12]. It first appeared as the International List of Causes of Death in 1893, adopted by the International Statistical Institute. Since then it has been revised according to advancements in medical science and healthcare. Since the creation of WHO in 1948, WHO has maintained ICD. WHO published ICD-6 in 1949, and it was the first coding system in which morbidity was incorporated [13]. It also included mental disorders for the first time. The U.S. Public Health Services issued International Classification of Diseases, Adapted for Indexing of Hospitals Records and Operation Classification (ICDA) in 1959. It was revised regularly and used to classify diseases and mortality until WHO published the ninth revision of ICD.

The 1967 WHO Nomenclature Regulations specified that the member nations should use the most recent ICD version for mortality and morbidity statistics. Along with the storage and retrieval of epidemiological and clinical information, it allows for the compilation of morbidity statistics for more than 100 WHO member nations. About 70% of the world's health expenditure in reimbursement and resource allocation is also done using ICD codes [14]. It is used to classify diseases and related problems, and provides a system of codes for a wide variety of diseases, signs, symptoms, abnormal findings, complaints, social circumstances, and external causes of injury or disease. It is the global foundation for providing common language in disease and health-related information and statistics exchange. ICD is comprehensive and organizes information into standard groups that allows for the following [15]:

- Easy storage, retrieval, and analysis of health information for evidence-based decision-making.
- Sharing and comparing health information between hospitals, regions, and countries.
- Data comparison in the same location across different time periods.

2.4.1.1 ICD-9

ICD ninth revision is the most popular coding system published by WHO in 1978. It was designed to promote comparability of classification, collection, processing, and presentation of mortality statistics. Its clinical modification, ICD-9-CM, was published by the U.S. Public Health Services in the following year to meet the statistical needs. The modified version had expanded the number of diagnostic codes and developed a procedure coding system. It has more than 13,000 codes and uses more digits representing the codes compared to ICD-9. It is the system that is used to encode all the diagnoses for healthcare services in the United States. It is maintained by the National Center for Health Statistics (NCHS) and the Center for Medicare and Medicaid Services (CMS). Both the departments are part of the federal department of Health and Human Services. The ICD-9-CM code set is organized in three volumes and consists of tabular lists and alphabetical indices.

- Volume 1: Disease and Injuries Tabular List
- Volume 2: Disease and Injuries Alphabetical Index
- Volume 3: Procedures Tabular List and Alphabetic Index

ICD-9-CM is updated every year to keep up-to-date with medical trends and diseases. NCHS has the responsibility to update Volumes 1 and 2, and CMS maintains Volume 3. Concerned parties from both the public and private sectors can propose changes to it. The major updates take effect on October 1 every year and minor updates occur on April 1. It is a statistical tool that converts the diagnoses and procedures into number codes. Its primary applications are

- Reporting and research
- Monitoring the quality of patient care
- Communication and transactions
- Reimbursement
- Administrative uses

2.4.1.2 ICD-10

The tenth version was endorsed by WHO in 1990 during the 43rd World Health Assembly. The first full version of ICD-10 was released in 1994. The first step of implementing ICD-10 was taken by NCHS awarding a contract to the Center for Health Policy Studies (CHPS) to evaluate ICD-10 for morbidity purposes within the United States. A prototype of clinically modified ICD-10 was developed after a thorough evaluation of ICD-10 by a technical advisory panel. After strong recommendations, NCHS proceeded with implementing a revised version of ICD-10-CM. During 1995–1996, further work on the enhancement of ICD-10-CM was done incorporating experiences from ICD-9-CM and through collaborating with many speciality groups like American Association of Dermatology, American Academy of Neurology, American Association of Oral and Maxillofacial Surgeons, American Academy of Orthopedic Surgeons, American Academy of Pediatrics, American College of Obstetricians and Gynecologists, American Urology Institution, and National Association of Children hospitals and other related institutions. In 1999, ICD-10 was implemented in the United States for mortality reporting. Death statistics and data regarding leading causes of death for the years 1999 and 2000 were published using ICD-10 [16]. In October 2002, ICD-10 was published in 42 languages. In June/July 2003, the American Health Information Management Association (AHIMA) and American Hospital Association (AHA) jointly conducted a pilot study to test ICD-10-CM. In their study, they have compared ICD-9-CM and ICD-10-CM and the initial results indicated ICD-10-CM is an improvement over ICD-9-CM; and ICD-10-CM is more applicable in non-hospital environments compared to ICD-9-CM. Canada, Australia, Germany, and others countries have their own revision of ICD-10 by adding country specific codes. The revisions are ICD-10-CA, ICD-10-AM, ICD-10-GM, and so on. The standard for procedure codes ICD-10-PCS was also developed during the same time frame to replace the Volume 3 of ICD-9-CM. The first revision of it was released in 1998.

ICD-9-CM is around thirty years old. Many of its categories are full, and there have been changes in technology. Some of them are also not descriptive enough. A newer coding system is needed, which would enhance reimbursement, better facilitate evaluation of medical processes and outcomes, and be flexible enough to incorporate emerging diagnoses and procedures. For example, in a scenario where a patient had a fractured left wrist and, after a month a fractured right wrist, ICD-9-CM cannot identify left versus right; additional information is required. However, ICD-10-CM can report distinguishing left from right. It can also characterize initial and subsequent encounters. Further, it can describe routine healing, delayed healing, nonunion, or malunion.

The major differences between ICD-10 and ICD-9-CM are [17]

- ICD-10 has 21 categories of diseases; while ICD-9-CM has only 19 categories.
- ICD-10 codes are alphanumeric; while ICD-9-CM codes are only numeric.
- ICD-9-CM diagnoses codes are 3–5 digits in length, while ICD-10-CM codes are 3–7 characters in length.
- Total diagnoses codes in ICD-9-CM is over 14,000; while ICD-10-CM has 68,000.
- ICD-10-PCS procedure codes are 7 characters in length; while ICD-9-CM procedure codes are 3–4 numbers in length.
- ICD-10-PCS total number of codes is approximately 87,000. The number of procedure codes in ICD-9-CM is approximately 4,400.

The Center for Medicare and Medicaid Services (CMS) guidelines mandated a conversion from ICD-9-CM to ICD-10-CM by October 1, 2014 in the United States. Adopting a new coding system will have the following benefits:

- Improve patient care. The increased detail in the coding system will improve the measurement of quality, safety, and efficacy of care, which will ultimately lead to improved patient care.

- Determine the severity of illness and prove medical necessity. ICD-10 codes are more granular and provide option to input the level of sickness along with complexity of disease of a patient in a code-based system.

- Improve research. The better and more accurate organization of code will be able to more precisely classify diseases and injuries, and correlate them with the cause, treatment, and outcome. The collected data will be less ambiguous and such a better-defined structure of the information will make data analysis easier. Information processing will be easier with newer coding system and it will open new opportunities for developing an intelligent prediction system. It will also allow the United States. to conduct comparative research with other countries that are already using ICD-10.

- Lend insight to the setting of health policy. With improved data analytics made possible through ICD-10, policy makers will be able to make informed policy decisions.

- Facilitate improved public health reporting and tracking. The comprehensive coding structure will allow concerned agencies to track public health risks and trends in greater detail.

- Improve clinical, financial, and administrative performance and resource allocation. The quality of data can reveal essential insights. It will allow the administrators to track time and workforce spent for procedures. This will help administrators to allocate resources more efficiently and achieve positive financial and managerial outcomes.

- Increase the accuracy of payment and reduce the risk that claims will be rejected for incorrect coding. Reduced number of claim denials is expected due to higher specificity of ICD-10. It will also create a better electronic record of evidence to receive proper payment from government payers, insurers, hospitals, health systems, and others.

- Make room for new procedures and techniques. The adaptation ability of ICD-9-CM is limited, where all the codes are already utilized and has no more room for new codes. The expanded coding of ICD-10 will be able to accommodate new procedures.

- It will have other facilities like reduced hassle of audits, help preventing and detecting healthcare fraud and abuse.

2.4.1.3 ICD-11

The World Health Organization is currently working on the eleventh revision of ICD. The final publication of ICD-11 is expected by 2017 [18]. The beta draft [19] was made public online for initial comments and feedback in May 2012. This development of ICD-11 revisions is taking place in a web-based platform called iCAT, where all the concerned parties collaborate. For interested groups or people, there are options to give structured input and field testing of revised editions. It will be available in multiple languages and free to download for personal use. In ICD-11, disease entries will have definitions and descriptions of the entry and category in human readable forms. The current version ICD-10 has only the title headings. There are 2,400 codes in ICD-11 that are different in the ICD-10 code set, where 1,100 codes are related to external causes and injury [20].

Although the beta version does not support any social network platforms, the support of websites such as Wikipedia, Facebook, Social Reader, LinkedIn, etc. is in the plan. The structure of definitions and other contents related to diseases and procedures will be defined more accurately. It will be more compatible with EHRs and other technologies.

2.4.2 Current Procedural Terminology (CPT)

Current Procedural Terminology (CPT) is a set of medical codes developed, maintained, and copyrighted by the American Medical Association (AMA). CPT codes are a list of descriptive terms, guidelines, and identifying codes of medical, surgical, and diagnostic services designed to provide uniform communication language among physicians, coders, patients, accreditation organizations, and payers for administrative, financial, and analytic purposes.

It was first created by the AMA in 1966. The first edition contained mainly surgical codes. A significant development took place for the second edition, which was published in 1970. The second edition contained 5 digits instead of 4 digits, and it included lab procedures. In 1983, the Health Claim Financial Administration (HCFA), which is now known as the Center for Medicine and Medicaid Services (CMS), merged its own Common Procedure Coding System (HCPCS) with CPT and mandated CPT would be used for all Medicare billing. Every year the new version is released in October. The Healthcare Common Procedures Coding System (HCPCS, often pronounced as "hick picks") is another set of codes developed by AMA based on CPT. Although the CPT coding system is similar to ICD-9 and ICD-10, it describes the treatment and diagnostic services provided while ICD codes describe the condition or the disease being treated. CPT is used only in inpatient settings.

2.4.3 Systematized Nomenclature of Medicine Clinical Terms (SNOMED-CT)

Systematized Nomenclature of Medicine Clinical Terms (SNOMED-CT) is a comprehensive, computer-processible, multilingual clinical and healthcare terminology, originally created by the College of American Pathologists (CAP). SNOMED was started as Systematic Nomenclature of Pathology (SNOP) in 1965 [21]. It was enhanced further and SNOMED was created in 1974. It had two major revisions in 1979 and 1993. In 1999, SNOMED-CT was created by the merger of SNOMED Reference Terminology (SNOMED-RT) developed by the CAP and Clinical Terms Version 3 (CTV3) developed by the National Health Services of the United Kingdom. This merged version was first released in 2002. SNOMED-RT had a vast coverage of medical specialities with over 12,000 concepts. It was designed for the retrieval and aggregation of healthcare information produced by multiple organizations or professionals. The strong suit of CTV3 was its coverage of terminologies for general practice. With more than 200,000 concepts, it was used to store primary care encounter information and patient-based records [22]. Currently SNOMED has more than 311,000 concepts with logic-based definitions organized into a hierarchy. In July 2003, the National Library of Medicine (NLM) on behalf of the U.S. Department of Health and Human Services signed a contract with CAP to make SNOMED-CT available for users. Since April 2007, it has been owned, maintained, and distributed by a newly formed Denmark-based nonprofit organization named International Health Terminology Standards Development Organization (IHTSDO) [9]. CAP collaborates with IHTSDO and continues to provide support for SNOMED-CT operations. More than 50 countries use SNOMED-CT.

SNOMED-CT is a valuable part of EHR. Its main purpose is to encode medical and healthcare-related concepts and support recording of data. It provides a consistent way to store, index, retrieve, and aggregate clinical data across different sites. It also helps to organize data in a more meaningful way and reduce the variability of the data collection and management process. Its extensive coverage includes clinical findings, symptoms, diagnoses, procedures, body structures, organisms and other etiologies, substances, pharmaceuticals, devices, and specimens [23].

SNOMED-CT has a logical and semantic relationship between concepts. It has a multiaxial hierarchy, which allows different level of details of information. Its extensible design permits the integration of national, local, and vendor specific requirements. It primarily consists of four components.

- Concept Codes: numerical codes to identify terms

- Descriptions: textual descriptions of the concept codes
- Relationships: represents relationships between the concept codes
- Reference Sets: used for grouping concept codes or descriptions. Supports cross mapping to other classification standards.

SNOMED-CT can be mapped to other well-known terminologies like ICD-9-CM, ICD-10, and LOINC. Renowned standards like ANSI, DICOM, HL7, and ISO are supported by it. In a joint project with WHO, it is providing insights for the upcoming ICD-11.

SNOMED-CT has some fundamental differences from ICD. It is mainly a terminology system while ICD is a classification system. SNOMED-CT is designed to encode and represent data for clinical purposes [24]. Information coded with ICD is used for statistical analysis, epidemiology, reimbursement, and resource allocation. SNOMED-CT facilitates the information input into the EHR and provides standardization for primary data purposes while ICD codes enable retrieval for secondary data purposes.

2.4.4 Logical Observation Identifiers Names and Codes (LOINC)

Logical Observation Identifiers Names and Codes (LOINC) is a universal code system for identifying laboratory observations and clinical test results. In response to the demand for electronic clinical data, it was created in 1994 by Regenstrief Institute Inc., an Indianapolis-based nonprofit research organization affiliated with Indiana University. It was originally called Laboratory Observations, Identifiers, Names, and Codes and the development was sponsored by NLM and other government and private agencies. Original sources of information include the following [25]:

- Silver book for International Union of Pure and Applied Chemistry
- International Federation of Clinical Chemistry
- Textbooks of Pathology
- EuCliD (European Clinical Database)
- Expertise and work of the LOINC members

LOINC coding system helps to improve the communication of information. In January 2009, Regenstrief Institute released a Windows operating system-based mapping software called Regenstrief LOINC Mapping Assistant (RELMA) where codes can be searched and local codes can be mapped to a LOINC database. The current version of LOINC is LOINC 2.46 released in December 2013. With more than 600 new users per month, it has 27,000 users from 158 different countries. LOINC vocabulary continues to grow till today.

Each LOINC record represents a single test result. A record consists of six fields [26].

- Component: what is measured and evaluated (e.g., glucose, hemoglobin)
- Kind of property: characteristics of the component that is measured (e.g., mass, length, concentration, volume, time stamp, etc.)
- Time: observation period of the measurement
- System: the specimen or the substance, in context of which the measurement was done (e.g., blood, urine)
- Scale: the measurement scale (e.g., quantitative, nominal, ordinal, or narrative)

- Method (optional): the procedure performed for measurement

Certain parameters and descriptors related to the test are explicitly excluded in LOINC from observation name. They are made as fields of test/observation report message [25]. These fields are

- The instrument used for testing
- Fine details of the sample or the site of collection
- The priority of the test
- Who verified the result
- Size of the sample
- Place of testing

LONIC's overall organization is divided into four categories: laboratory, clinical, attachments, and surveys. The laboratory component is further divided into subcategories such as chemistry, hematology, serology, microbiology (includes parasitology and virology), and toxicology. The clinical attributes are vital signs, hemodynamics, intake/output, EKG, obstetric ultrasound, cardiac echo, urologic imaging, gastroendoscopic procedures, pulmonary ventilator management, and other clinical observations [25]. It also contains information about nursing diagnoses and nursing interventions.

2.4.5 RxNorm

RxNorm is a drug vocabulary maintained and distributed by the National Library of Medicine [27]. It assigns standard names to the clinical drugs and drug delivery devices available in the United States. It is used as a basis for the capture and presentation of drug-related information in EHRs. In 2001, NLM started to develop RxNorm for modeling clinical drugs in the Unified Medical Language System (UMLS) in consultation with the HL7 vocabulary technical committee and the Veterans Administration [28]. It was developed to standardize the medication terminology that would reduce the missed synonymy in clinical drugs [29]. Additional goals were to facilitate electronic capture of related data, improve interoperability by supporting information exchange across platforms and systems, develop clinical decision support, and provide opportunity for research.

RxNorm follows a standard for naming drugs. The normalized name of a drug include the following components [28]:

- IN: Ingredient of the drug.
- DF: Dose form of the drug.
- SCDC: Semantic clinical drug component. It represents the ingredients and strength.
- SCDF: Semantic clinical drug form. It represents the ingredient and dose form.
- SCD: Semantic clinical drug. It represents the ingredient, strength, and dose form.
- BN: Brand name. This is the formal name for a group of drugs containing a specific active ingredient.
- SDBC: Semantic branded drug component. It represents the branded ingredient and strength.
- SBDF: Semantic branded drug form. It represents the branded ingredient and dose form.
- SDB: Semantic branded drug. It represents the branded ingredient, strength, and dose form.

RxNorm organizes drugs by concept. A concept is a set of names with similar meaning at a specific level of abstraction. It can distinguish similar drugs from different providers using concepts. The concepts and relationships between each other form a semantic network.

2.4.6 International Classification of Functioning, Disability, and Health (ICF)

The International Classification of Functioning, Disability, and Health, commonly known as ICF, is a classification of health-related components of function and disability. ICF concentrates on the functionality and body structure of people with a given health condition or disability rather than diagnosis or diseases. It does not account for the cause of disability. It is a unified and standard framework first developed by the World Health Organization (WHO) in 1980 [30]; initially it was known as International Classification of Impairments, Disabilities, and Handicaps (ICIDH). After years of coordinated revision, in May 2001, the 191 member states of WHO agreed to adopt ICF as the standard coding method of functioning and disability. In June 2008, the American Physical Therapy Association (APTA) joined WHO for endorsing ICF. ICF is the only method of its kind. It has been developed and tested for applicability in more than 40 countries.

Body functions and disability can be viewed as interactions between health condition and personal and environmental factors. ICF has mainly two parts: Functioning and disability, and Contextual factors. It can be categorized into further subparts. The components of ICF are listed below [31]:

- Functioning and disability
  - Body functions
    - Mental functions
    - Sensory functions and pain
    - Voice and speech functions
    - Functions of the cardiovascular, hematological, immunological, and respiratory systems
    - Genitourinary and reproductive functions
    - Neuromusculoskeletal and movement-related functions
    - Functions of the skin and related structures
  - Body structures
    - Structure of the nervous system
    - The eye, ear, and related structures
    - Structures involved in voice and speech
    - Structures related to cardiovascular, immunological, and respiratory systems
    - Structures related to digestive, metabolic, and endocrine systems
    - Structures related to genitourinary and reproductive systems
    - Structures related to movement
    - Skin and related structures
  - Activities and participation
    - Learning and applying knowledge
    - General tasks and demands
    - Communication
    - Self-care
    - Domestic life

    * Interpersonal interactions and relationships
    * Major life areas
    * Community, social, and civic life

- Contextual factors
  - Environmental factors
    * Products of technology
    * Natural environment and human-made changes to the environment
    * Support and relationships
    * Attitudes
    * Service, systems, and policies
  - Personal factors
    * Gender
    * Age
    * Coping styles
    * Social background
    * Education
    * Profession
    * Past and current experience
    * Overall behavior pattern
    * Character and other factors

ICF complements WHO's classification of disease scheme, ICD-10. ICD contains diagnosis and health condition-related information, but not functional status. Together they constitute the WHO Family of International Classifications (WHO-FIC) shown in Figure 2.2.

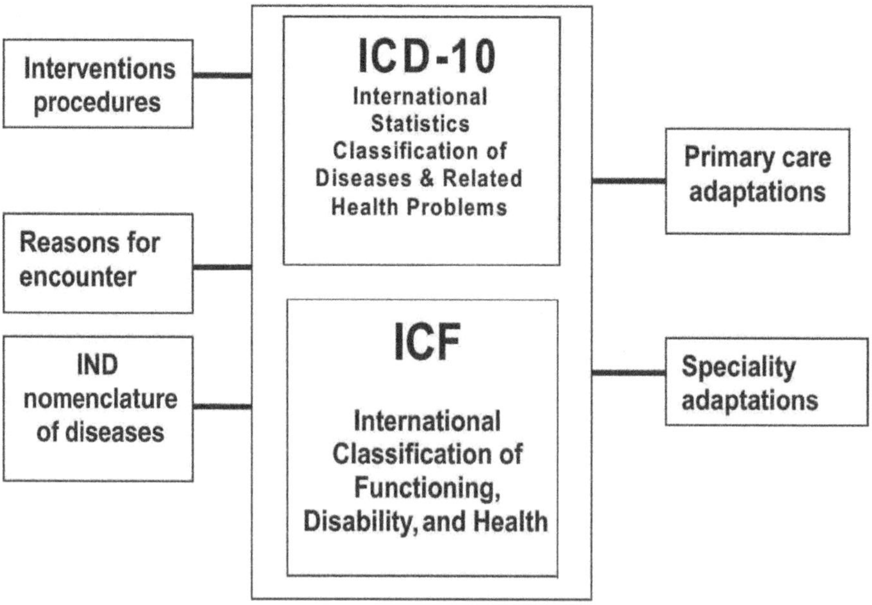

FIGURE 2.2: WHO Family of International Classifications taken from [32].

Diagnosis is used to define cause and prognosis of diseases, but by itself it does not predict service needs, length of hospitalization, or level of care of functional outcomes. Nor can it accurately provide support for disability. ICF allows incorporating all aspects of a person's life. The current ICF creates a more understandable and comprehensive profile of health forming of a person instead of focusing on a health condition [33]. It is used as a clinical, statistical, research, social policy, and educational tool. A common misconception about ICF is that it deals with only the disabled people. However, ICF has some limitations regarding the ability to classify the functional characteristics of developing children [34].

2.4.7 Diagnosis-Related Groups (DRG)

Diagnosis-Related Groups (DRG) are a patient classification scheme that group related patients and relate these groups with the costs incurred by the hospital. DRGs divide diagnosis and illness into 467 categories identified in ICD-9-CM [35]. The 467th group is "ungroupable." The classification is based on a patient's principal diagnosis, ICD diagnoses, gender, age, sex, treatment procedure, discharge status, and the presence of complications or comorbidities. The goals of developing DRGs were to reduce healthcare cost, and improve quality of care and efficiency of the hospitals. DRGs are by far the most important cost control and quality improvement tool developed [36].

It was first created at Yale University with the support from the Health Care Financing Administration, now known as the Center for Medicine and Medicaid Service (CMS). In 1980, it was first implemented in a small number of hospitals in New Jersey [37]. It is used to define the reimbursement amount of hospitals from Medicare. Medicare pays hospitals per patient and efficient hospitals receive better incentives. DRGs help to decide the efficiency of the hospital.

2.4.8 Unified Medical Language System (UMLS)

The Unified Medical Language System (UMLS) is a collection of comprehensive biomedical concepts and ontologies. It was developed by the U.S. National Library of Medicine (NLM) in 1986. It provides the development of computer-based systems that can behave as through they understand the biomedical and health concepts [38]. It is intended to be mainly used by medical informatics professionals. NLM maintains and distributes UMLS knowledge sources (database) and related software tools for developers to build enhanced electronic information system that can create process, retrieve, integrate, and/or aggregate health and biomedical-related information. The knowledge sources of UMLS are as follows [39]:

- Metathesaurus
  - Source Vocabularies
  - Concepts
- Relationships, Attributes
  - Semantic Network
  - Semantic Types (categories)
  - Semantic Relationships
- Lexical Resources
  - SPECIALIST Lexicon
  - Lexical Tools

Metathesaurus is a very large, multipurpose, and multilingual vocabulary database. It contains health and biomedical-related concepts of their various names and the relationships among them. It has 126 vocabularies in 17 languages [27]. It clusters similar terms into a concept. The semantic network provides consistent categorization of concepts defined in Metathesaurus. The network contains information regarding basic semantic types/categories that may be assigned to concepts and relationships between semantic types. In the semantic network, the semantic types are nodes and the relationships are links between them. In the current version of semantic network, there are 135 semantic types and 54 relationships [38]. The SPECIALIST Lexicon provides the lexical information needed for the SPECIALIST natural language processing tool.

2.4.9 Digital Imaging and Communications in Medicine (DICOM)

The Digital Imaging and Communications in Medicine (DICOM) is a medical imaging standard. It determines the data exchange protocol, digital image format, and file structure for biomedical images and related information [40]. DICOM was developed by the American College of Radiology (ACR) and National Electric Manufacturers Association (NEMA). The first version ACR/NEMA 300 was released in 1985. DICOM is generally used in the following application areas [40]

- Network image management
- Network image interpretation management
- Network print management
- Imaging procedure management
- Offline storage media management

DICOM allows the integration of scanners, servers, workstations, printers, and network hardware into a Picture Archiving and Communication Systems (PACS). It has been extensively used by the hospitals and other organizations. It provides a widely accepted foundation for medical imaging standards. It promotes interoperability between radiology systems.

2.5 Benefits of EHR

EHRs are transformational tools. The scope of paper-based systems is severely limited. We need EHRs to improve the quality of patient care and increase productivity and efficiency. In terms of the overall management and costs, EHRs are a better choice. They also help in complying with government regulations and other legal issues. The benefits of EHRs are described in this section.

2.5.1 Enhanced Revenue

An EHR system can capture the charges and bills for clinical services provided, laboratory tests, and medications more accurately. Utilization of electronic systems decrease billing errors [41]. They also provide a better documentation opportunity for these services that can be used to resolve financial disputes. Better management of information yield more accurate evaluation and increase reimbursements. According to experts, due to inaccurate coding systems, 3%–15% of a healthcare provider's total revenue is lost [42]. An EHR system can be programmed or configured to generate alerts for both patients and doctors when a healthcare service is due. This can aid better management of collecting revenue. It can be used to garner more revenues by incorporating services like telemedicine, e-visits, virtual office visits, etc. *It is true that all kinds of services are not possible over the Internet or telephone network, but not all diseases will require extensive diagnosis and laboratory testing.* Diseases commonly treated through telemedicine include acne, allergies, cold and flu, constipation, diabetes, fever, gout, headache, joint aches and pains, nausea and vomiting, pink eye, rashes, sinus infection, sore throat, sunburn and urinary tract infections, anxiety and depression, etc.

2.5.2 Averted Costs

After adopting electronic systems, some costs associated with the previous way of operating a business are eliminated. The Center for Information Technology leadership suggested that the use of EHRs will save a total of $44 billion each year [43]. Adopting EHR has the following averted costs [44].

- **Reduced paper and supply cost:** To maintain paper-based health records an organization will require a lot of paper, printing materials, and other supplies. Adopting EHR will reduce these costs. After adopting EHRs, one organization estimated a reduction of 90% of paper usage within a few months [45].

- **Improved utilization of tests:** In electronic systems, test results are better organized. A healthcare staff no longer needs to carry the reports from one place to another. Identifying redundancy or unnecessary tests is easier. This can reduce the loss of information and ensure improved utilization of tests. A study by Wang et al. [41] reports better utilization of radiology tests after adopting EHRs.

- **Reduced transcription costs:** An EHR can reduce transcription costs for manual administrative processes [46, 47]. It utilizes structured flow sheets, clinical templates, and point-of-care documentation. In a typical outpatient setting, physicians generate about 40 lines of transcription per encounter. For a group of three practicing physicians, treating 12,000 patients annually at the cost of $0.11 for each transcription line results in over $50,000 per year [46]. A study of fourteen solo or small-group primary care practices in twelve U.S. states reports the median transcription cost saving to be $10,800, where a minimum saving was $8,500 and a maximum was $12,000 for the year 2004–2005 [47]. Other related research work also describes saving $1,000–$3,000 per physician, per month [48].

- **Improved productivity:** EHR helps to improve workflows by utilizing resources more efficiently and reducing redundancies. As a result, the overall productivity of individuals increases.

- **Better availability of information and elimination of chart:** In EHR, all the charts are in digital format. It eliminates the need to pull, route, and re-file paper charts [46]. A significant amount of effort is spent on creating, filing, searching, and transporting paper charts [49]. A study estimated that the elimination of paper charts can save $5 per chart pull [41]. It is also comparatively easier to manage digital charts.

- **Improved clinician satisfaction:** Electronic technology can save time by reducing the paperwork burden, which can create additional time for patient encounters and delivery of care [3]. A study reports the use of EHR has reduced the physician's office visit time by 13% and a nurse's pre-exam interview time by 1 minute [50]. This can improve satisfaction for professionals, which can indirectly enhance revenue.

2.5.3 Additional Benefits

EHR offers many additional benefits that are discussed in more detail below.

- **Improved accuracy of diagnosis and care:** EHR provides comprehensive and accurate patient information to physicians that can help to quickly and systematically identify the correct problem to treat. EHRs do not just contain the patient information; they have the capability to perform computation and make suggestions. They can also present comparative results of the standard measurements. A U.S. national survey of doctors demonstrates the following [51]:

  - 94% of the providers report EHR makes records readily available at the point of care.
  - 88% report that EHR produces clinical benefits for their practice.
  - 75% report that EHR allowed them to deliver better patient care.

  The gathered information can guide a physician in the emergency department to take prudent and safer actions. Such services are unimaginable with paper-based systems. Diagnostic errors are difficult to detect and can be fatal to a patient. A new study suggests that EHR can help to identify potential diagnostic errors in primary care by using certain types of queries (triggers) [52].

- **Improved quality and convenience of care:** EHRs have the potential to improve the quality of care by embedding options such as Clinical Decision Support (CDS), clinical alerts, reminders, etc. Research suggests that EHRs are linked to better infection control [53], improved prescribing practices [12], and improved disease management [42] in hospitals. In such applications, convenience is also an important measure. EHRs greatly reduce the need for patients to fill out similar (or even sometimes the same) forms at each visit. Patients can have their e-prescriptions ready even before they leave the facility and can be electronically sent to a pharmacy. Physicians and staff can process claims insurance immediately. Following are the results of a study on the effects of e-prescribing reports [54].

  - 92% patients were happy with their doctor using e-prescribing.
  - 90% reported rarely or only occasionally having prescriptions not ready after going to the pharmacy.
  - 76% reported e-prescribing made obtaining medications easier.
  - 63% reported fewer medication errors.

- **Improved patient safety:** Just like improving the quality of care, clinical decision support systems (CDSS) and computerized physician order entry (CPOE) have the potential to improve patient safety. Medication errors are common medical mistakes and in the United States it is responsible for the death of a person every day on average as well as injuring more than a million annually [55]. Research shows that utilization of CPOE can reduce medication errors [56, 57]. Medication errors can occur at any stage of the medication administration process from a physician ordering the drug, followed by the dispensing of the drug by the pharmacist, and finally the actual administration of the drug by the nurse. CPOE is a technology that allows physicians to act on a computerized system that introduces structure and control. Along with patient information, EHR holds the medication records for a patient. Whenever a new medication is prescribed, it can check for potential conflicts and allergies related to the particular medication and alert the physician. The system also can provide the chemical entities present in the drug and cross-reference allergies, interactions, and other possible problems related to the specific drug. Introducing technologies such as Barcode Medication Administration can make the system even more accurate. The Institute of Medicine (IOM) recommends CPOE and CDS as main information technology mechanisms for increasing patient safety in the future [58].

- **Improved patient education and participation:** In an EHR system, certain features can provide simplified patient education [42]. EHRs can be used by the provider as a tool to illustrate procedures and explain a patient's conditions. It can increase a patient's participation by offering follow-up information, self-care instructions, reminders for other follow-up care, and links to necessary resources. Information technology affects every part of our life. In this digital era, patients may feel more comfortable with an electronic system.

- **Improved coordination of care:** EHRs are considered essential elements of care coordination. The National Quality Forum defines care coordination as the following [59]: "Care coordination is a function that helps ensure that the patient's needs and preferences for health services and information sharing across people, functions, and sites are met over time. Coordination maximizes the value of services delivered to patients by facilitating beneficial, efficient, safe and high-quality patient experiences and improved healthcare outcomes." For a patient with multiple morbidities, a physician is responsible for providing primary care services and coordinating the actions of multiple subspecialists [60]. According to a Gallup poll [61], it is a common scenario for older patients to have multiple doctors: no physician 3%, one physician 16%, two physicians 26%, three physicians 23%, four physicians 15%, five physicians 6%, and six or more physicians 11%. EHRs allow all clinicians to document services provided and access up-to-date information about their patient. It streamlines the transition process and knowledge sharing between different care settings. This facilitates an improved level of communication and coordination [62]. Research suggests that the clinicians having 6+ months use of EHRs reported better accessing and completeness of information than clinicians without EHRs. Clinicians having EHRs have also reported to be in agreement on treatment goals with other involved clinicians [63].

- **Improved legal and regulatory compliance:** As organizations develop their systems, it is important to understand and comply with many federal, state, accreditation, and other regulatory requirements. A health record is the most important legal and business record for a healthcare organization. The use of an EHR system will provide more security and confidentiality of a patient's information and thus, comply with regulations like HIPAA, Consumer Credit Act, etc. Moreover, the Center for Medicare and Medicaid Services (CMS) has financial incentive programs for hospitals regarding the meaningful use of health information technology. To receive the financial reimbursement, professionals have to meet a certain criteria and can get up to $44,000 through Medicare EHR Incentive Program and up to $63,750 through the Medicaid EHR Incentive Program [64]. Adaptation of certified EHR can help providers get reimbursed.

- **Improved ability to conduct research and surveillance:** In conjunction with the direct use of EHR in primary patient care, there is an increasing recognition that secondary use of EHR data can provide significant insights [65]. Using quantitative analysis of functional values, it has the potential to identify abnormalities and predict phenotypes. Pakhomov et al. demonstrated the use of text processing and NLP to identify heart failure patients [66]. EHR data can be used to predict survival time of patients [67]. Data from different EHRs can be integrated into a larger database and geo-location specific surveillance is also possible.

- **Improved aggregation of data and interoperability:** Standards play a crucial role in data aggregation and interoperability between different systems. EHRs maintain standard procedure and follow defined coding system while collecting data. This accommodates easier aggregation of data and greater interoperability, which offer the following benefits [68].
  - Manage increasingly complex clinical care
  - Connect multiple locations of care delivery

- Support team-based care
- Deliver evidence-based care
- Reduce errors, duplications, and delay
- Support ubiquitous care
- Empower and involve citizens
- Enable the move to the Personal Health Paradigm
- Underpin population health and research
- Protect patient privacy

We need high-quality aggregated data from multiple sources in order to make evidence-based decisions. The level of achievable interoperability using EHRs is unthinkable from paper-based systems. The American Medical Association recognizes that enhanced interoperability of EHRs will further help to attain the nation's goal of a high-performing healthcare system.

- **Improved business relationships:** A healthcare provider organization equipped a with superior EHR system can be in a better bargaining position with insurers and payers compared with less equipped ones. The next generation of business professionals will expect and demand a state-of-the-art information healthcare technology system.

- **Improved reliability:** Data is more reliable in a digital format. Due to the reduction of storage costs, having multiple copies of data is possible.

2.6 Barriers to Adopting EHR

Despite of having great potential of EHRs in medical practice, the adoption rate is quite slow and faces a range of various obstacles. Many other developed countries are doing far better than the United States. Four nations (United Kingdom, the Netherlands, Australia, and New Zealand) have almost universal use (each $\sim$90%) of EHRs among the general practitioners. In contrast, the United States and Canada have only around 10–30% of the ambulatory care physicians using EHRs [69]. Health informatics has been a high priority in other developed nations, while until recently, the degree of involvement and investment by the U.S. government in EHRs has not been significant. Major barriers to adopting EHRs are discussed below.

- **Financial barriers:** Although there are studies that demonstrate financial savings after adopting EHRs, the reality is that the EHR systems are expensive. Several surveys report that the monetary aspect is one of the major barriers of adopting EHRs [70, 71, 72, 73, 74, 75, 76]. There are mainly two types of financial costs, start-up and ongoing. A 2005 study suggests that the average initial cost of setting up an EHR is \$44,000 (ranging from a minimum of \$14,000 to a maximum of \$63,000) and ongoing costs average about \$8,500 per provider per year [47]. Major start-up costs include purchasing hardware and software. In addition, a significant amount of money is also required for system administration, control, maintenance, and support. Long-term costs include monitoring, modifying, and upgrading the system as well as storage and maintenance of health records. Besides, after the substantial amount of investment, physicians are worried that it could take up to several years for the return on the investment.

An EHR is not the only electronic system that exists in any healthcare provider like practice management. There might be other old systems that also need integration into the new system. It is important that an EHR system is integrated into other systems, and this integration can sometimes be very expensive. Surveys show that due to the high financial investment required, EHR adaptation was far higher in large physician practices and hospitals [77].

- **Physician's resistance:** To adopt EHRs, physicians have to be shown that new technology can return financial profits, saves time, and is good for their patients' well-being. Although research-based evidence is available, it is difficult to provide concrete proof of those benefits. As given in a report by Kemper et al. [76], 58% of physicians are without any doubt that EHR can improve patient care or clinical outcomes. Finally, adopting EHRs in a medical practice will significantly change the work processes that physicians have developed for years.

  Besides, physicians and staffs might have insufficient technical knowledge to deal with EHRs, which leads them to think EHR systems are overly complex. Many physicians complain about poor follow-up services regarding technical issues and a general lack of training and support from EHR system vendors [72]. A study reports that two-thirds of physicians expressed inadequate technical support as a barrier to adopting EHRs [75]. Some physicians are also concerned about the limitation of EHR capabilities. Under certain circumstances or as time passes, the system may no longer be useful [71, 74]. Besides, all physicians do not perform the same operations. EHR systems have to be customizable to best serve each purpose. Surveys suggest that one of the reasons for not adopting EHRs is that the physicians cannot find a system that meets their special requirements [71, 72, 73, 75, 78, 76]. However, an increased effort and support from vendors may play a role in motivating physicians towards adopting EHRs.

- **Loss of productivity:** Adoption of an EHR system is a time-consuming process. It requires a notable amount of time to select, purchase, and implement the system into clinical practice. During this period physicians have to work at a reduced capacity. Also, a significant amount of time has to be spent on learning the system. The improvement will depend on the quality of training, aptitude, etc. The fluent workflow will be disrupted during the transition period, and there will be a temporary loss of productivity [79].

- **Usability issues:** EHR software needs to be user-friendly. The contents of the software must be well-organized so that a user can perform a necessary operation with a minimal number of mouse clicks or keyboard actions. The interface of software workflow has to be intuitive enough. In terms of usability, a comprehensive EHR system may be more complex than expected. It has to support all the functionalities in a provider's setting. There might be a number of modules and submodules, so the user might get lost and not find what he is looking for. This has the potential to hamper clinical productivity as well as to increase user fatigue, error rate, and user dissatisfaction. Usability and intuitiveness in the system do not necessarily correlate to the amount of money spent. The Healthcare Information and Management Systems Society (HIMSS) has an EHR usability task force. A 2009 survey by the task force reported 1,237 usability problems, and the severity of 80% of them was rated "High" or "Medium" [80]. Apart from the workflow usability issue, other related issues are configuration, integration, presentation, data integrity, and performance. The task force defined the following principles to follow for effective usability [81]: simplicity, naturalness, consistency, minimizing cognitive load, efficient interactions, forgiveness and feedback, effective use of language, effective information presentation, and preservation of context.

- **Lack of standards:** Lack of uniform and consistent standards hinders the EHR adoption. Standards play an integral role in enabling interoperability. CMS reimbursement for meaningful use requires EHR systems to demonstrate the ability to exchange information. Many of the currently used systems have utility only for certain specific circumstances. Different vendors have developed systems in different programming languages and database systems. They do not have any defined best practice or design patterns. This makes the data exchange difficult or impossible between the systems [73, 74, 78]. This lack of standardization limits the proliferation of EHRs [82]. While large hospital systems have moved to EHRs, many others are skeptical about the available systems. They fear that the EHR software they buy now might not work with standards adopted by the healthcare industry or mandated by the government later on.

- **Privacy and security concerns:** Health records contain personal, diagnostics, procedures, and other healthcare related sensitive information. Due to the immense importance of this information, an EHR system may be subjected to attack. Some of the medical diagnoses are considered socially stigmatized, like sexually transmitted disease. Some information relates to direct life threats, like allergies. Employers as well as insurance companies may be interested to know more about a patient to make unethical decisions whether to cover a patient and/or his specific diagnosis. It can also influence some of the hiring decisions. EHRs contain information like social security numbers, credit card numbers, telephone numbers, home addresses, etc., which makes EHRs attractive target for attackers and hackers. A patient might even be motivated to alter his or her medical records to get worker's compensation or to obtain access to narcotics. Therefore, it is important that the privacy and security of EHRs are well maintained. The most used certification for privacy and security is given by the Certification Commission for Healthcare Information Technology (CCHIT). The CCHIT website claims that by mid-2009, 75% of EHR products in the marketplace were certified [83]. In addition to that, the Health Information Technology for Economic and Clinical Health (HITECH) Act introduced a new certification process sponsored by the Office of the National Coordination for Health Information Technology (ONC) in 2009. In January 2010, the ONC released the interim final rule that provides an initial set of standards, implementation specifications, and certification criteria of EHR technology. Its requirement includes database encryption, encryption of transmitted data, authentication, data integrity, audit logs, automatic log off, emergency access, access control, and account of HIPPA release of information [84]. Physicians doubt the level of security of patients' information and records. According to Simon et al. [74], physicians are more concerned about this issue than patients. The inappropriate disclosure of information might lead to legal consequences. Testing the security of EHR products, a group of researchers showed that they were able to exploit a range of common code-level and design-level vulnerabilities of a proprietary and an open source EHR [85]. These common vulnerabilities could not be detected by 2011 security certification test scripts used by CCHIT. EHRs pose new challenges and threats to the privacy and security of patient data. This is a considerable barrier to EHRs proliferation. However, this risk can be mitigated by proper technology, and maintaining certified standards with the software and hardware components.

- **Legal aspects:** Electronic records of medical information should be treated as private and confidential. Various legal and ethical questions obstruct adoption and use of EHRs. The legal system that relies on the paper-era regulations does not offer proper guidance regarding the transition to EHRs. EHRs may increase the physicians' legal responsibility and accountability [86]. With computer-based sophisticated auditing, it is easy to track what individuals have done. The documentation is comprehensive and detailed in EHRs. It can both defend and expose physicians regarding malpractice. According to a *Health Affairs* article, malpractice costs around $55 billion in the United States, which is 2.4% of total healthcare spending [87]. A 2010 research reveals that it was unable to determine whether the use of EHR increases or decreases malpractice liability overall [86]. HIPAA's privacy standards also present reasonable barriers to EHR adaptation.

2.7 Challenges of Using EHR Data

The primary purpose of EHR data is to support healthcare-related functionalities. As a vast amount of data is being collected every day, the secondary use of EHR data is gaining increased attention in research community to discover new knowledge. The main areas of use are clinical and transitional research, public health, and quality measurement and improvement. Using the EHR data, we can conduct both patient-oriented and public health research. EHR data can be used for the early detection of epidemics and spread of diseases, environmental hazards, promotes healthy behaviors, and policy development. The integration of genetic data with EHRs can open even wider horizons. But the data does not automatically provide us the knowledge. The quality and accuracy of the data is an issue to be taken care of. Beyley et al. [88] presents an excellent survey of the challenges posed by the data quality.

- **Incompleteness:** Data incompleteness or missingness is a widespread problem while using EHR data for secondary purpose [88, 89, 90]. Missing data can limit the outcomes to be studied, the number of explanatory factors to be considered, and even the size of population included [88]. Incompleteness can occur due to a lack of collection or lack of documentation [91]. Hersh [92] reports the following reasons for inaccurate reporting by professionals.

  - Unaware of legal requirements
  - Lack of knowledge of which diseases are reportable
  - Do not understand how to report
  - Assumption that someone else will report
  - Intentional failure for privacy reasons

  A pancreatic malignancies study using ICD-9-CM code at the Columbia University Medical Center found that 48% of the patients had corresponding diagnoses or disease documentation missing in their pathology reports [93]. Authors also report a significant amount of key variables missing (see Table 2.1).

  Patients' irregularity of communicating with the health system can also produce incompleteness. Based on the application in hand, type of data and proportion of data that is missing, certain strategies can be followed to reduce the missingness of data [91].

TABLE 2.1: Percentage of Incompleteness of Variables in a Pancreatic Malignancies Study

Variables	**Endocrine**
Necrosis	20%
Number of Mitoses	21%
Lymph Node Metastasis	28%
Perineural/Lymphovascula Invasion	15%
Differentiation	38%
Size	6%
Chronic Pancreatitis	14%
Smoking—Alcohol	27%–29%
History of Other Cancer	35%
Family History of Cancer	39%
Tumor Markers	46%

Source: Taken from Botsis et al. [93].

- **Erroneous Data:** EHR data can be erroneous as well. Data is collected from different service areas, conditions, and geographic locations. Data is collected by busy practitioners and staff. Therefore, the data can be erroneous due to human errors. Faulty equipment can also produce erroneous data. Validation techniques should be used to both identify and correct erroneous data. Both internal and external validation measures can be applied. Internal validation is a way to check the believability of the data, e.g., unrealistic blood pressure, BMI values, etc. Dates can be used to check whether the result generated before a test has taken place. External validation includes comparing the data with other patients or historical values.

- **Uninterpretable Data:** The captured EHR data might be uninterpretable to a certain extent. It is closely related with data incompleteness. It may occur when some part of the data is captured but the rest is missing. For example, if a specific quantitative or qualitative measurement unit is not provided with the result value, it will be difficult to interpret.

- **Inconsistency:** Data inconsistency can heavily affect the analysis or result. Data collection technologies, coding rules, and standards may change over time and across institutions, which may contribute to inconsistency. For multi-institutional studies this issue might be common, especially because different healthcare centers use different vendors for providing apparatus, softwares, and other technologies [88]. A study in Massachusetts of 3.7 million patients found that 31% of patients have visited two or more hospitals in the course of five years [94].

- **Unstructured Text:** In spite of having many defined structures for collecting the data, a large portion of the EHR data contain unstructured text. These data are present in the form of documentation and explanation. It is easy to understand them for humans, but in terms of automatic computational methods, detecting the right information is difficult. Sophisticated data extraction techniques like Natural Language Processing (NLP) are being used to identify information from text notes [95].

- **Selection Bias:** In any hospital, the patient group will mostly be a random collection. It varies depending on the nature of practice, care unit, and the geographical location of the institution. It will not contain the diversity of demography. This is an important challenge to overcome. Therefore, EHR data mining findings will not be generalizable. This problem must be addressed while working with the secondary use of data.

- **Interoperability:** Lack of EHR interoperability is a major impediment towards improved healthcare, innovation, and lowering costs. There are various reasons behind it. EHR software from commercial vendors are proprietary and closed systems. Most software were not built to support communication with a third party and developing new interfaces for that purpose might be a costly undertaking. Absence of standard also contributes to the problem. Many patients are not lenient towards sharing their information. Besides EHR systems must comply with the HIPAA Act [11] to ensure the security and privacy of the data.

  In a recent *JAMIA* (*Journal of the American Medical Informatics Association*) article, the authors have specified 11 specific areas that present barriers to interoperability of C-CDA documents by inspecting 91 C-CDA documents from 21 technologies [96]. In June 2014, the office of the National Coordinator for Health Information Technology (ONC) unveiled a plan for robust healthcare information sharing and aggregation and interoperability increase by 2024 [97]. Its three-year agenda includes "Send, Receive, Find, and Use Health Information to Improve Health Care Quality." Its six-year agenda states "Use Information to Improve Health Care Quality and Lower Cost," and finally, its 10-year agenda proposes to achieve a "Learning Health System." The mentioned building blocks for attaining the goals are the following:

  - Core technical standards and functions
  - Certification to support adoption and optimization of health IT products and services

- Privacy and security protections for health information
- Supportive business, clinical, cultural, and regulatory environments
- Rules of engagement and governance

2.8 Phenotyping Algorithms

Phenotyping algorithms are combinations of multiple types of data and their logical relations to accurately identify cases (disease samples) and controls (non-disease samples) from EHR as illustrated in Figure 2.3 [98]. Based on the structure, EHR data can be broadly divided into two parts, structured and unstructured data. Structured data exists in a name–value pair while unstructured data contains narrative and semi-narrative texts regarding descriptions, explanation, comments, etc. Structured data include billing data, lab values, vital signs, and medication information. Billing and diagnosis-related data are collected using various coding systems like ICD, CPT, and SNOMED-CT. These codes are important parts of the phenotyping process. ICD codes generally have high specificity but low sensitivity [99]. Table 2.2 lists different characteristics of EHR data.

The primary purpose of EHR data is to support healthcare and administrative services. Information is produced as a byproduct of routine clinical services. They are not a suitable format for performing research tasks. They often require further processing to be used for phenotyping algorithms. Within existing EHR systems, querying for a particular diagnosis or lab test across all patients can be a not-trivial task. An EHR can quickly pull the information related to a patient's current medications, and easily find any test results. But combining different data with a temporal relationship might require manual processing of data. From clinical operational settings, data are often extracted and reformatted to make them more convenient and suitable for doing research, typically storing them in relational databases. Researchers have created a number of Enterprise Data Warehouses (EDWs) for EHR data. Examples include Informatics for Integrating Biology and the Bedside (i2b2) [100], the Utah Population Database [101], Vanderbilt's Synthetic Derivative [102], etc. Commercial EHR vendors are also developing research repositories. For example, EPIC users can add the "Clarity" module to their system, which will convert the EHR data into SQL-based database for research purposes.

To build a phenotype algorithm, first we need to select the phenotype of interest, followed by the identification of key clinical elements that define the phenotype. It may contain billing codes, laboratory and test results, radiology reports, medication history, and NLP-extracted information. The gathered information may be combined with a machine learning method. For example, in [103], the authors have applied Support Vector Machine (SVM) to a both naive and well-defined collection of EHR features to identify rheumatoid arthritis cases. A medication record can be used to increase the accuracy of case and control identification of phenotyping algorithms. Patients who are believed to be controls must be having a different medication profile. They may not even have any medications prescribed to them at all. Sufficient dosage of a particular medication serves the confirmation that a person is having the disease of interest. For example, a patient treated with either oral or injectable hypoglycemic agents will be having diabetes. These medications are highly sensitive and specific for treating diabetes.

Studies have shown that CPT codes can accurately predict an occurrence of a given procedure [104]. The standard terminology codes for lab tests are LOINC. On the other hand, clinical notes are in free-text format. To be used for phenotyping algorithms, it has to undergo subsequent text processing. Certain procedures and test results may also exist in a combination of structured and unstructured form. For example, an electrocardiogram report typically contains structured interval

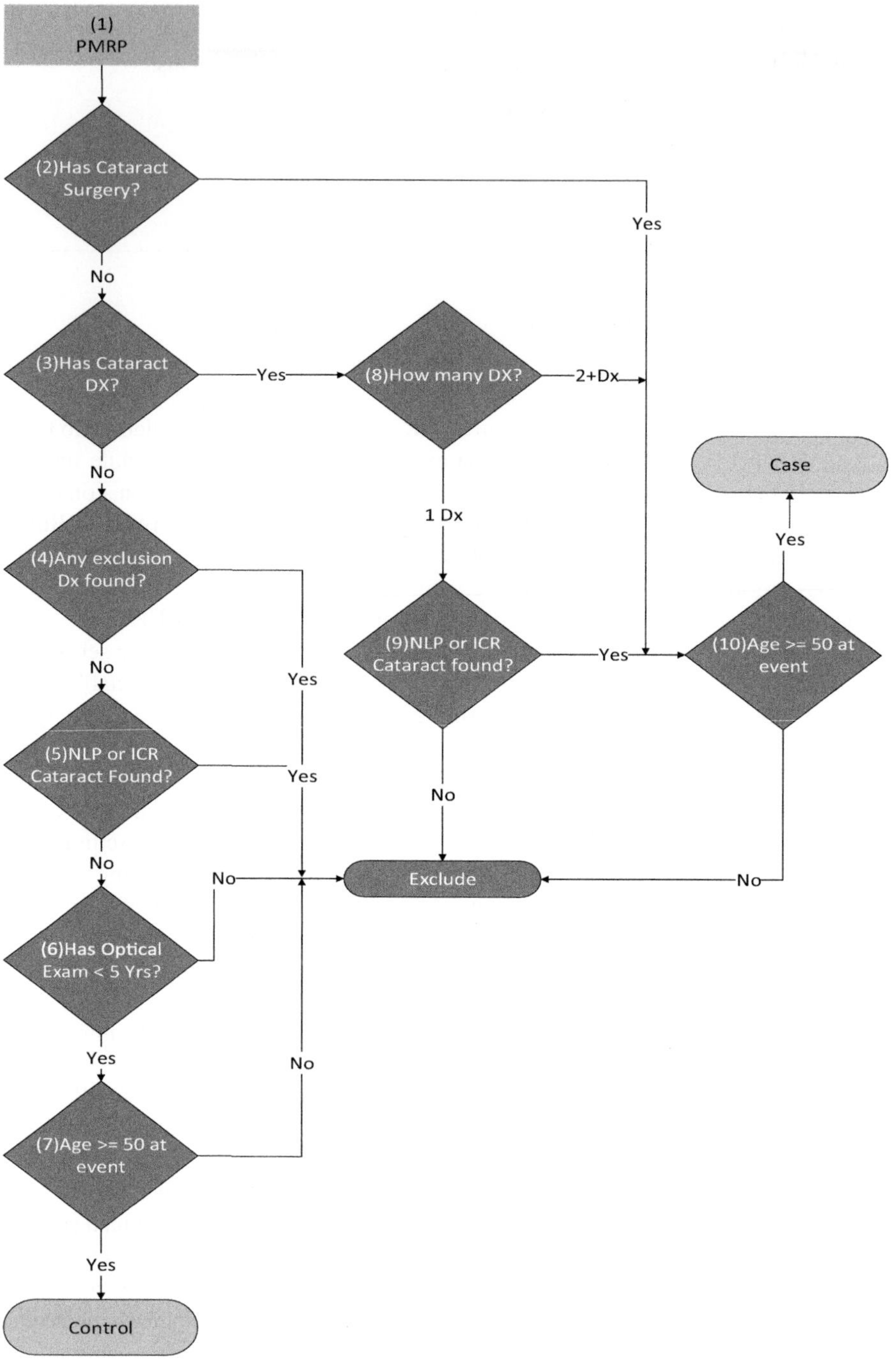

FIGURE 2.3: Flowchart for cataracts phenotyping algorithm taken from [98].

durations, heart rates, and overall categorization, along with a narrative text of cardiologist's interpretation of the result [105].

Recently, researchers have been linking EHR data with biological databanks (biobanks). The most popular biobanks are the collection of DNA samples. Hospitals and clinics can collect DNA

TABLE 2.2: Characteristics of Different EHR Data

	ICD	**CPT**	**Lab**	**Medication**	**Clinical notes**
Availability	High	High	High	Medium	Medium
Recall	Medium	Poor	Medium	Inpatient: High Outpatient: Variable	Medium
Precision	Medium	High	High	Inpatient: High Outpatient: Variable	Medium/High
Format	Structured	Structured	Mostly	Structured	Structured
Pros	Easy to work with, good approximation of disease status	Easy to work with, high precision	High data validity	High data validity	More details about the doctors' thoughts
Cons	Disease code often used for screening, therefore disease might not be there	Missing data	Data normalization and ranges	Prescribed not necessarily taken	Difficult to process

Source: Taken from Denny [106].

samples from a patient's blood sample that is used in routine tests. The Personalized Medicine Research Population (PMRP) project in Marshfield Clinic has a biobank of 20,000 individuals [107]. Similar DNA biobanks exist at eMERGE Network sites, Northwestern University, Geisinger Health System, Mount Sinai School of Medicine, and at other places. The eMERGE network is funded and organized by the National Human Genome Research Institute (NHGRI) and until today it has created and validated twenty-one EHR-derived phenotyping algorithms (see Table 2.3). Its mission is to develop, disseminate, and apply methods to combine DNA biorepositories and EHR systems for large scale and high throughput genetic research [108]. But the phenotype information extracted from EHRs may be challenging. Validation of phenotypes is important before integration of EHRs into genetic studies. By validating EHR-derived phenotypes from eMERGE network, Newton et al. report the following points [109]:

- Multisite validation improves phenotype algorithm accuracy
- Targets for validation should be carefully considered and defined
- Specifying time frames for review of variables eases validation time and improves accuracy
- Using repeated measures requires defining the relevant time period and specifying the most meaningful value to be studied
- Patient movement in and out of the health plan (transience) can result in incomplete or fragmented data
- The review scope should be defined carefully
- Particular care is required in combining EMR and research data
- Medication data can be assessed using claims, medications dispensed, or medications prescribed
- Algorithm development and validation will work best as an iterative process
- Validation by content experts or structured chart review can provide accurate results

TABLE 2.3: Phenotyping Algorithms Developed by eMERGE Network

Phenotype	**EHR data used to characterize phenotype**	**Institution**
Atrial Fibrillation — Demonstration Project	CPT Codes, ICD 9 Codes, Natural Language Processing	Vanderbilt University
Cardiac Conduction(QRS)	CPT Codes, ICD 9 Codes, Laboratories, Medications, Natural Language Processing	Vanderbilt University
Cataracts	CPT Codes, ICD 9 Codes, Medications, Natural Language Processing	Marshfield Clinic Research Foundation
Clopidogrel Poor Metabolizers	CPT Codes, ICD 9 Codes, Laboratories, Medications, Natural Language Processing	Denny's Group at Vanderbilt, VESPA — Vanderbilt Electronic Systems for Pharmacogenomic Assessment
Crohn's Disease — Demonstration Project	ICD 9 Codes, Medications, Natural Language Processing	Vanderbilt University
Dementia	ICD 9 Codes, Medications	Group Health Cooperative
Diabetic Retionapathy	CPT Codes, ICD 9 Codes, Laboratories, Medications, Natural Language Processing	Marshfield Clinic Research Foundation
Drug Induced Liver Injury	ICD 9 Codes, Laboratories, Medications, Natural Language Processing	Columbia University
Height	ICD 9 Codes, Laboratories, Medications	Northwestern University
High-Density Lipoproteins (HDL)	ICD 9 Codes, Laboratories, Medications, Natural Language Processing	Marshfield Clinic Research Foundation
Hypothyroidism	CPT Codes, ICD 9 Codes, Laboratories, Medications, Natural Language Processing	Vanderbilt University, Group Health Cooperative, Northwestern University
Lipids	ICD 9 Codes, Laboratories, Medications	Northwestern University
Multiple Sclerosis — Demonstration Project	ICD 9 Codes, Medications, Natural Language Processing	Vanderbilt University
Peripheral Arterial Disease	CPT Codes, ICD 9 Codes, Laboratories, Medications, Natural Language Processing	Mayo Clinic
Red Blood Cell Indices	CPT Codes, ICD 9 Codes, Laboratories, Medications, Natural Language Processing	Mayo Clinic
Rheumatoid Arthritis — Demonstration Project	ICD 9 Codes, Medications, Natural Language Processing	Vanderbilt University
Severe Early Childhood Obesity	ICD 9 Codes, Medications, Natural Language Processing, Vital Signs	Cincinnati Children's Hospital Medical Center
Type 2 Diabetes — Demonstration Project	ICD 9 Codes, Laboratories, Medications, Natural Language Processing	Vanderbilt University
Type 2 Diabetes Mellitus	ICD 9 Codes, Laboratories, Medications	Northwestern University
Warfarin dose/response	Laboratories, Natural Language Processing	Vanderbilt University
White Blood Cell Indices	CPT Codes, ICD 9 Codes, Laboratories, Medications	Group Health Cooperative

Source: Taken from [110].

Before the use of a phenotyping algorithm, data has to be normalized to standard representation. Natural Language Processing (NLP) based tools have gained much popularity to extract structured information from free text. Several studies have shown that coded data are not sufficient or accurate to identify disease cohorts [111, 112]. Information from narrative text complements the structured data. There are studies that report NLP-processed notes provide more valuable data sources. For example, Penz et al. reports ICD-9 and CPT codes identified less than 11% cases in detecting adverse events related to central venous catheters, while NLP methods achieved a specificity of 0.80 and sensitivity of 0.72 [113]. Widely used general-purpose NLP tools include MedLEE (Medical Language Extraction and Encoding System) [114], cTAKES (clinical Text Analysis and Knowledge Extraction System) [115], MetaMap [116], and KnowledgeMap [117]. All of them have been successfully applied to phenotyping using EHR data. Task-specific NLP methods are available that aim to extract specific concepts from clinical text.

The DNA sequence of a person can be huge in size (ranging from hundreds of gigabytes to terabytes) in raw format that exceeds the capability for using the current EHR systems. Storing, managing, and transferring a repository of such a large volume of data is difficult. Efficient data compression techniques can be applied to solve this problem. Genome Wide Association Study (GWAS) became the mainstay of genetic analysis over the last decade. In general, GWAS investigates around 500,000 genetic variants (Single Nucleotide Polymorphisms) or more to see the association of variations with observable traits. It compares the SNPs of cases versus controls to find meaningful knowledge. Besides traits, we can also identify SNPs that determine a particular drug response. One individual might react adversely to a particular drug while others might not. The genetic profile of an individual can be used for personalized medicine. One big advantage of genetic data is that the SNPs are the same for that individual and do not change based on a given/suspected disease. The same set of data can be used for different phenotype investigations as well. Researchers are working to integrate genetic information for enhanced clinical decision support. For example, researchers in Vanderbilt University are working on implementing Pharmacogenomic Resource for Enhanced Decisions in Care and Treatment (PREDICT) [118]. St. Jude Children's Research Hospital also has a multiplexed genotyping platform for providing decision support [119].

2.9 Conclusions

Electronic health records are the obvious and inevitable future of patient care in hospitals and medical practices. This chapter discusses several aspects of the EHRs. EHR systems are gaining nationwide popularity in the United States recently due to "Meaningful use legislation and reimbursement [120]. It is being widely installed in hospitals, academic medical centers," and outpatient clinics throughout the nation. Besides healthcare benefits like improved patient care, safety and reduced costs, it creates great opportunity for clinical and translational research. Widespread adoption of EHRs can foster the improvement of quality in healthcare services, safety and efficiency, and most importantly, public health. Having great potential for benefits, successful deployment of EHRs has several challenges to overcome. There are notable limitations of the use of EHR data in research purposes. In the era of technology, the necessary laws lag far behind. While other developed countries have showed widespread adoption, in the United States, the overall adoption is considerably low. Bigger Government initiatives and enhanced standardization today can lead to a brighter healthcare tomorrow.

Acknowledgments

This work was supported in part by the National Science Foundation Grant IIS-1231742.

Bibliography

[1] Eric Jamoom et al. *Physician Adoption of Electronic Health Record Systems: United States, 2011*, volume 98. US Department of Health and Human Services, Centers for Disease Control and Prevention, National Center for Health Statistics, 2012.

[2] Mark A. Musen and Jan Hendrik Bemmel. *Handbook of Medical Informatics*. MIEUR, 1999.

[3] Richard S. Dick and Elaine B. Steen. *The Computer-Based Patient Record: An Essential Technology for Health Care*. National Academics Press, 1991.

[4] http://yosemite.epa.gov/opa/admpress.nsf/8822edaadaba0243852572a000656841/66a4a31db7c1ae178525703d0067d18b!OpenDocument, September, 2003.

[5] George W. Bush. Transforming health care: The president's health information technology plan. Washington, DC, 2004.

[6] http://www.cnbc.com/id/28559492/Text_of_Obama_Speech_on_the_Econom.

[7] http://www.cdc.gov/osels/lspppo/healthcare_news.html.

[8] Hagop S. Mekhjian, Rajee R. Kumar, Lynn Kuehn, Thomas D. Bentley, Phyllis Teater, Andrew Thomas, Beth Payne, and Asif Ahmad. Immediate benefits realized following implementation of physician order entry at an academic medical center. *Journal of the American Medical Informatics Association*, 9(5):529–539, 2002.

[9] Electronic health records overview. National Institutes of Health National Center for Research Resources, MITRE Center for Enterprise Modernization, McLean, Virginia, 2006.

[10] Robert H. Dolin, Liora Alschuler, Sandy Boyer, Calvin Beebe, Fred M. Behlen, Paul V. Biron, and Amnon Shabo Shvo. Hl7 clinical document architecture, release 2. *Journal of the American Medical Informatics Association*, 13(1):30–39, 2006.

[11] Centers for Medicare & Medicaid Services et al. The health insurance portability and accountability act of 1996 (HIPAA). *Online at http://www. cms. hhs. gov/hipaa*, 1996.

[12] http://www.who.int/classifications/icd/en/.

[13] Heinz Katschnig. Are psychiatrists an endangered species? Observations on internal and external challenges to the profession. *World Psychiatry*, 9(1):21–28, 2010.

[14] http://www.who.int/classifications/icd/factsheet/en/index.html.

[15] http://www.ncvhs.hhs.gov/031105a1.htm.

[16] http://wonder.cdc.gov/wonder/help/mcd.html.

[17] Hude Quan, Bing Li, L. Duncan Saunders, Gerry A. Parsons, Carolyn I. Nilsson, Arif Alibhai, and William A. Ghali. Assessing validity of ICD-9-CM and ICD-10 administrative data in recording clinical conditions in a unique dually coded database. *Health Services Research*, 43(4):1424–1441, 2008.

[18] http://www.who.int/classifications/icd/revision/timeline/en/.

[19] World Health Organization et al. ICD-11 beta draft, 2013.

[20] http://www.who.int/classifications/icd/revision/icd11betaknownconcerns.pdf.

[21] Ronald Cornet and Nicolette de Keizer. Forty years of SNOMED: A literature review. *BMC Medical Informatics and Decision Making*, 8(Suppl 1):S2, 2008.

[22] Michael Q. Stearns, Colin Price, Kent A. Spackman, and Amy Y. Wang. SNOMED clinical terms: Overview of the development process and project status. In *Proceedings of the AMIA Symposium*, page 662. American Medical Informatics Association, 2001.

[23] http://www.ihtsdo.org/snomed-ct.

[24] Karen Kostick et al. SNOMED CT integral part of quality EHR documentation. *Journal of AHIMA/American Health Information Management Association*, 83(10):72–75, 2012.

[25] Clem McDonald, S.M. Huff, J. Suico, and Kathy Mercer. Logical observation identifiers names and codes (LOINC R) users' guide. *Indianapolis: Regenstrief Institute*, 2004.

[26] Alex A.T. Bui and Ricky K. Taira (Eds.). *Medical Imaging Informatics*. Springer New York, 2010.

[27] Casey C. Bennett. Utilizing RxNorm to support practical computing applications: Capturing medication history in live electronic health records. *Journal of Biomedical Informatics*, 45(4):634–641, 2012.

[28] Simon Liu, Wei Ma, Robin Moore, Vikraman Ganesan, and Stuart Nelson. RxNorm: Prescription for electronic drug information exchange. *IT Professional*, 7(5):17–23, 2005.

[29] https://www.nlm.nih.gov/research/umls/rxnorm/history.html.

[30] National Center for Health Statistics (US), World Health Organization, et al. *Classification of Diseases, Functioning, and Disability*. US Centers for Disease Control and Prevention.

[31] Alan M. Jette. Toward a common language for function, disability, and health. *Journal of American Physical Therapy Association*, 86(5):726–734, 2006.

[32] World Health Organization and others. Towards a common language for functioning, disability and health: ICF. *World Health Organization*, 2002.

[33] Helena Hemmingsson and Hans Jonsson. An occupational perspective on the concept of participation in the international classification of functioning, disability and healthsome critical remarks. *The American Journal of Occupational Therapy*, 59(5):569–576, 2005.

[34] Rune J. Simeonsson, Anita A. Scarborough, and Kathleen M. Hebbeler. ICF and ICD codes provide a standard language of disability in young children. *Journal of Clinical Epidemiology*, 59(4):365–373, 2006.

[35] http://www.ihtsdo.org/snomed-ct/snomed-ct0/.

[36] Norbert Goldfield. The evolution of diagnosis-related groups (DRGS): From its beginnings in case-mix and resource use theory, to its implementation for payment and now for its current utilization for quality within and outside the hospital. *Quality Management in Healthcare*, 19(1):3–16, 2010.

[37] W.C. Hsiao, H.M. Sapolsky, D.L. Dunn, and S.L. Weiner. Lessons of the New Jersey DRG payment system. *Health Affairs*, 5(2):32–45, 1986.

[38] Catherine Selden and Betsy L. Humphreys. *Unified Medical Language System (UMLS): January 1986 Through December 1996: 280 Selected Citations*, volume 96. US Dept. of Health and Human Services, Public Health Service, 1997.

[39] Donald A.B. Lindberg and Betsy L. Humphreys. Concepts, issues, and standards. current status of the nlm's umls project: The UMLS knowledge sources: Tools for building better user interfaces. In *Proceedings of the Annual Symposium on Computer Application in Medical Care*, page 121. American Medical Informatics Association, 1990.

[40] W. Dean Bidgood, Steven C. Horii, Fred W. Prior, and Donald E. Van Syckle. Understanding and using DICOM, the data interchange standard for biomedical imaging. *Journal of the American Medical Informatics Association*, 4(3):199–212, 1997.

[41] Samuel J. Wang, Blackford Middleton, Lisa A. Prosser, Christiana G. Bardon, Cynthia D. Spurr, Patricia J. Carchidi, Anne F. Kittler, Robert C. Goldszer, David G. Fairchild, Andrew J. Sussman et al. A cost-benefit analysis of electronic medical records in primary care. *The American Journal of Medicine*, 114(5):397–403, 2003.

[42] Tricia L. Erstad. Analyzing computer-based patient records: A review of literature. *Journal of Healthcare Information Management*, 17(4):51–57, 2003.

[43] Douglas Johnston, Eric Pan, and J. Walker. The value of CPOE in ambulatory settings. *Journal of Healthcare Information Management*, 18(1):5–8, 2004.

[44] Nir Menachemi and Robert G. Brooks. Reviewing the benefits and costs of electronic health records and associated patient safety technologies. *Journal of Medical Systems*, 30(3):159–168, 2006.

[45] T. Ewing and D. Cusick. Knowing what to measure. *Healthcare Financial Management: Journal of the Healthcare Financial Management Association*, 58(6):60–63, 2004.

[46] Abha Agrawal. Return on investment analysis for a computer-based patient record in the outpatient clinic setting. *Journal of the Association for Academic Minority Physicians: The Official Publication of the Association for Academic Minority Physicians*, 13(3):61–65, 2002.

[47] Robert H. Miller, Christopher West, Tiffany Martin Brown, Ida Sim, and Chris Ganchoff. The value of electronic health records in solo or small group practices. *Health Affairs*, 24(5):1127–1137, 2005.

[48] Jeff Mildon and Todd Cohen. Drivers in the electronic medical records market. *Health Management Technology*, 22(5):14, 2001.

[49] Karl F. Schmitt and David A Wofford. Financial analysis projects clear returns from electronic medical records. *Healthcare Financial Management: Journal of the Healthcare Financial Management Association*, 56(1):52–57, 2002.

[50] K. Renner. Electronic medical records in the outpatient setting (Part 1). *Medical Group Management Journal/MGMA*, 43(3):52–54, 1995.

[51] E. Jamoom. National perceptions of EHR adoption: Barriers, impacts, and federal policies. *National Conference on Health Statistics*, 2012.

[52] Hardeep Singh, Traber Davis Giardina, Samuel N. Forjuoh, Michael D. Reis, Steven Kosmach, Myrna M. Khan, and Eric J. Thomas. Electronic health record-based surveillance of diagnostic errors in primary care. *BMJ Quality & Safety*, 21(2):93–100, 2012.

[53] J. Michael Fitzmaurice, Karen Adams, and John M. Eisenberg. Three decades of research on computer applications in health care medical informatics support at the agency for healthcare research and quality. *Journal of the American Medical Informatics Association*, 9(2):144–160, 2002.

[54] R. Lamar Duffy, Shih Shen Angela Yiu, Ehab Molokhia, Robert Walker, and R. Allen Perkins. Effects of electronic prescribing on the clinical practice of a family medicine residency. *Family Medicine*, 42(5):358–63, 2010.

[55] Linda T. Kohn, Janet M. Corrigan, Molla S. Donaldson et al. *To Err is Human: Building a Safer Health System*, volume 627. National Academies Press, 2000.

[56] David W. Bates, Lucian L. Leape, David J. Cullen, Nan Laird, Laura A. Petersen, Jonathan M. Teich, Elizabeth Burdick, Mairead Hickey, Sharon Kleefield, Brian Shea et al. Effect of computerized physician order entry and a team intervention on prevention of serious medication errors. *JAMA*, 280(15):1311–1316, 1998.

[57] Ross Koppel, Joshua P. Metlay, Abigail Cohen, Brian Abaluck, A. Russell Localio, Stephen E. Kimmel, and Brian L. Strom. Role of computerized physician order entry systems in facilitating medication errors. *JAMA*, 293(10):1197–1203, 2005.

[58] Institute of Medicine (US). Committee on Quality of Health Care in America. *Crossing the Quality Chasm: A New Health System for the 21st Century*. National Academies Press, 2001.

[59] Elizabeth E Stewart, Paul A. Nutting, Benjamin F. Crabtree, Kurt C. Stange, William L. Miller, and Carlos Roberto Jaén. Implementing the patient-centered medical home: observation and description of the national demonstration project. *The Annals of Family Medicine*, 8(Suppl 1):S21–S32, 2010.

[60] Christopher J. Stille, Anthony Jerant, Douglas Bell, David Meltzer, and Joann G. Elmore. Coordinating care across diseases, settings, and clinicians: A key role for the generalist in practice. *Annals of Internal Medicine*, 142(8):700–708, 2005.

[61] Gallup serious chronic illness survey 2002. `http://poll.gallup.com/content/default.aspx?ci=6325&pg=1`.

[62] Lynda C. Burton, Gerard F. Anderson, and Irvin W. Kues. Using electronic health records to help coordinate care. *Milbank Quarterly*, 82(3):457–481, 2004.

[63] Ilana Graetz, Mary Reed, Thomas Rundall, Jim Bellows, Richard Brand, and John Hsu. Care coordination and electronic health records: Connecting clinicians. In *AMIA Annual Symposium Proceedings*, volume 2009, page 208. American Medical Informatics Association, 2009.

[64] Medicare and medicaid EHR incentive program basics. `http://www.cms.gov/Regulations-and-Guidance/Legislation/EHRIncentivePrograms/Basics.html`.

[65] Charles Safran, Meryl Bloomrosen, W. Edward Hammond, Steven Labkoff, Suzanne Markel-Fox, Paul C. Tang, and Don E. Detmer. Toward a national framework for the secondary use of health data: An American Medical Informatics Association white paper. *Journal of the American Medical Informatics Association*, 14(1):1–9, 2007.

[66] Serguei Pakhomov, James Buntrock, and Patrick Duffy. High throughput modularized NLP system for clinical text. In *Proceedings of the ACL 2005 on Interactive Poster and Demonstration Sessions*, pages 25–28. Association for Computational Linguistics, 2005.

[67] Bhanukiran Vinzamuri and Chandan K. Reddy. Cox regression with correlation based regularization for electronic health records *Proceedings of the 2013 IEEE International Conference on Data Mining*, pages 757–766.

[68] Dipak Kalra and BGME Blobel. Semantic interoperability of ehr systems. *Studies in Health Technology and Informatics*, 127:231, 2007.

[69] Ashish K. Jha, David Doolan, Daniel Grandt, Tim Scott, and David W. Bates. The use of health information technology in seven nations. *International Journal of Medical Informatics*, 77(12):848–854, 2008.

[70] Elizabeth Davidson and Dan Heslinga. Bridging the it adoption gap for small physician practices: An action research study on electronic health records. *Information Systems Management*, 24(1):15–28, 2006.

[71] Catherine M. DesRoches, Eric G. Campbell, Sowmya R. Rao, Karen Donelan, Timothy G. Ferris, Ashish Jha, Rainu Kaushal, Douglas E. Levy, Sara Rosenbaum, Alexandra E. Shields et al. Electronic health records in ambulatory carea national survey of physicians. *New England Journal of Medicine*, 359(1):50–60, 2008.

[72] Ebrahim Randeree. Exploring physician adoption of EMRS: A multi-case analysis. *Journal of Medical Systems*, 31(6):489–496, 2007.

[73] Robert H. Miller and Ida Sim. Physicians' use of electronic medical records: Barriers and solutions. *Health Affairs*, 23(2):116–126, 2004.

[74] Steven R. Simon, Rainu Kaushal, Paul D. Cleary, Chelsea A. Jenter, Lynn A. Volk, E John Orav, Elisabeth Burdick, Eric G. Poon, and David W. Bates. Physicians and electronic health records: A statewide survey. *Archives of Internal Medicine*, 167(5):507–512, 2007.

[75] Glenn A. Loomis, J. Scott Ries, Robert M. Saywell, and Nitesh R. Thakker. If electronic medical records are so great, why aren't family physicians using them? *Journal of Family Practice*, 51(7):636–641, 2002.

[76] Alex R. Kemper, Rebecca L. Uren, and Sarah J. Clark. Adoption of electronic health records in primary care pediatric practices. *Pediatrics*, 118(1):e20–e24, 2006.

[77] 2003 national survey of physicians and quality of care. `http://www.commonwealthfund.org/Surveys/2003/2003-National-Survey-of-Physicians-and-Quality-of-Care.aspx`.

[78] Arun Vishwanath and Susan D. Scamurra. Barriers to the adoption of electronic health records: using concept mapping to develop a comprehensive empirical model. *Health Informatics Journal*, 13(2):119–134, 2007.

[79] Nir Menachemi and Taleah H. Collum. Benefits and drawbacks of electronic health record systems. *Risk Management and Healthcare Policy*, 4:47–55, 2011.

[80] Clinicians and EHR usability. `http://www.himss.org/resourcelibrary/TopicList.aspx?MetaDataID=1721&navItemNumber=17121`.

[81] Jeffery L. Belden, Rebecca Grayson, and Janey Barnes. Defining and testing EMR usability: Principles and proposed methods of EMR usability evaluation and rating. Technical report, Healthcare Information and Management Systems Society (HIMSS), 2009.

[82] Ignacio Valdes, David C. Kibbe, Greg Tolleson, Mark E. Kunik, and Laura A. Petersen. Barriers to proliferation of electronic medical records. *Informatics in Primary Care*, 12(1): 3–9, 2004.

[83] About CCHIT. `https://www.cchit.org/about`.

[84] US Department of Health, Human Services, et al. Health information technology: Initial set of standards, implementation specifications, and certification criteria for electronic health record technology. *Federal Register*, 75(8):13, 2010.

[85] Ben Smith, Andrew Austin, Matt Brown, Jason T. King, Jerrod Lankford, Andrew Meneely, and Laurie Williams. Challenges for protecting the privacy of health information: Required certification can leave common vulnerabilities undetected. In *Proceedings of the Second Annual Workshop on Security and Privacy in Medical and Home-care Systems*, pages 1–12. ACM, 2010.

[86] Sandeep S. Mangalmurti, Lindsey Murtagh, and Michelle M. Mello. Medical malpractice liability in the age of electronic health records. *New England Journal of Medicine*, 363(21):2060–2067, 2010.

[87] Michelle M. Mello et al. National costs of the medical liability system. *Health Affairs*, 29(9):1569–1577, 2010.

[88] K. Bruce Bayley, Tom Belnap, Lucy Savitz, Andrew L. Masica, Nilay Shah, and Neil S. Fleming. Challenges in using electronic health record data for CER: Experience of 4 learning organizations and solutions applied. *Medical Care*, 51:S80–S86, 2013.

[89] Jionglin Wu, Jason Roy, and Walter F. Stewart. Prediction modeling using EHR data: challenges, strategies, and a comparison of machine learning approaches. *Medical Care*, 48(6):S106–S113, 2010.

[90] Chris Paxton, Alexandru Niculescu-Mizil, and Suchi Saria. Developing predictive models using electronic medical records: Challenges and pitfalls. *AMIA Annual Symposium Proceedings Archive*, pages 1109–1115, 2013.

[91] Brian J. Wells, Amy S. Nowacki, Kevin Chagin, and Michael W. Kattan. Strategies for handling missing data in electronic health record derived data. *Strategies*, 1(3):Article 7, 2013.

[92] William Hersh. Secondary Use of Clinical Data from Electronic Health Records. Oregon Health & Science University.

[93] Taxiarchis Botsis, Gunnar Hartvigsen, Fei Chen, and Chunhua Weng. Secondary use of EHR: Data quality issues and informatics opportunities. *AMIA Summits on Translational Science Proceedings*, 2010:1, 2010.

[94] Fabienne C. Bourgeois, Karen L. Olson, and Kenneth D. Mandl. Patients treated at multiple acute health care facilities: Quantifying information fragmentation. *Archives of Internal Medicine*, 170(22):1989–1995, 2010.

[95] Harvey J. Murff, Fern FitzHenry, Michael E. Matheny, Nancy Gentry, Kristen L. Kotter, Kimberly Crimin, Robert S. Dittus, Amy K. Rosen, Peter L. Elkin, Steven H. Brown et al. Automated identification of postoperative complications within an electronic medical record using natural language processing. *JAMA*, 306(8):848–855, 2011.

[96] John D. D'Amore, Joshua C. Mandel, David A. Kreda, Ashley Swain, George A. Koromia, Sumesh Sundareswaran, Liora Alschuler, Robert H. Dolin, Kenneth D. Mandl, Isaac S. Kohane et al. Are meaningful use stage 2 certified EHRS ready for interoperability? Findings from the smart C-CDA collaborative. *Journal of the American Medical Informatics Association*, 21(6):1060–1068, 2014.

[97] `http://www.healthit.gov/sites/default/files/ONC10yearInteroperabilityConceptPaper.pdf`.

[98] `http://www.phekb.org/phenotype/cataracts`.

[99] P. L. Elkin, A. P. Ruggieri, S. H. Brown, B. A. Bauer, D. Wahner-Roedler, S. C. Litin, J Beinborn, K. R. Bailey, and L. Bergstrom. A randomized controlled trial of the accuracy of clinical record retrieval using SNOMED-RT as compared with ICD-9-CM. *American Medical Informatics Association*, 2001.

[100] Shawn N. Murphy, Griffin Weber, Michael Mendis, Vivian Gainer, Henry C. Chueh, Susanne Churchill, and Isaac Kohane. Serving the enterprise and beyond with informatics for integrating biology and the bedside (i2b2). *Journal of the American Medical Informatics Association*, 17(2):124–130, 2010.

[101] John F. Hurdle, Stephen C. Haroldsen, Andrew Hammer, Cindy Spigle, Alison M. Fraser, Geraldine P. Mineau, and Samir J. Courdy. Identifying clinical/translational research cohorts: Ascertainment via querying an integrated multi-source database. *Journal of the American Medical Informatics Association*, 20(1):164–171, 2013.

[102] Dan M. Roden, Jill M. Pulley, Melissa A. Basford, Gordon R. Bernard, Ellen W. Clayton, Jeffrey R. Balser, and Dan R. Masys. Development of a large-scale de-identified DNA biobank to enable personalized medicine. *Clinical Pharmacology & Therapeutics*, 84(3):362–369, 2008.

[103] Robert J. Carroll, Anne E. Eyler, and Joshua C. Denny. Naïve electronic health record phenotype identification for rheumatoid arthritis. In *AMIA Annual Symposium Proceedings*, volume 2011, page 189. American Medical Informatics Association, 2011.

[104] Joshua C. Denny, Josh F. Peterson, Neesha N. Choma, Hua Xu, Randolph A. Miller, Lisa Bastarache, and Neeraja B. Peterson. Extracting timing and status descriptors for colonoscopy testing from electronic medical records. *Journal of the American Medical Informatics Association*, 17(4):383–388, 2010.

[105] Joshua C. Denny, Randolph A. Miller Anderson Spickard III, Jonathan Schildcrout, Dawood Darbar, S. Trent Rosenbloom, and Josh F. Peterson. Identifying UMLS concepts from ECG impressions using knowledgemap. In *AMIA Annual Symposium Proceedings*, volume 2005, page 196. American Medical Informatics Association, 2005.

[106] Joshua C. Denny. Mining electronic health records in the genomics era. *PLoS Computational Biology*, 8(12):e1002823, 2012.

[107] Catherine A. McCarty, Anuradha Nair, Diane M. Austin, and Philip F. Giampietro. Informed consent and subject motivation to participate in a large, population-based genomics study: The Marshfield Clinic personalized medicine research project. *Public Health Genomics*, 10(1):2–9, 2006.

[108] `http://emerge.mc.vanderbilt.edu/`.

[109] Katherine M. Newton, Peggy L. Peissig, Abel Ngo Kho, Suzette J. Bielinski, Richard L. Berg, Vidhu Choudhary, Melissa Basford, Christopher G. Chute, Iftikhar J. Kullo, Rongling Li et al. Validation of electronic medical record-based phenotyping algorithms: Results and lessons learned from the emerge network. *Journal of the American Medical Informatics Association*, 20(e1):e147–e154, 2013.

[110] `http://www.phekb.org/`.

[111] Elena Birman-Deych, Amy D. Waterman, Yan Yan, David S. Nilasena, Martha J. Radford, and Brian F. Gage. Accuracy of ICD-9-CM codes for identifying cardiovascular and stroke risk factors. *Medical Care*, 43(5):480–485, 2005.

[112] Elizabeth F.O. Kern, Miriam Maney, Donald R. Miller, Chin-Lin Tseng, Anjali Tiwari, Mangala Rajan, David Aron, and Leonard Pogach. Failure of ICD-9-CM codes to identify patients with comorbid chronic kidney disease in diabetes. *Health Services Research*, 41(2):564–580, 2006.

[113] Janet F.E. Penz, Adam B. Wilcox, and John F. Hurdle. Automated identification of adverse events related to central venous catheters. *Journal of Biomedical Informatics*, 40(2):174–182, 2007.

[114] Carol Friedman, George Hripcsak, William DuMouchel, Stephen B. Johnson, and Paul D. Clayton. Natural language processing in an operational clinical information system. *Natural Language Engineering*, 1(01):83–108, 1995.

[115] Guergana K. Savova, James J. Masanz, Philip V. Ogren, Jiaping Zheng, Sunghwan Sohn, Karin C. Kipper-Schuler, and Christopher G. Chute. Mayo clinical text analysis and knowledge extraction system (CTAKES): architecture, component evaluation and applications. *Journal of the American Medical Informatics Association*, 17(5):507–513, 2010.

[116] `http://metamap.nlm.nih.gov/`.

[117] Joshua C. Denny, Jeffrey D. Smithers, Randolph A. Miller, and Anderson Spickard. Understanding medical school curriculum content using knowledgemap. *Journal of the American Medical Informatics Association*, 10(4):351–362, 2003.

[118] Jill M. Pulley, Joshua C. Denny, Josh F. Peterson, Gordon R. Bernard, Cindy L. Vnencak-Jones, Andrea H. Ramirez, Jessica T. Delaney, Erica Bowton, Kyle Brothers, Kevin Johnson, et al. Operational implementation of prospective genotyping for personalized medicine: The design of the Vanderbilt predict project. *Clinical Pharmacology & Therapeutics*, 92(1):87–95, 2012.

[119] J. Kevin Hicks, Kristine R. Crews, James M. Hoffman, Nancy M. Kornegay, Mark R. Wilkinson, Rachel Lorier, Alex Stoddard, Wenjian Yang, Colton Smith, Christian A. Fernandez, et al. A clinician-driven automated system for integration of pharmacogenetic consults into an electronic medical record. *Clinical Pharmacology and Therapeutics*, 92(5):563, 2012.

[120] David Blumenthal and Marilyn Tavenner. The meaningful use regulation for electronic health records. *New England Journal of Medicine*, 363(6):501–504, 2010.

Chapter 3

Biomedical Image Analysis

Dirk Padfield
Biomedical Image Analysis Lab
GE Global Research
Niskayuna, NY
padfield@ge.com

Paulo Mendonca
Image Analytics Lab
GE Global Research
Niskayuna, NY
mendonca@ge.com

Sandeep Gupta
Biomedical Image Analysis Lab
GE Global Research
Niskayuna, NY
sandeep.n.gupta@ge.com

3.1 Introduction

In its broadest sense, an image is a spatial map of one or more physical properties of a subject where the pixel intensity represents the value of a physical property of the subject at that point. Imaging the subject is a way to record spatial information, structure, and context information. In this context, the subject could be almost anything: your family sitting for a family photo taken with your smartphone, the constellations of orion's belt viewed from a telescope, the roads of your neighborhood imaged from a satellite, a child growing inside of its mother viewed using an ultrasound probe. The list of possible subjects is endless, and the list of possible imaging methods is long and ever-expanding. But the idea of imaging is simple and straightforward: convert some scene of the world into some sort of array of pixels that represents that scene and that can be stored on a computer.

Naturally, if we wanted to describe all of the possible subjects and modalities, that would be an entire book of its own. But, for our purposes, we are interested in biomedical images, which are a subset of images that pertain to some form of biological specimen, which is generally some part of human or animal anatomy. The imaging modality used to acquire an image of that specimen generally falls into one of the categories of magnetic resonance imaging (MRI), computed tomography (CT), positron emission tomography (PET), ultrasound (U/S), or a wide range of microscopy modalities such as fluorescence, brightfield, and electron microscopy. Such modalities have various purposes: to image inside of the body without harming the body or to image specimens that are too small to be viewed with the naked eye. These modalities enable us to image biological structure, function, and processes.

While we often think of images as 2D arrays of pixels, this is an overly restrictive conception, especially as it pertains to biomedical images. For example, if you broke a bone in your leg, you might get a 3D MRI scan of the region, which would be stored as a three-dimensional array of pixel values on a disk. If that leg needed to be observed over time, there might be multiple MRI scans at different time intervals, thus leading to the fourth dimension of time. A fifth dimension of modality would be added if different types of MRI scans were used or if CT, PET, U/S, or biological images were added. When all of these time-lapse datasets of different modalities are registered to each other, a rich set of five-dimensional information becomes available for every pixel representing a physical region in the real world. Such information can lead to deeper insight into the problem and could help physicians figure out how to heal your leg faster.

Another multidimensional example is common in the area of microscopy. To visualize cellular dynamics and reactions to drugs (for example, for the purpose of discovering targets for treating cancer), a group of cells could be imaged in their 3D context using confocal microscopy, which enables optical sectioning of a region without harming the structure. This region could have multiple markers for different regions of the cell such as the nucleus, cytoplasm, membrane, mitochondria, endoplasmic reticulum, and so forth. If these are live cells moving over time, they can be imaged every few seconds, minutes, hours, or days, leading to time-lapse datasets. Such five-dimensional datasets are common and can elucidate structure-structure relationships of intracellular or extra-cellular phenomena over time in their natural 3D environment.

If we were to stop at this point in the description, we would be left in a rather frustrating position: having the ability to image complex structures and processes, to store them on a computer, and to visualize them but without any ability to generate any real quantitative information. Indeed, as the number of imaging modalities increases and the use of such modalities becomes ubiquitous coupled with increasing data size and complexity, it is becoming impossible for all such datasets to be carefully viewed to find structures or functions of interest. How is a physician supposed to find every single cancerous lesion in the CT scans of hundreds of patients every day? How is a biologist supposed to identify the one cell acting unusually in a field of thousands of cells moving around randomly? At the same time, would you want such events to be missed if you are the patient?

Being able to look inside of the body without hurting the subject and being able to view biological objects that are normally too small to see has tremendous implications on human health. These capabilities mean that there is no longer a need to cut open a patient in order to figure out the cause of an illness and that we can view the mechanisms of the building block of our system, the cell. But being able to view these phenomena is not sufficient, and generating quantitative information through image analysis has the capability of providing far more insight into large-scale and time-lapse studies. With these concepts in mind, the need for computationally efficient quantitative measurements becomes clear.

Biomedical image analysis is the solution to this problem of too much data. Such analysis methods enable the extraction of quantitative measurements and inferences from images. Hence, it is possible to detect and monitor certain biological processes and extract information about them. As one example, more than 50 years after the discovery of DNA, we have access to the comprehensive sequence of the human genome. But, while the chemical structure of DNA is now well understood, much work remains to understand its function. We need to understand how genome-encoded components function in an integrated manner to perform cellular and organismal functions. For example, much can be learned by understanding the function of mitosis in generating cellular hierarchies and its reaction to drugs: Can we arrest a cancer cell as it tries to replicate?

Such analysis has major societal significance since it is the key to understanding biological systems and solving health problems. At the same time, it includes many challenges since the images are varied, complex, and can contain irregular shapes. Furthermore, the analysis techniques need to account for multidimensional datasets $I(x,y,z,\lambda,t,...)$, and imaging conditions (e.g., illumination) cannot always be optimized.

In this chapter, we will provide a definition for biomedical image analysis and explore a range of analysis approaches and demonstrate how they have been and continue to be applied to a range of health-related applications. We will provide a broad overview of the main medical imaging modalities (Section 3.2) and a number of general categories for analyzing images including object detection, image segmentation, image registration, and feature extraction. Algorithms that fall in the category of object detection are used to detect objects of interest in images by designing a model for the object and then searching for regions of the image that fit that model (Section 3.3). The output of this step provides probable locations for the detected objects although it doesn't necessarily provide the segmented outline of the objects themselves. Such an output feeds directly into segmentation algorithms (Section 3.4), which often require some seeding from which to grow and segment the object borders. While some segmentation algorithms do not require seeding, accurate locations of the objects provides useful information for removing segmented regions that may be artifacts. Whereas detection and segmentation provide detailed information about individual objects, image registration (Section 3.5) provides the alignment of two or more images of either similar or different modalities. In this way, image registration enables information from different modalities to be combined together or the time-lapse monitoring of objects imaged using the same modality (such as monitoring tumor size over time). Feature extraction combines object detection, image segmentation, and image registration together by extracting meaningful quantitative measurements from the output of those steps (Section 3.6). Taken as a whole, these approaches enable the generation of meaningful analytic measurements that can serve as inputs to other areas of healthcare data analytics.

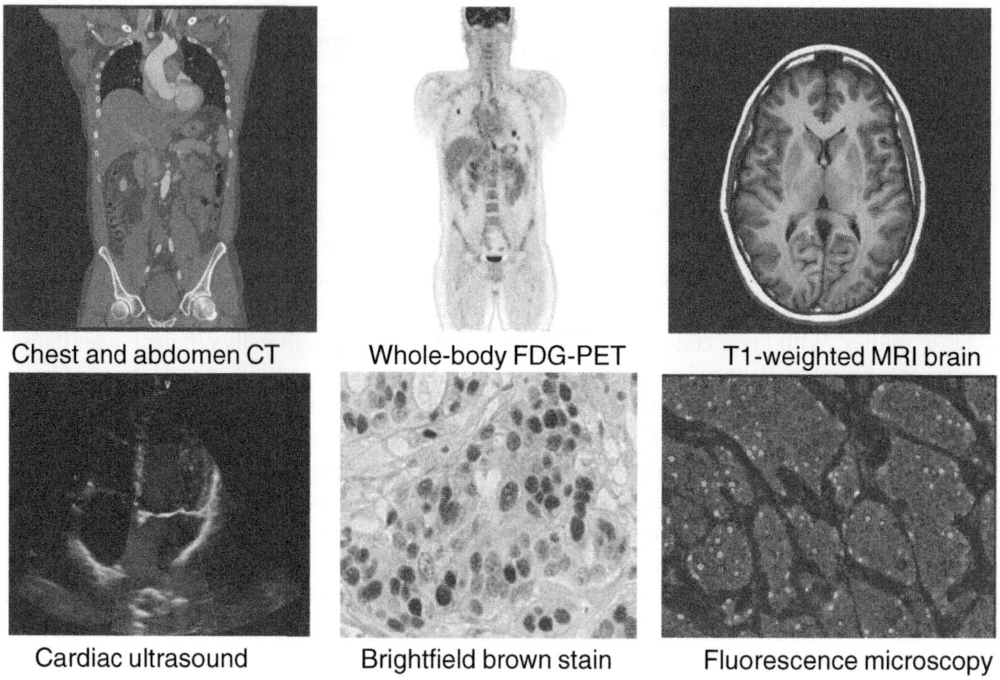

FIGURE 3.1 (See color insert.): Representative images from various medial modalities.

3.2 Biomedical Imaging Modalities

In this section, we provide a brief introduction to several biomedical imaging modalities with emphasis on unique considerations regarding image formation and interpretation. Understanding the appearance of images resulting from the different modalities aids in designing effective image analysis algorithms targeted to their various features. Representative images from the modalities discussed in this section are shown in Figure 3.1.

3.2.1 Computed Tomography

Computed Tomography (CT) creates 2D axial cross-section images of the body by collecting several 1D projections of conventional X-ray data using an X-ray source on one side and a detector on the other side. The 1D projection data are then reconstructed into a 2D image. Modern CT systems are capable of acquiring a large volume of data extremely fast by increasing the axial coverage. A CT image displays a quantitative CT number usually reported in Hounsfield units, which is a measure of the attenuation property of the underlying material at that image location. This makes CT inherently amenable to quantification. CT has become the mainstay of diagnostic imaging due to the very large number of conditions that are visible on CT images. A recent development has been the advent of so-called Dual Energy CT systems, where CT images are acquired at two different energy levels. This makes it possible to do a very rich characterization of material composition using differential attenuation of materials at two different energy levels. The simplest form of CT image reconstruction algorithms use variations of the filtered back-projection method, but modern iterative model-based methods are able to achieve excellent reconstruction while limiting doses to a patient. Common artifacts associated with CT images including aliasing, streaking, and beam hardening.

3.2.2 Positron Emission Tomography

Positron Emission Tomography (PET) is a nuclear imaging modality that uses radioactively labeled tracers to create activity maps inside the body based on uptake of a compound based on metabolic function. PET measures the location of a line on which a positron annihilation event occurs and as a result two simultaneous 511 keV photons are produced and detected co-linearly using co-incidence detection. PET allows assessment of important physiological and biochemical processes in vivo. Before meaningful and quantitatively accurate activity uptake images can be generated, corrections for scatter and attenuation must be applied to the data. Newer iterative reconstruction methods model attenuation, scatter, and blur and have sophisticated methods of dealing with motion that may take place during the image acquisition window.

3.2.3 Magnetic Resonance Imaging

Magnetic Resonance Imaging (MRI) is a high resolution, high contrast, noninvasive imaging modality with extremely rich and versatile contrast mechanisms that make it the modality of choice for looking at soft tissue contrast. In conventional MRI, signals are formed from nuclear magnetic response properties of water molecules that are manipulated using external static and varying magnetic fields and radio-frequency pulses. In addition to looking at anatomy and structure, image acquisition methods can be tailored to yield functional information such as blood flow. Images with very different contrasts can be created to selectively highlight and/or suppress specific tissue types. Spatially varying gradients of magnetic fields are used to localize the received signal from known anatomic locations and form 2D or 3D images. Received data is typically reconstructed using Fourier methods. Some common artifacts in MRI images are geometric distortion (warping) due to gradient nonlinearities, wraparound and aliasing, streaking, ghosts, chemical shift, and truncation artifacts.

3.2.4 Ultrasound

Ultrasound is one of the most ubiquitous imaging modalities due in large part to its low cost and completely noninvasive nature. Ultrasound imaging transmits high frequency sound waves using specialized ultrasound transducers, and then collects the reflected ultrasound waves from the body using specialized probes. The variable reflectance of the sound waves by different body tissues forms the basis of an ultrasound image. Ultrasound can also depict velocities of moving structures such as blood using Doppler imaging. Imaging a growing fetus in the womb and cardiovascular imaging are two of the most common ultrasound imaging procedures. Due to very fast acquisition times, it is possible to get excellent real-time images using ultrasound to see functioning organs such as the beating heart. Modern ultrasound systems employ sophisticated electronics for beam forming and beam steering, and have algorithms for pre-processing the received signals to help mitigate noise and speckle artifacts.

3.2.5 Microscopy

In addition to *in vivo* radiological imaging, clinical diagnosis as well as research frequently makes uses of *in vitro* imaging of biological samples such as tissues obtained from biopsy specimens. These samples are typically examined under a microscope for evidence of pathology. Traditional brightfield microscopy imaging systems utilize staining with markers that highlight individual cells or cellular compartments or metabolic processes in live or fixed cells. More rich proteomics can be captured by techniques such as fluorescence-based immunohistochemistry and images can be acquired that show expression of desired proteins in the sample. Images from such microscopy systems are traditionally read visually and scored manually. However, newer digital pathology platforms are emerging and new methods of automated analysis and analytics of microscopy data are enabling more high-content, high-throughput applications. Using image analysis algorithms, a multitude of features can be quantified and automatically extracted and can be used in data-analytic pipelines for clinical decision making and biomarker discovery.

3.2.6 Biomedical Imaging Standards and Systems

Development of image analytics and quantification methods is founded upon common standards associated with image formats, data representation, and capturing of meta-data required for downstream analysis. It would be extremely challenging to develop general-purpose solutions if the data produced by systems across platforms and manufacturers did not conform to standard formats and data elements. Digital Imaging and Communications in Medicine (DICOM, dicom.nema.org) is a widely used standard that helps achieve this for the purposes of handling, storing, printing, and transmitting medical imaging data. It defines a file format and a network communications protocol for these data types. Every device that deals with medical imaging data comes with a DICOM conformance statement which clearly states the DICOM classes that it supports and how it implements them. As an example, all the GE Healthcare devices DICOM conformance statements can be found in http://www3.gehealthcare.com/en/Products/Interoperability/DICOM.

While DICOM is the most commonly adopted industry wide standard for medical imaging data, HL7 (http://www.hl7.org) is a more general standard used for exchange, integration, sharing, and retrieval of electronic healthcare information. It defines standards not just for data but also application interfaces that use electronic healthcare data. The IHE (http://www.ihe.net) initiative drives the promotion and adoption of DICOM and HL7 standard for improved clinical care and better integration of the healthcare enterprise.

Medical imaging data is commonly stored and managed using specialized systems known as Picture Archiving and Communications System (PACS). PACS systems house medical images from most imaging modalities and in addition can also contain electronic reports and radiologist annotations in encapsulated form. Commercial PACS systems not only allow the ability to search, query-retrieve, and display and visualize imaging data, but often also contain sophisticated post-processing and analysis tools for image data exploration, analysis, and interpretation.

In this section, we have presented a number of the most common biomedical imaging modalities and described their key features. In the following sections, we will show how image analysis algorithms are applied to quantify these types of images.

3.3 Object Detection

We begin our discussion of image analysis algorithms with the topic of object detection. Detection is the process through which regions of potential interest, such as anatomical structures or localized pathological areas, are identified. Often associated with detection is the localization of the targeted structures. In the absence of such association, the problem of detecting a region of interest has a strong overlap with the problem of classification, in which the goal is simply to flag the presence (or absence) of an abnormal region. In this section the word "detection" is used specifically to designate the joint detection and localization of a structure of interest.

3.3.1 Template Matching

An often-used method to detect objects of interest in an image is to choose a representative template and apply some variant of template matching to find similar regions in the image of interest. Using an approach such as normalized cross-correlation (NCC) measures the similarity between the two signals f_1 and f_2. This yields an output map showing the magnitude of the match, and this can be thresholded to find the best detections in the image. If we define f_1 as the fixed image and f_2 as the moving image or template image, the normalized cross-correlation between images f_1 and f_2 at a given (u,v) is defined as

$$\frac{\sum\left[\left(f_1(x,y)-\overline{f_{1,u,v}}\right)\left(f_2(x-u,y-v)-\overline{f_{2,u,v}}\right)\right]}{\sqrt{\sum\left(f_1(x,y)-\overline{f_{1,u,v}}\right)^2}\sqrt{\sum\left(f_2(x-u,y-v)-\overline{f_{2,u,v}}\right)^2}} \tag{3.1}$$

Here $\overline{f_{1,u,v}}$ and $\overline{f_{2,u,v}}$ are the mean intensity of f_1 and f_2, respectively in the overlap region. The region of overlap is constantly shifting and represents the overlapping region of the correlation operation.

It is not difficult to see that such processing can become extremely computationally intensive as the size of the template grows because the sum of the product of the overlapping pixels must be computed for every location of the template relative to every pixel in the input image. Therefore, it is common to represent all terms of NCC in the Fourier domain, which leads not only to faster processing, but also enables a compact mathematical representation of the computation. The derivation of the following equation from Equation 3.1 can be found in [45, 44] along with an extension to masked regions.

$$\frac{\mathcal{F}^{-1}(F_1\cdot F_2^*)-\dfrac{\mathcal{F}^{-1}(F_1\cdot M_2^*)\cdot\mathcal{F}^{-1}(M_1\cdot F_2^*)}{\mathcal{F}^{-1}(M_1\cdot M_2^*)}}{\sqrt{\mathcal{F}^{-1}(\mathcal{F}(f_1\cdot f_1)\cdot M_2^*)-\dfrac{\left(\mathcal{F}^{-1}(F_1\cdot M_2^*)\right)^2}{\mathcal{F}^{-1}(M_1\cdot M_2^*)}}\sqrt{\mathcal{F}^{-1}(M_1\cdot\mathcal{F}(f_2'\cdot f_2'))-\dfrac{\left(\mathcal{F}^{-1}(M_1\cdot F_2^*)\right)^2}{\mathcal{F}^{-1}(M_1\cdot M_2^*)}}} \tag{3.2}$$

Here, $F_1=\mathcal{F}(f_1)$ and $F_2^*=\mathcal{F}(f_2')$, where $\mathcal{F}(\cdot)$ represents the FFT operation and F^* is the complex conjugate of the Fourier transform, which, by definition, is the Fourier transform of the rotated image (f_2' in this case) for real-valued images. Also, if m_1 and m_2 are images of ones the same size as f_1 and f_2, respectively, we define $M_1=\mathcal{F}(i_1)$ and $M_2^*=\mathcal{F}(i_2')$.

An example of the effectiveness of this approach can be seen in Figure 3.2, where a small template is matched with an entire image of cells imaged with differential interference contrast (DIC) microscopy, and the resulting NCC map is thresholding to yield strong detections in almost all of the cells.

3.3.2 Model-Based Detection

Model-based detection methods are a generalization of template matching, obtained by replacing the template and the NCC function with arbitrary models and figures of merit for the matching between the model and the data. In such methods, an arbitrary statistical model of features presumably found in the structure of interest is produced, often through the application of expert knowledge. When presented with an image, such methods compute the selected features throughout the image and evaluate a figure of merit that indicates whether the computed features are consistent with the presence of the structure of interest at any given location. If confounding structures, i.e., regions that could potentially be mistaken for the structure of interest, are also modeled, the figure of merit can be derived from a comparison of the output of different models as to their suitability as explanations for the observed data. Formally, we have a set of parametric models $\{\mathcal{M}_i, i=1,...,N\}$, where each

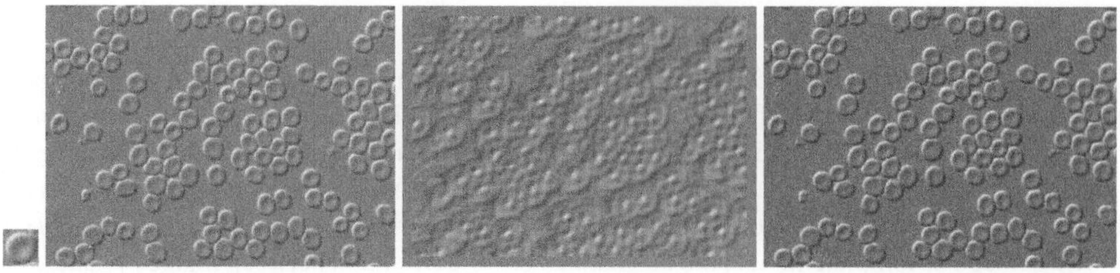

(a) Template (b) Input image (c) NCC map (d) Thresholded detections

FIGURE 3.2: Normalized cross-correlation (NCC) example for template matching. The thresholded NCC map serves as the detections for the cells in this DIC image.

$\mathcal{M}_i$ has parameters $\mathbf{m}_i$ in the domain $\mathbf{M}_i$. Given a choice of $\mathcal{M}_i$, if $\mathcal{D}$ can be *assumed* to be a set $\mathcal{D} = \{\mathcal{D}_j, j = 1, ..., M\}$ of *independent* features $\mathcal{D}_j$ computed at or in the vicinity of image location $\mathbf{x}$, we have, using Bayes' law and marginalizing over the model parameters,

$$P(\mathcal{M}_i|\mathcal{D},\mathbf{x}) = \frac{P(\mathcal{M}_i|\mathbf{x})}{p(\mathcal{D}|\mathbf{x})} p(\mathcal{D}|\mathcal{M}_i,\mathbf{x}) = \frac{P(\mathcal{M}_i|\mathbf{x})}{p(\mathcal{D}|\mathbf{x})} \prod_{j=1}^{M} p(\mathcal{D}_j|\mathcal{M}_i,\mathbf{x})$$
$$= \frac{P(\mathcal{M}_i|\mathbf{x})}{p(\mathcal{D}|\mathbf{x})} \prod_{j=1}^{M} \int_{\mathbf{M}_i} p(\mathcal{D}_j|\mathbf{m}_i,\mathcal{M}_i,\mathbf{x}) p(\mathbf{m}_i|\mathcal{M}_i,\mathbf{x})\, d\mathbf{m}_i, \tag{3.3}$$

an expression valid under the independence assumption.

Under this general framework for model-based detection, the development of different applications consists in identifying adequate parametric models $\mathcal{M}_i$ establishing adequate distributions for the prior distributions $p(\mathbf{m}_i|\mathcal{M}_i,\mathbf{x})$ and $P(\mathcal{M}_i|\mathbf{x})$, and solving (3.3). Two practical examples of these steps are sketched in the next paragraphs.

Lung-nodule detection. The detection of lung-nodules is a significant clinical problem. However, it has now been firmly established that mortality rates can be significantly reduced through CT screening [35]. Exploring curvature as an image feature and by developing knowledge-based priors for nodule, vessel, and vessel-junction modules, the work in [33] provides a canonical example for a model-based approach for lung nodule detection. Details of the algorithm can be found in that reference, but the central elements of the method are the use of geometric models built from ellipsoids and tori to represent the structure of interest (nodules) and the potential confounding structures (vessels and vessel junctions). The curvature of isosurfaces of the CT image at each location $\mathbf{x}$ was selected as the discriminative feature for detection. Probability distributions $p(\mathcal{D}_j|\mathbf{m}_i,\mathcal{M}_i,\mathbf{x})$ for the curvature were computed using elementary methods of differential geometry, and full exploitation of expert medical knowledge available in the literature was used in the derivation of the priors $p(\mathbf{m}_i|\mathcal{M}_i,\mathbf{x})$ for each model. The result was, essentially, a nonlinear filter that produced as output the ratio between the probability that a nodule is present at location $\mathbf{x}$ and the probability that either a vessel or a vessel junction is present at that same location. Qualitative and quantitative results for the algorithm are shown in Figure 3.3.

Colonic-polyp detection. Early detection of colonic polyps has been associated with reduction in the incidence of colorectal cancer [63], and optical colonoscopy has been shown to be an effective tool for polyp detection [59]. However, optical colonoscopy is an invasive procedure, and discomfort to the patient, in particular due to pre-examination colonic cleansing, has a negative impact on compliance [11]. In [32] the model-based method was applied to the detection of colonic polyps depicted in CT imaging. The use of cleansing materials and colonic fluids produces severe alterations

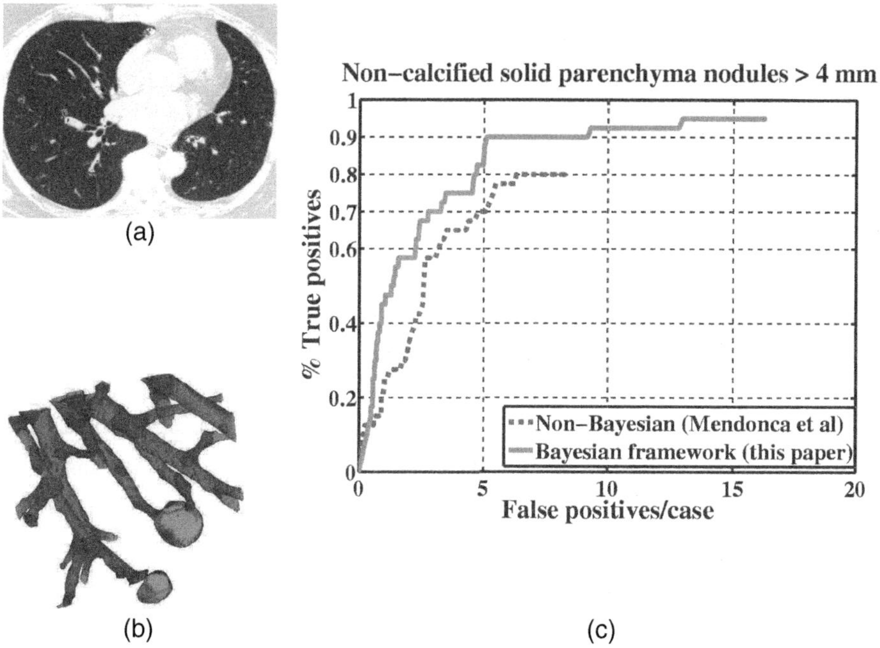

FIGURE 3.3 (See color insert.): Lung-nodule detection. (a) A 2D slice of a high-resolution CT scan with nodule labels overlaid in green on the intensity image. (b) A 3D rendering of the voxel labeling for a small region from the same case showing nodules (green), vessels (red), and junctions (blue). (c) fROC curves comparing performance of the Bayesian voxel labeling framework to a curvature-based non-probabilistic approach given in [31].

in the appearance of the image, and this poses a challenge to methods solely based on geometry, such as the one in [33]. Therefore, a joint modeling of shape and appearance was applied in [32]. In particular, the likelihood term $p(\kappa|\mathcal{M}_3,\mathbf{x})$ for the probability distribution of curvatures of the colon wall contained terms that were dependent on the amplitude of image noise, the image point-spread function, and the magnitude of the air-tissue or fluid-tissue gradient along the colon wall. The other elements of (3.3) were obtained using the same methods as in [33], i.e., through the judicious use of expert knowledge available in the medical literature. Results for the algorithm are shown in Figure 3.4.

3.3.3 Data-Driven Detection Methods

Model-based methods, although powerful, are difficult to apply when expert knowledge is not available or is not in a format that can be easily encoded in algorithmic form. To address this problem, data-driven methods apply machine learning techniques to automatically extract from labeled data the features and models relevant to the detection problem at hand. An additional difficulty of model-based methods is the need for explicit models for the structure or anatomical region of interest. Data-driven methods, on the other hand, can be used to construct models of normal regions, which are hopefully more common, and the detection problem is then translated into anomaly detection, where the objective is simply to locate structures or regions that do not conform to the norm, without explicit modeling of non-conforming structures. Unsupervised learning methods, such as PCA, can be used to discover and retain the more relevant modes of variation of the input, capturing the regularity of the input training data. When non-conforming data is presented to the algorithm, deviations from such regularity will become apparent, and abnormalities can therefore be detected.

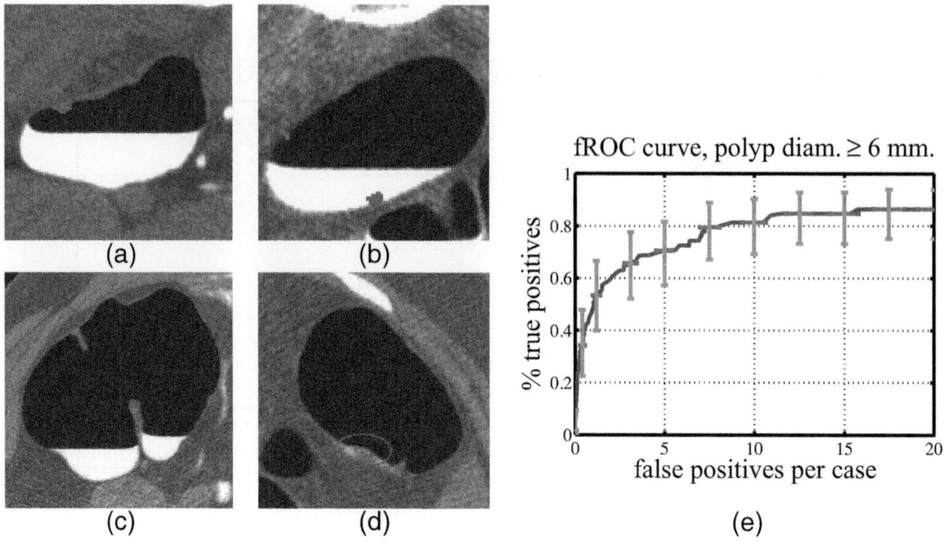

FIGURE 3.4 (See color insert.): Colonic-polyp detection. Examples of correctly detected polyps in air (a) and fluid (b) regions. The image in (c) shows a protruding tip on a fold incorrectly marked by the algorithm (a false positive), as shown in (c). (d) depicts a flat sessile polyp missed by the algorithm. Figure (e) is the fROC curve showing the performance of the algorithm for the WRAMC (http://imaging.nci.nih.gov) dataset.

Detection of carotid plaques. An example of an unsupervised data-driven method is found in the detection of carotid plaques. The availability of treatments that slow the progression of cardiovascular disease (CVD) increases the impact of early diagnosis in patient survival [4], and the presence of carotid plaque has been identified as a significant risk factor in the prognosis of CVD [37]. In [20], a data-driven detection method was applied to the problem of detecting carotid plaques depicted in ultrasound images. Seven hundred images of the cross sections of healthy carotids were used to build a normalcy model, from which an average image was extracted, as well as the first one-hundred modes of variation, obtained through PCA, as show in Figure 3.5. When a new image was presented to the algorithm, a reconstruction algorithm was applied to recover the image as a linear combination of the "eigencarotid" images obtained through PCA. The difference between the original and reconstructed images produced an anomaly map; the rationale for this is that normal images are well represented by the eigencarotids, whereas images containing plaque are not. Results of this operation are shown in Figure 3.6.

The detection methods and algorithms described in this section enable the detection and localization of objects of interest in images. The next section on segmentation will demonstrate how such detections can serve as seeds to enable accurate delineation of the borders of objects of interest.

3.4 Image Segmentation

The goal of image segmentation is to divide a digital image into separate parts or regions (sets of pixels) in such a manner that the regions have a strong correlation with objects or areas of the

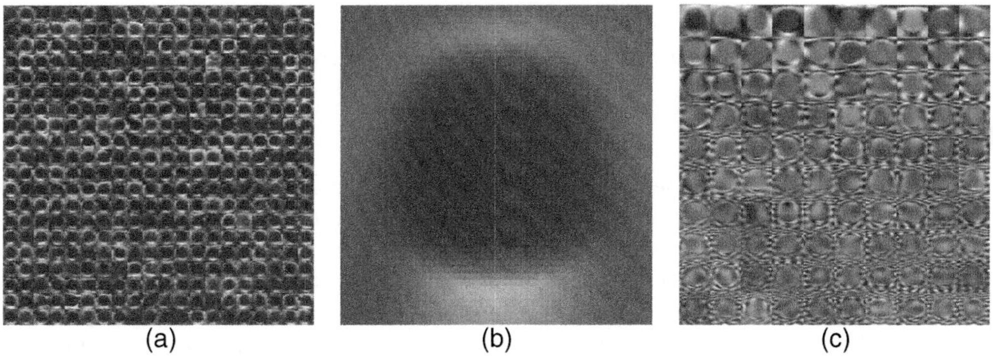

FIGURE 3.5: Eigencarotids. (a) Sample US cross-sectional images of healthy carotids, selected from over a dataset with 700 thousand images. (b) Average image after registration of data sampled in (a). (c) First 100 modes of variation of the complete dataset. Images courtesy of Shubao Liu.

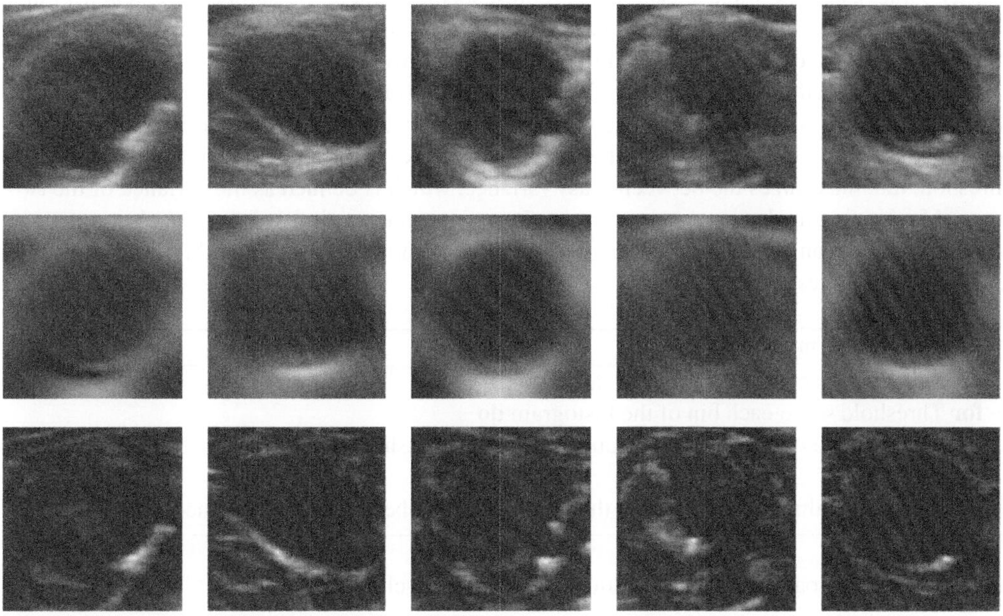

FIGURE 3.6: Detection of anomalies in the carotid. The top row shows input images of five different carotid cross sections. The middle row shows the reconstruction of the input images using the high-energy modes of variation of the input, as captured by PCA. The bottom row shows the residual image produced by the magnitude of the difference between each input image and its reconstruction. In each case, local peaks in the residual image correspond to plaque regions. Images courtesy of Shubao Liu.

real world contained in the image. This is used to locate objects and boundaries in images. Dividing the image into meaningful regions simplifies the representation of an image into something that is more meaningful and easier to analyze. Segmentation is one of the most important steps leading to the analysis of image data because it enables the further analysis of individual objects. While important, in general image segmentation is not well defined and is very challenging because of the difficulty of defining and identifying the particular shapes of the segmented objects. A large number of different segmentation algorithms exist in the literature and continue to be developed that fall into the broad categories of thresholding, watershed, region-growing, classification, wavelets, and level-sets. This section discusses a selection of these methods that are commonly used.

3.4.1 Thresholding

The most simple and intuitive segmentation approach is thresholding, which separates an image into foreground/background using a cutoff value, t. This can be accomplished through one simple loop over the image with the following operation: if a pixel value x_i is greater than t, set the new value to a foreground value (such as 255), and if it is less than t, set the new value to a background value (such as 0). The point is that the pixels are divided into two groups (creating a binary image) depending on their value relative to t. It is easy to see that increasing t increases the number of background pixels and vice versa.

Many thresholding approaches are based on the image histogram, which is a simple transformation of the image whereby pixels with the same or similar intensities are grouped together into a one-dimensional array. In this array, the index represents an intensity value (or a small range of intensity values), and the value at each index represents the count of the number of pixels with that intensity (or range of intensities). We can use the image statistics to separate the image background from the foreground. For certain types of images this will provide good results.

One effective method of finding a statistically optimal global threshold is using the Otsu algorithm [43], which is arguably the most common thresholding approach and certainly the baseline for comparison with other approaches. In Otsu's method, we exhaustively search the histogram for a threshold that maximizes the between-class variance, which is defined as the variance of the two classes. Maximizing the between-class variance is equivalent to minimizing the intraclass variance, and the algorithm can be structured using either of these formulations. Algorithm 1 outlines how the algorithm operates.

Algorithm 1 Otsu Thresholding

1: Create a histogram of the grayscale values.
2: **for** Threshold set to each bin of the histogram **do**
3:     Compute the between-class variance σ_B^2 for this threshold
4: **end for**
5: Set the optimal threshold as the one that maximizes the between class variance σ_B^2

The core of the approach is the computation of the between-class variance

$$\sigma_B^2 = w_1(\mu_1 - \mu_T)^2 + w_2(\mu_2 - \mu_T)^2 \tag{3.4}$$

where ω_1 and ω_2 are the percentage contribution (probability) of each class, μ_1 and μ_2 are the means of each class, and μ_T is the mean gray level of the entire image. Figure 3.7 shows an example of segmenting the lungs in a CT image using the Otsu thresholding algorithm.

In case more than one threshold is needed, the Otsu algorithm can be easily extended to handle multiple classes [19, 38]. For the multiclass problem, the between-class variance is defined as

$$\sigma_B^2 = \sum_{k=1}^{M} \omega_k (\mu_k - \mu_T)^2 \tag{3.5}$$

where M is the number of classes (number of thresholds + 1), ω_k is the probability of class k, μ_k is the mean of class k, and μ_T is the overall mean of the entire histogram.

These and many other global and local thresholding algorithms can be readily accessed in image analysis tools. For example in ImageJ [56] or FIJI [55], they are accessed from the "Image"-"Adjust"-"Auto Threshold" or "Image"-"Adjust"-"Auto Local Threshold."

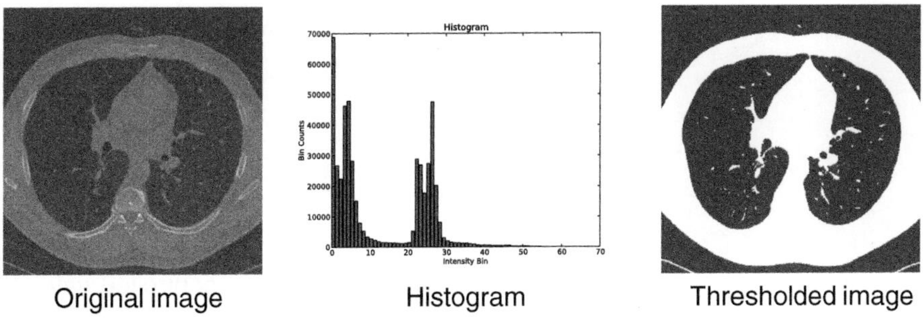

FIGURE 3.7: Segmenting the lungs in a CT image using Otsu thresholding.

The advantages of thresholding are speed, simplicity, and the ability to specify multiple thresholds. The disadvantages are that the objects must have similar appearance, it does not take into account any spatial information, it results in holes in objects, and it only works for simple tasks. Despite the simplicity of image thresholding approaches, they are widely used in image processing. The general rule is: Try thresholding first and only move on to more complicated approaches if it does not work.

3.4.2 Watershed Transform

The watershed transform [60] is an algorithm/solution framework that is very commonly used for image segmentation and for binary shape separation. It derives its name from the analogy to a topological watershed from nature where valleys flood progressively higher and eventually merge together as rain falls. Using this analogy, any grayscale image can be considered as a topographic surface where the gray level of a pixel is interpreted as its altitude in the relief. A drop of water falling on this topographic relief will first fill the local minima. If we flood this surface from its minima and, if we prevent the merging of the water coming from different sources, we partition the image into two different sets: the catchment basins and the watershed lines. Then, the watershed of the relief correspond to the limits of the adjacent catchment basins. From this standpoint, the watershed solution is related to Voronoi partitions.

The most difficult aspect of using the watershed transform is determining an appropriate speed image. Because the watershed transform is simply a solution framework, all of the work goes into creating an appropriate speed image. For example, the speed image could be based on image edges, or it could be based on object shape.

To segment based on image edges, watershed can be applied on a transformed image such as the image gradient. Ideally, the catchment basins should correspond to homogeneous gray level regions of image. However, in practice, this transform often produces oversegmentation due to noise or local irregularities in the gradient image. One of the most popular ways to correct this is the marker-controlled watershed, where seeds are selected in the image, and the watershed grows only from these seeds. For example, in [62], marker-controlled watershed is used for segmenting nuclei, where the seeds are defined using the H-maxima operation on the smoothed intensity image. The operation of the marker-controlled watershed is illustrated in the top part of Figure 3.8. The input image is transformed to an edge image by taking the gradient, which yields high intensities at the edges of the objects of interest. The watershed algorithm with a input height parameter is run on the gradient image using markers derived from the thresholded image. The height parameter can be adjusted to tradeoff between oversegmentation (objects broken into many pieces) and under-segmentation (objects merged or missing). This figure shows that some objects are missed for the chosen height value because the watershed algorithm floods into regions whose edge intensity is not high enough.

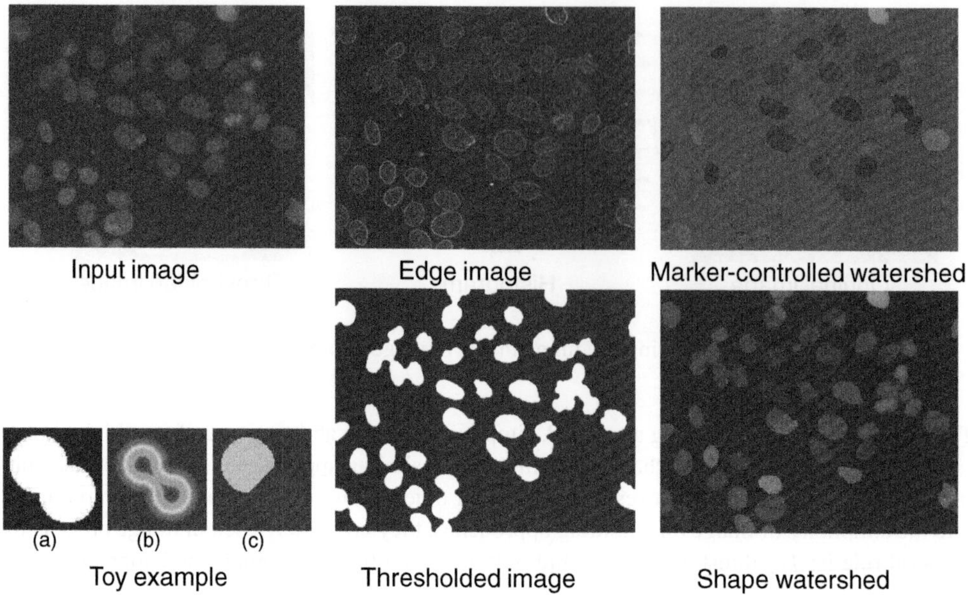

FIGURE 3.8 (See color insert.): Watershed segmentation examples. Top row: segmentation by marker-controlled watershed. Bottom row: segmentation by shape watershed.

To segment based on shape, the watershed can be applied to a distance transform instead. In particular, given an input image and a rough foreground/background segmentation, we can compute the distance map to the inside of each object and apply the watershed transform to this distance map. This is illustrated in the bottom left images of Figure 3.8, where the two overlapping circles in (a) are separated in (c) by running watershed on the distance map (b). Because this type of processing depends on the shape of the objects, it can be referred to as shape watershed. The bottom row of Figure 3.8 demonstrates the operation of shape watershed using a thresholded image. Notice that some objects are split into pieces; this can be avoided by merging together local maxima in the distance map at the risk of merging together some clustered objects.

The advantages of watershed are that it is an intuitive concept, it can be computed very quickly, and it is flexible since it can be applied to shape, intensity, gradient, etc. The disadvantages are that oversegmentation is common, it is difficult to incorporate any shape constraints, and its effectiveness depends on the preprocessed distance map.

3.4.3 Region Growing

Another class of segmentation algorithms involves choosing an initial seeded region and evolving some contour or region under given constraints that define the region of interest with the goal of obtaining more accurate region boundaries. Approaches like level-sets, active contours, and region growing algorithms fall under this general category, and all of these classes of approaches have been applied effectively to medical and biological image analysis problems. This class of algorithms depends on initial seeds, which can be derived from the detection algorithms from Section 3.3. Here we will discuss region growing as it forms the general intuitive framework for this class of algorithms. Algorithm 2 outlines the steps of the algorithm.

Region growing algorithms vary depending on the criteria used to decide whether a pixel should be included in the region. A broad range of options already exist (and many remain to be invented), but the simplest form is some kind of "threshold connected" approach. In such an approach, the

Algorithm 2 Region Growing

```
Choose one or many seeds inside of the object or objects to be segmented
Set the initial region to be the seeds and the neighbors to be the seed neighbors
while There exist neighbors to be processed do
    Add neighbor pixels to the region if they fulfill some criteria
    Set the new neighbors to be any not yet processed neighbors of the new region
end while
```

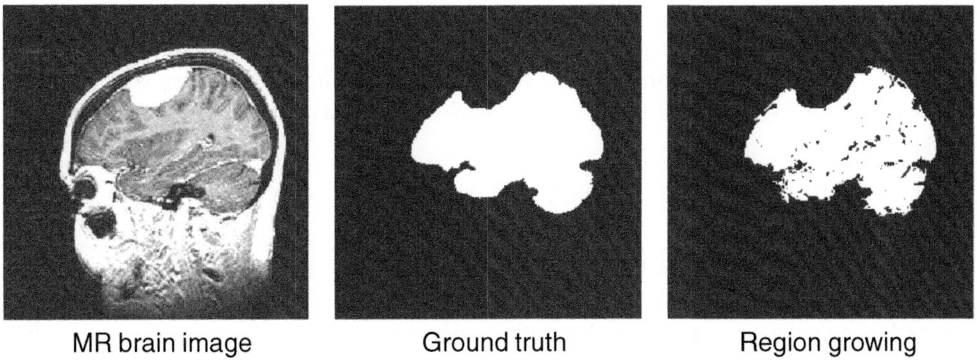

FIGURE 3.9: MR brain image segmented using confidence connected region growing by placing two seeds: one in the white matter and one in the gray matter. Adapted from Padfield and Ross [52].

user chooses a lower threshold and an upper threshold, and the algorithm starts from the seeds and grows as long as the neighbors of those seeds fall within the bounds of the threshold. This intuitively is similar to thresholding with the exception that only those regions that have a path to a seed are included in the segmentation.

Often, the lower and upper thresholds are not known beforehand, and a significant amount of experimentation is needed to determine them. To assist with this, one popular choice for automating the process is the "confidence connected" algorithm from the Insight Toolkit [15]. This algorithm is more intuitive and enables more robust parameter setting than global threshold based methods because it computes the thresholds from the region as it evolves. It computes the mean and standard deviation of the pixel values currently labeled as foreground and multiplies the standard deviation by a chosen factor in order to define a new interval as outlined in Algorithm 3. An example segmentation result image is shown in Figure 3.9 taken from [52].

Algorithm 3 Confidence Connected Region Growing

Set a multiplier k and the number of iterations n
Set the initial region to be a region around the seeds
for i = 0; i < n; i++ **do**
    Measure the mean μ and standard deviation σ of the region
    Compute the lower threshold $t_l = \mu - k\sigma$ and upper threshold $t_u = \mu + k\sigma$
    Add all neighbor pixels of the original seeds that have intensities between t_l and t_u
end for

3.4.4 Clustering

Another category of segmentation algorithms falls into the broad category of clustering or classification approaches. Clustering techniques are algorithms that separate the data into a set of different classes. They are broadly divided into two categories: supervised and unsupervised. Supervised classification approaches are ones that require training of some sort where the algorithm is fed a number of cases along with the labeled ground truth corresponding to those cases. The model resulting from the training of the classifier is then applied to unseen test data where labels are not known to the classifier. On the other hand, unsupervised classification approaches do not require a training step, and they instead seek to automatically find patterns and clusters in the data. This has the advantage that is removes the need for user training, but the results are generally not as accurate as supervised approaches, and there is less control over the output clusters.

A common unsupervised clustering algorithm is called K-means clustering [23, 61, 21]. Given an input parameter k and a set of points in a N-dimensional space, K-means seeks to divide the points into k clusters so as to minimize a cost function. In particular, the objective is to partition a set of observations $x_1, x_2, ..., x_N$ into k groups $S = S_1, S_2, ..., S_N$ so as to minimize the within-cluster sum of squares:

$$\underset{S}{\operatorname{argmin}} \sum_{i=1}^{k} \sum_{x_j \in S_i} ||x_j - \mu_i||_2 \tag{3.6}$$

where μ_j is the mean of cluster j. Obviously this is an iterative process since we don't know the clusters upfront and therefore cannot compute their means μ_j. To do this, we first randomly seed the centers, and then they are updated at each iteration using Algorithm 4, which is illustrated visually in Figure 3.10.

Algorithm 4 K-Means Clustering

procedure INITIALIZATION
    Randomly select k data points as cluster centers
    Set t = 0
    Determine S_0 and μ_i^t
end procedure
while $\mu_i^t \neq \mu_i^{t-1}$ for all i **do**
    procedure ASSIGNMENT
        Assign each observation x_j to the closest cluster mean using $\min_i ||x_j - \mu_i^t||_2$
        Determine S^t
    end procedure
    procedure UPDATE
        Compute the new cluster means μ_i^{t+1}
        t = t+1
    end procedure
end while

From this description it is clear that the accuracy of the algorithm depends heavily on the random initialization of the seeds: If this step yields seeds that poorly represent the true clusters, then the final clusters will not be accurate. To correct for this, the algorithm is generally run many times (perhaps 100), and each time the minimum within-cluster sum measure from Equation 3.6 is computed. The run that gives the best (lowest) score is chosen as the answer. The k must be decided beforehand, and it can be difficult to determine the best number of clusters k for some applications.

There are many ways to apply clustering algorithms to image data. Generally, several discriminative features can be computed on an image, and each pixel can be represented as a point in an N-dimensional space, where the number of dimensions corresponds to the number of features chosen. Figure 3.11 shows an illustrative approach that clusters the pixels using only the feature of intensity and using $k = 3$ intensity levels. Using such a feature yields results that are very similar to an Otsu threshold on intensity using 2 thresholds (2 thresholds leads to 3 regions). By calculating

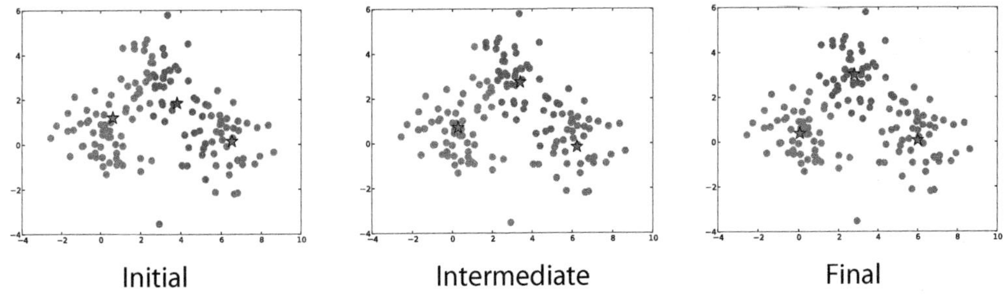

FIGURE 3.10 (See color insert.): *K*-means example. Three clusters are randomly initialized, and all points are assigned to one of these clusters. In each iteration, the cluster centers are recomputed and then the point assignments are recomputed. These steps are repeated until convergence. The data points are shown as colored dots, and the cluster centers are shown as stars.

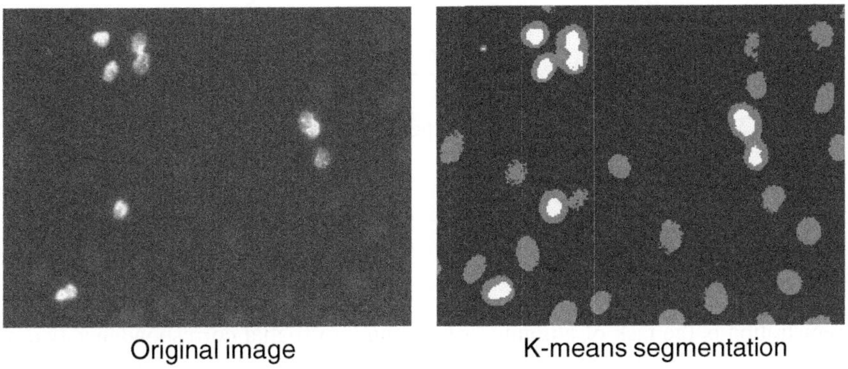

FIGURE 3.11: *K*-means segmentation of an image of cells where some cells undergoing mitosis are much brighter than others. Here K is set to 3, and the feature is intensity.

multiple features for each object (such as intensity, edges, texture) it is often easier to separate the different classes.

In this section, we discussed a number of common segmentation approaches including thresholding, watershed, region growing, and classification. There are myriads of variants of the use of these general approaches for segmenting specific image types and conditions, and there are many other common approaches such as wavelets, level-sets, and graph cuts. For example, [1, 36] introduce segmentation based on cost functions, [13] demonstrate a perceptual grouping approach, and the effectiveness of normalized cuts is shown in [26]. Level set methods [42, 57, 41] have been used for segmentation in [27], in [2] an edge attracting force was added to the formulation, and in [3], Chan and Vese present a model that can detect contours both with and without gradient. Such approaches have been applied to segmenting cells in 2D and 3D such as in [50, 51].

Wavelets are an effective tool for decomposing an image in the frequency and spatial domain. The underlying math for wavelets is described in [34], and the application of wavelets to signal processing is given by Mallat in [28, 29]. Statistical models for the wavelet distributions are given in [58], and Donoho introduced a de-noising approach using soft-thresholding in [7]. In [8, 40, 47, 48], a different wavelet variant called the à trous wavelet transform is used to combine coefficients at different decomposition levels to segment blob-like cells effectively.

Given that an extensive coverage of the segmentation topic could easily fill volumes of books, this section instead provided some examples of how some of these methods can be applied to the analysis of biomedical images.

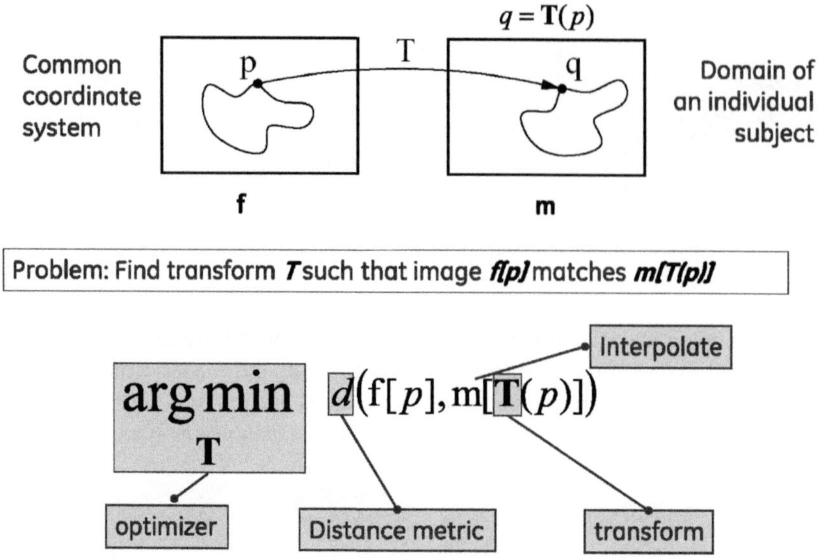

FIGURE 3.12: Schematic showing the components of an image registration problem.

3.5 Image Registration

Image registration is the task of aligning or bringing into spatial correspondence two different images or volumes. Image registration problems are encountered in the following types of applications among others:

- For motion correction or motion estimation, where two images contain the same anatomy but with some motion or deformation due to time difference between the two images.
- For multimodality registration, where two or more images represent different acquisition modalities for the same subject such as registering a CT image of a subject with an MRI image of the same subject. This is sometimes referred to as "Fusion."
- For intersubject comparisons, where images from two different subjects are registered to establish a spatial correspondence between the two images.

Image registration is often a critical step in biomedical data analytics since any kind of quantitative comparisons or analytics between images rely on image features or measurements being extracted from relevant, meaningful regions of the image that correspond to the same desired anatomic region of interest. In a mathematical sense, image registration can be considered as the problem of finding a transformation that maps the second image (often referred to as the "moving image") to a first image (referred to as the "fixed image"). Registration is treated as an optimization problem where we wish to find a transform that maps the moving image to the fixed image, yielding a transformed image that maximizes some similarity metric (or minimizes a distance metric) with respect to the original true fixed image. This is depicted in Figure 3.12. The following subsections describe some of the components of image registration and discuss some commonly used approaches. A more detailed description of image registration techniques can be found in [15, 25, 39].

3.5.1 Registration Transforms

The transform T is a function that maps physical points between the fixed and the moving image. The choice of the transform constrains the type of deformation that the image is allowed to undergo. Commonly used transforms are:

- **Rigid Body Transform:** A rigid body transform is comprised of image translation and rotation, and is represented by $T(x) = \mathbf{R} * x + \mathbf{t}$, where $\mathbf{R}$ and $\mathbf{t}$ are the rotation matrix and translation vector respectively. In a rigid body transformation, distances, and angles between points and lines are preserved.

- **Similarity Transform:** A similarity transform consists of an isotropic scaling factor in addition to the rigid body transformation of a rotation and translation. In a similarity tranformation, angles between lines are preserved, and objects change size proportionately in all dimensions.

- **Affine Transform:** An affine transform is a general linear transform in which straight lines remain straight lines after transformation but distances and angles may not be preserved, although ratios of distances between points are preserved. An affine transform is represented by the more general form $T(x) = \mathbf{M} * x + \mathbf{t}$, where $\mathbf{M}$ is any matrix and $\mathbf{t}$ is a vector.

- **B-spline Deformable Transform:** B-spline deformable transform is used for solving deformable registration problems where the image undergoes local deformations, and different parts of the image do not all obey the same transformation. In this case, one of the above transforms is assigned at a coarse set of grid points, and B-spline interpolation is used between the grid points to yield a deformable transform. Free form deformable transforms have very large degrees of freedom and result in very ill-posed problems. B-spline based interpolation makes the problem tractable by using basis functions of compact support.

3.5.2 Similarity and Distance Metrics

Perhaps the most important part of a registration problem is the image similarity metric that defines the "goodness" of registration. There are a wide variety of similarity or distance metrics with advantages and disadvantages. We describe here some representative metric examples:

- **Mean Squares Metric:** The mean squares metric is a distance metric that computes the mean-squared pixel-wise difference between two images A and B as follows

$$d(A,B) = \frac{1}{N}\sum_{i=1}^{N}(A_i - B_i)^2 \tag{3.7}$$

  where N is the number of pixels and A_i and B_i are the i-th pixels in images A and B, respectively. This metric is zero when the two images are identical and perfectly aligned, and has high values the more dissimilar the images are. This metric is easy to compute, but it assumes that image intensities do not change as pixel patches move from one image to the next. This metric does not handle intensity changes and is therefore not a good choice for multimodality registration.

- **Normalized Cross-Correlation Metric:** Normalized cross correlation, already described for object detection in Section 3.3.1, is a similarity metric that computes the pixel-wise cross-correlation of images and normalizes it using the autocorrelation of the two images as

$$s(A,B) = \frac{\sum_i [A_i - \mu_A][B_i - \mu_B]}{\sqrt{\sum_i [A_i - \mu_A]^2 \sum_i [B_i - \mu_B]^2}} \tag{3.8}$$

where μ_A and μ_B are the pixel-wise means of images A and B, respectively. This metric has a value of 1 when the two images are perfectly aligned, has smaller values as the images are increasingly mismatched, and has a minimum of -1 for perfectly uncorrelated images. Subtracting image means gives this metric robustness to intensity scaling between images, and it can handle a linear intensity variation model between images. The computational burden for this metric is also low. Cross-correlation based approaches have been used for addressing motion correction in medical image data [9].

- **Mutual Information Metric:** The mutual information (MI) metric between two images computes their similarity in an information theoretic sense and measures how much intensity information in one image informs the intensity information of the second image. Treating images A and B as random variables, with marginal probability distributions $p_A(a)$ and $p_B(b)$ and joint probability distribution $p_{AB}(a,b)$, the mutual information $I(A,B)$ is given by

$$I(A,B) = \sum_{a,b} p_{AB}(a,b) log \frac{p_{AB}(a,b)}{p_A(a)p_B(b)} \tag{3.9}$$

and it measures the difference in the joint distribution of A and B from the distribution in case of complete independence of A and B. The joint and marginal probability distributions can be estimated from the joint and marginal histograms of the two images. Because the MI metric does not make any assumptions about image intensity relationships in the two images and only requires that the two images explain each other well, this metric is very well suited for handling registration across modalities with very different intensity distributions and characteristics [24]. A detailed review of mutual information-based registration can be found in [53].

3.5.3 Registration Optimizers

After suitable choice of a registration similarity metric and registration transform, registration is solved as an optimization problem where the similarity metric is maximized (or a distance metric minimized) using an iterative optimization method. Optimizer method selection depends on several factors such as computational efficiency, robustness to local minima, and initialization, and may also depend on whether a fully automated registration method is desired or a semi-automated, user-guidance-based method is acceptable. Optimizers take as input a cost function and initialization of optimization parameters, and return optimized values of the parameters. Single-valued optimizers are used when working with single-valued cost functions. Conjugate gradient method and gradient descent method are among the most common single-valued optimizers. Multivalued cost functions generally employ non-linear least squares minimization techniques, and the Levenberg-Marquardt optimizer is one of the most widely used nonlinear optimization methods. The Insight Toolkit [15] contains a well-established and modular framework for testing different combinations of transforms, metrics, and optimizers.

Figure 3.13 shows results of registering two MRI brain images using rigid registration, affine registration, and deformable registration transforms. The mutual information similarity metric was used in all cases. The color images in the bottom row are shown using green for the registered image and red for the fixed image. Thus, the color image is yellow in the overlay, and areas of

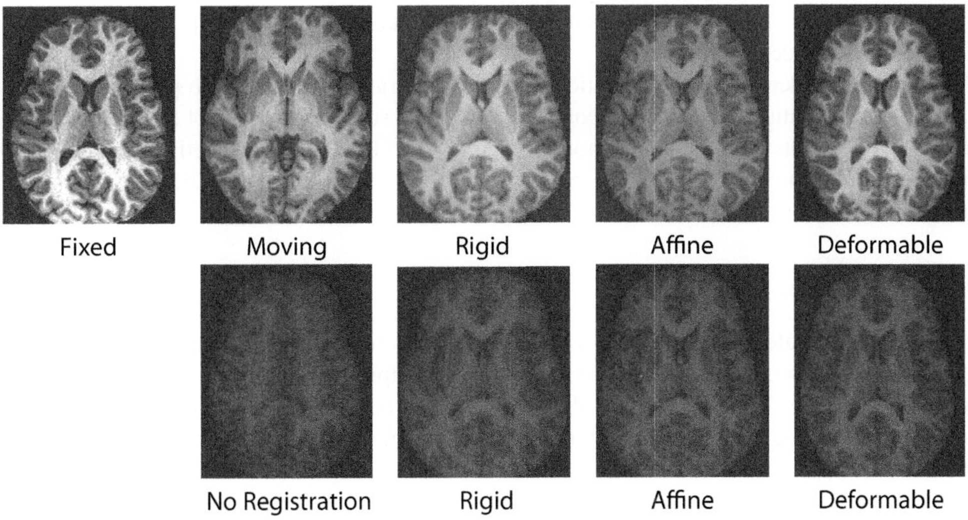

FIGURE 3.13 (See color insert.): Example showing registration of a moving image to a fixed image using various transforms (a single slice from a 3D volume is shown). Top row: fixed image, moving image, registered images using rigid body, affine, and deformable registration, respectively. Bottom row: image showing registered images and fixed image respectively to show accuracy of registration. Images courtesy of Xiaofeng Liu, GE Global Research.

incorrect registration are green or red. It is evident that the accuracy improves from rigid to affine to deformable registration. More examples of free-form deformable registration methods for medical imaging applications can be found in [30, 54].

Aligning images is a core requirement in many processing pipelines, and this section has outlined the main components of a registration framework. In combination with object detection and image segmentation, this leads to a powerful set of tools for analyzing images and for extracting features as demonstrated in the next section.

3.6 Feature Extraction

When a biological phenomenon is observed through an imaging device, the data collected contains a mix of effects, the most important of which are the characteristic biological phenomenon or object observed and the physical process that produces the images. For example, PET systems collect information about coinciding photon detections, which is the physical process that produces PET images. The underlying biological process of interest is the higher rate of consumption of glucose by cancer cells. The tagging of the glucose with a radioactive tracer initiates a chain of events that results in the emission of photons pairs with opposite moments, which reach the PET detectors virtually at the same time, producing the required coincident photon detections.

In a similar manner, feature extraction is the process of summarizing or converting raw image data into expressive representations that are more informative or show better association with an underlying biological phenomenon. The objective of such conversion is to highlight or make explicit in the data their most relevant elements with regard to a given task. For example, certain algorithms [18] rely on the extraction and matching of landmarks, e.g., SIFT features [22], for the purpose of image registration. Texture features such as Minkowski functionals [17] have been used for classification and detection tasks.

These examples demonstrate applications of carefully crafted features, with properties that are guaranteed by the feature design. Frequently, the design of such features is not feasible, since the most relevant elements of the data are not known *a priori*. In such cases, methods such as deep learning can reduce the burden of having to carefully design features and learn the most appropriate features for a given task from labeled data.

3.6.1 Object Features

In order to compute object features, a definition of an object must first be determined. Given a segmentation step such as those described earlier, the output is a set of foreground regions that are separated from the background. An algorithm such as connected components can be used to separate the foreground regions into individually labeled regions where each unique label indicates a unique object in the image.

Given individually segmented objects, a feature is a number that describes some aspect of an object. There are a large number of features that are defined in the literature, but they generally fall into the basic categories of shape, size, brightness, and texture. For example, in [10, 16] cells are classified into four phases of the cell life cycle using a number of extracted features followed by feature classification, and in [49] biologically relevant features are extracted that enable a range of biological studies based on these quantitative measures. We can use a function of one or more such features to model objects.

Table 3.1, adapted from [46], lists a number of common features and their mathematical definitions. In constructing features, it is convenient to first compute the image moments, which are particular averages of either binary objects (unweighted) or their pixel intensities (weighted). They are useful to describe objects and form the building blocks of many useful features of the objects. For example, they can be used to compute a variety of shape features such as volume and centroid, and they can also be used to compute the eigenvalues and eigenvectors of shapes, which can then be used to compute additional features such as eccentricity, elongation, and orientation.

For a discrete image $f(x,y)$, the discrete raw moment of order $(p+q)$ is defined as

$$M_{p,q}(f) = \sum_{y=0}^{Y-1} \sum_{x=0}^{X-1} x^p y^q f(x,y) \tag{3.10}$$

where x and y are indices of the first and second dimensions of the function and $f(x,y)$ is either a weighted (intensity) or unweighted (binary) image. For example, the volume (number of pixels or voxels) of an object can be computed as $M_{0,0}$ when $f(x,y)$ in Equation 3.10 is a binary image. And when $f(x,y)$ represents the intensity image itself, $M_{0,0}$ becomes the integrated intensity (sum of the intensities of an object). The mean of the intensity is simply the integrated intensity divided by the number of pixels, and other features of image intensity can also be easily computed such as standard deviation, min, max, median, and mode as well as features based on the intensity histogram.

The pixel locations of the object can be used to compute various bounding boxes as shown in Table 3.1. The bounding box is the smallest rectangle oriented along the x,y axes enclosing the object and is directly computed from the min and max locations of the image pixels. The oriented bounding box is the smallest rectangle (oriented along any direction) that encloses the shape. A brute force way to compute this would be to rotate the shape for a large number of angles and compute the angle that provides the smallest bounding box. But a much faster way is to use the eigenvectors and eigenvalues to compute the orientation of the object's major axis and then compute the bounding box along that axis.

Many other features, such as texture features, can be computed on objects and on full images, and new features continue to be designed and applied to problems in healthcare data analytics.

TABLE 3.1: Definitions of Several Features Derived from Image Moments

Feature Name	Definition
Shape Features (f is a binary image in Equation 3.10)	
Volume	$M_{0,0}$
Centroid	$\left[\frac{M_{1,0}}{M_{0,0}}, \frac{M_{0,1}}{M_{0,0}}\right]$
Axes length	$4\sqrt{\lambda_i}$, i = 0,...,D-1
Eccentricity	$\sqrt{\frac{\lambda_1 - \lambda_0}{\lambda_1}}$
Elongation	$\frac{\lambda_1}{\lambda_0}$
Orientation	$\tan^{-1}\left(\frac{\overline{v_1}(1)}{\overline{v_1}(0)}\right)$
Intensity Features (f is an intensity image in Equation 3.10)	
Integrated intensity	$M_{0,0}$
Intensity mean	$\frac{M_{0,0}}{\lvert X\rvert\lvert Y\rvert}$
Weighted centroid	$\left[\frac{M_{10}}{M_{00}}, \frac{M_{01}}{M_{00}}\right]$
Bounding Boxes	
Bounding box	[min(X), max(X), min(Y), max(Y), ...]
Bounding box size	[(max(X)-min(X)+1), (max(Y)-min(Y)+1), ...]
Oriented bounding box vertices	Bounding box along the major axis of the object
Oriented bounding box size	Bounding box size in rotated space

Notes: X and Y are the set of coordinates of the pixels inside of an object, $M_{p,q}$ are the image moments, $\lambda_1, \lambda_2, ..., \lambda_N$ are the eigenvalues, and $[\overline{v_0} \ \ \overline{v_1} \ \ ... \ \ \overline{v_N}]$ are the eigenvectors. Further descriptions are given in the text.

3.6.2 Feature Selection and Dimensionality Reduction

Given that a large number of size, shape, texture, and other features can be measured, this can result in an explosion of features and begs the question: How many features should be used? For example, if we can get 90% accuracy in separating various classes of objects (such as tumor versus benign nodules) with 3 features, it is worth using 4, 5, or 1,000 features? This depends on whether the additional features provide additional discriminatory value.

A good feature is (1) discriminatory: significantly different for each class, (2) information rich: has a small variance/spread within each class, (3) easy to compute, and (4) statistically independent: not correlated with another feature in use. The last point that features should be statistically independent is important because correlated features are redundant and increase dimensionality without adding value. Each feature increases the dimensionality of the features space, which increases the complexity of the search and the need for additional samples, known as the "curse of dimensionality." Thus, redundant and useless features unnecessarily add to the complexity. The dimensionality of the features and the complexity of the model can thus be viewed in light of Occam's Razor, which states that, when in doubt, choose the simpler model. For example, Figure 3.14 shows two classes of points and three different models for separating those points. While the more convoluted curve is more accurate than the line, it also may be overfitting the data.

The best approach for reducing the dimensionality of the features while retaining the most significant ones is to use an exhaustive approach that considers all subsets of features and picks the best one. While this yields the best approach, it is computationally expensive, especially for large numbers of features. A method referred to as a top-down approach that is much faster but not guar-

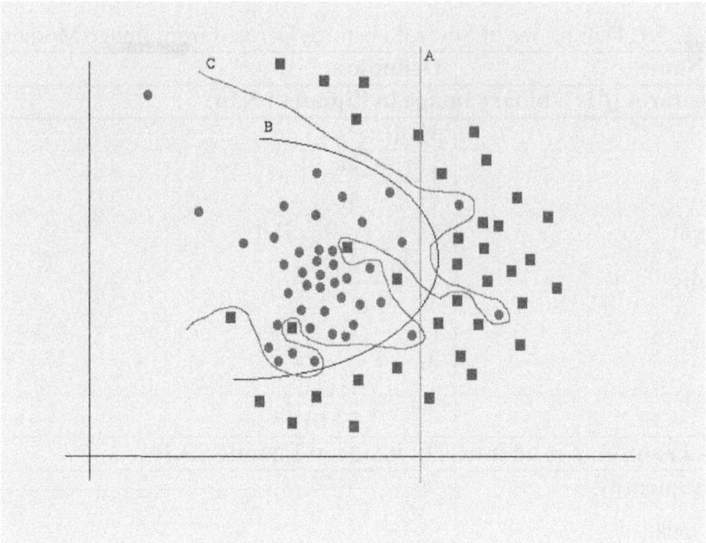

FIGURE 3.14: Two classes of points are shown in two different colors/shapes. The three curves show different models of increasing complexity.

anteed to be optimal is to start off with all features, remove one feature at a time (the feature that contributes the least to the discriminatory function), and continue until the performance is still acceptable or until the desired number of features have been removed. A bottom-up approach works in the opposite direction by sequentially adding features. A better approach is stepwise discriminant analysis, which is a method that combines the top-down and bottom-up approaches with the goal of selecting the most important features while keeping a high discrimination score. While this approach may work well, it is not guaranteed to find the optimal combination of features.

3.6.3 Principal Component Analysis

The goal of feature selection described in the last section is to reduce the complexity and dimensionality of the feature space in order to decrease the computational burden of the algorithms. It also enables the computation to focus on the most meaningful features while ignoring those that contribute little to the discriminatory power of the classifier. Another approach that has the same goal of dimensionality reduction is Principal Component Analysis (PCA) [14], which seeks to represent the underlying structure and variance of the data with as few dimensions as possible. It is the simplest of a class of eigenvector-based analysis approaches and has a simple closed-form analytical solution. It is an orthogonal transform of the data to a coordinate system where the coordinates are in descending order of importance.

A simple way to conceptualize the approach is to consider a 2D plot of points forming an ellipse that is oriented off the major x- and y-axes. If we fit an ellipse to the data and find its major and minor axes, the first principal component is the axis aligned with the major axis, and the second is that aligned with the minor axis. If we discard the minor axis by projecting the data on the major axis, we have preserved the largest variance of the data since the major axis of the ellipse is the widest part of the ellipse. This analogy can be extended to points in N-dimensions (although difficult to visualize), where the user can decide to keep k of the N principal components, where $k \leq N$. As fewer principal components are chosen, the complexity of the model is reduced but the accuracy of the representation also suffers. Such dimensionality reduction can be used to aid visualization since a high-dimensional space can be reduced to, for example, 2D or 3D which are easier to interpret visually while retaining the maximum variance of the original data. It is clear that PCA is sensitive to scaling of the features because if some features are naturally much larger than others, they will dominate the computation of the variances.

PCA can be computed using the eigenvalue decomposition of the covariance matrix of the data or using the singular-value decomposition (SVD). Consider the data as a matrix $\mathbf{X}$ with the rows representing the samples and the columns representing the features of each sample. When the means of each feature are subtracted from this matrix, then $\mathbf{X}^\mathbf{T}\mathbf{X}$ is proportional to the sample covariance of the data. If the eigenvectors of this covariance matrix are computed and stored as columns in a matrix $\mathbf{W}$, then the principal component decomposition is given by $\mathbf{T} = \mathbf{XW}$. At this point, the transformation still has the same dimension as the original data. But the structure of $\mathbf{W}$ is such that the eigenvectors are stored in decreasing order of the magnitude of their eigenvalues, which means that each additional eigenvector contributes a decreasing amount of variance to the total. Thus, if only the first k eigenvectors are chosen, the dimensionality of the problem is reduced to k dimensions, and the data is then approximated as $\mathbf{T_k} = \mathbf{XW_k}$. There is a tradeoff between the number of dimensions to remove versus the accuracy, and this tradeoff depends on the application and data.

In this section, we discussed the importance of feature extraction and showed how these features are computed from the output of detection and segmentation algorithms. We demonstrated a number of features and how they are computed, and also described the problem of feature selection and dimensionality reduction and showed some ways to approach this. The resulting features can then be used in machine learning algorithms for classification problems and for other applications in healthcare data analytics.

3.7 Conclusion and Future Work

In this chapter we have provided a broad overview of the main biomedical imaging modalities and a number of approaches for quantifying such images. We presented object detection algorithms that provide accurate location information for objects of interest. This lead into image segmentation algorithms that provide extraction of the borders of the objects and often rely on the object detection outputs for seeding the algorithms. We then demonstrated how image registration can be used to align intra- and intermodality images in order to enable combination of information across modalities or to provide time-lapse information. All of these algorithms culminated in the feature extraction algorithms, which compute meaningful analytics from these approaches that can serve as inputs to approaches such as machine learning algorithms. Thus, biomedical image analysis algorithms serve as valuable inputs to other approaches for healthcare data analytics.

The future of biomedical image analysis is looking bright. Given the broad range of modalities spanned by the topic, there is significant room for specific algorithm implementations and innovations to meet the needs of particular applications. At the same time, there are broad categories of algorithms that are being developed, such as deformable registration or model-based object detection methods, that span across modalities and can be applied to numerous applications by tuning the parameters. A theme that has permeated the algorithm developments over the years is model-based approaches, which seek to model the underlying acquisition physics and object appearance. Some examples are the applications discussed in the object detection section and many of the segmentation approaches, especially those in the literature that include shape models. However, another theme that has been rising in importance and influence is based on learning. With the emergence of machine learning topics such as big data [5], data science [6], and deep learning [12], much of the algorithm development community is increasingly investing in feature extraction methods, classification approaches, and data wrangling to be able to automatically extract meaningful patterns and insights out of images and data without explicitly modeling the objects of interest. This shows great promise for avoiding the bias that may be introduced by experts who miss important patterns in favor of finding the expected patterns from past experience. But at the same time, it has the potential to detect irrelevant patterns that may not be of clinical value. As the communities of engineers, computer scientists, statisticians, physicians, and biologists continue to integrate, this holds great promise for the development of methods that combine the best elements of modeling and learning approaches for solving new technical challenges. The future of the field is very promising, and it is ultimately the patient that will benefit.

Bibliography

[1] A. Blake and A. Zisserman. *Visual Reconstruction*. The MIT Press, 1987.

[2] V. Caselles, R. Kimmel, and G. Sapiro. Geodesic active contours. In *Proc. ICCV 1995*, Cambridge, M.A., 1995.

[3] T. Chan and L. Vese. Active contours without edges. *IEEE Transactions on Image Processing*, 10(2):266–277, February 2001.

[4] Jay N. Cohn. Arterial stiffness, vascular disease, and risk of cardiovascular events. *Circulation*, 113:601–603, February 2006.

[5] Kenneth Cukier. Data, data everywhere. *The Economist*, February 2010.

[6] Vasant Dhar. Data science and prediction. *Commun. ACM*, 56(12):64–73, December 2013.

[7] D. L. Donoho. De-noising by soft-thresholding. *IEEE Transactions on Information Theory*, 41(3):613–627, 1995.

[8] A. Genovesio, T. Liedl, V. Emiliani, W.J. Parak, M. Coppey-Moisan, and J.C. Olivo-Marin. Multiple particle tracking in 3-D+t microscopy: Method and application to the tracking of endocytosed quantum dots. *IEEE Trans. Image Proc.*, 15(5):1062–1070, 2006.

[9] Sandeep N. Gupta, Meiyappan Solaiyappan, Garth M. Beache, Andrew E. Arai, and Thomas K. F. Foo. Fast method for correcting image misregistration due to organ motion in time-series MRI data. *Magnetic Resonance in Medicine*, 49(3):506–514, 2003.

[10] N. Harder, F. Bermúdez, W.J. Godinez, J. Ellenberg, R. Eils, and K. Rohr. Automated analysis of the mitotic phases of human cells in 3D fluorescence microscopy image sequences. In R. Larsen, M. Nielsen, and J. Sporring, editors, *MICCAI '06*, LNCS, pages 840–848, 2006.

[11] Gavin C. Harewood, Maurits J. Wiersema, and L. Joseph Melton III. A prospective, controlled assessment of factors influencing acceptance of screening colonoscopy. *The American Journal of Gastroenterology*, 97(12):3186–3194, December 2002.

[12] Geoffrey E. Hinton. Learning multiple layers of representation. *Trends in Cognitive Sciences*, 11(10):428–434, 2007.

[13] A. Hoogs, R. Collins, R. Kaucic, and J. Mundy. A common set of perceptual observables for grouping, figure-ground discrimination and texture classification. *IEEE Transactions on Pattern Analysis and Machine Intelligence*, 25(4):458–474, April 2003.

[14] H. Hotelling. Analysis of a complex of statistical variables into principal components. *Journal of Educational Psychology.* 24:417–441, 1933.

[15] L. Ibanez, W. Schroeder, L. Ng, and J. Cates. *The ITK Software Guide.* Kitware, Inc. ISBN 1-930934-15-7, http://www.itk.org/ItkSoftwareGuide.pdf, second edition, 2005.

[16] V. Kovalev, N. Harder, B. Neumann, M. Held, U. Liebel, H. Erfle, J. Ellenberg, R. Eils, and K. Rohr. Feature selection for evaluating fluorescence microscopy images in genome-wide cell screens. In C. Schmid, S. Soatto, and C. Tomasi, editors, *Proc. IEEE CVPR*, pages 276–283, 2006.

[17] Xiaoxing Li and P. R. S. Mendonça. Texture analysis using Minkowski functionals. In *SPIE Proceedings*. Vol. 8314. San Diego, CA, USA, February 24, 2012.

[18] Zisheng Li, Tsuneya Kurhara, Kazuki Matsuzaki, and Toshiyuki Irie. Evaluation of medical image registration by using 3D SIFT and phase-only correlation. In *Abdomination Imaging — Computational and Clinical Applications*, Nice, France, October 2012.

[19] Ping-Sung Liao, Tse-Sheng Chen, and Paul-Choo Chung. A Fast Algorithm for Multilevel Thresholding. *Journal of Information Science and Engineering*, 17:713–727, 2001.

[20] S. Liu, D. Padfield, and P. Mendonca. Tracking of carotid arteries in ultrasound images. In *Medical Image Computing and Computer-Assisted Intervention MICCAI 2013*, volume 8150 of *Lecture Notes in Computer Science*, pages 526–533. Springer Berlin Heidelberg, 2013.

[21] S. Lloyd. Least square quantization in PCM. *IEEE Transactions on Information Theory*, 28:129–137, 1982.

[22] David G. Lowe. Object recognition from local scale-invariant features. In *International Conference in Computer Vision*, volume 2, pages 1150–1157, September 1999.

[23] J. Macqueen. Some methods for classification and analysis of multivariate observations. In *5th Berkeley Symposium on Mathematical Statistics and Probability*, pages 281–297, 1967.

[24] F. Maes, A. Collignon, D. Vandermeulen, G. Marchal, and P. Suetens. Multimodality image registration by maximization of mutual information. *IEEE Transactions on Medical Imaging*, 16(2):187–98, April 1997.

[25] J. B. Maintz and Max A. Viergever. A survey of medical image registration. *Medical Image Analysis*, 2(1):1–36, March 1998.

[26] J. Malik, S. Belongie, J. Shi, and T. Leung. Textrons, contours and regions: Cue integration in image segmantation. In *Proceedings of the 7th International Conference on Computer Vision*, pages 918–925, 1999.

[27] R. Malladi, J.A. Sethian, and B.C. Vemuri. Shape modeling with front propagation: A level set approach. *IEEE Transactions on Pattern Analysis and Machine Intelligence*, 17:158–175, 1995.

[28] S. Mallat. A theory for multiresolution signal decomposition : The wavelet representation. *IEEE Transactions on Pattern Analysis and Machine Intelligence*, 11:674–693, July 1989.

[29] S. Mallat. *A Wavelet Tour of Signal Processing*. Academic Press, 1997.

[30] David Mattes, D.R. Haynor, Hubert Vesselle, T.K. Lewellen, and William Eubank. PET-CT image registration in the chest using free-form deformations. *IEEE Transactions on Medical Imaging*, 22(1):120–128, 2003.

[31] P.R.S. Mendonça, R. Bhotika, Saad Sirohey, W.D. Turner, J.V. Miller, and R.S. Avila. Model-based analysis of local shape for lesion detection in CT scans. In *Medical Image Computing and Computer-Assisted Intervention*, pages 688–695, Palm Springs, CA, October 2005.

[32] Paulo R.S. Mendonça, R. Bhotika, Fei Zhao, John Melonakos, and Saad Sirohey. Detection of polyps via shape and appearance modeling. In *Proceedings of MICCAI 2008 Workshop: Computational and Visualization Challenges in the New Era of Virtual Colonoscopy*, pages 33–39, New York, NY, USA, September 2008.

[33] Paulo R.S. Mendonça, Rahul Bhotika, Fei Zhao, and James V. Miller. Lung nodule detection via Bayesian voxel labeling. In *Information Processing in Medical Imaging*, pages 134–145, Kerkrade, The Netherlands, July 2007.

[34] Y. Meyer. *Wavelets and Operators*. Cambridge University Press, 1992.

[35] Virginia A. Moyer. Screening for lung cancer: U.S. preventive services task force recommendation statement. *Annals of Internal Medicine*, 160(5):330–338, March 2013.

[36] D. Mumford and J. Shah. Boundary detection by minimizing functionals. In *Proceedings of the 1st International Conference on Computer Vision*, pages 22–26, 1987.

[37] Pieter Muntendam, Carol McCall, Javier Sanz, Erling Falk, and Valentin Fuster. The BioImage study: Novel approaches to risk assessment in the primary prevention of atherosclerotic cardiovascular disease — study design and objectives. *American Heart Journal*, 160(1):49–57, 2010.

[38] Hui-fuang Ng. Automatic thresholding for defect detection. *Pattern Recognition Letters*, 27:1644–1649, 2006.

[39] Francisco P. M. Oliveira and João Manuel R. S. Tavares. Medical image registration: A review. *Computer Methods in Biomechanics and Biomedical Engineering*, 17(2):73–93, January 2014.

[40] J.C. Olivo-Marin. Automatic detection of spots in biological images by a wavelet-based selective filtering technique. In *ICIP*, pages I:311–314, 1996.

[41] S.J. Osher and R.P. Fedkiw. *Level Set Methods and Dynamic Implicit Surfaces*. Springer, 2002.

[42] S.J. Osher and J.A. Sethian. Fronts propagating with curvature-dependent speed: Algorithms based on Hamilton–Jacobi formulations. *Journal of Computational Physics*, 79:12–49, 1988.

[43] N. Otsu. A threshold selection method from gray-level histogram. *IEEE Transactions on Systems Man Cybernetics*, 8:62–66, 1979.

[44] D. Padfield. Masked FFT Registration. In *Proc. CVPR*, 2010.

[45] D. Padfield. Masked object registration in the Fourier domain. *IEEE Transactions on Image Processing*, 21(5):2706–2718, 2012.

[46] D. Padfield and J. V. Miller. A label geometry image filter for multiple object measurement. *Insight Journal*, July-December:1–13, 2008.

[47] D. Padfield, J. Rittscher, and B. Roysam. Coupled minimum-cost flow cell tracking. In *Proc. IPMI*, pages 374–385, 2009.

[48] D. Padfield, J. Rittscher, and B. Roysam. Coupled minimum-cost flow cell tracking for high-throughput quantitative analysis. *Medical Image Analysis*, 15(4):650–668, 2011.

[49] D. Padfield, J. Rittscher, and B. Roysam. Quantitative biological studies enabled by robust cell tracking. In *2011 IEEE International Symposium on Biomedical Imaging: From Nano to Macro*, pages 1929–1934, March 2011.

[50] D. Padfield, J. Rittscher, T. Sebastian, N. Thomas, and B. Roysam. Spatio-temporal cell cycle analysis using 3D level set segmentation of unstained nuclei in line scan confocal fluorescence images. In *Proceedings of ISBI*, pages 1036–1039, 2006.

[51] D. Padfield, J. Rittscher, N. Thomas, and B. Roysam. Spatio-temporal cell cycle phase analysis using level sets and fast marching methods. *Medical Image Analysis*, 13(1):143–155, 2009.

[52] D. Padfield and J. Ross. Validation tools for image segmentation. In *Proceedings of SPIE Medical Imaging*, 2009.

[53] Josien P. W. Pluim, J. B. Antoine Maintz, and Max A. Viergever. Mutual-information-based registration of medical images: A survey. *IEEE Transactions on Medical Imaging*, 22(8):986–1004, August 2003.

[54] D. Rueckert, L.I. Sonoda, C. Hayes, D.L.G. Hill, M.O. Leach, and D.J. Hawkes. Nonrigid registration using free-form deformations: Application to breast MR images. *IEEE Transactions on Medical Imaging*, 18(8):712–721, 1999.

[55] Johannes Schindelin, Ignacio Arganda-Carreras, Erwin Frise, Verena Kaynig, Mark Longair, Tobias Pietzsch, Stephan Preibisch, Curtis Rueden, Stephan Saalfeld, Benjamin Schmid, Jean-Yves Tinevez, Daniel J. White, Volker Hartenstein, Kevin Eliceiri, Pavel Tomancak, and Albert Cardona. FIJI: An open-source platform for biological-image analysis. *Nature Methods*, 9(7):676–682, July 2012.

[56] Caroline A. Schneider, Wayne S. Rasband, and Kevin W. Eliceiri. NIH Image to ImageJ: 25 years of image analysis. *Nature Methods*, 9(7):671–675, July 2012.

[57] J.A. Sethian. *Level Set Methods and Fast Marching Methods.* Cambridge University Press, 1996.

[58] E.P. Simoncelli and O. Schwartz. Modelling surround suppression in v1 neurons via a statistically-derived normalistion model. In *Advances in Neural Information Processing Systems 11*, 1999.

[59] Robert A. Smith, Vilma Cokkinides, and Harmon J. Eyre. American cancer society guidelines for the early detection of cancer, 2006. *CA: A Cancer Journal for Clinicians*, 56(1):11–25, Jan/Feb 2006.

[60] P. Soille. *Morphological Image Analysis.* Springer-Verlag, Heidelberg, 2nd edition, 2003.

[61] H. Steinhaus. Sur la division des corp materiels en parties. *Bulletin of the Polish Academy of Sciences*, 1:801–804, 1956.

[62] C. Wahlby, I.-M. Sintorn, F. Erlandsson, G. Borgefors, and E. Bengtsson. Combining intensity, edge, and shape information for 2d and 3d segmentation of cell nuclei in tissue sections. *Journal of Microscopy*, 215:67–76, 2004.

[63] Sidney Winawer, Robert Fletcher, Douglas Rex, John Bond, Randall Burt, Joseph Ferrucci, Theodore Ganiats, Theodore Levin, Steven Woolf, David Johnson, Lynne Kirk, Scott Litin, and Clifford Simmang. Colorectal cancer screening and surveillance: Clinical guidelines and rationale — update based on new evidence. *Gastroenterology*, 124(2):544–560, February 2003.

Chapter 4

Mining of Sensor Data in Healthcare: A Survey

Daby Sow
IBM T. J. Watson Research Center
Yorktown Heights, NY
sowdaby@us.ibm.com

Kiran K. Turaga
Medical College of Wisconsin
Milwaukee, WI
kturaga@gmail.com

Deepak S. Turaga
IBM T. J. Watson Research Center
Yorktown Heights, NY
turaga@us.ibm.com

Michael Schmidt
Columbia University Medical Center
Neurological ICU
New York, NY
mjs2134@mail.cumc.columbia.edu

With progress in sensor technologies, the instrumentation of the world is offering unique opportunities to obtain fine grain data on patients and their environment. Turning this data into information is having a profound impact in healthcare. It not only facilitates design of sophisticated clinical decision support systems capable of better observing patients' physiological signals and helps provide situational awareness to the bedside, but also promotes insight on the inefficiencies in the healthcare system that may be the root cause of surging costs. To turn this data into information, it is essential to be able to analyze patient data and turn it into actionable information using data mining. This chapter surveys existing applications of sensor data mining technologies in healthcare. It starts with a description of healthcare data mining challenges before presenting an overview of applications of data mining in both clinical and nonclinical settings.

4.1 Introduction

Healthcare includes "efforts made to maintain or restore health, especially by trained and licensed professionals" [1]. These efforts are performed by various entities within a large ecosystem composed of patients, physicians, payers, health providers, pharmaceutical companies and more recently, IT companies. Medical informatics [2] is the science that deals with health information, its structure, acquisition, and use. A fundamental goal [3] of medical informatics is the improvement of healthcare by acquiring and transmitting knowledge for applications in a broad range of settings, across computational platforms, and in a timely fashion.

Reaching this goal can have far-reaching consequences on society. Historically, healthcare has been provided in a reactive manner that limits its effectiveness. A major issue with this is the inability to detect early or predict that a patient may be prone to develop complications associated with chronic diseases like cancer or diabetes. Even in an intensive care environment, care is often provided in response to the adverse events typically detected after the emergence of clinical symptoms, or after the interpretation of a lab test. In many cases, reacting after the detection of such events reduces the ability of physicians to drive patient trajectories towards good outcomes. As a result, there is an increasing push to transform medical care delivery from reactive to proactive.

This transformation necessitates better monitoring and understanding of patients, their physiological signals, and their context. Medical institutions and healthcare providers are collecting large amounts of data on their patients, and organizing this data into Electronic Medical Records (EMR) and Patient Health Records (PHR). Recently, with advances in sensor and wearable technologies, several new data sources are available to provide insights on patients. For instance, Bluetooth enabled scales, blood pressure cuffs, heart rate monitors, and even portable electrocardiogram monitors are now available off the shelves for the collection of important vitals that can be interpreted for early diagnosis. Using these advances in sensor technologies, several remote health monitoring solutions for chronic disease management, and wellness management have been proposed [4].

While rapid growth in healthcare sensor data offers significant promise to impact care delivery, it also introduces a data overload problem, for both systems and stakeholders that need to consume this data. It is, therefore necessary to complement such sensing capabilities with data mining and analytical capabilities to transform the large volumes of collected data into meaningful and actionable information. In this chapter, we survey the application of sensor data mining technologies in medical informatics. We divide this application space into two parts: clinical and nonclinical applications. Clinical applications are essentially clinical decision support applications for both in- and outpatient scenarios. Nonclinical applications include wellness management, activity monitoring, the use of smart environments (e.g., smart home scenarios) and reality mining. We provide a detailed survey of the sensors, systems, analytic techniques, and applications and challenges in these different areas, in this chapter.

This chapter is a revision of previously published work [120]. It is organized as follows. In Section 4.2, we present research challenges associated with the mining of sensor data in medical informatics. In Section 4.3, we consider the several challenges to obtaining and analyzing healthcare data. In Section 4.4, we review sensor mining applications and systems in clinical healthcare settings, while in Section 4.5 we describe several applications in nonclinical settings. We conclude in Section 4.6.

4.2 Mining Sensor Data in Medical Informatics: Scope and Challenges

Sensors measure physical attributes of the world and produce signals, i.e., time series consisting of ordered measurements of the form (timestamps, data elements). For example, in intensive care, respiration rates are estimated from measurements of the chest impedance of the patient. The resulting time series signals are consumed either by a human or by other sensors and computing systems. For instance, the output of the chest impedance sensor can be consumed by an apnea detection system to produce a signal measuring apnea episodes. The data elements produced by sensors range from simple scalar (numerical or categorical) values, to complex data structures. Examples of simple data elements include measures such as hourly average of temperature in a given geographical location, output by a temperature sensor. Examples of more complex data elements include summaries of vital signs and alerts measured by a patient monitor sensor in a medical institution. In this chapter, we focus on sensing challenges for medical informatics applications.

4.2.1 Taxonomy of Sensors Used in Medical Informatics

As shown in Figure 4.1, we categorize sensors in medical informatics as follows:

- *Physiological sensors*: These sensors measure patient vital signs or physiological statistics. They were first used to measure vitals on astronauts before appearing in medical institutions, at the bedside in the 1960s. Today, physiological sensors are also available outside medical institutions, even on pervasive devices (e.g., iPhone heart rate monitor applications that make use of smartphone cameras [5]).

- *Wearable activity sensors*: These sensors measure attributes of gross user activity, different from narrowly focused vital sign sensors. Good examples are accelerometers used for gait monitoring. Shoe manufacturers like Nike have enabled many of their running shoes with sensors capable of tracking walking or jogging activities [6]. Most smartphones are also equipped with accelerometers and several wellness management applications leverage these sensors.

- *Human sensors*: Humans play an integral role in the sensing process. For instance, physicians introduce important events that relate to the patient health status during examinations. Lab technicians follow rigorous processes to provide blood content information. Self-reporting (i.e., patients monitoring their health parameters) is also used in the management of chronic illnesses like diabetes. More recently, with the emergence of social media and pervasive computing, people use mechanisms like Web searches and Twitter to generate reports on important health-related events.

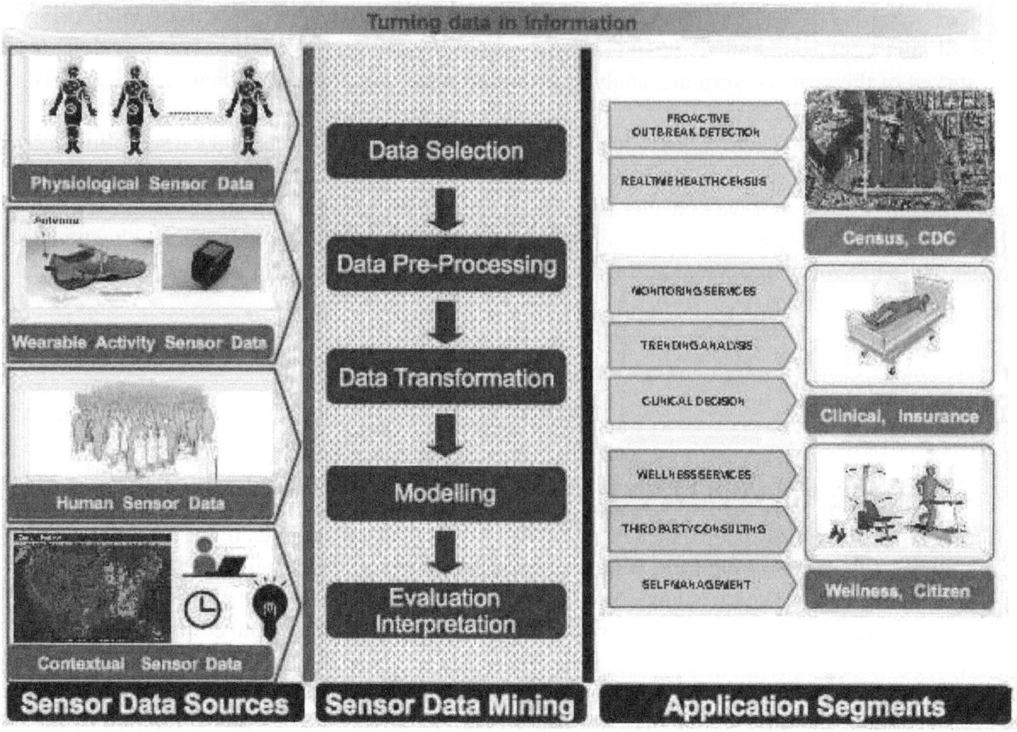

FIGURE 4.1: The sensor data mining process.

- *Contextual sensors*: These sensors are embedded in the environment around the user to measure different contextual properties. Examples include motion detection sensors, audio and video sensors, temperature sensors, weather sensors, etc.

4.2.2 Challenges in Mining Medical Informatics Sensor Data

As with standard data mining procedures [7] [8], healthcare mining is typically performed in five stages:

1. *Data Acquisition*: This includes operations involved in collecting data from external sensor data sources.

2. *Data Preprocessing*: This includes operations applied to the data to prepare it for further analysis. Typical preprocessing operations include data cleaning to filter out noisy data elements, data interpolation to cope with missing values, data normalization to cope with heterogeneous sources, temporal alignment, and data formatting.

3. *Data Transformation*: The includes operations for representing the data appropriately and selecting specific features from this representation. This stage is often called feature extraction and selection.

4. *Modeling*: This stage, also called mining applies knowledge discovery algorithms to identify patterns in the data. Modeling problems can be classified into six broad categories: (1) anomaly detection to identify statistically deviant data, (2) association rules to find dependencies and correlations in the data, (3) clustering models to group data elements according to

various notions of similarity, (4) classification models to group data elements into predefined classes, (5) regression models to fit mathematical functions to data, and (6) summarization models to summarize or compress data into interesting pieces of information.

5. *Evaluation*: This stage includes operations for evaluation and interpretation of the results of the modeling process.

There are several analytical challenges associated with each of these stages – specific to healthcare mining – that are listed in Table 4.1.

TABLE 4.1: Sensor Data Mining Analytical Challenges at Each Stage of the Data Mining Process

(I) Acquisition	*(II) Pre-processing*
lack of data standards	data formatting
lack of data protocols	data normalization
data privacy	data synchronization
(III) Transformation	*(IV) Modeling*
physiological feature extraction	sequential mining
feature time scales	distributed mining
unstructured data	privacy preserving modeling
	obtaining ground truth
	exploration-exploitation trade-offs
(V) Evaluation and Interpretation	
Model expressiveness	
Process and data provenance	

We present these analytical challenges in more detail in the rest of this chapter.

4.3 Challenges in Healthcare Data Analysis

Despite several standardization efforts, medical sensor manufacturers tend to design proprietary data models and protocols to externalize sensed signals. In healthcare, standard bodies like HL7 [9] and the Continua Health Alliance [10] address data modeling issues while several IEEE standard protocols address device interoperability issues [11]. However, there is a lack of incentives for sensor data manufacturers to adhere to these standards. With this lack of adherence to standards, mining medical sensor data across multiple data sources involves several nontrivial engineering challenges, and the design of custom solutions specific to each sensor data mining application.

Another key challenge in the acquisition process is related to the protection of user privacy. In the United States, the Health Insurance Portability and Accountability Act (HIPAA) defines regulations on access to health data. By law, data mining applications that leverage this data must comply with these regulations. Data de-identification and de-anonymization techniques are often required to comply with HIPAA. Privacy preserving data mining techniques [12], [13] may also be used to extract information from sensor data while preserving the anonymity of the data.

4.3.1 Acquisition Challenges

As discussed earlier, there are four different classes of sensors that generate and collect healthcare relevant information. In a clinical setting such as the ICU, these include different types of physiological sensors (e.g., ECG sensors, SpO2, Temperature sensors), contextual sensors (e.g., RFID sensors linked with care providers, video and cameras) and human sensors (e.g., care-provider notes, entries in the Electronic Medical Records). More recently, with the emergence of wearable devices, and network connectivity, additional information is provided (even in nonclinical settings) by activity sensors (e.g., wearable devices such as cell phones) and completely nontraditional sources of information (e.g., community discussions in healthcare-related sites, aggregated views of user searches, etc.).

Acquiring and integrating this data is nontrivial because of the inherent heterogeneity and lack of standards and protocols. Physiological sensor manufacturers have mostly designed proprietary data models and protocols to externalize sensed signals, despite the efforts of standard bodies like HL7 [9] and the Continua Health Alliance [10] to address data modeling issues, and IEEE standard protocols to address device interoperability issues [11]. Additionally, there is little standardization or interoperability studies of contextual and activity sensors, and data from healthcare providers is captured poorly, often requiring manual entry and transcription – all making the data acquisition task extremely complex. This has led to the emergence of data aggregators [121, 122, 123, 124] in ICU and EHRs for general clinical settings, however these aggregator solutions operate only on a narrow set of sources, and often do not interoperate with each other. Hence, mining medical sensor data across multiple data sources has involved several nontrivial engineering challenges, and the design of custom solutions specific to each sensor data mining application.

These acquisition challenges are compounded by the need to provide privacy protection for this often very sensitive personal information. This includes conforming with regulations such as the Health Insurance Portability and Accountability Act (HIPAA) act and providing appropriate controls with mechanisms for authentication, authorization, anonymization, and data de-identification. This also requires the design of privacy preserving data mining and analysis techniques [12], [13]. There are also several open, unresolved questions related to the privacy protection of data generated using nontraditional, contextual, and activity sensors.

4.3.2 Preprocessing Challenges

Data in the real world is inherently noisy. The preprocessing stage needs to address this problem with sophisticated data filtering, sampling, interpolation, and summarization techniques (such as sketches, descriptive statistics to minimize the effects of noise. The preprocessing also needs to account for the heterogeneity of data, and the lack of standards adoption by medical sensor manufacturers. Indeed, data generated in different formats needs to be syntactically aligned and synchronized before any analysis can take place. Sensors report data with timestamps based on their internal clocks. Given that clocks across sensors are often not synchronized, aligning the data across sensors can be quite challenging. In addition, sensors may report data at different rates. For instance while the ECG signal is generated at several 100s of Hz, the EMR may only be updated hourly. Aligning these datasets requires a careful design of strategies. These preprocessing techniques need to handle different types of structured data such as transactions, numeric measurements, and completely unstructured data such as text and images, often jointly. It is critical that the preprocessing of these sources retains the appropriate correlation structures across sources, so that meaningful and subtle indicators of patient health can be detected.

Furthermore, a semantic normalization is often required to cope with differences in the sensing process. As an illustration, a daily reported heart rate measure may correspond to a daily average heart rate in some cases, while in other cases it may represent a heart rate average measured every morning when the subject wakes up. Comparing these values in a data mining application can yield incorrect conclusions, especially if they are not semantically distinguished. All of these issues make the preprocessing task very complex.

4.3.3 Transformation Challenges

Data transformation involves taking the normalized and cleaned input data and converting it to a representation such that attributes or features relevant to the mining process can be extracted. This may include applying different types of linear (e.g., Fourier Transform, Wavelet Transform) and nonlinear transformations to numeric data, converting unstructured data such as text and images into numeric representations (e.g., using a bag of words representations, or extracting color, shape, and texture properties), and applying dimensionality reduction and de-correlation techniques (e.g., Principal Component Analysis), and finally summarizing the result with a set of representative features that can then be used for analysis and modeling. The choice of the appropriate transformations and representations for the features is heavily dependent on the task that needs to be performed. For instance a different set of features may be required for an anomaly detection task, as opposed to a clustering or classification task.

Additionally, the choice of appropriate features requires understanding of the healthcare problem at hand (e.g., the underlying physiology of the patient) and often requires inputs from domain experts. For instance, in neurological intensive care environments, spectral decomposition techniques for feature extraction have been defined, in conjunction with domain experts, to aid the interpretation of electroencephalograms (EEG) signals for brain activity monitoring and diagnosis of conditions such as seizures [14].

In addition to such signals, human sensing adds different types of unstructured data that need to be effectively integrated. This includes textual reports from examinations (by physicians or nurses) that need to be transformed into relevant features, and aligned with the rest of the physiological measurements. These inputs are important to the data mining process as they provide expert data, personalized to the patients. However, these inputs can be biased by physician experiences, or other diagnosis and prognosis techniques they use [15]. Capturing some of these aspects during the mining process is extremely challenging. Finally, there is a lot of external domain knowledge in open source repositories, medical journals, and patient guidelines that can be relevant to patient care, and features should be placed in context of this knowledge for appropriate interpretation.

4.3.4 Modeling Challenges

There are several challenges that need to be overcome in the modeling stage of the data mining process for medical sensor data. First of all, the time series nature of the data often requires the application of sequential mining algorithms that are often more complex than conventional machine learning techniques (e.g., standard supervised and unsupervised learning approaches). Nonstationarities in time series data necessitate the use of modeling techniques that can capture the dynamic nature of the state of the underlying processes that generate the data. Known techniques for such problems, including discrete state estimation approaches (e.g., dynamic Bayesian networks and hidden Markov models) and continuous state estimation approaches (e.g., Kalman filters or recurrent neural networks) have been used only in limited settings.

Another challenge arises due to the inherent distributed nature of these applications. In many cases, communication and computational costs, as well as sharing restrictions for patient privacy prevent the aggregation of the data in a central repository. As a result, the modeling stage needs to use complex distributed mining algorithms. In remote settings, there is limited control on the data acquisition at the sensor. Sensors may be disconnected for privacy reasons or for resource management reasons (e.g., power constraints), thereby affecting the data available for analysis. Modeling in these conditions may also require the distribution of analytic approaches between the central repository and the sensors. Optimizing the modeling process becomes a challenging distributed data mining problem that has received only limited attention in the data mining community.

Modeling in healthcare mining is also hindered by the ability to obtain ground truth on the data. Labels are often imprecise and noisy in the medical setting. For instance, a supervised learning approach for the early detection of a chronic disease requires well-labeled training data. However, domain experts do not always know exactly when a disease has started to manifest itself in a body, and can only approximate this time. Additionally, there are instances of misdiagnosis that can lead to incorrect or noisy labels that can degrade the quality of any predictive models.

In clinical settings, physicians do not have the luxury of being able to try different treatment options on their patients for exploration purposes. As a result, historical data sets used in the mining process tend to be quite sparse and include natural biases driven by the way care was delivered to the patient. Standard approaches are not well-equipped to cope with this bias in the data, especially as it is hard to quantify precisely. Furthermore, most studies in medical informatics are retrospective. Well-done prospective studies are hard to do, and are often done on small populations, limiting the statistical significance of any derived results.

4.3.5 Evaluation and Interpretation Challenges

Data mining results consist of models and predictions that need to be interpreted by domain experts. Many modeling techniques produce models that are not easily interpretable. For example, the weights of a neural network may be difficult to grasp for a domain expert. But for such a model to be adopted for clinical use, it needs to be validated with existing medical knowledge. It becomes imperative to track provenance metadata describing the process used to derive any results from data mining to help domain expert interpret these results. Furthermore, the provenance of the data sets, and analysis decisions used during the modeling are also required by the experts to evaluate the validity of the results. This imposes several additional requirements on the selected models and analysis.

4.3.6 Generic Systems Challenges

Beyond analytical challenges, sensor data mining also comes with a set of systems challenges that apply to medical informatics applications. The mining of sensor data typically requires more than conventional data management (database or data warehousing) technologies for the following reasons:

- The temporal aspect of the data produced by sensors sometimes generate large amounts of data that can overwhelm a relational database system. For example, a large population monitoring solution requiring the real-time analysis of physiological readings, activity sensor readings and social media interactions, cannot be supported with relational database technologies alone.

- Sensor mining applications often have real-time requirements. A conventional store-then-analyze paradigm leveraging relational database technologies may not be appropriate for such time-sensitive applications.

- The unstructured nature of some of the data produced by sensors coupled with the real-time requirements imposes requirements on the programming and analysis models used by developers of sensor data mining applications.

Hence, sensor mining in healthcare requires the use of emerging stream processing system technology in conjunction with database and data warehousing technologies. Stream processing systems are designed to cope with large amounts of real-time data, and their programming models are geared towards the analysis of structured and unstructured sensor data. They are also time sensitive and analyze data within small latency bounds. Figure 4.2 presents an extended architecture for sensor data mining that illustrates this integration. The rationale behind this architecture is to use a stream processing system for the real-time analysis of sensor data, including the preprocessing and transformation stages of the analytical data mining process. The sensor data acquisition is performed by

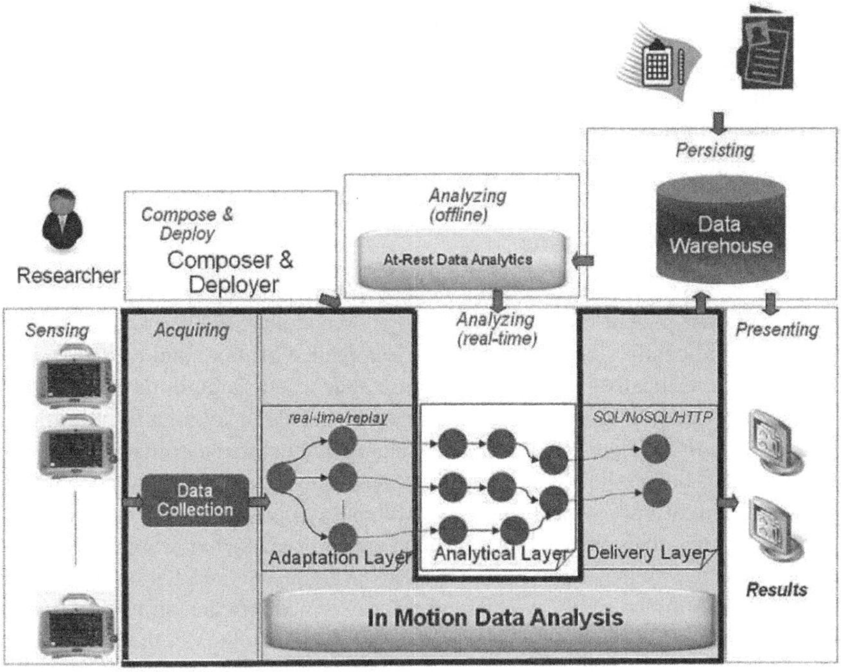

FIGURE 4.2: A generic architecture for sensor data mining systems.

a layer of software that interfaces with sensors and feeds into the stream processing system. The results of the transformation stage may be persisted in a data warehouse for offline modeling with machine learning techniques. The resulting models may be interpreted by analysts and redeployed on the stream processing platform for real-time scoring. In some cases, online learning algorithms may be implemented on the stream processing system. This integration of stream processing with data warehousing technologies creates a powerful architecture that addresses the system challenges outlined above.

4.4 Sensor Data Mining Applications

Most systems supporting clinical applications of data mining technologies in healthcare fall into the general class of Clinical Decision Support Systems (CDSS). Broadly speaking, CDSSs provide medical practitioners with knowledge and patient-specific information, intelligently filtered and presented at appropriate times, to improve the delivery of care [16]. As Robert Hayward from the Centre for Health Evidence says, "Clinical Decision Support systems link health observations with health knowledge to influence health choices by clinicians for improved health care."[1] Establishing links between observations or data and knowledge is one of the fundamental aspects of Data Mining. CDSS are either completely knowledge-driven, or completely data-driven or hybrid. Pure knowledge driven CDSS reason on a fix amount of existing knowledge represented in various ways (e.g., rules, state transition diagrams) to provide decision support. Data driven CDSS rely of data

[1] http://en.wikipedia.org/wiki/clinical_decision_support_system

mining and machine learning technologies to build inferencing models providing decision supports. Hybrid CDSS leverage existing knowledge and further enrich it using data driven techniques.

CDSSs have been used in both inpatient and outpatient scenarios.[2] In this section, we survey such systems with a focus on the ones that make extensive use of data mining to aid physicians in their decision-making process. We survey applications in intensive care, operating rooms, and in general clinical settings.

4.4.1 Intensive Care Data Mining

In 2003, it has been reported that intensivists have to handle over 200 variables, some of them being temporal, on a per patient basis to provide care. Anecdotal evidence tells us that this number has increased significantly since 2003 with the emergence of more and more sensing devices in critical care. Today, critically ill patients are often attached to large numbers of body sensors connected to sophisticated monitoring devices producing these large volumes of physiological data. These data streams originate from medical devices that include electrocardiogram, pulse oximetry, electroencephalogram, and ventilators, resulting in several kilobits of data each second. While these monitoring systems aim at improving situational awareness to provide better patient care with increased staff productivity, they clearly have introduced a data explosion problem. In fact, the vast majority of data collected by these monitoring systems in Intensive Care Units (ICUs) is transient. In talking with medical professionals, we learned that the typical practice in ICUs is for a nurse to eyeball representative readings and record summaries of these readings in the patient record once every 30–60 minutes. The rest of the data remains on the device for 72-96 hours (depending on the device's memory capacity) before it times out and is lost forever. Hospitals are simply not equipped with the right tools to cope with most of the data collected on their patients, prompting many to state that medical institutions are data rich but information poor.

The potential of data mining in this area has been recognized by many. Several efforts are underway to develop systems and analytics able for the modeling of patient states and the early detection of complications. In general, early detection of complications can lead to earlier interventions or prophylactic strategies to improve patient outcomes. Early detection rests on the ability to extract subtle yet clinically meaningful correlations that are often buried within several multimodal data streams and static patient information, spanning long periods of time.

4.4.1.1 Systems for Data Mining in Intensive Care

Modern patient monitors have evolved into complex system that not only measure physiological signals but also produce alerts when the physiological state of the patient appears to be out of range. State-of-the-art patient monitors allow physicians to program thresholds defining normality ranges for physiological systems. For example, one can program a patient monitor to produce an audible alert if the oxygen saturation level of the blood is below 85%. The values of these thresholds are typically obtained from general guidelines or from data mining processes. Such simple alerting schemes are well known to produce very large numbers of false alarms. In [17], it is reported that more than 92% of alarms generated in an ICU are of no consequence. Furthermore, there are many complex physiological patterns of interest to physicians that cannot be represented by a set of thresholds on sensor data streams. Several research initiatives [125] are addressing this problem with the design of platforms facilitating analysis beyond the simple thresholding capabilities of existing patient monitoring systems.

One example is BioStream [18], a system that performs real-time processing and analysis of physiological streams on a general purpose streaming infrastructure. The authors use ECG data along with temperature, oxygen saturation, blood pressure, and glucose levels as inputs into patient-

[2]Inpatient scenarios refer to scenarios for patients that are hospitalized for more than 24 hours. Outpatient scenarios refer to the rest of the clinical use-cases.

specific analytic applications. The system supports a different processing graph (for analysis) per patient, where the graph can be composed of system supplied operators (functions) and user implemented operators. The authors also state that BioStreams can be used to discover new patterns and hypotheses from the data and test them, however, there is limited discussion of the underlying analytics and use cases.

In [19] the authors describe an architecture for a system whose goals are data mining, fusion, and management of data streams for intensive care patients. The proposed system has online components for capture of physiological data streams and program execution along with offline components for data mining.

The SIMON (Signal Interpretation and MONitoring) platform [20] developed at Vanderbilt is a data acquisition system that continuously collects and processes bedside patient monitoring data. SIMON collects typical ICU monitoring vital signs including heart rate, blood pressures, oxygen saturations, intracranial and cerebral perfusion pressures, and EKG/ECG waveforms. This data collection is intended to support clinical research by enabling further analysis and mining. The system is also capable of producing alarms and has reporting capabilities though a Web interface and through event notification mechanisms.

The Online Healthcare Analytics infrastructure, also known as Artemis [22], is a programmable framework for real-time analysis of intensive care sensor data leveraging the IBM InfoSphere Streams (Streams) real-time high-performance stream analysis engine. OHA interfaces Streams with an open set of data collection systems (e.g., Excel Medical Electronics BedMasterEX system, the CapsuleTech data collection system), and leverages different data mining technologies and machine learning algorithms for the generation of models for prediction of the onset of complications in intensive care. OHA leverages Streams interface with well-known analytic software such as SPSS, SAS and R to provide data mining capabilities. Models learned with these data mining systems can be scored in real time, thus giving the analyst/physician the ability to test clinical hypotheses prospectively. This analytical loop is abstracted in Figure 4.2. It constitutes a general architecture for sensor data mining applications leveraging both at rest analytics for modeling and in motion analytics for the scoring of models in real time. The OHA system has been in use in live environments for the monitoring of neonates [22]. Its exploration capabilities are also used for the mining of sensor data for the early detection of complications in neurological ICUs [23].

OHA has been extended with patient similarity concepts to help physicians make decisions while leveraging past experiences gathered from similar patients who have been monitored in the past [24]. In [25], the MITRA system, introduced as an extension of OHA, allows physicians to query for similar patients and use records from these similar patients to make predictions on the health evolution of a patient of interest. An in-silico study using physiological sensor data streams from 1,500 ICU patients obtained from physionet [26] shows how MITRA may be used to forecast the trajectory of blood pressure streams and help predict acute hypotensive episodes in ICUs. In [27], similar approaches to time-series forecasting with applications to intensive care are also reported. Patient similarity techniques are described in this thesis as a way to extract robust features for forecasting purposes. Sequential learning techniques with Linear Dynamical Systems and Hidden Markov Models are proposed for the modeling stages.

4.4.1.2 State-of-the-Art Analytics for Intensive Care Sensor Data Mining

State-of-the-art analytics and mining approaches for in-hospital sensor data monitoring (Figure 4.3) tend to generate innovations on data preprocessing and transformation. Modeling is typically done with well-known families of machine learning techniques such as classification, clustering, and dynamic system modeling with sequential learning. These analytical techniques often attempt to derive features from physiological time series to model the *inflammatory response* of the body, as it is known to be highly correlated with early sign of complications in general. The inflammatory

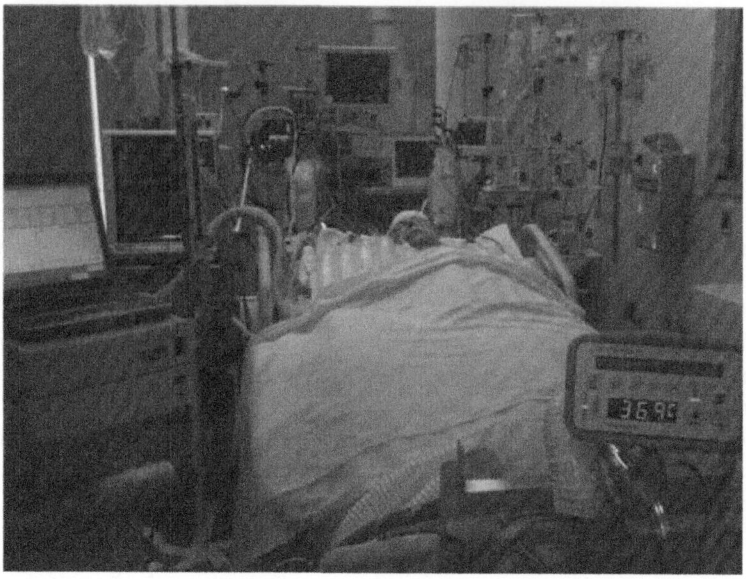

FIGURE 4.3 (See color insert.): Sensing in intensive care environments.

response is a reaction from the body to different harmful stimuli such as pathogens, various irritants, or even damaged cells. Hence, accurate modeling of it enables a wide range of early detection applications in intensive care. In particular, devastating complications such as sepsis are known to produce an inflammatory response well before the appearance of clinical symptoms [28].

The inflammatory response is controlled by the autonomic nervous system, consisting of the sympathetic and parasympathetic nervous systems [29]. These systems regulate several involuntary actions such heart beats, respiration, salivation, transpiration, etc. Inflammation results in poor regulation of these systems, and is often correlated with the Systemic Inflammatory Response Syndrome (SIRS) [30], [31]. The poor regulation manifests itself in loss of signal variability associated with physiological sensor streams. As a result, several researchers have attempted to model the inflammatory response using various measures estimating the signal variability of heart rate observations.[3] Monitoring reductions in Heart Rate Variability (HRV) has been a successful strategy for the early detection of disorders of the central and peripheral nervous system that induce a pro-inflammatory response [32].

Existing efforts to model the inflammatory response are focused primarily on the one-dimensional HRV analysis, due to a large body of work on ECG waveform processing. The Society for Complexity in Acute Illness (SCAI) [33] has devoted many efforts to model complexity and variability in the human body from ECG signals, as a way to model ICU patients and derive models predicting complications in ICUs. Variability metrics [34] typically used include spectral analysis techniques [35], approximations to uncomputable notions of randomness with the approximate and sample entropy [36],[37], and fractal analysis techniques like the Detrended Fluctuation Analysis (DFA) [38]. Surprisingly, classical information theoretic approaches to measure complexity with well understood concepts of compressibility and predictability [39] have received a modest amount of attention in acute care.

The success of variability analysis has been reported by many researchers. In [28], the authors perform a spectral analysis of heart rate measurements to show a relationship between heart rate

[3] Reductions in the variability of other vital signs such as respiration may also be correlated with the inflammatory response.

variability and sepsis. In [34], the potential of this approach is highlighted with a description of multiple clinical applications that use such complexity analysis. In [35] the authors derive several empirical links between heart rate variability and mortality in intensive care units. In [40], the prognostic potential of heart rate variability measures in intensive care is proposed. The authors in [41] have shown that reductions of heart rate variability are correlated with outcomes in pediatric intensive care. At the University of Virginia, Lake et al. [42] have used the sample entropy on heart rate measurements to predict the onset of sepsis in neonates. In [43] the predictive capability of heart rate variability on the prognosis of a large population of trauma patients is described.

Heart rate variability has also been used to determine when to extubate or remove patients from mechanical ventilation in intensive care [44]. A clinical trial is currently underway in Canada testing whether maintaining stable heart rate and respiratory rate variability throughout the spontaneous breathing trials, administered to patients before extubation, may predict subsequent successful extubation [44].

Besides heart rate variability analysis, there are many other applications of sensor data mining intensive care. Analysis of the dynamics of the ECG signal has enabled researchers to build systems for arrhythmia detection using standard machine learning and classification techniques. The work presented in [45] is illustrative of these systems.

Respiratory complications have also received a significant amount of attention in the intensive care community. In [46] the authors describe the use of sensor data from brain activity measured with electroencephalograms (EEG), eye movements measured with electrooculogram (EOG), muscle activity measured with electromyogram (EMG), and heart rhythm measured with ECGs during sleep, to detect obstructive sleep apnea episodes, that are known to be correlated with poor patient outcomes.

EEG signals have also been used beyond sleep apnea studies. In [47], EEG spectral analysis is performed to detect epileptic seizures with machine learning techniques, while in [48], continuous EEG spectral analysis for brain ischemia prediction is illustrated.

General predictive models for patient instability in intensive care have also been proposed in the literature. A notable example is the work in [49], where the authors extract several time series trending features from heart rate and blood pressure measurements collected every minute and build predictive models using a multivariable logistic regression modeling algorithm. This simple approach proves the ability to generate predictive alerts for hemodynamically unstable patients with high accuracy from trends computed on physiological signals.

In [50], a Bayesian belief network is developed to model ICU data and help caregivers interpret the measurements collected by patient monitors. The belief-network model represents knowledge of pathophysiologic or disease states in a causal probabilistic framework. The model is able to derive a quantitative description of the patient's physiological states as they progress through a disease by combining the information from both qualitative and quantitative or numerical inputs.

Another relevant body of work on sensor mining in intensive care environments has focused on the identification and removal of undesirable artifacts from sensor data streams. This includes mitigating the impact of missing and noisy events, as well as clinical interventions (e.g., drawing blood, medications) that complicate the data mining process (Section 13.2). In [51], a factorial switching Kalman Filtering approach is proposed to correct for artifacts in neonatal intensive care environments. In [52] the authors develop clever techniques leveraging dynamic Bayesian networks to analyze time-series sensor data in the presence of such artifacts.

4.4.2 Sensor Data Mining in Operating Rooms

Data mining applications that relate to operating rooms tend to focus on the analysis of Electronic Medical Record data where most sensor data inputs are filtered and summarized. For example, in [53], EMR data is used to improve the efficiency of operating rooms, in terms of scheduling (start times, turnover times) and utilization. In [54], knowledge management and data mining techniques are used to improve orthopedic operating room processes, yielding more effective decision making.

A few researchers have reported applications directly mining physiological sensor data produced by operating room monitoring systems. Exceptions are presented in [55] where the authors correlate EEG signals with cerebral blood flow measurements for patients undergoing carotid endarterectomy. This finding is quite valuable as it proves that EEG signals can be used to monitor complex mechanisms including cerebral blood flow for this patient population. In [56], machine learning techniques are proposed for the closed-loop control of anesthesia procedures. In [57], the authors present a prototype of a context-aware system able to analyze patient data streams collected in an operating room during surgical procedures, to detect medically significant events, and apply them in specific EMR systems.

4.4.3 General Mining of Clinical Sensor Data

Recent stimuli from the federal government and the increased ease of adoption of electronic health records system has led to widespread use of EHR in clinical practice. Large providers such as EPIC and McKesson have essentially unified the elements of data entry by having common platforms, although the use of free text and contextual rather than templated data is more common. EHR systems are a unique healthcare sensor, since real-time data and vast data troves are similar to other sensors, yet the relatively unstructured data makes it difficult to view this as a typical sensor. They typically contained structured and unstructured comprising of all the key administrative clinical data relevant to patients, demographics, progress notes, problems, medications, vital signs, past medical history, immunizations, laboratory data, diverse test results, and radiology reports [58]. Furthermore, there are no widely accepted standards for the representation of all these data points stored in EHR systems. Several code systems (e.g., ICD-9, ICD-10, CPT-4, SNOWMED-CT [59]) and interoperability standards (e.g., HL7, HIE) are in use by many systems but there are no overarching standards that EHR vendors are adhering to. Despite this lack of global standardization that is hindering the realization of very large-scale data mining, many researchers are spending considerable efforts to analyze these data sets to improve healthcare in general.

Mining of such sensors have been undertaken by various groups. The use of EHR mining to detect delays in cancer diagnosis, hospital-acquired complications, and the ability for groups to develop high throughput phenotyping to identify patient cohorts based on modular and consistent resources has been reported [127, 128, 129].

Demonstration of successful implementation of big data analytics in the Internet era coupled with the emergence of EHRs, has suddenly forced the healthcare industry to notice the use of large data in predicting patient outcomes, examining the effectiveness of policies and measures and healthcare prevention and improvement. Large cohorts maintained by insurance companies and in particular Medicare Claims data are easily accessible sources of data for researchers. The advantages of claims data include higher fidelity than EHR records given the emphasis on accuracy. Nevertheless, the lack of relevant clinical information and lower validity especially with bundling based on ICD-10 codes or Current Procedural Terminology (CPT) codes can lead to loss of granularity. While clinical trials remain the gold standard for the determination of efficacy of a form of treatment, the true effectiveness in the population is often unstudied. The use of a claims database lends itself to easy inclusion in Comparative Effectiveness Research (CER), which is a fairly innovative way of examining current evidence to detect best possible treatments.

For instance, Hospital Readmissions are an extremely important measure especially with the current pay for performance climate. An example of a claim-based algorithm developed at Johns Hopkins looks at patient specific risk factors to predict readmissions that they were able to perform with an AUC greater than 0.75 [133]. Similarly, a Bayesian Multi-Item Gamma Poisson Shrinkage algorithm applied to the Medicare Data examining the safety of the coxib class of drugs was able to confirm the association of these drugs with cardiac events and could be applied on a concurrent basis to identify and prevent harmful practices [134]. The lag time between the release of claims data and actual application can interfere with real-time interventions, although with improving EHR systems that can capture claims immediately, this may be avoided.

In [58], EHR data are mined to derive relationships between diabetic patients' usage of healthcare resources (e.g., medical facilities, physicians) and the severity of their diseases. In [60], Reconstructability Analysis (RA) is applied to EHR data to find risk factors for various complications of diabetes including myocardial infarction and microalbuminuria. RA is an information-theoretic technique used for mining of data sets of large dimensionality. In this setting, RA is used to induce relationships and correlations between EHR variables by identifying strongly related subsets of variables and to representing this knowledge in simplified models while eliminating the connections between all other weakly correlated subsets of variables. In [126], the authors propose an interesting framework for the mining of EHR data that models explicitly the temporal and sequential aspects present in longitudinal patient records.

In [61], data quality issues are reported while attempting to analyze EHR data for a survival analysis study on records of pancreatic cancer patients. Incomplete pathology reports for most of these patients forced the authors to exclude them from their study. The authors conclude this paper by suggesting complementing EHR data with more generic patient-related data to produce more complete patient representations where such data mining studies can be performed.

Batal et. al. present in [62] an approach to find temporal patterns in EHR data. At the core of their technique is the representation of longitudinal patient records with temporal abstractions. These abstractions are essentially summaries of intervals of time-series data. For example, patient body mass indices may be abstracted by increasing/decreasing/steady trend qualifiers. The authors also propose techniques for mining such EHR temporal abstraction using standard data mining schemes (e.g., apriori algorithm).

Neuvirth and his colleagues [63] proposed an interesting application of data mining techniques on EHR data for the management of chronic diseases. This application is able to predict patient future health states and identify high-risk patients for specific diseases where risk is a function of the likelihood of needing emergency care and the likelihood of receiving suboptimal treatments. They further explore the links between physicians treating these patient populations and outcomes to design a system that optimizes the matching between individual patients and physicians for better outcomes. Their analysis makes heavy use of standard machine learning techniques (e.g., logistic regression, K-Nearest Neighbor classification) and survival analysis (Cox modeling) and has generated interesting results for the management of diabetic patients.

The concept of patient similarity described above in Section 4.4.1 has also been on EHR data with the AALIM system [64], which uses content-based search techniques on different modality data to extract disease-specific patient information and find groups of similar patients. AALIM uses data from similar patients to help physicians make prognosis for a given patient and design care management strategies. Sensor data inputs into AALIM includes ECGs, videos, echocardiograms, MRIs, and text notes.

Social media is becoming more and more pervasive and the use of platforms such as Facebook (social networks), Twitter (microblogging sites), LinkedIn/Doximity (professional networks) and media platforms such as YouTube/Vimeo is also used extensively in healthcare. Social media has typically been a vehicle for dissemination of information, although the use of social media as a healthcare sensor is a very powerful tool. Recent use of an influenza surveillance system implented in the 2012–13 season demonstrated the use of social media as a healthcare sensor in detecting epidemics, which could then interface with public health efforts to contain them [130]. While the first three days of an epidemic are likely the most critical, the use of intelligent algorithms to mine this source of information can be critical to the successful implementation of strategies although there are no formal strategies in place currently [131, 132]. This media has also been used as a sensor to detect effectiveness of clinical trials, chronic disease control such as obesity, tobacco control, and sexual diseases among others.

With the emergence of question answering systems like IBM Watson [65], the potential to design systems able to ingest very large amounts of structured and unstructured clinical data to support clinical diagnosis and prognosis is emerging. Watson's ability to analyze the meaning and context of human language, and quickly process vast amounts of information to answer questions has wide applicability in healthcare. One can imagine applications where a properly trained Watson system can assist decision makers, such as physicians and nurses, in identifying the most likely diagnosis and treatment options for their patients. IBM and Wellpoint have partnered to develop such a system with applications to patient diagnosis [66]. A similar partnership with Memorial Sloan Kettering is in place for the diagnosis and management of cancer [67].

4.5 Nonclinical Healthcare Applications

The world is experiencing a rapid increase in its aging population, and a corresponding increase in the prevalence of chronic diseases and healthcare expenditure. For instance, the total Medicare expenditure in the United States has risen from $239.5 billion in 2000 to $524 billion in 2010. It is projected to be around $600 billion in 2014 and over a trillion by 2022. To react to these unprecedented rising costs, *Aging in place* has been proposed as one method to reduce costs and maintain quality of life for the aging population. The concept is to support older adults in the environment of their choice as opposed to placing them in traditional clinical settings or or nursing home environments. These initiatives also require city-wide technology allowing the elderly population to be mobile and live effectively in the society. Healthcare is being looked at as a continuum expanding outside of traditional clinical settings with goals to make it more proactive to reduce stress on medical institutions. Providing healthcare support outside of clinical environments with smart monitoring devices and e-health technology has been the focus of much research recently, especially in the ubiquitous computing research community.

Ubiquitous healthcare [68] is an emerging field of research that uses a large number of environmental and body sensors and actuators combined with sensor mining and analytic techniques to monitor and improve health of people in these types of settings. Ubiquitous healthcare approaches often employ several distributed and wireless sensors to gather information on bodily conditions such as temperature, heart rate, blood pressure, blood and urine chemical levels, breathing rate and volume, activity levels (derived from activity sensors such as pedometers, accelerometers, audio, and video cameras), and several other physiological characteristics that allow diagnosis of health problems. These sensors are either worn on or implanted in the body, or installed in the environment. Additionally, a subset of these sensors also include actuators that can trigger actions such as the release of small quantities of pharmaceutical drugs into the bloodstream, or the electrical stimulation of brain areas (e.g., those implicated in conditions such as Alzheimer's disease and Parkinson's disease or those associated with depression).

Ubiquitous healthcare has also relied heavily on the construction of *smart environments* where the environment itself is instrumented to capture the user behavior and their interaction with the external world. This includes several Radio Frequency Identification (RFID) tags and readers because of their durability, small size, and low costs. There is significant use of infrared sensors as well as video cameras and other sensors for motion detection, image processing, and control of in-home devices. Some environments also employ ultrasonic location tracking sensors, pressure sensors (deployed in various surfaces such as floors, etc.), and smart displays for information dissemination. These sensors are embedded in different parts of the home and workplace environment including on doors, beds, mirrors, bathrooms, mailboxes, in appliances such as microwaves and allow determining a comprehensive picture of user activities (Figure 4.4).

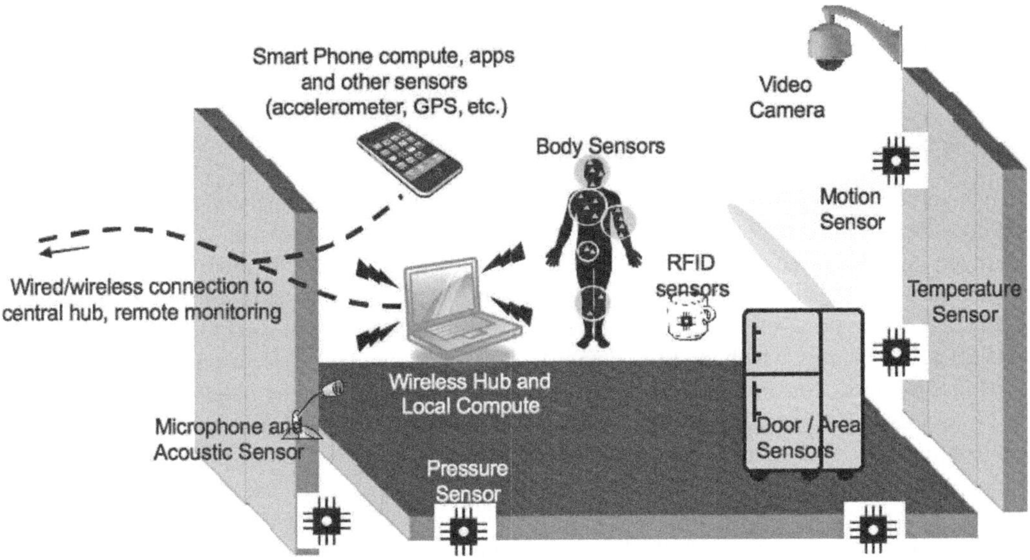

FIGURE 4.4: Sensing in home environments.

There are several trade-offs that need to be considered when deciding how many *smart environment* sensors are needed and where they should be placed in order to provide enough information for the analysis to accurately recognize activities. While a greater density of sensors provides more accurate information on the person position and their interactions with the environment, this comes with increased energy consumption, cost constraints, and intrusiveness. In addition, increasing sensors lead to increasing complexity, thus requiring a greater amount of data, large-scale algorithms, and systems to accurately learn activity models.

Reality mining [69] is also an emerging field complementing ubiquitous healthcare and leveraging data mining technologies. Reality mining processes all digital information available in the daily environments in which we evolve these days. Many of the daily activities we perform, such as checking our email, making phone calls, making a purchase, commuting, etc., leave digital traces and can be mined to capture records of our daily experiences. These human physical and social activity traces are captured by the multitude of sensors in mobile phones, cars, security cameras, RFID (smart card) readers, road-transport sensors, etc. Reality mining [69], is an emerging field of research that uses statistical analysis and machine learning methods on these digital traces to develop comprehensive pictures of our lives, both individually and collectively. Computational models based on this data, combined with any physiological information collected from body sensors and smart environments, can dramatically transform both individual as well as community health.

The different healthcare applications in nonclinical settings that we address in this chapter may be broadly categorized into:

- **Chronic Disease and Wellness Management Applications** that facilitate preventive care and chronic disease management and treatment, along with user programs to motivate happy and healthy behavior
- **Activity Monitoring Applications** that capture activities of daily living especially for elderly users, in remote healthcare settings
- **Reality Mining Applied to Healthcare** that applies machine learning techniques to data typically sensed with mobile phones to study complex social systems, including the study

of the distribution and patterns of health events, health characteristics, and their causes or influences in specific populations

4.5.1 Chronic Disease and Wellness Management

Several researchers have reported on remote patient monitoring systems with sensor mining capabilities for chronic disease and wellness management. In [70] the authors report on an interesting prototype streaming system called T2. T2 is designed to monitor remotely mobile patients' ECGs and accelerometers data streams. Using streaming analysis, the application is able to report periods of elevated heart rate to the clinician. The accelerometer data points are used to detect periods of physical activity during which the ECG data is filtered to account for different activity levels.

Holter Monitors constitute another class of sensors commonly used by patients with suspected cardiovascular problems. They are prescribed by physicians for several days during which a patient continuously wear them to have his/her ECG data continuously analyzed. The analysis of the recorded data is done offline to detect cardiac conditions of interest. The use of Holter Monitors is expanding as researchers seek ways to detect conditions and treat patients who have multiple diseases. In [71], researchers record both glucose and cardiac readings in diabetes patients with cardiac conditions to detect correlations between high glucose readings and ECG patterns.

A remote monitoring platform called Personal Care Connect (PCC) [72] has been extended with advanced distributed analytical capabilities. The resulting Harmoni platform allows for the distribution of analysis from back-end servers to remote devices located near the patient. Harmoni follows a three-tiered architecture with wearable sensors collecting data from the physical world, a data hub (typically a phone) aggregating and filtering the sensed data and a back-end server. Harmoni allows for the distribution and instantiation of monitoring rules on the data hub, triggered by changes in the context of the user being monitored. For example, while monitoring the heart rate of a user, thresholds for what constitute a normal heart rate are adjusted by inferring the activity of the user (e.g., sitting down vs. walking). Consequently, the system only reports contextually relevant information and the battery power of the sensors and the phone hub are extended with analytical rules requiring sensors to report measurement in a more granular way only in specific situations such as emergencies or during abnormal physiological episodes [73].

Several wireless Body Sensor Networks (BSNs) [74] [75] have been used in pilot applications for monitoring elderly patients with chronic conditions in outpatient settings. Using medical sensors such as ECG, several cardiovascular-related illnesses can be detected early by simply monitoring heartbeat rhythm (arrhythmias). Multiple heterogeneous sensor architecture can help, expanding the boundaries of BSNs application ranges. For instance, the DexterNet BSNs [76] use motion sensors (motes), GPS, and airborne particulate matter (PM) sensors to monitor as well as prevent asthma. Motion sensors (Accelerometer) combined with with Electromyogram (EMG) sensors that capture human motion balancing and muscular actives have been used to build postural stability and subject-independent classification models.

In the myHealthAssistant project [77], motion sensors data are integrated with general body sensors data to provide wellness and preventive healthcare services. This project focuses on the development of a system that helps reduce physical inactivity. The system captures individual user's activity throughout the day, and motivates users by calculating and suggesting new workout plans based on historical data on completed workouts.[4] In the base setup for daily activity monitoring, a single customized accelerometer, a smartphone, and a heart rate sensor are used together to identify five different activities, monitor the heart rate, and calculate the calorie expenditure. The system also allows the user to wear two additional accelerometers (strapped around the torso, and attached to the right weightlifting glove) while exercising in order to get a more accurate identification of 16

[4] Several studies [78] have shown that the Internet and phone-based user motivation systems can significantly increase the level of physical activity.

activities, and calorific expenditure. The analysis is performed at a local computer using a Gaussian model-based classifier.

Many other body sensor applications have been designed to monitor physical activities[5] as it is critical to maintain physical and psychological health, and reduce the risk of premature mortality, coronary heart disease, type II diabetes, colon cancer, and osteoporosis, and symptoms associated with mental health conditions such as depression and anxiety. Researchers [79] have developed the UbiFit Garden, which uses on-body sensing, activity inference, and a novel personal, mobile display to encourage physical activity. The UbiFit Garden system consists of three components: a fitness device, an interactive application, and a glanceable display. The fitness device automatically infers and communicates information about several types of physical activities to the glanceable display and interactive application. The interactive application includes detailed information about the individuals physical activities. The glanceable display, that resides on the background screen of a mobile phone uses a nonliteral, aesthetic representation of physical activities and goal attainment to motivate behavior. The UbiFit application includes the continuous monitoring of different fitness parameters and building statistical models of these to compute and project trends, and provide better information to users. Several other such fitness and physical activity monitoring applications are presented in [74].

The authors in [80] have shown how sensing body movements and eye movements can be used to generate data that provides contextual information to an adaptive hearing instrument. This instrument helps distinguishing different hearing needs in various acoustic environments. The authors record body movements, eye movements (using electrooculography), and hearing instrument sound in different simulated acoustic environments. They then use a Support Vector Machine (SVM) based classifier and person-independent training to show that these different sensor readings can accurately (in some cases up to 92%) determine the acoustic environment characteristics, and modify the settings of the hearing instrument appropriately.

Novel ways of correlating different body sensors to monitor dietary activities has been demonstrated in [81]. The authors' records include dietary parameters such as the rate of intake (in grams/sec), the number of chews for a food piece, etc., that capture palatability, satiety, and speed of eating. In particular, three core aspects of dietary activities were investigated using sensors: characteristic arm and trunk movement capture using inertial sensors, chewing of foods and food breakdown sounds using an ear microphone, and swallowing activity using a sensor-collar containing surface Electromyography (EMG) electrodes and a stethoscope microphone. The authors then build a recognition algorithm using time and frequency-domain features that addresses multiple challenges of continuous activity recognition, including the dynamic adaptability for variable-length activities and flexible deployment by supporting one to many independent classes. The approach uses a sensitive activity event search followed by a selective refinement of the detection using different information fusion schemes. The authors use selective fusion of detection results exploiting independent sources of error to filter out false positives and obtain an event classification in the same step, and achieve highly accurate activity recognition.

Recent work [82] has also focused on the use of body sensors for patient authentication. Credential-based authentication methods (e.g., passwords, certificates) are not well-suited for remote healthcare as these may be compromised. One-time authentication using credentials or trait-based biometrics (e.g., face, fingerprints, iris) do not cover the entire monitoring period and may lead to unauthorized postauthentication usage. Recent studies have shown that the human electrocardiogram (ECG) exhibits unique patterns that can be used to discriminate and authenticate individuals. However, perturbations of the ECG signal due to physical activity and other artifacts in real-world situations can lead to authentication failures. Sriram and Shin et al. [82] build an activity-aware bio-

[5]Commercial systems to encourage physical activity are used only while performing the target activity and are not trying to disambiguate that activity. Such technologies include Dance Dance Revolution, the Nintendo Wii Fit, the Nike+ system, Garmins Forerunner, Bones in Motions Active Mobile and Active Online, bike computers, heart rate monitors, MPTrain [17], Jogging over a distance [15], and mixed- and virtual-reality sports games [13, 14]

metric authentication system that combines ECG information with accelerometer data to handle the variability that arises from physical activity. The authors use the SHIMMER [83] sensing platform (with an integrated 3-axis accelerometer) developed by Intel Digital Health Advanced Technology Group to combine the motion and activity data with the ECG signal using a direct cable to a commercially available Polar WearLink Plus ECG chest strap. The sensor data is transmitted via a Bluetooth device to a computer running the BioMOBIOUS software for analysis. The mining uses different types of feature cleaning and preprocessing (beat-based linear interpolation) combined with K-Nearest Neighbor (KNN) and Bayesian network (BN) classification to obtain accurate user authentication under different activity levels.

The MIThril [84] project has focused on developing a next-generation wearable sensor research platform. The project includes the development and prototyping of new techniques of human-computer interaction (HCI) for body-worn applications, through the application of human factors, machine learning, hardware engineering, and software engineering. The MIThril project also involves research into constructing a new computing environment and developing prototype applications for health, communications, and just-in-time information delivery. The MIThril LiveNet [85] is a flexible distributed mobile platform that can be deployed for a variety of proactive healthcare applications. The LiveNet system allows people to receive real-time feedback from their continuously monitored and analyzed health state, as well as communicate health information with caregivers and other members of an individual's social network for support and interaction. Key components of this system include a PDA-centric mobile-wearable platform, the Enchantment software network and resource discovery API, and the MIThril real-time machine learning inference infrastructure. The LiveNet system is currently in use for multiple studies: capturing the effects of medication on the dyskinesia state of Parkinson's patients [86], a pilot epilepsy classifier study with the University of Rochester Center for Future Health, a depression medication study with the MGH Department of Neuroscience, and a hypothermia study with the Advanced Research in Environmental Medicine (ARIEM) at the Natick Army Labs [87].

The MyHeart [88] project funded by the IST program of the European Commission is a concerted effort aimed at developing intelligent systems for the prevention and monitoring of cardiovascular diseases using smart electronic and textile systems based wearable sensors, and appropriate services that empower the users to take control of their own health status. The MyHeart project integrates functional clothes with on-body sensors (textile and nontextile) and electronics to acquire, process, and evaluate physiological data. It also includes a wireless personal area network to transmit results to a mobile phone or PDA and from there to a server farm, to request professional medical services. Recently, there have also been several developments that combine on-body sensors with implantable sensors. The Healthy Aims [89] project of the European Commission focuses on developing a range of medical implants (Cochlear implant, retina implant and glaucoma sensor, implantable pressure sensor to monitor intracranial pressure, Sphincter sensor, and Inertial Measurement Unit) to assist aging people with disabilities.

The Wealthy [90] consortium was also established by the European Commission to fulfill the need to continuously monitor patient vital signs through novel-woven sensing interfaces that could be worn without any discomfort for the user. The focus of the project is on the development of smart material in fiber and yarn form endowed with a wide range of electrophysical properties (conducting, piezoresistive, etc.) for use as basic elements. The Alert Portable Telemedical Monitor (AMON), is another project whose aim is to develop a wrist-worn device encapsulating many sensors. Currently, blood pressure, pulse oximetry, ECG, accelerometer, and skin temperature are available. The device communicates directly to a telemedicine center via a GSM network, allowing direct contact with the patient if necessary. AMON enables patients that are not confined to a hospital to monitor continuously and analyze their vital signs.

The Motion Analysis Lab [91] is focused on researching rehabilitative tools in the treatment of mobility-limiting conditions in people with cerebral palsy, stroke, traumatic brain injury, spinal cord injury, Parkinson's Disease, and other neuromuscular disorders. In pursuit of this goal, the

MAL focuses on the rehabilitative possibilities of robotics and wearable sensor technology. The lab adopts these technologies for the purposes of retraining the gait in children with cerebral palsy and is leading research into development better prosthetics for amputees, interactive technology for stroke survivors, and traumatic brain injuries and people with burn-related contractures.

There is emerging interest in building Body Area Sensor Networks—large-scale BSNs across a public healthcare system such as a hospital. The miTag system [92] is a pilot public healthcare BSN deployed in the Baltimore Washington Metropolitan region. This system includes a wireless multi-sensor platform that collects information from GPS receivers, pulse oximeters, blood pressure cuffs, temperature sensors, and ECG sensors. The system supports two-way communication between patients and healthcare providers, to allow for feedback based on the monitored health and context information. Body Area Sensor Networks are also being developed to support disaster management in emergency response systems.

The maturity of sensor networks has allowed the development of smart environments for wellness and chronic disease management. For example, some researchers have used smart environments with combinations of wearable devices (RFID bracelets) and RFID tagged objects to detect indications of cognitive impairments such as dementia and traumatic brain injury (TBI) by monitoring individuals performing a well-defined routine task—making coffee [93]. The researchers define and compute a set of four domain specific features from the sensor data, that are increasingly representative of the task, and correlate with severity of cognitive impairment. These features include the Trial Duration, Action Gaps, Object Misuse, and Edit Distance. Trial Duration captures the total time taken for the activity while Action Gaps represent periods during which subjects were not interacting with any objects on the assumption that during those periods they are considering what step to take next. Object Misuse captures the number of times a subject interacts with each object used in the task—with failure to interact with a required object, or an excessive number of interactions indicates problems. Finally, the researchers manually define a representative plan[6] for the task, that represents a partial order (to allow alternate reasonable task executions) over object interaction. The Edit Distance, as used in natural language processing then captures deviations from this plan. Finally, these features are analyzed using Principal Component Analysis (PCA) to examine correlations between computed features and larger trends in the assessment data. They show that the first principal component includes a diverse set of measures of general intelligence, and appears to be a good proxy for general neuropsychological integrity, including measures of intellectual functioning, verbal and nonverbal reasoning, memory, and complex attention.

Researchers are developing several other techniques for the automatic detection of cognitive impairments, including automatically observing users play modified versions of different games. For instance, a modified version of the game FreeCell [94] is used in many studies. One study focuses on mouse movement during the game while others focus on the subject performance over time, comparing it to the performance of an automated solver. Using the results, it was possible to differentiate the three mildly cognitively impaired subjects from the six others. Work with several other computer games, specially created to perform assessments of cognitive impairments is underway with some promising early results. Researchers have also studied automatically monitoring mobility because slowed mobility may be a predictor of future cognitive decline. The time to answer a phone call was used to measure mobility, as were passive infrared detectors and several models to infer the mobility of subjects more directly as they move about a residence. More details on these may be obtained from [93].

Mining data from smart environments has also been used for sleep research [95] on a long-term basis, in a comfortable setting.[7] Inertial, ambient light, and time data are tracked from a wrist-

[6]Other research on activity recognition has addressed the question of automatically constructing plans for everyday activities by mining the Web for descriptions of these activities.

[7]The golden standard for observing sleep/wake patterns is polysomnography (PSG) that captures relevant sleep information with typically 20, mostly wired sensors attached to the patient's face, torso and limbs, making it costly, uncomfortable, and less feasible over longer periods.

worn sensor, and additional night vision footage is used for later expert inspection. The authors use two different classification techniques to monitor and classify the night sleep. Classifier 1 uses threshold-based segmentation on a Gaussian model-based classifier that calculates the variance and mean parameters for the light intensity and motion data from the training data, and uses a likelihood per minute of the awake state from the time-use database. Classifier 2 uses HMM-based segmentation to capture changes in sleep habits and state, and differentiate the awake state from the sleep state. The authors have shown that these techniques can be used for accurate sleep studies while minimizing the intrusiveness of the sensing environment for patients suffering from sleep disorders and psychiatric illnesses.

There has been a fair amount of work on using smart environments combined with body sensors for personal cardiac monitoring. This includes projects like Mobihealth [97] and PhMon [96]. Many of these solutions collect the physiological signals, but ECG analysis is performed remotely after transmission over a GPRS network. Recent work in multiple projects has enabled the processing of ECG data on a local device. MOLEC [98] analyses the ECG locally on a PDA and generates alarms to the hospital in case of high-risk arrhythmias. The authors in [99] develop an application whereby a heart patient is monitored using various types of sensors (ECG, accelerometer, Oxygen), and analyzed locally on a smartphone. The solution can be personalized by capturing location context, and includes rehabilitation applications for individual patients.

Additional efforts for wellness management include the Greenolive [100] platform, which is an open platform for a wellness management ecosystem. This platform provides a hosting environment for essential wellness management services using an elastic infrastructure to deal with scalability issues. Greenolive includes open APIs that allow new value-added services to be developed rapidly. The core platform consists of four components: Data Transformation and Routing Services, Wellness Monitoring Services, Wellness Analytic Services, and Wellness Record and Knowledge Repository. With these components, using a cloud-based computer infrastructure, developers can create different portals targeted towards both care assistants as well as portals that connect with the devices/sensors and provide end users wellness services based on the collected data. More details on the platform and the included mining and analytic capabilities can be obtained from [100].

4.5.2 Activity Monitoring

Several smart environments [101] have been built, deployed, and tested for pervasive healthcare applications focusing on activity monitoring. These applications, also called smart homes or offices, include combinations of environmental sensors—embedded in the home or the external environment—and body sensors for improved monitoring of people with different conditions and healthcare requirements.

One of the key roles of smart environments is to help researchers in this field monitor Activities of Daily Living (ADL), especially for the elderly population. In order to function independently at home, individuals need to be able to complete several ADLs such as eating, dressing, bathing, cooking, drinking, taking medicine, etc. Automating the recognition of these activities is an important step toward monitoring the functional health of a smart home resident. In addition to the ADL, researchers are also very interested in the interactions of users with the physical and social environment. This includes another set of activities such as using a telephone, shopping, housekeeping, doing laundry, transportation, handling finances, etc. These are collectively labeled Instrumental Activities of Daily Living (IADL) and also indicate different aspects of the functional health. In the absence of smart environments, the assessment of ADLs/IADLs has mostly been done manually through interviews and questionnaires. This is often a very time-consuming and error-prone process, and hence there is a strong need to automate the monitoring and recognition of these ADL/IADLs continuously via smart environments.

Some smart homes with healthcare technology for older adults have been developed as part of laboratory settings. The Smart Medical Home at the University of Rochester's Center for Future

Health [102] is one such example. The five-room house has infrared sensors, computers, biosensors, and video cameras. A large part of the research involves interactions of the research subjects (patients) with a medication advisor who provides advice on medication management and dietary adherence, memory assistance, and assistance with Smart Bandage. Smart Bandage is a program designed to decrease the burdens of chronic wound care at home. Future applications of this laboratory environment include gait monitoring, and observation of behavior and sleep. The Smart Medical Home is designed for adults of all ages, but it is not meant for actual habitation.

As described in [101], the Gator Tech Smart House at the University of Florida-Gainesville Mobile and Pervasive Computing Laboratory [103] is a laboratory-house created to assist older adults in maximizing independence. The house is equipped with (a) smart cameras for motion detection, image processing, and control of other in-home devices, (b) smart blinds that automatically close to block sunlight when the air conditioner is on, (c) ultrasonic location tracking transceivers that are installed on the ceiling corners of each room to detect movement, location, and orientation of the resident, (d) smart floor that uses pressure sensors embedded into each tile to detect falls and reports to emergency services, and (f) smart displays for entertainment media and information residents can follow from room to room. The house also includes a smart mailbox that senses and notifies the arrival of mail, a smart front door that identifies residents, using a radio-frequency identification tag among others, a smart bed that monitors sleeping patterns, a smart mirror that displays important messages or reminders such as when to take medication, and a smart bathroom that includes a toilet paper dispenser, a flush detector, and a water temperature regulating shower. The Gator Tech Smart House is adding healthcare technologies to assist diabetes management.

A set of smart home environments called CASAS has been setup in Washington State University. The CASAS home has five different testbed environments. The first, referred to as Kyoto [104], is a two-bedroom apartment that is equipped with motion sensors (positioned on the ceiling 1 m apart throughout the space), sensors to provide ambient temperature readings, and custom-built analog sensors to provide readings for hot water, cold water, and stove burner use. Voice-over IP captures phone usage, contact switch Q4 sensors monitor the open/closed status of doors and cabinets, and pressure sensors monitor usage of key items such as the medicine container, cooking tools, and telephone. The second testbed, referred to as Cairo is a two-bedroom, two-story home. There are three additional environments configured as single-resident apartments (Bosch1, Bosch2, and Bosch3) that are part of a single assisted-care facility. All of these environments contain motion sensors throughout the space as well as door contact sensors in key areas. Sensor data for each of the environments are captured using a sensor network and stored in a database. The data is analyzed for automatic ADL recognition, monitoring of a diabetic patient's diet, and exercise adherence. These environments also allow the presence of pets along with humans to simulate realistic settings. Researchers employ Hidden Markov Models (HMMs) to recognize possibly interleaved activities from a stream of sensor events, with the hidden states representing activities. There is also strong emphasis on questions pertaining to the selection, placement, and focus of sensors in a smart environment. In several studies conducted by researchers [104], they have employed mutual information (MI) based measures to rank sensors, and quantify the mutual dependence between the sensor reading and the activity of interest. They then use a filter-based sensor selection strategy to systematically evaluate the effect of removing sensors with low MI values on activity recognition performance. They also use hierarchical clustering to identify sensors with overlaps in the field of view in order to remove unnecessary sensors, and determine appropriate placements for the deployed sensors using a decision tree learner. They have shown that reductions on average of 20% of the sensors are possible for different types of activities and different configurations of the smart home.

Other laboratory smart environments include a two-story single-family house called Aware Home developed by the Georgia Institute of Technology. This is a living laboratory house designed primarily to assist adults with cognitive impairment [105]. For instance, the home includes a capture system on the kitchen countertop with a wall display that shows visual snapshots arranged as a series of panels to enable review of activities for users. A similar system can be used to support safe and complete medication adherence. This technology has also been used for diabetes management using a mobile phone to which a glucose meter can be connected via Bluetooth.

Besides these laboratory settings, there are also several smart homes that have been implemented in actual community settings, apartment complexes, and retirement housing units. These include a smart home in Vinson Hall Retirement Community in Missouri that is dedicated to serving former U.S. military officers and their families. Eskaton, Ltd. has created the National Demonstration Home in California with a range of technologies. The University of Missouri-Columbia has integrated sensor networks into privately owned apartments called TigerPlace II. A community-wide comprehensive smart home deployment is under development in McKeesport, Pennsylvania. The University at Buffalo, State University of New York, has utilized X10 devices to retrofit 50 homes for older adults with chronic conditions living alone in their own home. More details on these and other such smart home projects can be obtained from [101].

Researchers have recently investigated the use of domestic robots as a promising technology for persuasive telehealth [106]. Domestic robots have several unique features as compared against other devices in smart environments. One reason some technologies are difficult to use in persuasive telehealth systems is because they require the user to spend effort learning and becoming familiar with the technologies. Domestic robots are easier to use through their natural human-like communication, which can provide a pleasant experience for the user. Their friendliness can create an emotional bond that helps users, such as the elderly, feel more comfortable using them. Domestic robots are in fact effective informers, educators, reminders, and even readers of the users feelings and thoughts, which are hard to detect using other devices. While this effort is preliminary, and requires several technological advances, it is likely of significant interest for effective pervasive healthcare.

Multiple sensor mining technologies have been combined with such smart environment data gathering infrastructures to build healthcare applications targeting different requirements. The work in [107] uses frequent pattern mining to identify repeating structures in the routine patterns of human activity from environmental sensor data and detect changes in these patterns. This is important as the onset or complication of a life-threatening episode may be marked by changes in behavior and activity patterns. This has been shown to be true for several conditions including prostatism, degenerative joint disease, bursitis, and gastro-esophageal reflux, along with congestive heart failure, coronary artery disease, and chronic obstructive pulmonary disease.

Sensor mining, on data collected from a combination of body sensors and smart environments, has been used successfully for automatic assessment of ADL/IADL activities. In [108] RFID tags are attached to different key objects with which a person interacts for a specific set of activities. The data from these tags is augmented by accelerometers placed at diffrent strategic locations on the person (such as wrist, hip, and thigh). The combined dataset is analyzed using different feature extraction and mining and classification techniques. The computed features include statistical properties such mean, variance, energy, spectral entropy, pairwise correlation between the three axes, and the first ten FFT coefficients and exponential FFT bands, computed over sliding windows shifted in increments of 0.5 seconds. For classification of activities the authors use three different approaches, namely Naive Bayes, Hidden Markov Models (HMMs), and Joint Boosting. They show that Naive Bayes and HMM classifiers are well suited for low-level activities such as sitting, standing, walking, or woodworking activities. The Joint Boosting method is successfully applied to overcome limitations of the sensing and feature extraction. The results show that combined recognition helps in cases when tagged objects are being shared among the activities, as well as in periods when the RFID reader cannot detect interactions with objects due to its short range. The authors also consider extensions of this work to include techniques for accurate activity recognition with reduced supervision.

Researchers from the Imperial College [109] have developed an ear-based Activity Recognition (e-AR) sensor that identifies four different levels of activity ranging from almost no activity (during sleeping or sitting for example) to activities involving a lot of movement (running, exercising). The activity level is continuously detected using a classifier applied to the accelerometer measurements and streamed from the e-AR device every 4 seconds. While some activities may be described by a single activity level, many activities produce a sequence of activity levels. The work in [107] uses the output of the e-AR sensor to efficiently mine and update a concise variable-resolution synopsis routine for efficient behavior profiling in a home healthcare environment. The authors use the FP-Stream [110] and Closet+ [111] mining algorithms to describe behavior patterns using a routine tree data structure. The authors demonstrate that using this technique they can identify frequent patterns to describe the structure present in an individual's daily activity, and can then analyze both routine behavior as well as deviations.

4.5.3 Reality Mining

Reality mining [69] has recently been identified as one of 10 emerging technologies that could change the world. The scope of reality mining is very broad. It promises to allow us to build comprehensive pictures of our lives, with the potential of transforming our understanding of ourselves, our organizations, and our society. To reach this goal, reality mining pulls together any form of digital trace data that we generate as part of our daily activities. It then uses data mining and machine learning techniques on these data points to enable new nonintrusive applications in diagnosis, patient and treatment monitoring, health services use, surveillance of disease and risk factors, and public health investigation and disease control.

One of the key sensors employed by reality mining techniques is the mobile phone—that has become ubiquitous and a central part of our lives. Mobile phones being always carried by their users, they are able today to capture a lot of contextual information about them, including location (communication between the device and towers or GPS sensors) as well as data about their social connections (call and duration information). In addition, newer smartphones, e.g., the iPhone, include special sensors such as microphones, heart rate monitor, or accelerometers that allow the capture of important diagnostic and health-related data. These devices now also have the processing power of low-end desktop computers, allowing the deployment of several local analytics in support of healthcare applications.

Reality mining of these behavior signals may be correlated to the function of some major brain systems. It has been shown that arousal of the autonomic nervous system produces changes in activity levels. Hence, recent pilot projects have shown that it may be possible to diagnose depression from the way a person talks – depressed people tend to speak more slowly, a change that speech analysis software on a phone might recognize more readily than friends or family do [112]. Similarly, monitoring a phone with motion sensors can also reveal small changes in gait, which could be an early indicator of ailments such as Parkinson's disease.

The phone sensors may be used to measure time-coupling between people's speech and their movement, to capture indications of attention and screen for language development problems. The sensors can potentially capture the unconscious mimicry between people (e.g., reciprocated head nods, posture changes, etc.) as reliable predictors of trust and empathy, and improve compliance [113]. Similarly, the sensors can also be used to measure consistency or fluidity of movement or speech production to capture cognitive load. These different types of measurements of brain function have been shown to be predictive measures of human behavior [114], and play an important role in human social interactions thereby supporting new methods of diagnosis, treatment monitoring, and population health assessments.

In addition to these automated measurement streams from the phone sensors, these devices may also be used to collect self-reported data. Self-reported data from individuals during the course of their daily lives includes information such as symptoms, schedule, substance use, and mood that offer direct assessments of their cognitive and emotional states, perceptions of events, and general contextual information. By gathering self-reported data jointly with other reality mining data streams, accurate and dynamic aspects of various health phenomena can be revealed.

Besides information on individual health, cell phones can be also used to capture information about social relationships and social networks. Several pilot studies have shown how combined information on user location, proximity to other users, call and SMS patterns, and (with phones that have accelerometers) user motion can identify different patterns of behavior depending upon the social relationship between people. In [69] it has been shown that self-reported reciprocal friends (both persons report the other as a friend), nonreciprocal friends (only one of a pair reports the other as a friend), and reciprocal nonfriends (neither of a pair reports the other as a friend) exhibit very different patterns. It has been shown that coupled with appropriate statistical analysis, user social networks of friends and co-workers can be identified with average accuracies of up to 96% [115]. Such information has been shown to be useful for several healthcare applications including reinforcing active learning. In [116] the authors describe DiaBetNet, a computer game for young diabetics that leverages smartphone functionality to encourage young diabetics to keep track of their food intake, activity, and blood sugar level.

Several government health services rely on demographic data to guide service delivery. Reality mining also provides a way to characterize behavior, and thus provides a classification framework that is more directly relevant to health outcomes [114]. Reality mining research has shown that most people have only a small repertoire of behavior patterns, and that this small set of behavior patterns accounts for the vast majority of an individual's activity. Understanding the behavior patterns of different subpopulations and the mixing between them is critical to the delivery of public health services, because different subpopulations have different risk profiles and different attitudes about health-related choices. The use of reality mining to discover these behavior patterns can potentially provide great improvements in health education efforts and behavioral interventions.

Other attempts to model large-scale population health include Google Flu Trends [117] to detect influenza outbreaks indirectly by tracking the frequency of World Wide Web searches for terms related to influenza-like illnesses. For geographic areas as small as states in the United States, Google researchers have demonstrated that such search frequencies correlate strongly with estimated influenza incidence based on conventional surveillance of cases detected in a Centers for Disease Control and Prevention (CDC) network of sentinel laboratories and physicians. Similarly, the Automated Epidemiologic Geotemporal Integrated Surveillance System (AEGIS), developed by Children's Hospital Boston, involves Internet-based data collection, management, and analysis systems to produce timely estimates of incidence. Almost 30,000 residents of Belgium, the Netherlands, and Portugal voluntarily report on their influenza symptoms on a weekly basis at the Gripenet websites [118].

Reality mining can also have a significant impact on epidemiologic investigations that capture the impact of exposures to different types of environments and pathogens on population health.[8] For instance, traditional investigations attempting to find links between individual exposures to airborne pollutants (particulate matter, carbon monoxide, and nitric oxide) and health conditions have relied on comparisons of aggregates of persons, or static measures and snapshots of exposure. This has impacted the effectiveness of such studies, and the associated costs. As opposed to these aggregate or static approaches, reality mining can be used to capture dynamic measures of time-activity patterns in relation to exposures. The cell phone location data can be combined with existing air quality monitoring stations and/or inferred from vehicle traffic patterns and locations of industrial facilities to yield spatially precise measures of exposure suitable for studying large samples of individuals.

While the discussion on reality mining in this chapter has been dominated by information captured from individual mobile phones, additional data points can be obtained from several aspects of our cities that are getting more and more instrumented. This includes our transportation infrastructures, security infrastructures, energy and utility systems, food production and distribution. Combining all of this information at scale, overcoming the associated data ownership, privacy, and connectivity challenges, and analyzing it can provide significant benefits towards improving the delivery

[8]The Spatio-Temporal Epidemiological Modeler (STEM) [119] activity tool has recently been proposed as an open source application designed to help scientists and public health officials create and use models of emerging infectious diseases.

and advancement of healthcare both for personal healthcare as well as population health management.

4.6 Summary and Concluding Remarks

This chapter surveys the application of sensor data mining in medical informatics. With the general increased instrumentation of the world with sensors, the need to make healthcare delivery more proactive, the ability to mine sensor data in healthcare is receiving a significant amount of attention. Despite these efforts, several challenges both technical and nontechnical remain to be solved. We have surveyed these challenges in this chapter, before presenting illustrative applications of sensor data mining technologies, both for clinical and nonclinical applications.

Bibliography

[1] "Health care—Definition from the Merriam-Webster Dictionary" `http://www.merriam-webster.com/dictionary/health\%5C\%20care`

[2] William W. Stead, "Medical Informatics On the Path Toward Universal Truths," *Journal of the American Informatics Association*, 1998 Nov–Dec; 5(6): 583–584.

[3] Vimla L. Patel and David R. Kaufman,"Science and Practice: A Case for Medical Informatics as a Local Science of Design," *Journal of the American Medical Informatics Association.* 1998 Nov-Dec; 5(6): 489492.

[4] "HIMSS Analytics Survey Demonstrates Awareness and Usage of Remote Health Monitoring Devices," retrieved from `https://www.himssanalytics.org/about/NewsDetail.aspx?nid=79508`

[5] "Instant Heart Rate," retrieved from `http://www.azumio.com/apps/heart$-$rate/`

[6] "Using the Nike+iPod Sensor," retrieved from `http://walking.about.com/od/pedometer1/ss/nikeplussensor\_4.htm`

[7] "Data Mining: Concepts and Techniques, Second Edition," The Morgan Kaufmann Series in Data Management Systems, 2005.

[8] "CRISP DM 1.0, Step-by-Step Data Mining Guide," retrieved from `http://www.the-modeling-agency.com/crisp-dm.pdf`

[9] "Health Care Devices," retrieved from `http://www.hl7.org/special/committees/healthcaredevices/overview.cfm`

[10] "Continua Health Alliance," retrieved from `http://www.continuaalliance.org/index.html`

[11] Chan-Yong Park, Joon-Ho Lim, and Soojun Park, "ISO/IEEE 11073 PHD Standardization of Legacy Healthcare Devices for Home Healthcare Services," IEEE International Conference on Consumer Electronics (ICCE), 2011.

[12] Charu Aggarwal and Philip Yu (eds.), *Privacy Preserving Data Mining: Models and Algorithms*, Springer, 2008

[13] Rakesh Agrawal and Ramakrishnan Srikant, "Privacy Preserving Data Mining," SIGMOD '00 *Proceedings of the 2000 ACM SIGMOD International Conference on Management of Data*, 2000.

[14] Saeid Sanei and J.A. Chambers, *EEG Signal Processing*, Wiley-Interscience; 1st edition, 2007.

[15] John Saunders, "The Practice of Clinical Medicine as an Art and as a Science," *Medical Humanities* 2000; 26:18–22.

[16] Robert Trowbridge and Scott Weingarten, "Clinical Decision Support Systems," retrieved from `http://www.ahrq.gov/clinic/ptsafety/chap53.htm`

[17] C.L. Tsien and J.C. Fackler, "Poor prognosis for Existing Monitors in the Intensive Care Unit," *Critical Care Medicine*, 1997 Apr; 25(4): 614–619.

[18] A. Bar-Or, J. Healey, L. Kontothanassis, and J.M. Van Thong, "BioStream: A System Architecture for Real-Time Processing of Physiological Signals," IEEE Engineering in Medicine and Biology Society, 2004. IEMBS '04. 26th Annual International Conference, 2004.

[19] H. Hyoil, R. Han, and H. Patrick. "An Infrastructure of Stream Data Mining, Fusion and Management of Monitored Patients," in IEEE Symposium on Computer-Based Medical Systems, 2006.

[20] Patrick R. Norris and Benoit M. Dawant, "Knowledge-Based Systems for Intelligent Patient Monitoring and Management in Critical Care Environments," in *The Biomedical Engineering Handbook*, Second Edition. 2 Volume Set Edited by Joseph D. Bronzino, CRC Press 1999.

[21] D. Curtis, E. Pino, J. Bailey, E. Shih, J. Waterman, S. Vinterbo, T. Stair, J. Gutagg, R. Greenes, and L. Ohno-Machado, "Smart—An Integrated, Wireless System for Monitoring Unattended Patients," *Journal of the American Medical Informatics Association*, 15(1): 44–53, January–February 2008.

[22] M. Blount, M. Ebling, M. Eklund, A. James, C. McGregor, N. Percival, K. Smith, and D. Sow, "Real-Time Analysis for Intensive Care: Development and Deployment of the Artemis Analytic System," *IEEE Engineering in Medicine and Biology Magazine*, May 2010; 29(2): 110–118.

[23] Daby Sow, Michael Schmidt, David Alberts, Alina Beygelzimer, Alain Biem, Gang Luo, and Deepak Turaga, "Developing and Deploying Clinical Models for the Early Detection of Clinical Complications in Neurological Intensive Care Units," 2011 AMIA Clinical Research Informatics Summit.

[24] J. Sun, D. Sow, J. Hu, and S. Ebadollah,"A System for Mining Temporal Physiological Data Streams for Advanced Prognostic Decision Support," In 10th IEEE International Conference on Data Mining, December 2010.

[25] S. Ebadollahi, J. Sun, D. Gotz, J. Hu, D. Sow, and C. Neti, "Predicting Patient's Trajectory of Physiological Data Using Temporal Trends in Similar Patients: A System for Near-Term Prognostics," 2010 AMIA Annual Symposium.

[26] "MIMIC (Multiparameter Intelligent Monitoring in Intensive Care) II Database [Online]" available at `http://physionet.org/physiobank/database/mimic2db/`

[27] Lei Li, "Fast Algorithms for Mining Co-evolving Time Series," Ph.D. thesis, September 2011 CMU-CS-11-127.

[28] C. S. Garrard, D. A. Kontoyannis, and M. Piepoli, "Spectral Analysis of Heart Rate Variability in the Sepsis Syndrome," *Clinical Autonomic Research* official journal of the Clinical Autonomic Research Society 1993, 3(1): 5–13.

[29] "The Autonomic Nervous System," retrieved from `http://www.ndrf.org/ans.html`

[30] Elizabeth G. NeSmith, Sally P. Weinrich, Jeannette O. Andrews, BC, Regina S. Medeiros, Michael L. Hawkins, and Martin Weinrich, "Systemic Inflammatory Response Syndrome Score and Race as Predictors of Length of Stay in the Intensive Care Unit," *American Journal of Critical Care*, 2009; 18(4).

[31] U. Jaffer, R. Wade, and T. Gourlay, "Cytokines in the Systemic Inflammatory Response Syndrome: A Review," *Links* 2009.

[32] S. Ahmad, A. Tejuja, K.D. Newman, R. Zarychanski, and A.J. Seely, "Clinical Review: A Review and Analysis of Heart Rate Variability and the Diagnosis and Prognosis of Infection," *Critical Care*. 2009;13(6): 232. Epub 2009 Nov 24.

[33] "The Society for Complexity and Acute Illness," retrieved from `http://www.scai-med.org/`

[34] Timothy Buchman, Phyllis Stein, and Brahm Goldstein, "Heart Rate Variability in Critical Illness and Critical Care," *Current Opinion in Critical Care*, August 2002; 8(4): 113–115.

[35] R.J. Winchell and D.B. Hoyt, "Spectral Analysis of Heart Rate Variability in the ICU: A Measure of Autonomic Function," *Journal of Surgical Research*. 1996 Jun; 63(1): 11–16.

[36] Steve Pincus and Burton Singer, "Randomness and Degrees of Irregularity," *Proceedings of the National Academics of Science*; 93: 2083–2088, March 1996.

[37] J.S. Richman and R. Moorman, "Physiological Time-Series Analysis Using Approximate, Entropy and Sample Entropy," *American Journal of Physiology. Heart and Circulatory Physiology*, 2000; 278: H2039–H2049.

[38] R. Bryce and B. Sprague, "Revisiting Detrended Fluctuation Analysis," *Scientific Reports*. 2012/03/14/online Vol. 2.

[39] M. Feder, N. Merhav, and M. Gutman, "Universal Prediction of Individual Sequences," *IEEE Transactions on Information Theory*; 38: 1258–1270, July 1992.

[40] H. L. Kennedy, "Heart Rate Variability — A Potential, Noninvasive Prognostic Index in the Critically Ill Patient," *Critical Care Medicine*, 1998; 26(2): 213–214.

[41] B. Goldstein, D.H. Fiser, M.M. Kelly, D. Mickelsen, U. Ruttimann, and M.M. Pollack, "Decomplexification in Critical Illness and Injury: Relationship between Heart Rate Variability, Severity of Illness, and Outcome," *Critical Care Medicine*. 1998 Feb; 26(2): 352–357.

[42] D.E. Lake, J.S. Richman, P. Griffin, and R. Moorman, "Sample Entropy Analysis of Neonatal Heart Rate Variability," *American Journal of Physiology*. 2002; 283: R789–R797.

[43] William P. Riordan, Patrick R. Norris, Judith M. Jenkins and John A. Morris, "Early Loss of Heart Rate Complexity Predicts Mortality Regardless of Mechanism, Anatomic Location, or Severity of Injury in 2178 Trauma Patients," *Journal of Surgical Research* 2009; 156(2): 283–289.

[44] "Weaning and Variability Evaluation (WAVE)," retrieved from http://clinicaltrials.gov/ct2/show/NCT01237886

[45] N.V. Thakor and Y.S. Zhu, "Applications of Adaptive Filtering to ECG Analysis: Noise Cancellation and Arrhythmia Detection," *IEEE Transactions on Biomedical Engineering,* Aug. 1991; 38(8).

[46] Virend K. Somers, Mark E. Dyken, Mary P. Clary, and Francois M. Abboud, "Sympathetic Neural Mechanisms in Obstructive Sleep Apnea," *Journal of Clinical Investigation*, October 1995; 1897–1904.

[47] A. Shoeb. "Application of Machine Learning to Epileptic Seizure Onset Detection and Treatment," PhD Thesis, Massachusetts Institute of Technology, 2009.

[48] B. Foreman and J. Claassen,"Quantitative EEG for the Detection of Brain Ischemia," *Critical Care* 2012, 16: 216.

[49] H. Cao, L. Eshelman, N. Chbat, L. Nielsen, B. Gross, and M. Saeed, "Predicting ICU Hemodynamic Instability Using Continuous Multiparameter Trends," EMBS 2008, 30th Annual International Conference of the IEEE Engineering in Medicine and Biology Society, 2008.

[50] Geoffrey W. Rudedge, Stig K. Andersen, Jeanette X. Polaschek and Lawrence M. Fagan, "A Belief Network Model for Interpretation of ICU Data," *Proceedings of the Annual Symposium on Computer Application in Medical Care*, Nov 7, 1990: 785–789.

[51] J.A. Quinn and C.K.I. Williams, "Physiological Monitoring with Factorial Switching Linear Dynamical Systems," In *Bayesian Time Series Models*, eds. D. Barber, A. T. Cemgil, S. Chiappa, Cambridge University Press, 2011.

[52] Norm Aleks, Stuart Russell, Michael G. Madden, Diane Morabito, Kristan Staudenmayer, Mitchell Cohen, and Geoffrey Manley, "Probabilistic Detection of Short Events, with Application to Critical Care Monitoring," Neural Information Processing Systems (NIPS) 2008.

[53] B. Randall Brenn,"Using Your EMR to Improve Operational Efficiency," retrieved from http://www.pedsanesthesia.org/meetings/2009annual/syllabus/pdfs/submissions/Using\%20your\%20EMR\%20to\%20improve\%20operational\%20efficiency-B\%20Randall\%20Brenn\%20MD.pdf

[54] Nilmini Wickramasinghe, Rajeev K. Bali, M. Chris Gibbons, J.H. James Choi, and Jonathan L. Schaffer, "A Systematic Approach Optimization of Healthcare Operations with Knowledge Management," *JHIM* Summer 2009; 23(3): www.himss.org.

[55] F.W. Sharbrough, J.M. Messick and T.M. Sundt, "Correlation of Continuous Electroencephalograms with Cerebral Blood Flow Measurements during Carotid Endarterectomy," *Stroke* 1973, 4: 674–683.

[56] O. Caelen, G. Bontempi, E. Coussaert, L. Barvais, and F. Clement, "Machine Learning Techniques to Enable Closed-Loop Control in Anesthesia," 19th IEEE International Symposium on Computer-Based Medical Systems, 2006. CBMS 2006.

[57] S. Agarwal, A. Joshi, T. Finin, Y. Yesha, and T. Ganous, "A Pervasive Computing System for the Operating Room of the Future," *Journal Mobile Networks and Applications Archive*, March 2007; 12(2–3).

[58] Noah Lee, Andrew F. Laine, Jianying Hu, Fei Wang, Jimeng Sun, and Shahram Ebadollahi, "Mining Electronic Medical Records to Explore the Linkage Between Healthcare Resource Utilization and Disease Severity in Diabetic Patients," First IEEE International Conference on Healthcare Informatics, Imaging and Systems Biology (HISB) 2011.

[59] N. Ramakrishnan, "Mining Electronic Health Records," *IEEE Computer*, 2010; 43(10): 77–81.

[60] Adam Wright, Thomas N. Ricciardi, and Martin Zwick, "Application of Information-Theoretic Data Mining Techniques in a National Ambulatory Practice Outcomes Research Network," *AMIA Annual Symposium Proceedings*, 2005; 2005: 829–833.

[61] Taxiarchis Botsis, Gunnar Hartvigsen, Fei Chen, and Chunhua Weng, "Secondary Use of EHR: Data Quality Issues and Informatics Opportunities," *AMIA Summits Translational Science Proceedings*, 2010; 2010: 1–5.

[62] I. Batal, H. Valizadegan, G.F. Cooper, and M. Hauskrecht, "A Pattern Mining Approach for Classifying Multivariate Temporal Data," IEEE International Conference on Bioinformatics and Biomedicine, Atlanta, Georgia, November 2011.

[63] H. Neuvirth, M. Ozery-Flato, J. Hu, J. Laserson, M. Kohn, S. Ebadollahi, and M. Rosen-Zvi, "Toward Personalized Care Management of Patients at Risk: The Diabetes Case Study," Proceedings of the 17th ACM SIGKDD International Conference on Knowledge Discovery and Data Mining, 2011:395–403.

[64] Fei Wang, Tanveer Syeda-Mahmood, Vuk Ercegovac, David Beymer, and Eugene J. Shekita, "Large-Scale Multimodal Mining for Healthcare with MapReduce," ACM IHI Conference 2010.

[65] "IBM Watson," retrieved from `http://www-03.ibm.com/innovation/us/watson/index.html`

[66] "IBM's Watson Embarks on Medical Career," retrieved from `http://www.computerworld.com/s/article/358871/IBM\_s\_Watson\_to\_Diagnose\_Patients`

[67] L. Mearian, "IBM's Watson Expands Cancer Care Resume," retrieved from `http://www.computerworld.com/s/article/9225515/IBM\_s\_Watson\_expands\_cancer\_care\_resume`

[68] Ian Brown and Andrew Adams, "The Ethical Challenges of Ubiquitous Healthcare," *International Review of Information Ethics* Dec 2007; 8(12):53–60.

[69] A. Pentland, D. Lazer, D. Brewer, and T. Heibeck, "Improving Public Health and Medicine by Use of Reality Mining," *Studies in Health Technology Informatics* 2009; 149: 93–102.

[70] C.-M. Chen, H. Agrawal, M. Cochinwala, and D. Rosenblut, "Stream Query Processing for Healthcare Bio-sensor Applications," in 20th International Conference on Data Engineering, 2004, 791–794.

[71] C. Desouza, H. Salazar, B. Cheong, J. Murgo, and V. Fonseca, "Association of Hypoglycemia and Cardiac Ischemia," *Diabetes Care*, May 2003, 26(5): 1485–1489.

[72] M. Blount, V.M. Batra, A.N. Capella, M.R. Ebling, W.F. Jerome, S.M. Martin, M. Nidd, M.R. Niemi, and S.P. Wright, "Remote Health-Care Monitoring Using Personal Care Connect," *IBM Systems Journal* January 2007; 46(1): 95–113.

[73] I. Mohomed, A. Misra, M.R. Ebling, and W. Jerome, "HARMONI: Context-aware Filtering of Sensor Data for Continuous Remote Health Monitoring," Sixth Annual IEEE International Conference on Pervasive Computing and Communications (Percom 2008), Hong Kong, China, March 2008.

[74] M. Chen, S. Gonzalez et al., "Body Area Networks: A Survey," *Mobile Network Applications* (2011); 16: 171–193.

[75] M. Garg, D.-J. Kim, D.S. Turaga, B. Prabhakaran, "Multimodal Analysis of Body Sensor Network Data Streams for Real-Time Healthcare," ACM MIR 2010.

[76] E. Seto, A. Giani et al., "A Wireless Body Sensor Network for the Prevention and Management of Asthma, in *Proceedings of the IEEE Symposium on Industrial Embedded Systems*, (SIES), July, 2009.

[77] C. Seeger, A. Buchmann, and K. Van Laerhoven, "myHealthAssistant: A Phone-based Body Sensor Network that Captures the Wearers Exercises throughout the Day," The 6th International Conference on Body Area Networks, 2011.

[78] D. Tate, R. Wing, and R. Winett, "Using Internet Technology to Deliver a Behavioral Weight Loss Program," *JAMA*, 2001; 285(9): 1172–1177.

[79] S. Consolvo, D. McDonald et al., "Activity Sensing in the Wild: A Field Trial of UbiFit Garden," Conference on Human Factors in Computing Systems, 2008.

[80] B. Tessendorf, A. Bulling et al., "Recognition of Hearing Needs from Body and Eye Movements to Improve Hearing Instruments," International Conference on Pervasive Computing, 2011.

[81] O. Amft, and G. Troster, "Recognition of Dietary Activity Events Using On-Body Sensors," *Artificial Intelligence in Medicine*. 2008 Feb; 42(2): 121–136.

[82] J. Sriram, M. Shin et al., "Activity-Aware ECG-Based Patient Authentication for Remote Health Monitoring," ICMI-MLMI '09 Proceedings of the 2009 International Conference on Multimodal Interfaces.

[83] "The Shimmer Platform", retrieved from `http://shimmer-research.com/`

[84] R. DeVaul, M. Sung et al., "MIThril 2003: Applications and Architecture," International Symposium of Wearable Computers, October, 2003.

[85] M. Sung, and A. Pentland, "LiveNet: Health and Lifestyle Networking Through Distributed Mobile Devices," Mobisys 2004.

[86] J. Weaver, "A Wearable Health Monitor to Aid Parkinson Disease Treatment," MIT M.S. Thesis, June 2003.

[87] M. Sung, "Shivering Motion/Hypothermia Classification for Wearable Soldier Health Monitoring Systems," Technical Report, MIT Media Lab, Dec. 2003.

[88] "MyHeart—Fighting Cardio-Vascular Diseases by Prevention & Early Diagnosis," FP6 Integrated Project, `http://www.hitechprojects.com/euprojects/myheart/`

[89] "Healthy Aims," `http://www.healthyaims.org/`

[90] "Wearable Health Care System," `http://www.wealthy-ist.com/`

[91] "Motion Analysis Lab," http://www.spauldingnetwork.org/research/motion-analysis-lab.aspx

[92] T. Gao, C. Pesto et al., "Wireless Medical Sensor Networks in Emergency Response: Implementation and Pilot Results," in *Proceedings of the 2008 IEEE Conference on Technologies for Homeland Security*, pp:187-192, Waltham, MA, May 2008, 187–192.

[93] M. Hodges, N. Kirsch, M. Newman, and M. Pollack, "Automatic Assessment of Cognitive Impairment through Electronic Observation of Object Usage," *Pervasive Computing* 2010; 6030:192–209.

[94] H. Jimison, M. Pavel, and J. McKanna, "Unobtrusive Computer Monitoring of Sensory-Motor Function," *Proceedings of the 2005 IEEE Engineering in Medicine and Biology 27th Annual Conference* (September 2005).

[95] M. Borazio, and K. Van Laerhoven, "Combining Wearable and Environmental Sensing into an Unobtrusive Tool for Long-Term Sleep Studies," IHI 2012.

[96] "PhMon Personal Health Monitoring System with Microsystem Sensor Technology," retrieved from http://www.phmon.de/englisch/index.html

[97] V. Jones, A. van Halteren et al., "MobiHealth: Mobile Health Services Based on Body Area Networks," in *M-Health Emerging Mobile Health Systems*. Springer-Verlag, Berlin, 219–236.

[98] J. Rodriguez, A. Goni, and A. Illarramendi, "Real-time classification of ECGs on a PDA," *IEEE Transactions on Information Technology in Biomedicine*, March 2005; 9(1): 23–34.

[99] P. Leijdekkers, and V. Gay, "Personal Heart Monitoring and Rehabilitation System Using Smart Phones," Mobile Business, 2006. ICMB '06.

[100] L. Zeng, P.-Y. Hsueh, and H. Chang, "Greenolive: An Open Platform for Wellness Management Ecosystem," Service Operations and Logistics and Informatics (SOLI), 2010.

[101] Machiko R. Tomita, Linda S. Russ, Ramalingam Sridhar, Bruce J. Naughton M. (2010). "Smart Home with Healthcare Technologies for Community-Dwelling Older Adults," in *Smart Home Systems*, Mahmoud A. Al-Qutayri (Ed.), InTech.

[102] "Smart Medical Home Research Laboratory. University of Rochester," Retrieved from http://www.futurehealth.rochester.edu/smart;home/

[103] S. Helal, W. Mann et al, "The Gator Tech Smart House: A Programmable Pervasive Space," *IEEE Computer*, March 2005; 38(3): 64–74.

[104] D. Cook, and L. Holder, "Sensor Selection to Support Practical Use of Health-Monitoring Smart Environments," *Data Mining and Knowledge Discovery*, 2011 July; 1(4):339–351.

[105] "Georgia Institute of Technology (2009) Aware Home Research Institute," Retrieved from http://awarehome.imtc.gatech.edu

[106] D. Lee, S. Helal et al., "Participatory and Persuasive Telehealth," *Gerontology*, 2012; 58(3): 269–281.

[107] "Pattern Mining for Routine Behaviour Discovery in Pervasive Healthcare Environments," Proceedings of the 5th International Conference on Information Technology and Application in Biomedicine, May 2008.

[108] M. Stikic, T. Huynhy, K. Van Laerhoveny, and B. Schieley, "ADL Recognition Based on the Combination of RFID and Accelerometer Sensing," *Pervasive Computing Technologies for Healthcare*, 2008; 258–263.

[109] B. Lo, L. Atallah et al., "Real-Time Pervasive Monitoring for Postoperative Care," in *Proceedings of the 4th International Workshop on Wearable and Implantable Body Sensor Networks*, Aachen, 2007, 122–127.

[110] C. Giannella, J. Han, et al., "Mining Frequent Patterns in Data Streams at Multiple Time Granularities," Kargupta, A. Joshi, K. Sivakumar, and Y. Yesha (eds.), *Next Generation Data Mining*, AAAI/MIT Press, 2004.

[111] J. Wang, J. Han, and J. Pei, and CLOSET+: Searching for the Best Strategies for Mining Frequent Closed Itemsets," in *Proceedings of the 9th ACM SIGKDD*, 2003.

[112] W. Stoltzman, "Toward a Social Signaling Framework: Activity and Emphasis in Speech," Master's thesis, MIT EECS, 2006.

[113] J. Bailenson, and N. Yee, "Digital chameleons: Automatic Assimilation of Nonverbal Gestures in Immersive Virtual Environments," *Psychological Science*, 2005; 16(10): 814–819.

[114] A. Pentland, *Honest Signals: How They Shape Your World,* MIT Press, 2008.

[115] W. Dong, and A. Pentland, "Modeling Influence between Experts," *Lecture Notes on AI: Special Volume on Human Computing*, 4451: 170-189.

[116] V. Kumar, and A. Pentland, "DiaBetNet: Learning and Predicting Blood Glucose Results to Optimize Glycemic Control," 4th Annual Diabetes Technology Meeting, Atlanta, GA.

[117] J. Ginsberg, M.H. Mohebbi et al., "Detecting Influenza Epidemics Using Search Engine Query Data," *Nature* 2009; 457:1012–1014.

[118] S.P. Van Noort, M. Muehlen et al., "Gripenet: An Internet-Based System to Monitor Influenza-Like Illness Uniformly Across Europe," *Eurosurveillance*, 12(7): 2007. `http://www.eurosurveillance.org/ViewArticle.aspx?ArticleId=722`

[119] "Spatio Temporal Epidemiological Modeler," retrieved from `http://www.almaden.ibm.com/cs/projects/stem/`

[120] D. Sow, D. Turaga, and K. Turaga, "Mining Healthcare Sensor Data: A Survey, *Managing and Mining Sensor Data*, Charu C. Aggarwal (Ed.): Springer 2013.

[121] "Excel Medical Electronic," retrieved from: `http://www.excel-medical.com/`

[122] "Cardiopulmonary Corporation," retrieved from `http://www.cardiopulmonarycorp.com/`

[123] "Capsule," retrieved from `http://www.capsuletech.com/`

[124] "Moberg Research," retrieved from `http://www.mobergresearch.com/`

[125] "Battling the Alarm Fatigue," retrieved from `http://www.ucsf.edu/news/2013/10/109881/battling-alarm-fatigue-nursing-school-leads-research-dangerous-problem-hospitals`

[126] F. Wang, N. Lee, J. Hu, J. Sun, S. Ebadollahi, and A. Laine, "A Framework for Mining Signatures from Event Sequences and Its Applications in Healthcare Data," *IEEE Transactions on Pattern Analysis and Machine Intelligence*. 2013; 35(2): 272–285.

[127] D.R. Murphy, A. Laxmisan, B.A. Reis et al., "Electronic Health Record-Based Triggers to Detect Potential Delays in Cancer Diagnosis," *BMJ Quality and Safety* 2014; 23: 8–16.

[128] J.L. Warner, A. Zollanvari, Q. Ding, P. Zhang, G.M. Snyder, and G. Alterovitz, "Temporal Phenome Analysis of a Large Electronic Health Record Cohort Enables Identification of Hospital-Acquired Complications," *Journal of the American Medical Informatics Association* 2013; 20: E281–287.

[129] J. Pathak, K.R. Bailey, C.E. Beebe et al., "Normalization and Standardization of Electronic Health Records for High-Throughput Phenotyping: The SHARPn Consortium," *Journal of the American Medical Informatics Association* 2013; 20: E341-348.

[130] D.A. Broniatowski, M.J. Paul, and M. Dredze, "National and Local Influenza Surveillance through Twitter: An Analysis of the 2012-2013 Influenza Epidemic." *PLoS One* 2013; 8:e83672.

[131] H. Gu, B. Chen, and H. Zhu et al., "Importance of Internet Surveillance in Public Health Emergency Control and Prevention: Evidence from a Digital Epidemiologic Study During Avian Influenza A H7N9 Outbreaks," *Journal of Medical Internet Research* 2014;16:e20.

[132] E. Velasco, T. Agheneza, K. Denecke, G. Kirchner, and T. Eckmanns, "Social Media and Internet-Based Data in Global Systems for Public Health Surveillance: A Systematic Review," *Milbank* Q 2014; 92: 7–33.

[133] D. He, S.C. Mathews, A.N. Kalloo, S. Hutfless, "Mining High-Dimensional Administrative Claims Data to Predict Early Hospital Readmissions," *Journal of the American Medical Informatics Association* 2014; 21: 272–279.

[134] J.R. Curtis, H. Cheng, E. Delzell et al., "Adaptation of Bayesian Data Mining Algorithms to Longitudinal Claims Data: COXIB Safety as an Example," *Medical Care* 2008; 46: 969–975.

Chapter 5

Biomedical Signal Analysis

Abhijit Patil
John F. Welch Technology Centre
GE Global Research
Bangalore, India
abhijit.patil1@ge.com

Rajesh Langoju
John F. Welch Technology Centre
GE Global Research
Bangalore, India
Rajesh.langoju@ge.com

Suresh Joel
John F. Welch Technology Centre
GE Global Research
Bangalore, India
suresh.joel@ge.com

Bhushan D. Patil
John F. Welch Technology Centre
GE Global Research
Bangalore, India
Bhushan.Patil1@ge.com

Sahika Genc
GE Global Research
Niskayuna, NY
gencs@ge.com

5.1 Introduction

Biomedical Signal Analysis consists of measuring signals from biological sources, the origin of which lies in various physiological processes. These signals based on their origin are classified into different types, for instance, physiological signals originating because of electrical activity in the heart are called electrocardiogram (ECG), while those originating because of electrical activity in the brain are called electroencephalogram (EEG). Biological signals manifest themselves into different forms such as electrical, acoustic, chemical, and many others. The analysis of these signals is vital in diagnosing the pathological conditions and in deciding an appropriate care pathway. Many times the underlying pathological processes result in different signatures and a good understanding of the physiological system is necessary to understand the status of the system. For instance, a rise in the temperature of the human body can convey infections in the body. Sometimes it can be a consequence of a blood clot, which is good if it helps in stopping the bleeding but carries a risk of heart attack or stroke.

The measurement of physiological signals gives some form of quantitative or relative assessment of the state of the human body. The use of appropriate sensor and transducer is necessary to acquire these signals, which are acquired either invasively or non-invasively, are discrete or continuous, depending on the kind of care or severity of a particular pathological condition. The noteworthy point here is that many times the signals acquired from the sensor need to be teased out from the raw data so that meaningful information or features could be extracted. For instance, in case of ECG signals, measurement of the QT interval can reveal the condition of heart. Sometimes, the QT interval can get prolonged due to the induction of a drug, resulting in abnormal heart rhythm known as *torsade de pointes*, which is typically followed by sudden cardiac death. Thus, automatically processing of the ECG data by segmenting the electrocardiogram waveform is necessary so that appropriate features could be extracted. This needs the application of signal processing algorithms so that a constituent waveform feature could be separated in the presence of noise. In case of a fetal ECG signal, if a condition of fetal hypoxia (a condition in which the fetus has difficulty in breathing) is to be determined, then the ratio of amplitude of T segment to amplitude of QRS segment, commonly known as T/QRS ratio from PQRST waveform is considered as one of the useful indicators for this acute hypoxic situation.

The processing and interpretation of physiological signals sometimes exhibit challenges because of the low signal-to-noise ratio (SNR) or because of interdependency of the physiological systems. The human body system shows remarkable interaction between its constituents and is a classic example of a *control system* where various phenomena such as feedback, compensation, cause-and-effect, redundancy, and loading is working towards the most optimum performance. However, under pathological conditions, interpretation needs understanding of the complex interactions of the system to diagnose a particular condition. One classical example can be seen in the case of heart sound measurement. For a normal human subject, the second heart sound (S2), which is created by the closing of the aortic valve followed by the closing of the pulmonic valve, shows a split during inspiration but not during expiration; however, splitting of the second heart sound during both inspiration and expiration could indicate cardiac abnormalities. These interrelationships should be factored during the design of a feature extraction algorithm, which is sometimes a step after the signal has been processed.

Over the years several signal processing algorithms have been developed that have significantly enhanced the understanding of the physiological processes, which otherwise would have gone unnoticed if perceived by the naked eye. For instance, certain indications such as alternating changes in the amplitude of T-wave for the PQRST complex of an ECG waveform can indicate life-threatening arrhythmias. The challenge here is to detect a beat-to-beat T-wave alternans variance as small as $25\mu V^2$. The application of an appropriate signal processing algorithm is the key to estimating the signal of such a small magnitude [37].

The goal of this chapter is to present an overview of various signal processing techniques used for processing biomedical signals. This chapter first introduces the readers to a few biomedical signals in Section 5.2 and then focuses on various signal processing approaches commonly encountered in processing them. It is beyond the scope of this chapter to delve in depth into the myriads of signal processing frameworks that have been proposed over several decades to process signals originating from a particular system in the human body. Since several of the processing steps are common for many of the different kinds of physiological signals, the examples will primarily focus around ECG signals in Section 5.3. The reader will encounter classical filtering techniques, adaptive filtering, and non-stationary filtering in this section. In Section 5.4, we present a few denoising techniques based on principal component analysis, wavelet filtering, and wavelet-Wiener filtering. In Section 5.5, the readers are introduced to a source separation problem commonly seen during fetal health monitoring. Cross-correlation analysis is routinely applied in biomedical signal processing, and Section 5.6 presents its application to the resting state functional magnetic resonance imaging (fMRI) technique. Towards the end of this chapter in Section 5.7, a special emphasis on future trends in biomedical signal analysis will be presented.

5.2 Types of Biomedical Signals

This section discusses in brief a few types of biomedical signals, their origins and importance for diagnosis purpose [54]. The most basic form of measurement is body temperature, which although quite simplistic to measure can convey the well-being of the human system. This section looks into the signals originating from the cellular level, such as the action potential, to the macro level, for instance the heart sound, which is produced as a consequence of contractile activity of the cardiohemic system [104].

5.2.1 Action Potentials

A nerve impulse, or an action potential, is a series of electrical responses that occur in the cell as a consequence of mechanical contraction of a single cell, when stimulated by an electrical current [9]. Action potential is caused by the flow of certain ions such as sodium (Na^+), potassium (K^+), and chloride (Cl^-) along with other ions across the cell membrane. A cell in its resting state has a potential of −60 mV to −100 mV until some external stimulus or disturbance upsets the equilibrium. With the appropriate stimulation, the voltage in the dendrite of the neuron becomes somewhat less negative. This change in the membrane potential, known as depolarization, causes the voltage-gated sodium channels to open. As soon as the channels open, sodium ions flow inside the cell, resulting in a rapid change in the charge. At the peak of the action potential, that area of the neuron is about 40 mV positive. As the voltage becomes positive, the sodium channels close, and the voltage-gated potassium channels open, causing the potassium ions to rush out of the cell. As the potassium ions move out, the voltage becomes negative again. The potassium channels remain open until the membrane potential becomes at least as negative as the resting potential. In many cases, the membrane potential becomes even more negative than the resting potential for a brief period; this is called hyperpolarization. An action potential typically lasts a few milliseconds. Recording of the action potential needs a single cell to be isolated and a microelectrode with tips of the order of a few micrometers to stimulate the cell [9]. The action potential is the basic of all bioelectrical components in the human body. Next subsections discuss a few electrical signals such as the electroneurogram (ENG), electromyogram (EMG), electrocardiogram (ECG), electroencephalogram (EEG), event-related potentials (ERPs), and electrogastrogram (EGG). This section also discusses the measurement of sound signals produced by the contractile activity of the heart and blood together, using highly sensitive microphones.

5.2.2 Electroneurogram (ENG)

The active potential propagates along an unmyelinated nerve fiber or a muscle fiber. When a fiber is stimulated by an electrical current, the electrical current or action potential flows along the length of a fiber without attenuation by progressive depolarization of the membrane. Thus, the ENG is an electrical signal that is observed when the nerve is stimulated. The action potential propagates over the length of time and the velocity of propagation in a peripheral nerve is measured by stimulating a motor nerve at two points with a known distance apart along its course. Subtraction of the shorter latency from the longer latency gives the conduction time. ENGs are recorded at the surface of the body using two concentric needle electrodes or silver-silver chloride electrodes [30].

Typically, a pulse of 100 V and 100 μs to 300 μs duration is applied at a known separation distance between the stimulus sites. With the knowledge of the distance between the two stimulus sites, the conduction velocity is determined. ENG signals measured are of the order of 10 μV. These signals are susceptible to power line interference and instrumentation noise. Also, care needs to be taken to minimize the muscle contraction. For this, the limb is held in a relaxed posture. Neural diseases could cause a decrease in the conduction velocity. Nominal conduction velocities are 40–70 m/s in nerve fibers, 0.2–0.4 m/s in heart muscle, and 0.03–0.05 m/s in time-delay fibers between the atria and ventricles [56, 2, 31].

5.2.3 Electromyogram (EMG)

The basic functional unit for excitation and contraction in vertebrate skeletal muscle is the motor unit, whose activity can be controlled voluntarily by the brain. A motor unit is a single motor neuron plus all the muscle fibers to which it connects. When a motor neuron fires, all muscle fibers in the unit are simultaneously excited and produce an action potential, resulting in a brief, twitch-like contraction of the fibers. Skeletal muscles are made up of a collection of motor units, each of which contains an anterior horn cell or motor neuron, its axon extending peripherally from the spinal cord to a particular muscle, and all the muscle fibers innervated by that motor axon. The terminals of the motor axon are connected to this set of fibers by a chemical synapse. This synapse is usually referred to as the neuromuscular junction or motor end-plate. An electrical activity in a motor unit consists of a rhythmic series of action potentials [56].

When an action potential occurs simultaneously in all muscle fibers in one motor unit, the resulting external electrical effect is small, which can be detected with electrodes placed on the surface of the muscle. Each skeletal muscle is composed of many motor units. A large and powerful limb muscle, such as the gastrocnemius, may be composed of hundreds of motor units. Spatio-temporal summation of the motor unit action potentials of all the active motor units gives rise to an electromyogram (EMG) of the muscle, which can be recorded by placing needle electrodes on the surface of the body (Figure 5.1). EMG can assist in distinguishing myopathic from neurogenic muscle wasting and weakness. It can detect abnormalities such as chronic denervation or fasciculations in clinically normal muscle. By determining the distribution of neurogenic abnormalities, EMG can differentiate the focal nerve, plexus, or radicular pathology [90].

5.2.4 Electrocardiogram (ECG)

Electrocardiogram signals are generated as a consequence of electrical activity of the heart. These signals are typically recorded on the skin of the human body. However, there are instances when these electrical activities could be recorded directly on the epicardial surface [124, 105, 50]. Typically, 12 electrodes are placed at well-defined locations for the purpose of measuring the heart's conduction system, which is used to diagnose and monitor various cardiac conditions, including arrhythmias (irregularities of cardiac rhythm) and myocardial damage (such as myocardial infarction). The contraction of heart muscles results in the discharge of electrical charges known as "depolarization" and follows a standard pathway. The initiation of electrical discharge is at the sino-atrial (SA) node in the right atrium. This node acts as a *natural pacemaker* and discharges about 60–80 times per minute, resulting in a typical heart rate of 60–80 beats per minute (bpm) in adults. The depolarization spreads throughout the atrial muscle fibers and reaches the atrioventricular (AV) node, where its conduction to the ventricles in slightly delayed. Conduction then occurs rapidly down the "bundle of His" and its two branches, the left and right bundle branches. The left bundle further divides into anterior and posterior fascicles and conduction occurs more slowly through Purkinje fibers, resulting in ventricular muscle depolarization. During ventricular muscle depolar-

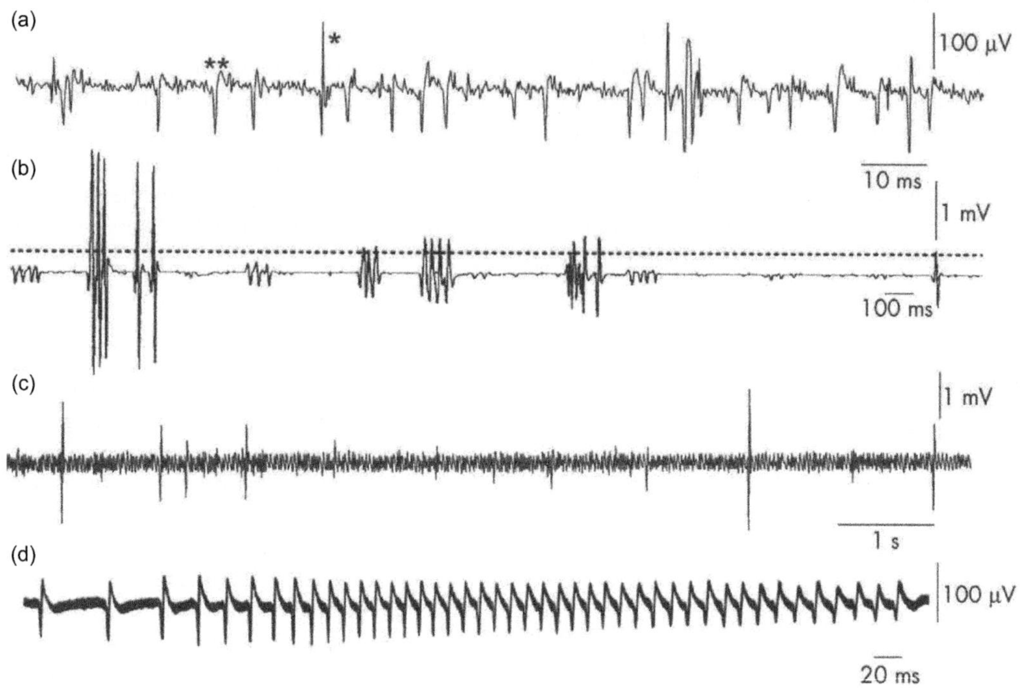

FIGURE 5.1: The figure shows abnormal spontaneous activity measured using EMG. (a) Fibrillations (*) and positive sharp waves (**) in an acutely denervated hand muscle. (b) Single, doublet, triplet, and multiplet motor unit neuromyotonic discharges. Bursts of discharge are irregular in frequency and the intra-burst frequency of discharge is up to 200 Hz. (c) Fasciculations in the tongue in a patient with amyotrophic lateral sclerosis. The single discharges are irregular and occur on a background of ongoing EMG activity caused by poor relaxation. (d) Myotonic discharges in a patient with dystrophia myotonica. Source: KR Mills, *Journal of Neurol. Neurosurg. Psychiatry* 76:ii32–ii35, 2005.

ization, atrial repolarization, i.e., a resting electrical state occurs. Ventricular repolarization occurs following ventricular depolarization and before the next cycle of SA discharge.

Conduction cycle abnormalities manifests with cardiac diseases and needs to be captured either through a 12-lead ECG, individual rhythm strips, or specialized ECGs that look at different parts of the heart. The placement of a 12-lead ECG is shown in Figure 5.2(a) and a typical ECG waveform is shown in Figure 5.2(b) along with the depolarization and repolarization cycle in the heart. Of the 12 leads, six are referred to as "limb leads." The limb leads are leads I, II, III, aVR, aVL, and aVF. The other six are referred to as "chest" or "precordial" leads. These leads are called V1, V2, V3, V4, V5, and V6. The signals recorded from these electrodes consist of a repeated PQRST segment along with a sometimes inverted U segment. The cycle of depolarization and repolarization of the electrical activity in the heart is embedded in this complex waveform.

In the PQRST complex, a P-waveform, representing atrial depolarization, lasts typically for 0.06 to 0.11 seconds, and its presence indicates "sinus rhythm" or the heart's normal rhythm. A P-R interval, representing conduction through the AV node and the "bundle of His," lasts for about 0.12 to 0.2 seconds. In the QRS complex, representing the depolarization of the ventricles, a Q wave

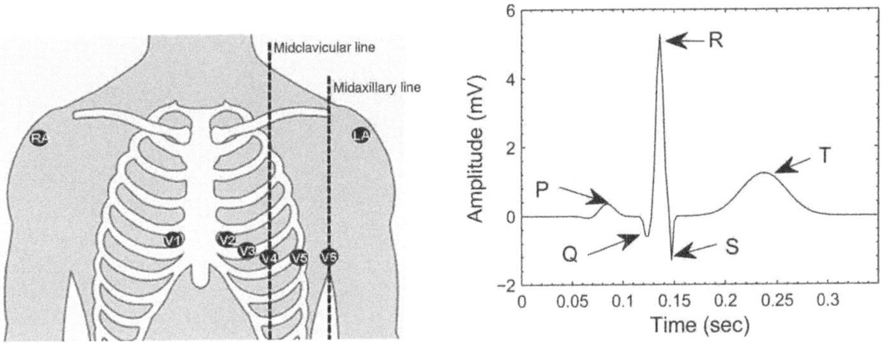

(a) (b)

FIGURE 5.2: (a) Typical placement of 12-lead ECG is shown in Figure 5.2(a). Only the chest electrodes are shown in the figure. (b) ECG waveform along with the depolarization and repolarization cycle in the heart.

shows a negative deflection at the beginning of the QRS segment. The noteworthy point is that small Q waves in some leads are normal, but large Q waves may be tagged as abnormal. The R wave is the first positive deflection, followed by an S wave that has a negative deflection. The QRS segment lasts less than 0.12 seconds. The ST segment, which is marked as the end of an S wave and the beginning of a T wave, is around 0.12 seconds in duration and should be isoelectric, i.e., at the same level as the part between the T wave and the next P wave. The T wave represents the repolarization of the ventricles.

5.2.5 Electroencephalogram (EEG)

The electroencephalogram (EEG) represents the electrical activity occurring at the surface of the brain. The organization of the brain is as follows (see Figure 5.3(a)): The main parts of the brain are the cerebrum, the cerebellum, the spinal cord, and the limbic system. The cerebrum is the largest portion of the brain, and contains tools that are responsible for most of the brain's function. It is divided into four sections: the temporal lobe, the occipital lobe, the parietal lobe, and the frontal lobe. The cerebrum is divided into two hemispheres, a right and a left hemisphere, which are separated by a connective band of fibers known as the corpus callosum. The outer surface of the cerebral hemisphere, known as cerebral cortex is made of nerve cells. Beneath the cortex lie nerve fibers that lead to other parts of the brain and the body.

EEG recorded from the surface of the scalp is in major part generated by the synchronous activity of neurons on the cerebral cortex. The main generators of the EEG are the postsynaptic potentials in the dendrites of large pyramidal neurons. Since several neurons activate synchronously through superposition, they generate a dipole moment, resulting in a measurable potential difference on the surface of the scalp. Nunez and Srinivasan in their study showed that approximately 6cm^2 of the cortical gyri tissue is necessary to activate synchronously to produce such a measurable potential at the scalp surface that can be detected without averaging [96]. The scalp EEG is an average of the multifarious activities of many small regions of the cortical surface beneath the electrode. EEG is characterized by a good temporal resolution on a submillisecond scale, but is poor in terms of spatial resolution. The reason for poor spatial resolution is blurring, which occurs as the EEG signals are volume conducted through the different tissues of the head. Typically, the number of electrodes is increased, followed by a spatial enhancement method to improve the spatial resolution.

The 10-20 system used to record the EEG is shown in Figure 5.3(b). The system contains 21 electrode locations positioned around four reference points, namely, the inion, the nasion, and the

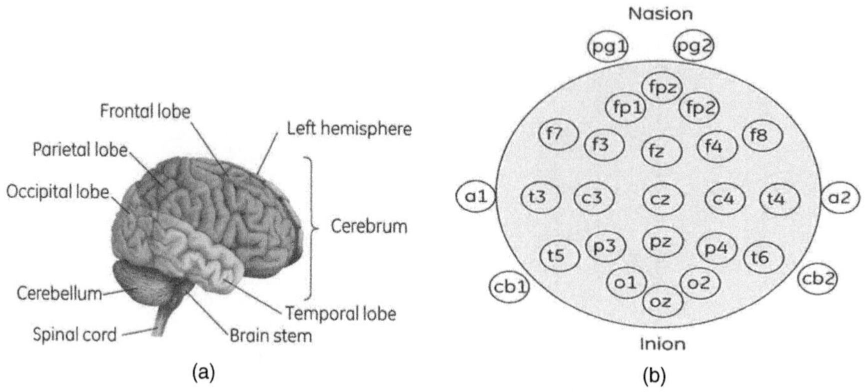

FIGURE 5.3: (a) The function parts of human brain, (b) The 10-20 arrangement of electrode placement for EEG recording. In the figure, the labels are as follows: pg- naso-pharyngeal, a-auricular (Ear lobes), fp-pre-frontal, f-frontal, p-pareital, c-central, o-occipital, t-temporal, cb-cerebellar, z-midline. Odd numbers and even numbers are on the left and the right side of the subject [70].

right and the left preauricular points. The reason why the system is called 10-20 is the fact that the actual distances between adjacent electrodes are either 10% or 20% of the total front-back or right-left distance of the skull. Recently, the trend has been to use over 100 electrodes for research purposes [42]. Oostenveld and Praamstra suggested a 10-5 electrode system that includes up to 345 electrode locations [100]. One of the aspects regarding spatial resolution with different electrode systems is the average interelectrode distance. According to study by Gevins et al., the typical average interelectrode distances are 6 cm in a standard 10-20 system, 3.3 cm with 64 electrodes, and 2.25 cm with 128 electrodes [43].

The signals measured using the electrode systems have a relevant frequency band of 0.1 Hz to 100 Hz. Amplitudes measured from the surface of the cortex can vary between 500 μV and 1500 μV peak-to-peak. However, because of strong attenuations when they are volume-conducted to the surface of the scalp, the amplitudes fall down to a range of a 10 μV to 100 μV peak-to-peak. The measurements are sensitive to the location of electrodes and inter-electrode distances [108].

EEG signals exhibit several patterns that occupy different frequency bands. Some of the commonly used terms for bands are: Delta (δ) 0.5 Hz to 4 Hz, Theta (θ) 4 Hz to 8 Hz, Alpha (α) 8 Hz to 13 Hz, and Beta (β) greater than 13 Hz. The EEG carries a signature of the level of consciousness of a person. As the activity increases, the EEG shifts to a higher dominating frequency and lower amplitude. When the eyes are closed, the alpha waves begin to dominate the EEG. When the person falls asleep, the dominant EEG frequency decreases. In a certain phase of sleep, rapid eye movement called (REM) sleep, the person dreams and has active movements of the eyes, which can be seen as a characteristic EEG signal. In deep sleep, the EEG has large and slow deflections called delta waves. The depression or absence of the normal response in a certain state of the subject could indicate abnormality. Sharp waves or spikes could indicate the presence of epileptogenic regions in the corresponding parts of the brain [83].

5.2.6 Electrogastrogram (EGG)

An EGG is a technique of recording gastric myoelectrical activity using cutaneous electrodes placed on the anterior abdominal wall [102]. The activity originates on the greater curvature at the junction between the proximal and distal stomach, and exhibits sinusoidal waveforms with a predominant frequency of 3 cycles per minute. Clinical studies have shown good correlation of

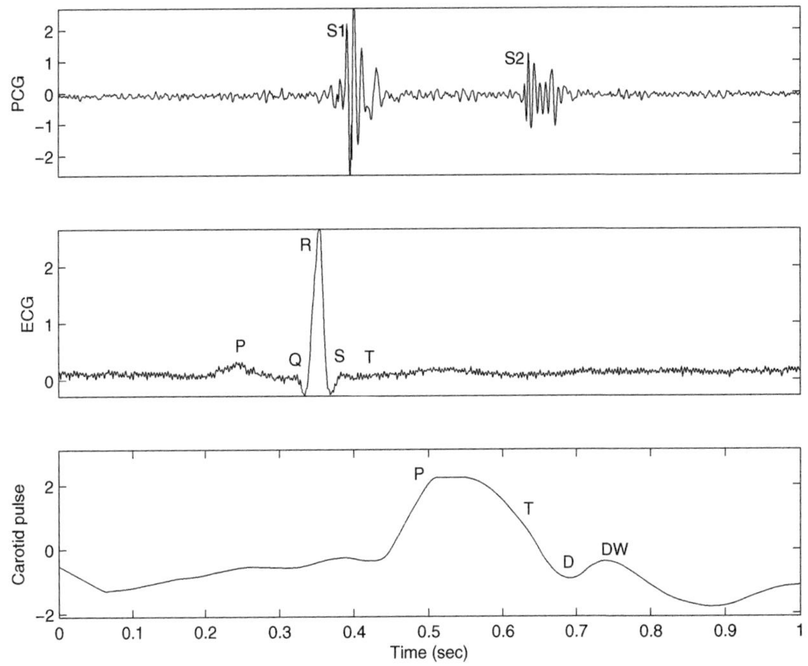

FIGURE 5.4: The figure shows simulated representation of simultaneous recordings of PCG, ECG, and carotid pulse signals for a normal male adult.

the cutaneous recordings with those acquired from serosally implanted electrodes [102]. The EGG recorded from the abdomen is supposed to reflect the electrical control activity and the electrical response activity of the stomach.

EGG signals are recorded with a patient in supine position and remaining motionless. Two main steps involved in EGG recordings are amplification and filtering. A typical EGG signal is in the range of 50–500 μV and needs adequate amplification. The signal is in the range of 0.0083 to 0.15 Hz and needs to be appropriately filtered, since the frequency range of the signal is much lower than that of most extracellular recordings. A wrong selection of filtering range may lead to a severe distortion or even disappearance of gastric slow waves in the EGG. Finally, since there are conflicting or inconclusive outcome-based investigations into the clinical utility of gastric motor and myoelectric testing, the performance of EGG for its clinical indication is still a subject of debate [128].

5.2.7 Phonocardiogram (PCG)

PCG is the measurement of a vibration or sound signal produced by the contractile activity of the heart and blood together. The PCG signal is recorded by placing a transducer (microphone) on the thorax. Heart sounds are an indicator of the general state of the heart in terms of rhythm and contractility. Variations or changes in the sound and murmurs could assist in diagnosing cardiovascular diseases.

Initially, it was believed that heart sounds are caused by valve leaflet movements, but it is now an accepted fact that recorded heart sounds are caused by vibrations of the whole cardiovascular system triggered by pressure gradients [104].

The origin of a heart sound in brief is as follows [104]: The heart sound contains two major components, the S1 and S2 as shown in Figure 5.4. When the first myocardial contractions in the ventricles move the blood towards the atria, the first vibrations in S1 occurs. The atrioventricular valves (AV) closes during this stage. When the AV valves closes, it results in a sudden increase in tension at the valves, resulting in deceleration of the blood. This is the point at which the second component of S1 occurs. The next stage is the opening of the aortic and pulmonary valves, resulting in ejection of blood out of the ventricles. Thus, the third component of S1 is attributed to the oscillations of blood between the root of the aorta and the ventricular walls. Finally, the fourth component of S1 may occur because of vibrations caused by turbulence in the ejected blood flowing rapidly through the ascending aorta and the pulmonary artery.

Similar signatures of sounds originating because of closure of semilunar (aortic and pulmonary) valves can be seen in the S2 component. S2 has two components: one because of closing of aortic valves, and two because of closing of pulmonary valves. The aortic valve closes before the pulmonary valves. The first heart sound is at the nearby position of the vertex of S wave of ECG. The time interval between the first and the second heart sound is from 0.280s to 0.300s [131]. Finally, the intervals between S1 and S2 and then S2 and S1 of the next cycle are typically silent. Certain defects in cardiovascular activity or disease may result in murmurs. The murmurs are characterized by high-frequency sounds. Extracting features from heart sounds and murmurs, such as intensity, frequency content, and timings can provide insight into the condition of the heart.

5.2.8 Other Biomedical Signals

Apart from the signals mentioned in the previous subsections, there are several other biomedical signals such as the carotid pulse (CP), the speech signals, signals recorded using catheter-tip sensors (signals such as left ventricular pressure, right atrial pressure, aortic pressure), the vibromyogram (vibration signals that accompanies EMG), and many others that are not discussed in this chapter. The reader is referred to reference [104] for a brief introduction to these signals. In the subsequent sections, the reader will be introduced to various signal processing tools that are commonly applied to process the biomedical signals. Since, the basic signal processing steps such as acquisition, filtering, and feature extraction or analysis remains the same for most of the biomedical signals, the objective of this chapter is not to deal with these signals in isolation, but rather to familiarize the reader with various signal processing algorithms that are applied in different scenarios. For instance, in case of denoising of signals, tools such as principal component analysis (second-order statistics) and independent component analysis (fourth-order statistics) can be applied, but there are certain cases where not only denoising is the objective, but also signal separation is the requirement. By the end of this chapter, the reader will have a good understanding of tools that could be applied for processing the biomedical signals.

5.3 ECG Signal Analysis

The recorded PQRST complex of the ECG waveform contains substantial information and certain features such as cardiac rate, rhythm, PR interval, QRS duration, ST segment, QT interval, and T waves indicate the underlying pathological condition of the patient. However, the ECG waveform is corrupted with several sources of noise and before any feature could be extracted, a proper signal conditioning is necessary. Various kinds of noise that affect the ECG signals are [40]:

(a) Power line interference

(b) Electrode contact noise

(c) Motion artifacts

FIGURE 5.5: Algorithm for processing ECG signal. The heart rate is estimated from successive QRS beats. Other features, for instance T-wave alternans, are estimated once the waves are delineated.

(d) Muscle contraction (electromyographic, EMG)

(e) Baseline drift and ECG amplitude modulation with respiration

(f) Instrumentation noise generated during signal acquisition

(g) Electrosurgical noises, and many other less significant noises

Common to all kinds of means by which an ECG signal is recorded, whether in an ambulatory or resting state or during a stress test, is the processing of an ECG signal. Figure 5.5 shows a frequently used signal processing routine deployed on ECG machines to minimize the interference due to the above-mentioned sources of noise. Signal processing has contributed immensely in deciphering information from an ECG signal and has substantially improved our understanding of the ECG signal and its dynamic properties as expressed by changes in rhythm and beat morphology (PQRST complex). For instance, detection of alternating changes in a T wave from one PQRST complex to another in the form of oscillations, an indicator of life-threatening arrhythmias cannot be perceived by the naked eye or from a standard ECG printout, but needs careful signal processing to unmask the information buried in noise.

While designing signal processing algorithms for reducing noises in the measurement, it is important to note that an electrocardiograph should meet or exceed the requirement of IEC 60601-2-51 (2003) and the ECG measuring devices should be programmed in accordance with American Heart Association (AHA) specifications [8]. For instance, according to the guidelines, the low frequency filter should be set no higher than 0.05 Hz to avoid distortion of the ST segment and the high frequency filter should be set no lower than 100 Hz to prevent loss of high frequency information.

The following subsections discuss various signal processing approaches applied to remove the noises affecting the ECG measurement and also the approaches commonly used for extracting certain morphological features from ECG, such as QRS detection, QT interval, etc.

5.3.1 Power Line Interference

Power line interference consists of 60 Hz/50 Hz pick up, depending upon where the instrument is operated (United States or Europe/Asia). Sometimes the harmonics also interfere with the measurements and the amplitudes can be up to 50 percent of peak-to-peak ECG amplitude. There are many sources of interference pick ups and alternating currents (AC) that are inherently present in the recording room can be a problem for many biopotential measurements. By properly shielding the cables as well as the device, effects due to AC interference can be minimized to a certain extent. However, these alternating currents still manage to interfere with the signals of interest by flowing through the system ground, thereby getting picked by the tissue or electrode [64].

In literature there are several approaches that mention reducing the effect of power line interference and could be broadly classified into adaptive and nonadaptive filtering. The first mention of adaptive filtering by using the external reference signal was proposed by Widrow et al. [125]. Ider and Koymen have also proposed a system for adaptive elimination of line interference using an external reference [67]. A different approach of using an internally generated reference signal on an adaptive 60-Hz filter for an ECG signal was proposed by Ahlstrom and Tompkins [5]. Interestingly, Glover [5] showed that Ahlstrom and Tompkins' filter of using an adaptive 60-Hz notch filter with an internally generated reference is approximately equivalent to a nonadaptive, second order, notch filter. The following section summarizes adaptive and nonadaptive filters for removal of power line pick up.

5.3.1.1 Adaptive 60-Hz Notch Filter

The algorithm proposed by Ahlstrom and Tompkins' maintains a running estimate of the 60-Hz noise [5]. At time t, the present noise estimate can be generated from the previous two noise estimates according to the equation

$$e(t) = \varepsilon e(t-nT) - e(t-2nT), \tag{5.1}$$

where, T is the sample period and $\varepsilon = 2\cos(2\pi 60T)$. The error in the noise estimate is

$$f(t) = [x(t) - e(t)] - [x(t-nT) - e(t-nT)], \tag{5.2}$$

where, the second term is an estimate of DC offset. If $f(t)<0$, the present noise estimate $e(t)$, is decreased by an increment d, whose units is in volts. If $f(t)>0$, the present noise estimate is decreased by d. The output of the filter is generated by subtracting the noise estimate $e(t)$ from the input ECG signal $x(t)$. Note that as d decreases, the filter adapts more slowly and exhibits a smaller bandwidth, however, as d increases the filter adapts more quickly and exhibits a larger bandwidth. In its simplest case of implementation, a sampling rate of 360 samples per second requires no multiplication because $\varepsilon = 1$ and all equation coefficients are equal to 1.

5.3.1.2 Nonadaptive 60-Hz Notch Filter

Design of a nonadaptive filter requires a transfer function $H(z)$ that has zero on the unit circle at 60 Hz and a pole at the same angle with a radius r. Such a transfer function that has notch at 60 Hz can be represented in the z domain as

$$H(z) = \frac{1 - 2\cos(2\pi\cdot 60\cdot T)z^{-1} + z^{-2}}{1 - 2r\cos(2\pi\cdot 60\cdot T)z^{-1} + r^2 z^{-2}} \tag{5.3}$$

In Equation 5.3, as r increases, the pole approaches the unit circle, the bandwidth of the notch decreases, and transient response time of the filter increases. The DC gain of the filter in Equation 5.3 is $1 - r + r^2$ and can be implemented using the following difference equation where ε has been defined previously. The adaptive and nonadaptive 60-Hz notch filters described by Equations. 5.2 and 5.3 have a similar frequency response but a different transient response. The nonadaptive filter continues to exhibit a similar transient response for signals of different amplitudes. On the contrary, the adaptive filter approach proposed by Ahlstrom and Tompkins is linearly related to input amplitudes and adapts more quickly to small amplitude signals and more slowly to large amplitude signals. The response of the filter to a QRS complex, which acts like an impulse input to filter, thus varies based on whether the filter is adaptive or nonadaptive. Noticeably, the adaptive filter produces less ringing and thus distortion of the ECG waveform to an input of the QRS complex, which has large amplitude and small pulse width, as compared to a nonadaptive filter, which tends to produce significant distortion in the ECG signal. Finally, the implementation of both of these filters is optimum for a sampling rate of 360 Hz, since the computational complexity is substantially reduced [51].

$$y(t) = r\varepsilon\cdot y(t-nT) - r^2 y(t-2nT) + x(t) - \varepsilon\cdot x(t-nT) + x(t-2nT), \tag{5.4}$$

5.3.1.3 Empirical Mode Decomposition

ECG signals are highly nonstationary, and use of an adaptive approach such as the empirical mode decomposition (EMD) has shown promise in reducing the effect of power line interference [14]. The EMD method was first presented by Huang et al. [63], and is an effective algorithm for time-frequency analysis of real-world signals. EMD is a fully data driven, unsupervised signal decomposition approach, and does not require any a priori-defined basis function, unlike the Fourier and wavelet-based methods that require predefined basis functions to represent a signal. The algorithm functions by decomposing the signal into finite and often small number of its intrinsic mode functions (IMF), which represents zero-mean amplitude and frequency modulated components. The Hilbert transform of intrinsic mode functions provide meaningful instantaneous frequency estimates. The EMD algorithm is as follows [14, 63]:

For a signal $x(t)$, the first step is to identify all local maxima and minima. All the local maxima are then connected by a cubic spline curve to form an upper envelope $E_u(t)$. A similar operation is performed on all the local minima to obtain $E_l(t)$. Given the envelope of upper and lower envelope, the next stage is to obtain the mean, denoted as $m_1(t) = 0.5 * [E_u(t) + E_l(t)]$. This mean $m_1(t)$ is subtracted from the signal $x(t)$. Thus, the first proto-IMF $h_1(t)$ is obtained as

$$h_1(t) = x(t) - m_1(t) \tag{5.5}$$

The process explained above is referred to as the *sifting process*. Note that $h_1(t)$ still contains multiple extremes between the zero crossings, and the sifting process is applied again to it. The process is repeated to the proto-IMF $h_k(t)$ until the first IMF $c_1(t)$, is obtained after satisfying a stopping criteria. The commonly used criteria is the sum of difference δ, given by

$$\delta = \sum_{t=0}^{T} \frac{|h_{k\text{-}1}(t) - h_k(t)|^2}{h^2{}_{k\text{-}1}(t)} \tag{5.6}$$

When δ is smaller than some threshold value, the first IMF $c_1(t)$ is obtained. The next step involves computing the residual signal $r_1(t)$, which is

$$r_1(t) = x(t) - c_1(t) \tag{5.7}$$

The residual signal still contains vital information, and is now treated as a new signal, i.e., $r_1(t) \to x(t)$. All the operations described above for processing $x(t)$ are applied again until the next IMF $c_2(t)$ is obtained. This process is repeatedly performed until $r_p(t)$ is either a constant, or a monotonic slope, or a function with only one extreme. A Hilbert transform can be applied to each of the IMFs to get a series of instantaneous frequency $\omega_i(t)$ and amplitude $a_i(t)$, where the subscript i corresponds to the ith IMF.

A Hilbert transform of each IMF $c_i(t)$ is given by:

$$u_i(t) = \frac{1}{\pi} \int_{-\infty}^{+\infty} \frac{c_i(\tau)}{t - \tau} d\tau \tag{5.8}$$

One can reconstruct an analytic signal $z_i(t)$ from $u_i(t)$ obtained in Equation 5.8 and $c_i(t)$.

$$z_i(t) = c_i(t) + ju_i(t) = a_i(t)e^{j\theta_i(t)} \tag{5.9}$$

where,

$$a_i(t) = \sqrt{c_i{}^2(t) + u_i{}^2(t)}, \theta_i(t) = \arctan(\frac{u_i(t)}{c_i(t)}) \tag{5.10}$$

The instantaneous frequency of $c_i(t)$ is defined as

$$\omega_i(t) = \frac{d\theta_i}{dt} \tag{5.11}$$

The original signal can be expressed in the form

$$x(t) = \sum_{i=1}^{n} c_i(t) + r_n(t) \tag{5.12}$$

where, $r_n(t)$ is the residual component. The other form of representation of signal $x(t)$ is

$$x(t) = Re \sum_{i=1}^{n} a_i(t) exp\{j \int \omega_i(t)dt\} \tag{5.13}$$

where, *Re* stands for the real part of the signal. Equation 5.13 allows us to represent signal $x(t)$ by the amplitude and the instantaneous frequency as a function of time in a three-dimensional plot: $\{t, \omega_i(t), a_i(t)\}$, in which usually the amplitude is contoured on the time-frequency plane. This three-dimensional distribution on the time-frequency plane is called the Hilbert amplitude spectrum: $H(\omega,t)$ or simply the Hilbert spectrum. One measure that is often useful is the *marginal spectrum* $h(\omega)$ in which the total amplitude contributed from each frequency value is summed up over time, given by:

$$h(\omega) = \int_{0}^{T} H(\omega,t)dt \tag{5.14}$$

Figure 5.6 shows a synthetic ECG signal processed using an EMD framework. The sampling frequency is 360 Hz. The figure shows thirteen different intrinsic modes. A 60-Hz power line hum is added to the signal. Clearly, the mode (IMF1) shows the signature of 60-Hz frequency and by removing this particular intrinsic mode and recombining all the other intrinsic modes using the equation shown below, one can get rid of this particular source of error.

$$x_{filt}(t) = \sum_{n=1;n\neq k}^{p} c_n(t) + r_p(t) \tag{5.15}$$

where, in Equation 5.15, $x_{filt(t)}$ is the filtered signal and $n = k$ is the intrinsic mode, we do not wish to consider reconstruction of the original signal.

5.3.2 Electrode Contact Noise and Motion Artifacts

Measurement of ECG depends to a certain extent on the placement of electrodes and how well the skin is prepared. The objective of good skin preparation involves using a medical grade abrasive pad to clean up the skin surface so that the impedance between the electrode (typically Ag/AgCl) and the skin's surface is minimized. Impedance is the measure of resistance to the flow of current in the electrical circuit. Notable reasons for the presence of high impedance are dry skin, dirt, long hair, or sometimes loss of skin tissues. Presence of high impedance invariably adds noise to the measured signal and thus skin preparation is necessary to reduce the impedance. In most of the ECG measurements, electrode gel is applied to the electrode to further reduce the impedance and increase the performance of ECG measurement. Most of the devices require impedance levels to be as low as 2 kΩ to 5 kΩ.

In spite of good skin preparation or other precautions during the ECG measurement, many times because of dryness of electrode gel with time, the contact between the electrode and skin loosens, causing transient interference with measurement. Figure 5.7 shows an example of ECG signal with loose electrode contact and respiratory movement, and also because of motion artifacts.

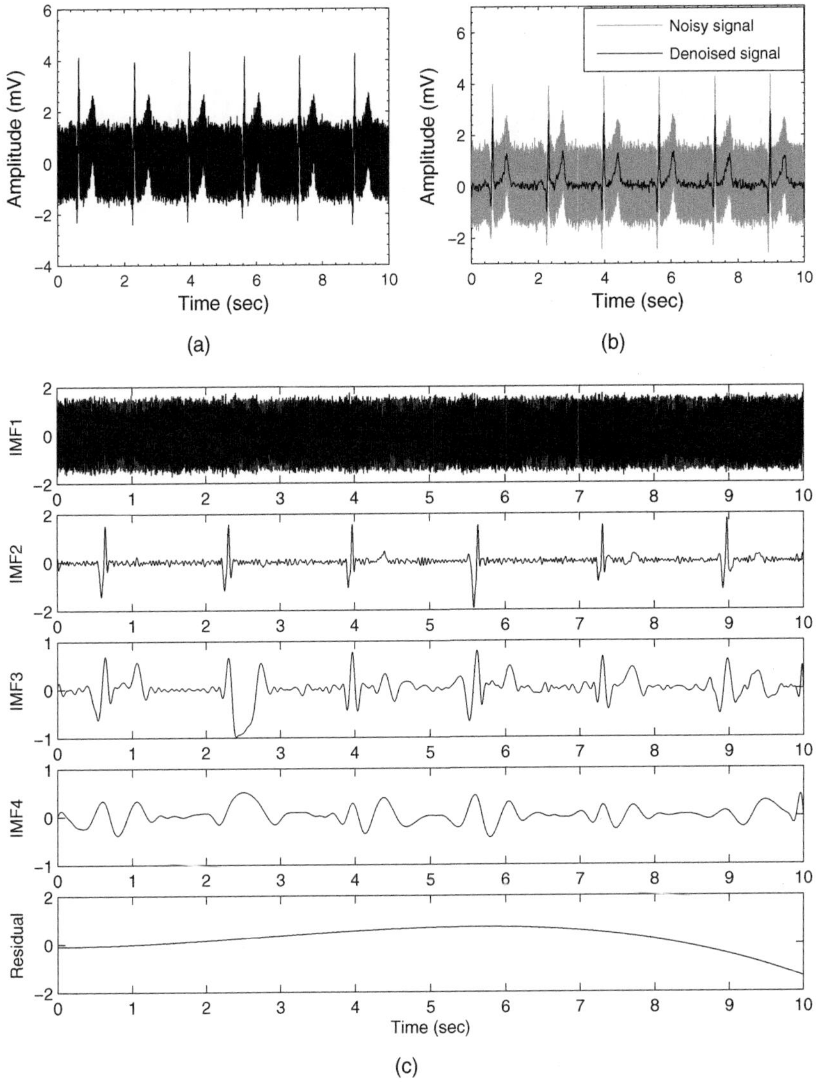

FIGURE 5.6: (a) ECG signal corrupted with 60-Hz powerline noise, (b) The processed signal is reconstructed by removing the IMF1 from the signal separated using EMD, and (c) EMD decomposition for noisy ECG signal.

During measurement, the electrode contact either can be permanent or can be intermittent, resulting in switching-like behavior. This switching action to the measurement system input causes large artifacts because the ECG signal is capacitively coupled to the system. Electrode contact noise manifests as a randomly occurring rapid baseline transition or step, which decays exponentially to the baseline value and has 60-Hz power line interference. The amplitude of the ECG signal during such a source of noise could be as large as the saturation level of the recorder. Most of the devices raise an alarm or indicate the condition of saturation so that an operator could intervene and ensure that such a source of noise is mitigated.

Unlike the electrode contact noise that shows a steep response, the motion artifact noise though transient in nature does not show a step-like behavior. Motion artifacts are baseline transitory behavior caused by changes in electrode–skin impedance with electrode motion. There can be several

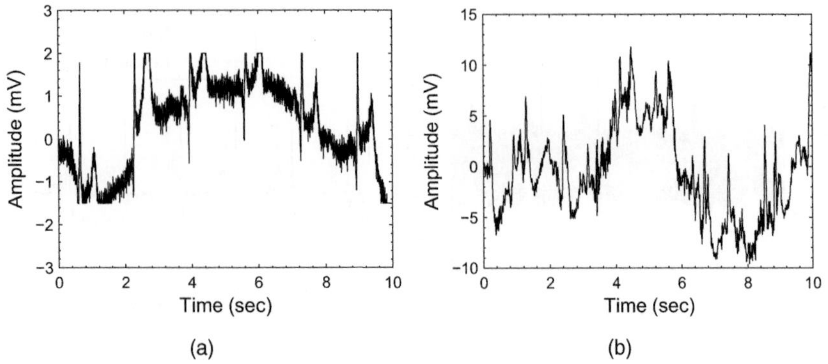

FIGURE 5.7: (a) An illustration of an ECG signal corrupted with slow varying respiration movement. The saturation of the ECG signal shows poor or open electrode contact with the skin, and (b) an ECG signal corrupted with motion artifact.

reasons for electrode motion apart from the one described in the previous paragraphs, such as ambulatory settings, vibrations, movement of the subject during the stress test or Holter recording. The baseline disturbance caused because of motion artifacts can be considered as a biphasic signal that resembles one cycle of a sine wave. The amplitudes of signals affected by motion artifacts can be as high as 500 percent of the peak-to-peak amplitude of the ECG signal, and could last as long as 100 to 500 ms [40].

5.3.2.1 The Least-Mean Squares (LMS) Algorithm

Adaptive filtering technique has been shown in the previous sections to be useful for removing the power line interference. One of the variants in the above-described method is the use of a reference signal representing power line interference tapped from some part of the body (not the region where ECG is recorded) and using the same to cancel the power line interference from the ECG signal. In case of motion artifact or to minimize the effect of electrode motion, the basic adaptive framework shown in Figure 5.8 can be employed.

In this framework, there are two ways by which the noise could be minimized. Figure 5.8(a) shows a filter implementation in which the main signal is the noise corrupted ECG signal (x_1+n_1), where n_1 is the additive noise, and n_2 is the reference signal, which in this particular case is a noise generated from some source. The requirement is that the noise n_2 is correlated in some way to noise n_1. In Figure 5.8(a), the desired signal x_1 is obtained by minimizing the objective function using the following formulation:

$$\varepsilon_r{}^2 = (x_1+n_1)^2 - 2y(x_1+n_1) + y^2 = (n_1-y)^2 + x_1{}^2 + 2x_1n_1 - 2ynx_1 \tag{5.16}$$

where, ε_r is the error signal. Since the signal and noise are assumed to be uncorrelated, the mean-squared error $\varepsilon_r{}^2$ in Equation 5.16 simplifies to

$$E[\varepsilon_r{}^2] = E(n_1-y)^2 + E[x_1{}^2] \tag{5.17}$$

Minimizing the mean squared error (MSE) in Equation 5.17 results in a filter error output ε_r that is the best least-squares estimate of the signal x_1. In this formulation, the adaptive filter is able to extract the signal from noise by iteratively minimizing the mean squared error between the input signal (x_1+n_1) and the reference noisy signal n_2.

There exists another scenario in which the ECG signal is recorded at several leads. One of the electrodes is considered as a reference electrode and also noise free. Thus, x_1+n_1 is the primary

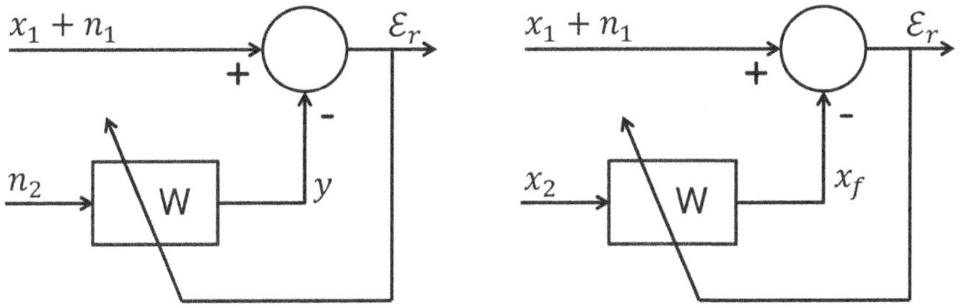

FIGURE 5.8: Basic adaptive filter structures. In (a), the reference input is noise n_2, which is correlated with noise n_1, the desired signal appears at E_r, in (b), the reference input is signal x_2 correlated with signal x_1. In this case, the desired signal appears at x_f.

input signal and x_2 is the signal from the reference electrode, as shown in Figure 5.8(b). The objective now is to extract x_1 from these two signals. This is accomplished by minimizing the MSE between the primary input signal and the reference signal. Using the formulations mentioned in Equation 5.17, we can show that

$$E[\varepsilon_r^2] = E(x_1 - y)^2 + E[n_1^2] \tag{5.18}$$

The next step involves estimating the filter coefficients so that the signal of interest could be extracted from the noise. For this different cost functions as a function of filter coefficients are possible. Let us consider a case shown in Figure 5.8(a) and obtain the filter coefficients using one of the MSE criterions. The following cost function can be written:

$$J = E\{\varepsilon_r^2[t]\} = (x_1[t] + n_1[t] - y[t])^2 \rightarrow min \tag{5.19}$$

Considering a filter with order N, this results in a quadratic cost function that has a global minimum. There are several methods to solve the minimization problem and due to the simplicity of implementation, the least-mean squares (LMS) algorithm will be explained here. The LMS algorithm [125] is an iterative algorithm, which minimizes the MSE between the primary and the reference signals, and results in filter coefficients or weights. The LMS algorithm can be written as:

$$\mathbf{W}_{k+1} = \mathbf{W}_k + 2\mu\varepsilon_k\mathbf{X}_k \tag{5.20}$$

where, $\mathbf{W}_k = [w1_k\ w2_k \ldots wj_k \ldots wN_k]^T$ is a set of filter weights and $\mathbf{X}_k = [x1_k\ x2_k \ldots xj_k \ldots xN_k]^T$ is the input vector at time k of the reference sample. The parameter ε_k is the difference between the input ECG and the filtered output y_k. Recall that the reference samples in this particular formulation is the noise signal. The parameter μ is empirically selected to produce a convergence at a desired rate. The larger its value, the faster is the convergence.

The time constant for the convergence is $1/(4\mu\alpha)$, where α is the largest eigenvalue of the autocorrelation matrix of the reference signal [117]. The LMS algorithm does not converge to the exact solution but to a sufficiently good approximation. Therefore, the selection of α becomes critical as a very large amplitude results in instability. The bound on α to ensure stability is $1/\alpha > \mu > 0$. Figure 5.9(b) shows the application of the LMS algorithm for the denoising signal. The ECG signal is corrupted with respiration artifacts, which manifests as a slow-moving component in the measured signal. The parameter $\mu = 1$ is selected. The filter starts adapting to the original signal after a few initial oscillations as could be seen from the denoised signal in Figure 5.9(b). The formulation

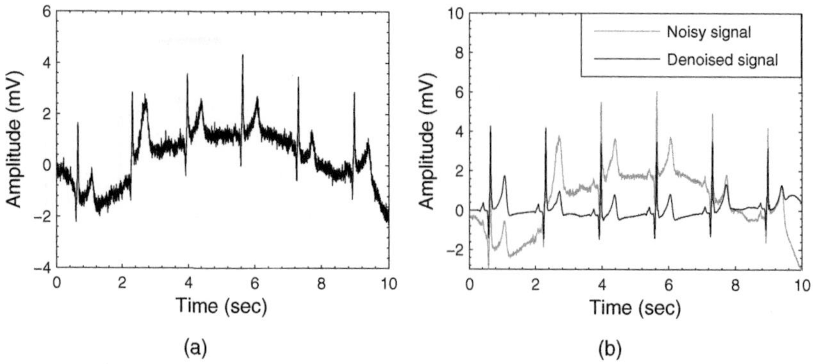

FIGURE 5.9: (a) Original ECG signal with baseline wander (b) filtered ECG signal using adaptive filter.

shown in Figure 5.8(b) is applied in which the reference input signal is derived from other lead so that the noise in the original signal can be minimized.

5.3.2.2 The Adaptive Recurrent Filter (ARF)

The other variants of adaptive filtering employed for ECG signal processing is the ARF technique [117], in which the objective is to adapt the filter coefficients or weights so that the impulse response of the desired signal is obtained. The ARF structure is shown in Figure 5.10. From the ECG signal, select the P-QRS-T signal that spans $k = 0 \cdots \cdot (J-1)$ samples. The transversal filter will require J coefficients. Thus, the ARF is implemented by first identifying a reference impulse train that is coincident with the QRS complexes. The reference impulse is implemented in such a way that the filter coefficients span the entire QRS-T complexes. The practical implementation for the QRS detection can be done through hardware or in software. The detection of the QRS complex will be discussed in the next section. The impulse is placed at the very beginning of the QRS complex. Thus, the reference signal is an impulse coincident in time with the first samples of the signal complex. Each recurrence of the ECG signal $i = 1, 2, \cdots \cdot$ results in a new reference impulse and the new update for the filter coefficients. The desired impulse response is obtained by minimizing the MSE between the noise-inflicted ECG signal and the reference inputs. For the ARF, the reference input vector is, $\mathbf{X}_\text{k} = [0, 0, 1, \cdots, 0]^\text{T}$. Therefore, at each time step only one weight is adapted, and can be written as, $w_{(\text{k}+1)} = w_\text{k} + 2\mu\varepsilon_\text{k}$. All the filter weights are adapted once at each recurring cycle of P-QRS-T complex i.

5.3.3 QRS Detection Algorithm

The QRS complex is the most prominent part in the ECG because of its high amplitude compared to the P and T waves. The QRS complex represents the depolarization of the ventricles of the heart and its presence or detection is most important for the calculation of heart rate. The design of QRS detector is critical because poor detection or no detection at all may severely limit the performance of the system as the error can propagate to the subsequent processing steps. One of the challenges while designing the QRS detector is its ability to not only detect a large number of different QRS morphologies, which are clinically relevant, but also to follow the sudden or gradual changes of the prevailing QRS morphology. The other difficulties associated with QRS detection is sometimes negative QRS polarities (because of extrasystoles, especially the ventricular extrasystole leading to a sudden polarity change), low SNR, nonstationarity, low QRS amplitudes,

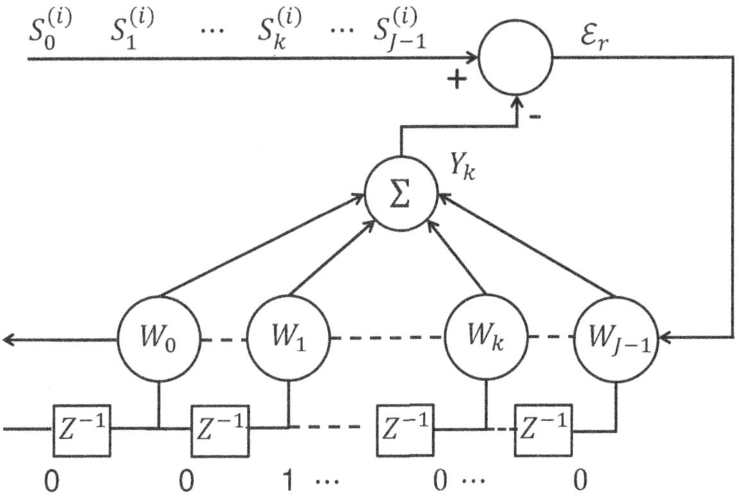

FIGURE 5.10: Schematic of adaptive recurrent filter. The input signal $S^i = S_0^{(i)}\ S_1^{(i)}\ ...S_k^{(i)}\ ...S_{j-1}^{(i)}$ is the vector for P-QRS-T signal complex that spans J samples. The reference input is an impulse sequence (indicated as 0, 0,1, ,0,0), which is coincident with the recurrence of the QRS complexes. Filter output Y_k is the desired output and error E_r is the used to adapt filter weights W_k [117].

and ventricular ectopics. Furthermore, the detector should not lock onto certain types of rhythm and be prepared to treat the next possible episode as if it could occur at almost any time after the most recently detected episode. The following subsection describes some of the common approaches for the detection of QRS complexes.

Pan–Tompkins Algorithm The real time detection of QRS was proposed by Pan and Tompkins [101], consisting of a bandpass filter, which is composed of a low pass filter followed by a high pass integer filter. Figure 5.11 shows different stages of a QRS detector algorithm proposed by Pan and Tompkins. Note that having integer coefficients in a digital filter allows real-time processing speed. Subsequent stages are differentiation, squaring, and time averaging.

(i) **Bandpass filter**

Before designing a bandpass filter it is important to analyze the power spectrum of various signal components in the ECG signal. Figure 5.12 shows the relative power spectra of ECG, P and T waves, motion artifact, QRS complex, and muscle noise [118]. From the figure, one can observe that a bandpass filter which has a pass band of approximately 5 to 15 Hz can maximize the QRS energy and reduce noise from other components of ECG signals by matching the spectrum of an average QRS complex.

The filters used in the algorithm are recursive filters that have poles located to cancel the zeros on the unit circle of the z-plane. The transfer function of a second-order low-pass filter is

$$H(z) = \frac{(1 - z^{-6})^2}{(1 - z^{-1})^2} \tag{5.21}$$

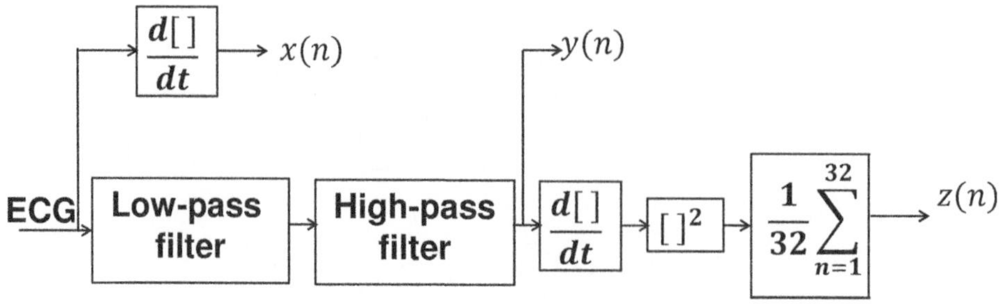

FIGURE 5.11: Different stages of Pan–Tompkins algorithm for QRS detection [101]. $z(n)$ is the time-averaged signal, $y(n)$ is the bandpassed signal, and $x(n)$ is the differentiated ECG.

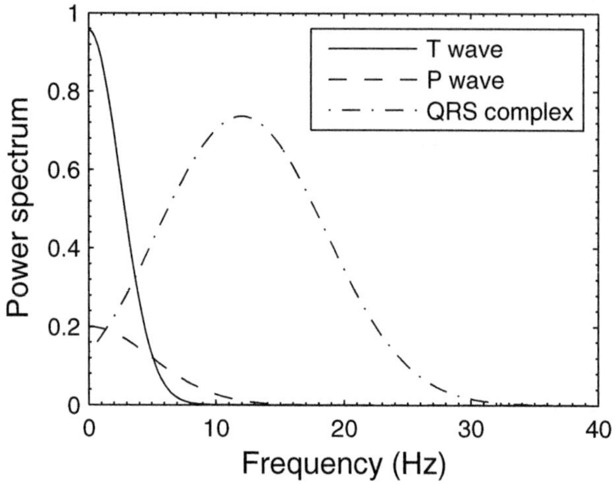

FIGURE 5.12: Typical relative power spectra of different components of ECG complex beats. A synthetic ECG is considered for spectral analysis.

The cut-off frequency of the filter is 11 Hz, the delay is 5 samples, and the gain is 36. The difference equation for this filter is

$$y(nT) = 2y(nT-T) - y(nT-2T) + x(nT) - 2x(nT-6T) + x(nT-12T) \tag{5.22}$$

In the above equation $x(T)$ is the input signal, T is the sampling period. The high-pass filter is implemented by subtracting a first-order low-pass filter from an all-pass filter with delay. The transfer function for a low-pass filter is

$$H_{\text{lp}}(z) = \frac{(1-z^{-32})}{(1-z^{-1})} \tag{5.23}$$

The transfer function of a high-pass filter is

$$H_{\text{hp}}(z) = z^{-16} - \frac{(1-z^{-32})}{32(1-z^{-1})} \tag{5.24}$$

The difference equation for the high-pass filter is

$$q(nT) = x(nT - 16T) - 0.0313[y(nT - T) + x(nT) - x(nT - 32T)] \qquad (5.25)$$

The low cut-off frequency of the filter is about 5 Hz and the delay is 80 ms. The gain of the filter is unity.

(ii) **Derivative**
This stage provides the slope of the QRS complex in which a five-point derivative is implemented using the following transfer function

$$H(z) = 0.1(2 + z^{-1} - z^{-3} - 2z^{-4}) \qquad (5.26)$$

The difference equation for this transfer function is given by

$$y(nT) = (1/8)[2x(nT) + x(nT - T) - x(nT - 3T) - 2x(nT - 4T)] \qquad (5.27)$$

The fraction (1/8) is an approximation for 0.1, since power-of-two facilitates real-time operation. This derivative approximates the ideal derivative in the DC through a 30-Hz frequency range, and it has a filter delay of 10 ms. The P and T waves are attenuated while the peak-to-peak amplitude of the QRS is further enhanced at the end of the derivative stage.

(iii) **Squaring**
The squaring is a nonlinear process and performed to get all the positive values so that once these samples are processed a square wave can be obtained. Also this step emphasizes the higher frequencies of the ECG signal, which are due to the presence of the QRS complexes. The point-by-point squaring of the samples is given by $y(nT) = [x(nT)]^2$.

(iv) **Moving Window Integral**
The slope of R wave only is not a definite way to detect QRS complexes in an ECG. There might be instances of abnormal QRS complexes that have large amplitudes and long durations. Thus, additional information from the signal needs to be extracted to reliably detect a QRS event. A moving average integrator extracts features apart from the slope of the R wave. The difference equation for the integrator with N samples is given by

$$y(nT) = (1/N)[x(nT - (N-1)T) + x(nT - (N-2)T) + \cdots + x(nT)] \qquad (5.28)$$

Selection of N is crucial and needs careful consideration. It is usually chosen from experimental observations. If the window is too large, then the integration waveform will merge the QRS and T complexes. If the window is too small then chances are that several peaks will result for a QRS complex. A typical time period for the window is about 150 ms.

(v) **Threshold Selection**
Pan and Tompkins have proposed a set of thresholds such that only the appropriate QRS complexes are detected. Two sets of thresholds—one corresponding to the signal and the other to the noise—are set. The peaks correspond to T wave, muscle artifact corresponds to the noise peaks, while the peaks corresponding to QRS correspond to signal peaks. Thus, the task narrows down to setting up the thresholds that are just above the noise peaks. The reader is referred to Hamilton and Tompkins [52] for more details on the formulation for setting up the threshold. Subsequently, the R to R interval is computed so that the heart rate can be determined.

A large number of QRS detection algorithms are described in the literature [93, 39, 58, 4, 35, 99, 126, 121, 88, 36, 47, 113, 45, 46, 97, 89, 17, 116, 16, 92] and it is beyond the scope of this chapter to discuss them in detail. However, these detection algorithms could be broadly classified into two categories, namely the performance and the complexity. Friesen et al. [40] have quantified the noise sensitivity of nine QRS detection algorithms. In their study, synthesized normal ECG data were used as a gold standard and different levels and types of noises were added to it. The noise types were electromyographic interference, 60-Hz power line interference, baseline drift due to respiration, abrupt baseline shift, and composite noise constructed from all the other noise types. They concluded that none of the algorithms was able to detect all QRS complexes without any false positives for all of the noise types at the highest noise level. Algorithms based on the amplitude and slope of the QRS complex are most immune to EMG noise. In practice, this type of noise is most common and likes to pose the greatest challenges; these algorithms have an advantage over the algorithms considered for the evaluation.

Apart from the standard threshold-based methods for the detection of QRS complexes, the other variants reported in the literature for QRS detection are based on adaptive matched filtering based on neural networks [127], wavelet transforms [77], continuous spline wavelet transforms using local maxima of the continuous wavelet transform (CWT) at different scales [6], CWT using fixed thresholds [129], first derivatives with adaptive quantized thresholds [25], and the filter banks approach [3] .

5.4 Denoising of Signals

The aim of signal denoising is to improve the measurement accuracy and reproducibility, which is otherwise not readily available from the signal through visual assessment. This section presents various denoising approaches commonly applied for processing biomedical signals. The ECG signal is considered for illustration; however, these techniques could be well applied for other signals too. Note that in the previous section a classical filtering approach was presented. This section introduces a statistical approach (principal component analysis), a nonstationary filtering technique (wavelet), and an optimum filter in wavelet domain (wavelet-Wiener).

The most common interference that occurs in ECG recording is the signal from the myopotentials, which arise in skeletal muscles. Since the frequency spectrum of ECGs coincides with the spectrum of myopotentials, a simple frequency selective filtering mentioned in the previous sections cannot be applied to remove the noise. Instead, approaches like principal component analysis (PCA) and filtering using wavelet transform are more preferable for denoising. Significant improvements in SNR could be achieved if these techniques are coupled, for instance wavelet and Wiener filtering. Finally a denoising approach known as the pilot estimation method will be presented.

5.4.1 Principal Component Analysis

For multivariate signal analysis, principal components analysis (PCA) is one of the oldest candidates in literature [71]. For electrocardiogram (ECG) signal enhancement, a robust extension of classical PCA is suggested [72] by analyzing shorter signal segments. PCA has been applied for data reduction, beat detection, classification, signal separation, and feature extraction [75, 71]. PCA can be used for the separation of respiratory and nonrespiratory segments in an ECG signal [75]. Noise reduction and data compression are closely related, as both require PCA to concentrate the original signal information within a few eigenvectors whose noise level is low. Classification of waveform morphologies in arrhythmia monitoring is another early application of PCA, in which a subset of the principal components serves as features, which are used to distinguish between normal sinus beats and abnormal waveforms, such as premature ventricular beats. A recent application of

PCA in ECG signal processing is robust feature extraction of various waveform properties for the purpose of tracking temporal changes due to myocardial ischemia. Historically, such tracking has been based on local measurements derived from the ST-T segment, however, such measurements are unreliable when the analyzed signal is noisy. With correlation as the fundamental signal processing operation, it has become clear that the use of principal components offer a more robust and global approach to the characterization of the ST-T segment [21].

In the following subsection, we present PCA-based denoising for single-channel and multichannel ECG signals. The methods are explained with some examples. We also present singular value decomposition (SVD) based method for ECG noise reduction.

5.4.1.1 Denoising for a Single-Channel ECG

Let us suppose that $x(n)$ is a mixture of noise-free single-lead ECG signal $s(n)$ corrupted with noise $w(n)$, where n represents $n = 0, 1, 2, ...N-1, N$.

$$x(n) = s(n) + w(n) \tag{5.29}$$

Both signals $s(n)$ and $w(n)$ are assumed to be uncorrelated. The first step in a single-channel ECG denoising is division of the beat data into time segments and accurate alignment of the different time segments. For this, the R peaks are first detected from the QRS complex and the Pan and Tompkins's method [101] mentioned in the previous section could be applied. The identification of R peaks is followed by measurement of all the R-R intervals (*Rint*) and the mean R-R interval for the selected time segment. Then the ECG signals with that particular time segment are aligned with the R peak locations as the centers with the range of $\pm Rint$. Any redundancy in the data is not a problem since in most cases the redundant data constitute isoelectric lines, which carry no significant information. The segmented signal of a beat is represented by a column vector given as [21]

$$\mathbf{x} = [x_1, x_2, ..., x_\mathrm{p}]^\mathrm{T} \tag{5.30}$$

where, P is the number of samples of the segment. The segments from several successive beats (say M beats) are ensembled to form a $P \times M$ data matrix $\mathbf{X}$,

$$\mathbf{X} = [\mathbf{x}_1, \mathbf{x}_2, ..., \mathbf{x}_\mathrm{M}] \tag{5.31}$$

The beats $\mathbf{x}_1, \mathbf{x}_2, ..., \mathbf{x}_\mathrm{M}$ can be viewed as M observations of a random process $\mathbf{x}$. Assuming the signal $\mathbf{x}$ is a zero-mean random process, the correlation matrix $\mathbf{R_x}$ can be obtained by

$$\mathbf{R_x} = \mathbf{E}\{\mathbf{x}\mathbf{x}^\mathbf{T}\} \tag{5.32}$$

Since $\mathbf{R_x}$ is rarely known in experiments, a sample correlation matrix $\hat{\mathbf{R}}_\mathbf{x}$ of size PXP is obtained using the data matrix $\mathbf{X}$ as

$$\hat{\mathbf{R}}_\mathbf{x} = \frac{\mathbf{1}}{\mathbf{M}} \mathbf{X}\mathbf{X}^\mathbf{T} \tag{5.33}$$

Next, the eigenvalue decomposition of the matrix $\hat{\mathbf{R}}_\mathbf{x}$ yields matrices $\mathbf{E}$ and $\mathbf{D}$ where E is the orthogonal matrix of eigenvectors of $\hat{\mathbf{R}}_\mathbf{x}$ and $\mathbf{D}$ is the diagonal matrix of its eigenvalues, represented as $\mathbf{D} = diag(d_1, d_2, ..., d_\mathrm{p})$. Now the principal components of the matrix $\mathbf{X}$ are obtained by applying orthonormal linear transformation to $\mathbf{X}$.

$$\mathbf{W} = \mathbf{E}^\mathbf{T}\mathbf{X} \tag{5.34}$$

The principal components, $\mathbf{W}$ reflects the degree of morphologic beat-to-beat variability: When the eigenvalue d_1 associated to the first principal component is much larger than those associated

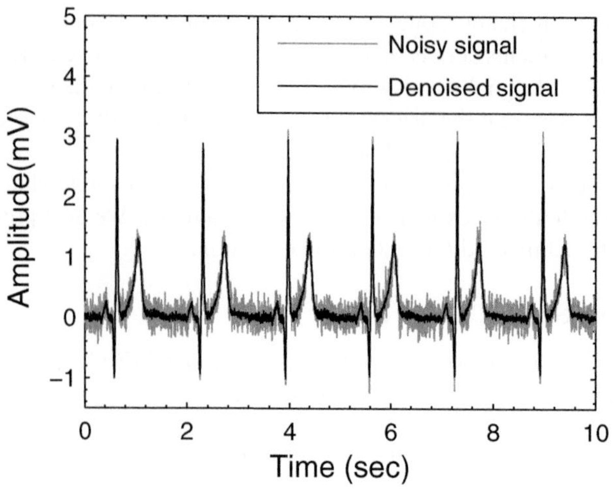

FIGURE 5.13: An example of PCA for ECG signal denoising. The signal is denoised by retaining only the first principal component.

to other components, the ensemble exhibits a low morphologic variability, whereas a slow fall-off of the principal component values indicates a large variability. Since there exists a correlation from one part of the signal **X** to another, the PCs with higher eigenvalues consists more of ECG and less of noise. Hence, the PCs that have significant eigenvalues are assumed to be part of the signal while the rest are assumed to be part of the noise. Therefore, by retaining only the higher eigenvalue PCs, it is possible to reduce most of the noise.

Let K principal components $w_1, w_2, ...w_K$, where $K < P$ is required to condense the information of **X** while retaining the physiological information. The choice of K may be guided by various statistical performance indices [71], of which one index is the degree of variation $\mathbf{R_K}$, reflecting how well the subset of K principal components approximates the ensemble in energy terms, given by

$$R_K = \frac{\sum_{k=1}^{K} d_k}{\sum_{k=1}^{N} d_k} \tag{5.35}$$

In practice, K is usually chosen so that the performance is clinically acceptable and no vital signal information is lost. The signal part of the ECG (without noise) can now be reconstructed from the selected PCs using

$$\hat{\mathbf{X}} = \hat{\mathbf{E}}\hat{\mathbf{W}} \tag{5.36}$$

where, $\hat{\mathbf{E}}$ and $\hat{\mathbf{W}}$ are the eigenvectors and PCs corresponding to the noise free signal, respectively. Finally a noise-reduced ECG signal is obtained by concatenating the columns of $\hat{\mathbf{X}}$. Figure 5.13 shows the application of PCA for signal denoising.

5.4.1.2 Denoising for a Multichannel ECG

Since considerable correlation exists between different ECG leads, for instance in 12-lead ECG, certain applications such as data compression and denoising of multichannel ECGs can benefit from exploring interlead information rather than just processing one lead at a time. In this section, a single-lead ECG signal of Equation 5.30 is extended to a multilead case by introducing the vector

$\mathbf{x}_{i,l}$, where the indices i and l denote beat and lead numbers, respectively. Then, a straightforward approach to applying PCA on multichannel ECGs is to pile up the leads $\mathbf{x}_{i,1}, \mathbf{x}_{i,2}, ..., \mathbf{x}_{i,L}$ of the ith beat into a $LP \times 1$ vector $\tilde{\mathbf{x}}_i$, defined by [21]

$$\tilde{\mathbf{x}}_i = \begin{bmatrix} \mathbf{x}_{i,1} \\ \cdot \\ \cdot \\ \cdot \\ \mathbf{x}_{i,L} \end{bmatrix} \tag{5.37}$$

For the ensemble of beats, M, the multichannel data matrix $\tilde{\mathbf{X}}$ is represented by a $LP \times M$ matrix, which is written as

$$\tilde{\mathbf{X}} = [\tilde{\mathbf{x}_1} ... \tilde{\mathbf{x}_M}] \tag{5.38}$$

Accordingly, $\tilde{\mathbf{X}}$ replaces $\mathbf{X}$ in the above calculations. The formulation of $\mathbf{X}$ discussed in the previous section for a single-channel ECG denoising is applied again for determining the eigenvectors of the sample correlation matrix. Once PCA has been performed on the piled vector, the resulting eigenvectors are "depiled" so that the desired principal components coefficients can be determined for each lead.

5.4.1.3 Denoising Using Truncated Singular Value Decomposition

Instead of performing PCA on data matrix $\mathbf{X}$, one can find the singular value decomposition of the $P \times M$ matrix $\mathbf{X}$, which is defined as

$$\mathbf{X} = \mathbf{USV}^{\mathrm{T}} \tag{5.39}$$

where, $\mathbf{U}$ is an $P \times P$ orthonormal matrix whose columns are the left singular vectors, and $\mathbf{V}$ is an $M \times M$ orthonormal matrix whose columns are the right singular vectors. The matrix $\mathbf{S}$ is a $P \times M$ nonnegative diagonal matrix containing the singular values $\sigma_1, \sigma_2, ...\sigma_p$, such that $\sigma_1 > \sigma_2 > ...\sigma_p \geq 0$. Singular values of the signal preserve the information like noise level, the amount of signal energy, and the number of elements that make up the signal. The greater the singular values are, the more important the corresponding singular vectors are in representing the matrix $\mathbf{X}$.

Since the segments of observed ECG signal are highly correlated, in the SVD domain, generally (for high SNR cases) higher valued singular values conserve the signal energy, whereas the lower singular values conserve the noise energy. Hence, by truncating the lower singular values, the effect of noise components in the signal reconstruction can be minimized. This technique is called the truncated singular value decomposition (TSVD) method [53]. The TSVD method involves the following steps.

1. Perform SVD on matrix $\mathbf{X}$, and identify the nonsignificant singular values in the matrix $\mathbf{S}$.
2. Set the nonsignificant singular values to zero and form a new diagonal matrix $\hat{\mathbf{S}}$.
3. Reconstruct a denoised matrix $\hat{\mathbf{X}} = \mathbf{U}\hat{\mathbf{S}}\mathbf{V}^{\mathrm{T}}$, which approximates matrix $\mathbf{X}$ in least squares sense.
4. Reconstruct a denoised ECG signal by concatenating the time segments.

One important aspect while applying the TSVD is the selection of singular values that belong to signal and noise subspace. For the lower SNR cases, the singular values of the signal and noise cannot be perfectly separated from each other (slow varying singular values). Assume that $M1$ singular values clearly belong to the signal subspace, next $M2$ singular values belong to both signal

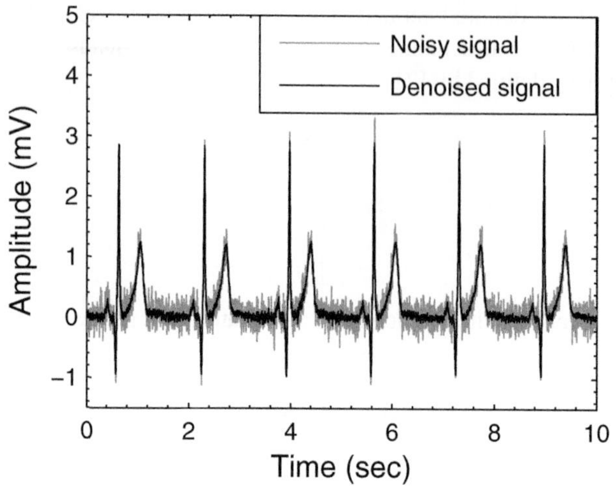

FIGURE 5.14: An example of SVD for ECG signal denoising. The signal is denoised by retaining only the first two singular values.

and noise subspaces, and the remaining $N-(M1+M2)$ singular values belong to the noise subspace. In such cases a filter **f** is designed in such a way that the singular values in the SVD mapping are modified. The expression for the filter function $f_i, i = 1,2,..,P$ is defined as [91]

$$f_i = \begin{cases} 1, & i \leq M1 \\ e^{-(i-\beta)/\beta} & M1 < i \leq M2 \\ 0, & i > M1+M2 \end{cases} \quad (5.40)$$

is applied to the singular values, $\hat{\sigma}_i = f_i * \sigma_i$, to obtain modified singular value matrix $\hat{\mathbf{S}}$. Here β is a weighting coefficient. Finally, the $\hat{\mathbf{S}}$ matrix is used to reconstruct the noise-free matrix $\mathbf{X}$ by $\hat{\mathbf{X}} = \mathbf{U}\hat{\mathbf{S}}\mathbf{V}^{\mathbf{T}}$. Figure 5.14 shows an application of SVD for signal denoising.

5.4.2 Wavelet Filtering

Discrete Wavelet Transform (DWT) is a method, which has the ability to represent a large class of well-behaved functions with a sparse representation in wavelet space. So, when DWT is applied to a noisy ECG signal, the noise-free component of the signal (true signal) will be concentrated in a small number of larger coefficients, while the noise will be distributed as smaller coefficients. So by applying simple threshold to the smaller coefficients and by performing the inverse wavelet transform (IDWT), noise-free ECG reconstruction can be obtained (Figure 5.14). However, choice of the threshold value and the thresholding scheme play a crucial role in denoising the ECG signal.

Let $y_m(n) = u_m(n) + v_m(n)$ be the wavelet coefficients obtained by performing DWT on the noisy signal, $x(n)$, in which $u_m(n)$ are the coefficients of the noise-free signal and $v_m(n)$ are the coefficients of the noise, m being the level of decomposition that denotes the mth frequency band. The threshold levels for modification of the wavelet coefficient should be set for each decomposition level m with respect to the noise level v_m (its standard deviation σ_{v_m}). When the noise level is low, the threshold values are low, and the risk of corrupting the true signal, $s(n)$ is low. Donoho [34] has proposed a universal thresholding method where the threshold value is given by $\sqrt{2logG}$, where G is the number of wavelet coefficients. Universal threshold yields near-optimal mean-squared error (MSE) rates over a range of signal smoothness classes, and produces visually appealing reconstruction irrespective of the size of the samples, G. However, it is well known that universal threshold

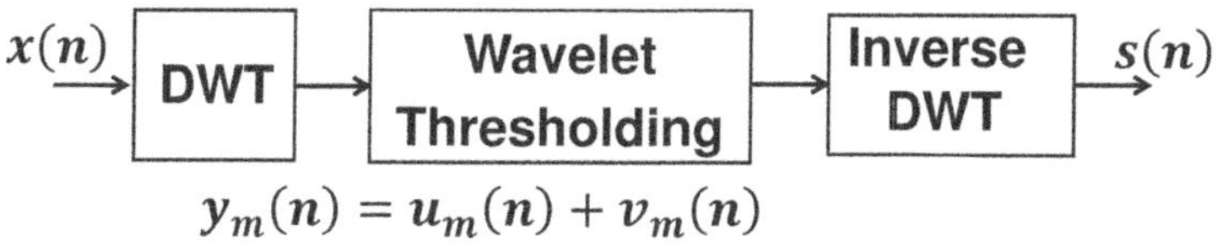

FIGURE 5.15: A typical block diagram for filtering ECG signal using wavelets.

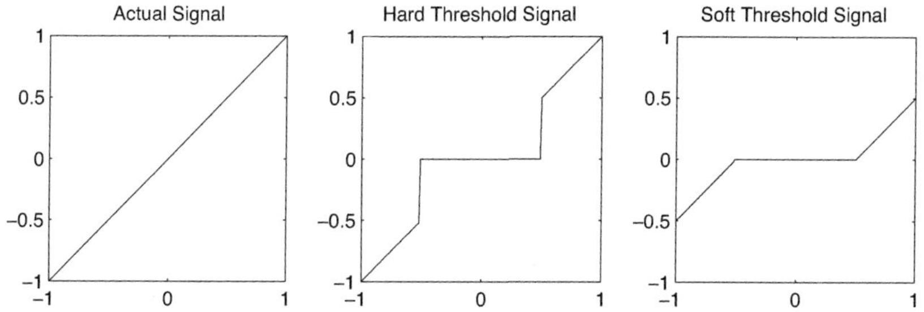

FIGURE 5.16: Wavelet thresholding methods (a) Actual signal (b) Hard thresholding (c) Soft thresholding.

oversmoothes the signal, $x(n)$, as it is often observed, and too much of signal components are killed in the process of thresholding. The reader is referred to [69] for methods for estimating the optimal threshold values.

The selection of a thresholding scheme is a problem of significant interest in wavelet thresholding. In general, the thresholding methods are categorized into two types, namely the hard thresholding and the soft thresholding, as shown in Figure 5.16. Performance of thresholding depends on the type of thresholding method and the rule used for a given application. The hard threshold function ($y_m{}^{ht}$) defined in Equation 5.41 tends to have bigger variance and is unstable (sensitive to even small changes in the signal), where y_m are the wavelet coefficients; Thr is a threshold value that is applied on the wavelet coefficients.

$$y_m{}^{ht} = \begin{cases} 0, & |y| < Thr \\ 1, & |y| \geq Thr \end{cases} \tag{5.41}$$

In contrary, soft thresholding function (y_{st}) is much more stable than hard thresholding and tends to have a bigger bias due to the shrinkage of larger wavelet coefficients described in Equation 5.42. In addition to these methods, the hypertrim shrinkage with α-trim thresholding is proposed for signal denoising [103]. In general, most of the researchers have proved that the soft thresholding method gives the best results with other methods on denoising the ECG signal [103].

$$(y_m{}^{st}) = \begin{cases} 0, & |y| < Thr \\ (y - Thr), & |y| \geq Thr \end{cases} \tag{5.42}$$

Finally, the steps of the denoising algorithm by wavelet thresholding are as follows:

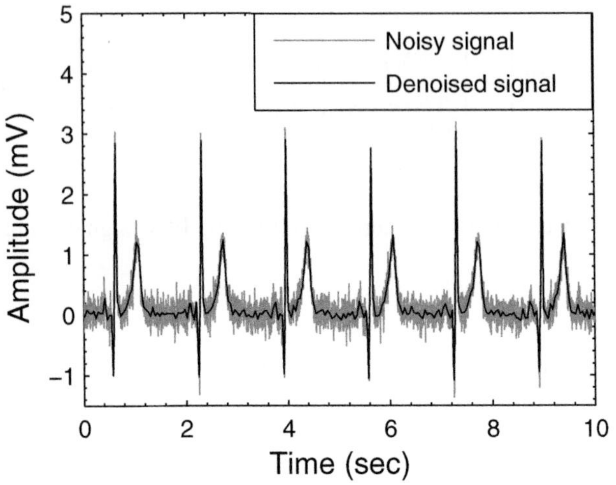

FIGURE 5.17: The noisy ECG signal is filtered using a wavelet filtering technique. A soft threshold is applied so that the morphology of the original signal is preserved.

(a) Transform the signal into a wavelet domain with a predefined level of decomposition using any standard orthogonal wavelet bases.

(b) Estimate the noise in the each subband.

(c) Calculate the soft threshold value for each subband.

(d) Apply the soft thresholding scheme to the wavelet coefficients with the subband level dependent threshold.

(e) Reconstruct the signal using IDWT.

The framework presented for denoising the signal using wavelet filtering is applied to the noisy ECG signal. Figure 5.17 shows the denoised signal using the wavelet filtering technique. A soft thresholding is applied so that the morphology of the original signal is maintained. Note that applying a hard threshold often results in altering the magnitudes of the PQRST complexes.

5.4.3 Wavelet Wiener Filtering

The technique is based on applying the Wiener filtering theory in the wavelet domain. As in traditional Wiener filtering, the signal in the wavelet domain $y_{\mathrm{m}}(n)$ has to be modified using a form factor $H_{\mathrm{m}}(n)$ to obtain filtered signal $HF_{\mathrm{m}}(n)$, which is defined as [24]

$$HF_{\mathrm{m}}(n) = H_{\mathrm{m}}(n) * y_{\mathrm{m}}(n) = H_{\mathrm{m}}(n) * [u_{\mathrm{m}}(n) + v_{\mathrm{m}}(n)] \tag{5.43}$$

The selection of the filter $H_{\mathrm{m}}(n)$ should be such a way that, the mean-squared error between the filtered signal $HF_{\mathrm{m}}(n)$ and the actual signal to be reconstructed, $u_{\mathrm{m}}(n)$ is minimum. The MSE is given by $e_{\mathrm{m}}{}^2(n) = [HF_{\mathrm{m}}(n) - u_{\mathrm{m}}(n)]^2$. The solution for minimum MSE gives an equation for the form factor, $H_{\mathrm{m}}(n)$ that

$$H_{\mathrm{m}}(n) = \frac{u_{\mathrm{m}}{}^2(n)}{u_{\mathrm{m}}{}^2(n) + v_{\mathrm{m}}{}^2(n)} \tag{5.44}$$

In the above expression both noise-free signal coefficients $u_{\mathrm{m}}(n)$ and the noise coefficients $v_{\mathrm{m}}(n)$

are unknown. For noise coefficients $v_{\mathrm{m}}(n)$, the values $v_{\mathrm{m}}^2(n)$ are replaced by the noise variance in the mth level. Now, the expression for $H_{\mathrm{m}}(n)$ gets modified to

$$H_{\mathrm{m}}(n) = \frac{u_{\mathrm{m}}^2(n)}{u_{\mathrm{m}}^2(n) + \sigma_{\mathrm{m}}^2(n)} \tag{5.45}$$

For low noise cases, $u_{\mathrm{m}}^2(n) >> \sigma_{\mathrm{m}}^2(n)$ such that the filter $H_{\mathrm{m}}(n) \approx 1$ and $|HF_{\mathrm{m}}(n)| \approx |y_{\mathrm{m}}(n)|$. On other hand, for high noise cases $u_{\mathrm{m}}^2(n) << \sigma_{\mathrm{m}}^2(n)$ and $H_{\mathrm{m}}(n) << 1$ and $|HF_{\mathrm{m}}(n)| < |y_{\mathrm{m}}(n)|$.

Hybrid Thresholding Literature [95] has shown that the noise-free coefficients $u_{\mathrm{m}}(n)$ can be estimated from signal $y_{\mathrm{m}}(n)$, and noise variance $\sigma_{\mathrm{m}}^2(n)$ in the form $u_{\mathrm{m}}^2(n) = max[\ ky_{\mathrm{m}}^2(n) - \sigma_{\mathrm{m}}^2(n), 0\ ]$ where k is a constant chosen as $k = 1/3$.

The result leads to form factor,

$$H_{\mathrm{m}}(n) = max[\frac{y_{\mathrm{m}}^2(n) - 3\sigma_{\mathrm{m}}^2(n)}{y_{\mathrm{m}}^2(n)}, 0] = max[1 - \frac{3\sigma_{\mathrm{m}}^2(n)}{y_{\mathrm{m}}^2(n)}, 0] \tag{5.46}$$

Now expressing $HF_{\mathrm{m}}(n)$ using Equation 5.46, we can conclude that filtering is nothing but thresholding of the coefficients $y_{\mathrm{m}}(n)$ with the threshold given by $Thr(m) = \sqrt{3}\sigma_{\mathrm{m}}(n)$. The filtered output $HF_{\mathrm{m}}(n)$ can be defined as

$$HF_{\mathrm{m}}(n) = \begin{cases} y_{\mathrm{m}}(n) - \dfrac{Thr^2(m)}{y_{\mathrm{m}}(n)}, & |y_{\mathrm{m}}(n)| > Thr(m) \\ 0, & |y_{\mathrm{m}}(n)| \leq Thr(m) \end{cases} \tag{5.47}$$

From Equation 5.47, it can be deduced that filtering is a combination of soft and hard thresholding: It is approached to soft thresholding for values $|y_{\mathrm{m}}(n)|$ approximately equal to $Thr(m)$ and hard thresholding for values $|y_{\mathrm{m}}(n)|$ much higher than $Thr(m)$. Therefore, this method is named the hybrid thresholding method.

However, an efficient alternative approach called the pilot estimation method can be used to estimate the noise-free signal coefficients $u_{\mathrm{m}}(n)$. The next subsection discusses the method in brief.

5.4.4 Pilot Estimation Method

The pilot estimation method [24] has two denoising blocks as shown in the block diagram in Figure 5.18. The first block of denoising is a wavelet filtering block that is discussed in Section 5.4.2. In brief, the DWT1 block performs the wavelet transform, followed by modifying the wavelet coefficients by wavelet thresholding. The modified coefficients are then fed to the inverse wavelet transform, IDWT1 to get an estimate $\hat{s}(n)$, which is a pilot signal that approximates the noise-free signal, $s(n)$. The pilot signal enters the DWT2 block and results in coefficients $\hat{u}_m(n)$.

The coefficients now form an estimate of $u_m(n)$ for the Wiener filtering block that is discussed in Section 5.4.3. The signal from DWT3 and $\hat{u}_m(n)$, and noise variance are fed to the wiener filtering block. The modified coefficients from the Wiener filter are then inverse transformed using IDWT2 to obtain noise-free reconstruction $s(n)$.

The choice of decomposition and reconstruction filters for WT1/WT2 and the method of thresholding and threshold value used in the first block have a large impact on the results. Analyses have proved that hybrid thresholding with the threshold value $\sqrt{3}\sigma_{\mathrm{m}}$ is optimal for the wavelet thresholding block in the pilot estimation method. Figure 5.19 shows one particular example of wavelet-Wiener filtering for signal denoising.

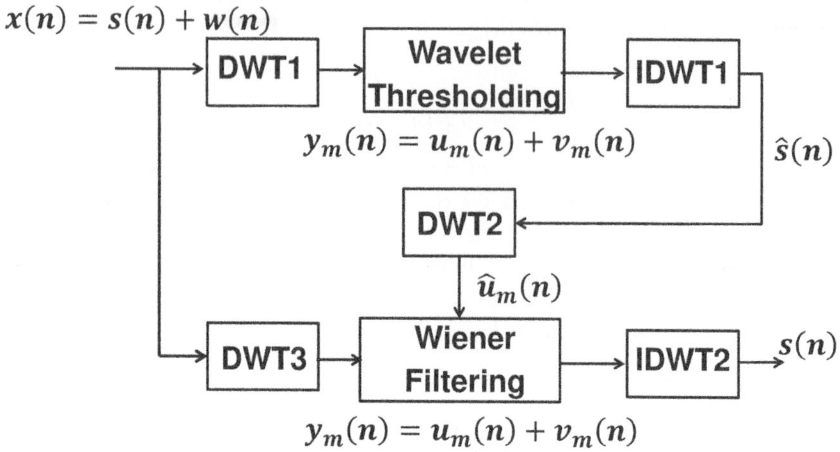

FIGURE 5.18: Pilot estimation method for wavelet-Wiener filtering.

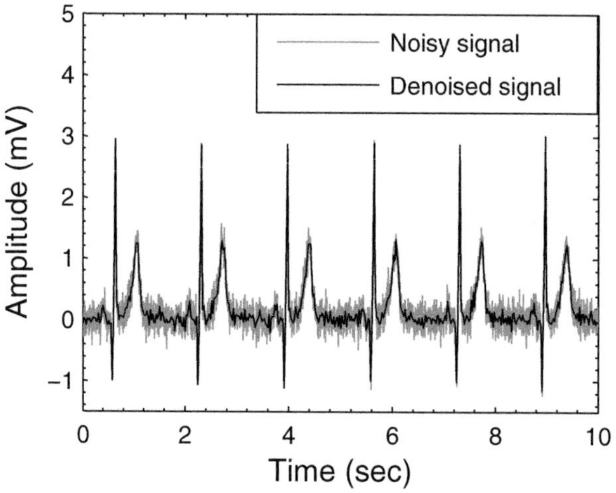

FIGURE 5.19: The noisy ECG signal is filtered using the wavelet-Wiener filtering technique.

5.5 Multivariate Biomedical Signal Analysis

Biomedical signal analysis of multivariate data has benefited immensely from the advances in research in other disciplines, for instance in neural network research, where the fundamental problem is to find a suitable representation of multivariate data, i.e., random vectors. Many times, for the sake of computational simplicity, a representation is desired that is a linear combination of the original data. Linear transformation allows each representation of data to be a linear combination of the original variables. Some of the well-known linear transformation methods are principal component analysis, factor analysis, projection pursuit, and independent component analysis. Independent component analysis (ICA) is a special class of blind source separation (BSS) techniques, in which

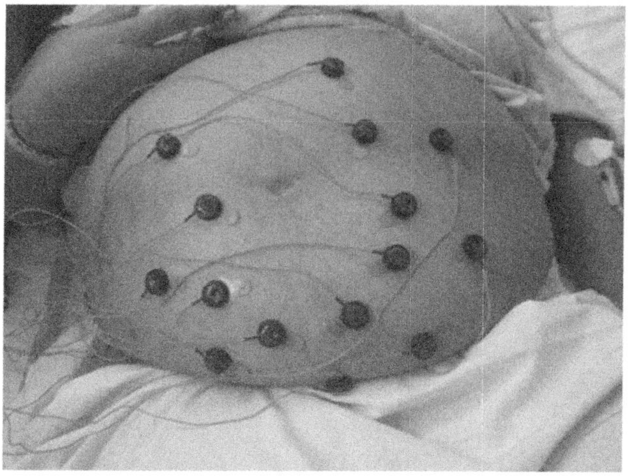

FIGURE 5.20: Multichannel recording of ECG from a maternal abdomen. The recorded signals contain maternal as well as fetal ECG along with other sources of noise.

the objective is to find a linear representation of non-Gaussian data so that each component is as independent as possible [57].

In the previous section, we discussed the use of principal component analysis to extract a statistical-based model of the signal and noise. This statistical technique allowed the removal of in-band noise by discarding the dimensions corresponding to noise. Independent component analysis has in recent times caught the imagination of several researchers to handle multiple channel data, where the features of interest overlap in bands but are statistically independent sources.

One of the applications of ICA is the separation of artifacts in magnetoencephalography (MEG) data. Magnetoencephalography (MEG) is a functional neuroimaging noninvasive technique for mapping brain activity by recording magnetic fields produced by electrical currents occurring naturally in the brain, using very sensitive magnetometers. Applications of MEG include basic research into perceptual and cognitive brain processes, localizing regions affected by pathology before surgical removal, determining the function of various parts of the brain, and neurofeedback. MEG can aid in finding locations of abnormalities by simply measuring the brain activity [28]. One of the issues while extracting the essential features from the brain signals is the presence of artifacts. To exacerbate the problem, the amplitude of disturbances can be higher than that of the signals from the brain, and also resemble pathological signals in shape. The artifacts commonly encountered during MEG recordings are eye movements or blinks, myographic or muscle artifacts, cardiac signals, or sensor noise. ICA techniques have been used successfully to isolate each sources of error and also to decompose evoked fields, enabling direct access to the underlying brain functioning [123].

Other area where ICA has been widely applied in the literature is the separation of fetal ECG from maternal ECG that is obtained through multiple sensor recordings from the maternal abdomen (Figure 5.20). This class of problem has become amenable with the fact that the signals originating from the mother and the fetus are statistically independent. In this particular case, a large set of multivariate data is measured from sensors placed on the abdomen. Each individual component is assumed to be mixed, either linearly or nonlinearly, and the components themselves along with the mixing system are assumed to be unknown. The task of ICA is now to demix or extract each individual component by exploiting the independence of sources. This technique is more powerful that classical methods such as principal component analysis. Figure 5.21 shows the ICA process involved in source separation of each individual component.

Essentially, the task of ICA is to recover N unknown underlying sources $\mathbf{S}(t) =$

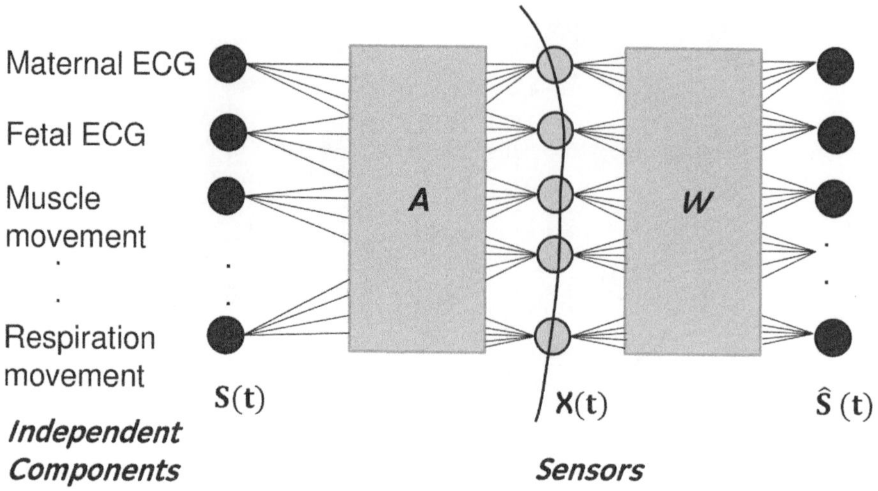

FIGURE 5.21: The extraction of individual components using ICA. The picture shows the individual components $\mathbf{S}(t)$, the mixing matrix **A**, the data recorded at the sensor $\mathbf{X}(t)$, and the demixing matrix **W**. In this model the inherent assumptions are linear mixing of the sources, a stationarity of mixing matrix and noiseless mixing [68]. In the figure, one particular example consisting of measurements from maternal abdomen is shown. The independent sources are maternal ECG, fetal ECG, motion artifacts, respiratory movement from the mother, and other noise sources.

$[s_1(t)\ s_2(t)\ s_3(t)\ ...\ s_N(t)]^T$ from a set of M measured data points at time instant t, $\mathbf{X}(t) = [x_1(t)\ x_2(t)\ x_3(t)\ ...\ x_M(t)]^T$. Some of the assumptions during the mixing of the sources are the linearity and the stationarity of the mixing process, and the mixing matrix **A** to be full rank of dimension NXM, such that

$$\mathbf{X}(t) = \mathbf{AS}(t) \tag{5.48}$$

It is also assumed that the number of sources is less than or equal to the number of measurement channels $N \leq M$. The task now reduces to recover the individual sources $s_i(t)$ from the observations $\mathbf{X}(t)$ and this essentially means finding a demixing or separating matrix **W** such that

$$\hat{\mathbf{S}}(t) = \mathbf{WX}(t) \tag{5.49}$$

where, $\hat{\mathbf{S}}(t)$ is the estimate of the underlying sources $\mathbf{S}(t)$. For estimating the demixing matrix **W**, various ICA algorithms based on higher-order statistics have been proposed and can be found in the literature [81, 27, 11, 66], though the list is not exhaustive.

The preprocessing step for estimating the $\hat{\mathbf{S}}(t)$ is centering and whitening the measured data $\mathbf{X}(t)$. Centering involves subtracting the signal with its mean value so as to make a zero mean variable. Whitening or decorrelation involves transforming the observed vector $\mathbf{X}(t)$ linearly so that one obtains a new vector $\hat{\mathbf{X}}(t)$, which is white, i.e., its components are uncorrelated and their variances equal unity. This implies that the covariance matrix $E\{\hat{\mathbf{X}}(t)\hat{\mathbf{X}}(t)^T\} = \mathbf{I}$, is an identity matrix. Whitening could be performed by performing the eigenvalue decomposition of the covariance matrix $E\{\hat{\mathbf{X}}(t)\hat{\mathbf{X}}(t)^T\} = \mathbf{EDE^T}$, where E is the orthogonal matrix of eigenvectors of $E\{\hat{\mathbf{X}}(t)\hat{\mathbf{X}}(t)^T\}$ and **D** is the diagonal matrix of it eigenvalues $\mathbf{D} = diag(d_1, d_2, ..., d_{N-1}, d_N)$. Whitening can be done by $\hat{\mathbf{X}} = \mathbf{ED}^{-1/2}\mathbf{E}^T\mathbf{X}$, where the matrix $\mathbf{D}^{-1/2}$ is computed by a simple component-wise operation on the diagonal matrix $\mathbf{D}^{-1/2} = diag(d_1^{-1/2}, d_2^{-1/2}, ..., d_{N-1}^{-1/2}, d_N^{-1/2})$. Decorrelation is essentially what a principal component analysis does.

Estimating the sources $\hat{\mathbf{S}}(t)$ is possible if and only if the sources are non-Gaussian. In theory the objective is now to make the estimates $\hat{\mathbf{S}}(t)$ as non-Gaussian as possible, as according to the central limit theorem, the sum of non-Gaussian random variables are closer to Gaussian than the original signals. One constraint that this formulation poses is that at most only one source with Gaussian distribution is possible [65]. The following paragraphs discuss three most commonly used approaches for implementing ICA using higher-order statistics.

5.5.1 Non-Gaussianity through Kurtosis: FastICA

Kurtosis or the fourth-order cumulant is the measure of non-Gaussianity of a signal. For a signal with Gaussian distribution the kurtosis is zero. FastICA works on the premise that the fast fixed point-iterative algorithm undertakes to find projections that maximize the non-Gaussianity of components by their kurtosis. Thus, the ICA formulation narrows down to an optimization problem with the sources as its solution. The kurtosis is used to describe the distribution of a zero mean random variable **X** and is defined as $kurt(\mathbf{X}) = E\{\mathbf{X}^4\} - \mathbf{3}(E\{\mathbf{X}^2\})^2$, where $E\{\cdot\}$ is the expectation operator. The reader is referred to the formulation by Hyvärinen amd Oja [66] for further details on FastICA.

5.5.2 Non-Gaussianity through Negentropy: Infomax

Bell and Sejnowski [11] have proposed an algorithm, which attempts to measure non-Gaussianity of the sources using negentropy. Entropy is the concept widely used in Information Theory. The entropy of a random variable is the degree of information that the observation variable gives. The more random or unpredictable the observation is, the larger is its entropy. The entropy H for a discrete random variable Y is defined as $H(Y) = \sum_i P(Y = a_i) \log P(Y = a_i)$, where a_i is the largest possible value of Y. The differential entropy H for a continuous-valued random vector y, is defined with density $f(y)$ as $H(Y) = -\int f(y) log f(y) dy$. It is a well-established fact in Information Theory that a Gaussian variable has the largest entropy among all random variables of equal variance [73]. Entropy is very small for a variable that is clearly clustered or has a probability density function that is very spiky. A slight variation of differential entropy called negentropy is often used as a measure of non-Gaussianity. Negentropy is defined as the difference between the entropy of a Gaussian random variable with the same variance as the observed random variable and the entropy of the random variable. This could be represented as $J(y) = H(Y_{\text{gauss}}) - H(y)$, where Y_{gauss} is a Gaussian random variable of the same covariance matrix as y.

The algorithm is a neural network gradient-based framework whose learning rule is based on the principle of information maximization (infomax), and it maximizes the output entropy of a neural network with nonlinear outputs. The learning criterion is the maximization likelihood estimation of an ICA model. In effect, it can be proved that ICA estimation by this criterion reduces to the maximization of the non-Gaussiantiy of the sources, and hence the separation of the sources s_i.

5.5.3 Joint Approximate Diagonalization of Eigenmatrices: JADE

The JADE algorithm [19] is slightly different to both the infomax and fixed-point algorithm in that the latter algorithms optimize a particular transform of the input data, whereas JADE optimizes a transform of a particular set of statistics about the data. The foundation for the JADE algorithm is the realization that blind source separation algorithms generally require an estimation of the distributions of the independent sources or have such an assumption built into the algorithm. Jean-François Cardoso [19] pointed out that optimizing cumulant approximations of data implicitly performs this.

The first step for the JADE-based ICA is prewhitening of $\mathbf{X(t)}$. Assume that the singular value decomposition of the mixing matrix **A** in Equation 5.48 is $= \mathbf{V}_0 \phi_0 \mathbf{U}$, where $\mathbf{V}_0$ and **U** are the unitary matrices, and ϕ_0 is the diagonal matrix of full column rank. The dimension of ϕ_0 can be made square if it is not a square matrix by pruning a few singular values that are either zero or are close to zero. Let the pruned matrix ϕ_0 be denoted as ϕ. Accordingly, the corresponding columns of $\mathbf{V}_0$ needs to be pruned. Let the pruned version of $\mathbf{V}_0$ be $\mathbf{V}$. Thus, the truncated matrix $\mathbf{A}$ can be written as $\mathbf{A} = \mathbf{V}\phi\mathbf{U}$, where ϕ is the $n \times n$ dimension matrix and $\mathbf{V}$ is the $m \times n$ dimension matrix. Substituting matrix $\mathbf{A}$ into Equation 5.48 results in

$$\mathbf{X}(t) = \mathbf{V}\phi\mathbf{U}\mathbf{S}(t) = \mathbf{V}\phi z(t) \tag{5.50}$$

where

$$\mathbf{z}(t) = \mathbf{U}\mathbf{S}(t), \tag{5.51}$$

is the whitened mixed signals and $\phi^{-1}\mathbf{V}^{\mathrm{T}}$ is the whitening matrix. The problem now reduces to solve Equation 5.51 using a following JADE criterion

$$JADE(\mathbf{U}) = \sum_{k,m,n=1}^{N} |cum[s_{\mathrm{k}}(t), s_{\mathrm{k}}^{*}(t), s_{\mathrm{n}}(t), s_{\mathrm{m}}^{*}(t)]|^2 \tag{5.52}$$

Equation 5.52 can be further simplified to

$$JADE(\mathbf{U}) = \sum_{r=1}^{N^2} \| \, diag(\mathbf{U}^{\mathrm{H}}\mathbf{Q}_{\mathrm{z}}(\mathbf{B}_{\mathrm{r}})\mathbf{U}) \, \|^2 = \sum_{k=1}^{N} \sum_{r=1}^{N^2} |\mathbf{u}_{\mathrm{k}}{}^{\mathrm{H}}\mathbf{Q}_{\mathrm{z}}(\mathbf{B}_{\mathrm{r}})\mathbf{u}_{\mathrm{k}}|^2 \tag{5.53}$$

where, $\mathbf{u}_{\mathrm{k}}$ is the k-th column of $\mathbf{U}$, $\mathbf{B}_{\mathrm{r}}$ with $r = 1, 2, ..., N^2$ constitute a set of orthonormal bases for the space of $N \times N$ matrices, $\mathbf{Q}_{\mathrm{z}}(\mathbf{B}_{\mathrm{r}})$ is the cumulant matrix defined element-wise as

$$[\mathbf{Q}_{\mathrm{z}}(\mathbf{B}_{\mathrm{r}})]_{\mathrm{ij}} = \sum_{p,q=1}^{N} cum[s_{\mathrm{k}}(t), s_{\mathrm{k}}^{*}(t), s_{\mathrm{n}}(t), s_{\mathrm{m}}^{*}(t)] b_{\mathrm{pq}}{}^{\mathrm{r}} \tag{5.54}$$

In Equation 5.54, cum$(\cdot)$ denotes cumulant, * denotes complex conjugate, and $b_{\mathrm{pq}}{}^{\mathrm{r}}$ the (p, q)-th element of $\mathbf{B}_{\mathrm{r}}$. Making the cumulant as diagonal as possible is making the data as independent as possible. The matrix that performs the diagonalization on cumulants can be translated to perform separation of the mixed data. Thus, if $\mathbf{R}$ is the rotation matrix that makes the cumulant matrices as diagonal as possible, then a demixing matrix can be estimated as $\mathbf{R}' \cdot \mathbf{z}$ [78].

As a case study, let us see how the JADE algorithm can be applied for the separation of fetal ECG from maternal ECG. For this the data sets from the Daisy database [62] was used. The raw channel consists of eight-channel raw data measured from a pregnant woman for 10 seconds. Channels 1 to 5 correspond to abdomen measurements, while Channels 6 to 8 are thoracic measurements. The data is sampled at 250 Hz. Figure 5.22 shows the raw channel mixed data. Note that the data shows clearly that the maternal and fetal ECG are mixed and needs to be separated in the presence of other sources of noises such as baseline wander. After initial preprocessing such as removal of baseline wander, which is a slow respiratory component dominating the measurement, Channels 1 to 5 are fed to the JADE algorithm. Figure 5.23 shows the separation of individual components, with maternal ECG and fetal ECG in Channels 1 and 3, respectively. The other channels consist of noise components. Some of the researchers have used the noise separation characteristics of ICA for signal denoising [1, 115].

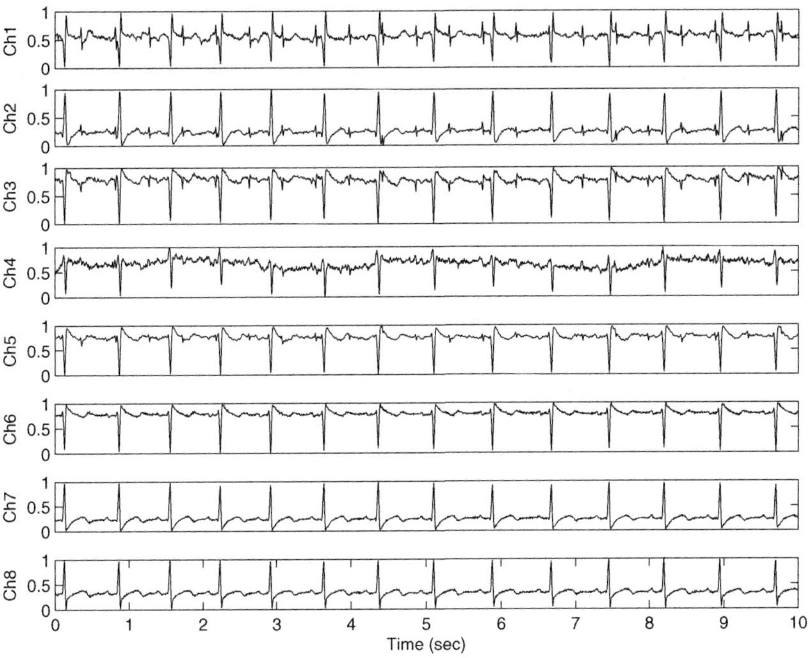

FIGURE 5.22: The eight-channel raw data measured from a pregnant woman for 10 seconds [62]. Channels 1 to 5 correspond to abdomen measurements, while Channels 6 to 8 are thoracic measurements. The data is sampled at 250 Hz.

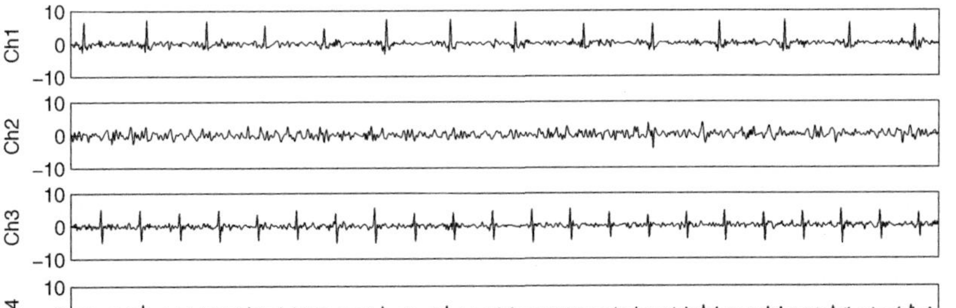

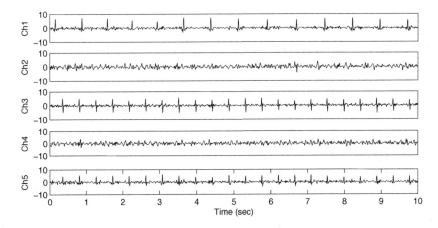

FIGURE 5.23: Extracted fetal and maternal ECG from the raw data shown in Figure 5.22. The algorithm applied for the extraction of fetal ECG is JADE. The magnitudes of original signals are not retained because of scaling ambiguity during separation. There also exists permutation ambiguity and each block of data processed might show fetal and maternal ECGs in different channels.

5.6 Cross-Correlation Analysis

This chapter until now focused on various signal processing approaches for processing biomedical signals, from basic filtering techniques, to exploiting the orthognality in a signal subspace to reduce noise, to source separation algorithms. However, in certain instances the signals originating from some physiological processes need to be compared so that certain features could be extracted. Cross-correlation analysis is sometimes a very useful tool to quantify the underlying relationship between two biosignals or for detecting a deterministic signal in a noisy environment. This analysis is also performed when one needs to estimate delay between two-signal propagation. This section describes one particular example involving resting state functional magnetic resonance imaging (rs-fMRI) as a case study and discusses various steps involved in processing the brain signals. The next few paragraphs introduces the reader to MRI, the resting state fMRI, and the various processing steps involved in fMRI. The noteworthy point is that several intermediate steps need to be performed before two biosignals are correlated. Thus, this section will first discuss a typical preprocessing step in fMRI and then show cross-correlation analysis.

Magnetic resonance imaging (MRI) is a medical imaging method to measure nuclear magnetic properties of tissues. MRI helps us noninvasively *view* internal parts of the human body using the difference in the magnetic properties of tissues. MRI is quite powerful since it can measure many different magnetic properties (such as T1, T2, and T2* relaxation) of several elements. In functional MRI (fMRI), magnetic resonance is used to indirectly measure the neuronal activity. Neuronal activity in one part of the brain changes local blood flow and blood oxygenation, which in turn changes the magnetic property of the area. This change in magnetic property is used to measure neuronal activity in fMRI. Since its discovery in the early 90s [98, 74], fMRI has dramatically increased our understanding of the brain in health and disease.

The simplest fMRI experiment is to measure blood oxygenation of the brain in two states: (a) while performing an explicit task (may be an active task such as tapping fingers or may be passive such as viewing a reverse checkerboard or a combination of both) and (b) while not performing the explicit task. By statistically contrasting the signal amplitude measured during the task and nontask, we can infer which regions in the brain were used to perform the task. It can be seen from this experiment that the baseline signal amplitude is not very important but the contrast between the two states is very important. Hence, in fMRI experiments, contrast to noise ratio (CNR) is very important.

A recently popular method of an fMRI experiment, known as resting state fMRI (rs-fMRI), involves measuring blood oxygenation while *not* performing any explicit task. This method was first described by Biswal et al. [13], in which he explored the relationships between brain regions rather than the application of explicit tasks to find regions associated with those tasks.

The signal strength in fMRI is low and requires elaborate processing to be able to extract useful information from the recorded data from an MR machine. Similar to any measurement system, there is system noise in the recorded signal. This includes thermal noise, RF-induced noise, noise introduced while signal amplification and other system-related processes that cause system instability. In addition to the system noise, there is also a physiological noise induced by changes in the physiology of the human (or animal) subject. This includes noise introduced due to motion (of the human) during scanning, signal fluctuations induced by cardiac pulsation, signal fluctuations due to magnetic field change induced by the amount of air in the lungs (respiration), and fluctuations in hematocrit content in the blood that influences the magnetic properties of the tissue and several others. While it is difficult to entirely eliminate noise, the attempt is to maximize sensitivity and specificity by reducing the effects of noise.

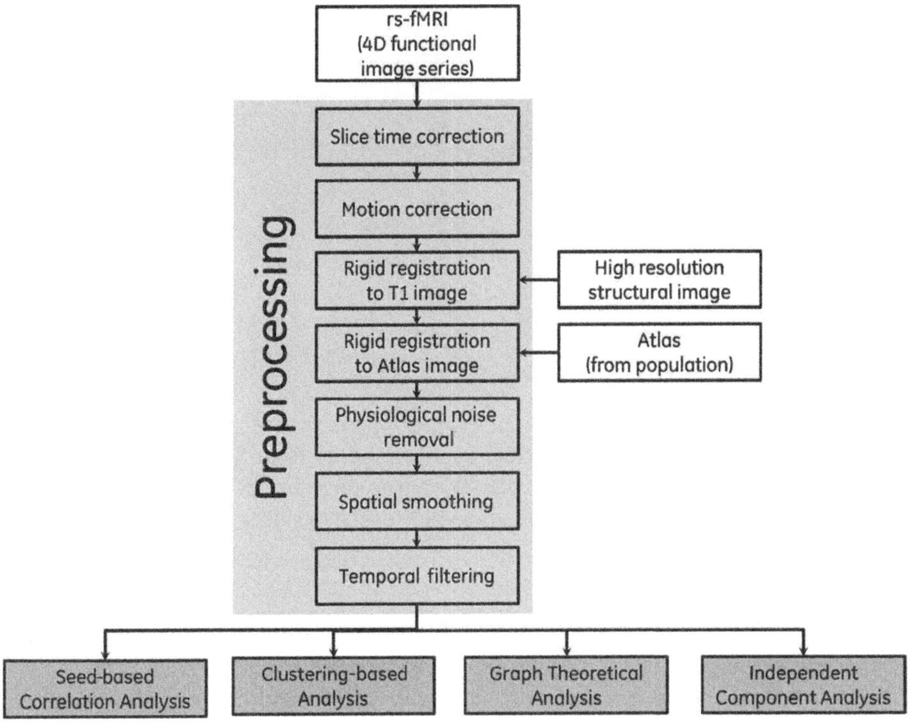

FIGURE 5.24: Typical processing pipeline for rs-fMRI processing.

5.6.1 Preprocessing of rs-fMRI

The overall processing pipeline for rs-fMRI analysis is shown in Figure 5.24. Each step in the preprocessing and the analysis stage will be discussed in subsequent subsections.

5.6.1.1 Slice Acquisition Time Correction

In rs-fMRI, a series of whole-brain 3D images are obtained over a period of 5 to 15 minutes, with each 3D brain image acquired with an approximate duration of 2 seconds. Each 3D brain image in turn is acquired as a stack of 2D images, i.e., the 3D image is not acquired in one instant but slice by slice over 2 seconds. Depending on the order of slices during acquisition, each slice will have a time shift relative to the other slices. This lag can be compensated by shifting the time courses by the difference in acquisition times with respect to a reference slice as shown in Figure 5.25. A fast implementation of shift in time domain is achieved by multiplication in the Fourier domain. A shift of δ in a signal x is achieved by transforming the signal to the Fourier domain, multiplying with a constant $e^{-j\omega\delta}$ and transforming it back to the time domain.

$$x(n-\delta) = F^{-1}\{X(\omega)e^{-j\omega\delta}\} \tag{5.55}$$

Boundary effects are minimized by making the signal circular by adding a linear trend of length $(2^M - N)$ from the initial to the final sample, where M is the n-point FFT used.

5.6.1.2 Motion Correction

Since the acquisition of multiple 3D images occurs over several minutes, the participant in the scanner is likely to move, introducing motion artifacts. Submillimeter motion can have profound

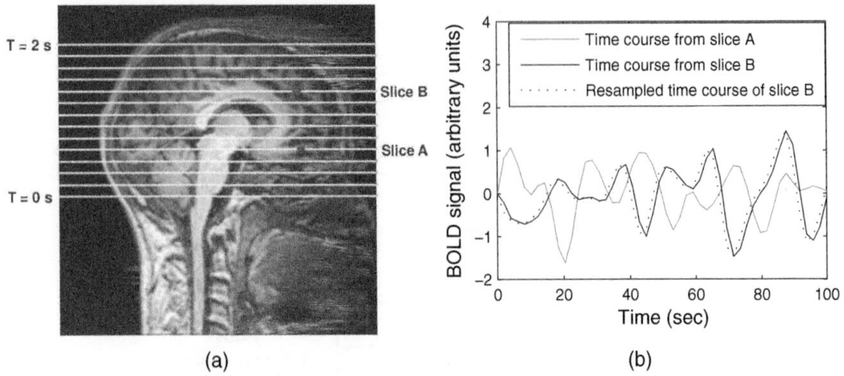

FIGURE 5.25: Slice time correction: (a) Time course acquired from Slice B (black solid line) is resampled at the same time as Slice A (reference slice) to produce the new shifted time course (black dotted line). In (b) BOLD corresponds to blood oxygen level dependent.

effects in estimating brain activation, especially near the edges. Even when the participant is very compliant, small motions can occur while breathing. In addition, since the brain is bathed in CSF within the skull, certain regions in the brain move with every cardiac pulse. Motion effects are worsened in pediatric participants, participants with motor problems (such as Parkinson's disease, epilepsy), and participants with psychiatric problems. The typical method to compensate for motion is to register every 3D brain image to the first brain image (or any one reference image). Registration is a process that finds the best match between two images by translations, rotations, shear, and warp (detailed discussion of registration is beyond the scope of this text). Since we expect motion to not cause shear or warp, rigid registration (allowing position shifting with only translation and rotations to find the best match) is performed between every image and the reference image to compensate for motion. Motion correction for a typical scan is shown in Figure 5.26. It can be seen from panels (c) and (d), that the residuals after motion correction are reduced. The six parameters of registration (3 rotations and 3 translations) are shown in panels (d) and (e). Registration-based motion correction only compensates for motion that occurs between acquisitions of two 3D brain images and does not correct for motion that occurs within acquisition of a single brain volume, which is not uncommon.

5.6.1.3 Registration to High Resolution Image

Since fMRI acquisitions are low resolution in space, it is often registered to a high-resolution T1-weighted image of the same subject. This aids to map anatomical landmarks onto the fMRI data and also map functional activation and connectivity onto the higher-resolution image. This registration is again using a rigid constraint (only position shifting with translation and rotation) since the images are from the same subject and hence do not have any shape or size difference. (There may be minor differences in shape due to distortion of fMRI acquisitions but these differences are typically ignored or corrected using methodologies that are irrelevant to the current scope.) An example of registration to a high-resolution image is shown in Figure 5.27.

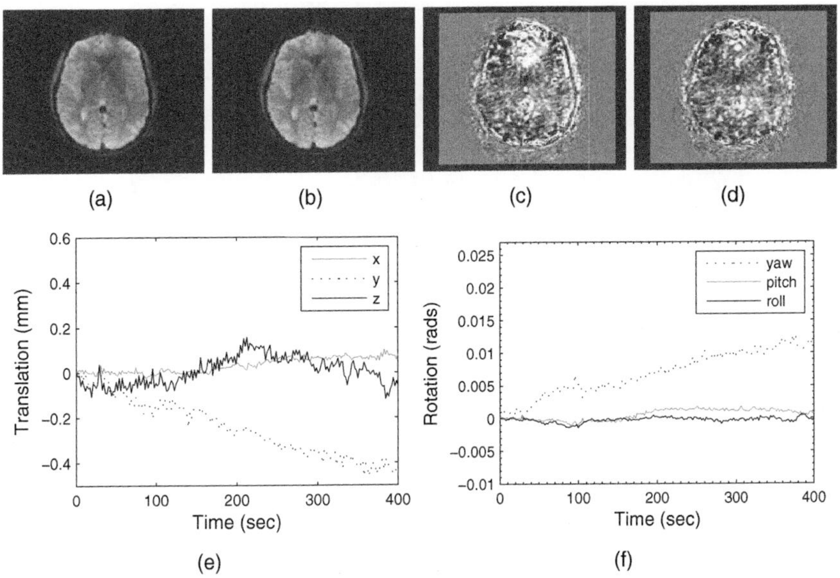

FIGURE 5.26: Motion correction: Raw images of the first time point (a) and the last time point (b) in an example acquisition. Though the raw images show little difference, the difference in the two images is large as seen in (c) before motion correction and this difference is reduced after motion correction (d). An example of estimated translations and rotations of the images over time is shown in (d) and (e).

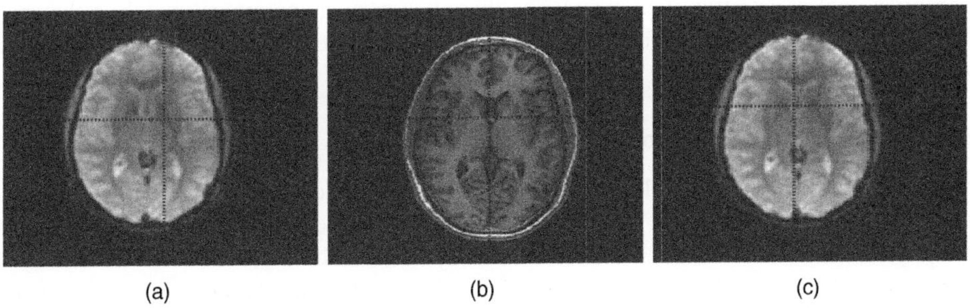

FIGURE 5.27: Registration to high resolution structural image. EPI image (a) is not always acquired with the same orientation as the high resolution structural image (b). Rigid registration between the two brings the rs-fMRI images in register with high resolution structural image as shown in (c).

5.6.1.4 Registration to Atlas

Labeling a region in the brain for each participant becomes tedious. To aid automated labeling, atlases (labeled average or typical brains) are available. Once the participant's brain is registered to an atlas brain, all the labels available on the atlas can be projected on the participant's brain. The registration in this case will be nonlinear and include shear and warp. A typical registration to an atlas is shown in Figure 5.28. Accurate registration is difficult since morphology and landmarks may not match between the participant and the atlas. Several registration methods have been proposed and it is an area of active research. It is to be noted at this point that anatomical registration does

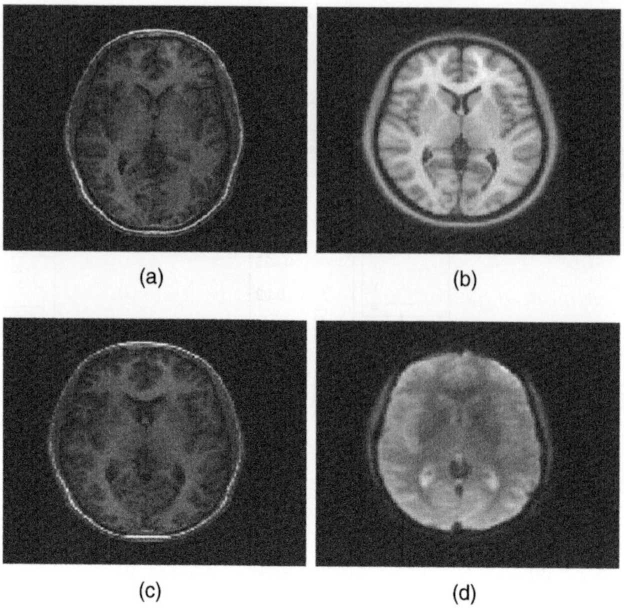

FIGURE 5.28: Registration of high resolution structural image (a) to atlas image (b) to produce a transformed structural image in atlas space (c). The same transformation can be applied to rs-fMRI images as shown in (d), thus taking the individual functional image to atlas space.

not mean functional registration, i.e., even when there is a perfect anatomical match in the spatial location between two subjects, the functional characteristic may be different for the two subjects at that location.

5.6.1.5 Physiological Noise Removal

Besides neuronal activity, signal fluctuations in fMRI data is caused by several noise sources. System noise is introduced by the electronics used to measure the magnetic signals. Several non-neuronal physiological activities such as cardiac activity and breathing give rise to altered magnetic tissue property in the brain, which in turn adds noise to the fMRI signal. Though physiological noise also plays a role in task-based fMRI, its effects are more pronounced in resting state fMRI. Noise introduced by cardiac activity includes a small motion of the brain induced by the pulsation. These motions are more pronounced in certain regions of the brain including the brain stem. Indirect effects of cardiac activity include modulation of blood flow over time that may appear as activation or connectivity. Respiration also influences fMRI signals measured in the brain. Changes in lung volume during the inhalation and exhalation of air change the magnetic field of the brain. End tidal volume of the lung has been shown to have large effects in fMRI signals [12, 22]. In addition to these, breathing patterns have also been shown to have significant effects. Breathing patterns may directly influence the lung air volume or may indirectly affect the amount of carbon dioxide in the blood. Small changes in carbon dioxide have been shown to have profound effects in fMRI signal fluctuations [119]. Indeed, breath holding has been proposed as a method to calibrate fMRI signals [76]. In addition to this, fMRI signals are modulated by other physiological factors including hematocrit content in the blood [29], neurovascular modifications due to certain drugs including caffeine [107], cocaine [79], alcohol [44], and a whole spectrum of prescription drugs. Motion effects that are not accounted for by motion correction using registration also fall under physiological nuisances. There are several methods proposed and used in the field to reduce the effects of these physiological artefacts. Two most popular methods are RETROICOR [10] and a COMPCOR [112].

In RETROICOR, the noise is assumed to be additive. Respiration and cardiac signals are concurrently recorded using a chest/abdomen strap and pulse oximeter, respectively. The phase of both of the signals are resampled at the same rate as the fMRI signal and then regressed out. The additive physiological noise component can be expressed as a Fourier series expansion given by

$$y_\delta(t) = \sum_{m=1}^{N} \{a_m{}^c \cos(m\varphi_c) + b_m{}^c \sin(m\varphi_c) + a_m{}^r \cos(m\varphi_r) + a_m{}^r \sin(m\varphi_r)\} \tag{5.56}$$

N = 2 was found to sufficiently capture most of the noise. The cardiac phase can be written as

$$\varphi_c(t) = \frac{2\pi(t - t_1)}{t_2 - t_1} \tag{5.57}$$

where, t_1 and t_2 are the times of the preceding and the succeeding R-wave peak (or any uniquely identifiable phase of the cardiac cycle). The respiratory phase is obtained using a histogram (H(b)) of the normalized respiratory signal, $R(t)$ normalized to a range of 0 to $R_{\max}$.

$$\varphi_r(t) = \pi \frac{\sum_{b=1}^{round(\frac{R(t)}{R_{\max}})} H(b)}{\sum_{b=1}^{Nbin} H(b)} sign\{\frac{dR}{dt}\} \tag{5.58}$$

The coefficients of Equation 5.56 can be calculated for every voxel using

$$a_m{}^x = \frac{\sum_{n=1}^{N} [y(t_n) - \bar{y}] \cos(m\varphi_x(t_n))}{\sum_{n=1}^{N} \cos^2(m\varphi_x(t_n))} \tag{5.59}$$

$$b_m{}^x = \frac{\sum_{n=1}^{N} [y(t_n) - \bar{y}] \sin(m\varphi_x(t_n))}{\sum_{n=1}^{N} \sin^2(m\varphi_x(t_n))}$$

where, x is either r or c, and $\bar{y}$ is the mean of the time series of the voxel.

In a COMPCOR, no extra physiological recording is performed. The physiological noise-related signals are extracted out of specific regions in the data itself and regressed out of the data. Deep white matter regions and deep lying cerebrospinal fluid (CSF) is assumed to have no neurovascular contribution to their signal, and hence the signals measured in these regions are exclusively noise. These nuisance anatomical regions can be identified using the high-resolution T1-weighted image and the signals from these regions can be extracted as nuisance signals. The set of time courses from these "nuisance" regions can be dimensionality reduced using PCA (or simply mean) and creating representative nuisance signals. These nuisance signals can regress out all regions in the brain using the general linear model, where if Y is the original signal and X is the nuisance signal, we can compute Y' after removing contributions by X, written as $Y' = Y - X\beta\, ,\, where\ \beta = (X^T X) * X^T * Y$. In literature, a COMPCOR is shown to perform at least as well as a RETROICOR without having to record respiration and cardiac waveforms [10].

In the nuisance signals, several other signals that are known to be associated with a noise source can be added. For example, the motion parameters (3 translations and 3 rotations per time point)

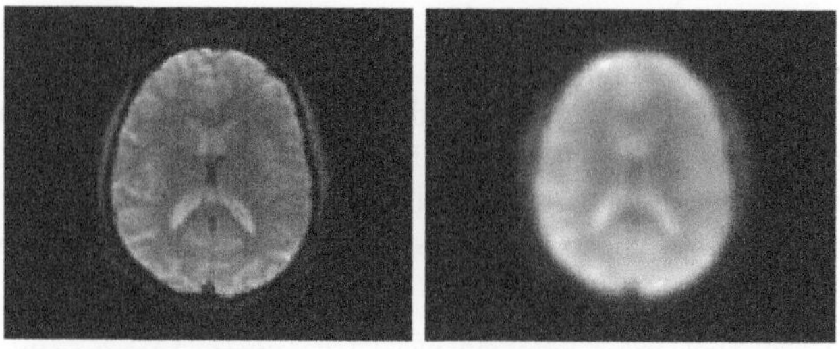

FIGURE 5.29: Spatial smoothing of rs-fMRI data (a) to increase SNR. As can be seen in the smoothed image (b), this comes at a loss in spatial resolution.

estimated by motion correction is typically added as a nuisance signal. In addition, to account for nonlinear effects of motion, squares of motion parameters and differentials of the motion parameters are also added as nuisance signals. The mean signal of the whole brain is also commonly used as a nuisance and is commonly termed as a global signal. Regressing out the global signal is controversial and the appropriateness of its usage is often debated. For each nuisance signal regressed, a degree of freedom is lost from the data. Hence, it is preferable to use fewer signals to accomplish maximal noise reduction.

5.6.1.6 Spatial Smoothing

Since the MR signal is proportional to the number of protons present in the voxel, a larger (*homogenous*) voxel would produce a larger signal. However, higher resolution provides tissue specificity that increases contrast to noise ratio. The spatial resolution of fMRI is set to maximize contrast to noise in the temporal domain, i.e., a maximal amplitude difference between task state and nontask state. In addition to selecting an optimal spatial resolution, typically fMRI signals are spatially smoothed to increase SNR and CNR. Typically, Gaussian smoothing in 3D is used to smooth fMRI data as shown in Figure 5.29.

Given noisy 4D fMRI data $I : \Omega \times [0,T] \rightarrow \Re$, we can denoise the data by smoothing the signal at each voxel, $u(x,t) = \frac{\sum_y w(x,y)I(y,t)}{\sum_y w(x,y)}$, where $w(x,y) = G_\sigma(|x-y|)$, and $G_\sigma(0,\sigma)$ is a Gaussian. It is also possible to incorporate anatomical priors (from a T1-weighted image) to the smoothing window to smooth only within tissue types [112] or to use functional priors from the data itself while smoothing [109]. Given noisy 4D fMRI data, $I : \Omega \times [0,T] \rightarrow \Re$, we can denoise I using a modified version of bilateral filtering [120],

$$u(x,t) = \frac{\sum_y w(x,y)I(y,t)}{\sum_y w(x,y)}, \tag{5.60}$$

where $w(x,y) = G_\sigma(|x-y|)G_v(R(x,y))$. Here, $G_\sigma(0,\sigma)$, and $G_v(0,v)$, are Gaussians, and $R(x,y)$ is the connectivity between x and y computed as the correlation coefficient.

5.6.1.7 Temporal Filtering

In rs-fMRI, functional connectivity in the brain has been found to be primarily contributed by signals between the frequencies of 0.01 and 0.1 Hz. The range has been experimentally found for the current state of the technology for investigating neuronal activity. This is not a theoretical limit

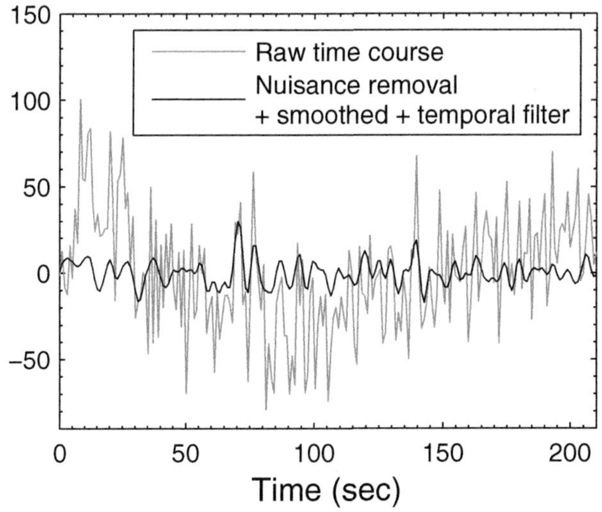

FIGURE 5.30: Raw time course (gray) and time course after nuisance removal, smoothing, and temporal band pass filtering (black).The Y-axis is in arbitrary units.

and a signal outside this band may play a significant role if sampled at better resolutions in time and space. A simple zero-phase bandpass filter is typically used to band-limit rs-fMRI signals. A zero-phase effect in the filter is obtained by filtering the signal in a forward direction once and filtering the signal in the reverse direction, essentially offsetting any phase effects caused by the forward filter. Transient effects at boundaries are minimized by using the mirror technique (padding the reverse signal at the boundaries). A typical signal after nuisance removal, smoothing, and temporal filtering is shown in Figure 5.30.

At this point, the fMRI signals are "preprocessed" and ready for estimating connectivity or correlation between signals from different regions.

5.6.2 Methods to Study Connectivity

Two regions in the brain are assumed to be functionally connected, if the temporal synchrony between the neural signals is high. In rs-fMRI, connectivity is measured as the synchrony of a BOLD signal between regions. Synchrony can be estimated by several methods including correlation and coherence. The most popular method to compute synchrony in fMRI is using the Pearsons correlation coefficient (PCC). PCC between two signals x and y is given by

$$C(x,y) = \frac{\Sigma(x-\bar{x})\cdot(y-\bar{y})}{\sqrt{\Sigma(x-\bar{x})^2}\sqrt{\Sigma(y-\bar{y})^2}} \tag{5.61}$$

PCC is 1 between two signals that are identical; -1 between two signals that are identical but sign reversed and 0 between two signals that are purely unrelated. Figure 5.31 shows example signals for each of the above cases.

Several properties of this correlation coefficient need to be considered for appropriate usage

1. Origin invariant, $\text{PCC}(x,y) = \text{PCC}(x+c_2, y+c_1)$.

2. Scale invariant, $\text{PCC}(x,y) = \text{PCC}(c_1 x, c_2 y)$.

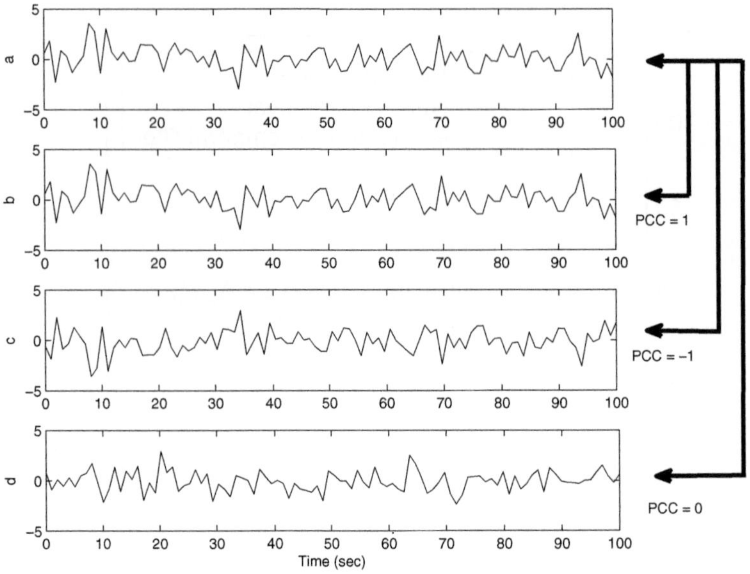

FIGURE 5.31: Examples of correlation coefficient between pairs of time courses. PCC between identical pairs of time courses (a) and (b) is 1; PCC between identical pairs but with opposite signs (a) and (c) is -1 and PCC between two unrelated time courses (a) and (d) is approximately 0.

3. Order insensitive, $\text{PCC}(x(t), y(t)) = \text{PCC}(x(u), y(u))$, where $t \neq u$.
4. Lag sensitive, $\text{PCC}(x(t), y(t)) \neq \text{PCC}(x(t+n), y(t))$, where n is nonzero and $x(t)$ and $y(t)$ is time varying.
5. Measures only linear synchrony, i.e., $\text{PCC}(x, y) \neq \text{PCC}(x^2, y^2)$.
6. For any two random signals, PCC is uniformly distributed between -1 and 1. Normality cannot be assumed.
7. Reliability or significance of PCC is dependent on several factors including the number of samples in the signals.
8. Independent variables are uncorrelated but uncorrelated variables are not always independent.

In some cases where linear synchrony cannot be assumed, Spearman's ranked correlation coefficient can be used. In this case, the samples of each signal are ranked and then correlation is computed for the ranks. If statistical tests that assume normality have to be used, PCC can be normalized using the Fisher transform [114]. Normal score, $z = \frac{1}{2} ln(\frac{1+r}{1-r})$, is where r is the PCC.

5.6.2.1 Connectivity between Two Regions

A small functionally homogeneous region is defined anatomically by drawing a region in the brain or by selecting a region from a brain atlas. The mean time course for this region is extracted as the mean of all the voxels within this region. PCC between time courses from two such regions provide a measure of functional connectivity between these regions.

5.6.2.2 Functional Connectivity Maps

A region in the brain (similar to the regions selected above) is selected as the seed region. Connectivity of this region with every voxel in the brain is computed using PCC and a map of connectivity is obtained [13]. This map is thresholded with statistically or empirically derived thresholds. These thresholded maps are called functional connectivity maps of the specified seed. By selecting seeds in specific locations in the brain, physiologically relevant functional brain networks that are associated with specific brain function can be extracted. For example, a seed in the primary visual region in the brain will show connections with several visual regions in the brain and a seed in the primary motor regions will reveal as connected several motor function-related areas such as the supplementary motor area, putamen, thalamus, and cerebellum. Functional connectivity maps so derived have been widely used to study brain function in healthy volunteers and changes during disease. Examples of a few typical functional connectivity maps are shown in Figure 5.32.

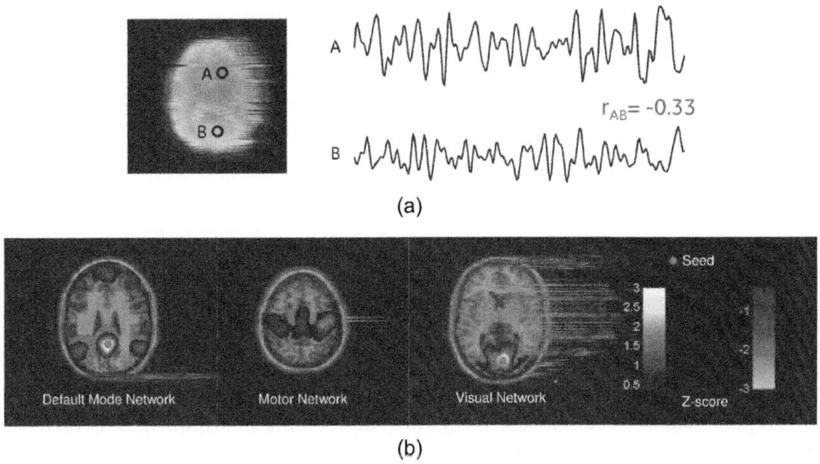

FIGURE 5.32 (See color insert.): Functional connectivity between two points, A and B shown in panel (a), is computed using correlation coefficient between their time courses. Connectivity to seed locations (shown as green dots in (b) can be computed for all voxels using Pearson correlation coefficient and converted to Z-scores. Functional networks can be extracted by placing the seeds at appropriate locations.

5.6.2.3 Graphs (Connectivity between Multiple Nodes)

In cases where interactions of specific brain regions need to be investigated, connectivity between each pair of these regions is computed. For example, PCC between pairs of time courses from several regions in the motor network can be computed. Networks thus formed can be viewed as a graph and graph theoretical methods can be applied to study these networks. In these networks, the regions become the nodes and the connectivity between the regions becomes the edge weights. A network formed using nodes placed in 264 functional locations in the brain is shown in Figure 5.33.

The edges are sometimes binarized (connected or unconnected) by applying a threshold and thus converting the graphs into binary graphs. Weighted graphs are also used where the edges are not binarized. Interesting organization of the brain networks have been revealed by studying it as a graph. The networks of the brain appear to be organized and are very similar to social networks, termed small world networks. Several properties of these graphs can be extracted as metrics such as centrality, degree, clustering coefficient, shortest path length, etc. Investigation of the disruption or deviation of brain function in diseases using these metrics is an area of active research [18].

FIGURE 5.33: A graph-based depiction of brain functional connectivity. Nodes are select regions in the brain and edge weights are the correlation coefficient between the time courses of the nodes. The thickness of the weight is proportional to the correlation coefficient and the size of the nodes is representative of the degree (number of connections) of that node.

5.6.2.4 Effective Connectivity

Functional connectivity in the brain is typically studied as being nondirectional, though the underlying connections may be directional. This is due to the limitations in the functional MR imaging technology. Since we indirectly measure a neuronal signal using a (varyingly) lagged vascular response, the temporal lag between different regions between the neuronal signals is difficult to ascertain. With certain assumptions and physiological constraints, claims have been made about the ability to find neuronal lags as short as 100 ms using Granger causality. Using Granger causality, activity in region A is said to be caused by region B when region B's current value can be predicted from the previous values of region A and region B. If x and y are the signals from region A and B respectively, x is caused by y when

$$x(n) = \sum_{i=-\infty}^{n-1} [a_i x(i) + b_i y(i)] \tag{5.62}$$

where, a_i and b_i are constants.

Despite several reports on how effective connectivity using Granger causality is more sensitive to differences between diseases than conventional functional connectivity [32], the field is controversial and active. The primary controversy arises from the theoretical inability to measure Granger causality from a signal whose delay is uncertain.

5.6.2.5 Parcellation (Clustering)

For rs-fMRI, since the correlation coefficient is computed for every pair of voxel independently, no spatial priors are used while using it in 3D functional imaging data. The relationship of the connectivity with spatial neighbors can be used to find functionally homogenous regions and functional boundaries. This method provides a way to functionally parcellate the brain. The parcellation itself has been shown to be changed over development and different in diseases [94].

5.6.2.6 Independent Component Analysis for rs-fMRI

ICA has already been discussed in previous sections. In fMRI, spatial ICA, sICA, has been shown to separate different networks in the brain. However, in fMRI, the dimension along which ICA is performed is not measured as illustrated in Section 5.5 for separating the fetal ECG signal from the maternal ECG signal. In spatial ICA (sICA), spatial patterns are decomposed based on their spatial independence. Consider the signal $S(x,t)$ at voxel x and time t; similar to temporal ICA, S can be decomposed using ICA as

$$S(x,t) = \sum_{k=1}^{K} c_{\mathrm{k}}(x) M_{\mathrm{k}}(t) \tag{5.63}$$

where M is the mixing matrix and C_{k} are the spatial independent maps or spatial sources. It has been well established that these sources are neurologically meaningful functional networks or noise sources. sICA was introduced for task-based fMRI [87] but was later used to extract networks in rs-fMRI [122]. A few typical brain networks obtained from ICA are shown in Figure 5.34.

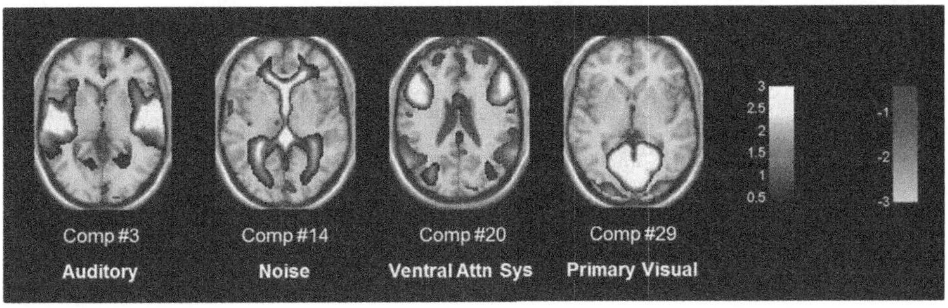

FIGURE 5.34 (See color insert.): Select subset of typical ICA components from rs-fMRI. ICA separates rs-fMRI signals to separate neuro-physiologically meaningful networks (sources). Some components are of neuronal origin (Comp 3, 20, 29) and some are noise related (Comp 14). Red and blue regions in the components have opposite directions of signal modulations.

One of the limitations of ICA is the difficulty in estimating the number of networks or sources, which is a common problem in dimensionality estimation of any data. ICA also produces components that are scale and sign ambiguous, i.e., C and M can be scaled by a and $1/a$ with no effect on S. This makes it difficult to estimate the amplitude of each network relative to others. This also implies no specific ordering of the components. In rs-fMRI, it is a significant problem to separate components of noise origin (such as physiological noise and system noise) from neurologically relevant components. Recently machine learning has been applied with reasonable success to address this problem [49, 7].

5.6.3 Dynamics of Networks

Conventionally rs-fMRI signals were measured over a period of several minutes and connectivity was computed assuming stationarity of the signals, even though nonstationarity of brain signals is well known. More recently, sliding window techniques have been applied to study the dynamics of brain networks and the dynamics of their interactions [23]. The difficultly to extract dynamics from a highly variable signal has made it an active area of research. Several methods of time-frequency analysis including wavelets and coherence have been used to study the dynamics of brain signals [23].

To summarize, data acquired from the MRI scanner needs rigorous preprocessing to be able to extract maximal information. The order of processing methods and the validity of the processing itself is an active area of research. The steps and order described above are accepted by the field for the current acquisition technology. Increasing field strengths of MR magnets and newer methods to measure neuronal activity will change the need for many of the processes above and may also introduce additional processing. Despite the complicated processing pipeline, there is little doubt that cross-correlation analysis in rs-fMRI has increased our understanding of brain function in health and disease.

5.7 Recent Trends in Biomedical Signal Analysis

Over the last two decades, there have been significant advancements in biomedical signal analysis with the growth of availability and access of biomedical data from a variety of devices ranging from medical devices in acute and intensive care areas in hospitals to wearable monitors such as heart rate monitor watches connecting to smartphones. The recent trends in biomedical signal analysis are across a variety of fundamental challenges and opportunities on processing and analysis of massive amounts of biomedical signals included but not limited to structured and robust time-series data such as waveforms and vitals and unstructured and disparate time-series data such as medication and laboratory tests as well as pervasive wearable sensor penetrating every aspect of our lives. It is a rather daunting task to confine the advancements in signal processing at the dawn of the "big biomedical data explosion" into a few pages. Our goal, in the following, is to provide a glimpse of recent trends in biomedical signal analysis within the fundamental construct of the signal processing field of study. More interested readers are recommended to refer to additional resources for a more comprehensive and in-depth coverage.

The theoretical foundations for "big biomedical data analysis and processing" include but are not limited to compressive sensing and dimensionality reduction, signal processing on graphs, robustness to outliers and missing data and imputation, scalability, convergence, and complexity issues, learning from very large (and sparse) matrix and graph data. Today, the massive volume of data processing often requires distributed processing with parallelized multiprocessors, and in general, the data is stored in a database over the cloud or is generated in real-time (streaming) and needs to be processed rapidly and accurately in a robust manner. Thus, there has been a growing need to develop theoretical foundations and algorithms for signal processing of "big biomedical data" as well as architecture and applications for large-scale data analysis and signal processing.

Compressive sensing theory has emerged recently to address the issue of simpler encoding and reconstruction of a sparse signal from fewer samples or measurements than the number of samples utilized by traditional methods. Compressive sensing can also be considered as part of a larger set of problems under dimensionality reduction, which is discussed next. One way to overcome challenges in analysis of large volumes of rapidly changing structured, unstructured, or semistructured data is to compress data fast and in large quantities while preserving its significant features to extract desired information and convert to actionable knowledge. The emerging compressive sensing theory had been successfully applied in acquisition and compression [84, 33] as well as noise and artifact reduction [41] of biomedical signals.

Dimensionality reduction can be combined into two groups: (1) unsupervised dimension reduction that includes principal component analysis (PCA) and singular value decomposition, and (2) supervised dimension reduction that includes Fisher linear discriminant analysis and hidden layers of neural networks to either select or extract features. One of the recent variants of these most commonly used methods include Latent Semantic Analysis that is a variant of PCA, which was first introduced as a text analysis technique but had been applied to image, video, music, audio, gene expression data, and biomedical signals [106, 111, 55]. Another recent variant is to include kernel functions to apply nonlinear transformations that may be more appropriate for the biomedical data. Recent trends also include extensions of deterministic methods to probabilistic approaches such as CUR matric decompositions that choose columns and rows that exhibit high "statistical leverage" and exert a large "influence" on the best low rank fit of the data matrix [80], random projection that is related to the compressed sensing and its computational complexity scales linearly with the problem size [38], the Latent Dirichlet Allocation (LDA) model that is a hierarchical Bayesian model where each item of a collection is modeled as a finite mixture over an underlying set of topics and each topic is modeled as an infinite mixture over an underlying set of topic probability [15]. It is worthwhile to note that in some cases the opposite of dimensionality reduction becomes critical in analysis, that is, one wishes to infer the high-dimensional structure from low-dimensional structure because the spaces are high-dimensional or too twisted to all allow projections to represent the features of the point cloud. One of the emerging approaches to address this issue is topological data analysis [20] that has been applied to several applications in various domains successfully. Another emerging analysis technique is signal processing on graphs that merges algebraic and spectral graph theoretic concepts with computational harmonic analysis to process such signals on graphs in application areas ranging from transportation to neuronal networks [110].

The statistical learning community contributes significantly to the signal processing research. The statistical learning theory and modeling are two complementary fields of study for analyzing signals, specifically, in the context of classification algorithms where a noisy signal or artifact is needed to be separated from the original biomedical signal (see [82] and references therein). Fundamental issues in statistical signal processing include the nature of basic probabilistic description, and the derivation of the probabilistic description of the output signal given that of the input signal and particular operation performed [48]. Recent trends in statistical learning theory include the study of a semisupervised learning problem where the objective is to classify unknown data with few labelled samples [e.g., [130]]. Recent trends in statistical learning and modeling theory expands into analysis and processing massive amounts of data including but not limited to a variety of biomedical signal data that requires learning from large incomplete data [e.g., [86, 26]].

One of the challenges in signal processing of "big data" originating from streaming sensors in various environments is that the data may be missing, contain outliers, or too noisy. In general, for the case of massive data from wearable sensors, the noise components may not fit into well-studied noise models such as Gaussian. Recent trends in accommodating for missing data, outliers, and untraditional noise components in biomedical signal processing include classical methods such as simple linear regression, trimmed means, and imputation of outliers with the neighboring high or low values as well as more advanced methods such as Kohonin self-organizing maps. Recent trends include identifying periods of low-quality data by designing signal quality indicators that merges domain knowledge with statistical measures to determine good signal quality periods and utilized the metric to drive high level decision making or incorporating auxiliary sensors such as accelerometer for adaptive filtering of the biomedical signal. Recent trends in imputation have been shaping around applying well-known techniques in single processing to massive streaming signals [e.g., [85]].

Real-time signal processing is a relatively mature field of signal processing while the main objective is to design and implement a variety of signal processing algorithms for real-word applications, the processing platform has been limited to single or a few digital signal processors (DSPs). In general, the analysis of the algorithms such as filtering is performed in MATLAB®, and the implementation is written in C, yet, for fast software development and maintenance, the mixing of C and assembly programs are recommended. The most recent focus of real-time signal processing is on massive amounts of streaming data collected at various velocities from a variety of data sources including but not limited to wearable sensors. Hadoop and its derivatives provide means to handle the volume and variety but not necessarily the rapid processing of the data. The rapid processing of the data can be critical in biomedical signal processing especially in clinical decision support. The real-time system should be a low-latency fault-tolerant system leveraging a distributed platform with near real-time response capability. Two popular open-source technologies to address these issues are Apache Kafka [59], which is a distributed messaging system and Storm [60], which is a distributed stream processing engines. The commercial technologies include but not limited to InfoSphere by IBM [61].

5.8 Discussions

Signal processing is an important step in analyzing and interpreting biomedical signals. The added advantage of processing a signal is an improvement in measurement accuracy when compared to the manual measurement and reproducibility. Certain signals or features that are not readily discernable using the naked eye have been made possible through various signal processing tools presented in this chapter. This chapter presented the origin of biomedical signals in the human body and demonstrated various signal processing approaches for ECG signals. These techniques are however, very generic and could be used in a wide variety of instances, provided there is a basic understanding of the nature of the signal and knowledge about the features one is looking for. The selection of algorithm depends upon the accuracy required and the complexity of the system, which varies for different applications.

Broadly, the chapter also discussed two different approaches through which a signal could be denoised. In one approach, various signal processing algorithms such as adaptive filtering and empirical mode decomposition were directly applied on the signal for denoising. In another instance, the signal was first transformed to a domain and denoised in another domain and then transformed back to the original domain. Principal component analysis is one such instance when such a transformation was applied. A few signal processing approaches such as JADE, INFOMAX, and FastICA based on blind source separation formulation showed that independent sources can be separated from composite signals using higher-order statistical techniques.

The chapter discussed future emerging trends in signal processing. One of the areas that are evolving in biomedical signal processing and not discussed in the chapter is data compression and transmission. Sometimes the data is not required immediately for assessment and needs to be stored for later use. In this case there is a need for the data to be stored and retrieved whenever required. Since some measurements can be performed over several hours and the data size can run into huge bytes, the data needs to be compressed efficiently so that the signal integrity is retained in subsequent analyses. In data compression, the overall goal is to accurately represent the data with a minimum number of bits, by applying either lossless compression in which the signal is reconstructed accurately or lossy compression, in which the signal is distorted. Many times the kind of compression required is dictated by the diagnostic value associated with a particular representation of the signal and distortion in the signal is accepted if it does not result in clinically altered diagnosis. Data transmission from a remote location to a central hub is another aspect that needs efficient data compression and data transfer network. Since huge amounts of data sometimes need to be transferred over the network, usually the data is first compressed and then transferred, since the transmission bandwidth is limited in low-income setting countries.

To summarize, the reader is encouraged to use these methods for processing various biomedical signals and care needs to be exercised to understand the nature of the signal and its diagnostic value so that an appropriate method can be used to deduce clinically relevant information.

Bibliography

[1] A Mansour, A Baros, and N Ohnishi. Removing artifacts from ECG signals using independent component analysis. *Neurocomputing*, 22:173–186, 1998.

[2] Edgar D Adrian and Detlev W Bronk. The discharge of impulses in motor nerve fibres part II. The frequency of discharge in reflex and voluntary contractions. *The Journal of Physiology*, 67(2):i3–151, 1929.

[3] Valtino X Afonso, Willis J Tompkins, Truong Q Nguyen, and Shen Luo. ECG beat detection using filter banks. *IEEE Transactions on Biomedical Engineering*, 46(2):192–202, 1999.

[4] Mark L Ahlstrom and Willis J Tompkins. Automated high-speed analysis of Holter tapes with microcomputers. *IEEE Transactions on Biomedical Engineering*, (10):651–657, 1983.

[5] ML Ahlstrom and WJ Tompkins. Digital filters for real-time ECG signal processing using microprocessors. *IEEE Transactions on Biomedical Engineering*, (9):708–713, 1985.

[6] Carlos Alvarado, Jesús Arregui, Juan Ramos, and Ramon Pallàs-Areny. Automatic detection of ECG ventricular activity waves using continuous spline wavelet transform. In *2005 2nd International Conference on Electrical and Electronics Engineering*, pages 189–192. IEEE, 2005.

[7] Ek Tsoon Tan Ashish A Rao, Hima Patel and Suresh E Joel. Automated classification of ICA networks from resting state fMRI using machine learning framework. In *Proceedings of the International Society of Magnetic Resonance in Medicine*. Milan, Italy, 2014.

[8] James J Bailey, Alan S Berson, Arthur Garson Jr, Leo G Horan, Peter W Macfarlane, David W Mortara, and Christoph Zywietz. Recommendations for standardization and specifications in automated electrocardiography: Bandwidth and digital signal processing: A report for health professionals by an ad hoc writing group of the committee on electrocardiography and cardiac electrophysiology of the council on clinical cardiology, American Heart Association. *Circulation*, 81(2):730, 1990.

[9] Mark W Barnett and Philip M Larkman. The action potential. *Practical Neurology*, 7(3):192–197, 2007.

[10] Yashar Behzadi, Khaled Restom, Joy Liau, and Thomas T Liu. A component based noise correction method (COMPCOR) for bold and perfusion based fMRI. *Neuroimage*, 37(1):90–101, 2007.

[11] Anthony J Bell and Terrence J Sejnowski. An information-maximization approach to blind separation and blind deconvolution. *Neural Computation*, 7(6):1129–1159, 1995.

[12] Rasmus M Birn, Jason B Diamond, Monica A Smith, and Peter A Bandettini. Separating respiratory-variation-related fluctuations from neuronal-activity-related fluctuations in fMRI. *Neuroimage*, 31(4):1536–1548, 2006.

[13] Bharat Biswal, F Zerrin Yetkin, Victor M Haughton, and James S Hyde. Functional connectivity in the motor cortex of resting human brain using echo-planar MRI. *Magnetic resonance in Medicine*, 34(4):537–541, 1995.

[14] Manuel Blanco-Velasco, Binwei Weng, and Kenneth E Barner. ECG signal denoising and baseline wander correction based on the empirical mode decomposition. *Computers in Biology and Medicine*, 38(1):1–13, 2008.

[15] David M Blei, Andrew Y Ng, and Michael I Jordan. Latent Dirichlet allocation. *The Journal of Machine Learning Research*, 3:993–1022, 2003.

[16] Per Ola Borjesson, Olle Pahlm, Leif Sornmo, and Mats-Erik Nygards. Adaptive QRS detection based on maximum a posteriori estimation. *Biomedical Engineering, IEEE Transactions on*, (5):341–351, 1982.

[17] FEM Brekelmans and CDR De Vaal. A QRS detection scheme for multichannel ECG devices. *Computers in Cardiology*, 8:437–440, 1981.

[18] Ed Bullmore and Olaf Sporns. Complex brain networks: Graph theoretical analysis of structural and functional systems. *Nature Reviews Neuroscience*, 10(3):186–198, 2009.

[19] Jean-François Cardoso and Antoine Souloumiac. Blind beamforming for non-Gaussian signals. In *IEE Proceedings F (Radar and Signal Processing)*, volume 140, pages 362–370. IET, 1993.

[20] Gunnar Carlsson. Topology and data. *Bulletin of the American Mathematical Society*, 46(2):255–308, 2009.

[21] Francisco Castells, Pablo Laguna, Leif Sörnmo, Andreas Bollmann, and José Millet Roig. Principal component analysis in ECG signal processing. *EURASIP Journal on Applied Signal Processing*, 2007(1):98–98, 2007.

[22] Catie Chang and Gary H Glover. Relationship between respiration, end-tidal CO_2, and BOLD signals in resting-state fMRI. *Neuroimage*, 47(4):1381–1393, 2009.

[23] Catie Chang and Gary H Glover. Time–frequency dynamics of resting-state brain connectivity measured with fMRI. *Neuroimage*, 50(1):81–98, 2010.

[24] L Chmelka and J Kozumplik. Wavelet-based Wiener filter for electrocardiogram signal denoising. In *Computers in Cardiology, 2005*, pages 771–774. IEEE, 2005.

[25] VS Chouhan and SS Mehta. Detection of QRS complexes in 12-lead ECG using adaptive quantized threshold. *International Journal of Computer Science and Network Security*, 8(1):155–163, 2008.

[26] Gari D Clifford and George B Moody. Signal quality in cardiorespiratory monitoring. *Physiological Measurement*, 33(9), 2012.

[27] Pierre Comon. Independent component analysis, a new concept? *Signal Processing*, 36(3):287–314, 1994.

[28] K Creath. *Physiology of Behavior*. Upper Saddle River, NJ: Pearson Education Inc., 2013.

[29] Stephen R Dager and Seth D Friedman. Brain imaging and the effects of caffeine and nicotine. *Annals of Medicine*, 32(9):592–599, 2000.

[30] JG Dusser de Barenne and JFG Brevée. The interpretation of the electromyogram of striated muscle during contractions set up by central nervous excitation. *The Journal of Physiology*, 61(1):81–97, 1926.

[31] Carlo J De Luca. Physiology and mathematics of myoelectric signals. *IEEE Transactions on Biomedical Engineering*, (6):313–325, 1979.

[32] Gopikrishna Deshpande and Xiaoping Hu. Investigating effective brain connectivity from fMRI data: Past findings and current issues with reference to granger causality analysis. *Brain Connectivity*, 2(5):235–245, 2012.

[33] Anna MR Dixon, Emily G Allstot, Daibashish Gangopadhyay, and David J Allstot. Compressed sensing system considerations for ECG and EMG wireless biosensors. *Biomedical Circuits and Systems, IEEE Transactions on*, 6(2):156–166, 2012.

[34] David L Donoho. De-noising by soft-thresholding. *IEEE Transactions on Information Theory*, 41(3):613–627, 1995.

[35] WAH Engelse and C Zeelenberg. A single scan algorithm for QRS detection and feature extraction. *Computers in Cardiology*, 6(1979):37–42, 1979.

[36] L Sornmo et al. A mathematical approach to QRS detection. In *Proceedings of IEEE Computing in Cardiology*, pages 205–208, 1980.

[37] Fabrice Extramiana, Charif Tatar, Pierre Maison-Blanche, Isabelle Denjoy, Anne Messali, Patrick Dejode, Frank Iserin, and Antoine Leenhardt. Beat-to-beat t-wave amplitude variability in the long QT syndrome. *Europace*, 12(9):1302–1307, 2010.

[38] Jianqing Fan, Fang Han, and Han Liu. Challenges of big data analysis. *National Science Review*, February, 2014. doi:10.1093/nsr/nwt032

[39] J Fraden and MR Neuman. QRS wave detection. *Medical and Biological Engineering and Computing*, 18(2):125–132, 1980.

[40] Gary M Friesen, Thomas C Jannett, Manal Afify Jadallah, Stanford L Yates, Stephen R Quint, and H Troy Nagle. A comparison of the noise sensitivity of nine QRS detection algorithms. *IEEE Transactions on Biomedical Engineering*, 37(1):85–98, 1990.

[41] Harinath Garudadri, Pawan K Baheti, Somdeb Majumdar, Craig Lauer, Fabien Massé, Jef van de Molengraft, and Julien Penders. Artifacts mitigation in ambulatory ECG telemetry. In *12th IEEE International Conference on e-Health Networking Applications and Services (Healthcom)*, pages 338–344. IEEE, 2010.

[42] Alan Gevins, Paul Brickett, Bryan Costales, Jian Le, and Bryan Reutter. Beyond topographic mapping: towards functional-anatomical imaging with 124-channel EEGs and 3-D MRIs. *Brain Topography*, 3(1):53–64, 1990.

[43] Alan Gevins, Jian Le, Nancy K Martin, Paul Brickett, John Desmond, and Bryan Reutter. High resolution EEG: 124-channel recording, spatial deblurring and MRI integration methods. *Electroencephalography and Clinical Neurophysiology*, 90(5):337–358, 1994.

[44] Gary H Glover, Tie-Qiang Li, and David Ress. Image-based method for retrospective correction of physiological motion effects in fMRI: RETROICOR. *Magnetic Resonance in Medicine*, 44(1):162–167, 2000.

[45] AL Goldberg and V Bhargava. Computerized measurement of the first derivative of the QRS complex. *Computers and Biomedical Research*, (14):464–471, 1981.

[46] A L Goldberg and V Bhargava. Detection of signal associated with noise. *Proceedings of IEEE Computing in Cardiology*, pages 343–346, 1981.

[47] Ary L Goldberger and Valmik Bhargava. Peak-to-peak amplitude of the high-frequency QRS: A simple, quantitative index of high-frequency potentials. *Computers and Biomedical Research*, 14(5):399–406, 1981.

[48] Robert M Gray and Lee D Davisson. *An Introduction to Statistical Signal Processing*, volume 49. Cambridge University Press Cambridge, 2004.

[49] Ludovica Griffanti, Gholamreza Salimi-Khorshidi, Christian F Beckmann, Edward J Auerbach, Gwenaëlle Douaud, Claire E Sexton, Enikő Zsoldos, Klaus P Ebmeier, Nicola Filippini, Clare E Mackay, et al. ICA-based artefact removal and accelerated fmri acquisition for improved resting state network imaging. *NeuroImage*, 95:232–247, 2014.

[50] RM Gulrajani. Models of the electrical activity of the heart and computer simulation of the electrocardiogram. *Critical Reviews in Biomedical Engineering*, 16(1):1–66, 1987.

[51] Patrick S Hamilton. A comparison of adaptive and nonadaptive filters for reduction of power line interference in the ECG. *IEEE Transactions on Biomedical Engineering*, 43(1):105–109, 1996.

[52] Patrick S Hamilton and Willis J Tompkins. Quantitative investigation of QRS detection rules using the MIT/BIH arrhythmia database. *IEEE Transactions on Biomedical Engineering*, (12):1157–1165, 1986.

[53] Per Christian Hansen. The truncated SVD as a method for regularization. *BIT Numerical Mathematics*, 27(4):534–553, 1987.

[54] Veena N Hegde, Ravishankar Deekshit, and PS Satyanarayana. A review on ECG signal processing and HRV analysis. *Journal of Medical Imaging and Health Informatics*, 3(2):270–279, 2013.

[55] Douglas R Heisterkamp. Building a latent semantic index of an image database from patterns of relevance feedback. In *Proceedings of the 16th International Conference on Pattern Recognition, 2002*, volume 4, pages 134–137. IEEE, 2002.

[56] KA Henneberg. Principles of electromyography, In JD Bronzino (ed.) *The Biomedical Engineering Handbook.* CRC Press,1995.

[57] Jeanny Herault and Christian Jutten. Space or time adaptive signal processing by neural network models. In *Neural Networks for Computing*, volume 151, pages 206–211. AIP Publishing, 1986.

[58] William P Holsinger, Kenneth M Kempner, and Martin H Miller. A QRS preprocessor based on digital differentiation. *IEEE Transactions on Biomedical Engineering*, (3):212–217, 1971.

[59] http://kafka.apache.org/.

[60] http://storm.incubator.apache.org/.

[61] http://www 01.ibm.com/software/data/infosphere/.

[62] http://www.esat.kuleuven.ac.be/sista/daisy.

[63] Norden E Huang, Zheng Shen, Steven R Long, Manli C Wu, Hsing H Shih, Quanan Zheng, Nai-Chyuan Yen, Chi Chao Tung, and Henry H Liu. The empirical mode decomposition and the Hilbert spectrum for nonlinear and non-stationary time series analysis. *Proceedings of the Royal Society of London. Series A: Mathematical, Physical and Engineering Sciences*, 454(1971):903–995, 1998.

[64] James C Huhta and John G Webster. 60-Hz interference in electrocardiography. *IEEE Transactions on Biomedical Engineering*, (2):91–101, 1973.

[65] Aapo Hyvärinen, Juha Karhunen, and Erkki Oja. *Independent Component Analysis*, volume 46. John Wiley & Sons, 2004.

[66] Aapo Hyvärinen and Erkki Oja. A fast fixed-point algorithm for independent component analysis. *Neural Computation*, 9(7):1483–1492, 1997.

[67] Yusuf Ziya Ider and Hayrettin Koymen. A new technique for line interference monitoring and reduction in biopotential amplifiers. *IEEE Transactions on Biomedical Engineering*, 37(6):624–631, 1990.

[68] Christopher J James and Christian W Hesse. Independent component analysis for biomedical signals. *Physiological Measurement*, 26(1):R15, 2005.

[69] Maarten Jansen. *Noise Reduction by Wavelet Thresholding*, volume 61. New York: Springer, 2001.

[70] Herbert Jasper. Report of the committee on methods of clinical examination in electroencephalography. *Electroencephalography and Clinical Neurophysiology*, 10:370–375, 1958.

[71] Ian Jolliffe. *Principal Component Analysis*. Wiley Online Library, 2005.

[72] M Kotas. Application of projection pursuit based robust principal component analysis to ECG enhancement. *Biomedical Signal Processing and Control*, 1(4):289–298, 2006.

[73] Roman W Swiniarski, Lukasz Andrzej Kurgan, Krzysztof J Cios, and Witold Pedrycz. *Data Mining: A Knowledge Discovery Approach*. Springer Science & Business Media, 2007.

[74] Kenneth K Kwong, John W Belliveau, David A Chesler, Inna E Goldberg, Robert M Weisskoff, Brigitte P Poncelet, David N Kennedy, Bernice E Hoppel, Mark S Cohen, and Robert Turner. Dynamic magnetic resonance imaging of human brain activity during primary sensory stimulation. *Proceedings of the National Academy of Sciences*, 89(12):5675–5679, 1992.

[75] Philip Langley, Emma J Bowers, and Alan Murray. Principal component analysis as a tool for analyzing beat-to-beat changes in ECG features: Application to ECG-derived respiration. *IEEE Transactions on Biomedical Engineering*, 57(4):821–829, 2010.

[76] Jonathan M Levin, Marjorie H Ross, Jonathan F Fox, Heidi L von Rosenberg, Marc J Kaufman, Nicholas Lange, Jack H Mendelson, Bruce M Cohen, Perry F Renshaw, et al. Influence of baseline hematocrit and hemodilution on bold fMRI activation. *Magnetic Resonance Imaging*, 19(8):1055–1062, 2001.

[77] Cuiwei Li, Chongxun Zheng, and Changfeng Tai. Detection of ECG characteristic points using wavelet transforms. *IEEE Transactions on Biomedical Engineering*, 42(1):21–28, 1995.

[78] Xuejun Liao and Lawrence Carin. A new algorithm for independent component analysis with or without constraints. In *Sensor Array and Multichannel Signal Processing Workshop Proceedings, 2002*, pages 413–417. IEEE, 2002.

[79] Michael Luchtmann, Katja Jachau, Daniela Adolf, Friedrich-Wilhelm Röhl, Sebastian Baecke, Ralf Lützkendorf, Charles Müller, and Johannes Bernarding. Ethanol modulates the neurovascular coupling. *Neurotoxicology*, 34:95–104, 2013.

[80] Michael W Mahoney and Petros Drineas. CUR matrix decompositions for improved data analysis. *Proceedings of the National Academy of Sciences*, 106(3):697–702, 2009.

[81] Scott Makeig, Tzyy-Ping Jung, Anthony J Bell, Dara Ghahremani, and Terrence J Sejnowski. Blind separation of auditory event-related brain responses into independent components. *Proceedings of the National Academy of Sciences*, 94(20):10979–10984, 1997.

[82] James D Malley, Karen G Malley, and Sinisa Pajevic. *Statistical Learning for Biomedical Data*. Cambridge University Press, 2011.

[83] Jaakko Malmivuo and Robert Plonsey. *Bioelectromagnetism: Principles and Applications of Bioelectric and Biomagnetic Fields*. Oxford University Press, 1995.

[84] Hossein Mamaghanian, Nadia Khaled, David Atienza, and Pierre Vandergheynst. Compressed sensing for real-time energy-efficient ECG compression on wireless body sensor nodes. *IEEE Transactions on Biomedical Engineering*, 58(9):2456–2466, 2011.

[85] Morteza Mardani, Gonzalo Mateos, and Georgios B Giannakis. Subspace learning and imputation for streaming big data matrices and tensors. *arXiv preprint arXiv:1404.4667*, 2014.

[86] Rahul Mazumder, Trevor Hastie, and Robert Tibshirani. Spectral regularization algorithms for learning large incomplete matrices. *The Journal of Machine Learning Research*, 11:2287–2322, 2010.

[87] Martin J McKeown, Terrence J Sejnowski, et al. Independent component analysis of fMRI data: Examining the assumptions. *Human Brain Mapping*, 6(5-6):368–372, 1998.

[88] Charles N Mead, Kenneth W Clark, Stephen J Potter, Stephen M Moore, and Lewis J Thomas Jr. Development and evaluation of a new QRS detector/delineator. In *Proceedings of IEEE Computers in Cardiology*, pages 251–254, 1979.

[89] CN Mead, HR Pull, JS Cheng, KW Clark, and LJ Thomas. A frequency-domain-based QRS classification algorithm. *IEEE Proceedings of Computers in Cardiology*, pages 351–354, 1981.

[90] KR Mills. The basics of electromyography. *Journal of Neurology, Neurosurgery & Psychiatry*, 76(suppl 2):ii32–ii35, 2005.

[91] B Mojtaba, K Mohammad Reza, A Amard, and G Jamal. ECG denoising using singular value decomposition. *Australian Journal of Basic and Applied Sciences*, 4:2109–2113, 2010.

[92] JCTB Moraes, MM Freitas, FN Vilani, and EV Costa. A QRS complex detection algorithm using electrocardiogram leads. In *Computers in Cardiology, 2002*, pages 205–208. IEEE, 2002.

[93] P Morizet-Mahoudeaux, C Moreau, D Moreau, and JJ Quarante. Simple microprocessor-based system for on-line ECG arrhythmia analysis. *Medical and Biological Engineering and Computing*, 19(4):497–500, 1981.

[94] Mary Beth Nebel, Suresh E Joel, John Muschelli, Anita D Barber, Brian S Caffo, James J Pekar, and Stewart H Mostofsky. Disruption of functional organization within the primary motor cortex in children with autism. *Human Brain Mapping*, 35(2):567–580, 2014.

[95] Robert D Nowak. Wavelet-based rician noise removal for magnetic resonance imaging. *IEEE Transactions on Image Processing,*, 8(10):1408–1419, 1999.

[96] Paul L Nunez and Ramesh Srinivasan. *Electric Fields of the Brain: The Neurophysics of EEG*. Oxford University Press, 2006.

[97] M Nygards and L Sornmo. A QRS delineation algorithm with low sensitivity to noise and morphology changes. In *Proceedings of IEEE Computers in Cardiology*, pages 347–350, 1981.

[98] Seiji Ogawa, David W Tank, Ravi Menon, Jutta M Ellermann, Seong G Kim, Helmut Merkle, and Kamil Ugurbil. Intrinsic signal changes accompanying sensory stimulation: Functional brain mapping with magnetic resonance imaging. *Proceedings of the National Academy of Sciences*, 89(13):5951–5955, 1992.

[99] Masahiko Okada. A digital filter for the ORS complex detection. *IEEE Transactions on Biomedical Engineering*, (12):700–703, 1979.

[100] Robert Oostenveld and Peter Praamstra. The five percent electrode system for high-resolution EEG and ERP measurements. *Clinical neurophysiology*, 112(4):713–719, 2001.

[101] Jiapu Pan and Willis J Tompkins. A real-time QRS detection algorithm. *IEEE Transactions on Biomedical Engineering*, (3):230–236, 1985.

[102] HP Parkman, WL Hasler, JL Barnett, and EY Eaker. Electrogastrography: A document prepared by the gastric section of the American Motility Society clinical GI motility testing task force. *Neurogastroenterology & Motility*, 15(2):89–102, 2003.

[103] S Poornachandra. Wavelet-based denoising using subband dependent threshold for ECG signals. *Digital Signal Processing*, 18(1):49–55, 2008.

[104] Rangaraj M Rangayyan. *Biomedical Signal Analysis*. IEEE Standards Office, 2001.

[105] Y Rudy and BJ Messinger-Rapport. The inverse problem in electrocardiography: Solutions in terms of epicardial potentials. *Critical Reviews in Biomedical Engineering*, 16(3):215–268, 1987.

[106] Emile Sahouria and Avideh Zakhor. Content analysis of video using principal components. *IEEE Transactions on Circuits and Systems for Video Technology*, 9(8):1290–1298, 1999.

[107] Karl F Schmidt, Marcelo Febo, Qiang Shen, Feng Luo, Kenneth M Sicard, Craig F Ferris, Elliot A Stein, and Timothy Q Duong. Hemodynamic and metabolic changes induced by cocaine in anesthetized rat observed with multimodal functional MRI. *Psychopharmacology*, 185(4):479–486, 2006.

[108] Donald L Schomer and Fernando Lopes Da Silva. *Niedermeyer's Electroencephalography: Basic Principles, Clinical Applications, and Related Fields*. Lippincott Williams & Wilkins, 2012.

[109] Suresh Joel, Dattesh Shanbhag, Sheshadri Thiruvenkadam, and Ek Tsoon Tan. Non-linear filtering using connectivity metrics. In *Proceedings of the Organization of Human Brain Mapping*. Hamburg, Germany, 2014.

[110] David I Shuman, Sunil K Narang, Pascal Frossard, Antonio Ortega, and Pierre Vandergheynst. The emerging field of signal processing on graphs: Extending high-dimensional data analysis to networks and other irregular domains. *IEEE Signal Processing Magazine*, 30(3):83–98, 2013.

[111] Paris Smaragdis, Bhiksha Raj, and Madhusudana Shashanka. A probabilistic latent variable model for acoustic modeling. *Advances in Models for Acoustic Processing, NIPS*, 148, 2006.

[112] Stephen M Smith and J Michael Brady. Susana new approach to low level image processing. *International Journal of Computer Vision*, 23(1):45–78, 1997.

[113] Leif Sornmo, P Ola Borjesson, Mats-erik Nygards, and Olle Pahlm. A method for evaluation of QRS shape features using a mathematical model for the ECG. *IEEE Transactions on Biomedical Engineering*, (10):713–717, 1981.

[114] James H Steiger. Tests for comparing elements of a correlation matrix. *Psychological Bulletin*, 87(2):245, 1980.

[115] GD Clifford, T He, and L Tarassenko. Application of ICA in removing artifacts from the ecg. *Neurocomputing*, 15:105–116, 2006.

[116] Jan L Talmon and Arie Hasman. A new approach to QRS detection and typification. *Computers in Cardiology*, pages 479–482, 1981.

[117] Nitish V Thakor and Yi-Sheng Zhu. Applications of adaptive filtering to ECG analysis: Noise cancellation and arrhythmia detection. *IEEE Transactions on Biomedical Engineering*, 38(8):785–794, 1991.

[118] NV Thakor, JG Webster, and WJ Tompkins. Optimal QRS detector. *Medical and Biological Engineering and Computing*, 21(3):343–350, 1983.

[119] Moriah E Thomason, Lara C Foland, and Gary H Glover. Calibration of BOLD fMRI using breath holding reduces group variance during a cognitive task. *Human Brain Mapping*, 28(1):59–68, 2007.

[120] Carlo Tomasi and Roberto Manduchi. Bilateral filtering for gray and color images. In *Sixth International Conference on Computer Vision*, pages 839–846. IEEE, 1998.

[121] GJH Uijen, JPC De Weerd, and AJH Vendrik. Accuracy of QRS detection in relation to the analysis of high-frequency components in the electrocardiogram. *Medical and Biological Engineering and Computing*, 17(4):492–502, 1979.

[122] Vincent G van de Ven, Elia Formisano, David Prvulovic, Christian H Roeder, and David EJ Linden. Functional connectivity as revealed by spatial independent component analysis of fMRI measurements during rest. *Human brain mapping*, 22(3):165–178, 2004.

[123] Ricardo Vigário, Jaakko Särelä, and Erkki Oja. Independent component analysis in wave decomposition of auditory evoked fields. In *ICANN 98*, pages 287–292. Springer, 1998.

[124] Lu Weixue and Xia Ling. Computer simulation of epicardial potentials using a heart-torso model with realistic geometry. *IEEE Transactions on Biomedical Engineering*, 43(2):211–217, 1996.

[125] Bernard Widrow, John R Glover Jr, John M McCool, John Kaunitz, Charles S Williams, Robert H Hearn, James R Zeidler, Eugene Dong Jr, and Robert C Goodlin. Adaptive noise cancelling: Principles and applications. *Proceedings of the IEEE*, 63(12):1692–1716, 1975.

[126] HK Wolf, ID Sherwood, and JD Kanon. The effect of noise on the performance of several ECG programs. *Proceedings of Computers in Cardiology*, pages 303–304, 1976.

[127] Qiuzhen Xue, Yu Hen Hu, and Willis J Tompkins. Neural-network-based adaptive matched filtering for QRS detection. *IEEE Transactions on Biomedical Engineering*, 39(4):317–329, 1992.

[128] Jieyun Yin and Jiande DZ Chen. Electrogastrography: Methodology, validation and applications. *Journal of Neurogastroenterology and Motility*, 19(1):5–17, 2013.

[129] Fei Zhang and Yong Lian. Novel QRS detection by CWT for ECG sensor. In *IEEE Biomedical Circuits and Systems Conference*, pages 211–214. IEEE, 2007.

[130] Dengyong Zhou, Olivier Bousquet, Thomas Navin Lal, Jason Weston, and Bernhard Schölkopf. Learning with local and global consistency. *Advances in Neural Information Processing Systems*, 16(16):321–328, 2004.

[131] Ping Zhou and Zhigang Wang. A computer location algorithm for ECG, PCG and CAP. In *Engineering in Medicine and Biology Society, 1998. Proceedings of the 20th Annual International Conference of the IEEE*, pages 220–222. IEEE, 1998.

Chapter 6

Genomic Data Analysis for Personalized Medicine

Juan Cui
Department of Computer Science & Engineering
University of Nebraska-Lincoln
Lincoln, NE
jcui@unl.edu

6.1 Introduction

Empowered by newly emerging biotechnologies and hence the fast generation of biological and medical information, advanced genomic research promises the whole field unprecedented opportunities and hopes for genome scale study of challenging problems in life science. For example, advances in genomic technology made it possible to study the complete genomic landscapes of healthy individuals or of any complex diseases [21, 20, 136], the genome-wide responses to certain genetic and chemical perturbations [72, 68, 92] or drug treatment [9], and the large-scale molecular changes that are associated to various disease phenotypes [54]. Many of such research efforts have proven to be highly promising to generate new insights into the biology of human disease and to predict the individual response to treatment, which therefore could enhances our understanding of the underlying mechanisms, promote the knowledge exchange between doctors and patients, and facilitate clinical decision making.

With increasingly rich data generated in recent years, our human ability of understanding the data has been outgrown in its entirety. While the whole community is still striving for better interpretation of these data, computational biologists have offered a suite of promising computational methods and information mining tools for analyzing the data, particularly focusing on elucidating novel connections between various biological entities and phenotypes. More often such data analyses will lead to novel discoveries and testable hypotheses. In the following sections of this chapter, we will introduce different kinds of computational approaches for tackling key research problems in life science such as identification of disease biomarkers and therapeutic targets and prediction of clinical outcomes. First, we use the analysis of genomic mutation to showcase how such data-driven approaches facilitate the generation of new discoveries and insights into biology. For instance, the genomic landscapes in complex diseases such as cancers are overwhelmingly complicated, revealing a high order of heterogeneity among different individuals. Then the natural questions wonder if any of these mutations are indeed responsible for the development of the diseases; if the answer is yes, how to identify these real contributors; when multiple mutations are involved, can we infer the evolutionary relation they may have against each other? To address such questions, a very simple and straightforward approach that has been used in cancer research during the past decade is to catalog all the genetic changes in many samples so that one can identify the common changes across individuals with the same or different cancers. With the common mutations, research focuses spread out subsequently from identifying the genetic changes linking to onset or progress of the disease to determining if the changes reflect genomic regions that are associated with clinical responses or can be targeted by a specific drug. The evolutionary patterns among these changes can be therefore studied based on the diverging lineages among different genetic populations.

With many decades of efforts in biomedical research, a substantial amount of knowledge has been gained about molecular- and cellular-level mechanisms of complex human diseases like cancers, typically accomplished using model systems. This rich background of knowledge serves as the foundation for computational biologists to study human diseases as evolving systems in their full complexity. It is the availability of the wide range of omic data collected on both model systems and human samples that makes such studies possible. More details about the genomic data generation along with some of the most popular and publicly available genomic data resources will be discussed in Section 6.2. The most fundamental computational algorithms and bioinformatics tools used for genomic data analysis is detailed out in Section 6.3. The author then illustrates in Section 6.4 what sort of health-related questions can be addressed through in-silico analysis of the genomic data through four typical data-driven studies and closes the chapter with the outlook of translating genetic discoveries into personalized medicine practice.

6.2 Genomic Data Generation

Different types of omics data including genomics, epigenetics, proteomics, and metabolomics data are generated by the state-of-the-art high throughput technologies as well as conventional biological experiments.

6.2.1 Microarray Data Era

During the past decade, microarray (also known as gene/protein-chips) and mass spectrometry (MS) are widely used to determine the presence and abundance of genes, proteins, and metabolites in biological samples including tissues, cells, blood, and urine. For example, Figure 6.1 shows the scanned image data generated from standard DNA microarray protocols, e.g., gene array platform

FIGURE 6.1: Scanned image data generated from standard DNA microarray protocols, e.g., gene array platform from Affymetrix, Agilent and ALMAC, where the signals extracted from the scanned array image reflect the gene abundance, after four major processes in the protocol including sample purification, Reverse-transcription (RT) and coupling, hybridization and wash, and scanning.

from Affymetrix, Agilent and ALMAC, where the signals extracted from the scanned array reflect the gene abundance.

Information about DNA replication timing and epigenetics such as DNA methylation can be derived through array-based assay as well. The comparative analyses of the qualitative data collected from samples of different conditions such as diseased versus healthy, early-stage disease versus late-stage disease, treated versus untreated, and others, allow researchers to identify abnormalities at different molecular levels that may be related to disease phenotypes, which in turn advances the discovery of biomarkers and therapeutic targets and improves health management in many different aspects including diagnosis, prognosis, treatment, and prevention. The microarray technology, for the first time, introduces to life science researchers a truly large amount of data and the need for quantitative training [6, 113, 76]. Many sophisticated computational tools have been developed for different analytical purposes, which have shown profound influences on the interpretation of array-based genomic data.

6.2.2 Next-Generation Sequencing Era

Since the advent of capillary electrophoresis (CE)-based Sanger sequencing, scientists have gained the ability to elucidate genetic information from any given biological system. The new technology-Next-Generation Sequencing (NGS) was introduced to overcome the inherent limitations of the previous techniques in throughput, scalability, speed, and resolution and then widely adopted in laboratories. Figure 6.2 illustrates how NGS works: Any given single genomics DNA is first fragmented into a library of small segments that can be uniformly and accurately sequenced in millions of parallel reactions. The identified strings of bases, called reads, are then assembled through aligning to a known reference genome (resequencing), or in the absence of a reference genome (de novo sequencing). The full set of aligned reads then reveals the entire sequence of the given gDNA sample.

Nowadays, with the increasingly mature NGS technologies, our understanding about diseased genomes has been revolutionized; however, the faster data generation makes the quantitative analysis more challenging. The "big data" generated by the sequencing experiments covers much broader molecular information including DNA genetic changes (using whole genome/exome sequencing [10]), quantification of protein-DNA binding or histone modifications (using chromatin immunoprecipitation followed by high-throughput sequencing (ChIPseq) [108]), transcript levels (using RNA sequencing (RNA-seq) [138]) and spatial interactions (using Hi-C [90]), allowing more applicable functional analysis than what microarray experiments can provide. Currently it becomes the norm that a single genome study can analyze a large set of genomes up to a few hundreds, even using combined sequencing techniques [113], and therefore, data interpretation, as well as data storage and management, particularly about how to organize this massive information into the database and share them in the public domain, becomes extraordinarily challenging than ever before.

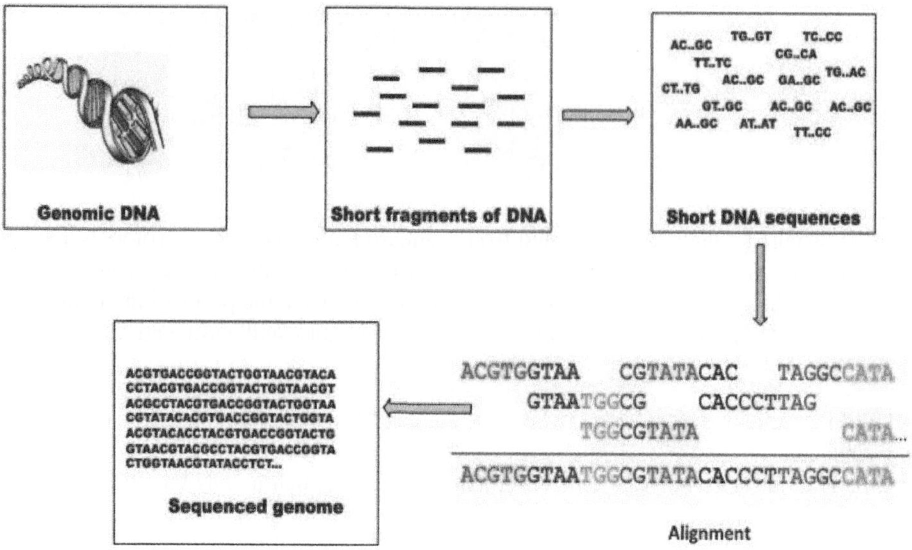

FIGURE 6.2: Conceptual overview of genome sequencing. The extracted gDNA is fragmented into a library of small segments that are each sequenced in parallel; individual sequence reads are reassembled by aligning to a reference genome; the whole-genome sequence is derived from the consensus of aligned reads.

6.2.3 Public Repositories for Genomic Data

Repositories of biological information are so essential for biomedical or bioinformatics studies as they organize a large variety of biological data and enable researchers to get access to the structured information and utilize them in their respective researches. Other than the most popular genomic databases for sequences and annotation such as the NCBI database (`http://www.ncbi.nlm.nih.gov/`) and GeneCards (`http://www.genecards.org/`), we will introduce in this section some other genomics databases that are broadly used, publicly available, and covering information of genetic mutations, sequences, expression and biological pathways.

Human genomes, mutations and epigenome databases: Two general genomic mutation databases on the Internet are HGMD (Human Genome Mutation Database) [27] that contains 141,161 germline mutations associated with human inheritable diseases and dbSNP database (Single Nucleotide Polymorphism Database) [126] that archives comprehensive genetic variation data across different species. TCGA (The Cancer Genome Atlas) [22] and ICGC (International Cancer Genome Consortium) [74] are two of the largest cancer genome projects to sequence thousands of whole genomes, along with other types of *omic* data, for many cancer types. Another highly useful large cancer genomic database is COSMIC (Catalog of Somatic Mutations In human Cancer) [47], which currently contains 1,592,109 gene mutations identified on 947,213 tumor samples. Other similar databases include the Cancer Gene Census database Census [49], CanProVar [88], and more specific ones such as the IARC TP53 database [101], CDKN2A [97], and the Androgen Receptor Gene Mutation database [104]. In Table 6.1, there are also a few epigenome databases such as MethyCancer [65] and the PubMeth database [102], which are at smaller scales.

Gene expression databases: Compared to other omics databases, there is a much larger collection of transcriptomic data on the Internet. Two of the most popular ones are GEO (Gene Expression Omnibus) at the NCBI that has more than 32,000 sets of gene-expression data collected from 800,000 samples of 1,600 organisms [12] and Arrayexpress at the EBI that consists of 1,245,005

TABLE 6.1: Human Genome, Mutation, and Epigenome Databases

Database	**Content**	**URL**
HGMD	A database for germline mutations that are associated with heritable diseases	`www.hgmd.org/`
dbSNP	A catalog for genome variations	`www.ncbi.nlm.nih.gov/projects/SNP/`
TCGA	A cancer *omic* data resource containing genomic, epigenomic, and transcriptomic data sponsored by NIH	`https://tcga-data.nci.nih.gov/tcga/`
ICGC	A cancer *omic* data resource containing genomic, epigenomic and transcriptomic data sponsored by ICGC	`http://icgc.org/`
COSMIC	A catalog of somatic mutations in human cancers containing > 50,000 mutations	`http://www.sanger.ac.uk/perl/genetics/CGP/cosmic`
Cancer gene census	A catalog of mutations in more than 400 cancer-related genes	`www.sanger.ac.uk/genetics/CGP/Census/`
CanProVar	A database for single amino-acid alterations including both germline and somatic variations	`http://bioinfo.vanderbilt.edu/canprovar/`
IARC TP53	A database for sequence-level variations in P53 identified in human population and tumor samples	`http://p53.iarc.fr`
CDKN2A	A database for variants of CDKN2A identified in human disease samples	`https://biodesktop.uvm.edu/perl/p16`
Androgen receptor gene mutations	A dataset of 374 mutations identified in patients with androgen insensitivity syndrome	`http://androgendb.mcgill.ca`
NIH roadmap epigenomics program	A database for human epigemomes now covering at least 23 cell types	`http://www.roadmapepigenomics.org/data`
Human epigenome project	A database for genome-wide DNA methylation patterns of all human genes in all major tissues	`http://www.epigenome.org/`
MethyCancer	A database for DNA methylation information in cancer-related genes, collected from public resource	`http://methycancer.genomics.org.cn`

sets of gene-expression data collected through 43,947 experiments using microarray and RNA sequencing. Table 6.2 lists some of such gene expression databases.

MicroRNAs and target databases: With intimate interaction with human mRNAs, micro RNAs have shown their important roles in regulating many major cellular processes such as cell growth, differentiation, and apoptosis [13, 7], as well as disease development [18, 144, 15, 121, 51, 142, 8, 30]. Many earlier researches in this field are focused on microRNA identification and targets prediction. MiRecords (`http://mirecords.biolead.org`) and miRBase (`http://www.mirbase.org`) are two databases archiving validated microRNAs with sequence, structure, and interaction information (Table 6.3). For example, MiRecords hosts, 2705 records of interactions between 644 microRNAs and, 1901 target genes in 9 animal species. TargetScan [83], Miranda [95] and MirTarBase [70] databases provide information of validated gene targets as well

TABLE 6.2: Gene Expression Databases

Database	Content	URL
NCBI GEO	A comprehensive collection of gene expression data	`http://www.ncbi.nlm.nih.gov/gds`
Arrayexpress	A database of functional genomics including gene expression data in both microarray and RNA-seq forms	`http://www.ebi.ac.uk/arrayexpress/`
SMD	Stanford microarray database for gene expression data covering multiple organisms	`http://smd.stanford.edu/`
Oncomine (research edition)	A commercial database for cancer transcriptomic and genomic data, with a free edition to academic and nonprofit organizations	`https://www.oncomine.org/resource/login.html`
ASTD	A database for human gene-expression data and derived alternatively spliced isoforms of human genes	`http://drcat.sourceforge.net/astd.html`

TABLE 6.3: MicroRNA Databases

Database	Content	URL
miRecords	A database for animal microRNA-target interactions	`http://mirecords.biolead.org`
miRBase	A database for published microRNA sequences and annotations covering numerous species	`http://www.mirbase.org`
TargetScan	A database for microRNA targets	`http://www.targetscan.org`
MiRanda	A databases for predicted microRNA targets	`http://www.microrna.org/microrna/home.do`
MirTarBase	A database for experimentally validated microRNA-target interactions	`http://mirtarbase.mbc.nctu.edu.tw`

as the ones from the computational perdition. Please note that microRNA expression data, although limited, are archived in GEO databases and TCGA.

6.3 Methods and Standards for Genomic Data Analysis

A big collection of different methods and algorithms have been developed for genomic data analysis, each serving a specific analytic step within the standard bioinformatics workflow (Figure 6.3) and are generally categorized into three groups including data preprocess, data analysis, and result interpretation. For example, microarray, sequencing slides, or phenotyping screening will have to be analyzed through the scanner using appropriate algorithms to quantify the raw signal, followed by data normalization to improve the signal-to-noise ratio. The quality of the data is checked at the level of both the image analysis and the normalization steps. After the preprocess, meaningful biological information will be extracted from the data and then subjected to further analysis using clinical statistics, classification or the systems biology approach, followed by the validation

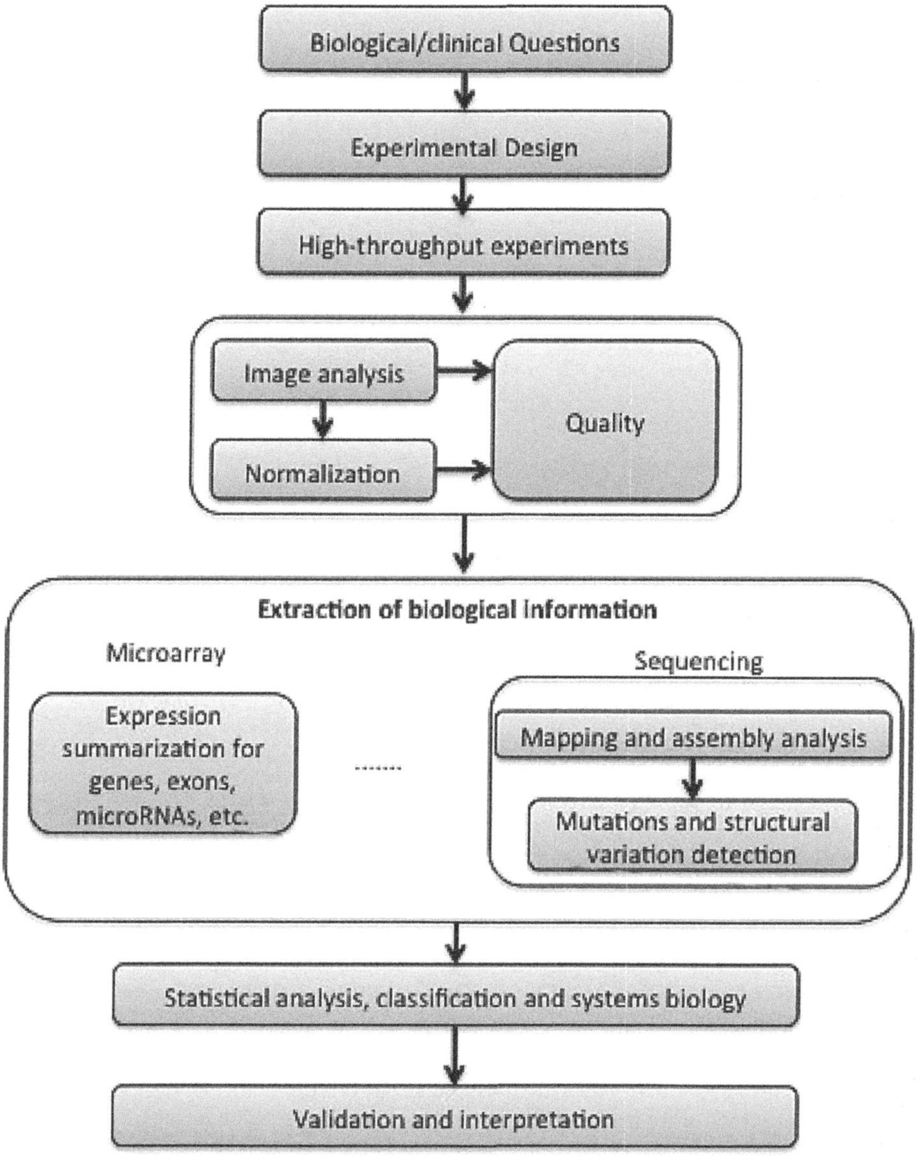

FIGURE 6.3: The standard bioinformatics workflow to analyze the genomic data.

and interpretation of the results. The next section will cover some methodologies used for the most fundamental analyses of the genomic data.

6.3.1 Normalization and Quality Control

Normalization is generally designed for correcting the systematic source of variability, first used in mRNA expression arrays to improve the signal-to-noise ratio for better gene expression extraction and thus more accurate biological interpretation. The first methods such as the *Lowess normalization* (for two-color microarrays), RMA, GC-RMA, MAS5, and PLIER (devoted to Affymetrix gene array and exon array) are still the most common methods used on microarray data. It is noted that normalization can be discussed at different levels other than the correction of the batch effect. For

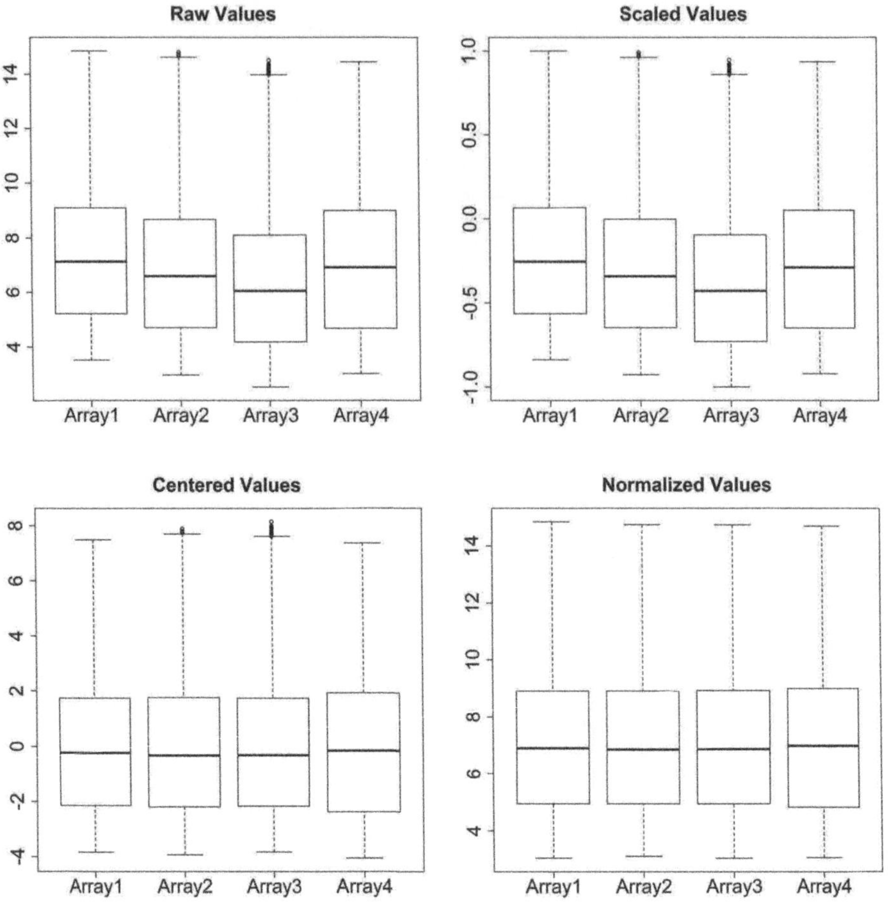

FIGURE 6.4: Gene expression profiles of four mice samples measured by Affymetrix chips. Boxplot of the top-left panel shows the raw expression of all the genes in these samples, which is then scaled into range $[-1, 1]$ (top-right), centered by the medium gene expression on the chip (bottom-left), and normalized using quartile normalization (bottom-right). R packages such as reshape, scales, and preprocess are used.

example, each experiment is singular and shows certain systematic variability that needs to be corrected, such as signal and spatial biases. Figure 6.4 shows the results of processing data using simple scaling and normalization approaches. Spatial normalization methods like MANOR [100] have been developed to correct spatial artifacts for gene expression, Comparative Genomic Hybridization (CGH) and DNA methylation microarrays. Similarly to GC-RMA, methods are designed to adjust the bias of GC-content, another major parameter that affects the signal measurement in microarray and NGS, among which ITALICS [115] represents one using multiple regression to correct the effect of GC-content for the Affymetrix SNP array. Overall, normalization is noted to be one of the most critical steps that needs to be considered carefully, as it will affect reliability, accuracy, and validity of the downstream analysis [129].

Also due to the experimental bias or uncontrolled variation that might be involved during high-throughput experiments, data quality control has to be performed adequately. The well-known MicroArray Quality Control (MAQC) project by the FDA (`http://www.fda.gov/`

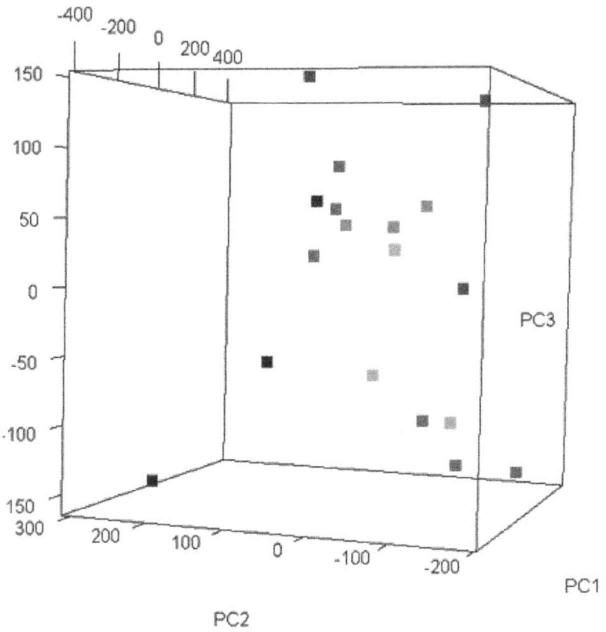

FIGURE 6.5: PCA analysis on a set of microarray data reported in Friedlin and McDonald [31]. Samples are from control ovarian cancer cells (LHR-), followed by LH-receptor expression (LHR+) and LH treatment in 1h (LH1), 4h (LH4), 8h (LH8), and 20h (LH20), which fall into six groups with three replicates for each.

`ScienceResearch/BioinformaticsTools/MicroarrayQualityControlProject/`) aims to provide QC tools to the microarray and sequencing community to avoid procedural failure and also establish QC metrics and thresholds for objectively assessing the performance achievable by various platforms. Outlier detection is one major step of QC, which aims to identify observations that are significantly different from the rest of the data and discard them. Statistical methods such as principal component analysis (PCA) (Figure 6.5) and hierarchical clustering [40] (discussed in the next section) can be used for this purpose.

6.3.2 Differential Expression Detection

For microarray analysis, one basic goal is to identify genes that show differential expression between two biological groups. Statistics such as the Student t-test and Mann-Whitney test can be used on each individual gene to test the null hypothesis that the means of two normally distributed populations (of the two biological groups) are equal; the latter one is more suitable for small sample size without requiring a normal distribution. Equal variance is normally considered if there are no evidential clues showing the two distributions are different. For those with multiple groups involved, ANOVA [2] can be used to examine if the gene expression is altered in any of the transition points when compared against others. Normally, only genes with a differential expression change more than 1.5- or 2-fold, with the P-value < 0.05 adjusted for multiple test or FDR < 0.1 were accepted for further analysis. Other approaches include bootstrap analysis, rank product, significance analysis of microarrays (SAM), and linear models of microarray (LMMA). Overall, the experimental design, coupled with the statistical significance and fold-change criteria employed, engenders high confidence in selecting reliable differential expressions.

6.3.3 Clustering and Classification

In order to identify meaningful expression patterns from the microarray, clustering methods can be applied to identify if some genes shows correlated expression across the given set of biological groups or if some samples share similar gene expression profiles. While an in-depth coverage of such clustering algorithms can be found in many publications and textbooks [57, 78], we briefly introduce the following techniques that are most popularly used.

- *Hierarchical clustering*: produce a gene/condition tree where the most similar expression profiles are joined together (Figure 6.6(a)). Strategies generally fall into two types:

  1. *agglomerative approach*, where each observation (expression profile for one gene or one sample) starts in its own cluster and pairs of clusters are merged as one moves up the hierarchy and
  2. *divisive approach*, where all observations start in one cluster and splits are performed recursively as one moves down the hierarchy.

  In general, the merge and splits are determined in a greedy manner. The measure of dissimilarity of observations can be calculated based on various distance functions including Euclidean distance, Manhattan distance, maximum distance, etc. Different strategies are used to calculate the distance between clusters including complete linkage, single linkage, average linkage, and centroid linkage.
- *K-mean clustering*: a representative partitioning method that needs to define k, the number of clusters in which to partition selected genes or conditions (Figure 6.6(b)). The algorithm attempts to minimize the mean-squared distance from each data point to its nearest center, the intracluster variability, and maximized intercluster variability.
- *SOM (Self-Organizing Map)*: artificial neural network-based. The goal is to find a set of centroids and to assign each object in the dataset to the centroid that provides the best approximation of that object, which is similar to k-means, but also produces information about the similarity between the clusters (Figure 6.6(c)).

Clustering 3.0, by Michael Eisen, is one of the earliest and most popular programs that implement hierarchical clustering algorithms, although many other updated versions have been developed. TreeView is a complementary tool to graphically browse results of clustering, which supports tree-based and image-based browsing of hierarchical trees, as well as multiple output formats for generation of images for publication. Bi-clustering methods such as the QUBIC (QUalitative BI-Clustering) program can be used to identify statistically significant bi-clusters in the data in a computationally efficient manner [84]. The basic idea of the algorithm is to find all subgroups of genes with similar expression patterns among some (to be identified) subsets of samples, and hence genes involved in each such pattern can possibly be used as signatures for sample subgrouping such as cancer subtyping or staging.

Like the clustering strategy for identifying gene expression patterns, classification methods can be used to identify gene signatures, which represent a set of genes that can differentiate different biological groups based on the gene expression. In Section 6.4.1 we will illustrate a classification application for disease biomarker identification in detail.

6.3.4 Pathway and Gene Set Enrichment Analysis

In order to derive the information about biological functions from the genomics changes such as alterations of gene expression, one can conduct functional enrichments analysis to identify the statistical associations between the gene expression changes and pathways. For each gene g in a gene-expression dataset D, the Spearman correlation is calculated between the expression levels of g and every other gene in D. If multiple gene-expression datasets are considered, one can use the Fisher transformation [46] to combine the calculated correlations across different datasets. The

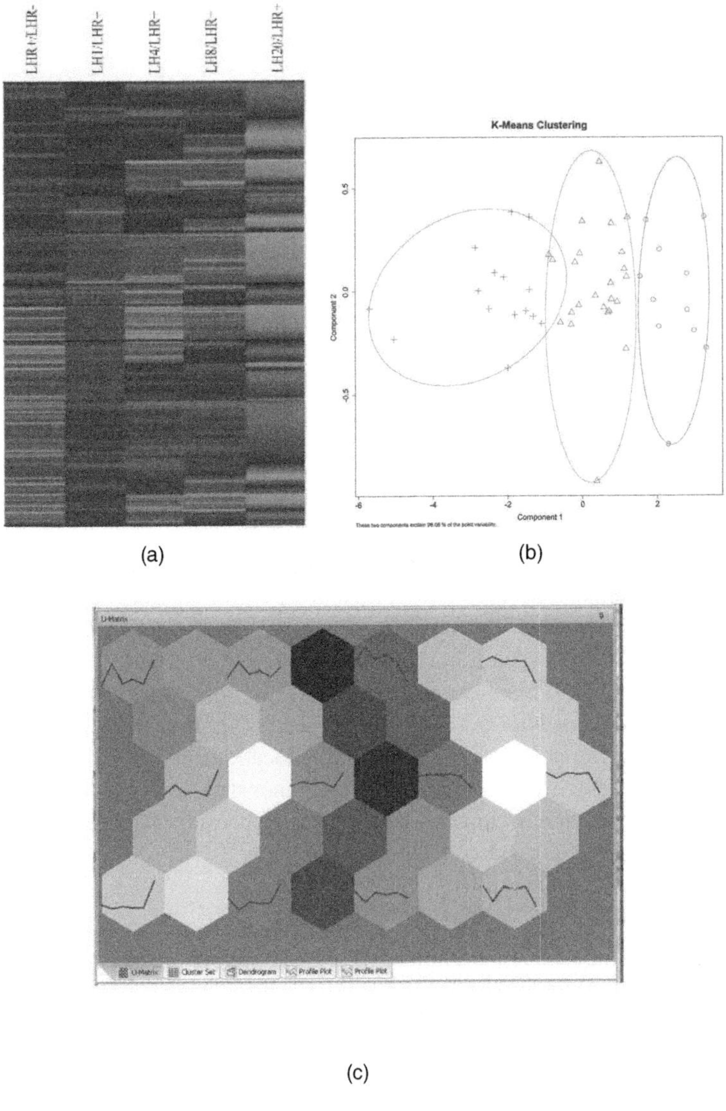

FIGURE 6.6: Results from three different clustering analyses including hierarchical clustering (a), K-mean clustering (b) and SOM (c), based on the same data from [31].

GSEA algorithm [130] can then be used for identification of pathways or more generally defined gene sets enriched in the expression changes. Similar methods are reviewed by Nam and Kim in [99], where pathway structure information are seldom considered. In this regard, Draghici et al. propose the "Impact Factor" (IF), which gives more weight to genes that are key regulators in the pathway [38].

6.3.5 Genome Sequencing Analysis

NGS data brings many challenging problems in every step of the analysis pipeline including read mapping, assembly and detection of SNP, copy number variants (CNVs) and other structural

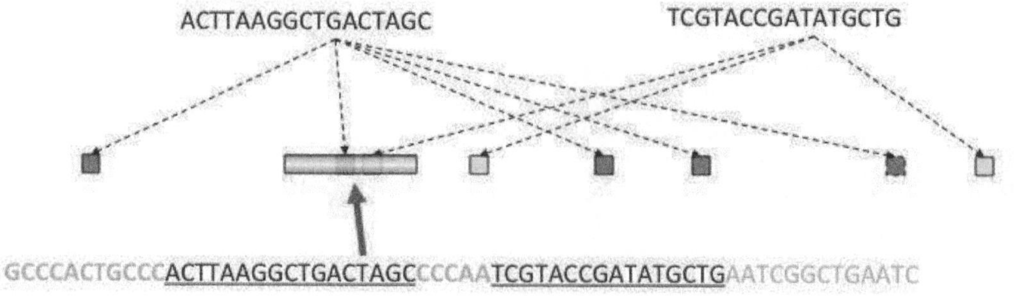

FIGURE 6.7: Paired-end short reads mapping. Both reads can map to multiple locations but the paired information, a fixed range of distance between two ends, can filter false mapping.

variations. In this section, we will introduce the major methods and tools applicable for tackling such problems.

Reads mapping represents the first computational task of aligning millions or billions of reads back to the reference genome. The two most efficient of these aligners, Bowtie and the BurrowsWheeler Aligner (BWA), achieve throughputs of 1040 million reads per hour on a single computer processor. Typically, 70-80% of the short reads (25 bp or longer) can map to a unique location on the human genome although this number varies depending on the read length, the availability of paired-end reads, and the sensitivity of the software used for alignment. So one major challenge remains when trying to assign reads that map to multiple locations, called multireads, which may lead to false inferences of SNP and CNVs. Figure 6.7 demonstrates how paired-end information facilitates the identification of right-mapping locations for multireads. Basically, an algorithm has three choices for dealing with multireads:

1. to ignore them, meaning that all multireads are discarded;
2. to only report the best match, the alignment with the fewest mismatches, either choosing one at random or report all of them if multiple equally good best matches are found;
3. to report all alignments up to a maximum number, d, regardless of the total number of alignments found.

One can use tools such as IGV (`http://www.broadinstitute.org/igv/`) and SAMtools [86] to manually resolve multireads sometimes, which is not usually a feasible strategy for very large NGS datasets.

SNP detection represents another analytical challenge where the accuracy is influenced by a few major factors including the error rate from NGS technologies, reliable read mapping, and assembles. For example, one known problem for short reads assemblers is reference sequence bias: Reads that more closely resemble the reference sequence are more likely to successfully map as compared with reads that contain valid mismatches. Proper care must be taken to avoid errors in these alignments, and is discussed in a recent review [111]. There is an inherent trade-off in allowing mismatches: The program must allow for mismatches without resulting in false alignments. The reference sequence bias problem is exacerbated with longer reads: Allowing for one mismatch per read is acceptable for 35 bp reads, but insufficient for 100 bp reads.

Sophisticated methods are required for novel SNP discovery: While the calling of common variants can be aided by their presence in a database such as dbSNP, accurate detection of rare and novel variants will require increased confidence in the SNP call. Current tools for SNP calling include MAQ [87], SAMtools [86], SOAPsnp [89], VarScan [81], and GATK [34]. Some recent methods attempt to handle multireads more explicitly. For example, Sniper calculates an alignment probability for each multiread using a Bayesian genotyping model that decomposes the likehood of a read mapping to a given locus into its component likelihoods [124].

Structural variant detection is performed for discovery of multiple types of variants including deletions, insertions, inversions, translocations, and duplications. One particular challenge for this analysis lies in detecting variants in repetitive regions that are longer than the read length. VariationHunter [69] represent one algorithm that incorporates both read-depth and read-pair data for accurate CNV discovery. A similar method was designed to find CNVs in a repeat-rich region [64] and both methods used the information of all mappings of the multireads to improve the estimation of the true copy number of each repeat.

De novo genome assembly represents one of the major challenging issues in NGS data analysis, especially with the short read length and repetitive sequence. Many new de novo assemblers have emerged to tackle this problem, a selection of which have been reviewed in [133]. These assemblers basically fall into two classes: overlap-based and de Bruijn graph-based, both applying graph theory. One very important step is about how to handle the repeats, which cause branches in the graphs and require the assemblers to make a decision as to which branch to follow. Incorrect guesses create false joins (chimeric contigs) and erroneous copy numbers. Normally, for assemblers that are more conservative, it will break the assembly at the branch points, leading to an accurate but fragmented assembly with fairly small contigs. A combination of strategies has been proposed to resolve the problems caused by the repeats including sequencing strategies that use fragment libraries of varying sizes [139], postprocessing that is for detecting misassemblies [110], analyzing coverage statistics and detecting and resolving tangles in a de Bruijn graph. Although leading NGS assemblers such as Allpaths-LG shows promising performance [55], the ultimate solution to completely resolve all of these problems require much longer read lengths.

Further information about methods and algorithms used for other types of sequencing data analysis such as RNA-seq, Chip-seq, and Metagenomics can be found in the nature reviews website (`http://www.nature.com/nrg/series/nextgeneration/index.html`).

6.3.6 Public Tools for Genomic Data Analysis

A variety of computational analysis and data mining tools have been published and deployed on the Internet, which can be used to analyze the databases presented in the previous section. We list a few in the following as examples to illustrate the types of tools that one can find on the Internet to analyze the different types of omics data.

Genome analysis tools: A number of tools provided at the Broad Institute's site [19] may be useful for the initial analysis of sequenced genomes, including ABSOLUTE for computing absolute copy number and mutation multiplicities in the genomes, MuTect for identifying point mutations, Breakpointer [131] for pinpointing the breakpoints of genomic rearrangements, dRanger for identifying genomic rearrangements, and Oncotator for annotations of the point mutations and INDELs in the sequenced genome. CREST [137] is another tool developed at St. Jude Children's Research Hospital, for mapping somatic structural variation in diseased genomes with high resolution. Specifically, a few hubs offer clusters of analysis tools for a cancer genome study, such as the Cancer Genomics Hub at UCSC, the TCGA site, the ICGC site, and the Cancer Genome Analysis suite at the Broad Institute. The Cancer Genomics Hub [23] is a good place to visualize cancer genomes mostly from the TCGA project and to retrieve simple analysis results such as genomic mutations.

Compared with the large number of genome analysis tools on the Internet, only a few tools for epigenomic analysis are available in the public domain, possibly reflecting the reality that the current understanding about the human epigenome is far less than that about human genomes. This is clearly understandable, knowing the current definition of "epigenetics" was not settled until a Cold Spring Harbor meeting in 2008 [14]. A few tools have been published for identifying differentially methylated regions in a given genome in comparison with reference epigenomes. R packages such as CHARM [77] and MethylKit [4] are for making such identifications. The similar ones also include EpiExplorer [61] and CpGassoc [11] for methylation analysis.

Transcriptome analysis tools: Numerous tools for transcriptomic data analysis have been published and deployed on the Internet, ranging from

1. identification of differentially expressed genes in cancer versus matching control tissues such as edgeR [118] and baySeq [63];

2. identification of co-expressed genes or genes with correlated expression patterns such as WGCNA [82] and GeneCAT [98];

3. transcriptome-based protein identification [42];

4. inference of splicing variants from RNA-seq data such as CUFFLINK [117];

5. elucidation of human signaling networks from gene-expression data [16];

6. de-convolution of gene expression data collected on tissue samples with multiple cell types to contributions from individual cell types [3]; and

7. development of predictive metabolic fluxes through integration of gene-expression data with flux balance analysis [39], among numerous other tools. Table 6.4 lists a few of these tools.

Statistical analysis tools: In addition to the above data type-specific tools, there are large collections of other statistical analysis tools on the Internet for boarder uses of analyzing different *omic* data types. The following sites provide a number of such tools. Bioconductor is a community-wide effort for developing and deploying open source bioinformatics software packages. All the deployed tools are written in the statistical programming language R. Currently the website has about 750 software tools, covering a wide range of analysis and inference capabilities [53]. Galaxy is another web-based platform that hosts a large collection of genomic data analysis tools [56]. The popular Gene Ontology website also hosts a wide range of analysis tools [52].

Pathway mapping and reconstruction tools: Various tools are currently available for pathway construction, annotation, analysis, and comparison on the Internet. Table 6.4 also listed a few such tools.

Visualization tools: Visualization tools may prove to be highly useful when analyzing complex biological data and inferring biological relationships among biomolecules or pathways. A number of visualization tools have been developed in support of such needs and made publicly available. Among these tools are CytoScape [122] for visualizing molecular interaction networks, PathView [93] for biological data integration and visualization, and iPATH [143] for visualization, analysis, and customization of pathway models.

6.4 Types of Computational Genomics Studies towards Personalized Medicine

After the introduction of computational methods and bioinformatics tools for genomic data analysis, we will discuss in this section about how to design a system biology approach or a genomic data-driven approach to tackle real biomedical problems through analyzing the genomic data one can generate, so that we can generate transformative knowledge that may bridge the gap between the basic research and clinical practice and derive novel insights in personalized medicine.

TABLE 6.4: Tools for Genomics Data Analysis and Pathway Prediction and Mapping

Database	Content	URL
edgeR	A tool for detection of differentially expressed genes	http://www.genomine.org/edge/
WGCNA	A tool for co-expression analysis of genes	http://labs.genetics.ucla.edu/horvath/CoexpressionNetwork
CUFFLINK	A tool for transcript assembly and identification of splicing variants	http://cufflinks.cbcb.umd.edu/index.html
DAVID	A tool for pathways enriched with differentially expressed genes (or any specified set of genes)	http://david.abcc.ncifcrf.gov/
CHARM	An early and widely used package for DNA methylation analysis.	http://www.bioconductor.org/packages/release/bioc/html/charm.html
EpiExplorer	A web-based tool for identification of comparing epigenetic markers in a specific genome to reference human epigenomes	http://epiexplorer.mpi-inf.mpg.de/
Pathway tools	A website providing a wide ranges of pathway-related tools, including pathway construction, editing, prediction, and flux analysis.	http://bioinformatics.ai.sri.com/ptools/
BioCyc and pathway tools	A database providing a list of reconstruction and analysis tools of metabolic pathways	http://biocyc.org/publications.shtml
PathoLogic pathway prediction	A tool for prediction of metabolic pathways based on BioCyc database	http://g6g-softwaredirectory.com/bio/cross-omics/pathway-dbs-kbs/20235SRIPathoLogicPathwPredict.php
Metabolic pathways	A website providing a large collection of pathway-related tools	http://www.hsls.pitt.edu/obrc/index.php?page=metabolic_pathway

6.4.1 Discovery of Biomarker and Molecular Signatures

The availability of the large quantities of omics data provided unprecedented opportunities for developing molecular-level signatures for each known disease phenotype, which could potentially lead to more accurate classifications of the disease into subtype, stage, or grade for the purpose of improved treatment-plan development and prognosis evaluation. With the capability of measuring thousands to millions of parameters, such as gene expression, protein and metabolite abundance, or DNA copy numbers, on a biological sample, the questions of which such features to use for designing the predictive models are crucial. The **feature selection** is an important step due to the following reasons:

(i) a predictive models with many parameters from a limited size of observed samples always lead to poor model in terms of ability to predict for future samples, often referred to as the curse of dimensionality [37];

(ii) smaller numbers of markers used for the predictive model allow the design of the diagnostic devices for cheaper and faster prediction;

(iii) predictive models with fewer markers can suggest biological interpretation that may potentially lead to better understanding of the molecular underpinnings of prognosis.

The problem of feature selection has been thoroughly studied in the statistics and machine learning communities [59]. In order to select a subset of the features G, called signature, which comprise q features selected from p candidates, the simplest way is to calculate a discriminative score for each candidate and then form the signature among the q top candidates with the largest scores. In the case of the binary classification where we predict binary phenotypes, i.e., $y = \{-1, 1\}$, the score of a feature typically measure how differentially distributed the feature is between the two subpopulation of samples S_{-1} and S_1, of respective sizes n_{-1} and n_1 , with different phenotypes. It can be calculated for each feature the normalized difference between its mean on both population

$$t = \frac{|u_1 - u_{-1}|}{\bar{\sigma}\sqrt{\frac{1}{n_1} + \frac{1}{n_{-1}}}}$$

where $\bar{\sigma}$ is an estimate of class-conditional variance of the feature. Methods such as Significance Analysis of Microarray (SAM) [134], regularized student's t-statistics [36], the randomized variance model [141], or limma [127] or nonparametric statistics such as the AUC and U-statistics of the Mann-Whitney test can be used for the similar analysis, all called univariate filer methods.

Instead of testing the features one by one and then taking the top q among them to form a signature, it is more interesting to directly select a subset of features that allow the inference of a good model. Here we use an example of identifying a gastric cancer subtype signature to illustrate how such a problem can be solved using machine learning-based feature selections [29].

Consider two subtypes of gastric cancers, the intestinal (C1) and diffuse (C2) subtypes, each having genome-scale gene-expression data collected using the same platform on paired cancer and control tissues from the same patients. Mathematically the goal is to find an SVM that has the best classification with its misclassification rate lower than a predefined threshold δ.

One way to solve this problem is by going through all combinations of K genes among all the human genes, from K = 1 up until an SVM classifier and a K-gene set G are found, which achieve the desired classification accuracy as defined by δ. Actually it does not need to search through all the genes encoded in the human genome since the majority of the human genes are not expressed for any specific tissue type. To get a sense about the amount of computing time it may need to exhaustively search through all K-gene combinations, consider the following typical scenario with two gene-expression datasets with C1 having 100 pairs of samples and C2 consisting of 150 pairs of samples and 500 genes consistently showing differential expressions between the two sets of samples. So one needs to go through $\binom{500}{k}$ combinations to find a K-gene combination having the optimal classification between the two datasets with misclassification lower than δ. For each K-gene combination, a linear SVM is trained to optimally classify the two datasets as discussed above. Our experience in analyses of differentially expressed genes in cancer tissues indicates that K should be no larger than 8 as otherwise the number $\binom{500}{k}$ may be too large for a desktop workstation to handle.

If one needs to search for a K-gene classifier with larger K's (> 8) for a specific application, a different type of search strategy may be needed to make it computationally feasible. Many wrapper methods are used for this purpose that usually follow greedy optimization procedures to find a "good" subset but not the best one. For example, a popular backward stepwise selection algorithm is the SVM recursive feature elimination (RFE) method that starts from all features and iteratively removes features with small weights estimated by a linear SVM [59]. Basically, one can search for the K most informative genes, for a specified K, to solve the above classification problem using a heuristic approach to achieve a desired computational efficiency. While the detailed information of an RFE-SVM procedure can be found in [75, 59], the basic idea is to start with a list of genes, each having some discerning power in distinguishing the two classes of samples, and train an optimal classifier with all the genes, followed with a procedure that repeatedly removes genes from the initial gene list as long as the classification accuracy is not affected until the desired number of K genes are left.

Numerous K-gene signatures have been identified for diagnostic use, mostly used in cancer cases, including a 70-gene panel for predicting the potential for developing breast cancers, developed by MammaPrint [125]; a 21-gene panel, termed *Oncotype* DX for a similar purpose [5]; a 71-gene panel for identification of cancers that are sensitive to TRAIL-induced apoptosis [24]; a 31-gene panel used to predict the metastasis potential of breast cancer, developed by CompanDX [25]; and a 16-gene panel for testing for non-small-cell lung cancer against other lung cancer types [123]. Having a test kit for a specific cancer type, e.g., metastasis prone or not, can help surgeons to make a quick and correct decision regarding what surgical procedures to take on the spot. Other test kits can help oncologists to make an informed decision regarding what treatment plans to use. For example, TRAIL (TNF-related apoptosis inducing ligand) is an anticancer agent, which can induce apoptosis in cancer cells but not in normal cells, hence making the drug highly desirable. However not all cancers are sensitive to TRAIL. Having a test using a simple kit can quickly determine if a patient should be treated using TRAIL or not.

One challenge in identifying signature genes for a specific type of disease using gene expression analysis lies in the proper normalization of transcriptomic data collected by different research labs using different platforms, to ensure that the identified signature genes are generally applicable. Some carefully designed normalization may be needed to correct any systematic effects on gene-expression levels caused by different sample-preparation and data-collection protocols.

6.4.2 Genome-Wide Association Study (GWAS)

GWAS has been the mainstay of genetic analysis over the last decade, especially when high-throughput genetic information can be collected through NGS techonologies. It has been a powerful tool for investigating the genetic architecture of human diseases or traits. For example, it has been applied in identification of genetic risk factors for common and complex diseases such as cataracts [106], hypothyroidism [33], schizophrenia, type II diabetes [79], and cancer.

The ultimate goal is to use genetic risk factors to make predictions about who is at risk and to identify the biological underpinnings of disease susceptibility for developing new prevention and treatment strategies. A few successful examples include the identification of the *Complement Factor H* gene as a major risk factor for age-related macular degeneration or AMD [60] and identification of several DNA sequence variations that have a large influence on warfarin dosing, which is a blood-thinning drug that helps prevent blood clots in patients [28]. The genetic tests results from these results can be used in a clinical setting that gives rise to a new field called personalized medicine that aims to tailor healthcare to individual patient based on their genetic background and other biological features. Here we will review some GWAS technology and analytical strategies as an important example of translational bioinformatics. Single nucleotide polymorphisms (SNPs), the single base-pair changes in the DNA sequence that occur with high frequency in the human genome, are currently used as the major genotype information for GWAS analysis, normally on a well-defined phenotype. Typically GWAS examines the effects of about 500,000 SNPs, using different approach like the de facto analysis to evaluate the association of each SNP independently to the phenotype. Multiple test corrections are necessary in such an analysis, considering the huge numbers of individual tests conducted. Bonferroni correction is one of the simplest approaches to adjusts the predefined threshold, alpha value from $\alpha = 0.05$ to $\alpha = (0.05/k)$ where k is the number of statistical tests conducted. For a typical GWAS using 500,000 SNPs, statistical significance of a

SNP association would be set at 1e-7. Furthermore, alternative measure, false discovery rate (FDR), and permutation testing can also be used for establishing significance.

Quantitative traits can be analyzed using generalized linear model (GLM) approaches like Analysis of Variance (ANOVA) while dichotomous case/control traits are studied using either contingency table methods or logistic regression. In some cases, covariate adjustment should be done for factors that may influence the trait, such as age, sex, and known clinical covariates. One major analysis of GWAS is to examine interactions among genetic variants throughout the genome, which represents numerous computational challenges [96]. In order to reduce the possible combinations of SNP that need analyzing, one possible strategy is to only examine the combinations that fall within an established biological context, such as a biochemical pathway or a protein family. As these techniques rely on electronic repositories of structured biomedical knowledge, they generally couple bioinformatics engines that generate SNP-SNP combinations with a statistical method that evaluates combinations in this dataset. For example, the Biofilter approach uses a variety of public data sources with logistic regression and multifactor dimensionality reduction methods [58, 17]. Similarly, INTERSNP uses logistic regression, log-linear, and contingency table approaches to assess SNP-SNP interaction models [66]. The results of multiple GWAS studies can be pooled together to perform a meta-analysis, a technique that was originally developed to examine and refine the significance and effect size estimates from multiple studies *examining the same hypothesis* in the published literature. With the development of large academic consortia, meta-analysis approaches allow the synthesis of results from multiple studies without requiring the transfer of protected genotype or clinical information to parties who were not part of the original study approval—only statistical results from a study need be transferred. Several software packages are available to facilitate such meta-analysis, including STATA products and METAL [120, 140].

We realize the greatest challenge in the "post-GWAS" era may be to understand the functional consequences of these identified loci associated with phenotypes. In a recent review article "Genetic heterogeneity in human disease" [94], the authors consider that "the vast majority of such [GWAS identified] variants have no established biological relevance to disease or clinical utility for prognosis or treatment." While the statement may be overly critical, it does point to one important issue that commonly observed genomic changes may not necessarily contain much disease-causing information. A generalized association study involving multiple omic data types such as trancriptomics and proteomics, as well as a massive amount of image data for phenotypes, needs to be done to better understand the genotype-phenotype relationship for the purpose of improving healthcare, which may require more general statistical frameworks than the GWAS type of analysis, hence creating challenges as well as opportunities for statistical analysts.

6.4.3 Discovery of Drug Targets

A typical system biology project aiming to identify drug targets starts with collection of data, such as genomic or transcriptomic data obtained with high-throughput technologies. After proper data process and statistical analysis, one often gets a list of genes that may be differentially expressed or muted in diseased versus normal cells or located in a genomic region found to be amplified or deleted in the diseased samples, which may contain good candidates to identify new drug targets. One of the strategies to find the most promising targets within this list is to prioritize these genes. The information for prioritization is often based on what we already know about the genes, for example, the biological function in a pathway that may be to the diseased cell, or if they share similarity such as co-expression with some known disease relevant genes. However, integration of such annotation information and knowledge that are normally fragmented in different forms in a multitude of databases become the most crucial and challenging step, for which some computational methods for heterogeneous data have emerged. For example, the functional annotation of each candidate gene was automatically compared to the description of the disease in order to automatize the target searching [109, 132]. Other similar methods include Endeavour [1, 32], which uses state-of-the-art machine-learning techniques to integrate heterogeneous information and ranks the candidate genes according to the similarity to know disease genes, and PRINCE [135] that uses label propagation over a PPI network and borrows information from known disease genes. An obvious limitation of these guilt-by-association strategies is that only genes sharing similarity to those known can be discovered, limiting the potential for disease with no or fewer-known causal genes.

Other types of drug targets can be master regulators out of the initiated differential gene list but regulate the expression of some genes on the list. One possible strategy to identify those regulators starts with the regulatory motif (i.e., DNA transcription factor binding sites) analysis on the promoters of the differentially expressed genes, which then predict the master regulator based on the transcriptional regulation network built among these genes. Software and databases such as JASPAR [112], Allegro [62], Weeder [105], and Pscan [145] can be used for this analysis.

More recently, some network methods have been used for target identifications, which require exploring network properties, in particular, the importance of individual network nodes (i.e., genes). There are many measures that consider the importance of nodes in a network and some may shed light on the biological significance and potential optimality of a gene or set of genes as therapeutic targets. With a little amount of prerequisite information, the simplest methods are to disrupt the network connectivity by attaching nodes with properties of hubs (with the highest connectivity) and routers (with the highest centrality). Intuitively, centrality is a measure of how far a node is located from the center of a graph where the graph center can be roughly defined as a node minimizing the sum of distances to all other nodes of the graph. Such an approach has been successfully applied in identifying targets in cancer [85] and infectious disease [43].

In addition to the single gene target identification, more and more research attention now has been put on finding multiple-gene combinations as therapeutic targets [107]. It has been shown that cancer therapeutics targeting a single gene often results in relapse since compensatory, feedback, and redundancy loops in the network may offset the activity associated with the targeted gene, thus multiple genes reflecting parallel functional cascades in a network should be targeted simultaneously. Although more discussion can be found in [107], the gene network analysis we introduce next can be also applied to address the problem here.

6.4.4 Discovery of Disease Relevant Gene Networks

A variety of gene network methods have been successfully used to elucidate the functional relationship between genes by modeling the pair-wise relationships reflected by experimental measures. Such approaches include Pearson's correlation-based approach [10, 108], Boolean network [138, 90], Bayesian network [27, 126], differential equations [76, 22], and model free approach [74]. With the advance of large-scale omics technologies, there is a clear need now to develop systematic approaches to unravel the high-order interacting patterns on the high-dimension chips (e.g., microarrays) in light of the Protein-Protein Interactions (PPI) network because they may point out possible interaction complexes or pathways related to the network dynamics of the disease.

The basic research question here is how to identify different subnetworks that are associated with disease phenotypes based on the gene expression data. One early idea to solve this problem was pioneered by Ideker et al. [73], who assigned a statistical Z-score z_g to each gene using expression data and then searched for subnetworks A that displayed a statistically significant amount of differential expression, with a combined Z-score defined by $Z_A = \frac{1}{\sqrt{|A|}} \sum_{g \in A} Z_g$. Such networks may correspond to small sets of gene/protein participating in a common complex or functional pathway. Many other methods used this idea and expanded. For example, Liu et al. [91] apply this method to identify differentially expressed network in diabetes. Sohler et al. [128] proposes a greedy heuristic method to identify subnetworks that are significant according to specified p-values, where individual p-value are combined using Fisher's inverse x^2 method. Specifically, this method starts with a set of seed genes and performs a greedy expansion by including the most significant gene neighbors in the current network. Chuang et al. [26] later defined an alternative to introduce gene ranking in the network by calculating the activity of each single gene in a network.

Several attempts have been made to identify the aberrant behavior in gene networks in disease conditions. For example, Ergun et al. [41] have applied a two-phase approach on primary and metastatic prostate cancer data, in which the AR pathway was identified as a highly enriched pathway for metastatic prostate cancer. Rhodes et al. [114] searched for transcriptional regulatory network related to cancer pathogenesis. In addition to revealing integrative effects of genes in the underlying genetic circuit for complex diseases, networking modeling also serves as a predictive tool for precise diagnosis and prognosis as to what biomarkers are used for. Since even the same disease have different prognosis and respond differently to different treatments, it is very important to predict as precisely as possible the prognosis and drug responsiveness of each individual at any levels, either individual genes or network, in order to be able to propose the most adapted treatment of each patient.

6.5 Genetic and Genomic Studies to the Bedside of Personalized Medicine

As molecular technologies to assay the whole genome and to profile various molecular activities have emerged and more important genetic associations have been identified through GWAS, it rapidly advances the implementation of personalized medicine. When genetic or genomic associations have been identified for a particular drug response such as drug efficacy, adverse events, toxicity, or variability in target or maintenance dose [116], for example, an individual with a certain genotype shows a higher risk to develop a serious drug event with certain drug exposure, this type of information can be immediately useful for patients and doctors in a clinic. Similarly, other genotypic information can be used to direct proper dosing for certain medications. Examples include chemotherapy medications such as trastuzumab and imatinib that target specific cancers [50, 71], a targeted pharmacogenetic dosing algorithm is used for warfarin [119, 80], and the incidence of adverse events is reduced by checking for susceptible genotypes for drugs like abacavir, carbamazepine and clozapine [35, 45, 67]. In 2012, one such bedside genetic test has been reported that used a simple cheek swab test to identify if patients have a generic variant known as CYP2C19*2. This test is useful for cardiac stent treatment, as patients with this particular variant are at risk of reacting poorly to standard anti-platelet therapy with Plavix® (clopidogrel). This study, among many others, has demonstrated that the tailed drug treatment therapy based on genetic testing successfully protects patients with the at-risk genetic variants from subsequent adverse events. Another example of the genomic guidance in current medications includes testing of thiopurine methyltransferse (TPMT) activity before prescribing thiopurines, since patients with reduced TPMT activity are at increased risk of potentially life-threatening bone marrow suppression with thiopurines. In addition to those recommended by the FDA, there are other ongoing efforts to determine the clinical utility of genetic variants for decision making. A few institutions such as Vanderbilt, St. Jude Children's Research Hospital, Mayo Clinic, and Scripps have been working on the implementation of a genotyping platform to support medications including clopidogrel (the most commonly prescribed antiplatelet medication), warfarin (the most commonly prescribed chronic anticoagulant), and simvastatin (one of the most commonly prescribed cholesterol lowering medications). Overall, it is very satisfying to the community about the progress of pharmacogenomics due to many success stories and high potential for translation to clinical practice.

Another major application of genomic information in personalized medicine is for accurate diagnosis, for example, using molecular signatures to differentiate specific subtypes or grades of a certain disease, as discussed in previous sections, or applying genome sequencing for typing and the characterization of hospital pathogens, so that patients can get more accurate clinical analysis and treatment. In this regard, the transformative potential of bacterial whole-genome sequencing for clinical diagnostics has been widely recognized in the scientific literature. Bioinformatics challenges have been also discussed when proposing whole-genome sequencing-based molecular diagnostics (MDx) in the clinic practice [48].

6.6 Concluding Remarks

This is an exciting time to study the extraordinarily complex problems in human diseases, specifically those dealing with the key drivers and facilitators at different developmental stages, disease diagnosis, and treatment in their full complexity. A tremendous amount of omic data has been generated and made publicly available, which enables us through analyzing and mining these data to extract useful information and generate new knowledge of the diseases and therefore to guide clinical diagnosis and personalized treatment. The bioinformatics challenges to realize personalized medicine, as discussed in this chapter, as well as in [44, 103], will lie in the development sophisticated new methods for

(i) more robust and accurate processing of the genomic data and interpretation of the functional impact of the genomic variations;

(ii) identification of the complex genetic interaction with phenotypes through integrated systems data;

(iii) translation of the genomic discoveries into medical practice.

It is the author's hope that the discussion in this chapter has prepared our readers to have a general idea about the types of omic data and analysis available for researchers in the modern biology era. The examples we listed represent only a small set of questions that one can address and possibly solve. The data resources and tools listed in this chapter represent but a small set of all the available tools and databases of which we are aware. A recommended reference to find a more comprehensive list of the relevant databases and tools is the special database and the server issues published annually by Nucleic Acids Research. There are undoubtedly many good problems for our reader to think about and to solve through analyzing the omics data, which hopefully will lead to progress that contributes to early detection, better prevention, or more successful personalized treatment of human diseases.

Bibliography

[1] S. Aerts, D. Lambrechts, S. Maity, P. Van Loo, B. Coessens, F. De Smet, L. C. Tranchevent, B. De Moor, P. Marynen, B. Hassan, P. Carmeliet, and Y. Moreau. Gene prioritization through genomic data fusion. *Nat Biotechnol*, 24(5):537–44, 2006.

[2] Affymetrix. Alternative transcript analysis methods for exon arrays. 2005-10-11.

[3] J. Ahn, Y. Yuan, G. Parmigiani, M. B. Suraokar, L. Diao, I. Wistuba, and W. Wang. Demix: deconvolution for mixed cancer transcriptomes using raw measured data. *Bioinformatics*, 29(15):1865–71, 2013.

[4] A. Akalin, M. Kormaksson, S. Li, F. E. Garrett-Bakelman, M. E. Figueroa, A. Melnick, and C. E. Mason. Methylkit: a comprehensive R package for the analysis of genome-wide DNA methylation profiles. *Genome Biol*, 13(10):R87, 2012.

[5] K. S. Albain, W. E. Barlow, S. Shak, G. N. Hortobagyi, R. B. Livingston, I. T. Yeh, P. Ravdin, R. Bugarini, F. L. Baehner, N. E. Davidson, G. W. Sledge, E. P. Winer, C. Hudis, J. N. Ingle, E. A. Perez, K. I. Pritchard, L. Shepherd, J. R. Gralow, C. Yoshizawa, D. C. Allred, C. K. Osborne, and D. F. Hayes. Prognostic and predictive value of the 21-gene recurrence score assay in postmenopausal women with node-positive, oestrogen-receptor-positive breast cancer on chemotherapy: a retrospective analysis of a randomised trial. *Lancet Oncol*, 11(1):55–65, 2010.

[6] D. B. Allison, X. Cui, G. P. Page, and M. Sabripour. Microarray data analysis: from disarray to consolidation and consensus. *Nat Rev Genet*, 7(1):55–65, 2006.

[7] V. Ambros. The functions of animal micrornas. *Nature*, 431(7006):350–5, 2004.

[8] S. Ambs, R. L. Prueitt, M. Yi, R. S. Hudson, T. M. Howe, F. Petrocca, T. A. Wallace, C. G. Liu, S. Volinia, G. A. Calin, H. G. Yfantis, R. M. Stephens, and C. M. Croce. Genomic profiling of microrna and messenger rna reveals deregulated microrna expression in prostate cancer. *Cancer Res*, 68(15):6162–70, 2008.

[9] G. F. Bammert and J. M. Fostel. Genome-wide expression patterns in saccharomyces cerevisiae: comparison of drug treatments and genetic alterations affecting biosynthesis of ergosterol. *Antimicrob Agents Chemother*, 44(5):1255–65, 2000.

[10] M. J. Bamshad, S. B. Ng, A. W. Bigham, H. K. Tabor, M. J. Emond, D. A. Nickerson, and J. Shendure. Exome sequencing as a tool for mendelian disease gene discovery. *Nat Rev Genet*, 12(11):745–55, 2011.

[11] R. T. Barfield, V. Kilaru, A. K. Smith, and K. N. Conneely. CpGassoc: an R function for analysis of DNA methylation microarray data. *Bioinformatics*, 28(9):1280–1, 2012.

[12] T. Barrett, S. E. Wilhite, P. Ledoux, C. Evangelista, I. F. Kim, M. Tomashevsky, K. A. Marshall, K. H. Phillippy, P. M. Sherman, M. Holko, A. Yefanov, H. Lee, N. Zhang, C. L. Robertson, N. Serova, S. Davis, and A. Soboleva. NCBI GEO: archive for functional genomics data sets–update. *Nucleic Acids Res*, 41(Database issue):D991–5, 2013.

[13] D. P. Bartel. Micrornas: genomics, biogenesis, mechanism, and function. *Cell*, 116(2):281–97, 2004.

[14] S. L. Berger, T. Kouzarides, R. Shiekhattar, and A. Shilatifard. An operational definition of epigenetics. *Genes Dev*, 23(7):781–3, 2009.

[15] M. Bloomston, W. L. Frankel, F. Petrocca, S. Volinia, H. Alder, J. P. Hagan, C. G. Liu, D. Bhatt, C. Taccioli, and C. M. Croce. Microrna expression patterns to differentiate pancreatic adenocarcinoma from normal pancreas and chronic pancreatitis. *JAMA*, 297(17):1901–8, 2007.

[16] R. Brandenberger, H. Wei, S. Zhang, S. Lei, J. Murage, G. J. Fisk, Y. Li, C. Xu, R. Fang, K. Guegler, M. S. Rao, R. Mandalam, J. Lebkowski, and L. W. Stanton. Transcriptome characterization elucidates signaling networks that control human ES cell growth and differentiation. *Nat Biotechnol*, 22(6):707–16, 2004.

[17] W. S. Bush, S. M. Dudek, and M. D. Ritchie. Biofilter: a knowledge-integration system for the multi-locus analysis of genome-wide association studies. *Pac Symp Biocomput*, pages 368–79, 2009.

[18] G. A. Calin, M. Ferracin, A. Cimmino, G. Di Leva, M. Shimizu, S. E. Wojcik, M. V. Iorio, R. Visone, N. I. Sever, M. Fabbri, R. Iuliano, T. Palumbo, F. Pichiorri, C. Roldo, R. Garzon, C. Sevignani, L. Rassenti, H. Alder, S. Volinia, C. G. Liu, T. J. Kipps, M. Negrini, and C. M. Croce. A microRNA signature associated with prognosis and progression in chronic lymphocytic leukemia. *N Engl J Med*, 353(17):1793–801, 2005.

[19] Cancer-Genome-Analysis. Absolute, 2013.

[20] N. Cancer Genome Atlas. Comprehensive molecular characterization of human colon and rectal cancer. *Nature*, 487(7407):330–7, 2012.

[21] N. Cancer Genome Atlas Research. Comprehensive genomic characterization of squamous cell lung cancers. *Nature*, 489(7417):519–25, 2012.

[22] N. Cancer Genome Atlas Research, J. N. Weinstein, E. A. Collisson, G. B. Mills, K. R. Shaw, B. A. Ozenberger, K. Ellrott, I. Shmulevich, C. Sander, and J. M. Stuart. The cancer genome atlas pan-cancer analysis project. *Nat Genet*, 45(10):1113–20, 2013.

[23] Cancer-Genomics-Hub. Cancer genomics hub, 2013.

[24] J. J. Chen, S. Knudsen, W. Mazin, J. Dahlgaard, and B. Zhang. A 71-gene signature of trail sensitivity in cancer cells. *Mol Cancer Ther*, 11(1):34–44, 2012.

[25] S. H. Cho, J. Jeon, and S. I. Kim. Personalized medicine in breast cancer: a systematic review. *J Breast Cancer*, 15(3):265–72, 2012.

[26] H. Y. Chuang, E. Lee, Y. T. Liu, D. Lee, and T. Ideker. Network-based classification of breast cancer metastasis. *Mol Syst Biol*, 3:140, 2007.

[27] D. N. Cooper, E. V. Ball, and M. Krawczak. The human gene mutation database. *Nucleic Acids Res*, 26(1):285–7, 1998.

[28] G. M. Cooper, J. A. Johnson, T. Y. Langaee, H. Feng, I. B. Stanaway, U. I. Schwarz, M. D. Ritchie, C. M. Stein, D. M. Roden, J. D. Smith, D. L. Veenstra, A. E. Rettie, and M. J. Rieder. A genome-wide scan for common genetic variants with a large influence on warfarin maintenance dose. *Blood*, 112(4):1022–7, 2008.

[29] C. Cortes and V. Vapnik. Support-vector networks. *Machine Learning*, 20(3):273–97, 1995.

[30] C. M. Croce. Causes and consequences of microrna dysregulation in cancer. *Nat Rev Genet*, 10(10):704–14, 2009.

[31] J. Cui, B. M. Miner, J. B. Eldredge, S. W. Warrenfeltz, P. Dam, Y. Xu, and D. Puett. Regulation of gene expression in ovarian cancer cells by luteinizing hormone receptor expression and activation. *BMC Cancer*, 11:280, 2011.

[32] T. De Bie, L. C. Tranchevent, L. M. van Oeffelen, and Y. Moreau. Kernel-based data fusion for gene prioritization. *Bioinformatics*, 23(13):i125–32, 2007.

[33] J. C. Denny, D. C. Crawford, M. D. Ritchie, S. J. Bielinski, M. A. Basford, Y. Bradford, H. S. Chai, L. Bastarache, R. Zuvich, P. Peissig, D. Carrell, A. H. Ramirez, J. Pathak, R. A. Wilke, L. Rasmussen, X. Wang, J. A. Pacheco, A. N. Kho, M. G. Hayes, N. Weston, M. Matsumoto,

P. A. Kopp, K. M. Newton, G. P. Jarvik, R. Li, T. A. Manolio, I. J. Kullo, C. G. Chute, R. L. Chisholm, E. B. Larson, C. A. McCarty, D. R. Masys, D. M. Roden, and M. de Andrade. Variants near foxe1 are associated with hypothyroidism and other thyroid conditions: using electronic medical records for genome- and phenome-wide studies. *Am J Hum Genet*, 89(4):529–42, 2011.

[34] M. A. DePristo, E. Banks, R. Poplin, K. V. Garimella, J. R. Maguire, C. Hartl, A. A. Philippakis, G. del Angel, M. A. Rivas, M. Hanna, A. McKenna, T. J. Fennell, A. M. Kernytsky, A. Y. Sivachenko, K. Cibulskis, S. B. Gabriel, D. Altshuler, and M. J. Daly. A framework for variation discovery and genotyping using next-generation dna sequencing data. *Nat Genet*, 43(5):491–8, 2011.

[35] M. Dettling, I. Cascorbi, C. Opgen-Rhein, and R. Schaub. Clozapine-induced agranulocytosis in schizophrenic caucasians: confirming clues for associations with human leukocyte class I and II antigens. *Pharmacogen*, 7(5):325–332, 2007.

[36] K. Dobbin, J. H. Shih, and R. Simon. Statistical design of reverse dye microarrays. *Bioinformatics*, 19(7):803–10, 2003.

[37] D. L. Donoho. High-dimensional data analysis: the curses and blessings of dimensionality, August 6-11 2000.

[38] S. Draghici, P. Khatri, A. L. Tarca, K. Amin, A. Done, C. Voichita, C. Georgescu, and R. Romero. A systems biology approach for pathway level analysis. *Genome Res*, 17(10):1537–45, 2007.

[39] N. C. Duarte, S. A. Becker, N. Jamshidi, I. Thiele, M. L. Mo, T. D. Vo, R. Srivas, and B. O. Palsson. Global reconstruction of the human metabolic network based on genomic and bibliomic data. *Proc Natl Acad Sci U S A*, 104(6):1777–82, 2007.

[40] M. B. Eisen, P. T. Spellman, P. O. Brown, and D. Botstein. Cluster analysis and display of genome-wide expression patterns. *Proc Natl Acad Sci U S A*, 95(25):14863–8, 1998.

[41] A. Ergun, C. A. Lawrence, M. A. Kohanski, T. A. Brennan, and J. J. Collins. A network biology approach to prostate cancer. *Mol Syst Biol*, 3:82, 2007.

[42] V. C. Evans, G. Barker, K. J. Heesom, J. Fan, C. Bessant, and D. A. Matthews. De novo derivation of proteomes from transcriptomes for transcript and protein identification. *Nat Methods*, 9(12):1207–11, 2012.

[43] R. M. Felciano, S. Bavari, D. R. Richards, J. N. Billaud, T. Warren, R. Panchal, and A. Kramer. Predictive systems biology approach to broad-spectrum, host-directed drug target discovery in infectious diseases. *Pac Symp Biocomput*, pages 17–28, 2013.

[44] G. H. Fernald, E. Capriotti, R. Daneshjou, K. J. Karczewski, and R. B. Altman. Bioinformatics challenges for personalized medicine. *Bioinformatics*, 27(13):1741–8, 2011.

[45] P. B. Ferrell and H. L. McLeod. Carbamazepine, HLA-B*1502 and risk of Stevens-Johnson syndrome and toxic epidermal necrolysis: US FDA recommendations. *Pharmacogenomics*, 9(10):1543–1546, 2008.

[46] R. A. Fisher. On the probable error of a coefficient of correlation deduced from a small sample. *Metron*, 1:3–32, 1921.

[47] S. A. Forbes, G. Bhamra, S. Bamford, E. Dawson, C. Kok, J. Clements, A. Menzies, J. W. Teague, P. A. Futreal, and M. R. Stratton. *The Catalogue of Somatic Mutations in Cancer (COSMIC)*. John Wiley & Sons, Inc., 2001.

[48] W. F. Fricke and D. A. Rasko. Bacterial genome sequencing in the clinic: bioinformatic challenges and solutions. *Nat Rev Genet*, 15(1):49–55, 2014.

[49] P. A. Futreal, L. Coin, M. Marshall, T. Down, T. Hubbard, R. Wooster, N. Rahman, and M. R. Stratton. A census of human cancer genes. *Nat Rev Cancer*, 4(3):177–83, 2004.

[50] C. Gambacorti-Passerini. Part I: Milestones in personalised medicine—imatinib. *Lancet Oncology*, 9(6):600, 2008.

[51] R. Garzon, S. Volinia, C. G. Liu, C. Fernandez-Cymering, T. Palumbo, F. Pichiorri, M. Fabbri, K. Coombes, H. Alder, T. Nakamura, N. Flomenberg, G. Marcucci, G. A. Calin, S. M. Kornblau, H. Kantarjian, C. D. Bloomfield, M. Andreeff, and C. M. Croce. Microrna signatures associated with cytogenetics and prognosis in acute myeloid leukemia. *Blood*, 111(6):3183–9, 2008.

[52] Gene-Ontology-Tools. Gene ontology tools, 2013.

[53] R. C. Gentleman, V. J. Carey, D. M. Bates, B. Bolstad, M. Dettling, S. Dudoit, B. Ellis, L. Gautier, Y. Ge, J. Gentry, K. Hornik, T. Hothorn, W. Huber, S. Iacus, R. Irizarry, F. Leisch, C. Li, M. Maechler, A. J. Rossini, G. Sawitzki, C. Smith, G. Smyth, L. Tierney, J. Y. Yang, and J. Zhang. Bioconductor: open software development for computational biology and bioinformatics. *Genome Biol*, 5(10):R80, 2004.

[54] C. Gilissen, A. Hoischen, H. G. Brunner, and J. A. Veltman. Unlocking Mendelian disease using exome sequencing. *Genome Biol*, 12(9):228, 2011.

[55] S. Gnerre, I. Maccallum, D. Przybylski, F. J. Ribeiro, J. N. Burton, B. J. Walker, T. Sharpe, G. Hall, T. P. Shea, S. Sykes, A. M. Berlin, D. Aird, M. Costello, R. Daza, L. Williams, R. Nicol, A. Gnirke, C. Nusbaum, E. S. Lander, and D. B. Jaffe. High-quality draft assemblies of mammalian genomes from massively parallel sequence data. *Proc Natl Acad Sci U S A*, 108(4):1513–8, 2011.

[56] J. Goecks, A. Nekrutenko, J. Taylor, and T. Galaxy. Galaxy: a comprehensive approach for supporting accessible, reproducible, and transparent computational research in the life sciences. *Genome Biol*, 11(8):R86, 2010.

[57] A. Gordon. *Classification*. Chapman and Hall/CRC, 1999.

[58] B. J. Grady, E. S. Torstenson, P. J. McLaren, D. E. B. PI, D. W. Haas, G. K. Robbins, R. M. Gulick, R. Haubrich, H. Ribaudo, and M. D. Ritchie. Use of biological knowledge to inform the analysis of gene-gene interactions involved in modulating virologic failure with efavirenz-containing treatment regimens in ART-naive ACTG clinical trials participants. *Pac Symp Biocomput*, pages 253–64, 2011.

[59] I. Guyon, J. Weston, S. Barnhill, and V. Vapnik. Gene selection for cancer classification using support vector machines. *Machine Learning*, 46(1-3):389–422, 2002.

[60] J. L. Haines, M. A. Hauser, S. Schmidt, W. K. Scott, L. M. Olson, P. Gallins, K. L. Spencer, S. Y. Kwan, M. Noureddine, J. R. Gilbert, N. Schnetz-Boutaud, A. Agarwal, E. A. Postel, and M. A. Pericak-Vance. Complement factor H variant increases the risk of age-related macular degeneration. *Science*, 308(5720):419–21, 2005.

[61] K. Halachev, H. Bast, F. Albrecht, T. Lengauer, and C. Bock. Epiexplorer: live exploration and global analysis of large epigenomic datasets. *Genome Biol*, 13(10):R96, 2012.

[62] Y. Halperin, C. Linhart, I. Ulitsky, and R. Shamir. Allegro: analyzing expression and sequence in concert to discover regulatory programs. *Nucleic Acids Res*, 37(5):1566–79, 2009.

[63] T. J. Hardcastle and K. A. Kelly. BaySeq: empirical Bayesian methods for identifying differential expression in sequence count data. *BMC Bioinformatics*, 11:422, 2010.

[64] D. He, F. Hormozdiari, N. Furlotte, and E. Eskin. Efficient algorithms for tandem copy number variation reconstruction in repeat-rich regions. *Bioinformatics*, 27(11):1513–20, 2011.

[65] X. He, S. Chang, J. Zhang, Q. Zhao, H. Xiang, K. Kusonmano, L. Yang, Z. S. Sun, H. Yang, and J. Wang. Methycancer: the database of human DNA methylation and cancer. *Nucleic Acids Res*, 36(Database issue):D836–41, 2008.

[66] C. Herold, M. Steffens, F. F. Brockschmidt, M. P. Baur, and T. Becker. INTERSNP: genome-wide interaction analysis guided by a priori information. *Bioinformatics*, 25(24):3275–81, 2009.

[67] S. Hetherington, A. R. Hughes, M. Mosteller, D. Shortino, K. L. Baker, W. Spreen, E. Lai, K. Davies, A. Handley, D. J. Dow, M. E. Fling, M. Stocum, C. Bowman, L. M. Thurmond, and A. D. Roses. Genetic variations in HLA-B region and hypersensitivity reactions to abacavir. *Lancet*, 359(9312):1121–1122, 2002.

[68] M. E. Hillenmeyer, E. Fung, J. Wildenhain, S. E. Pierce, S. Hoon, W. Lee, M. Proctor, R. P. St Onge, M. Tyers, D. Koller, R. B. Altman, R. W. Davis, C. Nislow, and G. Giaever. The chemical genomic portrait of yeast: uncovering a phenotype for all genes. *Science*, 320(5874):362–5, 2008.

[69] F. Hormozdiari, C. Alkan, E. E. Eichler, and S. C. Sahinalp. Combinatorial algorithms for structural variation detection in high-throughput sequenced genomes. *Genome Res*, 19(7):1270–8, 2009.

[70] S. D. Hsu, Y. T. Tseng, S. Shrestha, Y. L. Lin, A. Khaleel, C. H. Chou, C. F. Chu, H. Y. Huang, C. M. Lin, S. Y. Ho, T. Y. Jian, F. M. Lin, T. H. Chang, S. L. Weng, K. W. Liao, I. E. Liao, C. C. Liu, and H. D. Huang. mirtarbase update 2014: an information resource for experimentally validated miRNA-target interactions. *Nucleic Acids Res*, 42(Database issue):D78–85, 2014.

[71] C. A. Hudis. Drug therapy: trastuzumab—mechanism of action and use in clinical practice. *New England Journal of Medicine*, 357(1):39–51, 2007.

[72] T. R. Hughes, M. J. Marton, A. R. Jones, C. J. Roberts, R. Stoughton, C. D. Armour, H. A. Bennett, E. Coffey, H. Dai, Y. D. He, M. J. Kidd, A. M. King, M. R. Meyer, D. Slade, P. Y. Lum, S. B. Stepaniants, D. D. Shoemaker, D. Gachotte, K. Chakraburtty, J. Simon, M. Bard, and S. H. Friend. Functional discovery via a compendium of expression profiles. *Cell*, 102(1):109–26, 2000.

[73] T. E. Ideker, V. Thorsson, and R. M. Karp. Discovery of regulatory interactions through perturbation: inference and experimental design. *Pac Symp Biocomput*, pages 305–16, 2000.

[74] C. International Cancer Genome, T. J. Hudson, W. Anderson, A. Artez, A. D. Barker, C. Bell, R. R. Bernabe, M. K. Bhan, F. Calvo, I. Eerola, D. S. Gerhard, A. Guttmacher, M. Guyer, F. M. Hemsley, J. L. Jennings, D. Kerr, P. Klatt, P. Kolar, J. Kusada, D. P. Lane, F. Laplace, L. Youyong, G. Nettekoven, B. Ozenberger, J. Peterson, T. S. Rao, J. Remacle, A. J. Schafer, T. Shibata, M. R. Stratton, J. G. Vockley, K. Watanabe, H. Yang, M. M. Yuen, B. M. Knoppers, M. Bobrow, A. Cambon-Thomsen, L. G. Dressler, S. O. Dyke, Y. Joly, K. Kato, K. L.

Kennedy, P. Nicolas, M. J. Parker, E. Rial-Sebbag, C. M. Romeo-Casabona, K. M. Shaw, S. Wallace, G. L. Wiesner, N. Zeps, P. Lichter, A. V. Biankin, C. Chabannon, L. Chin, B. Clement, E. de Alava, F. Degos, M. L. Ferguson, P. Geary, D. N. Hayes, T. J. Hudson, A. L. Johns, A. Kasprzyk, H. Nakagawa, R. Penny, M. A. Piris, R. Sarin, A. Scarpa, T. Shibata, M. van de Vijver, P. A. Futreal, H. Aburatani, M. Bayes, D. D. Botwell, P. J. Campbell, X. Estivill, D. S. Gerhard, S. M. Grimmond, I. Gut, M. Hirst, C. Lopez-Otin, P. Majumder, M. Marra, J. D. McPherson, H. Nakagawa, Z. Ning, X. S. Puente, Y. Ruan, T. Shibata, M. R. Stratton, H. G. Stunnenberg, H. Swerdlow, V. E. Velculescu, R. K. Wilson, H. H. Xue, L. Yang, P. T. Spellman, G. D. Bader, P. C. Boutros, P. J. Campbell, et al. International network of cancer genome projects. *Nature*, 464(7291):993–8, 2010.

[75] I. Inza, P. Larranaga, R. Blanco, and A. J. Cerrolaza. Filter versus wrapper gene selection approaches in DNA microarray domains. *Artif Intell Med*, 31(2):91–103, 2004.

[76] J. P. Ioannidis, D. B. Allison, C. A. Ball, I. Coulibaly, X. Cui, A. C. Culhane, M. Falchi, C. Furlanello, L. Game, G. Jurman, J. Mangion, T. Mehta, M. Nitzberg, G. P. Page, E. Petretto, and V. van Noort. Repeatability of published microarray gene expression analyses. *Nat Genet*, 41(2):149–55, 2009.

[77] R. A. Irizarry, C. Ladd-Acosta, B. Carvalho, H. Wu, S. A. Brandenburg, J. A. Jeddeloh, B. Wen, and A. P. Feinberg. Comprehensive high-throughput arrays for relative methylation (CHARM). *Genome Res*, 18(5):780–90, 2008.

[78] A. K. Jain, M. N. Murty, and P. J. Flynn. Data clustering: a review. *ACM Computing Surveys*, 31(3):264–323, 1999.

[79] A. N. Kho, M. G. Hayes, L. Rasmussen-Torvik, J. A. Pacheco, W. K. Thompson, L. L. Armstrong, J. C. Denny, P. L. Peissig, A. W. Miller, W. Q. Wei, S. J. Bielinski, C. G. Chute, C. L. Leibson, G. P. Jarvik, D. R. Crosslin, C. S. Carlson, K. M. Newton, W. A. Wolf, R. L. Chisholm, and W. L. Lowe. Use of diverse electronic medical record systems to identify genetic risk for type 2 diabetes within a genome-wide association study. *J Am Med Inform Assoc*, 19(2):212–8, 2012.

[80] T. E. Klein, R. B. Altman, N. Eriksson, B. F. Gage, S. E. Kimmel, M. T. M. Lee, N. A. Limdi, D. Page, D. M. Roden, M. J. Wagner, M. D. Caldwell, J. A. Johnson, Y. T. Chen, M. S. Wen, Y. Caraco, I. Achache, S. Blotnick, M. Muszkat, J. G. Shin, H. S. Kim, G. Suarez-Kurtz, J. A. Perini, E. Silva-Assuncao, J. L. Andereson, B. D. Horne, J. F. Carlquist, M. D. Caldwell, R. L. Berg, J. K. Burmester, B. C. Goh, S. C. Lee, F. Kamali, E. Sconce, A. K. Daly, A. H. B. Wu, T. Y. Langaee, H. Feng, L. Cavallari, K. Momary, M. Pirmohamed, A. Jorgensen, C. H. Toh, P. Williamson, H. McLeod, J. P. Evans, K. E. Weck, C. Brensinger, Y. Nakamura, T. Mushiroda, D. Veenstra, L. Meckley, M. J. Rieder, A. E. Rettie, M. Wadelius, H. Melhus, C. M. Stein, U. Schwartz, D. Kurnik, E. Deych, P. Lenzini, C. Eby, L. Y. Chen, P. Deloukas, A. Motsinger-Reif, H. Sagreiya, B. S. Srinivasan, E. Lantz, T. Chang, M. Ritchie, L. S. Lu, and J. G. Shin. Estimation of the warfarin dose with clinical and pharmacogenetic data (vol 360, pg 753, 2009). *New Eng J Med*, 361(16):1613, 2009.

[81] D. C. Koboldt, K. Chen, T. Wylie, D. E. Larson, M. D. McLellan, E. R. Mardis, G. M. Weinstock, R. K. Wilson, and L. Ding. Varscan: variant detection in massively parallel sequencing of individual and pooled samples. *Bioinformatics*, 25(17):2283–5, 2009.

[82] P. Langfelder and S. Horvath. WGCNA: an R package for weighted correlation network analysis. *BMC Bioinformatics*, 9:559, 2008.

[83] B. P. Lewis, C. B. Burge, and D. P. Bartel. Conserved seed pairing, often flanked by adenosines, indicates that thousands of human genes are microrna targets. *Cell*, 120(1):15–20, 2005.

[84] G. Li, Q. Ma, H. Tang, A. H. Paterson, and Y. Xu. Qubic: a qualitative biclustering algorithm for analyses of gene expression data. *Nucleic Acids Res*, 37(15):e101, 2009.

[85] G. H. Li and J. F. Huang. Inferring therapeutic targets from heterogeneous data: HKDC1 is a novel potential therapeutic target for cancer. *Bioinformatics*, 30(6):748–52, 2014.

[86] H. Li, B. Handsaker, A. Wysoker, T. Fennell, J. Ruan, N. Homer, G. Marth, G. Abecasis, R. Durbin, and S. Genome Project Data Processing. The sequence alignment/map format and SAMtools. *Bioinformatics*, 25(16):2078–9, 2009.

[87] H. Li, J. Ruan, and R. Durbin. Mapping short DNA sequencing reads and calling variants using mapping quality scores. *Genome Res*, 18(11):1851–8, 2008.

[88] J. Li, D. T. Duncan, and B. Zhang. Canprovar: a human cancer proteome variation database. *Hum Mutat*, 31(3):219–28, 2010.

[89] R. Li, Y. Li, X. Fang, H. Yang, J. Wang, K. Kristiansen, and J. Wang. SNP detection for massively parallel whole-genome resequencing. *Genome Res*, 19(6):1124–32, 2009.

[90] E. Lieberman-Aiden, N. L. van Berkum, L. Williams, M. Imakaev, T. Ragoczy, A. Telling, I. Amit, B. R. Lajoie, P. J. Sabo, M. O. Dorschner, R. Sandstrom, B. Bernstein, M. A. Bender, M. Groudine, A. Gnirke, J. Stamatoyannopoulos, L. A. Mirny, E. S. Lander, and J. Dekker. Comprehensive mapping of long-range interactions reveals folding principles of the human genome. *Science*, 326(5950):289–93, 2009.

[91] M. Liu, A. Liberzon, S. W. Kong, W. R. Lai, P. J. Park, I. S. Kohane, and S. Kasif. Network-based analysis of affected biological processes in type 2 diabetes models. *PLoS Genet*, 3(6):e96, 2007.

[92] P. Y. Lum, C. D. Armour, S. B. Stepaniants, G. Cavet, M. K. Wolf, J. S. Butler, J. C. Hinshaw, P. Garnier, G. D. Prestwich, A. Leonardson, P. Garrett-Engele, C. M. Rush, M. Bard, G. Schimmack, J. W. Phillips, C. J. Roberts, and D. D. Shoemaker. Discovering modes of action for therapeutic compounds using a genome-wide screen of yeast heterozygotes. *Cell*, 116(1):121–37, 2004.

[93] W. Luo and C. Brouwer. Pathview: an r/bioconductor package for pathway-based data integration and visualization. *Bioinformatics*, 29(14):1830–1, 2013.

[94] J. McClellan and M. C. King. Genetic heterogeneity in human disease. *Cell*, 141(2):210–7, 2010.

[95] K. C. Miranda, T. Huynh, Y. Tay, Y. S. Ang, W. L. Tam, A. M. Thomson, B. Lim, and I. Rigoutsos. A pattern-based method for the identification of microRNA binding sites and their corresponding heteroduplexes. *Cell*, 126(6):1203–17, 2006.

[96] J. H. Moore and M. D. Ritchie. Studentjama: the challenges of whole-genome approaches to common diseases. *JAMA*, 291(13):1642–3, 2004.

[97] J. A. Murphy, R. Barrantes-Reynolds, R. Kocherlakota, J. P. Bond, and M. S. Greenblatt. The CDKN2A database: Integrating allelic variants with evolution, structure, function, and disease association. *Hum Mutat*, 24(4):296–304, 2004.

[98] M. Mutwil, J. Bro, W. G. T. Willats, and S. Persson. Genecatnovel webtools that combine blast and co-expression analyses. *Nucleic Acids Research*, 36(suppl 2):W320–W6, 2008.

[99] D. Nam and S. Y. Kim. Gene-set approach for expression pattern analysis. *Brief Bioinform*, 9(3):189–97, 2008.

[100] P. Neuvial, P. Hupe, I. Brito, S. Liva, E. Manie, C. Brennetot, F. Radvanyi, A. Aurias, and E. Barillot. Spatial normalization of array-CGH data. *BMC Bioinformatics*, 7:264, 2006.

[101] M. Olivier, R. Eeles, M. Hollstein, M. A. Khan, C. C. Harris, and P. Hainaut. The IARC TP53 database: new online mutation analysis and recommendations to users. *Hum Mutat*, 19(6):607–14, 2002.

[102] M. Ongenaert, L. Van Neste, T. De Meyer, G. Menschaert, S. Bekaert, and W. Van Criekinge. Pubmeth: a cancer methylation database combining text-mining and expert annotation. *Nucleic Acids Res*, 36(Database issue):D842–6, 2008.

[103] C. L. Overby and P. Tarczy-Hornoch. Personalized medicine: challenges and opportunities for translational bioinformatics. *Per Med*, 10(5):453–462, 2013.

[104] M. N. Patterson, I. A. Hughes, B. Gottlieb, and L. Pinsky. The androgen receptor gene mutations database. *Nucleic Acids Res*, 22(17):3560–2, 1994.

[105] G. Pavesi, P. Mereghetti, G. Mauri, and G. Pesole. Weeder web: discovery of transcription factor binding sites in a set of sequences from co-regulated genes. *Nucleic Acids Res*, 32(Web Server issue):W199–203, 2004.

[106] P. L. Peissig, L. V. Rasmussen, R. L. Berg, J. G. Linneman, C. A. McCarty, C. Waudby, L. Chen, J. C. Denny, R. A. Wilke, J. Pathak, D. Carrell, A. N. Kho, and J. B. Starren. Importance of multi-modal approaches to effectively identify cataract cases from electronic health records. *J Am Med Inform Assoc*, 19(2):225–34, 2012.

[107] Q. Peng and N. J. Schork. Utility of network integrity methods in therapeutic target identification. *Front Genet*, 5:12, 2014.

[108] S. Pepke, B. Wold, and A. Mortazavi. Computation for Chip-seq and RNA-seq studies. *Nat Methods*, 6(11 Suppl):S22–32, 2009.

[109] C. Perez-Iratxeta, P. Bork, and M. A. Andrade. Association of genes to genetically inherited diseases using data mining. *Nat Genet*, 31(3):316–9, 2002.

[110] A. M. Phillippy, M. C. Schatz, and M. Pop. Genome assembly forensics: finding the elusive mis-assembly. *Genome Biol*, 9(3):R55, 2008.

[111] J. E. Pool, I. Hellmann, J. D. Jensen, and R. Nielsen. Population genetic inference from genomic sequence variation. *Genome Res*, 20(3):291–300, 2010.

[112] E. Portales-Casamar, S. Thongjuea, A. T. Kwon, D. Arenillas, X. Zhao, E. Valen, D. Yusuf, B. Lenhard, W. W. Wasserman, and A. Sandelin. Jaspar 2010: the greatly expanded open-access database of transcription factor binding profiles. *Nucleic Acids Res*, 38(Database issue):D105–10, 2010.

[113] J. Quackenbush. Computational analysis of microarray data. *Nat Rev Genet*, 2(6):418–27, 2001.

[114] D. R. Rhodes, S. Kalyana-Sundaram, V. Mahavisno, T. R. Barrette, D. Ghosh, and A. M. Chinnaiyan. Mining for regulatory programs in the cancer transcriptome. *Nat Genet*, 37(6):579–83, 2005.

[115] G. Rigaill, P. Hupe, A. Almeida, P. La Rosa, J. P. Meyniel, C. Decraene, and E. Barillot. Italics: an algorithm for normalization and DNA copy number calling for affymetrix SNP arrays. *Bioinformatics*, 24(6):768–74, 2008.

[116] M. D. Ritchie. The success of pharmacogenomics in moving genetic association studies from bench to bedside: study design and implementation of precision medicine in the post-GWAS era. *Hum Genet*, 131(10):1615–26, 2012.

[117] A. Roberts, H. Pimentel, C. Trapnell, and L. Pachter. Identification of novel transcripts in annotated genomes using RNA-seq. *Bioinformatics*, 27(17):2325–9, 2011.

[118] M. D. Robinson, D. J. McCarthy, and G. K. Smyth. Edger: a bioconductor package for differential expression analysis of digital gene expression data. *Bioinformatics*, 26(1):139–40, 2010.

[119] H. Sagreiya, C. Berube, A. Wen, R. Ramakrishnan, A. Mir, and A. Hamilton. Extending and evaluating a warfarin dosing algorithm that includes CYP4F2 and pooled rare variants of CYP2C9 20(7): 407–13, 2010). *Pharmacogenetics and Genomics*, 20(10):645, 2010.

[120] S. Sanna, A. U. Jackson, R. Nagaraja, C. J. Willer, W. M. Chen, L. L. Bonnycastle, H. Shen, N. Timpson, G. Lettre, G. Usala, P. S. Chines, H. M. Stringham, L. J. Scott, M. Dei, S. Lai, G. Albai, L. Crisponi, S. Naitza, K. F. Doheny, E. W. Pugh, Y. Ben-Shlomo, S. Ebrahim, D. A. Lawlor, R. N. Bergman, R. M. Watanabe, M. Uda, J. Tuomilehto, J. Coresh, J. N. Hirschhorn, A. R. Shuldiner, D. Schlessinger, F. S. Collins, G. Davey Smith, E. Boerwinkle, A. Cao, M. Boehnke, G. R. Abecasis, and K. L. Mohlke. Common variants in the GDF5-UQCC region are associated with variation in human height. *Nat Genet*, 40(2):198–203, 2008.

[121] A. J. Schetter, S. Y. Leung, J. J. Sohn, K. A. Zanetti, E. D. Bowman, N. Yanaihara, S. T. Yuen, T. L. Chan, D. L. Kwong, G. K. Au, C. G. Liu, G. A. Calin, C. M. Croce, and C. C. Harris. Microrna expression profiles associated with prognosis and therapeutic outcome in colon adenocarcinoma. *JAMA*, 299(4):425–36, 2008.

[122] P. Shannon, A. Markiel, O. Ozier, N. S. Baliga, J. T. Wang, D. Ramage, N. Amin, B. Schwikowski, and T. Ideker. Cytoscape: a software environment for integrated models of biomolecular interaction networks. *Genome Res*, 13(11):2498–504, 2003.

[123] K. Shedden, J. M. Taylor, S. A. Enkemann, M. S. Tsao, T. J. Yeatman, W. L. Gerald, S. Eschrich, I. Jurisica, T. J. Giordano, D. E. Misek, A. C. Chang, C. Q. Zhu, D. Strumpf, S. Hanash, F. A. Shepherd, K. Ding, L. Seymour, K. Naoki, N. Pennell, B. Weir, R. Verhaak, C. Ladd-Acosta, T. Golub, M. Gruidl, A. Sharma, J. Szoke, M. Zakowski, V. Rusch, M. Kris, A. Viale, N. Motoi, W. Travis, B. Conley, V. E. Seshan, M. Meyerson, R. Kuick, K. K. Dobbin, T. Lively, J. W. Jacobson, and D. G. Beer. Gene expression-based survival prediction in lung adenocarcinoma: a multi-site, blinded validation study. *Nat Med*, 14(8):822–7, 2008.

[124] D. F. Simola and J. Kim. Sniper: improved SNP discovery by multiply mapping deep sequenced reads. *Genome Biol*, 12(6):R55, 2011.

[125] E. A. Slodkowska and J. S. Ross. Mammaprint 70-gene signature: another milestone in personalized medical care for breast cancer patients. *Expert Rev Mol Diagn*, 9(5):417–22, 2009.

[126] E. M. Smigielski, K. Sirotkin, M. Ward, and S. T. Sherry. dbSNP: a database of single nucleotide polymorphisms. *Nucleic Acids Res*, 28(1):352–5, 2000.

[127] G. K. Smyth. Linear models and empirical bayes methods for assessing differential expression in microarray experiments. *Stat Appl Genet Mol Biol*, 3:Article3, 2004.

[128] F. Sohler, D. Hanisch, and R. Zimmer. New methods for joint analysis of biological networks and expression data. *Bioinformatics*, 20(10):1517–21, 2004.

[129] P. Stafford. *Methods in Microarray Normalization*. CRC Press, 2007.

[130] A. Subramanian, P. Tamayo, V. K. Mootha, S. Mukherjee, B. L. Ebert, M. A. Gillette, A. Paulovich, S. L. Pomeroy, T. R. Golub, E. S. Lander, and J. P. Mesirov. Gene set enrichment analysis: a knowledge-based approach for interpreting genome-wide expression profiles. *Proceedings of the National Academy of Sciences of the United States of America*, 102(43):15545–15550, 2005.

[131] R. Sun, M. I. Love, T. Zemojtel, A. K. Emde, H. R. Chung, M. Vingron, and S. A. Haas. Breakpointer: using local mapping artifacts to support sequence breakpoint discovery from single-end reads. *Bioinformatics*, 28(7):1024–5, 2012.

[132] N. Tiffin, J. F. Kelso, A. R. Powell, H. Pan, V. B. Bajic, and W. A. Hide. Integration of text- and data-mining using ontologies successfully selects disease gene candidates. *Nucleic Acids Res*, 33(5):1544–52, 2005.

[133] T. J. Treangen and S. L. Salzberg. Repetitive DNA and next-generation sequencing: computational challenges and solutions. *Nat Rev Genet*, 13(1):36–46, 2012.

[134] V. G. Tusher, R. Tibshirani, and G. Chu. Significance analysis of microarrays applied to the ionizing radiation response. *Proc Natl Acad Sci U S A*, 98(9):5116–21, 2001.

[135] O. Vanunu, O. Magger, E. Ruppin, T. Shlomi, and R. Sharan. Associating genes and protein complexes with disease via network propagation. *PLoS Comput Biol*, 6(1):e1000641, 2010.

[136] B. Vogelstein, N. Papadopoulos, V. E. Velculescu, S. Zhou, J. Diaz, L. A., and K. W. Kinzler. Cancer genome landscapes. *Science*, 339(6127):1546–58, 2013.

[137] J. Wang, C. G. Mullighan, J. Easton, S. Roberts, S. L. Heatley, J. Ma, M. C. Rusch, K. Chen, C. C. Harris, L. Ding, L. Holmfeldt, D. Payne-Turner, X. Fan, L. Wei, D. Zhao, J. C. Obenauer, C. Naeve, E. R. Mardis, R. K. Wilson, J. R. Downing, and J. Zhang. Crest maps somatic structural variation in cancer genomes with base-pair resolution. *Nat Methods*, 8(8):652–4, 2011.

[138] Z. Wang, M. Gerstein, and M. Snyder. RNA-seq: a revolutionary tool for transcriptomics. *Nat Rev Genet*, 10(1):57–63, 2009.

[139] J. Wetzel, C. Kingsford, and M. Pop. Assessing the benefits of using mate-pairs to resolve repeats in de novo short-read prokaryotic assemblies. *BMC Bioinformatics*, 12:95, 2011.

[140] C. J. Willer, S. Sanna, A. U. Jackson, A. Scuteri, L. L. Bonnycastle, R. Clarke, S. C. Heath, N. J. Timpson, S. S. Najjar, H. M. Stringham, J. Strait, W. L. Duren, A. Maschio, F. Busonero, A. Mulas, G. Albai, A. J. Swift, M. A. Morken, N. Narisu, D. Bennett, S. Parish, H. Shen, P. Galan, P. Meneton, S. Hercberg, D. Zelenika, W. M. Chen, Y. Li, L. J. Scott, P. A. Scheet, J. Sundvall, R. M. Watanabe, R. Nagaraja, S. Ebrahim, D. A. Lawlor, Y. Ben-Shlomo, G. Davey-Smith, A. R. Shuldiner, R. Collins, R. N. Bergman, M. Uda, J. Tuomilehto, A. Cao, F. S. Collins, E. Lakatta, G. M. Lathrop, M. Boehnke, D. Schlessinger, K. L. Mohlke, and

G. R. Abecasis. Newly identified loci that influence lipid concentrations and risk of coronary artery disease. *Nat Genet*, 40(2):161–9, 2008.

[141] G. W. Wright and R. M. Simon. A random variance model for detection of differential gene expression in small microarray experiments. *Bioinformatics*, 19(18):2448–55, 2003.

[142] S. K. Wyman, R. K. Parkin, P. S. Mitchell, B. R. Fritz, K. O'Briant, A. K. Godwin, N. Urban, C. W. Drescher, B. S. Knudsen, and M. Tewari. Repertoire of micrornas in epithelial ovarian cancer as determined by next generation sequencing of small RNA cDNA libraries. *PLoS One*, 4(4):e5311, 2009.

[143] T. Yamada, I. Letunic, S. Okuda, M. Kanehisa, and P. Bork. ipath2.0: interactive pathway explorer. *Nucleic Acids Res*, 39(Web Server issue):W412–5, 2011.

[144] N. Yanaihara, N. Caplen, E. Bowman, M. Seike, K. Kumamoto, M. Yi, R. M. Stephens, A. Okamoto, J. Yokota, T. Tanaka, G. A. Calin, C. G. Liu, C. M. Croce, and C. C. Harris. Unique microRNA molecular profiles in lung cancer diagnosis and prognosis. *Cancer Cell*, 9(3):189–98, 2006.

[145] F. Zambelli, G. Pesole, and G. Pavesi. Pscan: finding over-represented transcription factor binding site motifs in sequences from co-regulated or co-expressed genes. *Nucleic Acids Res*, 37(Web Server issue):W247–52, 2009.

Chapter 7

Natural Language Processing and Data Mining for Clinical Text

Kalpana Raja
Department of Preventive Medicine
Feinberg School of Medicine
Northwestern University
Chicago, IL
kalpana.raja@northwestern.edu

Siddhartha R. Jonnalagadda
Department of Preventive Medicine
Feinberg School of Medicine
Northwestern University
Chicago, IL
sid@northwestern.edu

7.1 Introduction

Electronic health records (EHR) of patients are major sources of clinical information that are critical to improvement of health care processes. Automated approach for retrieving information from these records is highly challenging due to the complexity involved in converting clinical text that is available in free-text to a structured format. Natural language processing (NLP) and data mining techniques are capable of processing a large volume of clinical text (textual patient reports) to automatically encode clinical information in a timely manner. This chapter focuses on these techniques that map clinical information available in the clinical text to a structured form.

Advancement in health care relies on the integration, organization, and utilization of the huge amount of available genomic, pharmacological, and clinical information. The EHR with clinical information such as laboratory results, discharge diagnoses, pharmacy orders, etc., in a structured or coded form and the clinical data architecture (CDA), an XML standardized model for patient records further contribute to substantial improvements in health care [26]. The clinical information in EHR and CDA is the primary source on medical history of patients that is normally expressed using natural language. A major challenge in processing the clinical information is to deal with the massive increase in knowledge available in EHR and CDA.

The clinical information in EHR and CDA is commonly available in narrative form from the transcription of dictations, direct entry by providers, or use of speech recognition applications. However, manual encoding of this free-text form on a broad range of clinical information is too costly and time consuming, though it is limited to primary and secondary diagnoses, and procedures for billing purposes. Once the clinical information is encoded and made available as a structured data, there is a possibility to develop a wide range of automated high throughput clinical applications to support clinicians' information needs [70]. NLP (also called as medical language processing (MLP) in the medical domain) is accepted as a potential technology for mining the clinical information by the Institute of Medicine. The Institute of Medical Report, 2003 (`www.acmq.org/education/iomsummary.pdf`) defines NLP as a new level of functionality for health care applications that would not be otherwise possible. It provides automated methods with linguistic knowledge to improve the management of information in clinical text. The methods are capable of processing a large volume of clinical text (textual patient reports) to automatically encode the clinical information in a timely manner.

NLP application in the biomedical domain can be classified into two categories, namely biomedical text and clinical text. The text in natural language appearing in books, articles, literature abstracts, and posters is termed as biomedical text. Conversely, clinical text refers to reports written by the clinicians for describing patients, their pathologies, personal, social, and medical histories, findings made during interviews or procedures, and so on. The clinical text is the most abundant data type available for patients' medical history. Generally, the clinical text is written in clinical settings that either could be very short (e.g., a chief complaint) or quite long (a medical student history and physical). The processing of clinical text using NLP methods is more challenging when compared to the processing of biomedical text for several reasons: (1) clinical text are sometimes ungrammatical with short and telegraphic phrases; (2) text such as discharge summary are often dictated; (3) text related to progress notes are written mainly for documentation purposes and contain shorthand lexicons such as abbreviations, acronyms, and local dialectal phrases; (4) text may contain misspelled clinical terms especially when spell support is not available; (5) presence of alphabets other than English alphabets especially in prescriptions; (6) text is intentionally made as a structured template or pseudo table [59]. All these issues have a direct impact on the straightforward NLP tasks such as shallow or full parsing, sentence segmentation, text categorization, etc., thus making the clinical text processing highly challenging.

The data mining from free-text is a subfield of biomedical NLP that concerns directly with the extraction of information from the clinical text. The technique is meant to capture the information from the clinical records of a patient to make it available in a more structured form for various administrative processes and the delivery of care [62, 95]. The Cross Industry Standard Process for Data Mining (CRISP-DM) model offers a framework of six phases in which the order of phases is not fixed and the process is iterative: (1) business understanding phase concerns with the importance of patients' safety; (2) data understanding phase deals with the initial data collection and extends with the identification of data quality and data privacy/security problems; (3) data preparation phase is responsible for the extraction of relevant data and data quality assurance; (4) data modeling phase focuses on the knowledge discovery effort and consists of the construction of models using a variety of techniques; (5) evaluation phase with classification matrices and overall accuracy, sensitivity, and specificity; and finally (6) deploy phase [87].

Many approaches ranging from pattern-based matching [3], statistical and machine learning (ML) models [45] and graph-based methods [105] have been developed for extracting information from the vast amount of data available in the clinical text. The preliminary preprocessing task deals with spell checking, word sense disambiguation (WSD), and part of speech (POS) tag. The contextual feature detection and analysis task involves in the processing of important contextual information including negation (e.g., "denies the pain in the joints"), temporality (e.g., "...swelling in pancreas 4 months ago..."), and the event subject identification (e.g., "his grandfather had tuberculosis"). The extracted information can be linked to concepts in standard terminologies and used for coding as well as decision support to enrich EHR.

A wide range of NLP systems have been developed in the last decade for mining information available in the clinical text in natural language. Such systems convert the unstructured text into a structured form by applying a set of theories and technologies for successful realistic clinical applications including clinical decision support (CDS), surveillance of infectious diseases, research studies, automated encoding, quality assurance, indexing patient records, and tools for billing. Currently, NLP systems for clinical text are intended to process patients records to: (1) index or categorize reports, (2) extract, structure, and codify clinical information in the reports so that the information can be used by other computerized applications, (3) generate text to produce patient profiles or summaries, and (4) improve interfaces to health care systems [70].

This chapter will first focus on NLP and data mining techniques for extracting information from the clinical text and then describe the challenges in processing clinical reports along with the brief description of currently available clinical applications. We introduce natural language processing in Section 7.2 and further describe analyzers and core components of NLP. We explain about mining information from the clinical text in Section 7.3 with descriptions on information extraction and its tasks such as text preprocessing, context-based extraction, and extraction codes. We further focus on current methodologies, clinical corpora, and evaluation metrics available for mining clinical text. Additionally, the section provides an overview on contributions of Informatics for Integrating Biology and Bedside (i2b2) to clinical text processing and mining. In Section 7.4 we discuss various challenges involved in processing clinical text. Section 7.5 presents a discussion on clinical applications by addressing three most important areas applying the methodologies of clinical text mining.

Finally, in Section 7.6 we briefly talk about the applications of NLP and data mining techniques on clinical text.

7.2 Natural Language Processing

NLP emerges from two major disciplines: *Linguistics*, which focuses on the formal and structural models of the language, and *Computer Science*, which is concerned with the internal representations of data and efficient processing of the structures. NLP is often considered as a subfield of artificial intelligence (AI) [23]. *The Encyclopedia of AI* describes NLP as the formulation and investigation of computationally effective mechanisms for communication through natural language [107]. The term natural language is self-explanatory and related to any language used by human other than the programming languages and data representation languages used by the computers. The research in NLP focuses on building computational models for understanding natural language by combining the related techniques such as named entity recognition (NER), relation/event extraction, and data mining.

7.2.1 Description

Many problems within NLP apply for both generating and understanding the language; for example, a computer must be able to model morphology (the structure of words) in order to understand a sentence, and a model of morphology is also needed for producing a grammatically correct English sentence, i.e., natural language generator [3]. Research in NLP for clinical domain makes the computers to understand the free-form clinical text for automatic extraction of clinical information. The general aims of clinical NLP understandings include the theoretical investigation of human language to explore the details of language from computer implementation point of view and the more natural man-machine communications that aims at producing practical automated system.

Among the various approaches to NLP for clinical text, the syntactic and semantic language knowledge combined with the heuristic domain knowledge is the most commonly used method. The input for a NLP system is the unstructured natural text from a patient's medical record that is given to a report analyzer to identify segments and to handle textual irregularities such as tables, domain specific abbreviations, and missing punctuation. The core of the NLP engine is the text analyzer that uses the syntactic and semantic knowledge associated with the domain knowledge to extract information. In text analyzer a syntactic and semantic interpreter captures the respective details and generates a deeper structure such as a constituent tree or dependency tree. The conversion rules or ML algorithms accept this deep structure and encode the clinical information to make it compatible for the database storage. The database handler and inference rules work to generate a processed form from the storage point of view. The stored data in a structured format may be used by an automated clinical application. Figure 7.1 depicts the general workflow of a NLP system for the clinical text.

7.2.2 Report Analyzer

The clinical text differs from the biomedical text with the possible use of pseudo tables, i.e., natural text formatted to appear as tables, medical abbreviations, and punctuation in addition to the natural language. The text is normally dictated and transcribed to a person or speech recognition software and is usually available in free-text format. Some clinical texts are even available in the image or graph format [29]. In general, each type of clinical text serves a specific purpose to impose a semantic template on the information present in the text. For example, the radiology report is

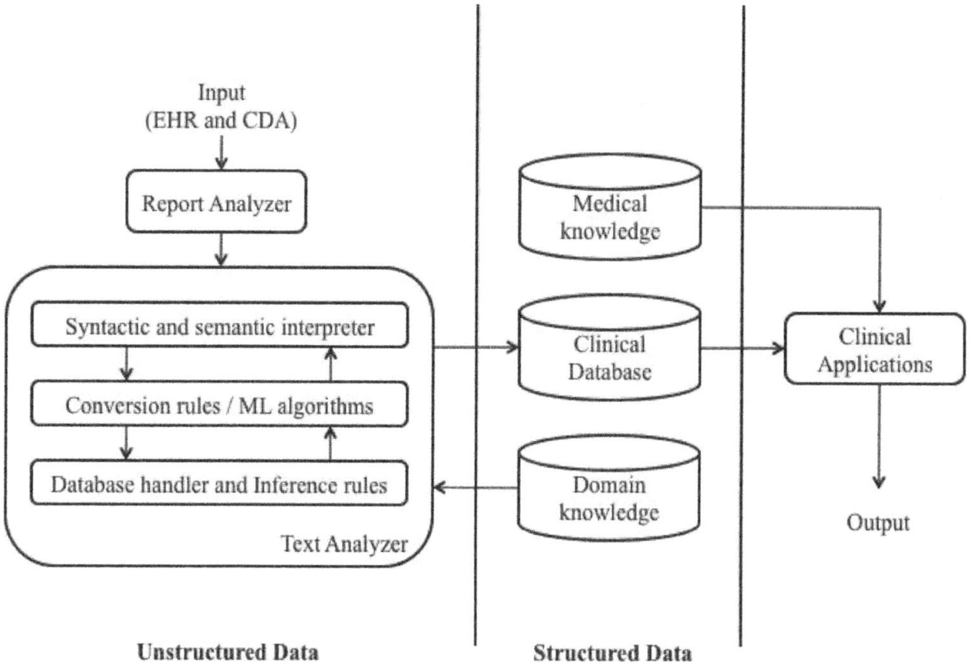

FIGURE 7.1: General workflow of a NLP system.

a primary means of communication between a radiologist and the referring physician. However, the data is required to be in a structured format for the purposes of research, quality assessment, interoperability, and decision support systems. As a result, NLP processing techniques are applied to convert the unstructured free-text into a structured format. Numerous NLP applications require preprocessing of the input text prior to the analysis of information available. The first and foremost task of report analyzer is to preprocess the clinical input text by applying NLP methodologies. The major preprocessing tasks in a clinical NLP include text segmentation, text irregularities handling, domain specific abbreviation, and missing punctuations [81].

7.2.3 Text Analyzer

Text analyzer is the most important module in clinical text processing that extracts the clinical information from free-text and makes it compatible for database storage. The analyzer is meant to perform an automatic structuring of clinical data into predefined sections in addition to text processing and extraction of clinical information [29]. An initial preprocessing of the text is necessary to map the medical concepts in narrative text to an unstructured information management architecture (UMLS) Metathesaurus [12]. The UMLS (`http://uima.apache.org`) is the most commonly employed application for a concept extraction pipeline. The components in the pipeline are tokenization, lexical normalization, UMLS Metathesaurus look-up, and concept screening and medical subject heading (MeSH) conversion [47] as described below:

- Tokenization component splits query into multiple tokens.

- Lexical normalization component converts words to their canonical form.
- UMLS Metathesaurus look-up for concept screening.
- Semantic grouping of UMLS concepts.
- Mapping of the screened concepts to MeSH headings.

The syntactic and semantic interpreter component of the text analyzer generates a deeper structure such as constituent or dependency tree structures to capture the clinical information present in the text. While each of these tree structures have marked advantages in processing the free-form text, a combination of tree structures with ML algorithms such as support vector machines (SVM) and word sequence kernels achieves high effectiveness [75]. The conversion rules or ML algorithms encode the clinical information from the deep tree structures. An advantage of the rule-based approach is that the predefined patterns are expert-curated and are highly specific. However, the sensitivity of the rule-based approach is usually low because of the incompleteness of the rules. The rule set or pattern templates are therefore not always applicable to other data they are not developed for [3]. One alternative to this limitation is to develop more sophisticated ML approaches for encoding information from clinical text. However, the requirement of a gold-standard training dataset is a constraint in ML algorithms [51]. The database handler and inference rules component generates a processed form of data from the database storage.

7.2.4 Core NLP Components

Research in NLP for clinical domain makes the computers understand the free-form clinical text for automatic extraction of clinical information. The general aims of clinical NLP understandings include the theoretical investigation of human language to explore the details of language from computer implementation point of view and the more natural man-machine communications that aims at producing a practical automated system. Due to the complex nature of the clinical text, the analysis is carried out in many phases such as morphological analysis, lexical analysis, syntactic analysis, semantic analysis, and data encoding (Figure 7.2).

7.2.4.1 Morphological Analysis

This is the process of converting a sentence into a sequence of tokens that are mapped to their canonical base form (e.g., cures = cure + s). This is the first stage of processing the input text in most of the NLP systems to reduce the number of words/tokens needed for the lexical analysis. An alternate approach is to implement a POS tagger to identify syntactic POS of the words and possibly their canonical forms.

7.2.4.2 Lexical Analysis

The words or phrases in the text are mapped to the relevant linguistic information such as syntactic information, i.e., noun, verb, adverb, etc., and semantic information i.e., disease, procedure, body part, etc. Lexical analysis is achieved with a special dictionary called a lexicon, which provides the necessary rules and data for carrying out the linguistic mapping. The development of maintenance of a lexicon requires extensive knowledge engineering and effort to develop and maintain. The National Library of Medicine (NLM) maintains the Specialist Lexicon [13] with comprehensive syntactic information associated with both medical and English terms.

7.2.4.3 Syntactic Analysis

The word "syntax" refers to the study of formal relationships between words in the text. The grammatical knowledge and parsing techniques are the major key elements to perform syntactic

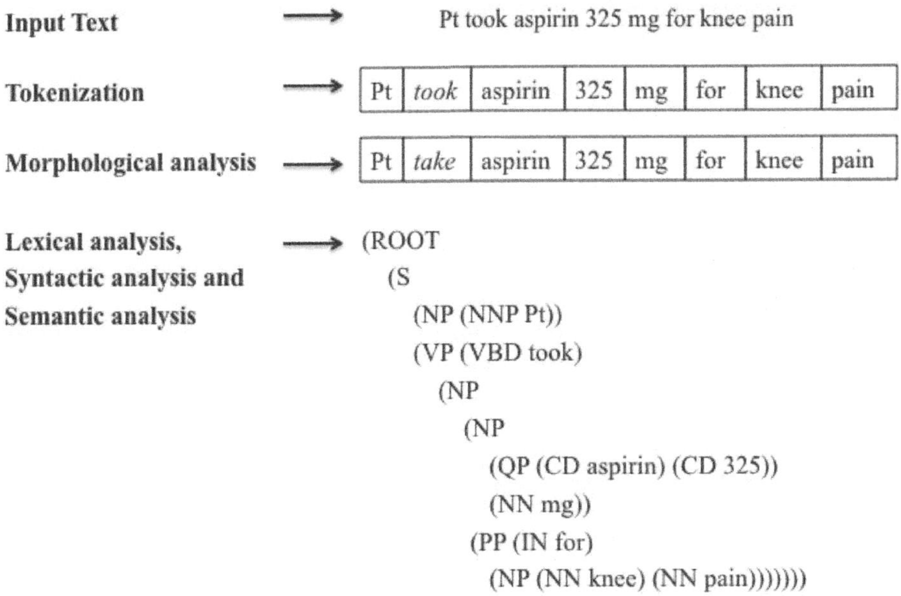

FIGURE 7.2: Core NLP components.

analysis. The context free grammar (CFG) is the most common grammar used for syntactic analysis. CFG is also known by various other terms including phrase structure grammar (PSG) and definite clause grammar (DCG). The syntactic analysis is done by using two basic parsing techniques called top-down parsing and bottom-up parsing to assign POS tags (e.g., noun, verb, adjective, etc.) to the sequence of tokens that form a sentence and to determine the structure of the sentence through parsing tools.

7.2.4.4 Semantic Analysis

It determines the words or phrases in the text that are clinically relevant, and extracts their semantic relations. The natural language semantics consists of two major features: (1) the representation of the meanings of a sentence, which can allow the possible manipulations (particularly inference) and (2) relating these representations to the part of the linguistic model that deals with the structure (grammar or syntax). The semantic analysis uses the semantic model of the domain or ontology to structure and encodes the information from the clinical text. The semantic model is either frame oriented [83] or conceptual graphs [9]. The generated structured output of the semantic analysis is subsequently used by other automated processes.

7.2.4.5 Data Encoding

The process of mining information from EHR requires coding of data that is achieved either manually or by using NLP techniques to map free-text entries with an appropriate code. The coded data is classified and standardized for storage and retrieval purposes in clinical research. Manual coding is normally facilitated with search engines or pick-up list [99]. NLP techniques make use of a wide range of available medical vocabularies such as ICD-10-CM [8], SNOMED [100], UMLS [78, 35], and even locally developed vocabularies [103]. The automatic ending of clinical text concepts to a standardized vocabulary is an area of interest for many NLP research teams.

7.3 Mining Information from Clinical Text

Clinical text mining is an interdisciplinary area of research requiring knowledge and skills in computer science, engineering, computational linguistics, and health science. It is a subfield of biomedical NLP to determine classes of information found in clinical text that are useful for basic biological scientists and clinicians for providing better health care [19]. Text mining and data mining techniques to uncover the information on health, disease, and treatment response support the electronically stored details of patients' health records. A significant chunk of information in EHR and CDA are text and extraction of such information by conventional data mining methods is not possible. The semi-structured and unstructured data in the clinical text and even certain categories of test results such as echocardiograms and radiology reports can be mined for information by utilizing both data mining and text mining techniques.

7.3.1 Information Extraction

Information extraction (IE) is a specialized field of NLP for extracting predefined types of information from the natural text. It is defined as the process of discovering and extracting knowledge from the unstructured text [40]. IE differs from information retrieval (IR) that is meant to be for identifying and retrieving relevant documents. In general, IR returns documents and IE returns information or facts. A typical IE system for the clinical domain is a combination of components such as tokenizer, sentence boundary detector, POS tagger, morphological analyzer, shallow parser, deep parser (optional), gazetteer, named entity recognizer, discourse module, template extractor, and template combiner. A careful modeling of relevant attributes with templates is required for the performance of high level components such as discourse module, template extractor, and template combiner. The high level components always depend on the performance of the low level modules such as POS tagger, named entity recognizer, etc. [41].

IE for clinical domain is meant for the extraction of information present in the clinical text. The Linguistic String Project–Medical Language Processor (LSP–MLP) [83], and Medical Language Extraction and Encoding system (MedLEE) [42] are the commonly adopted systems to extract UMLS concepts from clinical text. The Mayo clinical Text Analysis and Knowledge Extraction System (cTAKES) [85], Special Purpose Radiology Understanding System (SPRUS) [33], SymText (Symbolic Text Processor) [39], and SPECIALIST language-processing system [66] are the major systems developed by few dedicated research groups for maintaining the extracted information in the clinical domain. Other important systems widely used in the clinical domain are MetaMap [6], IndexFinder [106], and KnowledgeMap [24]. Among all, MetaMap is found to be useful with patients' EHR for automatically providing relevant health information. MetaMap and its Java version MMTx (MetaMap Transfer) were developed by the US NLM to index text or to map concepts in the analyzed text with UMLS concepts. Furthermore, NLP systems such as Lexical Tools and MetaMap [6] use UMLS with many other applications. Table 7.1 shows the major clinical NLP systems available along with their purpose and contents.

The researchers in the clinical NLP domain have contributed a wide range of methodologies for extracting information from the unstructured text. The simplest approach is the rule-based or

TABLE 7.1: Major Clinical NLP Systems

Clinical NLP system	Purpose
LSP-MLP	NLP system for extraction and summarization of signs/symptoms and drug information, and identification of possible medication and side effects
MedLEE	A semantically driven system used for (1) extracting information from clinical narrative reports, (2) participating in an automated decision-support system, and (3) allowing NLP queries
cTAKES	Mayo clinical Text Analysis and Knowledge Extraction System
SPRUS	A semantically driven IE system
SymText	NLP system with syntactic and probabilistic semantic analysis driven by Bayesian Networks
SPECIALIST	A part of UMLS project with SPECIALIST lexicon, semantic network, and UMLS Metathesaurus
IndexFinder	A method for extracting key concepts from clinical text for indexing
KnowledgeMap	A full-featured content management system to enhance the delivery of medical education contents
Lexical Tools	A set of fundamental core NLP tools for retrieving inflectional variants, uninflectional forms, spelling variants, derivational variants, synonyms, fruitful variants, normalization, UTF-8 to ASCII conversion, and many more
MetaMap	A highly configurable program to map biomedical text to UMLS Metathesaurus concepts

pattern-matching method that involves a set of predefined rules or patterns over a variety of structures such as text strings, POS tags, semantic pairs, and dictionary entries [77]. The rule-based or pattern-matching methods tend to give high precision and low recall for the specific domain they are generated. However, the main disadvantage of this approach is the lack of generalizability for other domains they are not developed for. The next well-known method for extracting information is with shallow or deep syntactic parsing of the natural text to generate a constituent or dependent tree that is further processed to extract specific information. The highly sophisticated ML approaches have been proven to produce remarkable results in clinical NLP with high recall and low precision scores. Unlike the rule-based or pattern-matching methods, ML approaches are applicable for other domains without much modification. Conversely, ML approaches require annotated corpora of relatively bigger size for training and the development of such a corpora is expensive, time consuming, and requires domain experts for manual verification. Apart from the approaches discussed, clinical NLP includes specific methods that are meant for the clinical text: the ontology-based IE method for free-text processing and a combination of syntactic and semantic parsing approach for processing the medical language [37]. A well-known fact is that the processing and extraction of information from the clinical text is still lagging behind when compared to general and biomedical text because of the following reasons: (1) limited access to clinical data as the patient's medical history is protected confidentially, (2) challenges involved in creating large volume of shared data, tasks, annotation guidelines, annotations, and evaluation techniques [70].

7.3.1.1 Preprocessing

The primary source of information in the clinical domain is the clinical text written in natural language. However, the rich contents of the clinical text are not immediately accessible by the clinical application systems that require input in a more structured form. An initial module adopted by various clinical NLP systems to extract information is the preliminary preprocessing of the unstructured text to make it available for further processing. The most commonly used preprocessing techniques in clinical NLP are spell checking, word sense disambiguation, POS tagging, and shallow and deep parsing [74].

Spell Checking
The misspelling in clinical text is reported to be much higher than any other types of texts. In addition to the traditional spell checker, various research groups have come out with a variety of methods for spell checking in the clinical domain: UMLS-based spell-checking error correction tool [93] and morpho-syntactic disambiguation tools [82].

Word Sense Disambiguation
The process of understanding the sense of the word in a specific context is termed as word sense disambiguation. The supervised ML classifiers [102] and the unsupervised approaches [59] automatically perform the word sense disambiguation for biomedical terms.

POS Tagging
An important preprocessing step adapted by most of the NLP systems is POS tagging that reads the text and assigns the parts of speech tag to each word or token of the text. POS tagging is the annotation of words in the text to their appropriate POS tags by considering the related and adjacent words in a phrase, sentence, and paragraph. POS tagging is the first step in syntactic analysis and finds its application in IR, IE, word sense disambiguation, etc. POS tags are a set of word-categories based on the role that words may play in the sentence in which they appear. The most common set contains seven different tags: Article, Noun, Verb, Adjective, Preposition, Number, and Proper Noun. A much more elaborated set of tags is provided by complete Brown Corpus tag-set (`www.hit.uib.no/icame/brown/bcm.html`) with eighty seven basic tags and Penn Treebank tag-set (`www.cis.upenn.edu/treebank`) with forty five tags. Table 7.2 lists a complete tag set used in most of the IE systems.

Shallow and Deep Parsing
Parsing is the process of determining the complete syntactic structure of a sentence or a string of symbols in a language. Parser is a tool that converts an input sentence into an abstract syntax tree such as the constituent tree and dependency tree, whose leafs correspond to the words of the given sentence and the internal nodes represent the grammatical tags such as noun, verb, noun phrase, verb phrase, etc. Most of the parsers apply ML approaches such as PCFGs (probabilistic context-free grammars) as in the Stanford lexical parser [50] and even maximum entropy and neural network. Few parsers even use lexical statistics by considering the words and their POS tags. Such taggers are well known for overfitting problems that require additional smoothing.

An alternative to the overfitting problem is to apply shallow parsing, which splits the text into nonoverlapping word sequences or phrases, such that syntactically related words are grouped together. The word phrase represents the predefined grammatical tags such as noun phrase, verb phrase, prepositional phrase, adverb phrase, subordinated clause, adjective phrase, conjunction phrase, and list marker [86]. The benefits of shallow parsing are the speed and robustness of processing. Parsing is generally useful as a preprocessing step in extracting information from the natural text.

TABLE 7.2: List of POS Tags

Tag	Description
$	Dollar
‘	open quotation mark
”	closing quotation mark
(	open parenthesis
)	closed parenthesis
,	comma
–	dash
.	sentence terminator
:	colon or ellipsis
CC	conjunction, coordinating
CD	numeral, cardinal
DT	determiner
EX	existential there
FW	foreign word
IN	preposition or conjunction, subordinating
JJ	adjective or numeral, ordinal
JJR	adjective, comparative
JJS	adjective, superlative
LS	list item marker
MD	model auxiliary
NN	noun, common, singular or mass
NNP	noun, proper, singular
NNPS	noun, proper, plural
NNS	noun, common, plural
PDT	predeterminer
POS	genitive marker
PRP	pronoun, personal
PRP$	pronoun, possessive
RB	adverb
RBR	adverb, comparative
RBS	adverb, superlative
RP	particle
SYM	symbol
TO	to as preposition or infinitive marker
UH	interjection
VB	verb, base form
VBD	verb, past tense
VBG	verb, present participle or gerund
VBN	verb, past participle
VBP	verb, present tense, not 3rd person singular
VBZ	verb, present tense, 3rd person singular
WDT	WH-determiner
WP	WH-pronoun
WP$	WH-pronoun, possessive
WRB	WH-adverb

7.3.1.2 Context-Based Extraction

The fundamental step for a clinical NLP system is the recognition of medical words and phrases because these terms represent the concepts specific to the domain of study and make it possible to understand the relations between the identified concepts. Even highly sophisticated systems of clinical NLP include the initial processing of recognizing medical words and phrases prior to the extraction of information of interest. While IE from the medical and clinical text can be carried out in many ways, this section explains the five main modules of IE.

Concept Extraction
Extracting concepts (such as drugs, symptoms, and diagnoses) from clinical narratives constitutes a basic enabling technology to unlock the knowledge within and support more advanced reasoning applications such as diagnosis explanation, disease progression modeling, and intelligent analysis of the effectiveness of treatment. The first and foremost module in clinical NLP following the initial text preprocessing phase is the identification of the boundaries of the medical terms/phrases and understanding the meaning by mapping the identified term/phrase to a unique concept identifier in an appropriate ontology [3]. The recognition of clinical entities can be achieved by a dictionary-based method using the UMLS Metathesaurus, rule-based approaches, statistical method, and hybrid approaches [52]. The identification and extraction of entities present in the clinical text largely depends on the understanding of the context. For example, the recognition of diagnosis and treatment procedures in the clinical text requires the recognition and understanding of the clinical condition as well as the determination of its presence or absence. The contextual features related to clinical NLP are negation (absence of a clinical condition), historicity (the condition had occurred in the recent past and might occur in the future), and experiencer (the condition related to the patient) [15]. While many algorithms are available for context identification and extraction, it is recommended to detect the degree of certainty in the context [23].

A baseline approach to concept extraction typically relies on a dictionary or lexicon of the concepts to be extracted, using string comparison to identify concepts of interest. Clinical narratives contain drug names, anatomical nomenclature, and other specialized names and phrases that are not standard in everyday English such as *"benign positional vertigo," "l shoulder inj," "po pain medications," "a c5-6 acdf," "st changes," "resp status,"* and others. There is also a high incidence of abbreviation usage, and many of the abbreviations have a different meaning in other genres of English. Descriptive expressions (such as coil embolization of bleeding vessel, a large bloody bowel movement, a tagged RBC scan and R intracerebral hemorrhage drainage) are commonly used to refer to concepts rather than using canonical terms. The specialized knowledge requirement and the labor-intensive nature of the task make it difficult to create a lexicon that would include all such expressions, particularly given that their use is often non-standard and varies across institutions and medical specialties, or even from one department to another in the same hospital, rendering dictionary-based approaches less adaptable in this domain [46]. An alternative to the dictionary-based approach is the use of ML methods such as conditional random fields (CRF) [55] and SVM [53] that have achieved excellent performance in concept extraction [11, 2, 65, 80]. Torii et al. studied the portability of ML taggers for concept extraction using the 2010 i2b2/VA Challenge. Furthermore, the authors examined the performance of taggers with the increase in size of the dataset [94]. While supervised ML approaches offer a promising alternative, a reliable system usually needs a large annotated corpus with as many relevant examples as possible. Therefore, clinical corpora generation is emerging as a specific branch of research in clinical NLP for the development of ML approaches.

Association Extraction
Clinical text is the rich source of information on patients' conditions and their treatments with additional information on potential medication allergies, side effects, and even adverse effects. Infor-

TABLE 7.3: Resources for Association Extraction

Resource	Purpose
UMLS Semantic Network	It defines the binary relations between the UMLS semantic types.
MedLEE	System to extract, structure, and encode clinical information in textual patient reports so that the data can be used by subsequent automated processes.
BioMedLEE	System for extracting phenotypic information underlying molecular mechanisms and their relationships.
SemRep	It maps syntactic elements (such as verbs) to predicates in the Semantic Network, such as TREATS and DIAGNOSIS.

mation contained in clinical records is of value for both clinical practice and research; however, text mining from clinical records, particularly from narrative-style fields (such as discharge summaries and progress reports), has proven to be an elusive target for clinical Natural Language Processing (clinical NLP), due in part to the lack of availability of annotated corpora specific to the task. Yet, the extraction of concepts (such as mentions of problems, treatments, and tests) and the association between them from clinical narratives constitutes the basic enabling technology that will unlock the knowledge contained in them and drive more advanced reasoning applications such as diagnosis explanation, disease progression modeling, and intelligent analysis of the effectiveness of treatment [46].

The clinical concepts appearing in the clinical text are related to one another in a number of ways. A better understanding of clinical text is possible through the identification and extraction of meaningful association or relationships between the concepts present in the text. However, the clinical text is not always written in a way that encodes the nature of the semantic relations. The two concepts are not likely to occur together in the same sentence or even in the same section of the clinical text. In other words, the association between the concepts is generally annotated explicitly to match the clinical narratives appearing in the clinical text. One possible approach to annotate the concepts and their association is by using the clinical text with strongly related concepts. However, it may not be possible to determine the exact nature of the association from clinical text. In such cases, the biomedical literature provides a rich source of associated concepts that are confirmed through various research groups (Table 7.3). Thus, the association between the concepts can be annotated by verifying with the association information available in the biomedical literature [61].

When the explicitly stated associations are not available, the association between the concepts is identified through co-occurrence between the two concepts in the same clinical text as the two concepts are not likely to occur together in the same sentence or even section of the note. The association between any pair of UMLS concepts can be calculated with similarity measurements. Mathur et al. [63] used the similarity measure to calculate the similarity between gene and disease. Sahay [84] used the word-level similarity measures offered by UMLS-similarity to provide contextual recommendations relevant to the health information conversation system.

Coreference Resolution

Coreferential expressions are common in clinical narratives and therefore understanding coreference relations plays a critical role in the discourse-level analysis of clinical documents, such as compiling a patient profile. Since the language and description style in clinical documents differ from common English, it is necessary to understand the characteristics of clinical text to properly perform coreference resolution. A comprehensive methodological review of coreference resolution developed for general English can be applied for coreference resolution in the clinical domain [48]. The existing methodologies for coreference resolution are:

1. Heuristics-based approaches based on linguistic theories and rules
2. Supervised machine learning approaches with binary classification of markable mention/entity pairs or classification by ranking markables
3. Unsupervised machine learning approaches, such as nonparametric Bayesian models or expectation maximization clustering.

The heuristics-based approaches are the early attempts for the coreference resolution task to incorporate a knowledge source to prune unlikely antecedent candidates to get the best candidate by employing a multitude of features such syntactic, semantic and pragmatic constraints and preferences [64]. The supervised ML approaches replaced the interest of researchers to use complete heuristics-based systems. The binary classification, ranking, anaphoricity and specialized models are the major methods available for supervised ML approaches [89]. On the other hand, the unsupervised approaches for coreference resolution adopt a fully generative, nonparametric Bayesian model based on hierarchical Dirichlet processes [36].

A multi-pass system that applies tiers of resolution models is applied for coreference analysis. Raghunathan et al. [79] developed a system that applies tiers of resolution models one at a time. Each tier (sieve) consists of similar deterministic rules and builds on outputs of previously applied sieves. On the other hand, Jonnalagadda et al. [48] employed a multi-pass sieve framework to exploit a heuristic-based approach along with a supervised ML method, specifically factorial hidden Markov models (FHMMs). Zheng et al. [104] provide a review of the approaches in the general English and biomedical literature domains and discuss challenges in applying those techniques in the clinical narrative. Furthermore, the 2011 i2b2/VA/Cincinnati challenge focuses on coreferential relations between common, clinically relevant classes in medical text. These classes include problem, treatment, test, person, and pronoun. Coreferring mentions are to be paired together, and the pairs are to be linked to form a chain that represents the entity being referenced. The aim of the challenge is to produce coreferential chains of these mentions at document level (i.e., coreference relations are made across paragraphs or sections within the same document, but not across documents).

Negation

"Negation" is an important context that plays a critical role in extracting information from the clinical text. Many NLP systems incorporate a separate module for negation analysis in text preprocessing [83, 33]. However, the importance of negation identification has gained much of its interest among the NLP research community in recent years. As a result, explicit negation detection systems such as NegExpander [4], Negfinder [73], and a specific system for extracting SNOMED-CT concepts [28] as well as negation identification algorithms such as NegEx [15] that uses regular expression for identifying negation and a hybrid approach based on regular expressions and grammatical parsing are developed by a few of the dedicated research community. While the NegExpander [4] program identifies the negation terms and then expands to the related concepts, Negfinder [73] is a more complex system that uses indexed concepts from UMLS and regular expressions along with a parser using LALR (look-ahead left-recursive) grammar to identify the negations.

Temporality Analysis

Temporal resolution for events and time expressions in clinical notes is crucial for an accurate summary of patient history, better medical treatment, and further clinical study. Discovery of a temporal relation starts with extracting medical events and time information and aims at building a temporal link (TLINK) between events or between events and time expressions. Clinical practice and research would benefit greatly from temporal expression and relation detection. Therefore, temporal expression and relation discovery in clinical NLP are timely and inevitable to improve clinical text mining. A comprehensive temporal information discovery in clinical text requires medical event extraction, time information, and temporal relation identification [88]. Temporal expression extraction is the first step to resolve temporal relations for any advanced natural language applications, such as text summarization, machine translation, and question answering. Several systems are available for extracting temporal expression. GUTime developed by Georgetown University is an extension of the TempEx tagger, which is a temporal tagger based on Perl regular expression. GUTime is now available as part of the TARSQI toolkit [98]. HeidelTime [90] is a rule-based system that is built in a UIMA framework and performed best for SemEval-2 (`http://semeval2.fbk.eu/`). SUTime [108] is also a rule-based system using regular expression and is implemented as one of the annotators in the Stanford CoreNLP pipeline.

The temporality information in clinical text represents the past medical history (e.g., history of congestive heart failure with shortness of left-sided chest pain), hypothetical or non-specific mentions (e.g., advise to patient to report on increased shortness of breath), and temporal course of disease (e.g., the chest pain of the patient is resolved after the administration of digoxin and diuretics). The temporality analysis is much more complicated when compared to negation analysis and an initial investigation for temporal information was carried out on discharge summaries by analyzing the temporal structure followed by the temporal constraint structure [42]. An NLP system called TimeText is available for detecting clinically important temporal relations. The system uses a temporal tagger, MedLEE and a set of postprocessing rules based on medical and linguistic knowledge to process implicit temporal information and uncertainty, and simple temporal constraint satisfaction problem for temporal reasoning [105]. Another temporal analysis system related to the context of the CLEF (Clinical eScience Framework) is used to extract the temporal information for building the patient chronicle to understand an overview of the significant events in the patients' medical history [38]. An interesting approach for temporality analysis uses ML techniques for automatic temporal segmentation and segment ordering with lexical, topical, positional, and syntactic features.

7.3.1.3 Extracting Codes

Extracting codes is a popular approach that uses NLP techniques to extract the codes mapped to controlled sources from clinical text. The most common codes dealing with diagnoses are the International Classification of Diseases (ICD) versions 9 and 10 codes. The ICD is designed to promote international comparability in the collection, processing, classification and presentation of mortality statistics. ICD-10 is the latest revised codes available with coding for diseases, signs and symptoms, abnormal findings, complaints, social circumstances, and external causes of injury (`http://apps.who.int/classifications/icd10/browse/2010/en`). Recently, a clinically modified form of ICD-10 version called ICD-10-CM is developed by the National Center for Health Statistics (NCHS). The entire draft of the tabular list of ICE-10-CM is available on the NCSH website for public comment. The specific clinical modifications incorporated in ICD-10-CM include many resources such as (1) the additional information related to ambulatory and managed care encounters, (2) expanded injury codes, (3) combined diagnosis/symptom codes to reduce the number of codes needed to describe a disease condition, (4) incorporation of common 4th and 5th digit sub-classifications, and (5) laterality and greater specificity in code assignment.

The medical NLP challenge in the year 2007 came out with a shared task exercise with a moderately large test/training corpus of radiology reports and their ICD-9-CM codes. Most of the teams utilized multi-component coding systems for extracting codes from the text. One of the participated group utilized NLM's Medical Text Indexer, a SVM classifier and a k-NN classifier for extracting and arranging the codes in a stack-like architecture [5]. Another team used ML, rule-based system and an automatic coding system based in human coding policies for extracting codes [20]. An interesting overview of ICD-10 encoding task can be found at *Baud 2004* [8].

A comprehensive clinical terminology similar to ICD is the Systematized Nomenclature of Medicine Clinical Terms (SNOMED–CT) that was originally created by the College of Amercian Pathologists (CAP) and distributed by the International Health Terminology Standards Development Organisation (IHTSDO) located in Denmark. It is one of the suites for use in US federal government systems for the electronic exchange of clinical health information. SNOMED CT is a required standard in interoperability specifications of the US Healthcare Information Technology Standards Panel. The SNOMED CT is also implemented as a standard code by many clinical researchers in the area of NLP for clinical text (`http://www.nlm.nih.gov/research/umls/Snomed/snomed_main.html`). In addition to the standard codes such as ICD and SNOMED, a widely adapted clinical NLP system called MedLEE is used as a code extractor in many clinical contexts [32]. Many NLP systems implement MedLEE for extracting the codes: an automated pneumonia severity score coding system [34], an NLP system for neuroradiology standard concept extraction [28], and an approach to code a standard for health and health-related states.

7.3.2 Current Methodologies

NLP as an intersection of artificial intelligence and linguistics was initially distinct from IR. However, NLP and IR have converged to a greater extent in recent years and applied together for indexing and searching large volumes of text. Currently, NLP adopts techniques and methodologies from several, very diverse fields to broaden its applications in various subtasks related to clinical text. Nadkarni et al. [74] describe the sub-tasks of NLP in two groups namely low-level and high-level tasks. According to them the low-level tasks are related to sentence boundary detection, tokenization, part-of-speech tagging, morphological decomposition, shallow parsing, and problem specific segmentations. The high-level tasks are usually problem specific and use the low-level subtasks for building the models. Some of the high-level tasks with wide range of application in NLP are spelling/grammatical error identification and recovery, NER, word sense disambiguation, negation and uncertainty identification, relationship extraction, temporal inferences/relationship extraction, and IE.

The various approaches applied for processing the clinical text range from simple rule-based methods to more sophisticated statistical, symbolic, or grammatical and hybrid approaches. Additionally, many researchers came out with more specific methods for specific NLP problems. Chard et al. [18] describe a system that leverages cloud-based approaches, i.e., virtual machines and representational state transfer (REST) to extract, process, synthesize, mine, compare/contrast, explore, and manage medical text data in a flexibly secure and scalable architecture. Zhou et al. [105] use a simple, efficient ontology-based approach to extract medical terms present in the clinical text. Huang and Lowe [43] present a novel hybrid approach for negation detection by classifying the negations based on the syntactical categories of negation signals and patterns, using regular expression.

7.3.2.1 Rule-Based Approaches

Rule-based approaches rely on a set of rules for possible textual relationships, called patterns, which encode similar structures in expressing relationships. The set of rules are expressed in the form of regular expressions over words or POS tags. In such systems, the rules extend as patterns by adding more constraints to resolve few issues including checking negation of relations and determining direction of relations. The rules are generated in two ways: manually constructed and automatically generated from the training dataset. Extension with additional rules can improve the performance of the rule-based system to a certain extent, but tend to produce much FP information. Thus, the rule-based systems tend to give high precision but low recall because the rules generated for a specific dataset cannot be generalized to other datasets. However, the recall of such systems can be improved by relaxing the constraints or by learning rules automatically from training data.

7.3.2.2 Pattern-Based Algorithms

The second popular approach for extracting information from the clinical text is the pattern-based algorithm. A set of word patterns are coded based on the biomedical entities and their relation keywords to extract special kinds of interactions. These approaches can vary from simple sentence-based extraction to more advanced extraction methods using POS tagging with additional linguistic information. Similar to the rule-based approaches, the patterns defined in any pattern-based system are either manually constructed or automatically generated using suitable algorithms such as bootstrapping. NLP systems based on manually constructed patterns require domain experts to define the related patterns. The concepts knowledge, the list of tokens between these concepts and their POS tags are mandatory to generate more sophisticated patterns. Few systems attempt to define patterns using syntactic analysis of a sentence, such as POS tags and phrasal structure (e.g., noun/verb/preposition phrases). On the whole, manually generated patterns always tend to produce high precision but low recall. Such patterns do not give good performance when applied for a new domain as well as in text with information not matching with any of the defined patterns.

7.3.2.3 Machine Learning Algorithms

Tom Dietterich says that the goal of ML is to build computer systems that can adapt and learn from their experience [25]. It is a type of AI that provides computers with the ability to learn without being explicitly programmed. The subfields of ML include supervised learning, unsupervised learning, semi-supervised learning, reinforcement learning, learning to learn, and developmental learning. In general, any ML system takes a set of input variables $\{x_1, x_2, \ldots x_m\}$ and gives a set of output variables $\{y_1, y_2, \ldots y_n\}$ after learning the hidden patterns $\{h_1, h_2, \ldots h_k\}$ from the input variables (Figure 7.3). ML approaches are not needed when the relationships between all system variables (input, output, and hidden) is completely understood. However, this is not the case in almost all real systems. There is a wide range of ML approaches and successful applications in clinical text mining. Among these, CRF is commonly accepted to perform well for NER and SVM has been proven to be the best classifier by many researchers.

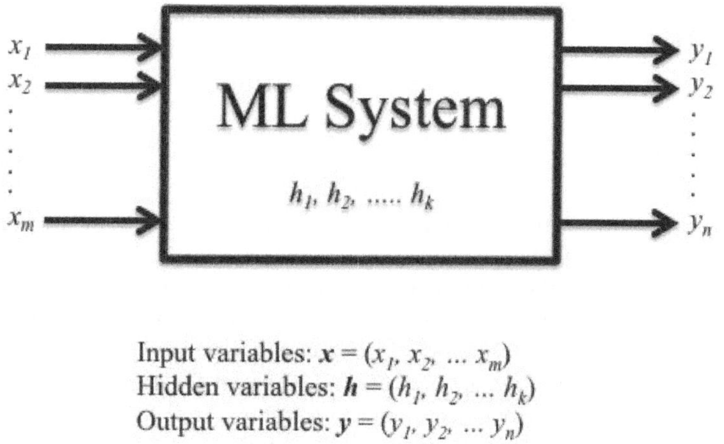

FIGURE 7.3: Block diagram of a generic ML System.

7.3.3 Clinical Text Corpora and Evaluation Metrics

The widespread usage of EHR in hospitals around the world promotes NLP community to create clinical text corpora for the evaluation of automatic language processing. The corpora of clinical text are the high quality gold standards annotated manually with the instances relevant to the specific NLP tasks. The performance of any NLP system depends heavily on the annotated corpus used for training and testing. The corpus for clinical text is developed based on the guidelines for annotation, identifying relevant features to annotate, and on the characterization of usability of the corpus. Albright et al. [1] discuss the task of creating a corpus of layered annotations and developing NLP components for the clinical domain. Their annotation layers include Treebank annotations consisting of POS, phrasal and function tags, and empty categories in the tree structure, PropBank annotations to mark the predicate-argument structure of sentences, and UMLS entities for semantic annotations.

The annotation schema presented by Chapman et al. [16] includes 40 clinical reports for training and 20 for testing, by focusing on the semantic categories of the words that are important. The corpus was later examined on the agreements among annotators after they were trained with the annotation schema. The five qualitative dimensions deciding the usefulness of the corpus in data mining applications are focus, polarity, certainty, evidence, and directionality and developed guidelines on how to annotate sentence fragments [101]. However, the difficulty of the annotation varies considerably depending on the dimension being annotated. The gold standard is used to test the performance and accuracy of the NLP system developed for a specific clinical task, i.e., retrieving a set of relevant documents automatically. The mismatches between the gold standard and system-retrieved document set can be due to system error and semantic disagreement between the original text and annotation. Thus, it is obvious that even the gold standard annotations available are difficult to interpret against the system-generated results due to the complexity of the language [60].

The quality of evaluation is given by three parameters namely, linguistic realism, accuracy, and consistency. Realism refers to the set of well-designed tags to bring the same category of words together, based on their similarity in syntactic distribution, morphological form, and/or semantic interpretation. Accuracy refers to the percentage of correctly tagged words or tokens in the corpus and calculated as precision and recall. Here, precision is the extent to which incorrect annotations are rejected from the output and recall is the extent to which all correct annotations are found in the output of the tagger. In corpus annotation, "correctness" is related to allows and disallows of the annotation scheme that corresponds closely with the linguistic realities recognized. The inter-annotator agreement on manual tagging is defined in terms of a consistency measure to determine the percentage of allows and disallows agreed by the annotators. A more sophisticated measure of inter-annotator consistency is given by kappa coefficient (K) to measure the proportion of assigning tags totally by chance.

$$K = \frac{P(A) - P(E)}{1 - P(E)} \tag{7.1}$$

where $P(A)$ is the proportion of time that the annotators agree and $P(E)$ is the proportion of times that we would expect them to agree by chance [14].

The accuracy of clinical NLP system can be measured with eight standard measures: precision, recall, F-measure, overgeneration, undergeneration, error, accuracy, and fallout [68]. The first three are the most common measures widely adopted in reporting the accuracy of a NLP system and defined as follows: In the accuracy measurement of a NLP system for document retrieval, precision quantifies the fraction of retrieved documents that are in fact relevant, i.e., belong to the target class (Equation 7.2), recall indicates which fraction of the relevant documents is retrieved (Equation 7.3), and F-measure is the harmonic mean of both for measuring the overall performance of classifiers (Equation 7.4). Likewise, the other measures are calculated as shown below: overgeneration as 1-precision (Equation 7.5), undergeneration as 1-recall (Equation 7.6), error (Equation 7.7), accuracy (equation 7.8), and fallout (Equation 7.9). The accuracy measurements are calculated by categorizing the retrieved information as true positive (TP) when the concept is present in the document and found by the system, false positive (FP) when the system finds a concept that is not present in the document, false negative (FN) when the concept present in the document is not found by the system and true negative (TN) when the concept absent in the document is not found by the system.

$$Precision = \frac{TP}{(TP+FP)} \tag{7.2}$$

$$Recall = \frac{TP}{(TP+FN)} \tag{7.3}$$

$$F-measure = \frac{2PR}{(P+R)} \tag{7.4}$$

$$Overgeneration = \frac{FP}{(TP+FP)} \tag{7.5}$$

$$Undergeneration = \frac{FN}{(TP+FN)} \tag{7.6}$$

$$Error = \frac{(FN+FP)}{(TP+FN+FP)} \tag{7.7}$$

$$Accuracy = \frac{(TP+TN)}{(TP+FN+FP+TN)} \tag{7.8}$$

$$Fallout = \frac{FP}{(FP+TN)} \tag{7.9}$$

7.3.4 Informatics for Integrating Biology and the Bedside (i2b2)

The Informatics for Integrating Biology and the Bedside (i2b2) is one among the National Institutes of Health (NIH) funded National Center for Biomedical Computing (NCBC) (`http://www.bisti.nih.gov/ncbc/`) for developing a scalable informatics framework to bridge clinical research data and basic science research data. The integration is helpful for better understanding of the genetic bases of complex diseases and the knowledge facilitates the design of targeted therapies for individual patients with diseases having genetic origins. The i2b2 is intended to serve various groups of clinical users including (1) clinical investigators who are interested to use the software available within i2b2, (2) bioinformatics scientists who wants the ability to customize the flow of data and interactions, and (3) biocomputational software developers who involve in the development of new software capabilities that can be integrated easily into the computing environment [72].

The 2010 i2b2/VA Workshop on Natural Language Processing Challenges for clinical text focused on three major tasks namely, (1) concept extraction task (2) assertion classification task for assigning assertion types for medical problem concepts, and (3) relation classification task for assigning relation types that exist between medical problems, tests, and treatments. Furthermore, i2b2 and VA provided an annotated reference standard corpus for all three tasks. There were 22 systems for concept extraction, 21 for assertion classification, and 16 for relation classification developed and presented in the workshop. The concepts extraction task was considered as an IE task to identify and extract the text corresponding to patient medical problems, treatments, and tests present in the corpus. The assertion classification was expected to classify the assertions made on the concepts as being present, absent or possible, conditionally present in the patient under certain circumstances, hypothetically present in the patient at some future point, and mentioned in the patient report but associated with other patient. The relation classification task was designed to classify relations between pairs of standard concepts present in a sentence. In general, the systems showed that ML approaches could be augmented with rule-based or pattern-based systems in determining the concepts, assertions, and relations [97].

7.4 Challenges of Processing Clinical Reports

The progress in NLP research in the clinical domain is slow and lagging behind when compared to the progress in general NLP due to multiple challenges involved in processing the clinical reports. The challenges to NLP development in the clinical domain are mainly due to the lack of access to shared data, lack of annotated datasets for training and benchmarking, insufficient common conventions and standards for annotations, the formidability of reproducibility, limited collaborations and lack of user-centered development and scalability. Shared tasks such as the i2b2/VA Challenge address such barriers by providing annotated datasets to participants for finding potential solutions [17].

7.4.1 Domain Knowledge

The most important criteria for an NLP researcher who is involved in the development of systems and methodologies for processing clinical reports is to have adequate knowledge in the domain. Many NLP systems are the sound knowledge representation of models for the domain of interest and use the model to achieve a semantic analysis. The primary importance of the domain knowledge arises from the fact that the system output is made available for the healthcare application. Thus, the system is always expected to have adequate recall, precision, and F-measure for the intended clinical application, with the possible adjustment of the performance according to the needs of the application. Interestingly, NLP techniques can be applied to capture the domain knowledge available in the free text. For example, the NLP approach for automated capturing of ontology-related domain knowledge applies a two-phase methodology to extract terms of linguistic representations of concepts in the initial phase followed by the semantic relations extraction [7].

7.4.2 Confidentiality of Clinical Text

A sample of training dataset is required for the development and testing of an NLP system. In a clinical domain, the training dataset is a huge collection of online patient records in textual forms. In the United States, the Health Insurance Portability and Accountability Act (HIPAA) protects the confidentiality of patient data. De-identification of personal information is necessary in order to make the records accessible for research purposes. However, automatic detection of identifying information such as names, addresses, phone numbers, etc. is a highly challenging task that often requires a manual review [91]. There are eighteen personal information identifiers, i.e., protected health information (PHI), in the clinical text required to be de-identified and found to be both time consuming and difficult to exclude as required by HIPAA [27]. Table 7.4 shows the list of PHI related to the clinical text.

The i2b2 de-identification challenge in 2006 took the largest effort to develop and evaluate automated de-identification tasks [21]. The approaches available for the de-identification include: (1) rule-based methods, which make use of dictionaries and manually crafted rules to match PHI patterns [71, 31], (2) machine learning methods, which automatically learn to detect PHI patterns based on training datasets [25, 92, 10], and (3) hybrid methods, which combine both the methods [96, 69].

7.4.3 Abbreviations

The clinical text is expected to contain many abbreviations related to the medical domain. The abbreviations are often interpreted easily by health care professionals based on their domain knowledge. However, abbreviations are found to be highly ambiguous when a clinical NLP system at-

TABLE 7.4: PHI Identifiers Related to Confidentiality of Clinical Text

PHI identifiers
1. Name of the patient
2. All geographical identifiers smaller than a state except for the initial three digits of a zip code
3. Dates (other than year)
4. Phone numbers
5. Fax numbers
6. Email addresses
7. Social Security numbers (SSN)
8. Medical record numbers
9. Health insurance beneficiary numbers
10. Account numbers
11. Certificate/license numbers
12. Vehicle identifiers and serial numbers
13. Device identifiers and serial numbers
14. Web URLs
15. Internet Protocol (IP) address numbers
16. Biometric identifiers, including finger, retinal, and voice prints
17. Full face photographic images/any comparable images
18. Any other unique identifying numbers, characteristics, or codes except for the unique codes assigned by the investigator to code the data

tempts to extract clinical information from the free-text. For example, the abbreviation PT in the clinical text could mean a patient, prothrombin, physical therapy, etc. The correct interpretation of clinical abbreviations is often challenging and involves two major tasks: detecting abbreviations and choosing the correct expanded forms. The most commonly employed methods for detecting abbreviations in the clinical domain are dictionary lookup and morphology-based matching and for choosing the correct expanded form is with machine-learning approaches. Researchers have contributed several methods to identify abbreviations present in the clinical texts, construct a clinical abbreviation knowledge base, and disambiguate ambiguous abbreviations [49]. Furthermore, the clinical NLP systems such as MedLEE, MetaMap, etc., are developed to extract medical concepts and related abbreviations from the clinical texts.

7.4.4 Diverse Formats

There is no standardized format for the clinical text, especially with the medical reports of patients: (1) The clinical text often contains the information in free-text format and as a pseudo table, i.e., text intentionally made to appear as a table. Though the contents of a pseudo table are easy to interpret by a human, it is very problematic for a general NLP program to recognize the formatting characteristics. (2) While the sections and subsections of the reports are important for many applications, in many occasions the section headers are either omitted or merged to similar headers. (3) Another problem commonly observed in the clinical text is the missing or inappropriate punctuation, i.e., a new line may be used instead of a period to signify the end of a sentence. The clinical document architecture (CDA) that aims to establish standards for the structure of clinical reports addresses the problem of diverse formats related to clinical text effectively [26].

7.4.5 Expressiveness

The language in the clinical domain is extremely expressive. The same medical concept can be described in a numerous ways, i.e., cancer can be expressed as tumor, lesion, mass, carcinoma, metastasis, neoplasm, etc. Likewise, the modifiers of the concept can also be described with many different terms, i.e., the modifier for certainty information would match with more than 800 MedLEE lexicons, thus making the retrieval process more complicated.

7.4.6 Intra- and Interoperability

A clinical NLP system is expected to function well in different health care as well as clinical applications and is easy to integrate into a clinical information system. In other words, the system needs to handle clinical text in different formats. For example, the formats of discharge summaries, diagnostic reports, and radiology reports are different. Furthermore, the NLP system is required to generate output that can be stored in an existing clinical repository. However, due to the complexity and nested relations of the output, it is almost unlikely to map the same to the clinical database schema. Additionally, the output from the NLP system is required to be available for comparison through widespread deployment across institutions for a variety of automated applications. To achieve this, the output needs to be mapped to a controlled vocabulary such as UMLS, ICD-10, SNOMED-CT, and to a standard representation for the domain. Finally, the construction of a representational model is considered to be essential to interpret the clinical information and relations between the concepts. For example, one of the relations between a drug and disease is "treats."

7.4.7 Interpreting Information

Interpretation of clinical information available in a report requires the knowledge of the report structure and additional medical knowledge to associate the findings with possible diagnoses. The complexity involved in interpreting information depends on the type of the report and section, i.e., retrieving information on the vaccination administered is more straightforward than retrieving information from a radiological report that contains patterns of lights (patchy opacity). An NLP system to interpret the patterns of lights to a specific disease should contain medical knowledge associated with findings [30].

7.5 Clinical Applications

NLP and data mining for clinical text mining is applied to discover and extract new knowledge from unstructured data. Mining information from clinical text includes finding association patterns such as disease-drug information and discharge summaries by applying techniques from NLP, data mining, text mining, and even statistical methodologies.

7.5.1 General Applications

NLP together with IR and IE approaches has been widely employed in a variety of clinical applications such as summarizing patient information in clinical reports [47], extracting cancer-related findings from radiology reports [76], ICD-10 encoding in a discharge summary [8], SNOMED encoding in a discharge summary [100], and many more.

7.5.2 EHR and Decision Support

The use of EHR in a hospital to store information about patients' health along with the details of drug usage, adverse effects, and so on requires the implementation of NLP to process large volumes of data such as discharge summaries. The clinical information in EHR is available as free-text as a result of transcription of dictations, direct entry by the providers, and use of speech recognition applications. While the information in free-text is convenient to express concepts and events, it is more complicated for searching, summarization, decision support, and statistical analysis [26]. NLP techniques are found to be highly successful to process EHR in terms of reducing errors and improving quality control and coded data. Many CDS systems have been developed in recent years to process and extract information from EHR. The goal of CDS is to help the health professionals in making clinical decisions through the interpretation of information available in EHR, i.e., to know the best possible treatment for a specific disease. In general, CDS is defined as any software that provides clinical decision making by matching the characteristics of an individual patient's information in EHR such as laboratory results, pharmacy orders, discharge diagnoses, radiology reports, operative notes, etc., with the computerized knowledge base, to provide patient specific assessments or recommendations [44].

Patients' medical history includes laboratory results, pharmacy orders, discharge diagnoses, etc., in EHR, which can be entered manually into a CDS system by clinicians. However, NLP is required to retrieve the required information from the data. Besides, NLP is also able to represent clinical knowledge and CDS interventions in standardized formats [57, 58, 54]. In other words, if CDS systems depend upon NLP, it would require reliable, high-quality NLP performance and modular, flexible, and fast systems. Such systems either are active NLP CDS applications that push the patient-specific information to users or passive NLP CDS applications that require input from user to generate the output. While active NLP CDS includes alerting, monitoring, coding, and reminding, passive NLP CDS focuses on providing knowledge and finding patient populations. Though the NLP CDS is meant for retrieving clinicians' information needs, the other active users of the system are researchers, patients, administrators, students, and coders [22].

7.5.3 Surveillance

The process of collecting, integrating, and interpreting information related to a specific disease is called surveillance. The activities of surveillance for public health professionals vary from standard epidemiological practices to advanced technological systems with more complicated algorithms. The health care officials are expected to have awareness of surveillance programs at the federal, state, and local levels. The National Strategy for Biosurveillance (NSB) brings together the government, private sectors, non-government organizations, and international partners to identify and understand the health-related threats at an early stage to provide accurate and timely information. On the other hand, the National Association of County and City Health Officials (NACCHO) supports the local surveillance by sharing critical information systems and resources to identify and prevent the spread of a disease in an effective and timely manner. Computers are known for their efficiency for performing repetitive tasks in processing the clinical text when humans face the problem of maintaining surveillance. For example, MedLEE is widely used to mount surveillance for a broad range of adverse drug events [67]. Similarly, Phase IV surveillance is a critical component of drug safety as all safety issues associated with drugs are not detected before approval. LePendu et al. describe an approach for processing clinical text to serve use cases such as drug safety surveillance [56]. The other important tasks include syndrome surveillance that concerns national security and pneumonia surveillance that extracts information from neonatal chest x-ray reports using MedLEE.

7.6 Conclusions

This chapter has summarized the techniques and applications of NLP and data mining on clinical text. We have discussed core components of NLP, information extraction, challenges involved in processing clinical reports, and related clinical applications. We have provided more emphasis on preprocessing, context-based extraction, and extracting codes while describing information extraction and on EHR, decision support, and surveillance while discussing clinical applications. The chapter provides information on current methodologies available for processing the natural text along with information on clinical text corpora and evaluation metrics. We have also discussed contributions of Informatics for Integrating Biology and Bedside (i2b2) in processing clinical text to support clinicians' decision on patients' treatment and diagnosis.

The challenges involved in processing the clinical text are many and provide ample opportunities for the NLP community for deriving new methodologies. We have discussed important challenges such as domain knowledge, confidentiality of clinical text, abbreviations, diverse formats, expressiveness, intra- and interoperability, and interpreting information. These discussions provide an opportunity to understand the complexity of clinical text processing and various approaches available. An important area of research from the understanding of the challenges involved in processing the clinical text is the development of methodologies for processing the diverse formats of clinical text. Each format by its own is a challenge for an NLP researcher and can be explored using traditional and hybrid methodologies.

Bibliography

[1] D. Albright, A. Lanfranchi, A. Fredriksen, W. F. T. Styler, C. Warner, J. D. Hwang, J. D. Choi, D. Dligach, R. D. Nielsen, J. Martin, W. Ward, M. Palmer, and G. K. Savova. Towards comprehensive syntactic and semantic annotations of the clinical narrative. *J Am Med Inform Assoc*, 20(5):922–30, 2013.

[2] Y. Altun, I. Tsochantaridis, and T. Hofmann. Hidden Markov support vector machines, *Proc ICML Washington, DC,* 2003.

[3] S. Ananiadou and J. McNaught. *Text Mining for Biology and Biomedicine*, volume 33. Artech House Publishers, 2005.

[4] D. B. Aronow, F. Fangfang, and W. B. Croft. Ad hoc classification of radiology reports. *J Am Med Inform Assoc*, 6(5):393–411, 1999.

[5] A. Aronson, O. Bodenreider, D. Fushman, K. Fung, V. Lee, J. Mork, A. Neveol, L. Peters, and W. Rogers. From indexing the biomedical literature to coding clinical text: experience with mti and machine learning approaches. In *Biological, Translational, and Clinical Language Processing*, pages 105–112. Association for Computational Linguistics.

[6] A. R. Aronson. Effective mapping of biomedical text to the UMLS metathesaurus: the MetaMap program. *Proc / AMIA ... Annu Symp. AMIA Symp*, pages 17–21, 2001.

[7] A. Auger. Applying natural language processing techniques to domain knowledge capture. In *Internat Conf on Intell Anal*, pages 1–2.

[8] R. Baud. A natural language based search engine for ICD-10 diagnosis encoding. *Med Arh*, 58(1 Suppl 2):79–80, 2004.

[9] R. H. Baud, A. M. Rassinoux, J. C. Wagner, C. Lovis, C. Juge, L. L. Alpay, P. A. Michel, P. Degoulet, and J. R. Scherrer. Representing clinical narratives using conceptual graphs. *Methods Inf Med*, 34(1-2):176–86, 1995.

[10] A. Benton, S. Hill, L. Ungar, A. Chung, C. Leonard, C. Freeman, and J. H. Holmes. A system for de-identifying medical message board text. *BMC Bioinform*, 12 Suppl 3:S2, 2011.

[11] D. Bikel. Nymble: a high-performance learning name-finder. *Proc ANLC*, 194–201, 1997.

[12] O. Bodenreider. The unified medical language system (UMLS): integrating biomedical terminology. *Nucl Acids Res*, 32(Database issue):D267–D270, 2004.

[13] A. C. Browne, G. Divita, A. R. Aronson, and A. T. McCray. Umls language and vocabulary tools. *AMIA Annu Symp Proc*, page 798, 2003.

[14] J. Carletta. Assessing agreement on classification tasks: the kappa statistic. *Comput Linguist*, 22(2):249–54, 1996.

[15] W. W. Chapman, W. Bridewell, P. Hanbury, G. F. Cooper, and B. G. Buchanan. A simple algorithm for identifying negated findings and diseases in discharge summaries. *J Biomed Inform*, 34(5):301–10, 2001.

[16] W. W. Chapman, D. Chu, and J. N. Dowling. Context: an algorithm for identifying contextual features from clinical text, *Proc NLP*, 81–88, 2007.

[17] W. W. Chapman, P. M. Nadkarni, L. Hirschman, L. W. D'Avolio, G. K. Savova, and O. Uzuner. Overcoming barriers to NLP for clinical text: the role of shared tasks and the need for additional creative solutions. *J Am Med Inform Assoc*, 18(5):540–3, 2011.

[18] K. Chard, M. Russell, Y. A. Lussier, E. A. Mendonca, and J. C. Silverstein. A cloud-based approach to medical NLP. *AMIA Annu Symp Proc*, 2011:207–16, 2011.

[19] B. Cohen and L. Hunter. Chapter 16: text mining for translational bioinformatics. *PLoS Comp Biol*, 9(4):e1003044, 2013.

[20] K. Crammer, M. Dredze, K. Ganchev, P. Talukdar, and S. Carroll. Automatic code assignment to medical text. In *Biological, Translational, and Clinical Language Processing*, pages 129–136, 2007. Association for Computational Linguistics.

[21] L. Deleger, K. Molnar, G. Savova, F. Xia, T. Lingren, Q. Li, K. Marsolo, A. Jegga, M. Kaiser, L. Stoutenborough, and I. Solti. Large-scale evaluation of automated clinical note de-identification and its impact on information extraction. *J Am Med Inform Assoc*, 20(1):84–94, 2013.

[22] D. Demner-Fushman, W. Chapman, and C. McDonald. What can natural language processing do for clinical decision support? *J Biomed Inform*, 42(5):760–72, 2009.

[23] J. C. Denny, J. F. Peterson, N. N. Choma, H. Xu, R. A. Miller, L. Bastarache, and N. B. Peterson. Development of a natural language processing system to identify timing and status of colonoscopy testing in electronic medical records. *AMIA Annu Symp Proc*, 2009:141, 2009.

[24] J. C. Denny, J. D. Smithers, R. A. Miller, and A. Spickard, "Understanding" medical school curriculum content using knowledgemap. *J Am Med Inform Assoc*, 10(4):351–62, 2003.

[25] T. Dietterich. Machine-learning research: four current directions. *AI Magazine*, 18:97–136, 1997.

[26] R. Dolin, L. Alschuler, C. Beebe, P. Biron, S. Boyer, D. Essin, E. Kimber, T. Lincoln, and J. Mattison. The HL7 clinical document architecture. *J Am Med Inform Assoc*, 8(6):552–69, 2001.

[27] D. A. Dorr, W. F. Phillips, S. Phansalkar, S. A. Sims, and J. F. Hurdle. Assessing the difficulty and time cost of de-identification in clinical narratives. *Meth Infor Med*, 45(3):246–52, 2006.

[28] J. S. Elkins, C. Friedman, B. Boden-Albala, R. L. Sacco, and G. Hripcsak. Coding neuro-radiology reports for the northern manhattan stroke study: a comparison of natural language processing and manual review. *Comput Biomed Res*, 33(1):1–10, 2000.

[29] E. Apostolova, D.S. Channin, D. Demner-Fushman, J. Furst, S. Lytinen, and D. Raicu. Automatic segmentation of clinical texts. In *Proc 31st Annu Internat Conf of the IEEE EMBS Minneapolis, Minnesota, USA*, pages 5905–08.

[30] M. Fiszman and P. J. Haug. Using medical language processing to support real-time evaluation of pneumonia guidelines. *Proc / AMIA ... Annu Symp. AMIA Symp*, pages 235–39, 2000.

[31] F. J. Friedlin and C. J. McDonald. A software tool for removing patient identifying information from clinical documents. *J Am Med Inform Assoc*, 15(5):601–10, 2008.

[32] C. Friedman. A broad-coverage natural language processing system. *Proc AMIA Symp*, pages 270–4, 2000.

[33] C. Friedman, S. B. Johnson, B. Forman, and J. Starren. Architectural requirements for a multipurpose natural language processor in the clinical environment. *Proc Annu Symp Comput Appl Med Care*, pages 347–51, 1995.

[34] C. Friedman, C. Knirsch, L. Shagina, and G. Hripcsak. Automating a severity score guideline for community-acquired pneumonia employing medical language processing of discharge summaries. *Proc AMIA Symp*, pages 256–60, 1999.

[35] H. Goldberg, D. Goldsmith, V. Law, K. Keck, M. Tuttle, and C. Safran. An evaluation of umls as a controlled terminology for the problem list toolkit. *Stud Health Technol Inform*, 52 Pt 1:609–12, 1998.

[36] A. Haghighi and D. Klein. Unsupervised coreference resolution in a nonparametric bayesian model. In *Proc 45th Annu Meeting Assoc Comput Ling*, pages 848–55. Association for Computational Linguistics.

[37] U. Hahn, M. Romacker, and S. Schulz. Creating knowledge repositories from biomedical reports: the medsyndikate text mining system. *Pacific Symp Biocomput*, pages 338–49, 2002.

[38] H. Harkema, A. Setzer, R. Gaizauskas, M. Hepple, R. Power, and J. Rogers. Mining and modelling temporal clinical data. In *4th UK e-Science All Hands Meeting*.

[39] P. J. Haug, S. Koehler, L. M. Lau, P. Wang, R. Rocha, and S. M. Huff. Experience with a mixed semantic/syntactic parser. *Proc Annu Symp Comput Appl Med Care*, pages 284–8, 1995.

[40] M. Hearst. Untangling text data mining. In *Proc 37th Annu Meeting Assoc Comput Ling*, volume 43, pages 3–10. Association for Computational Linguistics.

[41] J. R. Hobbs. Information extraction from biomedical text. *J Biomed Inform*, 35(4):260–64, 2002.

[42] G. Hripcsak, L. Zhou, S. Parsons, A. K. Das, and S. B. Johnson. Modeling electronic discharge summaries as a simple temporal constraint satisfaction problem. *J Am Med Inform Assoc*, 12(1):55–63, 2005.

[43] Y. Huang and H. J. Lowe. A novel hybrid approach to automated negation detection in clinical radiology reports. *J Am Med Inform Assoc*, 14(3):304–11, 2007.

[44] D. L. Hunt, R. B. Haynes, S. E. Hanna, and K. Smith. Effects of computer-based clinical decision support systems on physician performance and patient outcomes: a systematic review. *Jama*, 280(15):1339–46, 1998.

[45] M. Jiang, Y. Chen, M. Liu, S. T. Rosenbloom, S. Mani, J. C. Denny, and H. Xu. A study of machine-learning-based approaches to extract clinical entities and their assertions from discharge summaries. *J Am Med Inform Assoc*, 18(5):601–06, 2011.

[46] S. Jonnalagadda, T. Cohen, S. Wu, and G. Gonzalez. Enhancing clinical concept extraction with distributional semantics. *J Biomed Inform*, 45(1):129–40, 2012.

[47] S. R. Jonnalagadda, G. Del Fiol, R. Medlin, C. Weir, M. Fiszman, J. Mostafa, and H. Liu. Automatically extracting sentences from medline citations to support clinicians information needs. *J Am Med Inform Assoc*, 20(5):995–1000, 2013.

[48] S. R. Jonnalagadda, D. Li, S. Sohn, S. T. Wu, K. Wagholikar, M. Torii, and H. Liu. Coreference analysis in clinical notes: a multi-pass sieve with alternate anaphora resolution modules. *J Am Med Inform Assoc*, 19(5):867–74, 2012.

[49] Y. Kim, J. Hurdle, and S. M. Meystre. Using UMLS lexical resources to disambiguate abbreviations in clinical text. *AMIA Annu Symp Proc*, 2011:715–22, 2011.

[50] D. Klein and C. Manning. Accurate unlexicalized parsing. In *Proc 41st Annu Meeting Assoc Comput Ling – Volume 1*, pages 423–30. Association for Computational Linguistics.

[51] M. Krallinger, R. A.-A. Erhardt, and A. Valencia. Text-mining approaches in molecular biology and biomedicine. *Drug Discov Today*, 10(6):439–45, 2005.

[52] M. Krauthammer and G. Nenadic. Term identification in the biomedical literature. *J Biomed Inform*, 37(6):512–26, 2004.

[53] T. Kudo and Y. Matsumoto. Chunking with support vector machines. In *NAACL '01: Second Meeting N Am Chap Assoc Comput Ling Lang Techn 2001*, pages 1–8. Association for Computational Linguistics.

[54] I. J. Kullo, J. Fan, J. Pathak, G. K. Savova, Z. Ali, and C. G. Chute. Leveraging informatics for genetic studies: use of the electronic medical record to enable a genome-wide association study of peripheral arterial disease. *J Am Med Inform Assoc*, 17(5):568–74, 2010.

[55] J. D. Lafferty, A. McCallum, and F. C. N. Pereira. Conditional random fields: probabilistic models for segmenting and labeling sequence data *Proc ICML*, pages 282–89, San Francisco, CA, 2001.

[56] P. Lependu, S. V. Iyer, A. Bauer-Mehren, R. Harpaz, Y. T. Ghebremariam, J. P. Cooke, and N. H. Shah. Pharmacovigilance using clinical text. *AMIA Jt Summits Transl Sci Proc*, 2013:109, 2013.

[57] L. Li, H. S. Chase, C. O. Patel, C. Friedman, and C. Weng. Comparing ICD9-encoded diagnoses and NLP-processed discharge summaries for clinical trials pre-screening: a case study. *AMIA Annu Symp Proc*, pages 404–8, 2008.

[58] K. P. Liao, T. Cai, V. Gainer, S. Goryachev, Q. Zeng-treitler, S. Raychaudhuri, P. Szolovits, S. Churchill, S. Murphy, I. Kohane, E. W. Karlson, and R. M. Plenge. Electronic medical records for discovery research in rheumatoid arthritis. *Arthritis Care Res (Hoboken)*, 62(8):1120–7, 2010.

[59] H. Liu, Y. A. Lussier, and C. Friedman. Disambiguating ambiguous biomedical terms in biomedical narrative text: an unsupervised method. *J Biomed Inform*, 34(4):249–61, 2001.

[60] K. Liu, K. J. Mitchell, W. W. Chapman, and R. S. Crowley. Automating tissue bank annotation from pathology reports—comparison to a gold standard expert annotation set. *AMIA Annu Symp Proc*, pages 460–4, 2005.

[61] Y. Liu, R. Bill, M. Fiszman, T. Rindflesch, T. Pedersen, G. B. Melton, and S. V. Pakhomov. Using SemRep to label semantic relations extracted from clinical text. *AMIA Annu Symp Proc*, 2012:587–95, 2012.

[62] S. Loh, J. P. M. De Oliveira, and M. A. Gameiro. Knowledge discovery in texts for constructing decision support systems. *Appl Intell*, 18(3):357–66, 2003.

[63] S. Mathur and D. Dinakarpandian. Finding disease similarity based on implicit semantic similarity. *J Biomed Inform*, 45(2):363–71, 2012.

[64] C. Mayr. Focusing bound pronouns. *Nat Lang Seman*, 20(3): 299–48, 2012.

[65] A. McCallum and W. Li. Early results for named entity recognition with conditional random fields, feature induction and web-enhanced lexicons, *Proc CONLL*, 4:188–91, 2003.

[66] A. T. McCray, A. M. Razi, A. K. Bangalore, A. C. Browne, and P. Z. Stavri. The UMLS knowledge source server: a versatile internet-based research tool. *Proc AMIA Annu Fall Symp*, pages 164–8, 1996.

[67] G. B. Melton and G. Hripcsak. Automated detection of adverse events using natural language processing of discharge summaries. *J Am Med Inform Assoc*, 12(4):448–57, 2005.

[68] S. Meystre and P. Haug. Natural language processing to extract medical problems from electronic clinical documents: performance evaluation. *J Biomed Inform*, 39(6):589–99, 2006.

[69] S. M. Meystre, F. J. Friedlin, B. R. South, S. Shen, and M. H. Samore. Automatic de-identification of textual documents in the electronic health record: a review of recent research. *BMC Med Res Methodol*, 10:70, 2010.

[70] S. M. Meystre, G. K. Savova, K. C. Kipper-Schuler, and J. F. Hurdle. Extracting information from textual documents in the electronic health record: a review of recent research. *Yrbk of Med Inform*, pages 128–41, 2008.

[71] F. P. Morrison, L. Li, A. M. Lai, and G. Hripcsak. Repurposing the clinical record: can an existing natural language processing system de-identify clinical notes? *J Am Med Inform Assoc*, 16(1):37–9, 2009.

[72] S. N. Murphy, M. E. Mendis, D. A. Berkowitz, I. Kohane, and H. C. Chueh. Integration of clinical and genetic data in the i2b2 architecture. *AMIA Annu Symp Proc*, page 1040, 2006.

[73] P. G. Mutalik, A. Deshpande, and P. M. Nadkarni. Use of general-purpose negation detection to augment concept indexing of medical documents: a quantitative study using the UMLS. *J Am Med Inform Assoc*, 8(6):598–609, 2001.

[74] P. M. Nadkarni, L. Ohno-Machado, and W. W. Chapman. Natural language processing: an introduction. *J Am Med Inform Assoc*, 18(5):544–51, 2011.

[75] T.-V. T. Nguyen, A. Moschitti, and G. Riccardi. Convolution kernels on constituent, dependency and sequential structures for relation extraction, *Proc EMNLP*, 3: 1378–87, 2009.

[76] H.-S. Oh, J.-B. Kim, and S.-H. Myaeng. Extracting targets and attributes of medical findings from radiology reports in a mixture of languages, *Proc BCB*, pages 550–52, 2011.

[77] S. Pakhomov, J. Buntrock, and P. Duffy. High throughput modularized NLP system for clinical text, *Proc ACL*, pages 25–8, 2005.

[78] T. H. Payne and D. R. Martin. How useful is the UMLS metathesaurus in developing a controlled vocabulary for an automated problem list? *Proc Annu Symp Comput Appl Med Care*, pages 705–9, 1993.

[79] K. Raghunathan, H. Lee, S. Rangarajan, N. Chambers, M. Surdeanu, D. Jurafsky, and C. Manning. A multi-pass sieve for coreference resolution, *Proc EMNLP*, pages 492–501, 2010.

[80] L. Ratinov and D. Roth. Design challenges and misconceptions in named entity recognition, *Proc CoNLL*, 147–55, 2009.

[81] S. T. Rosenbloom, R. A. Miller, K. B. Johnson, P. L. Elkin, and S. H. Brown. Interface terminologies: facilitating direct entry of clinical data into electronic health record systems. *J Am Med Inform Assoc*, 13(3):277–88, 2006.

[82] P. Ruch, R. Baud, and A. Geissbühler. Using lexical disambiguation and named-entity recognition to improve spelling correction in the electronic patient record. *Artif Intell Med*, 29(1-2):169–84, 2003.

[83] N. Sager, C. Friedman, and E. Chi. The analysis and processing of clinical narrative. *Medinfo*, pages 1101–5, 1986.

[84] S. Sahay and A. Ram. Socio-semantic health information access. In *AI and Health Communication*, pages 57–60.

[85] G. K. Savova, J. J. Masanz, P. V. Ogren, J. Zheng, S. Sohn, K. C. Kipper-Schuler, and C. G. Chute. Mayo clinical text analysis and knowledge extraction system (cTAKES): architecture, component evaluation and applications. *J Am Med Inform Assoc*, 17(5):507–13, 2010.

[86] H. Shatkay and R. Feldman. Mining the biomedical literature in the genomic era: an overview. *J Comput Biol*, 10(6):821–55, 2003.

[87] C. Shearer. The CRISP-DM model: the new blueprint for data mining. *J Data Warehous*, 5(4):13–22, 2000.

[88] S. Sohn, K. B. Wagholikar, D. Li, S. R. Jonnalagadda, C. Tao, R. Komandur Elayavilli, and H. Liu. Comprehensive temporal information detection from clinical text: medical events, time, and tlink identification. *J Am Med Inform Assoc*, 20(5):836–42, 2013.

[89] W. Soon, H. Ng, and L. Daniel Chung Yong. A machine learning approach to coreference resolution of noun phrases. *Comput Linguist*, 27(4):521–44, 2001.

[90] J. Strötgen and M. Gertz. Heideltime: High quality rule-based extraction and normalization of temporal expressions, *Proc SemEval*, pages 322-24, 2010.

[91] L. Sweeney. Weaving technology and policy together to maintain confidentiality. *J Law, Med & Ethics*, 25(2-3):98–110, 1997.

[92] G. Szarvas, R. Farkas, and R. Busa-Fekete. State-of-the-art anonymization of medical records using an iterative machine learning framework. *J Am Med Inform Assoc*, 14(5):574–80, 2007.

[93] H. D. Tolentino, M. D. Matters, W. Walop, B. Law, W. Tong, F. Liu, P. Fontelo, K. Kohl, and D. C. Payne. A UMLS-based spell checker for natural language processing in vaccine safety. *BMC Med Inform Decis Mak*, 7:3, 2007.

[94] M. Torii, K. Wagholikar, and H. Liu. Using machine learning for concept extraction on clinical documents from multiple data sources. *J Am Med Inform Assoc*, 18(5):580–7, 2011.

[95] M. C. Tremblay, D. J. Berndt, S. L. Luther, P. R. Foulis, and D. D. French. Identifying fall-related injuries: text mining the electronic medical record. *Inf Technol and Mgmt*, 10(4):253–65, 2009.

[96] O. Uzuner, Y. Luo, and P. Szolovits. Evaluating the state-of-the-art in automatic de-identification. *J Am Med Inform Assoc*, 14(5):550–63, 2007.

[97] Ö. Uzuner, B. R. South, S. Shen, and S. L. DuVall. 2010 i2b2/va challenge on concepts, assertions, and relations in clinical text. *J Am Med Inform Assoc*, 18(5):552–56, 2011.

[98] M. Verhagen and J. Pustejovsky. Temporal processing with the tarsqi toolkit, *Proc COLING*, pages 189–92, 2008.

[99] S. J. Wang, D. W. Bates, H. C. Chueh, A. S. Karson, S. M. Maviglia, J. A. Greim, J. P. Frost, and G. J. Kuperman. Automated coded ambulatory problem lists: evaluation of a vocabulary and a data entry tool. *Int J Med Inform*, 72(1-3):17–28, 2003.

[100] H. Wasserman and J. Wang. An applied evaluation of SNOMED–CT as a clinical vocabulary for the computerized diagnosis and problem list. *AMIA Annu Symp Proc*, pages 699–703, 2003.

[101] J. Wilbur, A. Rzhetsky, and H. Shatkay. New directions in biomedical text annotation: definitions, guidelines and corpus construction. *BMC Bioinform*, 7(1):356, 2006.

[102] H. Xu, M. Markatou, R. Dimova, H. Liu, and C. Friedman. Machine learning and word sense disambiguation in the biomedical domain: design and evaluation issues. *BMC Bioinform*, 7:334, 2006.

[103] J. Zelingher, D. M. Rind, E. Caraballo, M. S. Tuttle, N. E. Olson, and C. Safran. Categorization of free-text problem lists: an effective method of capturing clinical data. *Proc Annu Symp Comput Appl Med Care*, pages 416–20, 1995.

[104] J. Zheng, W. W. Chapman, R. S. Crowley, and G. K. Savova. Coreference resolution: a review of general methodologies and applications in the clinical domain. *J Biomed Inform*, 44(6):1113–22, 2011.

[105] L. Zhou, S. Parsons, and G. Hripcsak. The evaluation of a temporal reasoning system in processing clinical discharge summaries. *J Am Med Inform Assoc*, 15(1):99–106, 2008.

[106] Q. Zou, W. W. Chu, C. Morioka, G. H. Leazer, and H. Kangarloo. Indexfinder: a method of extracting key concepts from clinical texts for indexing. *AMIA Annu Symp Proc*, pages 763–7, 2003.

[107] P. J. Hayes and J. Carbonell, Natural language understanding. *Encyclopedia of Artificial Intelligence*, pp. 660–77, 1987.

[108] Angel X C and C. Manning. SUTime: A library for recognizing and normalizing time expressions. *Language Resources and Evaluation* (LREC 2012); Istanbul, Turkey. pp. 3735–40.

Chapter 8

Mining the Biomedical Literature

Claudiu Mihăilă
National Centre for Text Mining
University of Manchester
Manchester, UK
claudiu.mihaila@manchester.ac.uk

Riza Batista-Navarro
National Centre for Text Mining
University of Manchester
Manchester, UK
riza.batista@manchester.ac.uk

Noha Alnazzawi
National Centre for Text Mining
University of Manchester
Manchester, UK
noha.alnazzawi@cs.man.ac.uk

Georgios Kontonatsios
National Centre for Text Mining
University of Manchester
Manchester, UK
georgios.kontonatsios@cs.man.ac.uk

Ioannis Korkontzelos
National Centre for Text Mining
University of Manchester
Manchester, UK
ioannis.korkontzelos@manchester.ac.uk

Rafal Rak
National Centre for Text Mining
University of Manchester
Manchester, UK
rafal.rak@manchester.ac.uk

Paul Thompson
National Centre for Text Mining
University of Manchester
Manchester, UK
paul.thompson@manchester.ac.uk

Sophia Ananiadou
National Centre for Text Mining
University of Manchester
Manchester, UK
sophia.ananiadou@manchester.ac.uk

8.1 Introduction

Human language is a complex, extremely powerful communication system. While people have an amazing ability to communicate with one another, understanding natural language is a daunting task for computers. The main difficulty is that although natural language provides the ability to signal, it also enables its users to express an infinite number of new meanings. Natural languages are inherently ambiguous, and thus become a problem for computers, which are not able to manage complex contextual situations.

Since the beginning of computational linguistics and natural language processing (NLP), it has been a known fact that scientific sublanguages exhibit specific properties that differentiate them from general language [100]. These differences can be observed at various levels, such as vocabulary, semantic relationships and, in some cases, even syntax [89], and often require domain-specialized knowledge sources to aid in the performed analysis.

Language is the medium in which, among others, health sciences education, research and practice operate. The language used in this domain, usually referred to as *biomedical language*, has also been studied from the sublanguage point of view [164, 179]. Their findings indicate that biomedical researchers need to be aware of the importance of subdomain variation when considering the practical use of NLP applications.

Another problem lies in the fact that the exponential growth of biomedical literature and the implementation of high-throughput methods for the generation of experimental data require the development of effective technologies for intelligent content creation and management, and for supporting the capture of knowledge, its sharing and re-use. The use of text mining methods for the long-term preservation, accessibility and usability of digitally available resources is a must for biomedical applications relying on evidence from scientific literature. Text mining methods and tools offer novel ways of applying new knowledge discovery methods in the biomedical field. Such tools offer efficient ways to search, extract, combine, analyze, and summarize big textual data, thus supporting researchers in knowledge discovery and generation [5, 45, 115, 255, 325].

Biomedical text mining offers numerous challenges and at the same time opportunities. One of the challenges can be attributed to is the multidisciplinary nature. For example, biologists describe chemical compounds using brand names, while chemists often use less ambiguous IUPAC-compliant names or unambiguous descriptors such as International Chemical Identifiers. While the latter, more precisely identified molecular entities, can be handled with cheminformatics tools, text mining techniques are required to extract less precisely defined entities and their relations from the literature. In addition, to support in-silico research, publicly available databases are needed to find biomedical entities and their interactions [7] from the literature. As the cost of curating such databases is too high, text mining methods offer new opportunities for their effective population, update and integration. The discovery, though, of specific entities and their interactions at different levels of granularity requires the adaptation of tools to different domains. Text mining brings about other benefits to biomedical research by linking textual evidence to biomedical pathways, reducing the cost of expert knowledge validation, and generating hypotheses. Through its discovery of previously unsuspected links, it provides a general methodology to enhance the way biomedical knowledge is organized.

This chapter aims to summarize the active research themes in biomedical text mining. We begin by describing in Section 8.2 the various resources (e.g., corpora) which serve as the sources of domain knowledge and enable the development of text mining methods. An overview of the fundamental tasks of terminology acquisition and management is then provided in Section 8.3. Central to text mining are methods for the automatic distillation of facts from unstructured data in a task known as information extraction. In this work we focus on named entity and event extraction, and discourse interpretation, which are focal points of Sections 8.4 and 8.5, respectively. In Section 8.6, we provide an overview of the different software environments that facilitate the integration of various biomedical text mining tools. Section 8.7 presents a discussion of several applications of text mining which address some of the most pressing biomedical information needs, while Section 8.8 expounds on how biomedical text mining methods can be applied and adapted to the clinical domain. Finally, in Section 8.9, we identify some of the current challenges in biomedical text mining and present prospective means for addressing them with the ultimate goal of advancing this important research field.

8.2 Resources

There exists a large variety of lexica, ontologies and databases encoding biomedical knowledge. However, biomedical language is one of the fastest evolving specialized languages, with old terms falling out of use and new terms being coined every day. Manually maintaining such knowledge bases is becoming more and more difficult as the sheer quantity of published work cannot be processed by humans, making it impossible for researchers to keep up to date with the relevant literature even for a specific topic [6]. In 2012 alone, for example, more than 500,000 articles were published in MEDLINE. Thus, it is important to teach machines how to automatically perform the tedious jobs of human experts, who can then dedicate their time to advancing science. To support their learning, machines need large collections of data annotated by humans to distinguish positive and negative cases. Such data sets, or *corpora*, are machine-readable collections of language material that are selected to represent a certain aspect of biomedicine, which can be subsequently used by text mining tools [6]. The GENIA corpus, for instance, is a collection of 2,000 journal abstracts from the molecular biology domain in which terms and associations relevant to human blood cell transcription factors were annotated [128].

Biomedical corpora have been traditionally constructed from abstracts sourced from MEDLINE,[1] a literature database maintained by the US National Library of Medicine (NLM). However, several studies have demonstrated the benefits of utilizing full-text articles instead of abstracts in information extraction tasks [265, 262, 46]. Their findings prompted a rise in interest towards the development of corpora containing full-text articles, e.g., BioScope [307], CRAFT [12] and the BioNLP 2011 Infectious Diseases data set [233]. The Open Access subset of PubMed Central[2] is one of the primary sources of publicly available full papers.

8.2.1 Corpora Types and Formats

Corpora of biomedical documents can be characterized according to various dimensions. They can be classified based on the domains they represent (e.g., molecular biology, anatomy, chemistry), the types of underlying documents (e.g., clinical reports, scientific articles, nano-texts), the intended language processing application and mode of use, i.e., information extraction (IE) or information retrieval (IR) [252]. Annotations add information over documents at different levels of analysis, such as syntactic (e.g., sentences [133], tokens [276], dependencies [230]), semantic (e.g., named entities [133], relations [233], events [128, 283]) and discourse (e.g., discourse relations [180, 227]). Figure 8.1 illustrates a sentence annotated at various levels. As most corpora were annotated based on the requirements of specific projects (e.g., GENIA [128] and PennBioIE [150]) or shared tasks (e.g., GENETAG from BioCreative I [275]), currently available biomedical document collections are highly heterogeneous. Table 8.1 presents a comparison of some of the well-known biomedical corpora according to the above-mentioned criteria.

Furthermore, biomedical corpora differ from each other in terms of the formats in which the annotated documents were encoded. Widely accepted within the community are representations based on boundary notation, in which any of a set of predefined labels is assigned to a basic unit (e.g., token) to indicate its position relative to the element being annotated (e.g., named entity). The BIO (begin-inside-outside) [242] and BILOU (begin-inside-last-outside-unit length) [244] formats are examples of this type of representation, which has been used to encode part-of-speech, phrase and named entity annotations [137, 129]. Although its simplicity has led to wide usability, its linear nature makes it unsuitable for more structured annotations such as nested entities, dependency trees,

[1] http://www.nlm.nih.gov/bsd/pmresources.html

[2] http://www.ncbi.nlm.nih.gov/pmc/tools/openftlist

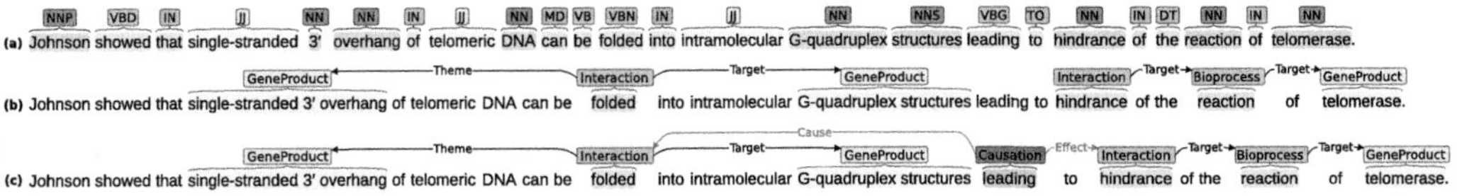

FIGURE 8.1: A sentence annotated with information pertaining to (a) syntax, i.e., parts of speech as defined in the Penn Treebank tag set [277], (b) semantics, i.e., named entities and events, and (c) discourse, i.e., causality.

relations and events. Furthermore, additional effort is required in reconstructing the original source text, even in the rare cases where character offsets have been supplied.

In some corpora, markup languages (e.g., XML, SGML) were exploited to encode annotations. Instances of defined markup language elements that hold annotated information are added to the source document in either an inline or stand-off manner. The former entails interspersing annotations within actual text while the latter leaves the source document untouched by using an indexing mechanism that allows for the elements to be stored separately. GENIA corpora with annotated parts-of-speech [276], named entities [133] and coreferring expressions [75] were encoded in inline XML, whereas GENIA events were stored as standoff XML elements [128]. Other XML-based representations include the generic XML Metadata Interchange (XMI) standard and the biomedically inspired BioC format [49]. While their tree-based model facilitates the storage of hierarchical and structured annotations (e.g., dependency trees, events), markup languages require the development of standards-conforming parsers for processing encoded documents. Due to the specifications of markup languages, it is also not possible to encode annotated text spans with partial intersections.

A much simpler yet flexible way of encoding annotations is by means of stand-off delimiter-separated values (DSV). Like stand-off markup language elements, indexed annotations in DSV formats leave the original text untouched, and can also be highly structured. Moreover, it has the additional flexibility of allowing partially overlapping/intersecting annotations. The increasingly popular BioNLP Shared Task (BioNLP ST) format [3] is one such format.

The last column of Table 8.1 indicates the specific formats employed in encoding the listed biomedical corpora.

TABLE 8.1: Some Biomedical Corpora and Their Characteristics

Corpus	Domain	Documents	Annotation	Format
GENETAG [275]	molecular biology	20,000 sent	entities	s/o DSV
CRAFT [12]	genomics	97 art	entities	s/o XML
PennBioIECYP[150]	molecular genomics	1,100 abstr	POS, entities, relations	s/o XML
BioNLP REL	molecular biology	1,210 abstr	entities, relations	s/o DSV
GENIA [128]	molecular biology	2,000 abstr	POS, entities, events	i/l XML
BioCause [180]	molecular biology	19 art	discourse relations	s/o DSV
BioScope [307]	radiology & molecular biology	1,954 rad. rep, 9 art, 1,273 abstr	negation, uncertainty and their scopes	i/l XML

Notes: s/o = stand-off, i/l = inline. All corpora listed support information extraction.

[3] http://2013.bionlp-st.org/file-formats

8.2.2 Annotation Methodologies

In terms of required effort, the information contained in corpora can be marked up in two ways: by means of automated methods, which employ tools to automatically generate annotations, and by manual annotation, in which highly qualified curators supply annotations starting from scratch. The latter is further grouped into three different schemes:

1. Traditional annotation. This scheme is followed in the development of almost all large-scale corpora and has been proven to be successful. An annotation team typically consists of at least two annotators, guideline designers, domain experts and technical support staff. Detailed guidelines for the annotation process are produced ahead of the beginning of the annotation phase and are revised during its progression as necessary. To build the Gene Regulation Event (GREC) corpus [283], for example, a comprehensive set of guidelines touching upon both the biomedical and linguistic aspects of the task were prepared before the domain experts proceeded with the annotation of biomedical events. This approach, however, is costly in terms of time and personnel. The two alternative approaches described next have thus been proposed [317].

2. Crowd-sourcing. Under this scheme, the annotation is carried out by members of online labor markets, e.g., Amazon's Mechanical Turk. This approach has been shown to work well on tasks that do not require a high level of domain expertise. Since it is not as costly as the traditional scheme, NLP researchers can afford to pay for multiple annotations of the same documents. Subsequently, voting mechanisms can be applied in order to obtain consensus annotations. This scheme was successfully employed in the annotation of medical conditions, medications and laboratory procedures in clinical trial documents [322].

3. Community annotation. This method requires annotation guidelines and some seed annotations, which are released to the research community. Multiple researchers then help complete the task at hand by contributing their own annotations. Based on this scheme, the 2009 i2b2 Challenge corpus was jointly annotated by the task organizers (who supplied the initial annotations) and the participating teams. This approach can prove to be fast, reliable and cheap if coordinated well [317].

On the one hand, while automated approaches produce consistent annotations within a minimal amount of time, the quality of generated annotations is questionable. With manual annotation, on the other hand, the high quality of annotations is ensured but with the expensive costs of time and personnel [209]. Combining the two approaches was shown to bring about benefits [209, 10]. In an interactive manner, annotators manually correct automatically generated annotations, leading to accelerated manual annotation rates, reduction in costs and increased inter-annotator consistency [209, 68, 10].

Supporting the development of corpora are various available annotation tools. The suitability of any tool for a given annotation task is dependent on the annotation methodology being employed. While traditional annotation, for instance, may not require features for real-time collaboration, these are most likely a must-have in crowd-sourcing and community annotation. In the meantime, for annotation efforts aiming to reduce time and personnel costs, platforms that can be integrated with custom automatic tools (e.g., WordFreak [195], MMAX [196], GATE Teamware [30], brat [272], Argo [239]) are desirable because of their capabilities to automatically generate annotations, which can then be manually validated. Table 8.2 presents the features offered by well-known annotation tools that have been employed in the development of biomedical corpora.

TABLE 8.2: Comparison of Various Annotation Tools

	WF [195]	C [63]	XConc [88]	MMAX [196]	K [218]	GT [30]	BN [38]	brat [272]	Argo [239]
Web-based	✗	✗	✗	✗	✗	✓	✓	✓	✓
Complex annotation structures	✓	✓	✓	✓	✓	✓	✗	✓	✓
Custom automatic tools	✓	✗	✗	✓	✗	✓	✗	✓	✓
Search	✓	✓	✓	✓	✓	✓	✗	✓	✗
Real-time collaboration	✗	✗	✗	✗	✗	✓	✓	✓	✓
Flexible output formats	✓	✓	✗	✓	✗	✗	✗	✗	✓
Sample corpus produced (citation)	[284]	[3]	[128]	[85]	[12]		[211]	[233]	[238]

Notes: WF=WordFreak, C=Callisto, K=Knowtator, GT=GATE Teamware, BN=BioNotate.

8.2.3 Reliability of Annotation

The contribution of annotations to the development of text mining methods is twofold. Firstly, they provide the samples that enable tools to effectively learn the task. Secondly, they serve as a gold standard that facilitates the systematic evaluation of developed methods [317]. Ensuring that the produced annotations are of high quality is thus of paramount importance.

Although it has been shown that linguists have been able to identify certain aspects in biomedical texts reliably, e.g., negation and speculation [307], they are likely to become overwhelmed in trying to understand the semantics. Identifying the entities, how they interact and what entities (or other events) are affected by certain events is a daunting task, as it requires vast, domain-specific background knowledge and an almost complete understanding of the topic. As biomedicine is highly specialized, it is necessary for annotators to have the required domain expertise. Furthermore, annotators ideally should be armed with near-native competency in the language, e.g., English.

Nevertheless, humans are likely to commit inconsistencies and to have different biases in judgment and understanding, usually due to varying education and expertise backgrounds [24]. To abstract away from any potential bias, at least two human experts are usually employed to provide annotations for the same set of documents. It has been shown that the reliability of a corpus increases together with the number of annotators (i.e., coders) who are involved in the annotation effort [10]. Also influencing coders are the guidelines provided prior to the annotation effort, outlining instructions, possible cases of ambiguity and resolutions to these. The more comprehensive the guidelines are, the fewer inconsistent annotations are created, leading to increased corpus reliability [6, 209].

In order to quantify the reliability of annotations, the value of a measure known as inter-annotator agreement (IAA) is calculated. It serves as an evaluation of the consistency of annotations produced by multiple coders carrying out the annotation task independently. The most straightforward manner of calculating IAA is by obtaining the percentage of absolute agreement, i.e., the ratio between the number of items the annotators agreed on and the total number of items [10]. However, this ratio does not consider chance agreement and is often misleading, as some portion of agreement between the two annotators could have been easily brought about by chance [108].

The most widely used coefficient of agreement that assesses the reliability of an annotated corpus and takes into account chance agreement is Cohen's kappa coefficient κ, which calculates the proportion of observed agreement corrected for chance agreement, as given in Equation 8.1.

$$\kappa = \frac{P(A) - P(E)}{1 - P(E)} \tag{8.1}$$

$P(E)$ is the expected agreement between the annotators by chance, while $P(A)$ is the observed absolute agreement. The resulting value of κ is 1 if the annotators generate identical annotations, positive if the observed agreement is greater than that expected by chance, and negative otherwise [6].

In several scenarios, the previously mentioned coefficient of agreement is unsuitable as the total number of annotated items is not known in advance. The evaluation of such cases is thus carried out by considering one set of annotations as reference (i.e., gold standard) and another as response. IAA is computed using the standard metrics of precision (P), recall (R) and balanced F-score (F_1). Precision pertains to the ratio of instances identified in the response that are relevant (according to the reference), while recall corresponds to the ratio of relevant instances that were identified in the response. To calculate the values of these two metrics, the following frequencies are initially tallied.

- TP is the number of instances in the reference that were correctly identified in the response (true positives).
- FP is the number of instances in the reference that were incorrectly identified in the response (false positives) .
- FN is the number of instances in the reference that were incorrectly rejected in the response (false negatives).

Precision and recall are then computed with Equations 8.2 and 8.3, respectively.

$$P = \frac{TP}{TP + FP} \tag{8.2}$$

$$R = \frac{TP}{TP + FN} \tag{8.3}$$

The combination of these two metrics is often expressed as the F_1 score (or balanced F-score), which is the harmonic mean of precision and recall (Equation 8.4).

$$F_1 = 2 \cdot \frac{P \cdot R}{P + R} \tag{8.4}$$

The values of these metrics over a set of documents may be reported by means of micro-averaging and/or macro-averaging. The former is accomplished by accumulating TP, FP and FN over all documents, and calculating precision (micro-P) and recall (micro-R) based on the sums. The value of micro-averaged F-score (micro-F_1) is then computed as the harmonic mean of micro-P and micro-R. Meanwhile, in macro-averaging, precision and recall are calculated for each document. The values of the macro-averaged metrics (macro-P and -R) are obtained by averaging over the precision and recall values over the entire set of documents. Calculating the harmonic mean of macro-P and -R results to the macro-averaged F-score (macro-F_1).

8.3 Terminology Acquisition and Management

In this section, we provide a discussion of two tasks involved in terminology acquisition and management, namely, term extraction and alignment.

Term extraction is the process of identifying terms automatically. Addressed mostly in the previous decade, it is an elementary natural language processing task that is genuinely useful for enriching existing ontologies with newly introduced terms, or creating lexica for new domains and unexploited languages. Due to the rich semantic content of identified terms, term extraction is used as a preprocessing step in a variety of text mining applications, e.g., document classification, named entity recognition, relation extraction and event extraction.

Term alignment is defined as the process of extracting translation correspondences between terms of a source and a target language. Techniques for term alignment are used to automatically or semi-automatically construct bilingual dictionaries of technical terms. Such resources play an important role in various applications including computer-aided translation (CAT) [55, 80], statistical machine translation (SMT) [216] and cross-language information retrieval (CLIR) [15].

8.3.1 Term Extraction

Terms are words or sequences of words that represent concepts closely related to a scientific or technical domain of knowledge [118, 70]. The property that distinguishes terms from other sequences that occur frequently in a collection of documents of a specific domain is that terms correspond to concepts, i.e., notions mentioned in a domain-specific ontology or dictionary. *Ecological pyramid*, *molecule* and *protein* are biological terms while *agoraphobia*, *bipolar disorder* and *group dynamics* are terms of psychology and psychiatry. Meanwhile, *annihilation*, *cosmic censor*, *white dwarf* and *yellow dwarf* are terms in the domain of astronomy. It is worth noting that terms are domain-specific, i.e., those of one domain are not another domain's terms. In addition, domain-specific terms might have different senses in that particular domain than in other domains or the general domain. For example, in contrast to their meaning in astronomy, *white* and *yellow dwarf* are tiny creatures in the domain of fairy tales. Apart from domains, there are several other crucial aspects of text that need to be considered for term extraction, among which language and style are the most important. Clearly, terms are different for different languages. In addition, text style, i.e., formal, colloquial and informal, might affect which term realization is chosen among synonyms.

A straightforward approach to extracting terms would be to use a domain-specific dictionary or term list and identify words and sequences that occur in the list as terms. However, this approach suffers several drawbacks: It cannot be used for domains and languages for which dictionaries are not available and also would not work for newly coined terms. For these reasons, unsupervised approaches are popular for this task. Term extraction methods can be divided into linguistic, dictionary-based, statistical and hybrid approaches, depending on the type of information that they take into account.

Linguistic methods inspect morphology, grammar and semantics related with words and sequences of words to identify terms. Linguistic approaches typically combine linguistic tools such as stop lists, sentence splitters, tokenizers, part-of-speech taggers, lemmatizers, parsers and part-of-speech (POS) patterns. In contrast, dictionary-based methods use existing dictionaries or lists of terms to recognize terms in running text [145]. An example of such method is LEXTER [31].

Statistical methods take advantage of statistical properties associated with the occurrences of words or sequences in text. They can be classified into termhood-based or unithood-based ones [118, 261]. Unithood-based approaches measure the attachment strength among the constituents of a candidate term. In other words, they quantify whether the words or sequences occur more frequently than chance. The most straightforward measure for this purpose is occurrence frequency.

However, more sophisticated methods, such as hypothesis testing, can be exploited to measure the significance of co-occurrence of constituents of sequences of words. Termhood-based approaches measure the degree to which a word or sequence refers to a specific ontology concept. Examples of termhood-based approaches are C-value and NC-value [76], the statistical barrier method [202] and the method of Shimohata et al. [267]. Most statistical methods are combined with some type of linguistic processing, such as considering words of specific parts-of-speech. Hybrid methods are combinations of components of linguistic, dictionary-based and statistical methods. Sometimes hybrid methods also combine classification models. Examples of hybrid methods are presented in Maynard and Ananiadou [169] and Vivaldi et al. [309].

The output of a term extractor is a list of candidate terms. Some term extractors, such as statistical ones, usually provide a score for each candidate indicating importance or confidence. This term list can be further exploited by other text mining components, such as a named entity recognizer, a relation extractor or an event extraction. A named entity recognizer would assess whether the term candidates are named entities of some type, i.e., person names, locations, proteins, cells, etc. A relation extractor would then receive the named entities and possibly also the term candidates that were not identified as named entities and would recognize relations among them. Similarly, an event extractor would identify complex relations, or in other words events, among the candidates. Terms that are not named entities might be identified as function parts of events, such as triggers. Apart from these uses, the output of a term extractor can be exploited by a multilingual term extractor or a term alignment tool that identifies correspondences of terms in different languages.

8.3.2 Term Alignment

Existing bilingual dictionaries of technical terms suffer from low coverage and they are only available for a limited number of language pairs. As an example, Figure 8.2 illustrates the percentage of English terms that are translated in various languages in the UMLS metathesaurus, a popular multilingual terminological resource of the biomedical domain. It can be observed that the widest coverage is achieved by the Spanish part of UMLS, albeit containing translations for only 14.2% of the total number of English terms. Given that UMLS indexes more than a million English terms, we count approximately 860,000 missing translations for Spanish. Hence, term alignment methods that discover new translations of terms are needed in order to automatically augment existing lexica.

Over the past two decades, researchers have proposed different solutions to term alignment. Existing term alignment approaches can be coarsely classified into first-generation methods that aimed to extract bilingual dictionaries from parallel corpora and an advancing second-generation group of techniques that focus on comparable corpora.

A parallel corpus is a collection of documents in a source language paired with their direct translation in a target language. Parallel corpora are considered invaluable resources for machine translation since current state-of-the-art methods, i.e., SMT, can only be trained on this type of data. Furthermore, parallel corpora were used by early term alignment algorithms to compile bilingual dictionaries of technical terms. At AT&T labs, Dagan and Church presented Termight [55], a multi-word term alignment tool. Termight initially extracts a bilingual word dictionary from the parallel corpus [56]. For each source multiword term, Termight then suggests candidate translations, i.e., target multiword terms, whose first and last words are aligned to any of the words in the source terms. While the dictionary extracted by Termight contained noisy translations (40% translation accuracy for the best translation candidates on an English-German parallel corpus), it was proven useful to human translators when translating technical manuals. Other approaches to term alignment from parallel corpora exploit statistical methods. They rely on the simple observation that a term and its translation tend to co-occur in a parallel, sentence-aligned corpus. Examples include methods based on the Dice coefficient [271], co-occurrence frequency [299] and mutual information [43].

A parallel corpus serves as an excellent resource for mining translation relationships between two languages because the source documents are directly translated in the target language. In addi-

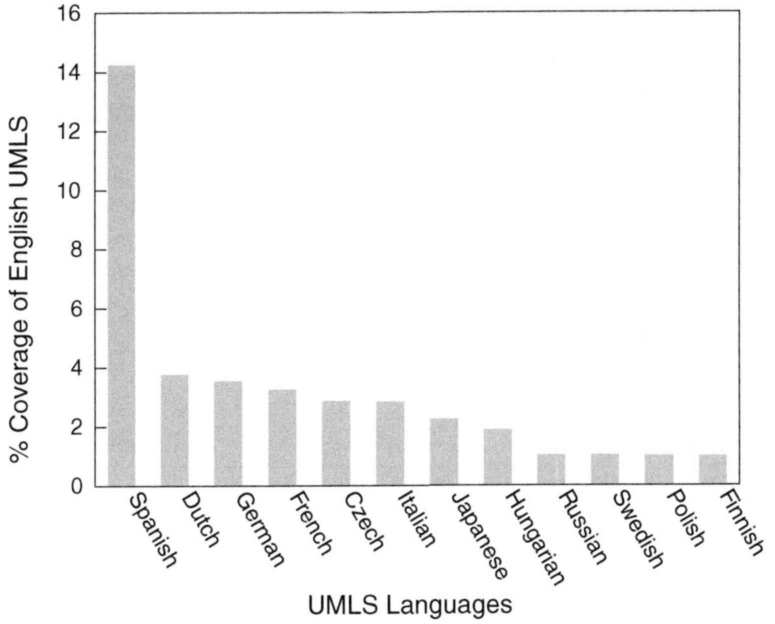

FIGURE 8.2: Percentage of English terms translated in foreign languages in the UMLS Metathesaurus.

tion to this, sentence alignments can be used to narrow down the search space of candidate translations (i.e., a translation is expected to appear in the corresponding target sentences) in order to facilitate the translation task. However, such resources are expensive to construct and they are not available for every domain or language pair. For this reason, the focus of term alignment has shifted to comparable corpora that are larger, cheaper to acquire and are more readily available to researchers. In contrast to a parallel corpus, the documents of a comparable corpus are not mutual translations of each other but they rather share one or more common characteristics (e.g., topic or domain). These second-generation term alignment algorithms that process comparable corpora can be coarsely classified into context-based and compositional translation algorithms.

Context-based (or context projection) approaches hypothesize that a term and its translation tend to appear in a similar lexical context [81, 243]. The lexical context of a term s is represented as a bag of words occurring within a window of N words around s. A seed bilingual dictionary is then used to project/translate the target lexical context (i.e., context vectors) into the source language feature space. In this way, the context vectors of source and target terms are directly comparable. The context projection method is perhaps the most widely used term alignment method from comparable corpora. However, its performance is largely dependent on a number of variables that require careful tuning. The size of the seed dictionary is one such variable. In general, the larger the seed dictionary is, the better the performance is since more target lexical context can be translated using the seed dictionary [194]. The quality of the comparable corpus is a second factor that directly affects the performance of context vectors. Li and Gaussier proposed a corpus comparability measure that estimates the probability of finding the corresponding translation in the target corpus for each source term [156]. They reported that for comparable corpora of higher corpus comparability, the performance of context vectors is increased. Finally, context projection methods are very robust when translating high frequency terms, but the translation accuracy significantly decreases for rare terms. As an example, Chiao and Zweigenbaum achieved an accuracy of 94% (on the top 20 ranked candidates) when translating terms that occur 100 times or more [40], while Morin and Daille reported an accuracy of 21% for multiword terms that occur 20 times or less [192].

While context projection methods use the surrounding context of terms to find translation correspondences, compositional translation algorithms exploit the internal structure of terms. Based on the "property of compositionality" [122] they hypothesize that a translation of a term is a function of the translation of its parts (e.g., words, morphemes, affixes, character *n*-grams). Hence, if we know the translation of the basic building blocks (i.e., textual units), we can extract the corresponding translation of a source term. Table 8.3 illustrates an example of the training and prediction process of a compositional translation algorithm. In this toy example, the compositional method is trained on two English-Greek and English-Romanian instances and learns how to translate the morphemes *cardio* and *vascular*. Once trained, the model uses the previously learned associations of textual units to extract new term translations, e.g., ⟨*cardio-vascular,* καρδι-αγγειακό, cardio-vascular⟩.

TABLE 8.3: Example of Training and Prediction Process of Compositional Methods

	English	Greek	Romanian
training	**cardio**-*myopathy*	*μυο*-**καρδιο**-*παθεια*	**cardio**-*miopatie*
	extra-**vascular**	*εξω*-**αγγειακό**	*extra*-**vascular**
prediction	**cardio-vascular**	**καρδι-αγγειακό**	**cardio-vascular**

Compositional translation methods can be decomposed into lexical and sublexical approaches according to the basic translation unit that they consider. Lexical algorithms exploit word correspondences to align multi-word terms [192, 193], while sublexical methods [67] work on the morpheme-level for single-word term translation. Morin and Daille introduced a lexical compositional method that uses a bilingual word dictionary to translate the individual words of a source multiword term [192]. Candidate translations are generated by considering all possible combinations of the translated words and the most frequently occurring candidate is selected as the correct translation. The authors note that the performance of the dictionary-based approach is bound to the coverage of the seed dictionary. In response to this, they employed morphosyntactic rules that map unknown words to the seed dictionary. In a more recent study, Morin and Daille used a context-based method to augment a bilingual word dictionary with new translation pairs [193]. By increasing the coverage of the seed dictionary, they achieved a significant improvement of the translation performance. Delpech et al. applied the same methodology as in previous lexical compositional methods for single-word term translation by considering morphemes instead of words as the basic translation unit [67]. The reported results showed that 30% of the untranslated terms was due to poor dictionary coverage.

Kontonatsios et al. introduced a supervised machine learning approach, a random forest (RF) classifier, that is able to learn translation correspondences of sublexical units, i.e., character *n*-grams, between terms of a source and target language [143]. An RF classifier is a collection of decision trees voting for the most popular class (i.e., whether or not an input pair of terms is a translation). The decision trees are the underlying mechanism that allows the model to learn a mapping of character *n*-grams between a source and a target language. The branches of a decision tree link together the character *n*-grams (nodes). Furthermore, the RF model ranks candidate translations using the classification confidence. The authors applied their method on a comparable corpus of Wikipedia articles that are related to the medical subdomain of "breast cancer." The RF classifier was shown to largely outperform context-based approaches when translating rare terms while for frequent terms, the two methods achieved approximately the same performance.

The idea of extracting bilingual dictionaries of technical terms from cheaply available comparable corpora is indeed attractive and for the past two decades, several researchers have proposed solutions to the problem. However, to our knowledge, no existing work has demonstrated large-scale experiments. Previous work restricted the evaluation task by translating only 100 [67] or 1,000 [143] terms, which are negligible amounts compared to the 860K missing translations from the Spanish

UMLS. Hence, it has yet to be confirmed how comparable corpora can be exploited to automatically update existing bilingual terminological resources.

8.4 Information Extraction

MEDLINE, the US National Library of Medicine's database of bibliographic references, currently contains over 22 million citations [292]. For the last five years, an average of about 740,000 citations have been added to MEDLINE annually. Based on the generally consistent rise in the number of new biomedical articles being published each year, this average is only bound to further increase in the coming years.

Text mining systems play a significant role in automatically distilling information from biomedical literature. With the goal of ultimately eliminating the need for a reader to manually examine documents for interesting pieces of information, the majority of text mining methods focused on information extraction (IE), an umbrella term for any task that involves the automatic extraction of information from unstructured data. Unlike information retrieval (IR) that finds documents matching a user-supplied search query, IE pertains to the selection of specific facts from text, as well as their human and machine-readable representation. In this section, we expound on three fundamental information extraction tasks, namely, named entity recognition, coreference resolution and relation/event extraction.

8.4.1 Named Entity Recognition

Named entities (NEs) are phrases or combinations of phrases that denote biomedical terms (e.g., proteins, genes, diseases, drugs, cells, chemicals) [6]. Automatically extracting them, a task known as named entity recognition (NER), involves the demarcation of entity names of a specific semantic type, e.g., proteins. It results in annotations corresponding to a name's in-text locations as well as the predefined semantic category it has been assigned to. Shown in Figure 8.3 is a sentence in which all disease, protein and drug names have been demarcated.

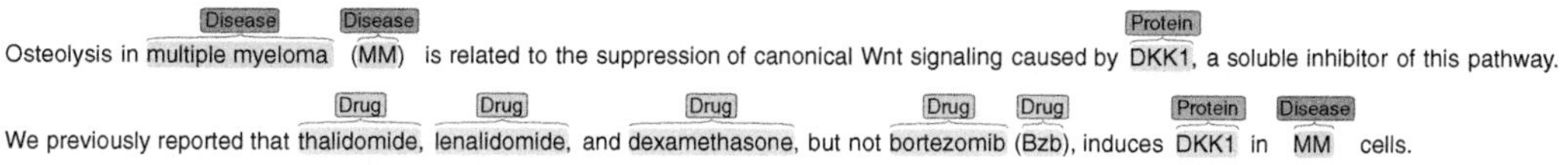

FIGURE 8.3: An excerpt taken from the paper of Qiang et al. [234] with recognized names of diseases, proteins and drugs.

Named entity recognition is fundamental to other tasks such as information extraction, summarization and question answering [57]. The successful recognition of biomedical entities allows for further extraction of useful associations described within text, e.g., protein-protein interactions, molecular events [44].

8.4.1.1 Approaches to Named Entity Recognition

Methods proposed to address NER can be grouped into dictionary-based, rule-based, machine learning-based and hybrid approaches.

Dictionary-based approaches are the most basic among NER methods. They rely on the use of existing biomedical resources containing a comprehensive list of terms, and determine whether expressions in the text match any of the biomedical terms in the provided list [270]. To recognize chemical substance names within patents, Kemp and Lynch [123] compiled stop word lists and a dictionary of chemical name fragments. Tokens in text that match any of the stop words (e.g., *episode* and *phobic*) are immediately eliminated as chemical name candidates. The remaining ones that match entries in the fragment list are then returned as chemical names, e.g., *ethanol, potassium carbonate, n-Propyl bromide*.

Dictionary-based approaches are generally characterized by good precision and low recall [270]. The low recall can be explained by lexical variation, or the fact that biomedical terms have multiple synonyms (e.g., *heart attack* and *myocardial infarction*). Tuason et al. [290] demonstrated that variation in gene names such as word order (e.g., *integrin alpha 4, alpha4 integrin*), punctuation (e.g., *bmp-4, bmp4*), spelling and the more complex case of synonyms account for 79% of false negatives [148]. Furthermore, significant progress in the biomedical domain has led to the rapid growth in the number of novel biomedical terms, making the available resources suffer from relatively lower coverage in some areas of interest. Some methods improved recall by partial rather than exact matching between terms in the biomedical resources and their mentions within text (e.g., BLAST) [270]. Other methods expand the dictionaries in advance by generating spelling variants for the terms in the resources [289]. Aside from these improvements, dictionary-based methods are often coupled with other approaches that employ rules and machine learning [148]. Nevertheless, these methods are still susceptible to low precision due to homonymy in which biomedical terms share the same lexical expressions with common English words (e.g., *dorsal, yellow*) [148, 106, 270]. For instance, abbreviated species names within text (e.g., *E. coli, S. aureus*) can be captured by a rule that requires the first token to be a capitalized, one-character noun, the second token to be a full stop and the last to be another noun. How rules are expressed depends on the syntax that a rule-based NER conforms with. In the Cafetière system [27], for example, the previously given rule can be realized as the following expression: `[orth=capitalized, syn=NN, token=‘‘?’’], [token=‘‘.’’], [syn=NN]`.

The earliest NER systems used rule-based approaches in which hand-crafted rules that capture common structures and patterns were developed [79, 110, 82]. While these methods yield satisfactory performance on the same corpora used to develop the rules, they are difficult to adapt to other domains and obtain lower performance on larger corpora. For example, precision dropped from 91% to 70% when Proux et al. [228] tested their method's performance on a corpus of 25,000 abstracts [201]. While the approach is simple, the construction of rules is time consuming, requires significant human effort and is unable to recognize terms that have not been seen before [201].

Machine learning-based approaches are grouped into supervised, semi-supervised and unsupervised methods. Supported by the availability of various annotated biomedical corpora, supervised machine learning methods have become popular, owing to the satisfactory performance they have demonstrated. Most of the machine learning-based NERs utilized hidden Markov models (HMMs) [48, 191], support vector machines (SVMs) [121], and conditional random fields (CRFs), which have especially shown reliable performance in the biomedical domain [172, 154, 19]. The performance of machine learning methods is highly dependent on the features employed, e.g., orthographic, morphological, lexical and semantic features [19]. It has been established in previous work that feature selection is as important as choosing the algorithm [321].

As supervised machine learning methods are reliant on the availability of annotated corpora for training and evaluating NERs, recent interest has been drawn towards semi-supervised methods that require fewer annotated examples. Semi-supervised methods use large amounts of unlabeled samples and only a small set of labelled ones. Many semi-supervised approaches have been utilized to tackle the NER task including co-training [29], self-training [293], active learning [198] and bootstrapping [310]. Semi-supervised methods are favored over supervised ones for two reasons: they require minimal human effort and usually obtain better classification performance compared to fully supervised learning, since the training is based on large unlabeled data [29, 310].

Hybrid approaches, combining different techniques, have also been successfully applied to named entity recognition. For example, Nichalin et al. combined semi-supervised and supervised methods (bootstrapping and CRFs) to recognize disease names from the literature and demonstrated that using combined approaches outperforms purely supervised CRFs for the same task [273]. In another work, rules, dictionaries and machine learning (i.e., SVMs) were combined to recognize protein names [181].

8.4.1.2 Progress and Challenges

Biomedical text mining community evaluations in the form of shared tasks showed that biomedical NERs have achieved satisfactory performance results. For example, F-scores of 73% and 77% were reported during the 2004 JNLPBA bio-entity [129] and BioNLP 2011 bacteria recognition [130] tasks, respectively. Furthermore, the top-ranked system in the BioCreative II gene mention task [147] achieved an F-score of 87%, which was also reported for chemical compound recognition in BioCreative IV [19].

However, a number of obstacles hamper the further advancement of methods for the task. The first challenge is the rapid proliferation of new biomedical terms, leading to the need for constantly updated biomedical resources. Synonymy (e.g., *PTEN* and *MMAC1* which refer to the same gene) is another challenge, as is the use of abbreviations and acronyms. Some biomedical terms consist of multiple words (e.g., *congestive heart failure*), which make task of identifying term boundaries more complex [44]. Normalization techniques that learn the similarity [153, 106] between mentions of biomedical terms and concepts have been proposed to tackle the challenges posed by acronyms, abbreviations and synonyms.

The performance of NER methods is conventionally evaluated using standard metrics of precision, recall and F-score. Evaluation is carried out based on the availability of annotated corpora that serve as ground truth. Strict and relaxed evaluation variants are typically conducted. In strict evaluation, an entity is counted as a true positive only if its left and right boundaries exactly match those in the ground truth. In contrast, relaxed matching only requires the recognized entity to overlap with the ground truth.

8.4.2 Coreference Resolution

Authors often use various linguistic elements to improve the readability and informativeness of their writing. Readability, on the one hand, is enhanced when the writing style avoids excessive repetition, e.g., by using substitutions such as pronouns in place of previously mentioned names. On the other hand, introducing new information into the discourse by means of coreferring noun phrases (e.g., appositives) helps boost informativeness. Text written with these elements, however, can become difficult to interpret for automated systems. This problem is addressed in a natural language processing task known as reference resolution that aims to bring out the meaning of a mention (referring expression) by determining the concept to which it refers (referent). It concerns the study of both coreference and anaphora. Coreference is characterized by coreferring expressions, i.e., any number of varying mentions referring to a unique referent. In contrast, anaphora involves only a referring expression called anaphor whose interpretation depends on another, previously occurring mention called antecedent [117].

Coreferring textual expressions can be linked together in a list known as a coreference chain. Whereas the automation of this task is known as coreference resolution, automatically determining the antecedent of an anaphor is referred to as anaphora resolution. The former produces a set of coreference chains, while the latter generates anaphor-antecedent pairs. Nevertheless, some overlaps between the results of these tasks can be observed. In many cases, an anaphor and its antecedent corefer or have the same referent, and thus belong to the same chain. From example (8.1) below, the following coreference chains can be formed: {*Krabbe disease, the degenerative disorder*}, {*galactosylceramidase, this enzyme*} and {*myelin*}. It can be observed that the anaphor and antecedent of each of the anaphoric pairs {*this enzyme*, *galactosylceramidase*} and {*the degenerative disorder*, *Krabbe disease*} belong to the same chain and thus, are coreferent.

(8.1) Krabbe disease has been linked to the deficiency of galactosylceramidase. The lack of this enzyme leads to impaired myelin production and brings about the symptoms of the degenerative disorder.

This does not hold, however, in certain cases, such as that of example (8.2). While the mentions *that* and *structure* are in an anaphoric relation, they are not necessarily coreferent since the chemical structure of *compound 3* could be completely different from the structure of the compound denoted by the number *2*.

(8.2) The structure of compound 3 was elucidated through NMR spectroscopic analysis while that of 2 was determined by mass spectrometry.

Conversely, an anaphoric relation does not always hold between a pair of coreferring expressions. Two mentions appearing in different documents may have the same referent, yet cannot be linked by an anaphoric relation since they come from multiple works of discourse. In this section, we focus on document-level coreference resolution, allowing us to cast any two coreferring mentions as anaphoric by treating the latter occurring one as an anaphor and the earlier one as its antecedent. Hence, the following discussion on coreference resolution touches on anaphora resolution as well.

Pioneering work on reference resolution was carried out mostly on general-domain documents. Most of them emerged in the mid-1990s with the organization of the 6th Message Understanding Conference (MUC-6) that introduced a community-wide shared task focusing on resolving coreferring expressions in news reports on the subject of labor dispute negotiation and corporate management succession [90]. The succeeding meeting, MUC-7, included the same task but focused on the domain of aircraft launches and crashes [166]. Much later on, researchers recognized the need to develop methods for biomedical reference resolution, a task which, until now, remains unsolved. The following is an overview of the state of the art in biomedical coreference resolution, touching upon known resources and methodologies.

8.4.2.1 Biomedical Coreference-Annotated Corpora

To support the development of biomedical coreference resolution methods, various annotated corpora have been developed. Both containing MEDLINE abstracts from the molecular biology domain, the MEDSTRACT [229] and MEDCo [75] corpora were annotated following schemes that represent coreferential expressions in a pairwise manner, i.e., through the linking of anaphoric mentions with their respective antecedents. Based on a similar scheme are the annotations of anaphoric relations in the DrugNerAr corpus [263]. As the biomedical text mining community recognized the need for investigating coreference within full-text documents [173], corpora containing full articles have also been made available. MEDCo, for example, was augmented with a set of coreference-annotated full-text articles, while the FlySlip [85] and HANAPIN [18] corpora consist entirely of full papers focused on fruit fly genomics and medicinal chemistry, respectively. Another full-text document collection is the Colorado Richly Annotated Full Text (CRAFT) corpus [47], which is unique in terms of its use of coreference chains (instead of anaphoric pairs) in representing coreferring mentions. Presented in Table 8.4 are more details on the above-mentioned biomedical coreference-annotated corpora, organized according to the following dimensions: topic domain, size, encoding format and inter-annotator agreement (IAA).

TABLE 8.4: Comparison of Coreference-Annotated Biomedical Corpora

Corpus	Domain	Size	Encoding	IAA
MEDSTRACT	molecular biology	100 abstracts	in-line XML	unknown
MEDCo abstracts	molecular biology	1,999 abstracts	in-line XML	83% α
MEDCo articles	molecular biology	1,999 articles	in-line XML	80.7% α
FlySlip	genomics	5 articles	in-line XML	83% κ
HANAPIN	medical chemistry	20 articles	in-line XML	84% α
CRAFT	genomics	97 articles	stand-off XML	61.9% α
DrugNerAr	pharmacology	49 nano-texts	stand-off XML	unknown

8.4.2.2 Approaches to Biomedical Coreference Resolution

A preliminary step to coreference resolution is mention extraction, i.e., the task of recognizing all textual expressions of interest [151]. Depending on the scope of the task at hand, mentions may include a wide range of mention types, e.g., names, pronouns, full phrases and abbreviations. Also, these expressions may pertain to nouns only or may include other parts of speech, e.g., verbs, which are covered by event coreference [47]. Links between these automatically generated mentions, often referred to as system mentions, are then created by coreference or anaphora resolution methods.

Various approaches to biomedical coreference resolution have been developed. Most common among them are methods that take a mention pair classification (MPC) approach, which forms a pair between the active mention (i.e., the expression that is being resolved) and each of several candidate referents. Each pair is then analyzed by a binary classifier that decides whether the two mentions are coreferent or not. Pustejovsky et al. [229] and Liang and Lin [161], for example, developed rule-based systems that employed salience scores to judge whether any two given expressions corefer. BioAR [134] similarly used salience-based scoring, but also incorporated ideas from the Centering Theory (CT) [91]. Also based on the said theory of discourse is the rule-based DrugNerAr [264], a tool for resolving anaphoric expressions pertaining to pharmacological substances. Among the MPC approaches, the machine learning-based method developed by Gasperin and Briscoe [84] is unique in utilizing a Naïve Bayes probabilistic model trained with domain-specific features.

Meanwhile, other approaches cast the coreference resolution problem as a mention pair ranking (MPR) task. Instead of deciding whether mention pairs are coreferent or not, these methods induce a ranking over the pairs formed for an active mention to determine the "most coreferent" candidate. In this way, the competition among the candidate referents for the active mention is captured, unlike in MPC approaches. The work by Nguyen and Kim [213] and Torii and Vijay-Shanker [287] explored maximum entropy ranking models to accomplish this task.

Quite different from both MPC and MPR methods are mention-chain classification (MCC) approaches. Although similar to MPC in its application of classification algorithms, MCC uses partially completed chains to represent candidate referents for an active mention, rather than just mentions. Instances for classification thus consist of mention-chain pairs. An advantage of this representation over mention pairs is increased expressivity – a coreference chain potentially holds more discriminative information, owing to the contribution of the attributes of several expressions. Yang et al. [319], for instance, employed decision trees in their MPC and MCC implementations, and demonstrated that the latter significantly outperformed the former.

Summarized in Table 8.5 are further details on each of the methods discussed above. For the column on reported performance, we indicate a range in cases where the proponents evaluated their method on individual mention types, e.g., pronouns, lexical noun phrases. We refer the reader to the respective cited publications for more information on the evaluation carried out. To date, there is no consensus on the standard measures for evaluating the performance of coreference resolution methods. While the scoring scheme formulated for the MUC conferences [306] has become popular, its failure to take singletons (i.e., one-member chains) into account motivated the development of metrics aiming to alleviate this weakness, including B3 [14], BLANC [247] and CEAF [165].

TABLE 8.5: Comparison of Biomedical Coreference Resolution Approaches

Approach	Proponent/ System	Key ideas	Evaluation corpus	Reported performance
MPC	Castaño et al.	salience-based scoring	MEDSTRACT	74-75% F_1
MPC	Liang & Lin	salience-based scoring	MEDSTRACT	78-92% F_1
MPC	BioAR	salience-based scoring, Centering Theory	120 MEDLINE interactions	61-64% F_1
MPC	DrugNerAr	Centering Theory	DrugNerAr	56-91% F_1
MPC	Gasperin & Briscoe	naïve Bayes problem model	FlySlip	68% F_1
MPR	Nguyen & Kim Briscoe	maximum entropy ranking model	MEDCo abstracts	80.85% success rate
MPR	Torii & Vijay-Briscoe	maximum entropy ranking model	297 MEDLINE abstracts	74% F_1
MCC	Yang et al.	decision trees	100 MEDCo abstracts	81% F_1

Notes: MPC=mention pair classification, MPR=mention pair ranking, MCC=mention chain classification.

8.4.2.3 Advancing Biomedical Coreference Resolution

Biomedical coreference resolution is considered a yet unsolved text mining problem. However, various approaches employed in other domains (which remain unexplored for biomedical applications) offer potential solutions. An example is mention-chain ranking, which has been proposed for general-domain coreference resolution [235] and adapted for medicinal chemistry domain in another work [17]. By representing candidate referents as chains and inducing a ranking among the instances, it combines MCC's expressivity and MPR's capability to capture competition between candidates. Another genre of approaches that has produced encouraging results for general-domain coreference resolution employs graph partitioning algorithms [214]. Under this approach, a document is represented as a graph whose nodes correspond to the mentions to be resolved. In a single step (i.e., without the intermediate steps of classification and ranking), these nodes are clustered by unsupervised methods, e.g., k-nearest neighbor [167] and spectral clustering [36]. Each resulting partition of nodes corresponds to a coreference chain.

Coreference resolution has applications in a number of other biomedical natural language processing tasks, including relation or event extraction [185]. In the BioNLP 2011 Shared Task, a supporting task focused on protein/gene coreference resolution [212] was organized with the aim of improving event extraction results. The levels of performance obtained by the various participating systems, however, validate that there is still plenty of room for improving the accuracy of biomedical coreference resolution methods.

8.4.3 Relation and Event Extraction

As explained in previous sections, biomedical text mining research has focused extensively on the automatic recognition, categorization and normalization of variant forms of biomedical entities, and mapping of these entities to unique identifiers in curated databases. Such tasks, which can now be carried out automatically to high levels of accuracy, can in themselves facilitate entity-based searching of documents, which can be far more effective than simple keyword-based searches (e.g., KLEIO [215], GeneView [281]).

However, when searching the literature, biologists are typically interested not in retrieving *all* instances of documents that mention a particular entity, but rather in locating specific pieces of *knowledge* involving the entity that are reported in the literature, and which can help them to answer research questions. An example of such a question is *Which proteins are positively regulated by IL-2.* Entity-based searching is only powerful enough to retrieve all documents that contain a mention of IL-2 or one or its variants. However, using such search mechanisms, it is not possible to place restrictions on the types of *relationships* in which the entity is involved. For example, to answer the question above, the researcher would only be interested in those documents that describe a positive regulation, and, more specifically, documents in which IL-2 is mentioned as being "responsible" for the regulation. An example of a sentence that would fulfill the researcher's information need is "p21ras proteins are activated by IL-2 in normal human T lymphocytes." In order to allow the results of search systems to more closely match the requirements of biologists, research into relationship and event extraction aims to carry out a deeper analysis of the text, with the aim of identifying and/or characterizing relationships and entities that participate in them. The output of such analyses can be used as the basis for developing advanced semantic search systems that allow queries to be performed over this *structured knowledge*, rather than over keywords or entities. This in turn helps to retrieve a more focused set of results in response to a query.

A simple method of detecting potential relationships is to find instances of sentences or abstracts in which different types of entities and/or interaction-indicating verbs co-occur [225, 83]. This method is sufficiently effective in uncovering unknown associations between different biomedical concepts to have been used in a number of semantic search applications. These include iHOP [107], which highlights terms and verbs in sentences retrieved by searching for a gene, and FACTA+ [288]. This system calculates and visualizes strengths of association between a search term and other important concepts (e.g., genes, diseases and chemical compounds), by finding abstract-level co-occurrences over the whole of the MEDLINE abstract database. Searches in FACTA+ can additionally be refined by specifying types of relationships that should occur in the retrieved abstracts, e.g., POSITIVE REGULATION. Although such methods can identify interesting relationships, they are also likely to retrieve many results in which valid relationships do not exist, e.g., only 30% of pairs of protein entities occurring in the same sentence as each other actually represent an interaction [41]. Improvements in the accuracy of relationship detection can only be obtained through a more in-depth analysis of the structural characteristics of texts.

To facilitate more accurate detection of relationships between biomedical entities in text, research has moved from the use of simple co-occurrence methods to the detection of more complex, structured, representations of actions, relations, processes or states that are expressed in text. Such representations, which are known as events [258], usually consist of several fragments from the text, which are categorized and linked together to create a semantically-oriented structure. Textual fragments included in an event representation typically consist of the trigger, i.e., a word or phrase (usually a noun or verb) that indicates the occurrence of the event, and participants, i.e., entities or secondary events that are involved in the event, or other phrases that are important in the description of the event. Examples of participants include the cause of the event, entities undergoing change during the event, locations/sites and experimental conditions. Participants are typically assigned semantic roles (e.g., AGENT, LOCATION) according to the part that they play in the description of the event. Each event is normally characterized through the assignment of a type (usually from an

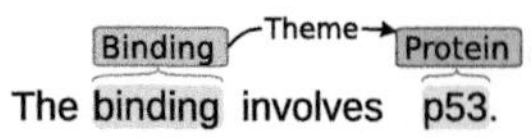

FIGURE 8.4: Simple bio-event example.

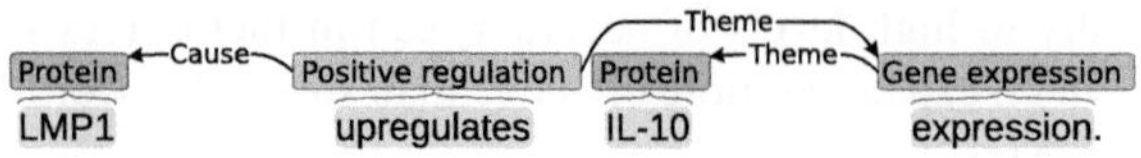

FIGURE 8.5: Sentence containing two events.

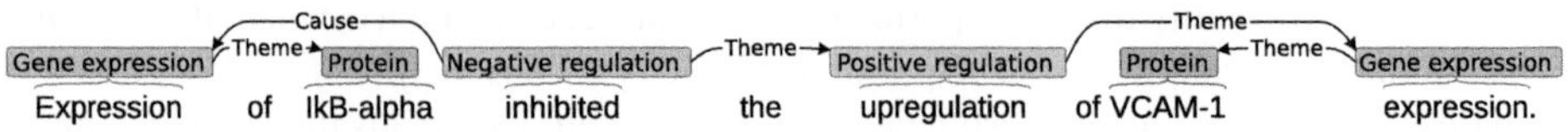

FIGURE 8.6: More complex sentence containing multiple events.

ontology) to denote the nature of the process described (e.g., positive regulation or binding). Figure 8.4 shows a simple example of a bio-event. The trigger (*binding*) allows the semantic event type BINDING to be assigned. A single participant, *p53*, is identified as an entity of type PROTEIN and has been assigned the semantic role THEME, since it undergoes change as part of the event.

Figure 8.5 shows a more complex example, involving 2 events. Firstly, the protein *IL-10* is identified as the THEME of the simple EXPRESSION event. The verb *upregulates* is the trigger for the second, complex event, which has been assigned the semantic event type POSITIVE REGULATION. This event has two participants. The protein *LMP1* has been identified as the CAUSE of the positive regulation event, while the THEME is the previously mentioned EXPRESSION event. Figure 8.6 shows a longer sentence, but demonstrates how event structures can encode complex semantics and normalize over different means of linguistic expression (e.g., the two different EXPRESSION events).

From the above examples, the central importance of analyzing textual structure to the automatic detection of events can be appreciated. Participants of events are typically structurally linked to the trigger verb or noun. For example, it is normally the case that the entity playing the role of AGENT in the event is the subject of the trigger verb, while the THEME is often the object. The detection of appropriate links between triggers and participants within complex biomedical descriptions is becoming increasing feasible, according to advances in the accuracy and robustness of language processing tools that have been adapted or tailored to biomedical text, such as deep syntactic parsers (e.g., Enju [188]).

To complete the event extraction process, structural analyses of the text must be mapped to appropriate semantic representations. Several types of mapping must be undertaken, e.g., to determine how different trigger words and phrases denote different event types, which may vary according to textual context. Additionally, correspondences must be determined between syntactic arguments of triggers and semantic participant types. Although some "typical" mappings between syntactic and semantic levels exist, such as those highlighted above, these are not universal, and they can vary, based both on the semantic type of the event and the idiosyncratic behavior of the specific verb or noun used to denote the event.

In order to address the issues of mapping from surface textual structure to semantic event representations, various resources have been created that provide direct evidence of how events manifest themselves in text. Event annotated corpora constitute collections of texts in which domain experts have manually identified and marked up events. They are used in training event extraction systems, usually through the application of machine learning techniques to the annotated data, and they can also act as a "gold standard" for evaluating the quality of events that are output by event extraction systems [104]. The features of biomedical event annotated corpora vary along a number of axes, including size, the complexity of annotated information and biomedical subdomain of the articles.

The GeneReg corpus [35] identifies 1,770 pairwise relations between genes and regulators in 314 MEDLINE abstracts that deal with the model organism *E. coli*. Relations correspond to three classes in the Gene Regulation Ontology [21]. The BioInfer [230] corpus is larger (2,662 events) and more complex, in that events are assigned to one of the 60 different classes of the BioInfer relationship ontology, and they can have more than two different participants. The GENIA Event Corpus [128] also uses a fairly complex ontology of 36 event types, based largely on a subset of classes from the Gene Ontology [11]. As one of the largest bio-event corpora, it consists of 1,000 abstracts concerning transcription factors in human blood cells, annotated with 36,858 events. Participants include LOCATION, TIME and EXPERIMENTAL CONTEXT, in addition to THEME and CAUSE. Negation and speculation information is also annotated. The Multi-Level Event Extraction (MLEE) corpus [232] aims to improving coverage of event extraction systems, through its annotation of information pertaining to multiple levels of biological organization, from the molecular to the whole organism.

The Gene Regulation Event Corpus (GREC) [283] is more restricted in terms of domain, size and event types (240 MEDLINE abstracts relating to the *E. coli* and human species, with 3,067 bio-events). However, its unique feature is its rich set of event arguments — 13 different semantic role types are annotated. GREC was instrumental in the creation of the BioLexicon [284], a comprehensive lexical resource that includes not only extensive coverage of biomedical terms and their variants, but also accounts for the syntactic and semantic behavior of verbs within biomedical text. As such, the BioLexicon can be an asset in the event extraction process.

The increasing availability of biomedically-oriented language processing tools and supporting resources has resulted in the growth of automatic event extraction into a rapidly maturing area of biomedical TM research. An major driving force behind the research interest in this area has been the organization of the BioNLP community Shared Tasks (STs) [132, 208]. Since 2009, these bi-annual STs have set increasingly ambitious tasks that have aimed to broaden the horizons of event extraction research and to encourage the development of practical and wide coverage event extraction systems. A further major contribution of the tasks has been the creation and release of 11 new event-annotated corpora, which complement those introduced above, in terms of their coverage of different text types (i.e., full papers as well as abstracts), new bio-medical subdomains and various target application areas.

A common theme running through each ST has been the inclusion of a GE (GENIA Event) task, involving the same textual subdomain as the original GENIA Event Corpus (i.e., molecular biology), and a subset of the original event types. The BioNLP'09 GE task [132] was largely based around a simplified subset of the original GENIA Event Corpus [128], using only nine of the original 36 event types. Subsequent GE tasks have added complexity, by supplementing abstracts with full papers (BioNLP'11) [135], or by using an exclusively full-paper corpus, annotated with an extended range of event types (BioNLP'13) [131]. Further tasks of the BioNLP'11 and BioNLP'13 STs have concentrated on different biomedical subdomains and/or target application areas, each defining a custom set of event types. These include Epigenetics and Post-translational modifications (EPI), Infectious Diseases (ID) [233] (BioNLP'11), Cancer Genetics (CG) [231] and Pathway Curation (PC) [219] (BioNLP'13).

The best performing systems extracting GENIA-style events have achieved accuracy levels between 50–57% F-score, depending on task and domain. The various tasks within the two latest STs have demonstrated the flexibility of event extraction technology, based on the finding that the best performing systems can maintain comparable levels to those achieved for the GE tasks, even when extraction is applied to full texts instead of abstracts, to new domains or to considerably extended ranges of event types. In addition, the evaluation criteria used for these tasks are more demanding than for the GE task.

Most state-of-the-art event extraction systems employ a machine-learning based pipeline, which carries out the event extraction process as a series of steps, implemented as different modules, i.e., a) identification of event triggers, b) detection of individual participants associated with these triggers and c) construction of complex event structures from the participant-argument pairs. Systems taking this general approach (particularly those employing SVMs as the learning model) have been shown to perform consistently well on many different event extraction tasks. Other approaches have demonstrated competitive performance for certain tasks, e.g., a rule-based approach (BioSEM [33]), and a joint model with minimal domain adaptation (UMass system [249]). The latter was particularly effective when combined with information from Stanford's parser-based model [171] in the stacking-based FAUST system [170].

EventMine [184] and the Turku Event Extraction System (TEES) [25] both employ SVM-based pipelines (each using different sets of features), which facilitates ease of portability to new tasks, through training on different corpora. Such flexibility has allowed both systems to be adapted to several tasks within the different BioNLP STs. Both systems have recently substantially decreased the overhead required to port them to new tasks and domains, alleviating the need for additional programming [182, 26]. The robustness of the systems has been demonstrated through their application to very large collections of biomedical literature. Both systems have been run over the entire PubMed collection of over 20 million biomedical abstracts, while TEES has additionally been applied to 460,000 full text articles from the PubMed Central open access database [302, 300, 301].

TEES has participated in the majority of tasks in each of the three STs, achieving the best performance in several of these, including the GE tasks of BioNLP'09 and BioNLP'13, the EPI task of BioNLP'11 and the GE task of BioNLP'13. EventMine participated formally in only the PC and CG tasks of the BioNLP'13 ST, for which it achieved the first and second place respectively, with the highest recall for both tasks [182]. Following the BioNLP'09 ST, EventMine was able to achieve better results than any of the originally participating systems, including significantly improved results for complex events (i.e., those that include other events as participants). Subsequent incorporation of a new coreference detection system and domain adaptation techniques [185], which allow features from multiple annotated corpora to be incorporated into the trained model, resulted in further improved results on the BioNLP'09 ST data, as well as the ability to outperform all original participants in the BioNLP'11 GE and ID tasks. In order to eliminate the need to train new versions of the system for each new domain, a recent improvement to EventMine allows the creation of a single event extraction system with broad semantic coverage, through training on multiple corpora with partial semantic annotation overlap [182].

8.5 Discourse Interpretation

As the previous sections in this chapter have demonstrated, biomedical text mining research has focused extensively on the extraction of entities and relations/events in which they are involved. Although event-based searching can retrieve many more relevant documents and distill essential factual knowledge from text than is possible using traditional keyword searches, the typical event representations (and the event extraction systems based on such representations) do not take into account all available information pertaining to the interpretation of the event. It is also important to consider that biomedical research articles have a discourse structure, and thus that the interpretation of information extracted will usually be affected by the discourse context in which it appears. Failure to take such context into account can result in the loss of vital information, which could result in incorrect assumptions being made about the information extracted. Furthermore, new knowledge can be obtained by connecting the newly extracted events with already existing information.

8.5.1 Discourse Relation Recognition

The connections between textual spans, also known as *discourse relations*, make the text coherent and cohesive, and their automatic discovery can lead to a better understanding of the conveyed knowledge. Although discourse relations have been studied for a long time in the general domain, a consensus on a specific set of relations has not emerged. The numerous theories define the relations at different levels of abstraction, from the more general to the more specific.

Discourse relations are usually composed of three elements: a discourse connective and two arguments. The relations can be either explicit or implicit, depending on whether or not they are expressed in text using overt *discourse connectives* (also known as *triggers*). For instance, example (8.3) shows two sentences between which a SPECIFICATION relation exists, but which is not overtly marked by the connective *specifically*.

(8.3) IL-10 signaling is impaired in macrophages upon chronic exposure to proinflammatory cytokines such as TNF-α and IL-1 and immune complexes.
Cell surface expression of IL-10R1 is decreased in synovial fluid dendritic cells due to the presence of TNF-α, IL-1, and granulocyte-macrophage colony-stimulating factor.

In the biomedical domain, the interest in discourse relations appeared only recently. In 2011, Prasad et al. published the BioDRB corpus [227], containing 24 full text articles manually annotated with 16 discourse relations, in a similar manner to the PDTB [226]. Following a similar approach, the BioCause corpus [180] contains annotations only for causal relations in 19 full text articles. This corpus also differs from BioDRB by the fact that it does not allow discontinuous textual spans for the connective and arguments.

This type of information could be leveraged by epidemiologists to identify patterns and predict disease outbreaks, health care professionals to provide personalized treatments based on patient history, etc. Nevertheless, discourse relations pose two main difficulties when trying to recognize them, one regarding discourse connectives, and the other regarding their arguments.

Firstly, discourse connectives are both highly ambiguous and highly variable. Take, for instance, the example (8.4) below, where the token *and* expresses causality. However, in most other contexts, the same token has a non-causal meaning, denoting only conjunctions.

(8.4) SsrB binds within SPI-2 *and* activates SPI-2 genes for transcription.

This is the usual case with most closed-class part-of-speech words, such as conjunctions and adverbials. Other examples of trigger types more commonly used as causal connectives and belonging to open-class parts-of-speech are *suggesting*, *indicating* and *resulting in*. For instance, example (8.5) contains two mentions of *indicating*, but neither of them implies discourse causality.

(8.5) Buffer treated control cells showed intense green staining with syto9 (*indicating* viability) and a lack of PI staining (*indicating* no dead/dying cells or DNA release).

Furthermore, their variability leads to numerous ways of expressing the same connective, due to the open-class properties of nouns and verbs. Take example (8.6), where the connective *this result suggests that* indicates a causal relation.

(8.6) The hilE mRNA level measured by real-time PCR also revealed that hilE expression was increased in SR1304 by about two-fold.

This result suggests that Mlc can act as a negative regulator of hilE.

The same idea can be conveyed using synonyms of these words, such as *observation*, *experiment*, *indicate*, *show*, *prove*, etc. The high variability reflects in obtaining a low recall, since there will be many false negatives.

With respect to the two arguments, they are more difficult to recognize than connectives. Firstly, the spans of text that make up the arguments are of arbitrary length, varying significantly from one case to another. Arguments can go up to 100 tokens in length in the case of CAUSE, and up to 70 in the case of EFFECT [180].

Secondly, the position of the two arguments around the connective can change. Although most of the relations follow a ARG1-CONN-ARG2 pattern, there is an important percentage of relations, 20%, which do not obey this rule [180]. Moreover, almost half of all relations have one argument in a different sentence than that of the connective. Thus, the search space increases significantly and the difficulty of a correct recognition increases too. The problem is further complicated by allowing discontinuous spans, such as those in BioDRB.

This leads to the third issue, which regards the distance between the trigger and the arguments. About half of the cases have the argument located in the previous sentence, but the rest spread up to the tenth previous sentence [180].

Despite the existence of the two previously mentioned corpora and importance and difficulty of the task, currently there are no end-to-end discourse parsers specifically designed for biomedical literature. Most existing work has been dedicated to discourse connectives, where the performance reaches values of around 0.80 F-score. However, it does not tackle the problem of disambiguating between the multiple relation types and is restricted to only identifying the textual span of the connective [241, 113]. Mihăilă and Ananiadou take it a step further and attempt to recognize causal discourse connectives using various machine learning algorithms [178], and then identify their argument using rule-based heuristics [177].

8.5.2 Functional Discourse Annotation

A coherent discourse structure is a vital element in the production of convincing research articles. Authors not only need to explain the new work/experiments carried out as part of their study, but also have to convince readers of the significance and novelty of their research. This is partly achieved by "framing" the description of new work within an appropriate context, e.g., by providing background knowledge as a solid grounding for new work being carried out, or by establishing links and comparisons to information found in previously published studies. In addition, experimental results must be interpreted and analyzed in order to draw appropriate conclusions. In order to maximize the significance and impact of any conclusions drawn, authors also need to "pitch" their interpretations carefully. This requires the consideration of various interacting factors, which can result in different nuances of information presentation. Often, authors will incorporate "hedging," i.e., uncertainty, into their descriptions of experimental outcomes, the degree and nature of which may depend on, e.g., an author's own confidence in the soundness of the methods he has used, or in the perceived reliability of his experimental interpretations.

Textual segments can thus be classified along a number of different dimensions, based upon:

a) Rhetorical function, e.g., whether the information in the textual segment relates to factual knowledge, results or analyses from previous studies, methods, new experimental results or analyses of these results.

b) Discourse-related features, e.g., the presence and level of hedging, the type of evidence that is used to support stated claims, etc.

8.5.2.1 Annotation Schemes and Corpora

Several different annotation schemes have been proposed that encode some or all of the above types of information. The schemes vary along several axes, including perspective, complexity and granularity of the textual units to which the scheme is applied, which range from complete sentences, down to events, of which there may be several in a single sentence.

In terms of schemes relating to the rhetorical function of sentences, a common approach has been to devise categories that characterize the contribution of sentences towards the logical structure of the document. The simplest of these concern biomedical abstracts [174, 254, 103], with only a small number of categories that reflect the focused and relatively fixed nature of the types of information expressed in abstracts, e.g., OBJECTIVE, METHOD, RESULT, CONCLUSION. Extensions of abstract-oriented models account for the wider range of information provided in full articles, through the addition of categories such as HYPOTHESIS, STRATEGY, EXPERIMENT AND DISCUSSION [65, 158]. The former scheme allows NEW/OLD attributes to be assigned, to distinguish between new knowledge and knowledge pertaining to previous work. The Argumentative Zoning (AZ) model [279] is also largely concerned with knowledge attribution, with a major aim being to distinguish between sentences that concern generally accepted BACKGROUND KNOWLEDGE, OTHER ideas that are attributed to other work outside of the study described in the current paper, and descriptions of the author's OWN new work. Encoding authors' attitudes towards other peoples' work is also an integral part of the scheme. The AZ scheme was originally designed for general scientific academic writing, but it has subsequently been extended and adapted for application to biomedical research articles [189]. In particular, the various types of information typically expressed about authors' OWN work motivated the creation of subcategories that are assigned to sentences corresponding to METHODS, RESULTS, INSIGHTS and IMPLICATIONS.

Other schemes and corpora have been created to capture other specific types of discourse features. These efforts include the classification of sentences according to whether they express negation [2] or speculation [175, 162] or the identification of negation/speculation scopes [307].

Although most schemes perform classification at the sentence level, others acknowledge that several discourse-level shifts can occur within the boundaries of a single sentence, by performing annotation at the level or clauses or sentence segments. Consider example (8.7) below.

(8.7) Inhibition of the MAP kinase cascade with PD98059, a specific inhibitor of MAPK kinase 1, may prevent the rapid expression of the alpha2 integrin subunit.

While the main purpose of the sentence is to report a speculative analysis, i.e., *Inhibition of the MAP kinase may prevent the expression of the alpha2 integrin subunit*, it also contains factual information, *PD98059* is *a specific inhibitor of MAPK kinase 1*. In the case of Wilbur et al. [313], a new segment is created whenever there is a change in the discourse-level information being expressed. The scheme is also more complex than those introduced five different features of each textual segment, i.e., focus (a simplified classification of rhetorical function), polarity, certainty, type of evidence and direction/trend (either increase or decrease in quantity/quality).

The assignment of discourse-level information to events also requires special consideration, since there may be several events within a single sentence, each of which may have a different interpretation. It has been shown that event-level discourse features cannot be inherited straightforwardly from the features of the textual spans in which they are contained. For example, a comparison of event annotation in the GENIA corpus with the linguistically-oriented scope annotation in the BioScope corpus showed it often the case that events falling within the linguistic scope of a speculated phrase are not necessarily speculated themselves [308].

In response to this, several of the event-annotated corpora introduced in Section 8.4.3 associate basic discourse-level features with annotated events, although these are generally limited to whether or not negation or speculation is specified towards the event. However, a more detailed scheme [207], which is tailored to biomedical events, recognizes that several different types of information may be specified within the textual contexts of events, which can affect their discourse interpretation. In common with the scheme of Wilbur et al. [313], this meta-knowledge scheme to encode the interpretation of bio-events is multidimensional, and encodes five different types of information, i.e., knowledge type (e.g., FACT, OBSERVATION, ANALYSIS), certainty level, information source (fact pertains to current or a previous study), polarity (POSITIVE/NEGATIVE) and biological manner (rate/strength of biological interaction). The scheme has been applied to create the GENIA-MK corpus [285], which is an enriched version of original GENIA corpus, and has also been used to annotate a set of full papers of full papers annotated according to the scheme [204]. While the knowledge type dimension encodes information relating to the rhetorical function of the event, its values are more abstract that those typically assigned by sentence-level schemes, which are more strongly tied to the structural aspects of the article. Thus, as demonstrated by Liakata et al. [160], event-level discourse information can complement sentence-level information by providing a finer-grained analysis.

8.5.2.2 Discourse Cues

The presence of specific cue words and phrases has been shown to be an important factor in classifying biomedical sentences automatically according to whether or not they express speculation [162, 175]. Corpus-based studies of hedging (i.e., speculative statements) in biological texts [111, 112] reinforce this, in that 85% of hedges were found to be conveyed lexically, i.e., through the use of particular words and phrases, which can be quite different to academic writing in general, with modal auxiliaries (e.g., may, could, would) playing a more minor role, and other verbs, adjectives and adverbs playing a more significant role [112]. It has additionally been shown that, in addition to speculation, specific lexical markers can denote other types of information pertinent to the identification of various types of discourse-level information [251]. As an example of the role of lexical cues in discourse interpretation, consider the following sentences, each of which contains the same event, but has a different discourse interpretation:

a) It is known that the narL gene product activates the nitrate reductase operon.

b) We examined whether the narL gene product activates the nitrate reductase operon.

c) The narL gene product did not activate the nitrate reductase operon.

d) These results suggest that the narL gene product might be activated by the nitrate reductase operon.

e) Previous studies have shown that the narL gene product activates the nitrate reductase operon.

In sentence (a), the word *known* tells us that the event is a generally accepted fact, while in (b), the word *examined* shows that the event is under investigation, and hence the truth value of the event is unknown. The presence of the word *not* in sentence (c) shows that the event is negated. In sentence (d), the word *suggest* indicates that the event is stated based on a somewhat tentative analysis. The level of speculation is further emphasized by the presence of the word *might*. Finally, the phrase *Previous studies* in (e) shows that the event is based on information available in previously published papers, rather than relating to new information from the current study. de Waard and Pander Maat [66] recognize that lexical cues relevant to discourse structure typically occur within certain formulaic phrases, which they call regulatory segments, since they regulate the discourse flow. For example, the phrase *It is known that* is used to introduce factual information. Various corpus-based studies have collected words and phrases relevant to identifying various discourse features of the text. Such lexical items have been shown to be domain-dependent, at least to a certain extent [282] and can be wide ranging, e.g., Kilicoglu and Bergler [124] identified 190 distinct hedging cues that are used in biomedical research articles. The interpretation of such cues can, however, be context-dependent [256], which provides motivation for their annotation within corpora, to facilitate learning and disambiguation of context-sensitive. Such annotation has been undertaken in a small number of the corpora introduced above. Features other than lexical clues can be important in determining discourse functions and features. For example, the main verb in the clause, tense, section type, position of the sentence within the paragraph and presence of citations in the sentence have all been identified as potentially important features [189].

8.5.2.3 Automated Recognition of Discourse Information

Various approaches have been taken to the automatic assignment of discourse information to textual segments and events. Approaches to abstract sentence classification have employed a range of different learning methods (e.g., Naïve Bayes [254], SVMs [174] and CRFs [103]) and have generally used a fairly simple sets of features, mainly based on either bags of words from the sentence or n-grams (possibly with stemming applied), combined with positional information about the sentence, and possibly the category assigned to the previous sentence [103]. All systems were able to achieve F-Scores of 0.85 or higher in predicting certain sentence categories, while sentence position was found to be essential to improving classification accuracy in all cases.

Systems aimed at predicting rhetorical sentence categories in full texts have used a wider range of feature types. Teufel and Moens [280] used a Naïve Bayes classifier to predict AZ categories, using 16 features including sentence position and length, presence of significant terms, verb syntax features and previous sentence category. The additional use of categorized lists of expressions and phrases typically found within different sentence types emphasizes the importance of lexical cues, as described above. The system was able to achieve F-scores of up to 0.61, according to the category being predicted. A similar set of features was used to train both SVM and CRF classifiers to predict the 11 categories of the CoreSC scheme [159], with F-scores ranging from 0.18 to 0.76 F-score, according to category, with only small differences being observed between SVM and CRF performance. The most important features were found to be n-grams, grammatical relations, the presence of specific verbs, lexical cues, in the form of section headings. Abstract sentence classification tasks were also found to benefit from such an extended set of features, with an average F-Score of 0.91 over the different categories being achieved by an SVM classifier [94]. The use of active learning has been demonstrated as a promising method to reduce the amount of training data needed for abstract sentence classification tasks [95].

In terms of the automated detection of discourse-related features, most work has focused on negation and/or speculation detection. For example, Agarwal and Yu [1] developed a CRF-based classifier to detect the scope of negations, using words and parts of speech as features. The participation of 23 teams in the CONLL-2011 shared task on detecting hedges and their scopes, stimulated a large amount of new research in this area. A variety of approaches were taken including purely rule-based [126], purely machine learning-based [190, 157] or hybrid approaches that combine machine learning classifiers with hand-crafted rules [305, 248].

Moving onto the recognition of discourse information for events, Nawaz et al. [205] tackled the problem of detecting negation within pre-annotated event structures. They found that a random forest classifier using a variety of syntactic, semantic and lexical features, coupled with a list of domain specific cue words, performed better than other learning algorithms, achieving an F-Score of 0.70 on the BioNLP'009 dataset. In the BioNLP STs, the more complex task of recognizing events and assigning negation and speculation information to them was addressed. Performance levels have been quite low, which is thought to be partly due to the lack of annotated cue words and phrases in the training corpora [132]. While a rule-based system, based on dependency parser output [125] achieved the best results for both negated and speculated events in the BIONLP'-09 ST (0.23 and 0.25 F-score, respectively) and for speculated events in the BioNLP-11 GE task (0.27 F-score) [127], the use of the SVM classifiers have recently exhibited slightly superior performance [26, 182].

EventMine-MK [186] incorporates an SVM-based module to assign features for the five different meta-knowledge dimensions introduced above. Features used in this module include the shortest dependency paths between event participants and meta-knowledge clue expressions, sentence position and citation information. Macro-averaged F-Scores for different dimensions range between 0.59 and 0.80, and the system could outperform the original participants of the BioNLP'09 ST in detecting negated and speculated events. Separate studies [203, 206] have shown that using custom sets of features to predict different meta-knowledge dimensions can achieve superior results.

A problem of similar complexity is the classification of textual segments according to the five dimensions of the scheme proposed by Wilbur et al. [313]. With an SVM classifier, using terms occurring within the textual fragments as features, performance levels of between 0.64 and 0.97 were achieved [266].

8.6 Text Mining Environments

Advanced text mining methods often build on top of existing preprocessing tools and form multistep pipelines, i.e., text mining workflows. For example, syntactic parsing must be preceded by part-of-speech tagging, named entity recognition by parsing and so forth. Hence, the ability to chain individual components into workflows is a requirement for the development of complex text mining applications. Text mining environments alleviate the requirement for programming and technical skill and allow users to "mix and match" components within workflows. Furthermore, text mining environments enable interoperability of tools and resources by defining a common and standard discipline for developing pipelined applications. For these reasons, an increasing number of workflow construction environments, or platforms, is becoming available to the community.

The General Architecture for Text Engineering (GATE) [53] is a long-standing workflow construction environment that has been used for the development of various biomedical text mining applications. It integrates a large number of text mining components, tuned for the biomedical domain [54]. GATE features a graphical user interface (GUI) and an integrated development environment (IDE) that aims to assist programming tasks. Furthermore, GATE implements a workflow management module, a central module of text mining environments, which is responsible for coordinating components and resources in pipelines and for the execution of the workflow. However, GATE offers a limited workflow management that lacks the iterative, parallel or nested execution of pipelines [16].

The Unstructured Information Management Architecture (UIMA) [72], an OASIS standard, is a robust and flexible framework with a special focus on reusability and interoperability of language resources (LRs). UIMA was originally developed by IBM, and subsequently donated as an Apache open source project. The underlying infrastructure implements a sophisticated workflow management that allows the development of conditional, iterative and parallel workflows. In addition to this, UIMA defines an analytic interoperability mechanism and common data structures abiding by annotation schemata or type systems. A comparative study of GATE and UIMA is given in a survey by Bank and Schierle [16].

Building on the interoperability of the UIMA framework, numerous researchers distribute their own text mining repositories as UIMA-compliant. Examples include U-Compare [119], DKPro [97], BioNLP UIMA [20], JCoRe [98] and cTAKES [259].

U-Compare [119] is a graphical text mining platform that builds on top of UIMA. Primarily, U-Compare focuses on the development of biomedical text mining workflows, but also supports the construction of a number of general-purpose applications such as machine translation, automatic summarization, and text-to-speech conversion [144]. U-Compare includes its own type system that covers a wide range of annotation types that are common to many text mining components. Furthermore, U-Compare implements a comparison and evaluation mechanism that is used to tune the performance of text mining workflows. As an example, Kolluru et al. [141] showed that tokenization is an important preprocessing component for chemical named entity recognition (NER). Using U-Compare's comparison mechanism, they were able to evaluate NER workflows that used different tokenizers and identified the optimal pipeline for their task.

Another UIMA-compliant text mining platform is the Web-based Argo workbench [239]. It provides its users with access to a wide range of elementary NLP components, which can be arranged into customizable workflows via a block diagramming tool. While similar to U-Compare in terms of a subset of available biomedical components and support for workflow evaluation, Argo is unique in its capabilities allowing for complex, graph-like workflows and the manual validation of automatically generated annotations. It is flexible in its support for type system customizations [240], but at the same time fosters interoperability by facilitating conversions between disparate type systems [237].

Some general-purpose scientific workflow construction platforms also provide support for text processing and analysis. Examples include the Konstanz Information Miner (KNIME) [22] and PipelinePilot [304]. Software dependencies of constructed workflows, however, pose a barrier to the wide applicability of text mining solutions. Although these platforms have functionalities for sharing and importing/exporting workflows, exchangeability is often limited to the same framework. Consequently, significant development effort is required to integrate workflows with external systems. To overcome these issues, more and more developers have turned to Web services as a means for deploying their text mining solutions. Due to their public availability and compliance with well-known standards, e.g., Representational State Transfer (REST) architecture, Web services have become extensively used and accepted, prompting the emergence of Web service registries. Examples include BioCatalogue [23], a repository of bioinformatics tools, and a library of biomedical concept recognizers known as Whatizit [246].

While the construction of tools using text mining platforms facilitates customization and eliminates the need for highly technical skills, their availability as Web services fosters reusability and interoperability across various platforms. These considerations prompted U-Compare to offer a mechanism to convert UIMA-only, standalone workflows into Web services that build on top of open standards (REST and SOAP protocols) [142]. Argo's Web service reader and writer components similarly allow for the invocation of its workflows as Web services. In this way, the UIMA workflows are decoupled from the platforms they originated from. These Web-based workflows can be reused in any application compliant with the above open standards. Taverna [220] is an example of an application that features a GUI for constructing workflows consisting of third-party Web services. Table 8.6 summarizes the features of the various platforms just described.

8.7 Applications

Having shown in the previous sections the different resources and methods that facilitate text mining, we demonstrate in this section its significance in addressing different information needs. Specifically, we provide a discussion of three timely applications, namely, semantic search, statistical machine translation and data curation.

8.7.1 Semantic Search Engines

The results of applying EventMine and TEES to PubMed document collections have been used to drive different semantic search applications. In the EVEX system [301], the user begins by searching for a gene, which causes the event types in which it participates to be displayed. Users can then

TABLE 8.6: Comparison of Platforms with Text Mining Capabilities

	GD	U-Compare	Argo	KNIME	Taverna	PP
Based on a standard interoperability framework	✗	✓	✓	✗	✗	✗
Web-based	✗	✗	✓	✗	✗	✗
GUI-based workflow construction	✓	✓	✓	✓	✓	✓
In-built library of components	✓	✓	✓	✓	✗	✓
Component-implementation independent	✗	✗	✗	✗	✓	✗
Focused on text mining	✓	✓	✓	✗	✗	✗
Focused on biomedical applications	✓	✓	✓	✗	✓	✗
Workflow sharing	✓	✓	✓	✓	✓	✓
Web service deployment	✗	✓	✓	✓	✓	✓

Notes: GD=GATE Developer, PP=PipelinePilot.

further "drill down" to information of interest in several ways, e.g., to discover all examples of given event type that have a specific Cause and Theme, or to find different types of events that include a specific pair of genes/proteins as participants. EventMine extraction results have been used to create an enhanced version of the MEDIE search system. While the original version of MEDIE [187] allows structured queries in the form of <subject, verb, object>, facilitated through the application of a deep syntactic analyzer tuned to the biomedical domain [99] to PubMed abstracts, the event extraction results produced by EventMine facilitate the provision of a more semantically-oriented search template, that further abstracts from the structure of the text. Queries are specified through the initial selection of an event type, with the ability to specify further restrictions on the participants of events. Event-based MEDIE search results are also used within PathText 2 [183], an integrated search system that links biological pathways with supporting knowledge in the literature. Formal pathway models are converted into queries that are submitted to three semantic search systems operating over MEDLINE, namely, KLEIO, FACTA+ and MEDIE (both the original and event-based versions). The accuracy of the event-based MEDIE retrieval methods means that documents retrieved by this method are ranked first by the system.

EvidenceFinder is a further search system, which utilizes information in the BioLexicon to allow event-based filtering of search results and efficient location of information within over 2.6 million articles from PubMed and PubMed Central contained within the Europe PubMed Central database. When an entity is entered as a search term, a list of questions is generated [28] that illustrate the most frequent types of events in which the search entity is involved in the underlying document collection. Events are extracted via a number of domain-specific tools and resources, namely the Enju Parser adapted to the biomedical domain [99], a named entity recognizer [257] and information about patterns of verb behavior from the BioLexicon.

Moving on to discourse, automatic detection of rhetorical categories and discourse features can assist researchers in writing literature reviews, by finding sentences in published articles relevant to authors' research questions, or by generating informative summaries [96, 50]. For database curators, discourse analysis can help them to find sentences containing new experimental evidence and methods is particularly important [320], and the analysis of discourse features can help to isolate new knowledge from previously reported knowledge. Identification of new knowledge can also be important in building and updating models of biological processes, such as pathways [217].

Discourse-level information can also be important in helping researchers to locate inconsistencies or contradictions in the literature, i.e., by finding events with similar participants but conflicting meta-knowledge values.

Discourse-level information has been incorporated into a number of semantic search applications. As part of its advanced search criteria, MEDIE allows users to restrict their searches to sentences of one of the following types: title, objective, method, result or conclusion. The classification is carried out according to the method described in [103]. Furthermore, a recently released update to the EvidenceFinder system, which is focused on anatomical entities, automatically assigns meta-knowledge information to the identified events. The events retrieved by question-based filtering display the discourse-level features assigned to them, while one or more meta-knowledge features can be used as a means to filter the initial set of results retrieved.

8.7.2 Statistical Machine Translation

In the beginning of 1990s, Jelinek's group at IBM labs proposed a statistical approach to machine translation (MT) [32], i.e., statistical machine translation (SMT), as opposed to the existing rule-based MT [303]. For over two decades now, SMT has been widely adopted by the MT community and researchers have made significant contributions to the first IBM models. Some of the most notable developments in SMT research include: (a) the automatic evaluation of MT systems using the BLEU score [222], (b) the evolution from a word-based [32] to a phrase-based translation model [140], which led to substantial improvement of the translation accuracy, (c) the release of the Europarl parallel corpus [138] which provides free data for training SMT systems for most of the European languages and (d) the release of Moses [139], a popular open-source SMT toolkit that is used as a benchmark, baseline system.

While research in SMT has been rapidly evolving (over 400 research papers were published only in 2013), the vast majority of state-of-the-art SMT approaches faces the same drawbacks since it builds on the same principles. Firstly, SMT systems can only be trained on parallel data that are only available for a limited number of language pairs and domains (see Term Alignment subsections for a detailed comparison of parallel and comparable corpora). In response to this, researchers have proposed to automatically mine parallel sentences from comparable corpora [200, 199, 245]. Secondly, current SMT technologies fail to translate unseen/out-of-vocabulary (OOV) words, i.e., words that do not occur in the training data. Daumé III and Jagarlamudi [61] showed that unseen words are responsible for half of the errors made by an SMT system when applied on a new domain. To address the OOV problem, term alignment techniques are used to mine OOV translations from comparable corpora. The extracted dictionary is then integrated in the phrase table of the SMT [114, 143]. The reported results show an improvement of 0.5 to 1.5 BLEU points over a baseline SMT system that only uses parallel data.

The use of MT technologies in the biomedical domain has many potential benefits. The United States Census of 2000 [268] counted approximately 47 million people living in the United States who spoke a language other than English at home and about 19 million people who are limited in English proficiency. This phenomenon poses severe limitations in doctor-patient dialogues. Flores et al. [74] noted that 63% of translation errors had possible clinical consequences. Hence, SMT systems that are adapted to the specialized medical language can facilitate the communication between doctors and patients. Additionally, MT technologies can largely benefit the non-English speaking population by making the vast amount of the biomedical literature published in English available to their native language.

Recently, several approaches have examined the use of MT technologies in the biomedical domain. Wu et al. [316] built biomedical SMT systems for 6 languages and they reported satisfactory results for high-resource language pairs, e.g., English-Spanish, for which enough parallel data exist in the biomedical domain. However, when only small training corpora are available, e.g., for English-Hungarian, the translation performance of the SMT system drastically decreases. Zeng-

Treitle et al. [324] investigated the use of a general MT tool, namely Babel Fish, to translate English medical records into four languages. Their findings showed that 76% to 92% of the translations were incomprehensible. Hence, it is clear that a general-purpose MT tool needs to be tuned, i.e., domain adapted, before applied on a domain specific corpus. As an example, Eck et al. [71] used a domain specific lexicon, namely UMLS, to domain adapt an SMT system for translating doctor-patient dialogues. The obtained results showed an improvement of the translation performance. Pecina et al. [224] used language models to identify in-domain parallel sentences that happen to occur in an out-domain corpus. Their adapted SMT system largely outperformed the baseline, general-purpose system when translating user search queries of the medical domain.

EMEA is one of the largest, freely available biomedical parallel corpora. EMEA is a collection of parallel documents in 22 European languages from the European Medicines Agency. The corpus has been sentence aligned using an automatic tool and is readily available for training SMT systems. MuchMore is a parallel corpus of journal medical abstracts available only for English-German. The automatic translation of patents is a challenging topic in SMT because patent documents tend to contain long sentences [278]. In the biomedical domain, available patent-related parallel corpora are: COPPA (English-French) and PatTR (English-French, English-German). Finally, the 9th Workshop on Statistical Machine Translation (ACL 2014 WMT) organizes a shared task with special interest in the medical domain and results yet to be reported. The outcome of the workshop will report the state-of-the-art on medical SMT and will provide benchmark evaluation datasets.

8.7.3 Semi-Automatic Data Curation

Most biomedical researchers rely on knowledge stored in substantially sized, structured information sources, i.e., databases, to guide the direction of their work. To address their information needs, numerous biological databases have been developed and continuously updated over the last few years. They support scientific research work in biomedically relevant areas, ranging from proteomics (e.g., ExPASy [86]) and genomics (e.g., Ensembl Genome [73]), to metabolomics (e.g., Human Metabolome Database [314]) and phylogenetics (e.g., PhylomeDB [109]), to chemoinformatics (e.g., ChEMBL [87]). The reader is referred to the the registry of the Nucleic Acids Research journal[4] for a listing of the currently available biological databases.

Together with results of scientific experiments and high-throughput computing, published scientific literature is one of the primary sources of information contained in these databases. Data from the literature had been traditionally curated by entirely manual methods in which a domain expert hand-picks and reviews scientific publications, and selects specific information that merits inclusion to the database of interest. The constantly increasing rate at which recent biomedical developments are being published, however, leads to a significant backlog of scientific publications that remain unexamined for notable information. In order to reduce the workload of curators, text mining methods have been incorporated into data curation pipelines. A relation extraction system, for instance, was employed in the curation of the Biomolecular Interaction Network Database (BIND) [13], leading to a 70% reduction in workload [69]. Meanwhile, time spent on curation was trimmed down by 20% upon the incorporation of a gene name recognizer [120] into the FlyBase pipeline [51]. Similarly, the efficiency of *C. elegans* protein curation was eight times improved [297] by the concept extractor of the Textpresso text mining tool [197]. Other databases which were semi-automatically populated by text mining tools include BRENDA [260], the Comparative Toxicogenomics Database (CTD) [62], STITCH [149] and SuperTarget [93].

Three tasks in typical data curation pipelines have been identified as focal areas in which text mining is most called for, namely, document triage, mark up of relevant biomedical concepts and annotation of the relationships between them [105]. To foster the advancement of tools that automatically perform these functions, members of the biomedical NLP community have organized

[4]http://www.oxfordjournals.org/nar/database/cap

shared tasks (e.g., the interactive tasks of the BioCreative 2012 [8] and BioCreative IV [168] workshops), which encouraged the development of text mining-enabled curation platforms. A feature that is required from any platform, apart from automated support, is a user-interactive interface to allow human curators to validate automatically generated results. With several international research groups rising up to the challenge, the last few years saw the emergence of an array of diverse text mining-assisted bio-curation platforms. Some participating systems come with capabilities for document triage, e.g., PubTator [312], T-HOD [59], Acetylation miner [274], BioQRator [152], SciKnowMine [34], while some offer support for the information extraction tasks of concept recognition (e.g., PCS [52], tagtog [39], T-HOD [59], TextPresso [298], CellFinder [210], Egas [37], BioQRator [152], MarkerRIF [58], RLIMS-P [286], Argo [238]) and interaction extraction (e.g., PPInterFinder [236], eFIP [291], MarkerRIF [58], ODIN [250]). While most of the proposed systems are highly domain-specific and tightly coupled with certain text mining analytics, a minority of them are more flexible and allow for customization of annotation types (e.g., tagtog, SciKnowMine, Egas, Argo) and underlying automatic tools (e.g., MarkerRIF, Egas, Argo). It is worth noting, however, that these tools are only meant to assist human curators rather than replace their contribution. Manual validation of text mining-generated results is indispensable in ensuring the high quality of curated scientific information.

8.8 Integration with Clinical Text Mining

In the last decade, Information Technology has been largely adopted in health care. The medical community has been increasingly realizing the applicability and usefulness of digitizing medical records. Clinical data records of patients on paper have been transformed rapidly into electronic health records (EHRs) [77, 78]. Electronic health records comprise a rich source of information about patients and may refer to a variety of aspects of health care [116].

EHRs contain structured and unstructured information. The structured part describes patient history details such as medication, laboratory results, imaging and pharmacy orders [92]. This part of the EHR consists of medical information fragments, each of which can be assigned a unique concept identifier from some medical controlled vocabulary, e.g., the International Classification of Diseases (ICD-10).

The unstructured part of electronic health records contains free narrative text of various content: progress notes, discharge summaries, pathology reports, operative reports and others [253]. In general, in the unstructured section, clinicians can enter natural language text to express patient conditions. For example, they can summarize the results of a physical examination or explain why specific drugs were prescribed or discontinued [253]. Clinicians prefer to use free text in writing reports because they can freely use the unlimited vocabulary of natural language with no need to map to ontological concepts. As a result, the unstructured part of EHRs usually contains valuable predictive information unavailable in a structured format [92]. Examples of valuable information expressed in free text are family history, risk factors, and signs and symptoms [315]. For instance, ejection fraction is a strong indicator of patients having congestive heart failure, and the information about ejection fraction is usually expressed in free text.

Structuring free text in medical records creates a rich resource for many healthcare professionals: clinical researchers, physicians, nurses and therapists [101]. It will release information hidden in the textual part of medical records, granting access to clinical practitioners and software applications [163].

For example, structured medical records can be processed automatically to summarize the medical history of patients and to compare a patient with others with the same or similar history. Structured medical records are also useful for clinical research. Combining many clinical records in a large repository allows for the investigation of research questions such as, *"How many patients with stage 2 adenocarcinoma who were treated with tamoxifen were symptom-free after 5 years*? One step further, patterns can be identified and new hypotheses can be generated, so as to be explored and validated later in clinical trials [253]. In addition, locating eligible candidates for clinical trials is much simpler and quicker, when electronic health records are available [223].

Evidence-based medicine (EBM) refers to the identification, adoption and integration of scientific evidence from the literature most suitable to a specific patient. The Evidence and Decision Support track of the 2000 AMIA Spring Symposium showed that the integration of clinical decision support systems (CDSS) with evidence-based medicine is very promising and it can potentially lead to improvements in health care quality and practice [269]. Currently, the adoption of evidence-based medicine is hampered by the overwhelming clinical information available in unstructured form, the low level of experience of clinicians and lack of time to find and synthesize evidence in the scientific literature [311].

Text mining methods can be applied to facilitate evidence-based medicine and exploit the rich, valuable clinical information that is locked in the clinical narratives of electronic health records. Then, extracted information can be linked to the literature to construct and generate associations that may be of interest to clinicians and are useful to assist in clinical decision making and evidence-based health care. Over the last decade, biomedical text mining has seen significant advances while clinical text mining has received less attention. The main reason is that the development or adaptation of text mining tools heavily relies on the availability of annotated training corpora. However, due to privacy and confidentiality issues, only limited corpora are available for text mining [176]. The majority of research work in clinical text mining has focused in structuring medical records. Medical concepts found within the records are mapped to medical terminologies by tools such as MetaMap [9], cTAKES [259], i2b2 HITEx [323] and MedLEE [77]. Only a small number of studies have utilized statistical machine-learning based approaches to extract medical information from electronic health records, and most of these efforts have been carried out within the context of i2b2 [295, 294, 296] and ShARe/CLEF eHealth shared tasks [155].

Integrating biomedical information from heterogeneous sources such as electronic health records and the scientific literature can expand and broaden the knowledge about patient health information, such as etiology of diseases and drug repurposing. An example of a corpus that integrates phenotypic information from both clinical notes and biomedical literature is PhenoCHF [4], which is relevant to the identification of phenotype information. The corpus includes annotations of causes, risk factors, signs and symptoms of congestive heart failure (CHF). It integrates electronic health records (300 discharge summaries) and scientific literature articles (5 full-text papers) from the PubMed Central Open Access database. Research has also focused on applying text mining methods to clinical trial protocols. Automatic terminology extraction, unsupervised clustering and distributional semantics have been employed to analyze and structure free text in protocols to support clinicians in searching the space of existing trials efficiently and creating new trials [146]. Moreover, visualizing information in clinical trials [102], linking clinical trial protocols to journal publications [64, 136], classifying clinical trials or their parts [221, 318, 42] are other important topics that have been investigated.

8.9 Conclusions

This chapter has summarized some of the most active research topics in the field of biomedical text mining. We have looked at various approaches to information extraction tasks such as named entity recognition, coreference resolution and event extraction, as well as methods for discourse interpretation. Despite the impressive amount of effort that has been invested in biomedical text mining, the research undertaken until now still leaves several unexplored aspects relating to techniques and resources. Nevertheless, they also pave the way for interesting new threads of research.

For instance, although significant work has been undertaken in extracting biomedical events from literature, the performance is still rather unsatisfactory. Several shared tasks have already attempted to address this issue and it is not yet clear whether more data is needed, meaning that the current resources are insufficient or too sparse, or other methods that do not rely on vast quantities of labeled data need to be explored and developed. In generating substantial amounts of annotated data, collaborative annotation methodologies such as crowd-sourcing and community annotation can be leveraged to distribute the required manual effort and to reduce the costs. If coordinated well, such annotation efforts could lead to large amounts of high-quality annotations. Another way of working around the data insufficiency problem is with the use of methods for unsupervised, semi-supervised, and deep learning, which discover patterns in biomedical text based only on a small amount of labeled samples.

Furthermore, based on the work briefly summarized in this chapter, several research opportunities exist. For instance, in the biomedical domain, epidemiologists study the patterns, as well as the causes and effects of health and disease conditions in specific populations. Epidemiology is thus the centerpiece of public health, being pivotal to health policy decision-making and evidence-based practice by identifying targets for preventive healthcare and risk factors for diseases. Being able to quickly analyze large amounts of documents and correctly recognize causal relations between relevant facts can improve significantly both the speed and quality of making decisions affecting the public. In order to achieve this, it is necessary to be able to recognize, extract and analyze, in an automatic manner, the patterns that occur in defined populations. For this mechanism to function in a realistic manner, several sources of information need to be brought together and combined. It is insufficient to consider studying only scientific articles, as these are published with several months' delay since the first observations were made and usually describe laboratory experiments performed under controlled conditions to test only specific aspects of larger problems. Integration with social media, such as Facebook and Twitter, is mandatory, since these environments are able to provide the most up-to-date situation in the real world. Users can supply first-hand information regarding their health status, primary or adverse effects of medication they are taking, public loci of infection, etc. This step is important especially in the context of the recent steep increase in the mobile share of media consumption, which is likely to continue in the following years [60].

However, most effects, whether they are diseases or even death, are not caused by a single cause, but by a chain or, in most cases, a web of many causal components. Take, for example, still incurable diseases such as cancer, for which a single cause does not exist. More specifically, in the case of pulmonary cancer, although smoking plays an important role, the disease cannot be attributed just to this factor. Thus, the interlinking of the various sources to analyze causal relations will eventually lead to the automatic creation of complex causal networks with various degrees of granularity. These networks can explain, to a certain degree or granularity, the aspects of everyday life. At a high, abstract level, the networks are addressed mostly to the general public, to advocate for both personal measures, like diet changing, and corporate measures, such as the taxation of junk food and banning its advertising. At a low, molecular level, causal networks are mostly useful for research performed in biochemistry, molecular biology, epigenetics, etc. Molecular and signaling pathways can be created and curated automatically, and linked to supporting evidence in the literature.

Bibliography

[1] S. Agarwal and H. Yu. Biomedical negation scope detection with conditional random fields. *Journal of the American Medical Informatics Association*, 17(6):696–701, 2010.

[2] S. Agarwal, H. Yu, and I. Kohane. BioN0T: A searchable database of biomedical negated sentences. *BMC Bioinformatics*, 12(1):420, 2011.

[3] B. Alex, C. Grover, B. Haddow, M. Kabadjov, W. Klein, M. Matthews, S. Roebuck, R. Tobin, and X. Wang. The ITI TXM corpora. In *Proceedings of the Sixth International Conference on Language Resources and Evaluation*, 2008.

[4] N. Alnazzawi, P. Thompson, and S. Ananiadou. Building a semantically annotated corpus for congestive heart and renal failure from clinical records and the literature. In *Proceedings of the 5th International Workshop on Health Text Mining and Information Analysis*, pages 69–74, 2014.

[5] S. Ananiadou, D. B. Kell, and J. Tsujii. Text mining and its potential applications in systems biology. *Trends in Biotechnology*, 24(12):571–579, 2006.

[6] S. Ananiadou and J. McNaught, editors. *Text Mining for Biology and Biomedicine*. Artech House, Inc., 2006.

[7] S. Ananiadou, P. Thompson, R. Nawaz, J. McNaught, and D.B. Kell. Event based text mining for biology and functional genomics. *Briefings in Functional Genomics*, 2014.

[8] C. Arighi, B. Carterette, K. Cohen, M. Krallinger, J. Wilbur, and C. Wu. An overview of the BioCreative Workshop 2012 Track III: Interactive text mining task. In *Proceedings of the 2012 BioCreative Workshop*, pages 110–120, 2012.

[9] A. Aronson. Effective mapping of biomedical text to the UMLS Metathesaurus: The MetaMap program. In *Proceedings of the AMIA Symposium*, page 17, 2001.

[10] R. Artstein and M. Poesio. Inter-coder agreement for computational linguistics. *Computational Linguistics*, 34(4):555–596, 2008.

[11] M. Ashburner, C. Ball, J. Blake, D. Botstein, H. Butler, M. Cherry, A. Davis, K. Dolinski, S. Dwight, J. Eppig, M. Harris, D. Hill, L. Issel-Tarver, A. Kasarskis, S. Lewis, J. Matese, J. Richardson, M. Ringwald, G. Rubin, and G. Sherlock. Gene ontology: Tool for the unification of biology. *Nature Genetics*, 25:25–29, 2000.

[12] M. Bada, M. Eckert, D. Evans, K. Garcia, K. Shipley, D. Sitnikov, W. Baumgartner, K. Cohen, K. Verspoor, J. Blake, and L. Hunter. Concept annotation in the CRAFT corpus. *BMC Bioinformatics*, 13(1):161, 2012.

[13] G. Bader, D. Betel, and C. Hogue. BIND: The Biomolecular Interaction Network Database. *Nucleic Acids Research*, 31(1):248–250, 2003.

[14] B. Baldwin, T. Morton, A. Bagga, J. Baldridge, R. Chandraseker, A. Dimitriadis, K. Snyder, and M. Wolska. Description of the UPENN CAMP system as used for coreference. In *Proceedings of the 7th Conference on Message Understanding*, 1998.

[15] L. Ballesteros and B. Croft. Phrasal translation and query expansion techniques for cross-language information retrieval. *SIGIR Forum*, 31(SI):84–91, 1997.

[16] M. Bank and M. Schierle. A survey of text mining architectures and the UIMA standard. In *Proceedings of the Eighth International Conference on Language Resources and Evaluation*, pages 3479–3486, 2012.

[17] R.T. Batista-Navarro and S. Ananiadou. Adapting the cluster ranking supervised model to resolve coreferences in the drug literature. In *Proceedings of the Fourth International Symposium on Languages in Biology and Medicine*, 2011.

[18] R.T. Batista-Navarro and S. Ananiadou. Building a coreference-annotated corpus from the domain of biochemistry. In *Proceedings of the 2011 Workshop on Biomedical Natural Language Processing*, pages 83–91, 2011.

[19] R.T. Batista-Navarro, R. Rak, and S. Ananiadou. Chemistry-specific features and heuristics for developing a CRF-based chemical named entity recogniser. In *BioCreative Challenge Evaluation Workshop vol. 2*, page 55, 2013.

[20] W. Baumgartner, K. Cohen, and L. Hunter. An open-source framework for large-scale, flexible evaluation of biomedical text mining systems. *Journal of Biomedical Discovery and Collaboration*, 3(1):1, 2008.

[21] E. Beisswanger, V. Lee, J. Kim, D. Rebholz-Schuhmann, A. Splendiani, O. Dameron, S. Schulz, and U. Hahn. Gene Regulation Ontology (GRO): Design principles and use cases. *Studies in Health Technology and Informatics*, 136:9–14, 2008.

[22] M. Berthold, N. Cebron, F. Dill, T. Gabriel, T. Kötter, T. Meinl, P. Ohl, C. Sieb, K. Thiel, and B. Wiswedel. KNIME: The Konstanz Information Miner. In *Studies in Classification, Data Analysis, and Knowledge Organization*, 2007.

[23] J. Bhagat, F. Tanoh, E. Nzuobontane, T. Laurent, J. Orlowski, M. Roos, K. Wolstencroft, S. Aleksejevs, R. Stevens, S. Pettifer, R. Lopez, and C. Goble. BioCatalogue: A universal catalogue of web services for the life sciences. *Nucleic Acids Research*, 38(suppl 2):W689–W694, 2010.

[24] P. Bhowmick, P. Mitra, and A. Basu. An agreement measure for determining inter-annotator reliability of human judgements on affective text. In *Proceedings of the Workshop on Human Judgements in Computational Linguistics*, pages 58–65, 2008.

[25] J. Björne, J. Heimonen, F. Ginter, A. Airola, T. Pahikkala, and T. Salakoski. Extracting complex biological events with rich graph-based feature sets. In *Proceedings of the Workshop on Current Trends in Biomedical Natural Language Processing: Shared Task*, pages 10–18, 2009.

[26] J. Björne and T. Salakoski. TEES 2.1: Automated annotation scheme learning in the BioNLP 2013 shared task. In *Proceedings of the BioNLP Shared Task 2013 Workshop*, pages 16–25, 2013.

[27] W.J. Black, R. Procter, S. Gray, and S. Ananiadou. A data and analysis resource for an experiment in text mining a collection of micro-blogs on a political topic. In *Proceedings of the Eighth International Conference on Language Resources and Evaluation (LREC 2012)*, pages 2083–2088, May 2012.

[28] W.J. Black, C. J. Rupp, C. Nobata, J. McNaught, J. Tsujii, and S. Ananiadou. High-precision semantic search by generating and testing questions. In *Proceedings of the UK e-Science All Hands Meeting*, 2010.

[29] A. Blum and T. Mitchell. Combining labeled and unlabeled data with co-training. In *Proceedings of the Eleventh Annual Conference on Computational Learning Theory*, pages 92–100, 1998.

[30] K. Bontcheva, H. Cunningham, I. Roberts, A. Roberts, V. Tablan, N. Aswani, and G. Gorrell. GATE Teamware: A web-based, collaborative text annotation framework. *Language Resources and Evaluation*, 47(4):1007–1029, 2013.

[31] D. Bourigault. Surface grammatical analysis for the extraction of terminological noun phrases. In *Proceedings of the 14th Conference on Computational Linguistics*, pages 977–981, 1992.

[32] P. Brown, J. Cocke, S. Pietra, V Pietra, F. Jelinek, J. Lafferty, R. Mercer, and P. Roossin. A statistical approach to machine translation. *Computational linguistics*, 16(2):79–85, 1990.

[33] Q. Bui, D. Campos, E. van Mulligen, and J. Kors. A fast rule-based approach for biomedical event extraction. In *Proceedings of the BioNLP Shared Task 2013 Workshop*, pages 104–108, 2013.

[34] G. Burns, M. Tallis, H. Onda, K. Cohen, J. Kadin, and J. Blake. Supporting document triage with the SciKnowMine system in the Mouse Genome Informatics (MGI) curation process. In *Proceedings of the Fourth BioCreative Challenge Evaluation Workshop vol. 1*, pages 234–240, 2013.

[35] E. Buyko, E. Beisswanger, and U. Hahn. The GeneReg corpus for gene expression regulation events—an overview of the corpus and its in-domain and out-of-domain interoperability. In *Proceedings of the Seventh International Conference on Language Resources and Evaluation (LREC'10)*, 2010.

[36] J. Cai and M. Strube. End-to-end coreference resolution via hypergraph partitioning. In *Proceedings of the 23rd International Conference on Computational Linguistics*, pages 143–151, 2010.

[37] D. Campos, J. Lourencço, T. Nunes, R. Vitorino, P. Domingues, S. Matos, and J. Oliveira. Egas—Collaborative biomedical annotation as a service. In *Proceedings of the Fourth BioCreative Challenge Evaluation Workshop vol. 1*, pages 254–259, 2013.

[38] C. Cano, T. Monaghan, A. Blanco, D.P. Wall, and L. Peshkin. Collaborative text-annotation resource for disease-centered relation extraction from biomedical text. *Journal of Biomedical Informatics*, 42(5):967 – 977, 2009.

[39] J. Cejuela, P. McQuilton, L. Ponting, S. Marygold, R. Stefancsik, G. Millburn, B. Rost, and the FlyBase Consortium. Tagtog: Interactive human and machine annotation of gene mentions in PLoS full-text articles. In *Proceedings of the Fourth BioCreative Challenge Evaluation Workshop vol. 1*, pages 260–269, 2013.

[40] Y. Chiao and P. Zweigenbaum. Looking for candidate translational equivalents in specialized, comparable corpora. In *Proceedings of the 19th International Conference on Computational Linguistics Vol. 2*, pages 1–5, 2002.

[41] H. Chun, Y. Tsuruoka, J. Kim, R. Shiba, N. Nagata, T. Hishiki, and J. Tsujii. Extraction of gene-disease relations from medline using domain dictionaries and machine learning. In *Proceedings of the Pacific Symposium on Biocomputing (PSB) 11*, pages 4–15, 2006.

[42] G. Chung. Sentence retrieval for abstracts of randomized controlled trials. *BMC Medical Informatics and Decision Making*, 9(1):10+, 2009.

[43] K. Church and P. Hanks. Word association norms, mutual information, and lexicography. *Computational Linguistics*, 16(1):22–29, 1990.

[44] A. Cohen and W. Hersh. A survey of current work in biomedical text mining. *Briefings in bioinformatics*, 6(1):57–71, 2005.

[45] K. Cohen and L. Hunter. Getting started in text mining. *PLoS Computational Biology*, 4(1):e20, 2008.

[46] K. Cohen, H. Johnson, K. Verspoor, C. Roeder, and L. Hunter. The structural and content aspects of abstracts versus bodies of full text journal articles are different. *BMC Bioinformatics*, 11(1):492, 2010.

[47] K. Cohen, A. Lanfranchi, W. Corvey, W.A. Jr. Baumgartner, C. Roeder, P.V. Ogren, M. Palmer, and L.E. Hunter. Annotation of all coreference in biomedical text: Guideline selection and adaptation. In *Proceedings of the Second Workshop on Building and Evaluating Resources for Biomedical Text Mining*, pages 37–41, 2010.

[48] N. Collier, C. Nobata, and J. Tsujii. Extracting the names of genes and gene products with a hidden Markov model. In *Proceedings of the 18th Conference on Computational Linguistics-Vol. 1*, pages 201–207, 2000.

[49] D. Comeau, R. Islamaj Dogan, P. Ciccarese, K. Cohen, M. Krallinger, F. Leitner, Z. Lu, Y. Peng, F. Rinaldi, M. Torii, A. Valencia, K. Verspoor, T. Wiegers, C. Wu, and J. Wilbur. BioC: A minimalist approach to interoperability for biomedical text processing. *Database*, 2013. doi: 10.1093/database/bat064

[50] D. Contractor, Y. Guo, and A. Korhonen. Using argumentative zones for extractive summarization of scientific articles. In *COLING*, pages 663–678, 2012.

[51] M. Crosby, J. Goodman, V. Strelets, P. Zhang, W. Gelbart, and The FlyBase Consortium. FlyBase: Genomes by the dozen. *Nucleic Acids Research*, 35(suppl 1):D486–D491, 2007.

[52] H. Cui, J. Balhoff, W. Dahdul, H. Lapp, P. Mabee, T. Vision, and Z. Chang. PCS for phylogenetic systematic literature curation. In *Proceedings of the BioCreative 2012 Workshop*, 2012.

[53] H. Cunningham, D. Maynard, K. Bontcheva, and V. Tablan. GATE: A framework and graphical development environment for robust NLP tools and applications. In *Proceedings of the 40th Anniversary Meeting of the Association for Computational Linguistics*, 2002.

[54] H. Cunningham, V. Tablan, A. Roberts, and K. Bontcheva. Getting more out of biomedical documents with GATE's full lifecycle open source text analytics. *PLoS Comput Biol*, 9(2):e1002854, 2013.

[55] I. Dagan and K. Church. Termight: Identifying and translating technical terminology. In *Proceedings of the Fourth Conference on Applied Natural Language Processing*, ANLC '94, pages 34–40, 1994.

[56] I. Dagan, K. Church, and W. Gale. Robust bilingual word alignment for machine aided translation. In *Proceedings of the Workshop on Very Large Corpora*, pages 1–8, 1993.

[57] H. Dai, J. Lin, C. Huang, P. Chou, R Tsai, and W. Hsu. A survey of state of the art biomedical text mining techniques for semantic analysis. In *Sensor Networks, Ubiquitous and Trustworthy Computing, 2008. SUTC'08. IEEE International Conference on*, pages 410–417, 2008.

[58] H. Dai, C. Wu, W. Lin, R. Tsai, and W. Hsu. MarkerRIF: An interactive curation system for biomarker. In *Proceedings of the Fourth BioCreative Challenge Evaluation Workshop vol. 1*, pages 224–233, 2013.

[59] H. Dai, J. Wu, R Tsai, W. Pan, and W. Hsu. T-HOD: A literature-based candidate gene database for hypertension, obesity and diabetes. *Database*, 2013. doi: 10.1093/database/bas061

[60] T. Danova. The mobile revolution is the biggest tech shift in years, and companies are in a race to keep up. *Business Insider*, 2014.

[61] H. Daumé III and J. Jagarlamudi. Domain adaptation for machine translation by mining unseen words. In *Proceedings of the 49th Annual Meeting of the Association for Computational Linguistics: Human Language Technologies: Short papers-Vol. 2*, pages 407–412, 2011.

[62] A.P. Davis, T.C. Wiegers, R.J. Johnson, J.M. Lay, K. Lennon-Hopkins, C. Saraceni-Richards, D. Sciaky, C.G. Murphy, and C.J. Mattingly. Text mining effectively scores and ranks the literature for improving chemical-gene-disease curation at the comparative toxicogenomics database. *PLoS ONE*, 8(4):e58201, 2013.

[63] D. Day, C. McHenry, R. Kozierok, and L. Riek. Callisto: A configurable annotation workbench. In *LREC*, 2004.

[64] B. de Bruijn, S. Carini, S. Kiritchenko, J. Martin, and I. Sim. Automated information extraction of key trial design elements from clinical trial publications. *Proceedings of AMIA Annual Symposium*, 2008.

[65] A. de Waard, L. Breure, J. Kircz, and H. Van Oostendorp. Modeling rhetoric in scientific publications. In *International Conference on Multidisciplinary Information Sciences and Technologies*, 2006.

[66] A. de Waard and H. Pander Maat. Categorizing epistemic segment types in biology research articles. In *Workshop on Linguistic and Psycholinguistic Approaches to Text Structuring*, pages 21–23, 2009.

[67] E. Delpech, B. Daille, E. Morin, and C. Lemaire. Extraction of domain-specific bilingual lexicon from comparable corpora: Compositional translation and ranking. In *Proceedings of COLING 2012*, pages 745–762, 2012.

[68] R. Doğan, R. Leaman, and Z. Lu. NCBI disease corpus: A resource for disease name recognition and concept normalization. *Journal of Biomedical Informatics*, 2014.

[69] I. Donaldson, J. Martin, B. de Bruijn, C. Wolting, V. Lay, B. Tuekam, S. Zhang, B. Baskin, G. Bader, K. Michalickova, T. Pawson, and C. Hogue. PreBIND and Textomy—mining the biomedical literature for protein-protein interactions using a support vector machine. *BMC Bioinformatics*, 4(1):11, 2003.

[70] P. Drouin. Term extraction using non-technical corpora as a point of leverage. *Terminology*, 9(1), 2003.

[71] M. Eck, S. Vogel, and A. Waibel. Improving statistical machine translation in the medical domain using the unified medical language system. In *Proceedings of the 20th International Conference on Computational Linguistics*, page 792, 2004.

[72] D. Ferrucci and A. Lally. UIMA: An architectural approach to unstructured information processing in the corporate research environment. *Natural Language Engineering*, 10(3-4):327–348, 2004.

[73] P. Flicek, M. Ridwan Amode, D. Barrell, K. Beal, K. Billis, S. Brent, D. Carvalho-Silva, P. Clapham, G. Coates, S. Fitzgerald, L. Gil, C. Girn, L. Gordon, T. Hourlier, S. Hunt, N. Johnson, T. Juettemann, A. Khri, S. Keenan, E. Kulesha, F. Martin, T. Maurel, W. McLaren, D.. Murphy, R. Nag, B. Overduin, M. Pignatelli, B. Pritchard, E. Pritchard, H. Riat, M. Ruffier, D. Sheppard, K. Taylor, AN. Thormann, S. Trevanion, A. Vullo, S. Wilder, M. Wilson, A. Zadissa, B. Aken, E. Birney, F. Cunningham, J. Harrow, J. Herrero, T. Hubbard, R. Kinsella, M. Muffato, A. Parker, G. Spudich, A. Yates, D. Zerbino, and S. Searle. Ensembl 2014. *Nucleic Acids Research*, 42(D1):D749–D755, 2014.

[74] G. Flores, B. Laws, S. Mayo, B. Zuckerman, M. Abreu, L. Medina, and E. Hardt. Errors in medical interpretation and their potential clinical consequences in pediatric encounters. *Pediatrics*, 111(1):6–14, 2003.

[75] Institute for Infocomm Research. MEDCo Annotation Project. http://nlp.i2r.a-star.edu.sg/medco.html. Accessed: August 2013.

[76] K. Frantzi, S. Ananiadou, and H. Mima. Automatic recognition of multi-word terms: The C-value/NC-value method. *International Journal on Digital Libraries*, 3(2):115–130, 2000.

[77] C. Friedman, P. Alderson, J. Austin, J. Cimino, and S. Johnson. A general natural-language text processor for clinical radiology. *JAMIA*, 1(2):161–174, 1994.

[78] C. Friedman, C. Knirsch, L. Shagina, and G. Hripcsak. Automating a severity score guideline for community-acquired pneumonia employing medical language processing of discharge summaries. In *Proceedings of the AMIA Symposium*, page 256, 1999.

[79] K. Fukuda, T. Tsunoda, A. Tamura, T. Takagi, et al. Toward information extraction: identifying protein names from biological papers. In *Pacific Symposium on Biocomputing*, volume 707, pages 707–718, 1998.

[80] P. Fung and K. McKeown. A technical word-and term-translation aid using noisy parallel corpora across language groups. *Machine Translation*, 12(1-2):53–87, 1997.

[81] S. Fung. Factors associated with breast self-examination behaviour among Chinese women in Hong Kong. *Patient Education and Counseling*, 33(3):233–243, 1998.

[82] R. Gaizauskas, D. Demetriou, P. Artymiuk, and P. Willett. Protein structures and information extraction from biological texts: The PASTA system. *Bioinformatics*, 19(1):135–143, 2003.

[83] Y. Garten and R. Altman. Pharmspresso: A text mining tool for extraction of pharmacogenomic concepts and relationships from full text. *BMC Bioinformatics*, 10(Suppl 2):S6, 2009.

[84] C. Gasperin and T. Briscoe. Statistical anaphora resolution in biomedical texts. In *Proceedings of the 22nd International Conference on Computational Linguistics*, pages 257–264, 2008.

[85] C. Gasperin, N. Karamanis, and R. Seal. Annotation of anaphoric relations in biomedical full-text articles using a domain-relevant scheme. *Proceedings of DAARC*, vol. 2007.

[86] E. Gasteiger, A. Gattiker, C. Hoogland, I. Ivanyi, R. Appel, and A. Bairoch. ExPASy: The proteomics server for in-depth protein knowledge and analysis. *Nucleic Acids Research*, 31(13):3784–3788, 2003.

[87] A. Gaulton, L. Bellis, A. Bento, J. Chambers, M. Davies, A. Hersey, Y. Light, S. McGlinchey, D. Michalovich, B. Al-Lazikani, and J. Overington. ChEMBL: A large-scale bioactivity database for drug discovery. *Nucleic Acids Research*, 2011.

[88] GENIA Project. XConc Suite. `http://www.nactem.ac.uk/genia/tools/xconc`. Accessed: July 2013.

[89] R. Grishman. Adaptive information extraction and sublanguage analysis. In *Proceedings of Workshop on Adaptive Text Extraction and Mining at Seventeenth International Joint Conference on Artificial Intelligence*, pages 1–4, 2001.

[90] R. Grishman and B. Sundheim. Message Understanding Conference-6: A brief history. In *Proceedings of the 16th Conference on Computational Linguistics, vol. 1*, pages 466–471, 1996.

[91] B. Grosz, S. Weinstein, and A. Joshi. Centering: A framework for modeling the local coherence of discourse. *Computational Linguistics*, 21:203–225, 1995.

[92] M. Gundersen, P. Haug, A. Pryor, R. van Bree, S. Koehler, K. Bauer, and B. Clemons. Development and evaluation of a computerized admission diagnoses encoding system. *Computers and Biomedical Research*, 29(5):351–372, 1996.

[93] S. Günther, M. Kuhn, M. Dunkel, M. Campillos, C. Senger, E. Petsalaki, J. Ahmed, E. Garcia Urdiales, A. Gewiess, L. Jensen, R. Schneider, R. Skoblo, R. Russell, P. Bourne, P. Bork, and R. Preissner. SuperTarget and Matador: Resources for exploring drug-target relationships. *Nucleic Acids Research*, 36(Database-Issue):919–922, 2008.

[94] Y. Guo, A. Korhonen, M. Liakata, I. Silins, L. Sun, and U. Stenius. Identifying the information structure of scientific abstracts: An investigation of three different schemes. In *Proceedings of the 2010 Workshop on Biomedical Natural Language Processing*, pages 99–107, 2010.

[95] Y. Guo, A. Korhonen, I. Silins, and U. Stenius. Weakly supervised learning of information structure of scientific abstracts—Is it accurate enough to benefit real-world tasks in biomedicine? *Bioinformatics*, 27(22):3179–3185, 2011.

[96] Y. Guo, I. Silins, U. Stenius, and A. Korhonen. Active learning-based information structure analysis of full scientific articles and two applications for biomedical literature review. *Bioinformatics*, 29(11):1440–1447, 2013.

[97] I. Gurevych, M. Mühlhäuser, C. Müller, J. Steimle, M. Weimer, and T. Zesch. Darmstadt knowledge processing repository based on UIMA. In *Proceedings of the First Workshop on Unstructured Information Management Architecture at Biannual Conference of the Society for Computational Linguistics and Language Technology*, 2007.

[98] U. Hahn, E. Buyko, R. Landefeld, M. Mühlhausen, M. Poprat, K. Tomanek, and J. Wermter. An overview of JCoRe, the JULIE lab UIMA component repository. In *LREC'08 Workshop "Towards Enhanced Interoperability for Large HLT Systems: UIMA for NLP,"* pages 1–7, 2008.

[99] T. Hara, Y. Miyao, and J. Tsujii. Adapting a probabilistic disambiguation model of an HPSG parser to a new domain. In R. Dale, K. F. Wong, J. Su, and O. Y. Kwong, editors, *Natural Language Processing IJCNLP 2005*, volume 3651, pages 199–210. Springer-Verlag, 2005.

[100] Z. Harris. *Mathematical Structures of Language*. John Wiley and Son, New York, 1968.

[101] P. Haug, S. Koehler, L. Lau, R. Wang, R. Rocha, and S. Huff. A natural language understanding system combining syntactic and semantic techniques. In *Proceedings of the Annual Symposium on Computer Application in Medical Care*, page 247, 1994.

[102] M. Hernandez, S. Carini, M. Storey, and I. Sim. An interactive tool for visualizing design heterogeneity in clinical trials. *Proceedings of AMIA Annual Symposium*, 2008.

[103] K. Hirohata, N. Okazaki, S. Ananiadou, and M. Ishizuka. Identifying sections in scientific abstracts using conditional random fields. In *Proceedings of the 3rd International Joint Conference on Natural Language Processing (IJCNLP 2008)*, pages 381–388, 2008.

[104] L. Hirschman and C. Blaschke. Evaluation of text mining in biology. In S. Ananiadou and John McNaught, editors, *Text Mining for Biology and Biomedicine*, pages 213–245. Artech House, Boston/London, 2006.

[105] L. Hirschman, G. Burns, M. Krallinger, C. Arighi, K. Cohen, A. Valencia, C. Wu, A. Chatr-Aryamontri, K. Dowell, E. Huala, A. Lourenco, R. Nash, A. Veuthey, T. Wiegers, and A. Winter. Text mining for the biocuration workflow. *Database: The Journal of Biological Databases and Curation*, http://database.oxfordjournals.org/cgi/doi/10.1093/database/bas020, 2012.

[106] L. Hirschman, M. Colosimo, A. Morgan, and A. Yeh. Overview of BioCreAtIvE task 1b: Normalized gene lists. *BMC Bioinformatics*, 6(Suppl 1):S11, 2005.

[107] R. Hoffmann and A. Valencia. Implementing the iHOP concept for navigation of biomedical literature. *Bioinformatics*, 21(suppl 2):ii252–ii258, 2005.

[108] G. Hripcsak and D. Heitjan. Measuring agreement in medical informatics reliability studies. *Journal of Biomedical Informatics*, 35(2):99–110, 2002.

[109] J. Huerta-Cepas, S. Capella-Gutierrez, L. Pryszcz, I. Denisov, D. Kormes, M. Marcet-Houben, and T. Gabaldón. PhylomeDB v3.0: An expanding repository of genome-wide collections of trees, alignments and phylogeny-based orthology and paralogy predictions. *Nucleic Acids Research*, 39(suppl 1):D556–D560, 2011.

[110] K. Humphreys, G. Demetriou, and R. Gaizauskas. Two applications of information extraction to biological science journal articles: Enzyme interactions and protein structures. In *Pacific Symposium on Biocomputing*, vol. 5, pages 505–516, 2000.

[111] K. Hyland. Talking to the academy forms of hedging in science research articles. *Written Communication*, 13(2):251–281, 1996.

[112] K. Hyland. Writing without conviction? Hedging in science research articles. *Applied linguistics*, 17(4):433–454, 1996.

[113] S. Ibn Faiz and R. Mercer. Identifying explicit discourse connectives in text. In O. Zaïane and S. Zilles, editors, *Advances in Artificial Intelligence*, volume 7884 of *Lecture Notes in Computer Science*, pages 64–76. Springer Berlin Heidelberg, 2013.

[114] A. Irvine and C. Callison-Burch. Combining bilingual and comparable corpora for low resource machine translation. In *Proceedings of the Eighth Workshop on Statistical Machine Translation*, pages 262–270, 2013.

[115] L. Jensen, J. Saric, and P. Bork. Literature mining for the biologist: From information retrieval to biological discovery. *Nature Reviews Genetics*, 7(2):119–129, 2006.

[116] P. Jensen, L. Jensen, and S. Brunak. Mining electronic health records: Towards better research applications and clinical care. *Nature Reviews Genetics*, 13(6):395–405, 2012.

[117] D. Jurafsky and J.H. Martin. Computational discourse. In *Speech and Language Processing: An Introduction to Natural Language Processing, Computational Linguistics, and Speech Recognition*, chapter 21. Prentice Hall, Upper Saddle River, New Jersey, USA, 2nd edition, 2008.

[118] K. Kageura and B. Umino. Methods of automatic term recognition: A review. *Terminology*, 3(2):259–289, 1996.

[119] Y. Kano, M. Miwa, K. Cohen, L.E. Hunter, S. Ananiadou, and J. Tsujii. U-Compare: A modular NLP workflow construction and evaluation system. *IBM Journal of Research and Development*, 55(3):11:1–11:10, 2011.

[120] N. Karamanis, I. Lewin, R. Seal, R. Drysdale, and E. Briscoe. Integrating natural language processing with flybase curation. In *Pacific Symposium on Biocomputing*, pages 245–256, 2007.

[121] J. Kazama, T. Makino, Y. Ohta, and J. Tsujii. Tuning support vector machines for biomedical named entity recognition. In *Proceedings of the ACL-02 workshop on Natural language processing in the biomedical domain-Vol. 3*, pages 1–8, 2002.

[122] E. Keenan and L. Faltz. *Boolean Semantics for Natural Language, vol. 23*. Springer, 1985.

[123] N. Kemp and M. Lynch. Extraction of information from the text of chemical patents. 1. Identification of specific chemical names. *Journal of Chemical Information and Modeling*, 38(4):544–551, Jan 1998.

[124] H. Kilicoglu and S. Bergler. Recognizing speculative language in biomedical research articles: A linguistically motivated perspective. *BMC Bioinformatics*, 9(Suppl 11):S10, 2008.

[125] H. Kilicoglu and S. Bergler. Syntactic dependency based heuristics for biological event extraction. In *Proceedings of the Workshop on Current Trends in Biomedical Natural Language Processing: Shared Task*, pages 119–127, 2009.

[126] H. Kilicoglu and S. Bergler. A high-precision approach to detecting hedges and their scopes. In *Proceedings of the Fourteenth Conference on Computational Natural Language Learning — Shared Task*, pages 70–77, 2010.

[127] H. Kilicoglu and S. Bergler. Biological event composition. *BMC Bioinformatics*, 13(11):1–19, 2012.

[128] J. Kim, T. Ohta, and J. Tsujii. Corpus annotation for mining biomedical events from literature. *BMC Bioinformatics*, 9(1):10, 2008.

[129] J. Kim, T. Ohta, Y. Tsuruoka, Y. Tateisi, and N. Collier. Introduction to the bio-entity recognition task at JNLPBA. In *Proceedings of the International Joint Workshop on Natural Language Processing in Biomedicine and Its Applications*, pages 70–75, 2004.

[130] J. Kim, S. Pyysalo, T. Ohta, R. Bossy, N. Nguyen, and J. Tsujii. Overview of BioNLP shared task 2011. In *Proceedings of the BioNLP Shared Task 2011 Workshop*, pages 1–6, 2011.

[131] J. Kim, Y. Wang, and Y. Yasunori. The GENIA event extraction Shared Task, 2013 edition - overview. In *Proceedings of the BioNLP Shared Task 2013 Workshop*, pages 8–15, 2013.

[132] J.-D. Kim, T. Ohta, S. Pyysalo, Y. Kano, and J. Tsujii. Extracting bio-molecular events from literature: The BioNLP'09 Shared Task. *Computational Intelligence*, 27(4):513–540, 2011.

[133] J.-D. Kim, T. Ohta, Y. Tateisi, and J. Tsujii. GENIA corpus: A semantically annotated corpus for bio-textmining. *Bioinformatics*, 19(suppl 1):i180–i182, 2003.

[134] J.-J. Kim and J.C. Park. BioAR: Anaphora resolution for relating protein names to proteome database entries. In *Proceedings of the Workshop on Reference Resolution and Its Applications*, pages 79–86, 2004.

[135] J.D. Kim, N. Nguyen, Y. Wang, J. Tsujii, T. Takagi, and A. Yonezawa. The GENIA event and protein coreference tasks of the BioNLP Shared Task 2011. *BMC Bioinformatics*, 13(Suppl 11):S1, 2012.

[136] S. Kiritchenko, B. de Bruijn, S. Carini, J. Martin, and I. Sim. ExaCT: Automatic extraction of clinical trial characteristics from journal publications. *BMC Medical Informatics and Decision Making*, 10(1):56+, 2010.

[137] R. Klinger, C. Kolářik, J. Fluck, M. Hofmann-Apitius, and C.M. Friedrich. Detection of IUPAC and IUPAC-like chemical names. *Bioinformatics*, 24(13):i268–i276, 2008.

[138] P. Koehn. Europarl: A parallel corpus for statistical machine translation. In *MT Summit, vol. 5*, pages 79–86, 2005.

[139] P. Koehn, H. Hoang, A. Birch, C. Callison-Burch, M. Federico, N. Bertoldi, B. Cowan, W. Shen, C. Moran, R. Zens, et al. Moses: Open source toolkit for statistical machine translation. In *Proceedings of the 45th Annual Meeting of the ACL on Interactive Poster and Demonstration Sessions*, pages 177–180, 2007.

[140] P. Koehn, F. Och, and D. Marcu. Statistical phrase-based translation. In *Proceedings of the 2003 Conference of the North American Chapter of the Association for Computational Linguistics on Human Language Technology-Vol. 1*, pages 48–54, 2003.

[141] B. Kolluru, L. Hawizy, P. Murray-Rust, J. Tsujii, and S. Ananiadou. Using workflows to explore and optimise named entity recognition for chemistry. *PLoS ONE*, 6(5):e20181, 2011.

[142] G. Kontonatsios, I. Korkontzelos, B. Kolluru, P. Thompson, and S. Ananiadou. Deploying and sharing U-Compare workflows as web services. *Journal of Biomedical Semantics*, 4:7, 2013.

[143] G. Kontonatsios, I. Korkontzelos, J. Tsujii, and S. Ananiadou. Using a random forest classifier to compile bilingual dictionaries of technical terms from comparable corpora. In *Proceedings of the 14th Conference of the European Chapter of the ACL, vol. 2: Short Papers*, pages 111–116, 2014.

[144] G. Kontonatsios, P. Thompson, R. T. B. Batista-Navarro, C. Mihăilă, I. Korkontzelos, and S. Ananiadou. Extending an interoperable platform to facilitate the creation of multilingual and multimodal NLP applications. In *Proceedings of the 51st Annual Meeting of the Association for Computational Linguistics: System Demonstrations*, pages 43–48, 2013.

[145] I. Korkontzelos. *Unsupervised Learning of Multiword Expressions*. PhD thesis, University of York, York, UK, 2011.

[146] I. Korkontzelos, T. Mu, and S. Ananiadou. ASCOT: A text mining-based web-service for efficient search and assisted creation of clinical trials. *BMC Medical Informatics and Decision Making*, 12 (Suppl 1)(S3), 2012.

[147] M. Krallinger, A. Morgan, L. Smith, F. Leitner, L. Tanabe, J. Wilbur, L. Hirschman, and A. Valencia. Evaluation of text-mining systems for biology: Overview of the second BioCreative community challenge. *Genome Biol*, 9(Suppl 2):S1, 2008.

[148] M. Krauthammer and G. Nenadic. Term identification in the biomedical literature. *Journal of Biomedical Informatics*, 37(6):512–526, 2004.

[149] M. Kuhn, D. Szklarczyk, A. Franceschini, C. von Mering, L. Jensen, and P. Bork. STITCH 3: zooming in on protein–chemical interactions. *Nucleic Acids Research*, 40(database issue): D876–880, 2011.

[150] S. Kulick, A. Bies, M. Liberman, M. Mandel, R. McDonald, M. Palmer, A. Schein, L. Ungar, S. Winters, and P. White. Integrated annotation for biomedical information extraction. In L. Hirschman and J. Pustejovsky, editors, *HLT-NAACL 2004 Workshop: BioLINK 2004, Linking Biological Literature, Ontologies and Databases*, pages 61–68, 2004.

[151] J. Kummerfeld, M. Bansal, D. Burkett, and D. Klein. Mention detection: Heuristics for the ontonotes annotations. In *Proceedings of the Fifteenth Conference on Computational Natural Language Learning: Shared Task*, pages 102–106, 2011.

[152] D. Kwon, S. Kim, S. Shin, and W. Wilbur. BioQRator: A web-based interactive biomedical literature curating system. In *Proceedings of the Fourth BioCreative Challenge Evaluation Workshop vol. 1*, pages 241–246, 2013.

[153] R. Leaman, R. Doğan, and Z. Lu. DNorm: disease name normalization with pairwise learning to rank. *Bioinformatics*, 29(22):2909–2917, 2013.

[154] R. Leaman, G. Gonzalez, et al. BANNER: An executable survey of advances in biomedical named entity recognition. In *Pacific Symposium on Biocomputing, vol. 13*, pages 652–663, 2008.

[155] R. Leaman, R. Khare, and Z. Lu. NCBI at 2013 ShARe/CLEF eHealth Shared Task: Disorder normalization in clinical notes with DNorm. http://www.ncbi.nim.nih.gov/CBBresearch/Lu/elef13task.pdf

[156] B. Li and E. Gaussier. Improving corpus comparability for bilingual lexicon extraction from comparable corpora. In *Proceedings of the 23rd International Conference on Computational Linguistics*, pages 644–652, 2010.

[157] X. Li, J. Shen, X. Gao, and X. Wang. Exploiting rich features for detecting hedges and their scope. In *Proceedings of the Fourteenth Conference on Computational Natural Language Learning—Shared Task*, pages 78–83, 2010.

[158] M. Liakata, S. Saha, S. Dobnik, C. Batchelor, and D. Rebholz-Schuhmann. Automatic recognition of conceptualisation zones in scientific articles and two life science applications. *Bioinformatics*, 28(7): 991–1000, 2012.

[159] M. Liakata, S. Saha, S. Dobnik, C. Batchelor, and D. Rebholz-Schuhmann. Automatic recognition of conceptualization zones in scientific articles and two life science applications. *Bioinformatics*, 28(7):991–1000, 2012.

[160] M. Liakata, P. Thompson, A. de Waard, R. Nawaz, H. Pander Maat, and S. Ananiadou. A three-way perspective on scientic discourse annotation for knowledge extraction. In *Proceedings of the ACL Workshop on Detecting Structure in Scholarly Discourse*, pages 37–46, 2012.

[161] T. Liang and Y.-H. Lin. Anaphora resolution for biomedical literature by exploiting multiple resources. In R. Dale, K.-F. Wong, J. Su, and O. Kwong, editors, *Proceedings of the Second International Joint Conference on Natural Language Processing, vol. 3651* of *Lecture Notes in Computer Science*, pages 742–753. Springer Berlin Heidelberg, 2005.

[162] M. Light, X. Qiu, and P. Srinivasan. The language of bioscience: Facts, speculations, and statements in between. In *HLT-NAACL 2004 Workshop: BioLINK 2004, Linking Biological Literature, Ontologies and Databases*, pages 17–24, 2004.

[163] R. Lin, L. Lenert, B. Middleton, and S. Shiffman. A free-text processing system to capture physical findings: Canonical phrase identification system (CAPIS). In *Proceedings of the Annual Symposium on Computer Application in Medical Care*, page 843, 1991.

[164] T. Lippincott, D. Seaghdha, and A. Korhonen. Exploring subdomain variation in biomedical language. *BMC Bioinformatics*, 12(1):212, 2011.

[165] X. Luo. On coreference resolution performance metrics. In *Proceedings of the Conference on Human Language Technology and Empirical Methods in Natural Language Processing*, pages 25–32, 2005.

[166] E. Marsh and D. Perzanowski. MUC-7 evaluation of IE technology: Overview of results. In *Proceedings of the Seventh Message Understanding Conference*, 1998.

[167] S. Martschat. Multigraph clustering for unsupervised coreference resolution. In *Proceedings of the 51st Annual Meeting of the ACL Proceedings of the Student Research Workshop*, pages 81–88, 2013.

[168] S. Matis-Mitchell, P. Roberts, C. Tudor, and C. Arighi. BioCreative IV interactive task. In *Proceedings of the Fourth BioCreative Challenge Evaluation Workshop, vol. 1*, pages 190–203, 2013.

[169] D. Maynard and S. Ananiadou. TRUCKS: A model for automatic term recognition. *Journal of Natural Language Processing*, 8(1): 101–125, 2000.

[170] D. McClosky, S. Riedel, M. Surdeanu, A. McCallum, and C. Manning. Combining joint models for biomedical event extraction. *BMC Bioinformatics*, 13(Suppl 11):S9, 2012.

[171] D. McClosky, M. Surdeanu, and C. Manning. Event extraction as dependency parsing. In *Proceedings of the 49th Annual Meeting of the Association for Computational Linguistics: Human Language Technologies–Vol. 1*, pages 1626–1635, 2011.

[172] R. McDonald and F. Pereira. Identifying gene and protein mentions in text using conditional random fields. *BMC Bioinformatics*, 6(Suppl 1):S6, 2005.

[173] T. McIntosh and J. Curran. Challenges for automatically extracting molecular interactions from full-text articles. *BMC Bioinformatics*, 10(1):311, 2009.

[174] L. McKnight and P. Srinivasan. Categorization of sentence types in medical abstracts. In *AMIA Annual Symposium Proceedings*, volume 2003, page 440, 2003.

[175] B. Medlock and T. Briscoe. Weakly supervised learning for hedge classification in scientific literature. In *Proceedings of ACL, vol. 2007*, pages 992–999, 2007.

[176] S. Meystre, G. Savova, K. Kipper-Schuler, J. Hurdle, et al. Extracting information from textual documents in the electronic health record: A review of recent research. *Yearbook of Medical Informatics*, 35:128–144, 2008.

[177] C. Mihăilă and S. Ananiadou. A hybrid approach to recognising discourse causality in the biomedical domain. In *Proceedings of the IEEE International Conference on Bioinformatics and Biomedicine (BIBM) 2013*, pages 361–366, 2013.

[178] C. Mihăilă and S. Ananiadou. Recognising discourse causality triggers in the biomedical domain. *Journal of Bioinformatics and Computational Biology*, 11(6):1343008, 2013.

[179] C. Mihăilă, R. T. B. Batista-Navarro, and S. Ananiadou. Analysing entity type variation across biomedical subdomains. In *Proceedings of the Third Workshop on Building and Evaluating Resources for Biomedical Text Mining (BioTxtM 2012)*, pages 1–7, May 2012.

[180] C. Mihăilă, T. Ohta, S. Pyysalo, and S. Ananiadou. BioCause: Annotating and analysing causality in the biomedical domain. *BMC Bioinformatics*, 14(1):2, 2013.

[181] S. Mika and B. Rost. Protein names precisely peeled off free text. *Bioinformatics*, 20(suppl 1):i241–i247, 2004.

[182] M. Miwa and S. Ananiadou. NaCTeM EventMine for BioNLP 2013 CG and PC tasks. In *Proceedings of the BioNLP Shared Task 2013 Workshop*, pages 94–98, 2013.

[183] M. Miwa, T. Ohta, R. Rak, A. Rowley, D. B. Kell, S. Pyysalo, and S. Ananiadou. A method for integrating and ranking the evidence for biochemical pathways by mining reactions from text. *Bioinformatics*, 29(13):i44–i52, 2013.

[184] M. Miwa, R. Sætre, J.-D. Kim, and J. Tsujii. Event extraction with complex event classification using rich features. *Journal of Bioinformatics and Computational Biology*, 8(1):131–146, 2010.

[185] M. Miwa, P. Thompson, and S. Ananiadou. Boosting automatic event extraction from the literature using domain adaptation and coreference resolution. *Bioinformatics*, 28(13):1759–1765, 2012.

[186] M. Miwa, P. Thompson, J. McNaught, D. B. Kell, and S. Ananiadou. Extracting semantically enriched events from biomedical literature. *BMC Bioinformatics*, 13:108, 2012.

[187] Y. Miyao, T. Ohta, K. Masuda, Y. Tsuruoka, K. Yoshida, T. Ninomiya, and J. Tsujii. Semantic retrieval for the accurate identification of relational concepts in massive textbases. In *Proceedings of COLING-ACL 2006*, pages 1017–1024, 2006.

[188] Y. Miyao and J. Tsujii. Feature forest models for probabilistic HPSG parsing. *Computational Linguistics*, 34(1):35–80, 2008.

[189] Y. Mizuta, A. Korhonen, T. Mullen, and N. Collier. Zone analysis in biology articles as a basis for information extraction. *International Journal of Medical Informatics*, 75(6):468–487, 2006.

[190] R. Morante, V. Van Asch, and W. Daelemans. Memory-based resolution of in-sentence scopes of hedge cues. In *Proceedings of the Fourteenth Conference on Computational Natural Language Learning—Shared Task*, pages 40–47, 2010.

[191] A. Morgan, L. Hirschman, A. Yeh, and M. Colosimo. Gene name extraction using FlyBase resources. In *Proceedings of the ACL 2003 Workshop on Natural Language Processing in Biomedicine–Vol. 13*, pages 1–8, 2003.

[192] E. Morin and B. Daille. Compositionality and lexical alignment of multi-word terms. *Language Resources and Evaluation*, 44(1-2):79–95, 2010.

[193] E. Morin and B. Daille. Revising the compositional method for terminology acquisition from comparable corpora. In *Proceedings of COLING 2012*, pages 1797–1810, 2012.

[194] E. Morin and E. Prochasson. Bilingual lexicon extraction from comparable corpora enhanced with parallel corpora. In *Proceedings of the 4th Workshop on Building and Using Comparable Corpora: Comparable Corpora and the Web*, pages 27–34, 2011.

[195] T. Morton and J. LaCivita. WordFreak: An open tool for linguistic annotation. In *Proceedings of the 2003 Conference of the North American Chapter of the Association for Computational Linguistics on Human Language Technology: Demonstrations–Vol. 4*, pages 17–18, 2003.

[196] C. Müller and M. Strube. Multi-level annotation of linguistic data with MMAX2. In S. Braun, K. Kohn, and J. Mukherjee, editors, *Corpus Technology and Language Pedagogy: New Resources, New Tools, New Methods*, pages 197–214. Peter Lang, Frankfurt a.M., Germany, 2006.

[197] H. Müller, E. Kenny, and P. Sternberg. Textpresso: An ontology-based information retrieval and extraction system for biological literature. *PLoS Biol*, 2(11):e309, 2004.

[198] T. Munkhdalai, M. Li, U. Yun, O. Namsrai, and K. Ryu. An active co-training algorithm for biomedical named-entity recognition. *Journal of Information Processing Systems*, 8(4): 575–588, 2012.

[199] D. Munteanu, A. Fraser, and D. Marcu. Improved machine translation performance via parallel sentence extraction from comparable corpora. In *HLT-NAACL*, pages 265–272, 2004.

[200] D. Munteanu and D. Marcu. Processing comparable corpora with bilingual suffix trees. In *Proceedings of the ACL-02 Conference on Empirical Methods in Natural Language Processing–Vol. 10*, pages 289–295, 2002.

[201] D. Nadeau and S. Sekine. A survey of named entity recognition and classification. *Lingvisticae Investigationes*, 30(1):3–26, 2007.

[202] H. Nakagawa. Automatic term recognition based on statistics of compound nouns. *Terminology*, 6(2):195–210, 2000.

[203] R. Nawaz, P. Thompson, and S. Ananiadou. Identification of manner in bio-events. In *Proceedings of the Eighth International Conference on Language Resources and Evaluation (LREC 2012)*, pages 3505–3510, 2012.

[204] R. Nawaz, P. Thompson, and S. Ananiadou. Meta-knowledge annotation at the event level: Comparison between abstracts and full papers. In *Proceedings of the Third Workshop on Building and Evaluating Resources for Biomedical Text Mining (BioTxtM 2012)*, pages 24–31, 2012.

[205] R. Nawaz, P. Thompson, and S. Ananiadou. Negated bioevents: Analysis and identification. *BMC Bioinformatics*, 14(1):14, 2013.

[206] R. Nawaz, P. Thompson, and S. Ananiadou. Something old, something new: Identifying knowledge source in bio-events. In *International Journal of Computational Linguistics and Applications, vol. 4*, pages 129–144, 2013.

[207] R. Nawaz, P. Thompson, J. McNaught, and S. Ananiadou. Meta-knowledge annotation of bio-events. In *Proceedings of the Seventh International Conference on Language Resources and Evaluation (LREC 2010)*, pages 2498–2505, 2010.

[208] C. Nédellec, R. Bossy, J. Kim, J. Kim, T. Ohta, S. Pyysalo, and P. Zweigenbaum. Overview of BioNLP shared task 2013. In *Proceedings of the BioNLP Shared Task 2013 Workshop*, pages 1–7, 2013.

[209] A. Névéol, R. Doğan, and Z. Lu. Semi-automatic semantic annotation of PubMed queries: A study on quality, efficiency, satisfaction. *Journal of Biomedical Informatics*, 44(2):310–318, 2011.

[210] M. Neves, J. Braun, A. Diehl, G. Hayman, S. Wang, U. Leser, and A. Kurtz. Evaluation of the CellFinder pipeline in the BioCreative IV User interactive task. In *Proceedings of the Fourth BioCreative Challenge Evaluation Workshop vol. 1*, pages 204–213, 2013.

[211] M. Neves, A. Damaschun, N. Mah, F. Lekschas, S. Seltmann, H. Stachelscheid, J. Fontaine, A. Kurtz, and U. Leser. Preliminary evaluation of the CellFinder literature curation pipeline for gene expression in kidney cells and anatomical parts. *Database*, 2013. doi: 10.1093/database/bat020

[212] N. Nguyen, J. Kim, and J. Tsujii. Overview of BioNLP 2011 protein coreference shared task. In *Proceedings of the BioNLP Shared Task 2011 Workshop*, pages 74–82, 2011.

[213] N.L.T. Nguyen and J.-D. Kim. Exploring domain differences for the design of pronoun resolution systems for biomedical text. In *Proceedings of the 22nd International Conference on Computational Linguistics, vol. 1*, pages 625–632, 2008.

[214] C. Nicolae and G. Nicolae. BestCut: A graph algorithm for coreference resolution. In *Proceedings of the 2006 Conference on Empirical Methods in Natural Language Processing*, pages 275–283, 2006.

[215] C. Nobata, P. Cotter, N. Okazaki, B. Rea, Y. Sasaki, Y. Tsuruoka, J. Tsujii, and S. Ananiadou. KLEIO: A knowledge-enriched information retrieval system for biology. In *Proceedings of the 31st Annual International ACM SIGIR Conference on Research and Development in Information Retrieval*, pages 787–788, 2008.

[216] F. Och and H. Ney. A systematic comparison of various statistical alignment models. *Computational Linguistics*, 29(1):19–51, 2003.

[217] K. Oda, J. Kim, T. Ohta, D. Okanohara, T. Matsuzaki, Y. Tateisi, and J. Tsujii. New challenges for text mining: Mapping between text and manually curated pathways. *BMC Bioinformatics*, 9(Suppl 3):S5, 2008.

[218] P. Ogren. Knowtator: A protégé plug-in for annotated corpus construction. In *Proceedings of the 2006 Conference of the North American Chapter of the Association for Computational Linguistics on Human Language Technology: Companion Volume: Demonstrations*, pages 273–275, 2006.

[219] T. Ohta, S. Pyysalo, R. Rak, A. Rowley, H.-W. Chun, S. J. Jung, S. P. Choi, and S. Ananiadou. Overview of the pathway curation (PC) task of BioNLP Shared Task 2013. In *Proceedings of the BioNLP Shared Task 2013 Workshop*, pages 67–75, 2013.

[220] T. Oinn, M. Greenwood, M. Addis, N. Alpdemir, J. Ferris, K. Glover, C. Goble, A. Goderis, D. Hull, D. Marvin, P. Li, P. Lord, M. Pocock, M. Senger, R. Stevens, A. Wipat, and C. Wroe. Taverna: Lessons in creating a workflow environment for the life sciences. *Concurrency and Computation: Practice and Experience*, 18(10):1067–1100, 2006.

[221] H. Paek, Y. Kogan, P. Thomas, S. Codish, and M. Krauthammer. Shallow semantic parsing of randomized controlled trial reports. *Proceedings of AMIA Annual Symposium*, 2006.

[222] K. Papineni, S. Roukos, T. Ward, and W. Zhu. BLEU: A method for automatic evaluation of machine translation. In *Proceedings of the 40th Annual Meeting on Association for Computational Linguistics*, pages 311–318, 2002.

[223] C. Parker and D. Embley. Generating medical logic modules for clinical trial eligibility criteria. *Proceedings of AMIA Annual Symposium*, 2003.

[224] P. Pecina, O. Dušek, L. Goeuriot, J. Hajič, J. Hlaváčová, G. Jones, L. Kelly, J. Leveling, D. Mareček, M. Novák, et al. Adaptation of machine translation for multilingual information retrieval in the medical domain. *Artificial Intelligence in Medicine*, 61(3): 165–185, 2014.

[225] C. Plake, T. Schiemann, M. Pankalla, J. Hakenberg, and U. Leser. AliBaba: PubMed as a graph. *Bioinformatics*, 22(19):2444–2445, 2006.

[226] R. Prasad, N. Dinesh, A. Lee, E. Miltsakaki, L. Robaldo, A. Joshi, and B. Webber. The Penn Discourse TreeBank 2.0. In *In Proceedings of the 6th International Conference on Language Resources and Evaluation (LREC)*, 2008.

[227] R. Prasad, S. McRoy, N. Frid, A. Joshi, and H. Yu. The biomedical discourse relation bank. *BMC Bioinformatics*, 12(1):188, 2011.

[228] D. Proux, F. Rechenmann, L. Julliard, V. Pillet, B. Jacq, et al. Detecting gene symbols and names in biological texts: A first step toward pertinent information extraction. *Genome Informatics Series*, pages 72–80, 1998.

[229] J. Pustejovsky, J. Castaño, R. Saurí, A. Rumshinsky, J. Zhang, and W. Luo. Medstract: Creating large-scale information servers for biomedical libraries. In *Proceedings of the ACL 2002 Workshop on Natural Language Processing in the Biomedical Domain*, volume 3, pages 85–92, 2002.

[230] S. Pyysalo, F. Ginter, J. Heimonen, J. Bjorne, J. Boberg, J. Jarvinen, and T. Salakoski. BioInfer: A corpus for information extraction in the biomedical domain. *BMC Bioinformatics*, 8(1):50, 2007.

[231] S. Pyysalo, T. Ohta, and S. Ananiadou. Overview of the cancer genetics (CG) task of BioNLP Shared Task 2013. In *Proceedings of the BioNLP Shared Task 2013 Workshop*, pages 58–66, 2013.

[232] S. Pyysalo, T. Ohta, M. Miwa, H. Cho, J. Tsujii, and S. Ananiadou. Event extraction across multiple levels of biological organization. *Bioinformatics*, 28(18):i575–i581, 2012.

[233] S. Pyysalo, T. Ohta, R. Rak, D. Sullivan, C. Mao, C. Wang, B. Sobral, J. Tsujii, and S. Ananiadou. Overview of the Infectious Diseases (ID) task of BioNLP Shared Task 2011. In *Proceedings of the BioNLP Shared Task 2011 Workshop*, pages 26–35, 2011.

[234] Y. W. Qiang, B. Hu, Y. Chen, Y. Zhong, B. Shi, B. Barlogie, and J.D. Shaughnessy Jr. Bortezomib induces osteoblast differentiation via Wnt-independent activation of β-catenin/TCF signaling. *Blood*, 113(18):4319–4330, 2009.

[235] A. Rahman and V. Ng. Supervised Models for Coreference Resolution. In *Proceedings of the 2009 Conference on Empirical Methods in Natural Language Processing*, pages 968–977, 2009.

[236] K. Raja, S. Subramani, and J. Natarajan. PPInterFinder—a mining tool for extracting causal relations on human proteins from literature. *Database*, 2013. doi: 10.1093/database/bas052

[237] R. Rak and S. Ananiadou. Making UIMA truly interoperable with SPARQL. In *Proceedings of the 7th Linguistic Annotation Workshop and Interoperability with Discourse*, pages 88–97, 2013.

[238] R. Rak, R. T. B. Batista-Navarro, A. Rowley, J. Carter, and S. Ananiadou. Customisable Curation Workflows in Argo. In *Proceedings of the Fourth BioCreative Challenge Evaluation Workshop, vol. 1*, pages 270–278, 2013.

[239] R Rak, A Rowley, W Black, and S Ananiadou. Argo: An integrative, interactive, text mining-based workbench supporting curation. *Database: The Journal of Biological Databases and Curation*, 2012. doi:10.1093/databse/bas010

[240] R. Rak, A. Rowley, J. Carter, R. T. B. Batista-Navarro, and S. Ananiadou. Interoperability and customisation of annotation schemata in Argo. In *Proceedings of the 9th Conference on Language Resources and Evaluation*, 2014.

[241] P. Ramesh, R. Prasad, T. Miller, B. Harrington, and H. Yu. Automatic discourse connective detection in biomedical text. *Journal of the American Medical Informatics Association*, 19(5):800–808, 2012.

[242] L. Ramshaw and M. Marcus. Text chunking using transformation-based learning. In *Proceedings of the Third ACL Workshop on Very Large Corpora*, 1995.

[243] R. Rapp. Automatic identification of word translations from unrelated English and German corpora. In *Proceedings of the 37th Annual Meeting of the ACL on Computational Linguistics*, pages 519–526, 1999.

[244] L. Ratinov and D. Roth. Design challenges and misconceptions in named entity recognition. In *Proceedings of the Thirteenth Conference on Computational Natural Language Learning*, pages 147–155, 2009.

[245] S. Rauf and H. Schwenk. Parallel sentence generation from comparable corpora for improved SMT. *Machine Translation*, 25(4):341–375, 2011.

[246] D. Rebholz-Schuhmann, M. Arregui, S. Gaudan, H. Kirsch, and A. Jimeno. Text processing through web services: Calling whatizit. *Bioinformatics*, 24(2):296–298, 2008.

[247] M. Recasens and E.H. Hovy. BLANC: Implementing the Rand index for coreference evaluation. *Natural Language Engineering*, 17(4):485–510, 2011.

[248] M. Rei and T. Briscoe. Combining manual rules and supervised learning for hedge cue and scope detection. In *Proceedings of the Fourteenth Conference on Computational Natural Language Learning—Shared Task*, pages 56–63, 2010.

[249] S. Riedel and A. McCallum. Robust biomedical event extraction with dual decomposition and minimal domain adaptation. In *Proceedings of the BioNLP Shared Task 2011 Workshop*, pages 46–50, 2011.

[250] F. Rinaldi, A. Davis, C. Southan, S. Clematide, T. Ellendorff, and G. Schneider. ODIN: A customizable literature curation tool. In *Proceedings of the Fourth BioCreative Challenge Evaluation Workshop vol. 1*, pages 219–223, 2013.

[251] V. Rizomilioti. Exploring epistemic modality in academic discourse using corpora. In *Information Technology in Languages for Specific Purposes*, volume 7, pages 53–71, 2006.

[252] A. Roberts, R. Gaizauskas, M. Hepple, G. Demetriou, Y. Guo, I. Roberts, and A. Setzer. Building a semantically annotated corpus of clinical texts. *Journal of Biomedical Informatics*, 42(5):950–966, 2009.

[253] A. Roberts, R. Gaizauskas, M. Hepple, G. Demetriou, Y. Guo, I. Roberts, and A. Setzer. Building a semantically annotated corpus of clinical texts. *Journal of Biomedical Informatics*, 42(5):950–966, 2009.

[254] P. Ruch, C. Boyer, C. Chichester, I. Tbahriti, A. Geissbühler, P. Fabry, J. Gobeill, V. Pillet, D. Rebholz-Schuhmann, C. Lovis, and A. Veuthey. Using argumentation to extract key sentences from biomedical abstracts. *International Journal of Medical Informatics*, 76(23):195–200, 2007.

[255] A. Rzhetsky, M. Seringhaus, and M. Gerstein. Seeking a new biology through text mining. *Cell*, 134(1):9–13, 2008.

[256] Á. Sándor. Modeling metadiscourse conveying the author's rhetorical strategy in biomedical research abstracts. *Revue Française de Linguistique Appliquée*, 12(2):97–108, 2007.

[257] Y. Sasaki, Y. Tsuruoka, J. McNaught, and S. Ananiadou. How to make the most of NE dictionaries in statistical NER. *BMC Bioinformatics*, 9(Suppl 11):S5, 2008.

[258] R. Saurí and J. Pustejovsky. FactBank: A corpus annotated with event factuality. *Language Resources and Evaluation*, 43(3):227–268, 2009.

[259] G. Savova, J. Masanz, P. Ogren, J. Zheng, S. Sohn, K. Kipper-Schuler, and C. Chute. Mayo clinical Text Analysis and Knowledge Extraction System (cTAKES): Architecture, component evaluation and applications. *Journal of the American Medical Informatics Association*, 17(5):507–513, 2010.

[260] I. Schomburg, A. Chang, C. Ebeling, M. Gremse, C. Heldt, G. Huhn, and D. Schomburg. BRENDA, the enzyme database: Updates and major new developments. *Nucleic Acids Research*, 32(suppl 1):D431–D433, 2004.

[261] P. Schone and D. Jurafsky. Is knowledge-free induction of multiword unit dictionary headwords a solved problem? In L. Lee and D. Harman, editors, *Proceedings of EMNLP*, pages 100–108, 2001.

[262] M. Schuemie, M. Weeber, B. Schijvenaars, E. van Mulligen, C. van der Eijk, R. Jelier, B. Mons, and J. Kors. Distribution of information in biomedical abstracts and full-text publications. *Bioinformatics*, 20(16):2597–2604, 2004.

[263] I. Segura-Bedmar, M. Crespo, C. de Pablo-Sanchez, and P. Martinez. Resolving anaphoras for the extraction of drug-drug interactions in pharmacological documents. *BMC Bioinformatics*, 11(Suppl 2):S1, 2010.

[264] I. Segura-Bedmar, P. Martínez, and C. de Pablo-Sánchez. A linguistic rule-based approach to extract drug-drug interactions from pharmacological documents. *BMC Bioinformatics*, 12(S-2):S1, 2011.

[265] P. Shah, C. Perez-Iratxeta, P. Bork, and M. Andrade. Information extraction from full text scientific articles: Where are the keywords? *BMC Bioinformatics*, 4(1):20, 2003.

[266] H. Shatkay, F. Pan, A. Rzhetsky, and J. Wilbur. Multi-dimensional classification of biomedical text: Toward automated, practical provision of high-utility text to diverse users. *Bioinformatics*, 24(18):2086–2093, 2008.

[267] S. Shimohata, T. Sugio, and J. Nagata. Retrieving collocations by co-occurrences and word order constraints. In P. Cohen and W. Wahlster, editors, *Proceedings of the 35th ACL and 8th EACL*, pages 476–481, 1997.

[268] H. Shin and R. Bruno. *Language Use and English-Speaking Ability, 2000.* US Department of Commerce, Economics and Statistics Administration, US Census Bureau, 2003.

[269] I. Sim, P. Gorman, R. Greenes, B. Haynes, B. Kaplan, H. Lehmann, and P. Tang. Clinical decision support systems for the practice of evidence-based medicine. *JAMIA*, 8(6):527–534, 2001.

[270] M. Simpson and D. Demner-Fushman. Biomedical text mining: A survey of recent progress. In *Mining Text Data*, pages 465–517. Springer, 2012.

[271] F. Smadja, K. McKeown, and V. Hatzivassiloglou. Translating collocations for bilingual lexicons: A statistical approach. *Computational Linguistics*, 22(1):1–38, 1996.

[272] P. Stenetorp, S. Pyysalo, G. Topić, T. Ohta, S. Ananiadou, and J. Tsujii. brat: A web-based tool for NLP-assisted text annotation. In *Proceedings of the Demonstrations at the 13th Conference of the European Chapter of the Association for Computational Linguistics*, pages 102–107, 2012.

[273] N. Suakkaphong, Z. Zhang, and H. Chen. Disease named entity recognition using semisupervised learning and conditional random fields. *Journal of the American Society for Information Science and Technology*, 62(4):727–737, 2011.

[274] C. Sun, M. Zhang, Y. Wu, J. Ren, Y. Bo, L. Han, and D. Li. Searching of information about protein acetylation system. In *Proceedings of the BioCreative 2012 Workshop*, 2012.

[275] L. Tanabe, N. Xie, L. Thom, W. Matten, and J. Wilbur. GENETAG: A tagged corpus for gene/protein named entity recognition. *BMC Bioinformatics*, 6(Suppl 1):S3, 2005.

[276] Y. Tateisi and J. Tsujii. Part-of-speech annotation of biology research abstracts. In *Proceedings of 4th LREC, vol. IV*, pages 1267–1270, 2004.

[277] A. Taylor, M. Marcus, and B. Santorini. The penn treebank: An overview. In A. Abeill, editor, *Treebanks*, volume 20 of *Text, Speech and Language Technology*, pages 5–22. Springer Netherlands, 2003.

[278] E. Terumasa. Rule based machine translation combined with statistical post editor for japanese to english patent translation. In *Proceedings of the MT Summit XI Workshop on Patent Translation, vol. 11*, pages 13–18, 2007.

[279] S. Teufel. *Argumentative Zoning*. PhD thesis, University of Edinburgh, 1999.

[280] S. Teufel and M. Moens. Summarizing scientific articles: Experiments with relevance and rhetorical status. *Computational Linguistics*, 28(4):409–445, 2002.

[281] P. Thomas, J. Starlinger, A. Vowinkel, S. Arzt, and U. Leser. GeneView: A comprehensive semantic search engine for PubMed. *Nucleic Acids Research*, 40(W1):W585–W591, 2012.

[282] P. Thompson, P. Cotter, J. McNaught, S. Ananiadou, S. Montemagni, A. Trabucco, and G. Venturi. Building a bio-event annotated corpus for the acquisition of semantic frames from biomedical corpora. In *Proceedings of the 6th LREC*, pages 2159–2166, 2008.

[283] P. Thompson, S. Iqbal, J. McNaught, and S. Ananiadou. Construction of an annotated corpus to support biomedical information extraction. *BMC Bioinformatics*, 10(1):349, 2009.

[284] P. Thompson, J. McNaught, S. Montemagni, N. Calzolari, R. del Gratta, V. Lee, S. Marchi, M. Monachini, P. Pezik, V. Quochi, C. J. Rupp, Y. Sasaki, G. Venturi, D. Rebholz-Schuhmann, and S. Ananiadou. The BioLexicon: A large-scale terminological resource for biomedical text mining. *BMC Bioinformatics*, 12:397, 2011.

[285] P. Thompson, R. Nawaz, J. McNaught, and S. Ananiadou. Enriching a biomedical event corpus with meta-knowledge annotation. *BMC Bioinformatics*, 12:393, 2011.

[286] M. Torii, G. Li, Z. Li, I. Çelen, F. Diella, R. Oughtred, C. Arighi, H. Huang, K. Vijay-Shanker, and C. Wu. RLIMS-P: Literature-based curation of protein phosphorylation information. In *Proceedings of the Fourth BioCreative Challenge Evaluation Workshop vol. 1*, pages 247–253, 2013.

[287] M. Torii and K. Vijay-Shanker. Sortal anaphora resolution in MEDLINE abstracts. *Computational Intelligence*, 23(1):15–27, 2007.

[288] Y. Tsuruoka, M. Miwa, K. Hamamoto, J. Tsujii, and S. Ananiadou. Discovering and visualizing indirect associations between biomedical concepts. *Bioinformatics*, 27(13):i111–i119, 2011.

[289] Y. Tsuruoka and Junichi Tsujii. Improving the performance of dictionary-based approaches in protein name recognition. *Journal of Biomedical Informatics*, 37(6):461–470, 2004.

[290] O. Tuason, L. Chen, H. Liu, J. Blake, and C. Friedman. Biological nomenclatures: A source of lexical knowledge and ambiguity. In *Proceedings of the Pacific Symposium of Biocomputing*, number 9, page 238, 2003.

[291] C. Tudor, C. Arighi, Q. Wang, C. Wu, and K. Vijay-Shanker. The eFIP system for text mining of protein interaction networks of phosphorylated proteins. *Database*, 2012. doi: 10.1093/database/bas044

[292] U.S. National Library of Medicine. Statistical Reports on MEDLINE/PubMed Baseline Data. `http://www.nlm.nih.gov/bsd/licensee/baselinestats.html`. Accessed: May 2014.

[293] Y. Usami, H. Cho, N. Okazaki, and J. Tsujii. Automatic acquisition of huge training data for bio-medical named entity recognition. In *Proceedings of BioNLP 2011 Workshop*, pages 65–73, 2011.

[294] Ö. Uzuner. Recognizing obesity and comorbidities in sparse data. *JAMIA*, 16(4):561–570, 2009.

[295] Ö. Uzuner, I. Goldstein, Y. Luo, and I. Kohane. Identifying patient smoking status from medical discharge records. *JAMIA*, 15(1):14–24, 2008.

[296] Ö. Uzuner, B. South, S. Shen, and S. DuVall. 2010 i2b2/VA challenge on concepts, assertions, and relations in clinical text. *JAMIA*, 18(5):552–556, 2011.

[297] K. Van Auken, J. Jaffery, J. Chan, H. Müller, and P. W. Sternberg. Semi-automated curation of protein subcellular localization: a text mining-based approach to gene ontology (GO) cellular component curation. *BMC Bioinformatics*, 10:228, 2009.

[298] K. Van Auken, Y. Li, J. Chan, P. Fey, R. Dodson, A. Rangarajan, R. Chisholm, P. Sternberg, and H. Müller. Textpresso text mining: Semi-automated curation of protein subcellular localization using the gene ontology's cellular component ontology. In *Proceedings of the BioCreative 2012 Workshop*, 2012.

[299] P. van der Eijk. Automating the acquisition of bilingual terminology. In *Proceedings of the Sixth Conference on European Chapter of the ACL*, pages 113–119, 1993.

[300] S. Van Landeghem, J. Björne, T. Abeel, B. De Baets, T. Salakoski, and Y. Van de Peer. Semantically linking molecular entities in literature through entity relationships. *BMC Bioinformatics*, 13(Suppl 11):S6, 2012.

[301] S. Van Landeghem, J. Björne, C. Wei, K. Hakala, S. Pyysalo, S. Ananiadou, H. Kao, Z. Lu, T. Salakoski, Y. Van de Peer, and F. Ginter. Large-scale event extraction from literature with multi-level gene normalization. *PLOS ONE*, 8(4):e55814, 2013.

[302] S. Van Landeghem, F. Ginter, Y. Van de Peer, and T. Salakoski. EVEX: A PubMed-scale resource for homology-based generalization of text mining predictions. In *Proceedings of BioNLP 2011 Workshop*, pages 28–37, 2011.

[303] B. Vauquois and C. Boitet. Automated translation at Grenoble University. *Computational Linguistics*, 11(1):28–36, 1985.

[304] S. G. Vellay, Miller E. Latimer, and G. Paillard. Interactive text mining with pipeline pilot: A bibliographic web-based tool for PubMed. *Infectious Disorders Drug Targets*, 9(3):366–374, 2009.

[305] E. Velldal, L. Øvrelid, and S. Oepen. Resolving speculation: Maxent cue classification and dependency-based scope rules. In *Proceedings of the Fourteenth Conference on Computational Natural Language Learning—Shared Task*, pages 48–55, 2010.

[306] M. Vilain, J. Burger, J. Aberdeen, D. Connolly, and L. Hirschman. A model-theoretic coreference scoring scheme. In *Proceedings of the 6th Conference on Message Understanding*, pages 45–52, 1995.

[307] V. Vincze, G. Szarvas, R. Farkas, G. Mora, and J. Csirik. The BioScope corpus: Biomedical texts annotated for uncertainty, negation and their scopes. *BMC Bioinformatics*, 9(Suppl 11):S9, 2008.

[308] V. Vincze, G. Szarvas, G. Möra, T. Ohta, and R. Farkas. Linguistic scope-based and biological event-based speculation and negation annotations in the BioScope and GENIA event corpora. *Journal of Biomedical Semantics*, 2(5):1–11, 2011.

[309] J. Vivaldi, L. Màrquez, and H. Rodríguez. Improving term extraction by system combination using boosting. *Lecture Notes in Computer Science*, 2167:515–526, 2001.

[310] A. Vlachos and C. Gasperin. Bootstrapping and evaluating named entity recognition in the biomedical domain. In *Proceedings of the HLT-NAACL BioNLP Workshop on Linking Natural Language and Biology*, pages 138–145, 2006.

[311] X. Wang, G. Hripcsak, M. Markatou, and C. Friedman. Active computerized pharmacovigilance using natural language processing, statistics, and electronic health records: A feasibility study. *JAMIA*, 16(3):328–337, 2009.

[312] C. Wei, H. Kao, and Z. Lu. PubTator: A web-based text mining tool for assisting biocuration. *Nucleic Acids Research*, 41(W1):W518–W522, 2013.

[313] J. Wilbur, A. Rzhetsky, and H. Shatkay. New directions in biomedical text annotation: Definitions, guidelines and corpus construction. *BMC Bioinformatics*, 7(1):356, 2006.

[314] D.S. Wishart, C. Knox, A.C. Guo, R. Eisner, N. Young, B. Gautam, D.D. Hau, N. Psychogios, E. Dong, S. Bouatra, R. Mandal, I. Sinelnikov, J. Xia, L. Jia, J.A. Cruz, E. Lim, C.A. Sobsey, S. Shrivastava, P. Huang, P. Liu, L. Fang, J. Peng, R. Fradette, D. Cheng, D. Tzur, M. Clements, A. Lewis, A. De Souza, A. Zuniga, M. Dawe, Y. Xiong, D. Clive, R. Greiner,

A. Nazyrova, R. Shaykhutdinov, L. Li, H.J. Vogel, and I. Forsythe. HMDB: A knowledgebase for the human metabolome. *Nucleic Acids Research*, 37(Suppl 1):D603–D610, 2009.

[315] A. Wright, E. Chen, and F. Maloney. An automated technique for identifying associations between medications, laboratory results and problems. *Journal of Biomedical Informatics*, 43(6):891–901, 2010.

[316] C. Wu, F. Xia, L. Deleger, and I. Solti. Statistical machine translation for biomedical text: Are we there yet? In *AMIA Annual Symposium Proceedings, vol. 2011*, page 1290, 2011.

[317] F. Xia and M. Yetisgen-Yildiz. Clinical corpus annotation: Challenges and strategies. In *Proceedings of the Third Workshop on Building and Evaluating Resources for Biomedical Text Mining (BioTxtM'2012)*, 2012.

[318] R. Xu, K. Supekar, Y. Huang, A. Das, and A. Garber. Combining text classification and hidden Markov modeling techniques for categorizing sentences in randomized clinical trial abstracts. *Proceedings of AMIA Annual Symposium*, 2006.

[319] X. Yang, J. Su, G. Zhou, and C.L. Tan. An NP-cluster based approach to coreference resolution. In *Proceedings of the 20th COLING*, 2004.

[320] A. Yeh, L. Hirschman, and A. Morgan. Evaluation of text data mining for database curation: Lessons learned from the KDD Challenge Cup. *Bioinformatics*, 19(suppl 1):i331–i339, 2003.

[321] A. Yeh, A. Morgan, M. Colosimo, and L. Hirschman. BioCreAtIvE task 1a: Gene mention finding evaluation. *BMC Bioinformatics*, 6(Suppl 1):S2, 2005.

[322] M. Yetisgen-Yildiz, I. Solti, F. Xia, and S. Halgrim. Preliminary experience with Amazon's Mechanical Turk for annotating medical named entities. In *Proceedings of the NAACL HLT 2010 Workshop on Creating Speech and Language Data with Amazon's Mechanical Turk*, pages 180–183, 2010.

[323] Q. Zeng, S. Goryachev, S. Weiss, M. Sordo, S. Murphy, and R. Lazarus. Extracting principal diagnosis, co-morbidity and smoking status for asthma research: Evaluation of a natural language processing system. *BMC Medical Informatics and Decision Making*, 6(1):30, 2006.

[324] Q. Zeng-Treitler, H. Kim, G. Rosemblat, and A. Keselman. Can multilingual machine translation help make medical record content more comprehensible to patients? *Studies in Health Technology and Informatics*, 160(Pt 1):73–77, 2009.

[325] P. Zweigenbaum, D. Demner-Fushman, H. Yu, and K. Cohen. Frontiers of biomedical text mining: Current progress. *Briefings in Bioinformatics*, 8(5):358–375, 2007.

Chapter 9

Social Media Analytics for Healthcare

Alexander Kotov
Department of Computer Science
Wayne State University
Detroit, MI
kotov@wayne.edu

9.1 Introduction

The emergence of social media resources in the form of social networking sites, blogs/microblogs, forums, question answering services, online communities and encyclopedias, which are often collectively referred to as Web 2.0, designated a move from passive consumption to active creation of diverse types of content by Internet users. Unlike newswire articles, social media goes beyond stating facts and describing events and provides a wealth of information about public opinion on virtually any topic, including healthcare. Recent studies [39] [38] report that 61% of American adults seek health information online and 37% have accessed or posted health information online. In addition to that, 72% of online adults in the United States are using social media. Of adult social media users, 23% follow their friends' personal health experiences or updates, 17% use social media to remember and memoralize people with a specific health condition and 15% obtain health information from social media sites [7].

Web 2.0 services and platforms have been designed to encourage frequent expression of people's thoughts and opinions on a variety of issues as well as random details of their lives. They have made possible open expression of opinions and exchange of ideas. They have also made measurable what was previously unmeasurable and shed additional light on important questions in public health that have been either too expensive or outright impossible to answer, such as distribution of health information in a population, tracking health information trends over time and identifying gaps between health information supply and demand. The fine granularity and pervasiveness of social media data models phenomena that were previously out of reach, including the probability of a given individual to get sick with a disease. Although most individual social media posts and messages contain little informational value, aggregation of millions of such messages can generate important knowledge. For example, knowing that a certain individual has contracted a flu based on his or her messages on social networking sites may not be an interesting fact by itself, but millions of such messages can be used to track influenza rate in a state or a country.

This chapter provides an overview of recent work that demonstrates that social media data can be mined for patterns and knowledge that can be leveraged in descriptive as well as predictive models of population health. It can also improve the overall effectiveness of public health monitoring and analysis and significantly reduce its latency. Previous research work on social media analytics for healthcare has focused on the following three broad areas:

1. Methods for capturing aggregate health trends from social media data, such as outbreaks of infectious diseases, and analyzing the mechanisms underlying the spread of infectious diseases;

2. Methods for fine-grained analysis and processing of social media data, such as methods to detect reports of adverse drug interactions and medical events and to model the health status and well-being of individuals;

3. Studying how social media can be effectively used as a communication medium between patients, between patients and doctors and how to effectively leverage social media in interventions and health education campaigns.

The primary goal of the first line of work, which we focus on in Section 9.2, is to detect and estimate the magnitude of an infectious disease outbreak in a particular geographical region from social media data, search logs of major Web search engines or access logs to medical Web sites. This direction views Web 2.0 users as the first responders to a disease outbreak in an information sense and attempts to capture the signals from those users to enable faster outbreak discovery. Timely detection of infectious disease outbreaks can significantly decrease their negative effect, while modeling "what-if" scenarios based on analysis of data from both social media and healthcare agencies can decrease public health response time and increase its effectiveness. A common theme for most early approaches proposed along this direction is establishing the degree of correlation between the data extracted from social media and official federal, state and local public health statistics.

The primary goal of the second line of work, which we focus on in Section 9.3, is to extract knowledge from social media that can be utilized to address specific healthcare problems, such as detecting reports of adverse medical events, summarizing the effects of recreational drugs use and predicting when a particular individual will become afflicted with an illness. Large-scale social media mining in combination with the analysis of online social networks, demographic analysis and predictive modeling of risk behaviors can improve our understanding of epidemiological mechanisms and allow public health professionals to tailor awareness, design more effective interventions and better predict their outcome.

The third line of work, which we overview in Section 9.4, is focused on studying how social media is used as a source of health information, such as how ordinary people and healthcare professionals use social media to answer their health-related questions or report their experiences in dealing with medical conditions. In particular, we discuss popular online communities for both patients and healthcare professionals and outline the findings that were made by analyzing the textual content posted on those communities.

The vast majority of approaches proposed as part of these three directions are based on combining social network analysis, machine learning, statistical modeling and computational linguistics with epidemiology, sociology, economics and public health research. Such an approach is best illustrated by the pyramid model of public health proposed by Sadilek and Kautz [71]. At the base of the pyramid is the entire population. In the middle of the pyramid are the users of online social media, whose data is publicly available. At the top of the pyramid is a small but strategically selected sample of individuals from the general population (which includes some of the social media users), for whom the detailed health records are available. This sample includes the subjects who respond to online medical surveys, actively monitor their health status at home (e.g., by using glucose or blood pressure monitors, HIV rapid tests, etc.) or at a nearby medical lab and are willing to share their personal health information with other people. Traditionally, epidemiological studies are based on the data collected from the top of this pyramid. Although the majority of the work discussed in this chapter uses the data from the middle of the pyramid, machine learning and statistical modeling techniques allow the knowledge gained at any level in the pyramid to "trickle down." For example, by applying machine learning techniques we can bootstrap from the top of the pyramid to make well-grounded predictions about the general population at the bottom of the pyramid. This will infuse epidemiological models with additional structure and parameters learned from detailed timely data, so that fewer factors need to be modeled via simulation. Information can also "trickle up" the pyramid, where the latent behavior of the general population may influence the predictions even for the individuals at the top. In the following sections, we will examine in detail each one of the three general directions outlined above.

9.2 Social Media Analysis for Detection and Tracking of Infectious Disease Outbreaks

Epidemics of infectious diseases, such as influenza and cholera, are a major public health concern that is difficult to anticipate and model [86]. Seasonal influenza epidemics result in about three to five million cases of severe illnesses and about 250,000 to 500,000 deaths worldwide each year. Although influenza reoccurs each season in regular cycles, geographic location, timing and size of each outbreak varies, complicating the efforts to produce reliable and timely estimates of influenza activity using traditional methods for time series analysis. In general, health organizations require accurate and timely disease surveillance techniques in order to respond to the emerging epidemics by better planning for surges in patient visits, therapeutic supplies and public health information dissemination campaigns. Additional early knowledge of an upward trend in disease prevalence can inform patient capacity preparations and increased efforts to distribute the appropriate vaccine or other treatments, whereas knowledge of a downward trend can signal the effectiveness of these efforts.

Public health monitoring has traditionally relied on surveys and aggregating primary data from healthcare providers and pharmacists (e.g., clinical encounters with healthcare professionals, sick-leave and drug prescriptions). Syndromic surveillance, the monitoring of clinical syndromes that have significant impact on public health, is particularly required for episodic and widespread infections, such as seasonal influenza. Many infectious disease surveillance systems, including those employed by Centers for Disease Control and Prevention (CDC) in the United States, Public Health Agency of Canada, Infectious Disease Surveillance Center in Japan, Health Protection Agency in the United Kingdom, Swedish Institute for Infectious Disease Control and the European Influenza Surveillance Scheme continuously collect virological and clinical reports from designated laboratories and physicians, in a process known as sentinel surveillance. For example, CDC operates the U.S. Outpatient Influenza-like Illness Surveillance Network (ILINet) and publishes the data collected and aggregated from it on-line via FluView.[1] ILINet is one of the most effective disease surveillance systems, which monitors 2,700 sentinel outpatient health providers and issues weekly reports of the proportion of all visits to those providers that are related to influenza-like illness (ILI) symptoms (temperature 100 degrees Fahrenheit or greater, cough and/or sore throat without any apparent cause). Although survey-based surveillance systems are effective tools in discovering disease outbreaks, they typically incur high operational costs and temporal lags in reporting the outbreaks, since an infectious disease case is recorded only after a patient visits a doctor's office and the information about it is sent to the appropriate public health agency. In the case of CDC, the typical lag times for influenza reporting are one to two weeks with even longer lags for less common diseases [29]. During the deadly infectious disease outbreaks, such as cholera, this delay can hinder early epidemiological assessment and result in a greater number of fatalities. Previous work in epidemiology [34] has also shown that the most effective way to fight an epidemic in urban areas is to quickly confine infected individuals to their homes. Since this strategy is effective only when applied early, it becomes important to be able to detect the outbreaks of infectious diseases in urban areas as quickly as possible. In general, methods for earlier outbreak detection allow more time to deploy interventions that can lower the morbidity and mortality resulting from the outbreak. Besides longer reporting time lag, sentinel-based surveillance systems suffer from population bias, since people who do not actively seek treatment or do not respond to surveys are virtually invisible to them, and tend to overreport population groups that are more vulnerable to diseases. By contrast, social media data are available in near real time and therefore can provide much earlier estimates of the magnitude and dynamics of an epidemic. Social media platforms, such as Twitter, offer virtually unlimited volumes of publicly available data and population sample sizes that exceed those of paper surveys by several orders of magnitude. Finding the key symptomatic individuals along with other people, who may have already contracted the disease, can also be done more effectively and in a timely manner by leveraging online social network data. Furthermore, geographical metadata in the form of the coordinates associated with some of the social media posts can play an important role in monitoring the impact and the geographical spread of an epidemic. In this section, we provide an extensive overview of the recently proposed methods for detection and tracking of infectious disease outbreaks based only on the analysis of the signals from social media.

9.2.1 Outbreak Detection

Experiments with unconventional methods using preclinical "health information seeking" for syndromic surveillance have been conducted before the advent of Web 2.0 and social media. For example, several surveillance systems have been introduced in the past to monitor indirect signals of influenza activity, such as the volume of calls to telephone health advisory lines [23] [33], over-the-counter drug sales [57] and school absenteeism rates [55]. The emergence and rapid widespread adoption of online services, such as search engines and social media platforms like Twitter and Facebook, presented an opportunity for nearly real-time Internet-based surveillance for disease outbreaks based only on the analysis of the data from these services. This led to the emergence of a new area of research at the intersection of computer science and public health known as "infodemiology" or "information epidemiology" [35]. Infodemiology is an umbrella term for methods that study the determinants and distribution of health information for public health purposes and are aiming at:

- developing methodologies and measures to understand patterns and trends for general public health research;
- identifying disease outbreaks based on the analysis of these trends;
- studying and quantifying knowledge translation gaps;

[1] `http://www.cdc.gov/flu/weekly/`

- understanding the predictive value of search and content generation behavior for syndromic surveillance and early detection of emerging diseases.

As a result, several lines of recent work have focused on developing new methods to detect outbreaks of infectious diseases using the data from different types of online services, such as query logs, microblogs and blogs.

9.2.1.1 Using Search Query and Website Access Logs

An increasing number of people around the world are using the Internet to seek and disseminate health-related information. People search for health information for a variety of reasons: concerns about themselves, their family or friends. According to the National Library of Medicine, an estimated 113 million people in the United States use the Internet to find health-related information with up to 8 million people searching for health-related information on a typical day [60]. About 90 million American adults are believed to search for online information about specific diseases or medical problems each year, making the Web search a unique source of information about health trends and major events, such as epidemics. Therefore, an interesting research question from both computer science and public health perspective is whether tracking health information-seeking behavior of people over time can be used to monitor public health in general and for syndromic surveillance, in particular.

The general idea behind the proposed methods for monitoring public health based on the analysis of query logs of search engines is that the interest of a general public in a certain public health topic can be approximated by the search query activity related to this topic. Therefore, health information-seeking behavior can be captured and transformed into indicators of disease activity. Since some search query data also carries geographical information (generally based on the IP address of the computer, from which a particular query was issued), it may also be possible to detect simple geo-spatial patterns. Eysenbach [36] explored whether an automated analysis of trends in Internet searches could be useful for predicting the outbreaks of infectious diseases, such as influenza. He created a Google advertisement campaign, in which the advertisements were triggered by the influenza-related search terms and experimented with different multivariate models to predict the number of ILI cases based on the advertisement campaign statistics. He found out that the number of clicks on online advertisements has the highest correlation with traditional surveillance measures. He also observed that the weekly number of flu-related advertisement clicks has even higher correlation with ILI reports from sentinel physicians for the following week, suggesting systematic mining of search engine logs could be a valuable addition to traditional surveillance methods for those conditions, when the patients consult the Internet before visiting a physician.

A joint study by CDC and Yahoo! suggested that Internet searches for specific cancers correlate with their estimated incidence, mortality and the volume of related news coverage [22]. They concluded that media coverage appears to play a powerful role in prompting online searches for cancer information. Ginsberg et al. [45] processed search logs containing hundreds of billions of search queries submitted to the Google search engine between 2003 and 2008 and estimated a simple linear regression model to predict the log-odds of the percentage of ILI-related physician visits in a geographical region based only on the log-odds of ILI-related queries for the same geographical region. Estimates produced by this model resulted in the Pearson correlation coefficient of 0.97 with the CDC-reported ILI statistics. This work resulted in creation of the Google Flu Trends service,[2] which estimates the current flu activity around the world based on the volume of search queries to the Google search engine. Google Flu Trends is used to successfully track influenza rates on a daily basis, up to 7 to 10 days faster than CDC's FluView [13]. Nevertheless, similar to sentinel surveillance, systems based on the analysis of search engine query logs also suffer from population

[2] `http://www.google.org/flutrends`

bias, as they are restricted to the sample of individuals, who search the Internet for certain types of content when sick.

Pelat et al. [66] compared the search trends related to 3 infectious diseases with clinical surveillance data from the French Sentinel Network and reported the correlation coefficients of 0.82 for influenza-like illnesses, 0.9 for gastroenteritis and 0.78 for chickenpox. They concluded that, for each of these three infectious diseases, one well-chosen query is sufficient to provide a time series of searches that is highly correlated with the actual incidence of those diseases reported through the sentinel surveillance system. The highest correlation between the best queries for influenza and gastroenteritis was achieved without any time lag, while the time series of searches for chickenpox was lagging one week behind the incidence time series.

Seifter et al. [80] explored the utility of using Google Trends to study seasonal and geographic patterns for Lyme disease. They found that the search traffic for the query "Lyme disease" reflected the increased likelihood of exposure to this disease during spring and summer months and that the cities and states with the highest search traffic for this query considerably overlapped with those, where Lyme disease was known to be endemic. Following a similar idea, Hulth et al. [50] explored the feasibility of using the queries submitted to a Swedish medical Web site[3] for the task of influenza outbreak detection and observed that certain influenza-related queries followed the same pattern as the data obtained by the two standard surveillance systems (based on the number of laboratory verified influenza cases and the proportion ILI-related patients visits to sentinel general practitioners). In particular, they used partial least-squares regression to identify the most indicative queries for influenza and achieved the correlation coefficients of 0.9 with the sentinel data and 0.92 with the laboratory data. Johnson et al. [51] used the access logs from Healthlink medical Web site[4] to measure the correlation between the number of accesses to selected Influenza-related pages on this Web site and influenza surveillance data from the CDC and reported such correlation to be moderately strong.

Although search data is confounded by media reports and "epidemics of fear," even crude (unadjusted) surges in increased search activity on a health topic not triggered by a real pandemic are still important measures for government health agencies and policy makers, as they may, even in the absence of a true epidemic, warrant a public health response into what may be causing an increased information demand. However, the major limitation of search query logs is that they do not provide any additional contextual information, therefore questions like why the search was initiated in the first place are difficult to answer.

9.2.1.2 Using Twitter and Blogs

The emergence and rapid increase in popularity of Twitter[5] opened up a new research direction in Internet-based disease surveillance. Twitter is a social networking and microblogging platform that enables users to create the posts limited to 140 characters and share them either with the general public or only with a specific group of people designated as "followers." Although the Twitter stream consists largely of useless chatter, self-promotion messages and user-to-user conversations that are only of interest to the parties involved, due to the sheer volume of tweets, it contains enough useful information for any task. For example, Twitter data has been used to measure political opinions [59], national sentiment [4], public anxiety related to stock prices [44] and to monitor the impact of earthquakes [74]. The advantages of Twitter-based approaches for disease outbreak detection over the ones that are based on search query and access logs are twofold. First, although Twitter messages are fairly short, they are still more descriptive and provide more contextual information than search engine queries. Second, Twitter profiles often contain rich meta-data associated with the users (e.g., their geographical location, gender, age and social network), enabling more sophisticated

[3]`http://www.vardguiden.se`
[4]`http://www.healthlink.com`
[5]`http://www.twitter.com`

and detailed analysis. Twitter also has an advantage over other social media services in that it offers a larger volume of mostly publicly available messages. In particular, as of January 2014, Twitter is estimated to have over 600 million active registered users worldwide, who create 58 million microblog posts every day. Frequent updates and public data availability open up opportunities for near real-time, demographically and geographically focused disease surveillance.

The work of Ritterman et al. [68] was one of the first to use Twitter for infectious disease surveillance. In particular, they used the dataset consisting of 48 million tweets collected over a period of two months, which covers the timespan between the first time when the news about H1N1 (or Swine Flu) virus first broke out and until the H1N1 pandemic was declared by the World Health Organization on May 11, 2009. They used the data from Hubdub,[6] an on-line prediction market, to model the public belief that H1N1 will become a pandemic using support vector machine (SVM) regression. Their analysis resulted in two major conclusions. The first conclusion is that simple bi-gram features extracted from the content of Twitter messages within historical contexts of different granularity (1 day, 3 days, 1 week, entire history) can accurately predict health-related beliefs and expectations of the general public. The second conclusion is that combining the features based on the content of Twitter messages and with the ones derived from the Hubdub data results in a more accurate prediction model than the one that relies on the prediction markets data alone. Quincey and Kostkova [31] have demonstrated the potential of Twitter outbreak detection by collecting and characterizing over 135,000 posts pertaining to H1N1 over a period of one week. Culotta [29] identified influenza-related Twitter posts by applying simple and multiple logistic regression-based document classifiers using the occurrence of predefined keywords such as “flu,” “cough,” “sore throat” and “headache” as features to a dataset of over 500,000 posts spanning 10 weeks. In a multiple regression model, each keyword had a different weight, whereas in a simple regression model all keywords had the same weights. He then calculated the Pearson correlation coefficient between the log-odds of a fraction of influenza-related messages in the overall daily volume of Twitter posts and the log-odds of a fraction of all outpatient visits with ILI-related symptoms reported by the CDC. Although multiple regression outperformed simple regression, he found that multiple regression began to overfit when too many keywords were used. The best model in his study achieved the correlation coefficient of 0.78 with CDC statistics. Culotta [30] applied similar methodology to estimate alcohol sales from the volume of tweets related to drinking and found that the most accurate model is the one, which relies only the keyword “drunk.” In particular, this model achieved the correlation coefficient of 0.932 with the U.S. Census Bureau data, which suggests that Twitter can also be used by public health researchers as a useful source for monitoring alcohol consumption trends. Signorini et al. [83] filtered 951,697 tweets containing flu-related keywords (“h1n1,” “swine,” “flu,” “influenza”) from 334,840,972 tweets posted during the H1N1 pandemic between April 29th and June 1st of 2009 and observed that that the percentage of such tweets rapidly declined over time as more and more H1N1 cases have been reported. They also constructed the time series of daily counts of tweets related to particular subtopics of the H1N1 pandemic, such as countermeasures (hand hygiene, protective face masks), treatments (antiviral medications used to treat influenza), travel-related issues, vaccination and vaccination side effects (Guillain-Barré syndrome) and food consumption-related concerns, and found that there was no evidence of sustained interest in those topics by Twitter users during the pandemic. They also applied SVM regression based on bag-of-words feature vectors to estimate the national ILI levels as well as ILI levels for specific geographical regions (states) by geo-locating the tweets based on user profiles and reported very high accuracy for both types of estimates.

Lampos and Cristianini [53] proposed a method to calculate the flu score for a given tweet (or a corpus of tweets) using the tweet’s n-grams as features (or “textual markers” in their terminology). A set of 1,560 stemmed candidate features was first extracted from both the Wikipedia article about influenza and an entry from an online medical directory describing flu symptoms along with the

[6] `http://www.hubdub.com`

comments from the patients who experienced flu. The most important features were then selected by the least-angle regression model (a variant of LASSO) using the daily flu scores reported by the U.K.'s Health Protection Agency as a dependent variable. The estimated regression model was used to determine the projected flu rates, which achieved the correlation coefficient of 0.94 with the actual rates. Additionally, they performed a geo-location of tweets and cross validation of regression models learned for one geographical region on all other regions and reported the total average correlation of 0.89.

Most of the early methods for infectious disease surveillance based on the content of Twitter posts relied on relatively simple methods (e.g., *n*-gram based models for classifying a tweet as flu-related or not). Although these methods were able to relatively accurately classify the tweets as being related or unrelated to influenza with promising surveillance results, they have ignored many subtle differences between the flu-related tweets. For example, many flu-related tweets express either beliefs related to the flu infection and preventative flu measures (e.g., flu shots) or concerned awareness of increased infections, including the fear of contracting the flu or even a widespread panic associated with a pandemic, as opposed to the actual infection-related tweets. Unlike search engine queries, Twitter posts provide more context, which can be leveraged by natural language processing tools to isolate more informative "self-diagnostic" posts from general discussions and opinions, caused by an increased attention towards the subject during the flu season and outright panic during the pandemic. In order to improve the accuracy of Twitter-based surveillance, Lamb et al. [52] proposed two methods for fine-grained classification of tweets based on a large number of lexical, syntactic and stylometric features. One method differentiates the flu awareness tweets from the flu infection-related ones, while the other method distinguishes the tweets that correspond to self-reported cases of flu by the people who are in fact infected from the tweets created by healthy people that refer to other individuals sick with flu. The tweets that were identified as flu-related based on their approach achieved higher correlation with the CDC ILI data than the tweets identified as flu-related based on using only lexical features. Achrekar et al. [1] approached the problem of improving the quality of an epidemiological signal from Twitter data from a different perspective. They observed that re-tweets and posts from the same users may distort the true number of self-reported cases of influenza infection and reported that excluding such messages improves the correlation coefficient and lowers the root mean-squared error of a linear regression between the number of unique Twitter users self-reporting flu infection and the CDC statistics. They also proposed an autoregression model combining the Twitter data for the current week with the CDC data from two weeks back (simulating a typical 2-week delay in CDC data reporting) to predict the percentage of ILI-related visits for the current week and observed that the addition of Twitter data improves the accuracy of prediction compared to using past CDC data alone.

In a recent work, Li and Cardie [56] focused on the early detection of the flu pandemic and introduced a Bayesian approach based on the spatio-temporal Markov Network (which they call Flu Markov Network), which takes into account both the spatial information and the daily fluctuations in the number of posted tweets, for early stage unsupervised detection of flu. Spatial proximity is an important factor in early-stage flu detection, since flu breakouts in many of the neighbors of a non-pandemic geographic location can be indicative of an imminent breakout in this location. Daily fluctuations in the number of tweets, depending on whether a certain day falls on a weekday, weekend or holiday, is a known phenomenon in social media analysis, which needs to be accounted for accurate interpretation of signals from Twitter. Spatial and temporal information is incorporated into a four-state Markov chain, in which the states correspond to non-epidemic, rising epidemic, stationary epidemic and declining epidemic phases and model the progression of a typical pandemic. In the non-epidemic and stationary phases, the number of flu-related tweets is modeled as a Gaussian process taking in account the daily tweet fluctuations, whereas in epidemic and declining epidemic phases the number of tweets is modeled as an autoregressive process incorporating the daily effect. In contrast to the standard Hidden Markov Model, in the Flu Markov Network, the state of the Markov chain for a given location at a given time point is not only dependent on the state of the

Markov chain for the same location, but also on the states of the Markov chains of the geographical neighbors of that location at a previous timestamp. For example, the number of ILI-related tweets in a state (country) is influenced by the number of ILI-related tweets in the neighboring states (countries). After filtering out flu-related tweets using SVM with polynomial kernel based on unigram and collocational features, removing re-tweets and tweets of the same user, they reported correlation coefficients with CDC data exceeding 0.98 for some geographical regions. Aramaki et al. [2] experimented with a large number of standard classifiers and feature generation techniques to determine the most accurate method for identifying the tweets about self-reported cases of flu infection and compared it with a simple frequency-based and search log analysis-based method. They separated an influenza season into periods of excessive and non-excessive news coverage and found that the performance of the Twitter-based surveillance method is sensitive to the intensity of news coverage. In particular, during the periods of non-excessive news coverage, the Twitter-based method slightly outperformed Google Flu Trends (achieving the correlation coefficient of 0.89 versus 0.847). However, the Twitter-based surveillance method exhibited a dramatic reduction in performance during the periods of excessive news coverage, indicating its vulnerability to "news wire bias." This observation is supported by social amplification of risk framework, which postulates that psychological, social, cultural and institutional factors interact with emergency events and intensify or attenuate risk perceptions. They also found that the Twitter-based method outperformed Google Flu Trends before the peak of the influenza season, but not afterwards, suggesting that the Twitter-based surveillance methods are better suited for early stage influenza detection.

While most research in this direction have correlated social media signals with influenza prevalence metrics in a retrospective way, Broniatowski et al. [8] demonstrated the potential for influenza surveillance with a system built and deployed before the influenza season even started. They found that the accuracy of most social media surveillance systems declines with media attention. The reason is that media attention increases Twitter "chatter"—tweets that are about flu, but do not pertain to the actual infection. They used a staged binary classifier, which first identified whether a tweet was relevant to health, then if it was relevant to influenza and, finally, if it was a report of an actual infection. They also correlated the weekly counts of tweets passing through all the filters with CDC ILI data from the 2012–2013 influenza season and reported the correlation coefficient of 0.93. In contrast, the correlation coefficient of the weekly number of tweets containing influenza keywords provided by the U.S. Department of Health and Human Services achieved the correlation coefficient with CDC data of only 0.75. They also applied their method at the level of municipality and reported the correlation coefficient of 0.88 between the number of weekly tweets that pass through all the filters and are geo-located to New York City and the number of weekly ILI-related emergency department visits reported by the New York City Department of Health and Mental Hygiene. Keyword-based selection of tweets resulted in the drop of the correlation correlation coefficient to 0.72. In addition, they analyzed the time series of national CDC ILI rates and counts of tweets related to the flu infection and tweets containing flu-related keywords using the Box-Jenkins procedure and found statistically significant effects for a lag of one week, while the lags of two weeks or more were insignificant.

Chew and Eysenbach [15] developed Infovigil, an open-source infoveillance system,[7] which continuously gathers flu-related tweets, automatically classifies them into predefined content categories and determines temporal trends for each category. Classification is performed according to a coding scheme consisting of three dimensions: the content of a tweet (whether a tweet contains a link to an informational resource, expresses an opinion, contains a joke or is about a personal experience, etc.); how the content was expressed (humor, relief, downplayed risk, concern, frustration, etc.); type of a link, if a tweet contains any (news, government Web sites, online stores, blogs, etc.) using a simple method based on matching the tweets with a set of predefined keywords, emoticons or example phrases for each content category. Despite its simplicity, this method was able to achieve

[7]`http://www.infovigil.com`

significant overlap with the manually created golden standard for most of the content categories. Furthermore, automatically classified tweets demonstrated a significant linear trend over time across different content categories, which was generally in the same direction as the manually classified tweets. They also found that the correlation coefficient between the number of tweets in each content category and the number of ILI cases reported by the CDC varies significantly depending on the content category (from 0.77 for personal experiences to 0.39 for concerns). Further comparison of the trends across different categories revealed that personal accounts of H1N1 increased over time, while the number of humorous comments decreased, possibly due to an increasing perceived seriousness of the situation and the declining popularity of the subject. Analysis of trends across different content categories indicated that the perceived severity, news coverage, viral dissemination of information and Twitter campaigns have considerable effect on tweet volume and posting behavior over time. Another interesting observation reported in this work is that, contrary to popular belief that misinformation is rampant in social media, only 4.5% of all tweets were manually classified as possible misinformation or speculation, while 90.2% of the tweets provided references to the sources of information they contained, allowing others to confirm its trustworthiness. Overall, this study demonstrated the potential of using Twitter to study public attitudes, perceptions and behaviors during pandemics.

Chunara et al. [19] estimated the correlation between the volume of Twitter posts, news media reports on HealthMap and the data reported by the Haitian Ministry of Public Health during the first 100 days of the 2010 Haitian cholera outbreak. They determined that the volume of information from these informal sources significantly correlated with the official reports during the initial phase of the outbreak (with 1 day lag, the correlation coefficients of HealthMap and Twitter data were 0.76 and 0.86, respectively). They also provided experimental results indicating that social media can be used to accurately estimate the reproductive number of an epidemic, which is used to determine the proportion of the population that needs to be immunized to contain an epidemic or the proportion that will be infected, when the disease reaches its endemic equilibrium.

Corley et al. [25] performed several types of analyses on a collection of 44 million blog posts to study the feasibility of using them for disease surveillance. First, they compared the trends for different types of blog posts with respect to the number of posts per day and observed a periodic pattern for both the general and influenza-related blog posts, when bloggers create more posts on a weekday than during the weekend, which was supported by fitting an autocorrelation function with a statistically significant weekly time lag. Second, they reported the correlation coefficient of 0.767 between the number of flu-related blog posts and the CDC ILI statistics. They also proposed a method for identification of blogger communities by leveraging the links between the blogs based on the closeness, betweenness centrality and PageRank. Closeness is the average of the shortest paths (geodesic distances) between a blog and all other blogs reachable from it via links. Betweenness centrality measures interpersonal influence. More specifically, a blog is central if it lies on a large number of shortest paths between other blogs. PageRank measures the importance of a blog assuming that the links pointing to it from more central blogs contribute to its ranking more than the links pointing from less central nodes. The general idea of this approach is to identify influential blogs, which can quickly disseminate and broker response strategies and interventions in their respective communities. Readers of these influential blogs can trigger an information cascade, spreading the response to vaccinate, quarantine and close public places. The blogs with high betweenness could broker information between the communities, synchronizing knowledge, while the blogs with greater closeness and PageRank can quickly disseminate outbreak response strategies.

Although Internet-based surveillance approaches may overcome some limitations of the traditional sentinel-based systems, integration of new and traditional approaches offers the greatest promise for future surveillance of influenza and other infectious diseases. Furthermore, social media, which inherently combines three different types of data (textual, geographical and network) opens up unique opportunities to study the interplay between human mobility, social structure and disease transmission. Although the Internet-based data streams as well as new efforts in syndromic surveillance from repurposed clinical data can fill in some of the critical gaps in traditional approaches to early disease outbreak detection (e.g., first cases or early reports of community-level transmission), they cannot completely describe the epidemiology and global impact of an emerging threat. Traditional surveillance is still necessary to estimate morbidity, mortality and shifts in the incidence of disease according to the demographic factors and changes in case fatality rates. Overall, syndromic surveillance using social media is the leading edge of what will almost certainly evolve into real-time surveillance of data from electronic medical records (EMRs).

9.2.2 Analyzing and Tracking Outbreaks

Besides near real-time surveillance through detection of self-reported cases of infectious diseases, social media analysis can also be used to analyze and track the spread of a pandemic. The lack of timely data and limited understanding of the emergence of global epidemics from day-to-day interpersonal interactions makes monitoring and forecasting the global spread of infectious diseases very difficult. Previous research in computational epidemiology has mostly concentrated on coarse-grained statistical analysis of populations, often using synthetic data. Although social media-based surveillance methods can effectively perform passive monitoring and produce coarse, aggregate statistics, such as the expected number of people afflicted by flu in a city or a state, their prediction capabilities are severely limited by the low resolution of the aggregate approach. Therefore, another line of work focused on developing new techniques to provide a detailed explanation of the mechanisms underlying infectious disease transmission and, given a pandemic, to predict how rapidly and where it will spread.

The bottom-up approaches proposed in [6] [73] [72] consist of two stages and take into account fine-grained interactions between individuals. In the first stage, a classifier is applied to detect sick individuals based on the content of their tweets. In the second stage, physical interactions between sick and healthy people are estimated via their online activities and the large-scale impact of these interactions on public health is predicted.

In particular, Brennan et al. [6] proposed a method to accurately predict the prevalence of an infectious disease in a geographical region (e.g., a city) by modeling fine-grained behavior and interactions of the residents in that region with the outside world. In the first stage of their method, individuals are classified as either healthy or symptomatic based on the content of their tweets using SVM. In the second stage, classification results for individual users are aggregated into two probabilistic variables capturing the flux of healthy and sick travelers as well as their physical interactions within predefined geographical locations based on using the GPS coordinates of their tweets and publicly available airline travel statistics to track geographical movements of people. They estimated that the first variable, which corresponds to the expectation of the number of sick users on a given day in a given geographical region has the correlation coefficients of 0.8 with the CDC statistics and 0.87 with Google Flu Trends. Additionally, they found that using only travel statistics in the regression model explains 56% of the variance in Google Flu Trends, while adding the expected number of sick travelers to the model explains 73% of the variance. Including the second variable, which models the number of physical interactions as a function of people traveling to the same airport at the same time, explains an additional 5% of the variance.

Sadilek et al. [72] focused on the fine-grained analysis of the spread of infectious diseases and studied how it is influenced by geographical co-location, social ties and interpersonal interactions. In their method, two individuals are considered to be co-located, if they visited the same 100 by 100 meter area within the same time window. To identify the tweets indicating that their author was infected by flu at the time of posting, they proposed a cascading process of training an SVM classifier working only with bag-of-words features (unigrams, bigrams and trigrams) that is optimized to overcome an imbalance between positive and negative samples and maximize the area under the ROC curve (i.e., to consistently have both high precision and recall). After identifying the tweets likely posted by the infected people, they used the GPS coordinates of these tweets and the Twitter friendships of their authors (in their work Twitter friendship is defined as two users, who follow each other) to quantify the effect of geographical co-locations and social ties on disease transmission. In both cases, they observed strong exponential dependencies: in case of co-locations, between probable physical encounters with sick individuals and ensuing sickness and in case of social ties, between the number of sick friends and the probability of getting sick. For example, they established that having 40 encounters with sick individuals within 1 hour or having 10 sick friends on a given day makes one ill with a 20% probability on the next day. At the same time, the number of friends in any health state (i.e., the size of a person's friends list) has no impact on that person's health status.

In [73] Sadilek et al. further developed their previous work [72] and proposed a model, which in addition to predicting whether an individual will fall ill can predict when exactly that will happen. Their method simultaneously captures the effect of collocations as well as their duration on disease transmission and the delay between contagion and the onset of symptoms. After applying SVM to detect individuals afflicted by flu based on the content of their posts, they used a dynamic conditional random field (CRF) model to predict an individual's health status in the future using the 7-day prior history of co-location events, the number of unique sick individuals encountered and the number of sick Twitter friends of this individual as features. They observed that the performance of CRF is significantly enhanced by including the features that are not only based on the health status of Twitter friends, but also on the estimated encounters with already sick, symptomatic individuals, including non-friends. Moreover, when using social ties and co-locations individually, CRF performs inconsistently when making predictions into the future. By contrast, when considering friendships and co-locations jointly, along with using the Viterbi algorithm to infer the most likely sequence of a person's health states over time, performance of the CRF improves and stabilizes, achieving up to 0.94 precision and 0.18 recall. The authors explained the low recall by the fact that about 80% of infections occur without any evidence in social media. They concluded that although many complex events and interactions take place "behind the scenes" and are not directly recorded in social media, they can still exhibit themselves in the activity of a sample of people we can observe. For example, although Twitter friendships themselves do not cause or even facilitate the spread of an infection, they can be proxies and indicators of a complex set of phenomena that may not be directly accessible. For example, friends often eat out together, meet in classes, share items and travel together. While most of these events are never explicitly mentioned online, they are crucial from the disease transmission perspective.

These results can have direct and immediate implications for public health. For example, a person predicted to be at high risk of contracting flu could be specifically encouraged to get a flu vaccination. Additionally, recommendations can be made regarding the places that pose a high risk of getting infected. Finally, the proposed models are not limited only to the healthcare domain. Similar approaches can be used to model and predict the transmission of political ideas, purchasing preferences and many other complex behavioral phenomena.

9.2.3 Syndromic Surveillance Systems Based on Social Media

Many of the techniques that we overviewed in this section have been implemented in existing online syndromic surveillance systems. InSTEDD's Riff[8] is an open source online platform for detection, prediction and response to health-related events (such as disease outbreaks) and humanitarian disasters. Riff synthesizes information about public health-related events from a variety of sources (e.g., news, social media, blogs) and visualizes them on a map to assist public health authorities with investigation and response (Figure 9.1).

HealthMap[9] [40] [11] is a system that monitors global media sources such as news wires and Web sites to provide a comprehensive view of ongoing disease activity around the world

[8] `http://instedd.org/technologies/riff`

[9] `http://www.healthmap.org`

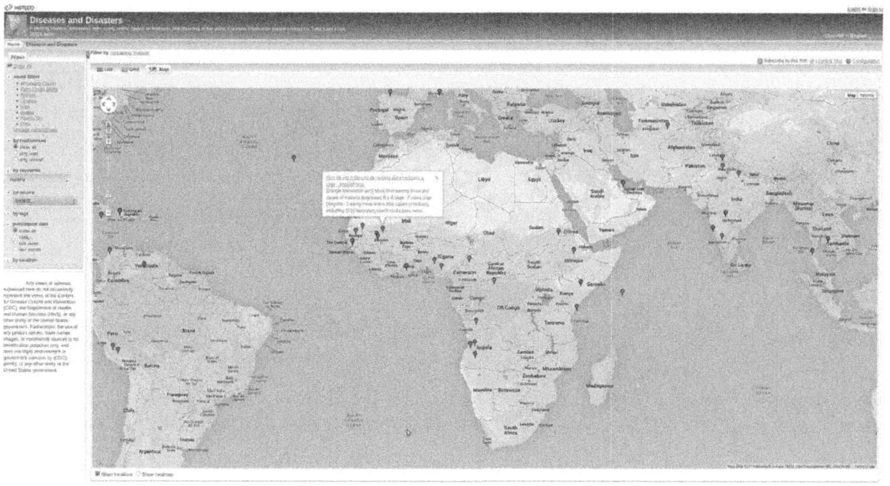

FIGURE 9.1: User interface of InSTEDD's Riff.

(Figure 9.2). It combines automated, around-the-clock data collection and processing with expert review and analysis. Visitors to the site could filter reports according to the suspected or confirmed cases of deaths from a disease and select a time interval to show its spread. All reports are entered into the HealthMap system along with their geographic location, allowing for easy tracking of both regional and global spread of infectious diseases. During the 2009 H1N1 pandemic, HealthMap created an interactive map [10] to provide information about disease outbreaks around the world using information from both informal sources (e.g., news media, mailing lists and contributions from individual users) and formal announcements (primarily from the World Health Organization, the Centers for Disease Control and Prevention and the Public Health Agency of Canada). Brownstein et al. [10] analyzed the geographical pattern for the spread of H1N1 and observed that the countries that are international travel hubs (e.g., France and the United Kingdom) reported flu infections earlier than the countries with less international traffic (e.g., Eastern European nations). They also found that the countries with a high Gross Domestic Product per capita tended to have shorter time lags between the issue dates of reports of suspected and confirmed cases of H1N1 influenza infection. Systems like HealthMap allow anyone with a mobile phone to get involved in responding to a epidemic or humanitarian crisis by contributing relevant information. As an example, during the 2010 Haitian earthquake and cholera outbreak, HealthMap allowed the individuals affected by this crisis to post information about their lost relatives and track the disease activity in their communities.

FluNearYou[10] is an online system that integrates different types of data (weekly surveys completed by volunteers, CDC Flu Activity data and Google Flu Trends ILI data) to visualize the current and retrospective flu activity in the United States and Canada (Figure 9.3). It is a joint project between HealthMap, the American Public Health Association, Skoll Global Threats Fund and Boston Children's Hospital.

Crowdbreaks[11] is a surveillance system that automatically collects the disease-related tweets, determines their location and visualizes them on a map (Figure 9.4). It employs a machine learning algorithm to assess whether a given tweet contains a reported case of a disease. Crowdbreaks uses crowdsourcing to generate the labeled training data for this algorithm by asking the site visitors to answer simple questions about randomly selected tweets. This system is based on the idea that

[10]`http://flunearyou.org`

[11]`http://www.crowdbreaks.com`

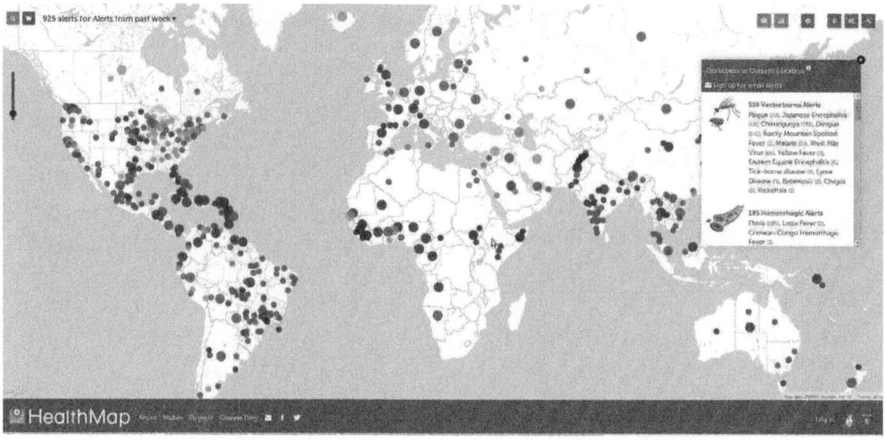

FIGURE 9.2: User interface of HealthMap.

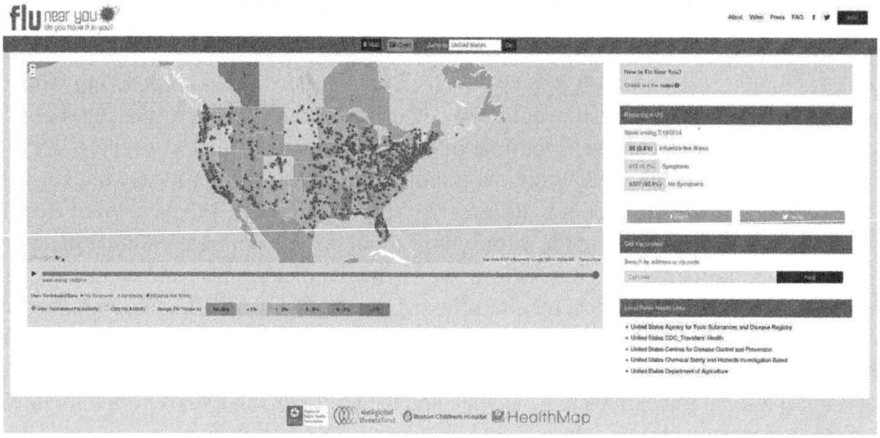

FIGURE 9.3: User interface of FluNearYou.

social media data are not only provided by the crowd, but can also be assessed and curated by the crowd for their relevance to the issue at hand.

9.3 Social Media Analysis for Public Health Research

While the majority of recent work on social media analysis for healthcare has focused on identifying posts related to particular diseases and correlating their volume with the data reported by the government healthcare agencies, social media analytics can potentially have a far greater impact on healthcare than just disease monitoring. Social media posts are not just isolated textual snippets – they are created at specific times and locations by users from a wide variety of socioeconomic groups, often with known social networks. In this section, we overview the proposed approaches addressing different public health research problems based on the analysis of the content generated by social media users and the structure of their online social networks.

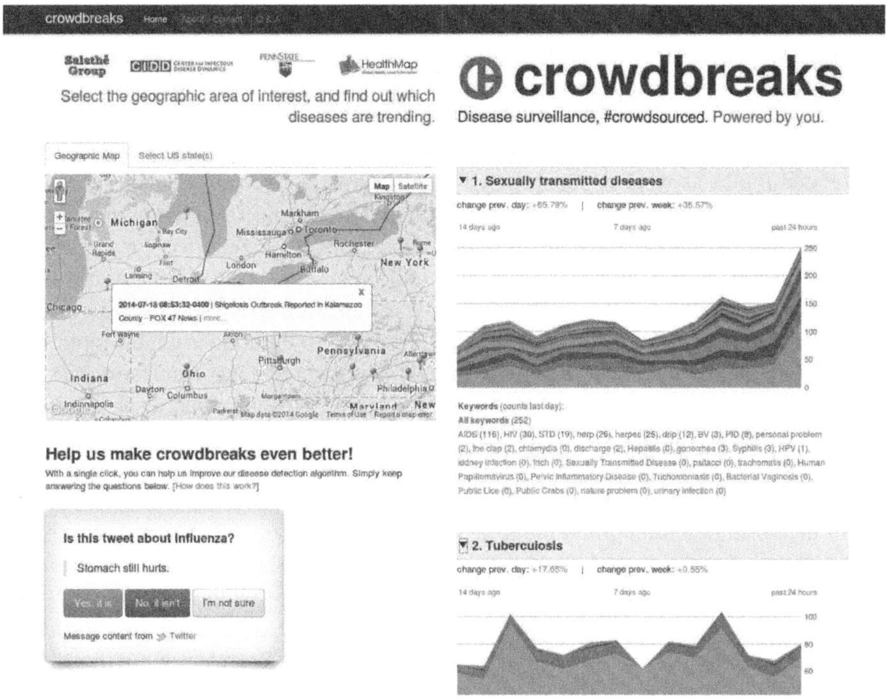

FIGURE 9.4: User interface of Crowdbreaks.

9.3.1 Topic Models for Analyzing Health-Related Content

Methods capable of aggregating healthcare-related content created by millions of social media users can provide extensive near real-time information about population health and different population characteristics, which is invaluable to public health researchers. Topic models, such as Latent Dirichlet Allocation (LDA) [5], are probabilistic latent variable generative models, which associate hidden variables controlling topical assignments with terms in document collections. They were designed to summarize information in large textual corpora by revealing their latent thematic structure in the form of clusters of semantically related words. In the generative process of topic models, topics are represented as multinomial distributions over the vocabulary of a given collection, such that more probability mass is allocated to the words that frequently co-occur within the same documents, and documents are represented as multinomial distributions over topics. Being an effective mechanism for textual data exploration, new and existing topic models have been extensively used to facilitate the analysis of social media data for healthcare research.

Prier et al. [67] applied LDA to a large corpus of health-related tweets and identified several prevalent topics: physical activity, obesity, substance abuse and healthcare. They observed that the topics related to obesity and weight loss correspond to advertisements, while healthcare topics mostly correspond to political discourse. Besides identifying general health-related topics in the Twitter stream, they also applied basic keyword filtering to create a corpus consisting only of the tweets related to tobacco use and determined the fine-grained topics in this corpus. By examining these topics they found out that besides tobacco promotions, smoking cigarettes or cigars and substance abuse (such as smoking marijuana and crack cocaine), Twitter users also typically discuss strategies to quit smoking and recover from smoking addiction.

Paul and Dredze [61] also applied standard LDA to a corpus of health-related tweets (filtered out from the general Twitter stream using an SVM classifier based on bag-of-words features) and reported that, although LDA was able to generate some disease-related topics, most of them did not clearly indicate specific ailments. For example, while many topics discovered by LDA contained surgery terms, it was not clear whether these surgeries were associated with a certain illness, physical injury or cancer. To overcome this problem, they proposed the Ailment Topic Aspect Model (ATAM), which assumes that each health-related tweet corresponds to a latent ailment (e.g., flu, allergy or cancer). Given a collection of such tweets, ATAM identifies a background topic, general health-related topics as well as general, symptom or treatment-related aspects (subtopics) for each latent ailment. Similar to standard LDA, topics and ailment aspects correspond to multinomial distributions over words. ATAM includes different topic types to account for the fact that even in the tweets about health topics, users often provide additional context, which may not fit into the symptom-treatment-ailment topic structure (e.g., in a tweet "sick today so playing video games" general topics account for "playing video games"). In order to determine which topic type each word is assigned to, the model relies on two binomially distributed latent switch variables. The first switch variable determines if a word is generated from a background topic. If it is not, then the second switch determines whether a word is generated from one of the general health topics or from one of the aspects of an ailment associated with the tweet.

Paul and Dredze later proposed ATAM+ [62], an extension to ATAM that incorporates prior knowledge in the form of multinomial language models, which correspond to the symptoms and treatments for 20 diseases obtained from the articles on WebMD.com, as asymmetric Dirichlet priors for the corresponding ailment aspects in ATAM. They reported the correlation coefficients between the CDC ILI statistics and the proportion of the tweets assigned to the flu ailment by ATAM and ATAM+ to be 0.935 and 0.968 respectively, while the correlation coefficient between Google Flu Trends data and the CDC statistics for the same time period was 0.932. They also evaluated the feasibility of applying ATAM+ to several population health analysis tasks. One such task is monitoring behavioral risk factors by geographical region. To demonstrate the potential of ATAM+ for this task, they calculated the correlation coefficient between the proportion of tweets in each U.S. state that were assigned to a particular ATAM ailment and the state's risk factor rate for the same ailment represented by the corresponding variable in the BRFSS dataset published by the National Center for Chronic Disease Prevention and Health Promotion at the CDC.[12] The strongest reported positive correlation was between the proportion of residents in each state, who are smokers, and the cancer ailment, while the strongest negative correlation was between exercise and the frequency of posting a tweet associated with any ailment, indicating that the Twitter users in the states, where people generally exercise more, are less likely to become sick. The other tasks include geographical syndromic surveillance, when the ailments are tracked both over time and per geographic region (ATAM+ was able to detect several known patterns of allergies) and analyzing correlation of symptoms and treatments with ailments. The latter task is particularly important, since for many health conditions patients prefer not to visit their doctors, managing an illness on their own. The illness, symptoms and chosen treatments for people not visiting healthcare providers remain unreported and obtaining these statistics requires extensive polling of large populations. Therefore, ATAM provides an opportunity to quickly and easily collect these statistics from Twitter. One disadvantage common to both ATAM and ATAM+, however, is that they require specifying the number of general health topics and ailments a priori, which is not always feasible.

Social media can also be a source of accurate and up-to-date information on recreational drugs, such as their usage profiles and side effects, which is crucial for supporting a wide range of healthcare activities, including addiction treatment programs, toxin diagnosis, prevention and awareness campaigns and public policy. Recreational drug use is an important public health problem, as it imposes a significant burden on businesses (via absenteeism or presenteeism of employees), healthcare infrastructure and society in general. Paul and Dredze proposed factorial LDA (f-LDA) [64], a topic model, in which each word is associated with a K-tuple of latent factors (e.g., topic, perspective), in contrast to LDA, which associates only one latent topic variable with each word. In

[12] `http://apps.nccd.cdc.gov/gisbrfss/`

f-LDA, each K-tuple corresponds to its own multinomial distribution over the collection vocabulary and each document is represented as a multinomial distribution over all possible K-tuples. f-LDA can jointly capture these factors as well as interesting interactions between them, producing fine-grained topical summaries of user discussions related to particular combinations of factors. Factorial LDA uses a novel hierarchical prior over model parameters and can be used to automatically extract textual snippets that correspond to fine-grained information patterns, a simple form of extractive multidocument summarization. In [63] and [65], Paul and Dredze reported the results of applying f-LDA to the task of mining recreational drug usage trends from online forums. In particular, they collected the data from drugs-forum.com and organized f-LDA topics along three dimensions: drug type (e.g., amphetamines, beta-ketones, LSD, etc.), route of intake (injection, oral, smoking, etc.) and aspect (cultural setting, drug pharmacology, usage and side effects). For example, in their three-dimensional model a tuple (*cannabis*, *smoking*, *effects*) corresponds to a topic summarizing the health effects of smoking cannabis. They focused on four drugs (mephedrone, Bromo-Dragonfly, Spice/K2 and salvia divinorum), which have been only recently discovered and studied, and used tuple-specific word distributions estimated by f-LDA to create a summary for each aspect of using these drugs.

9.3.2 Detecting Reports of Adverse Medical Events and Drug Reactions

Adverse drug reaction (ADR) is defined as a "harmful reaction, resulting from an intervention related to the use of medical product, which predicts hazard from future administration and warrants prevention of specific treatment, or alteration of the dosage regimen, or complete withdrawal of the product from the market" [32]. ADRs and drug-related adverse medical events (or adverse drug events, ADEs) pose substantial risks to patients, who consume postmarket or investigational drugs, since they can complicate their medical conditions, increase the likelihood of hospital admission and even cause death. Despite postmarket drug surveillance, ADEs remain the fourth leading cause of death in the United States. A large portion of adverse medical events have been ascribed to adverse interactions between different drugs, which are often caused by their shared action mechanisms and metabolic pathways. Unknown drug–drug interactions (DDIs) constitute a significant public health problem, as they account for up to 30% of unexpected ADRs. Most discovered adverse DDIs result in additional prescription precautions and contraindications or even complete withdrawal of a drug from the market. Traditionally, ADRs and DDIs have been detected based on four data sources: clinical trial data, chemical/pharmacological databases, EMRs and spontaneous reporting systems (SRSs), which have been developed and deployed by different countries around the world as part of their pharmacovigilance process. SRSs mostly rely on self-reports by patients: the Food and Drug Administration's MedWatch site[13] and Adverse Event Reporting System (AERS) in the United States, EudraVigilance by the European Medicines Agency and International Pharmacovigilance system by the World Health Organization. All of these sources, however, have inherent limitations, since clinical trials suffer from the cohort bias and passive nature of spontaneous reports that lead to low reporting ratios (only 1 to 10 percent of all reportable ADRs are normally reported through MedWatch). Although pharmaceutical companies are required to report all known adverse events and reactions, the majority of such events are detected by physicians and patients, for whom the reporting is voluntary. As a result, many serious or rare ADRs or DDIs may not be timely detected and their overall number may be significantly underestimated [92].

Due to the high frequency, diversity, public availability and volume, user posts on social media platforms have a great potential to become a new resource for Internet-based near real-time pharmacovigilance and complement the existing surveillance methods based on using natural language processing techniques to analyze electronic health records [41]. In particular, Chee et al. [14] proposed a machine learning method for identifying potential watchlist drugs from the messages on

[13]`http://www.fda.gov/Safety/MedWatch/`

Health and Wellness Yahoo! groups. They experimented with ensemble methods consisting of standard classifiers (Naïve Bayes and SVM) and two feature sets (bag-of-words lexical features and an expanded set based on drug and side-effect lexicons as well as sentiment vocabularies) and were able to identify the drugs that were actually withdrawn from the market. Bian et al. [3] proposed a method for large-scale mining of adverse drug events from Twitter consisting of two classification steps. In the first step, the tweets posted by the users of investigational drugs of interest are identified. In the second step, the historical posts of those users are accessed to identify their previous tweets about adverse side effects of using those drugs. They used SVM with the Gaussian radial basis kernel as a classification model and experimented with both standard bag-of-words lexical features and semantic features derived by mapping the tweet terms into the concept codes from the Unified Medical Language System Metathesaurus (UMLS) [77]. Despite using standard techniques to optimize the classification model, such as scaling, grid-based kernel parameter searching and feature selection using one-way analysis of variance F-test, they were only able to achieve the classification accuracy of 0.74 and the mean AUC of 0.82 for the the first classification step and the classification accuracy of 0.74 and the mean AUC of 0.74 for the second step. The relatively low performance of the classification models was attributed to the noisiness of Twitter data (the abundance of fragmented and non-grammatical sentences, misspellings and abbreviations), which degraded the performance of the standard part-of-speech tagger that was trained on proper medical documents and used to map the terms in tweets to the UMLS concepts. Scanfeld et al. [76] analyzed the tweets mentioning antibiotics to identify the major types of their proper use as well as misunderstanding and misuse. Yang and Yang [92] proposed a method to identify DDIs directly from social media content. In particular, they first extracted the n-grams from the posts and comments on the drug forums of MedHelp online patient community and identified the drug names and drug reactions by matching the extracted n-grams to the ADR lexicon derived from the Consumer Health Vocabulary (CHV) Wiki.[14] CHV is a collection of terms and phrases commonly used by non-specialists to refer to medical concepts (e.g., "irregular heartbeat" for "arrhythmia") that is compiled, reviewed and validated by healthcare professionals. After extracting drug names and reactions, adverse DDIs were identified by applying association rule mining. Using the data from the DrugBank database as a golden standard, this method was able to identify the known adverse DDIs between 10 popular drugs with 100% recall and 60% precision.

Frost et al. [43] proposed to use online patient communities to determine the prevalence of on-label versus off-label drug use (when healthcare providers prescribe a drug for a non-FDA approved purpose). In particular, they examined the patient data for amitriptyline and modafinil, two medications that are widely prescribed off-label, and conducted a post-hoc analysis of how patients reported using these drugs and their side effects that informed even broader understanding of these already well-understood medications. Nakhasi et al. [58] provided an analysis of preventable and adverse medical events that were reported and explicitly ascribed to the actions or procedures of healthcare professionals on Twitter. They classified such errors according to the type (procedural versus medication) and the source (physicians, nurses or surgeons) and reported the proportions of each error class. They also found out that the majority of such events are either self-reported by patients or reported by their relatives, demonstrating the potential of leveraging social media platforms to obtain the first-hand patient perspectives on the errors at different levels of the healthcare system. Such information is extremely valuable in developing the strategies to improve patient safety procedures for the entire healthcare teams. They also found that patients and relatives reacted to the safety errors in a wide variety of manners. While some people expressed anger and frustration in response to errors, others found them humorous and had an easy time moving on or used humor as a coping mechanism.

[14] `http://consumerhealthvocab.chpc.utah.edu/CHVwiki/`

9.3.3 Characterizing Life Style and Well-Being

While there is an ongoing argument among psychologists about how happiness should be defined, few would deny that people desire it. Governments around the world are starting to put more and more effort into measuring subjective well-being in their countries, moving beyond the common economic-based indicators, such as gross domestic product. Surveys by organizations like Gallup and government agencies are increasingly including one or more subjective well-being questions into their questionnaires. Subjective well-being, as measured by life satisfaction is also an important public health issue. Its importance goes far beyond the obvious attraction of positive emotion, as it affects the overall health, productivity and other positive life outcomes. Studying life satisfaction and well-being is conceptually different from predicting flu or allergies, since its goal is to not only predict regional variation in happiness, but to also understand the factors and mechanisms contributing to it. In particular, Schwartz et al. [79] focused on the cognitive-based estimation of overall life satisfaction by studying the language of well-being. They collected one billion tweets over nearly a one-year timespan and mapped them to the U.S. counties, from which the tweets were sent. They used LASSO linear regression to predict subjective life satisfaction scores derived from the questionnaires using the words from either clusters of semantically related words derived from Facebook status updates using LDA [78] or manually constructed word lists (based on LIWC [87] and PERMA dictionaries [82]) as features and controlling for demographic information (age, sex, ethnicity) and indicators of socioeconomic status (income and education). Based on the analysis of the estimated model, it was determined that socioeconomic status control variables are more predictive than the terms from social media-specific LDA topics alone, which are in turn more useful than hand-crafted lists of words from LIWC and PERMA dictionaries. However, all three feature sets combined produced significantly more accurate results than either of them alone, confirming that the words in tweets convey more information than just the control variables. The key conclusion of this work is that the words used in a sample of social media posts created by a particular community (e.g., county) reflect the well-being of individuals belonging to this community. In particular, the words belonging to categories and topics related to physical activity and exercise ("training," "gym," "fitness," "zumba"), pro-social activities ("money," "support," "donate"), community engagement ("meeting," "conference," "council," "board"), work and achievement ("skills," "management," "learning"), religion and spirituality ("universe," "existence," "spiritual," "nature") are the strongest positive predictors, while the words associated with disengagement (e.g., "sleepy," "tired," "bored") are the strongest negative predictors of life satisfaction.

Although to date there has been a wealth of behavioral science research examining the role of face-to-face interactions and real-life social networks in influencing a broad range of behavioral (such as alcohol consumption [70] and obesity [16]) and emotional (such as happiness [37], loneliness [12] and depression [69]) changes in individuals, very few works studied similar effects of online social networks. One notable exception is the work of Sadilek and Kautz [71], who applied a regression decision tree using 62 features derived from both the text of 16 million geo-tagged tweets authored by 630,000 unique users located in New York City and the social network structure of that sample to the task of predicting the cumulative probability of sickness of Twitter users based on the number of calendar days, during which they wrote at least one "sick" tweet in the past. They used several types of features covering different aspects of life and well-being: the online social status of individuals, their behavior and lifestyle, socioeconomic characteristics, intensity of contacts with sick individuals and exposure to pollution. The online social status of individuals was measured based on the properties of their Twitter social network, such as PageRank, reciprocity of following, various centrality measures (degree, communicability, eigenvector, betweenness, load, flow and closeness) and interactions with other users (e.g., how many times a person's messages got forwarded or "liked" and how many times other people mentioned that person in their messages). Lifestyle and behavior of users, such as how often they visit bars as opposed to gyms as well as how much time they spend in crowded public transportation, was measured by juxtaposing the GPS coordinates of their tweets with a database of 25,000 different venues and major public transportation routes in New York City. The main findings in this work are that physical encounters with sick individuals within different time windows (1, 4, 12, 24 hours) are strongly negatively correlated, while online social status is strongly positively correlated with a person's health status. Besides that, the distance to pollution sources and the visits to polluted cites are the two single features having the strongest positive and negative correlations with health status, respectively. Additionally, measures of social rank are highly cross correlated and have an almost identical high predictive power, together explaining over 24% of the variance in health status. Other highly predictive types of features include lifestyle, pollution, number of sick friends and encounters with sick individuals. At the same time, individual contributions of census-based features such as poverty, education and race were found to be small, jointly accounting only for 8.7% of the variance unexplained by other factors.

9.4 Analysis of Social Media Use in Healthcare

Communication between patients and clinicians is at the heart of healthcare. The emergence of new social media resources such as social networks, instant messaging platforms and video chats has the potential to completely change the way doctors and patients interact. Hawn [48] points out that using social media in health education "is about changing the locus of control to the patient" and altering the relationships between care givers and care receivers, in which patient portals, EHR platforms, blogs and microblogs won't merely substitute for many one-on-one encounters with providers, but will also allow for deeper doctor-patient relationships. Besides helping to establish better doctor-patient relationships, leveraging social media in healthcare has the following benefits:

- Social media platforms can make it easier for severely ill patients who are home-bound or bed-bound to regularly communicate with their providers, since written communication may take less energy/effort than phone calls and can be paused if the patient needs to take a break during the communication to rest;
- Such platforms can narrow the information gap between providers and patients and make patients more engaged in their healthcare management and decision making;
- Communications via social media would also be beneficial for patients who are seeing experts located in different parts of the state or even country for their health conditions.

The public health community is also considering how social media can be used to spread health information, with applications including health education and promotions, as well as larger scale scenarios, in which patients can "friend" their doctors and constantly share health information with them and receive advice.

9.4.1 Social Media as a Source of Public Health Information

Personal health data has been traditionally considered as private. However, with the emergence of collaboratively generated content platforms dedicated specifically to healthcare, that view started to change. While health information systems vary in complexity and purpose, the predominant model is that of a central repository for all health information generated within clinical contexts (health history, diagnoses, allergies, current treatments) that is kept securely for view only by patients and their healthcare providers. And while there is a growing demand by patients for access to their own health data, little is known about how other people with similar medical concerns can effectively use these data, if they are made available to them. A medical informatics working group asserted that the ideal personal health record is more than just a static repository for patient data. It should combine data, knowledge and software tools to help patients become active participants in their own care. Framing online patient interaction around sharing personal health information resulted in the emergence of healthcare-related Web 2.0 communities, in which the members exchange their knowledge and experience, educating each other. This way patients can be viewed as individual data stores, which if linked together with online social networks, can become part of a global, dynamic and shared healthcare knowledge repository.

The popularity of social media resources can be leveraged to disseminate health information and conduct interventions. For example, in the dermatology community, the Sulzberger Institute for Dermatologic Education is sponsoring an Internet contest for the best video promoting sun safe behavior. Other examples include Twitter groups dedicated to certain medical conditions (e.g., a group for mothers of children with attention deficit disorder), YouTube videos on tobacco cessation and human papillomavirus vaccination campaigns. Vance et al. [88] analyzed the pros and cons of using social media to spread public health information to young adults and concluded that the pros include low cost and rapid transmission, while the cons include blind authorship, lack of source citation and frequent presentation of opinions as facts.

Verhaag [89] studied experiences, expectations and strategies of 84 healthcare organizations in using social media for external communication. In particular, she studied the activity, popularity and presence of these organizations on Facebook, Twitter, LinkedIn, YouTube, Google+, and Pinterest as well as blogs and found that different social media platforms are not equally utilized and that the activity of organization on these platforms differs by their specific area. She found that health organizations generally have a Facebook and/or Twitter account, however, other social media platforms, such as Google+, blogs and YouTube are hardly used at all. In addition, health organizations most commonly use social media to spread information about themselves. Interviews with the employees of those organizations responsible for social media relations indicated that there is a need for "closed platforms," in which the members have different levels of access to the content. Such platforms will be more suitable for private and sensitive information, which is common in the healthcare industry.

As behavioral interventions are becoming increasingly important in public health, the potential of using social media to study dissemination of health behaviors, sentiments and rumors among very large populations is unparalleled. Salathé and Khandelwal [75] assessed the spread of vaccination sentiments from person to person during the unfolding of the H1N1 pandemic and found that anti-vaccination sentiments could be reliably assessed across time and that those sentiments tend to cluster in certain parts of online social networks. Their analysis also indicated that negative sentiments spread more effectively than positive ones. They also identified strong positive correlation between anti-vaccination sentiments and CDC estimates of H1N1 vaccination rates (i.e., vaccination coverage was higher in the regions with more positive sentiments).

9.4.2 Analysis of Data from Online Doctor and Patient Communities

Fast and easy access to online health information resulted in patients relying on social media and the Internet more frequently than their physicians as a source of health information. In particular, Lau et al. [54] conducted an extensive study of social media use by Generation Y, people with low socioeconomic status and chronically ill populations. Emerging healthcare-related social media platforms also play an increasing role in online health searches. In many cases, people prefer to turn to social media groups, discussion forums and patient communities to express and discuss their fears and concerns for several reasons. The patients either may not feel comfortable disclosing their fears to providers or may wish to find other individuals in similar situation, who will listen to them, provide support and address their everyday issues and fears that healthcare providers may not realize. This particularly applies to the issues that are traditionally related to stigma, ridicule and rejection in a society. Social interaction through computer-mediated communication services resembles face-to-face interactions, but offers greater anonymity and intimacy, which in turn results in higher levels of trust.

Both patients and doctors naturally seek to meet and interact with a community of other patients and doctors either to share their knowledge and experience or to receive support and advice. This type of dynamic online communication (called Health 2.0, by analogy with Web 2.0) now offers patients a unique opportunity to learn about their illness and gain support and knowledge from others with similar experiences. As a result, online patient communities can be used as a source of clinical data and patients' insights on the functioning of different aspects of the healthcare system. These platforms are based on two assumptions. First, given appropriate tools, patients will be able to interpret and learn from their own and others' health data. Second, sharing personal health data and collaboratively reviewing and critiquing it will enhance the utility of the data for each contributor. A list of popular on-line patient communities is provided in Table 9.1.

TABLE 9.1: Popular Online Patient Communities

Community	**Description**	**Website**
PatientsLikeMe	Online community for patients to share their experiences and progress or to get input from others, who suffer from the same condition	www.patientslikeme.com
MedHelp	Online patient community that partners with hospitals and medical research institutions to deliver on-line discussion boards on a variety of healthcare topics	www.medhelp.org
DailyStrength	Social networking platform centered on support groups, where users provide one another with emotional support by discussing their struggles and successes with each other	www.dailystrength.org
Inspire	Patient community organized around support groups related to medical conditions that are represented as a hierarchy	www.inspire.com
MediGuard	Patient and consumer network that helps patients to track their medications and exchange information with others	www.mediguard.org

PatientsLikeMe is an online platform built to support information exchange between the patients with life-changing diseases, which is organized around patient communities designated for specific conditions. PatientsLikeMe has more than 20 disease communities formed by more than 50,000 patients that anonymously share treatment options, symptoms, progression and outcome data for complex diseases. To make health information more accessible, this Web site provides visualization tools that help the patients understand and share information about their health status. Upon joining the site, patients enter a combination of structured and unstructured information about their health status and history, which is then processed and represented as a set of graphical displays on their profiles: a personal picture, an autobiographical statement, a diagram that maps a functional impairment to specific areas of the body, a diagnosis history and a series of charts. The "nugget" summary diagram displays the current function score as a color code mapped onto the affected areas of the body as well as the number of years with the disease, an iconic representation of the equipment currently used, and stars indicating the level of participation on the site. Each member can also see a graphical representation of their own and others' health status, treatments and symptoms over time and can view reports of aggregated data. The site includes an interactive report for each treatment, medication and intervention that patients add to the system. Such reports include dosages taken, time on treatment, evaluations of treatment, including perceived efficacy, side effects and burden. Members can locate other patients in similar circumstances and with shared medical experiences using searching and browsing tools and discuss the profiles, reports and general health concerns through the forum, private messages and comments they post on one another's profiles. Frost and Massagli [42] identified and analyzed how the users of PatientsLikeMe with incurable or rare life-altering diseases reference the personal health information of each other in patient-to-patient dialogues and found that discussions on the site fall into three major categories: targeted questions to other patients with relevant experience, proffering personally acquired disease-management knowledge or coping strategies, and forming and solidifying relationships based on shared health concerns.

Online patient networks open up new ways of testing treatments and can speed up patient recruitment into clinical trials for new drugs [9]. Recent studies have also demonstrated that using online patient network data in clinical studies can accelerate discoveries related to complex conditions such as Parkinson's disease [90], amyotrophic lateral sclerosis (ALS) [91] and rheumatoid arthritis [85]. These platforms can also be used to identify shifts in patients' perceptions and behaviors in response to public health policies.

Many disease-specific groups have arisen on Facebook, representing important sources of information, support and engagement for patients with chronic diseases. Greene et al. [46] identified the 15 largest groups focused on diabetes management and evaluated a sample of discussions within them. They found that Facebook diabetes communities contain a plurality of participants, including patients, their family members, advertisers and researchers, with divergent interests and modes of communication. They use Facebook to share personal clinical information, request disease-specific guidance and feedback and receive emotional support. They also found that users posted individual concerns about possible adverse effects of medications and diet supplements in an attempt to see if their own experiences correlated with those of others. Furthermore, nearly a quarter of all the posts shared sensitive aspects of diabetes management unlikely to be revealed in doctor–patient interactions.

Many blogging and Twitter communities are also dedicated to specific health conditions. Chung et al. [20] studied dietdiaries.com, the community of bloggers focused on weight management, and compared the effectiveness of two approaches for the task of predicting weight loss from natural language use in blogs. The first approach is based on manually categorizing blog posts based on the degree of weight loss or gain reported in them and then using standard multinomial Naïve Bayes textual classifier with bag-of-words features to classify them into those categories. The second approach is based on the detailed linguistic analysis of blog posts leveraging linguistic inquiry and word count (LIWC) [87] categories. In this method, textual feature vectors are mapped into linguistic categories that are known to be associated with psychological constructs. The proposed method first computes correlations between LIWC categories and weight change and then uses linear regression to predict the percent of body weight change based on the distribution of LIWC categories, which have statistically significant correlations with weight change. The authors observed that the LIWC-based regression approach generally outperformed the Naïve Bayes-based classification approach. In particular, they found that using more sadness-related words and fewer food ingestion-related words is a statistically significant predictor of weight loss, whereas the percent of body weight change was unrelated to the usage of positive emotion words (e.g., "awesome," "happy"), health words (e.g., "nausea," "sick") or social words (e.g., "friend," "hug"). The author's interpretation of these results was that sharing negative emotions is a more successful strategy in blogging about weight loss than simply keeping a food intake diary. Harris et al. [47] studied communication about childhood obesity on Twitter using descriptive statistics and exponential random graph modeling to examine the content of tweets, characteristics of users tweeting about childhood obesity and the types of Twitter followers receiving tweets about childhood obesity. They concluded that Twitter may provide an important channel for reaching traditionally difficult-to-reach populations, including lower income, Hispanic, and non-Hispanic Black groups facing significantly higher rates of childhood obesity than their higher income and non-Hispanic White counterparts.

Several researchers also focused on studying the content and social network structure of online communities for smoking cessation. Selby et al. [81] analyzed the content of the posts on StopSmokingCenter.net, an online social support network moderated by trained program health educators, as well as characteristics of the users who created them. They found that the majority of posters were female and that the most common theme of the posts was seeking support or advice with quitting. However, only 15% of the new members made at least one post on the support group boards and an even smaller fraction of users were active and consistent posters, suggesting that other self-quit program aspects (e.g., developing a strong sense of community) might be more appealing to the participants. Additional analysis revealed that 50% the the first-time posts were made relatively quickly (within three hours after joining the site). In their first posts, members most frequently conveyed that they were seeking support and advice. Replies to the first posts from other support group members were also quick, with 25% of the first posts receiving a reply within 12 minutes and 50% within 29 minutes. Responses were even faster for the posts from the members that were actively seeking support, revealing that the support group board did function to provide members with an immediate source of support not available with most traditional interventions. Cobb et al. [21] used network analysis techniques to identify structural and functional characteristics of QuitNet,[15] one of the largest and most popular continuously operating online communities focused on smoking cessation. They found that the members in the strongly and densely connected cores of QuitNet's social network are mostly older females (over 40 years old), that have been active and abstinent community members for more than a year. In a recent study by Corazza et al. [24], social media was also used to study a new drug, methoxetamine.

Chuang and Yang [18] [17] identified and compared the level of different types of social support (informational, emotional and instrumental) across three different types of computer-mediated communication tools (discussion forums, personal journals and notes) on the MedHelp alcoholism support community and found that the patients use these communication tools for different purposes. Forum users are more likely to seek and provide informational support, while journals and notes are primarily used to express higher levels of emotional support. Similar qualitative content analyses of posts on online communities for health conditions such as irritable bowel syndrome [26], Huntington's disease [27] and HIV [28] have been conducted and identified that all five subtypes of social support (emotional, informational, esteem and social network) are evident in the posts, with informational and emotional support being offered most frequently. Silenzio et al. [84] studied characteristics of the young lesbian, gay and bisexual population on Twitter and proposed several methods for effective peer-driven information diffusion and preventive care, specifically focusing on suicide prevention.

Besides patient communities, there is also a growing number of online communities for healthcare professionals, which foster and facilitate the exchange of information, insights and knowledge about current medical practices, treatments and medications and generate epidemiological and clinical data that were previously dispersed between the physicians' charts, EMRs and clinical histories. A list of popular online platforms dedicated to healthcare professionals is presented in Table 9.2. Sermo is the largest such community with over 200,000 registered licensed MDs and DOs. DataGenno is a Web portal for healthcare professionals and researchers along with patients and their relatives to exchange information about rare genetic and complex diseases. It provides a database with sample and disease information along with the images for each sign or symptom, a search engine for differential diagnosis and features for information exchange between healthcare professionals. It has been designed to bridge the gap between healthcare professionals, scientists, genetic counselors, nurses and patients by combining clinical, genetic and genomic information for specific diseases. eMERGE is an NIH-funded collaborative project linking medical records data with genomic data.

A community-based social network for health professionals that combines traditional drug dis-

[15] `http://www.quitnet.com`

TABLE 9.2: Popular Online Communities for Doctors and Clinical Researchers

Community	Description	Website
DataGenno	Interactive database containing molecular and clinical genetic information from diseases targeted to healthcare professionals, research scientists, and patients	`www.datagenno.com`
eMERGE	The Electronic Medical Records and Genomics (eMERGE) network combines DNA repositories with electronic medical record systems for large-scale genetic research	`emerge.mc.vanderbilt.edu`
Sermo	Online network for physicians with panel discussions about specific topics	`www.sermo.com`
Ozmosis	Provides several solutions for physicians to share their knowledge and clinical experiences with each other	`www.ozmosis.com`

covery informatics with Web 2.0 platforms and strong privacy is believed to be the key to facilitate richer collaborations between healthcare professionals with the same interests [49].

9.5 Conclusions and Future Directions

As we have seen in this chapter, social media can be considered both as a comprehensive source of individual-level experiences to be used by patients for health self-education or by providers to inform clinical practice and as a nearly unlimited source of aggregate data for large-scale population studies. The main advantages of social media-based approaches to public health research are that they do not require to explicitly recruit participants and can provide large volumes of data in near real time at virtually no cost. Their major disadvantages are sample bias and trustworthiness of the data.

The issue of sample bias has to do with the fact that the demographics of social media does not fully represent the general population, with the elderly and young children being particularly underrepresented. For example, previous studies reported that Twitter users tend to be younger (nearly half are under 35 and only 2% are 65 or older). Twitter is also known to be centric to the United States: as of June 2009, 62% of Twitter users were physically located in the United States Furthermore, the exact demographics of social media population that actively generates health-related content is generally unknown and not easy to estimate. As a result, population bias may limit the type of public health research questions that can be answered with the help of social media data. Therefore, an interesting future direction is to study how the estimates obtained from social media can be adjusted to reflect the properties of the general population.

Another challenge limiting the use of social media in healthcare is related to the inability of the existing methods to identify all health-related posts and messages with 100% accuracy as well as the general reliability of user-generated content. As more and more people become the users of social media, communication channels grow exponentially more diffused and the possibility of spreading inaccurate or problematic information increases accordingly. As a result, social media users have to aggregate often contradictory information from multiple sources and judge their credibility. It is also known that some users may never self-report any health condition no matter how serious it is (stoics), while others may report being sick even when in fact they are not (hypochondriacs). While some of this bias can be partially mitigated using heuristics, such as counting the number of days, during which a user posts "sick" tweets, it is very hard to remove it completely. Although for the purpose of identifying general population-level trends and important insights into an epidemic, the sample bias may not have a large effect, the lack of confirmation for the diagnosis presents certain challenges for validation, detailed analysis and interpretation of results obtained from smaller scale social media-based studies. Public health officials typically have reservations about integrating social media data into their reports as it could result in an additional burden to their surveillance responsibilities. However, social media is, by nature, a venue for two-way information exchange, where the users can verify and evaluate the quality of information shared by other users. Therefore, many existing online systems actively leverage this property of social social media by requiring the messages to be reviewed by a moderator (either before or after their public dissemination) and enabling the users to provide feedback and even corroboration of submissions, a strategy that has proven successful with Wikipedia. The initial work on automatically establishing the trustworthiness of social media data through cross validation with official sources was extensively discussed in this chapter. Nevertheless, this problem is far from being solved and constitutes another interesting and challenging future research direction.

Despite these limitations, social media-based methods clearly have the potential to become valuable additions to traditional public health monitoring and analysis systems, which can uncover the detailed biological mechanisms behind diseases and capture the signals that are presently too weak to be detected online.

Bibliography

[1] Harshavardhan Achrekar, Avinash Gandhe, Ross Lazarus, Ssu-Hsin Yu, and Benyuan Liu. Predicting flu trends using Twitter data. In *Workshop on Cyber-Physical Networking Systems (CPNS 2011)*, 2011.

[2] Eiji Aramaki, Sachiko Maskawa, and Mizuki Morita. Twitter catches the flu: Detecting influenza epidemics using Twitter. In *Proceedings of the Conference on Empirical Methods in Natural Language Processing (EMNLP'11)*, pages 1568–1576, 2011.

[3] Jiang Bian, Umit Topaloglu, and Fan Yu. Towards large-scale Twitter mining for drug-related adverse events. In *Proceedings of the 2012 International Workshop on Smart Health and Well-being*, pages 25–32, 2012.

[4] Celeste Biever. Twitter mood maps reveal emotional states of America. *The New Scientist*, 207(2771):14, 2010.

[5] David M. Blei, Andrew Y. Ng, and Michael I. Jordan. Latent Dirichlet allocation. *Journal of Machine Learning Research*, 3(12):993–1022, 2003.

[6] Sean Brennan, Adam Sadilek, and Henry Kautz. Towards understanding global spread of disease from everyday interpersonal interactions. In *Proceedings of the 23rd International Joint Conference on Artificial Intelligence (IJCAI'13)*, pages 2783–2789, 2013.

[7] Joanna Brenner and Aaron Smith. 72% of online adults are social networking site users. `http://www.pewinternet.org/2013/08/05/72-of-online-adults-are-social-networking-site-users/`, 2013. Accessed 08-08-2014.

[8] David A. Broniatowski, Michael J. Paul, and Mark Dredze. National and local influenza surveillance through Twitter: An analysis of the 2012–2013 influenza epidemic. *PLoS ONE*, 8(12):e83672, 2013.

[9] Catherine A. Brownstein, John S. Brownstein, Davis S. Williams, Paul Wicks, and James A. Heywood. The power of social networking in medicine. *Nature Biotechnology*, 27:888–890, 2009.

[10] John S. Brownstein, Clark C. Freifeld, Emily H. Chan, Mikaela Keller, Amy L. Sonricker, Sumiko R. Mekaru, and David L. Buckeridge. Information technology and global surveillance of cases of 2009 H1N1 influenza. *The New England Journal of Medicine*, 362(18):1731–1735, 2010.

[11] John S. Brownstein, Clark C. Freifeld, Ben Y. Reis, and Kenneth D. Mandl. Surveillance sans frontières: Internet-based emerging infectious disease intelligence and the HealthMap project. *PLoS Medicine*, 5(7):e151, 2008.

[12] John T. Cacioppo, James H. Fowler, and Nicholas A. Christakis. Alone in the crowd: The structure and spread of loneliness in a large social network. *Journal of Personality and Social Psychology*, 97(6):977–991, 2009.

[13] Herman Anthony Carneiro and Eleftherios Mylonakis. Google trends: A web-based tool for real-time surveillance of disease outbreaks. *Clinical Infectious Diseases*, 49(10):1557–1564, 2009.

[14] Brant W. Chee, Richard Berlin, and Bruce Schatz. Predicting adverse drug events from personal health messages. In *Proceedings of the 2011 AMIA Annual Symposium*, pages 217–226, 2011.

[15] Cynthia Chew and Gunther Eysenbach. Pandemics in the age of Twitter: Content analysis of tweets during the 2009 H1N1 outbreak. *PLoS ONE*, 5(11):e14118, 2010.

[16] Nicholas A. Christakis and James H. Fowler. The spread of obesity in a large social network over 32 years. *New England Journal of Medicine*, 357:370–379, 2007.

[17] Katherine Y. Chuang and Christopher C. Yang. Helping you to help me: Exploring supportive interaction in online health community. *Proceedings of the American Society for Information Science and Technology*, 47(1):1–10, 2010.

[18] Katherine Y. Chuang and Christopher C. Yang. Social support in online healthcare social networking. In *Proceedings of the 2010 iConference*, 2010.

[19] Rumi Chunara, Jason R. Andrews, and John S. Brownstein. Social and news media enable estimations of epidemiological patterns early in the 2010 Haitian cholera outbreak. *American Journal of Tropical Medicine and Hygiene*, 86(1):39–45, 2012.

[20] Cindy K. Chung, Clinton Jones, and Alexander Liu. Predicting success and failure in weight loss blogs through natural language use. In *Proceedings of the 2nd International AAAI Conference on Weblogs and Social Media (ICWSM'08)*, pages 180–181, 2008.

[21] Nathan K. Cobb, Amanda L. Graham, and David B. Abrams. Social network structure of a large online community for smoking cessation. *American Journal of Public Health*, 100(7):1282–1289, 2010.

[22] Crystale Purvis Cooper, Kenneth P. Mallon, Steven Leadbetter, Lori A. Pollack, and Lucy A. Peipins. Cancer Internet search activity on a major search engine. *Journal of Medical Internet Research*, 7(3):e36, 2005.

[23] D. L. Cooper, G. E. Smith, V. A. Hollyoak, C. A. Joseph, L. Johnson, and R. Chaloner. Use of NHS direct calls for surveillance of influenza—a second year's experience. *Communicable Diseases and Public Health*, 5(2):127–131, 2002.

[24] Ornella Corazza, Fabrizio Schifano, Pierluigi Simonato, Suzanne Fergus, Sulaf Assi, Jacqueline Stair, John Corkery, Giuseppina Trincas, Paolo Deluca, Zoe Davey, Ursula Blaszko, Zsolt Demetrovics, Jacek Moskalewicz, Aurora Enea, Giuditta di Melchiorre, Barbara Mervo, Lucia di Furia, Magi Farre, Liv Flesland, Manuela Pasinetti, Cinzia Pezzolesi, Agnieszka Pisarska, Harry Shapiro, Holger Siemann, Arvid Skutle, Elias Sferrazza, Marta Torrens, Peer van der Kreeft, Daniela Zummo, and Norbert Scherbaum. Phenomenon of new drugs on the Internet: The case of ketamine derivative methoxetamine. *Human Psychopharmacology: Clinical and Experimental*, 27(2):145–149, 2012.

[25] Courtney D. Corley, Armin R. Mikler, Karan P. Singh, and Diane J. Cook. Monitoring influenza trends through mining social media. In *Proceedings of the International Conference on Bioinformatics and Computational Biology (BIOCOMP'09)*, pages 340–346, 2009.

[26] Neil S. Coulson. Receiving social support on-line: An analysis of a computer-mediated support group for individuals living with irritable bowel syndrome. *Cyberpsychology and Behavior*, 8(6):580–584, 2005.

[27] Neil S. Coulson, Heather Buchanan, and Aimee Aubeeluck. Social support in cyberspace: A content analysis of communication within a Huntington's disease online support group. *Patient Education and Counseling*, 68(2):173–178, 2007.

[28] Constantinos K. Coursaris and Ming Liu. An analysis of social support exchanges in on-line HIV/AIDS self-help groups. *Computers in Human Behavior*, 25(4):911–918, 2009.

[29] Aron Culotta. Towards detecting influenza epidemics by analyzing Twitter messages. In *KDD 1st Workshop on Social Media Analytics*, 2010.

[30] Aron Culotta. Lightweight methods to estimate influenza rates and alcohol sales volume from Twitter messages. *Language Resources and Evaluation*, 47:217–238, 2013.

[31] Ed de Quincey and Patty Kostkova. Early warning and outbreak detection using social networking websites: The potential of Twitter. In *2nd International eHealth Conference*, pages 21–24, 2009.

[32] I. Ralph Edwards and Jeffrey K. Aronson. Adverse drug reactions: Definitions, diagnosis and management. *The Lancet*, 356(9237):1255–1259, 2000.

[33] Jeremy U. Espino, William R. Hogan, and Michael M. Wagner. Telephone triage: A timely data source for surveillance of influenza-like diseases. In *Proceedings of the 2003 AMIA Annual Symposium*, pages 215–219, 2003.

[34] Stephen Eubank, Hasan Guclu, V. S. Anil Kumar, Madhav V. Marathe, Aravind Srinivasan, Zoltan Toroczkai, and Nan Wang. Modelling disease outbreaks in realistic urban social networks. *Nature*, 429(6988):180–184, 2004.

[35] Gunther Eysenbach. Infodemiology: The epidemiology of (mis)information. *The American Journal of Medicine*, 113(9):763–765, 2002.

[36] Gunther Eysenbach. Infodemiology: Tracking flu-related searches on the web for syndromic surveillance. In *Proceedings of the 2006 AMIA Annual Symposium*, pages 244–248, 2006.

[37] James H. Fowler and Nicholas A. Christakis. Dynamic spread of happiness in a large social network: Longitudinal analysis over 20 years in the Framingham heart study. *BMJ*, 337:a2338, 2008.

[38] Susannah Fox. The social life of health information. `http://www.pewinternet.org/2011/05/12/the-social-life-of-health-information-2011/`, 2011. Accessed 08-08-2014.

[39] Susannah Fox and Sydney Jones. The social life of health information. `http://www.pewinternet.org/2009/06/11/the-social-life-of-health-information/`, 2009. Accessed 08-08-2014.

[40] Clark C. Freifeld, Kenneth D. Mandl, Ben Y. Reis, and John S. Brownstein. Healthmap: Global infectious disease monitoring through automated classification and visualization of Internet media reports. *Journal of the American Medical Informatics Association*, 15(2):150–157, 2008.

[41] Carol Friedman. Discovering novel adverse drug events using natural language processing and mining of the electronic health records. In *Proceedings of the 12th Conference on Artificial Intelligence in Medicine (AIME'09)*, pages 1–5, 2009.

[42] Jeana Frost and Michael P. Massagli. Social uses of personal health information within PatientsLikeMe, an online patient community: What can happen when patients have access to one another's data. *Journal of Medical Internet Research*, 10(3):e15, 2008.

[43] Jeana Frost, Sally Okun, Timothy Vaughan, James Heywood, and Paul Wicks. Patient-reported outcomes as a source of evidence in off-label prescribing: Analysis of data from PatientsLikeMe. *Journal of Medical Internet Research*, 13(1):e6, 2011.

[44] Jim Giles. Blogs and tweets could predict the future. *The New Scientist*, 206(2675):20–21, 2010.

[45] Jeremy Ginsberg, Matthew H. Mohebbi, Rajan S. Patel, Lynnette Brammer, Mark S. Smolinski, and Larry Brilliant. Detecting influenza epidemics using search engine query data. *Nature*, 457(7232):1012–1014, 2008.

[46] Jeremy A. Greene, Niteesh Choudhry, Elaine Kilabuk, and William H. Shrank. Dissemination of health information through social networks: Twitter and antibiotics. *Journal of General Internal Medicine*, 26(3):287–292, 2011.

[47] Jenine K. Harris, Sarah Moreland-Russell, Rachel G. Tabak, Lindsay R. Ruhr, and Ryan C. Maier. Communication about childhood obesity on Twitter. *American Journal of Public Health*, 104(7):e62–e69, 2014.

[48] Carleen Hawn. Take two aspirin and tweet me in the morning: How Twitter, Facebook and other social media are reshaping health care. *Health Affairs*, 28(2):361–368, 2009.

[49] Moses Hohman, Kellan Gregory, Kelly Chibale, Peter J. Smith, Sean Ekins, and Barry Bunin. Novel web-based tools combining chemistry informatics, biology and social networks for drug discovery. *Drug Discovery Today*, 14(5-6):261–270, 2009.

[50] Anette Hulth, Gustaf Rydevik, and Annika Linde. Web queries as a source for syndromic surveillance. *PLoS ONE*, 4(2):e4378, 2009.

[51] Heather A. Johnson, Michael M. Wagner, William R. Hogan, Wendy Chapman, Robert T. Olszewski, John Dowling, and Gary Barnas. Analysis of web access logs for surveillance of influenza. In *11th World Congress on Medical Informatics (MEDINFO 2004)*, pages 1202–1206, 2004.

[52] Alex Lamb, Michael J. Paul, and Mark Dredze. Separating fact from fear: Tracking flu infections on Twitter. In *Proceedings of the Conference of the North American Chapter of the Association for Computational Linguistics: Human Language Technologies (NAACL-HLT'13)*, pages 789–795, 2013.

[53] Vasileios Lampos and Nello Cristianini. Tracking the flu pandemic by monitoring the social web. In *IAPR 2nd Workshop on Cognitive Information Processing (CIP 2010)*, 2010.

[54] A. Y. S. Lau, K. A. Siek, L. Fernandez-Luque, H. Tange, P. Chhanabhai, S. Y. Li, P. L. Elkin, A. Arjabi, L. Walczowski, C. S. Ang, and G. Eysenbach. The role of social media for patients and consumer health. contribution of the IMIA consumer health informatics working group. *Yearbook of Medical Informatics*, 6(1):131–138, 2011.

[55] Dennis D. Lenaway and Audrey Ambler. Evaluation of a school-based influenza surveillance system. *Public Health Reports*, 110(3):333–337, 1995.

[56] Jiwei Li and Claire Cardie. Early stage influenza detection from Twitter. arXiv:1309.7340v3, 2013.

[57] Steven F. Magruder. Evaluation of over-the-counter pharmaceutical sales as a possible early warning indicator of human disease. *Johns Hopkins University APL Technical Digest*, 24:349–353, 2003.

[58] Atul Nakhasi, Ralph J. Passarella, Sarah G. Bell, Michael J. Paul, Mark Dredze, and Peter Pronovost. Malpractice and malcontent: Analyzing medical complaints in Twitter. In *AAAI Fall Symposium: Information Retrieval and Knowledge Discovery in Biomedical Text*, volume FS-12-05 AAAI Technical Report, 2012.

[59] Brendan O'Connor, Ramnath Balasubramanyan, Bryan R. Routledge, and Noah A. Smith. From tweets to polls: Linking text sentiment to public opinion time series. In *Proceedings of the 4th International AAAI Conference on Weblogs and Social Media (ICWSM'10)*, pages 122–129, 2010.

[60] National Library of Medicine / National Institutes of Health. NLM technical bulletin: MLA 2006, NLM online users' meeting remarks. `http://www.nlm.nih.gov/pubs/techbull/ja06/ja06_mla_dg.html`, 2006. Accessed 04-20-2014.

[61] Michael J. Paul and Mark Dredze. A model for mining public health topics from Twitter. Technical report, Johns Hopkins University, 2011.

[62] Michael J. Paul and Mark Dredze. You are what you tweet: Analyzing Twitter for public health. In *Proceedings of the 5th International AAAI Conference on Weblogs and Social Media (ICWSM'11)*, pages 265–272, 2011.

[63] Michael J. Paul and Mark Dredze. Experimenting with drugs (and topic models): Multi-dimensional exploration of recreational drug discussions. In *AAAI Fall Symposium: Information Retrieval and Knowledge Discovery in Biomedical Text*, 2012.

[64] Michael J. Paul and Mark Dredze. Factorial LDA: Sparse multi-dimensional text models. In *Proceedings of the Conference on Nueral Information Processing Systems (NIPS'12)*, pages 2591–2599, 2012.

[65] Michael J. Paul and Mark Dredze. Drug extraction from the web: Summarizing drug experiences with multi-dimensional topic models. In *Proceedings of the Conference of the North American Chapter of the Association for Computational Linguistics: Human Language Technologies (NAACL-HLT'13)*, pages 168–178, 2013.

[66] Camille Pelat, Clement Turbelin, Avner Bar-Hen, Antoine Flahault, and Alain-Jacques Valleron. More diseases tracked by using Google trends. *Emerging Infectious Diseases*, 15(8):1327–1328, 2009.

[67] Kyle W. Prier, Matthew S. Smith, Christophe Giraud-Carrier, and Carl L. Hanson. Identifying health-related topics on Twitter: an exploration of tobacco-related tweets as a test topic. In *Proceedings of the 4th International Conference on Social Computing, Behavioral-Cultural Modeling and Prediction (SBP'11)*, pages 18–25, 2011.

[68] Joshua Ritterman, Miles Osborne, and Ewan Klein. Using prediction markets and Twitter to predict a swine flu pandemic. In *1st International Workshop on Mining Social Analytics*, 2010.

[69] J. Niels Rosenquist, James H. Fowler, and Nicholas A. Christakis. Social network determinants of depression. *Molecular Psychiatry*, 16:273–281, 2011.

[70] J. Niels Rosenquist, Joanne Murabito, James H. Fowler, and Nicholas A. Christakis. The spread of alcohol consumption behavior in a large social network. *Annals of Internal Medicine*, 152(7):426–433, 2010.

[71] Adam Sadilek and Henry Kautz. Modeling the impact of lifestyle on health at scale. In *Proceedings of the 6th ACM International Conference on Web Search and Data Mining (WSDM'13)*, pages 637–646, 2013.

[72] Adam Sadilek, Henry Kautz, and Vincent Silenzio. Modeling spread of disease from social interactions. In *Proceedings of the 6th International AAAI Conference on Weblogs and Social Media (ICWSM'12)*, pages 322–329, 2012.

[73] Adam Sadilek, Henry Kautz, and Vincent Silenzio. Predicting disease transmission from geo-tagged micro-blog data. In *Proceedings of the 26th AAAI Conference on Artificial Intelligence (AAAI'12)*, pages 136–142, 2012.

[74] Takeshi Sakaki, Makoto Okazaki, and Yutaka Matsuo. Earthquake shakes Twitter users: Real-time event detection by social sensors. In *Proceedings of the 19th International Conference on World Wide Web (WWW'10)*, pages 851–860, 2010.

[75] Marcel Salathé and Shashank Khandelwal. Assessing vaccination sentiments with online social media: Implications for infectious disease dynamics and control. *PLoS Computational Biology*, 7(10):e1002199, 2011.

[76] Daniel Scanfeld, Vanessa Scanfeld, and Elaine L. Larson. Dissemination of health information through social networks: Twitter and antibiotics. *American Journal of Infection Control*, 38(3):182–188, 2010.

[77] Peri L. Schuyler, William T. Hole, Mark S. Tuttle, and David D. Sherertz. The UMLS metathesaurus: Representing different views of biomedical concepts. *Bulletin of the Medical Library Association*, 81(2):217–222, 1993.

[78] H. Andrew Schwartz, Johannes C. Eichstaedt, Lukasz Dziurzynski, Margaret L. Kern, Martin E. P. Seligman, Lyle Ungar, Eduardo Blanco, Michal Kosinski, and David Stillwell. Toward personality insights from language exploration in social media. In *Proceedings of the 7th International AAAI Conference on Weblogs and Social Media (ICWSM'13)*, pages 72–79, 2013.

[79] H. Andrew Schwartz, Johannes C. Eichstaedt, Margaret L. Kern, Lukasz Dziurzynski, Megha Agrawal, Gregory J. Park, Shrinidhi Lakshmikanth, Sneha Jha, Martin E. P. Seligman, Lyle Ungar, and Richard E. Lucas. Characterizing geographic variation in well-being using tweets. In *Proceedings of the 7th International AAAI Conference on Weblogs and Social Media (ICWSM'13)*, pages 583–591, 2013.

[80] Ari Seifter, Alison Schwarzwalder, Kate Geis, and John Aucott. The utility of Google trends for epidemiological research: Lyme disease as an example. *Geospatial Health*, 4(2):135–137, 2010.

[81] Peter Selby, Trevor van Mierlo, Sabrina C. Voci, Danielle Parent, and John A. Cunningham. Online social and professional support for smokers trying to quit: An exploration of first time posts from 2562 members. *Journal of Medical Internet Research*, 12(3):e34, 2010.

[82] Martin E. P. Seligman. *Flourish: A Visionary New Understanding of Happiness and Well-being*. Free Press, 2011.

[83] Alessio Signorini, Alberto Maria Segre, and Philip M. Polgreen. The use of Twitter to track levels of disease activity and public concerns in the U.S. during the influenza a H1N1 pandemic. *PLoS ONE*, 6(5):e19467, 2011.

[84] Vincent Michael Bernard Silenzio, Paul R. Duberstein, Xin Tu, Wan Tang, Naiji Lu, and Christopher M. Homan. Connecting the invisible dots: Network-based methods to reach a hidden population at risk for suicide. *Social Science and Medicine*, 69(3):469–474, 2009.

[85] Christof Specker, Jutta Richter, Ayako Take, Oliver Sangha, and Matthias Schneider. Rheumanet—a novel Internet-based rheumatology information network in Germany. *British Journal of Rheumatology*, 37(9):1015–1019, 1998.

[86] Donna F. Stroup, Stephen B. Thacker, and Joy L. Herndon. Application of multiple time series analysis to the estimation of pneumonia and influenza mortality by age 1962–1983. *Statistics in Medicine*, 7(10):1045–1059, 1988.

[87] Yla R. Tauszik and James W. Pennebaker. The psychological meaning of words: LIWC and computerized text analysis methods. *Journal of Language and Social Psychology*, 29(1):24–54, 2010.

[88] Karl Vance, William Howe, and Robert Dellavalle. Social Internet sites as a source of public health information. *Dermatologic Clinics*, 27(2):133–136, 2009.

[89] Melissa L. Verhaag. Social media and healthcare—hype or future? Master's thesis, University of Twente, 2014.

[90] Paul Wicks and Graeme J. A. MacPhee. Pathological gambling amongst Parkinson's disease and ALS patients in an online community (patientslikeme.com). *Movement Disorders*, 24(7):1085–1088, 2009.

[91] Paul Wicks, Timothy E. Vaughan, Michael P. Massagli, and James Heywood. Accelerated clinical discovery using self-reported patient data collected online and a patient-matching algorithm. *Nature Biotechnology*, 29:411–414, 2009.

[92] Haodong Yang and Christopher C. Yang. Harnessing social media for drug-drug interactions detection. In *Proceedings of the 2013 IEEE International Conference on Healthcare Informatics*, pages 22–29, 2013.

Part II

Advanced Data Analytics for Healthcare

Chapter 10

A Review of Clinical Prediction Models

Chandan K. Reddy
Department of Computer Science
Wayne State University
Detroit, MI
reddy@cs.wayne.edu

Yan Li
Department of Computer Science
Wayne State University
Detroit, MI
rock_liyan@wayne.edu

10.1 Introduction

Clinical prediction is one of the most important branches of healthcare data analytics. In this chapter, we will provide a relatively comprehensive review of the supervised learning methods that have been employed successfully for clinical prediction tasks. Some of these methods such as linear regression, logistic regression, and Bayesian models are basic and widely investigated in the statistics literature. More sophisticated methods in machine learning and data mining literature such as decision trees and artificial neural networks have also been successfully used in clinical applications. In addition, survival models in statistics that try to predict the time of occurrence of a particular event of interest have also been widely used in clinical data analysis.

Generally, supervised learning methods can be broadly classified into two categories: classification and regression. Both of these two classes of techniques focus on discovering the underlying relationship between covariate variables, which are also known as attributes and features, and a dependent variable (outcome). The main difference between these two approaches is that a classification model generates class labels while a regression model predicts real-valued outcomes. The choice of the model to be used for a particular application significantly depends on the outcomes to be predicted. These outcomes can fall into one of the five different categories: continuous outcomes, binary outcomes, categorical outcomes, ordinal outcomes, and survival outcomes.

The continuous outcomes can be seen in applications such as medical costs prediction [1, 2] and the estimation of some medical inspection [3]; linear regression and generalized additive models have been successfully employed for solving these kinds of problems. Binary outcomes are the most common outcomes in clinical prediction models; disease diagnostic [4], prediction of the patient's death or risk [5], and medical image segmentation [6] are some of the commonly studied binary classification problems in clinical medicine. Several statistical and machine learning methods such as logistic regression, binary classification trees, and Bayesian models have been designed to solve this binary classification problem.

Categorical outcomes are typically generated by multiclass classification problems, and usually there is no specific ordering among those classes. In the healthcare domain, categorical outcomes always appears in multiple disease diagnostics such as cancer [7] and tumor [8] classification. In clinical prediction, models such as polytomous logistic regression [9] and some ensemble approaches

[7, 10] are used to estimate the categorical outcomes. Ordinal outcomes are also quite common in clinical prediction and in several cases it is to predict the grade/severity of illness [11]. Finally, survival outcomes are particularly used for studying survival analysis that aims at analyzing the time to event data and the goal here is to predict the time to event of interest.

In this chapter we will provide more details about all these models and their applications in clinical medicine. In addition, we will also discuss different ways to evaluate such models in practice. The remainder of this chapter is organized as follows: In Section 10.2, we review some statistical prediction models. Some machine learning methods are introduced in Section 10.3, and the survival models are discussed in Section 10.4. We also provide some model evaluation and validation methods in Section 10.5, and finally, Section 10.6 concludes this chapter.

10.2 Basic Statistical Prediction Models

In this section, we review some of the well-known basic statistical models that are widely used in biomedical and clinical domains.

10.2.1 Linear Regression

In linear regression the dependent variable or outcome is assumed to be a linear combination of the attributes with corresponding estimated regression parameters [12]. In clinical data analysis, linear regression is often employed in clinical cost prediction [1, 2] and the estimation of some medical inspection [3]. Let us consider a sample of N subjects with p attributes, which can be represented as a $N \times p$ matrix X, and the observed output is a vector $Y^T = (y_1, y_2, ..., y_N)$. For a particular individual i, let $X_i = (x_{i1}, x_{i2}, ..., x_{ip})$ denote the covariate vector, and the output is a continuous real number denoted by Y_i. The linear regression model can be mathematically expressed as:

$$\hat{y}_i = \alpha + \sum_{j=1}^{p} x_{ij}\beta_j, \tag{10.1}$$

where $\beta^T = (\beta_1, \beta_2, ..., \beta_p)$ is the coefficient vector, α is the intercept, and $\hat{y}_i$ is the estimated output based on the linear regression model. It should be noted that all the input covariate values should be numeric; otherwise, the addition and multiplication computation of the covariate values is not feasible. In supervised learning, parameter estimation can be viewed as the minimization of a loss function over a training dataset. *Least squares* is the most commonly used coefficient estimation method in linear regression; the chosen loss function is the *residual sum of squares*, which is defined as the squared Euclidean distance between the observed output vector Y and the estimated output, $\hat{Y}$. It has the form

$$\begin{aligned} RSS(\beta) &= \sum_{i=1}^{N}(y_i - \hat{y}_i)^2 \qquad (10.2) \\ &= \sum_{i=1}^{N}(y_i - \alpha + \sum_{j=1}^{p} x_{ij}\beta_j)^2. \end{aligned}$$

It can be seen that the $RSS(\beta)$ is a quadratic equation in terms of β, and the minimization can be calculated by setting the first derivative of the $RSS(\beta)$ equal to 0. For convenience, the $RSS(\beta)$ can be rewritten in the matrix representation

$$RSS(\beta) = (Y - X\beta)^T(Y - X\beta). \tag{10.3}$$

It should be noticed that the X here is different from the definition above; here it is an $N \times (p+1)$ matrix where a unit column vector is added to the left of the original input matrix X, and correspondingly, the coefficient vector is $\beta^T = (\alpha, \beta_1, \beta_2, ..., \beta_p)$. The partial derivative of the $RSS(\beta)$ is

$$\frac{\partial RSS}{\partial \beta} = -2X^T Y + 2(X^T X)\beta, \tag{10.4}$$

By letting Equation 10.4 equal 0 we will get the estimated parameter to be

$$\hat{\beta} = (X^T X)^{-1} X^T Y. \tag{10.5}$$

For computational efficiency, usually the input covariant matrix X is normalized during preprocessing, hence $X^T X = \mathbf{1}$ and the estimated coefficient vector can be simplified as $\hat{\beta} = X^T Y$.

10.2.2 Generalized Additive Model

To model the continuous outcomes in regression, the popular choice is to use the generalized additive model (GAM) [13], which is a linear combination of smooth functions. It can be viewed as a variant of linear regression that can handle nonlinear distribution. In GAM, for individual X_i, the continuous outcome y_i can be estimated by:

$$\hat{y}_i = \alpha + f_1(x_{i1}) + f_2(x_{i2}) + \cdots + f_p(x_{ip}), \tag{10.6}$$

where $f_i(\cdot)$, $i = 1, 2, ..., p$ is a set of smooth functions, and p is the number of features.

Initially, the GAM was learned using the backfitting algorithm that was introduced in 1985 by Leo Breiman and Jerome Friedman [14]. It is an iterative method that can handle a wide variety of smooth functions; however, the termination criterion of the iterations is difficult to choose, and it almost always suffers from overfitting. An alternative method of GAM estimation is using the semi-parametric smoothing function and fit the model by penalized regression splines. More details about these models can be found in [15].

10.2.3 Logistic Regression

Logistic Regression is one of the most popular binary classification methods which is widely adopted for clinical prediction tasks [4, 16, 17]. Rather than directly predicting the output via a linear combination of features, it assumes that there is a linear relationship between the features and the log-odds of the probabilities. For simplicity, let us consider a two-class scenario with N-samples. For a certain individual $X_i = (x_{i0}, x_{i1}, x_{i2}, ..., x_{ip})$, the observed output y_i can be labeled as either 0 or 1; the formulation of the logistic regression is

$$log \frac{Pr(y_i = 1|X_i)}{Pr(y_i = 0|X_i)} = \sum_{k=0}^{p} x_{ik}\beta_k = X_i\beta. \tag{10.7}$$

Here, $x_{i0} = 1$ and β_0 is the intercept. Consider the fact that in a two-class classification $Pr(y_i = 1|X_i) + Pr(y_i = 0|X_i) = 1$; thus, from Equation (10.7), we have

$$Pr(y_i = 1|X_i) = \frac{exp(X_i\beta)}{1 + exp(X_i\beta)}. \tag{10.8}$$

The parameter estimation in logistic regression models is usually done by maximizing the likelihood function. The joint conditional probability of all N samples in the training data is

$$Pr(y = y_1|X_1) \cdot Pr(y = y_2|X_2) \cdot \ ... \ \cdot Pr(y = y_N|X_N) = \prod_{i=1}^{N} Pr(y = y_i|X_i), \tag{10.9}$$

where $y_i, i = 1, 2, ..., N$ is the actual observed labels in the training set; therefore, the log-likelihood for N observations is

$$\mathfrak{L}(\beta) = \sum_{i=1}^{N} \log[Pr(y = y_i|X_i)], \tag{10.10}$$

note that in the "$(0, 1)$ scenario," the logit transformation of conditional probability for an individual X_i is

$$\log[Pr(y = y_i|X_i)] = \begin{cases} X_i\beta - \log[1 + exp(X_i\beta)] & : \ y_i = 1 \\ -\log[1 + exp(X_i\beta)] & : \ y_i = 0 \end{cases}, \tag{10.11}$$

thus, Equation (10.10) can be rewritten as:

$$\mathfrak{L}(\beta) = \sum_{i=1}^{N} \{X_i\beta \cdot y_i - \log[1 + exp(X_i\beta)]\}. \tag{10.12}$$

Usually the Newton-Raphson algorithm is used to maximize this log-likelihood, where the coefficient vector is iteratively updated based on

$$\beta^{(t+1)} = \beta^{(t)} - \left[\frac{\partial^2 \mathfrak{L}(\beta)}{\partial\beta\partial\beta^T}\right]^{-1} \frac{\partial \mathfrak{L}(\beta)}{\partial\beta}, \tag{10.13}$$

where

$$\frac{\partial \mathfrak{L}(\beta)}{\partial\beta} = \sum_{i=1}^{N} X_i(y_i - \frac{exp(X_i\beta)}{1 + exp(X_i\beta)}) \tag{10.14}$$

$$\frac{\partial^2 \mathfrak{L}(\beta)}{\partial\beta\partial\beta^T} = -\sum_{i=1}^{N} X_i X_i^T \frac{exp(X_i\beta)}{[1 + exp(X_i\beta)]^2}. \tag{10.15}$$

The iteration always starts at $\beta = 0$. It is proven that the algorithm can guarantee the convergence towards the global optimum, but overshooting can occur.

10.2.3.1 Multiclass Logistic Regression

In multiclass logistic regression [18], conditional on one specific individual X_i, the probability that its observed output $y_i = j$ is

$$Pr(y_i = j|X_i) = \frac{exp(X_i\beta_j)}{\sum_{k \neq j} exp(X_i\beta_k)}, \tag{10.16}$$

where $j, k \in L$ and L is the label set. With this definition, the log-likelihood for N observations can be written as:

$$\mathfrak{L}(\beta) = \sum_{i=1}^{N} [(X_i\beta_j) - \log(\sum_{k \neq j} exp(X_i\beta_k))]. \tag{10.17}$$

This objective function can be minimized by the Broyden–Fletcher–Goldfarb–Shanno (BFGS) algorithm [19]. The BFGS is a kind of hill-climbing optimization technique [20], which solves the nonlinear optimization by iteratively updating the approximation to the Hessian using information gleaned from the gradient vector at each step [18].

10.2.3.2 Polytomous Logistic Regression

Polytomous logistic regression [21, 22] is an extension of the basic logistic regression, which is designed to handle multiclass problems. Polytomous logistic regression is used when there is no predefined order among the categories; in clinical analysis it has been used to deal with some complex datasets such as CT scans [9]. It learns different set of coefficients for different classes, in other words, each feature has a different coefficient value for each category; in addition, it also assumes that the output cannot be perfectly estimated by the covariate for any single class. It can be viewed as a simple combination of the standard two-class logistic regression. For a C-class problem, $C-1$ binary logistic regression will be fitted; for example, if we set the last category (C^{th} class) as the reference category, then the model will be:

$$\begin{aligned} \log \frac{Pr(y=1|X_i)}{Pr(y=C|X_i)} &= X_i\beta_1 \\ \log \frac{Pr(y=2|X_i)}{Pr(y=C|X_i)} &= X_i\beta_2 \\ &\vdots \\ \log \frac{Pr(y=C-1|X_i)}{Pr(y=C|X_i)} &= X_i\beta_{C-1}. \end{aligned} \tag{10.18}$$

Note that for individual X_i the sum of all the posterior probabilities of all C categories should be 1; thus, for each possible outcome we get:

$$\begin{aligned} Pr(y=k|X_i) &= \frac{exp(X_i\beta_k)}{1+\sum_{j=1}^{C-1} exp(X_i\beta_j)}, \; k=1,2,...,C-1 \\ Pr(y=C|X_i) &= \frac{1}{1+\sum_{j=1}^{C-1} exp(X_i\beta_j)}. \end{aligned} \tag{10.19}$$

The model can then be learned by maximum a posteriori (MAP). More details about the learning procedure can be found in [23].

10.2.3.3 Ordered Logistic Regression

Ordered logistic regression (or ordered logit) is an extension of the logistic regression that aims to solve an ordered output prediction. Here we will briefly introduce the two most popular logit models: proportional odds logistic regression and generalized ordered logit.

Proportional odds logistic regression Proportional odds logistic regression [24] was proposed based on the basic assumption that all the differences between different categories are introduced by different intercepts, while the regression coefficients among all levels are the same. In [25], proportional odds logistic regression was employed in the meta-analyses to deal with an increasing diversity of diseases and conditions. Consider a C-ordered output example; for an individual X_i the proportional odds logistic regression can be represented as:

$$logit[Pr(y \le j|X_i)] = \log \frac{Pr(y \le j|X_i)}{1-Pr(y \le j|X_i)} = \alpha_j - X_i\beta, \tag{10.20}$$

where $j = 1,2,...,C$, and $\alpha_1 < \alpha_2 < \cdots < \alpha_{C-1}$. The other thing to note is that the coefficient vector β here is a $P \times 1$ vector, where P is the number of features and $X_i = (x_{i1}, x_{i2}, ..., x_{iP})$. Apparently, this is a highly efficient model, and only one set of regression parameters has to be learned during the training process; however, this assumption is too restricted and thus is not applicable to a wide range of problems.

Generalized ordered logit The generalized ordered logit (gologit) [26] can be mathematically defined as:

$$Pr(y_i > j|X_i) = \frac{exp(X_i\beta_j)}{1+exp(X_i\beta_j)} = g(X_i\beta_j), \; j=1,2,...,C-1, \tag{10.21}$$

where C is the number of ordinal categories. From the Equation (10.21), the posterior probabilities that Y will take on each of the values $1,...,C$, conditional on X_i, are equal to

$$Pr(y_i = j|X_i) = \begin{cases} 1 - g(X_i\beta_1) & : \ j = 1 \\ g(X_i\beta_{j-1}) - g(X_i\beta_j) & : \ j = 2,...,C-1 \\ g(X_i\beta_{C-1}) & : \ j = C \end{cases}. \tag{10.22}$$

A popular Stata program "gologit2" [27] can be used to efficiently fit this model.

10.2.4 Bayesian Models

The Bayes theorem is one of the most important principles in probability theory and mathematical statistics; it provides a link between the *posterior probability* and the *prior probability*, so we can see the probability changes before and after accounting for a certain random event. The formulation of the Bayes theorem is

$$Pr(Y|X) = \frac{Pr(X|Y) \cdot Pr(Y)}{Pr(X)}, \tag{10.23}$$

where $Pr(Y|X)$ is the probability of event Y, conditional upon event X. Based on this theory, there are two widely used implementations: naïve Bayes and the Bayesian network. Both of these approaches are commonly studied in the context of clinical prediction [28, 29].

10.2.4.1 Naïve Bayes Classifier

The main intuition of the Bayesian classifiers is comparing $Pr(Y = y|X_i)$ for different $y \in Y$ where Y is the label set and choosing the most possible label (y_{chosen}) as the estimated label for individual $X_i = (x_{i1}, x_{i2}, ..., x_{ip})$. From Equation (10.23), we can see that, in order to calculate $Pr(Y = y|X_i)$ we need to know $Pr(X_i|Y = y)$, $Pr(Y = y)$, and $Pr(X_i)$. Among these three terms, $Pr(Y = y)$ can be easily estimated from the training dataset; $Pr(X_i)$ can be ignored because while comparing different y's; the denominator in the Equation (10.23) remains a constant. Thus, the main work in Bayesian classifiers is to choose the proper method to estimate $Pr(X_i|Y = y)$.

In naïve Bayes classifier, the elements in the covariate vector $(x_{i1}, x_{i2}, ..., x_{ip})$ of X_i are assumed to be conditionally independent; therefore, the $Pr(X_i|Y = y)$ can be calculated as:

$$Pr(X_i|Y = y) = \prod_{k=1}^{p} Pr(x_{ik}|Y = y), \tag{10.24}$$

where each $Pr(x_{ik}|Y = y)$, $k = 1, 2, ..., p$ can be separately estimated from the given training set. Thus, to classify a test record X_i based on the Bayes theorem and ignore the $Pr(X_i)$, the conditional probability for each possible output y in the label set Y can be represented as:

$$Pr(Y = y|X_i) \propto Pr(Y = y) \prod_{k=1}^{p} Pr(x_{ik}|Y = y). \tag{10.25}$$

Finally, the class label y_{chosen}, which maximizes the $Pr(Y = y)\prod_{k=1}^{p} Pr(x_{ik}|Y = y)$ is chosen to be the output.

10.2.4.2 Bayesian Network

Although the naïve Bayes classifier is a straightforward implementation of Bayesian classifier, in most real-word scenarios there are certain relationships that exist among the attributes. A Bayesian network introduces a *directed acyclic graph* (DAG), which represent a set of random variables by nodes and their dependency relationships by edges. Each node is associated with a probability function that gives the probability of the current node conditional on its parent nodes' probability. If the node does not have any parents, then the probability function will be the prior probability of the current node.

More specifically, in decision making or prediction problems, this Bayesian network can be viewed in terms of a hierarchical structure. Only the independent attributes that have prior probability are in the top level. For example, in Figure 10.1, there are 5 attributes that contribute to the output; among them "Smoking (Attribute 3)" and "Family history of heart disease (Attribute 5)" do not have any predecessors, so we can compute the prior probabilities $Pr(\text{Smoking})$ and $Pr(\text{Family history of heart disease})$ directly; "Aortic rupture (Attribute 1)" and "Hypertension (Attribute 4)" are in the second level, and their conditional probabilities are $Pr(\text{Aortic rupture}|\text{Smoking})$ and $Pr(\text{Hypertension}|\text{Smoking})$ respectively; "Stroke (Attribute 2)" is in the third level and its conditional probability is $Pr(\text{Stroke}|\text{Aortic rupture, Smoking, Hypertension})$. "Heart rate (Attribute 6)" and "Blood pressure (Attribute 7)" are two medical observations, and "Heart attacks" is the disease that needs to be predicted.

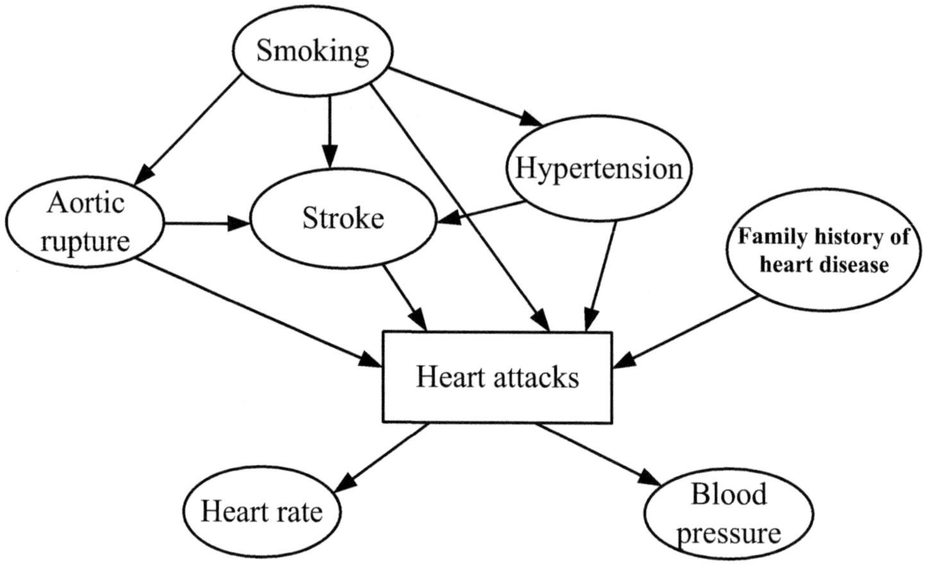

FIGURE 10.1: An example of a Bayesian network for decision making.

Based on this network, the joint probability function is computed as follows:

$$\begin{aligned} Pr(\text{Heart attacks}, 1,2,3,4,5,6,7) &= Pr(6|\text{Heart attacks}) \cdot Pr(7|\text{Heart attacks}) \\ &\cdot Pr(\text{Heart attacks}|1,2,3,4,5) \cdot Pr(2|1,3,4) \\ &\cdot Pr(1|3) \cdot Pr(4|3) \cdot Pr(3) \cdot Pr(5) \end{aligned} \tag{10.26}$$

Based on Equation(10.26), the $Pr(\text{Heart attacks}|1,2,3,4,5)$ for each kind of output can be calculated conditional on a specific combination of 5 different attributes.

10.2.5 Markov Random Fields

In the Bayesian network, the nodes are connected based on causality; however, in real-world applications, causality is not the only relationship. For example, in clinical inspection, although there is no causality between the quantity of blood leukocytes and the image of an X-ray, these two are correlated. It is awkward to represent the dataset by a directed acyclic graph in this scenario; thus, an undirected graphical model, which is also known as a *Markov random field* (MRF) or a *Markov network*, is needed. In the healthcare domain, Markov random fields were often adopted in medical image analyses such as magnetic resonance images [30] and digital mammography [31].

Given an undirected graph $G = (V,E)$, where V is the set of vertices and E is the set of edges; each vertex $v \in V$ represents a covariate vector X_v. In MRF, the conditional independence relationship is defined via the topology of the undirected graphical model. In total there are three categories of Markov properties: *global Markov property*, *local Markov property*, and *pairwise Markov property*. The global Markov property is defined as: $X_A \perp X_B | X_C$, where $A \subset V$, $B \subset V$, and $C \subset V$; that is, in the graph G, subset A and B are conditionally independent of the separating subset C; in other words, every path from a node in A to a node in B passes through C. From the global Markov property we can easily deduce that for a certain node (X_v, $v \in V$) all its neighbors ($X_{ne(v)}$, $ne(v) \subset V$) will separate the node from the nodes in the rest of graph G; this is called the local Markov property and can be represented as $X_v \perp X_{rest} | X_{ne(v)}$. It is obvious that two nonadjacent nodes, X_v and X_u, are conditionally independent of all the nodes in the rest of the graph, which is known as the pairwise Markov property, and can be mathematically represented as: $X_v \perp X_u | X_{rest}$.

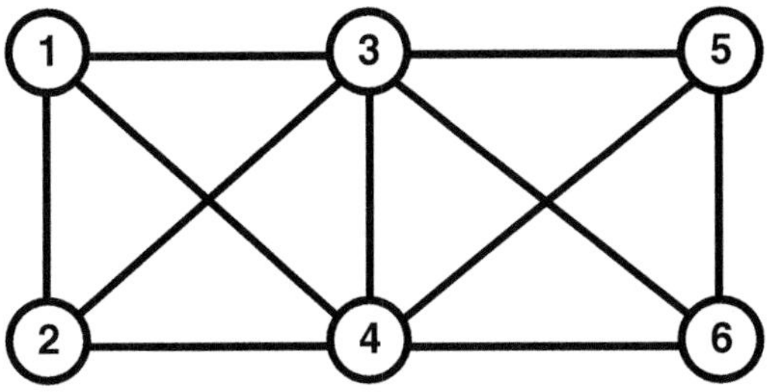

FIGURE 10.2: An example of an undirected graph.

In order to describe the Markov properties more intuitively, let us illustrate these conditional independence relations based on Figure 10.2.

1. **Global Markov property**, $\{1,2\} \perp \{5,6\} | \{3,4\}$.
2. **Local Markov property**, $\{1\} \perp \{5,6\} | \{2,3,4\}$.
3. **Pairwise Markov property**, $\{1\} \perp \{6\} | \{2,3,4,5\}$.

10.3 Alternative Clinical Prediction Models

In addition to the basic prediction models explained in the previous section, more recent developments in the machine learning and data mining literature allowed the biomedical researchers to apply other prediction models in clinical applications. These models include decision trees, artificial neural networks. While there are many other traditional prediction models that have been used in certain specific biomedical application, a complete discussion about the prediction models and their applications is out of scope of this chapter. We focus on the most widely used prediction models in this section. In addition, an important concept of cost-sensitive learning in the context of prediction which was motivated through some of the important biomedical problems will also be discussed in this section. In addition to these models and algorithm, more advanced clinical prediction methods such as multiple instance learning, reinforcement learning, sparse models, and kernel methods will also be discussed in this section.

10.3.1 Decision Trees

A decision tree is the most widely used clinical prediction model that has been successfully used in practice [32]. In a decision tree model, the predictions are made by asking a series of well-designed questions (splitting criteria) about a test record; based on the answers to these questions the test record hierarchically falls into a smaller subgroup where the contained individuals are similar to each other with respect to the predicted outcome. Choosing the proper splitting criteria, obviously, is a critical component for decision tree building. These criteria can help to find the locally optimum decisions that can minimize the within-node homogeneity or maximize the between-node heterogeneity in the current situation. In *C*4.5 [33] and *ID*3 [34], *information entropy* is used to determine the best splits, and multiple child nodes can be generated. In classification and regression tree (CART) [35], which can only produce binary splits, the best split is selected where the *gini* is minimized. The CHi-squared Automatic Interaction Detection (CHAID) [36] uses the statistical *Chi-square test* as its splitting criterion. Usually the tree is built by recursively choosing the best attribute to split the data to new subsets until meeting the termination criteria, which are designed to prevent *overfitting*.

Compared with other methods, a decision tree is more straightforward and can represent the actual human thinking process. Different from parametric methods, such as linear regression and logistic regression, constructing a decision tree does not require knowledge of the underlying distribution. In addition, a decision tree is very convenient for handling all kinds of data types for the input data. However, as finding an optimal decision tree is an NP-complete problem, usually a tree induction algorithm is a heuristic-based approach that makes the decision tree very unstable [37]. Decision trees have been heavily used in the medical decision making in a wide range of applications [38, 39].

10.3.2 Artificial Neural Networks

Inspired by biological neural systems, in 1958, Frank Rosenblatt published the first paper [40] about the artificial neural network (ANN), in which simple artificial nodes, called "neurons," are combined via a weighted link to form a network that simulates a biological neural network. A neuron is a computing element that consists of sets of adaptive weights and generates the output based on a certain kind of *activation function*. A simple artificial neural network named *perceptron* only has input and output layers. For a specific input attribute vector X_i the perception model can be written as: $\hat{y}_i = sign(X_i W)$ where $X_i = (x_{i0}, x_{i1}, ..., x_{ip})$ is the input attribute vector, W is the coefficient vector, and the sign function $sign(\cdot)$ is the activation function. We can see that this formulation is very similar to linear regression; however, here the model is fitted using an iterative algorithm that updates the weights using the following update rule: $w_j^{(t+1)} = w_j^{(t)} + \lambda(y_i - \hat{y}_i^{(t)})x_{ij}$ where λ is a parameter known as the *learning rate*.

General artificial neural networks are much more complex than the perceptron; they may consist of one or more intermediary layers, which are known as *hidden layers* and have multiple output. In addition, diverse mapping functions, such as the linear, logistic, and tanh function, can be chosen as the activation function. Therefore, a multilayer artificial neural network is capable of handling more complex nonlinear relationships between the input and output. An example of a multilayer artificial neural network is shown in Figure 10.3.

In ANN learning the commonly used cost function to minimize is the *mean-squared error*, which is the average squared difference between the estimated output and the real one. Because of

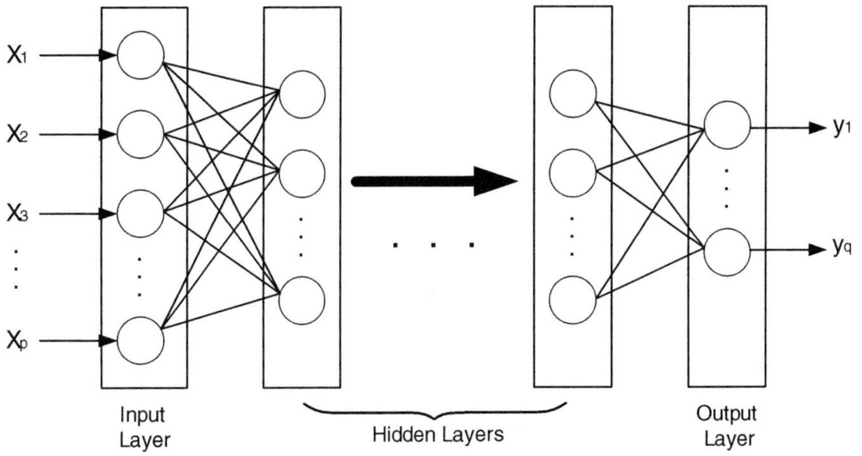

FIGURE 10.3: Example of a multilayer artificial neural network (ANN).

the complexity of finding the global minimum, the *gradient descent*, which finds a local minimum of a function, is involved in minimizing the cost function. As the hidden nodes do not influence the cost function directly, without the oupput information we can not identify its influence; thus, the common and well-known *backpropagation* technique is used for training neural networks. Due to their ability to model the complex mapping function and the rich literature in the machine learning community, the artificial neural networks have been widely used in various biomedical applications [41, 42]. Some of the prominent applications include decision support systems [43], medical intervention [44], and medical decision making [45]. A more detailed comparison of the performance of ANN with logistic regression is provided in this paper [16].

10.3.3 Cost-Sensitive Learning

A somewhat related concept that is extremely popular in the healthcare domain is the topic of *cost-sensitive learning*. Certain clinical prediction models [46] also can be viewed as cost-sensitive models. In the predictive model the learning process aims to minimize the sum of the total costs. Among different types of costs [47], computation cost and the cost of instability are two vital factors that need to be considered while designing various algorithms. In this section we only focus on two categories of cost that are widely used in the biomedical domain, namely, misclassification costs and test costs.

Misclassification cost is introduced by classification error. In the real world, the cost associated with each error is different, and for a certain error its costs change under different circumstances. For instance, in disease diagnosis there are two possible errors: the false negative error (a patient is wrongly predicted to be healthy) and the false positive error (a healthy person is wrongly predicted to be a patient). Obviously, in this scenario, compared with the false positive error, the false negative error is an even greater mistake because this places the patient in a very dangerous situation.

Some profound studies about the misclassification cost have been done in the literature [48, 49], and the basic idea of these works can be mathematically generalized as follows. Let L be the labelset, $a \in L$ is the actual label of a certain individual, and $p \in L$ is the predicted label; for each combination of a and p there is an element c_{ap} in the cost matrix C to represent the misclassification cost. Let us consider a set of N subjects. For each individual x_i, $i = 1, 2, ..., N$, the actual label is $y_i = a$, and $Pr(p|x_i, a)$ is the estimated probability that x_i belongs to the class p. Thus, for misclassification cost the cost-sensitive learning aims to minimize the following function $\min \sum_{i=1}^{N} \sum_{p \in L} Pr(p|x_i, a) c_{ap}$. In a two-class scenario, the cost matrix C is structured as in Table 10.1 below:

TABLE 10.1: Cost Matrix for the Two-Class Case

	Predict positive	Predict negative
Actual positive	c_{11}	c_{10}
Actual negative	c_{01}	c_{00}

The cost matrix can be used either during the learning process, such as re-selecting the threshold [49] and changing the splitting criteria during the tree induction [50], or after the learning phase during the performance evaluation of the model step [51] where we will just multiply the corresponding elements from the cost matrix and confusion matrix [51] and then calculate the sum of these products. This concept of learning in a cost-sensitive manner is very much related to the problem of imbalanced learning, which is heavily investigated in the biomedical literature [52]. Here the class with minority samples will be assigned a large misclassification cost.

Test cost or *the cost of obtaining the information* is incurred while obtaining the attribute values. For example, in disease diagnosis, a patient already had the X-ray test but did not have the nuclear magnetic resonance (NMR) test yet. Of course, a prediction can be made within the current information, but the NMR test will provide more information and may improve the performance of the predictive model. Thus, we have to make a trade-off between the costs and benefits of nuclear magnetic resonance. This test-cost sensitive learning is kind of a feature selection to factor into the cost of each attribute [53].

10.3.4 Advanced Prediction Models

More recent advances in the machine learning literature allowed the clinical researchers to apply complex prediction models to achieve better accuracy in nontrivial situations. Some examples of these methods include multiple instance learning, reinforcement learning, sparse methods, and kernel methods. We will now briefly discuss these approaches in this section.

10.3.4.1 Multiple Instance Learning

Unlike other prediction methods, in multiple instance learning [54], the exact label of each individual is actually unknown. Instead, the training data are packed into a set of labeled groups. A group is labeled positive if there is at least one positive instance in it; whereas, a group is labeled negative only when all the individuals in that group are negative. Multiple instance learning is often applied in diverse fields such as image classification, text mining, and the analysis of molecular activity. In clinical fields it is usually used to analyze radiology images especially when there are several hundreds of image slices for each patient. These slices are highly correlated and a patient is termed as having cancer even if a single image slice has a suspicious mass. In [55], researchers have successfully deployed the multiple instance learning algorithm based on convex hulls into practical computer-aided diagnostic tools to detect pulmonary embolism and colorectal cancer. In another study [56], for CT pulmonary angiography, multiple instance learning has been employed to detect pulmonary emboli.

10.3.4.2 Reinforcement Learning

Reinforcement learning aims to maximize the long-term rewards; it is particularly well suited to problems that include a long-term versus short-term reward trade-off [57]. In reinforcement learning, an action corresponds to any decision an agent might need to learn how to make, and a state is any factor that the agent might take into consideration in making that decision; in addition, associated with some states and state-action pairs, the rewards function is the objective feedback from the environment. The policy function is often a stochastic function that maps the possible states to the possible actions, and the value function reflects the long-term reward. Zhao et al. [58] used reinforcement learning to discover individualized treatment regimens. An optimal policy is learned from a single training set of longitudinal patient trajectories. Sahba et al. [59] proposed a reinforcement learning framework for medical image segmentation. In medical computer-aided detection (CAD) systems reinforcement learning could be used to incorporate the knowledge gained from new patients into old models.

10.3.4.3 Sparse Methods

Sparse methods perform feature selection by inducing the model coefficient vector to be sparse, in other words, contain many zero terms. The primary motivation for using sparse methods is that in high dimensions, it is wise to proceed under the assumption that most of the attributes are not significant, and it can be used to identify the the most important features [60]. Sparse methods can also be used to select a subset of features to prevent overfitting in the scenarios when $N \leq P$, where N is the number of training samples, and P is the dimension of feature space. An excellent survey on sparsity inducing norms and their utility in biomedical data analysis and prediction problems is available in [61]. With the availability of several high-dimensional genomic and clinical datasets in recent times, sparse methods have gained a lot of popularity in biomedical applications. Methods such as LASSO and Elastic Net are popular choices for penalty functions.

10.3.4.4 Kernel Methods

Kernel methods map the attributes from the original feature space to an abstract space where it is often much easier to distinguish multiple classes [62]. Kernel methods typically achieve a better performance by projecting the data into a higher-dimensional kernel space where a linear classifier can accurately separate the data into multiple categories. Choosing the right kernel is a challenging problem and in practice, researchers resort to some of the standard ones available in the literature and tune their parameters based on experimental results [18]. A kernel measures the similarity between two data objects: the more similar two objects X and X' are, the higher the value of a kernel $K(X,X')$ will be. Several kernel functions have been proposed in the literature. Polynomial kernels are well suited for problems where all the training data is normalized. The formulation of the polynomial kernel is:

$$K(X,X') = (\alpha X^T X' + c)^d, \tag{10.27}$$

where α is a constant coefficient, $c \geq 0$ is a constant trading off the influence of higher-order versus lower-order terms in the polynomial, and d is the polynomial degree. A Gaussian kernel is an example of radial basis function (RBF) kernel [63]; the definition of a Gaussian kernel is

$$K(X,X') = exp\left(-\frac{||X - X'||^2}{2\sigma^2}\right) \tag{10.28}$$

where σ^2 is known as the *bandwidth*, which plays a major role in the performance of the Gaussian kernel.

Kernel methods are an effective alternative to perform data integration in the presence of heterogeneous data sources. In such problems, one does not have to perform explicit feature extraction before combining data sources. The learning method can automatically learn the appropriate feature spaces in each of the data sources and effectively integrate them to provide a robust prediction model with better accuracy compared to the models built on individual data sources. The authors in [64] provided a comprehensive set of experimental results in several biomedical applications to demonstrate the power of multiple kernel learning. Such multiple kernel learning methods fall into the category of intermediate integration where the prediction models are simultaneously learned from heterogeneous data sources by choosing the optimal feature space. Wang et al. [65] proposed a colonic polyp detection framework where multiple kernels are used to extract and combine the features from different sources (such as statistical and geometric features).

10.4 Survival Models

Survival analysis [66, 67] aims at modeling the time to event data; the observation starts from a particular starting time and will continue until the occurrence of a certain event or the observed objects become missing (not observed) from the study. In the healthcare domain, the starting point of the observation is usually a particular medical intervention such as a hospitalization admission, the beginning of taking a certain medication or a diagnosis of a given disease. The event of interest might be death, discharge from the hospitalization, or any other interesting incident that can happen during the observation period. The missing trace of the observation is also an important characteristic of survival data. For example, during a given hospitalization some patients may be moved to another hospital and in such cases, that patient will become unobserved from the study with respect to the first hospital. Survival analysis is useful whenever we are interested not only in the frequency of occurrence of a particular type of event, but also in estimating the time for such an event occurrence. In healthcare applications, the survival prediction models mainly aim at estimating the failure time distribution and estimating the prognostic evaluation of different variables (jointly or individually considered) such as biochemical, histological, and clinical characteristics [68].

10.4.1 Basic Concepts

In this section, the basic concepts and characteristics of survival models will be introduced along with some examples. The examples come from real patient data about heart failure readmission problems collected at a major hospital in the southeastern Michigan region. In this problem, survival analysis is used to estimate the time between the discharge of a patient from hospitalization and the readmission of that patient for heart failure diagnosis. Here, the event of interest is hospital readmission, and the beginning of the observation starts from the discharge date of the previous hospitalization. From this section, we hope that the difference between survival analysis and the standard predictive models will become clear to the readers.

10.4.1.1 Survival Data and Censoring

In survival data the event of interest may not always be observed during the study; this scenario happens because of time limits or missing traces caused by other uninteresting events. This feature is known as censoring [66].

Let us consider a small number of N heart failure patients in the rehospitalization problem; suppose the observation terminates after 30 days of discharge. Thus, the time of the hospital readmission is known precisely only for those subjects for whom the event has occurred before the ending point (30 days in this case). For the remaining subjects, it is only known that the time to the event is greater than the observation time. Also during this observation time, we lose track of some patients because of death, moving out of the area, or being hospitalized due to other conditions. All of these scenarios are considered as censoring in this particular example. Figure 10.4 describes the concept of censoring in a more intuitive manner. Formally, let T be the time to event of interest, and U be the censoring variable, which is the time of the withdrawn, lost, or ended time of observation. For a certain subject if only the $Z = min(T, U)$ can be observed during the study, it is known as *Right*

Censoring; otherwise, if $Z = max(T,U)$, it is termed as *Left Censoring*. Practically, in the healthcare domain the majority of the survival data is right censored [68].

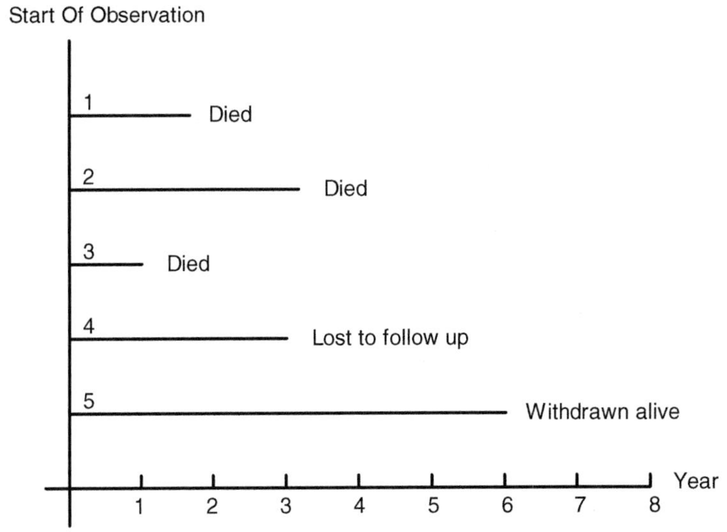

FIGURE 10.4: An illustration that demonstrates the concept of censoring.

In survival analysis, survival data are normally represented by a triple of variables (X, Z, δ), where X is the feature vector, and δ is an indicator. $\delta = 1$ if Z is the time to the event of interest and $\delta = 0$ if Z is the censored time; for convenience, Z is usually named the *observed time* [69]. An example of a small survival dataset, which is from our heart failure readmission problem, is shown in Table 10.2. In this dataset, for simplicity, we show only the patients' age and sex as our feature set (which is the X in the notation); the "status" is the indicator δ, and the "Gap" is the observed time.

10.4.1.2 Survival and Hazard Function

The object of primary interest of survival analysis is the ***survival function***, which is the probability that the time to the event of interest is no earlier than some specified time t [69, 66]. Conventionally, survival function is denoted as S, which is defined as:

$$S(t) = Pr(T \geq t). \tag{10.29}$$

It is certain that in the healthcare domain the survival function monotonically decreases with t, and the initial value is 1 when $t = 0$, which represents the fact that in the beginning of the observation 100% of the observed subjects survive; in other words, none of the events of interest are observed.

In contrast, the *cumulative death distribution function* $F(t)$ is defined as $F(t) = 1 - S(t)$, which represents the probability of time to the event of interest is less than t, and *death density function* $f(t)$ is defined as $f(t) = \frac{d}{dt}F(t)$ for continuous scenarios, and $f(t) = \frac{F(t+\Delta t)-F(t)}{\Delta t}$, where Δt is a short time interval, for discrete scenarios. The relationship among these functions is clearly described in Figure 10.5.

One other function commonly used in survival analysis is the ***hazard function*** ($\lambda(t)$), which is also known as the *force of mortality*, the *conditional failure rate*, or the *instantaneous death rate* [70]. The hazard function is not the chance or probability of the event of interest, but instead it is the event rate at time t conditional on survival until time t or later. Mathematically, the hazard function

TABLE 10.2: Survival Data on 40 Heart Failure Patients

Patient ID	Features: Sex	Age	Gap	Status	Patient ID	Features: Sex	Age	Gap	Status
1	F	91	29	1	21	M	77	82	1
2	M	70	57	1	22	M	69	615	1
3	F	91	6	1	23	F	79	251	0
4	M	58	1091	1	24	M	86	21	1
5	M	43	166	1	25	M	67	921	0
6	F	43	537	1	26	F	73	904	0
7	F	90	10	1	27	F	55	354	0
8	M	53	63	1	28	F	76	896	1
9	M	65	203	0	29	F	58	102	1
10	F	91	309	1	30	M	82	221	1
11	F	68	1155	1	31	F	54	1242	1
12	M	65	40	1	32	F	70	33	1
13	F	77	1046	1	33	F	38	272	0
14	F	40	12	1	34	M	57	136	1
15	F	42	48	1	35	F	55	424	1
16	F	68	86	1	36	F	59	110	1
17	F	90	126	1	37	M	74	173	1
18	M	58	1802	1	38	M	48	138	1
19	F	81	27	1	39	M	55	105	1
20	M	61	371	1	40	F	75	3	1

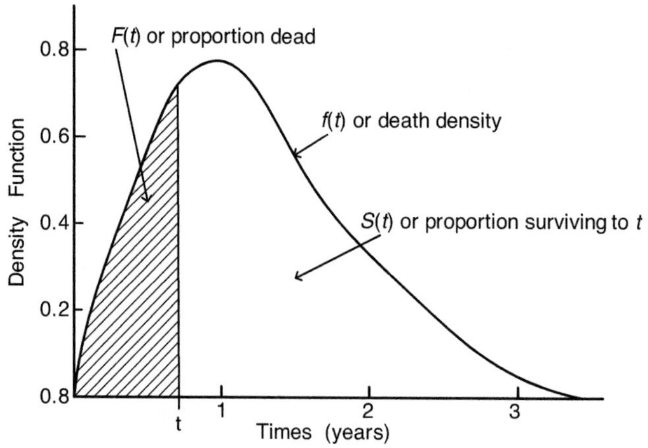

FIGURE 10.5: Relationship among $f(t)$, $F(t)$, and $S(t)$.

is defined as:

$$\begin{aligned}\lambda(t) &= \lim_{\Delta t \to 0} \frac{Pr(t \leq T < t + \Delta t \mid T \geq t)}{\Delta t} \\ &= \lim_{\Delta t \to 0} \frac{F(t+\Delta t) - F(t)}{\Delta t \cdot S(t)} \\ &= \frac{f(t)}{S(t)}. \end{aligned} \tag{10.30}$$

Similar to $S(t)$, $\lambda(t)$ is also a nonnegative function. Whereas all survival functions, $S(t)$, decrease over time, the hazard function can take on a variety of shapes. Consider the definition of $f(t)$, which can also be expressed as $f(t) = -\frac{d}{dt}S(t)$, so the hazard function can be represented as:

$$\lambda(t) = \frac{f(t)}{S(t)} = -\frac{d}{dt}S(t) \cdot \frac{1}{S(t)} = -\frac{d}{dt}[lnS(t)]. \tag{10.31}$$

Thus, the survival function can be rewritten as

$$S(t) = exp(-\Lambda(t)) \tag{10.32}$$

where $\Lambda(t) = \int_0^t \lambda(u)du$ is the *cumulative hazard function* (CHF) [69].

10.4.2 Nonparametric Survival Analysis

Nonparametric or distribution-free methods are quite easy to understand and apply. They are less efficient than parametric methods when survival times follow a theoretical distribution and more efficient when no suitable theoretical distributions are known.

10.4.2.1 Kaplan–Meier Curve and Clinical Life Table

In this section, we will introduce nonparametric methods for estimating the survival probabilities for censored data. Among all functions, the survival function or its graphical presentation, the *survival curve*, is the most widely used one. In 1958, Kaplan and Meier [71] developed the *product-limit estimator* or the *Kaplan–Meier Curve* to estimate the survival function based on the actual length of observed time. However, if the data have already been grouped into intervals, or the sample size is very large, or the interest is in a large population, it may be more convenient to perform a *Clinical Life Table* analysis [72]. We will describe both of these methods in this section.

Kaplan–Meier Curve Let $T_1 < T_2 < ... < T_K$, $K \leq N$, is a set of distinct ordered death (failure) times observed in N individuals; in a certain time T_j $(j = 1,2,...,K)$, the number $d_j \geq 1$ of deaths are observed, and the number r_j of subjects, whose either death or censored time is greater than or equal to T_j, are considered to be "at risk." The obvious conditional probability of surviving beyond time T_j can be defined as:

$$p(T_j) = \frac{r_j - d_j}{r_j} \tag{10.33}$$

and based on this conditional probability the survival function at t is estimated by the following product

$$\hat{S}(t) = \prod_{j:T_j<t} p(T_j) = \prod_{j:T_j<t} (1 - \frac{d_j}{r_j}) \tag{10.34}$$

and its variance is defined as:

$$Var(\hat{S}(t)) = \hat{S}(t)^2 \sum_{j:T_j<t} \frac{d_j}{r_j(r_j - d_j)}. \tag{10.35}$$

It is worth noting that because of the censoring, r_j is not simply equal to the difference between r_{j-1} and d_{j-1}; the correct way to calculate r_j is $r_j = r_{j-1} - d_{j-1} - c_{j-1}$, where c_{j-1} is the number of censored cases between T_{j-1} and T_j. Here, we illustrate the computation of Kaplan–Meier Curves with the example survival dataset, which is shown in Table 10.2. The calculated result is shown in Table 10.3, and the corresponding K–M survival curve is shown in Figure 10.6.

TABLE 10.3: Kaplan–Meier Estimator of 40 Heart Failure Patients in Table 10.2

						K–M Estimator								K–M Estimator	
j	T_j	δ_j	d_j	c_j	r_j	$\hat{S}(t)$	std.err	j	T_j	δ_j	d_j	c_j	r_j	$\hat{S}(t)$	std.err
1	3	1	1	0	39	0.975	0.025	21	166	1	1	0	19	0.475	0.079
2	6	1	1	0	38	0.95	0.034	22	173	1	1	0	18	0.45	0.079
3	10	1	1	0	37	0.925	0.042	23	203	0	0	1	17	.	.
4	12	1	1	0	36	0.9	0.047	24	221	1	1	0	16	0.424	0.078
5	21	1	1	0	35	0.875	0.052	25	251	0	0	1	15	.	.
6	27	1	1	0	34	0.85	0.056	26	272	0	0	1	14	.	.
7	29	1	1	0	33	0.825	0.06	27	309	1	1	0	13	0.393	0.078
8	33	1	1	0	32	0.8	0.063	28	354	0	0	1	12	.	.
9	40	1	1	0	31	0.775	0.066	29	371	1	1	0	11	0.361	0.078
10	48	1	1	0	30	0.75	0.068	30	424	1	1	0	10	0.328	0.078
11	57	1	1	0	29	0.725	0.071	31	537	1	1	0	9	0.295	0.077
12	63	1	1	0	28	0.7	0.072	32	615	1	1	0	8	0.262	0.075
13	82	1	1	0	27	0.675	0.074	33	896	1	1	0	7	0.229	0.072
14	86	1	1	0	26	0.65	0.075	34	904	0	0	1	6	.	.
15	102	1	1	0	25	0.625	0.077	35	921	0	0	1	5	.	.
16	105	1	1	0	24	0.6	0.077	36	1046	1	1	0	4	0.184	0.071
17	110	1	1	0	23	0.575	0.078	37	1091	1	1	0	3	0.138	0.066
18	126	1	1	0	22	0.55	0.079	38	1155	1	1	0	2	0.092	0.058
19	136	1	1	0	21	0.525	0.079	39	1242	1	1	0	1	0.046	0.044
20	138	1	1	0	20	0.5	0.079	40	1802	1	1	0	0	0	0

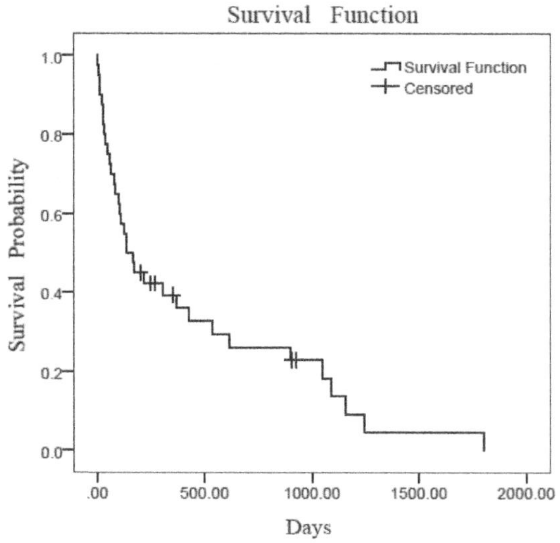

FIGURE 10.6: Kaplan–Meier survival curve of 40 heart failure patients in Table 10.2.

Clinical Life Table As mentioned above, the Clinical Life Table [72] is the application of the product-limit methods to the interval grouped survival data. The total number of N subjects are partitioned into J intervals based on the observed time. The jth interval, normally denoted I_j, is defined as $I_j = [t_j, t_{j+1}), j = 0, 1, \cdots, J-1$, and the length of I_j is $h_j = t_{j+1} - t_j$. For I_j, let

r'_j =number of survivors at the beginning of jth interval;
c_j =number of censored cases during the jth interval;
d_j =number of deaths in the jth interval;
$r_j = r'_j - c_j/2$ is assumed to be the number of survivors on average halfway through the interval.

Similarly, as in the case of the Kaplan–Meier estimator, the conditional probability of surviving during jth interval is estimated as

$$\hat{p}_j = 1 - \frac{d_j}{r_j} \tag{10.36}$$

and the corresponding survival function is estimated by the product

$$\hat{S}(I_j) = \prod_{i:i<j} (1 - \frac{d_i}{r_i}) \tag{10.37}$$

and the standard variation of this $\hat{S}(I_j)$ can be calculated in a similar way as it is in the Kaplan–Meier Curve. Table 10.4 illustrates the computation of the Clinical Life Table within 40 heart failure patients, which are shown in Table 10.2. In this example, we chose the interval length as 0.5 years (183 days), and all 40 patients are partitioned into 10 intervals.

TABLE 10.4: Clinical Life Table of 40 Heart Failure Patients

							Estimated	
j	jth interval(days)	r'_j	c_j	r_j	d_j	$\hat{p}_j$	$\hat{S}(I_j)$	std.err
0	0 to < 183	40	0	40	22	0.45	1	0
1	183 to < 366	18	4	16	2	0.88	0.45	0.08
2	366 to < 549	12	0	12	3	0.75	0.39	0.08
3	549 to < 732	9	0	9	1	0.89	0.3	0.08
4	732 to < 915	8	1	7.5	1	0.87	0.26	0.07
5	915 to < 1098	6	1	5.5	2	0.64	0.23	0.07
6	1098 to < 1281	3	0	3	2	0.33	0.14	0.07
7	1281 to < 1464	1	0	1	0	1	0.05	0.05
8	1464 to < 1647	1	0	1	0	1	0.05	0.05
9	1647 to < 1830	1	0	1	1	0	0.05	0.05

10.4.2.2 Mantel–Haenszel Test

In clinical research, one is concerned not only with estimating the survival probability but also, more often, with the comparison of the life experience of two or more groups of subjects differing for a given characteristic or randomly allocated to different treatments. The nonparametric approach is usually adopted also to compare survival curves. Among the various nonparametric tests that are available in the statistical literature, the Mantel–Haenszel (M–H) test [73] is one of the most frequently used statistical tools in medical reports for analyzing survival data (Table 10.5).

Let $T_1, T_2, ...T_J$ represent the J ordered, distinct death times, and in the jth death time, r_j number of patients survived, and d_j number of deaths occurred. Suppose that, based on certain characteristics, these patients can be divided into two groups, and at this T_j the data can be represented in a 2×2 contingency table.

Mantel and Haenszel suggested considering the distribution of the observed cell frequencies conditional on the observed marginal totals under the null hypothesis of no survival difference between these two groups. Under the null hypothesis, the d_{1j} follows hypergeometric distribution, so

TABLE 10.5: Mantel–Haenszel Test in 2 Groups

Group	Number of Deaths	Number of Survival	Total
0	d_{0j}	$r_{0j}-d_{0j}$	r_{0j}
1	d_{1j}	$r_{1j}-d_{1j}$	r_{1j}
Total	d_j	r_j-d_j	r_j

the expectation of d_{1j} is

$$E(d_{1j}) = r_{1j} \cdot \frac{d_j}{r_j}, \tag{10.38}$$

and the variance of d_{1j} is

$$Var(d_{1j}) = \left[r_{1j} \cdot \frac{d_j}{r_j}(1-\frac{d_j}{r_j}) \right] \frac{r_j - r_{1j}}{r_j - 1} = \frac{r_{1j} r_{0j} d_j (r_j - d_j)}{r_j^2 (r_j - 1)}. \tag{10.39}$$

The ratio is approximately distributed as a chi-square with one degree of freedom [74], and hence, for all J ordered distinct death times, the ratio is

$$X^2 = \frac{[\sum_{j=1}^{J} (d_{1j} - E(d_{1j}))]^2}{\sum_{j=1}^{J} Var(d_{1j})}. \tag{10.40}$$

Beside this Mantel–Haenszel test, there are also some nonparametric methods that have been used to compare the survival difference. In 1965, Gehan [75] proposed a generalized Wilcoxon test that is an extension of the Wilcoxon test of censored data. Later, Peto and Peto [76] suggested another version of the generalized Wilcoxon test. These nonparametric methods are less efficient than parametric methods when the baseline distributions of survival times are known and more efficient when no suitable theoretical distributions are known.

10.4.3 Cox Proportional Hazards Model

The Cox proportional hazards model [77] is the most commonly used model in survival analysis. Unlike parametric methods, this model does not require knowledge of the underlying distribution, but the attributes are assumed based on an exponential influence on the output. The baseline hazard function in this model can be an arbitrary nonnegative function, but the baseline hazard functions of different individuals are assumed to be the same. The estimation and hypothesis testing of parameters in the model can be calculated by minimizing the negative partial likelihood function rather than the ordinary likelihood function.

10.4.3.1 The Basic Cox Model

Let N be the number of subjects in the survival analysis, and as mentioned in Section 10.4.1, each of the individuals can be represented by a triple of variables (X, Z, δ). Considering an individual specific hazard function $\lambda(t, X_i)$ in the Cox model, the proportional hazards assumption is

$$\lambda(t, X_i) = \lambda_0(t) exp(X_i \beta), \tag{10.41}$$

for $i = 1, 2, ..., N$, where the $\lambda_0(t)$ is the *baseline hazard function*, which can be an arbitrary nonnegative function of time, $X_i = (x_{i1}, x_{i2}, ..., x_{ip})$ is the corresponding covariate vector for individual i, and $\beta^T = (\beta_1, \beta_2, ..., \beta_p)$ is the coefficient vector. The Cox model is a semiparametric model since it does not specify the form of $\lambda_0(t)$; in fact, the hazard ratio does not depend on the baseline hazard function; for two individuals, the hazard ratio is

$$\frac{\lambda(t,X_1)}{\lambda(t,X_2)} = \frac{\lambda_0(t)exp(X_1\beta)}{\lambda_0(t)exp(X_2\beta)} = exp[(X_1 - X_2)\beta]. \tag{10.42}$$

Since the hazard ratio is a constant, and all the subjects share the same baseline hazard function, the Cox model is a proportional hazards model. Based on this Cox assumption the survival function is given by

$$S(t) = exp(-\Lambda_0(t)exp(X\beta)) = S_0(t)^{exp(X\beta)} \tag{10.43}$$

where $\Lambda_0(t)$ is the *cumulative baseline hazard function*, and $S_0(t) = exp(-\Lambda_0(t))$ is the baseline survival function.

10.4.3.2 Estimation of the Regression Parameters

Because the baseline hazard function $\lambda_0(t)$ in the Cox proportional hazards model is not specified, it is impossible to fit the model using the standard likelihood function. To estimate the coefficients, Cox [77] proposed a partial likelihood that represents the data only depending on the β values. Consider the definition of the hazard function; the probability that an individual with covariate X fails at time t conditional on survival until time t or later can be expressed by $\lambda(t,X)dt, dt \to 0$. Again, let N be the number of subjects who have a total number of $J \leq N$ events of interest occurring during the observation period, and $T_1 < T_2 < ... < T_J$ is the distinct ordered time to the event of interest. Without considering the ties, let X_j be the corresponding covariate vector for the individual who fails at time T_j, and $R(T_j)$ be the set of subjects at time T_j. Thus, conditional on the fact that the event occurs at T_j, the probability of the individual's corresponding covariate is X_j can be formulated as

$$\frac{\lambda(T_j,X_j)dt}{\sum_{i\in R(T_j)} \lambda(T_j,X_i)dt}, \tag{10.44}$$

and the partial likelihood is the product of this probability; referring to the Cox assumption and the existence of the censoring, the definition of the partial likelihood is given by

$$L(\beta) = \prod_{j=1}^{N} \left[\frac{exp(X_j\beta)}{\sum_{i\in R_j} exp(X_i\beta)} \right]^{\delta_j}. \tag{10.45}$$

It should be noted that here $j = 1,2,...,N$; if $\delta_j = 1$, the jth term in the product is the conditional probability; otherwise, when $\delta_j = 0$, the corresponding term is 1 and has no effect on the result. The estimated coefficient vector $\hat{\beta}$ can be calculated by maximizing this partial likelihood; to achieve more time efficiency, it is usually equivalently estimated by minimizing the negative *log-partial likelihood*

$$LL(\beta) = \sum_{j=1}^{N} \delta_j \{X_j\beta - log[\sum_{i\in R_j} exp(X_i\beta)]\}. \tag{10.46}$$

10.4.3.3 Penalized Cox Models

Currently, with the development of medical procedures and detection methods, medical records tend to have more features than ever before. In some cases, the number of features (P) is almost equivalent to or even larger than the number of subjects (N); building the prediction model with all the features might provide inaccurate results because of the overfitting issues [78]. The primary motivation of using sparsity-inducing norms is that in high dimensions, it becomes appropriate to proceed under the assumption that most of the attributes are not significant, and it can be used to identify the vital features in prediction [60]. In biomedical data analysis the sparsity-inducing norms are also widely used to penalize the loss function of a prediction [61]. Consider the L_p norm penalty; the smaller the value of p that is chosen, the sparser the solution, but when $0 \leq P < 1$, the penalty is not convex, and the solution is difficult and often impossible to obtain. Commonly, the penalized methods have also been used to do feature selection in the scenarios when $N > P$. We will now introduce three commonly used penalty functions and their applications in the Cox proportional hazards model.

Lasso [79] is a L_1 norm penalty that can select at most $K = min(N,P)$ features while estimating the regression coefficient. In [80], the Lasso penalty was used along with the log-partial likelihood to obtain the Cox-Lasso algorithm.

$$\hat{\beta}_{lasso} = \min_{\beta}\{-\frac{2}{N}[\sum_{j=1}^{N} \delta_j X_j \beta - \delta_j log(\sum_{i \in R_j} e^{X_i \beta})] + \lambda \sum_{p=1}^{P} |\beta_p|\} \tag{10.47}$$

Elastic Net, which is a combination of the L_1 and squared L_2 norm penalties, has the potential to obtain both sparsity and handle correlated feature spaces [81]. The Cox-Elastic Net method was proposed by Noah Simon et al. [82] wherein the Elastic Net penalty term was introduced into the log-partial likelihood function

$$\begin{aligned} \hat{\beta}_{elastic\ net} &= \min_{\beta}\{-\frac{2}{N}[\sum_{j=1}^{N} \delta_j X_j \beta - \delta_j log(\sum_{i \in R_j} e^{X_i \beta})] \\ &+ \lambda[\alpha \sum_{p=1}^{P} |\beta_p| + \frac{1}{2}(1-\alpha) \sum_{p=1}^{P} \beta_p^2]\} \end{aligned} \tag{10.48}$$

where $0 \leq \alpha \leq 1$. Different from Cox-Lasso, Cox-Elastic Net can select more than N features if $N \leq P$.

Ridge regression was originally proposed by Hoerl and Kennard [83] and introduced to the Cox regression by Verweij and Van Houwelingen [84]. It is a L_2 norm regularization that tends to select all the correlated variables and shrink their values towards each other. The regression parameters of Cox-Ridge can be estimated by

$$\hat{\beta}_{ridge} = \min_{\beta}\{-\frac{2}{N}[\sum_{j=1}^{N} \delta_j X_j \beta - \delta_j log(\sum_{i \in R_j} e^{X_i \beta})] + \frac{\lambda}{2} \sum_{p=1}^{P} \beta_p^2\}. \tag{10.49}$$

Among three equations (10.47), (10.48), and (10.49), $\lambda \geq 0$ is used to adjust the influence introduced by the penalty term. The performance of these penalized estimator significantly depends on λ, and the optimal λ_{opt} can be chosen via cross-validation. Also, few other penalties based on kernel and graph-based similarities have been recently proposed to tackle the inherent correlations within the variables in the context of the Cox proportional hazards model [85].

10.4.4 Survival Trees

Survival trees are one form of classification and regression trees that are tailored to handle censored data. The basic intuition behind the tree models is to recursively partition the data based on a particular splitting criterion, and the objects that belong to the same node are similar to each other based on the event of interest. The earliest attempt at using tree structure analysis for survival data was made in [86].

10.4.4.1 Survival Tree Building Methods

The primary difference between a survival tree and the standard decision tree is the choice of splitting criterion. The splitting criteria used for survival trees can be grouped into two categories: minimizing within-node homogeneity or maximizing between-node heterogeneity. The first class of approaches minimizes a loss function based within-node homogeneity criterion. Gordon and Olshen [87] measured the homogeneity by using L_P, the L_P Wasserstein metric, and Hellinger distances between estimated distribution functions. Davis and Anderson [88] employed an exponential log-likelihood loss function in recursive partitioning based on the sum of residuals from the Cox model. LeBlanc and Crowley [89] measured the node deviance based on the first step of a full likelihood estimation procedure; Cho and Hong [90] proposed an L_1 loss function to measure the within-node homogeneity.

In the second category of splitting criteria, Ciampi et al. [91] employed log-rank test statistics for between-node heterogeneity measures. Later, Ciampi et al. [92] proposed a likelihood ratio statistic (LRS) to measure the dissimilarity between two nodes. Based on the Tarone-Ware class of two-sample statistics, Segal [93] introduced a procedure to measure the between-node dissimilarity.

10.4.4.2 Ensemble Methods with Survival Trees

To overcome the instability of a single tree, bagging [37] and random forests [94], proposed by Breiman, are commonly used to perform the ensemble-based model building. Hothorn et al. [95] proposed a general bagging method that was implemented in the R package "ipred." In 2008, Ishwaran et al. introduced a general random forest method, called random survival forest (RSF) [96] and implemented it in the R package "randomSurvivalForest".

***Bagging Survival Trees*:** Bagging is one of the oldest and most commonly used ensemble methods that typically reduces the variance of the base models being used. In survival analysis, rather than taking a majority vote, the aggregated survival function is generated by taking the average of the predictions made by each survival tree [95]. The main steps of this method are as follows:

1. Draw B booststrap samples from the original dataset.
2. Grow a survival tree for each bootstrap sample, and ensure that in each terminal node the number of events occurred is no less than d.
3. Compute the bootstrap aggregated survival function by averaging the leaf nodes' predictions.

For each leaf node the survival function is estimated by the Kaplan–Meier estimator [71], and all individuals within the same node are assumed to follow the same survival function.

***Random Survival Forests*:** Random forest is an ensemble method designed specifically for the tree structured prediction models [94]. It is based on a framework similar to bagging; the main difference between random forest and bagging is that at a certain node, rather than using all the attributes, random forest only uses a random subset of the residual attributes to select attributes based on the splitting criterion. Breiman proved that randomization can reduce the correlation among trees and thus improve the prediction performance.

In random survival forest, the Nelson–Aalen estimator [97, 98] is used to predict the cumulative hazard function (CHF). The definition of the Nelson–Aalen estimator is

$$\hat{\Lambda}(t) = \sum_{t_j \leq t} \frac{d_j}{r_j} \tag{10.50}$$

where d_j is the number of deaths at time t_j, and r_j is the number of individuals at risk at t_j. Based on this CHF, the ensemble CHF of OOB (out of bag) data can be calculated by taking the average of the corresponding CHF [96].

10.5 Evaluation and Validation

In this section, we will describe some of the widely studied evaluation metrics that are used in clinical medicine. We will also discuss different validation mechanisms used to obtain robust estimations of these evaluation metrics.

10.5.1 Evaluation Metrics

When we design and construct a new prediction model or apply an existing model to a particular clinical dataset, it is critical to understand whether the model is suitable for this data; thus, some evaluation metrics are needed to quantify the performance of the model. In this section, we will introduce some of the well-known metrics that are commonly used to evaluate the performance of the clinical prediction models.

10.5.1.1 Brier Score

Named after the inventor Glenn W. Brier, the Brier score [99] is designed to evaluate the performance of prediction models where the outcome to be predicted is either binary or categorical in nature. Note that the Brier score can only evaluate the prediction models that have probabilistic outcomes; that is, the outcome must remain in the range [0,1], and the sum of all the possible outcomes for a certain individual should be 1. Let us consider a sample of N individuals and for each X_i, $i = 1,2,...,N$, the predicted outcome is $\hat{y}_i$, and the actual outcome is y_i; therefore, the most common definition of the Brier score can be given by

$$\text{Brier score} = \frac{1}{N}\sum_{i=1}^{N}(\hat{y}_i - y_i)^2, \tag{10.51}$$

which only suits binary outcomes where the y_i can only be 1 or 0. In more general terms, the original Brier score, defined by Brier [99], has the form:

$$\text{Brier score} = \frac{1}{N}\sum_{i=1}^{N}\sum_{c=1}^{C}(\hat{y}_{ic} - y_{ic})^2, \tag{10.52}$$

for C-class output problem (categorical outcome), where $\sum_{c=1}^{C}\hat{y}_{ic} = 1$ and $\sum_{c=1}^{C} y_{ic} = 1$. From the above two definitions of the Brier score, it is evident that it measures the mean-squared difference between predictions made and the actual outcomes; therefore, the lower the Brier score, the better the prediction.

10.5.1.2 R^2

The R^2 or *coefficient of determination* [100] is used to measure the performance of regression models, which can be formalized as:

$$R^2 = 1 - \frac{RSS(\hat{Y})}{Var(Y)}, \tag{10.53}$$

where $RSS(\hat{Y})$ is the residual sum of squares, and $Var(Y)$ is the variance of actual outcomes. For a dataset with N samples, these two terms can be mathematically defined as:

$$RSS(\hat{Y}) = \sum_{i=1}^{N}(y_i - \hat{y}_i)^2, \text{ and } Var(Y) = \sum_{i=1}^{N}(y_i - \bar{y})^2, \tag{10.54}$$

where $\bar{y}$ is the mean value of the actual outcomes; in addition, for each individual X_i, y_i is the actual outcome, and $\hat{y}_i$ is the estimated outcome. Obviously, a good prediction model provides a small $RSS(\hat{Y})$; in other words, the closer the R^2 is to one, the better the prediction will be. At the same time, we should also note that the R^2 could be negative if the prediction model cannot well represent the distribution of the dataset and even worse than the mean value of the actual outcomes [101].

10.5.1.3 Accuracy

In general, the accuracy of measurement is defined as the closeness of agreement between a quantity value obtained by measurement and the true value of the measurand [102, 103]. Here we only consider its definition in the binary classification case where it can be used to measure the performance of the predicted model.

TABLE 10.6: Confusion Matrix for a 2-Class Problem

	Predict positive	Predict negative
Actual positive	TP	FN
Actual negative	FP	TN

Consider a confusion matrix [104] for a 2-class problem that is shown in Table 10.6, where the components can be separately defined as:

1. True positive (TP) is the number of positive individuals correctly predicted as positive.
2. False positive (FP) is the number of negative individuals incorrectly predicted as positive.
3. False negative (FN) is the number of positive individuals incorrectly predicted as negative.
4. True negative (TN) is the number of negative individuals correctly predicted as negative.

Based on this confusion matrix, the accuracy can be formalized as:

$$\text{Accuracy} = \frac{TP+TN}{TP+FP+FN+TN}, \tag{10.55}$$

which is the proportion of correct predictions over the entire set of samples.

10.5.1.4 Other Evaluation Metrics Based on Confusion Matrix

Even though accuracy is a good estimate of the model performance, it has some major drawbacks when applied in medical problems. For instance, one might be more interested in the performance of the model in prediction of the positive cases compared to the negative ones. Also, when the class distribution is imbalanced (i.e., one class completely dominates the other one), accuracy will not provide a good estimate of the model performance. Such class imbalance problems [105] are quite common in clinical applications. Let us consider a real-world example that demonstrates this class imbalance problem in a biomedical context. The World Health Organization (WHO) [106] indicated that in 2008 the Northern American incidence rate of lung cancer was 36 per 100,000 for females and 49 per 100,000 for males. In this case, the accuracy measure is no longer suitable. For such lung cancer diagnosis, the model that predicts no one getting lung cancer has an accuracy very close to 100%; however, it is clear that this is not a good prediction because we are more interested in a model that can accurately predict the lung cancer cases (which is a minority class in this application domain). We will now introduce some of the commonly studied evaluation metrics that are suitable for such problems especially in the 2-class scenario [51]. All the terms used in the definition of these metrics are already defined in the previous section. Figure 10.7 shows the popular evaluation metrics and the manner in which they are derived from the components of the confusion matrix.

<table>
<tr><td colspan="2"></td><td colspan="2">Actual Outcome</td><td></td></tr>
<tr><td colspan="2"></td><td>Positive</td><td>Negative</td><td></td></tr>
<tr><td rowspan="2">Prediction Model Outcome</td><td>Positive</td><td>True Positive (TP)</td><td>False Positive (FP)</td><td>Positive Predictive Value (Precision) = TP / (TP + FP)</td></tr>
<tr><td>Negative</td><td>False Negative (FN)</td><td>True Negative (TN)</td><td>Negative Predictive Value TN / (TN + FN)</td></tr>
<tr><td colspan="2"></td><td>Sensitivity (Recall) = TP / (TP + FN)</td><td>Specificity = TN / (FP + TN)</td><td>Accuracy = (TP + TN) /(TP + FP + TN + FN)</td></tr>
</table>

FIGURE 10.7: Various evaluation metrics derived from the confusion matrix.

Sensitivity Sensitivity, which is also known as the *true positive rate* (TPR) or *Recall*, measures the ratio of actual positives that are correctly identified. The formal definition of the sensitivity is

$$\text{Sensitivity} = \frac{TP}{TP+FN}. \tag{10.56}$$

Specificity Specificity, which is also known as the *true negative rate* (TNR), measures the ratio of actual negatives that are correctly identified [107]; this measurement can be employed in those problems where the negative individuals are more interesting, and it can be defined as:

$$\text{Specificity} = \frac{TN}{TN+FP}. \tag{10.57}$$

False positive rate The *false positive rate* (FPR) measures the ratio of actual negatives that are incorrectly identified, which is formalized as:

$$FPR = \frac{FP}{TN+FP}. \tag{10.58}$$

Precision Precision, which is also known as the *positive predictive value* (PPV), measures the ratio of true positives to predicted positives [108]; this measurement is suitable for those problems where the positive individuals are considered more important than the negatives, and it can be mathematically represented as:

$$\text{Precision} = \frac{TP}{TP+FP}. \tag{10.59}$$

F-measure F-measure [109] is the harmonic mean of recall and precision:

$$\text{F-measure} = \frac{2 \times Precision \times Recall}{Recall + Precision}. \tag{10.60}$$

Thus, a high value of F-measure indicates that both precision and recall are reasonably high [51]. F-measure varies in the range [0, 1] where the best value is reached at 1 and the worst score will be 0.

10.5.1.5 ROC Curve

The receiver operating characteristic (ROC) curve is a graphical technique that can be used to measure and visualize the performance of a prediction model over the entire range of possible cutoffs [110]. In the biomedical domain, the ROC curve has been employed in the evaluation of disease diagnosis [111]. In an ROC curve (see Figure 10.8), the x-axis is the false positive rate (FPR) and the y-axis is the true positive rate (TPR). The cutoff varies from the highest possible value, where all subjects are predicted as negative ($TPR = 0$, $FPR = 0$), to the lowest possible value, where all subjects are predicted as positive ($TPR = 1$, $FPR = 1$), and in each possible cutoff, the TPR and FPR are calculated based on the corresponding confusion matrix.

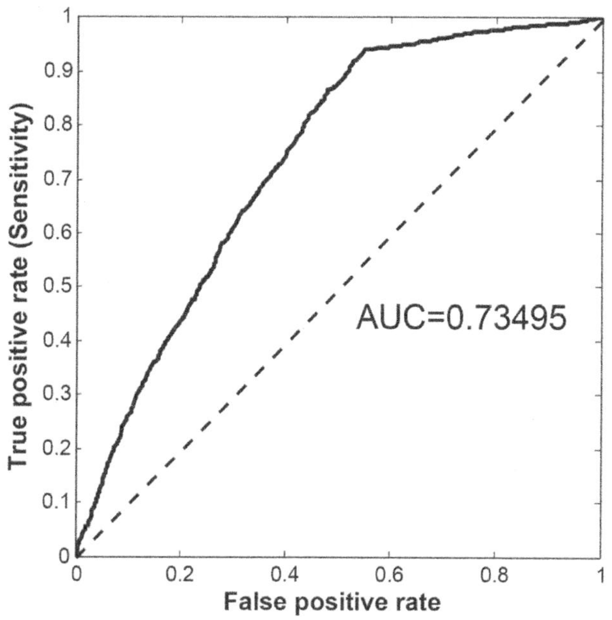

FIGURE 10.8: An example of a ROC curve.

For an ideal model, $TPR = 1$ and $FPR = 0$; that is, the area under the ROC curve (AUC) [112] will be equal to 1. In [112, 113], the meaning of AUC is thoroughly discussed in more detail, and it has been proved that AUC is equal to the probability that a binary classifier will give an arbitrary positive record a higher score than an arbitrary negative record, conditional on the assumption that the positive individual should receive a higher score than the negative one. A random classifier's AUC is 0.5, and when AUC is higher than 0.5, the higher the AUC value, the better the prediction model. When AUC is less than 0.5, it does not mean the prediction model is bad; however, it means the assumption made by the model is incorrect and hence, to solve this problem, we just need to exchange the definition of the positive individual and negative individual.

10.5.1.6 *C*-index

C-index, or the *concordance probability*, is used to measure the performance of a regression model [114]. Originally, it was designed to evaluate the performance of the survival estimation [115, 116]. Consider a pair of bivariate observations $(y_1, \hat{y}_1)$ and $(y_2, \hat{y}_2)$, where y_i is the actual observation, and $\hat{y}_i$ is the predicted value. The concordance probability is defined as:

$$c = Pr(\hat{y}_1 > \hat{y}_2 | y_1 \leq y_2). \tag{10.61}$$

Thus, we can see that if y_i is binary, then the C-index is the AUC. As this definition is not straightforward, in practice, there are multiple ways to calculate the C-index. In 1982, Harrell et al. proposed the first definition of the C-index [115]. Later, Heagerty and Zheng defined the c_τ in [117] which is calculated based on AUC values at all possible observation times. In [118], a c-index that is specific for the Cox model was designed. Among these three methods, Harrell et al.'s C-index [115] is suitable for all cases; in contrast, in [117] and [118] the C-index is designed specifically for the proportional hazards model, where $X_i\beta$ (see Section 10.4.3) is used instead of the estimated outcome $\hat{y}_i$.

10.5.2 Validation

In Section 14.6, we reviewed several quantitative metrics used for estimating the performance of clinical prediction models, and the model can be evaluated based on its performance on an unseen testing data. This section reviews some of the commonly used validation techniques that can provide an unbiased estimate for the evaluation of a predictive model. In general, these techniques fall into two categories: internal validation and external validation.

10.5.2.1 Internal Validation Methods

The internal validation works by randomly separating the training data and the testing data from the dataset where the labels of the individuals are already known. Here we briefly introduce two of the most commonly used internal validation methods: cross-validation and bootstrap validation.

Cross-Validation In k-fold cross-validation, first, the labeled dataset will be randomly partitioned into k equal-sized subsets based on uniform distribution. Then one subset is chosen as the testing dataset, while the remaining $k-1$ subsets are used to train the model [119]. This process is repeated k times and each time a different subset is used as the testing dataset; therefore, each individual is used for training exactly once, and each time the training dataset is different from the testing dataset. Finally, the model will be evaluated based on either the averaged performance of k subsets or the combined prediction of all samples. Using the cross-validation scheme, a model can achieve a relatively high performance by fully using all the datasets, and the variance of the estimated performance metric tends to be very low because of the multiple rounds. Through empirical analyses, Kohavi et al. indicated that the tenfold cross validation is the best choice in many practical situations [120].

Bootstrap Validation In cross-validation there are no duplicate samples in the training dataset, while in bootstrap the training records are sampled with replacement, and the number of bootstrap samples is the same as in the original samples [121]. In cross-validation, sampling is based on the uniform distribution; thus, it assumes that the data distribution of training data and testing data are the same, and the variance of the estimated performance metric is introduced by insufficient sampling. However, in bootstrap validation the data distribution of training data and testing data are not the same but are approximately similar; the training samples follow the empirical distribution of the original data. It has been proved that if the number of the original samples is sufficiently large, the training dataset will contain around 63.2% of the original samples, and the remaining 36.8% is called *OOB (out of bag)* data. In bootstrap validation, B bootstrap samples are repeatedly generated based on the above strategy; a prediction model is learned for each bootstrap sample, and the model is evaluated using both the original data and the corresponding OOB data. The final prediction error will be a combination of the training error and the testing error. This approach guarantees the stability of the performance estimate of the bootstrap validation.

10.5.2.2 External Validation Methods

In clinical data analysis, external validation methods are also used to validate whether the learned model can be generalized to other scenarios and other patients [122]. For example, a clinical prediction model is learned from the previous patients, and its performance is validated by the most recently treated patients; this validation method is known as the *temporal validation. Geographic validation* is another commonly used external validation technique, wherein the training data and testing data are separated not based on the random sampling but on the geographical location from where the data was collected. Once the prediction model has been learned from a local hospital, it will be interesting to see whether it can be viewed as a generalized model and if it will be applicable at other facilities and locations; thus, the geographic validation is needed. In general, if the model performance is similar, the larger the difference between the training and testing dataset, the more general the model is.

10.6 Conclusion

In this chapter, we reviewed some of the basic and advanced supervised learning methods that have been used for clinical prediction. Some of the widely used basic statistical methods include: (i) linear regression that is used to estimate a continuous outcome; (ii) logistic regression that is a linear binary classification method; (iii) decision trees that are more suitable for categorical inputs and outcomes; and (iv) survival models that are specifically designed for survival analysis. In addition, we also provided a few state-of-the art extensions for some of these basic models. These extensions include: (i) methods for handling sparse data and high-dimensional problems; (ii) kernel tricks to effectively handle nonlinear data distributions; (iii) ensemble approaches to improve the performance of the base models; and (iv) cost-sensitive learning methods to handle imbalanced data. By going through this chapter, we hope that the readers can get a general understanding of different models and pointers to articles that provide more details about effectively using prediction models in clinical medicine. In addition, we also discussed some of the popular evaluation metrics and validation schemes used for estimating the accuracy and utility of the prediction models when applied to healthcare applications.

Acknowledgments

This work was supported in part by National Science Foundation grant IIS-1231742 and the National Institutes of Health grant R21CA175974.

Bibliography

[1] Edwin Rietveld, Hendrik C.C. de Jonge, Johan J. Polder, Yvonne Vergouwe, Henk J. Veeze, Henriëtte A. Moll, and Ewout W. Steyerberg. Anticipated costs of hospitalization for respiratory syncytial virus infection in young children at risk. *The Pediatric Infectious Disease Journal*, 23(6):523–529, 2004.

[2] Michael A. Cucciare and William O'Donohue. Predicting future healthcare costs: how well does risk-adjustment work? *Journal of Health Organization and Management*, 20(2):150–162, 2006.

[3] P. Krijnen, B.C. Van Jaarsveld, M.G.M. Hunink, and J.D.F. Habbema. The effect of treatment on health-related quality of life in patients with hypertension and renal artery stenosis. *Journal of Human Hypertension*, 19(6):467–470, 2005.

[4] Daryl Pregibon. Logistic regression diagnostics. *The Annals of Statistics*, 9: 705–724, 1981.

[5] Taya V. Glotzer, Anne S. Hellkamp, John Zimmerman, Michael O. Sweeney, Raymond Yee, Roger Marinchak, James Cook, Alexander Paraschos, John Love, Glauco Radoslovich, et al. Atrial high rate episodes detected by pacemaker diagnostics predict death and stroke report of the atrial diagnostics ancillary study of the mode selection trial (most). *Circulation*, 107(12):1614–1619, 2003.

[6] Shijun Wang and Ronald M. Summers. Machine learning and radiology. *Medical Image Analysis*, 16(5):933–951, 2012.

[7] Li M. Fu and Casey S. Fu-Liu. Multi-class cancer subtype classification based on gene expression signatures with reliability analysis. *FEBS Letters*, 561(1):186–190, 2004.

[8] Yongxi Tan, Leming Shi, Weida Tong, G.T. Gene Hwang, and Charles Wang. Multi-class tumor classification by discriminant partial least squares using microarray gene expression data and assessment of classification models. *Computational Biology and Chemistry*, 28(3):235–243, 2004.

[9] Anila Wijesinha, Colin B. Begg, H. Harris Funkenstein, and Barbara J. McNeil. Methodology for the differential diagnosis of a complex data set. a case study using data from routine CT scan examinations. *Medical Decision Making: An International Journal of the Society for Medical Decision Making*, 3(2):133–154, 1982.

[10] Vladimir Vapnik. *The Nature of Statistical Learning Theory*. Springer, 2000.

[11] Frank E. Harrell, Peter A. Margolis, Sandy Gove, Karen E. Mason, E. Kim Mulholland, Deborah Lehmann, Lulu Muhe, Salvacion Gatchalian, and Heinz F. Eichenwald. Development of a clinical prediction model for an ordinal outcome: The World Health Organization multicentre study of clinical signs and etiological agents of pneumonia, sepsis and meningitis in young infants. *Statistics in Medicine*, 17(8):909–944, 1998.

[12] Trevor Hastie, Robert Tibshirani, and Jerome Friedman. *Linear Methods for Regression*. Springer, 2009.

[13] Trevor Hastie and Robert Tibshirani. Generalized additive models. *Statistical Science*, 1(3): 297–310, 1986.

[14] Leo Breiman and Jerome H. Friedman. Estimating optimal transformations for multiple regression and correlation. *Journal of the American Statistical Association*, 80(391):580–598, 1985.

[15] Simon Wood. *Generalized Additive Models: An Introduction with R*. CRC Press, 2006.

[16] Stephan Dreiseitl and Lucila Ohno-Machado. Logistic regression and artificial neural network classification models: A methodology review. *Journal of Biomedical Informatics*, 35(5):352–359, 2002.

[17] D.M. Wingerchuk, V.A. Lennon, S.J. Pittock, C.F. Lucchinetti, and B.G. Weinshenker. Revised diagnostic criteria for neuromyelitis optica. *Neurology*, 66(10):1485–1489, 2006.

[18] Kevin P. Murphy. *Machine Learning: A Probabilistic Perspective*. The MIT Press, 2012.

[19] Dimitri P. Bertsekas. *Nonlinear Programming*. Athena Scientific, 1999.

[20] Stephen M. Goldfeld, Richard E. Quandt, and Hale F. Trotter. Maximization by quadratic hill-climbing. *Econometrica: Journal of the Econometric Society*, 34(3): 541–551, 1966.

[21] J. Engel. Polytomous logistic regression. *Statistica Neerlandica*, 42(4):233–252, 1988.

[22] Balaji Krishnapuram, Lawrence Carin, Mario A. T. Figueiredo, and Alexander J. Hartemink. Sparse multinomial logistic regression: Fast algorithms and generalization bounds. *IEEE Transactions on Pattern Analysis and Machine Intelligence*, 27(6):957–968, 2005.

[23] Morris H. DeGroot. *Optimal Statistical Decisions*, volume 82. Wiley-Interscience, 2005.

[24] Rollin Brant. Assessing proportionality in the proportional odds model for ordinal logistic regression. *Biometrics*, 46(4): 1171–1178, 1990.

[25] Anne Whitehead, Rumana Z. Omar, Julian Higgins, Elly Savaluny, Rebecca M. Turner, and Simon G. Thompson. Meta-analysis of ordinal outcomes using individual patient data. *Statistics in Medicine*, 20(15):2243–2260, 2001.

[26] Richard Williams. Generalized ordered logit/partial proportional odds models for ordinal dependent variables. *Stata Journal*, 6(1):58–82, 2006.

[27] Richard Williams. Gologit2: Stata module to estimate generalized logistic regression models for ordinal dependent variables. *Statistical Software Components*, 2013.

[28] Igor Kononenko. Inductive and bayesian learning in medical diagnosis. *Applied Artificial Intelligence an International Journal*, 7(4):317–337, 1993.

[29] Margaret Sullivan Pepe. *The Statistical Evaluation of Medical Tests for Classification and Prediction*. Oxford University Press, 2003.

[30] Karsten Held, E. Rota Kops, Bernd J. Krause, William M. Wells III, Ron Kikinis, and H.W. Muller-Gartner. Markov random field segmentation of brain MR images. *IEEE Transactions on Medical Imaging*, 16(6):878–886, 1997.

[31] H.D. Li, M. Kallergi, L.P. Clarke, V.K. Jain, and R.A. Clark. Markov random field for tumor detection in digital mammography. *IEEE Transactions on Medical Imaging*, 14(3):565–576, 1995.

[32] Mary Jo Aspinall. Use of a decision tree to improve accuracy of diagnosis. *Nursing Research*, 28(3):182–185, 1979.

[33] John Ross Quinlan. *C4.5: Programs for Machine Learning*, volume 1. Morgan Kaufmann, 1993.

[34] J. Ross Quinlan et al. *Discovering Rules by Induction from Large Collections of Examples: Expert Systems in the Micro Electronic Age*. Edinburgh University Press, 1979.

[35] L. Breiman J. H. Friedman R. A. Olshen and Charles J. Stone. *Classification and Regression Trees*. Wadsworth International Group, 1984.

[36] Gordon V. Kass. An exploratory technique for investigating large quantities of categorical data. *Applied Statistics*, 29(2): 119–127, 1980.

[37] Leo Breiman. Bagging predictors. *Machine Learning*, 24(2):123–140, 1996.

[38] S.S. Gambhir, C.K. Hoh, M.E. Phelps, I Madar, and J Maddahi. Decision tree sensitivity analysis for cost-effectiveness of FDG-PET in the staging and management of non-small-cell lung carcinoma. *Journal of Nuclear Medicine: Official Publication, Society of Nuclear Medicine*, 37(9):1428–1436, 1996.

[39] William J. Long, John L. Griffith, Harry P. Selker, and Ralph B. D'Agostino. A comparison of logistic regression to decision-tree induction in a medical domain. *Computers and Biomedical Research*, 26(1):74–97, 1993.

[40] Frank Rosenblatt. The perceptron: A probabilistic model for information storage and organization in the brain. *Psychological Review*, 65(6):386, 1958.

[41] Leonardo Bottaci, Philip J. Drew, John E. Hartley, Matthew B. Hadfield, Ridzuan Farouk, Peter W. R. Lee, Iain Macintyre, Graeme S. Duthie, and John R. T. Monson. Artificial neural networks applied to outcome prediction for colorectal cancer patients in separate institutions. *The Lancet*, 350(9076):469–472, 1997.

[42] N. Ganesan, K. Venkatesh, M. A. Rama, and A Malathi Palani. Application of neural networks in diagnosing cancer disease using demographic data. *International Journal of Computer Applications*. http://www. ijcaonline. org/journal/number26/pxc387783. pdf, 2010.

[43] Paulo J. Lisboa and Azzam F.G. Taktak. The use of artificial neural networks in decision support in cancer: A systematic review. *Neural Networks*, 19(4):408–415, 2006.

[44] Paulo J.G. Lisboa. A review of evidence of health benefit from artificial neural networks in medical intervention. *Neural Networks*, 15(1):11–39, 2002.

[45] Maciej A. Mazurowski, Piotr A. Habas, Jacek M. Zurada, Joseph Y. Lo, Jay A. Baker, and Georgia D. Tourassi. Training neural network classifiers for medical decision making: The effects of imbalanced datasets on classification performance. *Neural Networks*, 21(2):427–436, 2008.

[46] Laurent G. Glance, Turner Osler, and Tamotsu Shinozaki. Intensive care unit prognostic scoring systems to predict death: A cost-effectiveness analysis. *Critical Care Medicine*, 26(11):1842–1849, 1998.

[47] Peter Turney. Types of cost in inductive concept learning. WCSL at ICML-2000. Stanford University, California.

[48] Pedro Domingos. Metacost: a general method for making classifiers cost sensitive. In *Proceedings of the Fifth ACM SIGKDD International Conference on Knowledge Discovery and Data Mining*, pages 155–164. ACM, 1999.

[49] Charles Elkan. The foundations of cost-sensitive learning. In *International Joint Conference on Artificial Intelligence*, volume 17, pages 973–978. Citeseer, 2001.

[50] Chris Drummond and Robert C. Holte. Exploiting the cost (in) sensitivity of decision tree splitting criteria. In *ICML*, pages 239–246, 2000.

[51] Pang-Ning Tan et al. *Introduction to Data Mining*. Pearson Education, 2005.

[52] Yusuf Artan, Masoom A. Haider, Deanna L. Langer, Theodorus H. van der Kwast, Andrew J. Evans, Yongyi Yang, Miles N. Wernick, John Trachtenberg, and Imam Samil Yetik. Prostate cancer localization with multispectral MRI using cost-sensitive support vector machines and conditional random fields. *IEEE Transactions on Image Processing*, 19(9):2444–2455, 2010.

[53] Susan Lomax and Sunil Vadera. A survey of cost-sensitive decision tree induction algorithms. *ACM Computing Surveys (CSUR)*, 45(2):16, 2013.

[54] Thomas G. Dietterich, Richard H. Lathrop, and Tomás Lozano-Pérez. Solving the multiple instance problem with axis-parallel rectangles. *Artificial Intelligence*, 89(1):31–71, 1997.

[55] Glenn Fung, Murat Dundar, Balaji Krishnapuram, and R. Bharat Rao. Multiple instance learning for computer aided diagnosis. *Advances in Neural Information Processing Systems*, 19:425, 2007.

[56] Jianming Liang and Jinbo Bi. Computer aided detection of pulmonary embolism with tobogganing and mutiple instance classification in ct pulmonary angiography. In *Information Processing in Medical Imaging*, pages 630–641. Springer, 2007.

[57] Richard S. Sutton and Andrew G. Barto. *Reinforcement Learning: An Introduction*, volume 1. Cambridge University Press, 1998.

[58] Yufan Zhao, Michael R Kosorok, and Donglin Zeng. Reinforcement learning design for cancer clinical trials. *Statistics in Medicine*, 28(26):3294–3315, 2009.

[59] Farhang Sahba, Hamid R. Tizhoosh, and Magdy M. A. Salama. A reinforcement learning framework for medical image segmentation. In *IJCNN'06. International Joint Conference on Neural Networks*, pages 511–517. IEEE, 2006.

[60] Trevor Hastie, Robert Tibshirani, and J. Jerome H. Friedman. *The Elements of Statistical Learning*, volume 1. Springer New York, 2001.

[61] Jieping Ye and Jun Liu. Sparse methods for biomedical data. *ACM SIGKDD Explorations Newsletter*, 14(1):4–15, 2012.

[62] Bernhard E. Boser, Isabelle M. Guyon, and Vladimir N. Vapnik. A training algorithm for optimal margin classifiers. In *Proceedings of the Fifth Annual Workshop on Computational Learning Theory*, pages 144–152. ACM, 1992.

[63] Bernhard Scholkopf, Kah-Kay Sung, Christopher J. C. Burges, Federico Girosi, Partha Niyogi, Tomaso Poggio, and Vladimir Vapnik. Comparing support vector machines with gaussian kernels to radial basis function classifiers. *IEEE Transactions on Signal Processing*, 45(11):2758–2765, 1997.

[64] Shi Yu, Tillmann Falck, Anneleen Daemen, Leon-Charles Tranchevent, Johan A.K. Suykens, Bart De Moor, and Yves Moreau. L2-norm multiple kernel learning and its application to biomedical data fusion. *BMC Bioinformatics*, 11(1):309, 2010.

[65] Shijun Wang, Jianhua Yao, Nicholas Petrick, and Ronald M. Summers. Combining statistical and geometric features for colonic polyp detection in CTC based on multiple kernel learning. *International Journal of Computational Intelligence and Applications*, 9(01):1–15, 2010.

[66] John P. Klein and Mei-Jie Zhang. *Survival Analysis Software*. Wiley Online Library, 2005.

[67] Rupert G. Miller Jr. *Survival Analysis*, volume 66. John Wiley & Sons, 2011.

[68] Ettore Marubini and Maria Grazia Valsecchi. *Analysing Survival Data from Clinical Trials and Observational Studies*. John Wiley & Sons, 414 pages ISBN 0–971-93987-0.

[69] Elisa T. Lee and John Wang. *Statistical Methods for Survival Data Analysis*, volume 476. Wiley.com, 2003.

[70] Olive Jean Dunn and Virginia A. Clark. *Basic Statistics: A Primer for the Biomedical Sciences*. Wiley.com, 2009.

[71] Edward L. Kaplan and Paul Meier. Nonparametric estimation from incomplete observations. *Journal of the American Statistical Association*, 53(282):457–481, 1958.

[72] Sidney J. Cutler and Fred Ederer. Maximum utilization of the life table method in analyzing survival. *Journal of Chronic Diseases*, 8(6):699–712, 1958.

[73] N. Mantel and W. Haenszel. Statistical aspects of the analysis of data from retrospective studies of disease. *Journal of the National Cancer Institute*, 22(4):719, 1959.

[74] Nathan Mantel. Chi-square tests with one degree of freedom: Extensions of the Mantel-Haenszel procedure. *Journal of the American Statistical Association*, 58(303):690–700, 1963.

[75] Edmund A. Gehan. A generalized Wilcoxon test for comparing arbitrarily singly-censored samples. *Biometrika*, 52(1-2):203–223, 1965.

[76] Richard Peto and Julian Peto. Asymptotically efficient rank invariant test procedures. *Journal of the Royal Statistical Society. Series A (General)*, pages 185–207, 1972.

[77] David R. Cox. Regression models and life-tables. *Journal of the Royal Statistical Society. Series B (Methodological)*, pages 187–220, 1972.

[78] Hans van Houwelingen and Hein Putter. *Dynamic Prediction in Clinical Survival Analysis*. CRC Press, Inc., 2011.

[79] Robert Tibshirani. Regression shrinkage and selection via the LASSO. *Journal of the Royal Statistical Society. Series B (Methodological)*, pages 267–288, 1996.

[80] Robert Tibshirani et al. The LASSO method for variable selection in the Cox model. *Statistics in Medicine*, 16(4):385–395, 1997.

[81] Hui Zou and Trevor Hastie. Regularization and variable selection via the elastic net. *Journal of the Royal Statistical Society: Series B (Statistical Methodology)*, 67(2):301–320, 2005.

[82] Noah Simon, Jerome Friedman, Trevor Hastie, and Rob Tibshirani. Regularization paths for Cox's proportional hazards model via coordinate descent. *Journal of Statistical Software*, 39(5):1–13, 2011.

[83] Arthur E. Hoerl and Robert W. Kennard. Ridge regression: Biased estimation for nonorthogonal problems. *Technometrics*, 12(1):55–67, 1970.

[84] Pierre J. M. Verweij and Hans C. Van Houwelingen. Penalized likelihood in Cox regression. *Statistics in Medicine*, 13(23-24):2427–2436, 1994.

[85] Bhanukiran Vinzamuri and Chandan K Reddy. Cox regression with correlation based regularization for electronic health records. In *IEEE 13th International Conference on Data Mining (ICDM)*, pages 757–766. IEEE, 2013.

[86] A. Ciampi, R. S. Bush, M. Gospodarowicz, and J. E. Till. An approach to classifying prognostic factors related to survival experience for non-Hodgkin's lymphoma patients: Based on a series of 982 patients: 1967–1975. *Cancer*, 47(3):621–627, 1981.

[87] L. Gordon and R. A. Olshen. Tree-structured survival analysis. *Cancer Treatment Reports*, 69(10):1065, 1985.

[88] Roger B. Davis and James R. Anderson. Exponential survival trees. *Statistics in Medicine*, 8(8):947–961, 1989.

[89] Michael LeBlanc and John Crowley. Relative risk trees for censored survival data. *Biometrics*, pages 411–425, 1992.

[90] Hyung Jun Cho and Seung-Mo Hong. Median regression tree for analysis of censored survival data. *IEEE Transactions on Systems, Man and Cybernetics, Part A: Systems and Humans*, 38(3):715–726, 2008.

[91] Antonio Ciampi, Johanne Thiffault, Jean-Pierre Nakache, and Bernard Asselain. Stratification by stepwise regression, correspondence analysis and recursive partition: A comparison of three methods of analysis for survival data with covariates. *Computational Statistics & Data Analysis*, 4(3):185–204, 1986.

[92] A. Ciampi, C. H. Chang, S. Hogg, and S. McKinney. Recursive partition: A versatile method for exploratory-data analysis in biostatistics. In *Biostatistics*, 38: 23–50. Springer, 1986.

[93] Mark Robert Segal. Regression trees for censored data. *Biometrics*, pages 35–47, 1988.

[94] Leo Breiman. Random forests. *Machine Learning*, 45(1):5–32, 2001.

[95] Torsten Hothorn, Berthold Lausen, Axel Benner, and Martin Radespiel-Tröger. Bagging survival trees. *Statistics in Medicine*, 23(1):77–91, 2004.

[96] Hemant Ishwaran, Udaya B. Kogalur, Eugene H. Blackstone, and Michael S. Lauer. Random survival forests. *The Annals of Applied Statistics*, 2(3): 841–860, 2008.

[97] Wayne Nelson. Theory and applications of hazard plotting for censored failure data. *Technometrics*, 14(4):945–966, 1972.

[98] Odd Aalen. Nonparametric inference for a family of counting processes. *The Annals of Statistics*, 6(4):701–726, 1978.

[99] Glenn W. Brier. Verification of forecasts expressed in terms of probability. *Monthly Weather Review*, 78(1):1–3, 1950.

[100] R. G. D. Steel and J. H. Torrie. *Principles and Procedures of Statistics with Special Reference to the Biological Sciences*. McGraw-Hill, 484 pages, 1960.

[101] A. Colin Cameron and Frank A. G. Windmeijer. An R-squared measure of goodness of fit for some common nonlinear regression models. *Journal of Econometrics*, 77(2):329–342, 1997.

[102] ISO 35341:2006. *Statistics Vocabulary and Symbols Part 1: General Statistical Terms and Terms Used in Probability*. Geneva, Switzerland: ISO, 2006.

[103] Antonio Menditto, Marina Patriarca, and Bertil Magnusson. Understanding the meaning of accuracy, trueness and precision. *Accreditation and Quality Assurance*, 12(1):45–47, 2007.

[104] Stephen V. Stehman. Selecting and interpreting measures of thematic classification accuracy. *Remote Sensing of Environment*, 62(1):77–89, 1997.

[105] Nathalie Japkowicz and Shaju Stephen. The class imbalance problem: A systematic study. *Intelligent Data Analysis*, 6(5):429–449, 2002.

[106] J. Ferlay, H. R. Shin, F. Bray, D. Forman, C. Mathers, and D. M. Parkin. Globocan 2008 v1. 2, Cancer Incidence and Mortality Worldwide: IARC Cancerbase No. 10 [Internet]. International Agency for Research on Cancer, Lyon, France, 2011.

[107] Douglas G. Altman and J. Martin Bland. Diagnostic tests. 1: Sensitivity and specificity. *British Medical Journal*, 308(6943):1552, 1994.

[108] Robert H. Fletcher, Suzanne W. Fletcher, Grant S. Fletcher et al. *Clinical Epidemiology: The Essentials.* Lippincott Williams & Wilkins, 2012.

[109] Gerard Salton and Michael J. McGill. *Introduction to Modern Information Retrieval.* McGraw-Hill, 1986.

[110] Tom Fawcett. An introduction to ROC analysis. *Pattern Recognition Letters*, 27(8):861–874, 2006.

[111] Mark H. Zweig and Gregory Campbell. Receiver-operating characteristic (ROC) plots: A fundamental evaluation tool in clinical medicine. *Clinical Chemistry*, 39(4):561–577, 1993.

[112] J. A. Hanely and B. J. McNeil. The meaning and use of the area under a receiver operating characteristic (ROC) curve. *Radiology*, 143(1):29–36, 1982.

[113] Donald Bamber. The area above the ordinal dominance graph and the area below the receiver operating characteristic graph. *Journal of Mathematical Psychology*, 12(4):387–415, 1975.

[114] Frank E. Harrell, Kerry L. Lee, Robert M. Califf, David B. Pryor, and Robert A. Rosati. Regression modelling strategies for improved prognostic prediction. *Statistics in Medicine*, 3(2):143–152, 1984.

[115] Frank E. Harrell Jr., Robert M. Califf, David B. Pryor, Kerry L. Lee, and Robert A. Rosati. Evaluating the yield of medical tests. *Journal of the American Medical Association*, 247(18):2543–2546, 1982.

[116] Michael J. Pencina and Ralph B. D'Agostino. Overall C as a measure of discrimination in survival analysis: Model specific population value and confidence interval estimation. *Statistics in Medicine*, 23(13):2109–2123, 2004.

[117] Patrick J. Heagerty and Yingye Zheng. Survival model predictive accuracy and ROC curves. *Biometrics*, 61(1):92–105, 2005.

[118] Mithat Gönen and Glenn Heller. Concordance probability and discriminatory power in proportional hazards regression. *Biometrika*, 92(4):965–970, 2005.

[119] Mervyn Stone. Cross-validatory choice and assessment of statistical predictions. *Journal of the Royal Statistical Society. Series B (Methodological)*, pages 111–147, 1974.

[120] Ron Kohavi et al. A study of cross-validation and bootstrap for accuracy estimation and model selection. In *IJCAI*, volume 14, pages 1137–1145, 1995.

[121] Bradley Efron and Robert Tibshirani. *An Introduction to the Bootstrap*, volume 57. CRC Press, 1993.

[122] Inke R. König, J.D. Malley, C. Weimar, H.C. Diener, and A. Ziegler. Practical experiences on the necessity of external validation. *Statistics in Medicine*, 26(30):5499–5511, 2007.

Chapter 11

Temporal Data Mining for Healthcare Data

Iyad Batal
Machine Learning Lab
General Electric Global Research
San Ramon, CA
iyad.batal@ge.com

11.1 Introduction

Hospitals and healthcare institutions nowadays are collecting large amounts of data about their patients. Utilizing these healthcare data requires developing advanced data mining and analytical capabilities that can transform data into meaningful intelligence. This can have far-reaching consequences on our society. A recent study [4] showed that the incorporation of current healthcare technology, such as automated records and clinical decision support systems led to reductions in mortality rates, costs, and complications in multiple hospitals. The premise is that mining and understanding healthcare data would transform medical care delivery from being reactive to become proactive (i.e., by predicting patients that are prone to medical complications and start treating them as early as possible).

Healthcare data almost always contain time information and it is inconceivable to reason and mine these data without incorporating the temporal dimension. The purpose of this chapter is to survey and summarize the literature on temporal data mining for healthcare data. But before we delve into the details of the different methods and techniques, it is important to first describe the major types of healthcare data and their temporal characteristics. For that, we differentiate between *electronic health records* (EHR) data and *sensor* data, which we will describe in the following.

EHR are becoming commonplace in most hospitals and medical practices. In fact, there is a U.S. government initiative for universal EHR adoption by the end of 2014. EHR contain longitudinal patient health information, including demographics, laboratory test results, medication orders, medical diagnoses, procedures, progress notes, radiology reports, etc. Mining the temporal dimension of EHR data is extremely promising as it may reveal patterns that enable a more precise understanding of disease manifestation, progression, and response to therapy. However, EHR data have several idiosyncrasies that make conventional methods inadequate to handle them. In particular, EHR data are:

1. *Multivariate*: A large number of clinical variables might be measured for a single patient (e.g., white blood counts, creatinine values, cholesterol levels, etc.).

2. *Heterogeneous*: The data contain multiple types of events; some events have numeric values (e.g., lab results), some events have categorical values (e.g., diagnosis/procedure codes), and some events may even have time durations (e.g., medications orders are usually associated with a time interval during which the patient should take the medication).

3. *Irregular in time*: The variables are measured asynchronously at irregular time intervals (i.e., data are collected whenever a patient visits a healthcare facility). The time intervals at which the variables are measured can greatly vary between different patients as well as within a specific patient.

4. *Sparse*: The data contain a lot of unknown/missing values because patients do not undergo all examinations every time.

In addition to EHR data, new sources of sensor data are emerging as a result of the advances in healthcare sensor technologies. Examples of these data are:

1. *Physiological parameters*: This data are often collected for critically ill patients in intensive care units (ICU). Examples of physiological parameters are temperature, blood pressure, oxygen saturation, respiration rate, and heart rate.

2. *Electrocardiogram (ECG)*: The recording of the electrical activity of the heart over a period of time. ECG translates impulses generated by the polarization and depolarization of cardiac tissue into a waveform, which are analyzed for the detection of arrhythmias and heart-related disorders.

3. *Electroencephalogram (EEG)*: The recording of the brain's spontaneous electrical activity over a period of time (typically 20–30 minutes). The activity is detected by electrodes placed on the scalp. EEG is often used for studying neurological disorders and assessing cognitive functions.

Unlike EHR data, sensor data are usually represented as numeric time series (the events are homogenous) that are regularly measured in time at a high frequency (e.g., physiological parameters are typically recorded at few Hz while EEG are recorded at several kHz). Moreover, sensor data for a specific subject are measured over a much shorter period of time (usually several minutes to several days) compared to the longitudinal EHR data (collected across the life span).

Given the different natures of EHR data and sensor data, the choice of appropriate temporal data mining methods for these types of data are often different. EHR data are usually mined using temporal pattern mining methods, which represent data instances (e.g., patients' records) as sequences

TABLE 11.1: 2×2 Contingency Table Containing Frequencies of Exposure to Drug i and Occurrences of Adverse Drug Reaction (ADR) j as Basis for Detection

DRUG i / ADR j	EVENT	NO EVENT	TOTAL
EXPOSED	n_{11}	n_{10}	$n_{1.}$
NOT EXPOSED	n_{01}	n_{00}	$n_{0.}$
TOTAL	$n_{.1}$	$n_{.0}$	$n_{..}$

of discrete events (e.g., diagnosis codes, procedures, etc.) and then try to find and enumerate statistically relevant patterns that are embedded in the data. On the other hand, sensor data are often analyzed using signal processing and time-series analysis techniques (e.g., wavelet transform, independent component analysis, etc.).

The rest of the chapter is organized as follows. We start by describing association analysis methods in Section 11.2, which look for strong pairwise associations among medical events (e.g., a drug and an adverse drug reaction). We also describe recent methods that incorporate the temporal information of EHR data to refine the analysis. In Section 11.3, we discuss in detail temporal pattern mining methods and their applications to EHR data. We start by describing sequential pattern mining, which is applicable to data for which all events are instantaneous (time-point events). After that, we describe methods that can handle events that have time durations. In Section 11.4, we survey the techniques that have been applied to analyze healthcare sensor data. In Section 11.5, we describe recent methods that apply other strategies to model the temporal dimension in healthcare data. In Section 11.6, we discuss useful public resources for researchers interested in temporal data mining for healthcare data. Lastly, in Section 11.7, we summarize the chapter and discuss challenges and future research opportunities.

11.2 Association Analysis

In this section, we discuss methods that aim to discover strong *pairwise* associations (correlations) between medical events. Such methods are widely used in pharmacovigilance for detecting unknown adverse drug reactions (ADRs) by analyzing a broad range of combinations of drug exposures and subsequent adverse events [48]. We start by discussing conventional methods that operate on atemporal snapshot data (e.g., spontaneous reports of ADRs). After that, we describe more recent methods that incorporate temporal information to perform more refined association analysis.

11.2.1 Classical Methods

Conventional association analysis, sometime referred to as *disproportionality analysis*, operates on frequencies collated in 2×2 contingency tables in order to identify event-event combinations that occur disproportionately often, compared to other event-event combinations. For example, for each drug-event combination (e.g., drug i and ADR j) in question, such a table is constructed and evaluated during the data mining process (see Table 11.1). Several disproportionality measures have been proposed in the literature, which can be generally divided into two main categories: *frequentist* and *Bayesian*, both relying on the aforementioned 2×2 contingency tables. In pharmacovigilance, the most popular frequentist methods are the proportional reporting rate [17] and the reporting odds ratio [51]; and the most popular Bayesian methods are the Bayesian confidence propagation neural network [9] and the Gamma-Poisson shrinker [15].

A major limitation of the above methods is the lack of temporal reasoning and ability to hypothesize about potential cause-and-effect relations. This necessitates the need for more advanced temporal association analysis methods.

11.2.2 Temporal Methods

Hanauer and Ramakrishnan [19] described an exploratory data analysis approach to model pairwise temporal associations and applied it to find relationships between ICD-9 (International Classification of Diseases, ninth revision) diagnosis codes in EHR data. The authors assessed the temporal direction of the association using the following simple logic: Given two codes X and Y, count the number of times code X appears before code Y, and vice versa (using only the initial encounter of each code); and then compare these counts using an exact binomial test with a hypothesized probability of success equals to 0.5. The direction of the association is determined by the code that appeared first more often and the magnitude is represented by the p-value of the binomial test. In order to explore relationships across different time scales, this analysis was conducted using several time frames for the difference between each pair of codes, e.g., ≥ 1 day apart, 1-30 days apart, ≥ 1 year apart, etc. For instance, when the time frame is set to ≥ 1 year, only time differences that are 1 or more years apart are considered (i.e., all time differences shorter than 1 year are not counted).

Network graphs were used to visualize the results. In these graphs, a node represented an ICD-9 code and a directed edge represents a significant temporal relationship between two codes, with the arrowhead pointing to the lagged code. Note that the directed edges should be interpreted only *individually*, not as longer chains of cascades. For example, if the network graph contains chain $a \rightarrow b \rightarrow c$, patients with codes $a \rightarrow b$ are not necessarily the same patients who have codes $b \rightarrow c$. This approach was applied on a dataset that contains 41.2 million time stamped ICD-9 codes from 1.6 million patients. It discovered around 400,000 highly associated pairs of ICD-9 codes with varying number of strong temporal associations ranging from ≥ 1 day to ≥ 10 years.

Norén et al. [36] proposed a method for identifying temporal associations between the prescription of a drug and the occurrence of an ADR. Basically, the method contrasts the observed number of an ADR in a certain time period t to an expected number based on the overall frequency of the ADR relative to other drugs. This is done using the *information component* (IC) disproportionality measure [9]. IC is a regularized version of the raw log observed-to-expected ratio that shrinks the estimation towards 0 for rare events to reduce the volatility and achieve better variance properties.

A temporal drug-ADR association was visualized using a *chronograph*, which displays IC values (along with the 95% confidence interval) for different time periods relative to prescriptions of the drug of interest (see Figure 11.1 for an example). Chronographs can help identifying different types of temporal associations. For example, a transient increase in the IC value immediately *before* the prescription may indicate that the medical event triggers the prescription, whereas an increase in the IC value immediately *after* the prescription may indicate that the drug triggers the medical event. However, it is important to note that such temporal associations do not necessarily imply causality, as there could be a number of other possible explanations for why one event tends to occur soon after the other.

Chronographs only show IC values for specific time periods and do not account for temporal variations. To overcome this shortcoming, the authors introduced the IC_Δ measure, which is the contrast between the IC values in two different time periods: a follow-up period u (immediately after the prescription of a drug) and a control period v against which u is to be contrasted. The IC_Δ is used to identify medical events that are registered more often in the period after the prescription of a given drug (u) than in the control period (v), which may correspond to suspected ADRs.

The authors applied their approach on an EHR dataset that contains 3,445 drug substances and 5,753 medical events including diagnoses, clinical symptoms and signs, and administrative notes. They presented examples of several temporal associations that were discovered from data including suspected ADRs, potential beneficial effects of drugs, medical events related to an underlying disease, periodic patterns and trends, and drug co-prescription patterns.

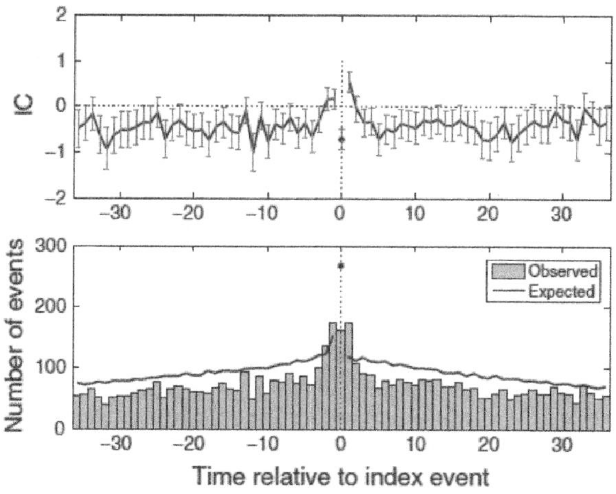

FIGURE 11.1: Example of a chronograph (taken from Norén et al. [36]). The bottom panel displays the observed and expected numbers of a medical event in different time periods relative to the prescription of the drug. The top panel displays the corresponding variation in the IC value.

11.3 Temporal Pattern Mining

The methods discussed in the previous section are limited in that they only evaluate the association between two events (e.g., one drug and one ADR). However, in real-world healthcare data, patterns are often more complex than simple pairwise associations (e.g., the joint exposure to two drugs poses a safety risk, but the exposure to one of them alone is not problematic). Therefore, it is crucial to develop tools and techniques for mining complex temporal patterns that are embedded in large clinical data. Examples of such patterns are common sequences of lab tests/medications that are prescribed for a specific disease [6], clinically relevant sequences of medical diagnosis [39], temporal patterns that indicate the onset of a disease [7], and so on.

Temporal pattern mining (TPM) aims to find statistically relevant patterns in temporal data for which the instances are represented as sequences of events (discrete symbols). The first class of TPM methods is known as sequential pattern mining, which is applicable to temporal data for which all events are represented as *time points* (i.e., events are instantaneous). For example, clinical diagnoses, lab exams, and ambulatory visits are often represented as time-point events. Later on, a new class of TPM methods emerged to handle temporal data for which the events have *time durations* (time-interval events). Examples of such events in the healthcare domain are medication orders (e.g., the period during which heparin medication was administered) or abstract events that are derived from data (e.g., the period during which there was a decreasing trend in platelet counts).

In the rest of this section, we describe the most popular TPM methods and present an overview of their applications for mining EHR data. We start by discussing sequential pattern mining and then we discuss time-interval pattern mining.

11.3.1 Sequential Pattern Mining

The *sequential pattern mining* (SPM) problem was first introduced by Agrawal and Srikant [2] for analyzing market basket data and customer shopping behavior. For instance, a market basket sequential pattern would be something like "customers who buy a Canon digital camera are likely to buy an HP color printer within a month." Later on, SPM has been applied to analyze temporal data in a variety of other domains and it recently gained a lot of popularity in medical data mining [12, 26, 21, 6, 39]. In the following, we first introduce the main concepts and definitions of SPM and then survey several papers that applied it on healthcare data.

11.3.1.1 Concepts and Definitions

In SPM, each data instance S_i is represented as a sequence of timestamped events:

$$S_i = \langle\, (e_1,t_1),(e_2,t_2),...,(e_{|S_i|},t_{|S_i|})\rangle$$

where e_j denotes a specific event that belongs to a finite alphabet Σ (the space of all possible events) and t_i denotes the time event e_j appeared in instance S_i. All events are instantaneous (have zero duration) and the events in S_i are conventionally ordered according to their timestamps, i.e., $t_j \leq t_{j+1}$ for $j \in \{1,...,|S_i|-1\}$. For instance, if the task is to analyze clinical diagnosis sequences, S_i would represent the medical record for the i-th patient and each event (e_j) would denote a specific diagnosis code.

A *sequential pattern* is a sequence of events $P = \langle a_1,a_2,\ldots a_k\rangle$, where $a_j \in \Sigma$. We say that instance S_i supports (satisfies) P if the events of P appear in the same order in S_i. Additionally, we may want to impose temporal constraints to further restrict the definition of sequential patterns. For instance, a *maximum gap* constraint can be specified to define the maximum allowed time between consecutive events in a pattern. For example, we may specify that the time difference between consecutive diagnosis codes in a pattern should not exceed 6 months.

The *support* of a sequential pattern P is the fraction of instances in the data that support it. We say that P is *frequent* if its support is at least equal to *minsup*, where *minsup* is a user-specified parameter of the mining process. Similar to itemsets [1], sequential patterns obey the *apriori* (downward closure) property, which states that all subpatterns (generalizations) of a frequent pattern are also frequent. For example, if sequence $\langle A,D,B\rangle$ is frequent, all its subsequences (e.g., $\langle D,B\rangle$) are also frequent.

Once frequent sequential patterns are found, interesting sequential rules may be identified. A sequential rule is usually defined as $X \Rightarrow Y$, where both X and Y are frequent sequential patterns and Y follows X in time. For example, suppose that sequence $\langle A,D,B\rangle$ is frequent, we may derive rule $\langle A,D\rangle \Rightarrow B$, which means that if we observe sequence $\langle A,D\rangle$, we expect to also observe B later on. Rules are usually characterized by the *support* and *confidence* quality measures. The support of $X \Rightarrow Y$ is the support of X followed by Y (i.e., the support of sequential pattern $\langle X,Y\rangle$). The confidence of $X \Rightarrow Y$ is the support of the rule divided by the support of X (the antecedent), which represents the likelihood of Y occurring after X (i.e., the conditional probability of Y given X). The support is usually used to identify statistically significant rules, while the confidence represents the strength of the rule. Note that in addition to the support and confidence, a variety of other measures have been proposed to evaluate the quality of rules (see [18] for more details).

Several SPM algorithms have been proposed in the literature to efficiently generate all frequent sequential patterns in the data. These algorithms can be generally categorized into three main classes: (i) level-wise algorithms based on horizontal data representation, such as the GSP (generalized sequential patterns) algorithm [46]; (ii) level-wise algorithms based on vertical data representation, such as the SPADE (sequential pattern discovery using equivalent class) algorithm [57]; and (iii) projection-based pattern growth algorithms, such as the PrefixSpan (prefix-projected sequential pattern growth) algorithm [40]. Furthermore, algorithms to efficiently incorporate temporal constraints (such as the maximum gap constraint) into the mining were also introduced [41].

11.3.1.2 Medical Applications

Several research papers have applied SPM to discover sequential patterns in EHR data. For example, SPM has been used to find the common sets/sequences of medical exams that are ordered in a specific situation or to find sequences of observations that are often associated with a particular disease. Moreover, the original SPM framework has been extended to mine time-annotated sequential patterns, unexpected temporal association rules, and partial order episodes.

Frequent Sequences of Clinical Exams Baralis et al. [6] analyzed patients' exam log data to rebuild from operational data an image of the steps of the medical treatment process (medical pathways). The analysis was performed on the treatment of diabetic patients provided by a local sanitary agency in Italy. Detected medical pathways include both the set of exams frequently done together, and the sequences of exam sets frequently followed by patients. The proposed approach is based on mining closed sequential patterns using a modified version of the PrefixSpan algorithm [56]. The extracted knowledge allows highlighting medical pathways typically adopted for a specific disease. Moreover, it can also help identifying non-compliant pathways (pathways that deviate from predefined guidelines), which may be due to patient negligence in following the prescribed treatment, medical ignorance of the predefined guidelines, or incorrect procedures for data collection.

Sequential Patterns for Predicting Cardiovascular Disease Klema et al. [26] applied SPM to a longitudinal preventive study of atherosclerosis where the data consist of a series of long-term observations recording the development of risk factors and associated conditions. The purpose was to find frequent sequential patterns and to identify possible relations between these patterns and the onset of a cardiovascular disease. The paper compared three different SPM methods based on windowing, episode rules, and inductive logic programming. Patterns mined by each method were used to extract classification rules for predicting whether or not there is risk of cardiovascular disease. The experiments showed that all compared methods require a lot of pre-processing (using domain knowledge to adjust their parameters) in order to find useful patterns and none of them clearly outperforms the others.

Time-Annotated Sequences for Medical Data Mining Berlingerio et al. [12] argued that classical SPM is not expressive enough to describe medical data because it only considers on the order of events, without specifying the typical time elapsing between consecutive events. To address this shortcoming, they advocated using *time-annotated sequences* (TAS), which are sequential patterns where the transition between two events is annotated with a typical transition time that is found frequently in the data. An example of a TAS is $\langle A\ [t_1,t_2]\ B \rangle$, where A and B are events and t_1 and t_2 are the minimum and maximum time delay allowed between A and B. TAS mining was applied to a set of patients in the follow-up of a liver transplantation (the study involved 50 patients and 38 clinical variables). The aim was to assess the effectiveness of the extracorporeal photopheresis (ECP) as a therapy to prevent rejection in solid organ transplantation. The approach received positive feedback from physicians as the extracted patterns represented additional evidence of the effectiveness of the applied therapy.

Unexpected Temporal Association in Detecting Drug Reactions In medical applications, it might be useful to mine unanticipated episodes, where certain event patterns unexpectedly lead to outcomes. These unanticipated episodes are usually unexpected and *infrequent*, which makes standard SPM techniques (mainly designed to find frequent patterns) ineffective. Jin et al. [21] studied mining unexpected temporal association rules to detect adverse drug reactions from healthcare administrative data. The extracted rules are of the form $A \Rightarrow C\ [T]$, which means that an event A (e.g., a drug) unexpectedly occurs in a T-sized period prior to another event C (e.g., a condition). Note that mining unexpected temporal associations is computationally very expensive because it needs to explore many infrequent patterns without being able to apply the pruning strategies that are used in frequent pattern mining. To make computation tractable, the authors limit their rules to have length 2.

Partial-Order Episodes of Clinical Diagnosis Patnaik et al. [39] studied how to extract clinically relevant sequences of diagnosis codes that are embedded in EHR data. They argued that a straightforward application of SPM does not effectively solve the problem because the resulting sequences are too many for human consumption and they are nearly permutations of each other (representing several alternate serializations of the same sets of codes). To overcome this limitation, the authors proposed mining *partial order* patterns from frequent sequences of codes using the following three steps:

1. *Mining parallel episodes*: Parallel episodes are very similar to itemsets [1] but take temporal information into account in the form of expiry constraints (an expiry constraint T specifies that the symbols of a pattern should occur no further than T time units apart from each other). These parallel episodes are ranked based on their significance using the maximum entropy principle [50].

2. *Tracking serial extensions*: After mining the lattice of frequent parallel episodes, another pass through the data is made to record the number of times different serial extensions of each frequent parallel episode occur in the data. The intuition behind this step is to unearth potential evidence (or lack thereof) for sequentiality in the data.

3. *Learning partial orders*: The set of all serial extensions determined in the previous step is compacted into a partial order using a specialized PQ tree algorithm [13]. This step of the procedure is interactive in that the medical professional can iteratively generalize or specialize partial orders to arrive to an understanding of the underlying orders.

This mining system, called EMRView, was applied on a large EHR data of more than 1.6 million subjects of the University of Michigan's health system to discover partial order relations of frequent ICD-9 diagnosis code sequences.

11.3.2 Time-Interval Pattern Mining

SPM methods described in the previous section only deal with *time-point* events (i.e., instantaneous events). In this section, we describe *time-interval pattern mining* (TIPM), a relatively young research field that aims to mine data for which the events have time durations (i.e., an event has specific start time and end time). We start by introducing the main concepts and definitions and then we survey several papers that applied TIPM on healthcare data.

11.3.2.1 Concepts and Definitions

In TIPM, a data instance S_i is represented as a sequence of time-interval events:

$$S_i = \langle\ (e_1, s_1, f_1), (e_2, s_2, f_2), ..., (e_{|S_i|}, s_{|S_i|}, f_{|S_i|})\rangle$$

where e_j denotes a specific event from a finite alphabet Σ that starts at time s_j and finishes at time f_j. By convention, the events of S_i are sorted according to their start time [20], i.e., $s_j \leq s_{j+1}$ for $j \in \{1, ..., |S_i| - 1\}$. The intervals of consecutive events are not necessarily disjoint (we do not require f_i to be less than s_{i+1}). Time-interval events appear abundantly in medical data. They might be either part of the original raw data (e.g., the period during which a cancer patient underwent chemotherapy) or they might be derived from data using temporal abstractions, which we will discuss in the following.

Temporal abstractions (TA) is a way of transforming raw numeric time-series variables into a higher level qualitative form [43, 44]. More specifically, TA converts a time-series clinical variable into a sequence of time-interval events, where each event represents a property of the time series (e.g., instead of a series of hemoglobin measurements, TA derives characterizations of the series such as "3 weeks of moderate anemia"). A survey of the use of temporal abstractions in medicine can be found in [47]. The most commonly used TA types are:

1. *Trend abstractions*, which segment the time series based on its local trends in order to capture increasing, decreasing, or stationary courses in the series. Trend abstractions are usually obtained by first applying piecewise linear approximation [24] to represent the time series with straight lines and then defining the abstractions based on the slopes of the fitted lines.

2. *Value abstractions*, which segment the time series based on its values in order to create states corresponding to, for example, low, high, and normal values. The thresholds used for defining value abstractions (e.g., which values of hemoglobin are considered to be "high") can be either obtained from medical experts or automatically extracted from data using discretization techniques such as symbolic aggregate approximation (SAX) [28] or persist [33].

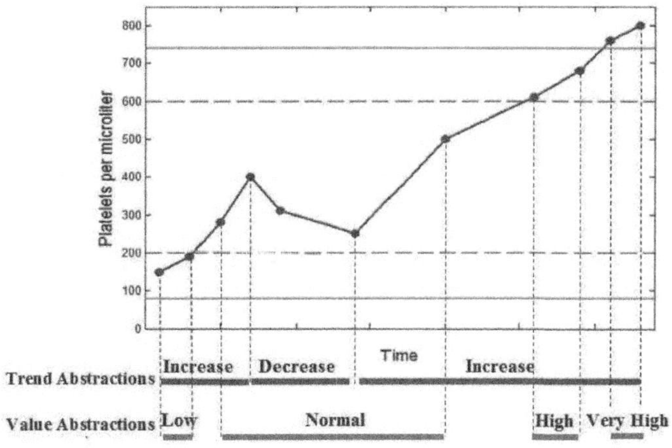

FIGURE 11.2: An example illustrating trend abstractions and value abstractions.

Figure 11.2 shows an example of trend and value abstractions applied on a series of platelet counts. In the following, we will describe how basic temporal abstractions can be combined to create time-interval patterns in order to capture complex multivariate temporal behavior in patients' data.

Defining temporal patterns for time-interval events is more complicated than that for time-point events (i.e., sequential patterns). To illustrate this, consider describing the temporal relation between only two events. If the events are instantaneous, the relation is simply one of the following: *before*, *equals* (at the same time), or *after*. However, when the events have time durations, the relationship becomes more complex. Commonly, time-interval relations are described using Allen's temporal operators [3], which consist of the following 13 relations: *before*, *meets*, *overlaps*, *is-finished-by*, *contains*, *starts*; their corresponding inverses; and the *equals* relation (see Figure 11.3).

Several representations have been proposed in the literature for describing temporal patterns that consist of multiple time-interval events. Examples of such representations are the nested A1 patterns

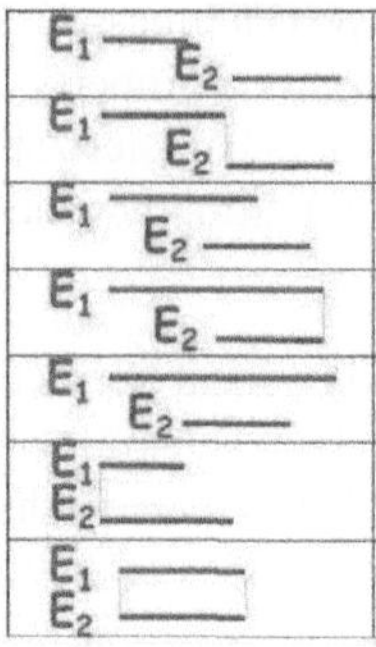

E_1 before E_2	E_2 after E_1
E_1 meets E_2	E_2 is-met-by E_1
E_1 overlaps E_2	E_2 is-overlapped-by E_1
E_1 is-finished-by E_2	E_2 finishes E_1
E_1 contains E_2	E_2 during E_1
E_1 starts E_2	E_2 is-started-by E_1
E_1 equals E_2	E_2 equals E_1

FIGURE 11.3: Allen's temporal relations.

[23], Höppner's representation [20], time-series knowledge representation (TSKR) [31], interval boundaries sequential patterns [55], and semi-interval sequential patterns (SISP) [32]. Among them, Höppner's representation [20] is still the most popular because it is non-ambiguous, intuitive, and easy to interpret. Therefore, it has been adopted by several recent TIPM methods [37, 54, 34, 8, 7].

According to Höppner representation, a *time-interval pattern* P is defined as $P = (\langle a_1, ..., a_k \rangle, R)$, where $a_1, ..., a_k$ are the pattern's time-interval events sorted in the normalized form[1] and R is a matrix that specifies Allen's relations between all pairs of events (i.e., $R_{i,j}$ is the temporal relation between event a_i and event a_j). Note that it suffices to only specify the relations between each event and all of its following events (only using the upper triangular matrix of R) since the other relations are simply their inverses. Figure 11.4 shows an example of a time-interval pattern $(\langle A, B, D \rangle, R_{1,2} = overlaps, R_{1,3} = before, R_{2,3} = contains)$.

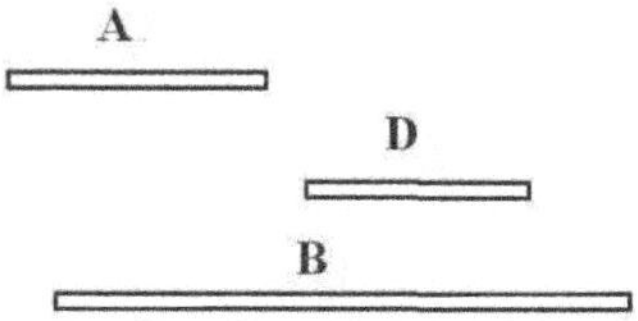

	A	B	D
A	Equals	**Overlaps**	**Before**
B	Overlapped-by	Equals	**Contains**
D	After	During	Equals

FIGURE 11.4: A time-interval pattern represented using Höppner's representation.

Once we have defined the representation for time-interval patterns, we can define the *support* of a pattern (see Section 11.3.1.1) and design algorithms for mining frequent time-interval patterns. Note that, similar to sequential patterns, time-interval patterns also obey the apriori property. For example, if the pattern in Figure 11.4 is frequent, all its subpatterns, such as $(\langle B, D \rangle, R_{1,2} = contains)$, are guaranteed to be frequent.

11.3.2.2 Medical Applications

There has been a lot of interest recently in applying TIPM to EHR data. The reason is that many concepts of EHR data are naturally represented as time-interval events and hence cannot be adequately mined using SPM. In this section, we describe methods for finding temporal association

[1] The events are sorted in increasing index according to their start times, end times, and value.

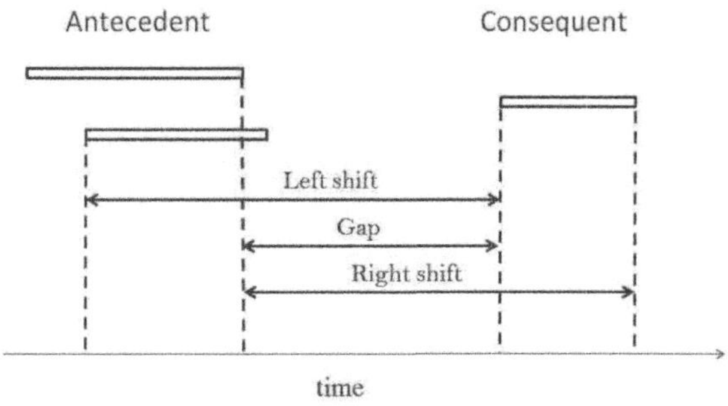

FIGURE 11.5: Illustrating the three parameters of the *precedes* relation for a rule that has two *AoI*s in the antecedent.

rules and frequent time-interval patterns in abstracted data. After that, we discuss a method for mining a concise set of time-interval patterns for classification. Lastly, we describe an efficient TIPM algorithm for event detection.

Temporal Rules with Abstractions of Interest Sacchi et al. [42] proposed a method for mining temporal association rules from medical data. In this approach, the user should define beforehand a set of complex patterns of interest, called *abstractions of interest* (AoI), which constitute the basis for the construction of the rules. The method mines rules of the form $A \Rightarrow c$, where A (the antecedent) is a set of *AoIs*, c (the consequent) is a single *AoI*, and *A precedes c*. In order to define the *precedes* relationship, the user should specify the following three context-dependent parameters: (i) the *left shift*, which is the maximum allowed time between the start of c and the maximum start of the patterns in A, (ii) the *gap*, which is the maximum allowed time between the start of c and the minimum end of the patterns in A, and (iii) the *right shift*, which is the maximum allowed time between the end of c and the minimum end of the patterns in A (see Figure 11.5 for an illustration). Once the user specifies the set of *AoIs* and the parameters of the *precedes* relation, an apriori-like algorithm searches the data to find strong temporal association rules (i.e., rules that have high support and high confidence). The authors applied their method to find temporal rules for time-series variables monitored during hemodialysis sessions and to reconstruct gene regulatory relationships from gene expression data.

Frequent Time-Interval Patterns for Exploratory Analysis Moskovitch and Shahar [34] studied the problem of mining frequently occurring temporal patterns in abstracted EHR data. The approach applies temporal abstraction to convert the raw clinical variables into time-interval events and uses Höppner's representation to define complex time-interval patterns (see Figure 11.4). The authors presented an efficient algorithm called *karma-lego* for constructing an enumeration tree that contains all frequent time-interval patterns (see Figure 11.6 for an example). Briefly, the algorithm operates in two phases by first generating and indexing all frequent 2-sized patterns (composed of two abstractions), and then recursively extending the 2-sized patterns into a tree of longer frequent patterns. The authors applied their method on a dataset of diabetic patients and developed a visualization tool to facilitate exploring and navigating the enumeration tree.

Minimal Predictive Temporal Patterns for Classification Most existing TIPM methods [20, 37, 31, 42, 54, 55, 34, 32] have been applied in an unsupervised setting to generate all frequent patterns or to find strong temporal association rules. Unlike these methods, Batal et al. [8] proposed a method for mining time-interval patterns that are most useful for *classification* (e.g., patterns that

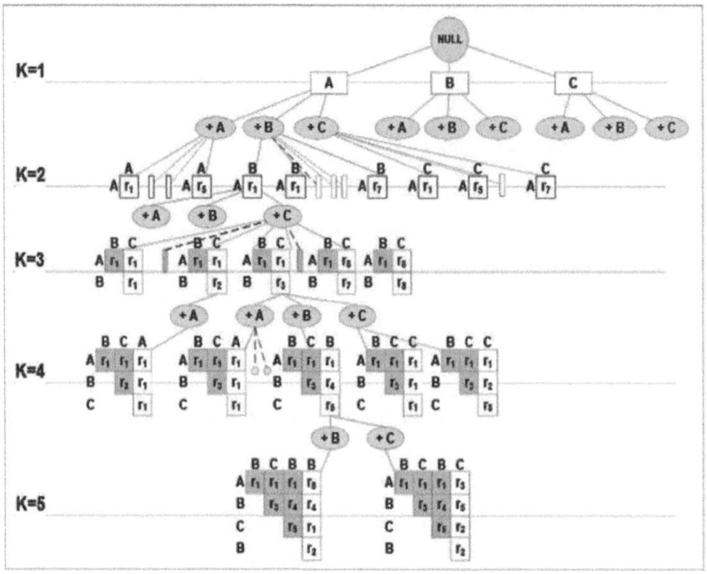

FIGURE 11.6: An enumeration tree constructed by karma-lego (taken from [34]). Each node represents a time-interval pattern using Höppner's representation (only the upper triangular matrix of the temporal relations matrix is shown). The level *K* contains the frequent time-interval patterns of size *K*.

discriminate well between sick patients and healthy patients). This method was applied to the clinical task of predicting patients who are at risk of developing heparin induced thrombocytopenia (HIT), a life-threatening condition that may develop in patients treated with heparin [53].

The proposed *minimal predictive temporal pattern* (MPTP) mining framework attempts to find a concise set of patterns that are most predictive of the class variable (e.g., whether or not the patient will develop HIT) and at the same time contain low redundancy among the patterns. To achieve this, MPTP applies a statistical significance test to ensure that every pattern in the result predicts the class label significantly better than all of its subpatterns. For example, consider pattern *P* =*heparin-on before platelet-decreasing* (heparin was administered and after that there was a decreasing trend in platelet counts). For *P* to be an MPTP for predicting HIT, the patient population that satisfies *P* should have a significantly higher rate of HIT compared to the population that satisfies only *heparin-on*, the population that satisfies only *platelet-decreasing*, as well as the entire population in the data. An efficient algorithm was presented to directly mine MPTPs without having to generate all frequent time-interval patterns (i.e., the algorithm applies pruning strategies to further reduce the search space of frequent patterns).

Recent Temporal Patterns for Adverse Event Detection Batal et al. [7] studied applying TIPM for detecting adverse medical events (e.g., onsets of diseases or drug toxicity) as early as possible. In this setting, an adverse event is associated with a specific time point during the patient's record (e.g., a specific patient developed an adverse drug reaction on the fifth day he/she was hospitalized). The goal is to learn temporal patterns that indicate the development of the adverse event of interest and use these patterns to monitor future patients (i.e., detect if that event is developing for new patients).

For event detection, temporal measurements that are observed recently before the occurrence of the event are typically the most important for predicting it (e.g., recent lab values are usually more indicative of the patient's current health status compared to old lab values). To incorporate this local nature of decision into TIPM, *recent temporal pattern* (RTP) mining was introduced. The method mines frequent time-interval patterns backward in time starting from patterns related to the most recent observations before the events. Applying this technique, patterns that extend far into the past are likely to have low support in the data and hence would not be considered during the mining.

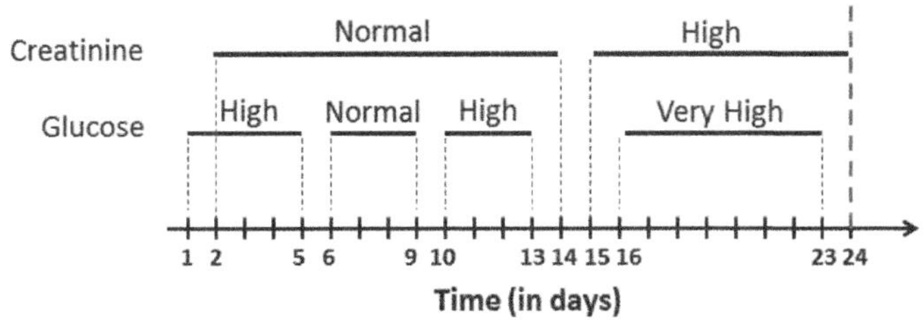

FIGURE 11.7: A example of an EHR with two variables (creatinine and glucose) that are abstracted using value abstractions.

For illustration purposes, consider the example in Figure 11.7, which shows an EHR instance with two clinical variables (creatinine and glucose) that are abstracted using value abstractions (see Section 11.3.2.1). For instance, creatinine values were "normal" from day 2 until day 14, then became "high" after that. Assume the event of interest happened at the end of the instance (the red dashed line at day 24).[2] For a time-interval pattern P to be an RTP in an instance, the last interval of P should be "close" to the end of the instance (within a specific gap) and all intervals of P should be "close" to each other. For example, assume the maximum gap parameter g is 3 days. Pattern *creatinine-normal before glucose-very high* is an RTP in the example EHR because the gap between *glucose-very high* and the end of the instance is less than g $(24-23 \leq g)$ and the gap between *creatinine-normal* and *glucose-very high* is also less than g $(16-14 \leq g)$. On the other hand, pattern *glucose-high before glucose-normal* is not an RTP because the gap between *glucose-normal* and the end of the record is more than g $(24-9 > g)$.

RTP mining was evaluated on large-scale data that contain records of more than 13K adult diabetic patients. The results demonstrated its benefit in finding time-interval patterns that are important for detecting and diagnosing several disorders that are commonly associated with diabetes, such as cardiological, renal, or neurological disorders. Furthermore, they showed that RTP mining is more scalable compared to existing TIPM methods.

11.4 Sensor Data Analysis

TPM methods discussed in the previous section have been mostly used in the healthcare domain for mining observational EHR data, which are usually heterogeneous, irregularly sampled in time, and sparse. In this section, we describe methods that are used to analyze sensor healthcare data (e.g., physiological parameters, EEG signals, etc.). In contrast to EHR data, sensor data are usually represented as numeric time series (either univariate or multivariate) that are measured at regular time intervals and at a high frequency. Not surprisingly, techniques used to analyze sensor data are different from those used to analyze EHR data. In the following, we outline several signal processing and time-series analysis methods that have been successfully applied to healthcare sensor data.

The *wavelet transform* is a popular signal processing technique that maps a signal from the time domain into a joint *time-frequency* domain (i.e., revealing the frequency content while at the same

[2]For learning the patterns, we only consider the EHR instances up to the time of the event.

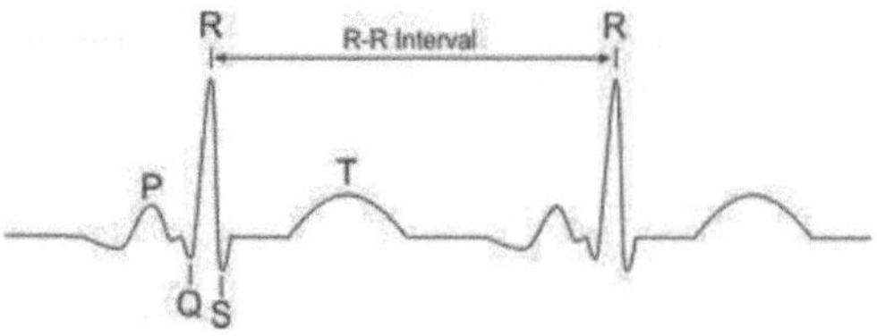

FIGURE 11.8: Typical ECG waveform.

time preserving the temporal locality). Basically, wavelets perform a multiresolution analysis of the signal using dilated windows such that wide windows provide good frequency resolution (and bad time resolution) and narrow windows provide good time resolution (and bad frequency resolution). In the healthcare domain, wavelets have been widely applied to analyze ECG signals for detecting different types of arrhythmias (abnormal rates of heart contraction that are dangerous and may cause death). A typical ECG signal is characterized by a recurrent waveform associated with each beat, which consists of the following perceptually important points: P, Q, R, S, and T (see Figure 11.8). Arrhythmias manifest themselves in ECG signals as deformations or irregularities in the observed waveform. In [22], Joshi et al. applied wavelet transform and support vector machines for arrhythmia detection. In [25], Kim and Yang studied ECG characteristics using wavelets and neural networks. The wavelet transform was first applied to preprocess the signals and the backpropagation algorithm was then used for classification.

Multiscale entropy (MSE) analysis [14] is a useful method to analyze complexity in signals that exhibit correlations at multiple (time) scales. MSE is based on the observation that the output of real-world complex systems is far from the extremes of perfect regularity and complete randomness. Instead, such systems generally reveal structures with long-range correlations across multiple temporal scales. In [5], MSE was applied on three physiological signals (heart rate, blood pressure, and lung volume) to differentiate between healthy subjects and subjects with chronic heart failure. The results showed that MSE is able to produce statistically significant differences between the two populations.

Fractal geometry is a tool to quantitatively characterize and describe objects that are considered very complex. Fractals are objects that have a similar appearance when viewed at different scales (they are copies of themselves buried deep within the original). Paramanathan and Uthayakumar [38] applied fractal analysis to EEG time-series data and showed that detection of fractal patterns in each electrode positions can be useful for analyzing and understanding different brain activity signals.

Independent component analysis (ICA) is a computational method for separating a multivariate signal into additive subcomponents by assuming that the subcomponents are non-Gaussian signals and are all statistically independent from each other. In [30], Melissant et al. used ICA for detecting EEG patterns that are indicative of Alzheimer's disease. Basically, ICA was applied prior to classification in order to remove unwanted artifacts from the EEG signals. The experiments showed that this preprocessing improved the classification accuracy, especially for patients that are in the initial stage of the disease. Furthermore, ICA was applied to functional magnetic resonance imaging (fMRI) data. fMRI is a functional neuroimaging procedure that uses MRI technology to measure hemodynamic changes (the change in blood flow) in the brain as a result of a stimulation. The data can be viewed as a 4-D data cube (3-D space+time), where each data cube is known as a voxel. Esposito et al. [16] used ICA on fMRI data for revealing modes of signal variability in brain activity patterns. Two types of ICA were performed: *spatial ICA* and *temporal ICA*. A similarity measure that combines both spatial and temporal similarity based on the Pearson correlation coefficient was used to cluster the data. The main advantage of this method is that it exploits commonalities across multiple subject-specific patterns, while at the same time it addresses the intersubject variability of the measured responses. The experiments demonstrated the validity of the approach in extracting meaningful activity and functional connectivity groups.

11.5 Other Temporal Modeling Methods

This section describes some recent methods for modeling the temporal dimension of healthcare data, which apply other strategies compared to the methods discussed in the previous sections. We outline three different approaches. The first applies an optimization framework to extract event patterns that summarize important temporal relations in EHR data (in a convolutional sense). The second approach reaches a patient prognostic by reasoning over patients that have similar temporal trajectories to the query patient (case-based reasoning). Lastly, the third approach applies multi-task regression for predicting disease progression at multiple future time points (using a temporal smoothness assumption for the predictions).

11.5.1 Convolutional Event Pattern Discovery

Wang et al. [52] proposed a non-negative matrix factorization framework using a convolutional approach for temporal pattern discovery in EHR data. This approach models each patient's record as an image matrix, where the x-axis corresponds to the timestamps and the y-axis corresponds to the event types. The (i, j)-th element of the patient matrix is 1 if the i-th event happens at time j; and it is 0 otherwise. Note that this representation only deals with binary event values (e.g., it only models whether or not a particular laboratory test was ordered for a patient but does not model its actual value).

Based on this matrix representation, the authors presented a method called *one-sided convolutional non-negative matrix factorization* (OSC-NMF), which assumes that each patient matrix is generated by the superposition and concatenation of a set of temporal pattern matrices over the time axis. The method is called *one-sided* because the convolution only occurs along the time axis but not on the event axis. Figure 11.9 gives an intuitive graphical illustration of the procedure of one-side convolution, where the bottom image (the patient matrix) is obtained through the one-side convolution of the pattern on the top left and the time vector on the top right.

To carry out the convolutional decomposition, the authors presented a methodology for minimizing the β-divergence[3] between the convoluted matrix and the original patient matrix in order to obtain the optimal pattern matrices under non-negativity constraints. Furthermore, they presented a multiplicative updates procedure to solve the optimization and proved its convergence.

OSC-NMF was tested on an EHR dataset consisting of records from around 21K diabetes patients collected over a period of up to one year. The evaluation was done in a classification setting in which the patients were stratified into the following three groups: (i) patients with no complications, (ii) patients with chronic disease complications, and (iii) patients with acute complications. The results showed that including OSC-NMF patterns as additional features for classification can improve the performance compared to simple baselines that use only aggregate features without considering any temporal information. In a related work, Lee et al. [27] applied OSC-NMF for exploratory analysis to link temporal patterns of healthcare resource utilization against diabetic disease complications in order to better understand the relationships between disease severity and care delivery.

[3]β-divergence is a family of cost functions that includes many common measures such as Euclidean distance and KL-divergence as special cases.

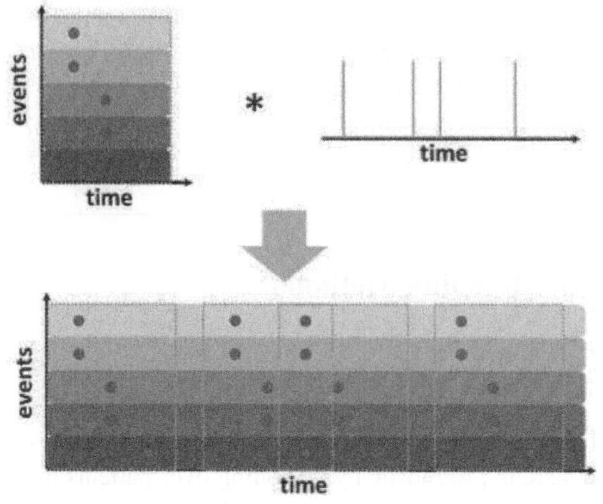

FIGURE 11.9: A graphical illustration of one-side convolution (taken from Wang et al. [52]).

11.5.2 Patient Prognostic via Case-Based Reasoning

Nilsson et al. [35] described a clinical decision support system for aiding clinicians in the detection of respiratory sinus arrhythmia. Their approach extracts patterns from time series using the wavelet transform (see Section 11.4) and matches them for similarity against preclassified cases stored in a database. Matching of cases is performed by matching individual wavelet coefficients. The authors argued that smaller oscillations are often more informative for finding irregularities within signals and hence they assigned higher weights to higher frequency bands. Specifically, the weight for frequency band ψ is defined as follows:

$$W(\psi) = \frac{1}{2^{\psi}}$$

The Fourier transform was also tried for extracting the patterns. However, doing so decreased the detection rate by 20% compared to using wavelets.

Sun et al. [49] presented a mining system for predicting the future health status of ICU patients using the temporal trajectories of health status of a set of similar patients. The proposed system implements the following components:

1. *Feature extraction*: Features are computed by applying the wavelet transform with a sliding window. More specifically, the raw physiological parameters for every ICU patient on every sliding window are converted into feature vectors that correspond to the top k wavelet coefficients.

2. *Offline data analysis*: This component involves performing metric learning in the context of patient similarity and applying subsequent clustering to facilitate fast execution of online data analysis. To capture the notion of similarity, the authors developed a metric learning method called *locally supervised metric learning*. This method leverages labeled data to learn a distance metric that maximizes both the within-class compactness (patients with the same label are close together) and the between-class scatterness (patients with different labels are far away from each other).

3. *Online data analysis*: This component assesses the query patient's prognosis based on the trajectories of similar patients. When a new query patient with available observations up to a decision point is presented, the system performs the following steps: (i) extract the query

patient's features, (ii) retrieve a subset of similar reference patients, (iii) perform temporal alignment between the query patient and each reference patient to identify the window in the reference patient's history that best matches the query patient's assessment window, and (iv) use the observations of the retrieved and "properly aligned" reference patients to predict the prognosis of the query patient. The last step is done by applying a regression model to account for the difference in patient characteristics in the pre-anchor/decision point observations.

This system was tested on the MIMIC II database (see Section 11.6), which consists of physiological waveforms and accompanying clinical data obtained for ICU patients. The study was carried out on 1500 patients from this database, which were categorized into two groups: (i) patients who experienced Acute Hypotensive Episode (AHE) and (ii) patients who did not experience any AHE. The experiments showed that using supervised metric learning improves classification and retrieval performance compared to using unsupervised approaches.

11.5.3 Disease Progression Modeling

Zhou et al. [59] proposed a method for predicting disease progression and applied it to predict the progression of Alzheimer's disease (AD). Because a definite diagnosis of AD requires autopsy confirmation, cognitive measures including mini mental state examination (MMSE) and Alzheimer's disease assessment scale cognitive subscale (ADAS-cog) were used to evaluate the cognitive status of the patients. That is, MMSE and ADAS-cog were used as criteria for clinical diagnosis of "probable AD."

The problem was formulated as *multi-task regression* by considering the prediction of the cognitive scores (MMSE or ADAS-cog) at each time point as one task. Specifically, the data is of the form $\{(x_1,y_1),\ldots(x_n,y_n)\}$, where each $x_i \in \mathbb{R}^d$ is the features for the i-th patient (e.g., his/her neuroimages and baseline clinical assessments) and $y_i \in \mathbb{R}^t$ is the corresponding clinical scores at different future time points. The goal is to learn from data how to predict future clinical scores for new patients (e.g., predicting the value of ADAS-cog after 6 months, after 12 months, etc.).

In order to capture the intrinsic relatedness among different tasks at different time points, a *temporal smoothness prior* was incorporated into the model. This prior penalizes large deviations of predictions at neighboring time points, resulting in the following formulation:

$$\min_W ||XW - Y||_F^2 + \lambda_1||W||_F^2 + \lambda_2 \sum_{i=1}^{t-1} ||w^i - w^{i+1}||_2^2$$

where $X = [x_1,\ldots x_n]^T \in \mathbb{R}^{n\times d}$ is the data matrix, $Y = [y_1,\ldots y_n]^T \in \mathbb{R}^{n\times t}$ is the target matrix, $W = [w_1,\ldots w_t] \in \mathbb{R}^{d\times t}$ is the weight matrix (linear models are used for prediction), and $||.||_F$ is the Frobenius norm of a matrix. Note that finding the weight matrix that minimizes the first two terms corresponds to the standard ridge regression model, which assumes the tasks at different time points are independent of each other. By adding the last term, the tasks become *dependent* and $\lambda_2 \geq 0$ is a regularization parameter that controls the temporal smoothness assumption. Furthermore, the authors proposed using *temporal group lasso* regularization ($\ell_{2,1}$-norm penalty) for feature selection to ensure that the regression models at different time points share a common set of features. The experimental evaluation showed that this method can better capture the progression trends of AD compared to learning independent models and that features identified using temporal group lasso are consistent with findings from existing AD studies.

In a related work, Zhang et al. [58] studied AD progression by learning how to predict future clinical changes for mild cognitive impairment (MCI) patients, including both qualitative changes (i.e., conversion from MCI to AD) and quantitative change (i.e., MMSE and ADAS-cog cognitive scores). The authors proposed a feature selection method to jointly select brain regions related to

AD across multiple time points. Specifically, for each time point, a sparse linear regression model is trained using the imaging data and the corresponding clinical scores, with an extra "group regularization" to group together weights that correspond to the same brain region across multiple time points. After that, longitudinal features are extracted and features of the selected brain regions are combined for prediction (multikernel support vector machines was used for classification). The method was evaluated on 88 MCI subjects and the results showed that it can achieve better performance in predicting future clinical changes of MCI patients compared to other conventional baseline methods.

11.6 Resources

PhysioNet (http://www.physionet.org) is an excellent resource for researchers interested in temporal data mining for healthcare data. PhysioNet is the gateway to PhysioBank and PhysioToolkit. The former is a large and growing archive of well-characterized digital recordings of physiological signals and related temporal healthcare datasets, while the latter is a library of algorithms for analyzing and mining the data.

PhysioBank currently contains over 50 publicly available datasets[4] from a variety of healthcare domains. Examples of these datasets are:

1. *MIMIC II Clinical Database*: This dataset contains clinical records for 32,536 subjects. The records contain results of laboratory tests, medications, ICD9 diagnosis codes, admission notes, discharge summaries, and more. Many records span multiple ICU admissions for the same subject, including available medical history between ICU stays.

2. *MIMIC II Waveform Database*: This dataset contains record sets for approximately 13,500 ICU patients. The record sets include digitized signals, such as ECG, arterial blood pressure, respiration, and pulse oximetry. They also include numeric time series recording of vital signs throughout an ICU stay.

3. *ECG datasets*: These datasets contain labeled ECG signals for studying the detection of arrhythmias that are associated with different types of heart diseases, such as congestive heart failure and atrial fibrillation.

4. *Neuroelectric datasets*: These datasets contain EEG recordings and other brain signals for assessing a variety of cognitive functions.

5. *Gait and Balance Databases*: These databases contain stride interval (gait cycle duration) time series for studying gait dynamics in subjects suffering from a neurodegenerative disorder (e.g., Parkinson's disease).

PhysioToolkit contains open source algorithms for processing, visualizing and analyzing physiological and biomedical signals. These algorithms are divided into several categories, including physiologic signal processing (e.g., QRS detector for ECG or blood pressure pulse detector), general signal processing (e.g., linear and nonlinear filters), frequency domain analysis of time series (Fourier and other algorithms for spectral density estimation), and nonlinear analysis of time series (e.g., multiscale entropy analysis and multifractal analysis). The unifying theme of these algorithms is the extraction of "hidden" information from biomedical signals, which may have diagnostic/prognostic value in medicine, or explanatory/predictive power in basic research.

[4]The support provided to PhysioBank by the NIH allowed providing free access to these databases.

11.7 Summary

The vast amounts of data collected nowadays by hospitals prompts the development of advanced data mining methods for extracting useful and actionable knowledge from data. Most of healthcare data contain time information (e.g., lab values and medications that are recorded over time). Therefore, it is crucial for the mining algorithm to adequately represent the temporal dimension of the data in order to discover meaningful patterns that can potentially enhance our knowledge about disease manifestation, progression, and response to therapy.

In this chapter, we surveyed and summarized temporal data mining methods for healthcare data. We started by discussing methods for finding simple pairwise temporal associations between medical events (e.g., a drug and an adverse drug reaction), which are often used to hypothesize about potential cause-and-effect relations. After that, we discussed methods that use temporal pattern mining for discovering more complex temporal relations in electronic health records. These methods represent data instances (e.g., patient records) as sequences of events (e.g., diagnoses, procedures, or abstractions of lab values) and look for temporal patterns (whether sequential patterns or time-interval patterns) that are useful for a variety of data mining tasks, such as temporal rule extraction (e.g., describing complex temporal dependence among medical events), classification (e.g., discriminating between sick patients and healthy patients), event detection (e.g., early detection of diseases), data summarization (e.g., summarizing most common medical practices), or anomaly detection (e.g., identifying instances that deviate from the norm). We also discussed methods for analyzing healthcare sensor data, such as physiological, ECG, EEG, and fMRI signals. These methods typically apply signal processing techniques to extract hidden information from the high-frequency signals. Lastly, we discussed methods for convolutional event pattern discovery, case-based reasoning, and disease progression prediction.

Despite the progress that has been made in mining and understanding healthcare data, there are still several challenges that face both researchers and practitioners in this domain. In the following, we examine some major challenges and point out promising research directions.

- *Large volume of the data*: A fundamental challenge is to scale data mining algorithms to deal with the huge amounts of healthcare data that are nowadays collected and stored. This requires developing novel data mining techniques that can better utilize big data technologies, such as distributed architecture and parallel computation, to handle the data explosion. Moreover, as healthcare data is constantly expanding (by adding new lab results or new ECG signals for patients), we need methods that can update the learned models/patterns "on the fly" at low cost as opposed to relearning them on the entire data. Therefore, methods that use online learning or stream data mining (e.g., mining temporal patterns from data streams [29]) might become more popular in the healthcare domain.

- *Multimodality of the data*: Healthcare data are representative examples of multimodal/multisource data; including demographics, measurements (e.g., lab values), sensor time series, textual reports (examinations written by physicians or nurses), medical images (e.g., X-ray or MRI images), gene expression data, etc. Developing methods that can understand and mine the different modalities of medical data is extremely important for advancing personalized medicine. For instance, there have been several recent studies on combining DNA biorepositories with EHR data for improving genetic risk assessment, prevention, diagnosis, and treatment.[5]

- *Imprecise ground truth*: Mining healthcare data is often hindered by the ability to obtain accurate ground truth on the data [45]. For example, the task of learning early detection of diseases

[5] See the eMERGE network at http://emerge.mc.vanderbilt.edu/

assumes well-labeled data that indicate, for different patients, the time when the disease has started manifesting itself in the body. However, in reality, obtaining this data is hard because physicians can only approximate the time of the disease based on their experience and how often the patient is being examined. Moreover, the data may contain instances of misdiagnosis (i.e., incorrect labels). Therefore, it is important for the data mining method to be robust against noise in the data.

- *Bias of the data*: Physicians do not have the luxury of trying different treatment options on their patients for exploration purposes. Consequently, historical data often tend to include natural biases driven by the way care is typically delivered to patients [45], which might be suboptimal (e.g., overly conservative in some cases). So if we naively mine the data, we would fail to learn more effective and personalized treatment options. An important research direction is designing computational methods that can simulate alternative sequential clinical decisions while capturing conflicting and synergistic interactions of various components in the healthcare system [11]. Such simulation modeling may improve decision making compared to the "treat-as-usual" approach in terms of reducing costs and increasing patient outcomes.

- *Interpretation and knowledge discovery*: Understanding the results of data mining is especially imperative in healthcare applications. For example, for a decision support system to be adopted in clinical practice, its output (whether a prediction or a recommended action) must be easy to interpret by the domain expert in order to be validated with existing medical knowledge. For this reason, methods based on temporal pattern mining (Section 11.3) are often favored in medicine because they present the discovered knowledge in a form that is intuitive and easy to understand by the user. However, because these methods search through a large space of possible patterns, they inherently suffer from the multiple comparisons problem [10], which may eventually lead to false discoveries in the results. Note that the larger the search space, the higher the chance of reporting false discoveries. As an example, consider a comparison between sequential patterns and time-annotated sequences (TAS) [12] (explained in Section 11.3.1.2). TAS are more expressive than sequential patterns (i.e., TAS can represent more complex temporal concepts). However, the search space of TAS is much larger than that of sequential patterns and so they are more prone to false discoveries. Therefore, it is important to incorporate domain knowledge when designing the mining algorithm in order to choose the appropriate pattern language. Moreover, the results of automatic pattern discovery must be viewed as hypothetical, exploratory in nature, and subject to a careful validation analysis (both statistical and clinical) before they are relied on for practical applications.

Bibliography

[1] R. Agrawal, T. Imielinski, and A. Swami. Mining Association Rules between Sets of Items in Large Databases. In *Proceedings of the International Conference on Management of Data (SIGMOD)*, 1993.

[2] R. Agrawal and R. Srikant. Mining Sequential Patterns. In *Proceedings of the International Conference on Data Engineering (ICDE)*, 1995.

[3] F. Allen. Towards a General Theory of Action and Time. *Artificial Intelligence*, 23:123–154, 1984.

[4] R. Amarasingham, L. Plantinga, M. Diener-West, D. Gaskin, and N. Powe. Clinical Information Technologies and Inpatient Outcomes: A Multiple Hospital Study. *Archives of Internal Medicine*, 169(2), 2009.

[5] L. Angelini, R. Maestri, D. Marinazzo, L. Nitti, M. Pellicoro, G. D. Pinna, S. Stramaglia, and S. Tupputi. Multiscale Analysis of Short Term Heart Beat Interval, Arterial Blood Pressure, and Instantaneous Lung Volume Time Series. *Artificial Intelligence in Medicine*, 41:237–250, 2009.

[6] E. Baralis, G. Bruno, S. Chiusano, V. Domenici, N. Mahoto, and C. Petrigni. Analysis of Medical Pathways by Means of Frequent Closed Sequences. *Knowledge-Based and Intelligent Information and Engineering Systems*, 6278:418–425, 2010.

[7] I. Batal, D. Fradkin, J. Harrison, F. Moerchen, and M. Hauskrecht. Mining Recent Temporal Patterns for Event Detection in Multivariate Time Series Data. In *Proceedings of the International Conference on Knowledge Discovery and Data Mining (SIGKDD)*, 2012.

[8] I. Batal, H. Valizadegan, G. F. Cooper, and M. Hauskrecht. A Temporal Pattern Mining Approach for Classifying Electronic Health Record Data. *ACM Transaction on Intelligent Systems and Technology (ACM TIST), Special Issue on Health Informatics*, 2013.

[9] A. Bate, M. Lindquist, I. R. Edwards, S. Olsson, R. Orre, A. Lansner, and R. M. de Freitas. A Bayesian Neural Network Method for Adverse Drug Reaction Signal Generation. *European Journal of Clinical Pharmacology*, 54(4):315–321, 1998.

[10] Y. Benjamini and Y. Hochberg. Controlling the False Discovery Rate: A Practical and Powerful Approach to Multiple Testing. *Journal of the Royal Statistical Society. Series B (Methodological)*, pages 289–300, 1995.

[11] C. Bennett and K. Hauser. Artificial Intelligence Framework for Simulating Clinical Decision-Making: A Markov Decision Process Approach. *Artificial Intelligence in Medicine*, 2013.

[12] M. Berlingerio, F. Bonchi, F. Giannotti, and F. Turini. Time-Annotated Sequences for Medical Data Mining. In *Proceedings of the 7th IEEE International Conference on Data Mining*, 2007.

[13] K. Booth and GeorgeLueker. Testing for the Consecutive Ones Property, Interval Graphs, and Graph Planarity Using PQ-Tree Algorithms. *Journal of Computer and System Sciences*, 13(3):335–379, 1976.

[14] M. Costa, A. L. Goldberger, and C.-K. Peng. Multiscale Entropy Analysis of Biological Signals. *Physical Review. E*, 71, 2005.

[15] W. DuMouchel. Bayesian Data Mining in Large Frequency Tables with an Application to the FDA Spontaneous Reporting System. *The American Statistician*, 53(3):177–190, 1999.

[16] F. Esposito, T. Scarabino, A. Hyvarinen, J. Himberg, E. Formisano, S. Comani, G. Tedeschi, R. Goebel, E. Seifritz, and F. D. Salle. Independent Component Analysis of fMRI Group Studies by Self-Organizing Clustering. *NeuroImage*, 25(1):193–205, 2005.

[17] S. J. Evans, P. C. Waller, and S. Davis. Use of Proportional Reporting Ratios (PRRs) for Signal Generation from Spontaneous Adverse Drug Reaction Reports. *Pharmacoepidemiology and Drug Safety*, 10(6):483–486, 2001.

[18] L. Geng and H. J. Hamilton. Interestingness Measures for Data Mining: A Survey. *ACM Computing Surveys*, 38(3): Article 9, 2006.

[19] D. A. Hanauer and N. Ramakrishnan. Modeling Temporal Relationships in Large Scale Clinical Associations. *Journal of the American Medical Informatics Association*, 20(2):332–341, 2013.

[20] F. Höppner. Discovery of Temporal Patterns. Learning Rules about the Qualitative Behaviour of Time Series. In *Proceedings of the European Conference on Principles of Data Mining and Knowledge Discovery (PKDD)*, 2001.

[21] H. Jin, J. Chen, H. He, G. J. Williams, C. Kelman, and C. M. O'Keefe. Mining Unexpected Temporal Associations: Applications in Detecting Adverse Drug Reactions. *IEEE Transactions on Information Technology in Biomedicine*, 12(4):488–500, 2008.

[22] A. Joshi, A. Rajshekhar, S. Chandran, S. Phadke, V. Jayaraman, and B. Kulkarni. Arrhythmia Classification Using Local Holder Exponents and Support Vector Machine. In *Proceedings of Pattern Recognition and Machine Intelligence*, 2005.

[23] P.-S. Kam and A. W.-C. Fu. Discovering Temporal Patterns for Interval-Based Events. In *Proceedings of the International Conference on Data Warehousing and Knowledge Discovery (DaWaK)*, 2000.

[24] E. Keogh, S. Chu, D. Hart, and M. Pazzani. Segmenting Time Series: A Survey and Novel Approach. *Data Mining in Time Series Databases*, World Scientific Publishing, 1993.

[25] M. S. Kim and H. Yang. A Study of ECG Characteristics by Using Wavelet and Neural Networks. In *Proceedings of the IEEE International Conference on Computer Systems and Applications*, 2007.

[26] J. Klema, L. Novakova, F. Karel, O. Stepankova, and F. Zelezny. Sequential Data Mining: A Comparative Case Study in Development of Atherosclerosis Risk Factors. *IEEE Transactions on Systems, Man, and Cybernetics, Part C*, 38(1):3–15, 2008.

[27] N. Lee, A. Laine, J. Hu, F. Wang, J. Sun, and S. Ebadollahi. Mining Electronic Medical Records to Explore the Linkage between Healthcare Resource Utilization and Disease Severity in Diabetic Patients. In *Proceedings of the First IEEE International Conference on Healthcare Informatics, Imaging and Systems Biology*, 2011.

[28] J. Lin, E. J. Keogh, S. Lonardi, and B. Y. chi Chiu. A Symbolic Representation of Time Series, with Implications for Streaming Algorithms. In *Proceedings of the SIGMOD Workshop on Research Issues in Data Mining and Knowledge Discovery*, 2003.

[29] A. Marascu and F. Masseglia. Mining Sequential Patterns from Data Streams: A Centroid Approach. *Journal of Intelligent Information Systems*, 27(3):291–307, 2006.

[30] C. Melissant, A. Ypma, E. E. Frietman, and C. J. Stam. A Method for Detection of Alzheimer's Disease Using ICA-enhanced EEG Measurements. *Artificial Intelligence in Medicine*, 33(3):209–222, 2005.

[31] F. Moerchen. Algorithms for Time Series Knowledge Mining. In *Proceedings of the International Conference on Knowledge Discovery and Data Mining (SIGKDD)*, 2006.

[32] F. Moerchen and D. Fradkin. Robust Mining of Time Intervals with Semi-Interval Partial Order Patterns. In *Proceedings of the SIAM International Conference on Data Mining (SDM)*, 2010.

[33] F. Moerchen and A. Ultsch. Optimizing Time Series Discretization for Knowledge Discovery. In *Proceedings of the International Conference on Knowledge Discovery in Data Mining (SIGKDD)*, 2005.

[34] R. Moskovitch and Y. Shahar. Medical Temporal-Knowledge Discovery via Temporal Abstraction. In *Proceedings of the American Medical Informatics Association (AMIA)*, 2009.

[35] M. Nilsson, P. Funk, and N. Xiong. Clinical Decision Support by Time Series Classification using Wavelets. In *Proceedings of the 7th International Conference on Enterprise Information Systems*, 2005.

[36] G. Norén, J. Hopstadius, A. Bate, K. Star, and I. Edwards. Temporal Pattern Discovery in Longitudinal Electronic Patient Records. *Data Mining and Knowledge Discovery*, 20(3):361–387, 2010.

[37] P. Papapetrou, G. Kollios, S. Sclaroff, and D. Gunopulos. Discovering Frequent Arrangements of Temporal Intervals. In *Proceedings of the International Conference on Data Mining (ICDE)*, 2005.

[38] P. Paramanathan and R. Uthayakumar. Detecting Patterns in Irregular Time Series with Fractal Dimension. In *International Conference on Computational Intelligence and Multimedia Applications*, volume 2, pages 323–327, 2007.

[39] D. Patnaik, P. Butler, N. Ramakrishnan, L. Parida, B. J. Keller, and D. A. Hanauer. Experiences with Mining Temporal Event Sequences from Electronic Medical Records: Initial Successes and Some Challenges. In *Proceedings of the 17th ACM SIGKDD International Conference on Knowledge Discovery and Data Mining*, 2011.

[40] J. Pei, J. Han, B. Mortazavi-Asl, H. Pinto, Q. Chen, U. Dayal, and M. Chun Hsu. PrefixSpan: Mining Sequential Patterns Efficiently by Prefix-Projected Pattern Growth. In *Proceedings of the International Conference on Data Engineering (ICDE)*, 2001.

[41] J. Pei, J. Han, and W. Wang. Constraint-based Sequential Pattern Mining: The Pattern-growth Methods. *Journal of Intelligent Information Systems*, 28:133–160, 2007.

[42] L. Sacchi, C. Larizza, C. Combi, and R. Bellazzi. Data mining with Temporal Abstractions: Learning Rules from Time Series. *Data Mining and Knowledge Discovery*, 2007.

[43] Y. Shahar. A Framework for Knowledge-Based Temporal Abstraction. *Artificial Intelligence*, 90:79–133, 1997.

[44] Y. Shahar. Timing Is Everything: Temporal Reasoning and Temporal Data Maintenance in Medicine. In *Artificial Intelligence in Medicine*, volume 1620 of *Lecture Notes in Computer Science*, pages 30–46, 1999.

[45] D. Sow, D. Turaga, and M. Schmidt. Mining of Sensor Data in Healthcare: A Survey. In *Managing and Mining Sensor Data*, pages 459–504. Springer, 2013.

[46] R. Srikant and R. Agrawal. Mining Sequential Patterns: Generalizations and Performance Improvements. In *Proceedings of the International Conference on Extending Database Technology (EDBT)*, 1996.

[47] M. Stacey and C. McGregor. Temporal Abstraction in Intelligent Clinical Data Analysis: A Survey. *Artificial Intelligence in Medicine*, 39(1):1–24, 2007.

[48] M. Suling and I. Pigeot. Signal Detection and Monitoring Based on Longitudinal Healthcare Data. *Pharmaceutics*, 4(4):607–640, 2012.

[49] J. Sun, D. Sow, J. Hu, and S. Ebadollahi. A System for Mining Temporal Physiological Data Streams for Advanced Prognostic Decision Support. In *Proceedings of the 10th International Conference on Data Mining*, 2010.

[50] N. Tatti. Maximum Entropy Based Significance of Itemsets. *Knowledge and Information Systems*, 17(1):57–77, 2008.

[51] E. P. van Puijenbroek, A. Bate, H. G. Leufkens, M. Lindquist, R. Orre, and A. C. Egberts. A Comparison of Measures of Disproportionality for Signal Detection in Spontaneous Reporting Systems for Adverse Drug Reactions. *Pharmacoepidemiology and Drug Safety*, 11(1):3–10, 2002.

[52] F. Wang, N. Lee, J. Hu, J. Sun, and S. Ebadollahi. Towards Heterogeneous Temporal Clinical Event Pattern Discovery: A Convolutional Approach. In *Proceedings of the 18th ACM SIGKDD International Conference on Knowledge Discovery and Data Mining*, 2012.

[53] T. Warkentin. Heparin-Induced Thrombocytopenia: Pathogenesis and Management. *British Journal of Haematology*, 121:535–555, 2000.

[54] E. Winarko and J. F. Roddick. ARMADA - An Algorithm for Discovering Richer Relative Temporal Association Rules from Interval-based Data. *Data and Knowledge Engineering*, 63:76–90, 2007.

[55] S.-Y. Wu and Y.-L. Chen. Mining Nonambiguous Temporal Patterns for Interval-Based Events. *IEEE Transactions on Knowledge and Data Engineering*, 19:742–758, 2007.

[56] X. Yan, J. Han, and R. Afshar. CloSpan: Mining Closed Sequential Patterns in Large Datasets. In *Proceedings of the SIAM International Conference on Data Mining (SDM)*, 2003.

[57] M. J. Zaki. SPADE: An Efficient Algorithm for Mining Frequent Sequences. *Machine Learning*, 42:31–60, 2001.

[58] D. Zhang and D. Shen. Predicting Future Clinical Changes of MCI Patients Using Longitudinal and Multimodal Biomarkers. *PLoS One*, 7, 2012.

[59] J. Zhou, L. Yuan, J. Liu, and J. Ye. A Multi-Task Learning Formulation for Predicting Disease Progression. In *Proceedings of the 17th ACM SIGKDD International Conference on Knowledge Discovery and Data Mining*, 2011.

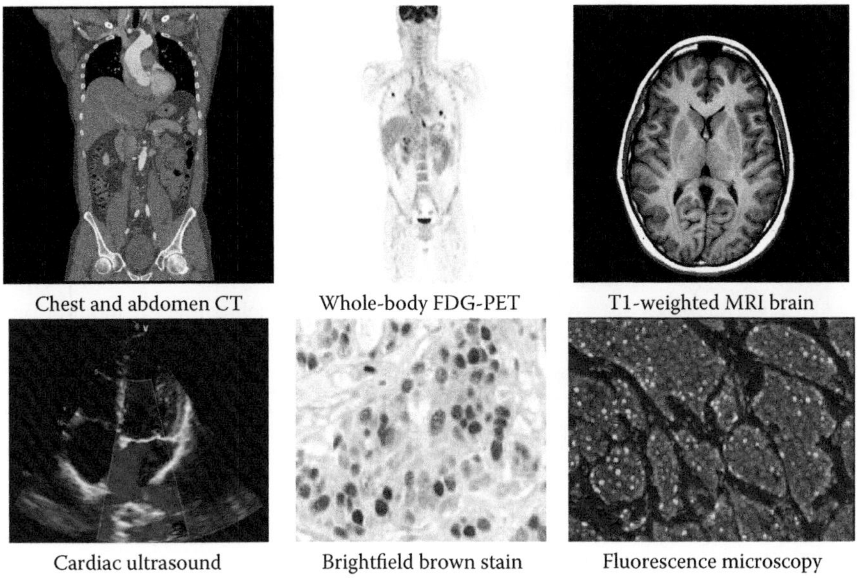

FIGURE 3.1: Representative images from various medial modalities.

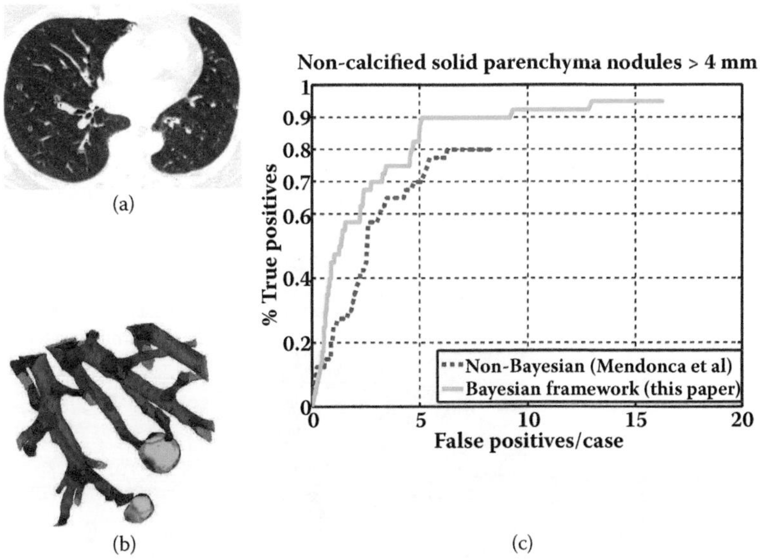

FIGURE 3.3: Lung-nodule detection. (a) A 2D slice of a high-resolution CT scan with nodule labels overlaid in green on the intensity image. (b) A 3D rendering of the voxel labeling for a small region from the same case showing nodules (green), vessels (red), and junctions (blue). (c) fROC curves comparing performance of the Bayesian voxel labeling framework to a curvature-based non-probabilistic approach given in [31]

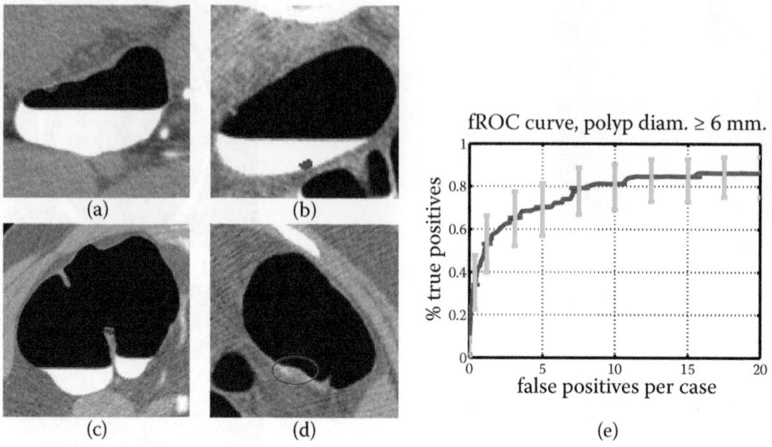

FIGURE 3.4: Colonic-polyp detection. Examples of correctly detected polyps in air (a) and fluid (b) regions. The image in (c) shows a protruding tip on a fold incorrectly marked by the algorithm (a false positive), as shown in (c). (d) depicts a flat sessile polyp missed by the algorithm. Figure (e) is the fROC curve showing the performance of the algorithm for the WRAMC (http://imaging.nci.nih.gov) dataset.

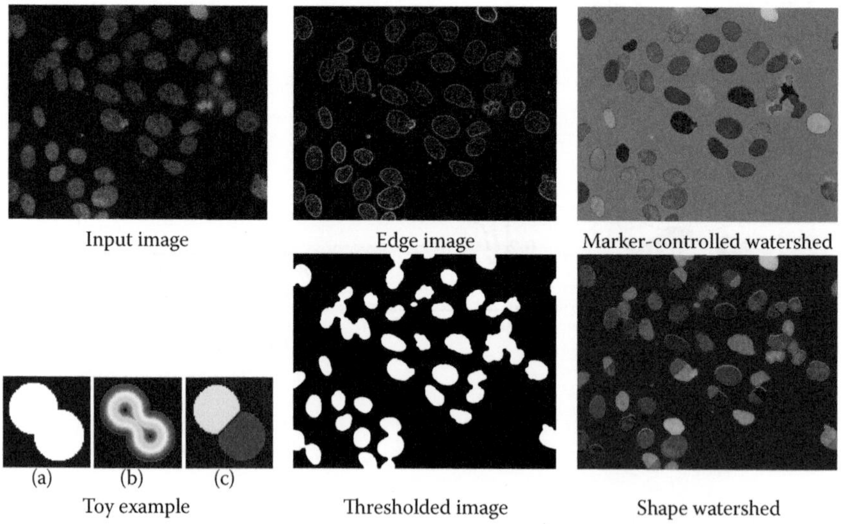

FIGURE 3.8: Watershed segmentation examples. Top row: segmentation by marker-controlled watershed. Bottom row: segmentation by shape watershed.

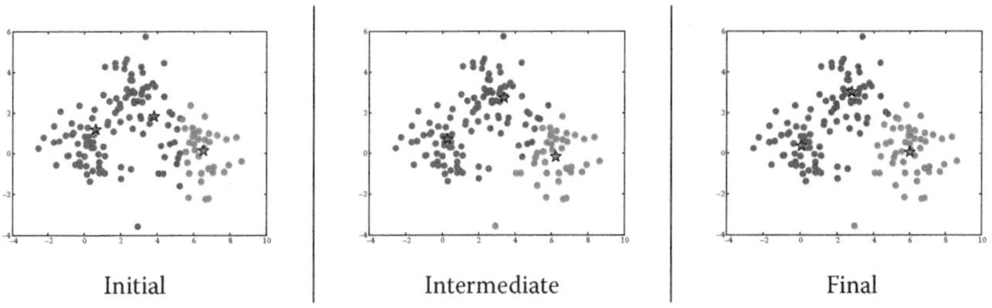

FIGURE 3.10: K-means example. Three clusters are randomly initialized, and all points are assigned to one of these clusters. In each iteration, the cluster centers are recomputed and then the point assignments are recomputed. These steps are repeated until convergence. The data points are shown as colored dots, and the cluster centers are shown as stars.

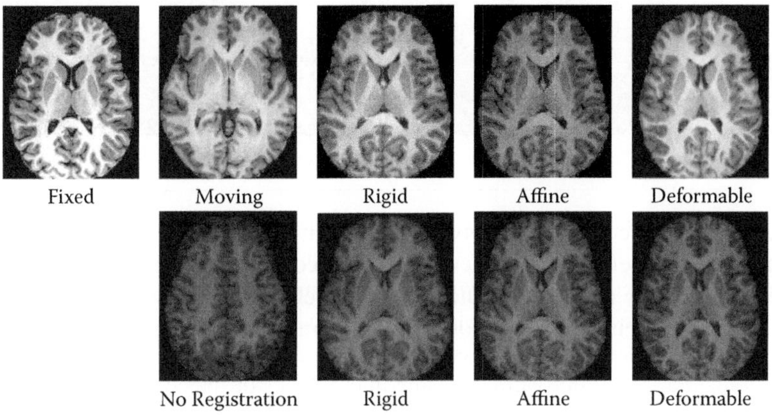

FIGURE 3.13: Example showing registration of a moving image to a fixed image using various transforms (a single slice from a 3D volume is shown). Top row: fixed image, moving image, registered images using rigid body, affine, and deformable registration, respectively. Bottom row: image showing registered images and fixed image respectively to show accuracy of registration. Images courtesy of Xiaofeng Liu, GE Global Research.

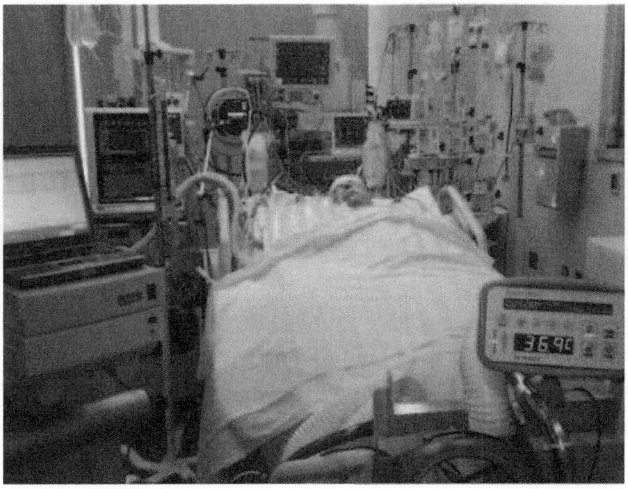

FIGURE 4.3: Sensing in intensive care environments.

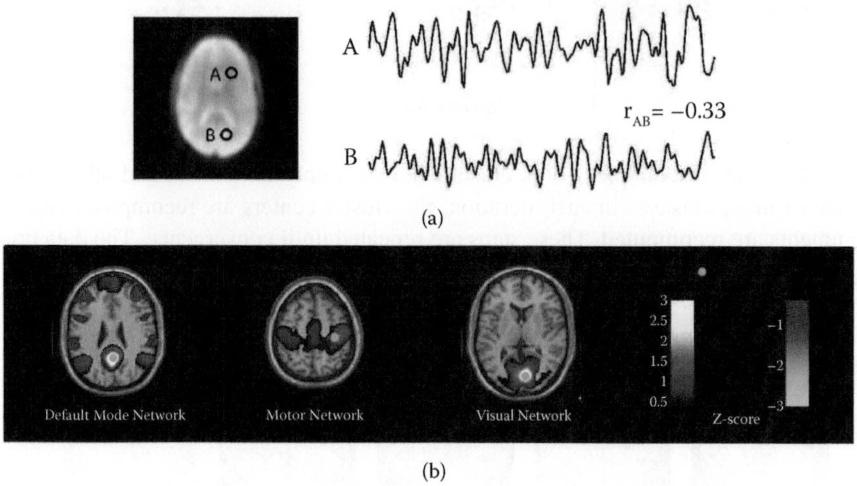

FIGURE 5.32: Functional connectivity between two points, A and B shown in panel (a), is computed using correlation coefficient between their time courses. Connectivity to seed locations (shown as green dots in (b) can be computed for all voxels using Pearson correlation coefficient and converted to Z-scores. Functional networks can be extracted by placing the seeds at appropriate locations.

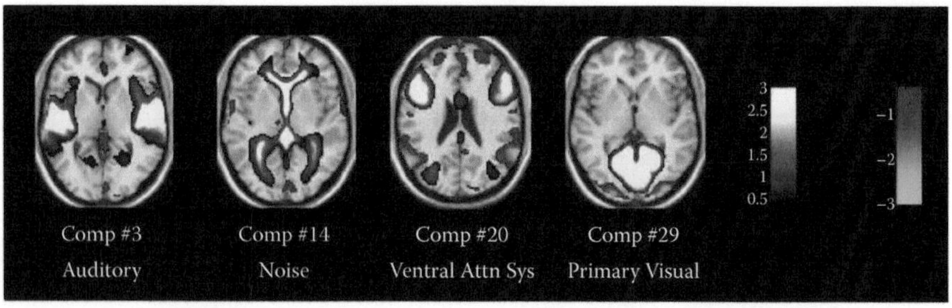

FIGURE 5.34: Select subset of typical ICA components from rs-fMRI. ICA separates rs-fMRI signals to separate neuro-physiologically meaningful networks (sources). Some components are of neuronal origin (Comp 3, 20, 29) and some are noise related (Comp 14). Red and blue regions in the components have opposite directions of signal modulations.

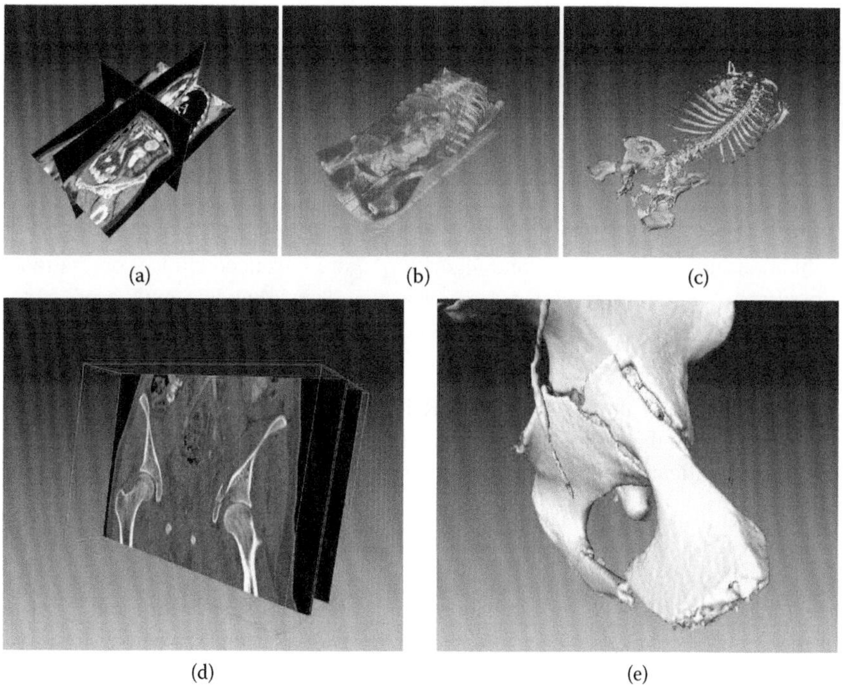

FIGURE 12.7: (a) A CT image displayed using the *axial, sagittal*, and *coronal* image planes. (b) A volume rendering of the same dataset. (c) An iso-surface representation of the bone structures. (d) An X-ray rendering of a 3D volume of a fractured hip bone. (e) An iso-surface of the same dataset that can be used to analyze the different fragments caused by the fracture.

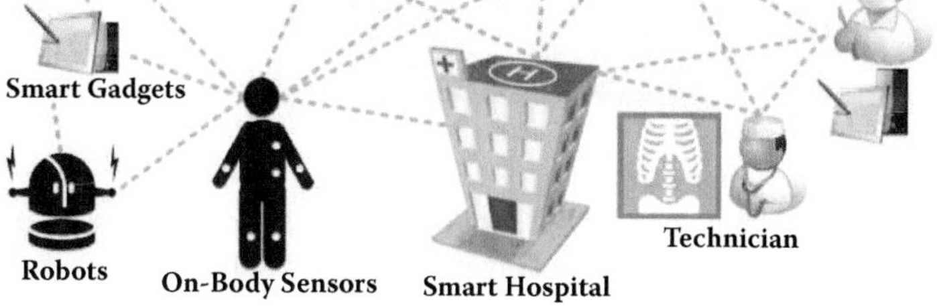

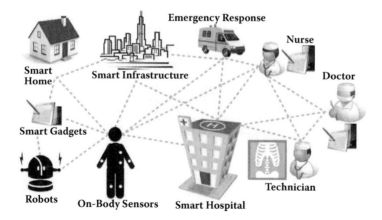

FIGURE 16.1: Interconnected world of intelligent health services.

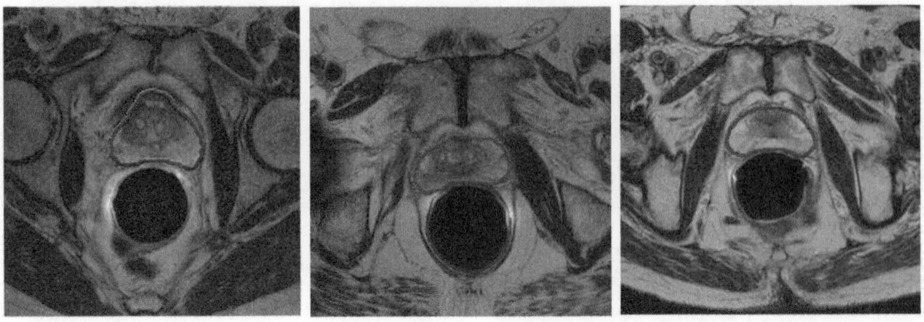

FIGURE 20.1: Examples of the prostate T2 MR images obtained from three different patients, where the red contours are the segmentation groundtruth provided by an experienced radiation oncologist. Note that significant image appearance variations of the prostate can be observed across the three patients.

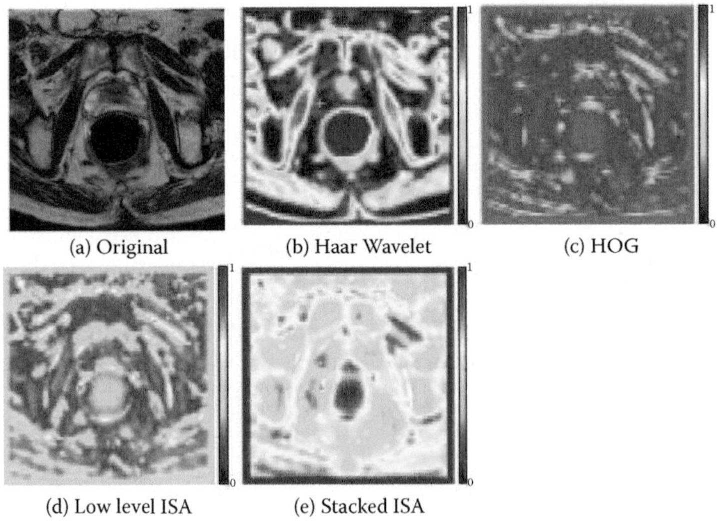

FIGURE 20.2: A typical example of a neural network, where the perceptrons in the hidden layer are learnt to weight the features from the input layer in order to predict the correct class label in the output layer.

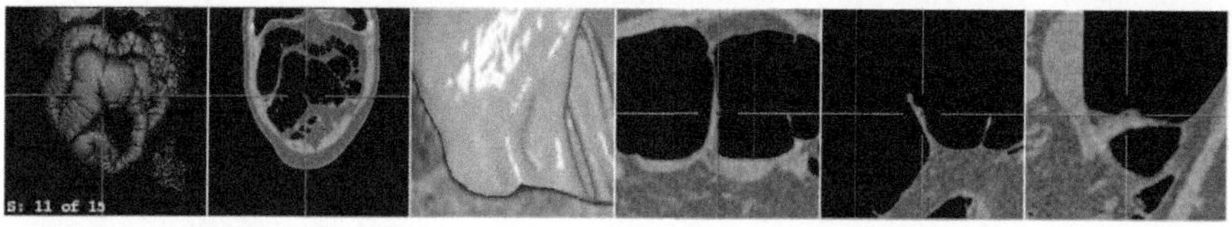

FIGURE 20.16: Example of a false-positive finding. With the help of the additional images it can be easily identified as a fold.

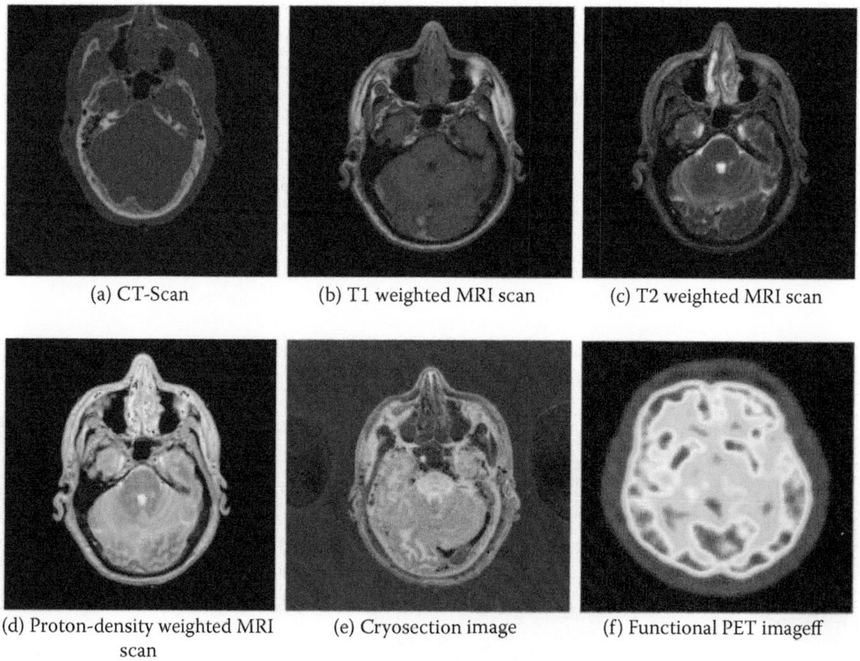

FIGURE 21.5: Cross-sectional images of a male person taken with different imaging modalities. [56].

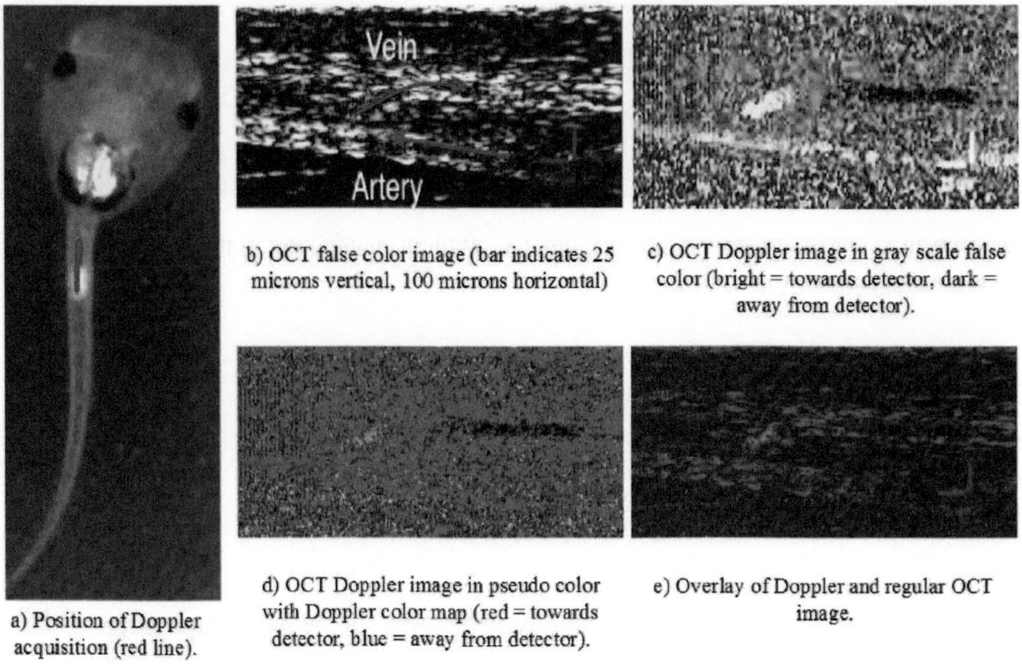
Vein
Artery
a) Position of Doppler acquisition (red line).
b) OCT false color image (bar indicates 25 microns vertical, 100 microns horizontal)
c) OCT Doppler image in gray scale false color (bright = towards detector, dark = away from detector).
d) OCT Doppler image in pseudo color with Doppler color map (red = towards detector, blue = away from detector).
e) Overlay of Doppler and regular OCT image.

FIGURE 21.7: False and pseudo coloring applied in diagnostics OCT image data of frog embryo. [55].

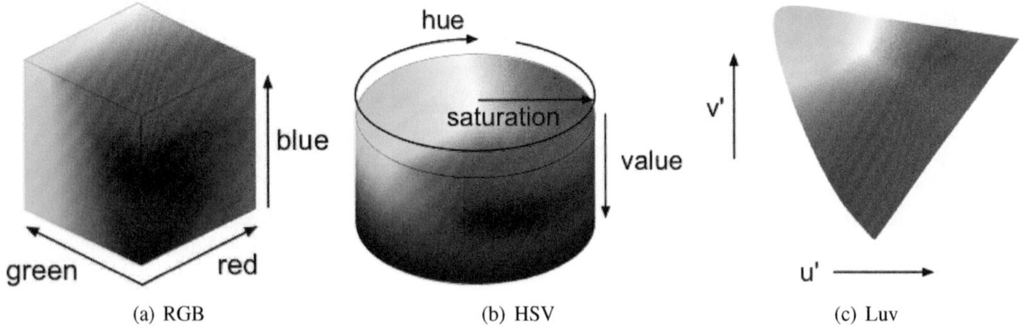

FIGURE 21.8: Color spaces frequently used in biomedical imaging: red, green, blue (RGB); hue, saturation, value (HSV); and Luv, a colorspace with percepted uniformity (Wikipedia, modified).

Chapter 12

Visual Analytics for Healthcare

David Gotz
School of Information and Library Science
University of North Carolina at Chapel Hill
Chapel Hill, NC
gotz@unc.edu

Jesus Caban
National Intrepid Center of Excellence (NICoE)
Walter Reed National Military Medical Center
Bethesda, MD
jesus.j.caban.civ@health.mil

Annie T. Chen
School of Information and Library Science
University of North Carolina at Chapel Hill
Chapel Hill, NC
atchen@email.unc.edu

12.1 Introduction

Visual analytics is a science that involves the integration of interactive visual interfaces with analytical techniques to develop systems that facilitate reasoning over, and interpretation of, complex data. As the volume of health-related information continues to increase at unprecedented rates, there is a critical need to study effective ways to support the analysis of large amounts of data by leveraging human-computer interaction and graphical interfaces. This need is particularly evident in healthcare organizations where information overload could result in different diagnoses and interpretations.

Information overload is the problem of simultaneously trying to analyze a number of variables that surpass the limits of human cognition. Information overload can result in incorrect interpretations of data, omission of modest changes, and confusion with missing or noisy elements. Any large dataset includes objective measurements, redundant data, irrelevant measurements, errors, non-normalized data, missing elements, and subjective evaluations. The multimodal, heterogeneous, and uncertain properties of data pose significant challenges to users trying to synthesize the information and obtain insights from the dataset under consideration. As medical centers, clinics, and small clinical practice offices continue to embrace health information technology (HIT) and join electronic health information exchange (HIE) programs, the amount of data available to clinicians is unprecedented, which can yield to information overload.

Studies in psychology have shown that humans can correctly analyze up to four variables [41], and this upper limit decreases with increasing complexity of the relations being analyzed [42]. In the evaluation of many diseases, clinicians are presented with datasets that often contain hundreds of clinical and diagnostic variables. To be able to evaluate a patient, clinicians unconsciously employ dimensionality reduction techniques such as segmentation or conceptual chunking. *Segmentation* is when a problem is broken into smaller components that do not exceed the human processing capacity and *conceptual chunking* is when different concepts are analyzed independently to reduce the dimensionality of the task. Unfortunately, dimensionality reduction techniques neglect relationships among components that may be necessary for accurate diagnosis. The ability to analyze and identify meaningful patterns in multimodal clinical data must be addressed in order to produce significant breakthroughs in our understanding of diseases and to identify patterns that could be affecting the clinical workflow.

The amount of information being produced by healthcare organizations opens up opportunities to design new interactive interfaces to explore large-scale databases, to validate clinical data and coding techniques, and to increase transparency within different departments, hospitals, and organizations.

This chapter is structured as follows. Section 12.2 discusses some of the popular data visualization techniques used in clinical settings. Section 12.3 describes areas in healthcare that benefit from visual analytics, including applications of visual analytics for public health, for patients, for clinicians, to improve clinical workflow, and for clinical research. Finally, Section 12.4 presents a conclusion, discussing the present and future impact of visual analytics in healthcare.

12.2 Introduction to Visual Analytics and Medical Data Visualization

Visual analytics provides a way to combine the strengths of human cognition with interactive interfaces and data mining techniques that can facilitate the exploration of complex datasets [84]. John W. Tukey [83] showed the importance of supportive data analysis through the use of illustrations and other interactive visual representations to present results. The increasing popularity of visual analytics tools has been driven by their effectiveness to enable users to detect patterns, correlations, and anomalies not obvious with other forms of data representations. In general, visual analytics tools seek to present information in ways that let the human brain detect meaningful patterns using expert knowledge. In the clinical domain, the value and usability of the tools lies in customizing them to act as an intermediary between the multiple clinical variables, databases, and the specific goals of the clinicians or researchers.

In order to successfully prototype visual data analysis interfaces to display results, core concepts from multiple disciplines must be incorporated. This fact has made research in visual analytics a highly interdisciplinary domain that combines various related research areas including visualization, data mining, data processing, graphics, data fusion, statistics, and cognition.

Tools, techniques, and approaches from information and scientific visualization are the single most important component for creating effective visual analytics interfaces to explore complex clinical datasets. During the last ten years, many graphing and plotting software applications such as Excel, SAS, SPSS, Tableau, Spotfire, and QlikView have successfully been used to analyze complex datasets [34, 48]. However, most of these applications are limited when trying to illustrate the relationship between more than three variables and are not optimized for clinical and healthcare applications.

The following three subsections will discuss the data types commonly found in clinical systems or warehouses, the visualization techniques that are frequently used in clinical practice, and some of the visualization techniques used to illustrate high-dimensional clinical data.

12.2.1 Clinical Data Types

The predominant data type found within electronic health records (EHRs) is unstructured free text that generally requires natural language processing (NLP) or text analysis to be standardized into a computable form. However, there is also structured data found within EHRs that can take one of several forms. First, *quantitative data* refers to elements and/or measurements stored using numerical representations. These are values on which arithmetic operations can be performed such as blood test results or imaging data. Closely related, *interval data* refers to data types such as date ranges (e.g., months or years) or test result intervals (above normal, normal, below normal) that include ordered ranges of quantitative measures. Similar to interval data, *ordinal data* refers to ordered measures such as classifying a patient's condition as mild, moderate, and severe. However, with ordinal data the ordered measures do not have to map to specific numerical ranges. *Categorical data* are discretely defined nominal measures that have no inherent ordering. For example, patient gender and country of citizenship are categorical values. Finally, *hierarchical data* is that which can be represented using a tree-like structure in which the parent-child structure of the tree captures containment relationships within the data. For instance, the International Classification of Diseases, Ninth Revision (ICD-9) is a hierarchy in which a primary disease is represented by the first part of the code, and secondary characteristics are captured by a numeric sequence that is appended to the primary code. For example, the parent level of the code ICD-9-722.52 is Intervertebral Disc Disorders (722), the second level is Degeneration of Lumbar Intervertebral Disc (722.5), and the third level of hierarchy is Degenerative Disc Disease, Lumbar (722.52). In clinical settings, such a hierarchical model is effective because providers can add specificity to a diagnosis without precluding higher-level interpretation, reimbursement, or analysis.

12.2.2 Standard Techniques to Visualize Medical Data

Electronic medical records (EMRs), clinical devices, and many software applications used in hospital organizations provide basic plotting capabilities including *histograms, line plots, pie charts, scatter plots*, and other techniques to display clinical data. In addition, most EHRs pro-

Date	Pain
15-Nov-13	4
18-Nov-13	4
19-Nov-13	3
19-Nov-13	3
20-Nov-13	3
21-Nov-13	4
22-Nov-13	3
25-Nov-13	3
25-Nov-13	2
26-Nov-13	2
27-Nov-13	0
2-Dec-13	2
2-Dec-13	0
3-Dec-13	0
3-Dec-13	2
3-Dec-13	0
4-Dec-13	4

(a)

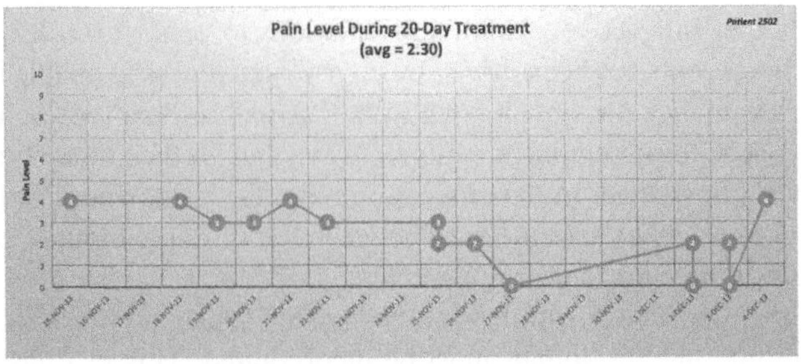

(b)

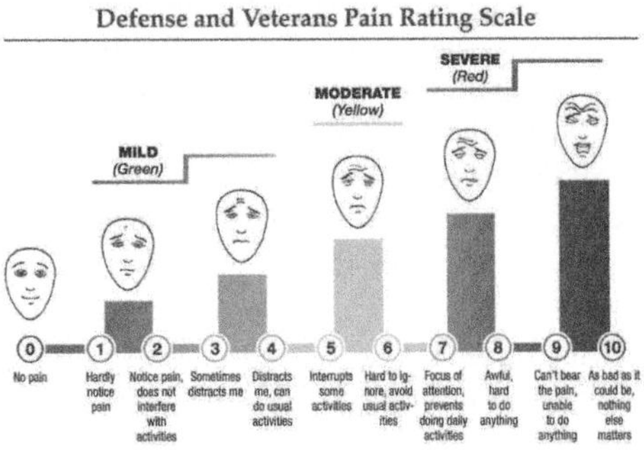

(c)

FIGURE 12.1: The most common technique to show structured clinical data within EHRs are *tables*. (a) Table with a colormap showing the pain scale values for a given patient that went through an intensive 20-day treatment. (b) Graphical illustration showing the pain scale for a given patient that went through an intensive 20-day treatment. (c) Illustration of the DoD/VA pain rating scale shown to patients to better standardize pain assessments.

vide *heatmaps, maximum intensity projection* (MIP), and other mechanisms to illustrate tabular and imaging data.

The most common technique to show structured clinical data within EHRs are *tables*. The primary benefit of arranging the data in rows and columns is that it allows the provider to display the results of multiple variables within a single tabular structure. Tables have the benefit of illustrating the raw data while mixing variables of different types and ranges. Unfortunately, one of the key limitations of using tables to illustrate clinical data is that as the number of columns and rows increases, the reader quickly becomes overwhelmed with the amount of information.

To overcome some of those limitations, tables often support features such as sorting, filtering, and coloring. A *heatmap* is a graphical representation of the data where each cell is assigned to a particular color. Such an approach is often used to quickly illustrate trends and to highlight values of interest. Figure 12.1a shows the pain scale values for a given patient that went through an intensive 20-day treatment. A colormap is a way to show the data to quickly illustrate a pattern.

Among plotting techniques, *line charts* are the most common visualization technique available within EHRs [80]. Even though there are differences between EHR vendors, the vital signs tab for most platforms allows the plotting of measurements such a body temperature, heart rate, and blood pressure, among other elements. Figure 12.1b shows the pain scale for a given patient that went through an intensive 20-day treatment. This plot allows referring providers to better understand how the treatment is affecting the patient's overall pain. In addition to EHRs, many of the widely used medical devices employ basic visualization techniques to illustrate clinical data. For instance, electrocardiogram (EKG) devices used to monitor the heart electrical activity and the cardiotocog-

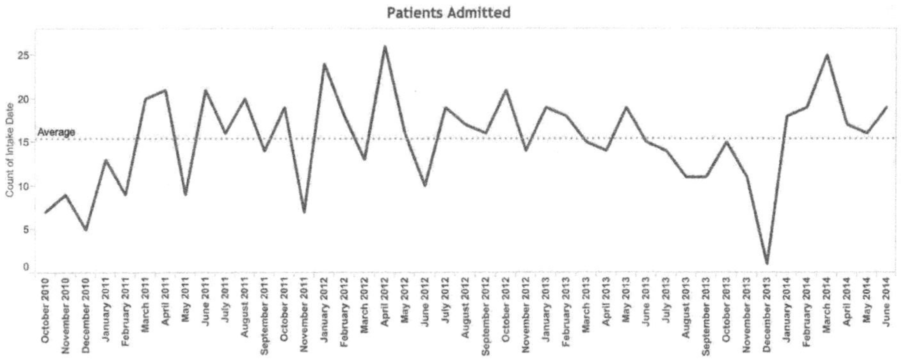

(a)

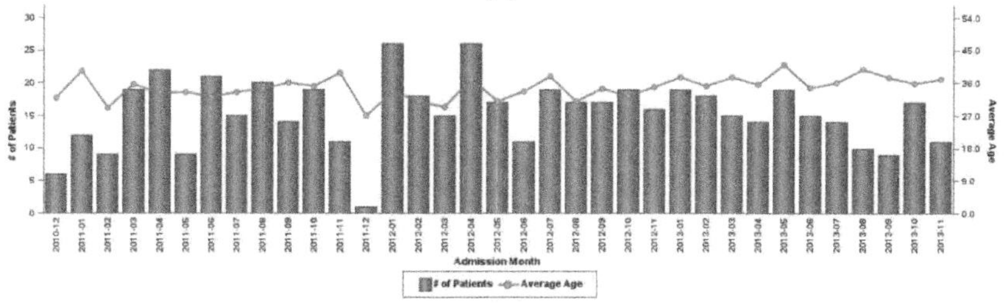

(b)

FIGURE 12.2: Sample visualization techniques commonly used to illustrate clinical data. Visual analytics techniques often incorporate interactive interfaces to allow the user to engage in data exploration and analysis. (a) A line plot illustrating the number of specific patients that a particular provider admitted during a 45-month period. (b) A plot that combines bar charts and line plots. The bar charts illustrate the number of patients a provider admitted per month and the line chart in the right axis illustrates the average age of those patients.

raphy (CTG) devices used to monitor contractions during delivery rely on line plots of temporal data to illustrate progression and show patterns [58].

When basic plotting techniques like line plots incorporate dynamic and interactive interfaces, users become more engaged with the data analysis and are able to obtain a significant amount of insight about the data more quickly. Figure 12.2 shows samples of visual analytics tools used in clinical settings that employ basic plotting techniques to illustrate clinical patterns and interactively allow the user to explore larger longitudinal datasets. Figure 12.2a shows a line plot illustrating the number of specific patients that a particular provider admitted during a 45-month period. Such a plot is used to see patterns, measure productivity, and justify additional clinical resources.

In general, basic visualization techniques are used to display a single variable or a small set of elements that are of the same type and range. However, multiple basic charting techniques can be incorporated into a single plot, thus allowing the illustration of multiple variables or data types simultaneously. For instance, Figure 12.2b combines bar charts and line plots. The bar charts are used to illustrate the number of specific patients that visited a provider during a 36-month period and a line chart in the right axis illustrates the average age of those patients.

Another commonly used approach to display multiple variables within a single chart is by doing a stacked plot. Figure 12.3(a) shows a stacked plot illustrating the monthly patient encounters that took place within a given department versus those encounters where patients were transferred to a different location. By stacking the variables within a single chart the user can obtain three measurements: (a) the number of encounter per month within the hospital department under consideration, (b) the number of encounters per month that require a patient's transfer, and (c) the total number of

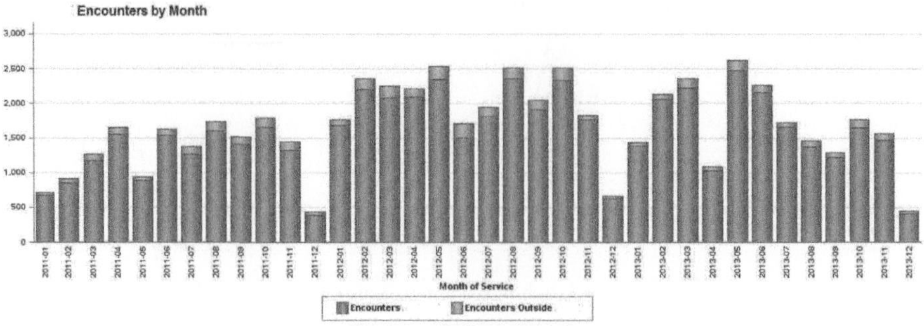

(a)

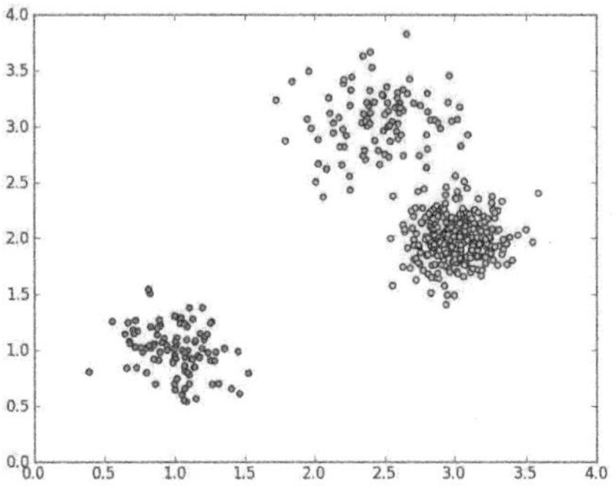

(b)

FIGURE 12.3: Often providers are interested in comparing two related variables within a single illustration. (a) Stacked bars are used to illustrate three values: the total number of encounters for a given month, the total number of encounters that happened within a department, and the total number of appointments that happened outside the department. (b) A scatter plot illustrating a particular classification for a group of patients.

encounters providers of the department under consideration are involved in. In addition, the temporal aspect of the chart helps users to analyze the changes of each of those three measurements over time.

Another widely used chart to compare two related variables is a *scatter plot*. Figure 12.3(b) shows a scatter plot illustrating a particular classification for patients.

The inherent complexity, variability, and uncertainty associated with many clinical elements have motivated clinicians and providers to find effective ways to communicate findings, patterns, and ask questions of patients. *Infographics* are visual representations of information that try to simplify the data or questions into something that is visually appealing and easy to understand. Figure 12.1 shows how the Department of Defense (DoD) and U.S. Department of Veterans Affairs (VA) use an *infographics* approach to better standardize the collection of a subjective data point such as pain.

As seen in this section, most of the widely popular charts are effective at illustrating one or two or three elements. More advanced visualization techniques are needed to enable the exploration of high-dimensional, multivariable datasets.

12.2.3 High-Dimensional Data Visualization

Over the last several years, multiple high-dimensional data visualization techniques have been proposed including *parallel coordinates, star glyphs, tree graphs, treemaps*, and *dependency graphs*, to enable interactive exploration of complex clinical datasets and help users identify previously unknown patterns [44, 88].

Parallel coordinates are a powerful method for visualizing multidimensional data [49]. Given an $N \times M$ spreadsheet with N patients containing M clinical variables, a parallel coordinate visualization is created by displaying M equally spaced vertical axes with individual ranges. Each of the N patients are illustrated as a line that passes through each of the axes. Once generated, the visualization technique allows the users to interactively define a range within a single or multiple variables (axes) and explore correlations between variables for the selected patients.

Figure 12.4(a) shows a diagram illustrating how parallel coordinates plots are created and used. This particular example is to show how the human eye can quickly look at multiple variables and immediately find sample lines (e.g., patients) that are outside the normal range.

Figure 12.4(b) shows results of using parallel coordinates to explore the relationship between imaging and neuropsychological measurements. When the user selects subjects with a specific range of brain lesions (see gray region at which the arrow points), we can see that only lines corresponding to those subjects are highlighted while the rest of the lines are grayed out. Then if we compare the first axis describing the number of brain lesions with the second axis describing the neuropsychology test "Symbol Search," we can see that most of the relationships between these two variables are linear. Thus, from this data it seems that as the number of lesions increases, subjects' Symbol Search scores also increase. In addition, by observing the relationship between the selected variable and "Visual Puzzle" (second to last axis) we can see that patients are clustered between 12–22; however, there seems to be an outlier of a patient that scored in the 70s. This shows that parallel coordinates can also be used to identify errors and study outliers that might require additional attention.

Another technique to analyze the relationship between many variables is by using a *chord* visualization plot [57]. These plots are generated by creating a circular plot consisting of boundaries, where each boundary is a variable. Connections are drawn between boundaries and the thickness of each connection represents the strength of the correlation. Hovering the mouse over a connection displays the corresponding R-value to help the researcher understand the associations between individual variables. Figure 12.5(a) shows how a chord visualization technique can be used to study

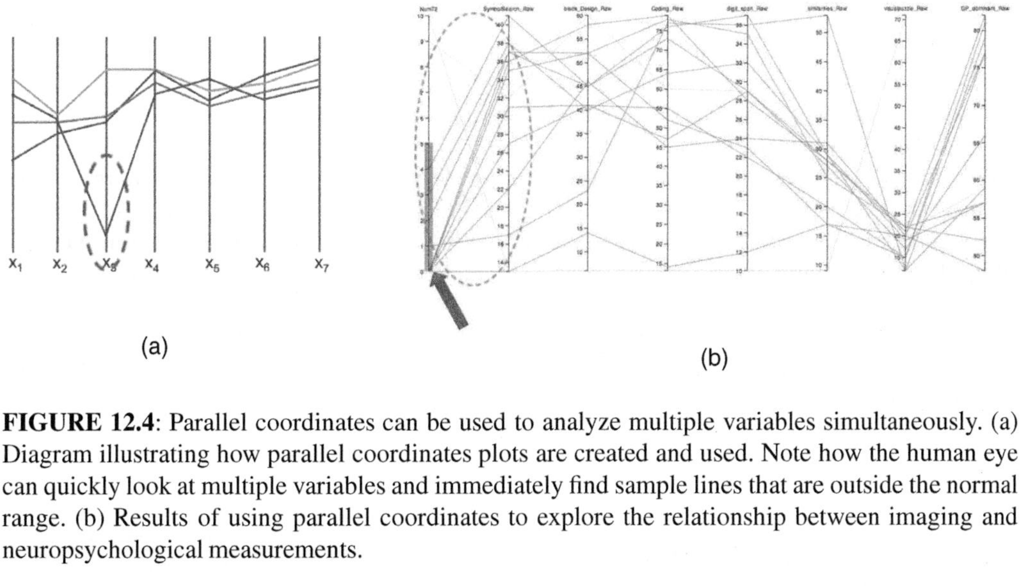

FIGURE 12.4: Parallel coordinates can be used to analyze multiple variables simultaneously. (a) Diagram illustrating how parallel coordinates plots are created and used. Note how the human eye can quickly look at multiple variables and immediately find sample lines that are outside the normal range. (b) Results of using parallel coordinates to explore the relationship between imaging and neuropsychological measurements.

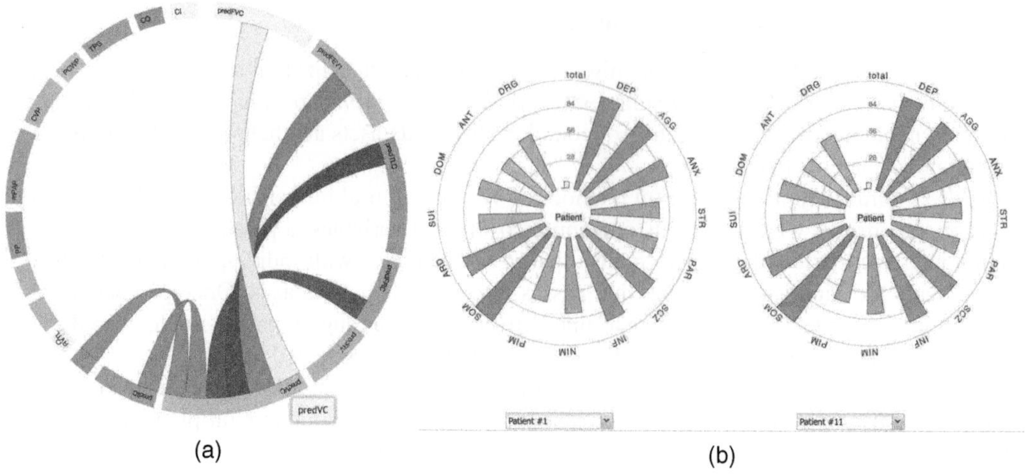

FIGURE 12.5: (a) Chord visualization technique can be used to study the associations between multiple clinical variables. In this particular example, 18 clinical elements are displayed and the associations between predictive volume capacity (predVC) of the lungs and other clinical elements is being illustrated. (b) Star glyphs are visualization techniques that can be used to compare patients based on multiple clinical variables.

the associations between multiple clinical variables. In this particular example, 18 clinical elements are displayed and the associations between predictive volume capacity of the lungs (predVC) and other clinical elements is being illustrated. The *star glyph* [82] is a visualization technique that can be used to compare multiple variables at the same time. For example, given M clinical variables for a patient, a star glyph representation is constructed by creating M axes following a radial configuration (i.e., the axes share a common central origin and are arranged like spokes on a wheel). For each data element, the value for each variable is normalized between 0.0 and 1.0 and drawn using either a series of bars, or a single connected shape that traverses each axis in the glyph (also called a *spider* chart). From this depiction, a user can quickly obtain an overview of the values for a single record in the dataset (e.g., a patient). Figure 12.5(b) shows a star glyph being used to compare multiple clinical elements between two different patients. From the illustration we can see that the two subjects follow a similar distribution, thus resulting in a similar shape. When the pattern or shape of two plots is different, the human eye can quickly notice the contrast and immediately engage in analyzing the differences between patients. The same technique for detecting differences can be applied to compare two samples of data for the same patient (e.g., samples recorded at two different points in time to examine patient stability).

Two of the most widely used techniques to explore hierarchical data are *hierarchical trees* and *treemaps*. The treemap visualization places the top layer of the data (e.g., patients) in a grid as individual rectangles. The area of the rectangle corresponds to a given measurement, such as the height of the subtree or the amount of data under that specific node. Clicking on a particular rectangle (i.e. patient) will zoom into the corresponding subtree, thus producing subtreemaps representing the variables under that specific node. Figure 12.6(a) shows an example of the treemap visualization chart. Another way to visualize hierarchical data is using trees. Figure 12.6(b) shows an example of how a large collection of data can be explore by traversing the tree.

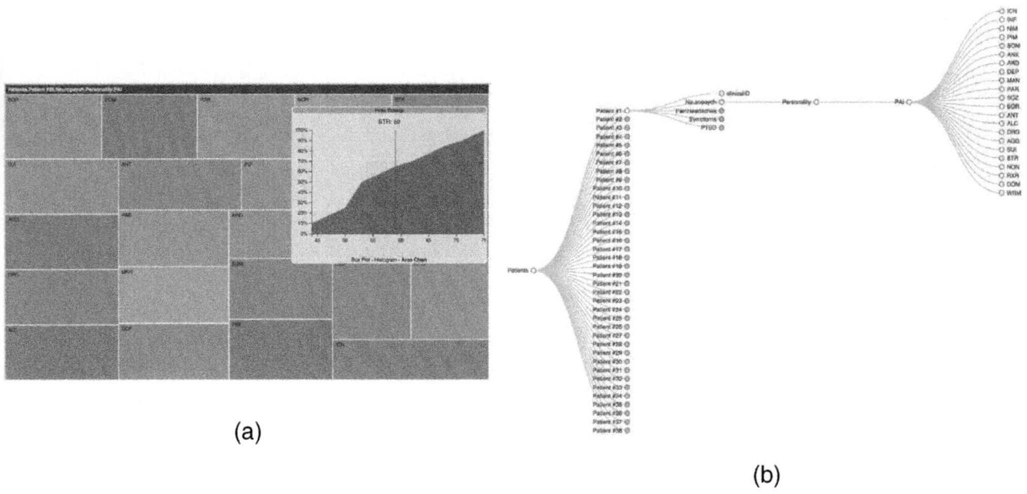

FIGURE 12.6: Two of the most widely used techniques to explore hierarchical data are *hierarchical tree* and *treemaps*.

12.2.4 Visualization of Imaging Data

Most hospital organizations have different systems that they use to display and analyze medical images, and these are seamlessly integrated with EHRs. The *picture archiving and communication system* (PACS) is the primary system used to store, manipulate, and visualize clinical scans. A comprehensive review of visualization techniques used to illustrate medical images is out of the scope of this chapter. Readers are referenced to existing publications that focus on this specific topic [72, 12, 43]. As a brief overview, some of the most widely used visual analytical techniques to illustrate medical images are *Maximum Intensity Projection, X-Ray Rendering, Direct Volume Rendering,* and *Iso-surfaces.*

Most of the imaging data collected in hospital organizations is comprised of either 2D images or 3D volumes such as MR, CT, or PET scans. The easiest way to display 3D images is by visualizing three images corresponding to each of the planes: *axial, sagittal,* and *coronal.* Figure 12.7(a) shows a CT image being displayed using these three image planes.

Direct volume rendering, a technique used to construct a 2D projection of a 3D image, has proven to be effective at rendering different materials. In volume rendering, a combination of color and opacity are assigned to each 3D point (voxel), to allow simultaneous visualization of external and internal structure. To accomplish this, a transfer function is used to map intensity values of the image to colors and opacities, thus making it possible for the user to define the appearances of the volume and create visualizations such as translucent skin, opaque skulls, and red vessels. Figure 12.7(b) shows a volume rendering of a CT scan. In this case, we can simultaneously visualize skins, internal organs, and bone structures.

Iso-surface visualization is a technique that uses contours/boundaries of the volume to generate an approximate polygonal structure and surface. Figure 12.7(c) shows an iso-surface that was generated for the bone structures of a CT dataset.

Other widely used techniques used to visualize 3D medical images are *maximum intensity projection* (MIP) and *X-ray rendering*. MIP is a way to interpolate 3D images in which only the largest value is written to the pixel. It is often used to illustrate vascular structures. Another approach is *X-ray rendering*, which renders an overview image where interpolated samples are simply summed. Some of the limitations of mapping 3D volumetric data into 2D images is that a significant amount of the measurements, 3D structures, and relationships between different structures can be missed.

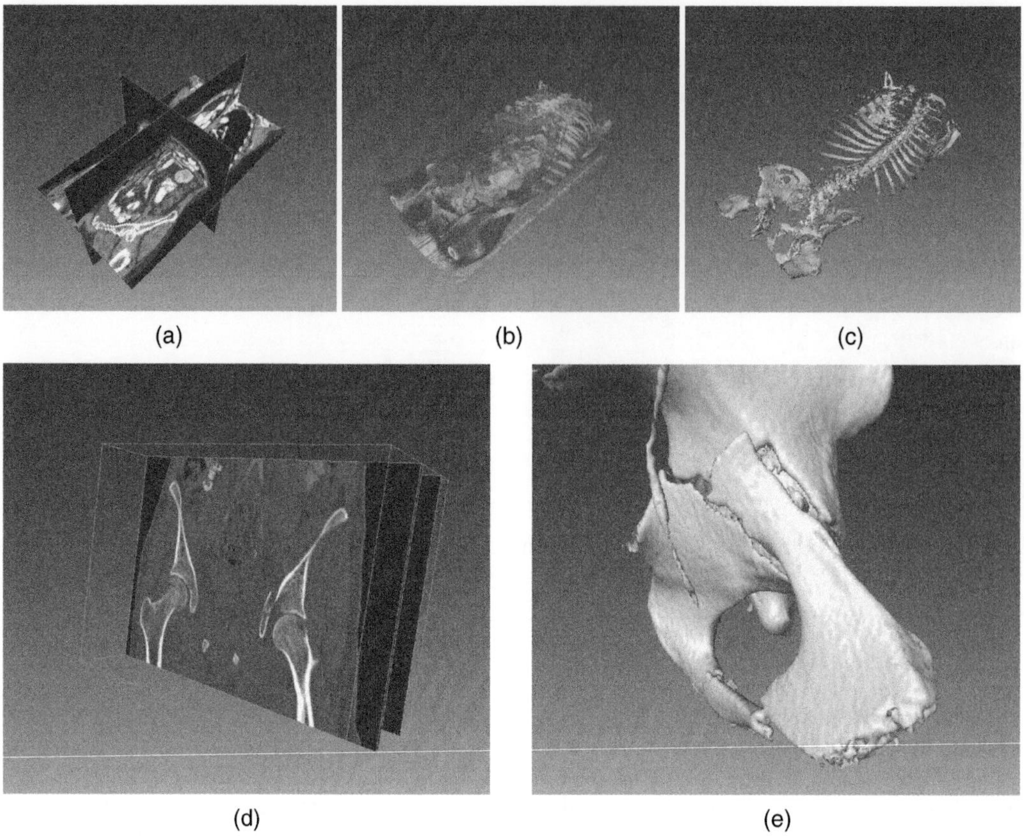

FIGURE 12.7 (See color insert.): (a) A CT image displayed using the *axial, sagittal*, and *coronal* image planes. (b) A volume rendering of the same dataset. (c) An iso-surface representation of the bone structures. (d) An X-ray rendering of a 3D volume of a fractured hip bone. (e) An iso-surface of the same dataset that can be used to analyze the different fragments caused by the fracture.

Figure 12.7(d–e) shows a fractured hip; when the information is visualized using an iso-surface, the provider can easily see fragments of the bone.

12.3 Visual Analytics in Healthcare

Medicine is a field driven by data. Basic research is conducted by designing experiments, collecting data, and analyzing the results. Scientists studying human health gather a wide variety of different types of data, and they do it at scales that range from an individual's genomic fingerprint to large-scale surveys of global populations. Data is often collected over time, then analyzed, summarized, and inspected to draw out clinically significant findings. These insights translate to the bedside where healthcare providers gather yet more data about their patients, examine this data in light of the known literature, and make treatment decisions. Policy makers define guidelines and regulations, develop economic models, and design clinical workflows to match this information. The system is monitored for quality assurance by observing, analyzing the gathered data, and—ideally—feeding the insights back to the healthcare system for continuous improvement.

At the center of this enterprise sit healthcare professionals who are tasked with making clinically significant decisions based on an ever-increasing pool of complex, often conflicting, electronic medical data: epidemiologists, biostatisticians, patients and their families, clinicians, nurses, social workers, medical directors, and policy makers. It is this group of people—not computers or automated algorithms—that are responsible for making the clinically important decisions that affect individuals as well as entire populations.

The visual analytics techniques described earlier provide a powerful framework for supporting information analysts of all types. The application of such methods to the field of healthcare has therefore been broadly explored in areas ranging from public health and population research, clinical workflow, clinical practice, and patient engagement and communication. In this section, we provide an overview of the visual analytics literature in these areas, and we attempt to further categorize the variety of research topics that have been explored.

12.3.1 Visual Analytics in Public Health and Population Research

Public health and population research are critical components of the healthcare system. These fields focus on understanding the health of a population as a whole, on specific subpopulations, or on the efficacy of specific interventions within those groups. As such, public health and outcomes research professionals regularly work with large collections of patient data gathered from sources such as electronic medical systems, large-scale surveys, and health surveillance or monitoring infrastructures.

12.3.1.1 Geospatial Analysis

Given the spatial distribution of populations across geographic areas, geospatial analysis is one of the most widely used techniques in support of public health applications. Examples of such work date back to as early as the 1850s, when John Snow—often considered a founding father of modern epidemiology—plotted deaths by location during a cholera outbreak. The resulting map, shown in Figure 12.8, has become a canonical example used in both the scientific and popular literature to illustrate how graphical representations can yield epidemiological insights [51].

Snow's Broad Street map is an example of a *dot map*, a technique where sets of similar data points are represented as repeated, spatially located, graphical marks such that the quantity and location of the marks convey the spatial distribution of the data. In this example, individual fatalities are represented with short, black, linear strokes that are arranged to form histograms along the streets, indicating how many individuals had died at each given location.

For larger datasets with variables valued too large to draw each point individually, the graphical marks in a dot map can be used to represent groups of data points (e.g., one mark for every 1000 fatalities). Moreover, the data represented by each mark need not directly reflect the raw source data as was done in Figure 12.8. Rather, dot maps can be used to represent any scalar variable, be it a simple native attribute of your dataset or the scalar result of a complex statistical computation. This makes the dot map technique very flexible. However, dot maps are less effective when used displaying non-scalar attributes, such as categorical or ordinal values.

In contrast, chloropleth maps can be used to represent a wide range of data including scalar, ordinal, and categorical variables. Such maps have a long history, with the term *chloropleth map* dating back to 1938 [96]. This technique represents a map as a collection of non-overlapping spatial regions, each of which is rendered with a color (or texture) that represents the value to be visualized. For example, Figure 12.9 shows a chloropleth map being used as part of the Institute of Health Metrics and Evaluation's US Health Map system [2]. The map shows United States counties, each of which is shaded a specific color that represents the prevalence of smoking among females according to a dataset from 2012. The color coding adheres to a gradient from blue to yellow to red, and similarities among spatially proximate counties become apparent via clusters of similarly colored

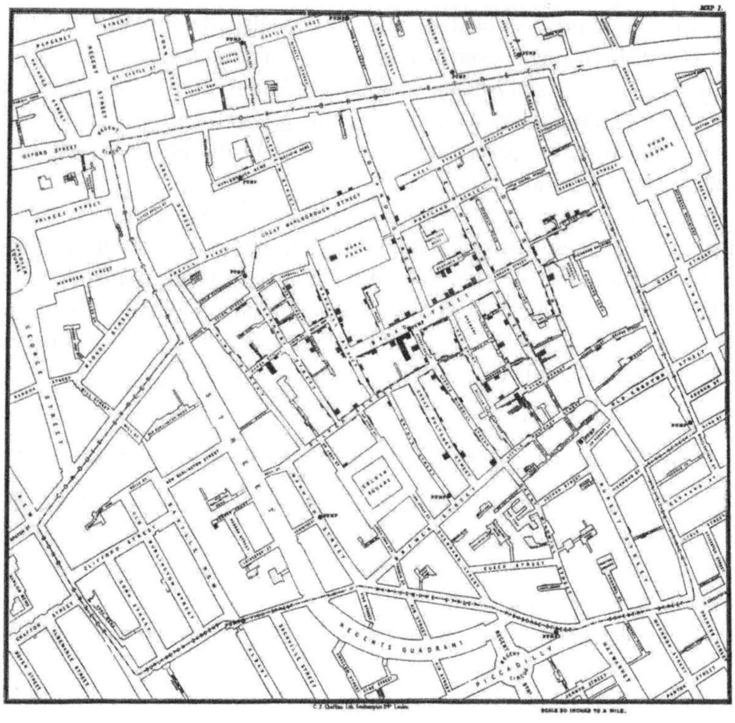

FIGURE 12.8: John Snow developed this map to illustrate the spatial distribution of fatalities during an outbreak of cholera in 1854 London. The cluster of deaths were centered around the Broad Street pump.

regions. The map in the figure shows high smoking rates in Appalachian counties, with lower rates in the Northeast, Pacific, and lower West.

Static dot and chloropleth maps are effective tools for geospatial analysis because they tap in to the powerful spatial perception capabilities we possess as humans. Through effective visual representations, patterns in the data quickly become apparent. The utility of these techniques is clear even in static form. However, adding interaction, as in the US Health Map [2] example, allows users to dynamically explore the data by applying filters, comparing subsets, and adjusting visual parameters (e.g., the minimum and maximum threshold values for the color scale). Combining geospatial techniques with traditional statistical charts including line and bar charts—as done in the US Health Map and Disease View [27]—provides coordinated views that enable an even richer—interactive analysis experience.

In practice, such geospatial representations are often used in combination with statistical analyses or automated data mining/machine learning algorithms that process the raw underlying data. For example, Lavrač et al. [59] combine data mining and statistical analysis techniques with both dot and chloropleth maps (along with other statistical charts) to model metrics such as healthcare availability. Sopan et al. follow a similar path in their Community Health Map initiative [75].

With chloropleth maps, geographic area is preserved within the visualized map. However, population density is not uniformly distributed. As a result, such maps can be misleading. Alternatives are therefore sometimes used. For instance, Freifeld et al. [32] describe a system for monitoring global infectious disease that uses maps to display the results of automated classification algorithms applied to online media (news stories, official alerts, and curated accounts). The system can plot events individually (following the "push pin" metaphor popularized by Google Maps) or in aggregate (as size-encoded circles positioned by latitude and longitude on the map.

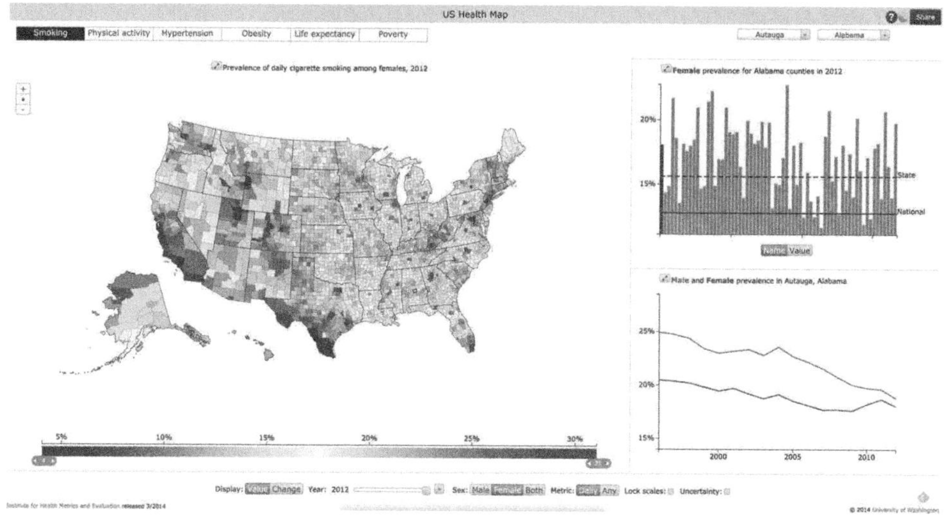

FIGURE 12.9: The US Health Map [2], developed by the Institute for Health Metrics and Evaluation, uses the chloropleth map technique to support the visual analysis of spatial public health data. This example employs county data across the United States to show the patterns associated with cigarette smoking for females in 2012. Other coordinated views and controls allow for exploratory analysis.

Cartograms are another geospatial technique designed to overcome the mismatch between geographic area and population distributions. Cartogram-based techniques warp the boundaries of geographic regions so that areas more closely represent populations, while preserving adjacency during the warping process. This approach has been adopted, for example, by Merrill et al. [64] in geospatial analysis of childhood cancer rates.

12.3.1.2 Temporal Analysis

The concept of time is a central and essential element of many health-related analyses. In the public health domain, investigators are often concerned with how a population evolves over time. For example, are incidence rates of a disease increasing or decreasing? Do the symptoms associated with an outbreak change over time? How well is an intervention working for a given group of people?

Given the critical nature of time in many investigations, charting of temporal data for cohorts of patients has been a key practice for many years and predates the computational era. For example, the famed statistician and matriarch of modern nursing Florence Nightingale used a unique temporal visualization known as the Rose Diagram (Figure 12.10) to demonstrate the seasonal impact on soldier mortality at a field hospital that was in her command. The cyclical nature of the calendar year is captured by the radial nature of the chart, a technique that is still in use today for analysts seeking repeating temporal patterns (e.g., by hours of day, days of the week, or months of the year).

However, temporal trends are not always correlated with a cyclical time structure. Many temporal patterns play out over time marked by a "starting event." This may be the index case in a disease outbreak, or the date of diagnosis for a population-based outcomes study. In these cases, a linear timeline-based visualization technique can be most effective. Most relevant to public health applications are visual analysis techniques that handle large cohorts of patients. For example, Wang et al. developed Lifelines2 [89, 90, 91], a visual analysis method designed to support alignment and ranking across multiple patient records. While basic aggregation was supported in the form of event-type histograms, this approach visualizes each patient as an individual horizontal timeline. When

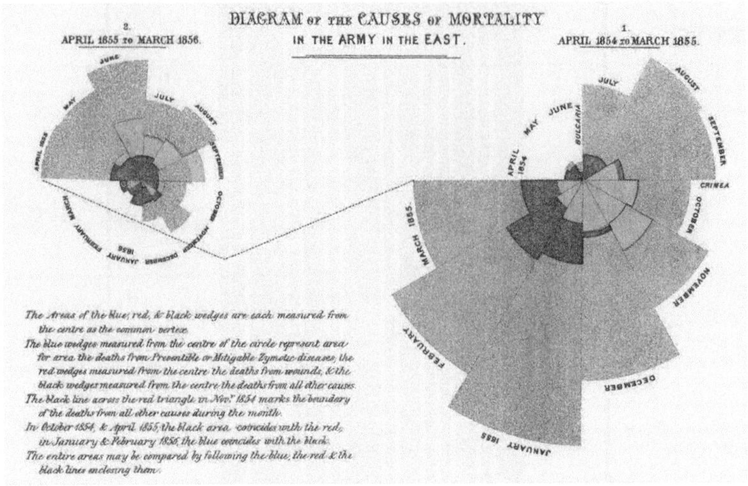

FIGURE 12.10: Florence Nightingdale developed this so-called Rose Diagram to visualize the seasonal nature of soldier mortality at her field hospital. The cyclical nature of the 12 months is captured by the circular arrangement of the visualization.

multiple patients are viewed at the same time, the corresponding individual timelines are stacked vertically. Users can scroll through the stack to view individual timelines.

Recognizing that lengthy stacks of individual timelines can be hard to navigate and interpret for large populations, more recent work has explored the use of aggregate methods. This approach captures population proportions by grouping similar patient timelines into event *pathways* which no longer graphically represent each patient individually. The common pattern in these visual analysis methods [40, 39, 95, 94] includes a three-step process of (a) temporal alignment designed to adjust all patients around a common *time zero*, (b) an aggregation process designed to uncover common temporal patterns through data manipulation and statistical analysis, and (c) interactive visualization to support exploratory analysis.

These methods scale well when applied to large populations, but are still challenged by datasets with large numbers of event types. To address this limitation, simplification methods can be applied to the underlying event sequences. Such an approach was adopted by Monroe et al. [65], who proposed a series of manual interactions designed to iteratively reduce the visual complexity of a visualized aggregate event timeline. Automated data mining techniques can also be used to derive patterns and temporal abstractions, thereby reducing complexity of the aggregate data structure that drives the visualization [45, 54].

An alternative technique to event sequence aggregation is to eschew the notion of a formal timeline altogether, focusing instead on a segmented timeline that shows the change in value of individual measures over time. For example, medical event data can be analyzed for co-occurrences over time. The pairwise co-occurrences can be plotted as line chart or matrix-based heatmaps as in [67]. These approaches allow the analyst to view changes in pairwise relationships over time (e.g., correlations between symptoms growing more intense as a disease progresses) without introducing the complexities that result when visually depicting sequential event ordering.

12.3.1.3 Beyond Spatio-Temporal Visualization

While much of the visual analysis work in public health has focused on advanced techniques for geospatial and temporal data, other types of data have been studied as well. One other important area is network visualization, which can be used, for instance, to view social network structures, disease propagation models [24, 25], or medication use within online communities [17].

Interactive variants of traditional statistical charts, including scatter plots, dendrograms (for hierarchies), and parallel coordinates are also widely employed [14, 73]. And finally, a range of more novel techniques for other data types have also been proposed (e.g., [36]).

The most powerful visual analysis methods employ more than one of these visualization types in combination through a technique known as *multiple coordinated views*. For example, as seen in Figure 12.9, spatio-temporal visualizations are often used together with a variety of other visualization types through an integrated user interface. In such systems, selections in one view are automatically propagated to other views. As a result, users can quickly discover correlated patterns that span across different views of the dataset. Examples of such integrated systems that address public health challenges include Epinome by Livnat et al. [61] and the space-time system developed by Avruskin et al. [8].

These sorts of interactive, coordinated, multiview visual analysis environments can provide domain experts experts with powerful platforms for exploratory data analysis and decision making. However, like all user-facing technology, they must be designed carefully to match the needs of the target user population. User-centered design (UCD) is one method that can be effectively employed to ensure that users needs are met. For example, UCD was used by Sutcliffe et al. [4] to inform their design of ADVISES, a visualization-based decision-support tool for public health experts that included chloropleth maps linked to other types of interactive visualization components.

ADVISES is just one example of how visual analytics can be tied to the practices of public health professionals. To gain a more comprehensive view, Carroll et al. [21] cataloged methods that have been proposed across three decades of public health literature. In addition to specific visualization and analysis techniques, Carroll et al. identified a number of key challenges moving forward, including (a) understanding users' needs, visual literacy, and numeracy; (b) integrating tightly into the analysis workflow; (c) the need to support collaborative and interdisciplinary analysis; and (d) uncertain and missing data. Not surprisingly, these challenges closely parallel the concerns highlighted by Thomas and Cook in their research agenda that helped define the modern conception of visual analytics [81].

In one recent example of work toward this larger goal, Streit et al. [77] outlined a model-driven design process aimed at connecting data, views, analytics, and tasks within a comprehensive multistep analysis process. A prototype visual analysis system for biomedical data was developed that links data from a variety of sources including tissue samples, MR/CT/X-ray sources, genetic data, lab results, biochemical pathways, and more. They use their system to link disparate data sources, apply a series of analytical algorithms, and define a wide range of key views of the data to enable decision making.

This example hints at the richness of data available for such analyses, and the range of visualization types that are often custom designed for specific types of data and analysis tasks. In particular, while much of the work in public health and outcomes research has focused on population survey data, administrative data (e.g., claims), electronic medical records, and genomic data is quickly emerging as an enormously valuable yet complex resource. As a result, a wide variety of visual analysis techniques are being developed for such purposes. While a detailed survey is beyond the scope of this chapter, we refer readers to the proceedings from the BioVis [1] and VIZBI [3] conferences.

12.3.2 Visual Analytics for Clinical Workflow

As clinical centers continue to embrace new health information technology (HIT), hospital administrators and leadership groups are interested in ways to better understand the overall workflow of their organizations including billings, coding patterns, waiting times, patient outcomes, differences/similarities between providers, frequencies of specific diagnoses, effectiveness of particular treatments, and many other details that could be used to obtain insight about the organization. Ef-

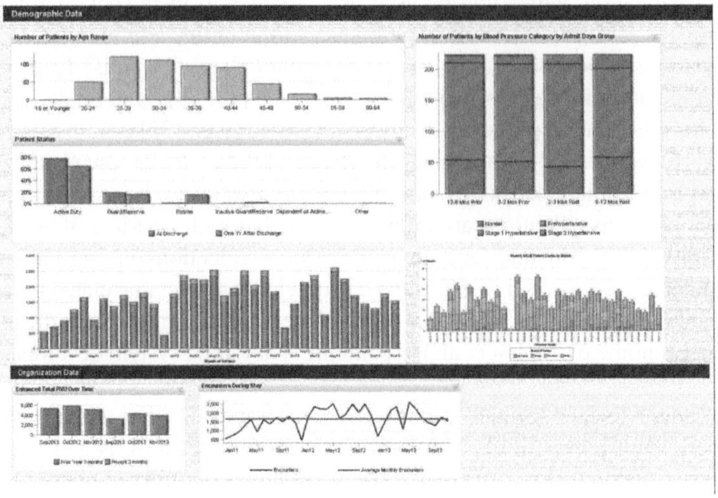

FIGURE 12.11: Different visual analytics techniques can be combined within a single dashboard to provide hospital administrators with detailed information about the organization, clinical workflows, coding standards, and other information that can be used to improve the efficiency of the clinic.

fective methods to obtain that information, generate reports, and identify trends can help hospital administrators better justify resources, determine areas of improvement, increase transparency between providers and patients, compare the performance between different departments, and reduce the overall cost of treatment.

Hospital administrators are one of the groups that, remarkably, have most aggressively accepted new data visualization tools and visual analytics within healthcare organizations. In hospital settings, visual analytics systems are often deployed as *business intelligence* (BI) *dashboards* or *clinical decision dashboards*. Such applications can either display real-time data about the utilization of different resources (e.g., operating rooms, MRIs, etc.) or display data for a particular time frame (i.e., monthly, quarterly) and compare it against historical norms. An example dashboard is shown in Figure 12.11. To help engage users with the data and allow exploratory analysis, clinical dashboards are often created as interactive tools that allow drilling down to more detailed information from high level summaries. These summary displays are designed with the purpose of advancing the quality of the care, increasing medication safety, managing patient flow, monitoring patient handovers between departments, and many other applications.

For example, Aydin et al. [18] presented a dashboard that leverages visual analytics techniques to monitor and quickly analyze multiple metrics related to nurses. In particular, they focused on different ways of presenting and reporting the California Nursing Outcomes Coalition (CalNOC) data, including comparison reports, summary statistics, facility-specific reports, and trends. Some of the metrics included in their dashboard were total hours of work per day, number of patients per nurse, hours of care with a patient, as well as patient outcome variables such as falls after discharge. The authors explain how visual analytics helped in their understanding of the large number of measurements collected for their staff and their patients.

Such dashboard techniques have proven useful for a range of workflow applications. For instance, Dolan et al. [26] performed a user study to measure the effectiveness of visual analytics and interactive clinical dashboards in supporting operational decision making. They found that interactive decision dashboards are effective at illustrating clinical workflow data and have the potential to foster an informed decision-making process. Most importantly, they found that visual analytics techniques can reduce the cognitive effort needed to understand the daily flow of hospital organizations.

In related work, Ferranti et al. [31] conducted a user study at the Duke University Health System to evaluate the impact of a dashboard system used to display six specific performance improvement metrics. The study results and subsequent analysis estimated that using the dashboard helped the system identify and prevent 157.8 potential cases of *noscomially acquired C difficile* per year. Moreover, the improvements went beyond outcomes. The authors estimated, for example, that in one case study the identification and correction of process flaws uncovered by the system resulted in improved financial performance saving millions of dollars within just four months.

In other case studies, dashboards have been applied to a range of settings from surgical wards to radiology units. For example, Hugine et al. [47] show how treemaps, the hierarchical visualization technique discussed in Section 12.2.3, were used to explore and analyze surgical quality data. In their study, they found that treemaps were effective at illustrating the surgical quality data. However, they emphasized that more research was needed to develop a wider range of additional techniques that could be flexibly applied to support outcomes-based quality monitoring and analysis. In a somewhat similar work, both Kohli et al. [55] and Nagy et al. [66] used web-based visual analytics-based dashboards to monitor and improve the effectiveness of radiology departments.

Overall, visual analytics are transforming healthcare services and management by depicting key operational measures in ways that are interpretable and actionable. These trends has been especially evident in recent years as a wide range of data visualization systems and dashboards have emerged for use in clinical settings [10, 15, 37, 56, 85, 86, 97]. These systems have had a great impact on clinical workflow improvement, outcomes, and patient safety.

12.3.3 Visual Analytics for Clinicians

In contrast to the applications described earlier in this chapter, clinical use cases for visual analytics typically focus on understanding data about an individual patient. Such index patients are often visualized in the context of a larger background population to demonstrate deviations (or lack thereof) from a peer group, but the goal is to provide a clinician with individualized insights and—potentially—support personalized-care decisions.

12.3.3.1 Temporal Analysis

Given the temporal nature of disease and patient progression, a wide variety of visual analysis techniques for clinical use are centered around a temporal presentation of patient data. These techniques are similar in some ways to the temporal methods described in Section 12.3.1.2. However, clinical applications focus on individual patient records rather than broad populations.

For example, early pioneering work from Plaisant et al. [69] employed a multithreaded, hierarchical graphical timeline to summarize a single patient's medical record. The Lifelines approach allowed clinicians to spot trends over time across disparate data points that were displayed separately in traditional medical record user interface designs. Moreover, the visualization provided a central location from which clinicians could access more detailed information across multiple modalities. For example, as shown in Figure 12.12, ultrasound or x-ray imaging could be integrated for viewing in context within the graphical timeline.

More recent work has continued to explore the use of visualization to integrate data from multiple sources [28], summarize and diagnose [71], and aid in decision support for individual patients [46, 62]. For example, MidGaard [9] uses a variety of methods to summarize temporal trends in intensive care data in the context of guideline information. It includes a series of temporal plots showing a variety of quantitative intensive care data streams. The plots are reminiscent of traditional line charts. However, they include several additional features including pan and zoom capabilities to support navigation of the time dimension at different scales. They also have a unique visual encod-

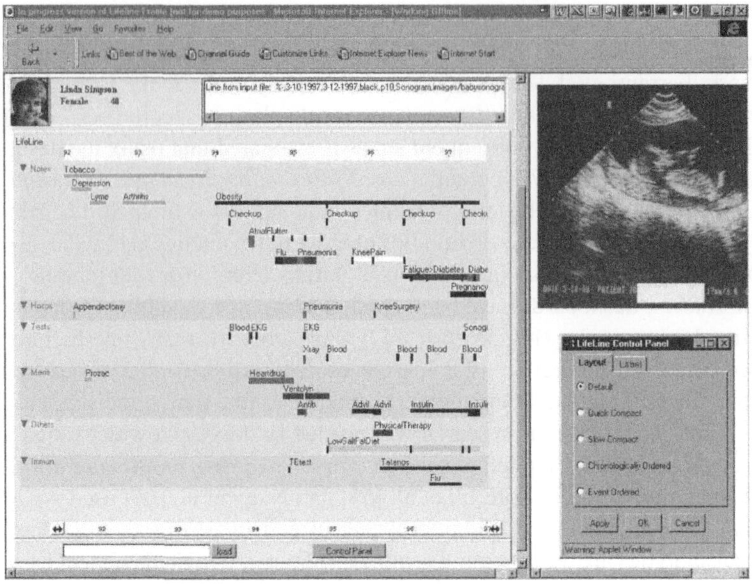

FIGURE 12.12: Lifelines from Plaisant et al. [69] emerged in the late 1990s as an early example of visualization applied to personal medical records.

ing designed to support *focus in context*, a visual analysis technique in which small scale features are visualized at the same time as wider-scale contextual information that provides a context for interpretation. This is achieved by employing slightly different visual representations at different scales, and a rendering engine that can switch dynamically between those methods as users interact with the visualization.

12.3.3.2 Patient Progress and Guidelines

Patient progress is often evaluated in the context of clinical guidelines that capture best practices for care and common disease progression pathways. For this reason, a number of visual analysis techniques have been developed to show patient data in the context of guideline information [6]. These technique are often applied in combination with temporal visual analysis methods.

For example, Aigner and Miksch developed CareVis [7], an interactive visual analysis environment that uses multiview methods to depict the logical and sequential structure of patient care plans. They coordinate display and navigation of data through both nested flow-chart diagrams and a timeline view similar to Gantt charts (commonly found in project management software). A key feature of CareVis is the use of *focus in context* methods. This approach is used for both the care plan structural diagrams as well as the timeline, enabling the visual analysis of large and complex care plans.

12.3.3.3 Other Clinical Methods

While temporal visual analysis methods generally focus on trends and changes over time, another common use case is understanding the current set of values in a complex, multivariate information space. A common approach toward this challenge is the multivariate glyph [92]. Glyphs are graphical objects that are mapped to multivariate data such that specific attributes of the graphical representation are determined by values of individual dimensions within the data. For example, the VIE-VISU [93] system uses a glyph-based method to visualize multiple continuous streams of data from an ICU environment. The benefit of a well-designed glyph-based approach is that users can learn to see patterns across multidimensional data very quickly and "at-a-glance," making it ideal for situation awareness applications such as those commonly found in acute care settings.

Glyphs can help convey a patient's current condition, but often that is not enough to make clinical decisions. Contextualization—placing a patient's data in the context of her/his past and peers—is important to understand how a patient is progressing. Data analytics can be used to process large sets of data and extract statistical measures from a population of similar patients to provide such context. These contextual insights can then be visualized along with patient-specific data to help explain a variety of patient risk factors. This pattern is followed in ICDA [35], a visual analysis system that identifies at-risk patients. ICDA analyzes a large patient population and assigns patients simple-to-read risk scores that measure the magnitude of various types of medical risk. Two patients may have the same risk of developing a particular disease but for very different reasons that require different interventions. ICDA provides a suite of interactive visualization tools to help convey why a patient is at risk as context for the simplified risk scores assigned by the underlying risk models.

ICDA is just one example of class of visual analysis methods developed around the notion of patient similarity. These methods all aim to contextualize the data for a patient undergoing clinical care via data derived from historical records for a cohort of similar patients. For example, Stubbs et al. [78] uses a highly interactive visualization-based interface to let clinicians query, explore, analyze, and compare sets of similar patients for decision support purposes. Simple toggles are used to allow users to navigate multivariate categorical dimensions, enabling fast and efficient exploration of the data. Interactive elements of the visualization are also used to let users control parameters of the underlying analytics, making it possible for clinicians to experiment with alternative models while working to judge the merits of different interventions.

Similarity analytics have also been used to help understand patient symptom progression and treatment response for heart failure patients [40, 94], using temporal methods similar to those identified in Section 12.3.1.2. Glyph-based methods have also been used with patient similarity analytics. For example, DICON [38] uses treemap-based glyphs to represent subgroups of similar patients. The glyphs support direct manipulation, allowing clinicians to refine a cohort of similar patients based on expertise or contextual knowledge. Using simple mouse-based gestures, clinicians can merge patient subgroups, apply algorithmic clustering algorithms, or pivot between alternative spatial mappings to better understand a population of similar patients.

Complementing the above methods, which use patient similarity to provide quantitative evidence for decision support, a final set of clinical visual analysis applications focuses on presenting medical literature in a more informative way. For example, search results returned from PubMed can be visualized based on metadata in a two-dimensional space to facilitate improved navigation and comprehension over the traditional ranked lists returned by search engines. For example, Boulous [16] demonstrates a variety of mapping techniques, each of which projects a set of search results into a two-dimensional plane for visualization. The specifics of the mapping function can be controlled to optimize certain informational constraints (e.g., maintain geographic collocation, or maximize item separation) during the projection. Similar methods are used by Sun et al. [79] who employ a multidimensional scaling (MDS) technique to visualize data from online medical information portals.

12.3.4 Visual Analytics for Patients

Interfaces that are helpful to patients may be very different from the ones that are helpful to clinicians. At the outset, the intended uses may be different. Major uses include assisting patients to comprehend health information, to manage their health condition, and to serve as a communication platform within particular healthcare contexts.

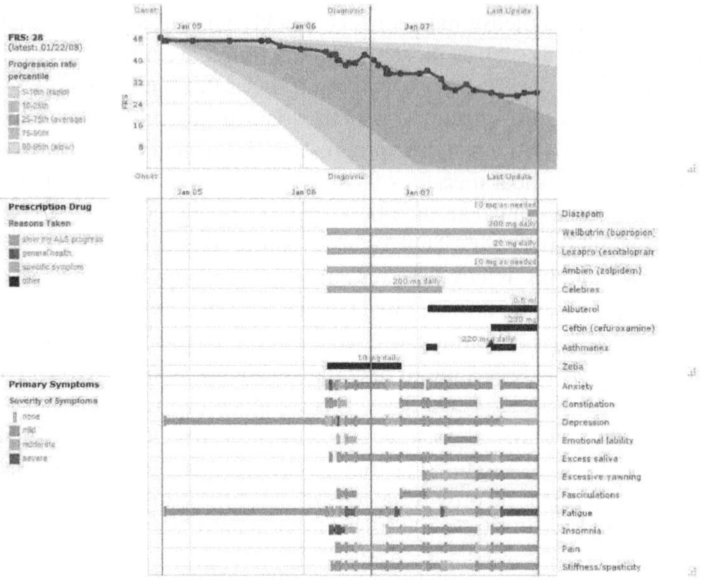

FIGURE 12.13: The individual summary visualization used within PatientsLikeMe.

12.3.4.1 Assisting Comprehension

Given the vast amount of health information that is available today, patients may become overwhelmed and wish there were a way to make sense of it all, particularly those with chronic and nebulous conditions, such as fibromyalgia [22]. For controversial topics for which opposing viewpoints are represented, interfaces may help patients sort through these viewpoints [63].

Visualizations can help patients to make sense of health information. Websites for health consumers are increasingly featuring visual displays to help patients understand their own information. For example, PatientsLikeMe employs the "nugget" (see Figure 12.13) to summarize and represent a patients' current status, and Gantt charts are used to display changes in their treatment and symptoms over time [33]. Visualizations can also help patients to explore and reflect upon relationships between their behavior and objective health measures, such as blood sugar.

Though one's own data is important, it is not as valuable with additional information from other sources to contextualize it. For example, Chun and MacKellar [5] provide an example of how experiential data from blogs can be integrated with other sources including PatientsLikeMe, WebMD, and PubMed. In the future, integration of information from disparate sources, including patient-generated data with expert-curated data, is likely to become increasingly prevalent.

With regard to this task, it may be particularly important to leverage existing research concerning health consumers' information seeking patterns and ways of evaluation. Previous research has reported that health consumers often base credibility judgments of websites on heuristics such as the presence of structural features such as navigation menus, and links to external websites [70]; and that consumers often seek information which confirms their own pre-existing beliefs [52]. Developing visual interfaces collaboratively with consumers could lead to insights about how they might interpret and use them to make health decisions.

12.3.4.2 Condition Management

Other important aims include helping patients capture and manage different aspects of their daily lives [30]. Visualization can encourage patient involvement in their own healthcare. PatientsLikeMe allows patients to enter custom values for symptoms such as "late for everything" [19].

One example of an application with visual tools to facilitate tracking is Pain Squad, a pain assessment application designed for adolescents with cancer [76]. The application employs a selectable body map and visual analogue slider to facilitate data collection. Another tool, BodyDiagrams, enables patients to describe their symptoms visually via drawings and text [50].

One of the particular challenges of design of mobile devices is the incorporation of sensors that collect information about physical activity and social interactions. Such information can be used to understand aspects of a person's daily routines such as exercise levels and sleep patterns. For example, a mobile phone with a built-in accelerometer and Wellness Dairy software can be used to support outpatient cardiac rehabilitation [87]. Patients receive motivational and educational multimedia content via their phone. The phone also facilitates weekly discussions between the patient and a personal mentor who will help them to reach their goals.

In recent years, there has been a particular increase in the use of mobile apps to promote behavioral changes such as smoking cessation, diet change, medication adherence and exercise, often through the use of gamification, where desirable behaviors are rewarded [20]. One active area of development is the design of peripheral displays that require low cognitive effort and promote awareness of one's activities [11]. A "glanceable display" can serve as a persistent reminder to engage in exercise or some other healthful behavior [53].

Mobile apps can also facilitate goal setting and progress assessment. BeWell+, an application that employs an ambient design, conveys well-being scores to users through an aquatic ecosystem visualization [60]. Mobile apps may also assist users overcome decision inertia. The *Bant* app detects when a user's blood glucose levels have been out of range for three consecutive days, and then helps the user to identify the cause of the trend and adjust their behavior [20].

12.3.4.3 Integration into Healthcare Contexts

Information technology can also be integrated into healthcare environments. In one example, data from EMRs has been pulled into patients' phones in order to provide them real-time information about activities that concern them in the hospital. They also have access to information about their care team, and any medications and tests that are administered. This information can help to reduce their anxiety during their stay [68]. Other than anxiety reduction, patients reported positive benefits such as increased understanding, better memory, and a sense of information ownership.

Interfaces can also help patients to understand treatments and procedures. In one intervention, it was reported patients who received explanations that included visualizations scored higher on the knowledge scale than those who did not see visualizations [29]. In another example, embodied conversation agents were used to present information to patients with low health literacy [13]. Two different ECAs, one with Caucasian and the other with African American features were designed to provide patients' medical information. Hand gestures and voices with different accents were also used to help patients understand. Patients liked the ECAs because they could take more time digesting the information than they felt comfortable doing if there were a live clinician in front of them.

One last example is InnoMotion, a web-based application that integrates motion sensing technology to help patients with occupational therapy [23]. The system provides different levels of feedback, including instant feedback during exercise, performance feedback after exercise completion, aggregate summary feedback and a timeline visualization to view overall progress. This system also enables a healthcare provider to view and communicate with patients on their progress.

In summary, visualizations that have been designed for patients generally have very different goals than those designed for clinicians. In many situations, the focus is on helping patients to understand their own data and track their own progress. There is also a proliferation of mobile applications, particularly focused on health behaviors such as diet, exercise, sleep, and smoking cessation. With regard to mobile apps, there has been a focus on sensor integration, the design of ambient displays that are motivational and provide a great deal of information at a glance. Interfaces have also been designed for patients in particular healthcare contexts, e.g., to support them in healthcare environments such as hospitals, to prepare them for treatments and procedures, and also as actual parts of the treatment, as in the case of occupational therapy.

With regard to assisting comprehension, some of the particular challenges that lie ahead include how to effectively incorporate semantic information to contextualize patient data, and how to assist patients to sense-make about the information that they see. With regard to the design of mobile devices, current research is focused on how to minimize cognitive effort and motivate patients to engage in healthful behaviors. This often involves gamification and social feedback. Lastly, patient-centered interfaces in healthcare contexts can facilitate communication between patients and their healthcare teams. These interfaces can fill in information gaps that currently exist in healthcare settings by providing patients with more information about the care that they are receiving, and spend more time providing explanations than clinicians might otherwise be able to give. Interfaces can also provide visual feedback for particular tasks, such as occupational therapy.

12.4 Conclusion

Visual analytics technologies combine visual interactive interfaces with analytical techniques to create systems that can facilitate the reasoning and interpretation of complex data. Given the high volume of complex, heterogeneous, and high-dimensional data used across a range of healthcare application areas, visual analytics techniques have been widely deployed. This chapter has provided a general overview of the field of visual analytics and introduced a variety of basic methodologies commonly used in the field.

Following the general introduction, this chapter surveyed a range of healthcare applications for visual analytics including public health and medical research, clinical workflow, clinical practice, and patient communication and engagement. As the many examples in these sections show, visualization and interactive technologies have been successfully applied to a range of complex information problems in which visual analysis methods have facilitated direct human participation in the analysis process. These methods have proven most effective when tasks require a combination of human intelligence with the power of computation to analyze and summarize large volumes of complex data: topics such as clinical decision making, hypothesis formulation in medical research, and patients' communications with physicians, information resources, and their peers. When the right methods are applied to appropriate problems, the results can be dramatic.

However, despite the great strides that have been made in developing visual analysis methods that make complex healthcare information more accessible to users in many roles and use cases, a number of challenges remain unsolved. As a result, advances in this area are being explored by a vibrant and growing research community. As the volume and complexity of electronic data in the healthcare domain grows, so too must our ability as human practitioners and thinkers to touch, explore, and derive insights from data that improve our medical decisions and understanding. Visual analytics is in a position to play a crucial role as we drive toward a more evidenced-based healthcare system [74].

Bibliography

[1] About BioVis | BioVis, http://www.biovis.net, April 2014.

[2] US health map, http://viz.healthmetricsandevaluation.org/us-health-map/, March 2014.

[3] VIZBI - visualizing biological data, http://vizbi.org, April 2014.

[4] Alistair Sutcliffe, Oscar de Bruijn, Sarah Thew, et al. Developing visualization-based decision support tools for epidemiology. *Information Visualization*, 2012.

[5] Soon Ae Chun and Bonnie MacKellar. Social health data integration using semantic web. In *Proceedings of the 27th Annual ACM Symposium on Applied Computing*, pages 392–397. ACM, 2012.

[6] Wolfgang Aigner, Katharina Kaiser, and Silvia Miksch. Visualization methods to support guideline-based care management. *Studies in Health Technology and Informatics*, 139:140, 2008.

[7] Wolfgang Aigner and Silvia Miksch. CareVis: Integrated visualization of computerized protocols and temporal patient data. *Artificial Intelligence in Medicine*, 37(3):203–218, July 2006.

[8] Gillian A Avruskin, Geoffrey M Jacquez, Jaymie R Meliker, Melissa J Slotnick, Andrew M Kaufmann, and Jerome O Nriagu. Visualization and exploratory analysis of epidemiologic data using a novel space time information system. *International Journal of Health Geographics*, 3:26, November 2004.

[9] Ragnar Bade, Stefan Schlechtweg, and Silvia Miksch. Connecting time-oriented data and information to a coherent interactive visualization. In *Proceedings of the SIGCHI Conference on Human Factors in Computing Systems*, CHI '04, page 105–112, New York, NY, USA, 2004. ACM.

[10] Jakob E Bardram. Activity-based computing for medical work in hospitals. *ACM Transactions on Computer-Human Interaction*, 16(2):1–36, June 2009.

[11] Jared Bauer, Sunny Consolvo, Benjamin Greenstein, Jonathan Schooler, Eric Wu, Nathaniel F Watson, and Julie Kientz. ShutEye: Encouraging awareness of healthy sleep recommendations with a mobile, peripheral display. In *Proceedings of the 2012 ACM Annual Conference on Human Factors in Computing Systems*, page 1401–1410. ACM, 2012.

[12] Jacob Beutel, J Michael Fitzpatrick, Steven C Horii, Yongmin Kim, Harold L Kundel, Milan Sonka, and Richard L Van Metter. *Handbook of Medical Imaging, Volume 3. Display and PACS*. Washington, DC: SPIE Press, 2002.

[13] Timothy W Bickmore, Laura M Pfeifer, and Brian W Jack. Taking the time to care: Empowering low health literacy hospital patients with virtual nurse agents. In *Proceedings of the SIGCHI Conference on Human Factors in Computing Systems*, page 1265–1274. ACM, 2009.

[14] Oliver Bieh-Zimmert, Claudia Koschtial, and Carsten Felden. Representing multidimensional cancer registry data. *Proceedings of i-Know '13*, Article 35, ACM Press, 2013.

[15] Peter Bodesinsky, Paolo Federico, and Silvia Miksch. Visual analysis of compliance with clinical guidelines. In *Proceedings of the 13th International Conference on Knowledge Management and Knowledge Technologies, i-Know '13*, page 12:112:8, New York, NY, USA, 2013. ACM.

[16] Maged NK Boulos. The use of interactive graphical maps for browsing medical/health internet information resources. *International Journal of Health Geographics*, 2(1):1, January 2003.

[17] Brant W Chee, Richard Berlin, and Bruce R. Schatz. *Information Visualization of Drug Regimens from Health Messages*. pages 282–287, 2009.

[18] Diane Storer Brown, Carolyn E Aydin, and Nancy Donaldson. Quartile dashboards: Translating large data sets into performance improvement priorities. *Journal for Healthcare Quality*, 30(6):18–30, November 2008.

[19] Jed Brubaker, Caitlin Lustig, and Gillian Hayes. PatientsLikeMe: Empowerment and representation in a patient-centered social network. In *CSCW10; Workshop on Research in Healthcare: Past, Present, and Future*, 2010.

[20] Joseph A Cafazzo, Mark Casselman, Nathaniel Hamming, Debra K Katzman, and Mark R Palmert. Design of an mHealth app for the self-management of adolescent type 1 diabetes: A pilot study. *Journal of Medical Internet Research*, 14(3):e70, May 2012.

[21] Lauren N Carroll, Alan P Au, Landon Todd Detwiler, Tsung-chieh Fu, Ian S. Painter, and Neil F. Abernethy. Visualization and analytics tools for infectious disease epidemiology: A systematic review. *Journal of Biomedical Informatics*, 51:287–298, 2014.

[22] Annie T. Chen. Information seeking over the course of illness: The experience of people with fibromyalgia: Information seeking in people with fibromyalgia. *Musculoskeletal Care*, 10(4):212–220, December 2012.

[23] Luxi Chen, Ni Yan, Miranda Kiang, Anna S Muth, and Kruthi Sabnis Krishna. Innomotion: a web-based rehabilitation system helping patients recover and gain self-awareness of their body away from the clinic. *Proceedings of CHI EA '14*, pages 233–238. ACM Press, 2014.

[24] Nicholas A. Christakis and James H. Fowler. Social network visualization in epidemiology. *Norwegian Journal of Epidemiology*, 9(1):5–16, 2009.

[25] Victoria J Cook, Sumi J Sun, Jane Tapia, Stephen Q Muth, D Fermn Argello, Bryan L Lewis, Richard B Rothenberg, and Peter D McElroy. Transmission network analysis in tuberculosis contact investigations. *Journal of Infectious Diseases*, 196(10):1517–1527, November 2007.

[26] James G Dolan, Peter J Veazie, and Ann J Russ. Development and initial evaluation of a treatment decision dashboard. *BMC Medical Informatics and Decision Making*, 13(1):51, April 2013.

[27] Timothy Driscoll, Joseph L Gabbard, Chunhong Mao, Oral Dalay, Maulik Shukla, Clark C Freifeld, Anne Gatewood Hoen, John S Brownstein, and Bruno W Sobral. Integration and visualization of hostpathogen data related to infectious diseases. *Bioinformatics*, 27(16):2279–2287, August 2011.

[28] B Drohan, G Grinstein, and K Hughes. Oncology lifeline - a timeline tool for the interdisciplinary management of breast cancer patients in a surgical clinic. In *Information Visualisation (IV), 2010 14th International Conference*, pages 233–238, 2010.

[29] Manuel Enzenhofer, Hans-Bernd Bludau, Nadja Komm, Beate Wild, Knut Mueller, Wolfgang Herzog, and Achim Hochlehnert. Improvement of the educational process by computer-based visualization of procedures: Randomized controlled trial. *Journal of Medical Internet Research*, 6(2):e16, June 2004.

[30] Sarah Faisal, Ann Blandford, and Henry WW Potts. Making sense of personal health information: Challenges for information visualization. *Health Informatics Journal*, 19(3):198–217, 2013.

[31] Jeffrey M Ferranti, Matthew K Langman, David Tanaka, Jonathan McCall, and Asif Ahmad. Bridging the gap: Leveraging business intelligence tools in support of patient safety and financial effectiveness. *Journal of the American Medical Informatics Association*, 17(2):136–143, March 2010.

[32] Clark C Freifeld, Kenneth D Mandl, Ben Y Reis, and John S Brownstein. HealthMap: Global infectious disease monitoring through automated classification and visualization of internet media reports. *Journal of the American Medical Informatics Association*, 15(2):150–157, March 2008.

[33] Jeana H Frost and Michael P Massagli. Social uses of personal health information within PatientsLikeMe, an online patient community: What can happen when patients have access to one anothers data. *Journal of Medical Internet Research*, 10(3):e15, May 2008.

[34] Miguel García and Barry Harmsen. *QlikView 11 for Developers*. Packt Publishing Ltd, 2012.

[35] D Gotz, H Stavropoulos, J Sun, and F Wang. ICDA: A platform for intelligent care delivery analytics. In *AMIA Annual Symposium Proceedings*, 2012.

[36] D H Gotz, J Sun, and N Cao. Multifaceted visual analytics for healthcare applications. *IBM Journal of Research and Development*, 56(5):6:1–6:12, 2012.

[37] David Gotz, Cao Nan, Esther Goldbraich, and Carmeli Boaz. GapFlow: Visualizing gaps in care for medical treatment plans. In *IEEE VIS Posters*, 2013.

[38] David Gotz, Jimeng Sun, Nan Cao, and Shahram Ebadollahi. Visual cluster analysis in support of clinical decision intelligence. *AMIA ... Annual Symposium Proceedings / AMIA Symposium.* 2011:481–490, 2011.

[39] David Gotz, Fei Wang, and Adam Perer. A methodology for interactive mining and visual analysis of clinical event patterns using electronic health record data. *Journal of Biomedical Informatics*, 48:148–159, April 2014.

[40] David Gotz and Krist Wongsuphasawat. Interactive intervention analysis. *AMIA ... Annual Symposium Proceedings / AMIA Symposium.* 2012:274–280, 2012.

[41] Graeme S Halford, Rosemary Baker, Julie E McCredden, and John D Bain. How many variables can humans process? *Psychological Science*, 16(1):70–76, 2005.

[42] Graeme S Halford, William H Wilson, and Steven Phillips. Processing capacity defined by relational complexity: Implications for comparative, developmental, and cognitive psychology. *Behavioral and Brain Sciences*, 21(06):803–831, 1998.

[43] Charles D Hansen and Chris R Johnson. *The Visualization Handbook*. Academic Press, 2005.

[44] Jeffrey Heer, Jock Mackinlay, Chris Stolte, and Maneesh Agrawala. Graphical histories for visualization: Supporting analysis, communication, and evaluation. *IEEE Transactions on Visualization and Computer Graphics*, 14(6):1189–1196, 2008.

[45] Tu Bao Ho, Trong Dung Nguyen, Saori Kawasaki, Si Quang Le, Dung Duc Nguyen, Hideto Yokoi, and Katsuhiko Takabayashi. Mining hepatitis data with temporal abstraction. In *Proceedings of the Ninth ACM SIGKDD International Conference on Knowledge Discovery and Data Mining*, page 369–377. ACM, 2003.

[46] W Hsu, R K Taira, S El-Saden, Hooshang Kangarloo, and A A T Bui. Context-based electronic health record: Toward patient specific healthcare. *IEEE Transactions on Information Technology in Biomedicine*, 16(2):228–234, March 2012.

[47] Akilah L Hugine, Stephanie A Guerlain, and Florence E Turrentine. Visualizing surgical quality data with treemaps. *Journal of Surgical Research*, 191(1):74–83, 2014.

[48] Tableau Inc. Tableau software: Business intelligence and analytics, May 2014.

[49] Alfred Inselberg and Bernard Dimsdale. *Parallel coordinates for Visualizing Multi-dimensional Geometry*. Springer, 1987.

[50] Amy Jang, Diana L MacLean, and Jeffrey Heer. *BodyDiagrams: Improving Communication of Pain Symptoms Through Drawing*, pages 1153–1162. ACM Press, 2014.

[51] Steven Johnson. *The Ghost Map: The Story of London's Most Terrifying Epidemic–and How It Changed Science, Cities, and the Modern World*. Riverhead Trade, New York, 1 reprint edition edition, October 2007.

[52] A Keselman, A C Browne, and D R Kaufman. Consumer health information seeking as hypothesis testing. *Journal of the American Medical Informatics Association*, 15(4):484–495, April 2008.

[53] Predrag Klasnja, Sunny Consolvo, David W McDonald, James A Landay, and Wanda Pratt. Using mobile & personal sensing technologies to support health behavior change in everyday life: lessons learned. In *AMIA Annual Symposium Proceedings*, volume 2009, page 338. American Medical Informatics Association, 2009.

[54] Denis Klimov, Yuval Shahar, and Meirav Taieb-Maimon. Intelligent visualization and exploration of time-oriented data of multiple patients. *Artificial Intelligence in Medicine*, 49(1):11–31, May 2010.

[55] Marc D Kohli, Max Warnock, Mark Daly, Christopher Toland, Chris Meenan, and Paul G Nagy. Building blocks for a clinical imaging informatics environment. *Journal of Digital Imaging*, 27(2):174–181, April 2014.

[56] Robert Kosara and Silvia Miksch. Metaphors of movement: A visualization and user interface for time-oriented, skeletal plans. *Artificial intelligence in Medicine*, 22(2):111–131, 2001.

[57] Martin Krzywinski, Jacqueline Schein, İnanç Birol, Joseph Connors, Randy Gascoyne, Doug Horsman, Steven J Jones, and Marco A Marra. Circos: An information aesthetic for comparative genomics. *Genome Research*, 19(9):1639–1645, 2009.

[58] Mahantapas Kundu, Mita Nasipuri, and Dipak Kumar Basu. Knowledge-based ECG interpretation: A critical review. *Pattern Recognition*, 33(3):351–373, 2000.

[59] Nada Lavrač, Marko Bohanec, Aleksander Pur, Bojan Cestnik, Marko Debeljak, and Andrej Kobler. Data mining and visualization for decision support and modeling of public health-care resources. *Journal of Biomedical Informatics*, 40(4):438–447, August 2007.

[60] Mu Lin, Nicholas D Lane, Mashfiqui Mohammod, Xiaochao Yang, Hong Lu, Giuseppe Cardone, Shahid Ali, Afsaneh Doryab, Ethan Berke, and Andrew T Campbell. BeWell+: Multi-dimensional wellbeing monitoring with community-guided user feedback and energy optimization. In *Proceedings of the Conference on Wireless Health*, page 10. ACM, 2012.

[61] Y Livnat, T Rhyne, and M Samore. Epinome: A visual-analytics workbench for epidemiology data. *IEEE Computer Graphics and Applications*, 32(2):89–95, March 2012.

[62] Ketan K Mane, Chris Bizon, Charles Schmitt, Phillips Owen, Bruce Burchett, Ricardo Pietrobon, and Kenneth Gersing. VisualDecisionLinc: A visual analytics approach for comparative effectiveness-based clinical decision support in psychiatry. *Journal of Biomedical Informatics*, 45(1):101–106, February 2012.

[63] Jennifer Mankoff, Kateryna Kuksenok, Sara Kiesler, Jennifer A Rode, and Kelly Waldman. Competing online viewpoints and models of chronic illness. In *Proceedings of the SIGCHI Conference on Human Factors in Computing Systems*, page 589–598. ACM, 2011.

[64] D W Merrill, S Selvin, E R Close, and H H Holmes. Use of density equalizing map projections (DEMP) in the analysis of childhood cancer in four california counties. *Statistics in Medicine*, 15(17-18):1837–1848, September 1996.

[65] Megan Monroe, Rongjian Lan, Hanseung Lee, Catherine Plaisant, and Ben Shneiderman. Temporal event sequence simplification. *Visualization and Computer Graphics, IEEE Transactions on*, 19(12):2227–2236, 2013.

[66] Paul G Nagy, Max J Warnock, Mark Daly, Christopher Toland, Christopher D Meenan, and Reuben S Mezrich. Informatics in radiology: Automated web-based graphical dashboard for radiology operational business intelligence. *Radiographics: A Review Publication of the Radiological Society of North America, Inc.*, 29(7):1897–1906, November 2009.

[67] Adam Perer and Jimeng Sun. MatrixFlow: Temporal network visual analytics to track symptom evolution during disease progression. *AMIA Annual Symposium Proceedings*, 2012:716–725, November 2012.

[68] Laura Pfeifer Vardoulakis, Amy Karlson, Dan Morris, Greg Smith, Justin Gatewood, and Desney Tan. Using mobile phones to present medical information to hospital patients. In *Proceedings of the 2012 ACM Annual Conference on Human Factors in Computing Systems*, page 14111420. ACM, 2012.

[69] C Plaisant, R Mushlin, A Snyder, J Li, D Heller, and B Shneiderman. LifeLines: Using visualization to enhance navigation and analysis of patient records. *Proceedings of the AMIA Symposium*, pages 76–80, 1998.

[70] Stephen A Rains and Carolyn Donnerstein Karmikel. Health information-seeking and perceptions of website credibility: Examining web-use orientation, message characteristics, and structural features of websites. *Computers in Human Behavior*, 25(2):544–553, March 2009.

[71] Alexander Rind, Wolfgang Aigner, Silvia Miksch, Sylvia Wiltner, Margit Pohl, Thomas Turic, and Felix Drexler. Visual exploration of time-oriented patient data for chronic diseases: Design study and evaluation. In *Information Quality in e-Health*, page 301–320. Springer, 2011.

[72] Richard A Robb. *Biomedical Imaging, Visualization, and Analysis*. John Wiley & Sons, Inc., 1999.

[73] Jack Schryver, Mallikarjun Shankar, and Songhua Xu. Moving from descriptive to causal analytics: Case study of discovering knowledge from us health indicators warehouse. In *Proceedings of the 2012 International Workshop on Smart Health and Wellbeing*, SHB '12, page 18, New York, NY, USA, 2012. ACM.

[74] Mark Smith, Robert Saunders, Leigh Stuckhardt, and J Michael McGinnis. *Best Care at Lower Cost: The Path to Continuously Learning Health Care in America*. The National Academies Press, 2013.

[75] Awalin Sopan, Angela Song-Ie Noh, Sohit Karol, Paul Rosenfeld, Ginnah Lee, and Ben Shneiderman. Community health map: A geospatial and multivariate data visualization tool for public health datasets. *Government Information Quarterly*, 29(2):223–234, April 2012.

[76] Jennifer N Stinson, Lindsay A Jibb, Cynthia Nguyen, Paul C Nathan, Anne Marie Maloney, L Lee Dupuis, J Ted Gerstle, Benjamin Alman, Sevan Hopyan, Caron Strahlendorf, Carol Portwine, Donna L Johnston, and Mike Orr. Development and testing of a multidimensional iPhone pain assessment application for adolescents with cancer. *Journal of Medical Internet Research*, 15(3):e51, March 2013.

[77] M Streit, H Schulz, A Lex, D Schmalstieg, and H Schumann. Model-driven design for the visual analysis of heterogeneous data. *IEEE Transactions on Visualization and Computer Graphics*, 18(6):998–1010, June 2012.

[78] Brendan Stubbs, David C. Kale, and Amar Das. Sim TwentyFive: An interactive visualization system for data-driven decision support. In *AMIA Annual Symposium Proceedings*, volume 2012, page 891. American Medical Informatics Association, 2012.

[79] Jimeng Sun, David Gotz, and Nan Cao. A visualization tool for navigation of online disease literature. In *American Medical Informatics Association Annual Symposium Posters*, 2010.

[80] Rhys Tague, Anthony Maeder, and Quang Vinh Nguyen. Interactive visualisation of time-based vital signs. In *Advances in Visual Computing*, pages 545–553. Springer, 2010.

[81] James Thomas and Kristin Cook. *Illuminating the Path: The Research and Development Agenda for Visual Analytics*. National Visualization and Analytics Center, 2005.

[82] Christian Tominski, James Abello, and Heidrun Schumann. Axes-based visualizations with radial layouts. In *Proceedings of the 2004 ACM Symposium on Applied Computing*, pages 1242–1247. ACM, 2004.

[83] John W Tukey. *Exploratory Data Analysis*. Pearson, 1977.

[84] Kathleen Tyner. *Development of Mental Representation: Theories and Applications*. Psychology Press, 2013.

[85] Mithra Vankipuram, Kanav Kahol, Trevor Cohen, and Vimla L Patel. Visualization and analysis of activities in critical care environments. In *AMIA Annual Symposium Proceedings*, volume 2009, page 662. American Medical Informatics Association, 2009.

[86] Mithra Vankipuram, Kanav Kahol, Trevor Cohen, and Vimla L Patel. Toward automated workflow analysis and visualization in clinical environments. *Journal of Biomedical Informatics*, 44(3):432–440, June 2011.

[87] Darren L Walters, Antti Sarela, Anita Fairfull, Kylie Neighbour, Cherie Cowen, Belinda Stephens, Tom Sellwood, Bernadette Sellwood, Marie Steer, and Michelle Aust. A mobile phone-based care model for outpatient cardiac rehabilitation: The care assessment platform (CAP). *BMC Cardiovascular Disorders*, 10(1):5, 2010.

[88] Jing Wang, Wei Peng, Matthew O Ward, and Elke A Rundensteiner. Interactive hierarchical dimension ordering, spacing and filtering for exploration of high dimensional datasets. In *Information Visualization, 2003. INFOVIS 2003. IEEE Symposium on*, pages 105–112. IEEE, 2003.

[89] Taowei David Wang, Catherine Plaisant, Alexander J Quinn, Roman Stanchak, Shawn Murphy, and Ben Shneiderman. Aligning temporal data by sentinel events: Discovering patterns in electronic health records. In *Proceedings of the SIGCHI Conference on Human Factors in Computing Systems*, page 457–466. ACM, 2008.

[90] Taowei David Wang, Catherine Plaisant, Ben Shneiderman, Neil Spring, David Roseman, Greg Marchand, Vikramjit Mukherjee, and Mark Smith. Temporal summaries: Supporting temporal categorical searching, aggregation and comparison. *Visualization and Computer Graphics, IEEE Transactions on*, 15(6):1049–1056, 2009.

[91] Taowei David Wang, Krist Wongsuphasawat, Catherine Plaisant, and Ben Shneiderman. Visual information seeking in multiple electronic health records: Design recommendations and a process model. In *Proceedings of the 1st ACM International Health Informatics Symposium*, IHI '10, page 46–55, New York, NY, USA, 2010. ACM.

[92] Matthew O Ward. Multivariate data glyphs: Principles and practice. In *Handbook of Data Visualization*, Springer Handbooks Comp. Statistics, pages 179–198. Springer Berlin Heidelberg, January 2008.

[93] Christian Popow, Werner Horn, and Lukas Unterasinger, Metaphor graphics to visualize ICU data over time. In *Workshop Notes of the ECAI-98 Workshop*, 1998.

[94] Krist Wongsuphasawat and David Gotz. Exploring flow, factors, and outcomes of temporal event sequences with the outflow visualization. *Visualization and Computer Graphics, IEEE Transactions on*, 18(12):2659–2668, 2012.

[95] Krist Wongsuphasawat, John Alexis Guerra Gmez, Catherine Plaisant, Taowei David Wang, Meirav Taieb-Maimon, and Ben Shneiderman. LifeFlow: Visualizing an overview of event sequences. In *Proceedings of the SIGCHI Conference on Human Factors in Computing Systems*, CHI '11, page 1747–1756, New York, NY, USA, 2011. ACM.

[96] John Kirtland Wright. Problems in population mapping. In *Notes on Statistical Mapping, with Special Reference to the Mapping of Population Phenomena*. American Geographical Society; Population Association of America, 1938.

[97] K Zheng, H M Haftel, R B Hirschl, M O'Reilly, and D A Hanauer. Quantifying the impact of health IT implementations on clinical workflow: A new methodological perspective. *Journal of the American Medical Informatics Association*, 17(4):454–461, July 2010.

Chapter 13

Predictive Models for Integrating Clinical and Genomic Data

Sanjoy Dey
Department of Computer Science
University of Minnesota
Minneapolis, MN
sanjoy@cs.umn.edu

Rohit Gupta
Department of Computer Science
University of Minnesota
Minneapolis, MN
rohit@cs.umn.edu

Michael Steinbach
Department of Computer Science
University of Minnesota
Minneapolis, MN
steinbac@cs.umn.edu

Vipin Kumar
Department of Computer Science
University of Minnesota
Minneapolis, MN
kumar@cs.umn.edu

13.1 Introduction

Until the last decade, traditional clinical care and management of complex diseases mainly relied on different clinico-pathological data, such as signs and symptoms, demographic data, pathology results, and medical images. In addition, efforts have been made to capture genetic factors by examining the family history of patients. The effect of such clinical and histo-pathological markers is assessed by cohort-based studies conducted on large populations [115] and the knowledge obtained from these studies is summarized in clinical guidelines for the diagnosis, prognosis, monitoring, and treatment of human disease, e.g., NPI [50] and Adjuvant! Online [56, 119] for breast cancer and palmOne [12] for prostate cancer. However, this approach still falls short. For example, there are adverse drug reactions for some patients who have risk factors similar to those patients who have been cured by the same therapeutic treatment. This issue stems from the strategy of one drug fits all and motivates the need to improve on conclusions drawn from cohort-based studies so that the underlying mechanism of complex diseases can be understood at the individual patient level.

The recent advancement of high-throughput technology has led to an abundance of information for each individual at the micro-molecular level. A myriad of genetic, genomic, and metabolomics data have been collected to capture different aspects of cell mechanisms that shed light on human physiology. Examples include SNPs, which provide information about the genetic polymorphism of an individual; gene expressions, which measure transcription; and protein and metabolite abundance, which captures protein abundance and post-translational modifications. These high-throughput datasets have helped answer some complex biological questions for different diseases, such as assessing the prognosis [109, 38, 97, 51], epistasis effects on diseases [5], and discovering new sub-phenotypes of complex diseases [58, 4, 9]. The use of genetic information in epidemiology helped design effective diagnostics, new therapeutics, and novel drugs, which have led to the recent era of personalized medicine (genomic medicine) [112, 40, 118]. However, these genetic factors alone cannot explain all the intricacies of complex diseases. For example, the incidences of cancer vary widely among different countries due to the environmental factors, even for the same ethnic groups, as is illustrated by changes in incidence when people of different ethnicities migrate from one country to another [99, 133].

In recent studies [101, 87], it has been hypothesized that most complex diseases are caused by the combined effects of many diverse factors, including different genetic, genomic, behavioral, and environmental factors. For example, cancer, which is the most widely studied disease phenotype in last few decades, is extremely heterogeneous. Different clinical endpoints of cancer, such as the idiosyncrasy of individual tumors, the survival rate of cancer patients after chemotherapy or surgical treatment, development of metastasis, and the effectiveness of drug therapy are governed by different risk factors including multiple mutations of genetic factors (e.g., RAS, RTK, TGF-β, Wnt/signaling pathways), behavioral factors (e.g., tobacco exposure, diet, lifestyle) [133], long-time environmental effects (e.g., stresses, temperature, radiation, oxygen tensions, hydration and tonicity, micro- and macro-nutrients, toxins) [84] and germline variations (e.g., BRCA1/2) [134]. Therefore, clinico-pathological and genomic datasets capture the different effects of these diverse factors on complex diseases in a complementary manner rather than a supplementary nature. In a more complicated scenario, a complex genetic network can evolve dynamically under various environmental factors [101]. Using the two diverse perspectives provided by both types of data can potentially reveal disease complexities in greater detail.

It is essential to build integrative models considering both genomic and clinical variables simultaneously so that they can combine the information present in clinical and genomic data [101]. In most of the cases, the goal of the integrative study is biomarker discovery, i.e., finding the clinical and genomic factors related to a particular disease phenotype such as cancer vs. no cancer, tumor vs. normal tissue samples, metastasis vs. non-recurrent cancer, the survival time after chemotherapy. Therefore, the information present in each dataset is assessed by its capabilities to predict the disease endpoint, and the integrative studies mainly aim at building a predictive model by combining clinical and genomic datasets, so that they can provide better prediction power than the individual datasets. This has led to an emerging research area of integrative predictive models by combining clinical and genomic data, which we will refer to as clinicogenomic integration. In this review, we survey not only different issues and challenges existing in such clinicogenomic integrative studies, but also different approaches that aim to address those issues. Finally, we conclude with a general discussion on future research directions in this topic.

13.1.1 What Is Clinicogenomic Integration?

Clinicogenomic integration means building models by integrating clinical and genomic data. Clinical data refers to a broad category of patients pathological, behavioral, demographic, familial, environmental and medication history, while genomic data refers to any kind of patients genomic information including SNPs, gene expression, protein, and metabolite profiles (Figure 13.1). More

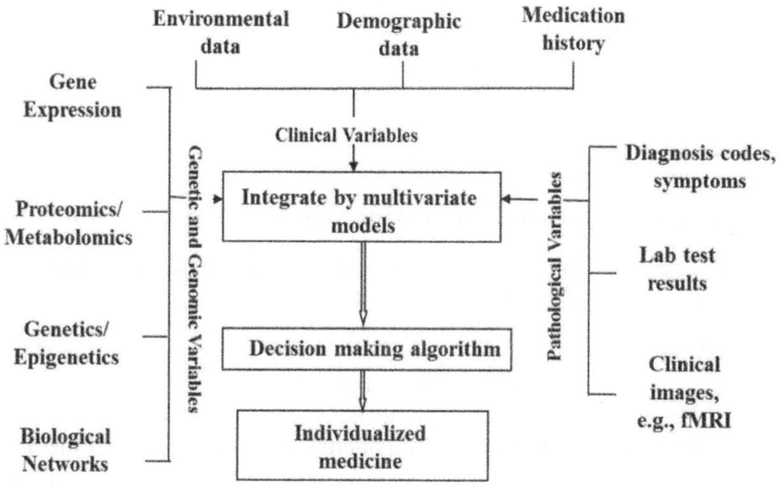

FIGURE 13.1: The integrative multivariate approach for clinical decision making by combining multiple types of data.

specifically, the clinicogenomic studies should have at least one clinical dataset and one genomic dataset for a group of people who are assessed for an outcome of a phenotype of a disease. Furthermore, we survey only integrative models with an emphasis on biomarker discovery. Therefore, each sample of datasets is assessed for a particular disease phenotype. The phenotype can be either binary class labels such as cancer vs. no cancer, tumor vs. normal tissue samples, metastasis vs. non-recurrent cancer, or continuous variables, e.g., the survival time after chemotherapy or other types of therapeutic treatments. Achieving the goal of biomarker discovery requires identifying the clinical and genomic features from the data that are significantly associated with the disease phenotype.

13.1.2 Different Aspects of Clinicogenomic Studies

Integration of diverse biomedical datasets is a vast research topic that has been studied widely in many different domains. Although some initial efforts have been made by researchers for clinicogenomic integration, most of these studies are scattered throughout the literature and were developed from a clinical perspective for different disease phenotypes with their own limitations and advantages. Moreover, the issues and challenges related to this field are not yet well understood. In this article, we first identify the overall issues and challenges of this field with an emphasis on the methodological perspective (Section 13.2) and then discuss how the existing clinicogenomic methods address these challenges (Section 13.3 and Section 13.4). In particular, we categorize existing predictive models from two perspectives: stage of integration (Section 13.3.1) and how disparate dimensionality is addressed (Section 13.3.2). We also discuss the different goals that these predictive methods try to achieve (Section 13.4) and the validation techniques used in each category (Section 13.5). Moreover, the scope of the article is the integrative model development of clinical and genomic data, rather than the simple incorporation of genomic data into clinical practice for designing genomic medicine.

There are some existing articles that focus on a few aspects of the clinicogenomic studies. Boulesteix and Sauerbrei [17] performed a recent survey on how to validate the additional predictive power of genomic markers over traditional clinical variables with a focus on external data. However, they did not aim at reviewing all types of predictive clinicogenomic models and the generic challenges on this topic. There are several other reviews on studies that integrate diverse genetic, genomic, proteomic, metabolomics, interactome, phylogeneic, and phenome data (abbreviated as omic data) [22, 60, 67]. However, they do not cover the integration of clinical data with genomic datasets. To the best of our knowledge, currently there is no study that aims at reviewing integrative approaches combining genomic and clinical/environmental data from a methodological perspective.

13.2 Issues and Challenges in Integrating Clinical and Genomic Data

The integration of genomic and clinical studies is difficult as the two fields have different perspectives. Several key technical challenges are described below.

- *Difference in Nature of the Datasets:* As the datasets being integrated are collected from two different perspectives, the difference in the nature of the data being integrated creates several challenges for developing integrative models. First, clinical data are usually record-based where each patient is represented by a record of clinical variables. On the other hand, genetic and genomic data sets vary widely in terms of formats. Besides record-based data, there are many network-based datasets where the relationships among several biomolecular entities are represented as features. Second, clinical variables are available in diverse data types such as text, categorical, and numeric values, but on the other hand genomic variables are mostly numeric. Third, some datasets may contain structure, e.g., measurements across time or across a genetic sequence, that are not present in others. Fourth, genomic and genetic datasets are high-dimensional in comparison with clinical data that often contain 10–20 variables. Fifth, genetic and genomic data contains a higher level of missing values because of technological issues [71]. In contrast, clinical data are easy and inexpensive to collect, and so contain fewer missing values. Integrating variables with such different formats, types, structure, dimensionality, and missing values is a challenging problem in the data mining and machine learning domain.

- *Statistical Significance:* The high dimensionality of genomic datasets combined with low-sample size poses challenges for finding statistically significant biomarkers (classical statistical n<<p problem) [137]. Combining such high-dimensional features with low-dimensional clinical data creates a further challenge for statistical and data mining methods. Even after pre-selecting significant genes, genomic features (which usually number a few hundred) still dominate the traditional clinical variables in number (which usually are around 10–20), due to the over-fitting problem. Unless the whole experimental setup is performed cautiously, the clinical markers can be lost in the vast number of genomic variables and thus, the predictive power of the genomic data could be overestimated [16], [121].

- *Different Biases and Assumptions:* Since the corresponding datasets are collected independently, the biases and assumptions of each of the datasets being integrated may be different due to the difference in experimental designs and protocols. For example, since clinical variables are gathered more systematically over a large period of time, they contain less noise. In addition, they are validated rigorously by numerous epidemiology studies [16, 123, 91]. Also, clinical data are cheap and easy to collect [91]. In contrast, gene expression data (and also other genomic data) are less reproducible over independent cohorts because of the high noise, different experimental biases, high dimensionality and small sample sizes of microarray datasets [42, 43, 89, 27]. Integrative studies need to be aware of the differing degrees of information present in different datasets. Otherwise, the role of clinical variables may be underestimated in the prognostic model when compared with noisy genomic variables [123].

- *Interpretability:* Another generic challenge for biomarker studies is that the obtained model has to be interpretable, i.e., the effect of individual markers on the disease phenotype must be identified. Otherwise, the domain experts cannot use the potential risk factors for further validations. Similarly, clinicogenomic integrative models must be easily interpretable to be treated as biomarkers. For example, if the original genes or clinical variables cannot be interpreted by the model, then drugs cannot be designed targeting genes or the proteins encoded by those genes.

Some of the technical challenges (e.g., the disparate natures of the data) described above are quite general and are applicable for any type of integrative studies in any domain, while some others (e.g., statistical significance due to high dimensionality and interpretability) are applicable mainly for biomarker discovery. We will first describe how the clinicogenomic studies aim to address these three challenges in Section 13.3. Then, we will discuss the predictive models integrating clinical and genomic datasets with different goals in Section 13.4, which mainly aim at addressing the challenges of interpretability and a different amount of information present in the two types of datasets. It is difficult to address all these challenges. In fact, most clinicogenomic studies aim to address only a few of the challenges described earlier. Several of the studies were motivated by integrative models from different research communities including biostatistics, data mining, and machine learning, which can handle the generic challenges mentioned above. Of course, many of these models were further modified, and sometimes completely new methods were designed to address the specific challenges of clinicogenomic data integration. The main goal of the review is to analyze the clinicogenomic models from a methodological perspective.

Besides these technical challenges, there are several domain challenges as well. First, there are differences in the terminologies used in epidemiology and genetics studies, even for the same topic. For example, association studies (genetics) and case-control studies (epidemiology) deal with the same concept of finding causative factors of diseases. [86]. This makes the automatic extraction of information from healthcare and genetics data difficult. Second, the genomic data have been collected from a research perspective solely according to solid scientific theories and models. However, the healthcare data is collected slowly over a longer period of time in a retrospective manner, from different sources spanning broad areas such as medical observations, patient management data, healthcare providers, doctors notes, and a patient's life history. Thus, clinical data collected from electronic medical records (EMR) may contain redundant information, which has to go through several preprocessing steps to extract useful information about a patient that can be later integrated with genomic data. Lastly, privacy issues related to the healthcare domain [69, 88] create a serious bottleneck to the availably of clinical data. The data collection related challenges require several preprocessing steps such as building data warehouses, integrating multiple sources of data, extracting information, text mining, and natural language processing (NLP). Such data collection and preprocessing steps are out of the scope of this review, since the focus of this review is on developing integrative models.

13.3 Different Types of Integration

In this section, we discuss several aspects of integrative model development in the context of biomarker discovery. In particular, we will first describe different stages of integration to address the differences in natures of data. Second, we will describe how the clinicogenomic models address the difference in dimensionalities of clinical and genomic data to enhance the statistical significance of the studies. Furthermore, we will categorize the existing clinicogenomic studies based on those aspects and discuss how they address different challenges as described in the last section.

13.3.1 Stages of Data Integration

Integration of multiple heterogeneous datasets in general can be performed in several stages depending on how disparate the natures of the data in terms of type, format, properties, and so on. In particular, either individual datasets can be integrated first before developing any model or the decisions coming from models built on each dataset independently can be integrated. Alternatively, each dataset can be transformed to a common intermediate structure such as a graph or kernel and then these structures can be merged before developing models. Pavlidis et al. [95] performed seminal work on these three types of integration and called them early, late, and intermediate integration, respectively. Figure 13.2 shows the detailed steps of the three stages of data integration. We will categorize all clinicogenomic integration into these three broad conceptual categories.

13.3.1.1 Early Integration

In general, early integrative approaches merge the independent data sources together before performing any kind of data analysis. In a simplistic case, the individual data matrices are simply combined into a larger matrix if both of the datasets have the same set (or subset) of samples. Thus, the integration of the individual datasets, which are clinical and genomic data in our case, is performed at an early stage of the overall analysis. Once the combined data matrix is prepared, any types of models can be developed based on the two goals of the clinicogenomic studies described in Section 13.4. The unique assumption of this type of integration is that both of the datasets are similar in nature, i.e., most of the properties of the datasets such as data type, formats, structure, and dimensionality, are either similar or preprocessed to be as similar as possible. Otherwise, a significant amount of preprocessing such as dimensionality reduction, missing value imputation, and data discretization is required before integrating individual datasets.

Advantage: Early integration is the simplest approach, since any standard model can be applied on the integrated dataset to achieve any of the objectives. Therefore, most of the clinicogenomic studies fall in this category (Table 13.1). Moreover, they can preserve any kind of inter-data relationships. For example, if some clinical and genomic variables are correlated, the model developed after data integration can take the correlation structure into account.

Disadvantage: Early integration loses the individual properties of each dataset such as the structure and the different degree of information when merged together into an augmented dataset. The dimensionality of the augmented dataset also increases. Thus, the model may also suffer from high dimensionality and low statistical significance of the obtained results.

13.3.1.2 Late Integration

Late integration first develops predictive models separately for each of the individual data sources and then merges the individual decisions of all predictive models into a final score as the prediction for the outcome variable. As opposed to early integration, this type of integration actually merges the classifier decision rather than the original dataset. The main assumption of late integration is that the individual datasets are independent and there is no inter-dataset relationship.

The biggest challenge of late integration is how to merge the decision of classifiers obtained from individual datasets. Several strategies like majority voting, linear aggregation, and weighted average have been applied for this purpose. For example, two breast cancer studies conducted by Campone et al. 2008 [24] and Silhava and Smrz 2009 [106] simply summed up the individual decision coming from genomic and clinical data. Campone et al. applied the Cox regression model

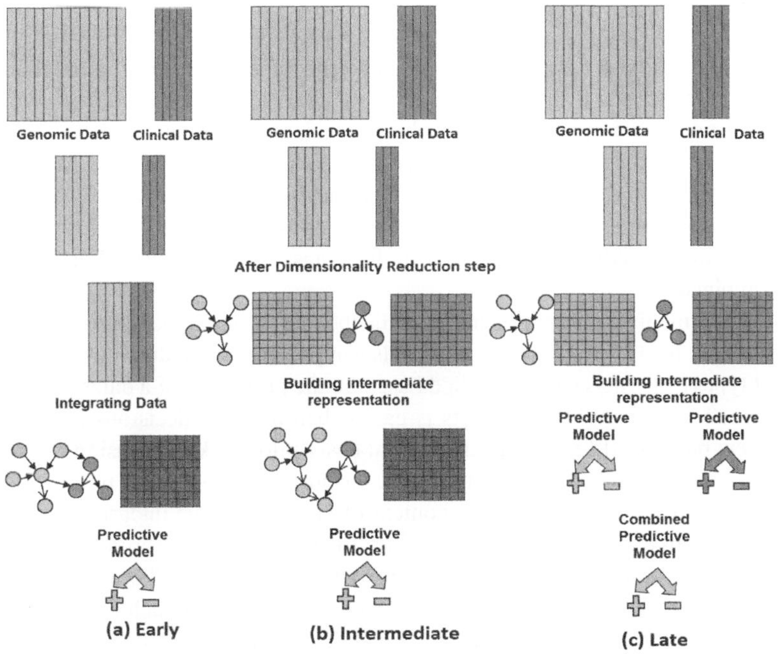

FIGURE 13.2: Pictorial representation of three stages of integrations inspired by Pavlidis et al. [95].

to summarize the topmost 15 discriminating genes into a single genomic score and then added it to the traditional clinical score of breast cancer, NPI, to get the final score for assessing the effect of adjuvant chemotherapy. On the other hand, Silhava and Smrz [106] applied two different predictive models: logistic regression and bionomial boosting (BB) [21] to get the genomic and clinical score, respectively, before summing them. However, simple summation is not always appropriate because the contribution of the individual data sources to the overall clinicogenomic model may be different. Alternatively, the contribution from each individual dataset towards the disease phenotype can be assessed and the scores obtained from the individual models can be weighted accordingly. For example, Futschik et al. [49] used parameterized learning for merging the individual decisions of the clinical (Bayesian classifier) and genomic data (evolutionary fuzzy artificial neural network (EFuNN [74])) into a final decision. Furthermore, they also tested statistical independence of the outputs of two independent models using the mutual information [31], which is a key assumption for late integration. In a more complicated scenario, with many datasets being integrated, the more general problem arises when some of the models built on individual datasets produce binary class decisions and some of the predictive models generate continuous-valued scores. Several approaches, including majority vote and its more generic version called consensus learning [30], have been studied in many other domains such as image processing and social networks.

Advantage: The individual structure and the nature of each dataset are preserved in late integration, since the model is developed on each dataset separately. Moreover, different models can be used for different datasets depending on the individual nature of each dataset. Late integration is particularly useful when each of the datasets is completely heterogeneous, i.e., the datasets cannot be transformed into a common format for integration.

Disadvantage: Late integration misses any kind of possible relationship, such as correlation or interactions, which may be present among the datasets. Moreover, late integration generates a different hypothesis for each of the datasets as opposed to a single hypothesis for the integrated dataset. Interpretation and validation of these different types of hypotheses is not trivial.

13.3.1.3 Intermediate Integration

Early and late integration are opposite in nature in terms of their advantages and disadvantages. Intermediate integration tries to overcome the limitations of both approaches. It first represents each dataset with a common structure, such as a graph or kernel, and then merges these representations before developing any models. Therefore, it generates one hypothesis, but can retain the structure of each dataset and take into account the possible relationships between the datasets to some extent. The main assumption of this approach is that there is an appropriate intermediate representation for each dataset preserving the individual properties of that dataset and the intermediate representations can be easily combined.

Kernel-based intermediate integration has become the most popular technique for data fusion in many domains mainly for two reasons. First, kernels can preserve the individual properties of data easily. Different types of kernels can be applied based on the properties of a dataset. Second, merging kernels obtained from individual datasets is easier than merging decisions in late integration (refer to the review paper [54] for a more theoretical description of kernel fusion methodologies). Followed by the seminal work of Pavlidis et al. [95], this idea of kernel-based intermediate integration was used by Daemen et. al. [32] in this context of clinicogenomic integration for classifying metastasis vs. relapse free survival of breast cancer. In particular, two normalized linear kernels were developed for both clinical and gene expression data and then, those kernels were fused using a weight before applying the final predictive model. One advantage of such kernel-based integration is that the weights corresponding to an individual dataset can denote the relative contribution towards the final prediction. However, choosing an appropriate kernel for a particular dataset is not trivial. Moreover, kernels are not easily interpretable so that they are not readily used as biomarkers.

Graph-based techniques can provide more interpretable models for intermediate integration. In an similar effort to develop such techniques, Gevaert et. al. [53] used a Bayesian network as the intermediate representation. A Bayesian network can represent the dependency among the variables by a directed acyclic graph (DAG) in a probabilistic manner. In brief, there are two independent stages in Bayesian modeling: learning the structure of the DAG and learning the parameters of the probability distribution. The authors attempted three types of Bayesian integration: early, late, and partial integration using the two independent steps of Bayesian learning. Partial integration is conceptually similar to intermediate integration. For example, first, structure learning is performed on both datasets separately (using the heuristic model search algorithm K2 [29]) and then, these two structures are merged through the outcome variable, which is the only common variable in the two datasets. In a second step, Bayesian parameter estimation of the model (learning of conditional probability tables) is performed using a Dirichlet distribution. Finally, the factors within the Markov blankets of the outcome variable are defined as the biomarkers. Although such graph-based intermediate integration provides more interpretable models, merging the structures (DAGs) obtained from each dataset is not as straightforward as fusing the kernels. In both studies, intermediate and partial integration showed better performance than early and late integration.

Advantage: Intermediate integration can preserve the individual properties of a dataset. Moreover, inter-dataset relationships such as correlation and redundancy can also be taken into account during final model creation, although this depends on many issues such as the choice of kernel and how such relationships are preserved during kernel fusion.

Disadvantage: Finding appropriate intermediate representations that are interpretable and easily fusible at the same time is difficult. Moreover, finding interactions and causal relationships across datasets is difficult due to the transformation of the original feature space.

13.3.2 Stage of Dimensionality Reduction

Clinicogenomic integrative models have to be aware of the disparate dimensionalities of the clinical and genomic datasets. Otherwise, low-dimensional clinical variables will be lost among the thousands of genomic variables [16]. We categorize existing clinicogenomic studies into two categories based on how they handle this issue, each of which has its own assumptions, advantages, and disadvantages.

13.3.2.1 Two-Step Methods

The easiest way to handle the disparate dimensionalities of individual datasets is to first perform dimensionality reductions for each dataset separately and then, build predictive models on them in a second step. In the context of clinicogenomic integration, dimension-reduction techniques are applied solely on the genomic dataset assuming that clinical variables are already low dimensional. Most of the techniques select topmost discriminative genomic features, while others methods combine those features into a combined score for future model development (Appendix of [35] detailed description of several dimensionality reduction steps used by clinicogenomic studies). In the second step, the selected genomic variables are merged with the clinical variables to build the prognosis model on the combined dataset.

Advantages: The two-steps models are very flexible. Any types of dimensionality reduction technique and any predictive modeling techniques can be incorporated in building the clinicogenomic model.

Disadvantages: There are few disadvantages of the two-step methods. First, determining the appropriate number of genomic features in the first step is hard. The number of features may impact the comparison between the additive performances of clinical and genomic variables. For example, if too many features are selected from genomic data, it may overfit the clinicogenomic model in the second phase. On the other hand, if too few genomic factors are retained, then the predictive capability of the genomic factor can be underestimated. This overfitting issue is even more serious if the dimensionality reduction techniques take response variables into account in the first step. In this scenario, the genomic features fed into the second stage will have strong prediction power for the response variable. Hence, comparing those genomic features with the clinical variable is not completely fair [16]. Second, performing dimensionality reduction only on genomic data cannot account for the relationship existing between the two datasets. For example, even the right number of genomic variables selected in the first step may be redundant in the second step for model development given the clinical variables used. Moreover, the subtle contributions of many genes to prediction can be missed by the dominant genomic features that are correlated with the clinical variables [15]. This is especially important when the goal is to assess the additional power of genomic data over clinical variables (Section 13.4.2).

13.3.2.2 Combined Clinicogenomic Models

The second type of approach merges the two steps of dimensionality reduction and model development into a single step by leveraging regularization-based statistical models with possible modifications. Regularized models can increase the generalization power of a predictive model by preferring a less complex model and thus are very effective for reducing the possible overfitting problem for high-dimensional data such as gene expression. In general, regularized techniques introduce an extra penalty term for the model complexity ($P_\lambda(\beta)$) in addition to the original loss function ($L(\beta|X)$) of the objective function as shown below.

$$\min_{\beta} L(\beta|X) + P_\lambda(\beta). \tag{13.1}$$

Here, X is the clinicogenomic dataset, β is the coefficient that represents the corresponding weight of each of the variables present in X, and λ is the regularization parameter that controls the tradeoff between the loss function and model complexity. The most popular regularization approaches used in statistical learning are L_2 (ridge [64]) and L_1 (lasso [120]) regularization, which impose penalty as the square ($P_\lambda(\beta) = \lambda\sum_{i=1}^{p}\beta_i^2$) and absolute value ($P_\lambda(\beta) = \lambda\sum_{i=1}^{p}|\beta_i|$) of the regression coefficients in Equation 13.1, respectively. Moreover, L_1 penalization shrinks most of the coefficients of the regression model to zero and hence, it is widely used to perform feature selection simultaneously with model development. However, the disparate dimensionalities of clinical and genomic datasets pose new challenges to the generic regularization problem. Several modifications have been proposed to impose different penalty structures for different datasets and discussed in more details in Section 13.4.1.

Advantage: The main advantage of the one-step models is that they can take the redundancy present between genomic and clinical datasets implicitly, since both datasets are considered together during model development. This property makes the single-step approach most suitable for assessing additional predictive performances of genomic features over the clinical variables [15]. Moreover, most of the coefficients of the sparse regularized model are zeros with few non-zero entries that precludes the explicit variable selection step. So, the number of genomic features to retain for model development is not required to be specified upfront.

Disadvantage: Each of the regularized models has their own model assumptions and requires learning several parameters. This sometimes yields to higher computational complexity. Moreover, the regression-based models are mostly applicable to building predictive models. Finding inter-dataset relationships like correlation is hard using these models.

13.4 Different Goals of Integrative Studies

In the previous section, we described the methodological differences between several integration methods based on how they address the generic challenges of data fusion. Moreover, the clinicogenomic integration can also be categorized based on the goals that they want to achieve through using those models. More or less, the overall goal of clinicogenomic studies can be divided into three broad categories from a medical perspective. Some studies aim at achieving more than one clinical goal in a single study either implicitly or explicitly.

13.4.1 Improving the Prognostic Power Only

Predictive clinicogenomic models aim at improving the clinical prediction of diseases by integrating clinical and genomic datasets. Thus, the main research question addressed by this type of clinicogenomic model is whether the datasets contain complementary information. To assess the improvement of prognosis power, the combined clinicogenomic method is compared with the models built on either clinical or genomic data independently. We will first describe the two-step approach that performs explicit dimensionality reduction followed by the creation of combined single-step predictive models.

13.4.1.1 Two-Step Linear Models

The choice of the particular predictive model differs based on the clinical endpoints of the disease, i.e., whether the target variable is discrete or continuous. If the response variable is continuous, such as survival of patients after a particular therapeutic treatment or the development of metastasis after surgery, then the regression-based methods are deployed for model development. For example, the Cox proportional hazard model estimates the lifetime (survival or failure) of an event associated with the covariates using two parameters: a hazard function describing the changes of hazard (risk) over time at the baseline level of covariates and the co-efficients describing the effect of each variable on survival. In one such clinicogenomic study, Lexin Li [81] used the Cox model for predicting the survival of the patients with diffuse large-B-Cell lymphoma (DLBCL) after chemotherapy. In addition to the genomic features (selected by a supervised dimensionality reduction [80]), they included a well-established clinical factor called the international prognosis index (IPI) [105], which combines different clinical factors of DLBCL.

Classification techniques are used to build clinicogenomic models when the output variable has discrete categories. This includes mostly binary two-class variables, e.g., diseased vs. healthy group, successful vs. unsuccessful treatment, recurrent vs. non-recurrent, survival vs. death after certain time point, and metastasis vs. relapse free outcome. Among the wide variety of classification schemes, discriminant models, which aim at learning a discriminative function to separate the two classes, are widely used. Discriminant models learn a discriminant function $L = g(x) = w^T x + w_0$, where w is the coefficients for each variable of x (as shown in Figure 13.3) for two-dimensional dataset x (x denotes the genomic variables here, but can also denote the clinical variables c and clinicogenomic variables z). Linear Discriminant Analysis (LDA) chooses the parameters $\mathbf{w}$ and w_0, such that the samples from the two classes are well separated, maximizing the between class variances [11]. Sun et al. [114] used LDA [11] for combining the current clinical guidelines for breast cancer prognosis such as St. Gallen [56], [57], and NIH [41] with genomic information to predict the survival of breast cancer.

In addition to learning linear decision boundary, logistic regression [39], [11] learns the posterior probability of the outcome variable by a logistic function y = sigmoid ($g(x)$). Logistic regression is a generalized linear model that summarizes the contributions of all predictors into a single variable, which is fed into a sigmoid transfer function to produce the final predicted probability of outcome event y. Most of the clinicogenomic studies [112, 7] use a stepwise logistic regression model where each predictive variable is added successively in the model until the optimal model is achieved. In one such model, Beane et al. [7] combined the gene expression profiles of lung epithelial cells of potential lung cancer patients using bronchoscopy [111] with the clinical and demographic data to make better diagnostic decisions. Similarly, Stephenson et. al. [112] used stepwise logistic regression to predict the recurrence of prostate cancer after a radical prostatectomy (RP) using a well-established clinical marker called nomogram [61, 94, 75, 13, 59] that includes diagnostic variables such as the PSA level, Gleason grade, margin status, and pathological stage along with gene expression data. For avoiding model overfitting, a goodness of fit measure like Akaikes information criteria [3] is used to select the optimal model.

On the other hand, support vector machines (SVM) try to learn the decision boundary in such a way that maximizes the separation between the two classes (measured by the soft margin). Li et al. [82] applied SVM with a linear kernel to predict the survival of advanced-stage ovarian cancer after platinum-based chemotherapy.

13.4.1.2 Two-Step Nonlinear Models

Although logistic regression and LDA provide simpler discriminant models, they are typically confined in finding linear decision boundary only. Support vector machines [130] can circumvent this problem to learn more generalized non-linear decision boundary, by utilizing the power of kernel machines. The kernel machines first transfer the original feature space into higher dimensions by a non-linear mapping function and then, linear SVM is applied in that higher-dimensional space. Thus, learning linear decision boundary in the higher-dimensional space yields a non-linear decision boundary in the original space, which was used for developing an intermediate integration described earlier (Section 13.3.1).

Other types of non-linear models have also been applied for the integrative purpose. For example, tree-based methods [62] are very popular because of their two properties. First, they can be easily represented as classification rules, which are more interpretable to clinicians and can be tested for inferring new domain knowledge. Second, these methods are based on recursive partitioning of all available samples into more homogeneous subgroups with respect to the binary class variable,

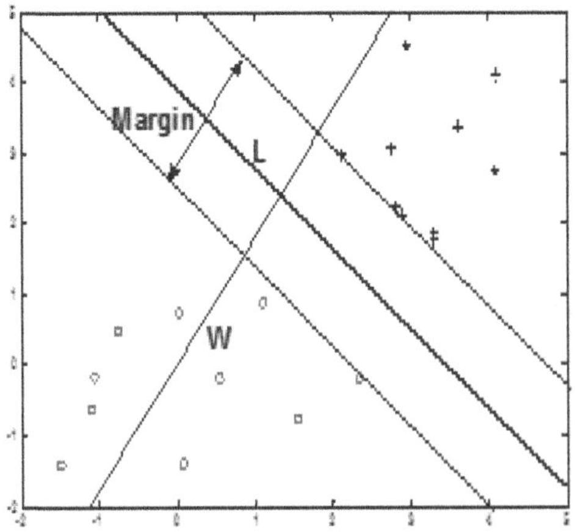

FIGURE 13.3: Discriminant models with linear decision boundary. SVM tries to maximize the separation between the two classes (red and black).

therefore they can capture the non-linear interaction between the variables of a tree. Because of these two properties, [135] used the multi-step decision tree to find the interaction between 81 clinical covariates and genomic variables to predict asthma patients. Other clinicogenomic studies include Pittman et al. 2004 [90, 96] for enhancing the prognostic power of breast cancer patients relative to long-term recurrence and Clarke and West 2008 [28] for the survival prediction of ovarian cancer. One problem with tree-based methods is that there is no single optimal tree because they are built using heuristic search criteria. To circumvent this problem, all these clinicogenomic studies used ensemble learning [68], [76] and model averaging [93, 98, 65] techniques to generate a forest of trees and then, estimate the final prediction by taking the weighted average of the individual predictions of each tree. Such techniques not only boost the predictive performances by combining many weak learners (trees), but also provide a confidence interval for the prediction estimated from the individual models. This property is extremely useful in the context of an integrative clinicogenomic study for capturing the clinical uncertainties [138, 23] arising from different clinical processes such as variability of tissue processing, hybridization measures, small sample size, and sample selection [90, 96]. Also, such model uncertainty may capture potential conflicting predictions either within or between the clinical and genomic factors, which can be very important for complex heterogeneous diseases. Similarly, mixture of expert (ME) is another non-linear method that combines several expert trees using a convex weighted sum of all the outputs produced by them. However, each expert can be trained on different partitions of the input data with possible overlaps among them (soft split) as opposed to hard split of the data used by CART. Cao et al. [79] applied the ME method for integrating categorical clinical variables directly with continuous-valued gene expression data without any discretization. Furthermore, ME provided a better result than the random forest-based approach used by Boulesteix, Porzelius, and Daumer [16].

13.4.1.3 Single-Step Sparse Models

Some clinicogenomic studies leverage the strength of the sparse modeling technique to perform model development and feature selection in a single step by considering clinical and genomic data simultaneously. For example, Ma and Huang 2007 [85] extended one such iterative boosting approach called threshold gradient directed regularization (TGDR [48]) into a more generalized framework (Cov-TGDR) for two generalized linear models: logistic regression and the Cox survival model. Cov-TGDR iteratively optimized the gradient of negative log-likelihood considered as the loss function ($L(\beta|X)$ in Equation 13.1). Moreover, in each iteration the component-wise gradient was updated only for only a few variables controlled by a regularization parameter λ. Thus, the components with lower gradient values are not updated in each iteration and these results in a sparse representation of the solution (β). Moreover, variable selection was performed separately for the two datasets to respect their individual properties of the data using two parameters L_1 and L_2 for the two datasets in Equation 13.1. Finally, this study applied the Cox proportional model for the survival of follicular lymphoma [34] and logistic regression for the binary prediction of the development metastasis of breast cancer ([129]).

13.4.1.4 Comparative Studies

van Vliet et al. [128] performed a recent comparative study of the two-step predictive models to systematically assess whether combining clinical and genomic data help improve the prediction power of breast cancer. They consider three simple classifiers such as nearest-mean classifier (NMC), Naive Bayes, Nearest neighbor, and two more complex classifiers such as SVM (similar to [32]) and the tree-based classifier. All of these models were developed in three different stages (early, intermediate, and late) along with no integration (built on clinical and genomic variables). The original tree-based classifiers proposed by [96] were modified for intermediate integration by restricting one dataset at the top node. For all these classifiers, integration improved the prediction power for breast cancer significantly, and simple classifiers performed better than complex classifiers (with NMC with OR-type late integration performing the best), which may be an effect of small sample size. Moreover, either late or intermediate strategies performs the best, which confirms the previous studies [53, 32]). Unlike the previous study by [129], this study found that clinical data has slightly better information than genomic data, which they believe that is mainly because of more comprehensive clinical features such as matrix information, central fibrosis, etc. Moreover, the genomic and clinical features obtained from this study perform better than the markers found by the previous four studies in different cell lines [129, 25, 110, 83]. However, they did not assess the effect of different feature selection techniques in the model development stage. Bøvelstad et al. [18] provided a methodological comparison of different dimensionality reduction techniques designed for Cox regression in survival studies. They covered both two-step and one-step approaches (Section 13.3.2) in their model development and they observed that modified ridge regression performed the best when applied to three different clinicogenomic datasets. However, they did not compare it to the Cov-TGDR methods.

Advantages and Disadvantages of the Predictive Models: The main advantage of predictive models is that they are easy to develop and simple from a methodological perspective. Any model that is applicable on either clinical or genomic data can be applied directly (for two-step approaches) or with minor modifications (for regularized methods) to the combined dataset. These models build unbiased models on clinical and genomic datasets without any prior information and bias towards any of the datasets being integrated. Therefore, the predictive model can test whether the datasets being integrated are complementary in nature based on the improvement of the predictive power of the combined model over the individual models. However, the final clinicogenomic models may select a completely different set of clinical and genomic variables than those selected by independent models. Hence, comparing the predictive power of clinical and genomic features grossly in the dataset level cannot assess directly how much additional power genomic features possess given the traditional clinical variables.

13.4.2 Assessing the Additive Prognostic Effect of Clinical Variables over the Genomic Factors

The generic predictive clinicogenomic models described so far treats clinical and genomic datasets similarly. However, clinical variables are considered more important than genomic variables by many studies for two reasons. First, clinical variables are well-validated through independent studies unlike genomic factors. Second, clinical factors are easy to collect and currently used in the healthcare system, and thus reuse of those clinical variables will also reduce healthcare costs. Therefore, treating both datasets similarly may underestimate the clinical variables and overestimate the performance of the genomic variables significantly. Trutzner et al. [123] performed a systematic study to assess such optimistic use of genomic markers over the clinical variables. Using the synthetic datasets, the authors showed that the genes selected by the unbiased predictive models are less reproducible in the independent test datasets. They used both the two-step methods and the threshold gradient directed regularization (TGDR [48]) described in Section 13.3.2, and concluded that such over-estimation of the value of genomic data increases because of the estimation of too many free-parameters for large number of genes with small samples. The two-step methods containing separate supervised dimensionality reduction step are even more prone to over-estimation (Section 13.3.2). For such two-step methods, Tibshirani and Efron [121] performed some seminal works and proposed the prevalidation framework to compare the genomic markers to clinical markers more rigorously. In particular, they suggested that the genes should be selected by a separate cross-validation framework rather than the same cross-validation framework used for assessing the predictive performance of the final model (more detail in the validation Section 13.5). In contrast, for models built for the one-step combined clinicogenomic study, it is less difficult to remove such overestimation.

In addition to categorization based on how dimensionality reduction is performed, clinicogenomic studies can be further categorized into two groups based on how the additive power is assessed. One type of study builds clinicogenomic models that are biased to the clinical markers by including the clinical variables (or clinical index built thereof) as a mandatory variable in the model development phase. The second type of study focuses directly on assessing the additional power of the genomic data given the clinical variables using a hypothesis testing framework. Strictly speaking, they answer the question of "Do genomic variables boost the performance of models given the clinical variables?" in comparison to the null-hypothesis of "no additional value."

13.4.2.1 Developing Clinicogenomic Models Biased Towards Clinical Variables

The easiest way to look for the additional prediction power of the genomic data over clinical data is by developing a predictive model only on the samples that cannot be classified well by the clinical variables. A few studies [131, 33, 132, 118, 117, 91] used traditional clinical variables, such as age, tumor grade, tumor status, vascular invasion in liver, and so on for stratifying the breast cancer population, and then incorporating genomic variables only to those patients, who cannot be improved by these clinical variables. Using the prevalidation framework provided by Tibshirani et al., Boulesteix et al. [16] developed a two-step clinicogenomic model that can assess the additional predictive power of genomic data using two separate cross-validation loops, one for each of the two steps. The first cross validation was used to reduce the genomic features to a few unbiased prevalidated components [121] using the supervised partial least square (PLS) method [136]. Second, they built a random forest [20] that first selected all clinical variables as mandatory variables and then added PLS genomic components one by one, as long as the predictive power improved as assessed by the out-of-bag (OOB) error [20] using a bootstrapping strategy. Therefore, the additional performance was assessed by the number of genomic components selected automatically by the predictive model in addition to the clinical features. In another recent study, Choi et al. [26] developed a similar CV-based framework for removing over optimism of the genomic dataset, where the internal CV was used for choosing a parsimonious model based on its model complexity. When applying this framework for the Cox model, it outperformed ridge and lasso Cox models in breast cancer data.

As discussed in Section 13.3.2, the above-mentioned two-step methods are only partially successful in removing a potential redundancy that can be present between the clinical and genomic features. For example, in the previous study, some of the PLS components that have marginal predictive power are non-redundant compared to the clinical variables that may be missed in the first phase. Alternatively, a single-step sparse Cox model called CoxBoost has been proposed by Binder and Schumacher [10] to assess the additional power of genomic data for a survival study using a component-wise offset-based boosting approach [124]. In particular, they optimize the log-likelihood of the model via component-wise gradient boosting updates using a Neuton-Raphson method. Moreover, all the clinical variables were included in the model as the mandatory variables using a customized diagonal penalty matrix with zero entries (in the second term of Equation 13.1) while feature selection was performed on the genomic features using one entry in the penalty matrix to assess the additional predictive power. In a similar study, Kammers et al. [72] used other types of sparse models such as L_1 and L_2 regularization techniques only on gene expression data and included clinical variables as mandatory variables into the model.

13.4.2.2 Hypothesis Testing Frameworks

All the biased clinicogenomic models discussed so far assess the additional power of genomic features indirectly using how many genomic features are included in the model. However, some of the selected components may be statistically insignificant. The more effective way to address this issue is to assess the additive performance of genes in a hypothesis-testing framework. In a seminal study, Tibshirani and Efron [121] first summarized the genomic variables into a single unbiased genomic score using the prevalidation framework (LASSO internal model). In a second step, a hypothesis-testing framework was designed based on a linear regression model (or any GLM) built on the clinical variables and the prevalidated genomic (PVG) markers used as pseudo-predictors. In particular, the added predictive value was assessed by whether the regression coefficients of the genomic marker was statistically significant, i.e., $\beta_{PVG} > 0$ compared to the null-hypothesis $\beta_{PVG} = 0$ using t-test or z-tests. In a later study [66], Hofling and Tibshirani showed that this test was biased because of the violation of the i.i.d. assumption by the sampling procedure used in the PVG framework. Alternatively, they proposed a random permutation-based empirical p-value estimation. In both cases, it was shown that the prevalidated genomic score was less significant than the genomic score without prevalidation using a landmark breast cancer study [129], which actually overestimated the performance of gene expression data. However, any two-step approach cannot remove the potential redundancy between the clinical and genomic data completely (Section 13.3.2). For example, if clinical and genomic markers are correlated, then both types of markers will have significant coefficients by the above approach.

A more rigorous hypothesis-testing framework has been proposed by Boulesteix and Hothorn [15] considering both types of datasets simultaneously in a similar way as CoxBoost [10] to remove any types of redundancy between the two types of variables completely. The main idea of the method was to include not only the clinical variables, but also the contribution of those clinical variables as the mandatory variable in the clinicogenomic model, so that genomic variables cannot influence the clinical contribution. More specifically, this method first fits a generalized linear model on the clinical variables only, and then the clinical predictor is used in the final combined clinicogenomic model built by least-square boosting strategy [47] as a fixed offset such that its coefficient is not changed during the iterative learning process. Thus, the genomic features cannot affect the contribution of the clinical features in the final model, unlike the CoxBoost and Prevalidation methods. Finally, the likelihood of the boosting method was tested for the statistical significance by randomly permuting the genomic variables to estimate the additive performance similar to [66]. Although this approach did not perform any feature selection for genomic features similar to CoxBoost, it can be easily generalized to a regularization-based framework, as argued in the later study [92]. In this later study, they also compared both prevalidation testing and Globalboosttest by generating several synthetic datasets with different amounts of correlation between clinical and genomic markers. As expected, if the informative genes are perfectly correlated with the clinical variables, Globalboosttest is more conservative in selecting genomic features (p-values uniformly distributed in [0, 1]) than prevalidation. Note that the prevalidation framework not only removes the bias associated with genomic variables, but can compare the two datasets in a more generic fashion. In contrast, Globalboosttest is completely biased to clinical variables with the sole purpose of rigorously testing the additional power of the genomic marker, but the opposite properties of the two datasets cannot be tested.

13.4.2.3 Incorporating Prior Knowledge

One issue with including gene expression data directly into the model is that the selected genes do not necessarily yield to biologically interpretable pathways. Moreover, each of the genes belonging in a pathway may have weak association and thus missed by the model, but their aggregate association may be large. Testing the association of the pathways with disease directly, rather than in a post-processing stage has become popular to aid clinical interpretability [113]. Kammers et al. [72] recently also used gene ontologies (GO) for grouping the genes and then the combined effect of each GO group (assessed by the first principal component) as the predictor in a Cox survival model. However, some GO groups are very generic and only part of a GO process can be activated in a particular disease due to disease heterogeneity [87]. Alternatively, the author also further clustered the genes belonging to each GO group into several subgroups before including them in the model. From a methods perspective, they followed the combined one-step model development where both L_1 and L_2 penalization schemes (Equation 13.1) were used for handling high-dimensional genomic data by including clinical variables as mandatory variables. All the three types of genomic data, i.e., the original gene expressions, GO groups, and preclusters of GO groups when combined with the clinical variables provided similar performance assessed by the p-value of the final prognostic model and Brier score. Since the preclustering technique is unsupervised here and guided by GO, no prevalidation-like framework was necessary to reduce the bias of the genomic data as well.

Advantages and Disadvantages: The main advantage of the prevalidation-based framework is that it can compare the genomic and clinical features more directly by removing any sort of redundancy among them and thus can assess the additional predictive power of the genomic features in an unbiased manner. However, the prevalidation-based framework combines the genomic features into one or more newly developed features, which make the interpretation of the final model difficult for biomarker discovery. Another problem with such models is that they assume that clinical variables are important and thus the predictive models should be biased towards clinical variables. However, this assumption may not be true in the future as genomic data become more easily available and are validated in multiple independent studies. Moreover, sometimes the clinical variables, such as pathological and behavioral effects, can be the downstream effect of causal genomic features. In that case, genomic features may not provide additional predictive power over clinical variables. However, knowing such relationships among different types of markers can be useful knowledge. Neither the original predictive models nor these unbiased models aim to assess the relationships present among different types of data.

13.5 Validation

In this section, we discuss the validation procedures of the clinicogenomic models described so far. Since the main goal of all these clinicogenomic models is to improve the prognostic power of disease, they compare the combined clinicogenomic model with the models built on either genomic data or clinical data alone. We will first discuss several performance metrics used for this purpose. Then we will discuss different validation techniques to assess the effectiveness of obtained results from clinicogenomic models.

13.5.1 Performance Metrics

The most common metrics for performance measurement of the binary classification based models [7], [114] are accuracy, precision, recall, and area under the ROC curve [116]. On the other hand, the studies that want to predict continuous outcome variable such as survival time and disease progression-free probability (PFP) use different metrics, e.g., c-index, to assess [112] how well the model discriminates between patients with different survival probabilities. C-index measures the concordance between the predicted and observed responses [61] in a scale between 0–1. Another popular measure used by [81] is the time-dependent area under the curve (AUC) defined by [63]. On the other hand, instead of using cross-validation, Binder and Schumacher [10] used a bootstrap sampling strategy, as in [102], for performance evaluation using the Brier score [52]. Some studies [7], [121] also used the coefficient of the genomic and clinical markers to estimate their relative contribution towards the predictive model. However, the performance gain can be obtained by random chance as a mere data artifact, thus yielding overoptimistic results unless they are validated for statistical significance or repeatedly observed in multiple datasets [14]. Permutation-based techniques have also been used by many studies to get the statistical significance of the observed result. For example, [66] randomly permutated a genomic marker X to get the statistical significance of the observed coefficient of genomic marker. Similarly, [112] permutated the class label to get the statistical significance of the classification accuracy of the predictive model. Some studies [82, 7] also used standard hypothesis tests—Wilcoxon test, t-test, and z-score—to get the statistical significance of the improvement in performance of combined model over the individual models. Beside all these measures, the Kaplan-Meier curve [73] is a popular visualization technique to visualize the survival probabilities of different groups of population along the progression of time. All clinicogenomic survival studies used this technique to visualize the prognostic separations of subpopulations defined by the final model.

Besides estimating the performance of the predictive model empirically using the above-mentioned metrics, some clinicogenomic studies validated their obtained results from a domain perspective as well. Some studies wanted to investigate which groups of patients benefitted the most by the integration of clinical and genomic markers. For example, Stephenson et al. [112] observed that their clinicogenomic model can significantly improve the prediction of a subsample (30% of the whole prostate cancer dataset) where the prediction of well-established clinical monogram is in middle range (7-year PFP, 30%–70%). On the other hand, [7] validated their observed combined clinicogenomic model by three expert pulmonary physicians. Some studies, e.g., [112], tried to find biological information about the obtained predictors in previous literature. The breast cancer studies [96, 28] found that the important clinical factors (lymph node status and estrogen receptor [ER] status) and metagenes selected by the topmost trees were well recognized in clinical practice and had been validated through previous study. For example, all of these studies identified some of the metagenes that are related to estrogen pathways or growing signal pathways, or are correlated with the ER status. The breast cancer study by Sun et al. [114] compared their obtained model with the 70-gene signature built by Van't Veer et. al. [129]. Ma and Huang [85] also confirmed the obtained significant genes from previous studies.

13.5.2 Validation Procedures for Predictive Models

The ideal technique for testing the obtained model is to use an external validation dataset that is collected independently [17] of the training dataset on which the model was built. For example, Beane et al. [7] compared the performances of clinicogenomic models on independent test datasets that did not have a definite diagnosis following bronchoscopy as a part of the diagnosis for lung carcinoma. However, in most of the practical cases, data is scarce and expensive to collect. It is also hard to design similar experimental setups for collecting both validation data and the training data in an unbiased manner. The simplest way to solve this problem is to divide the original data into two disjoint sets: training and test data. The training data is used to develop the model while test data tries to mimic the independent validation data. For example, some clinicogenomic studies [81], [6, 7] use a simple setup of random splitting of available data based on previous studies. Alternatively, such random splitting is repeated several times by some studies to avoid selection bias [28, 18].

K-fold cross-validation [62, 77] provides a more systematic framework by dividing the available data into K parts, where each of these K parts is considered as a test set while the rest of K-1 datasets are considered as the training set. Bootstrapping [62], which is another useful validation technique, samples the original data with replacement to estimate the variance of the result. Applying standard techniques such as cross-validation or bootstrapping for the one-step regularization-based techniques is straightforward. However, applying them for two-step approaches is not straightforward because of the separate supervised dimensionality reduction step. In the simplest setting for

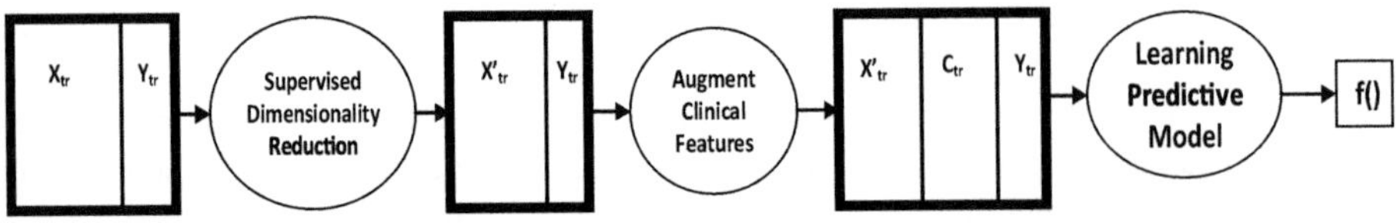

FIGURE 13.4: The training phase for the clinicogenomic model.

building a two-step predictive model, the first step of dimensionality reduction is performed on the whole dataset and the second step of predictive model development is performed using two separate datasets: a training dataset for learning the model and a test dataset for assessing the performance of the observed model. However, as mentioned in [108], [107], performing supervised dimensionality reduction on the whole dataset provides biased results because of the use of the test dataset, on which the performance of the final predictive model is estimated in the second step. In order to get an unbiased estimate of the performance, both the supervised dimensionality reduction step and predictive model development (Section 13.3.2) should be performed solely on the training dataset. More specifically, the whole two-step development process of predictive modelling (i.e., dimensionality reduction and model building) should be performed on the training data only, which is shown in detail in Figure 13.4. In particular, the dimensionality reduction is only performed for the genomic dataset and then the obtained features (some selected genes or some newly developed features) are combined with the clinical marker using a predictive model. Several studies [112], [96], [82], [114], [85], [96] are aware of the fact and used this step to assess the predictive models correctly.

Sometimes, models have a few parameters that need to be learned from the data itself. In those cases, one more inner CV is used to select the optimal parameters for the classifier for the training data obtained from the outer CV framework [114], [85], [10], [18]. In subsequent discussions, we will ignore this inner CV for simplicity and assume only one CV for estimating the final performance of the predictive model.

13.5.3 Assessing Additional Predictive Values

The experimental design of methods with the goal of assessing additional predictive power should be performed carefully; otherwise the prognosis effect of the genomic marker may be overestimated. For example, if supervised feature selection techniques are used in the dimensionality reduction step, another issue arises. Specifically, the genomic features are either selected or created in such a way so that they are the most discriminating features in the original genomic dataset **X**. Comparing such discriminative genomic features with the clinical variables can lead to overestimation of the predictive power of the genomic features. If we look at the last training phase of model development, the genomic data $X_t r$ already have seen the label $y_t r$ but the clinical features have not.

Tibshirani and Efron proposed a variant of the cross-validation framework (called prevalidation) to remove such a bias toward the genomic variable. In particular, they proposed one more k-fold CV for supervised dimensionality reduction even before developing the predictive model using the second CV framework. The available training data ($X_t r$) will be further divided into two sets as mentioned by [121]. One set will be used for the dimensionality reduction step to select and/or create the genomic feature out of the original data, and then the other set of data will be used for building a predictive model on the combined clinical and the obtained features from the previous step. The detailed steps are described below (Figure 13.5):

1. Divide the available training data into K separate parts.

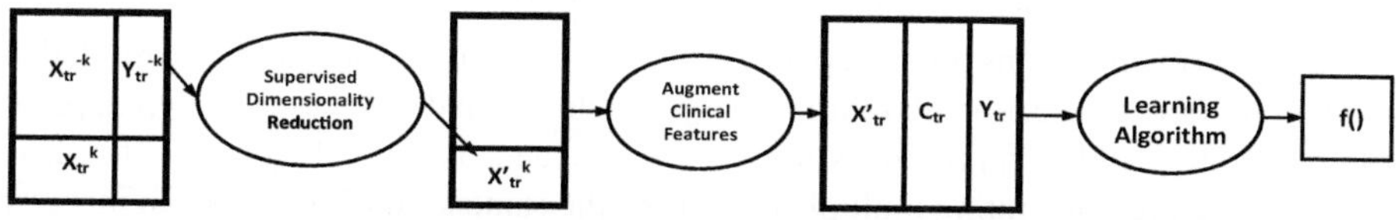

FIGURE 13.5: Schematic diagram of prevalidation as suggested by Tibshirani and Efron. The first three phases are repeated here k times to get the full X matrix. Here X_{tr}^k represents the k-th part of the training set.

2. The first (k-1) parts are used to learn the dimensionality reduction to select and/or create a genomic feature out of the original data.

3. Afterward, the same set of selected genes or feature creation rules will be applied to the left-out k-th samples to predict the label of them.

4. Repeat the steps 2 and 3 for each k-th part to get the unbiased predictor of genomic variables for all samples.

5. Build the predictive model on the combined clinical and the prevalidated genomic features. Comparison between the clinical and genomic factors can be done as well here.

Tibshirani and Efron [121] provided both theoretical and empirical evidence that the prevalidated genomic score has fewer degrees of freedom (ideally one) than the non-validated version. So, this score can be treated as a fairer pseudo-predictor as if it was built on an independent dataset, and hence the whole dataset can be used for model development in step 5. They also empirically showed that a prevalidated genomic factor is less significant than that of a non-prevalidated predictor when compared to the clinical variables. Although the authors used the above technique for summarizing all genomic factors into a single predictor, it can be easily generalized for selecting more than one feature as performed in [16]. In summary, the right setup for both developing the predictive model and assessing an additional predictive power of the genomic features is as follows:

1. To estimate the performance of a two-step predictive model along with a supervised dimensionality reduction technique, separate training and testing data are required as shown in Figure 13.4.

2. To compare the clinical and reduced genomic factors fairly, the supervised dimensionality reduction and comparison of genomic variables with the classical clinical predictors should be done in separate datasets or the prevalidation technique should be used to build a fairer version of the genomic predictor (Figure 13.5). This step is critical for assessing the additional performance gain from genomic data.

Here, in both of the steps where separate training and testing sets are required several alternative techniques like repeated sampling or boosting can be used along with cross-validation. Boulesteix et al. [16] performed these two steps using two separate cross-validation loops. The first CV was for the pre-validation of selected genes as mentioned by Tibshirani and Efron [121] with the second one for estimating the classification error rate of the random forest [20] model built on the selected gene signature component from the previous step and the clinical data.

13.5.4 Reliability of the Clinicogenomic Integrative Studies

Oftentimes the markers obtained from clinicogenomic studies are not replicable across studies. Especially, genomic data are often criticized for the lack of reproducibility among the independent cohorts. For example, very few overlapping genes were observed between the biomarker genes of the two well-known breast cancer studies by [129] and [132] by other independent studies [43], [42], [27], [89]. The main reasons for such poor consistency of genomic signature across studies are small sample cohorts size, selection bias during sample inclusion and annotation, different protocols for sample preparation and data preprocessing, and heterogeneous clinical endpoints for different studies [104]. Therefore, integrating multiple cohorts of the same kind of patients can increase the sample size significantly and thus, is very popular to develop reproducible genomic biomarkers [44]. Such multi-site integration can be performed in many ways: either keeping the most common features among all datasets (data level early integration), or by learning a more sophisticated Bayesian method to fuse information available in individual datasets [122], [78]. Inspired by such multi-site studies, some clinicogenomic studies integrated not only multiple gene expression datasets, but also multiple clinical datasets to build multi-site universal clinicogenomic models and finally assess the improvement of prediction power of such models over that of individual multi-site clinical and genomic biomarkers.

Predictive multi-site studies use some of the available independent cohorts for developing clinicogenomic model and then use the rest of the cohorts for testing the reproducibility of the predictive model. The existing multi-site clinicogenomic models proceed in two steps. First, most of the studies take the simplistic approach of retaining only those features (both clinical and genomic) that are common in all of the datasets (the homogeneous integration). Then, the clinical and genomic data are integrated using any of the techniques described earlier (the heterogeneous integration). For example, Teschendorff et al. [118] built a universal molecular prognosis marker from five publicly available gene expression datasets including their own collected gene expression data for breast cancer survival prediction. They used three cohorts for building a Cox regression-based predictive model and reserved the other three as independent test sets. However, instead of using classification accuracy for validation, they used a recently developed statistical distribution-based evaluation measure called the D-index [100], which depends only on the relative risk ordering of the test samples rather than relying on the absolute value of outcome variable. Thus the prediction power remains unchanged as long as the relative ranking of the test samples are not changed. This property makes the D-index suitable for assessing the performances over test samples coming from different cohorts with diverse characteristics. On the other hand, Shedden et al. [104] tried to minimize the experimental bias in multi-site studies directly by generating their own datasets from six different institutions using a uniform robust and reproducible protocol [37]. Moreover, several different gene selection methods along with different classifiers were applied on two out of four datasets collected for predicting the survival of lung adenocarcenomas patients. Congruent with most of other clinicogenomic studies, clinical variables like cancer stage and age added some prognostic power to gene expression, especially for more heterogeneous stage-1 lung cancer patients.

13.6 Discussion and Future Work

Clinicogenomic integration has received wide attention from different communities recently, because of its great potential of integrating diverse perspectives from clinical and genomic sources to reveal complex disease mechanisms. Because of the multi-disciplinary nature of the topic, the approaches taken by all these clinicogenomic efforts are quite diverse, although the objective is the same: improving the prognosis power of predictive models for complex diseases. In this article, we survey these clinicogenomic studies with emphasis on, but not restricted to the methodological perspective. We aimed at finding the existing challenges in integrating heterogeneous datasets such as clinical and genomic data, and understanding how these challenges were handled by the methods in the clinicogenomic context. Table 13.1 categorizes the examplary studies based on these challenges. This review can also be relevant for some other integrative studies, as well, where the challenges are similar to those for the integration of clinical and genomic data. For example, Hamid et al. [60] surveyed the studies that integrate different kinds of genomic data that address a few challenges that are common in clinicogenomic integrative efforts. Thus, some of the integrative methods can be shared between both areas.

The main purpose of most of the clinicogenomic studies was to develop a better predictive model for complex diseases through integration. In general, most of the clinicogenomic studies reduce the dimensionality of the data in a first step and then develop some predictive models on the selected features. A few studies merge these two steps into a single step taking advantage of regularization-based predictive models. Several statistical metrics were used to compare the performance of the

TABLE 13.1: Taxonomy of Different Clinicogenomic Models

Main Categories		Predictive Modelling	Testing Additional Power
Explicit Dimensionality Reduction	Early Integration	Regression (Li [81], Teschendorff et al. [118], Shedden et al. [104]); Classification (Stephenson et al. [112], Sun et al. [114], Li et al. [82], Beane et al. [7]); Tree-based method (Nevins et al. [90], Pittman et al. [96], Clarke and West [28], Cao et al. [79])	Tibshirani and Efron [121]; Hofling and Tibshirani [66]; Boulesteix et al. [16]; Acharya et al. [1], Wang et al. [131], Obulkashim et al. [91]
	Intermediate Integration	Daemen et al. [32], Gevaert et al. [53]	
	Late Integration	Campone et al. [24], Silvaha and Smrz [106], Futschik et al. [49]	
Sparse Model	Early Integration	Bøvelstad et al. [18], Ma and Huang [85]	Binder and Schumacher [10], Boulesteix et al. [15], Kammers and Hothorn [72]

Note: Some branches are missing indicating no studies were observed in that category.

combined clinicogenomic model with that of the clinical and genomic model. In most of the cases, the predictive power of the combined models was improved over that of individual clinical and genomic models, which justifies the usefulness of integration. However, in some cases, the combined model provided only marginal improvement; sometimes the performance of the genomic model was even worse than that of well-established clinical prognostic markers. This means that the value of traditional clinical variables should not be underestimated. Moreover, unlike genomic variables, the clinical variables are well established and validated through independent studies on multiple cohorts. These observations motivated second sets of clinicogenomic studies, which aimed at including the genomic variables into the prognosis models only if they provide some additional prognosis power. Thus, these models are biased towards clinical variables somehow. However, there are some additional issues with these kinds of approaches as well. If the models are biased too much towards the clinical variables, then the importance of genomic data may be subdued. This will hinder the discovery of potential new knowledge about complex diseases and thus may deviate from the main goal of elucidating new knowledge through integration. As a result, there is a tradeoff between how much the combined model should be biased towards the clinical dataset. Deciding this tradeoff is not trivial, more systematic studies are required for this purpose.

Each of the data sources being integrated do not provide the same amount of information, so the integration method should be cognizant of this difference in the datasets in terms of amount of information and the inherent properties in each dataset. Very few studies such as kernel-based methods [32] tried to preserve the individual properties available in each data source explicitly. However, this method used the vector-based records only for both clinical and genomic data. On the other hand, the plethora of other types of medical, genetic, and genomic data contains rich information with different types of structures such as time sequences, networks, and replicates. Integrating such diverse types of data requires developing new computational techniques.

Interpretability of the obtained clinicogenomic models is a much-desired property for personalized medicine. However, predictive models mainly focus on improving the prediction power by combining the clinical and genomic data rather than interpretability. Therefore, most of the predictive models use those models that are more useful for improving the prediction power rather than producing interpretable models that can infer useful knowledge. Although tree-based methods have been applied in this context, most of the studies applied more complex ensemble tree-based models that are less interpretable than the original tree-based rules. Moreover, a separate dimensionality reduction step before developing the clinicogenomic model may also reduce the interpretability of the model. For example, all these studies first combine the effect of genomic markers into a single score by either unsupervised techniques like PCA or a separate prevalidation step, or some supervised techniques like PLS before developing any clinicogenomic model. The components do not provide information about the obtained genes, and thus the pathways are involved in the disease progression, which is important for defining drug targets. Thus, incorporating the prevalidation framework for the feature selection step is an open issue.

Very few studies validate the obtained clinicogenomic models extensively. Most of the studies did not compare the obtained model with other clinicogenomic models, even those developed for the same disease. For example, only one out of seven breast cancer studies [114] compared their final genomic signature with previous studies [129, 132, 126]. Although the multi-site clinicogenomic studies aim at improving the reliability of the obtained markers, the difference in experimental setups and biological conditions of the independent studies may a cause difference in probe design and final available gene expression profiles. In all multi-site clinicogenomic studies, a simplistic approach was taken during integrating multiple genomic datasets by including only those genes as features that are significantly expressed (performed by the t-test or other similar statistical test) in all cohorts. However, this reduces the number of features dramatically, because it is very less likely that genes will be simultaneously expressed in all independent cohorts. Moreover, it is biologically not meaningful, because different pathways may be disrupted for different groups of patients, even different groups of genes can be mutated for the same pathway during different environmental factors. So, it may be better to loosen the restriction a little bit to include genes that are not significantly expressed. More intelligently, genes can be selected from cohorts if they belong to a known pathway but do not meet the threshold of statistical significance.

Most clinicogenomic studies were not designed from a methodological perspective. Most of the clinicogenomic studies applied different simple statistical and data-mining predictive models rather than applying and comparing different methodologies to get the best predictive model. Some studies [104], [18] tried to compare several dimensionality reduction techniques for a regression-based predictive model. On the other hand, the best way to integrate this uniform number of clinical and genomic variables after dimensionality reduction is not well understood. Some studies proposed intermediate integration for handling the challenges of heterogeneous data integration. Though in theory, kernel-SVM-based intermediate integration is supposed to be more generalized, it did not provide significant improvement in the clinicogenomic context [32]. Moreover, it is not clear how to represent the individual data using an intermediate format in the best possible way during intermediate integration. Kernel-based models also cannot find relationships among variables both within and across datasets. Alternatively, a graph-based approach can be utilized to address these issues. More systematic studies are required in this space to develop new methods to best leverage the diverse information available from both the clinical and gene expression data.

There may exist several types of relationships between the clinical and genomic data, which can have different implications from domain perspectives [36]. For example, if both datasets contain many correlated variables, then they contain similar types of information of a supplementary nature that cannot provide value to integrative studies. These types of correlations between datasets can be induced through other hidden factors [16], e.g., the effect of a drug on gene expression [109] during the treatment process. Besides correlation, more complicated relationships like interactive or causal relationships may also exist between the clinical and genomic variables [101]. For example, the intricate interaction between some genomic markers and environmental factors can make the disease phenotype more severe beyond their additive levels [84]. Furthermore, there may be some genomic factors that have causal effects on some clinical variables. In that case, drugs can target those genomic variables in an early stage for better treatment design. For example, tumor surgery can be avoided if some causative genomic markers of tumor grade can be targeted in the early stage of breast cancer. Another interesting factor is that the clinical factors are not the causal factors of a disease phenotype unlike the genomic factors. Rather, most of the clinico-pathological variables are the observational properties of disease phenotype. Beside all these inter-dataset relationships, there may be also intra-dataset relationship among the variables within the same dataset representing the interactions or synergy between similar variables [19], [70]. For example, familial hypertrophic cardiomyopathy is caused by mutations in several genes responsible for coding sarcomeric proteins [84], where each gene or protein is marginally inexplicable. Though some studies [15] seek to develop robust clinicogenomic models even in the presence of correlated variables, none of the clinicogenomic studies aim at elucidating this kind of inter- and intra-relationships between the clinical and genomic datasets. Further investigation is required to understand and utilize the potential broader relationships among different clinical and genomic variables when developing integrative models.

Another important issue with most clinicogenomic studies is that most of these models consider only gene expression data as the genomic data from widely available public datasets. However, gene expression data contains information about transcriptional regulation only, and thus cannot provide any information about other aspects of vast complex cell mechanisms like post-transcriptional modification, protein synthesis and phosphorylation, copy number variation, random mutation in the genome, and so on. Recent technological advancements have led to the advent of various high-throughput genomic data like protein abundance data, genome-wide association (GWA) data, genetic interaction data, protein-protein interaction data, epigenomic data, and so on. It is important to note that these datasets are inherently related and each of them covers one particular aspect of cellular activity. Overlooking the inherent relationship could result in the discovery of biologically spurious associations, albeit statistically significant. For example, a gene that is differentially expressed can be spurious if the resultant protein is not differentially abundant due to post-transcriptional modifications. Integrating these enriched genomic data in the context of clinicogenomic studies pose further challenges. For example, the formats of other kinds of genomic data are not uniform—gene expressions or SNPs are vector based, while PPI is networkgraph-based containing relationships among different genomic entities. Moreover, some of the datasets may contain multiple replicates or time-points. Integrating such diverse types of data with vector-based clinical data is not trivial and needs further research.

In spite of great potential of clinicogenomic integration, the topic is still in a rudimentary phase. In general, integrating heterogeneous datasets like clinical and genomic data is a hard problem. The existing clinicogenomic models address these challenges partly. More detailed research is necessary especially to handle different kinds of relationships among variables and datasets: design a robust model to handle the disparate nature, structure, dimensionality, and amount of information present in each dataset; incorporate prior knowledge into account; integrate diverse genomic and medical data besides gene expression and histo-pathological and demographic data; and finally validate the obtained clinicogenomic biomarkers rigorously in multiple independent cohort studies before final deployment for personalized medicine.

Bibliography

[1] C. R. Acharya, D. S. Hsu, C. K. Anders, A. Anguiano, K. H. Salter, K. S. Walters, R. C. Redman, S. A. Tuchman, C. A. Moylan, and S. Mukherjee. Gene expression signatures, clinicopathological features, and individualized therapy in breast cancer. *JAMA*, 299(13):1574, 2008.

[2] R. Agrawal, T. Imielinski, and A. Swami. Mining association rules between sets of items in large databases. *Proceedings of the 1993 ACM SIGMOD International Conference on Management of Data*, pages 207–216. ACM, 1993.

[3] H. Akaike. A new look at the statistical model identification. *IEEE Transactions on Automatic Control*, 19(6):716–723, 1974.

[4] A. A. Alizadeh, M. B. Eisen, R. E. Davis, C. Ma, I. S. Lossos, A. Rosenwald, J. C. Boldrick, H. Sabet, T. Tran, and X. Yu. Distinct types of diffuse large b-cell lymphoma identified by gene expression profiling. *Nature*, 403(67–69):503–511, 2000.

[5] D. Anastassiou. Computational analysis of the synergy among multiple interacting genes. *Molecular Systems Biology*, 3(1), 2007.

[6] E. Bair, T. Hastie, D. Paul, and R. Tibshirani. Prediction by supervised principal components. *Journal of the American Statistical Association*, 101(473):119–137, 2006.

[7] J. Beane, P. Sebastiani, T. H. Whitfield, K. Steiling, Y. M. Dumas, M. E. Lenburg, and A. Spira. A prediction model for lung cancer diagnosis that integrates genomic and clinical features. *Cancer Prevention Research*, 1(1):56, 2008.

[8] M. Berlingerio, F. Bonchi, M. Curcio, F. Giannotti, and F. Turini. Mining clinical, immunological, and genetic data of solid organ transplantation. *Biomedical Data and Applications*, pages 211–236, 2009.

[9] A. Bhattacharjee, W. G. Richards, J. Staunton, C. Li, S. Monti, P. Vasa, C. Ladd, J. Beheshti, R. Bueno, and M. Gillette. Classification of human lung carcinomas by mRNA expression profiling reveals distinct adenocarcinoma subclasses. *Proceedings of the National Academy of Sciences of the United States of America*, 98(24):13790, 2001.

[10] H. Binder and M. Schumacher. Allowing for mandatory covariates in boosting estimation of sparse high-dimensional survival models. *BMC Bioinformatics*, 9(1):14, 2008.

[11] C. M. Bishop and SpringerLink. *Pattern Recognition and Machine Learning*, volume 4. Springer New York, 2006. (Online service).

[12] J. W. Blumberg. PDA applications for physicians. *ASCO News*, 16:S4–S6, 2004.

[13] M. L. Blute, E. J. Bergstralh, A. Iocca, B. Scherer, and H. Zincke. Use of Gleason score, prostate specific antigen, seminal vesicle and margin status to predict biochemical failure after radical prostatectomy. *The Journal of Urology*, 165(1):119–125, 2001.

[14] A. L. Boulesteix. Over-optimism in bioinformatics research. *Bioinformatics*, 26(3):437, 2010.

[15] A. L. Boulesteix and T. Hothorn. Testing the additional predictive value of high-dimensional molecular data. *BMC Bioinformatics*, 11(1):78, 2010.

[16] A. L. Boulesteix, C. Porzelius, and M. Daumer. Microarray-based classification and clinical predictors: On combined classifiers and additional predictive value. *Bioinformatics*, 24(15):1698, 2008.

[17] A. L. Boulesteix and W. Sauerbrei. Added predictive value of high-throughput molecular data to clinical data, and its validation. *Briefings in Bioinformatics*, 12(3):215–229, 2011.

[18] H. Bøvelstad, S. Nygård, and O. Borgan. Survival prediction from clinico-genomic models-A comparative study. *BMC Bioinformatics*, 10:413, 2009.

[19] R. Braun, L. Cope, and G. Parmigiani. Identifying differential correlation in gene/pathway combinations. *BMC Bioinformatics*, 9(1):488, 2008.

[20] L. Breiman. Random forests. *Machine Learning*, 45(1):5–32, 2001.

[21] P. Buhlmann and T. Hothorn. Boosting algorithms: Regularization, prediction and model fitting. *Statistical Science*, 22(4):477–505, 2007.

[22] E. Bullmore and O. Sporns. Complex brain networks: Graph theoretical analysis of structural and functional systems. *Nature Reviews Neuroscience*, 10(3):186–198, 2009.

[23] M. Calnan. Clinical uncertainty: Is it a problem in the doctor-patient relationship? *Sociology of Health and Illness*, 6(1):74–85, 2008.

[24] M. Campone, L. Campion, H. Roch, W. Gouraud, C. Charbonnel, F. Magrangeas, S. Minvielle, J. Genve, A. L. Martin, and R. Bataille. Prediction of metastatic relapse in node-positive breast cancer: establishment of a clinicogenomic model after FEC100 adjuvant regimen. *Breast Cancer Research and Treatment*, 109(3):491–501, 2008.

[25] J. T. Chi, Z. Wang, D. S. A. Nuyten, E. H. Rodriguez, M. E. Schaner, A. Salim, Y. Wang, G. B. Kristensen, A. Helland, and A. L. Brresen-Dale. Gene expression programs in response to hypoxia: Cell type specificity and prognostic significance in human cancers. *PLoS Medicine*, 3(3):e47, 2006.

[26] I. Choi, M. W. Kattan, B. J. Wells, and C. Yu. A hybrid approach to survival model building using integration of clinical and molecular information in censored data. *IEEE/ACM Transactions on Computational Biology and Bioinformatics (TCBB)*, 9(4):1091–1105, 2012.

[27] H. Y. Chuang, E. Lee, Y. T. Liu, D. Lee, and T. Ideker. Network-based classification of breast cancer metastasis. *Molecular Systems Biology*, 3(1), 2007.

[28] J. Clarke and M. West. Bayesian weibull tree models for survival analysis of clinico-genomic data. *Statistical Methodology*, 5(3):238–262, 2008.

[29] G. F. Cooper and E. Herskovits. A Bayesian method for the induction of probabilistic networks from data. *Machine Learning*, 9(4):309–347, 1992.

[30] N. M. Correa, T. Adali, Y. O. Li, and V. D. Calhoun. Canonical correlation analysis for data fusion and group inferences. *Signal Processing Magazine, IEEE*, 27(4):39–50, 2010.

[31] T. M. Cover and J. A. Thomas. *Elements of Information Theory*. Wiley, 2006.

[32] A. Daemen, O. Gevaert, and B. De Moor. Integration of clinical and microarray data with kernel methods. *Proceedings of the Annual International Conference of the IEEE Engineering in Medicine and Biology Society*, pages 5411–5415, 2007.

[33] H. Dai, L. van't Veer, J. Lamb, Y. D. He, M. Mao, B. M. Fine, R. Bernards, M. van de Vijver, P. Deutsch, and A. Sachs. A cell proliferation signature is a marker of extremely poor outcome in a subpopulation of breast cancer patients. *Cancer research*, 65(10):4059–4066, 2005.

[34] S. S. Dave, G. Wright, B. Tan, A. Rosenwald, R. D. Gascoyne, W. C. Chan, R. I. Fisher, R. M. Braziel, L. M. Rimsza, and T. M. Grogan. Prediction of survival in follicular lymphoma based on molecular features of tumor-infiltrating immune cells. *New England Journal of Medicine*, 351(21):2159, 2004.

[35] S. Dey, R. Gupta, M. Steinbach, and V. Kumar. Integration of clinical and genomic data: A methodological survey. Technical Report, Department of Computer Science and Engineering, University of Minnesota, 2013.

[36] S. Dey, K. Lim, G. Atluri, A. MacDonald III, M. Steinbach, and V. Kumar. A pattern mining based integrative framework for biomarker discovery. In *Proceedings of the ACM Conference on Bioinformatics, Computational Biology and Biomedicine*, pages 498–505. ACM, 2012.

[37] K. K. Dobbin, D. G. Beer, M. Meyerson, T. J. Yeatman, W. L. Gerald, J. W. Jacobson, B. Conley, K. H. Buetow, M. Heiskanen, and R. M. Simon. Interlaboratory comparability study of cancer gene expression analysis using oligonucleotide microarrays. *Clinical Cancer Research*, 11(2):565, 2005.

[38] K. Driouch, T. Landemaine, S. Sin, S. X. Wang, and R. Lidereau. Gene arrays for diagnosis, prognosis and treatment of breast cancer metastasis. *Clinical and Experimental Metastasis*, 24(8):575–585, 2007.

[39] R. O. Duda, P. E. Hart, and D. G. Stork. *Pattern Classification*, 2nd edition, Wiley-Interscience, Citeseer, 2001.

[40] P. Edn, C. Ritz, C. Rose, M. Fern, and C. Peterson. Good old clinical markers have similar power in breast cancer prognosis as microarray gene expression profilers. *European Journal of Cancer*, 40(12):1837–1841, 2004.

[41] P. Eifel, J. A. Axelson, J. Costa, J. Crowley, W. J. Curran Jr, A. Deshler, S. Fulton, C. B. Hendricks, M. Kemeny, and A. B. Kornblith. National institutes of health consensus development conference statement: Adjuvant therapy for breast cancer, November 1–3, 2000. *Journal of the National Cancer Institute*, 93(13):979, 2001.

[42] L. Ein-Dor, I. Kela, G. Getz, D. Givol, and E. Domany. Outcome signature genes in breast cancer: Is there a unique set? *Bioinformatics*, 21(2):171, 2005.

[43] L. Ein-Dor, O. Zuk, and E. Domany. Thousands of samples are needed to generate a robust gene list for predicting outcome in cancer. *Proceedings of the National Academy of Sciences USA*, 103(15):5923–5928, 2006.

[44] C. Fan, D. S. Oh, L. Wessels, B. Weigelt, D. S. A. Nuyten, A. B. Nobel, L. J. van't Veer, and C. M. Perou. Concordance among gene-expressionbased predictors for breast cancer. *New England Journal of Medicine*, 355(6):560–569, 2006.

[45] G. Fang, R. Kuang, G. Pandey, M. Steinbach, C. L. Myers, and V. Kumar. Subspace differential coexpression analysis: Problem definition and a general approach. *Pacific Symposium on Biocomputing*, 15:145–56, 2010.

[46] G. Fang, G. Pandey, W. Wang, M. Gupta, M. Steinbach, and V. Kumar. Mining low-support discriminative patterns from dense and high-dimensional data. *IEEE Transactions on Knowledge and Data Engineering*, 24(2):279–294, 2010.

[47] J. Friedman, T. Hastie, and R. Tibshirani. Additive logistic regression: A statistical view of boosting (with discussion and a rejoinder by the authors). *The Annals of Statistics*, 28(2):337–407, 2000.

[48] J. Friedman and B. E. Popescu. Gradient directed regularization for linear regression and classification. Stanford University Department of Statistics. Technical Report, 2004.

[49] M. E. Futschik, M. Sullivan, A. Reeve, and N. Kasabov. Prediction of clinical behaviour and treatment for cancers. *Applied Bioinformatics*, 2:53–58, 2003.

[50] M. H. Galea, R. W. Blamey, C. E. Elston, and I. O. Ellis. The Nottingham prognostic index in primary breast cancer. *Breast Cancer Research and Treatment*, 22(3):207–219, 1992.

[51] M. E. Garber, O. G. Troyanskaya, K. Schluens, S. Petersen, Z. Thaesler, M. Pacyna-Gengelbach, M. Van De Rijn, G. D. Rosen, C. M. Perou, and R. I. Whyte. Diversity of gene expression in adenocarcinoma of the lung. *Proceedings of the National Academy of Sciences of the United States of America*, 98(24):13784, 2001.

[52] T. A. Gerds and M. Schumacher. Consistent estimation of the expected Brier score in general survival models with right-censored event times. *Biometrical Journal*, 48(6):1029–1040, 2006.

[53] O. Gevaert, F. D. Smet, D. Timmerman, Y. Moreau, and B. D. Moor. Predicting the prognosis of breast cancer by integrating clinical and microarray data with Bayesian networks. *Bioinformatics*, 22(14):e184, 2006.

[54] M. Gnen and E. Alpaydn. Multiple kernel learning algorithms. *Journal of Machine Learning Research*, 12:2211–2268, 2011.

[55] K. I. Goh, M. E. Cusick, D. Valle, B. Childs, M. Vidal, and A. L. Barabsi. The human disease network. *Proceedings of the National Academy of Sciences*, 104(21):8685, 2007.

[56] A. Goldhirsch, A. S. Coates, R. D. Gelber, J. H. Glick, B. Thrlimann, and H. J. Senn. First-select the target: Better choice of adjuvant treatments for breast cancer patients. *Annals of Oncology*, 17(12):1772, 2006.

[57] A. Goldhirsch, W. C. Wood, R. D. Gelber, A. S. Coates, B. Thurlimann, and H. J. Senn. Meeting highlights: Updated international expert consensus on the primary therapy of early breast cancer. *Journal of Clinical Oncology*, 21(17):3357–3365, 2003.

[58] T. R. Golub, D. K. Slonim, P. Tamayo, C. Huard, M. Gaasenbeek, J. P. Mesirov, H. Coller, M. L. Loh, J. R. Downing, and M. A. Caligiuri. Molecular classification of cancer: Class discovery and class prediction by gene expression monitoring. *Science*, 286(5439):531, 1999.

[59] M. Graefen, P. I. Karakiewicz, I. Cagiannos, E. Klein, P. A. Kupelian, D. I. Quinn, S. M. Henshall, J. J. Grygiel, R. L. Sutherland, and P. D. Stricker. Validation study of the accuracy of a postoperative nomogram for recurrence after radical prostatectomy for localized prostate cancer. *Journal of Clinical Oncology*, 20(4):951, 2002.

[60] J. S. Hamid, P. Hu, N. M. Roslin, V. Ling, C. M. T. Greenwood, and J. Beyene. Data integration in genetics and genomics: Methods and challenges. *Human Genomics and Proteomics*, 2009. doi:10.4061/2009/869093

[61] F. E. Harrell Jr., R. M. Califf, D. B. Pryor, K. L. Lee, and R. A. Rosati. Evaluating the yield of medical tests. *JAMA*, 247(18):2543, 1982.

[62] T. Hastie, R. Tibshirani, and J. H. Friedman. *The Elements of Statistical Learning: Data Mining, Inference, and Prediction*. Springer Verlag, 2009.

[63] P. J. Heagerty, T. Lumley, and M. S. Pepe. Time-dependent ROC curves for censored survival data and a diagnostic marker. *Biometrics*, 56(2):337–344, 2000.

[64] A. E. Hoerl and R. W. Kennard. Ridge regression: Biased estimation for nonorthogonal problems. *Technometrics*, 12(1):55–67, 1970.

[65] J. A. Hoeting, D. Madigan, A. E. Raftery, and C. T. Volinsky. Bayesian model averaging: A tutorial. *Statistical Science*, 14(4):382–401, 1999.

[66] H. Hofling and R. Tibshirani. A study of pre-validation. *Annals*, 2(2):643–664, 2008.

[67] C. J. Honey, O. Sporns, Leila Cammoun, Xavier Gigandet, Jean-Philippe Thiran, Reto Meuli, and Patric Hagmann. Predicting human resting-state functional connectivity from structural connectivity. *Proceedings of the National Academy of Sciences*, 106(6):2035–2040, 2009.

[68] T. Hothorn, P. Buhlmann, S. Dudoit, A. Molinaro, and M. J. Van Der Laan. Survival ensembles. *Biostatistics*, 7(3):355–373, 2005.

[69] V. Hristidis. *Information Discovery on Electronic Health Records*. Chapman and Hall, 2009.

[70] T. H. Hwang, H. Sicotte, Z. Tian, B. Wu, J. P. Kocher, D. A. Wigle, V. Kumar, and R. Kuang. Robust and efficient identification of biomarkers by classifying features on graphs. *Bioinformatics*, 24(18):2023, 2008.

[71] J. P. Ioannidis. Microarrays and molecular research: Noise discovery? *Lancet*, 365(9458):454, 2005.

[72] K. Kammers, M. Lang, J. G. Hengstler, M. Schmidt, and J. Rahnenfhrer. Survival models with preclustered gene groups as covariates. *BMC Bioinformatics*, 12(1):478, 2011.

[73] E. L. Kaplan and P. Meier. Nonparametric estimation from incomplete observations. *Journal of the American Statistical Association*, 53(282):457–481, 1958.

[74] N. K. Kasabov. On-line learning, reasoning, rule extraction and aggregation in locally optimized evolving fuzzy neural networks. *Neurocomputing*, 41(1-4):25–45, 2001.

[75] M. W. Kattan, T. M. Wheeler, and P. T. Scardino. Postoperative nomogram for disease recurrence after radical prostatectomy for prostate cancer. *Journal of Clinical Oncology*, 17(5):1499, 1999.

[76] J. Kittler. Combining classifiers: A theoretical framework. *Pattern Analysis and Applications*, 1(1):18–27, 1998.

[77] R. Kohavi. A study of cross-validation and bootstrap for accuracy estimation and model selection. *Proceedings of the 14th International Joint Conference on Artificial Intelligence*, pages 1137–1145, 1995.

[78] P. A. Konstantinopoulos, S. A. Cannistra, H. Fountzilas, A. Culhane, K. Pillay, B. Rueda, D. Cramer, M. Seiden, M. Birrer, and G. Coukos. Integrated analysis of multiple microarray datasets identifies a reproducible survival predictor in ovarian cancer. *PloS One*, 6(3):e18202, 2011.

[79] K. A. Le Cao, E. Meugnier, and G. J. McLachlan. Integrative mixture of experts to combine clinical factors and gene markers. *Bioinformatics*, 26(9):1192–1198, 2010.

[80] K. C. Li. Sliced inverse regression for dimension reduction. *Journal of the American Statistical Association*, 86(414):316–327, 1991.

[81] L. Li. Survival prediction of diffuse large-b-cell lymphoma based on both clinical and gene expression information. *Bioinformatics*, 22(4):466, 2006.

[82] L. Li, L. Chen, D. Goldgof, F. George, Z. Chen, A. Rao, J. Cragun, R. Sutphen, and J. M. Lancaster. Integration of clinical information and gene expression profiles for prediction of chemo-response for ovarian cancer. *Conference Proceedings: Annual International Conference of the IEEE Engineering in Medicine and Biology Society*, 5:4818–4821, 2005.

[83] R. Liu, X. Wang, G. Y. Chen, P. Dalerba, A. Gurney, T. Hoey, G. Sherlock, J. Lewicki, K. Shedden, and M. F. Clarke. The prognostic role of a gene signature from tumorigenic breast-cancer cells. *New England Journal of Medicine*, 356(3):217–226, 2007.

[84] J. Loscalzo, I. Kohane, and A. L. Barabasi. Human disease classification in the postgenomic era: A complex systems approach to human pathobiology. *Molecular Systems Biology*, 3(1), 2007.

[85] S. Ma and J. Huang. Combining clinical and genomic covariates via Cov-TGDR. *Cancer Informatics*, 3:371, 2007.

[86] V. Maojo and F. Martin-Sanchez. Bioinformatics: Towards new directions for public health. *Methods of Information in Medicine*, 43(3):208–214, 2004.

[87] J. McClellan and M. C. King. Genetic heterogeneity in human disease. *Cell*, 141(2):210–217, 2010.

[88] M. Meingast, T. Roosta, and S. Sastry. Security and privacy issues with health care information technology. *Conference Proceedings: Annual International Conference of the IEEE Engineering in Medicine and Biology Society*, 1:5453–5458, 2006.

[89] A. Naderi, A. E. Teschendorff, N. L. Barbosa-Morais, S. E. Pinder, A. R. Green, D. G. Powe, J. F. R. Robertson, S. Aparicio, I. O. Ellis, and J. D. Brenton. A gene-expression signature to predict survival in breast cancer across independent data sets. *Oncogene*, 26(10):1507–1516, 2006.

[90] J. R. Nevins, E. S. Huang, H. Dressman, J. Pittman, A. T. Huang, and M. West. Towards integrated clinico-genomic models for personalized medicine: Combining gene expression signatures and clinical factors in breast cancer outcomes prediction. *Human Molecular Genetics*, 12(Review Issue 2):R153, 2003.

[91] A. Obulkasim, G. A. Meijer, and M. A. van de Wiel. Stepwise classification of cancer samples using clinical and molecular data. *BMC Bioinformatics*, 12(1):422, 2011.

[92] M. R. Oelker and A. L. Boulesteix. On the simultaneous analysis of clinical and omics data-a comparison of globalboosttest and pre-validation techniques. *Proceedings of the 8th Scientific Meeting of the Classification and Data Analysis Group of the Italian Statistical Society,* pages 259–268, 2013.

[93] J. J. Oliver and D. J. Hand. On pruning and averaging decision trees, In *Proceedings of the 12th International Conference on Machine Learning*, pages 430–437, Morgan Kaufman, 1995.

[94] A. W. Partin, J. L. Mohler, S. Piantadosi, C. B. Brendler, M. G. Sanda, P. C. Walsh, and J. I. Epstein. Selection of men at high risk for disease recurrence for experimental adjuvant therapy following radical prostatectomy. *Urology*, 45(5):831–838, 1995.

[95] P. Pavlidis, J. Weston, J. Cai, and W. N. Grundy. Gene functional classification from heterogeneous data. In *Proceedings of the 5th Annual International Conference on Computational Biology*, April 22–25, 2001, pages 242–248.

[96] J. Pittman, E. Huang, H. Dressman, C. F. Horng, S. H. Cheng, M. H. Tsou, C. M. Chen, A. Bild, E. S. Iversen, and A. T. Huang. Integrated modeling of clinical and gene expression information for personalized prediction of disease outcomes. *Proceedings of the National Academy of Sciences of the United States of America*, 101(22):8431, 2004.

[97] A. Potti, S. Mukherjee, R. Petersen, H. K. Dressman, A. Bild, J. Koontz, R. Kratzke, M. A. Watson, M. Kelley, and G. S. Ginsburg. A genomic strategy to refine prognosis in early-stage non-small-cell lung cancer. *New England Journal of Medicine*, 355(6):570, 2006.

[98] A. E. Raftery, D. Madigan, and J. A. Hoeting. Bayesian model averaging for linear regression models. *Journal of the American Statistical Association*, 92(437):179–191, 1997.

[99] D. E. Redmond Jr. Tobacco and cancer: The first clinical report, 1761. *New England Journal of Medicine*, 282(1):18–23, 1970.

[100] P. Royston and W. Sauerbrei. A new measure of prognostic separation in survival data. *Statistics in Medicine*, 23(5):723–748, 2004.

[101] E. E. Schadt. Molecular networks as sensors and drivers of common human diseases. *Nature*, 461(7261):218–223, 2009.

[102] M. Schumacher, H. Binder, and T. Gerds. Assessment of survival prediction models based on microarray data. *Bioinformatics*, 23(14):1768, 2007.

[103] E. Schwarz, F. M. Leweke, S. Bahn, and P. Li. Clinical bioinformatics for complex disorders: A schizophrenia case study. *BMC Bioinformatics*, 10(Suppl 12):S6, 2009.

[104] K. Shedden, J. M. G. Taylor, S. A. Enkemann, M. S. Tsao, T. J. Yeatman, W. L. Gerald, S. Eschrich, I. Jurisica, T. J. Giordano, and D. E. Misek. Gene expressionbased survival prediction in lung adenocarcinoma: A multi-site, blinded validation study. *Nature Medicine*, 14(8):822–827, 2008.

[105] M. A. Shipp, D. P. Harrington, J. R. Anderson, J. O. Armitage, G. Bonadonna, G. Brittinger, F. Cabanillas, G. P. Canellos, B. Coiffier, and J. M. Connors. A predictive model for aggressive non-hodgkins lymphoma the international non-hodgkins lymphoma prognostic factors project. *New England Journal of Medicine*, 329(14):987–994, 1993.

[106] J. Silhava and P. Smrz. Additional predictive value of microarray data compared to clinical variables. *4th IAPR International Conference on Pattern Recognition in Bioinformatics*, 2009.

[107] R. Simon, M. D. Radmacher, K. Dobbin, and L. M. McShane. Pitfalls in the use of dna microarray data for diagnostic and prognostic classification. *Journal of the National Cancer Institute*, 95(1):14, 2003.

[108] P. Smialowski, D. Frishman, and S. Kramer. Pitfalls of supervised feature selection. *Bioinformatics*, 26(3):440, 2010.

[109] C. Sotiriou and M. J. Piccart. Taking gene-expression profiling to the clinic: when will molecular signatures become relevant to patient care? *Nature Reviews Cancer*, 7(7):545–553, 2007.

[110] C. Sotiriou, P. Wirapati, S. Loi, A. Harris, S. Fox, J. Smeds, H. Nordgren, P. Farmer, V. Praz, and B. Haibe-Kains. Gene expression profiling in breast cancer: understanding the molecular basis of histologic grade to improve prognosis. *JNCI Cancer Spectrum*, 98(4):262, 2006.

[111] A. Spira, J. E. Beane, V. Shah, K. Steiling, G. Liu, F. Schembri, S. Gilman, Y. M. Dumas, P. Calner, and P. Sebastiani. Airway epithelial gene expression in the diagnostic evaluation of smokers with suspect lung cancer. *Nature Medicine*, 13(3):361–366, 2007.

[112] A. J. Stephenson, A. Smith, M. W. Kattan, J. Satagopan, V. E. Reuter, P. T. Scardino, and W. L. Gerald. Integration of gene expression profiling and clinical variables to predict prostate carcinoma recurrence after radical prostatectomy. *Cancer*, 104(2):290, 2005.

[113] A. Subramanian, P. Tamayo, V. K. Mootha, S. Mukherjee, B. L. Ebert, M. A. Gillette, A. Paulovich, S. L. Pomeroy, T. R. Golub, and E. S. Lander. Gene set enrichment analysis: A knowledge-based approach for interpreting genome-wide expression profiles. *Proceedings of the National Academy of Sciences of the United States of America*, 102(43):15545, 2005.

[114] Y. Sun, S. Goodison, J. Li, L. Liu, and W. Farmerie. Improved breast cancer prognosis through the combination of clinical and genetic markers. *Bioinformatics*, 23(1):30, 2007.

[115] M. Szklo. Population-based cohort studies. *Epidemiologic Reviews*, 20(1):81, 1998.

[116] P. N. Tan, M. Steinbach, and V. Kumar. *Introduction to Data Mining*. Pearson Addison Wesley Boston, 2006.

[117] A. E. Teschendorff, A. Miremadi, S. E. Pinder, I. O. Ellis, and C. Caldas. An immune response gene expression module identifies a good prognosis subtype in estrogen receptor negative breast cancer. *Genome Biol*, 8(8):R157, 2007.

[118] A. E. Teschendorff, A. Naderi, N. L. Barbosa-Morais, S. E. Pinder, I. O. Ellis, S. Aparicio, J. D. Brenton, and C. Caldas. A consensus prognostic gene expression classifier for ER positive breast cancer. *Genome Biology*, 7(10):R101, 2006.

[119] D. Thomas. Geneenvironment-wide association studies: Emerging approaches. *Nature Reviews Genetics*, 11(4):259–272, 2010.

[120] R. Tibshirani. Regression shrinkage and selection via the lasso. *Journal of the Royal Statistical Society Series B (Methodological)*, 58:267–288, 1994.

[121] R. Tibshirani and B. Efron. *Pre-Validation and Inference in Microarrays*. Stanford University, Department of Biostatistics, 2002.

[122] O. G. Troyanskaya, K. Dolinski, A. B. Owen, R. B. Altman, and D. Botstein. A Bayesian framework for combining heterogeneous data sources for gene function prediction (in saccharomyces cerevisiae). *Proceedings of the National Academy of Sciences of the United States of America*, 100(14):8348, 2003.

[123] C. Truntzer, D. Maucort-Boulch, and P. Roy. Comparative optimism in models involving both classical clinical and gene expression information. *BMC Bioinformatics*, 9(1):434, 2008.

[124] G. Tutz and H. Binder. Boosting ridge regression. *Computational Statistics and Data Analysis*, 51(12):6044–6059, 2007.

[125] I. Ulitsky, R. Karp, and R. Shamir. Detecting disease-specific dysregulated pathways via analysis of clinical expression profiles. *Research in Computational Molecular Biology*, 4955:347–359. Springer, 2008.

[126] M. J. van de Vijver, Y. D. He, L. J. van't Veer, H. Dai, A. A. M. Hart, D. W. Voskuil, G. J. Schreiber, J. L. Peterse, C. Roberts, and M. J. Marton. A gene-expression signature as a predictor of survival in breast cancer. *The New England Journal of Medicine*, 347(25):1999, 2002.

[127] S. Van Dongen. A cluster algorithm for graphs. *Report-Information Systems*, (10):1–40, 2000.

[128] M. H. van Vliet, H. M. Horlings, M. J. van de Vijver, M. J. T. Reinders, and L. F. A. Wessels. Integration of clinical and gene expression data has a synergetic effect on predicting breast cancer outcome. *PloS One*, 7(7), 2012.

[129] L. J. van't Veer, H. Dai, M. J. Van de Vijver, Y. D. He, A. A. M. Hart, M. Mao, H. L. Peterse, K. van der Kooy, M. J. Marton, A. T. Witteveen, G. J. Schreiber, R. M. Kerkhoven, and C. Roberts. Gene expression profiling predicts clinical outcome of breast cancer. *Nature*, 415(6871):530–536, 2002.

[130] V. N. Vapnik. *The Nature of Statistical Learning Theory*. Springer Verlag, 2000.

[131] S. M. Wang, L. L. P. J. Ooi, and K. M. Hui. Identification and validation of a novel gene signature associated with the recurrence of human hepatocellular carcinoma. *Clinical Cancer Research*, 13(21):6275, 2007.

[132] Y. Wang, J. G. M. Klijn, Y. Zhang, A. M. Sieuwerts, M. P. Look, F. Yang, D. Talantov, M. Timmermans, M. E. Meijer-van Gelder, and J. Yu. Gene-expression profiles to predict distant metastasis of lymph-node-negative primary breast cancer. *The Lancet*, 365(9460):671–679, 2005.

[133] R. A. Weinberg. *The Biology of Cancer*. Garland Science, 2007.

[134] M. West, G. S. Ginsburg, A. T. Huang, and J. R. Nevins. Embracing the complexity of genomic data for personalized medicine. *Genome Research*, 16(5):559, 2006.

[135] C. R. Williams-DeVane, D. M. Reif, E. C. Hubal, P. R. Bushel, E. E. Hudgens, J. E. Gallagher, and S. W. Edwards. Decision tree-based method for integrating gene expression, demographic, and clinical data to determine disease endotypes. *BMC Systems Biology*, 7(1):119, 2013.

[136] H. Wold. Partial least squares. In *Encyclopedia of Statistical Sciences*, 6:581–591. S. Kots and N.L. Johnson (Eds). Wiley, 1985.

[137] L. Zhang and X. Lin. Some considerations of classification for high dimension low-sample size data. *Statistical Methods in Medical Research*, 22(5):537–550, 2013.

[138] W. Zhou, G. Liu, D. P. Miller, S. W. Thurston, L. L. Xu, J. C. Wain, T. J. Lynch, L. Su, and D. C. Christiani. Gene-environment interaction for the ERCC2 polymorphisms and cumulative cigarette smoking exposure in lung cancer. *Cancer Research*, 62(5):1377–1381, 2002.

Chapter 14

Information Retrieval for Healthcare

William R. Hersh
Department of Medical Informatics & Clinical Epidemiology (DMICE)
Oregon Health & Science University
Portland, OR
hersh@ohsu.edu

14.1 Introduction

Although most work in Healthcare Data Analytics focuses on mining and analyzing data from patients, another vast trove of information for use in this process includes scientific data and literature. The techniques most commonly used to access this day include those from the field of *information retrieval* (IR), sometimes called *search*. IR is the field concerned with the acquisition, organization, and searching of knowledge-based information, which is usually defined as information derived and organized from observational or experimental research [60, 66]. Although IR in biomedicine traditionally concentrated on the retrieval of text from the biomedical literature, the purview of content covered has expanded to include newer types of media that include images, video, chemical structures, gene and protein sequences, and a wide range of other digital media of relevance to biomedical education, research, and patient care. With the proliferation of IR systems and online content, even the notion of the library has changed substantially, with the new *digital library* emerging [90].

Figure 14.1 shows a basic overview of the IR process and forms the basis for most of this chapter. The overall goal of the IR process is to find *content* that meets a person's information needs. This begins with the posing of a *query* to the IR system. A *search engine* matches the query to content items through metadata. There are two intellectual processes of IR. *Indexing* is the process of assigning metadata to content items, while *retrieval* is the process of the user entering his or her query and retrieving content items.

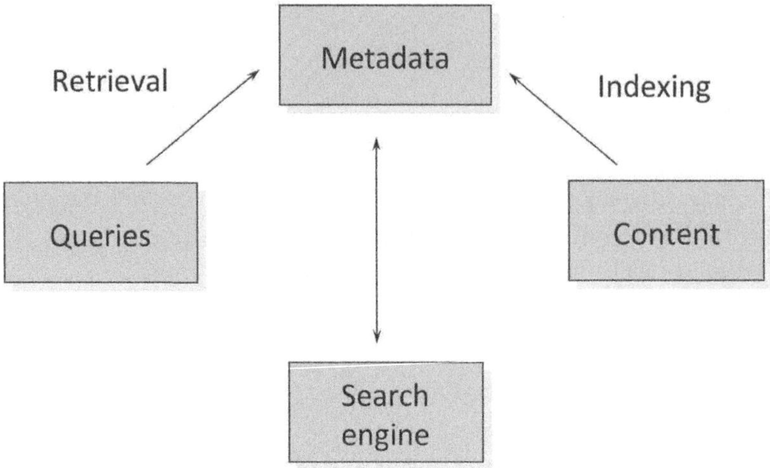

FIGURE 14.1: Basic overview of information retrieval (IR) process. (Copyright, William Hersh)

The use of IR systems has become essentially ubiquitous. It is estimated that among individuals who use the Internet in the United States, over 80 percent have used it to search for personal health information [50]. Virtually all physicians use the Internet [102]. Furthermore, access to systems has gone beyond the traditional personal computer and extended to new devices, such as smartphones and tablet devices.

Other evidence points to the importance of IR and biomedicine. One author now defines biology as an "information science" [76]. Another notes that pharmaceutical companies compete for informatics and library talent [28]. Clinicians can no longer keep up with the growth of the literature, as an average of 75 clinical trials and 11 systematic reviews are published each day [9]. *Search* is even part of the "meaningful use" program to incentivize adoption of the electronic health record, as text search over electronic notes is a requirement for obtaining incentive funding [94].

14.2 Knowledge-Based Information in Healthcare and Biomedicine

IR tends to focus on knowledge-based information, which is information based on scientific research and in distinction to patient-specific information that is generated in the care of the patient. Knowledge-based information is typically subdivided into two categories. Primary knowledge-based information (also called primary literature) is original research that appears in journals, books, reports, and other sources. This type of information reports the initial discovery of health knowledge, usually with either original data or reanalysis of data (e.g., systematic reviews and meta-analyses). Secondary knowledge-based information consists of the writing that reviews, condenses, and/or synthesizes the primary literature. The most common examples of this type of literature are books, monographs, and review articles in journals and other publications. Secondary literature also includes opinion-based writing such as editorials and position or policy papers. It also encompasses clinical practice guidelines, narrative reviews, and health information on Web pages. In addition, it includes the plethora of pocket-sized manuals that were formerly a staple for practitioners in many professional fields. As will be seen later, secondary literature is the most common type of literature used by physicians. Secondary literature also includes the growing quality of patient/consumer-oriented health information that is increasingly available via the Web.

14.2.1 Information Needs and Seeking

It is important when designing IR systems to consider the needs of various users and the types of questions they bring to the system. Different users of knowledge-based information have differing needs based on the nature of what they need the information for and what resources are available. The information needs and information seeking of physicians have been most extensively studied. Gorman and Helfand [57] has defined four states of information need in the clinical context:

- Unrecognized need—clinician unaware of information need or knowledge deficit.
- Recognized need—clinician aware of need but may or may not pursue it.
- Pursued need—information seeking occurs but may or may not be successful.
- Satisfied need—information seeking successful.

Studies of physician information needs find that they are likely to pursue only a minority of unanswered questions. A variety of studies over several decades have demonstrated that physicians in practice have unmet information on the order of two questions for every three patients seen and only pursue answers for about 30 percent of these questions [25, 57, 39]. When answers to questions are actually pursued, these studies showed that the most frequent source for answers to questions was colleagues, followed by paper-based textbooks. Therefore, it is not surprising that barriers to satisfying information needs remain [40]. It is probably likely that physicians use electronic sources more now than were measured in these earlier studies, with the widespread use of the electronic health record (EHR) as well as the ubiquity of portable smartphones and tablets. One possible approach to lowering the barrier to knowledge-based information is to link it more directly with the context of the patient in the EHR [22].

The information needs of other users are less well-studied. As noted above, surveys find about 80 percent of all Internet users have searched for personal health information [50]. About 4.5 percent of all queries to Web search engines are health-related [43]. Analyses show that consumers tend to search on the following categories of topics [49]:

- Specific disease or medical problem—66%
- Certain medical treatment or procedure—56%
- Doctors or other health professionals—44%
- Hospitals or other medical facilities—36%
- Health insurance, private or government—33%
- Food safety or recalls—29%

- Environmental health hazards—22%
- Pregnancy and childbirth—19%
- Medical test results—16%

14.2.2 Changes in Publishing

Profound changes have taken place in the publishing of knowledge-based information in recent years. Virtually all scientific journals are published electronically now. In addition, there is great enthusiasm for electronic availability of journals, as evidenced by the growing number of titles to which libraries provide access. When available in electronic form, journal content is easier and more convenient to access. Furthermore, since most scientists have the desire for widespread dissemination of their work, they have incentive for their papers to be available electronically. Not only is there the increased convenience of redistributing reprints, but research has found that freely available on the Web have a higher likelihood of being cited by other papers than those that are not [12]. As citations are important to authors for academic promotion and grant funding, authors have an incentive to maximize the accessibility of their published work.

The technical challenges to electronic scholarly publication have been replaced by economic and political ones [69, 113]. Printing and mailing, tasks no longer needed in electronic publishing, comprised a significant part of the "added value" from publishers of journals. There is still however value added by publishers, such as hiring and managing editorial staff to produce the journals, and managing the peer review process. Even if publishing companies as they are known were to vanish, there would still be some cost to the production of journals. Thus, while the cost of producing journals electronically is likely to be less, it is not zero, and even if journal content is distributed "free," someone has to pay the production costs. The economic issue in electronic publishing, then, is who is going to pay for the production of journals [113]. This introduces some political issues as well. One of them centers around the concern that much research is publicly funded through grants from federal agencies such as the National Institutes of Health (NIH) and the National Science Foundation (NSF). In the current system, especially in the biomedical sciences (and to a lesser extent in other sciences), researchers turn over the copyright of their publications to journal publishers. The political concern is that the public funds the research and the universities carry it out, but individuals and libraries then must buy it back from the publishers to whom they willingly cede the copyright. This problem is exacerbated by the general decline in funding for libraries.

Some proposed models of "open access" scholarly publishing keep the archive of science freely available [98, 121, 129]. The basic principle of open access publishing is that authors and/or their institutions pay the cost of production of manuscripts up front after they are accepted through a peer review process. After the paper is published, it becomes freely available on the Web. Since most research is usually funded by grants, the cost of open access publishing should be included in grant budgets. The uptake of publishers adhering to the open access model has been modest, with the most prominent being *Biomed Central* (BMC,`www.biomedcentral.com`) and the *Public Library of Science* (PLoS, `www.plos.org`).

Another model that has emerged is *PubMed Central* (PMC, `pubmedcentral.gov`). PMC is a repository of life science research articles that provides free access while allowing publishers to maintain copyright and even optionally keep the papers housed on their own servers. A lag time of up to 6 months is allowed so that journals can reap the revenue that comes with initial publication. The National Institutes of Health (NIH, `www.nih.gov`) now requires all research funded by its grants to be submitted to PMC, either in the form published by publishers or as a PDF of the last manuscript prior to journal acceptance (`publicaccess.nih.gov`). Publishers have expressed concern that copyrights give journals more control over the integrity of the papers they publish [35]. An alternative approach advocated by non-commercial (usually professional society) publishers is the

DC Principles for Free Access to Science (www.dcprinciples.org), which advocates reinvestment of revenues in support of science, use of open archives such as PMC as allowed by business constraints, commitment to some free publication, more open access for low-income countries, and no charges for authors to publish.

14.3 Content of Knowledge-Based Information Resources

The previous sections of this chapter have described some of the issues and concerns surrounding the production and use of knowledge-based information in biomedicine. It is useful to classify the information to gain a better understanding of its structure and function. In this section, we classify content into bibliographic, full-text, annotated, and aggregated categories, although some content does not neatly fit within them.

14.3.1 Bibliographic Content

The first category consists of bibliographic content. It includes what was for decades the mainstay of IR systems: literature reference databases. Also called bibliographic databases, this content consists of citations or pointers to the medical literature (i.e., journal articles). The best-known and most widely used biomedical bibliographic database is MEDLINE, which contains bibliographic references to all of the biomedical articles, editorials, and letters to the editors in approximately 5,000 scientific journals. The journals are chosen for inclusion by an advisory committee of subject experts convened by NIH. At present, about 750,000 references are added to MEDLINE yearly. It now contains over 22 million references. A Web page devoted to MEDLINE size and searches statistics is at https://www.nlm.nih.gov/bsd/bsd_key.html.

The MEDLINE record may contain up to 49 fields. A user wanting just an overview on a topic may be interested in just a handful of these fields, such as the title, abstract, and indexing terms. But other fields contain specific information that may be of great importance to other audiences. For example, a genome researcher might be highly interested in the Supplementary Information (SI) field to link to genomic databases. A clinician may, however, derive benefit from some of the other fields. For example, the Publication Type (PT) field can help in the application of EBM, such as when one is searching for a practice guideline or a randomized controlled trial. MEDLINE is accessible by many means and available without charge via the PubMed system (http://pubmed.gov), produced by the National Center for Biotechnology Information (NCBI, www.ncbi.nlm.nih.gov) of the NLM, which provides access to other databases as well. A number of other information vendors, such as Ovid Technologies (www.ovid.com) and Aries Systems (www.ariessys.com), license the content of MEDLINE and other databases and provide value-added services that can be accessed for a fee by individuals and institutions.

MEDLINE is only one of many databases produced by the NLM. Other more specialized databases are also available, including textbooks, gene sequences, protein structures, and so forth. There are several non-NLM bibliographic databases that tend to be more focused on subjects or resource types. The major non-NLM database for the nursing field is the *Cumulative Index to Nursing and Allied Health Literature* (CINAHL, CINAHL Information Systems, http://www.ebscohost.com/cinahl/), which covers nursing and allied health literature, including physical therapy, occupational therapy, laboratory technology, health education, physician assistants, and medical records.

Another well-known bibliographic database is EMBASE (www.embase.com), which is sometimes referred to as the "European MEDLINE." It contains over 24 million records and covers many of the same medical journals as MEDLINE but with a more international focus, including more non-English-language journals. These journals are often important for those carrying out meta-analyses and systematic reviews, which need access to all the studies done across the world.

A second, more modern type of bibliographic content is the Web catalog. There are increasing numbers of such catalogs, which consist of Web pages containing mainly links to other Web pages and sites. It should be noted that there is a blurry distinction between Web catalogs and aggregations (the fourth category). In general, the former contain only links to other pages and sites, while the latter include actual content that is highly integrated with other resources. Some well-known Web catalogs include:

- *HealthFinder* (`www.healthfinder.gov`)–consumer-oriented health information maintained by the Office of Disease Prevention and Health Promotion of the U.S. Department of Health and Human Services.

- *HON Select* (`www.hon.ch/HONselect`)–a European catalog of quality-filtered, clinician-oriented Web content from the HON foundation.

- *Translating Research into Practice* (TRIP, `www.tripdatabase.com`)–a database of content deemed to meet high standards of EBM.

- *Open Directory* (`www.dmoz.org`)–a general Web catalog that has significant health content.

An additional modern bibliographic resource is the *National Guidelines Clearinghouse* (NGC, www.guideline.gov). Produced by the Agency for Healthcare Research and Quality (AHRQ), it contains exhaustive information about clinical practice guidelines. Some of the guidelines produced are freely available, published electronically, and/or on paper. Others are proprietary, in which case a link is provided to a location at which the guideline can be ordered or purchased. The overall goal of the NGC is to make evidence-based clinical practice guidelines and related abstract, summary, and comparison materials widely available to healthcare and other professionals.

A final kind of bibliographic-like content consists of RSS feeds, which are short summaries of Web content: typically news, journal articles, blog postings, and other content. Users set up an RSS aggregation, which can be through a Web browser, email client, or standalone software, configured for the RSS feed desired, with an option to add a filter for specific content. There are two versions of RSS (1.0 and 2.0) but both provide:

- Title–name of item

- Link–URL to content

- Description–a brief description of the content

14.3.2 Full-Text Content

The second type of content is full-text content. A large component of this content consists of the online versions of books and periodicals. As already noted, most traditionally paper-based medical literature, from textbooks to journals, is now available electronically. The electronic versions may be enhanced by measures ranging from the provision of supplemental data in a journal article to linkages and multimedia content in a textbook. The final component of this category is the Web site. Admittedly, the diversity of information on Web sites is enormous, and sites may include every other type of content described in this chapter. However, in the context of this category, "Web site" refers to the vast number of static and dynamic Web pages at a discrete Web location.

Electronic publication of journals allows additional features not possible in the print world. Journal Web sites may provide supplementary data of results, images, and even raw data. A journal

Web site also allows more dialog about articles than could be published in a "Letters to the Editor" section of a print journal. Electronic publication also allows true bibliographic linkages, both to other full-text articles and to the MEDLINE record.

The Web also allows linkage directly from bibliographic databases to full text. PubMed maintains a field for the Web address of the full-text paper. This linkage is active when the PubMed record is displayed, but users may be met by a "paywall" if the article is not available for free. Many sites allow both access to subscribers or a pay-per-view facility. Many academic organizations now maintain large numbers of subscriptions to journals available to faculty, staff, and students. Other publishers, such as Ovid and MDConsult (`www.mdconsult.com`), provide access within their own password-protected interfaces to articles from journals that they have licensed for use in their systems.

The most common secondary literature source is traditional textbooks, which have essentially made a complete transition to publication in electronic form. A common approach with textbooks is bundling them, sometimes with linkages across the bundled texts. An early bundler of textbooks was Stat!-Ref (Teton Data Systems, `www.statref.com`) that, like many, began as a CD-ROM product and then moved to the Web. Stat!-Ref offers over 30 textbooks. Most other publishers have similarly aggregated their libraries of textbooks and other content. Another collection of textbooks is the NCBI Bookshelf, which contains many volumes on biomedical research topics (`http://www.ncbi.nlm.nih.gov/books`). One textbook that was formerly produced by NCBI but now is a standalone Web site is Online Mendelian Inheritance in Man (OMIM, `http://omim.org`), which is continually updated with new information about the genomic causes of human disease.

Electronic textbooks offer additional features beyond text from the print version. While many print textbooks do feature high-quality images, electronic versions offer the ability to have more pictures and illustrations. They also have the ability to provide sound and video. As with full-text journals, electronic textbooks can link to other resources, including journal references and the full articles. Many Web-based textbook sites also provide access to continuing education self-assessment questions and medical news. Finally, electronic textbooks let authors and publishers provide more frequent updates of the information than is allowed by the usual cycle of print editions, where new versions come out only every 2 to 5 years.

As noted above, Web sites are another form of full-text information. Probably the most effective provider of Web-based health information is the U.S. government. Not only do they produce bibliographic databases, but the NLM, AHRQ, the National Cancer Institute (NCI), Centers for Disease Control (CDC), and others have also been innovative in providing comprehensive full-text information for healthcare providers and consumers. One example is the popular CDC Travel site (`http://www.cdc.gov/travel/`). Some of these will be described later as aggregations, since they provide many different types of resources.

A large number of commercial biomedical and health Web sites have emerged in recent years. On the consumer side, they include more than just collections of text; they also include interaction with experts, online stores, and catalogs of links to other sites. Among the best known of these are Intelihealth (`www.intelihealth.com`) and NetWellness (`www.netwellness.com`). There are also Web sites, either from medical societies or companies, that provide information geared toward healthcare providers, typically overviews of diseases, their diagnosis, and treatment; medical news and other resources for providers are often offered as well.

Other sources of online health-related content include encyclopedias, the body of knowledge, and Weblogs or blogs. A well-known online encyclopedia with a great deal of health-related information is Wikipedia, which features a distributed authorship process whose content has been found to be reliable [56, 99] and frequently shows up near the top in health-related Web searches [86]. A growing number of organizations have a body of knowledge, such as the American Health Information Management Association (AHIMA, `http://library.ahima.org/bok/`). Blogs tend to carry a stream of consciousness but often high-quality information is posted within them.

14.3.3 Annotated Content

The third category consists of annotated content. These resources are usually not stored as free-standing Web pages but instead are often housed in database management systems. This content can be further subcategorized into discrete information types:

- Image databases—collections of images from radiology, pathology, and other areas.
- Genomics databases—information from gene sequencing, protein characterization, and other genomic research.
- Citation databases—bibliographic linkages of scientific literature.
- EBM databases—highly structured collections of clinical evidence.
- Other databases—miscellaneous other collections.

A great number of biomedical image databases are available on the Web. These include:

- Visible Human–`http://www.nlm.nih.gov/research/visible/visible_human.html`
- Lieberman's eRadiology–`http://eradiology.bidmc.harvard.edu`
- WebPath–`http://library.med.utah.edu/WebPath/webpath.html`
- Pathology Education Instructional Resource (PEIR)–`www.peir.net`
- DermIS–`www.dermis.net`
- VisualDX–`www.visualdx.com`

Many genomics databases are available on the Web. The first issue each year of the journal *Nucleic Acids Research* (NAR) catalogs and describes these databases, and is now available by open access means [55]. NAR also maintains an ongoing database of such databases, the Molecular Biology Database Collection (`http://www.oxfordjournals.org/nar/database/a/`). Among the most important of these databases are those available from NCBI [111]. All their databases are linked among themselves, along with PubMed and OMIM, and are searchable via the GQuery system (`http://www.ncbi.nlm.nih.gov/gquery/`).

Citation databases provide linkages to articles that cite others across the scientific literature. The earliest citation databases were the *Science Citation Index* (SCI, Thomspon-Reuters) and *Social Science Citation Index* (SSCI, Thomspon-Reuters), which are now part of the larger *Web of Science*. Two well-known bibliographic databases for biomedical and health topics that also have citation links include SCOPUS (`www.scopus.com`) and Google Scholar (http://scholar.google.com). These three were recently compared for their features and coverage [80]. A final citation database of note is CiteSeer (`http://citeseerx.ist.psu.edu/`), which focuses on computer and information science, including biomedical informatics. Evidence-based medicine (EBM) databases are devoted to providing annotated evidence-based information. Some examples include:

- *The Cochrane Database of Systematic Reviews*–one of the original collections of systematic reviews (`www.cochrane.org`).
- *Clinical Evidence*–an "evidence formulary" (`www.clinicalevidence.com`).
- *UpToDate*–content centered around clinical questions (`www.uptodate.com`).
- *InfoPOEMS*–"patient-oriented evidence that matters" (`www.infopoems.com`).

- *ACP Smart Medicine* (formerly Physicians' Information and Education Resource, PIER) "practice guidance statements" for which every test and treatment has associated ratings of the evidence to support them (pier.acponline.org).

There is a growing market for a related type of evidence-based content in the form of clinical decision support order sets, rules, and health/disease management templates. Publishers include EHR vendors whose systems employ this content as well as other vendors such as Zynx (www.zynxhealth.com) and Thomson Reuters Cortellis (http://cortellis.thomsonreuters.com).

There are a variety of other annotated content. The ClinicalTrials.gov database began as a database of clinical trials sponsored by NIH. In recent years it has expanded its scope to a register of clinical trials [30, 82] and to containing actual results of trials [131, 130]. Another important database for researchers is NIH RePORTER (http://projectreporter.nih.gov/reporter.cfm), which is a database of all research funded by NIH.

14.3.4 Aggregated Content

The final category consists of aggregations of content from the first three categories. The distinction between this category and some of the highly linked types of content described above is admittedly blurry, but aggregations typically have a wide variety of different types of information serving the diverse needs of users. Aggregated content has been developed for all types of users from consumers to clinicians to scientists.

Probably the largest aggregated consumer information resource is *MedlinePlus* (http://medlineplus.gov) from the NLM. MedlinePlus includes all of the types of content previously described, aggregated for easy access to a given topic. MedlinePlus contains health topics, drug information, medical dictionaries, directories, and other resources. Each topic contains links to health information from the NIH and other sources deemed credible by its selectors. There are also links to current health news (updated daily), a medical encyclopedia, drug references, and directories, along with a preformed PubMed search, related to the topic.

Aggregations of content have also been developed for clinicians. Most of the major publishers now aggregate all of their content in packages for clinicians. Another aggregated resource for clinicians is *Merck Medicus* (www.merckmedicus.com), developed by the well-known publisher and pharmaceutical house, is available for free to all licensed U.S. physicians, and includes a number of well-known resources, including some described above.

Another well-known group of aggregations of content for genomics researchers is the model organism databases. These databases bring together bibliographic databases, full text, and databases of sequences, structure, and function for organisms whose genomic data have been highly characterized. One of the oldest and most developed model organism databases is the Mouse Genome Informatics resource (www.informatics.jax.org).

14.4 Indexing

As described at the beginning of the chapter, indexing is the process of assigning metadata to content to facilitate its retrieval. Most modern commercial content is indexed in two ways:

1. Manual indexing–where human indexers, usually using a controlled terminology, assign indexing terms and attributes to documents, often following a specific protocol.

2. Automated indexing–where computers make the indexing assignments, usually limited to breaking out each word in the document (or part of the document) as an indexing term.

Manual indexing is done most commonly for bibliographic databases and annotated content. In this age of proliferating electronic content, such as online textbooks, practice guidelines, and multimedia collections, manual indexing has become either too expensive or outright unfeasible for the quantity and diversity of material now available. Thus, there are increasing numbers of databases that are indexed only by automated means. Before covering these types of indexing in detail, let us first discuss controlled terminologies.

14.4.1 Controlled Terminologies

A controlled terminology contains a set of terms that can be applied to a task, such as indexing. When the terminology defines the terms, it is usually called a vocabulary. When it contains variants or synonyms of terms, it is also called a thesaurus. Before discussing actual terminologies, it is useful to define some terms. A concept is an idea or object that occurs in the world, such as the condition under which human blood pressure is elevated. A term is the actual string of one or more words that represent a concept, such as *Hypertension* or *High Blood Pressure*. One of these string forms is the preferred or canonical form, such as Hypertension in the present example. When one or more terms can represent a concept, the different terms are called synonyms.

A controlled terminology usually contains a list of terms that are the canonical representations of the concepts. If it is a thesaurus, it contains relationships between terms, which typically fall into three categories:

- Hierarchical–terms that are broader or narrower. The hierarchical organization not only provides an overview of the structure of a thesaurus but also can be used to enhance searching (e.g., MeSH tree explosions that add terms from an entire portion of the hierarchy to augment a search).
- Synonym–terms that are synonyms, allowing the indexer or searcher to express a concept in different words.
- Related–terms that are not synonymous or hierarchical but are somehow otherwise related. These usually remind the searcher of different but related terms that may enhance a search.

The MeSH terminology is used to manually index most of the databases produced by the NLM [23]. The latest version contains over 26,000 subject headings (the word MeSH uses for the canonical representation of its concepts). It also contains over 170,000 synonyms to those terms, which in MeSH jargon are called entry terms. In addition, MeSH contains the three types of relationships described in the previous paragraph:

- Hierarchical–MeSH is organized hierarchically into 16 trees, such as Diseases, Organisms, and Chemicals and Drugs.
- Synonym–MeSH contains a vast number of entry terms, which are synonyms of the headings.
- Related–terms that may be useful for searchers to add to their searches when appropriate are suggested for many headings.

The MeSH terminology files, their associated data, and their supporting documentation are available on the NLM's MeSH Web site (`http://www.nlm.nih.gov/mesh/`). There is also a browser that facilitates exploration of the terminology (`http://www.nlm.nih.gov/mesh/MBrowser.html`). Figure 14.2 shows a slice through the MeSH hierarchy for certain cardiovascular diseases.

There are features of MeSH designed to assist indexers in making documents more retrievable.

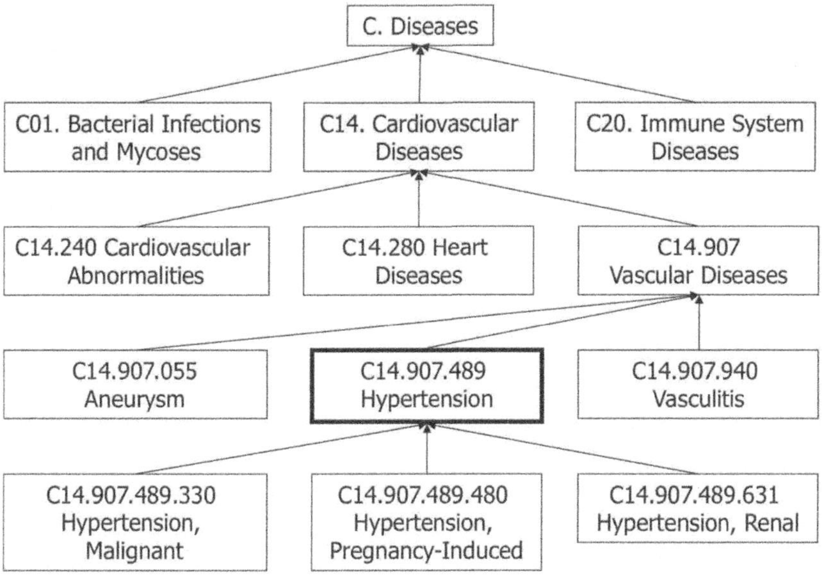

FIGURE 14.2: Portion of MeSH hierarchy for Cardiovascular Diseases. (Courtesy of NLM)

One of these is subheadings, which are qualifiers of subject headings that narrow the focus of a term. In Hypertension, for example, the focus of an article may be on the diagnosis, epidemiology, or treatment of the condition. Another feature of MeSH that helps retrieval is check tags. These are MeSH terms that represent certain facets of medical studies, such as age, gender, human or nonhuman, and type of grant support. Related to check tags are the geographical locations in the Z tree. Indexers must also include these, like check tags, since the location of a study (e.g., Oregon) must be indicated. Another feature gaining increasing importance for EBM and other purposes is the publication type, which describes the type of publication or the type of study. A searcher who wants a review of a topic may choose the publication type *Review* or *Review Literature*. Or, to find studies that provide the best evidence for a therapy, the publication type *Meta-Analysis, Randomized Controlled Trial,* or *Controlled Clinical Trial* would be used.

MeSH is not the only thesaurus used for indexing biomedical documents. A number of other thesauri are used to index non-NLM databases. CINAHL, for example, uses the CINAHL Subject Headings, which are based on MeSH but have additional domain-specific terms added. EMBASE has a terminology called EMTREE, which has many features similar to those of MeSH (`http://www.embase.com/info/helpfiles/emtree-tool/emtree-thesaurus`).

One problem with controlled terminologies, not limited to IR systems, is their proliferation. There is great need for linkage across these different terminologies. This was the primary motivation for the Unified Medical Language System (UMLS, `http://www.nlm.nih.gov/research/umls/`) Project, which was undertaken in the 1980s to address this problem [74]. There are three components of the UMLS Knowledge Sources: the Metathesaurus, the UMLS Semantic Network, and the Specialist Lexicon. The Metathesaurus component of the UMLS links parts or all of over 100 terminologies [13].

In the Metathesaurus, all terms that are conceptually the same are linked together as a concept. Each concept may have one or more terms, each of which represents an expression of the concept from a source terminology that is not just a simple lexical variant (i.e., differs only in word ending or order). Each term may consist of one or more strings, which represent all the lexical variants that are represented for that term in the source terminologies. One of each term's strings is designated as the preferred form, and the preferred string of the preferred term is known as the canonical form of the concept. There are rules of precedence for determining the canonical form, the main one being that the MeSH heading is used if one of the source terminologies for the concept is MeSH.

Each Metathesaurus concept has a single concept unique identifier (CUI). Each term has one term unique identifier (LUI), all of which are linked to the one (or more) CUIs with which they are associated. Likewise, each string has one string unique identifier (SUI), which likewise are linked to the LUIs in which they occur. In addition, each string has an atomic unique identifier (AUI) that represents information from each instance of the string in each vocabulary. Figure 14.3 depicts the English-language concepts, terms, and strings for the Metathesaurus concept atrial fibrillation. (Each string may occur in more than one vocabulary, in which case each would be an atom.) The canonical form of the concept and one of its terms is atrial fibrillation. Within both terms are several strings, which vary in word order and case.

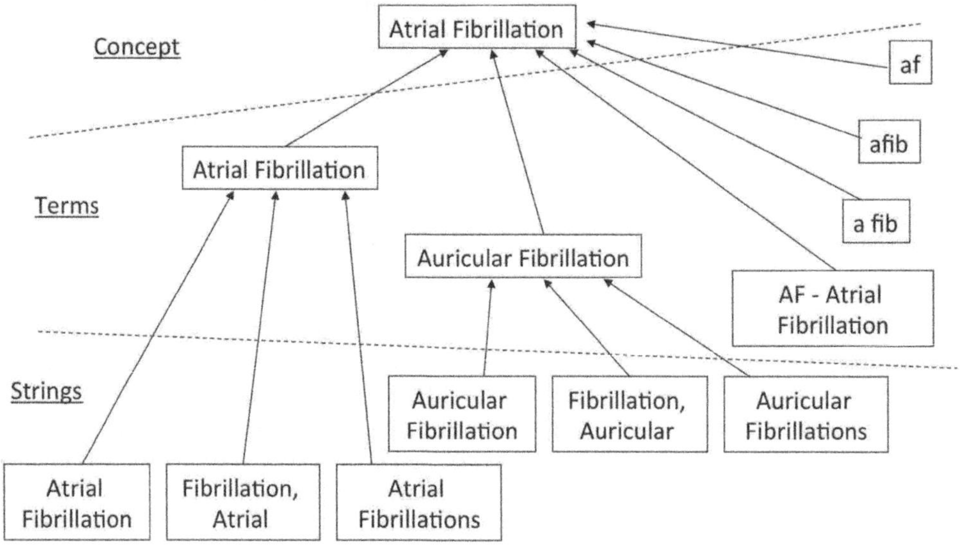

FIGURE 14.3: Unified Medical Language System Metathesaurus concept of atrial fibrillation. (Courtesy of NLM)

The Metathesaurus contains a wealth of additional information. In addition to the synonym relationships between concepts, terms, and strings described earlier, there are also nonsynonym relationships between concepts. There are a great many attributes for the concepts, terms, strings, and atoms, such as definitions, lexical types, and occurrence in various data sources. Also provided with the Metathesaurus is a word index that connects each word to all the strings it occurs in, along with its concept, term, string, and atomic identifiers.

14.4.2 Manual Indexing

Manual indexing is most commonly done for bibliographic and annotated content, although it is sometimes for other types of content as well. Manual indexing is usually done by means of a controlled terminology of terms and attributes. Most databases utilizing human indexing usually have a detailed protocol for assignment of indexing terms from the thesaurus. The MEDLINE database is no exception. The principles of MEDLINE indexing were laid out in the two-volume MEDLARS Indexing Manual [21]. Subsequent modifications have occurred with changes to MEDLINE, other databases, and MeSH over the years. The major concepts of the article, usually from two to five headings, are designed as main headings, and designated in the MEDLINE record by an asterisk. The indexer is also required to assign appropriate subheadings. Finally, the indexer must also assign check tags, geographical locations, and publication types. Although MEDLINE indexing is still manual, indexers are aided by a variety of electronic tools for selecting and assigning MeSH terms.

Few full-text resources are manually indexed. One type of indexing that commonly takes place with full-text resources, especially in the print world, is that performed for the index at the back of the book. However, this information is rarely used in IR systems; instead, most online textbooks rely on automated indexing (see below). One exception to this is MDConsult, which uses back-of-book indexes to point to specific sections in its online books.

Manual indexing of Web content is challenging. With billions of pages of content, manual indexing of more than a fraction of it is not feasible. On the other hand, the lack of a coherent index makes searching much more difficult, especially when specific resource types are being sought. A simple form of manual indexing of the Web takes place in the development of the Web catalogs and aggregations as described earlier. These catalogs contain not only explicit indexing about subjects and other attributes, but also implicit indexing about the quality of a given resource by the decision of whether to include it in the catalog.

Two major approaches to manual indexing have emerged on the Web, which are often complementary. The first approach, that of applying metadata to Web pages and sites, is exemplified by the Dublin Core Metadata Initiative (DCMI, `www.dublincore.org`) [125]. The second approach, to build directories of content, was popularized initially by the Yahoo! search engine (`www.yahoo.com`). A more open approach to building directories was taken up by the Open Directory Project (`www.dmoz.org`), which carries on the structuring of the directory and entry of content by volunteers across the world.

The goal of the DCMI has been to develop a set of standard data elements that creators of Web resources can use to apply metadata to their content. The DCMI was recently approved as a standard by the National Information Standards Organization (NISO) with the designation Z39.85. It is also a standard with the International Organization for Standards (ISO), ISO Standard 15836:2009. The specification has 15 defined elements:

- DC.title—name given to the resource
- DC.creator—person or organization primarily responsible for creating the intellectual content of the resource
- DC.subject—topic of the resource
- DC.description—a textual description of the content of the resource
- DC.publisher—entity responsible for making the resource available in its present form
- DC.date—date associated with the creation or availability of the resource
- DC.contributor—person or organization not specified in a creator element who has made a significant intellectual contribution to the resource, but whose contribution is secondary to any person or organization specified in a creator element
- DC.type—category of the resource
- DC.format—data format of the resource, used to identify the software and possibly hardware that might be needed to display or operate the resource
- DC.identifier—string or number used to uniquely identify the resource
- DC.source—information about a second resource from which the present resource is derived
- DC.language—language of the intellectual content of the resource
- DC.relation—identifier of a second resource and its relationship to the present resource

- DC.coverage—spatial or temporal characteristics of the intellectual content of the resource
- DC.rights—rights management statement, an identifier that links to a rights management statement, or an identifier that links to a service providing information about rights management for the resource

There have been some medical adaptations of the DCMI. The most developed of these is the Catalogue et Index des Sites Mèdicaux Francophones (CISMeF, `www.cismef.org`) [27]. A catalog of French-language health resources on the Web, CISMeF has used DCMI to catalog over 40,000 Web pages, including information resources (e.g., practice guidelines, consensus development conferences), organizations (e.g., hospitals, medical schools, pharmaceutical companies), and databases. The Subject field uses the French translation of MeSH but also includes the English translation. For Type, a list of common Web resources has been enumerated.

While Dublin Core Metadata was originally envisioned to be included in Hypertext Markup Language (HTML) Web pages, it became apparent that many non-HTML resources exist on the Web and that there are reasons to store metadata external to Web pages. For example, authors of Web pages might not be the best people to index pages or other entities might wish to add value by their own indexing of content. A standard for cataloging metadata is the Resource Description Framework (RDF) [1]. A framework for describing and interchanging metadata, RDF is usually expressed in Extensible Markup Language (XML), a standard for data interchange on the Web. RDF also forms the basis of what some call the future of the Web as a repository not only of content but also of knowledge, which is also referred to as the Semantic Web [1]. Dublin Core Metadata (or any type of metadata) can be represented in RDF.

Manual indexing has a number of limitations, the most significant of which is inconsistency. Funk and Reid [54] evaluated indexing inconsistency in MEDLINE by identifying 760 articles that had been indexed twice by the NLM. The most consistent indexing occurred with check tags and central concept headings, which were only indexed with a consistency of 61 to 75 percent. The least consistent indexing occurred with subheadings, especially those assigned to noncentral concept headings, which had a consistency of less than 35 percent. A repeat of this study in more recent times found comparable results. Manual indexing also takes time. While it may be feasible with the large resources the NLM has to index MEDLINE, it is probably impossible with the growing amount of content on Web sites and in other full-text resources. Indeed, the NLM has recognized the challenge of continuing to have to index the growing body of biomedical literature and is investigating automated and semiautomated means of doing so [7].

14.4.3 Automated Indexing

In automated indexing, the indexing is done by a computer. Although the mechanical running of the automated indexing process lacks cognitive input, considerable intellectual effort may have gone into development of the system for doing it, so this form of indexing still qualifies as an intellectual process. In this section, we will focus on the automated indexing used in operational IR systems, namely the indexing of documents by the words they contain.

Some might not think of extracting all the words in a document as "indexing," but from the standpoint of an IR system, words are descriptors of documents, just like human-assigned indexing terms. Most retrieval systems actually use a hybrid of human and word indexing, in that the human-assigned indexing terms become part of the document, which can then be searched by using the whole controlled term or individual words within it. Most MEDLINE implementations have always allowed the combination of searching on human indexing terms and on words in the title and abstract of the reference. With the development of full-text resources in the 1980s and 1990s, systems that allowed only word indexing began to emerge. This trend increased with the advent of the Web.

Word indexing is typically done by defining all consecutive alphanumeric sequences between white space (which consists of spaces, punctuation, carriage returns, and other non-alphanumeric characters) as words. Systems must take particular care to apply the same process to documents and the user's query, especially with characters such as hyphens and apostrophes. Many systems go beyond simple identification of words and attempt to assign weights to words that represent their importance in the document [107].

Many systems using word indexing employ processes to remove common words or conflate words to common forms. The former consists of filtering to remove *stop words*, which are common words that always occur with high frequency and are usually of little value in searching. The stop word list, also called a negative dictionary, varies in size from the seven words of the original MEDLARS stop list (and, an, by, from, of, the, with) to the list of 250 to 500 words more typically used. Examples of the latter are the 250-word list of van Rijsbergen, the 471-word list of Fox [48], and the PubMed stop list [3]. Conflation of words to common forms is done via *stemming*, the purpose of which is to ensure words with plurals and common suffixes (e.g., -ed, -ing, -er, -al) are always indexed by their stem form [51]. For example, the words cough, coughs, and coughing are all indexed via their stem cough. Both stop word remove and stemming reduce the size of indexing files and lead to more efficient query processing.

A commonly used approach for term weighting is *TF*IDF* weighting, which combines the inverse document frequency (IDF) and term frequency (TF). The *IDF* is the logarithm of the ratio of the total number of documents to the number of documents in which the term occurs. It is assigned once for each term in the database, and it correlates inversely with the frequency of the term in the entire database. The usual formula used is:

$$IDF(term) = log\frac{number\ of\ documents\ in\ database}{number\ of\ documents\ with\ term} + 1 \tag{14.1}$$

The TF is a measure of the frequency with which a term occurs in a given document and is assigned to each term in each document, with the usual formula:

$$TF(term, document) = frequency\ of\ term\ in\ document \tag{14.2}$$

In $TF*IDF$ weighting, the two terms are combined to form the indexing weight, $WEIGHT$:

$$WEIGHT(term, document) = TF(term, document) * IDF(term) \tag{14.3}$$

Experiments from the Text Retrieval Conference (TREC, `trec.nist.gov`) (see section 14.6), led to the discovery of two other term-weighting approaches that have yielded consistently improved results. The first of these was based on a statistical model known as Poisson distributions and has been more commonly called *BM*25 weighting [105]. This weighting scheme is an improved document normalization approach, yielding up to 50% improvement in mean average precision (MAP) in various TREC collections [104]. One version of TF for $BM25$ is:

$$BM25TF = \frac{(f_{td})(k_1+1)}{k_1(1-b) + k_1 b\frac{length\ of\ document}{average\ document\ length} + f_{td}} \tag{14.4}$$

f_{td}—frequency of terms in document

The variables k_1 and b are parameters set to values based on characteristics of the collection. Typical values for k_1 are between 1 and 2 and for b are between 0.6 and 0.75. A further simplification of this weighting often used is [104]:

$$BM25TF = \frac{(f_{td})}{0.5 + 1.5\frac{length\ of\ document}{average\ document\ length} + f_{td}} \tag{14.5}$$

f_{td}—frequency of terms in document

Okapi weighting has its theoretical foundations in probabilistic IR, to be described shortly. As such, its $TF{*}IDF$ weighting uses a "probabilistic" variant of IDF:

$$BM25IDF = log \frac{t_d - number\,of\,documents\,with\,term + 0.5}{number\,of\,documents\,with\,term + 0.5} \tag{14.6}$$

t_d—total number of documents

The probabilistic model has also led to the newest theoretical approach to term weighting, known as language modeling, which will be described later in this section. Other techniques for term weighting have achieved varying amounts of success. One approach aimed to capture semantic equivalence of words in a document collection. Called latent semantic indexing (LSI), it uses a mathematically complex technique called singular-value decomposition (SVD) [31]. In LSI, an initial two-dimensional matrix of terms and documents is created, with the terms in one dimension and the documents in the other. The SVD process creates three intermediate matrices, the two most important being the mapping of the terms into an intermediate value, which can be thought to represent an intermediate measure of a term's semantics, and the mapping of this semantic value into the document. The number of intermediate values can be kept small, which allows the mapping of a large number of terms into a modest number of semantic classes or dimensions (i.e., several hundred). The result is that terms with similar semantic distributions (i.e., distributions that co-occur in similar document contexts) are mapped into the same dimension. Thus, even if a term does not co-occur with another, if it occurs in similar types of documents it will be likely to have similar semantics. While the optimal number of dimensions is not known, it has been shown for several of the small standard test collections that a few hundred is sufficient [31]. Some early evaluation studies showed small performance enhancements for LSI with small document collections [31, 73], but these benefits were not realized with larger collections such as TREC [36]. A better use for this technique may be with the automated discovery of synonymy [83].

Another approach to term weighting has been to employ probability theory. This approach is not necessarily at odds with the vector-space model, and in fact its weighting approaches can be incorporated into the vector-space model. The theory underlying probabilistic IR is a model to give more weight to terms likely to occur in relevant documents and unlikely to occur in nonrelevant documents. It is based on Bayes' theorem, a common probability measure that indicates likelihood of an event based on a prior situation and new data. Probabilistic IR is predominantly a relevance feedback technique, since some relevance information about the terms in documents is required. However, it did not show improvement over vector modification techniques in six older test collections [108]. In the TREC experiments, as noted earlier, some variants on the probabilistic approach were shown to perform better than vector-space relevance feedback with the addition of query expansion [15, 24, 81, 104, 124].

One modification to probabilistic IR was the inference model of Turtle and Croft [119], where documents were ranked based on how likely they are to infer belief they are relevant to the user's query. This method was also not necessarily incompatible with the vector-space model, and in some ways just provided a different perspective on the IR problem. One advantage of the inference model was the ability to combine many types of "evidence" that a document should be viewed by the user, such as queries with natural language and Boolean operators, as well as other attributes, such as citation of other documents. Combining some linguistic techniques, described later in this chapter, with slight modifications of TF*IDF weighting, passage retrieval, and query expansion, this approach performed consistently well in the TREC experiments [15].

A more recent application of probabilistic IR has been the use of language modeling [70]. This approach was adapted from other computer tasks, such as speech recognition and machine translation, where probabilistic principles are used to convert acoustic signals into words and words from one language to another, respectively. A key aspect of the language modeling approach is "smoothing" of the probabilities away from a purely deterministic approach of a term being present or absent in a document in a binary fashion. Theoretically, the language modeling approach measures the probability of a query term given a relevant document.

Language modeling was introduced to the IR community by Ponte and Croft [101], who showed modest performance gains with TREC collections. A variety of enhancements were subsequently found to improve retrieval performance further [11]. Zhai and Lafferty [132] investigated smoothing models and derived a number of new conclusions about this approach to IR. Subsequent work processing text into topic signatures based on mapping to Unified Medical Language System (UMLS) Metathesaurus terms and using those instead of words found 10–20% performance gains with ad hoc retrieval data from the TREC Genomics Track [134].

Language models also allow the measurement of query "clarity," which is defined as a measure of the deviation between in the query and document language models from the general collection model [26]. Cronen-Townsend et al. found that query clarity was a good predictor of retrieval results from topics in the TREC ad hoc test collections, although application of this technique to real user queries from the TREC Interactive Track failed to uphold this association [118].

Another automated approach to pre-computing metadata about documents involves the use of link-based methods, which is best known through its use by the Google search engine (`www.google.com`). This approach gives weight to pages based on how often they are cited by other pages. The PageRank (PR) algorithm is mathematically complex, but can be viewed as giving more weight to a Web page based on the number of other pages that link to it [14]. Thus, the home page of the NLM or a major medical journal is likely to have a very high PR, whereas a more obscure page will have a lower PR. Google has also had to develop new computer architectures and algorithms to maintain pace with indexing the Web, leading to a new paradigm for such large-scale processing called MapReduce [29, 89].

In a simple description, *PR* can be viewed as giving more weight to a Web page based on the number of other pages that link to it. Thus, the home page of the NLM or JAMA is likely to have a very high *PR*, whereas a more obscure page will have a lower *PR*. The *PR* algorithm was developed by Brin and Page [14]. To calculate it for a given page *A*, it is assumed that there is a series of pages $T_1 \ldots T_n$ having links to *A*. There is another function C(A) that is the count of the number links going out of page *A*. There is also a "damping factor" d that is set between 0 and 1, by default at 0.85. Then *PR* is calculated for *A* as:

$$PR(A) = (1-d) + d\left(\frac{PR(T_1)}{C(T_1)} + \ldots + \frac{PR(T_n)}{C(T_n)}\right) \tag{14.7}$$

The algorithm begins by assigning every page a baseline value (such as the damping factor) and then iterates on a periodic basis. When implemented efficiently on a moderately-powered workstation, *PR* can be calculated for a large collection of Web pages.

It is often stated simplistically that *PR* is a form of measuring the in-degree, or the number of links, that point to a page. In reality, *PR* is more complex, giving added weight to pages that are pointed to by those that themselves have higher *PR*. Fortunato et al. [47] assessed how closely *PR* is approximated by simple in-degree, finding that the approximation was relatively accurate, allowing Web content creators to estimate their *PR* of their content by knowing the in-degree to their pages.

General-purpose search engines such as Google and Microsoft Bing (`www.bing.com`) use word-based approaches and variants of the PageRank algorithm for indexing. They amass the content in their search systems by "crawling" the Web, collecting and indexing every object they find on the Web. This includes not only HTML pages, but other files as well, including Microsoft Word, Portable Document Format (PDF), and images.

Word indexing has a number of limitations, including:

- Synonymy—different words may have the same meaning, such as high and elevated. This problem may extend to the level of phrases with no words in common, such as the synonyms *hypertension* and *high blood pressure*.

- Polysemy—the same word may have different meanings or senses. For example, the word *lead* can refer to an element or to a part of an electrocardiogram machine.
- Content—words in a document may not reflect its focus. For example, an article describing *hypertension* may make mention in passing to other concepts, such as *congestive heart failure* (CHF) that are not the focus of the article.
- Contex—words take on meaning based on other words around them. For example, the relatively common words *high, blood*, and *pressure*, take on added meaning when occurring together in the phrase *high blood pressure*.
- Morphology—words can have suffixes that do not change the underlying meaning, such as indicators of plurals, various participles, adjectival forms of nouns, and nominalized forms of adjectives.
- Granularity—queries and documents may describe concepts at different levels of a hierarchy. For example, a user might query for *antibiotics* in the treatment of a specific infection, but the documents might describe specific *antibiotics* themselves, such as *penicillin*.

A second purpose of indexing is to build structures so that computer programs can rapidly ascertain which documents use which indexing terms. Whether indexing is by terms in a thesaurus or words, IR systems are feasible only if they can rapidly process a user's query. A timely sequential search over an indexed text database is infeasible if not impossible for any large document collection. In IR, the usual approach involves the use of inverted files, where the terms are "inverted" to point to all the documents in which they occur. The algorithms for building and maintaining these structures have been used for decades [52]. An inverted file group for a sample document collection as it would be stored on a computer disk is shown in Figure 14.4. The first file is the *dictionary file*, which contains each indexing term along with a number representing how many documents contain

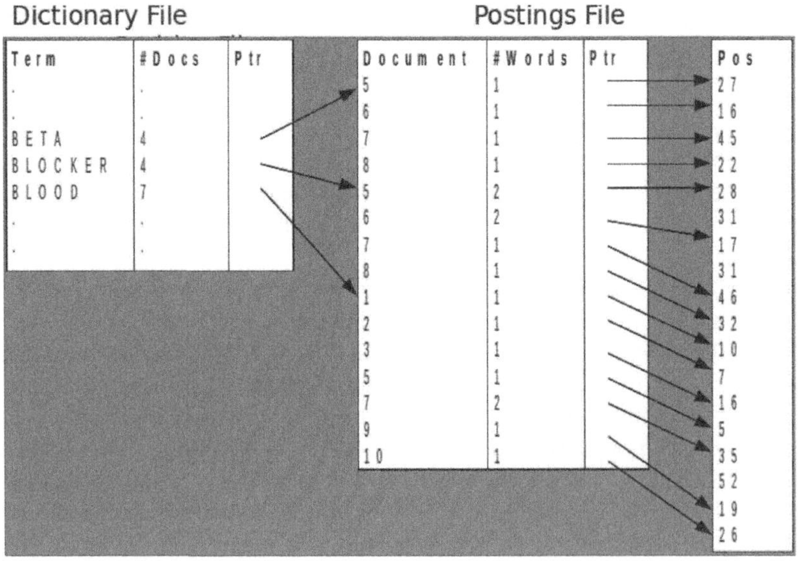

FIGURE 14.4: Inverted file structure used by information retrieval systems. Each term in the document collection occurs in the Dictionary File, which has a pointer to the Postings File, which has a pointer to each position of the word in the document in the Postings File. (Copyright, William Hersh)

the term and a pointer to the postings file. The *postings file* consists of a sequential list of all the documents that contain the indexing term. If it is desired to keep positional information for the indexing term (to allow proximity searching), then the postings file will also contain a pointer to the *position file*, which sequentially lists the positions of each indexing term in the document. The structure of the position file depends on what positional information is actually kept. The simplest position file contains just the word position within the document, while more complex files may contain the not only the word number, but also the sentence and paragraph number within the document.

The final component of inverted files is a mechanism for rapid lookup of terms in the dictionary file. This is typically done with a B-tree, which is a disk-based method for minimizing the number of disk accesses required to find a term in an index, resulting in fast lookup. The B-tree is very commonly used for keys in a DBMS. Another method for fast-term lookup is hashing [52].

Of course, with the need to process millions of queries each minute, just having an efficient file and look-up structure is not enough. Systems must be distributed across many servers in disparate geographic locations. Although the details of its approach are proprietary, Google has published some on how it maintains its subsecond response time to queries from around the globe [8, 29].

14.5 Retrieval

There are two broad approaches to retrieval. Exact-match searching allows the user precise control over the items retrieved. Partial-match searching, on the other hand, recognizes the inexact nature of both indexing and retrieval, and instead attempts to return the user content ranked by how close it comes to the user's query. After general explanations of these approaches, we will describe actual systems that access the different types of biomedical content.

14.5.1 Exact-Match Retrieval

In exact-match searching, the IR system gives the user all documents that exactly match the criteria specified in the search statement(s). Since the Boolean operators AND, OR, and NOT are usually required to create a manageable set of documents, this type of searching is often called Boolean searching. Furthermore, since the user typically builds sets of documents that are manipulated with the Boolean operators, this approach is also called set-based searching. Most of the early operational IR systems in the 1950s through the 1970s used the exact-match approach, even though Salton and McGill was developing the partial-match approach in research systems during that time [110]. In modern times, exact-match searching tends to be associated with retrieval from bibliographic and annotated databases, while the partial-match approach tends to be used with full-text searching.

Typically the first step in exact-match retrieval is to select terms to build sets. Other attributes, such as the author name, publication type, or gene identifier (in the secondary source identifier field of MEDLINE), may be selected to build sets as well. Once the search term(s) and attribute(s) have been selected, they are combined with the Boolean operators. The Boolean AND operator is typically used to narrow a retrieval set to contain only documents with two or more concepts. The Boolean OR operator is usually used when there is more than one way to express a concept. The Boolean NOT operator is often employed as a subtraction operator that must be applied to another set. Some systems more accurately call this the ANDNOT operator.

Some retrieval systems allow terms in searches to be expanded by using the wild-card character, which adds all words to the search that begin with the letters up until the wild-card character. This approach is also called truncation. Unfortunately, there is no standard approach to using wild-card characters, so syntax for them varies from system to system. PubMed, for example, allows a single asterisk at the end of a word to signify a wild-card character. Thus, the query word can* will lead to the words cancer and Candid, among others, being added to the search.

14.5.2 Partial-Match Retrieval

Although partial-match searching was conceptualized very early, it did not see widespread use in IR systems until the advent of Web search engines in the 1990s. This is most likely because exact-match searching tends to be preferred by "power users" whereas partial-match searching is preferred by novice searchers. Whereas exact-match searching requires an understanding of Boolean operators and (often) the underlying structure of databases (e.g., the many fields in MEDLINE), partial-match searching allows a user to simply enter a few terms and start retrieving documents.

The development of partial-match searching is usually attributed to Salton and McGill [110], who pioneered the approach in the 1960s. Although partial-match searching does not exclude the use of non-term attributes of documents, and for that matter does not even exclude the use of Boolean operators (e.g., [109]), the most common use of this type of searching is with a query of a small number of words, also known as a natural language query. Because Salton's approach was based on vector mathematics, it is also referred to as the vector-space model of IR. In the partial-match approach, documents are typically ranked by their closeness of fit to the query. That is, documents containing more query terms will likely be ranked higher, since those with more query terms will in general be more likely to be relevant to the user. As a result this process is called relevance ranking. The entire approach has also been called lexical-statistical retrieval.

The most common approach to document ranking in partial-match searching is to give each a score based on the sum of the weights of terms common to the document and query. Terms in documents typically derive their weight from the TF*IDF calculation described above. Terms in queries are typically given a weight of one if the term is present and zero if it is absent. The following formula can then be used to calculate the document weight across all query terms:

$$Document\ weight = \sum_{all\ query\ terms} WT_q * WT_d \tag{14.8}$$

WT_q—Weight of terms in query
WT_d—Weight of terms in document

This may be thought of as a giant OR of all query terms, with sorting of the matching documents by weight. The usual approach is for the system to then perform the same stop word removal and stemming of the query that was done in the indexing process. (The equivalent stemming operations must be performed on documents and queries so that complementary word stems will match.)

One problem with TF*IDF weighting is that longer documents accumulate more weight in queries simply because they have more words. As such, some approaches "normalize" the weight of a document. The most common approach is cosine normalization:

$$Document\ weight = \frac{\sum_{all\ query\ terms} WT_q * WT_d}{\sqrt{(\sum_{all\ query\ terms} WT_q^2) * (\sum_{all\ document\ terms} WT_q^2)}} \tag{14.9}$$

WT_q—Weight of terms in query
WT_d—Weight of terms in document

A variety of other variations to the basic partial-matching retrieval approach have been developed. One important addition is *relevance feedback*, a feature allowed by the partial-match approach, permits new documents to be added to the output based on their similarity to those deemed relevant by the user. This approach also allows reweighting of relevant documents already retrieved to higher positions on the output list. The most common approach is the modified Rocchio equation employed by Buckley et al. [17]. In this equation, each term in the query is reweighted by adding value for the term occurring in relevant documents and subtracting value for the term occurring in nonrelevant documents. There are three parameters, α, β, *and* γ, which add relative value to the original weight, the added weight from relevant documents, and the subtracted weight from nonrelevant documents, respectively. In this approach, the query is usually expanded by adding a specified number of query terms (from none to several thousand) from relevant documents to the query. Each query term takes on a new value based on the following formula:

$$\begin{aligned}
&New\ query\ weight = \\
&\alpha * Original\ query\ weight \\
&+\beta * \frac{1}{Number\ of\ relevant\ documents} * \sum_{All\ relevant\ documents} Weight\ in\ document \\
&-\gamma * \frac{1}{Number\ of\ Nonrelevant\ documents} * \sum_{All\ non-relevant\ documents} Weight\ in\ document \qquad (14.10)
\end{aligned}$$

When the parameters, α, β, *and* γ, are set to one, this formula simplifies to:

$$\begin{aligned}
&New\ query\ weight = \\
&Original\ query\ weight \\
&+Average\ term\ weight\ in\ relevant\ documents \\
&-Average\ term\ weight\ in\ nonrelevant\ documents \qquad (14.11)
\end{aligned}$$

A number of IR systems offer a variant of relevance feedback that finds similar documents to a specified one. PubMed allows the user to obtain "related articles" from any given one in an approach similar to relevance feedback but which uses a different algorithm [127]. A number of Web search engines allow users to similarly obtain related articles from a specified Web page.

One enduring successful retrieval technique has been *query expansion*, where the relevance feedback technique is used without relevance information. Instead, a certain number of top-ranking documents are assumed to be relevant and the relevance feedback approach is applied. Query expansion techniques have been shown to be among the most consistent methods to improve performance in TREC. In TREC-3, Buckley et al. [18] used the Rocchio formula with parameters 8, 8, and 0 (which perform less reweighting for expansion terms than in the relevance feedback experiments cited earlier) along with the addition of the top 500 terms and 10 phrases to achieve a 20% performance gain. Others in TREC have also shown benefit with this approach [42, 15, 18, 78, 104]. Additional work by Mitra et al. [95] has shown that use of manually created Boolean queries, passage-based proximity constraints (i.e., Boolean constraints must occur within 50–100 words), and term co-occurrences (i.e., documents are given more weight when query terms co-occur) improves MAP performance further still. The value of query expansion (and other approaches) has been verified by Buckley [16], who has constructed a table comparing different features of TREC systems with each year's ad hoc retrieval collection (p. 311).

Whether using exact-match or partial-match approaches, efficiency in merging sets of documents or sorting individual documents based on weighting is achieved through the use of inverted files described previously. The indexing terms can be rapidly found in the dictionary file, with document collections merged in Boolean operations and/or weighted in partial-matching operations in the postings file.

14.5.3 Retrieval Systems

There are many different retrieval interfaces, with some of the features reflecting the content or structure of the underlying database. As noted above, PubMed is the system at NLM that searches

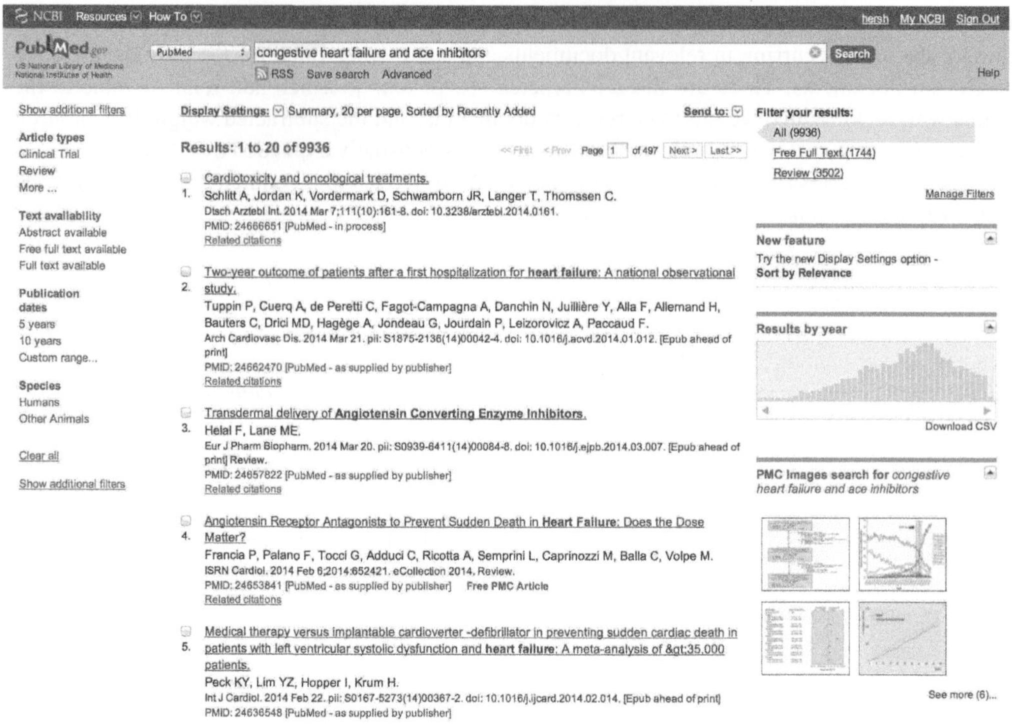

FIGURE 14.5: Screen shot of PubMed search. (Courtesy of NLM)

MEDLINE and other bibliographic databases. Although presenting the user with a simple text box, PubMed does a great deal of processing of the user's input to identify MeSH terms, author names, common phrases, and journal names (described in the online help system of PubMed). In this automatic term mapping, the system attempts to map user input, in succession, to MeSH terms, journals names, common phrases, and authors. Remaining text that PubMed cannot map is searched as text words (i.e., words that occur in any of the MEDLINE fields). Figure 14.5 shows the PubMed search results screen. The system allows a basic search and then provides access to a wealth of features around the results. The left-hand side of the screen allows setting of limits, such as to study type (e.g., randomized controlled trial), species (e.g., human or others), and age group (e.g., age >65 years). The right-hand side provides filters for free full-text article and reviews, as well as other features that include the details of the search. As in most bibliographic systems, users can search PubMed by building search sets and then combining them with Boolean operators to tailor the search. This is called the "advanced search" or "search builder" of PubMed, as shown in Figure 14.6. PubMed also has a specialized query interface for clinicians seeking the best clinical evidence (called Clinical Queries) as well as several "apps" that allow access via mobile devices (e.g., iOS or Android).

Another recent addition to PubMed is the ability to sort search results by relevance ranking rather than the long-standing default reverse-chronological ordering. Choosing this option leads to MEDLINE records being sorted based on a formula that includes IDF, TF, a measure for which field in which the word appears (more for title and abstract), and a measure of recency of publication [4].

As noted already, a great number of biomedical journals use the Highwire system for online access to their full text. The Highwire system provides a retrieval interface that searches over the complete online contents for a given journal. Users can search for authors, words limited to the title and abstract, words in the entire article, and within a date range. The interface also allows searching

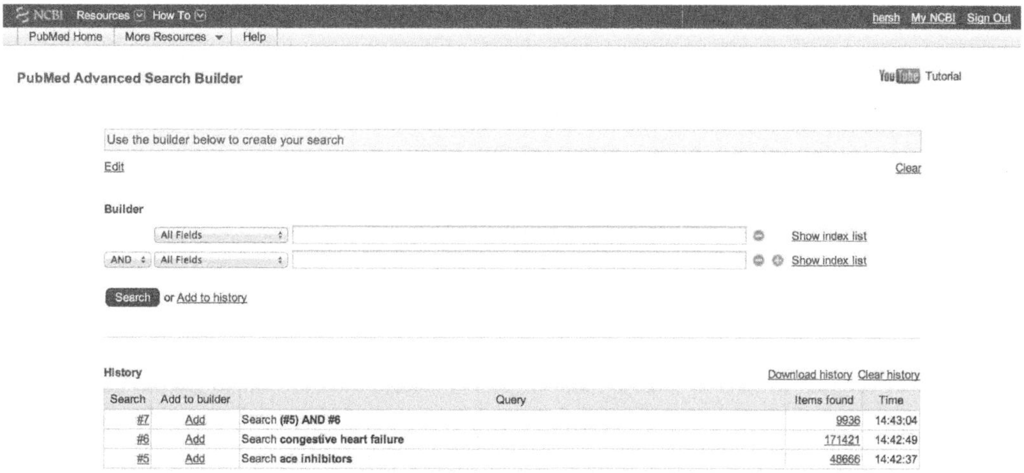

FIGURE 14.6: Screen shot of advanced search interface of PubMed. (Courtesy of NLM)

by citation by entering volume number and page as well as searching over the entire collection of journals that use Highwire. Users can browse through specific issues as well as collected resources.

Once an article has been found, a wealth of additional features is available. First, the article is presented both in HTML and PDF form, with the latter providing a more readable and printable version. Links are also provided to related articles from the journal as well as the PubMed reference and its related articles. Also linked are all articles in the journal that cited this one, and the site can be configured to set up a notification email when new articles cite the item selected. Finally, the Highwire software provides for "Rapid Responses," which are online letters to the editor. The online format allows a much larger number of responses than could be printed in the paper version of the journal. Other journal publishers use comparable approaches.

A growing number of search engines allow searching over many resources. The general search engines Google, Microsoft Bing, and others allow retrieval of any types of documents they index via their Web-crawling activities. Other search engines allow searching over aggregations of various sources, such as NLM's GQuery (`https://www.ncbi.nlm.nih.gov/gquery/gquery.fcgi`), which allows searching over all NLM databases and other resources in one simple interface.

14.6 Evaluation

There has been a great deal of research over the years devoted to the evaluation of IR systems. As with many areas of research, there is a controversy as to which approaches to evaluation best provide results that can assess searching in the systems they are using. Many frameworks have been developed to put the results in context. One of those frameworks organized evaluation around six questions that someone advocating the use of IR systems might ask [68]:

1. Was the system used?
2. For what was the system used?
3. Were the users satisfied?

4. How well did they use the system?

5. What factors were associated with successful or unsuccessful use of the system?

6. Did the system have an impact?

A simpler means for organizing the results of evaluation, however, groups approaches and studies into those which are system-oriented, i.e., the focus of the evaluation is on the IR system, and those which are user-oriented, i.e., the focus is on the user.

14.6.1 System-Oriented Evaluation

There are many ways to evaluate the performance of IR systems, the most widely used of which are the relevance-based measures of recall and precision. These measures quantify the number of relevant documents retrieved by the user from the database and in his or her search. Recall is the proportion of relevant documents retrieved from the database:

$$Recall = \frac{number\ of\ retrieved\ and\ relevant\ documents}{number\ of\ relevant\ documents\ in\ database} \tag{14.12}$$

In other words, recall answers the question, for a given search, what fraction of all the relevant documents have been obtained from the database?

One problem with Equation (14.5) is that the denominator implies that the total number of relevant documents for a query is known. For all but the smallest of databases, however, it is unlikely, perhaps even impossible, for one to succeed in identifying all relevant documents in a database. Thus, most studies use the measure of relative recall, where the denominator is redefined to represent the number of relevant documents identified by multiple searches on the query topic.

Precision is the proportion of relevant documents retrieved in the search:

$$Precision = \frac{number\ of\ retrieval\ and\ relevant\ documents}{number\ of\ documents\ retrieved} \tag{14.13}$$

This measure answers the question, for a search, what fraction of the retrieved documents are relevant?

One problem that arises when one is comparing systems that use ranking versus those that do not is that nonranking systems, typically using Boolean searching, tend to retrieve a fixed set of documents and as a result have fixed points of recall and precision. Systems with relevance ranking, on the other hand, have different values of recall and precision depending on the size of the retrieval set the system (or the user) has chosen to show. Often we seek to create an aggregate statistic that combines recall and precision. Probably the most common approach in evaluative studies is the mean average precision (MAP), where precision is measured at every point at which a relevant document is obtained, and the MAP measure is found by averaging these points for the whole query.

A good deal of evaluation in IR is done via challenge evaluations, where a common IR task is defined and a test collection of documents, topics, and relevance judgments are developed. The relevance judgments define which documents are relevant for each topic in the task, allowing different researchers to compare their systems with others on the same task and improve them. The longest running and best-known challenge evaluation in IR is the Text Retrieval Conference (TREC, `trec.nist.gov`), which is organized by the U.S. National Institute for Standards and Technology (NIST, `www.nist.gov`). Started in 1992, TREC has provided a testbed for evaluation and a forum for presentation of results. TREC is organized as an annual event at which the tasks are specified and queries and documents are provided to participants. Participating groups submit "runs" of their systems to NIST, which calculates the appropriate performance measure(s). TREC is organized into tracks geared to specific interests. A book summarizing the first decade of TREC grouped the tracks into general IR tasks [122]:

- Static text—ad hoc
- Streamed text—routing, filtering
- Human in the loop—interactive
- Beyond English (cross-lingual)—Spanish, Chinese, and others
- Beyond text—optical character recognition (OCR), speech, video
- Web searching—very large corpus
- Answers, not documents—question-answering
- Domain-specific—genomics, legal

While TREC has mostly focused on general-subject domains, there have been a couple of tracks that have focused on the biomedical domain. The first track to do so was the Genomics Track, which focused on the retrieval of articles as well as question-answering in this domain [64]. A second track to do focused on retrieval from medical records, with a task devoted to identifying patients who might be candidates for clinical studies based on criteria to be discerned from their medical records [123].

The TREC Genomics Track initially focused on improving MEDLINE retrieval. The ad hoc retrieval task modeled the situation of a user with an information need using an IR system to access the biomedical scientific literature. The document collection was based on a ten-year subset of MEDLINE. The rationale for using MEDLINE was that despite being in an era of readily available full-text journals (usually requiring a subscription), many users still entered the biomedical literature through searching MEDLINE. As such, there were still strong motivations to improve the effectiveness of searching MEDLINE.

The MEDLINE subset consisted of 10 years of completed citations from the database inclusive from 1994 to 2003. This provided a total of 4,591,008 records, which was about one-third of the full MEDLINE database. The data included all of the PubMed fields identified in the MEDLINE Baseline record. The size of the file uncompressed was about 9.5 gigabytes. In this subset, there were 1,209,243 (26.3%) records without abstracts.

Topics for the ad hoc retrieval task were based on information needs collected from real biologists. For both the 2004 and 2005 tracks, the primary measure of performance was MAP. Research groups were also required to classify their runs into one of three categories:

- Automatic—no manual intervention in building queries
- Manual—manual construction of queries but no further human interaction
- Interactive—completely interactive construction of queries and further interaction with system output

In the 2004 track, the best results were obtained by a combination of Okapi weighting (BM25 for term frequency but with standard inverse document frequency), Porter stemming, expansion of symbols by LocusLink and MeSH records, query expansion, and use of all three fields of the topic (title, need, and context) [53]. These achieved a MAP of 0.4075. When the language modeling technique of Dirichlet-Prior smoothing was added, an even higher MAP of 0.4264 was obtained. Another group achieved high-ranking results with a combination of approaches that included Okapi weighting, query expansion, and various forms of domain-specific query expansion (including expansion of lexical variants as well as acronym, gene, and protein name synonyms) [19]. Approaches that attempted to map to controlled vocabulary terms did not fare as well [6, 97, 112]. As always in

TREC, many groups tried a variety of approaches, beneficial or otherwise, but usually without comparing common baseline or running exhaustive experiments, making it difficult to discern exactly what techniques provided benefit.

Somewhat similar results were obtained in the 2005 track. As with 2004, the basic Okapi with good parameters gives good baseline performance for a number of groups. Manual synonym expansion of queries gave the highest MAP of 0.302 [72], although automated query expansion did not fare as well [2, 5]. Relevance feedback was found to be beneficial, but worked best without term expansion [133].

Follow-up research with the TREC Genomics Track ad hoc retrieval test collection has yielded a variety of findings. One study assessed word tokenization, stemming, and stop word removal, finding that varying strategies for the first resulted in substantial performance impact while changes in the latter two had minimal impact. Tokenization in genomics text can be challenging due to the use of a wide variety of symbols, including numbers, hyphens, super- and subscripts, and characters in non-English languages (e.g., Greek) [77].

Another TREC track focused on the biomedical domain was introduced in 2011 and run again in 2012, the TREC Medical Records Track [123]. The use case for the track TREC Medical Records Track was identifying patients from a collection of medical records who might be candidates for clinical studies. This is a real-world task for which automated retrieval systems could greatly aid in ability to carry out clinical research, quality measurement and improvement, or other "secondary uses" of clinical data [106]. The metric used to measure systems employed was inferred normalized distributed cumulative gain (infNDCG), which takes into account some other factors, such as incomplete judgment of all documents retrieval by all research groups.

The data for the track was a corpus of de-identified medical records developed by the University of Pittsburgh Medical Center. Records containing data, text, and ICD-9 codes are grouped by "visits" or patient encounters with the health system. (Due to the de-identification process, it was impossible to know whether one or more visits might emanate from the same patient.) There were 93,551 documents mapped into 17,264 visits.

A number of research groups used a variety of techniques, such as synonym and query expansion, machine learning algorithms, and matching against ICD-9 codes, but still had results that were not better than manually constructed queries employed by groups from NLM [32] or OHSU [10] (although the NLM system had a number of advanced features, such as document field searching [75]). Although the performance of systems in the track was "good" from an IR standpoint, they also showed that identification of patient cohorts would be a challenging task even for automated systems. Some of the automated features that had variable success included document section focusing, and term expansion, term normalization (mapping into controlled terms).

A number of approaches have been found to achieve modest improvement in results using data from this track. These include:

- Query expansion of normalized terms [103] and related terms [20, 79, 87]
- Detection of negation in records [88]
- Use of machine learning algorithms for ranking output [88, 135]

A failure analysis over the data from the 2011 track demonstrated why there are still many challenges that need to be overcome [37]. This analysis found a number of reasons why visits frequently retrieved were not relevant:

- Notes contain very similar term confused with topic
- Topic symptom/condition/procedure done in the past
- Most, but not all, criteria present

- All criteria present but not in the time/sequence specified by the topic description
- Topic terms mentioned as future possibility
- Topic terms not present–can't determine why record was captured
- Irrelevant reference in record to topic terms
- Topic terms denied or ruled out

The analysis also found reasons why visits rarely retrieval were actually relevant:

- Topic terms present in record but overlooked in search
- Visit notes used a synonym for topic terms
- Topic terms not named and must be derived
- Topic terms present in diagnosis list but not visit notes

Some researchers have criticized or noted the limitations of relevance-based measures. While no one denies that users want systems to retrieve relevant articles, it is not clear that the quantity of relevant documents retrieved is the complete measure of how well a system performs [115, 58]. Hersh [65] has noted that clinical users are unlikely to be concerned about these measures when they simply seek an answer to a clinical question and are able to do so no matter how many other relevant documents they miss (lowering recall) or how many nonrelevant ones they retrieve (lowering precision).

What alternatives to relevance-based measures can be used for determining performance of individual searches? Harter admits that if measures using a more situational view of relevance cannot be developed for assessing user interaction, then recall and precision may be the only alternatives. Some alternatives have focused on users being able to perform various information tasks with IR systems, such as finding answers to questions [38, 96, 61, 128, 63]. For several years, TREC featured an Interactive Track that had participants carry out user experiments with the same documents and queries [62]. Evaluations focusing on user-oriented evaluation of biomedical IR will be described in the next section.

14.6.2 User-Oriented Evaluation

A number of user-oriented evaluations have been performed over the years looking at users of biomedical information. Most of these studies have focused on clinicians.

One of the original studies measuring searching performance in clinical settings was performed by Haynes et al. [59]. This study also compared the capabilities of librarian and clinician searchers. In this study, 78 searches were randomly chosen for replication by both a clinician experienced in searching and a medical librarian. During this study, each original ("novice") user had been required to enter a brief statement of information need before entering the search program. This statement was given to the experienced clinician and librarian for searching on MEDLINE. All the retrievals for each search were given to a subject domain expert, blinded with respect to which searcher retrieved which reference. Recall and precision were calculated for each query and averaged. The results showed that the experienced clinicians and librarians achieved comparable recall in the range of 50%, although the librarians had better precision. The novice clinician searchers had lower recall and precision than either of the other groups. This study also assessed user satisfaction of the novice searchers, who despite their recall and precision results said that they were satisfied with their search outcomes. The investigators did not assess whether the novices obtained enough relevant articles to answer their questions, or whether they would have found additional value with the ones that were missed.

A follow-up study yielded some additional insights about the searchers [93]. As was noted, different searchers tended to use different strategies on a given topic. The different approaches replicated a finding known from other searching studies in the past, namely, the lack of overlap across searchers of overall retrieved citations as well as relevant ones. Thus, even though the novice searchers had lower recall, they did obtain a great many relevant citations not retrieved by the two expert searchers. Furthermore, fewer than 4 percent of all the relevant citations were retrieved by all three searchers. Despite the widely divergent search strategies and retrieval sets, overall recall and precision were quite similar among the three classes of users.

Recognizing the limitations of recall and precision for evaluating clinical users of IR systems, Hersh and co-workers [67] have carried out a number of studies assessing the ability of systems to help students and clinicians answer clinical questions. The rationale for these studies is that the usual goal of using an IR system is to find an answer to a question. While the user must obviously find relevant documents to answer that question, the quantity of such documents is less important than whether the question is successfully answered. In fact, recall and precision can be placed among the many factors that may be associated with ability to complete the task successfully.

The first study by this group using the task-oriented approach compared Boolean versus natural language searching in the textbook *Scientific American Medicine* [61]. Thirteen medical students were asked to answer 10 short-answer questions and rate their confidence in their answers. The students were then randomized to one or the other interface and asked to search on the five questions for which they had rated confidence the lowest. The study showed that both groups had low correct rates before searching (average 1.7 correct out of 10) but were mostly able to answer the questions with searching (average 4.0 out of 5). There was no difference in ability to answer questions with one interface or the other. Most answers were found on the first search to the textbook. For the questions that were incorrectly answered, the document with the correct answer was actually retrieved by the user two-thirds of the time and viewed more than half the time.

Another study compared Boolean and natural language searching of MEDLINE with two commercial products, CD Plus (now Ovid) and KF [63]. These systems represented the ends of the spectrum in terms of using Boolean searching on human-indexed thesaurus terms (Ovid) versus natural language searching on words in the title, abstract, and indexing terms (KF). Sixteen medical students were recruited and randomized to one of the two systems and given three yes/no clinical questions to answer. The students were able to use each system successfully, answering 37.5 percent correctly before searching and 85.4 percent correctly after searching. There were no significant differences between the systems in time taken, relevant articles retrieved, or user satisfaction. This study demonstrated that both types of systems can be used equally well with minimal training.

A more comprehensive study looked at MEDLINE searching by medical and nurse practitioner (NP) students to answer clinical questions. A total of 66 medical and NP students searched five questions each [67]. This study used a multiple-choice format for answering questions that also included a judgment about the evidence for the answer. Subjects were asked to choose from one of three answers:

- Yes, with adequate evidence.
- Insufficient evidence to answer question.
- No, with adequate evidence.

Both groups achieved a pre-searching correctness on questions about equal to chance (32.3 percent for medical students and 31.7 percent for NP students). However, medical students improved their correctness with searching (to 51.6 percent), whereas NP students hardly did at all (to 34.7 percent).

This study also attempted to measure what factors might influence searching. A multitude of factors, such as age, gender, computer experience, and time taken to search, were not associated with successful answering of questions. Successful answering was, however, associated with answering the question correctly before searching, spatial visualization ability (measured by a validated instrument), searching experience, and EBM question type (prognosis questions easiest, harm questions most difficult). An analysis of recall and precision for each question searched demonstrated a complete lack of association with ability to answer these questions.

Two studies have extended this approach in various ways. Westbook et al. [126] assessed use of an online evidence system and found that physicians answered 37% of questions correctly before use of the system and 50% afterwards, while nurse specialists answered 18% of questions correctly and also 50% afterwards. Those who had correct answers before searching had higher confidence in their answers, but those not knowing the answer initially had no difference in confidence whether their answer turned out to be right or wrong. McKibbon and Fridsma [92] performed a comparable study of allowing physicians to seek answers to questions with resources they normally use employing the same questions as Hersh et al. [67]. This studies found no difference in answer correctness before or after using the search system. Clearly these study show a variety of effects with different IR systems, tasks, and users.

Pluye and Grad [100] performed a qualitative study assessing impact of IR systems on physician practice. The study identified 4 themes mentioned by physicians:

- Recall—of forgotten knowledge.
- Learning—new knowledge.
- Confirmation—of existing knowledge.
- Frustration—that system use not successful.

The researchers also noted two additional themes:

- Reassurance—that system is available.
- Practice improvement—of patient-physician relationship.

The bulk of more recent physician user studies have focused on ability to users to answer clinical questions. Hoogendam et al. compared UpToDate with PubMed for questions that arose in patient care among residents and attending physicians in internal medicine [71]. For 1305 questions, they found that both resources provided complete answers 53% of the time, but UpToDate was better at providing partial answers (83% full or partial answer for UpToDate compared to 63% full or partial answer for PubMed).

A similar study compared Google, Ovid, PubMed, and UpToDate for answering clinical questions among trainees and attending physicians in anaesthesiology and critical care medicine [117]. Users were allowed to select which tool to use for a first set of four questions to answer, while 1–3 weeks later they were randomized to only a single tool to answer another set of eight questions. For the first set of questions, users most commonly selected Google (45%), followed by UpToDate (26%), PubMed (25%), and Ovid (4.4%). The rate of answering questions correctly in the first set was highest for UpToDate (70%), followed by Google (60%), Ovid (50%), and PubMed (38%). The time taken to answer these questions was lowest for UpToDate (3.3 minutes), followed by Google (3.8 minutes), PubMed (4.4 minutes), and Ovid (4.6 minutes). In the second set of questions, the correct answer was most likely to be obtained by UpToDate (69%), followed by PubMed (62%), Google (57%), and Ovid (38%). Subjects randomized a new tool generally fared comparably, with the exception of those randomized from another tool to Ovid.

Another study compared searching UpToDate and PubMed Clinical Queries at the conclusion of a course for 44 medical residents in an information mastery course [41]. Subjects were randomized to one system for two questions and then the other system for another two questions. The correct answer was retrieved 76% of the time with UpToDate versus only 45% of the time with PubMed

Clinical Queries. Median time to answer the question was less for UpToDate (17 minutes) than PubMed Clinical Queries (29 minutes). User satisfaction was higher with UpToDate.

Fewer studies have been done assessing nonclinicians searching on health information. Lau et al. found that use of a consumer-oriented medical search engine that included PubMed, Medline-PLUS, and other resources by college undergraduates led to answers being correct at a higher rate after searching (82.0%) than before searching (61.2%) [85, 84]. Providing a feedback summary from prior searches boosted the success rate of using the system even higher, to 85.3%. Confidence in one's answer was not found to be highly associated with correctness of the answer, although confidence was likely to increase for those provided with feedback from other searchers on the same topic.

Despite the ubiquity of search systems, many users have skill-related problems when searching for information. van Duersen assessed a variety of computer-related and content-related skills from randomly selected subjects in the Netherlands [120]. Older age and lower educational level were associated with reduced skills, including use of search engines. While younger subjects were more likely to have better computer and searching skills than older subjects, they were more likely to use nonrelevant search results and unreliable sources in answering health-related questions. This latter phenomenon has also been seen outside the health domain among the "millennial" generation, sometimes referred to as "digital natives" [116].

14.7 Research Directions

The above evaluation research shows that there is still plenty of room for IR systems to improve their abilities. In addition, there will be new challenges that arise from growing amounts of information, new devices, and other new technologies.

There are also other areas related to IR where research is ongoing in the larger quest to help all involved in biomedicine and health–from patients to clinicians to researchers–better use information systems and technology to improve the application of knowledge to improve health. This has resulted in research taking place in a number of areas related to IR, which include:

- Information extraction and text mining–usually through the use of natural language processing (NLP) to extract facts and knowledge from text. These techniques are often employed to extract information from the EHR, with a wide variety of accuracy as shown in a recent systematic review [114]. Among the most successful uses of these techniques have been studies to identify diseases associated with genomic variations [33, 34].

- Summarization–Providing automated extracts or abstracts summarizing the content of longer documents [91, 46]

- Question-answering–Going beyond retrieval of documents to providing actual answers to questions, as exemplified by the IBM Corp. Watson system [44], which is being applied to medicine [45].

14.8 Conclusion

There has been considerable progress made in IR. Seeking online information is now done routinely not only by clinicians and researchers, but also by patients and consumers. There are still considerable challenges to make this activity more fruitful to users. They include:

- How do we lower the effort it takes for clinicians to get to the information they need rapidly in the busy clinical setting?
- How can researchers extract new knowledge from the vast quantity that is available to them?
- How can consumers and patients find high-quality information that is appropriate to their understanding of health and disease?
- Can the value added by the publishing process be protected and remunerated while making information more available?
- How can the indexing process become more accurate and efficient?
- Can retrieval interfaces be made simpler without giving up flexibility and power?

Although *search* has become a ubiquitous activity for many, there is still required research to answer these questions, move interaction to new devices, and discover how it will be implemented in the unforeseen advances in computing that will occur in the future.

Bibliography

[1] R. Akerkar. *Foundations of the Semantic Web: XML, RDF & Ontology*. Alpha Science International, Ltd., 2009.

[2] R. K. Ando, M. Dredze, and T. Zhang. TREC 2005 Genomics Track experiments at IBM Watson. In *TREC*, 2014. http://trec.nist.gov/pubs/trec14/papers/ibm-tjwatson.geo.pdf

[3] Stopwords. In *PubMed Help*. National Library of Medicine, Bethesda, MD, 2007. http://www.ncbi.nlm.nih.gov/books/bv.fcgi?highlight=stopwords&rid=helppubmed.table.pubmedhelp.T43

[4] PubMed Help, 2014. http://www.ncbi.nlm.nih.gov/books/NBK3827/

[5] A. R. Aronson, D. Demner-Fushman, S. M. Humphrey, J. J. Lin, P. Ruch, M. E. Ruiz, L. H. Smith, L. K. Tanabe, W. J. Wilbur, and H. Liu. Fusion of knowledge-intensive and statistical approaches for retrieving and annotating textual genomics documents. In *TREC*, 2005. http://trec.nist.gov/pubs/trec14/papers/nlm-umd.geo.pdf

[6] A. R. Aronson, S. M. Humphrey, N. C. Ide, W. Kim, R. R. Loane, J. G. Mork, L. H. Smith, L. K. Tanabe, W. J. Wilbur, N. Xie, et al. Knowledge-intensive and statistical approaches to the retrieval and annotation of genomics MEDLINE citations. In *TREC*, 2004. http://trec.nist.gov/pubs/trec13/papers/nlm-umd-ul.geo.pdf

[7] A. R. Aronson, J. G. Mork, C. W. Gay, S. M. Humphrey, and W. J. Rogers. The NLM Indexing Initiative's Medical Text Indexer. *Medinfo*, 11(Pt 1):268–272, 2004.

[8] L. A. Barroso, J. Dean, and U. Holzle. Web search for a planet: The Google cluster architecture. *Micro, IEEE*, 23(2):22–28, 2003.

[9] H. Bastian, P. Glasziou, and I. Chalmers. Seventy-five trials and eleven systematic reviews a day: How will we ever keep up? *PLoS Medicine*, 7(9):e1000326, 2010.

[10] S. Bedrick, T. Edinger, A. Cohen, and W. Hersh. Identifying patients for clinical studies from electronic health records: TREC 2012 Medical Records Track at OHSU. In *The Twenty-First Text REtrieval Conference Proceedings (TREC 2012) [NIST Special Publication: SP 500-298]*. National Institute of Standards and Technology-NIST, 2012. http://trec.nist.gov/pubs/trec20/papers/OHSU.medical.update.pdf

[11] A. Berger and J. Lafferty. Information retrieval as statistical translation. In *Proceedings of the 22nd Annual International ACM SIGIR Conference on Research and Development in Information Retrieval*, pages 222–229. ACM, 1999.

[12] B.-C. Björk and D. Solomon. Open access versus subscription journals: A comparison of scientific impact. *BMC Medicine*, 10(1):73, 2012. http://www.biomedcentral.com/1741-7015/10/73

[13] O. Bodenreider. The Unified Medical Language System (UMLS): Integrating biomedical terminology. *Nucleic Acids Research*, 32(suppl 1):D267–D270, 2004.

[14] S. Brin and L. Page. The anatomy of a large-scale hypertextual web search engine. *Computer Networks and ISDN Systems*, 30(1):107–117, 1998.

[15] J. Broglio, J. Callan, W. Croft, and D. Nachbar. Document retrieval and routing using the Inquery system. In D. Harman, editor, *Overview of the Third Text REtrieval Conference (TREC-3)*, pages 29–38, Gaithersburg, MD, 1994. National Institute of Standards and Technology.

[16] C. Buckley. The Smart project at TREC. *Voorhees and Harman [2005]*, 2005.

[17] C. Buckley, G. Salton, and J. Allan. The effect of adding relevance information in a relevance feedback environment. In *Proceedings of the 17th Annual International ACM SIGIR Conference on Research and Development in Information Retrieval*, pages 292–300. Springer-Verlag New York, Inc., 1994.

[18] C. Buckley, G. Salton, J. Allan, and A. Singhal. Automatic query expansion using SMART: TREC 3. *NIST special publication*, pages 69–80, 1994.

[19] S. Buttcher, C. L. Clarke, and G. V. Cormack. Domain-specific synonym expansion and validation for biomedical information retrieval (Multitext experiments for TREC 2004). In *Proceedings of the 13th Text Retrieval Conference*, 2004.

[20] P. Callejas, A. Miguel, Y. Wang, and H. Fang. Exploiting domain thesaurus for medical record retrieval. In *The Twenty-First Text REtrieval Conference Proceedings (TREC 2012) [NIST Special Publication: SP 500-298]*. National Institute of Standards and Technology-NIST, 2012. http://trec.nist.gov/pubs/trec21/papers/udel_fang.medical.nb.pdf

[21] T. Charen. *MEDLARS Indexing Manual. Part 1: Bibliographic Principles and Descriptive Indexing*. National Library of Medicine, 1977.

[22] J. Cimino and G. Del Fiol. Infobuttons and point of care access to knowledge. *Clinical Decision Support—The Road Ahead*, pages 345–372, 2007.

[23] M. H. Coletti and H. L. Bleich. Medical Subject Headings used to search the biomedical literature. *Journal of the American Medical Informatics Association*, 8(4):317–323, 2001.

[24] W. Cooper, A. Chen, and F. Gey. Experiments in the probabilistic retrieval of documents. In D. Harman, editor, *Overview of the Third Text REtrieval Conference (TREC-3)*, pages 127–134, Gaithersburg, MD, 1994. National Institute of Standards and Technology.

[25] D. G. Covell, G. C. Uman, and P. R. Manning. Information needs in office practice: Are they being met? *Annals of Internal Medicine*, 103(4):596–599, 1985.

[26] S. Cronen-Townsend, Y. Zhou, and W. B. Croft. Predicting query performance. In *Proceedings of the 25th Annual International ACM SIGIR Conference on Research and Development in Information Retrieval*, pages 299–306. ACM, 2002.

[27] S. Darmoni, J. Leroy, F. Baudic, M. Douyere, J. Piot, and B. Thirion. CISMEF: A structured health resource guide. *Methods of Information in Medicine*, 39(1):30–35, 2000.

[28] K. Davies. Search and deploy. Bio–IT World, October 16, 2006. http://www.bio-itworld.com/issues/2006/oct/biogen-idec/

[29] J. Dean and S. Ghemawat. MapReduce: Simplified data processing on large clusters. *Communications of the ACM*, 51(1):107–113, 2008.

[30] C. D. DeAngelis, J. M. Drazen, F. A. Frizelle, C. Haug, J. Hoey, R. Horton, S. Kotzin, C. Laine, A. Marusic, A. J. P. Overbeke, et al. Is this clinical trial fully registered?: A statement from the International Committee of Medical Journal Editors. *JAMA*, 293(23):2927–2929, 2005.

[31] S. C. Deerwester, S. T. Dumais, T. K. Landauer, G. W. Furnas, and R. A. Harshman. Indexing by latent semantic analysis. *Journal of the American Society for Information Science*, 41(6):391–407, 1990.

[32] D. Demner-Fushman, S. Abhyankar, A. Jimeno-Yepes, R. Loane, F. Lang, J. G. Mork, N. Ide, and A. R. Aronson. NLM at TREC 2012 medical records track. In *The Twenty-First Text REtrieval Conference Proceedings (TREC 2012) [NIST Special Publication: SP 500-298]*. National Institute of Standards and Technology-NIST, 2012. http://trec.nist.gov/pubs/trec21/papers/NLM.medical.final.pdf

[33] J. C. Denny. Mining electronic health records in the genomics era. *PLoS Computational Biology*, 8(12):e1002823, 2012. http://www.ploscompbiol.org/article/info%3Adoi%2F10.1371%2Fjournal.pcbi.1002823

[34] J. C. Denny, L. Bastarache, M. D. Ritchie, R. J. Carroll, R. Zink, J. D. Mosley, J. R. Field, J. M. Pulley, A. H. Ramirez, E. Bowton, et al. Systematic comparison of phenome-wide association study of electronic medical record data and genome-wide association study data. *Nature Biotechnology*, 31(12):1102–1111, 2013.

[35] J. M. Drazen and G. D. Curfman. Public access to biomedical research. *New England Journal of Medicine*, 351(13):1343–1343, 2004.

[36] S. T. Dumais et al. Latent semantic indexing (LSI): TREC-3 report. *Overview of the Third Text REtrieval Conference*, pages 219–230, 1994.

[37] T. Edinger, A. M. Cohen, S. Bedrick, K. Ambert, and W. Hersh. Barriers to retrieving patient information from electronic health record data: failure analysis from the TREC Medical Records Track. In *AMIA Annual Symposium Proceedings*, volume 2012, pages 180–188. American Medical Informatics Association, 2012.

[38] D. E. Egan, J. R. Remde, L. M. Gomez, T. K. Landauer, J. Eberhardt, and C. C. Lochbaum. Formative design evaluation of Superbook. *ACM Transactions on Information Systems (TOIS)*, 7(1):30–57, 1989.

[39] J. W. Ely, J. A. Osheroff, M. H. Ebell, G. R. Bergus, B. T. Levy, M. L. Chambliss, and E. R. Evans. Analysis of questions asked by family doctors regarding patient care. *BMJ*, 319(7206):358–361, 1999.

[40] J. W. Ely, J. A. Osheroff, M. H. Ebell, M. L. Chambliss, D. C. Vinson, J. J. Stevermer, and E. A. Pifer. Obstacles to answering doctors' questions about patient care with evidence: Qualitative study. *BMJ*, 324(7339):710, 2002.

[41] L. S. Ensan, M. Faghankhani, A. Javanbakht, S.-F. Ahmadi, and H. R. Baradaran. To compare PubMed clinical queries and UpToDate in teaching information mastery to clinical residents: A crossover randomized controlled trial. *PLoS ONE*, 6(8):e23487, 2011.

[42] D. Evans and R. Lefferts. Design and evaluation of the CLARIT TREC-2 system. *NIST special publication*, pages 137–150, 1993.

[43] G. Eysenbach and C. Köhler. Health-related searches on the internet. *JAMA*, 291(24):2946–2946, 2004.

[44] D. Ferrucci, E. Brown, J. Chu-Carroll, J. Fan, D. Gondek, A. A. Kalyanpur, A. Lally, J. W. Murdock, E. Nyberg, J. Prager, et al. Building Watson: An overview of the DeepQA project. *AI Magazine*, 31(3):59–79, 2010.

[45] D. Ferrucci, A. Levas, S. Bagchi, D. Gondek, and E. T. Mueller. Watson: Beyond Jeopardy! *Artificial Intelligence*, 199–200:93–105, 2013.

[46] M. Fiszman, T. C. Rindflesch, and H. Kilicoglu. Summarization of an online medical encyclopedia. *Medinfo*, 11(Pt 1):506–510, 2004.

[47] S. Fortunato, M. Boguna, A. Flammini, and F. Menczer. How to make the top ten: Approximating PageRank from in-degree, 2005. http://arxiv.org/pdf/cs.IR/0511016

[48] C. Fox. Lexical analysis and stoplists. In *Information Retrieval*, pages 102–130. Prentice-Hall, Inc., 1992.

[49] S. Fox. Health topics. *Pew Internet & American Life Project*, 2011. http://www.pewinternet.org/Reports/2011/HealthTopics.aspx

[50] S. Fox and M. Duggan. Health online. *Health*, 2013. http://www.pewinternet.org/Reports/2013/Health-online.aspx

[51] W. Frakes. Stemming algorithms. In *Information Retrieval*, pages 131–160. Prentice-Hall, Inc., 1992.

[52] W. B. Frakes and R. Baeza-Yates. *Information Retrieval: Data Structures and Algorithms*, Prentice Hall, 1992.

[53] S. Fujita. Revisiting again document length hypotheses—TREC 2004 Genomics Track experiments at Patolis. In *TREC*, 2004. Available at http://trec.nist.gov/pubs/trec13/t13_proceedings.html

[54] M. Funk and C. Reid. Indexing consistency in MEDLINE. *Bulletin of the Medical Library Association*, 71(2):176–183, 1983.

[55] M. Y. Galperin and G. R. Cochrane. The 2011 nucleic acids research database issue and the online Molecular Biology Database Collection. *Nucleic Acids Research*, 39(suppl_1):D1–D6, 2011.

[56] J. Giles. Internet encyclopaedias go head to head. *Nature*, 438(7070):900–901, 2005.

[57] P. N. Gorman and M. Helfand. Information seeking in primary care how physicians choose which clinical questions to pursue and which to leave unanswered. *Medical Decision Making*, 15(2):113–119, 1995.

[58] S. P. Harter. Psychological relevance and information science. *Journal of the American Society for Information Science*, 43(9):602–615, 1992.

[59] R. B. Haynes, K. A. McKibbon, C. J. Walker, N. Ryan, D. Fitzgerald, and M. F. Ramsden. Online access to MEDLINE in clinical settings: A study of use and usefulness. *Annals of Internal Medicine*, 112(1):78–84, 1990.

[60] W. Hersh. *Information Retrieval: A Health and Biomedical Perspective.* Springer, 2009.

[61] W. Hersh and D. Hickam. An evaluation of interactive Boolean and natural language searching with an on-line medical textbook. *Journal of the American Society for Information Science*, 46:478–489, 1995.

[62] W. Hersh and P. Over. Interactivity at the Text REtrieval Conference (TREC). *Information Processing & Management*, 37(3):365–366, 2001.

[63] W. Hersh, J. Pentecost, and D. Hickam. A task-oriented approach to information retrieval evaluation. *Journal of the American Society for Information Science*, 47(1):50–56, 1996.

[64] W. Hersh and E. Voorhees. TREC Genomics special issue overview. *Information Retrieval*, 12(1):1–15, 2009.

[65] W. R. Hersh. Relevance and retrieval evaluation: perspectives from medicine. *Journal of the American Society for Information Science*, 45(3):201–206, 1994.

[66] W. R. Hersh. Information retrieval and digital libraries. In *Biomedical Informatics: Computer Applications in Healthcare and Biomedicine*, pages 613–641. Springer, 2014.

[67] W. R. Hersh, M. K. Crabtree, D. H. Hickam, L. Sacherek, C. P. Friedman, P. Tidmarsh, C. Mosbaek, and D. Kraemer. Factors associated with success in searching MEDLINE and applying evidence to answer clinical questions. *Journal of the American Medical Informatics Association*, 9(3):283–293, 2002.

[68] W. R. Hersh and D. H. Hickam. How well do physicians use electronic information retrieval systems? A framework for investigation and systematic review. *JAMA*, 280(15):1347–1352, 1998.

[69] W. R. Hersh and T. C. Rindfleisch. Electronic publishing of scholarly communication in the biomedical sciences. *Journal of the American Medical Informatics Association*, 7(3):324–325, 2000.

[70] D. Hiemstra and W. Kraaij. A Language-Modeling Approach to TREC. In *TREC: Experiment and Evaluation in Information Retrieval.* E. Voorhees and D. Harman (editors). MIT Press, Cambridge, MA. 2005.

[71] A. Hoogendam, A. F. Stalenhoef, P. F. de Vries Robbé, and A. J. P. Overbeke. Answers to questions posed during daily patient care are more likely to be answered by UpToDate than PubMed. *Journal of Medical Internet Research*, 10(4):e29–e29, 2008.

[72] X. Huang, M. Zhong, and L. Si York University at TREC 2005: Genomics Track. In *The Fourteenth Text REtrieval Conference Proceedings (TREC 2005)*. National Institute of Standards & Technology, 2005. http://trec.nist.gov/pubs/trec14/papers/yorku-huang2.geo.pdf

[73] D. Hull. Improving text retrieval for the routing problem using latent semantic indexing. In *SIGIR'94*, pages 282–291. Springer, 1994.

[74] B. L. Humphreys, D. A. Lindberg, H. M. Schoolman, and G. O. Barnett. The Unified Medical Language System: An informatics research collaboration. *Journal of the American Medical Informatics Association*, 5(1):1–11, 1998.

[75] N. C. Ide, R. F. Loane, and D. Demner-Fushman. Essie: A concept-based search engine for structured biomedical text. *Journal of the American Medical Informatics Association*, 14(3):253–263, 2007.

[76] T. R. Insel, N. D. Volkow, T.-K. Li, J. F. Battey Jr., and S. C. Landis. Neuroscience networks. *PLoS Biology*, 1(1):e17, 2003.

[77] J. Jiang and C. Zhai. An empirical study of tokenization strategies for biomedical information retrieval. *Information Retrieval*, 10(4-5):341–363, 2007.

[78] D. Knaus, E. Mittendorf, and P. Schäuble. Improving a basic retrieval method by links and passage level evidence. *TREC 3*, pages 241–246, 1994.

[79] B. Koopman, G. Zuccon, A. Nguyen, D. Vickers, L. Butt, and P. D. Bruza. Exploiting SNOMED CT concepts and relationships for clinical information retrieval: Australian e-health Research Centre and Queensland University of Technology at the TREC 2012 Medical Track. In *The Twenty-First Text REtrieval Conference Proceedings (TREC 2012)[NIST Special Publication: SP 500-298]*. National Institute of Standards and Technology-NIST, 2012. http://trec.nist.gov/pubs/trec21/papers/AEHRC.medical.nb.pdf

[80] A. V. Kulkarni, B. Aziz, I. Shams, and J. W. Busse. Comparisons of citations in Web of Science, Scopus, and Google Scholar for articles published in general medical journals. *JAMA*, 302(10):1092–1096, 2009.

[81] K. L. Kwok, L. Grunfeld, D. D. Lewis TREC-3 ad-hoc, routing retrieval, and thresholding experiments using PIRCS. *TREC 3*, pages 247–255, 1994.

[82] C. Laine, R. Horton, C. D. DeAngelis, J. M. Drazen, F. A. Frizelle, F. Godlee, C. Haug, P. C. Hébert, S. Kotzin, A. Marusic, et al. Clinical trial registration: Looking back and moving ahead. *JAMA*, 298(1):93–94, 2007.

[83] T. K. Landauer and S. T. Dumais. A solution to Plato's problem: The latent semantic analysis theory of acquisition, induction, and representation of knowledge. *Psychological Review*, 104(2):211–240, 1997.

[84] A. Lau, T. Kwok, and E. Coiera. How online crowds influence the way individual consumers answer health questions–an online prospective study. *Applied Clinical Informatics*, 2:177–189, 2011.

[85] A. Y. Lau and E. W. Coiera. Impact of web searching and social feedback on consumer decision making: A prospective online experiment. *Journal of Medical Internet Research*, 10(1):e2–e2, 2008.

[86] M. R. Laurent and T. J. Vickers. Seeking health information online: Does Wikipedia matter? *Journal of the American Medical Informatics Association*, 16(4):471–479, 2009.

[87] N. Limsopatham, C. Macdonald, and I. Ounis. Inferring conceptual relationships to improve medical records search. In *Proceedings of the 10th Conference on Open Research Areas in Information Retrieval*, pages 1–8, 2013.

[88] N. Limsopatham, C. Macdonald, and I. Ounis. Learning to handle negated language in medical records search. In *Proceedings of the 22nd ACM International Conference on Information & Knowledge Management*, pages 1431–1440. ACM, 2013.

[89] J. Lin and C. Dyer. *Data-Intensive Text Processing with MapReduce*. Morgan & Claypool, San Rafael, CA, 2010.

[90] D. A. Lindberg and B. L. Humphreys. 2015-The future of medical libraries. *New England Journal of Medicine*, 352(11):1067–1070, 2005.

[91] I. Mani. *Automatic Summarization*, Volume 3. John Benjamins Publishing, 2001.

[92] K. McKibbon and D. B. Fridsma. Effectiveness of clinician-selected electronic information resources for answering primary care physicians? Information needs. *Journal of the American Medical Informatics Association*, 13(6):653–659, 2006.

[93] K. McKibbon, R. B. Haynes, C. J. Walker Dilks, M. F. Ramsden, N. C. Ryan, L. Baker, T. Flemming, and D. Fitzgerald. How good are clinical MEDLINE searches? A comparative study of clinical end-user and librarian searches. *Computers and Biomedical Research*, 23(6):583–593, 1990.

[94] J. Metzger and J. Rhoads. Summary of Key Provisions in Final Rule for Stage 2 HITECH Meaningful Use. Falls Church, VA. *Computer Sciences Corp*, 2012. http://assets1.csc.com/health_services/downloads/CSC_Key_Provisions_of_Final_Rule_for_Stage_2.pdf

[95] M. Mitra, A. Singhal, and C. Buckley. Improving automatic query expansion. In *Proceedings of the 21st Annual International ACM SIGIR Conference on Research and Development in Information Retrieval*, pages 206–214. ACM, 1998.

[96] B. T. Mynatt, L. M. Leventhal, K. Instone, J. Farhat, and D. S. Rohlman. Hypertext or book: Which is better for answering questions? In *Proceedings of the SIGCHI Conference on Human Factors in Computing Systems*, pages 19–25. ACM, 1992.

[97] P. Nakov, A. S. Schwartz, E. Stoica, and M. A. Hearst. Biotext team experiments for the TREC 2004 Genomics Track. http://trec.nist.gov/pubs/trec13/papers/ucal-berkeley.geo.pdf

[98] C. Neylon. Science publishing: Open access must enable open use. *Nature*, 492(7429):348–349, 2012.

[99] D. T. Nicholson. *An Evaluation of the Quality of Consumer Health Information on Wikipedia*. PhD thesis, Oregon Health & Science University, 2006.

[100] P. Pluye and R. Grad. How information retrieval technology may impact on physician practice: An organizational case study in family medicine. *Journal of Evaluation in Clinical Practice*, 10(3):413–430, 2004.

[101] J. M. Ponte and W. B. Croft. A language modeling approach to information retrieval. In *Proceedings of the 21st Annual International ACM SIGIR Conference on Research and Development in Information Retrieval*, pages 275–281. ACM, 1998.

[102] K. Purcell, J. Brenner, and L. Rainie. Search engine use 2012. 2012. http://www.pewinternet.org/Reports/2012/Search-Engine-Use-2012.aspx

[103] Y. Qi and P.-F. Laquerre. Retrieving medical records with sennamed: NEC Labs America at TREC 2012 Medical Records Track. In *The Twenty-First Text REtrieval Conference Proceedings (TREC 2012) [NIST Special Publication: SP 500-298]*. National Institute of Standards and Technology-NIST, 2012. http://trec.nist.gov/pubs/trec21/papers/sennamed.medical.final.pdf

[104] S. E. Robertson, S. Walker, S. Jones, M. M. Hancock-Beaulieu, and M. Gatford Okapi at TREC-3. In *Overview of the Third Text REtrieval Conference (TREC-3)*. National Institute of Standards and Technology, 1994.

[105] S. E. Robertson and S. Walker. Some simple effective approximations to the 2-Poisson model for probabilistic weighted retrieval. In *Proceedings of the 17th Annual International ACM SIGIR Conference on Research and Development in Information Retrieval*, pages 232–241. Springer-Verlag New York, 1994.

[106] C. Safran, M. Bloomrosen, W. E. Hammond, S. Labkoff, S. Markel-Fox, P. C. Tang, and D. E. Detmer. Toward a national framework for the secondary use of health data: An American Medical Informatics Association white paper. *Journal of the American Medical Informatics Association*, 14(1):1–9, 2007.

[107] G. Salton. Developments in automatic text retrieval. *Science*, 253(5023):974–980, 1991.

[108] G. Salton and C. Buckley. Improving retrieval performance by relevance feedback. *Journal of the American Society for Information Science*, 41(4):288–297, 1990.

[109] G. Salton, E. A. Fox, and H. Wu. Extended Boolean information retrieval. *Communications of the ACM*, 26(11):1022–1036, 1983.

[110] G. Salton and M. McGill. *Introduction to Modern Information Retrieval.* McGraw-Hill, New York, 1983.

[111] E. W. Sayers, T. Barrett, D. A. Benson, E. Bolton, S. H. Bryant, K. Canese, V. Chetvernin, D. M. Church, M. DiCuccio, S. Federhen, et al. Database resources of the National Center for Biotechnology Information. *Nucleic Acids Research*, 39(suppl 1):D38–D51, 2011.

[112] K. Seki, J. C. Costello, V. R. Singan, and J. Mostafa. TREC 2004 Genomics Track experiments at IUB. In *TREC*, 2004. http://trec.nist.gov/pubs/trec13/papers/indianau-seki.geo.pdf

[113] H. C. Sox. Medical journal editing: Who shall pay? *Annals of Internal Medicine*, 151(1):68–69, 2009.

[114] M. H. Stanfill, M. Williams, S. H. Fenton, R. A. Jenders, and W. R. Hersh. A systematic literature review of automated clinical coding and classification systems. *Journal of the American Medical Informatics Association*, 17(6):646–651, 2010.

[115] D. R. Swanson. Historical note: Information retrieval and the future of an illusion. *Journal of the American Society for Information Science*, 39(2):92–98, 1988.

[116] A. Taylor. A study of the information search behaviour of the millennial generation. *Information Research: An International Electronic Journal*, 17(1):n1, 2012. http://informationr.net/ir/17-1/paper508.html

[117] R. H. Thiele, N. C. Poiro, D. C. Scalzo, and E. C. Nemergut. Speed, accuracy, and confidence in Google, Ovid, PubMed, and UpToDate: Results of a randomised trial. *Postgraduate Medical Journal*, 86(1018):459–465, 2010.

[118] A. Turpin and W. Hersh. Do clarity scores for queries correlate with user performance? In *Proceedings of the 15th Australasian Database Conference-Volume 27*, pages 85–91. Australian Computer Society, 2004.

[119] H. Turtle and W. B. Croft. Evaluation of an inference network-based retrieval model. *ACM Transactions on Information Systems (TOIS)*, 9(3):187–222, 1991.

[120] A. J. van Deursen. Internet skill-related problems in accessing online health information. *International Journal of Medical Informatics*, 81(1):61–72, 2012.

[121] R. Van Noorden. The true cost of science publishing. *Nature*, 495(7442):426–429, 2013.

[122] D. Hiemstra and W. Kraaij. A language-modeling approach to trec. In E. Voorhees and D. Harman, editors, *TREC: Experiment and Evaluation in Information Retrieval.* MIT Press, Cambridge, MA, 2005.

[123] E. M. Voorhees. The TREC Medical Records Track. In *Proceedings of the International Conference on Bioinformatics, Computational Biology and Biomedical Informatics*, pages 239–246. ACM, 2013.

[124] N. Walczuch, N. Fuhr, M. Pollmann, and B. Sievers. Routing and ad-hoc retrieval with the TREC-3 collection in a distributed loosely federated environment. *TREC-3*, 135–144.

[125] S. L. Weibel and T. Koch. The Dublin Core Metadata Initiative. *D-lib Magazine*, 6(12), 2000.

[126] J. I. Westbrook, E. W. Coiera, and A. S. Gosling. Do online information retrieval systems help experienced clinicians answer clinical questions? *Journal of the American Medical Informatics Association*, 12(3):315–321, 2005.

[127] W. J. Wilbur and Y. Yang. An analysis of statistical term strength and its use in the indexing and retrieval of molecular biology texts. *Computers in Biology and Medicine*, 26(3):209–222, 1996.

[128] B. M. Wildemuth, R. de Bliek, C. P. Friedman, and D. D. File. Medical students' personal knowledge, searching proficiency, and database use in problem solving. *Journal of the American society for Information Science*, 46(8):590–607, 1995.

[129] A. J. Wolpert. For the sake of inquiry and knowledge? The inevitability of open access. *New England Journal of Medicine*, 368(9):785–787, 2013.

[130] D. A. Zarin and T. Tse. Trust but verify: Trial registration and determining fidelity to the protocol. *Annals of Internal Medicine*, 159(1):65–67, 2013.

[131] D. A. Zarin, T. Tse, R. J. Williams, R. M. Califf, and N. C. Ide. The clinicaltrials.gov results database? Update and key issues. *New England Journal of Medicine*, 364(9):852–860, 2011.

[132] C. Zhai and J. Lafferty. A study of smoothing methods for language models applied to information retrieval. *ACM Transactions on Information Systems (TOIS)*, 22(2):179–214, 2004.

[133] Z. Zheng, S. Brady, A. Garg, and H. Shatkay. Applying probabilistic thematic clustering for classification in the TREC 2005 Genomics Track. In *TREC*, 2005.

[134] X. Zhou, X. Hu, and X. Zhang. Topic signature language models for ad hoc retrieval. *IEEE Transactions on Knowledge and Data Engineering,*, 19(9):1276–1287, 2007.

[135] D. Zhu and B. Carterette. An adaptive evidence weighting method for medical record search. In *Proceedings of the 36th Annual International ACM SIGIR Conference on Research and Development in Information Retrieval*, pages 1025–1028. ACM, 2013.

Chapter 15

Privacy-Preserving Data Publishing Methods in Healthcare

Yubin Park
Department of Electrical and Computer Engineering
The University of Texas at Austin
Austin, TX
`yubin.park@utexas.edu`

Joydeep Ghosh
Department of Electrical and Computer Engineering
University of Texas at Austin
Austin, TX
`ghosh@ece.utexas.edu`

15.1 Introduction

In 2009, the United States government enacted the Health Information Technology for Economic and Clinical Health Act (HITECH) that includes an incentive program totaling up to $27 billion for the adoption and meaningful use of Electronic Health Records (EHRs). Health information exchanges have emerged to facilitate the meaningful use of health information by sharing and exchanging somewhat disparate and distributed EHRs. According to HITECH, the meaningful use of EHRs can help "improve care coordination, reduce disparities, engage patients and their families, and improve population and public health" [12]. Such meaningful use can only be achieved through carefully controlled sharing and exchanging of personal health information and complying with existing regulations such as the Health Insurance Portability and Accountability Act (HIPAA), otherwise the privacy of patients may be severely damaged. In the United States, 75% of patients have expressed concerns about uninformed sharing of their health information [44], possibly due to the frequent data breaches in medical institutions [27].

Sharing personal health information can bring enormous economical benefits. In fact, several legal theorists have argued that privacy is overrated. Judge Posner viewed that privacy can be used "to manipulate the world around them by selective disclosure of facts about themselves" [41]. Professor Epstein stated that regulations on data privacy may create "an elaborate set of cross-subsidies that reduces the total level of social wealth as it transfers wealth between parties" [22]. In a complex healthcare system, however, the negative consequences for open access of health information overwhelm the idealistic economical benefits [53]. For example, insurance companies and employers can maliciously utilize such data to increase their revenues, discriminating out unhealthy subpopulations. Thus, there exists a delicate equilibrium point between utility and privacy, and an extreme point cannot be a solution.

Privacy is a subjective and contextual concept, and it conveys different connotations and interpretations in different fields; e.g., banking and healthcare sectors focus on different privacy aspects [20]. In the healthcare sector, the definition of privacy is commonly accepted as "a person's right and desire to control the disclosure of their personal health information" [47], where the type of health information ranges from a person's identity to disease/medication history. The concept of healthcare data privacy sometimes extends to cover organizational information such as hospitals and insurance companies, not just patient information [7]. Contrary to the systemic views on medical privacy, in the computer science and statistics literature, privacy is often approached from an information theoretic perspective in an attempt to quantify the level of privacy [60, 6]. Popular privacy metrics include k-anonymity [55], l-diversity [34], and ε-differential privacy [19]. Different privacy measures assume different access settings and attack scenarios; for example, k-anonymity and l-diversity fit in a data publication setting, and ε-differential privacy is motivated from the statistical database literature. Privacy, especially in healthcare, should be interpreted from both systemic and information perspectives to clearly understand potential breaches and consequences [28].

The appropriateness and settings for different privacy measures also need to be carefully considered. For example, legal frameworks such as the U.S. HIPAA safe harbor rule typically require protection of individually identifiable data. If differential privacy is being used, the probability of identification can vary substantially depending on actual data values even for the same value of ε, and moreover this privacy measure does not correspond well with the ability to infer private data values for an individual. It has been forcefully argued that an alternative measure such as differential identifiability is more suitable for such privacy criteria [29]. Also access to data should depend on a variety of other aspects such as provenance, who is seeing the data and for what purpose, and so on. A report by [42] suggests and XML-based approach to privacy, where the tags capture all the nuances required for proper data access and release.

In this chapter, we primarily focus on applying privacy-preserving algorithms to healthcare data for secondary-use data publishing. Using an actual subset of Texas Inpatient Public Use Data File, we will demonstrate step-by-step how to apply privacy-preserving algorithms, and interpret the usefulness and implications of the processed data. Although details may vary, in general, the steps for privacy-preserving data publication algorithms are as follows:

1. Identifying an appropriate privacy metric and level for a given access setting and data characteristics

2. Applying one or multiple privacy-preserving algorithm(s) to achieve the desired privacy level

3. Postanalyzing the utility of the processed data

4. Repeating this cycle (from 1 to 3) until the desired utility and privacy levels are jointly met

In practice, multiple privacy-preserving algorithms are applied before publishing. For example, Centers for Medicare and Medicaid Services[1] recently published synthetic data that are processed by 6

[1]`http://www.cms.gov/Research-Statistics-Data-and-Systems/Statistics-Trends-and-Reports/SynPUFs/Downloads/SynPUF_DUG.pdf`

different methods: (1) variable reduction, (2) suppression, (3) substitution, (4) imputation, (5) data perturbation, and (6) coarsening [11]. We will also apply a series of privacy-preserving algorithms: starting with variable reduction and coarsening, and then generalization/suppression, and finally applying imputation and perturbation techniques.

15.2 Data Overview and Preprocessing

We use the Texas Inpatient Public Use Data File from the Texas Department of State Health Services ([56]) to concretely illustrate various approaches described in the chapter. Hospital billing records collected from 1999 to 2007 are publicly available through their website. Each yearly dataset contains about 2.8 millions events with more than 250 features. Except for a few exempt hospitals, all the hospitals in Texas reported inpatient discharge events to DSHS. This chapter uses the inpatient records from the fourth quarter of 2006, and we specifically focus on the natural delivery events from Parkland Memorial Hospital. The dataset is already anonymized, and does not contain any identifiable information such as name, social security number, and driver license number.

Outlier Removal, Variable Reduction, and Coarsening. Let us assume that a group of researchers submitted a pilot study proposal about modeling the relationship between demographic factors (sex, address), insurance, and hospital charges. Our objective is to publish this dataset for the specified research objective while protecting patients' privacy. We first remove irrelevant variables for the research objective except for five research-related variables: sex (of an infant), zip code, payment source (primary insurance), length of stay, and total charges. Before applying actual privacy-preserving algorithms, the first step is to check the characteristics of the data. Figure 15.1 shows the cross-scatter plots of the original data. As can be seen, there is one missing zip code record (`zipcode=0`), and very few paticnts paid more than $10K. Such outliers and rare events can

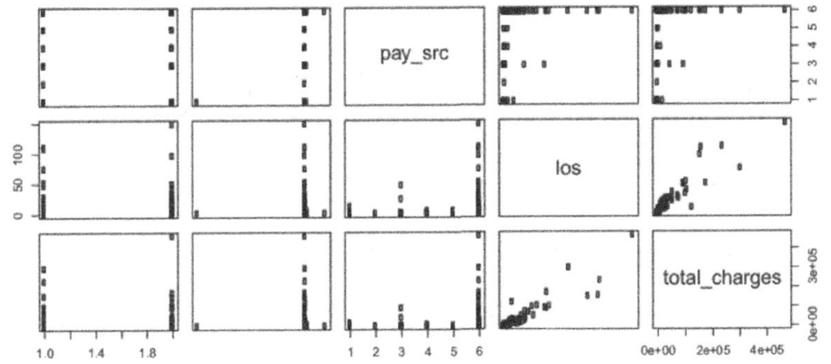

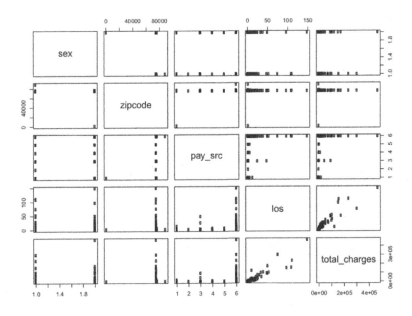

FIGURE 15.1: Cross-scatter plots of the original Texas inpatient data.

be vulnerable to a linking attack (see Section 15.3.1), thus we filter out these records. The "total charges" variable contains the original numeric scale dollar values. Such numeric variables tend to have many unique entries, which can be easily utilized in a linking attack as well. Therefore, we bin the original numeric values of total charges into 20 ranges: $[0, 500), [500, 1000), \ldots [9500, 10000)$.

Table 15.1 illustrates overall summary statistics of this preprocessed dataset. From the total 1432 patients, 1298 patients were paid by the Medicaid program (`pay_src=MC`), and 155 patients self-paid (`pay_src=09`). On average, patients stayed 1.068 days (`Mean los=1.068`), and paid 1160 dollars (`Mean total_charges=1160`). Figure 15.2 shows the cross-scatter plots of the preprocessed data. As can be seen, we effectively removed easily identifiable data points by coarsening and truncating data.

These simple procedures are, however, not sufficient for comprehensive privacy protection. For example, we can observe that only one patient is paid by a non-federal program (`pay_src=11`). If an attacker has a list of beneficiaries from this non-federal program, then the patient identity of the record can be easily hacked. Figure 15.3 shows the histogram of duplicate records from the dataset. With the full combination of five variables, 134 (about 10%) records are unique. Population

TABLE 15.1: Summary Statistics of Texas Inpatient Data

sex	zipcode	pay_src	los	total_charges
F:648	75217 : 82	09: 155	Min. :0.000	Min. : 0
M:844	75211 : 79	11: 1	1st Qu.:1.000	1st Qu.:1000
	75220 : 79	12: 30	Median :1.000	Median :1000
	75061 : 68	15: 3	Mean :1.068	Mean :1160
	75228 : 54	HM: 5	3rd Qu.:1.000	3rd Qu.:1000
	75231 : 54	MC:1298	Max. :6.000	Max. :9500
	(Other):1076			

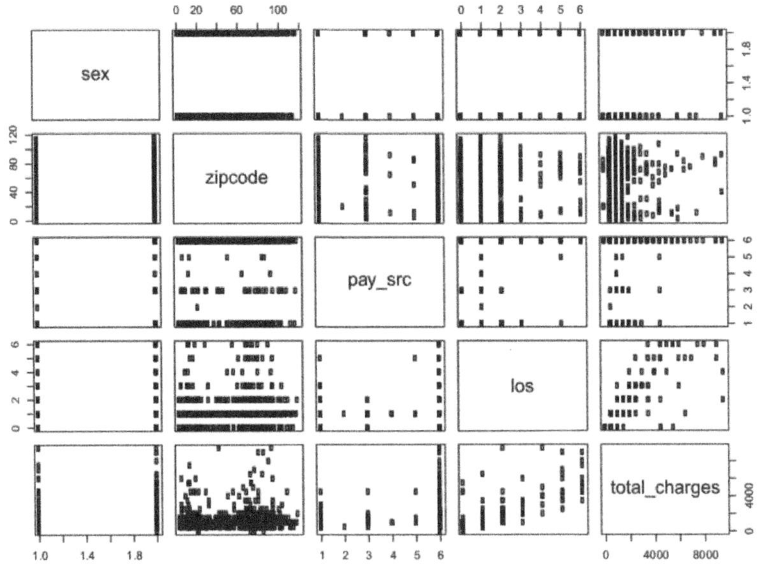

FIGURE 15.2: Scatter plots of the preprocessed Texas inpatient data.

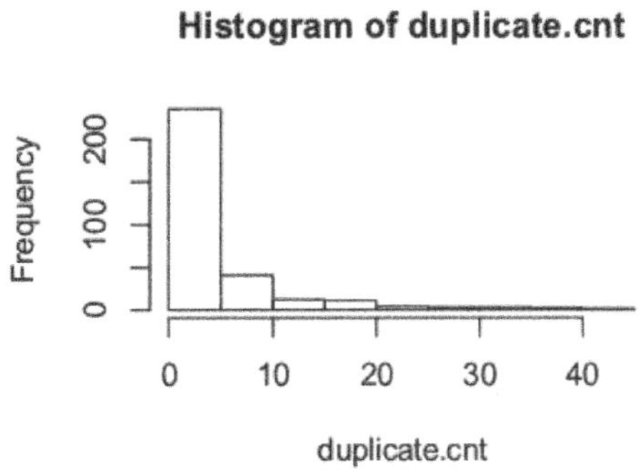

FIGURE 15.3: Histogram of duplicate records.

uniqueness is a very important concept in privacy-preserving algorithms. In Section 15.3.1, we will illustrate the potential threats for unique records, and algorithms to prevent such attacks.

15.3 Privacy-Preserving Publishing Methods

In this section, we apply three different kinds of privacy-preserving algorithms: generalization/suppression, creation of synthetic data, and perturbed synthetic data. First, we show how generalization/suppression techniques can be applied to the categorical variables of the Texas inpatient data. Using the generalized/suppressed data, we synthesize numeric columns: length of stay and total charges. Finally, we introduce a cutting-edge synthesizing technique that can synthesize both categorical and numeric variables while adhering to ε-differential privacy.

15.3.1 Generalization and Suppression

The most basic step before publishing sensitive data is to remove any personal identifiable variables such as name, telephone number, social security number, and driving license number. For the Texas inpatient data, the Texas Department of State Health Services has already removed these explicit identifiers, and assigned an arbitrary record number to each row. As another example, the Synthetic Data from Centers for Medicare and Medicaid Services replaced explicit identifiers with random hash codes, so that users can link and match the records from the same patient, but not with external data sources. This seemingly intuitive process, however, is not sufficient to protect the patient identities from a "linking attack."

Sweeney [54, 55] provided a simple example by linking two datasets: a dataset from the Group Insurance Commission (GIC) in Massachusetts and the voter registration list for Cambridge. The GIC dataset does not include explicit identifiers, but the voter registration list does; it contains name and address. These two datasets have three common variables: zip code, birth date, and sex. By linking the two datasets using these three variables, she demonstrated that the governor of Massachusetts can be identified from the GIC data. This type of privacy attack is called a linking attack. Figure 15.4 visualizes the potential links between two datasets. A linking attack is difficult to foresee and prevent, since it is almost impossible to check all the external linking datasets before publishing.

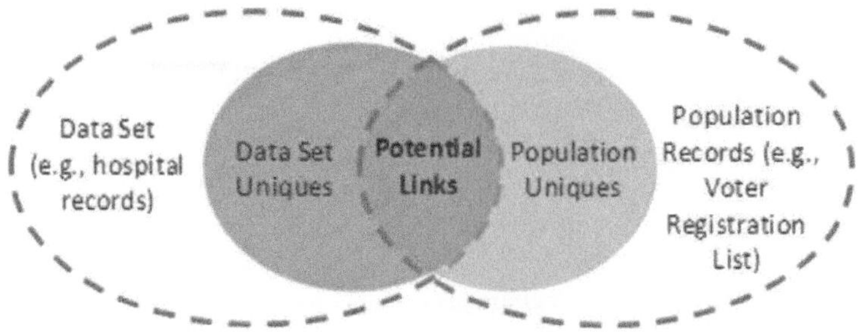

FIGURE 15.4: Link Attack Diagram. Source: `http://www.hhs.gov/ocr/privacy/hipaa/understanding/coveredentities/De-identification/guidance.html`

Generalization and suppression techniques alleviate the disclosure risks that may arise from linking attacks [51, 54]. Generalization replaces a value with a less specific but semantically consistent value. For example, a zip code can be generalized into city or county. On the other hand, suppression replaces a value to a non-informative value, e.g., 70512 $\rightarrow$ *. In Figure 15.5, we demonstrated two types of generalization: city-level generalization, and three-digit zip code generalization by removing the last two digits. Parkland Memorial Hospital is located in Dallas, and of course, most of the patients live in Dallas (the zip codes of Dallas start with 752). As can be seen, the Dallas population is shown as the peaks on both bar charts. We are, however, more interested in low-count categories such as Waco and 761** (high-risk values).

Even if identifiable variables, such as name or social security number, are removed from a dataset, a certain combination of variables can be unique, and this may potentially lead to privacy breach incidents. From the suppression example, there is only one female who lives in 761** (suppressed zip code). The city-level generalized dataset is not an exception; the dataset also shows only one male in Waco. With the city-level generalized data, an attacker can easily identify who this male in Waco is, and how much this person paid for his hospital charges.

As can be seen, data uniqueness may arise from a set of seemingly non-private variables. Dalenius (1986) formally defined the set of such variables as "quasi-identifier."

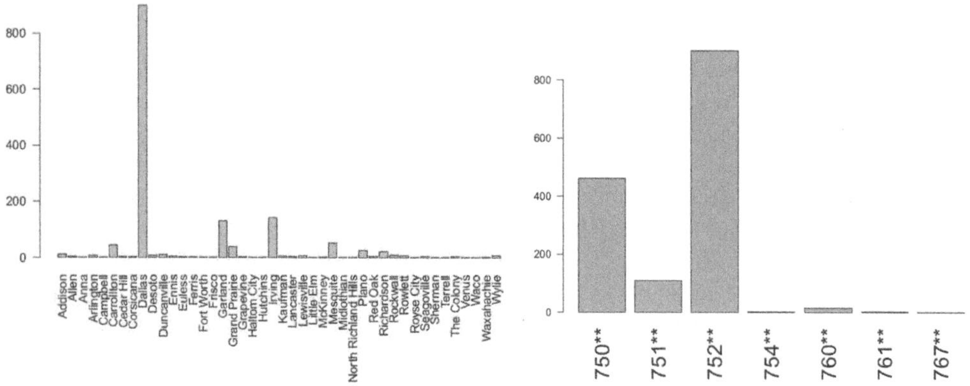

(a) Generalization (city-level)

(b) Generalization (three-digit zip code)

FIGURE 15.5: Generalization of the zip code from the Texas inpatient dataset.

Definition 15.3.1 (Quasi-identifier) *A quasi-identifier is a set of variables within a dataset that may be empirically unique. Therefore, in principle, such a quasi-identifier can be used to uniquely identify a population unit.*

As an illustrative example, from our Texas discharge dataset example, a quasi-identifier can be a set of sex, geographical code, and payment source.

Sweeney [54, 55] proposed k-anonymity to formalize and quantify the disclosure risk of unique populations. The definition of k-anonymity is as follows:

Definition 15.3.2 (k-anonymity) *A table is said to satisfy k-anonymity if and only if the quasi-identifier of the table appears with at least k occurrences.*

In other words, to adhere to the k-anonymity principle, each row in a dataset should be indistinguishable with at least $k-1$ other rows.

Suppose that we want to publish a dataset that satisfies 3-anonymity. Figure 15.6 shows mosaic plots of the quasi-identifiers for two different zip code generalization methods. Mosaic plots visualize multi-way contingency tables. The vertical axis (y-axis) represents the generalized zip codes, and the horizontal axis (x-axis) shows the cross-tabulation of sex (top) and payment source (bottom). The areas of the rectangles specify the number of entries with the corresponding attribute values; bigger rectangles mean more data points. For example, the Medicare population in Dallas is shown as two big boxes in Figure 15.6 (a), and the HMO populations are shown as tiny boxes ($\odot$ represents no entry). Mosaic plots are useful not only in categorical variable analysis, but also in visual diagnostics for data privacy assessment. For more information about mosaic plots, see [24, 25]. As can be seen, there exist many unique data points even if we generalize the address variable into either city or three-digit zip code. The three-digit zip code generalization has less unique data points i.e. small-sized rectangles, but the address resolution became overly coarsened.

To achieve 3-anonymity ($k = 3$), we combine generalization and suppression. Using the city-level generalized data, we collect the data points that are unique or appearing only two times. We suppress these rare data points to *. Figure 15.7 shows the mosaic plot of the generalized and suppressed quasi-identifiers. As can be seen, there are no more unique data points, and at the same time, the original data properties are reasonably preserved. Note that generalization and suppression should not be abused, otherwise the utility of data can be seriously damaged. As an illustrative example, k-anonymity with higher k values can be easily obtained by generalizing the address variable to a state-level variable, or suppressing all the rows; the address variable does not contain any information. Therefore, generalization and suppression should be minimally applied to the extent that the transformed data satisfy k-anonymity.

Achieving the optimal k-anonymity is, in fact, NP-hard, so several heuristic and greedy algorithms have been developed. The pioneering work of Sweeney [54, 55] introduced the Preferred Minimal Generalization (MinGen) algorithm. The principal idea in this algorithm is to transform the original dataset with (1) minimal generalization and (2) minimal distortion. To formally address the notion of minimal generalization, a concept of generalization hierarchy needs to be introduced. Generalization hierarchy is simply a semantic structure of generalization concepts. For example, for the zip code variable in our example, one can generalize through a geographical hierarchy as follows:

$$\underbrace{\text{ZIP}}_{\text{lv0-geo}} \rightarrow \underbrace{\text{City}}_{\text{lv1-geo}} \rightarrow \underbrace{\text{County}}_{\text{lv2-geo}} \rightarrow \underbrace{\text{State}}_{\text{lv3-geo}} \rightarrow \underbrace{\text{Nation}}_{\text{lv4-geo}}$$

Similarly, the payment source variable can be grouped as:

$$\underbrace{\text{Payment Source Code}}_{\text{lv0-pay}} \rightarrow \underbrace{\text{National vs. Private}}_{\text{lv1-pay}}$$

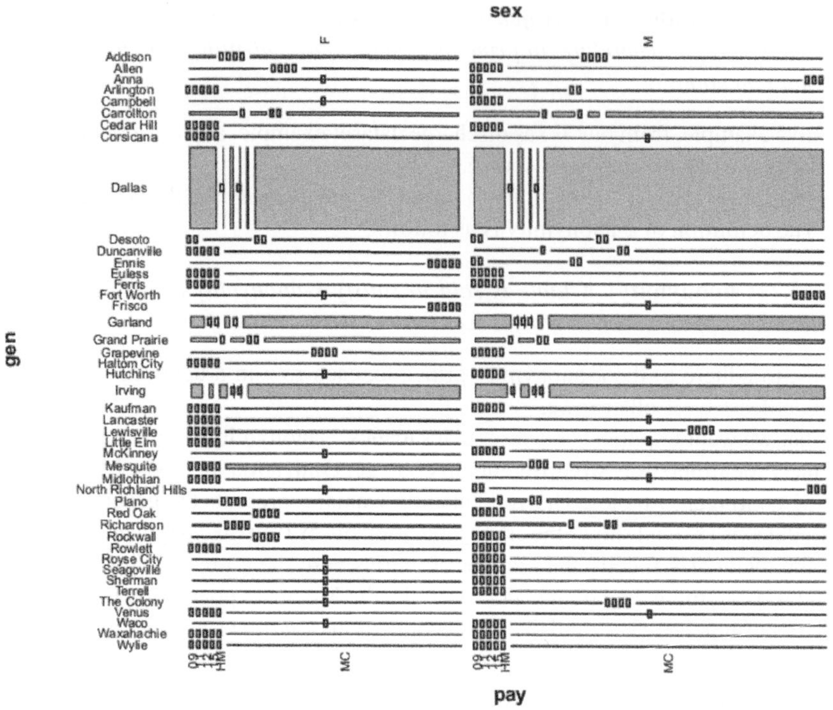

(a) City-level codes

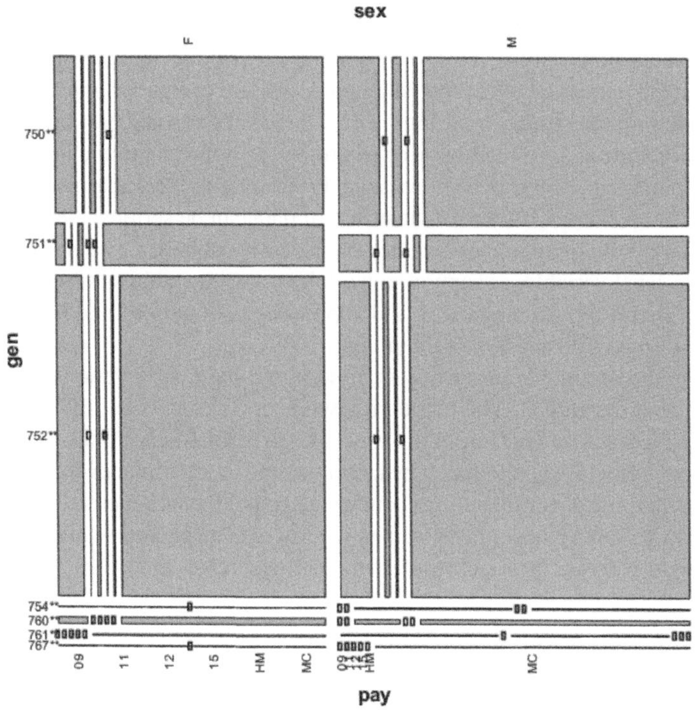

(b) Three-digit zip codes

FIGURE 15.6: Mosaic plots of the quasi-identifiers (sex, payment source, address).

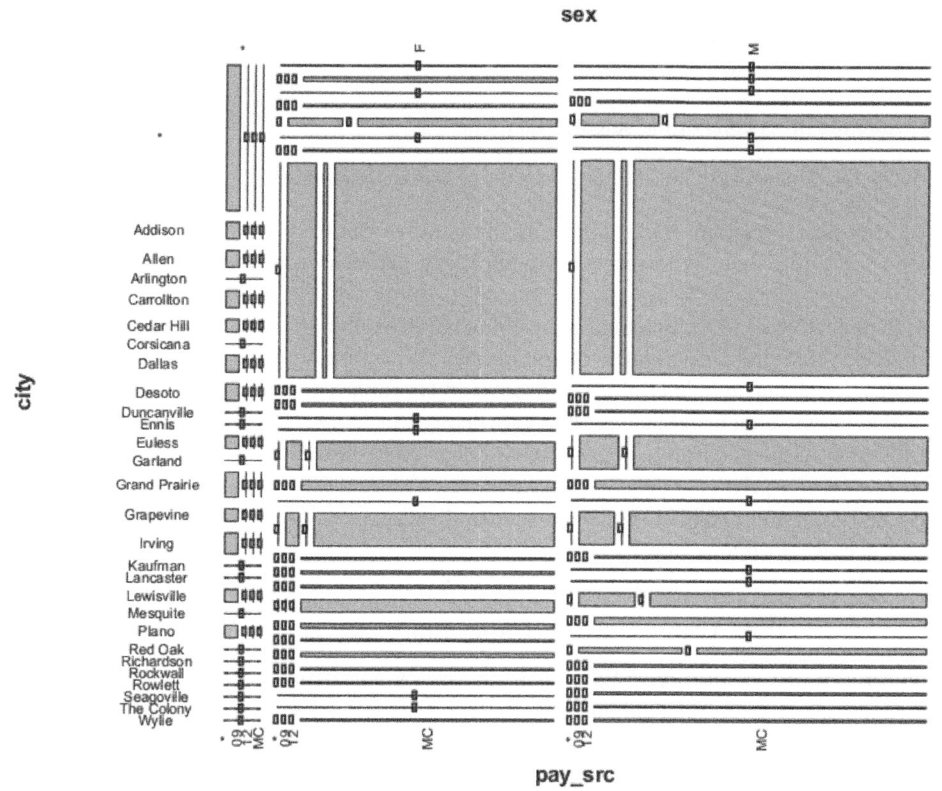

FIGURE 15.7: Mosaic plot of the generalized and suppressed quasi-identifiers.

which is a simple two-level hierarchy. One can obtain 10 different generalized datasets (including the original dataset) based on these two variables:

- (lv0-geo, lv0-pay): original dataset
- (lv1-geo, lv0-pay): city-level geo code and the original payment source code
- (lv2-geo, lv0-pay): county-level geo code and the original payment source code
- (7 more combinations)

Clearly, the (lv1-geo, lv0-pay) dataset is less generalized than the (lv2-geo, lv0-pay) dataset. If both datasets happen to satisfy k-anonymity, then the (lv1-geo, lv0-pay) dataset is said to be a k-minimally generalized dataset.

Note that, in the notion of k-minimal generalization, there can be multiple k-minimally generalized datasets. For example, it is possible that both (lv1-geo, lv0-pay) and (lv0-geo, lv1-pay) can be k-minimal generalizations. To differentiate among multiple k-minimally generalized datasets, Sweeney (54, 55) proposed to measure the cell distortion that are induced by generalization using a precision metric. The precision value is 1 if the generalized dataset maintains the same resolution as the original dataset, and it is 0 if the generalized dataset provides no distinguishable rows. If two datasets both satisfy the k-minimal generalization principle, it is desirable to choose the dataset that gives a higher precision. Using these two notions, minimal generalization and minimal distortion, the MinGen algorithm is outlined as follows:

1. Construct generalization hierarchies for the quasi-identifier.

2. Generate all possible generalized datasets based on the generalization hierarchies.

3. Select k-minimally generalized datasets.

4. Measure the precisions of the selected datasets.

5. Choose the generalized dataset that gives the maximum precision.

As can be seen, the algorithm scales exponentially with respect to the number of variables. Even Sweeney herself wrote that "With respect to complexity, MinGen makes no claim to be efficient" [54].

Subsequently several more practical algorithms have been proposed, e.g., Incognito [30] and Mondrian [31]. Satisfying k-anonymity is not a perfect protective solution, and there exist several failure modes. Machanavajjhala et al. [34] discovered two attack scenarios in which k-anonymity can fail: homogeneity attack and background knowledge attack, and suggested an extended privacy metric, l-diversity. Xiao and Tao [61] proposed a linear-time algorithm that satisfies l-diversity. Li et al. [32] proposed a privacy metric, t-closeness, that overcomes limitations of k-anonymity and l-diversity, and Xiao and Tao [62] suggested a generalization principle, m-invariance, that caters to re-publication issues of microdata.

15.3.2 Synthetic Data Using Multiple Imputation

The generation of synthetic data [49] is an alternative (and sometimes complementary) approach to data transforming disclosure techniques. Multiple imputation, which was originally developed to impute missing values in survey responses [48], can also be used to generate either partially or fully synthetic data. Abowd and Woodcock [2] synthesized a French longitudinal-linked database, and Raghunathan et al. [43] provided general methods for obtaining valid inferences using multiply imputed data. Markov Chain Monte Carlo simulation methods and generalized linear models are typically used for sampling. Decision trees models, such as CART and Random forests, can also be used as imputation models in multiple imputation [45, 9]. Some illustrative empirical studies have used U.S. census data [18], a German business database [46], and a U.S. American Community Survey [50].

Let us start from the missing value imputation setting. Consider a survey with two variables x and z, $\mathcal{D} = \{(x,z)\}$, where some of the x responses are missing. Let x_{obs} be the observed subset of x. In the multiple imputation approach, the unobserved responses are imputed using samples from a predictive posterior model as follows:

$$x \sim \Pr(x \mid x_{\text{obs}}, z)$$

Note that the predictive posterior can be modeled using the observed subset, and often obtained using generalized linear models, Bayesian Bootstrapping methods, or Markov Chain Monte Carlo simulations [52, 45]. For example, an R package for multivariate imputation for a chained equation [58] provides nine different imputation models including predictive mean matching, Bayesian linear regression, Linear regression, Unconditional mean imputation, etc. Generating fully synthetic data is straightforward from this framework.[2] First, z is drawn from $\Pr(z)$, then x is drawn from the predictive posterior distribution. Typically, this entire process is repeated independently K times to obtain K different synthetic datasets.

Raghunathan et al. [43] showed that valid inferences can be obtained from multiply imputed synthetic data. Let Q be a function of (x,z). For example, Q may represent the population mean of (x,z) or the population regression coefficients of x on z. Let q_i and v_i be the estimate of Q and

[2]To see the difference between partially and fully synthetic datasets, see [17] .

its variance obtained from the ith synthetic dataset. Then, valid inferences on Q can be obtained as follows:

$$\bar{q}_K = \sum_{i=1}^{K} q_i / K$$

$$T_s = (1 + \frac{1}{K}) b_K - \bar{v}_K$$

where $b_K = \sum_{i=1}^{K} (q_i - \bar{q}_K)^2/(K-1)$ and $\bar{v}_K = \sum_{i=1}^{K} v_i/K$. These two quantities $\bar{q}_K$ and T_s estimate the original Q and the variance from sampling.

For our Texas inpatient example, we fit simple imputation models based on linear regression. Note that, in theory, multiple imputation for fully/partially synthetic data requires sampling from predictive posterior distributions, and our approach can be viewed as a pseudo-multiple imputation implementation.[3] We build two regression models for length of stay and total charges, respectively. The other three variables—sex, payment source, and address—are categorical variables, and can also be modeled using generalized linear models, but we skip the process since (1) the goodness of fit of the fitted generalized linear models are poorly measured, and (2) these three variables are already k-anonymized. Specifically, for the two numeric variables, we build regression models as follows:

$$\text{length of stay} \sim \text{sex} + \text{payment source} + \text{city} + \text{total charges}$$

$$\text{total charges} \sim \text{sex} + \text{payment source} + \text{city} + \text{length of stay (los)}$$

We estimate regression coefficients and residual variances shown in Table 15.2 (length of stay) and Table 15.3 (total charges). As can be seen, the length of stay variable is primarily determined by the total charges variable, and vice versa. Interestingly, the total charges are slightly affected by the city variable e.g., see, the coefficients of cityDesoto and cityPlano. Male infants generally cost more, since many of them receive circumcision. Figure 15.8 shows the goodness of fit of the regression models: the fitted values (y-axis) and the original values (x-axis). From the fitted data, synthetic data can be obtained by adding Gaussian noise with the estimated residual variances.

15.3.3 PeGS: Perturbed Gibbs Sampler

The two competing requirements for public use data also apply to synthetic data disclosure. Synthetic data need to be accurate enough to answer relevant statistical queries without revealing private information to third parties. Statistical properties of synthetic data are primarily determined by imputation models [45], and models that are too accurate tend to leak private information [1].

The disclosure risks of multiply imputed synthetic datasets are typically measured after synthetic datasets are generated, i.e., using *post hoc* risk analysis. Multiple imputation is a general imputation methodology, and the choice of posterior model is usually up to statisticians. This flexibility makes it difficult to apply and analyze rigorous privacy measures, such as differential privacy and l-diversity, in a unified framework. Park and Ghosh (2014) were able to address this limitation by deriving the relationship between the amount of Laplace smoothing and privacy measures (ε in differential privacy and l in l-diversity) using a simple non-parametric model. They then directly incorporated these privacy measures in the synthesizing process, guaranteeing the desired level of privacy for synthetic data.

The resulting Perturbed Gibbs Sampler (PeGS) is a *practical* multidimensional categorical data synthesizer that satisfies ε-differential privacy. It can handle multidimensional data that are not practical to be represented as contingency tables. In our example, to sample from a multi-dimensional

[3] Multiple imputation is a sophisticated Bayesian methodology, and there are several different aspects from the example we presented. Our example is designed to convey the overall idea of multiple imputation. For more information, see [17].

TABLE 15.2: Regression Coefficients for the "Length of Stay" Model

	Estimate	Std. Error	t value	Pr(>|t|)
(Intercept)	0.1759	0.0889	1.98	0.0481
sexF	-0.0049	0.1002	-0.05	0.9610
sexM	-0.1198	0.1007	-1.19	0.2342
pay_src09	0.0101	0.0470	0.21	0.8302
pay_src12	-0.1005	0.1489	-0.67	0.4999
cityAddison	0.1015	0.1839	0.55	0.5813
cityAllen	0.0666	0.2703	0.25	0.8053
cityArlington	0.2729	0.2471	1.10	0.2696
cityCarrollton	0.1263	0.1473	0.86	0.3913
cityCedar Hill	0.1475	0.3080	0.48	0.6321
cityCorsicana	0.0715	0.3239	0.22	0.8253
cityDallas	0.0812	0.1327	0.61	0.5405
cityDesoto	-0.7054	0.2072	-3.40	0.0007
cityDuncanville	-0.1657	0.2241	-0.74	0.4597
cityEnnis	0.2673	0.3240	0.82	0.4096
cityEuless	-0.3476	0.3082	-1.13	0.2596
cityGarland	0.1374	0.1394	0.99	0.3245
cityGrand Prairie	0.1048	0.1459	0.72	0.4727
cityGrapevine	0.1929	0.3081	0.63	0.5314
cityIrving	0.0394	0.1363	0.29	0.7725
cityKaufman	0.1290	0.2472	0.52	0.6019
cityLancaster	0.0443	0.2645	0.17	0.8670
cityLewisville	0.0153	0.2196	0.07	0.9444
cityMesquite	0.0999	0.1498	0.67	0.5052
cityPlano	0.1227	0.1593	0.77	0.4414
cityRed Oak	0.3240	0.3241	1.00	0.3176
cityRichardson	0.1738	0.1748	0.99	0.3203
cityRockwall	-0.0763	0.2240	-0.34	0.7333
cityRowlett	0.1025	0.2343	0.44	0.6618
citySeagoville	0.1107	0.2647	0.42	0.6760
cityThe Colony	-0.1469	0.3241	-0.45	0.6504
cityWylie	0.0960	0.2241	0.43	0.6684
total_charges	0.0008	0.0000	48.54	0.0000

joint distribution, PeGS utilizes Gibbs sampling as follows:

$$\begin{aligned}
\text{sex} &\sim \Pr(\text{sex} \mid \text{payment source}, \text{address}, \text{los}, \text{charges}) \\
\text{payment source} &\sim \Pr(\text{payment source} \mid \text{sex}, \text{address}, \text{los}, \text{charges}) \\
\text{address} &\sim \Pr(\text{address} \mid \text{sex}, \text{address}, \text{los}, \text{charges}) \\
\text{los} &\sim \Pr(\text{los} \mid \text{sex}, \text{payment source}, \text{address}, \text{charges}) \\
\text{charges} &\sim \Pr(\text{charges} \mid \text{sex}, \text{payment source}, \text{address}, \text{los})
\end{aligned}$$

A sample from this iterative sampling scheme asymptotically converges to the sample from the original joint distribution. To satisfy ε-differential privacy, each conditional distribution is now perturbed

TABLE 15.3: Regression Coefficients for the "Total Charges" Model

	Estimate	Std. Error	t value	Pr(>|t|)
(Intercept)	359.1373	91.9207	3.91	0.0001
sexF	27.3817	103.9231	0.26	0.7922
sexM	174.8796	104.3848	1.68	0.0941
pay_src09	-48.5822	48.7065	-1.00	0.3187
pay_src12	95.4214	154.4706	0.62	0.5368
cityAddison	-234.4290	190.7568	-1.23	0.2193
cityAllen	-174.5079	280.3842	-0.62	0.5338
cityArlington	-297.4287	256.3879	-1.16	0.2462
cityCarrollton	-159.3104	152.7674	-1.04	0.2972
cityCedar Hill	-112.9648	319.5768	-0.35	0.7238
cityCorsicana	-201.8896	336.0570	-0.60	0.5481
cityDallas	-175.0181	137.5925	-1.27	0.2036
cityDesoto	897.3799	214.5596	4.18	0.0000
cityDuncanville	-76.4373	232.5305	-0.33	0.7424
cityEnnis	-287.8444	336.1882	-0.86	0.3920
cityEuless	35.7392	319.8752	0.11	0.9111
cityGarland	-196.9284	144.5687	-1.36	0.1734
cityGrand Prairie	-98.2934	151.3952	-0.65	0.5163
cityGrapevine	-341.1746	319.5782	-1.07	0.2859
cityIrving	-192.8540	141.3302	-1.36	0.1726
cityKaufman	-275.6385	256.4033	-1.08	0.2825
cityLancaster	-64.9637	274.4042	-0.24	0.8129
cityLewisville	-118.7260	227.8391	-0.52	0.6024
cityMesquite	-204.3538	155.3656	-1.32	0.1886
cityPlano	-264.5943	165.1621	-1.60	0.1094
cityRed Oak	-535.2229	336.0570	-1.59	0.1115
cityRichardson	-226.1209	181.3205	-1.25	0.2126
cityRockwall	-67.1545	232.4419	-0.29	0.7727
cityRowlett	-312.5497	243.0179	-1.29	0.1986
citySeagoville	-249.3875	274.6011	-0.91	0.3639
cityThe Colony	-77.5973	336.3026	-0.23	0.8176
cityWylie	-231.5758	232.4009	-1.00	0.3192
los	815.3706	16.7967	48.54	0.0000

by a derived privacy parameter $\alpha = f(\varepsilon)$, resulting in:

$$\begin{aligned} \text{sex} &\sim \Pr_\alpha(\text{sex} \mid \text{payment source}, \text{address}, \text{los}, \text{charges}) \\ \text{payment source} &\sim \Pr_\alpha(\text{payment source} \mid \text{sex}, \text{address}, \text{los}, \text{charges}) \\ \text{address} &\sim \Pr_\alpha(\text{address} \mid \text{sex}, \text{address}, \text{los}, \text{charges}) \\ \text{los} &\sim \Pr_\alpha(\text{los} \mid \text{sex}, \text{payment source}, \text{address}, \text{charges}) \\ \text{charges} &\sim \Pr_\alpha(\text{charges} \mid \text{sex}, \text{payment source}, \text{address}, \text{los}) \end{aligned}$$

The samples from this iterative mechanism satisfies ε-differential privacy. Figure 15.9 shows the overall algorithmic steps of PeGS. The statistical building blocks refer to the estimated conditional distributions, the noise injection step is basically $\Pr \rightarrow \Pr_\alpha$, and finally the synthesis step is the illustrated Gibbs sampling procedure.

Differential privacy [19] is a mathematical measure of privacy that quantifies disclosure risks

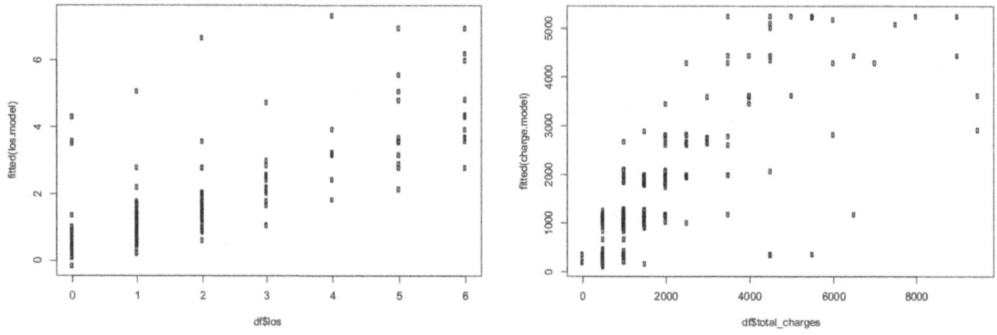

(a) Fitted vs. original length of stay (b) Fitted vs. original total charges

FIGURE 15.8: Scatter plots of the original and fitted data for synthetic data.

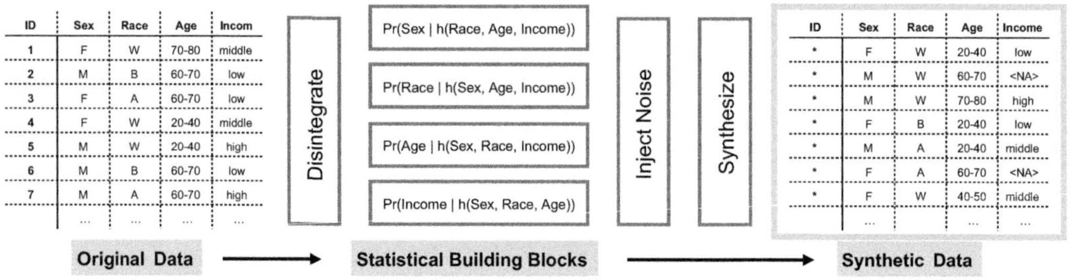

FIGURE 15.9: PeGS conceptual diagram.

of statistical functions. To satisfy ε-differential privacy, the inclusion or exclusion of any particular record in data cannot affect the outcome of functions by much. Specifically, a randomized function $f : \mathcal{D} \rightarrow f(\mathcal{D})$ provides ε-differential privacy, if it satisfies:

$$\frac{\Pr(f(\mathcal{D}_1) \in \mathcal{S})}{\Pr(f(\mathcal{D}_2) \in \mathcal{S})} \leq \exp(\varepsilon)$$

for all possible $\mathcal{D}_1, \mathcal{D}_2 \in \mathcal{D}$ where $\mathcal{D}_1$ and $\mathcal{D}_2$ differ by at most one element, and $\forall \mathcal{S} \in \text{Range}(f(\mathcal{D}))$. For a synthetic sample, this definition can be interpreted as follows [37]:

$$\frac{\Pr_{\mathcal{D}_1}(\mathbf{x})}{\Pr_{\mathcal{D}_2}(\mathbf{x})} \leq \exp(\varepsilon) \tag{15.1}$$

where $\mathbf{x}$ represents a random sample from synthesizers. In other words, a data synthesizer $\Pr_{\mathcal{D}}(\mathbf{x})$ is ε-differentially private, if the probabilities of generating $\mathbf{x}$ from $\mathcal{D}_1$ and $\mathcal{D}_2$ are indistinguishable to the extent of $\exp(\varepsilon)$.

Several mechanisms have been developed to achieve differential privacy. For numeric outputs, the most popular technique is to add Laplace noise with mean 0 and scale $\Delta f/\varepsilon$ where Δf is the L_1 sensitivity of function f. Exponential mechanism [38] is a general differential privacy mechanism that can be applied to non-numeric outputs. For categorical data, a Dirichlet prior can be used as a noise mechanism to achieve differential privacy [33, 37]. PeGS also uses this Dirichlet prior mechanism, also known as Laplace smoothing, to achieve ε-differential privacy.

Figure 15.10 compares three datasets: the original k-anonymized data, multiple imputation synthetic data, and PeGS synthetic data. As can be seen, the multiple imputation synthetic data follow

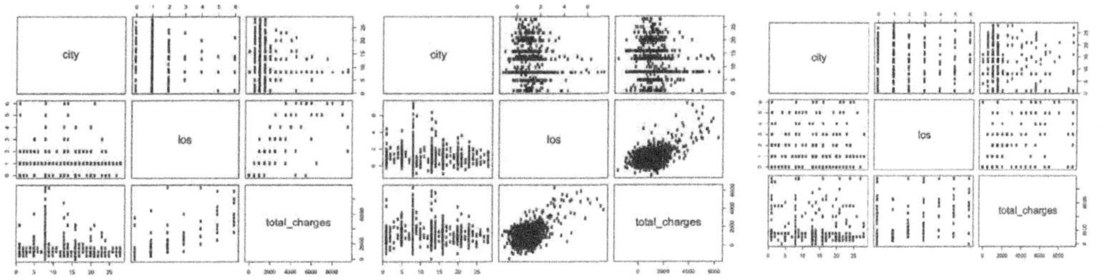

(a) Original Data (b) Synthesized Data (c) PeGS Data (ε = 10)

FIGURE 15.10: Scatter plots of the original, multiple-imputation synthetic, and PeGS synthetic data.

the specified additive Gaussian noise linear models. On the other hand, the PeGS synthetic data capture non-linear relationships in the original data. Furthermore, we can observe that the PeGS data points are more dispersed (perturbed) than the original data points. This perturbation is carefully calibrated to meet the specified differential privacy level.

Unlike general synthesizing mechanisms, PeGS provides an extra knob, $\alpha = f(\varepsilon)$, that can control the level of privacy when synthesizing data points. Figure 15.11 shows two synthetic datasets with different privacy level specifications: $\varepsilon = 100$ (utility-oriented) and $\varepsilon = 1$ (privacy-oriented). The value of ε can range from 0 to ∞. Smaller values of ε generate more perturbed synthetic data points guaranteeing better confidentiality and privacy protection. On the other hand, larger values of ε synthesize data points that are similar to the original data points, thus exhibiting low level privacy-protection but enhanced utility.

Stochastic perturbation is a critical component of the PeGS algorithm. Table 15.4 shows the first 10 data points from the original and PeGS synthetic data points. As can be seen, some data points changed to new points, and some did not. For example, the five attributes of the first row (F, MC, Dallas, 0.00, 500.00) changed to a completely new data (M, 09, Garland, 1.00, 1000.00). On the other hand, the 10th row remained unchanged. Since the synthesizing process is stochastic, attackers cannot be certain about which row is unchanged, and which row is completely synthesized. Thus,

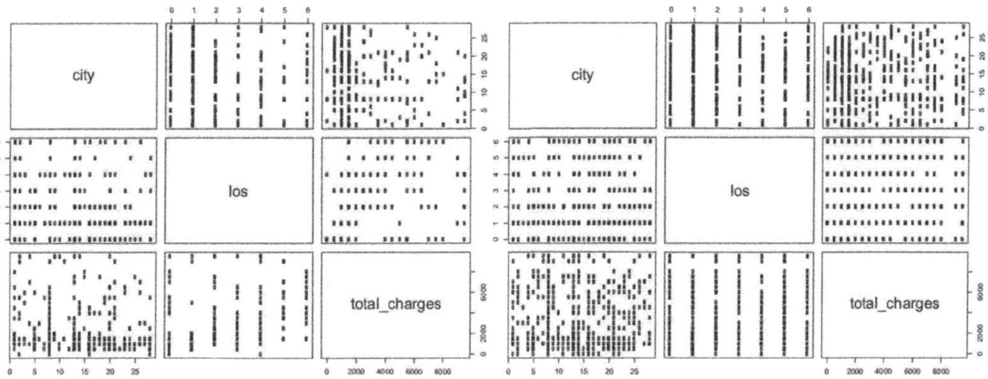

(a) Utility oriented ($\varepsilon = 100$) (b) Privacy oriented($\varepsilon = 1$)

FIGURE 15.11: PeGS can control the level of privacy by changing the privacy parameter α.

TABLE 15.4: Original and PeGS Synthetic Data

Original Data					
row id	sex	pay_src	city	los	total_charges
1	F	MC	Dallas	0.00	500.00
2	M	MC	Grand Prairie	2.00	4500.00
3	M	MC	Dallas	0.00	5500.00
4	*	*	*	0.00	4500.00
5	F	MC	Dallas	3.00	3000.00
6	M	MC	Dallas	1.00	1000.00
7	M	MC	Dallas	1.00	1000.00
8	F	MC	Garland	6.00	7500.00
9	F	MC	Dallas	6.00	4500.00
10	F	MC	Garland	1.00	1000.00
PeGS Data					
row id	sex	pay_src	city	los	total_charges
1	M	09	Garland	1.00	1000.00
2	M	MC	Grand Prairie	5.00	4500.00
3	M	MC	Dallas	1.00	500.00
4	*	*	*	1.00	5000.00
5	M	MC	Dallas	2.00	2000.00
6	M	MC	Dallas	1.00	1000.00
7	F	MC	Grand Prairie	1.00	1000.00
8	M	MC	Garland	6.00	7500.00
9	F	MC	Irving	3.00	9500.00
10	F	MC	Garland	1.00	1000.00

this stochastic perturbation enhances the protection from linking attack. Figure 15.12 shows the perturbed city values in comparison with the original city values. With no perturbation, the mosaic plot should show a thick diagonal band as shown in Figure 15.12 (a). The stochastic perturbation of PeGS disperse the data values, and as a result, we obtain a smoothed-out diagonal band as shown in Figure 15.12 (b). Note that the level of dispersion is determined by the privacy parameter, $\alpha = f(\varepsilon)$.

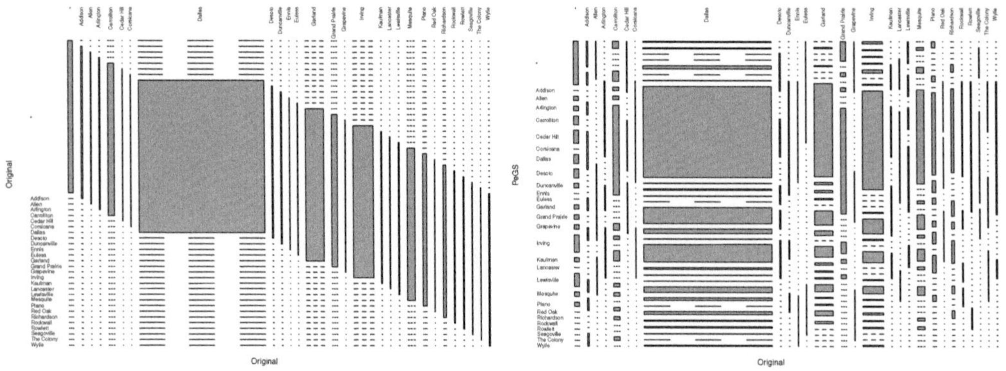

(a) Original vs. original city variables.

(b) PeGS vs. original city variables.

FIGURE 15.12: Original and perturbed data.

15.3.4 Randomization Methods

The generation of synthetic data can be viewed as a special case of the "randomization method." Although the term "randomization method" has been traditionally used in the context of survey design [59], in this chapter, a randomization method refers to a privacy-preserving algorithm that involves a degree of randomness in its mechanism [6]; for example, additive noise, probabilistic value mapping and suppression, and sampling from (perturbed) distributions. However, unlike multiple imputation and other synthetic data mechanisms, randomization methods been mainly developed in the database and data mining communities.

Although randomization methods are straightforward and easy to apply, it is difficult to quantify the level of privacy. Inspired by k-anonymity, [5] quantified the degree of randomization, i.e., k-randomization, required to guarantee a desired level of privacy. The authors pointed out that such randomization methods may be susceptible to outliers and data-specific properties.

The utility of such randomized data can be enhanced by using special types of data mining algorithms. [4] demonstrated that the actual distributions of the original data can be reconstructed from randomized data. Furthermore, the authors showed that reasonable decision trees can be also trained on such randomized data. [3] extended this reconstruction framework by applying an Expectation Maximization algorithm.

15.3.5 Data Swapping

Although little used in practice, data swapping is an important algorithm that has influenced various subsequent privacy-preserving algorithms. The original idea of data swapping was proposed by [14] as a method for preserving confidentiality in categorical datasets. In data swapping, sensitive values are exchanged among individuals while maintaining lower-order frequency counts and marginals. This transformation not only protects confidentiality by de-correlating sensitive values with the other values, but also keeps a certain level of data utility by preserving summary statistics of the data. [23] extensively surveyed the influence of data swapping in the field of statistical disclosure limitation. Subsequent variations include: rank swapping by [39], simplified rank swapping in [15] and [16], data swapping for continuous and ordinal variables by [10], and the Post Randomization Method (PRAM) by [26].

We have visited various types of privacy-preserving algorithms, from generalization and suppression to data swapping. Each method exhibits distinct utility and risk perspectives. In practice, we recommend practitioners to use a combination of multiple privacy-preserving methods to mitigate potential risks.

15.4 Challenges with Health Data

Thus far, we have demonstrated various statistical disclosure limitation techniques using the Texas discharge dataset. However, in practice, health data privacy is not just about the statistical identifiability, and its impact needs to be carefully interpreted within a healthcare system. In this section, we briefly discuss some of such challenges, specifically:

1. Are health datasets more vulnerable to privacy attacks compared to other kinds of datasets?
2. Can we estimate re-identification risks in the HIPAA regulations?
3. Is there an alternative method to the Safe Harbor Standard?
4. What are future directions for health data privacy research?

Compared to other types of datasets, health datasets inherently contain more privacy-sensitive variables, and they tend to be person-specific. Thus, the first natural question is whether health datasets are more at risk than other kinds of datasets. [21] collected 1498 academic papers related to re-identification from IEEE Xplore, ACM Digital Library, and PubMed. The authors carefully selected 14 most relevant articles, of which six articles were about health data re-identification. Although the mean re-identification rate on health data was slightly higher than the rate on the others (0.34 versus 0.26), they observed that the re-identification rate was dominated by small-scale studies. Most notably, the authors found that "most re-identified data were not de-identified according to existing standards."

The Health Insurance Portability and Accountability Act (HIPAA) Privacy Rule delineates several routes to de-identify health data. Among many others, the Safe Harbor Standard in HIPAA is "an easily followed cookbook approach" to anonymize secondary use datasets, which essentially removes 18 types of identifiable variables including names, geographic subdivisions smaller than a state, all elements of dates that are directly related to an individual, etc. However, in many cases, this guideline is often applied without knowledge of the risk of "re-identification." [8] estimated the re-identification risk for data sharing policies by linking voter registration lists. The authors separately measured the re-identification rates for each state dataset, and found that the measured re-identification rates ranged from 0.01% to 0.25% if the Safe Harbor Standard was applied. Sparsely populated states, such as Delaware and Rhode Island, were shown to be more vulnerable to privacy attacks. The authors concluded that blanket protection policies, such as the Safe Harbor Standard, should be followed by locally performed re-identification risk studies to accurately quantify potential privacy risks.

An alternative route to the Safe Harbor Standard is the Statistical Standard. According to the HIPAA de-identification guideline[4] (§164.514(b)), this criterion is defined as follows:

> A person with appropriate knowledge of and experience with generally accepted statistical and scientific principles and methods for rendering information not individually identifiable:
>
> 1. Applying such principles and methods, determines that the risk is very small that the information could be used, alone or in combination with other reasonably available information, by an anticipated recipient to identify an individual who is a subject of the information; and
> 2. Documents the methods and results of the analysis that justify such determination.

This regulation points to various statistical methods including suppression, generalization, randomization, and perturbation, which are all covered in this chapter. [35] designed five alternative policies that are different from the Safe Harbor Standard, and compared the re-identification risks of the six different privacy-processed datasets (including the Safe Harbor Standard). The authors found that these alternatives have shown equal or lesser re-identification risk than the Safe Harbor Standard. The advantage of the alternatives is that they can provide different levels of granularity in patient demographics. For example, the Safe Harbor Standard specifies that any age above 90 years old must be suppressed, while the alternative rules allow keeping the age variable with 5 years and 10 years age binning but suppressing other variables such as ethnicity and sex. Using the suggested alternatives, a healthcare organization can apply customized de-identification standards that are best suitable for specific research objectives.

Note that this chapter specifically focused on privacy-preserving algorithms for publishing secondary use health data. In a recent special focus issue of the *Journal of the American Medical Informatics Association* on biomedical data privacy, [36] categorized three different types of privacy notions based on the health data life-cycle:

---

[4]`http://www.hhs.gov/ocr/privacy/hipaa/understanding/coveredentities/De-identification/guidance.html#guidancedetermination`

- **Privacy in Collection Zone** deals with who can collect health information, how much, when, and for what purposes.
- **Privacy in Primary Use Zone** is closely related to confidentiality and security.
- **Privacy in Secondary Use Zone** focuses on anonymity and de-identification methods.

As can be seen, the scope of health data privacy is broad and multidisciplinary. Privacy research, especially in the health domain, should comprehensively cover all these multifaceted aspects. Also, privacy research should keep eyes on the emergence and adoption of new technologies such as cloud computing [57] and mobile devices, as they are transforming the way data are collected and stored. Finally, it would be worthwhile to compare the U.S. system to foreign jurisdictions with different privacy laws and regulations.

15.5 Conclusion

In this chapter, we presented a short walk-through of basic privacy-preserving data transformation techniques: variable reduction, elimination of rare cases, coarsening, generalization and suppression, and imputation. Each method has distinct utility and risk aspects. In practice, domain experts and statisticians should carefully choose privacy preserving algorithms depending on the publishing objectives. For example, generalization and suppression techniques can provide truthful data, but the resultant variable resolution may not be useful for some applications. Synthetic data can preserve the original variable resolution, but more efforts are needed to obtain valid inferences.

As privacy is a subjective and contextual concept, so is "utility." Utility can be measured in multiple ways, depending on the research objectives. For our Texas inpatient example, if we want to find out relevant variables and their coefficients that affect hospital charges, we can measure the utility as follows:

$$\text{Utility} = \exp(-||\beta_{\text{original}} - \beta_{\text{synthetic}}||^2)$$

where β_{original} and $\beta_{\text{synthetic}}$ are regression coefficients from the original and synthetic data, respectively. This utility metric is maximized when $\beta_{\text{original}} = \beta_{\text{synthetic}}$. Note that this utility metric is one of many other utility metrics that can measure similar quantities. As an another example, if aggregate statistics are the primary concerns, the utility can be measured as follows:

$$\text{Utility} = \exp(-||E[x_{\text{original}}] - E[x_{\text{synthetic}}]||^2)$$

where x is the variable of interest. It is recommended to try several different utility metrics before publishing transformed data.

Even if there exist theoretical privacy guarantees for transformed datasets, rigorous risk analyses should be performed before actual publishing. Researchers need to consider possible and worst-case attack scenarios, and try simulating such attacks. Matching internal databases, and searching already published external databases are good practices as well. By doing so, data publishers can estimate the potential consequences of privacy breaches. Privacy breaches may result in a significant amount of legal and social costs, and data publishers should to be aware of the worst-case scenarios.

Privacy must be interpreted both contextually and through information theoretic ways. In healthcare systems, some variables may be more sensitive than others. For example, an address or name can be less sensitive than a disease or medication history. Domain knowledge and data exploration steps are exceptionally important because of the complex healthcare ecosystem. Furthermore, perceptions on privacy also changes over time with new technologies: for example, social network services. Therefore, for successful privacy-preserving data publishing in healthcare, one needs to understand social infrastructures as well as information-theoretic or statistical privacy concepts.

Bibliography

[1] John M. Abowd and Lars Vilhuber. How protective are synthetic data? *Privacy in Statistical Databases*, 5262:239–246, 2008.

[2] John M. Abowd and Simon D. Woodcock. Disclosure limitation in longitudinal linked data. In *Confidentiality Dislosure and Data Access: Theory and Practical Applications for Statistical Agencies*, Amsterdam: NorthHolland, pages 215–277, 2001.

[3] Dakshi Agarwal and Charu C Aggarwal. On the design and quantification of privacy preserving data mining algorithms. In *PODS '01 Proceedings of the Twentieth ACM SIGMOD-SIGACT-SIGART Symposium on Principles of Database Systems*, pages 247–255, 2001.

[4] Rakesh Agarwal and Ramakrishnan Srikant. Privacy-preserving data mining. In *Proceedings of the 2000 ACM SIGMOD International Conference on Management of Data*, 2000.

[5] Charu C. Aggarwal. On randomization, public information and the curse of dimensionality. In *IEEE 23rd International Conference on Data Engineering*, pages 136–145, 2007.

[6] Charu C. Aggarwal and Philip S. Yu. A general survey of privacy-preserving data mining models and algorithms. In Charu C. Aggarwal and Philip S. Yu, editors, *Privacy-Preserving Data Mining*, volume 34 of *Advances in Database Systems*, pages 11–52. Springer US, 2008.

[7] Ajit Appari and M. Eric Johnson. Information security and privacy in healthcare: Current state of research. *International Journal of Internet and Enterprise Management*, 6(4):279–314, 2010.

[8] Kathleen Benitez and Bradley Malin. Evaluating re-identification risks with respect to the hipaa privacy rule. *Journal of the American Medical Informatics Association*, 17(2):169–177, 2010.

[9] Gregory Caiola and Jerome P. Reiter. Random forests for generating partially synthetic, categorical data. *Transactions on Data Privacy*, 3:27–42, 2010.

[10] Michael Carlson and Mickael Salabasis. A data-swapping technique for generating synthetic samples; a method for disclosure control. *Research in Official Statistics*, 5:35–64, 2002.

[11] Centers for Medicare and Medicaid Services. Medicare Claims Synthetic Public Use Files (SynPUFs). `http://www.cms.gov/Research-Statistics-Data-and-Systems/Statistics-Trends-and-Reports/SynPUFs/`, 2013.

[12] Centers for Medicare and Medicaid Services. CMS EHR Meaningful Use Overview. *EHR Incentive Programs*, Octorber 2011.

[13] Tore Dalenius. Finding a needle in a haystack—or identifying anonymous census record. *Journal of Official Statistics*, 2:329–336, 1986.

[14] Tore Dalenius and Steven P. Reiss. Data-swapping: A technique for disclosure control. *Journal of Statistical Planning and Inference*, 6:73–85, 1982.

[15] Josep Domingo-Ferrer and Vincenc Torra. *Theory and Practical Applications for Statistical Agencies*, chapter "Disclosure control methods and information loss for microdata", pages 91–110. Elsevier, 2001.

[16] Josep Domingo-Ferrer and Vincenc Torra. *Theory and Practical Applications for Statistical Agencies*, chapter "A quantitative comparison of disclosure control methods for microdata", pages 111–133. Elsevier, 2001.

[17] Jorg Drechsler, Stefan Bender, and Susanne Rassler. Comparing fully and partially synthetic datasets for statistical disclosure control in the German IAB establishment panel. *Transactions on Data Privacy*, 1:105–130, 2008.

[18] Jorg Drechsler and Jerome P. Reiter. Sampling with synthesis: A new approach for releasing public use census microdata. *Journal of the American Statistical Association*, 105(492):1347–1357, 2010.

[19] Cynthia Dwork. Differential privacy. In *Proceedings of the 33rd International Colloquium on Automata, Languages and Programming*, volume 4052, pages 1–12, 2006.

[20] Julia Brande Earp and Fay Cobb Payton. Information privacy in the service sector: An exploratory study of health care and banking professionals. *Journal of Organizational Computing and Electronic Commerce*, 16(2):105–122, 2006.

[21] Khaled El Emam, Elizabeth Jonker, Luk Arbuckle, and Bradley Malin. A systematic review of re-identification attacks on health data. *PLoS One*, 6(12):e28071, 2011.

[22] Richard A. Epstein. The legal regulation of genetic discrimination: Old responses to new technology. *Boston University Law Review*, 74(1):1–24, 1994.

[23] Stephen E. Fienberg and Julie McIntyre. Data swapping: Variations on a theme by Dalenius and Reiss. *Journal of Official Statistics*, 21:309–323, 2005.

[24] Michael Friendly. Mosaic displays for multi-way contingency tables. *Journal of the American Statistical Association*, 89(425):190–200, 1994.

[25] Michael Friendly. Extending mosaic displays: Marginal, conditional, and partial views of categorical data. *Journal of Computational and Graphical Statistics*, 8(3):373–395, 1999.

[26] J. M. Gouweleeuw, P. Kooiman, L. C. R. J. Willenborg, and P. P. de Wolf. Post randomization for statistical disclosure control: Theory and implementation. *Journal of Official Statistics*, 14:463–478, 1998.

[27] Ragib Hassan and William Yurcik. A statistical analysis of disclosed storage security breaches. In *Proceedings of the Second ACM Workshop on Storage Security and Survivability*, pages 1–8, 2006.

[28] Rashid Hussain Khokhar, Rui Chen, Benjamin C.M. Fung, and Siu Man Lui. Quantifying the costs and benefits of privacy-preserving health data publishing. *Journal of Biomedical Informatics*, 50:107–121, 2014.

[29] Jaewoo Lee and Chris Clifton. Differential identifiability. In *Proceedings of the ACM SIGKDD International Conference on Knowledge Discovery and Data Mining*, pages 1041–1049, 2012.

[30] K. LeFevre, D. J. DeWitt, and R. Ramakrishnan. Incognito: Efficient full-domain k-anonymity. In *Proceedings of the 2005 ACM SIGMOD International Conference on Management of Data*, pages 46–60, 2005.

[31] K. LeFevre, D. J. DeWitt, and R. Ramakrishnan. Mondrian multidimensional k-anonymity. In *Proceedings of the 22nd International Conference on Data Engineering*, 2006.

[32] Ninghui Li, Tiancheng Li, and Suresh Venkatasubramanian. t-closeness: Privacy beyond k-anonymity and l-diversity. In *Proceedings of International Conference on Data Engineering*, 2007.

[33] Ashwin Machanavajjhala, Daniel Kifer, John Abowd, Johannes Gehrke, and Lars Vilhuber. Privacy: Theory meets practice on the map. In *Proceedings of the 24th International Conference on Data Engineering*, 2008.

[34] Ashwin Machanavajjhala, Daniel Kifer, Johannes Gehrke, and Muthuramakrishnan Venkitasubramanian. l-diversity: Privacy beyond k-anonymity. *Transactions on Knowledge Discovery from Data*, 1, 2007.

[35] Bradley Malin, Kathleen Benitez, and Daniel Masys. Never too old for anonymity: A statistical standard for demographic data sharing via the HIPAA privacy rule. *Journal of the American Medical Informatics Association*, 18(1):3–10, 2011.

[36] Bradley A. Malin, Khaled El Emam, and Christine M. O'Keefe. Biomedical data privacy: Problems, perspectives, and recent advances. *Journal of the American Medical Informatics Association*, 20(1):2–6, 2013.

[37] David McClure and Jerome P. Reiter. Differential privacy and statistical disclosure risk measures: An investigation with binary synthetic data. *Transactions on Data Privacy*, 5:535–552, 2012.

[38] Frank McSherry and Kunal Talwar. Mechanism design via differential privacy. In *Proceedings of the 48th Annual Symposium of Foundations of Computer Science*, 2007.

[39] Richard A. Moore. Controlled data-swapping techniques for masking public use microdata sets. Technical report, U.S. Bureau of the Census, 1996.

[40] Yubin Park and Joydeep Ghosh. PeGS: Perturbed Gibbs Samplers that Generate Privacy-Compliant Synthetic Data. arXiv:1312.5370, 2014.

[41] Richard A. Posner. The right of privacy. *Georgia Law Review*, 4(1):393–422, 1978.

[42] President Obama's Council of Scientific Advisors. PCAST Health IT Report. `http://www.whitehouse.gov/sites/default/files/microsites/ostp/pcast-health-it-report.pdf`, 2010.

[43] T. E. Raghunathan, Jerome P. Reiter, and Donald B. Rubin. Multiple imputation for statistical disclosure limitation. *Journal of Official Statistics*, 19(1):1–16, 2003.

[44] A. Raman. Enforcing privacy through security in remote patient monitoring ecosystems. In *6th International Special Topic Conference on Information Technology Applications in Biomedicine*, pages 298–301, 2007.

[45] Jerome P. Reiter. Releasing multiply imputed, synthetic public use microdata: An illustration and empirical study. *Journal of the Royal Statistical Society, Series A*, 168:185–205, 2005.

[46] Jerome P. Reiter and Jorg Drechsler. Releasing multiply imputed synthetic data generated in two stages to protect confidentiality. *Statistica Sinica*, 20:405–421, 2010.

[47] Thomas C. Rindfieisch. Privacy, information technology, and health care. *Communications of the ACM*, 40(8):92–100, 1997.

[48] Donald B. Rubin. *Multiple Imputation for Nonresponse in Surveys*. Wiley, 1987.

[49] Donald B. Rubin. Discussion: Statistical disclosure limitation. *Journal of Official Statistics*, 9:462–468, 1993.

[50] Joseph W. Sakshaug and Trivellore E. Raghunathan. Synthetic data for small area estimation. *Privacy in Statistical Databases*, 6344:162–173, 2011.

[51] Pierangela Samarati. Protecting respondents' identities in microdata release. *IEEE Transactions on Knowledge and Data Engineering*, 1998.

[52] J. L. Schafer. *Analysis of Incomplete Multivariate Data*. Chapman and Hall, 1997.

[53] Paul M. Schwartz. Privacy and the economics of personal health care information. *Texas Law Review*, 76(1):1–76, 1997.

[54] Latanya Sweeney. Achieving k-anonymity privacy protection using generalization and suppression. *International Journal on Uncertainty, Fuzziness and Knowledge-Based Systems*, 10(5):571–588, 2002.

[55] Latanya Sweeney. k-anonymity: A model for protecting privacy. *International Journal on Uncertain, Fuzziness and Knowledge-Based Systems*, 10:557–570, October 2002.

[56] Texas Department of State Health Services. Texas hospital inpatient discharge public use data file. `http://www.dshs.state.tx.us/thcic/hospitals/Inpatientpudf.shtm`, 2006.

[57] Yue Tong, Jinyuan Sun, Sherman S M Chow, and Pan Li. Cloud-assisted mobile-access of health data with privacy and auditability. *IEEE Journal of Biomedical and Health Informatics*, 18(2):419–429, 2014.

[58] Stef van Buuren and Karin Groothuis-Oudshoorn. MICE: Multivariate imputation by chained equations in R. *Journal of Statistical Software*, 45(3), 1–67, 2011.

[59] S L Warner. Randomized response: A survey technique for eliminating evasive answer bias. *Journal of American Statistical Association*, 60(309):63–69, 1965.

[60] L. Willenborg and T. de Waal. *Elements of Statistical Disclosure Control*, volume 155. Springer, 2001.

[61] Xiaokui Xiao and Yufei Tao. Anatomy: Simple and effective privacy preservation. In *Proceedings of the 32nd International Conference on Very Large Data Bases*, pages 139–150, 2006.

[62] Xiaokui Xiao and Yufei Tao. m-invariance: Towards privacy preserving re-publication of dynamic datasets. In *Proceedings of SIGMOD*, 2007.

Part III

Applications and Practical Systems for Healthcare

Chapter 16

Data Analytics for Pervasive Health

Giovanni Acampora
School of Science and Technology
Nottingham Trent University
Nottingham, UK
giovanni.acampora@ntu.ac.uk

Diane J. Cook
School of Electrical Engineering and Computer Science
Washington State University
Pullman, WA
cook@eecs.wsu.edu

Parisa Rashidi
Department of Biomedical Engineering
University of Florida
Gainesville, FL
parisa.rashidi@ufl.edu

Athanasios V. Vasilakos
Department of Computer and Telecommunications Engineering
University of Western Macedonia
Kozani, Greece
vasilako@ath.forthnet.gr

16.1 Introduction

Nowadays, the majority of industrialized nations are facing significant complications regarding the quality and cost of various healthcare and well-being services. These difficulties will exacerbate even more due to an increasing aging population, which translates into a multitude of chronic diseases and tremendous demand for various healthcare services. As a result, the cost of the healthcare sector might not be sustainable and therefore industrialized countries need to find and plan policies and strategies to use the limited economical resources more efficiently and effectively. This need for sustainable healthcare systems translates into a range of challenges in science and technology, which if solved, ultimately could benefit our global society and economy. In particular, the exploitation of information and communication technology for implementing autonomous and pro-active healthcare services will be extremely beneficial.

In the face of such challenges, there has been an increasing interest in applying analytics techniques to healthcare problems. Analytics techniques can be applied in scenarios such as assisted living for individuals with disabilities, aging in place, and remote health monitoring. The need for developing healthcare applications based on analytics techniques is not just underscored by researchers, but also governments are trying to use such techniques to lower the cost of healthcare in the United States and elsewhere. With recent advances in analytics as well as sensor technology, we are embarking on the path of revolutionary low cost intelligent health systems embedded within the home and living environments [24, 121]. Some examples include cognitive health monitoring systems based on activity recognition, persuasive systems for motivating users to change their health and wellness habits, and abnormal health condition detection systems. Figure 16.1 depicts how intelligent health systems might be used as cohesive services integrated into different environments and devices.

A wide variety of sensor modalities can be used when developing intelligent health systems, including wearable and ambient sensors [45]. In the case of wearable sensors, sensors are attached to the body [258] or woven into garments [86, 154]. For example, 3-axis accelerometers distributed over an individual's body can provide information about the orientation and movement of the corresponding body part. Researchers commonly use these inertial measurement units to recognize ambulatory movements (e.g., walking, running, sitting, climbing, and falling) [150, 222], posture [138], and gestures [4, 120, 128, 148].

Ambient sensors such as infrared motion detectors, magnetic door sensors, break-beam sensors, and pressure mats [22, 251] also have been used to gather information about health status and user

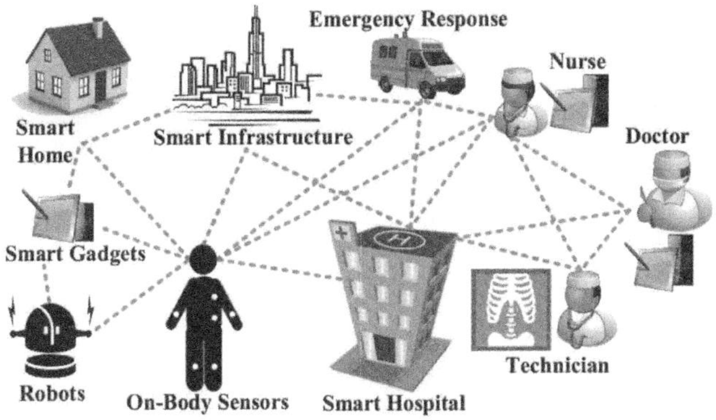

FIGURE 16.1 (See color insert.): Interconnected world of intelligent health services.

activities in indoor environments [50, 169]. Because this approach embeds sensors within environments, it is well suited to creating intelligent health systems such as smart environments and has been widely adopted for health monitoring and ambient assisted living [239]. Other sensors include RFID tags [34, 179], shake sensors [186], video cameras [32, 62, 158, 248], microphones [99, 146], and GPS locators [143, 178].

In this chapter, we will explore how different analytics techniques can be used for supporting the development of intelligent health systems and sensor data analysis.[1] First, we will provide an overview of supporting infrastructure and technology including different types of sensors that can be used for collecting data, then in the next two sections we will cover basic and advanced analytics techniques including different types of supervised and unsupervised machine learning techniques. Application in different healthcare domains will be discussed in its next section, and finally we will close the chapter with our conclusions and a brief discussion of the our outlook in this area.

16.2 Supporting Infrastructure and Technology

This section will introduce and describe the supporting infrastructure and technologies used in intelligent health systems in the context of the healthcare domain. In particular, we will explain *Body Area Networks* (BANs) and *Dense/Mesh Sensor Networks in Smart Homes*, and we point to some recent trends in sensor technology, such as epidermal electronics and MEMS sensors, among others.

16.2.1 BANs: Body Area Networks

The widespread use of wireless networks and the constant miniaturization of electrical devices has empowered the development of Body Area Networks (BANs) [46]. In a BAN, various sensors are attached on clothing or on the body or even implanted under the skin [137]. This new communication approach offers numerous new, practical, and innovative applications for improving human health and the quality of life by continuously monitoring health features such as heartbeat, body temperature, physical activity, blood pressure, ECG (electrocardiogram), EEG (electroencephalog-

[1] This chapter is partially based on an article published in the Proceedings of IEEE, titled "A Survey on Ambient Intelligence in Healthcare." The full version of this paper can be found at the IEEE Website.

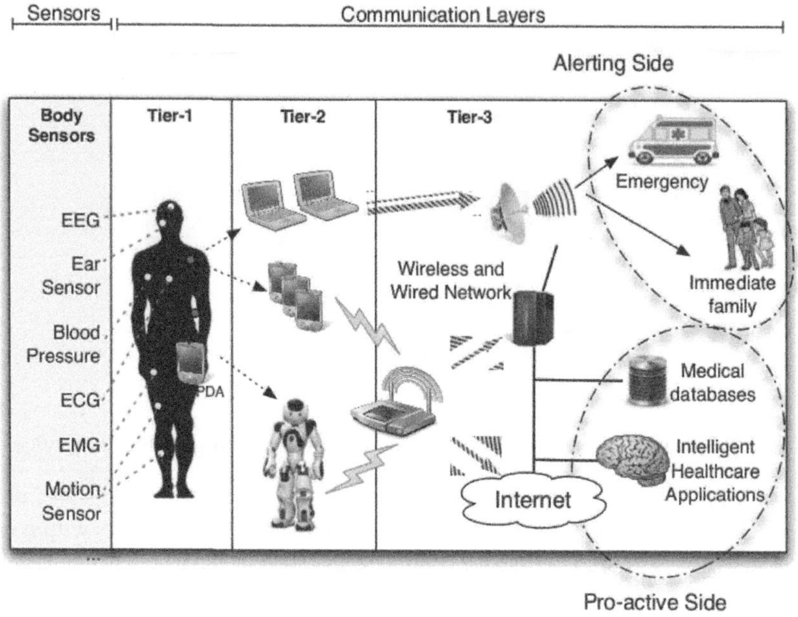

FIGURE 16.2: A three-tier architecture of the BAN communication system.

raphy), and EMG (electromyography). BANs provide a technological infrastructure for remotely streaming sensored data to a medical doctor's site for a real-time diagnosis, to a medical database for record keeping, or to a corresponding technological equipment that, pro-actively and autonomously, can issue an emergency alert or intelligently manage this information for taking suitable actions and improving the quality of human life [44].

There are several benefits of using wireless BANs in healthcare applications; mainly *communication efficiency* and *cost-effectiveness*. Indeed, physiological signals obtained by body sensors can be effectively processed to obtain reliable and accurate physiological estimations. At the same time, the ultra-low power consumption provision of such sensors makes their batteries long-lasting. Moreover, with the increasing demand of body sensors in the consumer electronics market, more sensors will be mass-produced at a relatively low cost, especially for medical purposes. Another important benefit of BAN is their scalability and integration with other network infrastructure. BANs may interface with Wireless Sensor Networks (WSNs), radio frequency identification tags (RFIDs) [109, 110], Bluetooth, Bluetooth Low Energy (BLE, previously called WiBree) [106], video surveillance systems, wireless personal area network (WPAN), wireless local area networks (WLANs), Internet, and cellular networks. All of these important benefits are opening and expanding new marketing opportunities for advanced consumer electronics in the field of ubiquitous computing for health care applications.

Figure 16.2 better depicts BANs' communication architecture in terms of three different layers: *Tier-1-Intra BAN*, *Tier-2-Inter BAN*, and *Tier-3- beyond-BAN communications*. These architectural layers cover multiple aspects of communication that range from low-level to high-level design issues, and facilitate the creation of a component-based, efficient BAN system for a wide range of applications.

The term "intra-BAN communications" refers to radio communications of about 2 meters around the human body, which can be further subcategorized as: (1) communications between body sensors, and (2) communications between body sensors and a portable Personal Server (PS) device (i.e., a PDA), as shown in in Figure 16.2. Due to the direct relationship with body sensors and BANs, the design of intra-BAN communications is very critical. Furthermore, the intrinsically battery-operated and low bit-rate features of existing body sensor devices make it a challenging issue to design an energy-efficient MAC protocol with QoS provisioning.

The "inter-BAN communications" enables the communications between the body sensors and one or more access points (APs). The APs can be deployed as part of the infrastructure, or be strategically placed in a dynamic environment for handling emergency situations. Similarly, the functionality of a tier-2-network (as shown in Figure 16.2) is used to interconnect BANs with various networks that are easy to access in daily life, such as the Internet and cellular networks. We divide the paradigms of inter-BAN communications into two categories, infrastructure-based architecture and ad hoc-based architecture. While the infrastructure-based architecture provides larger bandwidth with centralized control and flexibility, the ad hoc-based architecture facilitates fast deployment when encountering a dynamic environment, such as medical emergency care response, or at a disaster site (e.g., AID-N system [74]).

Most BAN applications use infrastructure-based, inter-BAN communications that assumes an environment with limited space, e.g., a waiting room in a hospital, home and office, etc. Compared to its ad-hoc networks counterpart, infrastructure-based networks offer the advantage of centralized management and security control. Due to this centralized structure, the AP also works as the database server in some applications, such as SMART [56], or CareNet [116].

Tier 3 is intended for streaming body sensor data to metropolitan areas. Sensor data are moved from an inter-BAN network to a beyond-BAN network by using a gateway device; for instance a PDA could be employed to create a wireless link between these two networks, transfer body information between geographical networks and, consequently, enhance the application and coverage range of healthcare systems by enabling authorized healthcare personnel (e.g., doctor or nurse) to remotely access a patient's medical information through a cellular network or the Internet. A database is also an important component of the "beyond-BAN" tier in the scenario of healthcare. This database maintains the user's profile and medical history. According to a user's service priority and/or doctor's availability, the doctor may access the user's information as needed. At the same time, automated notifications can be issued to his/her relatives based on this data via various means of telecommunications. The design of beyond-BAN communication is application-specific, and should adapt to the requirements of user-specific services. For example, if any abnormalities are found based on the up-to-date body signal transmitted to the database, an alarm can be notified to the patient or the doctor through email or short message service (SMS). In fact, it might be possible for the doctor to remotely diagnose a problem by relying on both video communications with the patient and the patient's physiological data information stored in the database or retrieved by a BAN worn by the patient.

16.2.2 Dense/Mesh Sensor Networks for Smart Living Environments

Besides BAN, sensors can be embedded into our environments, resulting in intelligent and proactive living environments capable of supporting and enhancing daily life, especially in case of elderly or individuals suffering from mental or motor deficiencies. In particular, *Wireless Mesh Sensor Networks* (WMSNs) could be used for designing unobtrusive, interconnected, adaptable, dynamic, and intelligent environments where processors and sensors are embedded in everyday objects (clothes, household devices, furniture, and so on) [92]. The sensors embedded into daily environments are usually called "ambient sensors" (as opposed to body sensors). The ambient sensors will collect various types of data to deduce the activities of inhabitants and to anticipate their needs in order to maximize their comfort and quality of life [181]. WMSNs are based on mesh networking topology, a type of networking where each node must not only capture and disseminate its own data, but also serve as a relay for other nodes. In other words, each sensor must collaborate to propagate the data in the network. The main benefits of WMSNs is their capability to be dynamically self-organized and self-configured, with the network automatically establishing and maintaining mesh connectivity among sensors [6]. WMSNs do not require centralized access points to mediate the wireless communication and they are particularly suitable to be used in complex and dynamic environments such as the living spaces [80].

The general architecture of WMSNs, described in [242], is composed of three distinct wireless network elements:

1. Network Gateways
2. Access Points
3. Mobile and Stationary Nodes

These elements are usually referred to as mesh nodes (MNs). In WMSNs, each node acts not only as a client but also as a router. Unlike WiFi hotspots, which need a direct connection to the Internet, mesh networks pass a data request until a network connection is found. The architecture of WMSNs can be classified into three classes: Infrastructure/BackBone WMNs, Client WMSNs and Hybrid WMSNs. In Infrastructure WMSNs, mesh routers form an infrastructure for clients; in Client WMSNs, all client nodes constitute the actual network to perform routing and configuration functionalities; Hybrid networks are a combination of the former two; as a result, mesh clients can perform mesh functions with other ones as well as access the network.

The innovative WMSNs networking platform allows smart environments to offer new solutions that provide high reliability and power efficiency. WMSNs also enable high adaptability and scalability, since low-profile mesh modules can be easily embedded and integrated with existing sensing devices throughout a building to form seamless networks. In general, WMSNs enable intelligent environments [80] to be characterized by:

- *Faster retrofitting*: One of the main reasons of increasing costs and time delays in retrofitting office space is caused by the labor-intensive movement of utility wiring to conform to the new wall organization. By means of WMSNs, systems' designers can relocate sensors quickly and conveniently without intrusive, disruptive, and costly rewiring efforts [225].

- *Simplified maintenance*: Low maintenance costs are a key concern in designing a sensor network. The self-configuring and self-healing capabilities of WMSNs combined with its low power usage yield an effective solution to the maintenance issue.

- *Reduced life-cycle costs*: WMSNs continuously lead to economic benefits because they are easy to maintain, move, or replace resulting in a distributed system with life-cycle costs that are significantly less than traditional wired installations.

- *Seamless upgrades, transitions*: With the convergence and coordination between principal standard communication corporations, such as ZigBee Alliance [110] and the ASHRAE BACnet Committee[105], the transition to a wireless solution is not an all-or-nothing proposition. In this way WMSNs can be phased in easily—one room, area, floor, or building at a time.

- *Flexibility*: Free from wiring problems, systems' designers can install a WMSN by placing wireless controllers virtually anywhere. This approach results in easily reconfigurable systems to create adaptable workspaces or less intrusively retrofit the existing network infrastructures while saving time and reducing costs.

Some examples of WMSNs for intelligent living environments have been provided by the Siemens APOGEE project [104] and by the HomeMesh project [93]. Both projects highlight that, starting from WMSNs features, it will be possible to design living spaces particularly suitable for supporting the capabilities of elderly or individuals with disabilities in order to enhance their quality of life.

16.2.3 Sensor Technology

Both BANs and WMSNs can be viewed as a collection of interconnected wireless sensors based on a particular processing and communication technology. In general, a wireless sensor is characterized by its small size and its capability of sensing environmental (in the case of ambient sensors) or physiological information (in the case of body sensors).

16.2.3.1 Ambient Sensor Architecture

Ambient sensors typically consist of transducers for measuring the quantity of interest (e.g., room temperature), and transceivers for communicating the collected information.

Different approaches can be taken for designing the transducer hardware. The most common and scalable approach is based on development of transducer boards that can be attached to the main processor board by the means of an expansion bus. A typical transducer board can provide light, temperature, microphone, sounder, tone detector, 2-axis accelerometer, and 2-axis magnetometer devices. Alternatives include economical versions that provide a reduced set of transducers or more expensive versions that boast GPS, for instance. Special boards are also available that carry no transducers, but provide I/O connectors that custom developers can use to connect their own devices. The alternative design approach puts transducers directly on the micro-controller board. Transducers are soldered or can be mounted if needed but the available options are very limited and generality and expandability is affected. However, the on-board transducers design can cut production costs and provides more robustness than stand-alone transducer boards that may detach from the micro-controller board in harsh environments.

Through a transceiver circuitry, a sensor device communicates the sensed information to nearby units using a physical layer based on RF communication. Over the physical layer, different protocols have been implemented for allowing sensors to communicate among themselves [58]. The higher number of supported protocols makes it easier for a BAN to be integrated with other applications. Bluetooth is a popular wireless protocol for short-range communications, but BANs need protocols that support low energy consumption and the self-organizing feature seen in ad-hoc networks. Even though Bluetooth has a very good communications mechanism over a short range, it is not a very feasible solution for BANs. To overcome these problems, most of the BAN applications use the ZigBee protocol. A key component of the ZigBee protocol is its ability to support mesh networks. ZigBee is used nowadays for communications among sensors in a network. Some of the advantages of using ZigBee are: (1) it incurs low energy consumption for communications between the nodes, (2) it has a low duty cycle that enables it to provide longer battery life, (3) its communications primitives enable low-latency communications, (4) and it supports 128-bit security [263]. In addition, it has all the basic features required for communications between the sensors in wireless nodes. ZigBee also enables broad-based deployment of sensor networks in a cost-effective manner.

Some of the most widely used ambient sensors are summarized in Table 16.1.

16.2.3.2 BANs: Hardware and Devices

A body sensor node mainly consists of two parts: the physiological signal sensor and the radio platform to which multiple body sensors can be connected in order to create a complex communication network. The general functionality of body sensors is to collect analog signals that correspond to a human's physiological activities or body actions. The analog signal is later digitized by an Analog to Digital converter (A/D), and is forwarded to the network to be analyzed.

Different body sensors for measuring physiological signs are summarized in Table 16.2 where depending on the captured physiological signal, high or low data sampling rate might be needed.

More specifically, some of the most important body sensors include:

- *Accelerometer/Gyroscope*: Accelerometers are used in the field of healthcare for recognizing body postures (e.g., sitting, kneeling, crawling, laying, standing, walking, running, and

TABLE 16.1: Ambient Sensors Used in Smart Environments

Sensor	Measurement	Data Format
PIR[1]	Motion	Categorical
Active Infrared	Motion/Identification	Categorical
RFID[2]	Object Information	Categorical
Pressure	Pressure on Mat, Chair, etc.	Numeric
Smart Tiles	Pressure on Floor	Numeric
Magnetic Switches	Door/Cabinet Opening/Closing	Categorical
Ultrasonic	Motion	Numeric
Camera	Activity	Image
Microphone	Activity	Sound

[1] Passive Infrared Motion Sensor
[2] Radio Frequency Identification

TABLE 16.2: Body Sensors

Sensor	Measurement	Data Rate
Accelerometer	Direction	High
Gyroscope	Orientation	High
Image/video	Activity	Very high
Glucometer	Blood Sugar	High
Blood Pressure	Oscillometric	Low
CO2 gas sensor	CO2 Concentration	Very low
ECG[1]	Cardiac Activity	High
EEG[2]	Brain Activity	High
EMG[3]	Muscle Activity	Very high
EOG[4]	Eye Movement	High
Pulse oximetry	Blood Oxygen Saturation	Low
GSR (Galvanic Skin Response)	Perspiration	Very low
Thermal	Body Temperature	Very Low

[1] Electrocardiography [2] Electroencephalography
[3] Electromyography [4] Electrooculography

so on). The accelerometer-based posture monitoring for BANs typically consists of 3-axis accelerometers (or tri-axial accelerometers) positioned on well-defined locations on a human body. They can also be used to measure the vibration or acceleration due to gravity, useful for recognizing, for example, elderly falls. Gyroscopes are used for measuring orientation, based on the principle of conservation of angular momentum. Gyroscopes are typically used together with accelerometers for physical movement monitoring.

- *Blood glucose*: Glucose, also referred to as blood sugar, refers to the amount of glucose circulating in the blood. Traditionally, glucose measurements are done by pricking a finger and extracting a drop of blood, which is applied to a test strip composed of chemicals sensitive to the glucose in the blood sample [107]. An optical meter (glucometer) is used to analyze the blood sample and gives a numerical glucose reading. Recently, noninvasive glucose monitoring is available through infrared technology and optical sensing.

- *Blood pressure*: The blood pressure sensor is a noninvasive sensor designed to measure systolic and diastolic human blood pressure, utilizing the oscillometric technique.

FIGURE 16.3: The scalable electronic sensate skin from MIT.

- *CO_2 gas sensor*: This sensor measures gaseous carbon dioxide levels to monitor changes in CO_2 levels, as well as to monitor oxygen concentration during human respiration.
- *ECG sensor*: ECG is a graphic record of the heart's electrical activity. Healthcare providers use it to help diagnose a heart disease. They can also use it to monitor how well different heart medications are working. In order to obtain an ECG signal, several electrodes are attached at specific sites on the skin (e.g., arms, and chest), and the potential differences between these electrodes are measured.
- *EEG sensor*: This sensor measures electrical activity within the brain by attaching small electrodes to the human's scalp at multiple locations. Then, information of the brain's electrical activities sensed by the electrodes is forwarded to an amplifier for producing a pattern of tracings. Synchronous electrical activities in different brain regions are generally assumed to imply functional relationships between these regions. In a hospital, the patient may be asked to breathe deeply or to look at a flashing light during the recording of EEG.
- *EMG sensor*: EMG measures electrical signals produced by muscles during contractions or at rest. Nerve conduction studies are often done together while measuring the electrical activity in muscles, since nerves control the muscles in the body by electrical signals (impulses), and these impulses make the muscles react in specific ways. Nerve and muscle disorders cause the muscles to react in abnormal ways.
- *Pulse Oximetry*: This sensor measures oxygen saturation using a noninvasive probe. A small clip with a sensor is attached to the person's finger, earlobe, or toe. The sensor gives off a light signal that passes through the skin. According to the light absorption of oxygenated hemoglobin and total hemoglobin in arterial blood, the measurement is expressed as a ratio of oxygenated hemoglobin to the total amount of hemoglobin.
- *Humidity and temperature sensors*: They are used for measuring the temperature of the human body and/or the humidity of the immediate environment around a person. An alarm signal can be issued if a certain amount of changes are measured.

16.2.3.3 Recent Trends in Sensor Technology

Since body sensors are in direct contact with body tissue or might even be implanted, their size and physical compatibility with human tissues are crucial. This motivates the research and synthesis of novel materials and technologies, such as the *Micro-Electro Mechanical Systems* (MEMS)

[108]. MEMS is an innovative technology for sensors design based on miniaturized mechanical and electro-mechanical elements (i.e., devices and structures) that are made using the techniques of micro-fabrication. The physical dimensions of MEMS devices can vary from well below one micron on the lower end of the dimensional spectrum, all the way to several millimeters. As a consequence, they open up new scenarios for ubiquitous healthcare applications. Recently MEMS technology has been used for the design of different kinds of sensors such as the accelerometer, blood glucose, blood pressure, carbon dioxide (CO_2) gas sensor, ECG, EEG, EMG, gyroscope, pulse oximetry, as well as some sensors typically used in WSNs. For example, in case of ECG bedside monitoring, disposable electrodes are traditionally made of silver chloride (AgCl). However, long-term usage of these types of electrodes may cause failure of electrical contacts, as well as skin irritation problems. MEMS technology can alleviate this problem by using textile-structured electrodes that are embedded into clothes fabrics. These textile-structure electrodes, possibly woven into clothes, will not cause any skin irritation and thus are comfortable and suitable for long-term monitoring. Compared to the conventional electrodes, they are also much more flexible, since their shape can be adapted to human motion.

Other research directions are also considering the possibility of innovative and noninvasive sensors. For example, MIT researchers have designed a scalable electronic sensate skin by using a collection of flexibly interconnected small (1" x 1") rigid circuit boards (Figure 16.3). Each board contains an embedded processor together with a suite of thirteen sensors, providing dense, multimodal capture of proximate and contact phenomena. Other important results have been obtained in the field of computer vision, thanks to the advancement of charge-coupled devices (CCD) and complementary metal-oxide-semiconductor (CMOS) active-pixel sensors [37]. The recent advancements are allowing cameras to be made so small as to be embedded into eyeglasses, as a consequence enhancing the capabilities of BANs with vision features. The captured images can be mapped to audible outputs in order to assist people who have eyesight problems. The images can even be translated to other kinds of formats, e.g., gentle electrical impulses on the tongue. Together with a lollipop-sized electrode array in their mouths, blind people can also be trained to regain "vision."

16.3 Basic Analytic Techniques

Among data analytics methods, machine learning techniques, have been heavily used in pervasive health applications in recent years. Machine learning is a subdiscipline of artificial intelligence, which allows real-world systems to learn from data. Machine learning algorithms are able to generalize in case of new, unseen data examples by learning from a set of observed data examples called a *training set*. For example, after being trained on a training set of sample accelerometer data marked as `walking` or `jogging`, a machine learning algorithm will be able to classify the future data points into `walking` and `jogging` classes.

Machine learning methods are prevalent in modern applications, and they have been successfully implemented and deployed into many real-world applications. In the healthcare domain, these methods also have gained vast popularity by being used in numerous applications such as electronic health record analysis for predicting life expectancy [155], computer-aided diagnosis [60], DNA sequence classification [246], medical imaging [249], pharmacovigilance and postmarketing adverse drug reaction detection [87, 88], and early prediction of diseases [182], among many other healthcare applications.

Machine learning also has become quite ubiquitous in many pervasive health applications. Many current pervasive health applications rely on machine learning to analyze the sensor data. These algorithms make it possible to obtain insights from the wealth of sensor data, and to support decision making in pervasive health applications. Some example applications include activity recognition algorithms for monitoring dementia patients [198], or physical activity monitoring algorithms for fitness and well-being applications [130]. More examples can be found in Section 16.3.3.

16.3.1 Supervised Techniques

Two common forms of machine learning techniques are *supervised* learning and *unsupervised* learning algorithms. The former focuses on predicting the known properties of data, while the second focuses on discovering unknown knowledge from data.

Supervised learning techniques construct an internal model of the observed data, which is used to predict the label of future examples. Supervised learning methods predict the label of a previously unseen data point based on the model's properties learned from the training data. Typically, if the predicted label is discrete, the supervised technique is called a *classifier*. If the predicted attribute is a continuous value, it is called a *regression* task.

Supervised algorithms require a labeled training set, where each training data point is annotated with its predictive label. Each data point itself is described in terms of a number of features. For example, if the goal is to distinguish between `walking` and `jogging` using accelerometer data, then each data point in the training set can be described by features such as the mean and the standard deviance of points in the surrounding window, peak value in this window, and other relevant features. Each one of the data points in the training set also needs to be annotated with one of the two labels: `jogging` or `walking`. The annotated training dataset is then used as input in the training stage of the algorithm, thus allowing the machine learning algorithm to make generalizations and predictions in case of future unseen data points. To test the performance of a machine learning algorithm, part of the annotated data is usually set aside, and is used to test the performance of the algorithm. If the performance is satisfactory, the machine learning algorithm can be deployed and integrated with the rest of the system.

Figure 16.4 shows how a supervised machine learning method works. In general, processing data is a multistage process. First, data are captured and annotated with their corresponding labels. Then, preprocessing tasks are performed on data. For example, accelerometer data might be filtered to remove high frequency noises and is segmented into shorter segments. Next, statistical and morphological features are extracted from data. This step might also reduce the number of features by applying feature selection and dimensionality reduction techniques. Finally, the classification step predicts the class of activity according to the features.

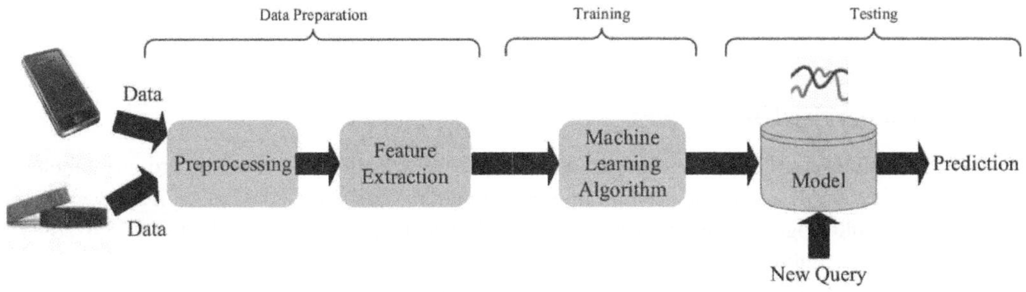

FIGURE 16.4: Machine learning often involves a number of steps, including data preparation, training, and testing.

Classification techniques are one of the most widely used type of supervised machine learning techniques in the context of pervasive health applications. As mentioned before, if the predicted label is a discrete value, such as predicting whether the user is `walking` or `jogging`, it is called a *classification* task, and the algorithm that performs the classification is called a *classifier*. Some famous classification techniques include naive Bayes [141], decision trees [193, 208], support vector machines [53], logistic regression [101], and neural networks [83].

Figure 16.5 shows how a classification algorithm works for a toy problem. Here, each data point is represented in terms of two features (i.e., the *x*- and *y*-axis). In the real world, most datasets have tens, hundreds, or even thousands of features. As can be seen in Figure 16.5, the decision boundary separates the first class from the second class. In reality, we do not know what the true boundary looks like, therefore machine learning algorithms try to reconstruct an approximate boundary based on extracting information from the training set. Some algorithms might only reconstruct a liner boundary such as the perceptron algorithm [206], or a recti-linear boundary such as decision trees [193], or a nonlinear boundary such as the nearest neighborhood [40] and kernel machines [250]. Some algorithms might also assign a confidence value to each prediction, such as the logistic regression algorithm.

If the predicted value is a continuous value, the supervised machine learning technique is called a *regression* task. For example, if our goal is to predict blood pressure value in the next few days based on current food intake and activity level, then a regression algorithm is needed. Similar to classification techniques, regression algorithms might be linear or nonlinear in nature.

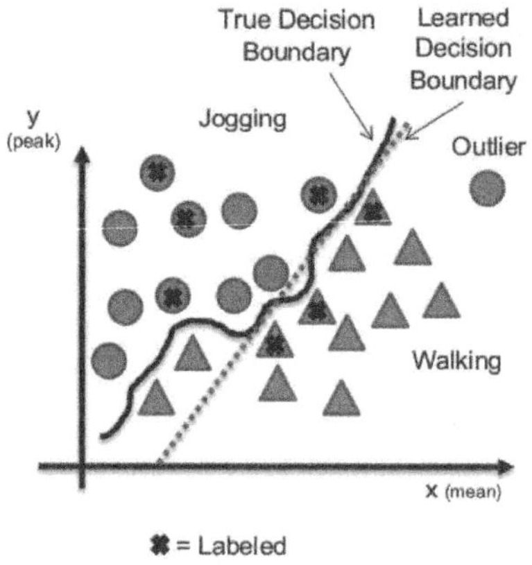

FIGURE 16.5: The true decision boundary is typically unknown; machine learning algorithms try to reconstruct an approximate boundary.

16.3.2 Unsupervised Techniques

Unlike the supervised learning algorithms, unsupervised methods do not require any labeled data. Instead, they try to automatically find interesting patterns in unlabeled data, such as by grouping similar examples together into a cluster. For example, sequence mining can be used to discover user activities from ambient sensor data obtained in a smart home. Some of the unsupervised machine learning techniques includes cluster analysis [124], as well as a large class of data mining methods including association rule mining [261], frequent item-set mining [29], and sequence mining [159].

Frequent pattern mining is an area of data mining that involves finding frequently observed patterns in data. Pattern mining algorithms might look for different types of patterns: frequent itemsets, frequent sequences, frequent trees, or frequent graphs, among others. Frequent pattern mining algorithms can be useful in many pervasive health applications. For example, activity recognition is often used in monitoring the activities of the elderly with dementia. While recognizing predefined activities often relies on supervised learning techniques, frequent pattern mining is valuable for its ability to discover recurring sequences of unlabeled sensor activities that may comprise activities of interest.

The pioneering work of Agrawal's Aprori algorithm [5] was the starting point in this area. Apriori finds frequent itemsets and uses a bottom-up approach, where frequent subsets are extended one item at a time in a step known as candidate generation, and then groups of candidates are tested against the data; the algorithm terminates when no further successful extensions are found. There have been many extensions and variations of frequent pattern mining algorithms [75, 85, 84, 3]. For more information, refer to surveys on frequent pattern mining [159, 29].

16.3.3 Example Applications

There are many examples of using both supervised and unsupervised machine learning techniques in pervasive health technology in the literature [2], here we mention two prominent examples: continuous health monitoring and emergency detection.

Continuous Health Monitoring: Machine learning techniques can be used in continuous health monitoring applications, where a variety of noninvasive sensors monitor various physiological parameters such as ECG, EEG, respiration, and even biochemical processes such as wound healing. For example, Jin et al. [117] describe a cell phone-based real-time monitoring technology for cardiovascular disease (CVD), which automatically detects and classifies abnormal CVD conditions using neural networks. The training data is a combination of both an individual's cardiac characteristics and information from clinical ECG databases. Similar research has been done using sensors to monitor EEG to predict onset of epilepsy [214], or in spirometry sensing using the built-in microphone of cell phones [135]. In addition to monitoring physiological signs, one can also monitor and track activity as an indicator of physical and cognitive function. Activity might refer to activities of daily living (ADL) when monitoring dementia patients and the elderly [199], or to physical activity in the context of fitness and well-being applications [130], or to online activity when monitoring patients with mental disorders [35]. Both supervised and unsupervised approaches have been used quite frequently in activity recognition, especially supervised techniques [2, 134].

Emergency Detection: While it is valuable to monitor common normal events, we are also very interested in abnormal events. These abnormal events may indicate a crisis or an abrupt change in a regimen that is associated with health difficulties. Classification techniques can be used to detect abnormal events from normal events based on incoming sensor data. There have been solutions for detecting emergency situations using PIR sensor network [33], for detecting possible falls in the elderly using ambient sound and sensors [262, 9], or for classifying cane usage and walking patterns, in case of a high risk of falling [257].

16.4 Advanced Analytic Techniques

In this section we introduce the set of more advanced analytics techniques that enable us to develop sophisticated intelligent healthcare systems, as summarized in Table 16.3.

16.4.1 Activity Recognition

Intelligent health systems focus on the needs of a human and therefore require information about the activities being performed by the human [218]. At the core of such technologies is activity recognition, which is a challenging and well-researched problem. The goal of activity recognition

TABLE 16.3: Advanced Analytics Techniques Used in Intelligent Health Systems

Component	Example Techniques	Example Applications
Activity recognition	Graphical models	Health monitoring
Behavior discovery	Sequence mining	Behavior monitoring
Anomaly detection	Statistical methods	Emergency detection
Planning	D-HTN	Prompting
Decision support	Knowledge-based	Communication of care personnel
Anonymization	K-Anonymity	Privacy preservation

is to identify activities as they occur based on data collected by sensors. There exist a number of approaches to activity recognition [43, 196] that vary depending on the underlying sensor technologies that are used to monitor activities, the machine learning algorithms that are used to model the activities, and the complexity of the activities that are being modeled.

In terms of sensor technology, besides using wearable and ambient sensors, researchers have used a varity of other sensors for activity recognition. Some activities such as washing dishes, taking medicine, and using the phone are characterized by interacting with unique objects. In response, researchers have explored the usage of RFID tags [34, 179] and accelerometers or shake sensors [186] for tagging these objects and using the data for activity recognition. The challenge with this modality is deciding which objects to tag with sensors. One approach that has been investigated [173, 184] is to mine web page description of activities to determine which objects are instrumental to the activity and help differentiate the activity from others. Other sensor modalities that have been researched for activity recognition include video cameras [32, 62, 158, 248], microphones [99, 146], and GPS locators [143, 178]. Each of these does face a unique challenge for use in healthcare applications. Cameras and microphones need to be carefully positioned and robust in the presence of occlusion. Furthermore, these technologies are not always well accepted because of privacy concerns. Smartphones are increasing in popularity for activity recognition [81, 133] because sensors in the phone collect all of the gyroscope, accelerometer, magnetometer, GPS, acoustic, and video data found in the other methods, as long as they are on the individual while they perform activities.

16.4.1.1 Activity Models

The methods that are used to model and recognize activities are as varied as the sensor modalities used to observe activities. Existing methods can be broadly categorized into template matching/transductive techniques, generative, and discriminative approaches. Template matching techniques employ a nearest-neighbor classifier based on Euclidean distance or dynamic time warping [21, 223]. Generative approaches such as naïve Bayes classifiers where activity samples are modeled using Gaussian mixtures have yielded promising results for batch learning [32, 226, 238]. Generative probabilistic graphical models such as hidden Markov models [31, 226, 237, 38] and dynamic Bayesian networks [143, 251] have been used to model activity sequences and to smooth recognition results of an ensemble classifier [51]. Decision trees as well as bagging and boosting methods have been tested [150]. Discriminative approaches, including support vector machines [32] and conditional random fields [103, 147, 239, 234], which attempt to maximally separate activity clusters, have also been effective.

16.4.1.2 Activity Complexity

Many of these methods analyze presegmented activity sequences that have been collected in controlled settings. More recently, attempts have been made to perform automatic segmentation of the data into sensor events that belong to the same activity class [79, 173, 197]. Still others have focused on recognizing activities in real time from continuous sensor streams [197]. In addition, researchers have also investigated methods of leveraging information or models in one setting to boost activity recognition for a new sensor network [236], a new environmental setting [198, 195, 50], or new activity labels [111]. Another level of complexity for activity recognition is analyzing data for interwoven activities [157, 219] or concurrent activities [247]. Humans often make efficient use of time by performing a step for one activity while still in the middle of another activity, causing the sensor streams to interweave. Concurrent activities may occur if a single sensor event contributes to more than one activity. This situation may also indicate that multiple residents are in the space, which can be a challenge for activity recognition algorithms [54, 189].

16.4.2 Behavioral Pattern Discovery

While recognizing predefined activities often relies on supervised learning techniques, unsupervised learning is valuable for its ability to discover recurring sequences of unlabeled sensor activities that may comprise activities of interest. Methods for activity discovery build on a rich history of discovery research, including methods for mining frequent sequences, mining frequent patterns using regular expressions [22], constraint-based mining [183], and frequent-periodic pattern mining [200, 94].

More recent work extends these early approaches to look for more complex patterns. Ruotsalainen et al. [207] design the GAIS genetic algorithm to detect interleaved patterns in an unsupervised learning fashion. Other approaches have been proposed to mine more complex discontinuous patterns [196, 183], from streaming data over time [197], in different types of sequence datasets, and to allow variations in occurrences of the patterns [183]. Discovered behavioral patterns are valuable to interpret sensor data, and models can be constructed from the discovered patterns to recognize instances of the patterns when they occur in the future.

16.4.3 Anomaly Detection

While it is of value to characterize and recognize common normal events that account for the majority of the sensor events that are generated, for health applications we are also very interested in abnormal events. These abnormal events may indicate a crisis or an abrupt change in a regimen that is associated with health difficulties.

Abnormal event detection, or anomaly detection, is also important in security monitoring where suspicious activities need to be flagged and handled. Anomaly detection is most accurate when it is based on behaviors that are frequent and predictable. There are common statistical methods to automatically detect and analyze anomalies including the box plot, the chart, and the CUSUM chart [233]. Anomalies can be captured at different population scales. For example, while most of the population may exhibit condition A, one person might exhibit condition B, which pinpoints a condition needing further investigation [57]. Anomalies may also be discovered at different temporal scales, including single events, days, or weeks [221].

Little attention has been devoted to anomaly detection in intelligent health systems. This is partly because the notion of an anomaly is somewhat ill-defined. Many possible interpretations of anomalies have been offered and use cases have even been generated for intelligent health systems [229]. Some algorithmic approaches have been suggested that build on the notion of expected temporal relationships between events and activities [114]. Others tag events are anomalies if they occur rarely and they are not anticipated for the current context [259].

16.4.4 Planning and Scheduling

Automatic planning and scheduling can be useful in many intelligent health systems applications. Automatic planning techniques achieve a goal state by starting from an initial known state and choosing among possible actions at each state. Planning can be useful in a number of different intelligent health scenarios. For example, planning can be used to schedule daily activities in a flexible manner for reminding dementia patients about their daily activities. It also can be used in order to detect any possible deficiencies in task execution, and to help dementia patients to complete those steps. Another use of planning is in automating daily routines, in order to allow users with physical limitations to live a more independent lifestyle.

In the past, many planning techniques have been proposed. Some techniques include decision-theoretic techniques (e.g., Markov Decision Processes [23]), search methods (e.g., forward and backward search [28]), graph-based techniques (e.g., GraphPlan [25]), hierarchal techniques (e.g., O-Plan [227]), and reactive planning techniques (e.g., [69]). For example, graph-based planning techniques represent search space of possible actions in the form of a graph, hierarchal planning techniques use hierarchies to predefine groups of actions, and reactive planning techniques adjust the plan based on sensed information.

Intelligent health systems pose many new challenges to the classical planning techniques. For example, the planner has to be functional in a dynamic environment where the outcome of the actions and their duration is not deterministic. Also, the availability of resources might change due to user mobility or other factors. Therefore, more advanced planning techniques have been proposed by extending classical planning techniques [216]. One example is the distributed hierarchal task network (D-HTN) technique [10], which extends the hierarchal task network (HTN). It uses a centralized approach to manage the distributed capabilities provided by the distributed devices. The distributed devices might be available in a permanent or transient manner. D-HTN has been studied in the context of care for diabetic patients at home, where different home devices communicate and coordinate plans with each other in a distributed manner. For example, data from monitoring devices might require actions such as adjusting the room temperature, suggesting insulin injection, or contacting medical help.

Several intelligent health systems have been reported in the literature that use automated planning and scheduling, especially to help dementia patients. COACH is one such system that provides task guidance to Alzheimer's disease patients [156]. It uses a hand-coded representation of detailed steps of hand-washing, and relies on vision techniques to recognize user steps. If the user is unable to complete a particular step, detailed instructions are provided. Another example is PEAT, which also provides task guidance to the user [140]. It maintains a detailed model of the daily plan in terms of hierarchal events, and tracks their execution. PEAT has the capability of rescheduling activities in case of unexpected events, however it lacks any real sensory information from the world, except for user feedback. Autominder by Pollack et al. [191] is another system that provides users with reminders about their daily activities by reasoning about any disparities between what the client is supposed to do and what she is doing, and makes decisions about whether and when to issue reminders.

16.4.5 Decision Support

Decision Support Systems (DSSs) [63, 67, 66] have been widely used in the field of healthcare for assisting physicians and other healthcare professionals with decision-making tasks, for example for analyzing patient data [172, 19, 20, 145, 220, 205, 185]. DSS systems are mainly based on two mainstream approaches: *knowledge-based* and *nonknowledge-based.*

The knowledge-based DSS consists of two principal components: the knowledge database and the inference engine. The knowledge database contains the rules and associations of compiled data that often take the form of IF-THEN rules, whereas the inference engine combines the rules from the knowledge database with the real patients' data in order to generate new knowledge and to propose a set of suitable actions. Different methodologies have been proposed for designing healthcare knowledge databases and inference engines, such as the ontological representation of information [123].

The nonknowledge-based DSS have no direct clinical knowledge about a particular healthcare process, however they learn clinical rules from past experiences and by finding patterns in clinical data. For example, various machine learning algorithms such as decision trees represent methodologies for learning healthcare and clinical knowledge.

Both of these approaches could be used in conjunction with intelligent health systems. Indeed, the sensitive, adaptive, and unobtrusive nature of intelligent health systems is particularly suitable for designing decision support systems capable of supporting medical staffs in critical decisions. In particular, intelligent health systems enable the design of the third generation of *telecare systems*. The first generation was the *panic-alarms gadgets*, often worn as pendants or around the wrist to allow a person to summon help in the case of a fall or other kinds of health emergency. The second generation of telecare systems uses sensors to automatically detect situations where assistance or medical decisions are needed. Finally, the third generation represents intelligent health systems that move away from the simple reactive approach and adopt a proactive strategy capable of anticipating emergency situations. As a result, DSSs could be used with *multimodal sensing* and *wearable computing* technologies for constantly monitoring all vital signs of a patient and for analyzing such data in order to take real-time decisions and opportunely support that people.

Finally, DSSs are jointly used with the intelligent health systems paradigm for enhancing communications among health personnel such as doctors and nurses. For example, Anya et al. have introduced a DSS system based on context aware knowledge modeling aimed at facilitating the communication and improving the capability to take decisions among healthcare personal located in different geographical sites [15].

16.4.6 Anonymization and Privacy Preserving Techniques

As intelligent health systems become more ubiquitous, more information will be collected about individuals and their lives. While the information is intended to promote the well-being of individuals, it may be considered an invasion of privacy and, if intercepted by other parties, could be used for malicious purposes.

While some privacy concerns focus on the perception of intrusive monitoring [59], many heavily-deployed Internet gadgets and current intelligent systems are nearly devoid of security against adversaries, and many others employ only crude methods for securing the system from internal or external attacks. The definition of privacy will continue to evolve as ambient intelligent systems mature [90]. This is highlighted by the fact that even if personal information is not directly obtained by an unwanted party, much of the information can be inferred even from aggregated data. For this reason, a number of approaches are being developed to ensure that important information cannot be gleaned from mined patterns [136, 245].

16.5 Applications

Different kinds of intelligent health applications for healthcare have been developed in academia and industry, as summarized in Table 16.4. This section discusses about each application class by presenting both scientific and real-world frameworks and highlights the benefits provided to patients, elderly, and so on.

TABLE 16.4: Ambient Intelligence Applications in Healthcare

Application	Goals	Ambient[1]	Body[1]	Methodologi
Continuous Health Monitoring	Using sensor networks for monitoring physiological measures (ECG, EEG, etc.)	●	○	Activity Recognition
Continuous Behavioral Monitoring	Using sensor networks for monitoring human behaviors (watching TV, sitting, etc.)	●	●	Activity Recognition
Monitoring for Emergency Detection	Using sensor networks for detecting hazards, falls, etc.	○	●	Activity Recognition
Assisted Living	Creating smart environments for supporting patients and elderly during their daily activities	●	×	Activity Recognition, Decision Support
Therapy and Rehabilitation	Supporting people who require rehabilitation services with remote and autonomous systems	○	●	Activity Recognition, Decision Support
Persuasive Well-Being	Systems aimed at changing persons attitudes in order to motivate them to lead a healthier lifestyle	●	×	Activity Recognition, Decision Support
Emotional Well-Being	Ubiquitous systems based on neurological and psychological insights to analyze emotions and improve well-being	●	●	Activity Recognition
Smart Hospitals	Improving communication among hospital stakeholders through ubiquitous technology	●	×	Decision Support

[1] ●: Mandatory - ○: Optional - ×: Not required (e.g., they could increase the intrusiveness of the system without additional benefits)

[2] All application classes use *Anonymization and Privacy Preserving Techniques* for ensuring personal data hiding

16.5.1 Continuous Monitoring

One of the first and most important application of analytics in healthcare has been monitoring the health status of the users in a noninvasive manner. In the following subsection, we will also discuss other monitoring applications such as continuous behavior monitoring as well as monitoring for detecting emergency situations.

16.5.1.1 Continuous Health Monitoring

In the past decade, a variety of noninvasive sensors have been developed for measuring and monitoring various physiological parameters such as ECG, EEG, EDA, respiration, and even biochemical processes such as wound healing. Some of those sensors are in the form of wearable devices such as wristbands, while others are embedded into textiles, known as E-textile or smart fabrics. The majority of these sensors allow for noninvasive monitoring of physiological signs, though some physiological measurements such as EEG still require the use of invasive devices and sensors (e.g., measuring EEG requires the use of electrodes). Regardless of the form of the sensors, such sensors allow the patients with chronic diseases to be in control of their health condition by benefiting from continuous monitoring and anomalous situation detection. Achieving continuous monitoring is almost impossible in conventional healthcare settings, where typical measures are taken only during occasional doctor visits. The use of such sensors will also allow the healthy adults to keep track of their health status and to take the necessary steps for enhancing their lifestyle.

Gouaux et al. [78] describe a wearable personal ECG monitoring device (PEM) for early detection of cardiac events, which detects and reports anomalies by generating different alarm levels. Another example is AMON which is in the form of a wristband and measures various physiological signals [14]. Nowadays, there are several commercially available health monitoring devices, such as HealthBuddy by Bosch [30], TeleStation by Philips [187], HealthGuide by Intel [113], and Genesis by Honeywell [100]. A number of academic projects also have tried to integrate monitoring devices with clothing fabrics, including the WEALTHY project [174], BIOTEX project [176], and MagIC project [202]. For example, BIOTEX monitors sore conditions based on pH changes and inflammatory proteins concentration [176]. Other projects have tried to provide a variety of accessible medical implants, for example the "Healthy Aims" project focuses on developing a range of medical implants to help the aging population [97]. Developing completely noninvasive methods for health monitoring is another active research area. For example, Masuda et al. [149] measure physiological signs such as respiration rate and heartbeat by measuring perturbations in the pressure of an air-filled mattress and relying on the low frequency characteristics of heart and respiration. Similarly, Andoh et al. have developed a sleep monitoring mattress to analyze respiration rate, heart rate, snoring, and body movement [11]. The SELF smart home project also monitors various factors such as posture, body movement, breathing, oxygen in the blood, airflow at mouth and nose and apnea, using pressure sensor arrays, cameras, and microphones [167].

16.5.1.2 Continuous Behavioral Monitoring

In addition to monitoring physiological measures, another potential monitoring application is behavioral monitoring. Behavioral monitoring especially can be useful in assisted living settings and monitoring of individuals with mental disabilities. Such systems can assess mental health and cognitive status of inhabitants in a continual and naturalistic manner. They can also provide automated assistance and can decrease the caregiver burden. In some cases a single activity is monitored, for example, Nambu et al. [165] monitor watching TV for diagnosing health conditions. The majority of research projects monitor a subset of daily tasks. For example, the CASAS project [200] monitors a subset of daily tasks to identify consistency and completeness in daily activities of dementia patients. The IMMED project monitors instrumented activities of daily living (IADL) in dementia patients by using a wearable camera to monitor the loss of motor or cognitive capabilities

[153]. Other researchers have worked on recognizing social activity, especially in nursing homes [41, 48]. Identifying any changes in activities might be an indicator of cognitive or physical decline. For example, indicators such as changes in movement patterns, walking speed, number of outgoings, and sleep rhythm have been identified as early signs of dementia [224, 91, 71].

16.5.1.3 Monitoring for Emergency Detection

There also have been some projects to monitor emergency situations. In the UK, British Telecom (BT) and Liverpool City Council have developed a project on telecare technology that monitors residents using a variety of sensors such as PIR sensors [33]. In case of any detected hazards, the system asks the residents if they are OK, otherwise the selected personnel are notified. Another important area of emergency detection is fall detection, which can be especially useful for the elderly, as falls contribute to a high rate of morbidity and mortality in the elderly. Fall detection techniques rely on several technologies: wearable devices, ambient sensors, and cameras [160]. Wearable fall detection systems measure posture and motion using sensors such as an accelerometer and gyroscope and by measuring orientation and acceleration [256, 131]. Ambient fall detection systems use ambient sensors such as passive infrared (PIR) sensors and pressure sensors to detect falls. They also rely on techniques such as floor vibration detection and ambient audio analysis to detect possible falls [262, 9]. Finally, vision-based fall detection systems extract video features such as 3D motion, shape, and inactivity to detect falls [70, 212]. There are also some preventive fall detection tools, such as the smart cane developed by Wu et al., which classify cane usage and walking patterns, and informs the elderly in case of a high risk of falling [257].

It should be noted that there is a huge potential for combining and fusing data from various sensors such as physiological sensors with electronic health records (EHRs) or daily activity information [89]. This will allow the healthcare to shift from cure to prevention by early detection of diseases using continuous monitoring, as well as to reduce the need for institutional care by shifting the care to a personalized level.

16.5.2 Assisted Living

Intelligent health technology can allow individuals with disabilities to maintain a more independent lifestyle using home automation, it can offer them continuous cognitive and physical monitoring, and can provide them with real-time assistance, if needed. Those services especially can be useful for older adults who are suffering from physical and cognitive decline [171].

We already have discussed how behavioral monitoring and fall detection methods can be useful for the elderly. Medication management is another area that can provide great benefit to the elderly [168, 161, 240]. The majority of older adults take many different medications and they usually forget medication dosage and timing due to cognitive decline. Using appropriate contextual information obtained from various sensors, medication reminders can be delivered in a context aware and flexible manner. Care personnel can be contacted, if non-compliance is detected.

For example, John will be reminded about his medications right after finishing his breakfast, but he will not be reminded if he is watching his favorite program on TV or if he is talking on the phone. If John forgets to take his medication more than a certain number of times (depending on the medication), his doctor will be automatically contacted.

Current medication management systems are not yet fully context aware, though there has been some great progress. For example, iMat is a user friendly medication management system [231]. An iMat user has no need to understand the directions of her/his medications, rather iMAT enables the pharmacist of each user to extract a machine readable medication schedule specification from the user's prescriptions or over-the-counter descriptions. Once loaded into an iMAT dispenser or schedule manager, the tool automatically generates a medication schedule. Other medication management tools also have been proposed by researchers, such as the "Magic Medicine Cabinet," which can provide a reminder and can interact with healthcare professionals [243], or the "Smart Medicine Cabinet," which uses RFID tags to monitor medication usage and can communicate with a cell phone [215].

Besides medication management, other cognitive orthotics tools can be quite useful for people with mental disabilities, especially older adults suffering from dementia. COACH is a cognitive orthotics tool that relies on planning and vision techniques to guide a user through hand a washing task [156]. Other cognitive orthotics tools such as PEAT [140] and Autominder [191] also use automated planning to provide generic reminders about daily activities. They can adjust their schedules in case of any changes in the observed activities. Cognitive orthotics tools also can be used for cognitive rehabilitation. SenseCam is a small wearable camera developed by Microsoft, which captures a digital record of the wearer's day in terms of images in addition and a log of sensor data [96]. It has been shown to help dementia patients to recollect aspects of earlier experiences that have subsequently been forgotten, thereby acting as a retrospective memory aid. Hoey et al. [98] also describe the development of a cognitive rehabilitation tool to assist art therapists working with older adults with dementia.

Intelligent health tools also can be useful for preventing wandering behavior of older adults who suffer from dementia. There are a number of outdoor wandering prevention tools. KopAL [73] and OutCare [244] support issues related to disorientation by contacting the caregiver in case of leaving predefined routes or deviating from daily signature routes. A number of tools have also been developed for preventing indoor wandering. For example, Lin et al. [144] use RFID technology to detect if people prone to disorientation (e.g., children or elderly) have approached a dangerous area, and Crombag [55] proposes using virtual indoor fencing. Some commercially available products for wandering prevention include safeDoor and SafetyBed [65]; for example, safeDoor raises an alarm if a person walks out a door without opening it, to prevent nighttime wandering. Navigation assistance tools also have been developed to help elderly suffering from early signs of dementia. "Opportunity Knocks" is a mobile application that provides public transit system guidance by learning user's routes [180].

A number of Intelligent health projects try to provide comprehensive assistance through a variety of services. "RoboCare" is an assisted living project providing assistance to people with disabilities using a combination of software, robots, intelligent sensors, and humans [18]. It uses a tracking system for tracking people and robots by exploiting vision techniques to determine various 3D positions. It also relies on a task execution and monitoring component to recognize a current situation and to compare it with the expected schedule. The "Aware Home Research Initiative" (AHRI) at Georgia Tech includes a number of different projects focused on providing assistance to elderly, such as the "Independent LifeStyle Assistant" project that monitors the behavior of the elderly in a passive manner and alerts caregivers in case of emergency (e.g., fall) [125]. The " Technology Coach" is another AHRI project that watches the use of home medical devices by the elderly and provides appropriate feedback and guidance for better use [163]. Smart home projects such as CASAS also try to provide comprehensive monitoring and assistance services in a noninvasive manner by relying on various machine learning and data mining techniques to make sense of sensor data.

Intelligent health systems also can provide great help to visually impaired people. A number of different systems have been proposed for blind navigation, relying on various sensors such as RFID tags, infrared sensors, and GPS technology. Chumkamon et al. [47] used RFID tags to develop a tracking system for indoor guidance of blind persons. Chen et al. [42] embed RFID tags in the tiles of a blind path for better navigation. Some systems also use audio interface to communicate the name of important locations to the user, e.g., the SAWN system [252]. There are also applications to facilitate daily tasks such as shopping, e.g., the ShopTalk project [166].

Finally, several intelligent assisted living environments have been designed by using decision support methodologies. For example, the ALARM-NET project [7] is an assisted living and residential monitoring network for pervasive healthcare developed at the University of Virginia. It integrates environmental and physiological sensors in a scalable, heterogeneous architecture to support real-time data collection and processing. The ALARM-NET network creates a continuous medical history while preserving resident comfort and privacy by using unobtrusive ambient sensors combined with wearable interactive devices [255, 254]. The project CAALYX (Complete Ambient Assisted Living Experiment) [36] is another project for increasing elderly autonomy and self-confidence by developing a wearable light device capable of measuring specific vital signs and detecting falls, and for communicating in real time with care providers in case of an emergency. MyHeart [162] is an integrated project for developing smart electronic and textile systems and services that empower the users to take control of their own health status [82]. The system uses wearable technology and smart fabrics to monitor' patients vital body signs in order to provide proper well-being recommendations to the user. The SAPHIRE [211] project develops an intelligent healthcare monitoring and decision support system by integrating the wireless medical sensor data with hospital information systems [132]. In the SAPHIRE project the patient monitoring will be achieved by using agent technology complemented with intelligent decision support systems based on clinical practice guidelines. The observations received from wireless medical sensors together with the patient medical history will be used in the reasoning process. The patients' history stored in medical information systems will be accessed through semantically enriched web services.

16.5.3 Therapy and Rehabilitation

According to the Disability and Rehabilitation Team at the World Health Organization (WHO), the estimated number of people who require rehabilitation services is continuously growing (1.5% of the entire world population) [203]. Nevertheless, the current healthcare solutions and technologies are not nearly sufficient to fulfill the rehabilitation needs. In such scenarios, intelligent health can shape innovative rehabilitative approaches that support individuals to have access to rehabilitation resources. This can be achieved by developing ad-hoc rehabilitation systems based on sensor networks and other technological approaches such as *robotics* and *brain-computer interfaces* (BCIs).

Sensor networks have the potential to greatly impact many aspects of medical care, including rehabilitation [177]. For example, Jarochowski et al. [115] propose the implementation of a system, the *Ubiquitous Rehabilitation Center*, which integrates a Zigbee-based wireless network with sensors that monitor patients and rehabilitation machines. These sensors interface with Zigbee motes, which in turn interface with a server application that manages all aspects of the rehabilitation center and allows rehabilitation specialists to assign prescriptions to patients. Another system proposed by Piotrowicz et al. [190] describes the requirements of a system for cardiac tele-rehabilitation at home, and in particular it discusses the different components controlling a physical exercise training session, which needs to recognize and identify critical patient states through a continuous monitoring and react accordingly. As a side effect, the health-related data gathered during the tele-rehabilitation session are used for providing cardiologists with useful information for patient care. The rehabilitation systems proposed by Helmer et al. [95] improves the quality of life for patients suffering from chronic obstructive pulmonary disease (COPD). The system includes a component for monitoring the rehabilitation training and automatically. As a consequence, it controls the target load for the exercise on the basis of his or her vital data.

Moreover, by equipping patients with wireless, wearable, or environmental vital sign sensors, collecting detailed real-time data on physiological status can enable innovative activities as autonomous rehabilitation and therapy [213][192][253]. The Stroke Rehab Exerciser by Philips Research [188] guides the patient through a sequence of exercises for motor retraining, which are prescribed by the physiotherapist and uploaded to a patient unit. The system lies on a wireless inertial sensor system aimed at recording the patient's movements, analyzes the data for deviations from a personal movement target, and provides feedback to the patient and the therapist [209]. The Stroke Rehab Exerciser coaches the patient through a sequence of exercises for motor retraining, which are prescribed by the physiotherapist and uploaded to a patient unit. A wireless inertial sensor system

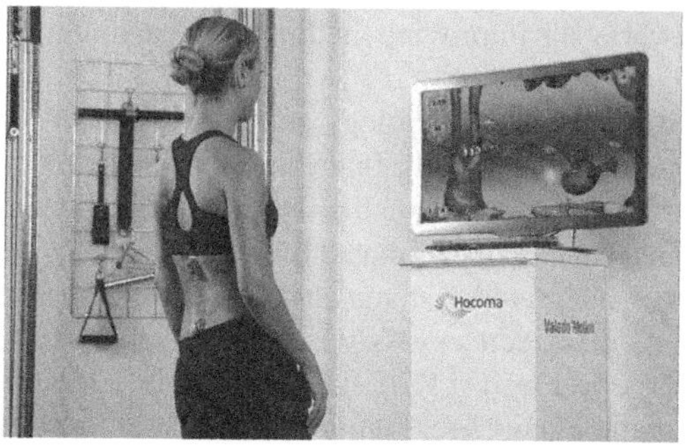

FIGURE 16.6: The Hocoma AG Valedo at work [235].

records the patient's movements, analyzes the data for deviations from a personal movement target, and provides feedback to the patient and the therapist. The Hocoma AG Valedo system [235] (see Figure 16.6) is a medical back training device, which improves a patient's compliance and allows one to achieve increased motivation by real-time Augmented Feedback based on trunk movements. It transfers trunk movements from two wireless sensors into a motivating game environment and guides the patient through exercises specifically designed for low back pain therapy. In order to challenge the patient and to achieve more efficient training, the exercises can be adjusted according to the patient's specific needs. Finally, GE Healthcare [76] is developing a wireless medical monitoring system that is expected to allow one to gather physiological and movement data thus facilitating rehabilitation interventions in the home setting. Several other systems are currently under research and development. As an example, Jovanov et al. [118] have developed a computer-assisted physical rehabilitation applications and ambulatory monitoring based on a Wireless Body Area Network (WBAN). This system performs real-time analysis of sensors' data, providing guidance and feedback to the user in different therapy fields such as stroke rehabilitation, physical rehabilitation after hip or knee surgeries, myocardial infarction rehabilitation, and traumatic brain injury rehabilitation. A practical application example is given by the Tril [230] project that, by means of its subcomponent named BASE [61], provides a home-based interactive technology solution to deliver and validate the correctness of a personalized, physiotherapist-prescribed exercise program to older adults. BASE uses a sensor network to gather data necessary to deliver the exercise program and it exploits computer vision algorithms for validating the correctness of these rehabilitation experiences. One of the main aims of the Active Care [64] project is related to the support of at-risk elders [194]. This project exploits two environmental cameras for extracting human silhouettes and investigating about the human gait by analyzing shoulder level, spinal incline, and silhouette centroid. This analysis could be precious for remotely or autonomously aiding elder or impaired people [142]. Other interesting work based on sensors networks are related to the design of rehabilitation systems for degenerative pathologies such as Parkinson's disease [77]. The authors present the results of a pilot study to assess the feasibility of using accelerometer data to estimate the severity of symptoms and motor complications in patients with Parkinson's disease. This system is based on a support vector machine (SVM) classifier used for estimating the severity of tremor, bradykinesia and dyskinesia from accelerometer data features and, as a consequence, optimizing the patient's therapy. Bachlin et al. [17] also introduce a wearable assistant for Parkinson's disease patients with the freezing of gait (FOG) symptom. This wearable system uses on-body acceleration sensors to measure the patients' movements to detect FOG and automatically provide a rhythmic auditory signal that stimulates the patient to resume walking. In the future, by using the wearable sensor networks together with haptic hardware, it will be possible to design medical training systems based on augmented reality frameworks for improving medical staff capabilities to support the elderly or patients during their rehabilitation [1].

The combination of sensor network technology and robots is also a very recent development in the field of rehabilitation systems [27][253]. Interest in this approach originates from the observation that subjects with chronic conditions (such as hemiparesis following a stroke) could benefit from therapeutic interventions that can be facilitated by robotic systems and enhanced by wearable technology [26]. Indeed, these integrated systems could be used in a variety of healthcare scenarios. A concrete application of these concepts is the human-friendly assistive home environment, Intelligent Sweet Home (ISH) developed at KAIST, South Korea [175][119]. The system considers the residents' lifestyle by continuously checking their intention or health status; the home itself is seen as an intelligent robot actively supporting the appropriate services for people with disabilities. Kubota et al. [129] also propose a similar hybrid Robotic systems for aiding disabled people with quadriplegia.

Recently, there has been some attempt to further improve the sensor networks rehabilitation capabilities by sensing electroencephalography (EEG) signals directly using BCI technology. BCI systems represent a natural extension for intelligent health environments. Indeed, they are envisioned to be typically used for allowing smart environments habitants to deal with their surrounding space in a transparent way. This effortlessly interaction approach is particularly suitable for enhanced rehabilitation systems. The ASPICE [49] and DAT [13] projects are examples of this kind of technology that allow the temporary or permanent neuro-motor disabled persons to improve or recover their mobility (directly or by emulation), as well as their communication skills.

16.5.4 Persuasive Well-Being Applications

Persuasive technology [241], represents computing systems, devices, or applications intentionally designed to change a person's attitude or behavior in a predetermined way in order to motivate people to lead a healthier lifestyle by mediating prevention and treatment [112]. Although the field of persuasive technologies has lately attracted lots of attention, the notion of *ambient persuasive technology* was introduced only recently [39][201][123]. Ambient persuasive technology constitutes a radically new category of relationships between human beings and technological artifacts by blending insights from the behavioral sciences with computing technology [122]. One of the first examples of a computerized persuasion system for healthy living is the *Persuasive Mirror* [12]. This system uses ubiquitous sensors for continuously gathering information about human behaviors and provides users with continuous visual and nonintrusive feedback matching the psychological strategy (see Figure 16.7). Other applications of the ambient persuasive mirror are introduced in [164].

Another seminal application of ambient persuasive technology is provided by the HygieneGuard projector [126]. This environmental persuasive system is used in restaurants and hospitals to motivate employees or workers to wash their hand before leaving the restrooms. The equipment is installed in the restrooms and every employee is required to wear a badge. Whenever the employee goes to the restroom, she has to use the sink for a period of time. De Carolis and Mazzotta [39] presents an approach to ambient persuasion based on a combination of pervasive and distributed computation to motivate users in a fitness center. The user is surrounded by several connected devices that cooperate during the persuasion process. Another interesting intelligent health application based on persuasive technologies is PerCues [232]. Different from the previous applications, PerCues is oriented to achieve a collective human well-being by persuading users to reach a common goal like decreasing environmental pollution. The project perFrame [170] implements a persuasive interface in the form of an interactive picture frame that integrates unobtrusively into the working environment and provides affective feedback in order to persuade employees to adapt better healthy habits while working with a computer.

Etiobe [8] is another project devoted to treat child obesity. Its architecture merges ubiquitous,

FIGURE 16.7: The Persuasive Mirror project at work [12].

intelligent, and persuasive features for implementing a cyber-therapy approach. It is based on virtual and augmented reality, and attempts to persuade children to avoid poor eating habits. The system uses a collection of environmental sensors for capturing important information such as contextual, physiological, and psychological data.

Lastly, some game-based ambient persuasive systems for well-being have been introduced or they are under development [228]. For an example, the project Dance Dance Revolution connects a sensor-enabled dance floor with a video interface and provides stimulating exercise as dance competition [102]. A recent trend is the use of motion sensing controllers such as the WiiMote or Kinect sensor, allowing individuals to naturally manipulate digital worlds in persuasive games. Taken together, this body of work demonstrates that games and social competition can be used to establish long-term commitments. For example, such games can be used by elders or individuals with physical impairments during their rehabilitation sessions.

16.5.5 Emotional Well-Being

Recent advances in neurology and psychology have demonstrated the importance of emotions in various aspects of our lives and, in particular, in the field of healthcare and well-being. Indeed, it has been demonstrated that negative emotions have adverse effects on the immune system of a person [139]. Emotions are typically communicated through three channels: audio (speech), face and body gestures (visual), and internal physiological changes such as blood pressure, heartbeat rate, or respiration.

Intelligent sensor-based infrastructures may represent a suitable tool for recognizing and managing emotions, as well as for improving well-being. McNaney et al. [152] have designed a Wearable Acoustic Monitor (WAM) device, which provides support in various aspects of social and emotional well-being by inferring level of a social interaction and vocal features of emotionality. It can monitor and evaluate the level of a wearer's voice by identifying vocal features such as amplitude, pitch, rate of speech, and pause length in order to provide insight into the emotionality of the wearer at a given time. This feature allows the individual to reflect on the contexts or situations that prove particularly stressful or pleasurable, and may affect future behaviors. Another interesting application of environmental sensors to emotional well-being is the AffectAura [151] project. This system continuously predicts users' valence, arousal, and engagement based on information gathered from a webcam, kinect sensor, microphone, electrodermal activity sensor, GPS, file activity sensor, and calendar scraper. The users were allowed to leverage cues from AffectAura to construct stories about their days, even after they had forgotten particular incidents or their related emotional tones. Another project, EmoSoNet [260], introduces an emotion-aware social network for the purpose of increasing emotional well-being. The framework uses sensors and behavior analysis methods in order to infer users' stress level automatically with minimal user effort. It also uses audio, animation, and vibro-tactile feedback for enhanced engagement. Another system named MONARCA [72] develops and validates solutions for multiparametric, long-term monitoring of behavioral and physiological information relevant to bipolar disorder. In particular, the system consists of a sensor-enabled mobile phone, a wrist worn activity monitor, a physiological sensor (GSR, pulse), a stationary EEG system for periodic measurements, and a home gateway. Combining the sensor information with patients' medical records and established psychiatric knowledge, a prediction of depressive and manic episodes is given.

The Emo&Pain project [217] is an intelligent system that enables ubiquitous monitoring and assessment of patients' pain-related mood and movements. Specifically, this system aims to develop a collection of methods for automatically recognizing audiovisual cues related to pain, behavioral patterns typical of low back pain, and affective states influencing pain. Aziz et al. [16] also propose an animated conversational agent providing emotional support and companionship in order to promote the emotional well-being of patients and enhance patient care and outcomes during a hospital stay.

16.5.6 Smart Hospitals

Intelligent health technology can be also useful for other stakeholders such as nurses, doctors, and other healthcare personnel, especially for facilitating communication among them. Sánchez et al. have developed the iHospital project that provides context-aware communication based on activity recognition [210]. Various pieces of contextual information are collected and used, including location, time, the roles of the people present, and RFID-tagged artifacts, in order to help in decision making and communication.

There have been some efforts to create middleware for healthcare. Rodriguez et al. [204] describe the development of SALSA, an agent-based middleware to facilitate responding to the particular demands of patients and hospital personnel. SALSA takes into account the distributed access nature of doctors, which is a result of their high mobility. A doctor has to access patients' clinical records, access medical devices distributed throughout the premises, and communicate with colleagues spread throughout the hospital. In order to track the location of people, Rodriguez et al. use radio frequency signal strength between mobile devices and access points and build a signal propagation model to estimate the distance.

Favela et al. [68] describe several possible scenarios for using intelligent health in hospitals and build their frameworks around those scenarios.

> For example, Dr. Garcia is checking the patient in bed 234, when he is alerted that a new message has arrived. His handheld device displays a hospital floor map informing him that the X-ray results of another patient are available. He approaches the nearest public display that detects his presence and provides him with a personalized view. Dr. Garcia selects the message on bed 225, which opens windows displaying the patient's medical record and the X-ray image recently taken. Aware of the context of the situation, the system automatically opens a window with the hospital's medical guide that relates to the patient's current diagnosis, and an additional one with previous similar cases to support

the physicians' analysis. While Dr. Garcia is analyzing the X-ray image, he notices on the map that a resident physician is nearby and calls him up to show him this interesting clinical case.

Kofod-Petersen and Anmodt [127] also describe using intelligent health technology for supporting health workers cooperating in patient diagnosis and treatment by using context information, goal recognition, and case-based reasoning. GerAmi (Geriatric Ambient Intelligence) is another hospital project that helps doctors and nurses to monitor patients and to better manage theirs tasks [52]. For example, it keeps track of the patients' locations using RFID technology and generates alarms, if needed. It also allocates tasks to nurses based on various contextual information such as the availability of nearby nurses and their profile information.

16.6 Conclusions and Future Outlook

With the help of analytics techniques, intelligent health systems promise to enhance our health and well-being in many aspects in a radical manner by successful acquisition and interpretation of contextual information. By relying on various computing and networking techniques, as well as different sensor modalities, intelligent health systems have the potential to enhance our healthcare system in the near future.

In this chapter, we explored the application of analytics to healthcare from various perspectives. We discussed the use of analytics in healthcare based on individuals' medical conditions, such as physical or mental disabilities, chronic disease, or rehabilitation situations. From a different perspective, we discussed current technology and infrastructure, such as smart environments, wearable sensors, and smart fabrics. More importantly, we provided a high-level description of various analytics techniques in the healthcare domain, such as automated decision making, planning techniques, activity recognition, and other numerous techniques.

Despite their inarguable values for improving our health system, there are also many ethical and social concerns that need to be addressed. Overreliance on intelligent health systems might have its own dangers for the individuals with health needs and might result in the early loss of the ability and confidence to manage their life. Care must be taken to ensure that intelligent health is not limited to the affluent individuals, because less privileged individuals can also benefit from the benefits of intelligent health systems. Fear of decreased communication and patient isolation is another ethical issue that many researchers have brought up. Identifying where the problem lies in a misdiagnosis will become more and more difficult in such complex systems and will result in many ethical and legal discussions.

We are aware that the goals set up for analytics techniques in intelligent health systems are not easily reachable and there are still many challenges to face and, consequently, this research field is getting more and more impetus. Researchers with different backgrounds are enhancing the current state of the art of intelligent health systems by addressing fundamental problems not only in analytics, but also related to human factors, design and implementation, security, as well as social and ethical issues. As a result, we are confident that this synergistic approach will materialize the complete vision of intelligent health systems and its full application to healthcare and human well-being.

Bibliography

[1] A.F. Abate, G. Acampora, V. Loia, S. Ricciardi, and A.V. Vasilakos. A pervasive visual haptic framework for virtual delivery training. *Information Technology in Biomedicine, IEEE Transactions on*, 14(2):326–334, March 2010.

[2] G. Acampora, D.J. Cook, P. Rashidi, and A.V. Vasilakos. A survey on ambient intelligence in healthcare. *Proceedings of the IEEE*, 101(12):2470–2494, 2013.

[3] Charu C. Aggarwal, Yan Li, Jianyong Wang, and Jing Wang. Frequent pattern mining with uncertain data. In *Proceedings of the 15th ACM SIGKDD International Conference on Knowledge Discovery and Data Mining*, pages 29–38. ACM, 2009.

[4] R. Agrawal and R. Srikant. Mining sequential patterns. In *Proceedings of the Eleventh International Conference on Data Engineering*, pages 3–14. IEEE, 1995.

[5] Rakesh Agrawal, Ramakrishnan Srikant, et al. Fast algorithms for mining association rules. In *Proceedings of the 20th International Conference on Very Large Data Bases, VLDB*, volume 1215, pages 487–499, 1994.

[6] Ian F. Akyildiz, Xudong Wang, and Weilin Wang. Wireless mesh networks: A survey. *Computer Networks*, 47(4):445–487, 2005.

[7] alarmnet. `http://www.cs.virginia.edu/wsn/medical/`, 2014.

[8] M. Alcaniz, C. Botella, R.M. Banos, I. Zaragoza, and J. Guixeres. The intelligent e-therapy system: A new paradigm for telepsychology and cybertherapy. *British Journal of Guidance & Counselling*, 37(3):287–296, 2009.

[9] M. Alwan, P.J. Rajendran, S. Kell, D. Mack, S. Dalal, M. Wolfe, and R. Felder. A smart and passive floor-vibration based fall detector for elderly. In *Information and Communication Technologies, 2006. ICTTA'06. 2nd*, volume 1, pages 1003–1007. IEEE, 2006.

[10] F. Amigoni, N. Gatti, C. Pinciroli, and M. Roveri. What planner for ambient intelligence applications? *IEEE Transactions on Systems, Man and Cybernetics, Part A: Systems and Humans*, 35(1):7–21, 2005.

[11] Hisanori Andoh, Takayuki Ishikawa, Keita Kobayashi, Kazuyuki Kobayashi, Kajiro Watanabe, and Testuo Nakamura. Home health monitoring system in the sleep. In *SICE Annual Conference*, pages 2416–2419, 2003.

[12] A. Andrés del Valle and A. Opalach. The persuasive mirror: Computerized persuasion for healthy living. In *Human Computer Interaction International, HCI International*, 2005.

[13] Renzo Andrich, Valerio Gower, Antonio Caracciolo, Giovanni Del Zanna, and Marco Di Rienzo. The DAT project: A smart home environment for people with disabilities. In Klaus Miesenberger, Joachim Klaus, Wolfgang Zagler, and Arthur Karshmer, editors, *Computers Helping People with Special Needs*, volume 4061 of *Lecture Notes in Computer Science*, pages 492–499. Springer Berlin / Heidelberg, 2006.

[14] U. Anliker, J.A. Ward, P. Lukowicz, G. Troster, F. Dolveck, M. Baer, F. Keita, E.B. Schenker, F. Catarsi, L. Coluccini, A. Belardinelli, D. Shklarski, M. Alon, E. Hirt, R. Schmid, and M. Vuskovic. Amon: A wearable multiparameter medical monitoring and alert system. *IEEE Transactions on Information Technology in Biomedicine*, 8(4):415–427, 2004.

[15] O. Anya, H. Tawfik, S. Amin, A. Nagar, and K. Shaalan. Context-aware knowledge modelling for decision support in e-health. In *The 2010 International Joint Conference on Neural Networks (IJCNN)*, pages 1–7, July 2010.

[16] Maryam Aziz, Timothy W. Bickmore, Laura Pfeifer Vardoulakis, Christopher Shanahan, and Michael K. Paasche-Orlow. Using computer agents to improve emotional wellbeing of hospital patients. In *CHI2012 Workshop Interaction Design and Emotional Well-Being*, 2012.

[17] M. Bachlin, M. Plotnik, D. Roggen, I. Maidan, J.M. Hausdorff, N. Giladi, and G. Troster. Wearable assistant for Parkinson's disease patients with the freezing of gait symptom. *IEEE Transactions on Information Technology in Biomedicine*, 14(2):436–446, March 2010.

[18] S. Bahadori, A. Cesta, G. Grisetti, L. Iocchi, R. Leone, D. Nardi, A. Oddi, F. Pecora, and R. Rasconi. Robocare: Pervasive intelligence for the domestic care of the elderly. *Intelligenza Artificiale*, 1(1):16–21, 2004.

[19] P. Bakonyi, A. Bekessy, J. Demetrovics, P. Kerekfy, and M. Ruda. Microcomputer-network based decision support system for health-care organizations. In *IFAC Proceedings Series*, pages 1651–1658, 1985.

[20] R.A. Bankowitz, J.R. Lave, and M.A. McNeil. A method for assessing the impact of a computer-based decision support system on health care outcomes. *Methods of Information in Medicine*, 31(1):3–10, 1992.

[21] L. Bao and S. Intille. Activity recognition from user-annotated acceleration data. *Pervasive Computing*, pages 1–17, 2004.

[22] T.S. Barger, D.E. Brown, and M. Alwan. Health-status monitoring through analysis of behavioral patterns. *IEEE Transactions on Systems, Man and Cybernetics, Part A: Systems and Humans*, 35(1):22–27, 2005.

[23] R. Bellman. A Markovian decision process. Technical report, DTIC Document, 1957.

[24] J. P. Black, W. Segmuller, N. Cohen, B. Leiba, A. Misra, M. R. Ebling, and E. Stern. Pervasive computing in health care: Smart spaces and enterprise information systems. In *Proceedings of the MobiSys 2004 Workshop on Context Awareness*, Boston, June 2004.

[25] A.L. Blum and M.L. Furst. Fast planning through planning graph analysis. *Artificial Intelligence*, 90(1-2):281–300, 1997.

[26] P. Bonato. Wearable sensors and systems. *Engineering in Medicine and Biology Magazine, IEEE*, 29(3):25–36, May-June 2010.

[27] P. Bonato, F. Cutolo, D. De Rossi, R. Hughes, M. Schmid, J. Stein, and A. Tognetti. Wearable technologies to monitor motor recovery and facilitate home therapy in individuals post stroke. In *XVII Congress of the International Society of Elecectrophysiology and Kinesiology*, 2008.

[28] B. Bonet and H. Geffner. Planning as heuristic search. *Artificial Intelligence*, 129(1):5–33, 2001.

[29] Christian Borgelt. Frequent item set mining. *Wiley Interdisciplinary Reviews: Data Mining and Knowledge Discovery*, 2(6):437–456, 2012.

[30] Bosch. Healthbuddy. `www.bosch-telehealth.com/`, 2010.

[31] M. Brand, N. Oliver, and A. Pentland. Coupled hidden Markov models for complex action recognition. In *Proceedings of the IEEE Computer Society Conference on Computer Vision and Pattern Recognition*, pages 994–999. IEEE, 1997.

[32] O. Brdiczka, J.L. Crowley, and P. Reignier. Learning situation models in a smart home. *IEEE Transactions on Systems, Man, and Cybernetics, Part B: Cybernetics*, 39(1):56–63, 2009.

[33] M. Buckland, B. Frost, and A. Reeves. Liverpool telecare pilot: Telecare as an information tool. *Informatics in Primary Care*, 14(3):191–196, 2006.

[34] M. Buettner, R. Prasad, M. Philipose, and D. Wetherall. Recognizing daily activities with rfid-based sensors. In *Proceedings of the 11th International Conference on Ubiquitous Computing*, pages 51–60. ACM, 2009.

[35] Michelle Nicole Burns, Mark Begale, Jennifer Duffecy, Darren Gergle, Chris J. Karr, Emily Giangrande, and David C. Mohr. Harnessing context sensing to develop a mobile intervention for depression. *Journal of Medical Internet Research*, 13(3), 2011.

[36] caalyx. `http://www.caalyx.eu/`, 2014.

[37] Huasong Cao. A novel wireless three-pad ECG system for generating conventional 12-lead signals. Master's thesis, The University of British Columbia, 2010.

[38] X.-Q. Cao and Z.-Q. Liu. Human motion detection using Markov random fields. *Journal of Ambient Intelligence and Humanized Computing*, 1(3):211–220, 2010.

[39] Berardina De Carolis and Irene Mazzotta. Motivating people in smart environments. In *UMAP Workshops*, pages 368–381, 2011.

[40] Chin-Liang Chang. Finding prototypes for nearest neighbor classifiers. *IEEE Transactions on Computers*, 100(11):1179–1184, 1974.

[41] Datong Chen, Jie Yang, and Howard D. Wactlar. Towards automatic analysis of social interaction patterns in a nursing home environment from video. In *International Workshop on Multimedia Information Retrieval*, pages 283–290, 2004.

[42] Jinying Chen, Zhi Li, Min Dong, and Xuben Wang. Blind path identification system design base on RFID. In *Electrical and Control Engineering (ICECE), 2010 International Conference on*, pages 548–551. IEEE, 2010.

[43] L. Chen, J. Hoey, C. Nugent, D. Cook, and Z. Hu. Sensor-based activity recognition. *IEEE Transactions on Systems, Man, and Cybernetics, Part C*, 42(6):790–808, 2010.

[44] Min Chen, Sergio Gonzalez, Athanasios Vasilakos, Huasong Cao, and Victor Leung. Body area networks: A survey. *Mobile Networks and Applications*, 16:171–193, 2011. 10.1007/s11036-010-0260-8.

[45] Min Chen, Sergio Gonzalez, Athanasios Vasilakos, Huasong Cao, and Victor C. Leung. Body area networks: A survey. *Mobile Networks and Applications*, 16(2):171–193, April 2011.

[46] Min Chen, Sergio Gonzalez, Athanasios Vasilakos, Huasong Cao, and Victor C. Leung. Body area networks: A survey. *Mobile Networks and Applications*, 16(2):171–193, April 2011.

[47] S. Chumkamon, P. Tuvaphanthaphiphat, and P. Keeratiwintakorn. A blind navigation system using RFID for indoor environments. In *ECTI-CON 2008. 5th International Conference on Electrical Engineering/Electronics, Computer, Telecommunications and Information Technology*, volume 2, pages 765–768. IEEE, 2008.

[48] Pau-Choo Chung and Chin-De Liu. A daily behavior enabled hidden Markov model for human behavior understanding. *Pattern Recognition*, 41:1589–1597, 2008.

[49] F. Cincotti, F. Aloise, F. Babiloni, M.G. Marciani, D. Morelli, S. Paolucci, G. Oriolo, A. Cherubini, S. Bruscino, F. Sciarra, F. Mangiola, A. Melpignano, F. Davide, and D. Mattia. Brain-operated assistive devices: The ASPICE project. In *The First IEEE/RAS-EMBS International Conference on Biomedical Robotics and Biomechatronics, BioRob 2006.* pages 817–822, Feb. 2006.

[50] D. Cook. Learning setting-generalized activity models for smart spaces. *Intelligent Systems, IEEE*, (99):1–1, 2010.

[51] D. Cook, K. D. Feuz, and N. C. Krishnan. Transfer learning for activity recognition: A survey. *International Journal on Knowledge and Information Systems*, 36:537–556, 2013.

[52] J.M. Corchado, J. Bajo, and A. Abraham. Gerami: Improving healthcare delivery in geriatric residences. *Intelligent Systems, IEEE*, 23(2):19–25, 2008.

[53] Corinna Cortes and Vladimir Vapnik. Support vector machine. *Machine Learning*, 20(3):273–297, 1995.

[54] A.S. Crandall and D.J. Cook. Coping with multiple residents in a smart environment. *Journal of Ambient Intelligence and Smart Environments*, 1(4):323–334, 2009.

[55] Erik Crombag. Monitoring the elderly using real time location sensing. Master's thesis, Radboud University, March 2009.

[56] Dorothy Curtis, Eugene Shih, Jason Waterman, John Guttag, Jacob Bailey, Thomas Stair, Robert A. Greenes, and Lucila Ohno-Machado. Physiological signal monitoring in the waiting areas of an emergency room. In *Proceedings of the ICST 3rd International Conference on Body Area Networks*, BodyNets '08, pages 5:1–5:8, ICST, Brussels, Belgium, Belgium, 2008. ICST (Institute for Computer Sciences, Social-Informatics and Telecommunications Engineering).

[57] P. Dawadi, D. Cook, C. Parsey, M. Schmitter-Edgecombe, and M. Schneider. An approach to cognitive assessment in smart home. In *Proceedings of the 2011 Workshop on Data Mining for Medicine and Healthcare*, pages 56–59. ACM, 2011.

[58] Franca Delmastro and Marco Conti. *Wearable Computing and Sensor Systems for Healthcare*, pages 113–133. John Wiley & Sons, 2011.

[59] G. Demiris, D.P. Oliver, G. Dickey, M. Skubic, and M. Rantz. Findings from a participatory evaluation of a smart home application for older adults. *Technology and Health Care*, 16(2):111–118, 2008.

[60] Kunio Doi. Computer-aided diagnosis in radiological imaging: current status and future challenges. In *Sixth International Symposium on Multispectral Image Processing and Pattern Recognition*, pages 74971A–74971A. International Society for Optics and Photonics, 2009.

[61] J. Doyle, C. Bailey, B. Dromey, and C.N. Scanaill. BASE—an interactive technology solution to deliver balance and strength exercises to older adults. In *2010 4th International Conference on Pervasive Computing Technologies for Healthcare (PervasiveHealth)*, pages 1–5, March 2010.

[62] L. Duan, D. Xu, I.W. Tsang, and J. Luo. Visual event recognition in videos by learning from web data. In *Computer Vision and Pattern Recognition (CVPR), 2010 IEEE Conference on*, pages 1959–1966. IEEE, 2010.

[63] Turban Efraim. Implementing decision support systems: A survey. In *Proceedings of the IEEE International Conference on Systems, Man and Cybernetics*, volume 4, pages 2540–2545, 1996.

[64] ElderTech. `http://eldertech.missouri.edu/`, 2014.

[65] EmFinders. Emfinder. `www.emfinders.com/`, 2011.

[66] S. Eom and E. Kim. A survey of decision support system applications (1995–2001). *Journal of the Operational Research Society*, 57(11):1264–1278, 2006.

[67] S.B. Eom, S.M. Lee, E.B. Kim, and C. Somarajan. A survey of decision support system applications (1988–1994). *Journal of the Operational Research Society*, 49(2):109–120, 1998. cited By (since 1996) 30.

[68] J. Favela, M. Rodríguez, A. Preciado, and V.M. González. Integrating context-aware public displays into a mobile hospital information system. *Information Technology in Biomedicine, IEEE Transactions on*, 8(3):279–286, 2004.

[69] R.J. Firby. An investigation into reactive planning in complex domains. In *Proceedings of the Sixth National Conference on Artificial Intelligence*, volume 202, page 206, 1987.

[70] H. Foroughi, A. Naseri, A. Saberi, and H.S. Yazdi. An eigenspace-based approach for human fall detection using integrated time motion image and neural network. In *ICSP 2008. 9th International Conference on Signal Processing*, pages 1499–1503. IEEE, 2008.

[71] Céline Franco, Jacques Demongeot, Christophe Villemazet, and Vuiller Nicolas. Behavioral telemonitoring of the elderly at home: Detection of nycthemeral rhythms drifts from location data. In *Advanced Information Networking and Applications Workshops*, pages 759–766, 2010.

[72] Mads Frost and Jakob E. Bardram. Personal monitoring for bipolar patients: An overview of the MONARCA self-assessment system. In *CHI2012 Workshop Interaction Design and Emotional Wellbeing*, 2012.

[73] Sebastian Fudickar and Bettina Schnor. Kopal: A mobile orientation system for dementia patients. In *Intelligent Interactive Assistance and Mobile Multimedia Computing*, volume 53, pages 109–118, 2009.

[74] Tia Gao, T. Massey, L. Selavo, D. Crawford, Bor-rong Chen, K. Lorincz, V. Shnayder, L. Hauenstein, F. Dabiri, J. Jeng, A. Chanmugam, D. White, M. Sarrafzadeh, and M. Welsh. The advanced health and disaster aid network: A light-weight wireless medical system for triage. *IEEE Transactions on Biomedical Circuits and Systems*, 1(3):203–216, Sept. 2007.

[75] Minos N. Garofalakis, Rajeev Rastogi, and Kyuseok Shim. Spirit: Sequential pattern mining with regular expression constraints. In *VLDB*, 99:7–10, 1999.

[76] GE. `http://www.gehealthcare.com`, 2012.

[77] Daniele Giansanti, Velio Macellari, and Giovanni Maccioni. Telemonitoring and telerehabilitation of patients with Parkinson's disease: Health technology assessment of a novel wearable step counter. *Telemedicine Journal and E-Health*, 14(1):76–83, 2008.

[78] F. Gouaux, L. Simon-Chautemps, J. Fayn, S. Adami, M. Arzi, D. Assanelli, M.C. Forlini, C. Malossi, A. Martinez, J. Placide, et al. Ambient intelligence and pervasive systems for the monitoring of citizens at cardiac risk: New solutions from the EPI-medics project. In *Computers in Cardiology*, pages 289–292. IEEE, 2002.

[79] T. Gu, S. Chen, X. Tao, and J. Lu. An unsupervised approach to activity recognition and segmentation based on object-use fingerprints. *Data & Knowledge Engineering*, 69(6):533–544, 2010.

[80] Wenqi (Wendy) Guo, William M. Healy, and MengChu Zhou. Wireless mesh networks in intelligent building automation control: A survey. *The International Journal of Intelligent Control and Systems*, 16(1):28–36, March 2011.

[81] N. Győrbíró, Á. Fábián, and G. Hományi. An activity recognition system for mobile phones. *Mobile Networks and Applications*, 14(1):82–91, 2009.

[82] J. Habetha. The MyHeart project - fighting cardiovascular diseases by prevention and early diagnosis. In *Engineering in Medicine and Biology Society, 2006. EMBS '06. 28th Annual International Conference of the IEEE*, volume Supplement, pages 6746–6749, 2006.

[83] Martin T. Hagan, Howard B. Demuth, Mark H. Beale, et al. *Neural Network Design*. Pws Pub. Boston, 1996.

[84] Jiawei Han, Hong Cheng, Dong Xin, and Xifeng Yan. Frequent pattern mining: Current status and future directions. *Data Mining and Knowledge Discovery*, 15(1):55–86, 2007.

[85] Jiawei Han, Jian Pei, Behzad Mortazavi-Asl, Qiming Chen, Umeshwar Dayal, and Mei-Chun Hsu. Freespan: Frequent pattern-projected sequential pattern mining. In *Proceedings of the Sixth ACM SIGKDD International Conference on Knowledge Discovery and Data Mining*, pages 355–359. ACM, 2000.

[86] H. Harms, O. Amft, G. Tröster, and D. Roggen. Smash: A distributed sensing and processing garment for the classification of upper body postures. In *Proceedings of the ICST 3rd International Conference on Body Area Networks*, page 22. ICST (Institute for Computer Sciences, Social-Informatics and Telecommunications Engineering), 2008.

[87] Rave Harpaz, Santiago Vilar, William DuMouchel, Hojjat Salmasian, Krystl Haerian, Nigam H. Shah, Herbert S. Chase, and Carol Friedman. Combing signals from spontaneous reports and electronic health records for detection of adverse drug reactions. *Journal of the American Medical Informatics Association*, 20(3):413–419, 2013.

[88] Manfred Hauben, David Madigan, Charles M. Gerrits, Louisa Walsh, and Eugene P. Van Puijenbroek. The role of data mining in pharmacovigilance. *Expert Opinion on Drug Safety*, 4(5):929–948, 2005.

[89] R. Haux. Individualization, globalisation and healthabout sustainable information technologies and the aim of medical informatics. *International Journal of Medical Informatics*, 75:795–808, 2006.

[90] G.R. Hayes, E.S. Poole, G. Iachello, S.N. Patel, A. Grimes, G.D. Abowd, and K.N. Truong. Physical, social, and experiential knowledge in pervasive computing environments. *IEEE Pervasive Computing*, pages 56–63, 2007.

[91] Tamara L. Hayes, Francena Abendroth, Andre Adami, Misha Pavel, Tracy A. Zitzelberger, and Jeffrey A. Kaye. Unobtrusive assessment of activity patterns associated with mild cognitive impairment. *Journal of the Alzheimer's Association*, 4(6):395–405, 2008.

[92] Daojing He, Chun Chen, S. Chan, Jiajun Bu, and A.V. Vasilakos. Retrust: Attack-resistant and lightweight trust management for medical sensor networks. *Information Technology in Biomedicine, IEEE Transactions on*, 16(4):623–632, July 2012.

[93] Ting He, S.-H. Chan, and Chi-Fai Wong. Homemesh: A low-cost indoor wireless mesh for home networking. *Communications Magazine, IEEE*, 46(12):79–85, December 2008.

[94] E.O. Heierman III and D.J. Cook. Improving home automation by discovering regularly occurring device usage patterns. In *ICDM 2003. Third IEEE International Conference on Data Mining*, pages 537–540. IEEE, 2003.

[95] A. Helmer, Bianying Song, W. Ludwig, M. Schulze, M. Eichelberg, A. Hein, U. Tegtbur, R. Kayser, R. Haux, and M. Marschollek. A sensor-enhanced health information system to support automatically controlled exercise training of COPD patients. In *4th International Conference on Pervasive Computing Technologies for Healthcare (PervasiveHealth)*, pages 1–6, March 2010.

[96] Steve Hodges, Lyndsay Williams, Emma Berry, Shahram Izadi, James Srinivasan, Alex Butler, Gavin Smyth, Narinder Kapur, and Ken Wood. Sensecam: A retrospective memory aid. In *Ubicomp*, pages 177–193, 2006.

[97] D. Hodgins, A. Bertsch, N. Post, M. Frischholz, B. Volckaerts, J. Spensley, J.M. Wasikiewicz, H. Higgins, F. von Stetten, and L. Kenney. Healthy aims: Developing new medical implants and diagnostic equipment. *Pervasive Computing, IEEE*, 7(1):14–21, 2008.

[98] Jesse Hoey, Krists Zutis, Valerie Leuty, and Alex Mihailidis. A tool to promote prolonged engagement in art therapy: Design and development from arts therapist requirements. In *Conference on Computers and Accessibility*, pages 211–218, 2010.

[99] D. Hollosi, J. Schroder, S. Goetze, and J.E. Appell. Voice activity detection driven acoustic event classification for monitoring in smart homes. In *3rd International Symposium on Applied Sciences in Biomedical and Communication Technologies (ISABEL)*, pages 1–5. IEEE, 2010.

[100] Honeywell. Genesis dm. `http://hommed.com/`, 2011.

[101] David W. Hosmer Jr., Stanley Lemeshow, and Rodney X. Sturdivant. *Applied Logistic Regression*. Wiley.com, 2013.

[102] Johanna Hoysniemi. International survey on the dance revolution game. *Computers in Entertainment*, 4(2):Article 8, 2006.

[103] K.C. Hsu, Y.T. Chiang, G.Y. Lin, C.H. Lu, J. Hsu, and L.C. Fu. Strategies for inference mechanism of conditional random fields for multiple-resident activity recognition in a smart home. *Trends in Applied Intelligent Systems*, pages 417–426, 2010.

[104] https://www.hqs.sbt.siemens.com/. `https://www.hqs.sbt.siemens.com/`, 2014.

[105] http://www.bacnet.org. `http://www.bacnet.org`, 2014.

[106] http://www.csr.com/bc7/. `http://www.csr.com/bc7/`, 2014.

[107] http://www.healthopedia.com/. `http://www.healthopedia.com/`, 2014.

[108] http://www.memsnet.org. `http://www.memsnet.org`, 2014.

[109] http://www.rfid.org/. `http://www.rfid.org/`, 2014.

[110] http://z wavealliance.org. `http://z-wavealliance.org`, 2014.

[111] J. Iglesias, P. Angelov, A. Ledezma, and A. Sanchis. Creating evolving user behavior profiles automatically. *Knowledge and Data Engineering, IEEE Transactions on*, (99):1–1, 2011.

[112] Wijnand Ijsselsteijn, Yvonne de Kort, Cees Midden, Berry Eggen, and Elise van den Hoven. Persuasive technology for human well-being: Setting the scene. In *Persuasive Technology*, pages 1–5. Springer, 2006.

[113] Intel. Healthguide. `www.intel.com/corporate/healthcare/`, 2011.

[114] V. Jakkula and D.J. Cook. Anomaly detection using temporal data mining in a smart home environment. *Methods of Information in Medicine*, 47(1):70–75, 2008.

[115] Bartosz P. Jarochowski, SeungJung Shin, DaeHyun Ryu, and HyungJun Kim. Ubiquitous rehabilitation center: An implementation of a wireless sensor network based rehabilitation management system. In *Proceedings of the 2007 International Conference on Convergence Information Technology*, ICCIT '07, pages 2349–2358, Washington, DC, USA, 2007. IEEE Computer Society.

[116] Shanshan Jiang, Yanchuan Cao, Sameer Iyengar, Philip Kuryloski, Roozbeh Jafari, Yuan Xue, Ruzena Bajcsy, and Stephen Wicker. Carenet: an integrated wireless sensor networking environment for remote healthcare. In *Proceedings of the ICST 3rd International Conference on Body Area Networks*, BodyNets '08, pages 9:1–9:3, ICST, Brussels, Belgium, Belgium, 2008. ICST (Institute for Computer Sciences, Social-Informatics and Telecommunications Engineering).

[117] Zhanpeng Jin, Yuwen Sun, and Allen C Cheng. Predicting cardiovascular disease from real-time electrocardiographic monitoring: An adaptive machine learning approach on a cell phone. In *Conference Proceedings of the IEEE Engineering in Medicine and Biology Society*, pages 6889–6892. IEEE, 2009.

[118] Emil Jovanov, Aleksandar Milenkovic, Chris Otto, and Piet de Groen. A wireless body area network of intelligent motion sensors for computer assisted physical rehabilitation. *Journal of NeuroEngineering and Rehabilitation*, 2(1):6, 2005.

[119] Jin-Woo Jung, Jun-Hyeong Do, Young-Min Kim, Kwang-Suhk Suh, Dae-Jin Kim, and Z.Z. Bien. Advanced robotic residence for the elderly/the handicapped: Realization and user evaluation. In *ICORR 2005. 9th International Conference on Rehabilitation Robotics*, pages 492–495, June–1 July 2005.

[120] H. Junker, O. Amft, P. Lukowicz, and G. Tröster. Gesture spotting with body-worn inertial sensors to detect user activities. *Pattern Recognition*, 41(6):2010–2024, 2008.

[121] A. Kameas and I. Calemis. Pervasive Systems in Health Care. In H. Nakashima, H. Aghajan, and J. C. Augusto, editors, *Handbook of Ambient Intelligence and Smart Environments*, page 315. Springer, 2010.

[122] Maurits Clemens Kaptein, Panos Markopoulos, Boris E. R. de Ruyter, and Emile H. L. Aarts. Persuasion in ambient intelligence. *Journal of Ambient Intelligence and Humanized Computing*, 1(1):43–56, 2010.

[123] M.C. Kaptein, P. Markopoulos, B. de Ruyter, and E. Aarts. Persuasion in ambient intelligence. *Journal of Ambient Intelligence and Humanized Computing*, 1(1):43–56, 2010.

[124] Leonard Kaufman and Peter J. Rousseeuw. *Finding Groups in Data: An Introduction to Cluster Analysis*, volume 344. Wiley.com, 2009.

[125] L. Kiff, K. Haigh, and X. Sun. Mobility monitoring with the independent lifestyle assistant?(ILSA). In *International Conference on Aging, Disability and Independence (ICADI)*, December 4–6 2003. Washington, DC.

[126] Phillip King and Jason Tester. The landscape of persuasive technologies. *Communications of the ACM*, 42(5):31–38, May 1999.

[127] A. Kofod-Petersen and A. Aamodt. Contextualised ambient intelligence through case-based reasoning. *Advances in Case-Based Reasoning*, pages 211–225, 2006.

[128] N.C. Krishnan, P. Lade, and S. Panchanathan. Activity gesture spotting using a threshold model based on adaptive boosting. In *IEEE International Conference on Multimedia and Expo (ICME)*, pages 155–160. IEEE, 2010.

[129] Naoyuki Kubota, Takenori Obo, and Honghai Liu. Human behavior measurement based on sensor network and robot partners. *JACIII*, pages 309–315, 2010.

[130] Jennifer R. Kwapisz, Gary M. Weiss, and Samuel A. Moore. Activity recognition using cell phone accelerometers. *ACM SIGKDD Explorations Newsletter*, 12(2):74–82, 2011.

[131] C.F. Lai, S.Y. Chang, H.C. Chao, and Y.M. Huang. Detection of cognitive injured body region using multiple triaxial accelerometers for elderly falling. *Sensors Journal, IEEE*, 11(3):763–770, 2011.

[132] Gokce B. Laleci, Asuman Dogac, Mehmet Olduz, Ibrahim Tasyurt, Mustafa Yuksel, and Alper Okcan. SAPHIRE: A multi-agent system for remote healthcare monitoring through computerized clinical guidelines. In Roberta Annicchiarico, Ulises Cortés, Cristina Urdiales, Marius Walliser, Stefan Brantschen, Monique Calisti, and Thomas Hempfling, editors, *Agent Technology and e-Health*, Whitestein Series in Software Agent Technologies and Autonomic Computing, pages 25–44. Birkhäuser Basel, 2008.

[133] N.D. Lane, Y. Xu, H. Lu, S. Hu, T. Choudhury, A.T. Campbell, and F. Zhao. Enabling large-scale human activity inference on smartphones using community similarity networks (CSN). *Ubicomp11*, pages 355–364, 2011.

[134] Nicholas D. Lane, Emiliano Miluzzo, Hong Lu, Daniel Peebles, Tanzeem Choudhury, and Andrew T. Campbell. A survey of mobile phone sensing. *Communications Magazine, IEEE*, 48(9):140–150, 2010.

[135] Eric C. Larson, Mayank Goel, Gaetano Boriello, Sonya Heltshe, Margaret Rosenfeld, and Shwetak N. Patel. Spirosmart: Using a microphone to measure lung function on a mobile phone. In *Proceedings of the 2012 ACM Conference on Ubiquitous Computing*, pages 280–289. ACM, 2012.

[136] M. Laszlo and S. Mukherjee. Minimum spanning tree partitioning algorithm for microaggregation. *IEEE Transactions on Knowledge and Data Engineering*, 17(7):902–911, 2005.

[137] Benoît Latré, Bart Braem, Ingrid Moerman, Chris Blondia, and Piet Demeester. A survey on wireless body area networks. *Wireless Networks*, 17(1):1–18, January 2011.

[138] S.W. Lee and K. Mase. Activity and location recognition using wearable sensors. *Pervasive Computing, IEEE*, 1(3):24–32, 2002.

[139] Enrique Leon, Iraitz Montalban, Sarah Schlatter, and Inigo Dorronsoro. Computer-mediated emotional regulation: Detection of emotional changes using non-parametric cumulative sum. *Conference Proceedings of the IEEE Engineering in Medicine and Biology Society*, 1:1109–12, 2010.

[140] R. Levinson. The planning and execution assistant and trainer (PEAT). *The Journal of Head Trauma Rehabilitation*, 12(2):85, 1997.

[141] David D. Lewis. Naive (Bayes) at forty: The independence assumption in information retrieval. In *Machine Learning: ECML-98*, pages 4–15. Springer, 1998.

[142] Jun Liang, C.C. Abbott, M. Skubic, and J. Keller. Investigation of GAIT features for stability and risk identification in elders. In *Conference Proceedings of the IEEE Engineering in Medicine and Biology Society*, pages 6139–6142, Sept. 2009.

[143] L. Liao, D.J. Patterson, D. Fox, and H. Kautz. Learning and inferring transportation routines. *Artificial Intelligence*, 171(5):311–331, 2007.

[144] Chung-Chih Lin, Ming-Jang Chiu, Chun-Chieh Hsiao, Ren-Guey Lee, and Yuh-Show Tsai. Wireless health care service system for elderly with dementia. *IEEE Transactions on Information Technology in Biomedicine*, 10(4):696–704, 2006.

[145] R. Linnarsson. Drug interactions in primary health care: A retrospective database study and its implications for the design of a computerized decision support system. *Scandinavian Journal of Primary Health Care*, 11(3):181–186, 1993.

[146] P. Lukowicz, J. Ward, H. Junker, M. Stäger, G. Tröster, A. Atrash, and T. Starner. Recognizing workshop activity using body worn microphones and accelerometers. *Pervasive Computing*, pages 18–32, 2004.

[147] M. Mahdaviani and T. Choudhury. Fast and scalable training of semi-supervised CRFS with application to activity recognition. *Advances in Neural Information Processing Systems*, 20:977–984, 2007.

[148] J. Mantyjarvi, J. Himberg, and T. Seppanen. Recognizing human motion with multiple acceleration sensors. In *IEEE International Conference on Systems, Man, and Cybernetics*, volume 2, pages 747–752. IEEE, 2001.

[149] Y. Masuda, M. Sekimoto, M. Nambu, Y. Higashi, T. Fujimoto, K. Chihara, and Y. Tamura. An unconstrained monitoring system for home rehabilitation. *Engineering in Medicine and Biology Magazine, IEEE*, 24(4):43–47, 2005.

[150] U. Maurer, A. Smailagic, D.P. Siewiorek, and M. Deisher. Activity recognition and monitoring using multiple sensors on different body positions. In *International Workshop on Wearable and Implantable Body Sensor Networks, 2006. BSN 2006*, pages 113–116, IEEE, 2006.

[151] Daniel McDuff, Amy Karlson, Ashish Kapoor, Asta Roseway, and Mary Czerwinski. Affectaura: Emotional wellbeing reflection system. In *6th International Conference on Pervasive Computing Technologies for Healthcare (PervasiveHealth)*, pages 199–200, May 2012.

[152] R. McNaney, A. Thieme, B. Gao, C. Ladha, P. Olivier, D. Jackson, and K. Ladha. Objectively monitoring wellbeing through pervasive technology. In *CHI2012 Workshop Interaction Design and Emotional Wellbeing*, 2012.

[153] Rémi Mégret, Vladislavs Dovgalecs, Hazem Wannous, Svebor Karaman, Jenny Benois-Pineau, Elie El Khoury, Julien Pinquier, Philippe Joly, Régine André-Obrecht, Yann Gaëstel, and Jean-François Dartigues. The IMMED project: Wearable video monitoring of people with age dementia. In *International Conference on Multimedia*, pages 1299–1302, 2010.

[154] C. Metcalf, S. Collie, A. Cranny, G. Hallett, C. James, J. Adams, P. Chappell, N. White, and J. Burridge. Fabric-based strain sensors for measuring movement in wearable telemonitoring applications. In *IET Conference on Assisted Living*, pages 1–4. The Institution of Engineering and Technology, 2009.

[155] Stéphane M. Meystre, Guergana K. Savova, Karin C. Kipper-Schuler, and John F. Hurdle. Extracting information from textual documents in the electronic health record: A review of recent research. *Yearbook of Medical Informatics*, 35:128–144, 2008.

[156] A. Mihailidis, B. Carmichael, and J. Boger. The use of computer vision in an intelligent environment to support aging-in-place, safety, and independence in the home. *IEEE Transactions on Information Technology in Biomedicine*, 8(3):238–247, 2004.

[157] J. Modayil, T. Bai, and H. Kautz. Improving the recognition of interleaved activities. In *Proceedings of the 10th International Conference on Ubiquitous Computing*, pages 40–43. ACM, 2008.

[158] T.B. Moeslund, A. Hilton, and V. Krüger. A survey of advances in vision-based human motion capture and analysis. *Computer Vision and Image Understanding*, 104(2):90–126, 2006.

[159] Carl H. Mooney and John F. Roddick. Sequential pattern mining–Approaches and algorithms. *ACM Computing Surveys (CSUR)*, 45(2):19, 2013.

[160] M. Mubashir, L. Shao, and L. Seed. A survey on fall detection: Principles and approaches. *Neurocomputing*, 100:144–152, 2012.

[161] M.D. Murray. Automated medication dispensing devices. In *Making Health Care Safer: A Critical Analysis of Patient Safety Practices*, chapter 11, 2001.

[162] myheart. `http://www.hitech-projects.com/euprojects/myheart/`, 2012.

[163] A.L. Mykityshyn, A.D. Fisk, and W.A. Rogers. Learning to use a home medical device: Mediating age-related differences with training. *Human Factors: The Journal of the Human Factors and Ergonomics Society*, 44(3):354–364, 2002.

[164] Tatsuo Nakajima and Vili Lehdonvirta. Designing motivation using persuasive ambient mirrors. *Personal and Ubiquitous Computing*, pages 1–20, 2011.

[165] M. Nambu, K. Nakajima, M. Noshiro, and T. Tamura. An algorithm for the automatic detection of health conditions. *Engineering in Medicine and Biology Magazine, IEEE*, 24(4):38–42, 2005.

[166] J. Nicholson, V. Kulyukin, and D. Coster. Shoptalk: Independent blind shopping through verbal route directions and barcode scans. *The Open Rehabilitation Journal*, 2:11–23, 2009.

[167] Y. Nishida, T. Hori, T. Suehiro, and S. Hirai. Sensorized environment for self-communication based on observation of daily human behavior. In *International Conference on Intelligent Robots and Systems*, pages 1364–1372, 2000.

[168] C. Nugent, D. Finlay, R. Davies, M. Mulvenna, J. Wallace, C. Paggetti, E. Tamburini, and N. Black. The next generation of mobile medication management solutions. *International Journal of Electronic Healthcare*, 3(1):7–31, 2007.

[169] C.D. Nugent, M.D. Mulvenna, X. Hong, and S. Devlin. Experiences in the development of a smart lab. *International Journal of Biomedical Engineering and Technology*, 2(4):319–331, 2009.

[170] Christoph Obermair, Wolfgang Reitberger, Alexander Meschtscherjakov, Michael Lankes, and Manfred Tscheligi. perframes: Persuasive picture frames for proper posture. In Harri Oinas-Kukkonen, Per Hasle, Marja Harjumaa, Katarina Segerstahl, and Peter Ohrstrom, editors, *Persuasive Technology*, volume 5033 of *Lecture Notes in Computer Science*, pages 128–139. Springer Berlin / Heidelberg, 2008.

[171] M.J. O'Grady, C. Muldoon, M. Dragone, R. Tynan, and G.M.P. O'Hare. Towards evolutionary ambient assisted living systems. *Journal of Ambient Intelligence and Humanized Computing*, 1(1):15–29, 2010.

[172] M. Omichi, Y. Maki, T. Ohta, Y. Sekita, and Fujisaku S. A decision support system for regional health care planning in a metropolitan area. *Japan-hospitals: The Journal of the Japan Hospital Association*, 3:19–23, 1984.

[173] P. Palmes, H.K. Pung, T. Gu, W. Xue, and S. Chen. Object relevance weight pattern mining for activity recognition and segmentation. *Pervasive and Mobile Computing*, 6(1):43–57, 2010.

[174] R. Paradiso, G. Loriga, and N. Taccini. A wearable health care system based on knitted integrated sensors. *Information Technology in Biomedicine, Transactions on*, 9(3):337–344, 2005.

[175] Kwang-Hyun Park, Zeungnam Bien, Ju-Jang Lee, Byung Kim, Jong-Tae Lim, Jin-Oh Kim, Heyoung Lee, Dimitar Stefanov, Dae-Jin Kim, Jin-Woo Jung, Jun-Hyeong Do, Kap-Ho Seo, Chong Kim, Won-Gyu Song, and Woo-Jun Lee. Robotic smart house to assist people with movement disabilities. *Autonomous Robots*, 22:183–198, 2007. 10.1007/s10514-006-9012-9.

[176] Stephanie Pasche, Silvia Angeloni, Real Ischer, Martha Liley, Jean Luprano, and Guy Voirin. AMON: A wearable multiparameter medical monitoring and alert system. *IEEE Transactions on Information Technology in Biomedicine*, 57(80):80–87, 2008.

[177] Shyamal Patel, Hyung Park, Paolo Bonato, Leighton Chan, and Mary Rodgers. A review of wearable sensors and systems with application in rehabilitation. *Journal of NeuroEngineering and Rehabilitation*, 9(1):21, 2012.

[178] D. Patterson, L. Liao, D. Fox, and H. Kautz. Inferring high-level behavior from low-level sensors. In *UbiComp 2003: Ubiquitous Computing*, pages 73–89. Springer, 2003.

[179] D.J. Patterson, D. Fox, H. Kautz, and M. Philipose. Fine-grained activity recognition by aggregating abstract object usage. In *Proceedings of the Ninth IEEE International Symposium on Wearable Computers*, pages 44–51. IEEE, 2005.

[180] Donald J. Patterson, Lin Liao, Krzysztof Gajos, Michael Collier, Nik Livic, Katherine Olson, Shiaokai Wang, Dieter Fox, and Henry Kautz. Opportunity knocks: A system to provide cognitive assistance with transportation services. In *International Conference on Ubiquitous Computing (UbiComp)*, pages 433–450. Springer, 2004.

[181] E.J. Pauwels, A.A. Salah, and R. Tavenard. Sensor networks for ambient intelligence. In *MMSP 2007. IEEE 9th Workshop on Multimedia Signal Processing*, pages 13–16, Oct. 2007.

[182] Callum B. Pearce, Steve R. Gunn, Adil Ahmed, and Colin D. Johnson. Machine learning can improve prediction of severity in acute pancreatitis using admission values of APACHE II score and C-reactive protein. *Pancreatology*, 6(1):123–131, 2006.

[183] J. Pei, J. Han, and W. Wang. Constraint-based sequential pattern mining: The pattern-growth methods. *Journal of Intelligent Information Systems*, 28(2):133–160, 2007.

[184] M. Perkowitz, M. Philipose, K. Fishkin, and D.J. Patterson. Mining models of human activities from the web. In *Proceedings of the 13th International Conference on World Wide Web*, pages 573–582. ACM, 2004.

[185] M.R. Perwez, N. Ahmad, M.S. Javaid, and M. Ehsan Ul Haq. A critical analysis on efficacy of clinical decision support systems in health care domain. *Advanced Materials Research*, 383-390:4043–4050, 2012.

[186] M. Philipose, K.P. Fishkin, M. Perkowitz, D.J. Patterson, D. Fox, H. Kautz, and D. Hahnel. Inferring activities from interactions with objects. *Pervasive Computing, IEEE*, 3(4):50–57, 2004.

[187] Philips. Telestation. `www.healthcare.philips.com/`, 2011.

[188] Philips. `http://research.philips.com`, 2012.

[189] C. Phua, K. Sim, and J. Biswas. Multiple people activity recognition using simple sensors. In *International Conference on Pervasive and Embedded Computing and Communication Systems*, pages 313–318, 2011.

[190] Ewa Piotrowicz, Anna Jasionowska, Maria Banaszak-Bednarczyk, Joanna Gwilkowska, and Ryszard Piotrowicz. ECG telemonitoring during home-based cardiac rehabilitation in heart failure patients. *Journal of Telemedicine and Telecare*, 18(4):193–197, 2012.

[191] Martha E. Pollack, Laura Brown, Dirk Colbry, Colleen E. McCarthy, Cheryl Orosz, Bart Peintner, Sailesh Ramakrishnan, and Ioannis Tsamardinos. Autominder: An intelligent cognitive orthotic system for people with memory impairment. *Robotics and Autonomous Systems*, 44(3-4):273–282, 2003.

[192] C.C.Y. Poon, Yuan-Ting Zhang, and Shu-Di Bao. A novel biometrics method to secure wireless body area sensor networks for telemedicine and m-health. *Communications Magazine, IEEE*, 44(4):73–81, April 2006.

[193] J. Ross Quinlan. Induction of decision trees. *Machine Learning*, 1(1):81–106, 1986.

[194] M. Rantz, M. Aud, G. Alexander, D. Oliver, D. Minner, M. Skubic, J. Keller, Z. He, M. Popescu, G. Demiris, and S. Miller. Tiger place: An innovative educational and research environment. *AAAI in Eldercare: New Solutions to Old Problems*, Washington, DC, November 7–9, 2008.

[195] P. Rashidi and D. Cook. Domain selection and adaptation in smart homes. *Toward Useful Services for Elderly and People with Disabilities*, pages 17–24, 2011.

[196] P. Rashidi, D. Cook, L. Holder, and M. Schmitter-Edgecombe. Discovering activities to recognize and track in a smart environment. *IEEE Transactions on Knowledge and Data Engineering*, 23(4):527–539, 2011.

[197] P. Rashidi and D.J. Cook. Mining sensor streams for discovering human activity patterns over time. In *IEEE 10th International Conference on Data Mining (ICDM)*, pages 431–440. IEEE, 2010.

[198] P. Rashidi and D.J. Cook. Activity knowledge transfer in smart environments. *Pervasive and Mobile Computing*, 7(3):331–343, 2011.

[199] P. Rashidi, D.J. Cook, L.B. Holder, and Maureen Schmitter-Edgecombe. Discovering activities to recognize and track in a smart environment. *IEEE Transactions on Knowledge and Data Engineering*, 23(4):527–539, 2011.

[200] Parisa Rashidi and Diane J. Cook. The resident in the loop: Adapting the smart home to the user. *IEEE Transactions on Systems, Man, and Cybernetics Journal, Part A*, 39(5):949–959, 2009.

[201] Wolfgang Reitberger, Manfred Tscheligi, Boris de Ruyter, and Panos Markopoulos. Surrounded by ambient persuasion. In *CHI '08 Extended Abstracts on Human Factors in Computing Systems*, CHI EA '08, pages 3989–3992, New York, NY, USA, 2008. ACM.

[202] M. Di Rienzo, F. Rizzo, G. Parati, G. Brambilla, M. Ferratini, and P. Castiglioni. Magic system: A new textile-based wearable device for biological signal monitoring; applicability in daily life and clinical setting. In *EMBS*, pages 7167–7169, 2005.

[203] G. Riva, F. Vatalaro, F. Davide, and M. Alcañiz. *Ambient Intelligence: The Evolution of Technology, Communication and Cognition Towards The Future of Human-Computer Interaction*. Emerging communications: studies in new technologies and practices in communication. IOS, 2005.

[204] Marcela D. Rodríguez, Jesus Favela, Alfredo Preciado, and Aurora Vizcaíno. Agent-based ambient intelligence for healthcare. *AI Communications*, 18(3):201–216, 2005.

[205] M.J. Romano and R.S. Stafford. Electronic health records and clinical decision support systems: Impact on national ambulatory care quality. *Archives of Internal Medicine*, 171(10):897–903, 2011.

[206] Frank Rosenblatt. The perceptron: A probabilistic model for information storage and organization in the brain. *Psychological review*, 65(6):386, 1958.

[207] M. Ruotsalainen, T. Ala-Kleemola, and A. Visa. GAIS: A method for detecting interleaved sequential patterns from imperfect data. In *IEEE Symposium on Computational Intelligence and Data Mining, CIDM 2007*, pages 530–534. IEEE, 2007.

[208] S. Rasoul Safavian and David Landgrebe. A survey of decision tree classifier methodology. *IEEE Transactions on Systems, Man and Cybernetics*, 21(3):660–674, 1991.

[209] Privender Saini, Richard Willmann, Ruth Huurneman, Gerd Lanfermann, Juergen te Vrugt, Stefan Winter, and Jaap Buurke. Philips stroke rehabilitation exerciser: A usability test. In *Proceedings of the IASTED International Conference on Telehealth/Assistive Technologies*, Telehealth/AT '08, pages 116–122, Anaheim, CA, USA, 2008. ACTA Press.

[210] Dairazalia Sánchez, Monica Tentori, and Jesús Favela. Activity recognition for the smart hospital. *IEEE Intelligent Systems*, 23(2):50–57, 2008.

[211] saphire. `http://www.srdc.metu.edu.tr/projects/saphire/`, 2012.

[212] G. Shi, C.S. Chan, W.J. Li, K.S. Leung, Y. Zou, and Y. Jin. Mobile human airbag system for fall protection using MEMS sensors and embedded SVM classifier. *Sensors*, 9(5):495–503, 2009.

[213] Victor Shnayder, Bor-rong Chen, Konrad Lorincz, Thaddeus R. F. Fulford Jones, and Matt Welsh. Sensor networks for medical care. In *Proceedings of the 3rd International Conference on Embedded Networked Sensor Systems*, SenSys '05, pages 314–314, New York, NY, USA, 2005. ACM.

[214] Ali H. Shoeb and John V. Guttag. Application of machine learning to epileptic seizure detection. In *Proceedings of the 27th International Conference on Machine Learning (ICML-10)*, pages 975–982, 2010.

[215] F. Siegemund and C. Florkemeier. Interaction in pervasive computing settings using bluetooth-enabled active tags and passive RFID technology together with mobile phones. In *IEEE International Conference on Pervasive Computing and Communications*, pages 378–387. IEEE, 2003.

[216] Richard Simpson, Debra Schreckenghost, Edmund LoPresti, and Ned Kirsch. Plans and planning in smart homes. In *Designing Smart Homes*, volume 4008 of *Lecture Notes in Computer Science*, pages 71–84, 2006.

[217] Aneesha Singh, Tali Swann-Sternberg, Nadia Berthouze, Amanda C. de C. Williams, Maja Pantic, and Paul Watson. Emotion and pain: Interactive technology to motivate physical activity in people with chronic pain. In *CHI2012 Workshop Interaction Design and Emotional Wellbeing*, 2012.

[218] G. Singla, D.J. Cook, and M. Schmitter-Edgecombe. Recognizing independent and joint activities among multiple residents in smart environments. *Journal of Ambient Intelligence and Humanized Computing*, 1(1):57–63, 2010.

[219] G. Singla, D.J. Cook, and M. Schmitter-Edgecombe. Recognizing independent and joint activities among multiple residents in smart environments. *Journal of Ambient Intelligence and Humanized Computing*, 1(1):57–63, 2010.

[220] R. Snyder-Halpern. Assessing health care setting readiness for point of care computerized clinical decision support system innovations. *Outcomes Management for Nursing Practice*, 3(3):118–127, 1999.

[221] C. Song, T. Koren, P. Wang, and A.L. Barabási. Modelling the scaling properties of human mobility. *Nature Physics*, 6(10):818–823, 2010.

[222] R. Srinivasan, C. Chen, and D.J. Cook. Activity recognition using actigraph sensor. In *Proceedings of the 4th International Workshop on Knowledge Discovery from Sensor Data (ACM SensorKDD'10), Washington, DC, July*, pages 25–28, 2010.

[223] M. Stikic and B. Schiele. Activity recognition from sparsely labeled data using multi-instance learning. *Location and Context Awareness*, pages 156–173, 2009.

[224] T. Suzuki, S. Murase, T. Tanaka, and T. Okazawa. New approach for the early detection of dementia by recording in-house activities. *Telemedicine Journal and E-Health*, 13(1):41–44, 2007.

[225] T.A.C. Wireless controller networks for building automation benefits and opportunities for facility owners, 2006. http://www.tac.com/data/internal/data/07/39/1220381406396/TAC+Wireless+WP_A4.pdf

[226] E. Tapia, S. Intille, and K. Larson. Activity recognition in the home using simple and ubiquitous sensors. *Pervasive Computing*, pages 158–175, 2004.

[227] A. Tate, J. Dalton, and J. Levine. O-plan: A web-based AI planning agent. In *Proceedings of the National Conference on Artificial Intelligence*, pages 1131–1132. Menlo Park, CA; Cambridge, MA; London; AAAI Press; MIT Press; 1999, 2000.

[228] Monica Tentori, Gillian R. Hayes, and Madhu Reddy. Pervasive computing for hospital, chronic, and preventive care. *Foundations and Trends in Human-Computer Interaction*, 5(1):1–95, 2012.

[229] A. Tran, S. Marsland, J. Dietrich, H. Guesgen, and P. Lyons. Use cases for abnormal behaviour detection in smart homes. *Aging Friendly Technology for Health and Independence*, pages 144–151, 2010.

[230] Tril. `http://www.trilcentre.org`, 2012.

[231] P.H. Tsai, C.Y. Yu, M.Y. Wang, J.K. Zao, H.C. Yeh, C.S. Shih, and J.W.S. Liu. iMat: Intelligent medication administration tools. In *12th IEEE International Conference on e-Health Networking Applications and Services (Healthcom)*, pages 308–315. IEEE, 2010.

[232] Manfred Tscheligi, Wolfgang Reitberger, Christoph Obermair, and Bernd Ploderer. perCues: Trails of persuasion for ambient intelligence. In *Proceedings of the First International Conference on Persuasive Technology for Human Well-Being*, PERSUASIVE'06, pages 203–206, Berlin, Heidelberg, 2006. Springer-Verlag.

[233] J.W. Tukey. *Exploratory Data Analysis*. Pearson, Reading, MA, 1977.

[234] D.L. Vail, M.M. Veloso, and J.D. Lafferty. Conditional random fields for activity recognition. In *Proceedings of the 6th International Joint Conference on Autonomous Agents and Multiagent Systems*, page 235. ACM, 2007.

[235] valedo. `http://www.hocoma.com/en/products/valedo/`, 2012.

[236] T. van Kasteren, G. Englebienne, and B. Kröse. Transferring knowledge of activity recognition across sensor networks. *Pervasive Computing*, pages 283–300, 2010.

[237] T. van Kasteren, G. Englebienne, and B. Kröse. Hierarchical activity recognition using automatically clustered actions. *Ambient Intelligence*, pages 82–91, 2011.

[238] T. van Kasteren and B. Krose. Bayesian activity recognition in residence for elders. In *IE 07. 3rd IET International Conference on Intelligent Environments*, pages 209–212. IET, 2007.

[239] T.L.M. van Kasteren, G. Englebienne, and B.J.A. Kröse. An activity monitoring system for elderly care using generative and discriminative models. *Personal and Ubiquitous Computing*, 14(6):489–498, 2010.

[240] U. Varshney. Wireless medication management system: Design and performance evaluation. In *Wireless Telecommunications Symposium (WTS)*, pages 1–8. IEEE, 2011.

[241] Peter-Paul Verbeek. Ambient intelligence and persuasive technology: The blurring boundaries between human and technology. *Nanoethics*, 3(3):231–242, 2009. Open Access.

[242] S. Waharte and R. Boutaba. Tree-based wireless mesh networks: Topology analysis. In *First International Workshop on Wireless Mesh Networks (MeshNets)*, 2005.

[243] D. Wan. Magic medicine cabinet: A situated portal for consumer healthcare. In *Handheld and Ubiquitous Computing*, pages 352–355. Springer, 1999.

[244] Jie Wan, Caroline Byrne, Gregory M.P. O'Hare, and Michael J. O'Grady. Orange alerts: Lessons from an outdoor case study. In *5th International Conference on Pervasive Computing Technologies for Healthcare (PervasiveHealth)*, pages 446–451, 2011.

[245] J. Wang, Y. Luo, Y. Zhao, and J. Le. A survey on privacy preserving data mining. In *First International Workshop on Database Technology and Applications*, pages 111–114. IEEE, 2009.

[246] Jason T.L. Wang, Steve Rozen, Bruce A. Shapiro, Dennis Shasha, Zhiyuan Wang, and Maisheng Yin. New techniques for DNA sequence classification. *Journal of Computational Biology*, 6(2):209–218, 1999.

[247] L. Wang, T. Gu, X. Tao, and J. Lu. Sensor-based human activity recognition in a multi-user scenario. *Ambient Intelligence*, pages 78–87, 2009.

[248] D. Weinland, R. Ronfard, and E. Boyer. A survey of vision-based methods for action representation, segmentation and recognition. *Computer Vision and Image Understanding*, 115(2):224–241, 2011.

[249] Miles Wernick, Yongyi Yang, Jovan Brankov, Grigori Yourganov, and Stephen Strother. Machine learning in medical imaging. *Signal Processing Magazine, IEEE*, 27(4):25–38, 2010.

[250] Christopher Williams and Matthias Seeger. Using the Nyström method to speed up kernel machines. In *Advances in Neural Information Processing Systems 13*. Citeseer, 2001.

[251] D. Wilson and C. Atkeson. Simultaneous tracking and activity recognition (STAR) using many anonymous, binary sensors. *Pervasive Computing*, pages 329–334, 2005.

[252] J. Wilson, B.N. Walker, J. Lindsay, C. Cambias, and F. Dellaert. Swan: System for wearable audio navigation. In *11th IEEE International Symposium on Wearable Computers*, pages 91–98. IEEE, 2007.

[253] J.M. Winters and Yu Wang. Wearable sensors and telerehabilitation. *Engineering in Medicine and Biology Magazine, IEEE*, 22(3):56–65, May-June 2003.

[254] A. Wood, J. Stankovic, G. Virone, L. Selavo, Zhimin He, Qiuhua Cao, Thao Doan, Yafeng Wu, Lei Fang, and R. Stoleru. Context-aware wireless sensor networks for assisted living and residential monitoring. *Network, IEEE*, 22(4):26–33, July-Aug. 2008.

[255] A. Wood, G. Virone, T. Doan, Q. Cao, L. Selavo, Y. Wu, L. Fang, Z. He, S. Lin, and J. Stankovic. Alarm-net: Wireless sensor networks for assisted-living and residential monitoring. Technical report, Department of Computer Science, University of Virginia, 2006.

[256] G. Wu and S. Xue. Portable preimpact fall detector with inertial sensors. *IEEE Transactions on Neural Systems and Rehabilitation Engineering*, 16(2):178–183, 2008.

[257] Winston Wu, Lawrence Au, Brett Jordan, Thanos Stathopoulos, Maxim Batalin, William Kaiser, Alireza Vahdatpour, Majid Sarrafzadeh, Meika Fang, and Joshua Chodosh. The smartcane system: an assistive device for geriatrics. In *International Conference on Body Area Networks*, pages 1–4, 2008.

[258] A.Y. Yang, R. Jafari, S.S. Sastry, and R. Bajcsy. Distributed recognition of human actions using wearable motion sensor networks. *Journal of Ambient Intelligence and Smart Environments*, 1(2):103–115, 2009.

[259] J. Yin, Q. Yang, and J.J. Pan. Sensor-based abnormal human-activity detection. *IEEE Transactions on Knowledge and Data Engineering*, 20(8):1082–1090, 2008.

[260] Zerrin Yumak-Kasap, Yu Chen, and Pearl Pu. Emosonet: An emotion-aware social network for emotional wellbeing. In *CHI2012 Workshop Interaction Design and Emotional Wellbeing*, 2012.

[261] Chengqi Zhang and Shichao Zhang. *Association Rule Mining: Models and Algorithms*. Springer-Verlag, 2002.

[262] X. Zhuang, J. Huang, G. Potamianos, and M. Hasegawa-Johnson. Acoustic fall detection using Gaussian mixture models and gmm supervectors. In *IEEE International Conference on Acoustics, Speech and Signal Processing, ICASSP 2009*, pages 69–72. IEEE, 2009.

[263] ZigBee. Zigbee. `http://www.digi.com/technology/rf-articles/wireless-zigbee.jsp`, 2014.

Chapter 17

Fraud Detection in Healthcare

Varun Chandola
Department of Computer Science & Engineering
State University of New York at Buffalo
Buffalo, NY
chandola@buffalo.edu

Jack Schryver
UT-Battelle LLC
Oak Ridge National Laboratory
Oakridge, TN
schryverjc@ornl.gov

Sreenivas Sukumar
UT-Battelle LLC
Oak Ridge National Laboratory
Oakridge, TN
sukumarsr@ornl.gov

17.1 Introduction

Healthcare fraud has been one of the biggest problem faced by United States, and almost every other nation, costing tens of billions of dollars a year. With growing healthcare expenditure, currently estimated to exceed $3 trillion in 2014 [21], the threat of healthcare fraud is increasing at an alarming pace. The complexity of the healthcare domain, which includes multiple sets of participants, including healthcare providers, beneficiaries (patients), and insurance companies, makes the problem of detecting healthcare fraud equally challenging and sets it apart from other similar areas such as credit card [7] and auto insurance fraud detection [16].

Healthcare spending in the United States is one of the key issues targeted by policy makers, owing to the fact that it is a major contributor to the high national debt levels that are projected for next two decades. In 2008, the total healthcare spending in the United States was 15.2% of its GDP (highest in the world) and is expected to reach as much as 19.5% by 2017 [3]. But while the healthcare costs have risen (by as much as 131% in the past decade), the quality of healthcare in the United States has not seen comparable improvements (see Figure 17.1) [32].

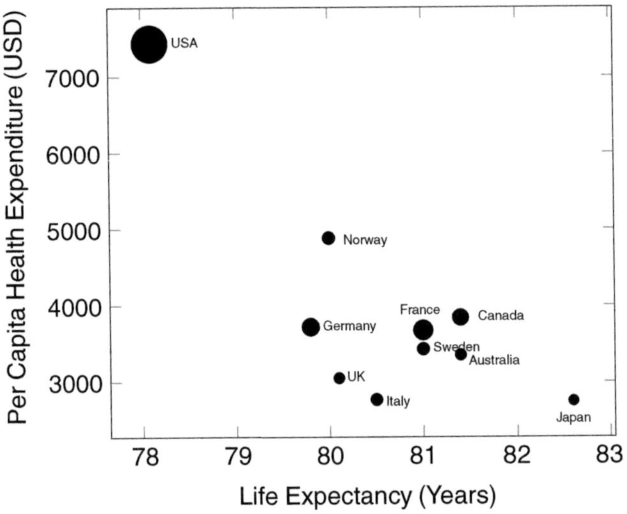

FIGURE 17.1: Life expectancy compared to per-capita healthcare spending for 2008, in the United States and the next 19 most wealthy countries by total GDP [22]. Size of the bubbles indicate the relative healthcare costs as a percent of GDP.

Experts agree that inefficiencies in the current healthcare system, resulting in unprecedented amounts of waste, is the primary driver for the discrepancy between the spending and the returns in the healthcare domain [17]. Recent studies estimate that close to 30% ($\sim$ $765 billion in 2009) of total healthcare spending in the United States is wasted. Some reports show even higher proportion of waste (closer to 50%) [15]. This waste can be attributed to many factors such as unnecessary services, fraud, excessive administrative costs, and inefficiencies in healthcare delivery. Recent policy changes such as the *Patient Protection and Affordable Care Act* and the emphasis on greater transparency and accessibility into federal programs have underscored the importance of understanding the healthcare data to address this wastage.

Data is an integral part of healthcare. In fact, the recent McKinsey report on Big Data [25] values the potential of healthcare data at $300 billion per year. A significant portion of this value is attributed to the ability to combat healthcare fraud. The problem of healthcare fraud coupled with the available data has been a very attractive target for data analysis and data mining community. The major advantages of data-driven fraud detection system are: (i) automatic extraction of fraud patterns from data, (ii) prioritization of suspicious cases for law enforcement agencies, and (iii) identification of new types of fraud for which no known "signatures" exist.

We discuss the problem of fraud in healthcare and existing data-driven methods for fraud detection in this chapter. Given the recent scrutiny of the inefficiencies in the US healthcare system, identifying fraud has been on the forefront of the efforts towards reducing the healthcare costs. In this chapter we will focus on understanding the issue of healthcare fraud in detail, and review methods that have been proposed in the literature to combat this issue using data-driven approach. The rest of the chapter is organized as follows: Section 17.2 introduces the problem of healthcare fraud detection including the relationship between different entities within the healthcare ecosystem. Section 17.3 discusses the different ways in which fraud is committed. We describe the available data in Section 17.4. We provide an overview of existing methods for healthcare fraud detection in Section 17.5.

17.2 Understanding Fraud in the Healthcare System

One of the key factors for the inefficiencies mentioned above is the presence of rampant fraud in the healthcare system. Several estimates have pointed out that close to 10% of the total money wasted in the healthcare sector in the United States can be attributed to healthcare fraud [2] (see Figure 17.2). For the year 2009 this amounted to nearly 75 Billion USD! Similar estimates have been reported for recent years as well. While policy makers are careful in distinguishing between *fraud* and *abuse*, the latter being the exploitation of the weaknesses in the system while not explicitly breaking any laws, one can argue that the two forms of wastage can be considered as fraud in general. Abuse may be considered as fraud, which is even more challenging to detect. In fact, in 1996 the US *Department of Health and Human Services* (HHS) established[1] the *Health Care Fraud and Abuse Control* (HCFAC) program to combat fraud and abuse as a single problem. Overall, the combination of fraud and abuse constitute one of the primary drivers of inefficiencies in the healthcare system, costing the healthcare system in the range of $100 to $175 billion annually.

While the other reasons shown in Figure 17.2 have only recently attracted attention, detecting healthcare fraud and abuse has been on the radar of the healthcare lawmakers and enforcement agencies for many years [34]. Unfortunately, owing to the complexity of the healthcare sector, only a small fraction of the losses are recovered by steps taken by enforcement programs such as HCFAC. Recent estimates suggest that less than 5% of losses from fraud and abuse are recovered every year. For example, in 2007, HCFAC collected $1.8 billion in fraudulent claims [1], which is close to 1% of the total fraud committed that year. While such estimates portray a dismal picture of the state of art in healthcare fraud detection, they also indicate the opportunities for innovations in the fraud detection area. Before investigating the issue of healthcare fraud we first describe how the healthcare system is typically setup. While, the healthcare system varies across countries, we are going to focus on the US healthcare system. The healthcare ecosystem can be divided into three groups of actors:

1. **Beneficiaries**—The individuals who seek medical attention in the form of medical services, drugs, and equipment (commonly known as healthcare). Most individuals in the United States (close to 84% in 2010) are covered through some type of "insurance" to pay for their medical needs for a monthly premium.

[1]Health Insurance Portability and Accountability Act of 1996 (HIPAA)

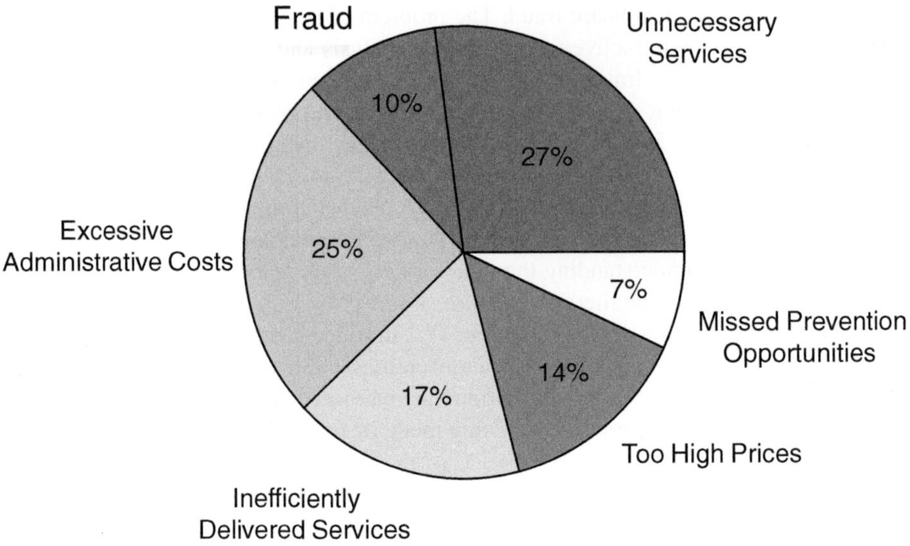

FIGURE 17.2: Breakup of Annual Waste in the U.S. healthcare System [2]. Total wasteful spending is estimated to be around \$750 billion every year (nearly 30% of total healthcare spending). The total estimates and the breakup has been roughly consistent over the last 5 years.

2. **Providers**—Organizations that provide healthcare including hospitals, physicians and other medical staff, pharmacies, and medical equipment dealers. Healthcare facilities in the United States are primarily managed by the private sector (close to 80%).

3. **Insurance Agencies**—Organizations that actually pay the providers for administering "care" to the beneficiaries. Close to 84% of the U.S. population (over 250 million individuals) have some kind of health insurance to cover all or some of their healthcare needs. In the United States, almost 28% of the population (83 million) is covered under government health insurance programs. Two of the biggest such programs are *Medicare* and *Medicaid*. Medicare is a federal program administered by the *Center for Medicare & Medicaid* (CMS) and provides health benefits for Americans over 65 and younger people with disabilities. Medicaid is a program jointly funded by federal and state governments and managed by states to provide health benefits to a low income population.

There is a fourth group as well—the policy makers and enforcement agencies, but since they are not *active* participants in fraud, we will not focus on them in this chapter.

The healthcare model works as follows. A beneficiary visits a healthcare provider who supports his/her insurance plan to seek medical services. The provider performs the services and sends a "bill" (or an insurance *claim*) to the corresponding insurance agency. Sometimes the beneficiary has to a pay a lesser amount (co-pay) to the provider. The insurance agency reimburses the provider for the rendered services based on a payment model (*capitation*, *bundled payments* or *fee for service*).

17.3 Definition and Types of Healthcare Fraud

As per HIPAA, the federal government defines healthcare fraud [4] as follows:

Definition 17.3.1 *Healthcare fraud is committed when, an individual or a group of individuals acting together or an organization, knowingly, and willfully executes or attempts to execute a scheme to defraud any healthcare benefit program or to obtain by means of false or fraudulent pretenses, representations, or promises any of the money or property owned by any healthcare benefit program.*

The reason that fraud and abuse is so rampant in the US healthcare system can be attributed to a large extent to three key aspects of the healthcare insurance system. The first is the *pay and chase* model adopted by many insurance agencies, which means that the agencies first pay the claimant and then investigate the claim. Such a model is clearly attractive to fraudsters who can disappear after defrauding the system and reappear in another state or with a different identity. This leads to the second reason which is *the presence of many insurance organizations* (both private and government). Most of these organizations do not collaborate with each other, due to business and other reasons, making them easy targets for fraudsters who can "move" from one system to another without getting detected. The third reason is the *fee for service* payment model adopted by many insurance organizations, where the providers are paid for individual medical services given to the beneficiaries. This model encourages both fraud (see example below) and abuse, since the providers can charge for more expensive but unnecessary services.

Among the three groups of actors listed earlier, the majority of healthcare fraud is committed by organized crime groups and dishonest healthcare providers. The most common types of health care fraud include:

1. Billing for services that were never provided. This is typically done in two ways. First is to create "fake patients" through identity theft and fabricate entire claims (See the dead patients example below). The second method is to "pad" an existing claim with expensive services that were not provided at all.

2. Falsely billing for a higher-priced treatment that was actually administered. This is also known as **upcoding**. Most insurance agencies associate a medical condition (characterized by a *diagnosis code*) with a particular procedure or service. In a upcoding fraud, the fraudster typically "inflates" the patient's diagnosis code to a more serious condition and charge for the corresponding service, which is typically more expensive. Upcoding is also rampant in abuse, where providers diagnose patients with more serious conditions than necessary to justify more expensive treatments.

3. Administering medically unnecessary services solely for the purpose of generating insurance payments.

4. Showing noncovered medical services as medically necessary. Many insurance plans cover only some medical services. For example, Medicare insurance does not cover cosmetic surgery. But fraudsters can misrepresent the uncovered services as medically necessary and bill the insurance agency. For example, a "nose job" can be billed to the insurance agency as a deviated-septum repair.

5. Changing a patient's diagnosis to justify for medically unnecessary services.

6. **Unbundling**—billing each step of a procedure as if it were a separate procedure.

7. Billing the beneficiary (through co-pay) and the insurance agency for the same service even when the service might be fully covered by the insurance. Another type of fraud is to not charge any co-pay and overbill the insurance agency.

8. Accepting kickbacks for patient referrals.

9. Illegal acquisition of prescription drugs for personal use or profit (also known as *prescription fraud* [8]).

The following is an example of a fraud case discovered in Florida:[2]

Example: Florida Dermatologist Case Since 1997 a doctor in Florida had an arrangement with a local medical laboratory to increase the lab's referral business. The doctor sent patients (covered under the U.S. Federal Medicare insurance program) to the lab for testing and diagnosis of skin-related issues. The lab provided an unsigned pathology report to the doctor for each referral. The doctor then made it appear that he himself had conducted the tests and charged Medicare for the lab's work. The doctor was paid by Medicare for these services, which he had not actually performed! The doctor received more than $6 million in Medicare payments and he shared part of his fraudulent profits with the lab. Moreover, the doctor substantially increased the number of skin biopsies and other **medically unnecessary** procedures that he performed on the Medicare patients thereby defrauding the system more.

Another case of healthcare fraud was uncovered in 2011:[3]

Example: Counseling Dead Patients A licensed physician in Atlanta, Georgia, filed close to 100,000 claims to Medicare and Georgia Medicaid for group psychological therapy sessions, amounting to close to a million dollars. An investigation of the physician's claims revealed that many of these services were provided to beneficiaries who were dead at the time the purported care was rendered! Many other beneficiaries were hospitalized at the time of service and could not have possibly been part of the group services rendered at the physician's nursing home.

17.4 Identifying Healthcare Fraud from Data

From the types and examples of fraud mentioned above, one can clearly see that many, if not all, types of healthcare fraud can be identified through data-driven analytical methods. In recent years, several experts as well as the federal government[4] have stressed the role of big data analytics in addressing the issues with healthcare including identifying fraud. The 2011 report by the McKinsey Global Institute [25] estimate that the potential value that can be extracted from data in the healthcare sector in the United States could be more than $300 billion per year. The same report lists out several areas within the healthcare sector that can benefit from using big data analytics. These include segmentation of patients based on their health profiles to identify target groups for proactive care or lifestyle changes, development of fraud resistant payment models, creating information transparency and accessibility around healthcare data, and conducting comparative effectiveness research across providers, patients, and geographies.

Healthcare fraud detection can be broadly conducted in two ways. The first way is to place regulatory checks during the claim processing phase. Many such checks already exist and act as the first line of defense against fraudsters. But many types of fraud cannot be detected using such checks because of organized crime where the criminals are aware of the regulations and commit multistep fraud designed to avoid such checks. The second way is to detect fraud in a retrospective

[2] http://www.justice.gov/opa/pr/2013/February/13-civ-183.html

[3] http://www.fbi.gov/atlanta/press-releases/2011/doctor-pleads-guilty-to-billing-medicare-and-medicaid-for-counseling-sessions-with-dead-patients

[4] http://www.whitehouse.gov/sites/default/files/microsites/ostp/big_data_press_release_final_2.pdf

manner by examining the data related to the financial transactions (insurance claims). We will focus on the second fraud detection approach.

Healthcare insurance claims have the potential of answering many of the questions currently faced by the healthcare sector, In fact, until shareable *electronic health records* become a reality, healthcare claims, especially from organizations with a large spatial and demographic coverage such, which is the case with many of the government-run health insurance programs in the country, are the most reliable resource for understanding the current healthcare landscape, from conditions, care, and cost perspective. But the transactional format of claims data is not amenable for advance analytics that the state-of-art KDD methodologies have to offer for fraud detection. In this chapter we will explore transformations of the healthcare claims data to facilitate healthcare fraud detection.

Healthcare claims-related data is tied to the type of insurance payment model currently being used. In the United States, the typical health insurance payment model is a *fee-for-service* (FFS) model in which the providers (doctors, hospitals, etc.) render services to the patients and are paid for each service by the payer or the insurance agency. The providers record the details of each service, including the cost and justification and submit the record to the payer. The payer decides to either pay or reject the claim based on the patient's eligibility for the particular services that are determined by the policy guidelines.

17.4.1 Types of Data

In the past, researchers and policy makers have tapped into a variety of data to understand the healthcare system. Figure 17.3 shows the different pertinent sources. Data that is useful for identifying healthcare fraud is collected by the providers (hospitals or individual practitioners) and the insurance agencies. The insurance agency typically maintains three types of data for their operations:

1. *Claim information* that captures the information about the service transaction including the nature of the service and the cost.

2. *Patient enrollment and eligibility data* that captures demographic information about the patients (or beneficiaries of the system) and their eligibility for different services.

3. *Provider enrollment data* that captures the information about the physicians, hospitals, and other healthcare-providing organizations.

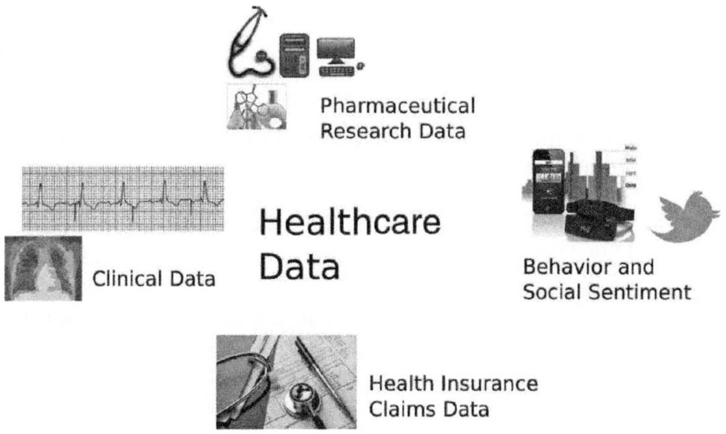

FIGURE 17.3: Different types of data relevant for healthcare fraud detection.

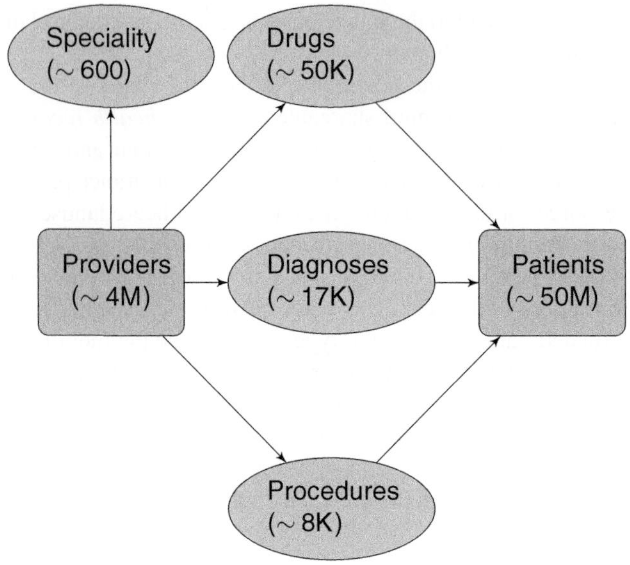

FIGURE 17.4: Entities and relationships in Medicare healthcare claims data along with approximate number of entries in each entity set.

4. *Blacklists* that enumerate the providers and other entities who have been previously indicted as fraudsters.

The data collected by the providers is typically shared with the insurance agencies to facilitate payment of claims. Additionally, the providers also maintain detailed health records for the patients, more of which now are being stored as *electronic medical records* (EMRs). There are other static databases that encode the different types of drugs, diagnoses, and procedures that are used for treatments.

Figure 17.4 shows the relationships between different entities within the healthcare ecosystem. The numbers associated with each entity is an approximate size encountered within the US healthcare system. The numbers will vary in a different context (a single hospital, a private insurance agency, etc.).

17.4.2 Challenges

Healthcare fraud detection from data is a challenging task. Here we list some of the key challenges associated with identifying fraud in the healthcare data:

1. **Modality**: Claims and enrollment data is stored in databases or data warehouses as multiple linked database tables. Data consists of patient-specific (demographics, physiological measurements, etc.), disease-specific (type, severity, etc.), and treatment-specific (type, cost, etc.) information. Often, the provider information is in the form of networks (referral network, affiliation network, etc.). A provider's activities can be considered as a time series.

2. **Data size**: As noted in Figure 17.4, the size of the data poses a big challenge. For the entire United States, analyzing fraud requires processing claims corresponding to interaction between the patients (of the order of the population of the entire country) and providers (few million) through diseases, treatments, and drugs.

3. **Privacy concerns**: Perhaps the biggest challenge for applying data-driven methods for healthcare fraud detection is the relative unavailability of data due to strong privacy requirements. Health information is protected under the *Health Insurance Portability and Accountability Act of 1996 (HIPAA), Privacy, Security and Breach Notification Rules*[5] (HIPAA), which imposes strict restrictions on the sharing of such data, even in an anonymized form. So researchers either need to develop methods based on highly anonymized/partial data or synthetic versions of the real data.

The claims and the provider enrollment data comes from transactional data warehouses. Each claim, consists of several data elements with information about the beneficiary, provider, the health condition (or diagnosis), the service provided (procedure or drug), and the associated costs. Figure 17.4 shows the different entities and their relationships that are present in the healthcare claims data. Note that the providers typically are affiliated to each other through organizations such as hospitals. This information and additional data about the providers is present in the provider data.

17.5 Knowledge Discovery-Based Solutions for Identifying Fraud

In this section we will discuss existing methods for identifying healthcare fraud. Many methods exist for fraud detection in other communities, such as credit card and telecommunications fraud [7, 16, 9]. Most of such methods rely on constructing profiles for the users based on the historical data and monitor deviations in the behavior of the user from the profile. For healthcare, such approaches are not applicable, because the users in the healthcare setting are the beneficiaries, who typically are not the fraud perpetrators. Thus, more sophisticated analysis is required in the healthcare sector to identify fraud.

Note that several data-driven solutions for detecting healthcare fraud have been developed in the private sector. But given the proprietary nature of the underlying algorithms, we are not including them in our discussion in this chapter. We refer the reader to surveys on this topic for a more comprehensive coverage of existing methods [24, 35, 5, 12].

Data-driven methods for healthcare fraud detection can be employed to answer the following questions:

- Is a given episode of care fraudulent or unnecessary? Note that an *episode of care* is essentially the collection of healthcare provided to a patient under the same health issue. Thus, an episode corresponds to a single health condition and may contain multiple claims.
- Is a given claim within an episode fraudulent or unnecessary?
- Is a provider or a network of providers fraudulent?

The rest of this chapter discusses some possible approaches to answer the above questions.

17.5.1 Identifying Fraudulent Episodes

A healthcare episode can be considered as a sequence of steps, where each step corresponds to a healthcare activity (procedure, test, prescription, etc.). These sequences are often also referred to as *clinical pathways*. A clinical pathway is a standardized sequence of care administered for a specific situation. For example, for a procedure such as cholecystectomy (gall bladder removal), healthcare organizations follow a clinical pathway that might begin with preadmission testing and

[5] `http://www.hhs.gov/ocr/privacy/`

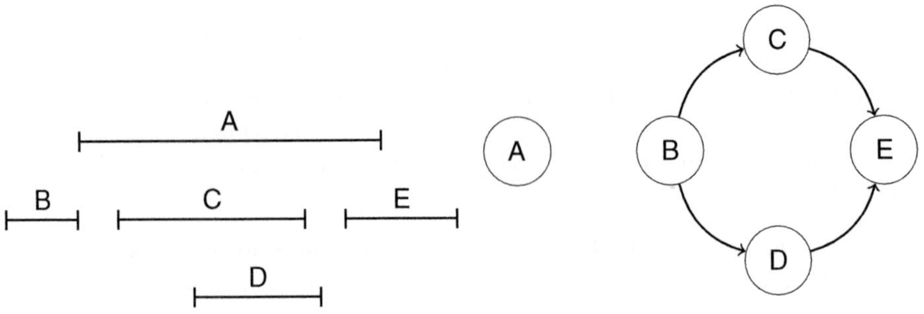

FIGURE 17.5: Example of a clinical pathway and the corresponding graph representation [38].

an anesthesia consult, then a set of assessments, surgery, and physicians' orders, and finally ending with a follow-up visit in the surgeon's office. While clinical pathways are designed to serve as "best practices" for a caregiver, they can also be used for identifying suspicious episodes by detecting irregular pathways. For example, a single ambulant visit in a particular pathway might be acceptable but multiple such visits might be suspicious.

One way to identify fraud is by analyzing a patient's episode under the assumption that episodes for the same type of health condition exhibit common patterns [38]. For example, Yang [38] uses the episodes for known normal and fraudulent episodes and extract structural patterns in the episodes. These patterns are used as features and a classifier is trained on the labeled episodes. The classifier is then used to determine if a new episode is fraudulent or not. The key data representation in the proposed method is a temporal graph in which each activity is represented as a vertex and links are added based on the order in which the activities are performed. An example is shown in Figure 17.5.

Identifying fraudulent episodes, as discussed above, can be further reduced into two subproblems. The first is to discover common patterns from episodes. If the episodes are represented as temporal graphs, one could apply temporal subgraph mining [37] or frequent episodes mining methods to identify frequently occuring patterns [6]. The second subproblem is to use the discovered patterns as features and train a classifier that can identify fraudulent from nonfraudulent episodes using a labeled training data set. Yan and Han [37] applied this approach to detect fraudulent episodes in the area of pelvic inflammatory disease (PID) and reported close to 80% accuracy in identifying fraudulent episodes from a set of 906 fraudulent and 906 normal episodes collected from several hospitals in Taiwan.

17.5.2 Identifying Fraudulent Claims

A healthcare claim typically has following types of information:

1. Patient demographics
2. Provider information
3. Health issue (disease)
4. Healthcare provided (procedures, drugs)
5. Costs

One could analyze such claims along different dimensions to identify fraud. For instance, one could ask the following question: *Is the claim for the given disease legitimate, given the patient?* To answer such a question, one needs to build models from historical data that can provide a likelihood or probability score of observing a claim conditioned on the diagnosis and the patient demographics. One possible Bayesian approach can be described as follows.

17.5.2.1 A Bayesian Approach to Identifying Fraudulent Claims

Consider a simple Bayesian network that captures the relationships between disease and patient information as shown in Figure 17.6. The patient information is captured in three random variables, *gender* (G), *age* (A), and *location* (L). The disease information is represented as a random variable D, which could correspond to the diagnosis code associated with the claim. Note that we have assumed conditional independence for G, A, L, and D though this may be modified based on expert input.

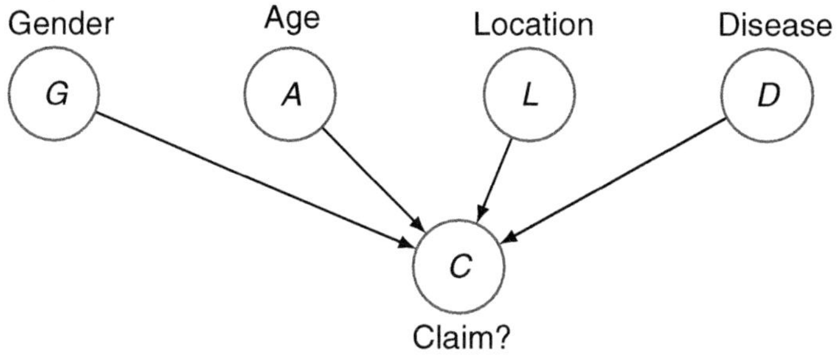

FIGURE 17.6: A simple Bayesian network for modeling dependencies between disease, patient, and claims.

We model the occurrence of a claim as a binary random variable $C \in \{yes, no\}$. Given a claim, one can compute the probability of an occurrence of a claim, using the Bayesian network in Figure 17.6, as follows:

$$\begin{aligned} P(C=yes|G=g,A=a,L=l,D=d) &= P(C=yes|G=g) \\ &\times P(C=yes|A=a) \\ &\times P(C=yes|L=l) \\ &\times P(C=yes|D=d) \end{aligned} \tag{17.1}$$

The individual probabilities in (17.1) can be computed using the Bayes rule. For example:

$$P(C=yes|G=g) = \frac{P(G=g|C=yes)P(C=yes)}{\sum_{g'} P(G=g'|C=yes)P(C=yes)} \tag{17.2}$$

If the gender random variable, G, is modeled as a *Bernoulli* random variable, then $P(G=g|C=yes)$ is the parameter for the class-conditional Bernoulli random variable and can be estimated from historical data by simply computing the fraction of the number of claims observed for the gender g from the total number of claims.

One can extend the simple Bayesian algorithm described above in many ways. One extension is to add more variables. The second extension is to introduce dependence in the Bayesian network. Some variants are given in Figures 17.7 and have been proposed earlier [28, 11, 36].

17.5.2.2 Non-Bayesian Approaches

The Bayesian approach discussed above models the probability of observing a claim for a given patient. This can also be approached as an anomaly detection problem [12]. Let us consider each

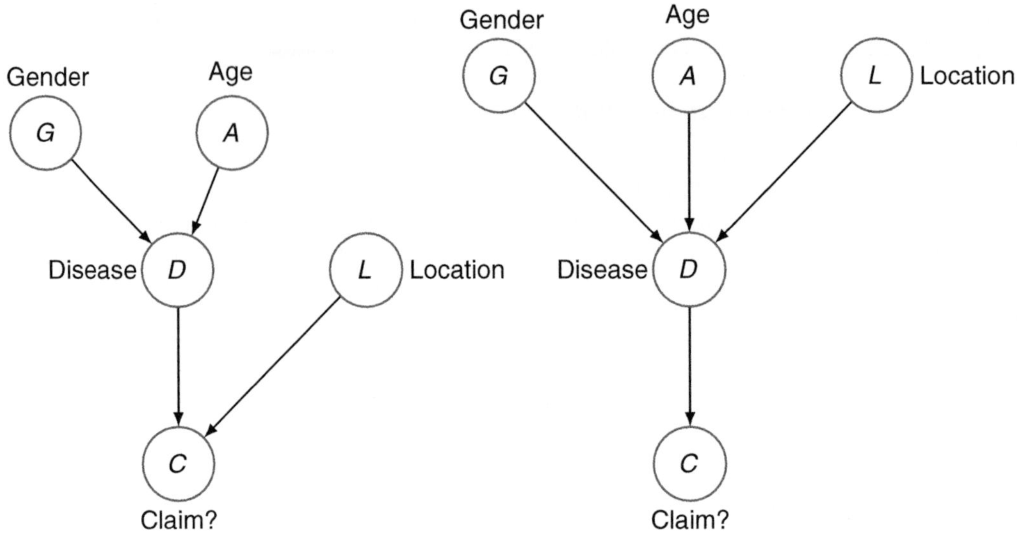

(a) Demographics-dependent disease (b) Demographics- and location-dependent disease

FIGURE 17.7: Extensions to the simple Bayesian network shown in Figure 17.6.

claim as a multivariate data instance with attributes $\langle g, a, l, d \rangle$ corresponding to gender, age, location, and disease. Given a data set $\mathcal{D}$ of such examples, one can then apply an unsupervised anomaly detection method to assign an anomaly score to each claim.

Proximity-based anomaly detection methods such as the k-nearest neighbor-based anomaly detection, *local outlier factor* (lof) and many variants thereof have been proposed in the literature to detect such anomalies. Proximity-based methods rely on a similarity kernel (or an equivalent distance metric) that allows comparison of data examples. If all variables in the data vector are continuous, one could employ widely used *Euclidean* or *Mahalanobis* Distance, but for nonmetric variables (such as categorical or ordinal) one needs to use appropriate similarity measures [10].

17.5.3 Identifying Fraudulent Providers

Given that almost all healthcare fraud is committed through a malicious party acting as a healthcare provider, identifying fraudulent providers is perhaps the most important objective of healthcare fraud detection. Note that the approaches discussed earlier to identify fraudulent claims can be applied to identify fraudulent providers by identifying providers who are generating multiple fraudulent claims. In this part, we will focus on two types of direct methods to identify fraudulent providers. The first class of methods will focus on analyzing provider networks while the second class of methods will be based on analyzing the temporal behavior of providers.

17.5.3.1 Analyzing Networks for Identifying Coordinated Frauds

We motivate network-based methods using the following real example.[6]

[6] `http://www.npr.org/blogs/health/2014/04/16/303704523/medicare-kept-paying-indicted-sanctioned-doctors`

Example: Case of Paying Indicted Doctors In August 2011, a psychiatrist and a podiatrist were among those providers who were arrested and subsequently suspended from Michigan's Medicaid program for running a defrauding scheme. In 2012, it was found out that the federal Medicare program paid $862,000 to the psychiatrist and $155,000 to the podiatrist after getting suspended from Medicaid. In all, the same report estimates around $6 million paid to such indicted doctors in 2012.

The biggest issue highlighted in the above example is the fact that same provider might be enrolled into multiple health insurance programs. Getting indicted in one program might not automatically mean that the provider is identified as fraudulent in other programs. One of the biggest reasons for this is the lack of a unifying identifier across programs. This leads to the following question: *Can we match providers across programs?* In other words, given an indicted provider from one program, can we detect if the same provider is operating in a different program?

One possible way to identify such cross-program connections is to study the relationship between providers. The relationship should be available from a source independent of any program. Two possibilities are **patient referral networks** and **hospital affiliation networks**. In both cases, the healthcare system is realized as a social network in which providers are nodes. For patient referral networks, two providers are connected if they refer patients to each other. For hospital affiliation networks, the providers are connected to hospitals or practices to which they are affiliated.

As health insurance companies shift focus from fraud detection to fraud prevention, building a predictive model to **estimate the risk of a provider before making any claims** has been a challenging problem. Furthermore, a substantial amount of healthcare fraud is expected to be hidden in the relationships among providers and between providers and beneficiaries making insurance claims. In this section we will study how modeling relationships of providers as a social network [27] can belp us identify fraudulent providers, especially when "black lists" of known perpetrators are added to the normal data.

17.5.3.2 Constructing a Provider Social Network

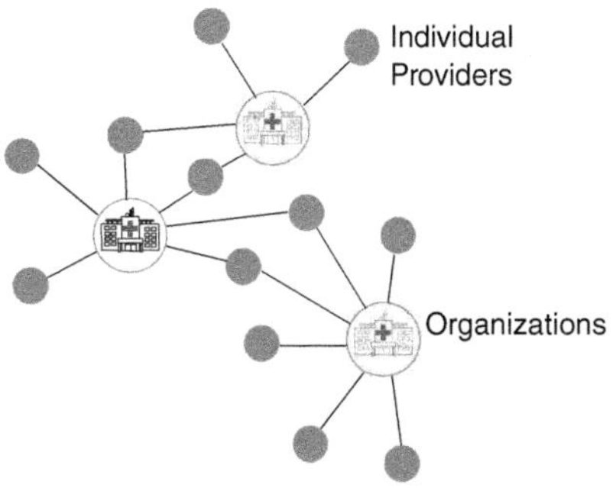

FIGURE 17.8: A sample provider network.

Providers in the US healthcare system are typically associated with multiple hospitals and health organizations. The information about the providers can be obtained from multiple sources. Some of such data sources are public[7] while others may be purchased.[8] We use data from such sources to construct a social network in which providers (both individual and organizations) are the nodes. The edges are between individual and organization nodes (see Figure 17.8). A graph, when constructed

[7] `https://nppes.cms.hhs.gov/NPPES/`
[8] `http://www.healthmarketscience.com/`

for all providers in the United States, is expected to have nearly 35 million nodes and more than 100 million edges. For instance, a graph constructed for providers in the state of Texas displayed almost 1 million nodes and close to 3 million edges [13].

One can also construct a network using the patient referrals to join a pair of providers with an edge; two providers have an edge in the network if one of them refers a patient to the other. Such referral data can be constructed from claims information or by corralling health records across practices. A snapshot of the provider network in the state of Texas is shown in Figure 17.9. This provider

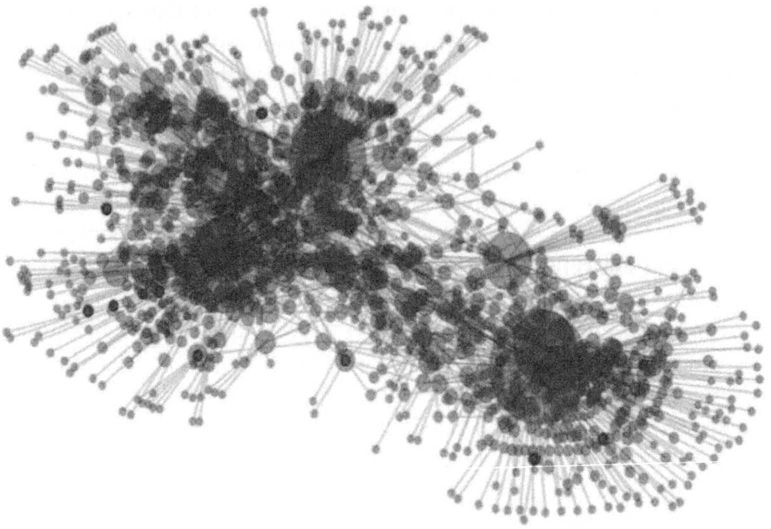

FIGURE 17.9: Snapshot of the provider network for Texas. The width of the circle at each node denotes the number of affiliations. The large circles indicate organizations, such as hospitals. Nodes in red are fraudulent providers.

network is different from a typical "social network" in the following ways: (i) the networks consist of both organizations and individuals. This introduces a latent hierarchy in the network because several individual physicians work for organizations and can also own group practices; (ii) the network is a collection of disconnected graphs, the largest being a network of a few 100,000 providers and the smallest as little as 3; and, (iii) the network is constructed based on self-reported data and inferred data based on subject matter expertise and may be subject to omissions, errors, and quality issues. To differentiate between normal and fraudulent providers, one could study the network using a "guilt-by-association" principle. The idea is to understand each node in the network based on its association with known malicious (fraudulent) nodes. One can extract multiple features for every node in the network and use them for discriminating between fraudulent and non-fraudulent providers. Most network-based features [27, 31] (see Table 17.1) can be broadly categorized into the following groups:

- **Centrality**: Such features identify the most important vertices (or providers) in the graph. One fundamental centrality feature is the **degree**. Vertices with a higher number of *links* with other vertices are considered to be more important than the vertices with very few links.

- **Eigenvector**: centrality measures the influence of a vertex on the graph. If A is the $n \times n$ adjacency matrix of a given graph $G = (V, E)$ with n vertices, then the eigenvector centrality for any vertex v is equal to the vth component of the eigenvector of A corresponding to the largest eigenvalue.

- **Assortativity**: Such features measure the *preference* of a vertex to attach to another vertex. In the healthcare domain, it essentially measures the probability of a provider to get linked with other providers. **Average neighbor degree** or **neighbor connectivity** is one such feature that is equal to the average degree of neighbors of a given vertex.
- **Clustering**: Such features measure the extent to which each vertex is part of localized structures, such as **triangles**. The triangle structure is particularly interesting from the healthcare fraud perspective. A triangle in a referral graph denotes a situation where three providers refer patients to each other.
- **Communities, cores**: Similar to clustering, community-based features such as the *k*-**community** feature measures the participation of a node in (near) *cliques* or densely connected components within the graph that could identify the presence of a collusion of fraudulent providers. Measures such as *k*-**cores** have a similar effect, i.e., they measure the participation of each vertex in subgraphs in which all vertices have a minimum degree of *k*.
- **Distance Measures**: Such features, like **eccentricity**, measure the *distance* of each vertex from other vertices. For example, eccentricity of a vertex is the maximum graph distance between that vertex and any other vertex in the graph.
- **Link Analysis**: Such features, such as the widely used **Page Rank**, measure the *importance* of vertices by recursively scoring them based on the importance of the vertices that are linked to them.
- **Vitality**: Such features measure the importance of each vertex in terms of how much impact they have on the general connectivity of the graph. For example, the **closeness vitality** feature is defined as the change in the sum of distances between all vertex pairs when excluding that vertex from the graph.

TABLE 17.1: Network Features Studied for the Provider Network [27]

Centrality	Degree, Closeness, Betweenness, Load
	Current Flow Closeness, Communicability
	Current Flow Betweenness, Eigenvector
Assortativity	Average Neighbor Degree
	Average Degree Connectivity
Clustering	Triangles, Average Clustering
	Square Clustering
Communities	*K*-Clique
Cores	Core number, *k*-Core
Distance Measures	Eccentricity
	Periphery, Radius
Link Analysis	PageRank, Hits
Vitality	Closeness Vitality

17.5.3.3 Relevance for Identifying Fraud

The first question that comes up is: Are any of the features listed in Table 17.1 discriminative enough to distinguish between fraudulent and nonfraudulent nodes in the network? One way to test this is to compute the *Information Complexity* (ICOMP) measure [23] for each feature. For the affiliation network data for Texas, the top five features that were the most *discriminative* using the ICOMP measure are:

1. **Node degree**
2. **Number of fraudulent providers in a 2-hop network**
3. **Page rank**
4. **Eigenvector centrality**
5. **Current-flow closeness centrality**

For each feature, we estimated its capability to distinguish between fraudulent and nonfraudulent nodes using the *Information Complexity* (ICOMP) measure [23], which compares the distribution of the features for the fraudulent and nonfraudulent populations. Figure 17.10 shows the distribution of the five most discriminative features with respect to the fraudulent and nonfraudulent populations.

For instance, the gray line in Figure 17.10(a) indicates the node degree distribution for providers previously identified as fraudulent. The black lines are for a random sample of nonfraudulent providers. We observe that an increase in degree of provider correlates to a higher risk of fraud. Similar conclusions can be drawn from analyzing the 2-hop network (see Figure 17.10(b)). In fact, the chance of finding other fraudulent providers within the 2-hop network of a fraudulent provider is $\sim$40% compared to the chance of finding a fraudulent provider within the 2-hop network of a random provider ($\sim$2%).

Given the ability of the above features to distinguish between fraudulent and nonfraudulent providers, one can utilize them within either an unsupervised multivariate anomaly detection algorithm [12] for automatic detection of such providers or in a binary classification algorithm that learns from the available labeled data.

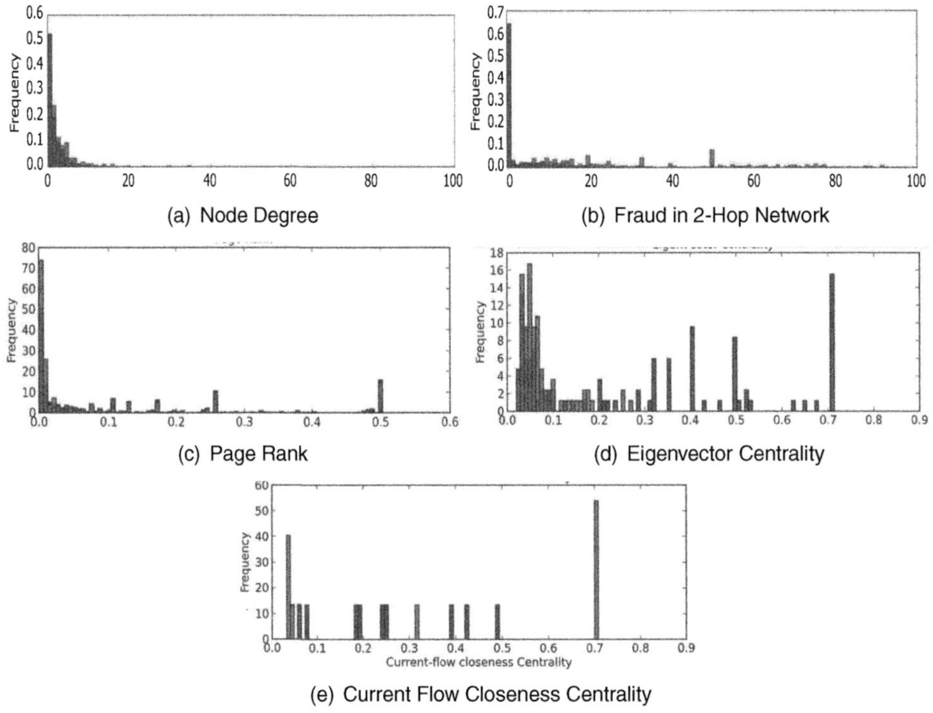

FIGURE 17.10: Distribution of top distinguishing features for fraudulent (gray) vs. nonfraudulent providers (black).

17.5.4 Temporal Modeling for Identifying Fraudulent Behavior

While network-based methods are effective in analyzing providers with respect to their associations with known providers, another possible approach to identifying fraudulent providers is to *monitor* their behavior. This monitoring can be done in two ways:

1. Monitoring provider behavior over time (temporal modeling)
2. Classifying provider behavior over time as fraudulent or not (supervised learning)
3. Comparing provider behavior with peers (anomaly detection)

Here we will discuss the first approach that involves temporal modeling of provider behavior to address the following two questions:

1. How can we identify the transition of a *good* provider into a *bad* actor in an online fashion using the temporal sequence of claims?
2. How can the temporal sequence be used to discriminate fraudulent providers from others?

The first question is essentially a *change-point detection problem.* Such formulation can allow deployment of a statistical process control-based approach to identify when a provider transitions from a normal to a fraudulent provider. The strength of this method is that it can be implemented online to examine each claim as it enters a processing queue for payment.

For the second question one can compare the temporal claim submission patterns of every provider to estimated population norms for similar providers (e.g., by specialty and geographic location) and define features from these comparisons. Classifiers can subsequently be trained to learn the differences between known fraudsters and presumed normal providers.

17.5.4.1 Change-Point Detection with Statistical Process Control Techniques

The statistical process control (SPC) literature [26] has evolved into a fairly mature methodology for implementation of a temporal approach to processing data sequences. A number of methods have been proposed in SPC theory to monitor processes for exceedance of control limits. One popular metric is the cumulative sum (CUSUM) statistic [30]. Here we illustrate an application of CUSUM to identify changes in patient enrollment. A useful assumption in this approach is that fraudulent providers often start "taking" more patients than usual [34].

Consider a time-ordered sequence of n claims $X = x_1, x_2, \ldots, x_n$. This sequence could represent all insurance claims submitted by a single provider over a fixed time interval (e.g., one year). One of the simplest SPC statistics is the Bernoulli CUSUM [33], where X is simply a vector of zeros and ones. For example, we can define x_i according to the following:

$$x_i = \begin{cases} 1 & \text{if the } i^{th} \text{ claim has a new beneficiary number} \\ 0 & \text{otherwise} \end{cases} \tag{17.3}$$

This vector tracks the introduction of new beneficiaries in the stream of claims submitted by a specific claimant, and provides a basis for estimating whether a large number of new beneficiaries were seen by a provider during a particular time interval. The Bernoulli CUSUM statistics to analyze this vector are:

$$S_t = \max(0, S_{t-1} + L_t), t = 1, 2, \ldots, \tag{17.4}$$

where $S_0 = 0$ and the chart signals if $S_t > h$. The values of the log-likelihood scores are

$$L_t = \begin{cases} \ln\left(\frac{1-p_1}{1-p_0}\right) & \text{if } X_t = 0 \\ \ln\left(\frac{p_1}{p_0}\right) & \text{if } X_t = 1 \end{cases} \tag{17.5}$$

A more common form of fraud occurs when providers start taking patients with conditions different from their past profile. Given that the condition codes can have multiple categories, the above method needs to be generalized to a multinomial case. The multinomial CUSUM statistic [20] can be applied here as follows:

$$L_t = \ln\left(\frac{p_{i1}}{p_{i0}}\right) \text{ when } X_t = i \tag{17.6}$$

Where p_{i1} is the ith alternative hypothesis, and p_{i0} is the ith null hypothesis. A typical multinomial/categorical CUSUM for a "presumed normal" is shown in Figure 17.11(a). The CUSUM statistic spikes when the provider uses different condition codes than the typical, but falls back to 0 since the atypical behavior is sporadic. On the other hand, Figure 17.11(b) shows the CUSUM statistic for an unusual (potentially fraudulent) physician who uses many condition codes that are not typical for his specialty; the CUSUM statistic captures this unusual behavior.

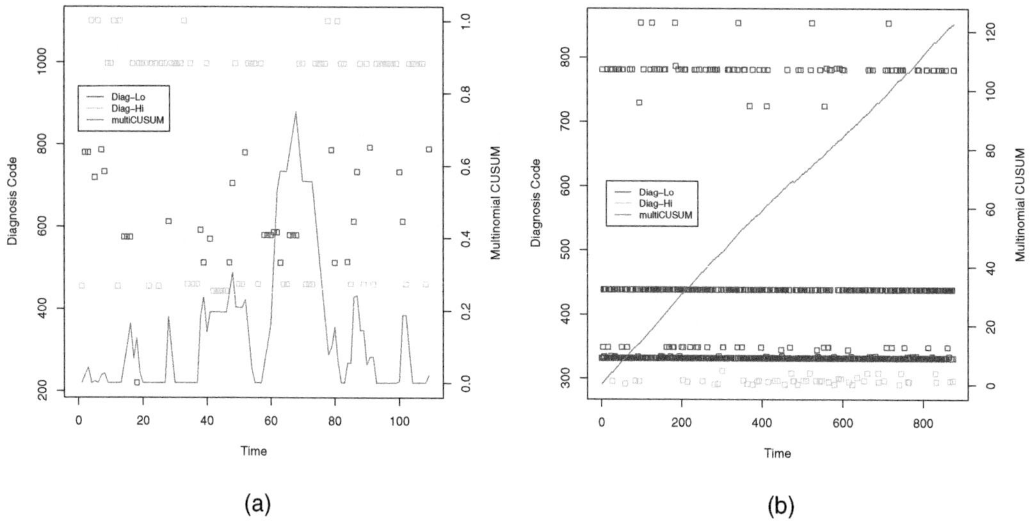

FIGURE 17.11: Multinomial CUSUM chart to track time-ordered condition codes from insurance claims. Green squares indicate the typical codes and blue squares indicate the atypical codes for the given speciality.

A complete set of out-of-control probabilities are selected for the multinomial CUSUM. In the absence of a specific alternative hypothesis, a simple method of formulating the out-of-control probabilities is to assume that every probability reverses direction to become less extreme, i.e., probabilities migrate in the direction of the grand mean. We specify a proportional change constant to compute the exact probabilities. The alternative hypothesis $\mathbf{p_1}$ is then

$$\mathbf{p_1} = \mathbf{p_0} + c * (m - \mathbf{p_0}) \tag{17.7}$$

where $0 \leq c \leq 1$ and the mean m is simply the reciprocal of the number of categories.

17.5.4.2 Anomaly Detection Using the CUSUM Statistic

One promising metric for screening anomalies is the maximum value of a CUSUM statistic over a fixed time interval. However, this statistic is biased by the number of claims submitted by a provider during that interval. Some outlier providers exhibit continuously anomalous behavior, even over a large time interval, and their CUSUM statistics often resemble a linear function. This pattern suggests another metric that is not similarly biased by the length of the claims sequence—the

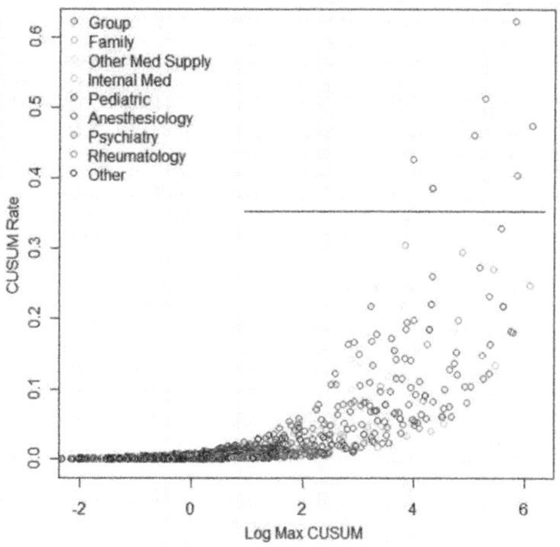

FIGURE 17.12: Distribution of CUSUM metrics for a provider population.

average CUSUM rate. Figure 17.12 shows a scatter plot using these metrics for a typical provider population color-coded by specialty. The scatter plot displays a cornucopia-shaped pattern with the tail originating at the lowest CUSUM values, and the mouth arcing upward toward the highest CUSUM rates. Anomalies are separated from the main cluster near the top of the scatter plot. Further analysis is required to determine whether these anomalies are normal in a statistical sense, or whether they are more likely members of an anomalous cluster. A horizontal line boundary is drawn at a CUSUM rate of about 0.35 to suggest a possible division of outliers from normals.

17.5.4.3 Supervised Learning for Classifying Provider Profiles

The previous section explored the possibility that a provider presumed to be normal up to some position within a temporal claims sequence is diverted either temporarily or permanently to anomalous behavior. Additionally we expect that some providers are either fraudsters from the moment they enroll in an insurance program, or that they revert to fraudulent activity permanently at some time before the beginning of a limited claims sequence. In this case the availability of provider ground truth affords the analyst an opportunity to go beyond anomaly detection as a method of identifying potential bad actors. In particular, if every provider can be labeled as either "bad actor" or "presumed normal," we can discriminate between temporally stable characteristics of normal and bad actors. Here we assume that providers naturally cluster into a main normal group and a main bad actor group. This assumption may only be approximately correct, especially for the class of bad actors if multiple paths exist to fraudulent behaviors.

The key step for such analysis is the construction of features from a provider's profile that can be discriminative between fraudulent and normal behavior. One such feature could be *the proportion of initial-to-subsequent consultations*. Another could be *the number of new patients admitted every year*. He et al. [19], used 28 such features, though they did not release the actual features for legal reasons.

Given a set of features, the next step is to create a labeled training data set in which each profile in the training data is labeled as either fraudulent or not. He et al. [19] actually used 4 labels ("1","2","3","4") where "1" denotes fraudulent provider and "4" denotes normal provider while "2" and "3" denote profiles in between. Obtaining labels is often the most challenging step and is either done manually [19] or uses providers who have been previously indicted by law enforcement agencies [29]. In the absence of labels one could use anomaly detection methods such as the one described in Section 17.5.4.2.

Given a training data set, one can then train any suitable classifier (both He et al. [19] and Ortega et al. [29], use a Multi-Layered Perceptron), which can assign a label to an unseen provider profile. Such approaches have also been integrated into several commercial fraud detection products [14, 18].

17.6 Conclusions

In the context of identifying healthcare fraud perpetrated by providers, two generic response mechanisms are possible: (1) identify and prosecute providers *after* claims are submitted (*pay and chase*), and (2) timely denial of payment for a submitted claim based on the associated risk. Whereas legal prosecution is expensive, time-consuming and difficult to wage, a policy of *selective denial* of payment by identifying fraudulent claims and fraud-perpetrating providers through analytics.

In this chapter we have surveyed existing methods for healthcare fraud detection using data-driven approaches. In particular we have elaborated upon two broad approaches. The first approach is to identify anomalous claims by comparing the claim properties with historical or contextual information. The second approach is to analyze behavior of providers with respect to their peers or their history to identify fraudulent providers.

An important observation that one can make is that identifying fraud in the healthcare sector requires analyzing data that has broad coverage in terms of geographical, temporal, and demographic extents. While most hospitals or single providers collect and maintain data relevant to their practice, effective fraud detection can be achieved by analyzing data collected at higher levels, such as health insurance programs. With the changes proposed in the recent *Patient Protection and Affordable Care Act*, more data at the national scale is going to be available and will present an enormous opportunity for the data analytics community.

Bibliography

[1] Health care fraud and abuse control program annual report for FY 2007. U.S. Department of Health and Human Services and Department of Justice, 2008.

[2] *The Healthcare Imperative: Lowering Costs and Improving Outcomes.* National Academies Press, 2010.

[3] World health statistics. WHO Library Cataloguing-in-Publication Data, 2011.

[4] Medicare fraud and abuse: Prevention, detection, and reporting. `http://www.cms.gov/Outreach-and-Education/Medicare-Learning-Network-MLN/MLNProducts/downloads/Fraud_and_Abuse.Pdf`, 2014.

[5] C. C. Aggarwal. *Outlier Analysis.* Springer, 2013.

[6] R. Agrawal and R. Srikant. Mining sequential patterns. In *Proceedings of the Eleventh International Conference on Data Engineering*, ICDE '95, pages 3–14, Washington, DC, USA, 1995. IEEE Computer Society.

[7] E. Aleskerov, B. Freisleben, and B. Rao. Cardwatch: A neural network based database mining

system for credit card fraud detection. In *Proceedings of IEEE Computational Intelligence for Financial Engineering*, pages 220–226, 1997.

[8] K. D. Aral, H. A. Güvenir, I. Sabuncuoğlu, and A. R. Akar. A prescription fraud detection model. *Computer Methods and Programs in Biomedicine*, 106(1):37–46, Apr. 2012.

[9] F. Bonchi, F. Giannotti, G. Mainetto, and D. Pedreschi. A classification-based methodology for planning audit strategies in fraud detection. In *Proceedings of the Fifth ACM SIGKDD International Conference on Knowledge Discovery and Data Mining*, KDD '99, pages 175–184, New York, NY, USA, 1999. ACM.

[10] S. Boriah, V. Chandola, and V. Kumar. Similarity measures for categorical data: A comparative evaluation. In *SDM 2008: Proceedings of the eighth SIAM International Conference on Data Mining*, pages 243–254, 2008.

[11] C. L. Chan and C. H. Lan. A data mining technique combining fuzzy sets theory and Bayesian classifieran application of auditing the health insurance fee. In *Proceedings of the International Conference on Artificial Intelligence*, pages 402–408, 2001.

[12] V. Chandola, A. Banerjee, and V. Kumar. Anomaly detection – a survey. *ACM Computing Surveys*, 41(3), July 2009.

[13] V. Chandola, S. R. Sukumar, and J. C. Schryver. Knowledge discovery from massive healthcare claims data. In *Proceedings of the 19th ACM SIGKDD International Conference on Knowledge Discovery and Data Mining*, KDD '13, pages 1312–1320, New York, NY, USA, 2013. ACM.

[14] C. Cooper. Turning information into action. `http://www.ca.com`, 2003.

[15] PricewaterhouseCoopers. The price of excess: Identifying waste in healthcare spending, PricewaterhouseCoopers LLP. Health Research Institute 2008.

[16] T. Fawcett and F. Provost. Activity monitoring: noticing interesting changes in behavior. In *Proceedings of the 5th ACM SIGKDD International Conference on Knowledge Discovery and Data Mining*, pages 53–62. ACM Press, 1999.

[17] A. M. Garber and J. Skinner. Is American health care uniquely inefficient? Working Paper 14257, National Bureau of Economic Research, August 2008.

[18] C. Hall. Intelligent data mining at IBM: New products and applications. *Intelligent Software Strategies*, 7(5):1–11, 1996.

[19] H. He, J. Wang, W. Graco, and S. Hawkins. Application of neural networks to detection of medical fraud. *Expert Systems with Applications*, 13(4):329–336, 1997. Selected Papers from the PACES/SPICIS'97 Conference.

[20] M. Hhle. Online change-point detection in categorical time series. In T. Kneib and G. Tutz, editors, *Statistical Modelling and Regression Structures*, pages 377–397. Physica-Verlag HD, 2010.

[21] P. Keckley, S. Coughlin, and L. Korenda. The hidden costs of U.S. health care. *Deloitte Center for Health Solutions Report*, 2012.

[22] L. Kenworthy. Americas inefficient health-care system: Another look. http://lanekenworthy.net/2011/07/10/americas-inefficient-health-care-system-another-look/, 2011.

[23] S. Konishi and G. Kitagawa. *Information Criteria and Statistical Modeling (Springer Series in Statistics)*. Springer, 2007.

[24] J. Li, K.-Y. Huang, J. Jin, and J. Shi. A survey on statistical methods for health care fraud detection. *Health Care Management Science*, 11(3):275–287, 2008.

[25] J. Manyika, M. Chui, B. Brown, J. Bughin, R. Dobbs, C. Roxburgh, and A. H. Byers, McKinsey Global Institute. Big data: The next frontier for innovation, competition, and productivity, May 2011.

[26] D. C. Montgomery. *Introduction to Statistical Quality Control*. John Wiley and Sons, 4th. edition, 2001.

[27] M. Newman. *Networks: An Introduction*. Oxford University Press, Inc., New York, NY.

[28] T. Ormerod, N. Morley, L. Ball, C. Langley, and C. Spenser. Using ethnography to design a mass detection tool (MDT) for early discovery of insurance fraud. In *Proceedings ACM CHI Conference*, 2003.

[29] P. A. Ortega, C. J. Figueroa, and G. A. Ruz. A medical claim fraud/ abuse detection system based on data mining: A Case study in Chile. In *International Conference on Data Mining*, 2006.

[30] E. S. Page. On problems in which a change can occur at an unknown time. *Biometrika*, 44(1-2):248–252, 1957.

[31] L. Page, S. Brin, R. Motwani, and T. Winograd. The pagerank citation ranking: Bringing order to the web. Technical Report 1999-66, Stanford InfoLab, November 1999.

[32] S. H. Preston and J. Ho. Low life expectancy in the United States: Is the health care system at fault? In E. M. Crimmins, S. H. Preston, and B. Cohen, editors, *National Research Council (US) Panel on Understanding Divergent Trends in Longevity in High-Income Countries*. National Academies Press (US), 2010.

[33] M. Reynolds and Z. Stoumbos. A cusum chart for monitoring a proportion when inspecting continuously. *Journal of Quality Technology*, 31(1):87, 1999.

[34] M. Sparrow. *License to Steal: How Fraud Bleeds America's Health Care System*. Westview Press, 2000.

[35] D. Thornton, R. M. Mueller, P. Schoutsen, and J. van Hillegersberg. Predicting healthcare fraud in medicaid: A multidimensional data model and analysis techniques for fraud detection. *Procedia Technology*, 9(0):1252–1264, 2013.

[36] K. Yamanishi, J. Takeuchi, G. Williams, and P. Milne. On-line unsupervised outlier detection using finite mixtures with discounting learning algorithms. *Data Mining and Knowledge Discovery*, 8(3):275–300, 2004.

[37] X. Yan and J. Han. Closegraph: Mining closed frequent graph patterns. In *Proceedings of the Ninth ACM SIGKDD International Conference on Knowledge Discovery and Data Mining*, KDD '03, pages 286–295, New York, NY, USA, 2003. ACM.

[38] W.-S. Yang. *A Process Pattern Mining Framework for the Detection of Healthcare Fraud and Abuse*. PhD thesis, National Sun Yat-sen University, 2003.

Chapter 18

Data Analytics for Pharmaceutical Discoveries

Shobeir Fakhraei
Department of Computer Science
University of Maryland
College Park, MD
shobeir@cs.umd.edu

Eberechukwu Onukwugha
Department of Pharmaceutical Health Services Research
University of Maryland
Baltimore, MD
eonukwug@rx.umaryland.edu

Lise Getoor
Department of Computer Science
University of California
Santa Cruz, CA
getoor@soe.ucsc.edu

18.1 Introduction

Interdisciplinary computational approaches that combine statistics, computer science, medicine, chemoinformatics, and biology are becoming highly valuable for drug[1] discovery and development. Data mining and machine learning methods are being more commonly used to properly analyze the emerging high volumes of structured and unstructured biomedical and biological data from several sources including hospitals, laboratories, pharmaceutical companies, and even social media. These data may include sequencing and gene expression, drug molecular structures, protein and drug interaction networks, clinical trial and electronic patient records, patient behavior and self-reporting data in social media, regulatory monitoring data, and biomedical literature.

Data mining methods can be used in several stages of drug discovery and development to achieve different goals. Figure 18.1 summarizes the drug development and FDA[2] approval process diagram. Most new compounds fail during this approval process in clinical trials or cause adverse side effects. The cost of successful novel chemistry-based drug development often reaches millions of dollars, and the time to introduce the drug to market often comes close to a decade [1]. The high failure rate of drugs during this process, make the trial phases known as the "valley of death" [2].

Similar to many other domains, pharmaceutical data mining algorithms aim to limit the search space and provide recommendations to domain experts for hypothesis generation and further analysis and experiments. One way to categorize data mining and machine learning approaches is based on their application to pre-marketing and post-marketing stages. In the pre-marketing stage, data mining methods focus on discovery activities, including but not limited to, finding signals that indicate relations between drugs and targets, drugs and drugs, genes and diseases, protein and diseases, and finding bio-markers. In this stage potential interactions that could cause therapeutic or adverse effects are studied. Most of the chemical compounds under study at this stage have not been through clinical trails, and the *in silico* experiments serve as a basis for further explorations for them. In the post-marketing stage an important application of data analytics is in finding indications of adverse side effects for approved drugs. These algorithms provide a list of potential drug side-effect associations that can be used for further studies.

In this chapter we provide a brief overview of some data analytics applications in this domain, and mainly focus on two major tasks from each stage. We first summarize some of the main methods for drug-target interaction prediction that is highly important during the pre-marketing stage. We then provide an overview of *pharmacovigilance* (or drug safety surveillance), which is an important focus in the post-marketing stage.

18.1.1 Pre-marketing Stage

In the pre-marketing stage, data mining algorithms primarily focus on drug discovery and predicting potential adverse effects using characteristics of the compounds (e.g., drug targets, chemical structure) or screening data (e.g., bioassay data) [4]. One of the important challenges where data mining and machine learning methods could be very beneficial is drug-target interaction prediction. This task is also highly important for drug repurposing and drug adverse reactions prediction [5]. *In vitro* identification of drug-target associations is a labor-intensive and costly procedure. Hence, *in silico* prediction methods are promising approaches for focusing *in vitro* investigations [6].

Most drugs affect multiple targets, and *polypharmacology*, the study of such interactions, is an area of growing interest [7]. These multi-target interactions potentially result in adverse side effects or unintentional therapeutic effects, and is the main cause in the high failure rate of drug

[1] Organic molecules that bind to bio-molecular targets and inhibit or activate their functions.

[2] U.S. Food and Drug Administration.

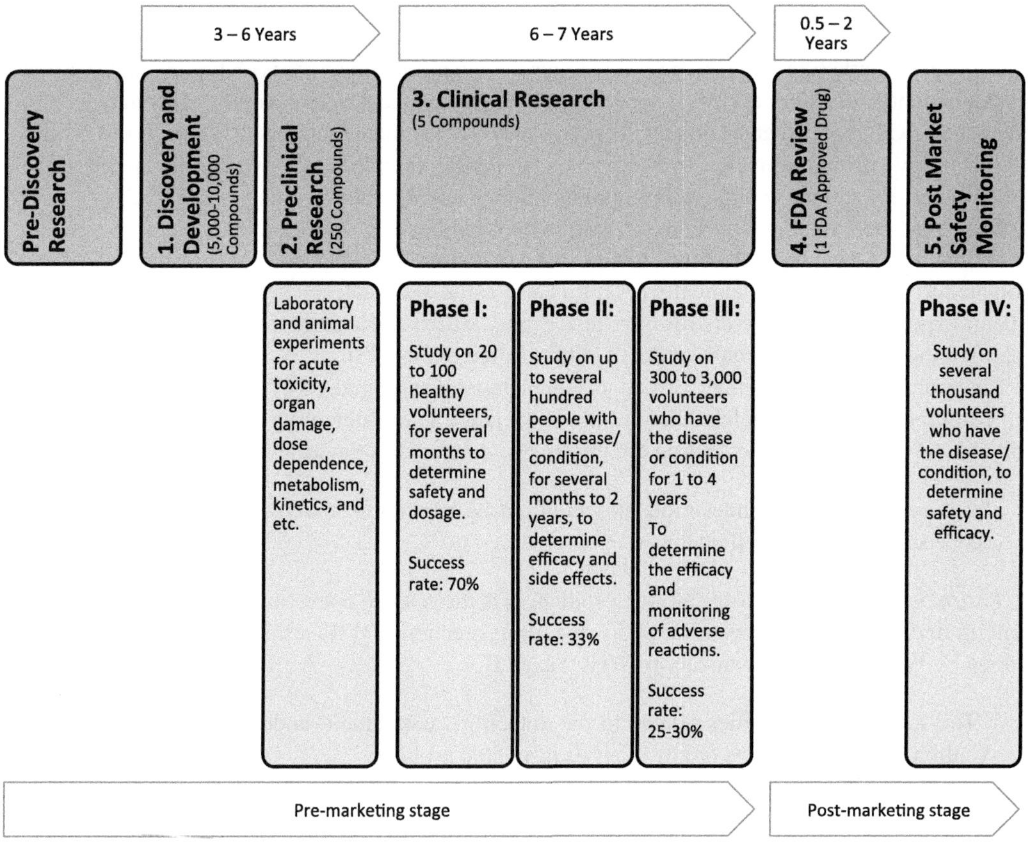

FIGURE 18.1: The drug development process [3].

candidates in clinical trials. Unacceptable toxicities resulting from these interactions account for approximately 30% of the failures [8]. Predicting these interactions during the drug developmental phase can reduce the high cost of clinical trials and can be crucial for the commercial success of new drugs.

Moreover, due to the high cost and low success rate of novel drug development, pharmaceutical companies are also interested in *drug repositioning* or *repurposing*, which involves finding new therapeutic effects of pre-approved drugs. For example, *Sildenafil*, which was originally developed for pulmonary arterial hypertension treatment, was re-purposed and branded as *Viagra*, based on its side effect of treating erectile dysfunction in men [9].

Another important task where data mining algorithms can also be effective is drug-drug interaction prediction, which may account for up to 30% of unexpected adverse drug events and close to 50% in hospitalized patients [10]. For example, *Tramadol* (a pain reliever) can enhance the effect of *Fluoxetine (Prozac)*, increasing Serotonin levels and potentially leading to seizures [11]. The National Health and Nutrition Examination Survey [12] reports that over 76% of elderly Americans are taking two or more drugs each day. Another study estimated that 29.4% of elderly patients are taking six or more drugs [13]. The drug-drug interactions can be predicted in the pre-marketing stage from compounds profiles [14, 15] or identified in the post-marketing stage using signals from several sources [16, 17]. For example, Gottlieb et al. [18] infer drug-drug interactions based on several similarities between the drugs and the previously known interactions between them.

18.1.2 Post-marketing Stage

In the post-marketing stage an important focus of data mining methods is on finding patterns that indicate potential drug-related adverse events [4]. Undiscovered severe adverse events may lead to drug withdrawals, which can be financially detrimental for the manufacturers [4]. Several drugs have been withdrawn from the market over the years [19]. For example, *Vioxx*, which was considered a powerful anti-inflammatory drug was withdrawn due to an increased coronary risk [20, 21].

Each year more than two million hospitalizations and injuries, and 700,000 emergency visits in the United States have been estimated to be caused by these effects [22, 4, 23]. They have also been estimated to cost $75 billion annually [11]. It is also estimated that each year 6–7% of hospitalized patients experience severe adverse drug-related events, which can lead to a potential 100,000 deaths, making it the fourth largest cause of death in the United States [23].

Since only a limited number of patient characteristics are studied in clinical trials and for a limited duration, often complex safety issues associated with a new drug cannot be fully studied with clinical trials [11]. Adverse drug effects are often defined as the following [24]:

> "Any unintended and undesirable effects of a drug beyond its anticipated therapeutic effects occurring during clinical use."

Pharmacovigilance (or drug safety surveillance) is the science concerning the detection, assessment, understanding and prevention of adverse drug reactions [4]. Pharmacovigilance is formally defined by World Health Organization (WHO) as [25]:

> "The science and activities related to the detection, assessment, understanding and prevention of adverse effects or any other drug-related problems."

Data analysis algorithms are crucial to narrow the search space and detect the hidden patterns. Harpaz et al. [11] define data mining algorithms for pharmacovigilance as:

> "Automated high-throughput methods to uncover hidden relationships of potential clinical significance to drug safety."

They report that volume of publications on data mining methods for Pharmacovigilance index in PubMed[3] has grown from less than 40 in the year 2000 to about 200 a year in 2011. An important focus of data mining algorithms in the post-marketing stage is on computing measures of statistical association between pairs of drugs and clinical outcomes recorded in underlying data sources [26].

18.1.3 Data Sources and Other Applications

There are several important data mining applications that we do not address in this chapter. For example, another area of growing interest where data mining algorithms play a significant role is predicting individual drug responses and personalized medicine [27, 28]. Personalized medicine or pharmacogenomics, is using an individual's genetic profile to make the best therapeutic choice by facilitating predictions about whether that person will benefit from a particular medicine or will suffer serious side effects [29]. For example, Pharmacogenomics Knowledgebase (PharmGKB) is a resource that collects, curates, and disseminates information about the impact of human genetic variation on drug responses [30].

Data mining algorithms in different stages of drug development use different data sources. Chemical and biological data are mainly used in the pre-marketing stage for tasks such as hypothesis generation and prediction, while spontaneous reporting systems, electronic health records,

[3] A search engine accessing primarily the MEDLINE database of references and abstracts on life sciences and biomedical topics.

and administrative claims data are often used in post-marketing data mining tasks mainly to detect signals of association. Biomedical literature and patient-generated data in health-related Internet forums has also received considerable research interest in recent years [11].

In the rest of the chapter, we highlight some of the related data mining tasks and methods based on the data resource they are applied to. First, we summarize some of the methods that use chemical and biological data focusing on approaches that predict drug-target and drug-drug interactions. We then highlight methods that detect patterns of drug-related adverse events using spontaneous reports, electronic health records, and patient-generated data such as web search engine logs. We also mention some of the advances in application of data mining in biomedical literature that can facilitate pharmaceutical discoveries.

There is a plethora of high quality research recently published related to data analytics in pharmaceutical discoveries that we could not cover in this chapter. We did not aim to provide a complete or comprehensive survey; our goal was to provide highlights of some of the important data analytics methods in this domain.

18.2 Chemical and Biological Data

One of the important goals of data mining methods that use chemical and biological data is predicting interactions between chemical compounds (e.g., drugs) and biological targets (e.g., proteins), which could cause therapeutic or adverse effects, or interactions between two or more chemical compounds that could cause potential adverse effects. Openly available databases, including multiple resources available on the Internet that include drug-related data and information about their targets are highly used for this task. These databases are used to study properties of drugs for several purposes, including drug-target and drug-drug interaction elucidation. Table 18.1 summarizes some of the more commonly used databases that contain information about drugs, their targets, and interactions between them.

There are several methods to model the drug-target interaction prediction task [38]. They can be separated into two categories based on their explicit emphasis on the graph or network representation of drugs and targets interactions. The first category constructs a network structure to predict interactions [39], while others make predictions based on other factors. In this section, we mainly cover network-based approaches.

Among the methods that do not use a network representation, the *similarity ensemble approach* (SEA), used ligands[4] to predict interactions between drugs and targets. They used ligands for target representation and chemical similarities between drugs and ligand sets as potential interaction indicators [6]. In CMap, Lamb [40] used RNA expressions to represent diseases, genes, and drugs [35]. They compared up- and down-regulations of the gene-expression profiles from cultured human cells treated with bioactive molecules and provided cross-platform comparisons. They predicted new potential interactions based on opposite-expression profiles of drugs and diseases.

Methods that consider the network structure address two important factors. The first one is how to construct the network and what information to include, and the other is how to predict new interactions. In the following sections, we summarize the main approaches for each task.

18.2.1 Constructing a Network Representation

A number of research publications study network structures to predict interactions. Cockell et al. [9] described how to integrate drugs, targets, genes, proteins, and pathways into a network for

[4] A small molecule, that forms a complex with a biomolecule to serve a biological purpose.

TABLE 18.1: Databases Containing Chemical and Biological Data

Name	URL	Description
Drugbank [31]	www.drugbank.ca	Drug (i.e., chemical, pharmacological and pharmaceutical) data with their targets (i.e., sequence, structure, and pathway) information.
KEGG Drug [32]	www.genome.jp/kegg/drug	Chemical drug structures with their targets.
MATADOR (Manually Annotated Targets and Drugs Online Resource)[33]	matador.embl.de	Drugs and their target interactions.
DCDB (Drug Combination Database) [34]	www.cls.zju.edu.cn/dcdb	Drug combinations and their targets.
DBPedia	www.dbpedia.org	Drugs, diseases, and proteins information extracted from Wikipedia.
ChEMBL	www.ebi.ac.uk/chembl	Trial drugs with their targets.
Connectivity Map (CMAP) [35]	www.broadinstitute.org/cmap	Genetic profile information about diseases and drugs.
Pubchem [36]	pubchem.ncbi.nlm.nih.gov	Biological activities of small molecules (i.e., drugs).
Therapeutic Target Database	bidd.nus.edu.sg/group/cjttd	Therapeutic protein and nucleic acid targets, disease, pathway information, and the corresponding drugs.
PDTD (Potential Drug Target Database)	www.dddc.ac.cn/pdtd	Drug targets information, focused on the ones with known 3D-structures.
Drug2Gene [37]	www.drug2gene.com	A knowledge base combining the compound/drug-gene/protein information from several publicly available databases.

different tasks. Nodes in this network usually include drugs, proteins and diseases, and edges include their interactions and similarities, where similarities could be extracted from several sources such as chemical structure of the compounds [5]. Figure 18.2 shows an example of a schematic overview of such networks.

Lee et al. [41] described drug repurposing, multi-agent drug development, and estimation of drug effects on target perturbations via network-based solutions. Yildirim et al. [39] explained trends in the drug-discovery industry over time using a network-based analysis and showed that sequencing the genome is changing the traditional trends of drug development. They also discussed different structural aspects of this network including preferential attachment and cluster formation.

A common approach to predict new interactions is to construct a bipartite interaction network where nodes represent drugs and targets, and edges denote interactions. Drug–drug and target–target similarities can augment this network on each side. Data from multiple publicly accessible

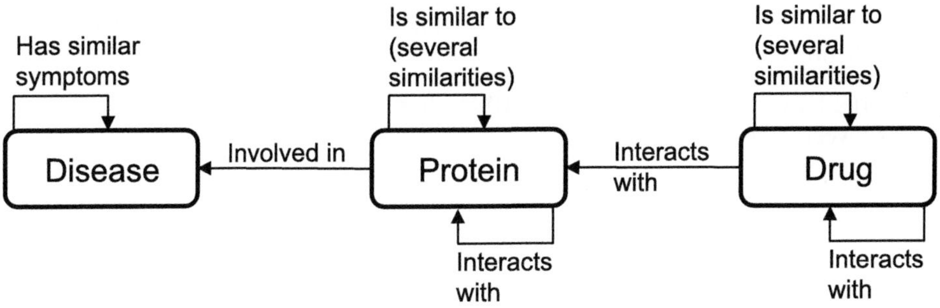

FIGURE 18.2: Network representation example of drugs, targets, and diseases.

datasets can be integrated to build these networks [41]. The similarities between drugs and between targets can have different semantics. For example, targets can have similarity measures based on their sequences and their ontology annotations [5, 42]. Another example is drug side effects; while potential drug side effects can be predicted via the drug-target interaction predictions [43] they can also be used as similarities between drugs to predict new targets [44]. There are a few databases that contain information about the drugs' known side effects. Table 18.2 summarizes a few datasets that contain this information.[5]

TABLE 18.2: Databases That Include Drug Side Effects

Name	URL	Description
SIDER [45]	sideeffects.embl.de	Information on marketed drugs and their recorded adverse drug reactions.
Drugs.com	www.drugs.com/sfx	Information about drugs and their side effects.
MedlinePlus	www.nlm.nih.gov/ medlineplus/ druginformation.html	National Library of Medicine's website containing drugs and their side effects.

18.2.2 Interaction Prediction Methods

In the drug–target interaction network, similar targets tend to interact with the same drugs, and similar drugs tend to interact with the same targets [9]. Using variations of this intuition, a link prediction method can predict new potential drug–target interactions in a drug–target interaction network [46].

18.2.2.1 Single Similarity–Based Methods

Network-based approaches integrate drug-drug and target-target similarities extracted via different methods (e.g., SEA and CMap) with the drug-target interactions network [38]. The following methods proposed a single similarity measure for drugs and targets to predict interactions.

Cheng et al. [47] predicted potential interactions using drug-drug and target-target similarities and a bipartite interaction graph. Using SIMCOMP [48], they computed the 2D chemical drug simi-

[5] These databases mainly do not focus on chemical and biological data.

larities and sequence similarities for targets via the Smith–Waterman score. They used the following three link-prediction methods:

1. Drug-based similarity inference (DBSI) where they only considered similarities between drugs for prediction.
2. Target-based similarity inference (TBSI) where they only considered target similarities for prediction.
3. Network-based inference (NBI) where they combined both drug-drug and target-target similarities.

Alaimo et al. [49] extended this approach by proposing a hybrid drug-target method that integrated prior domain knowledge.

Yamanishi et al. [50] proposed three methods for interaction prediction, including a nearest neighbor approach, a weighted *k*-nearest neighbors approach, and a space integration. In their space integration method, they described a genomic space, using the Smith–Waterman score, and a pharmaceutical space, using the SIMCOMP score. They proposed a method to integrate drugs and targets in a unified latent *pharmacological space*, and they predicted interactions based on the proximity of drugs and targets in that space. Figure 18.3 shows an overview of their method. They separated out four categories of targets, namely enzymes, ion channels, GPCR, and nuclear receptors for their experiments, which was adopted by most subsequent drug–target interaction prediction methods [38]. Overall steps in their method include:

1. Embed compounds and proteins on the interaction network into a unified space called "pharmacological space."
2. Learn a model between the chemical/genomic space and the pharmacological space, and map any compounds/proteins onto the pharmacological space.
3. Predict interacting compound–protein pairs by connecting compounds and proteins that are closer than a threshold in the pharmacological space.

Bleakley and Yamanishi [51] extended this method by constructing local models for graph inference. They classified each interaction twice and combined the results to provide predictions. First, they built a classifier based on drugs and then based on targets. They used the similarities as the *support vector machine* (SVM) kernels. Further extending this method, Mei et al. [52] proposed an approach to infer training data from neighbors' interaction profiles to make predictions for new drug or target candidates that do not have any interactions in the network. Wang and Zeng [53] proposed a method based on restricted Boltzmann machines for a drug–target interaction prediction.

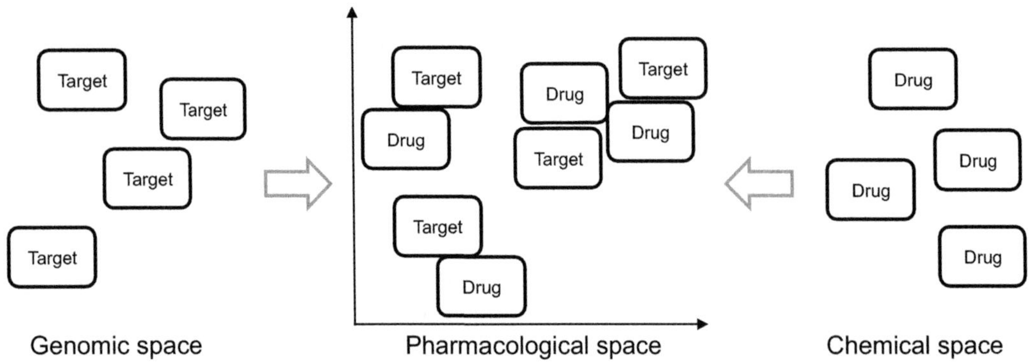

FIGURE 18.3: Overview of Yamanishi et al.'s [50] method.

18.2.2.2 Multiple Similarity–Based Methods

More complex methods can predict interactions based on multiple heterogeneous similarities. Chen et al. [54] reasoned about the possibility of a drug-target interaction in relation with other linked objects. They used distance, shortest paths, and other topological properties in the network to assess the strength of a relation. Their method assigned scores to paths between drugs and targets and combined path scores for each drug-target pair.

Perlman et al. [42] proposed a supervised learning method along with a feature-engineering approach based on combinations of drug-drug and target–target similarities to predict interactions, called *similarity-based inference of drug targets (SITAR)*. They built their model based on five drug–drug and three target–target similarities. For each potential drug–target interaction, they built a feature based on how similar that potential drug–target interaction is to one of the observed interactions in the network, and computed the interaction similarity based on the weighted combination of the drug–drug and target–target similarities. Overall steps of their method include:

1. They considered chemical-based, ligand-based, expression-based, side-effect-based, and annotation-based similarities between drugs, and computed target similarities using sequence-based, protein–protein interaction network-based, and gene ontology-based information.
2. They built a dataset where each link (i.e., drug–target pair) is a sample (i.e., row) and computed 15 (i.e., 5×3) features for each link based on the similarities. The sample was labeled with class 1 if the drug–target pair was a known interaction, and 0 otherwise.
3. Their model computed the value of each feature based on how similar the potential drug–target interaction is to the closest observed interaction in the network, and computed the similarity of the interaction based on the weighted combination of the drug–drug and target–target similarities.
4. A logistic regression classifier on this dataset was then used to predict new interactions.

Fakhraei et al. [5, 55] proposed a drug-target interaction prediction framework based on *probabilistic soft logic* (PSL), to collectively predict interactions using a structured representation of the network. Their interpretable model captured the multi-relational characteristics of the drug-target interaction network (i.e., nodes and edges with different semantics). They proposed PSL models that reason over rules, based on triad and tetrad structural intuitions, and improved the prediction result of Perlman et al. [42]. Figure 18.4 shows how similarities were used in their method for new drug-target interaction prediction in their triad-based rules, which captures the tendency of similar targets interacting with the same drugs, and similar drugs interacting with the same targets. They used the following steps for their predictions:

1. Similar to SITAR [42], they used five drug-drug and three target-target similarities.
2. They used a blocking threshold to only include the k most similar drugs or targets for each entity in their model.
3. They defined rules based on triad structures with the overall intuition that similar drugs tend to interact with the same target, and a drug tends to interact with similar targets. They introduced a rule for each similarity measure (i.e., eight rules in total).
4. They defined tetrad based rules with the intuition that similar drugs tend to interact with similar targets.

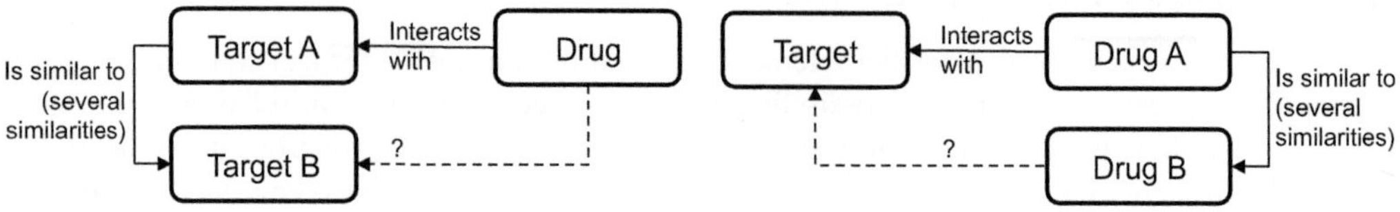

FIGURE 18.4: Predicting new drug-target interactions based on drug–drug and target–target similarities.

5. They considered a negative prior to capture the sparsity of the network.
6. They studied the effect of collective inference and combination of similarities in improving the performance.

18.3 Spontaneous Reporting Systems (SRSs)

Spontaneous reporting systems (SRSs) are important data sources for post-marketing analysis and data mining, and up until recent years they have been the main resource for pharmacovigilance (or drug safety surveillance) [56, 57].

> "Spontaneous reporting systems are passive systems composed of reports of suspected adverse drug events collected from health-care professionals, consumers, and pharmaceutical companies, and maintained largely by regulatory and health agencies [11]."

They have supported regulatory decisions for a long list of marketed drugs since their inception. There are two main spontaneous reporting systems administrated by the *U.S. Food and Drug Administration* (FDA) and *World Health Organization* (WHO), which are described in Table 18.3.

Spontaneous reporting systems have a structured format and include information on the drug suspected to cause the adverse reaction. They also contain limited demographic information [11]. There are multiple advantages in using them for pharmacovigilance. They are centralized sources of information focused on drug-adverse event relationships and cover large populations. They are also accessible for analysis and research [58].

TABLE 18.3: Spontaneous Reporting Systems Dataset

Name	**URL**	**Description**
FDA Adverse Event Reporting System (FAERS)	www.fda.gov/Drugs/GuidanceComplianceRegulatoryInformation/Surveillance/AdverseDrugEffects	Information on adverse event and medication error reports submitted to FDA.
VigiBase	www.umc-products.com/vigibase_services	World Health Organizations global individual case safety reports database.

While spontaneous reporting systems are the main source of post-market drug-adverse effect identification, they have several limitations [59]. Only a fraction of adverse drug events are identified and reported in these systems because reporting to them is on a voluntary basis, except for pharmaceutical companies, which are required to report suspected adverse drug reactions. They may also contain biased reporting rates and missing patient data [60, 61].

There are many reasons causing such limitations in spontaneous reporting systems. Physicians may worry about possible legal issues after disclosure of medical errors, or may not clearly understand the definition of an adverse event. They may consider that the circumstances of a case or its outcome do not warrant reporting, or do not believe that reporting will lead to improvement. They may also not see what added value the growing body of quality and safety guidelines provide in terms of patient outcomes [21]. Amalberti et al. [21] and Strom [20] suggest several improvements to the spontaneous reporting systems to address some of these challenges and also introduce further categories to better organize the reports for analysis.

The main methods that focus on spontaneous reporting systems data are designed to generate measures of statistical association for large sets of drug–outcome pairs. These signals can be used to prioritize and identify risks for further evaluations. Newer approaches have been designed to facilitate identification of higher-order or multivariate associations that represent more complex safety phenomena such as drug–drug interactions [11]. The main methods for signal identification using the spontaneous reporting systems data are summarized in the following sections.

18.3.1 Disproportionality Analysis

Disproportionality analysis plays an important role in most methods applied to spontaneous reporting systems data. Frequency analysis of 2 × 2 contingency tables (shown in Figure 18.4) is used to estimate measures of statistical association between specific drug–event combinations mentioned in spontaneous reports. Disproportionality analysis methods differ in statistical adjustments for low numbers, and their assumptions. Two main categories of them are frequentist and Bayesian methods [4, 11].

TABLE 18.4: Contingency Table Used in Disproportionality Analysis of Spontaneous Reporting Systems Data

	With target adverse event	**Without target adverse event**	**Total**
With target drug	a	b	n = a + b
Without target drug	c	d	c + d
Total	m = a + c	b + d	t = a + b + c + d

The *relative reporting ratio* is the most widely discussed measure for disproportionality analysis and is defined as the ratio of the observed incidence rate of a drug–event combination to its *baseline* expected rate under the assumption that the drug and event occur independently. Both the U.S. Food and Drug Administration and the World Health Organization use a Bayesian version of the relative reporting ratio as a basis for monitoring safety signals in their spontaneous reporting systems [11]. Frequentist approaches use one of the measures listed in Table 18.5 to estimate associations and are typically accompanied by hypothesis tests of independence. The hypothesis tests are used as an extra precautionary measure to take into account the sample size used while computing an association.

The uncertainty associated with small counts in Bayesian approaches is addressed by *shrinking* the measure towards no association by a proportional amount [11]. Among the Bayesian approaches the *multi-item gamma Poisson shrinker* is a predominant algorithm used in the United States by the FDA, the United Kingdom, and several pharmaceutical companies. An empirical Bayes geometric

TABLE 18.5: Mathematical Definitions of Measures of Association

Measure of association	Mathematical definition
Relative reporting ratio (RRR)	$\frac{t \times a}{m \times n}$
Proportional reporting ratio	$\frac{a \times (t-n)}{c \times n}$
Reporting odds ratio	$\frac{a \times d}{c \times b}$
Information component	$\log_2(RRR)$

mean is used in this method, which is a centrality measure of the posterior distribution of the true relative reporting ratio. The World Health Organization uses a similar Bayesian approach, called the *Bayesian Confidence Propagation Neural Network* [11]. However, due to the lack of a gold standard to evaluate the performances of these methods, it is accepted that none of them is universally better than any other. Also, their results differences tend to fade with the increase in the number of reports of a specific drug-event combination [11].

18.3.2 Multivariate Methods

Traditional disproportionality analysis approaches do not properly support the discovery and analysis of higher-dimensional drug safety phenomena that involve more than one drug or event, and the confounding issue [4, 11]. Hauben and Bate [62] report the importance and difficulties with more complex drug safety phenomena detections. Methods that aim to identify signals of adverse events based on multiple drugs, should be able to detect hidden drug–drug interactions [16].

Confounding is another challenge in these analyses. A confounder is an observed or unobserved variable that mediates an association between other variables. Many related research publications have focused on confounding by drug co-administration. In these cases a drug that is frequently co-prescribed with another drug could be mistakenly associated with an event rather than the correct one [11]. Several multivariate approaches have been proposed to address these issues. We summarized some of them in this section.

- **Disproportionality analysis extensions:** This method has been applied mostly to three-dimensional associations corresponding to drug–drug interactions [63], for which observed-to-expected ratios are calculated in a similar manner but based on three elements (i.e., $drug_1$–$drug_2$–*event*).

- **Multivariate logistic regression:** Stratification is traditionally used to address confounding; however, this method is not effective for studying a large number of potential confounders [64]. Multiple logistic regressions can be a more appropriate approach to deal with confounding. It can estimate the drug–event association by controlling or adjusting for the presence of other potential confounders [64]. Caster et al. [65] applied Bayesian logistic regression [66], which can carry out regression analyses with millions of covariates, to address confounding in World Health Organization spontaneous reporting system data.

- **Associations rule learning:**[6] This method is well established for discovering relations between variables in large databases using specific measures of interestingness. Agrawal et al. [67] introduced association rules for discovering regularities between products in large-scale transaction data in supermarkets. The *Apriori* algorithm is usually used to deal with the huge

[6] Also referred to as association rule mining.

search space in association rule learning. Rouane-Hacene et al. [68] applied association rule learning to find association of up to three anti-HIV drugs. Harpaz et al. [69] extended this method to capture associations of up to six drugs.

- **Bi-clustering:** Bi-clustering is simultaneous clustering of the data matrix rows and columns to find sub-matrices that exhibit highly correlated activities [70]. Harpaz et al. [71] used a bi-clustering algorithm to identify associations between multiple drugs and adverse effects.

- **Network analysis:** Another approach to adverse event identification from spontaneous reporting systems are based on constructions and analysis of network structures. Ball and Botsis [72] constructed a network for vaccine adverse events where nodes in the network correspond to vaccines and reported events. They observed this network is *scale-free*[7] and proposed using *hubs* in this network to identify patterns of adverse events caused by *HPV4* vaccines. Zhang et al. [73] also constructed bipartite networks of vaccines, diseases and genes to analyze vaccine-adverse event data.

In any of the above methods, there are several factors that one should consider in the analysis of spontaneous reporting systems data. Amalberti et al. [21] identified examples of incorrect conclusion due to the fact that the studies were performed with simplistic assumptions and only looking for the cause in the researchers' own specialty. They also identified that many studies consider a short time frame and thus miss many adverse events, and proposed three different time frames to study the effect of adverse events. They also highlighted that many studies of adverse events are influenced by emotions and media coverage and are often insurance-driven, while the ones that may have an impact on a larger population are left without much attention.

18.4 Electronic Health Records

As mentioned in the previous section there are multiple limitations with spontaneous reports, that encouraged the use of several other sources to identify drug-adverse events signals. One source is electronic health records and administrative claims data. Electronic health records have some advantages when compared to spontaneous reporting systems data. They are captured during the usual course of care and contain more detailed medical data, such as patients' clinical history, and the timing of symptom development and medication administration. There is also no need to estimate the reporting frequency as events are captured as part of the standard care [61].

Electronic health records are being increasing used throughout the United States, potentially providing more data [74]. Initiatives like the *Observational Medical Outcomes Partnership* in the United States and the *Exploring and Understanding Adverse Drug Reactions* project in Europe are focusing on building electronic health records-based surveillance systems [13]. The efficacy of electronic health records to identify adverse drug events was shown by Ramirez et al. [10]. They used abnormal laboratory signals to identify patients with adverse drug events. Via retrospective studies, Brown et al. [75] have also shown that the adverse events caused by *Vioxx* could have been found sooner based on electronic health records.

Electronic health records can be categorized into structured coded data, and unstructured clinical notes [4]. ICD[8] codes [76], laboratory data, and vital measurements [77] are among the structured coded data that have been used to detect association of drugs and adverse events. Wang et al. [78] proposed one of the early methods to use unstructured clinical notes to detect drug-adverse event

[7] A network with power law degree distribution.

[8] International Classification of Diseases.

associations. In addition to the challenges with structured coded data, unstructured clinical notes require methods that can extract relevant information from free-text clinical narratives. We discuss some details of the natural language processing and text mining methods in Section 18.6.

Since electronic health records are mainly captured for diagnoses (usually based on billing codes) and not adverse drug event detection, they often require pre-processing to support analysis. Healthcare providers often use different solutions for documentation and encoding the data. There are also legal and privacy concerns in accessing patients data causing logistical issues in sharing, accessing, and storing data.

There is a need for methods that can address confounding in the observational studies. There are methods to apply disproportionality analysis on electronic health records data, and also methods that are based on cohort designs, case-control designs, and self-controlled designs [11]. Cohort designs partition the subject cohorts based on their exposure to the drug, case-control designs divide them based on the event, and self-controlled designs compare the same subjects before and after they were exposed to the drug.

Electronic health records can also be used to detect more complex signals for drug–drug interactions. Iyer et al. [13] proposed adjusted disproportionality ratios to identify significant drug-drug-event associations among 1165 drugs and 14 adverse events. They published the database of population event rates among patients on drug combinations based on the electronic health records corpus from *Stanford Translational Research Integrated Database Environment.* Their method's overall steps include:

1. They first annotated the clinical text, extracting drugs and events of interest, which focused on 14 adverse events.
2. They then constructed a 2×2 contingency table based on cohort design, where the exposed group are patients who have taken both drugs, and the comparison group include patients who have taken one or none of the drugs.
3. Then they computed the population event rate for patients who have taken both drugs.

They found that the interaction between Amiodarone and Haloperidol known to cause QT prolongation could have been detected based on signals from *Stanford Translational Research Integrated Database Environment* data as early as 2007. The *FDA Adverse Event Reporting System* started receiving reports for this interaction in 2009 [13]. They also showed that signals from electronic health records can be as useful as signals from spontaneous reporting systems. However, most methods do not indicate causality, instead they only show correlation and are means to provide early warning to focus more extensive investigations.

Harpaz et al. [26] proposed an empirical Bayes model to combine signals extracted from electronic health records and spontaneous reports. They showed an average 40% improvement by combining results from these sources in comparison to using each source independently.

18.5 Patient-Generated Data on the Internet

Patient-generated data such as web search logs, social networks, and health-care related forums are resources that contain medical-related information on the Internet. Surveys suggest about 60–70% of adults search for health and medical information online, and about 80% of online health inquiries start at a search engine [79]. Table 18.6 summarizes some of the resources that contain patient-generated medical data.

TABLE 18.6: Online Resources with Patient-Generated Medical Information

Name	URL	Purpose
Ask a Patient	www.askapatient.com	To share and compare medication experiences.
DailyStrength	www.dailystrength.org	Support group forum to discuss medical conditions.
PatientsLikeMe	www.patientslikeme.com	To find patients with similar conditions and share experiences.

Several systems that make medical predictions based on these types of data have received recent attention from the research community that either support or question their findings. For example, Google Flu trends [80] that uses aggregated Google search data to estimate flu activity has been both perceived positively [81] and also criticized [82] by the research community.

Although the information provided by patients may be inaccurate or even questionable, such forums can provide valuable supplementary information on drug effectiveness and side effects because they cover large and diverse populations and contain unsolicited, uncensored data directly from patients [11]. However, extracting such information is very challenging and requires statistical and linguistic models to interpret conversational styles, correct spelling and grammatical errors, and separate gossip from real experiences.

Noise, influence of experiences, different bias factors, profession, and online content exposure are some examples that can contaminate the search engine log signals. There could be several reasons for users to search for symptoms and medications; for example, medical professionals could search for these information regularly [79].

Leaman et al. [83] extracted information from DailyStrength posts and found high correlation between user reported drug-adverse events and the documented cases. White et al. [84] showed that the interaction of Paroxetine and Pravastatin that can cause hyperglycemia could have been detected based on web search logs prior to its identification. In another example, Freifeld et al. [85] showed the efficacy of the Twitter data for pharmacovigilance.

White et al. [79] combined the signals from search engines logs of 80 million users over 18 months with the FDA's adverse event reporting system, and showed that the detection performance can be improved by 19%. In their analysis they applied the following steps to detect signals from the search queries:

1. They performed entity recognition and resolution to map synonym search terms into a unified representation for drugs, conditions, and symptoms.
2. They excluded a portion (approximately 9%) of users from their analysis, based on the frequency of their queries (for Internet bots) and the time they first started submitting medical queries (for healthcare professionals).
3. For a drug of interest, they considered a surveillance window around the first occurrence of a query (defined as t_0).
4. To exclude exploratory searches and the queries influenced by reading the online articles related to the drug they defined an exclusion window around t_0.
5. They defined and computed a measure for a self-controlled study design called the *query rate ratio* (QRR) as the ratio of number of after to before symptom- or condition-related queries around t_0 to indicate the association of drug–symptom conditions.

18.6 Biomedical Literature

Natural language processing and text mining can be used for knowledge representation and hypothesis generation based on biomedical literature. For example, Shetty and Dalal [86] used research articles indexed on Pubmed[9] that mentioned specific drugs and adverse events to rank potential drugs-adverse event relations. They applied several preprocessing steps and disproportionality analysis for their approach and showed that the association between Vioxx and myocardial infarction could have been found sooner. Haerian et al. [61] used the *Medical Language Extraction and Encoding System* (MedLEE) [87], a clinical NLP system developed at Columbia University, to analyze electronic health records and detect drug-adverse events. MedLEE has also been used for automated knowledge acquisition from text, extracting adverse events from health records, and quality of care assessment [88, 89, 90].

Text mining could be beneficial to the pharmaceutical industry in several ways; For example, it could facilitate literature reviewing for medical professionals, and identify and extract relevant information. Such information can be extracted from unstructured clinical notes, like those in electronic health records and also biomedical research articles [91, 92]. However, biomedical literature is a very rich resource of information that can be used for discoveries beyond drug-adverse events predictions. Mining the biomedical literature has been successfully used to discover new relationships among genes, biological pathways, diseases, or even for drug repurposing [93, 11].

Information extraction from a huge volume of available research literature is a challenging task. For example, Thorn et al. [94] highlight this problem as one of their main challenges in maintaining a *pharmacogenomics knowledge base* (PharmGKB). They have developed a natural language processing framework to streamline the identification of articles of interest and speed up the annotation process [95]. Due to these challenges, biomedical literature mining has increasingly become a focus of active research in recent years. *BioCreative*[10] (Critical Assessment of Information Extraction systems in Biology) is an international community-wide effort that evaluates text mining and information extraction systems applied to the biomedical domain. *BioNLP*[11] is organizing events to support application of natural language processing on biomedical literature. There is a considerable amount of research literature and methods addressing the biomedical text mining challenges that we could not summarize in this section. Demner-Fushman et al. [96] and Krallinger et al. [97] provided a survey of biomedical and clinical text mining research, and Hahn et al. [93] summarized the recent advances in text mining for pharmacogenomics.

In this section we briefly highlight some of the main related tasks and resources to pharmaceutical discoveries and pharmacogenomics. Pharmacogenomics publications span the intersection of research in genotypes, phenotypes, and pharmacology. Some of the applications of pharmacogenomics text mining includes guiding human database curation, discovering interactions, and potential cause–effect phenomena such as candidate gene ranking, drug–drug interaction and adverse drug interaction prediction, and drug repurposing [93]. An interesting application of biomedical text mining, pioneered by Don Swanson, is literature-based discovery and hypothesis generation [98], where the goal is to find implicit and novel information relating entities that are not explicitly spelled out in the underlying documents. Some of the main tasks in biomedical literature mining includes corpus development, entity recognition and resolutions, relation extraction, and creation and use of ontologies.

There are three main types of entities of interest for recognition and resolutions in biomedical literature for pharmacogenomics: genotypes, phenotypes, and pharmacological entities. The most important genotype entity types are genes and proteins. Phenotype entities mainly include

[9]www.ncbi.nlm.nih.gov/pubmed
[10]http://www.biocreative.org
[11]http://bionlp.org

pathological phenomena and diseases in particular, as well as their anatomical sites, conditions, and treatment. Pharmacological entities are drugs and other chemicals that are functionally important in treating or causing medically significant phenotypes in the course of treatments and therapies. One of the challenges in biomedical literature mining is entity recognition and resolution. Several databases are used as canonical resources for entity resolution in biomedical literature, some of which are highlighted in Table 18.7.

TABLE 18.7: Canonical Databases for Entity Resolution

Name	**URL**	**Entities**
EntrezGene	www.ncbi.nlm.nih.gov/gene	genotype
UniProt	www.uniprot.org	genotype
Medical Subject Headings (MeSH)	www.ncbi.nlm.nih.gov/mesh	phenotypes, pharma-ceutical
Unified Medical Language System (UMLS)	www.nlm.nih.gov/research/umls	phenotypes, pharma-ceutical
International Classification of Diseases (ICD-10)	www.who.int/classifications/icd/en	phenotypes
Systematized Nomenclature of Medicine – Clinical Terms (SNOMED–CT)	www.ihtsdo.org/snomed-ct	phenotypes
Medical Dictionary for Regulatory Activities (MedDRA)	www.meddramsso.com	phenotypes
DrugBank	www.drugbank.ca	pharmaceutical
Chemical Entities of Biological Interest (ChEBI)	www.ebi.ac.uk/chebi	pharmaceutical
KEGG	www.genome.jp/kegg	pharmaceutical, genotype
Human Metabolome Database (HMDB)	www.hmdb.ca	pharmaceutical, genotype
ChemIDplus	chem.sis.nlm.nih.gov/chemidplus	pharmaceutical

More complex tasks in biomedical text mining deal with finding relations between entities. Genotype–phenotype relation extraction aims to identify which genotypes can play a role in which diseases [97]. Genotype–pharmaceutical relation extraction focuses on personalized medicine and possibility of tailoring drugs given a genetic context [99]. Phenotype–pharmaceutical relation extraction mostly concentrates on finding drug side effect and associated adverse effects [100]. Genotype–phenotype–pharmaceutical relations are more complex relations that aim to find genetic information and relate them to the phenotype–pharmaceutical level. Typically, studies in this area combine text mining with other sources of information, to derive better conclusions [101].

18.7 Summary and Future Challenges

Data mining and data analytics are becoming more widely used in pharmaceutical discoveries. From proposing new hypotheses to detecting adverse event patterns, data mining methods are used to analyze chemical and biological data, spontaneous reports, electronic health records, biomedical literature, and most recently patient-generated Internet data. But only in recent years new opportunities and interests have emerged to analyze data that have not been traditionally available and used for pharmaceutical discoveries.

These methods can advance pharmaceutical discoveries by potentially allowing for personalized medicine, drug re-purposing, more effective drug design and developments, and also active and proactive paradigms of surveillance. These new horizons also introduce new interesting challenges that should be addressed by the research community. There is a need for methods that can better address confounding and detect multi-drug interactions and adverse events related to them. Combining different sources of information to provide better predictions and hypotheses is also an interesting area of research.

Most tasks and data in the pharmaceutical domain that data mining algorithms can be effective on, lack negative samples. For example, in drug-target interaction prediction, while positive interactions are well documented, a lack of interactions is not properly captured in the commonly used databases. Hence, it is not really known whether the absence of interaction data is due to a lack of real interaction, or it is due to the fact that such an interaction has not been properly studied yet. In addition to challenges for standard supervised learning in data mining methods, this limitation introduces problems for standard evaluations.

In addition, further research is needed to understand the relative benefits and limitations of each data source and effectively integrate information from multiple data sources, including biomedical literature, biological/chemical data, user-generated data on the Internet for pharmaceutical discoveries and pharmacovigilance. The application and development of data mining and machine learning methods to facilitate and help advance pharmaceutical discoveries, has great potential and needs to be further investigated.

Acknowledgments

We are thankful to the editors, anonymous reviewers, and James Foulds for their valuable comments, insightful suggestions, and constructive feedback that greatly helped improving this chapter. We also gratefully acknowledge funding provided by The University of Maryland/Mpowering the State through the Center for Health-related Informatics and Bioimaging, and by the National Science Foundation (NSF) under contract number IIS0746930. Any opinions, findings, and conclusions or recommendations expressed in this material are those of the author(s) and do not necessarily reflect the views of the National Science Foundation.

Bibliography

[1] Steven M. Paul, Daniel S. Mytelka, Christopher T. Dunwiddie, Charles C. Persinger, Bernard H. Munos, Stacy R. Lindborg, and Aaron L. Schacht. How to improve R&D productivity: the pharmaceutical industry's grand challenge. *Nature Reviews Drug Discovery*, 9 (3):203–214, 2010.

[2] David J. Adams. The valley of death in anticancer drug development: a reassessment. *Trends in Pharmacological Sciences*, 33(4):173–180, 2012.

[3] FDA drug development process. http://www.patientnetwork.fda.gov/learn-how-drugs-devices-get-approved/drug-development-process

[4] Mei Liu, Michael E. Matheny, Yong Hu, and Hua Xu. Data mining methodologies for pharmacovigilance. *ACM SIGKDD Explorations Newsletter*, 14(1):35–42, 2012.

[5] Shobeir Fakhraei, Bert Huang, Louiqa Raschid, and Lise Getoor. Network-based drug-target interaction prediction with probabilistic soft logic. *IEEE/ACM Transactions on Computational Biology and Bioinformatics*, 2014.

[6] Michael J. Keiser, Vincent Setola, John J. Irwin, Christian Laggner, Atheir I. Abbas, Sandra J. Hufeisen, Niels H. Jensen, Michael B. Kuijer, Roberto C. Matos, Thuy B. Tran, Ryan Whaley, Richard A. Glennon, Jérôme Hert, Kelan L. H. Thomas, Douglas D. Edwards, Brian K. Shoichet, and Bryan L. Roth. Predicting new molecular targets for known drugs. *Nature*, 462 (7270):175–181, November 2009.

[7] Aislyn D.W. Boran and Ravi Iyengar. Systems approaches to polypharmacology and drug discovery. *Current Opinion in Drug Discovery & Development*, 13(3):297, 2010.

[8] Andrew L Hopkins. Network pharmacology: the next paradigm in drug discovery. *Nature Chemical Biology*, 4(11):682–690, 2008.

[9] S. J. Cockell, J. Weile, P. Lord, C. Wipat, D. Andriychenko, M. Pocock, D. Wilkinson, M. Young, and A. Wipat. An integrated dataset for in silico drug discovery. *Journal of Integrative Bioinformatics*, 7(3):116, 2010.

[10] E. Ramirez, A.J. Carcas, A.M. Borobia, S.H. Lei, E. Piñana, S. Fudio, and J. Frias. A pharmacovigilance program from laboratory signals for the detection and reporting of serious adverse drug reactions in hospitalized patients. *Clinical Pharmacology & Therapeutics*, 87 (1):74–86, 2010.

[11] Rave Harpaz, William DuMouchel, Nigam H. Shah, David Madigan, Patrick Ryan, and Carol Friedman. Novel data-mining methodologies for adverse drug event discovery and analysis. *Clinical Pharmacology & Therapeutics*, 91(6):1010–1021, 2012.

[12] National health and nutrition examination survey. http://www.cdc.gov/NCHS/NHANES.htm.

[13] Srinivasan V. Iyer, Rave Harpaz, Paea LePendu, Anna Bauer-Mehren, and Nigam H. Shah. Mining clinical text for signals of adverse drug-drug interactions. *Journal of the American Medical Informatics Association*, 21(2):353–362, 2014.

[14] Sean Ekins and Steven A. Wrighton. Application of in silico approaches to predicting drug–drug interactions. *Journal of Pharmacological and Toxicological Methods*, 45(1):65–69, 2001.

[15] Jialiang Huang, Chaoqun Niu, Christopher D. Green, Lun Yang, Hongkang Mei, and Jing-Dong J. Han. Systematic prediction of pharmacodynamic drug-drug interactions through protein-protein-interaction network. *PLoS Computational Biology*, 9(3):e1002998, 2013.

[16] Nicholas P. Tatonetti, Guy Haskin Fernald, and Russ B. Altman. A novel signal detection algorithm for identifying hidden drug-drug interactions in adverse event reports. *Journal of the American Medical Informatics Association*, 19(1):79–85, 2012.

[17] Nicholas P. Tatonetti, P. Ye Patrick, Roxana Daneshjou, and Russ B. Altman. Data-driven prediction of drug effects and interactions. *Science Translational Medicine*, 4(125):125ra31–125ra31, 2012.

[18] Assaf Gottlieb, Gideon Y. Stein, Yoram Oron, Eytan Ruppin, and Roded Sharan. INDI: a computational framework for inferring drug interactions and their associated recommendations. *Molecular Systems Biology*, 8(1):592, July 2012.

[19] Kathleen M. Giacomini, Ronald M. Krauss, Dan M. Roden, Michel Eichelbaum, Michael R. Hayden, and Yusuke Nakamura. When good drugs go bad. *Nature*, 446(7139):975–977, 2007.

[20] Brian L. Strom. How the US drug safety system should be changed. *Journal of the American Medical Association*, 295(17):2072–2075, 2006.

[21] René Amalberti, Dan Benhamou, Yves Auroy, and Laurent Degos. Adverse events in medicine: easy to count, complicated to understand, and complex to prevent. *Journal of Biomedical Informatics*, 44(3):390–394, 2011.

[22] Adam L. Cohen, Daniel S. Budnitz, Kelly N. Weidenbach, Daniel B. Jernigan, Thomas J. Schroeder, Nadine Shehab, and Daniel A. Pollock. National surveillance of emergency department visits for outpatient adverse drug events in children and adolescents. *The Journal of Pediatrics*, 152(3):416–421, 2008.

[23] Jason Lazarou, Bruce H. Pomeranz, and Paul N. Corey. Incidence of adverse drug reactions in hospitalized patients: a meta-analysis of prospective studies. *Journal of the American Medical Association*, 279(15):1200–1205, 1998.

[24] Munir Pirmohamed, Alasdair M. Breckenridge, Neil R. Kitteringham, and B. Kevin Park. Adverse drug reactions. *British Medical Journal*, 316(7140):1295–1298, 1998.

[25] World Health Organization. *The Importance of Pharmacovigilance-Safety Monitoring of Medicinal Products*. World Health Organization, Geneva, 2002.

[26] Rave Harpaz, William DuMouchel, Paea LePendu, and Nigam H. Shah. Empirical Bayes model to combine signals of adverse drug reactions. In *Proceedings of the 19th ACM SIGKDD International Conference on Knowledge Discovery and Data Mining*, pages 1339–1347. ACM, 2013.

[27] Margaret A. Hamburg and Francis S. Collins. The path to personalized medicine. *New England Journal of Medicine*, 363(4):301–304, 2010.

[28] William E. Evans and Howard L. McLeod. Pharmacogenomics drug disposition, drug targets, and side effects. *New England Journal of Medicine*, 348(6):538–549, 2003.

[29] Jill U. Adams. Pharmacogenomics and personalized medicine. *Nature Education*, 1(1):194, 2008.

[30] M. Whirl-Carrillo, E.M. McDonagh, J.M. Hebert, L. Gong, K. Sangkuhl, C.F. Thorn, R.B. Altman, and Teri E. Klein. Pharmacogenomics knowledge for personalized medicine. *Clinical Pharmacology & Therapeutics*, 92(4):414–417, 2012.

[31] Vivian Law, Craig Knox, Yannick Djoumbou, Tim Jewison, An Chi Guo, Yifeng Liu, Adam Maciejewski, David Arndt, Michael Wilson, Vanessa Neveu, Alexandra Tang, Geraldine Gabriel, Carol Ly, Sakina Adamjee, Zerihun T. Dame, Beomsoo Han, You Zhou, and David S. Wishart. Drugbank 4.0: shedding new light on drug metabolism. *Nucleic Acids Research*, 2013.

[32] Minoru Kanehisa, Susumu Goto, Miho Furumichi, Mao Tanabe, and Mika Hirakawa. Kegg for representation and analysis of molecular networks involving diseases and drugs. *Nucleic Acids Research*, 38(suppl 1):D355–D360, 2010.

[33] Stefan Günther, Michael Kuhn, Mathias Dunkel, Monica Campillos, Christian Senger, Evangelia Petsalaki, Jessica Ahmed, Eduardo Garcia Urdiales, Andreas Gewiess, Lars Juhl Jensen, et al. Supertarget and matador: resources for exploring drug-target relationships. *Nucleic Acids Research*, 36(suppl 1):D919–D922, 2008.

[34] Yanbin Liu, Bin Hu, Chengxin Fu, and Xin Chen. DCDB: Drug combination database. *Bioinformatics*, 26(4):587–588, 2010.

[35] Justin Lamb, Emily D. Crawford, David Peck, Joshua W. Modell, Irene C. Blat, Matthew J. Wrobel, Jim Lerner, Jean-Philippe Brunet, Aravind Subramanian, Kenneth N. Ross, Michael Reich, Haley Hieronymus, Guo Wei, Scott A. Armstrong, Stephen J. Haggarty, Paul A. Clemons, Ru Wei, Steven A. Carr, Eric S. Lander, and Todd R. Golub. The connectivity map: using gene-expression signatures to connect small molecules, genes, and disease. *Science*, 313(5795):1929–1935, September 2006.

[36] Yanli Wang, Jewen Xiao, Tugba O. Suzek, Jian Zhang, Jiyao Wang, and Stephen H. Bryant. Pubchem: a public information system for analyzing bioactivities of small molecules. *Nucleic Acids Research*, 37(suppl 2):W623–W633, 2009.

[37] Helge G. Roider, Nadia Pavlova, Ivaylo Kirov, Stoyan Slavov, Todor Slavov, Zlatyo Uzunov, and Bertram Weiss. Drug2gene: an exhaustive resource to explore effectively the drug-target relation network. *BMC Bioinformatics*, 15(1):68, 2014.

[38] Hao Ding, Ichigaku Takigawa, Hiroshi Mamitsuka, and Shanfeng Zhu. Similarity-based machine learning methods for predicting drug–target interactions: a brief review. *Briefings in Bioinformatics*, 15(5):734–747, 2013.

[39] Muhammed A. Yildirim, Kwang-Il Goh, Michael E. Cusick, Albert-Laszlo Barabasi, and Marc Vidal. Drug–target network. *Nature Biotechnology*, 25(10):1119–1126, October 2007.

[40] Justin Lamb. The connectivity map: a new tool for biomedical research. *Nature Reviews Cancer*, 7(1):54–60, January 2007.

[41] Soyoung Lee, Keunwan Park, and Dongsup Kim. Building a drug–target network and its applications. *Expert Opinion on Drug Discovery*, 4(11):1177–1189, November 2009.

[42] Liat Perlman, Assaf Gottlieb, Nir Atias, Eytan Ruppin, and Roded Sharan. Combining drug and gene similarity measures for drug-target elucidation. *Journal of Computational Biology*, 18(2):133–145, February 2011.

[43] Eugen Lounkine, Michael J. Keiser, Steven Whitebread, Dmitri Mikhailov, Jacques Hamon, Jeremy L. Jenkins, Paul Lavan, Eckhard Weber, Allison K. Doak, Serge Côté, et al. Large-scale prediction and testing of drug activity on side-effect targets. *Nature*, 486(7403):361–367, 2012.

[44] Monica Campillos, Michael Kuhn, Anne-Claude Gavin, Lars Juhl Jensen, and Peer Bork. Drug target identification using side-effect similarity. *Science*, 321(5886):263–266, 2008.

[45] Michael Kuhn, Monica Campillos, Ivica Letunic, Lars Juhl Jensen, and Peer Bork. A side effect resource to capture phenotypic effects of drugs. *Molecular Systems Biology*, 6(1):343, 2010.

[46] Linyuan Lu and Tao Zhou. Link prediction in complex networks: a survey. *Physica A: Statistical Mechanics and its Applications*, 390(6):1150–1170, March 2011.

[47] Feixiong Cheng, Chuang Liu, Jing Jiang, Weiqiang Lu, Weihua Li, Guixia Liu, Weixing Zhou, Jin Huang, and Yun Tang. Prediction of drug-target interactions and drug repositioning via network-based inference. *PLoS Computational Biology*, 8(5):e1002503, May 2012.

[48] Masahiro Hattori, Yasushi Okuno, Susumu Goto, and Minoru Kanehisa. Heuristics for chemical compound matching. *Genome Informatics Series*, pages 144–153, 2003.

[49] Salvatore Alaimo, Alfredo Pulvirenti, Rosalba Giugno, and Alfredo Ferro. Drug-target interaction prediction through domain-tuned network based inference. *Bioinformatics*, 2013.

[50] Yoshihiro Yamanishi, Michihiro Araki, Alex Gutteridge, Wataru Honda, and Minoru Kanehisa. Prediction of drug–target interaction networks from the integration of chemical and genomic spaces. *Bioinformatics*, 24(13):i232–i240, July 2008.

[51] Kevin Bleakley and Yoshihiro Yamanishi. Supervised prediction of drug–target interactions using bipartite local models. *Bioinformatics*, 25(18):2397–2403, September 2009.

[52] Jian-Ping Mei, Chee-Keong Kwoh, Peng Yang, Xiao-Li Li, and Jie Zheng. Drug–target interaction prediction by learning from local information and neighbors. *Bioinformatics*, 29 (2):238–245, 2013.

[53] Yuhao Wang and Jianyang Zeng. Predicting drug-target interactions using restricted Boltzmann machines. *Bioinformatics*, 29(13):i126–i134, 2013.

[54] Bin Chen, Ying Ding, and David J. Wild. Assessing drug target association using semantic linked data. *PLoS Computational Biology*, 8(7):e1002574, July 2012.

[55] Shobeir Fakhraei, Louiqa Raschid, and Lise Getoor. Drug-target interaction prediction for drug repurposing with probabilistic similarity logic. In *ACM SIGKDD 12th International Workshop on Data Mining in Bioinformatics (BIOKDD)*. ACM, 2013.

[56] Marie Lindquist and I. Ralph Edwards. The who programme for international drug monitoring, its database, and the technical support of the uppsala monitoring center. *The Journal of Rheumatology*, 28(5):1180–1187, 2001.

[57] Marie Lindquist. Vigibase, the WHO global ICSR database system: basic facts. *Drug Information Journal*, 42(5):409–419, 2008.

[58] Diane K. Wysowski and Lynette Swartz. Adverse drug event surveillance and drug withdrawals in the united states, 1969-2002: the importance of reporting suspected reactions. *Archives of Internal Medicine*, 165(12):1363–1369, 2005.

[59] Dianne L. Kennedy, Stephen A. Goldman, and Ralph B. Lillie. Spontaneous reporting in the united states. *Pharmacoepidemiology, Third Edition*, pages 149–174, 2000.

[60] Stephen A. Goldman. Limitations and strengths of spontaneous reports data. *Clinical Therapeutics*, 20:C40–C44, 1998.

[61] K. Haerian, D. Varn, S. Vaidya, L. Ena, H.S. Chase, and C. Friedman. Detection of pharmacovigilance-related adverse events using electronic health records and automated methods. *Clinical Pharmacology & Therapeutics*, 92(2):228–234, 2012.

[62] M. Hauben and A. Bate. Decision support methods for the detection of adverse events in post-marketing data. *Drug Discovery Today*, 14(7):343–357, 2009.

[63] June S. Almenoff, William DuMouchel, L. Allen Kindman, Xionghu Yang, and David Fram. Disproportionality analysis using empirical Bayes data mining: a tool for the evaluation of drug interactions in the post-marketing setting. *Pharmacoepidemiology and Drug Safety*, 12 (6):517–521, 2003.

[64] Nicholas P. Jewell. *Statistics for Epidemiology*. CRC Press, 2004.

[65] Ola Caster, G. Niklas Norén, David Madigan, and Andrew Bate. Large-scale regression-based pattern discovery: the example of screening the who global drug safety database. *Statistical Analysis and Data Mining*, 3(4):197–208, 2010.

[66] Alexander Genkin, David D. Lewis, and David Madigan. Large-scale Bayesian logistic regression for text categorization. *Technometrics*, 49(3):291–304, 2007.

[67] Rakesh Agrawal, Tomasz Imieliński, and Arun Swami. Mining association rules between sets of items in large databases. In *ACM SIGMOD Record*, volume 22, pages 207–216. ACM, 1993.

[68] Mohamed Rouane-Hacene, Yannick Toussaint, and Petko Valtchev. Mining safety signals in spontaneous reports database using concept analysis. In *Artificial Intelligence in Medicine*, pages 285–294. Springer, 2009.

[69] Rave Harpaz, Herbert S. Chase, and Carol Friedman. Mining multi-item drug adverse effect associations in spontaneous reporting systems. *BMC Bioinformatics*, 11(Suppl 9):S7, 2010.

[70] Sara C. Madeira and Arlindo L. Oliveira. Biclustering algorithms for biological data analysis: a survey. *IEEE/ACM Transactions on Computational Biology and Bioinformatics*, 1(1):24–45, 2004.

[71] Rave Harpaz, Hector Perez, Herbert S. Chase, Raul Rabadan, George Hripcsak, and Carol Friedman. Biclustering of adverse drug events in the FDA's spontaneous reporting system. *Clinical Pharmacology & Therapeutics*, 89(2):243–250, 2011.

[72] R. Ball and T. Botsis. Can network analysis improve pattern recognition among adverse events following immunization reported to VAERS? *Clinical Pharmacology & Therapeutics*, 90(2):271–278, 2011.

[73] Yuji Zhang, Cui Tao, Yongqun He, Pradip Kanjamala, and Hongfang Liu. Network-based analysis of vaccine-related associations reveals consistent knowledge with the vaccine ontology. *Journal of Biomedical Semantics*, 4(1):33, 2013.

[74] R.A. Wilke, H. Xu, J.C. Denny, D.M. Roden, R.M. Krauss, C.A. McCarty, R.L. Davis, T. Skaar, J. Lamba, and G. Savova. The emerging role of electronic medical records in pharmacogenomics. *Clinical Pharmacology & Therapeutics*, 89(3):379–386, 2011.

[75] Jeffrey S. Brown, Martin Kulldorff, K. Arnold Chan, Robert L. Davis, David Graham, Parker T. Pettus, Susan E. Andrade, Marsha A. Raebel, Lisa Herrinton, Douglas Roblin, et al. Early detection of adverse drug events within population-based health networks: application of sequential testing methods. *Pharmacoepidemiology and Drug Safety*, 16(12):1275–1284, 2007.

[76] Yanqing Ji, Hao Ying, Peter Dews, Ayman Mansour, John Tran, Richard E. Miller, and R. Michael Massanari. A potential causal association mining algorithm for screening adverse drug reactions in postmarketing surveillance. *IEEE Transactions on Information Technology in Biomedicine*, 15(3):428–437, 2011.

[77] Jonathan S. Schildcrout, Sebastien Haneuse, Josh F. Peterson, Joshua C. Denny, Michael E. Matheny, Lemuel R. Waitman, and Randolph A. Miller. Analyses of longitudinal, hospital clinical laboratory data with application to blood glucose concentrations. *Statistics in Medicine*, 30(27):3208–3220, 2011.

[78] Xiaoyan Wang, George Hripcsak, Marianthi Markatou, and Carol Friedman. Active computerized pharmacovigilance using natural language processing, statistics, and electronic health records: a feasibility study. *Journal of the American Medical Informatics Association*, 16(3): 328–337, 2009.

[79] Ryen W. White, Rave Harpaz, Nigam H. Shah, William DuMouchel, and Eric Horvitz. Toward enhanced pharmacovigilance using patient-generated data on the Internet. *Clinical Pharmacology & Therapeutics*, 96(2):239–246, 2014.

[80] Herman Anthony Carneiro and Eleftherios Mylonakis. Google trends: a web-based tool for real-time surveillance of disease outbreaks. *Clinical Infectious Diseases*, 49(10):1557–1564, 2009.

[81] John S. Brownstein, Clark C. Freifeld, and Lawrence C. Madoff. Digital disease detection harnessing the web for public health surveillance. *New England Journal of Medicine*, 360 (21):2153–2157, 2009.

[82] David M. Lazer, Ryan Kennedy, Gary King, and Alessandro Vespignani. The parable of Google flu: traps in big data analysis. *Science*, 343(6176):1203–1205, 2014.

[83] Robert Leaman, Laura Wojtulewicz, Ryan Sullivan, Annie Skariah, Jian Yang, and Graciela Gonzalez. Towards internet-age pharmacovigilance: extracting adverse drug reactions from user posts to health-related social networks. In *Proceedings of the Workshop on Biomedical Natural Language Processing*, pages 117–125. Association for Computational Linguistics, 2010.

[84] Ryen W. White, Nicholas P. Tatonetti, Nigam H. Shah, Russ B. Altman, and Eric Horvitz. Web-scale pharmacovigilance: listening to signals from the crowd. *Journal of the American Medical Informatics Association*, 20(3):404–408, 2013.

[85] Clark C. Freifeld, John S. Brownstein, Christopher M. Menone, Wenjie Bao, Ross Filice, Taha Kass-Hout, and Nabarun Dasgupta. Digital drug safety surveillance: monitoring pharmaceutical products in Twitter. *Drug Safety*, 37(5):343–350, 2014.

[86] Kanaka D. Shetty and Siddhartha R. Dalal. Using information mining of the medical literature to improve drug safety. *Journal of the American Medical Informatics Association*, 18 (5):668–674, 2011.

[87] George Hripcsak, Carol Friedman, Philip O. Alderson, William DuMouchel, Stephen B. Johnson, and Paul D. Clayton. Unlocking clinical data from narrative reports: a study of natural language processing. *Annals of Internal Medicine*, 122(9):681–688, 1995.

[88] Genevieve B. Melton and George Hripcsak. Automated detection of adverse events using natural language processing of discharge summaries. *Journal of the American Medical Informatics Association*, 12(4):448–457, 2005.

[89] Jung-Hsien Chiang, Jou-Wei Lin, and Chen-Wei Yang. Automated evaluation of electronic discharge notes to assess quality of care for cardiovascular diseases using medical language extraction and encoding system (MEDLEE). *Journal of the American Medical Informatics Association*, 17(3):245–252, 2010.

[90] Xiaoyan Wang, Amy Chused, Noémie Elhadad, Carol Friedman, and Marianthi Markatou. Automated knowledge acquisition from clinical narrative reports. In *AMIA Annual Symposium Proceedings*, volume 2008, page 783. American Medical Informatics Association, 2008.

[91] Carol Friedman, George Hripcsak, Lyuda Shagina, and Hongfang Liu. Representing information in patient reports using natural language processing and the extensible markup language. *Journal of the American Medical Informatics Association*, 6(1):76–87, 1999.

[92] Hua Xu, Shane P. Stenner, Son Doan, Kevin B. Johnson, Lemuel R. Waitman, and Joshua C. Denny. MEDEX: a medication information extraction system for clinical narratives. *Journal of the American Medical Informatics Association*, 17(1):19–24, 2010.

[93] Udo Hahn, K. Bretonnel Cohen, Yael Garten, and Nigam H. Shah. Mining the pharmacogenomics literaturea survey of the state of the art. *Briefings in Bioinformatics*, 13(4):460–494, 2012.

[94] Caroline F. Thorn, Teri E. Klein, and Russ B. Altman. Pharmacogenomics and bioinformatics: PharmGKB. *Pharmacogenomics*, 11(4):501–505, 2010.

[95] Yael Garten and Russ B. Altman. Pharmspresso: a text mining tool for extraction of pharmacogenomic concepts and relationships from full text. *BMC Bioinformatics*, 10(Suppl 2):S6, 2009.

[96] Dina Demner-Fushman, Wendy W. Chapman, and Clement J. McDonald. What can natural language processing do for clinical decision support? *Journal of Biomedical Informatics*, 42 (5):760–772, 2009.

[97] Martin Krallinger, Florian Leitner, and Alfonso Valencia. Analysis of biological processes and diseases using text mining approaches. In *Bioinformatics Methods in Clinical Research*, pages 341–382. Springer, 2010.

[98] Tanja Bekhuis. Conceptual biology, hypothesis discovery, and text mining: Swanson's legacy. *Biomedical Digital Libraries*, 3(1):2, 2006.

[99] Jeffrey T. Chang and Russ B. Altman. Extracting and characterizing gene-drug relationships from the literature. *Pharmacogenetics and Genomics*, 14(9):577–586, 2004.

[100] Pernille Warrer, Ebba Holme Hansen, Lars Juhl-Jensen, and Lise Aagaard. Using text-mining techniques in electronic patient records to identify ADRS from medicine use. *British Journal of Clinical Pharmacology*, 73(5):674–684, 2012.

[101] Thomas C. Rindflesch, Lorraine Tanabe, John N. Weinstein, and Lawrence Hunter. EDGAR: extraction of drugs, genes and relations from the biomedical literature. In *Pacific Symposium on Biocomputing. Pacific Symposium on Biocomputing*, pages 517–528. NIH Public Access, 1999.

Chapter 19

Clinical Decision Support Systems

Martin Alther
Department of Computer Science
Wayne State University
Detroit, MI
martin.alther@wayne.edu

Chandan K. Reddy
Department of Computer Science
Wayne State University
Detroit, MI
reddy@cs.wayne.edu

19.1 Introduction

Clinical Decision Support Systems (CDSS) are computer systems designed to assist clinicians with patient-related decision making, such as diagnosis and treatment. Ever since the seminal *To Err Is Human* [1] was published in 2000, CDSS (along with Computer-Based Physician Order Entry systems) have become a crucial component in the evaluation and improvement of patient treatment. CDSS have shown to improve both patient outcomes and cost of care. They have demonstrated to minimize analytical errors by notifying the physician of potentially harmful drug interactions, and their diagnostic procedures have been shown to enable more accurate diagnoses. There are a wide variety of uses for CDSS in clinical practice. Some of the main uses include:

- Assisting with patient-related decision making.
- Determining optimal treatment strategies for individual patients.
- Aiding general health policies by estimating the clinical and economic outcomes of different treatment methods.
- Estimating treatment outcomes under circumstances where methods like randomized trials are either impossible or infeasible.

In 2005, Garg et al. [2] conducted a review of 100 patient studies and concluded that CDSS improved diagnosis in 64% and patient outcomes in 13% of the studies tested. That same year, Duke University conducted a systematic review of 70 different cases and concluded that decision support systems significantly improved clinical practice in 68% of all trials. The CDSS features attributed to the analysis' success included:

- natural integration with clinical workflow.
- electronic nature.
- providing decision support at the time/location of care rather than before or after the patient encounter.
- use of recommended care rather than assessments of care.

Two particular fields of healthcare where CDSS have been hugely influential are the pharmacy and billing. Pharmacies now use batch-based order checking systems that look for negative drug interactions and then report them to the corresponding patient's ordering professional. Meanwhile, in terms of billing, CDSS have been used to examine both potential courses of treatment and conventional Medicare conditions in order to devise treatment plans that provide an optimal balance of patient care and financial expense.

In this chapter, we will provide a survey of different aspects of CDSS along with various challenges associated with their usage in clinical practice. This chapter is organized as follows: Section 19.2 provides a brief historical perspective including the current generation CDSS. Various types of CDSS will be described in Section 19.3. Decision support during care provider order entry is described in 19.4 while the diagnostic decision support is given in 19.5. Description of the human-intensive techniques that can be used to build the knowledge base is given in Section 19.6. The primary challenges with the usage of CDSS are studied in Section 19.7 while the legal and ethical issues concerned is discussed in Section 19.8. Section 19.9 concludes our discussion.

19.2 Historical Perspective

In this section, we provide a historical perspective on the development of CDSS. We will first describe the most popular early CDSS that were developed several decades ago and then we will discuss the current generation CDSS. For each of the CDSS, we will give the high-level idea of its functioning and also mention the primary drawbacks.

19.2.1 Early CDSS

Ever since the birth of the medical industry, health scientists have recognized the importance of informed clinical decision making. Unfortunately, for a long time, efficient methods for researching and evaluating such methods were quite rarc. Clinicians often relied on extensive research and handwritten records to establish the necessary knowledge for a well-informed decision. Naturally, this proved to be both error prone and very time consuming. Fortunately, the evolution of business-related computing in the 1970s and 1980s gave clinicians an easy mechanism for analyzing patient data and recommending potential courses of treatment and thus, CDSS were born.

Early systems rigidly decided on a course of action, based on the user's input [3]. The user would input any necessary information, and the CDSS would output a final decision, which in turn would be the user's course of action:

- **Caduceus (aka The Internist) [4]:** This system was developed in the 1970s as a means of implementing an artificial intelligence model for use in CDSS, with the central goal of the physician using a "hypothetico-deductive" approach to medical diagnosis. One of the system's unique features was its use of a probabilistic method for ranking diagnoses. It evaluated patient symptoms and then searched its knowledge base for the most likely disease, based on the statistics of existing patients with the specified symptoms. Unfortunately, Caduceus' diagnostic accuracy was not good. For instance, in 1981, a study using pre-existing clinicopathological conference cases was conducted and then published in *The New England Journal of Medicine*. Caduceus was unable to match the diagnostic accuracy of real-life experts in this study, due to its limited knowledge base and small number of diagnostic algorithms. Thus, the system was unable to gain widespread acceptance with the medical community.

  In the mid 1980s, Caduceus evolved into **QMR (Quick Medical Reference)**. QMR differed significantly from Caduceus in that, while Caduceus was used mainly for diagnostic consultation (i.e., suggesting rigid courses of treatment to clinicians), QMR was more flexible. It allowed clinicians to modify and manipulate its suggested diagnoses/treatments in whichever way they wished, while allowing them to utilize its knowledge base to establish their own hypotheses with regards to the treatment of more complex and difficult cases [4]. While QMR contained an extensive medical database (approximately 570 diseases in all), it had the major disadvantage of requiring frequent updates whenever new diseases were discovered. Furthermore, according to a 1994 study comparing QMR with three other clinical decision support systems, the system gave considerably fewer "correct" patient diagnoses (by the standards of a group of physicians) than the three competing systems [5]. Thus, by 2001, QMR was largely abandoned in favor of less cumbersome and more accurate CDSS.

- **MYCIN [6]:** This was originally developed in the 1970s as a means for identifying infectious diseases and recommending antibiotics for treatment. A unique aspect of MYCIN was its emphasis on artificial intelligence (AI). Its AI model was constructed through a rule-based system, in which roughly 200 decision rules (and counting) were implemented into the system, forming the knowledge base. To determine possible patient diagnoses, MYCIN's internal decision tree was consulted, and diagnostic options were reached by running through its various branches. The rule-based system was very flexible in that it allowed clinicians to either modify existing rules or devise new ones as they saw fit, making MYCIN adaptable to changing medical trends and discoveries. Therefore, it was considered an expert system, since its AI component allowed for results that were theoretically similar to those of a real-life expert.

  Unfortunately, there were many significant problems with MYCIN. First, it worked very slowly, with a typical analysis requiring upwards of 30 minutes. Second, there was concern over whether physicians ran the risk of putting too much trust in computerized results at the expense of their own judgment and inquiry. Third, there was the issue of accountability: Who would be held liable if the machine made an error in patient diagnosis? Perhaps the most important problem was how ahead of its time MYCIN was. It was developed before desktop computing and the Internet existed, so the system was based on a rather dated model for computer interaction [7]. Nonetheless, its influence was far reaching and is still felt to this day, with many systems either combining it with other expert systems (Shyster-MYCIN [8]) or using it as an influence on the development of new systems (GUIDON [9]).

- **Iliad [10]:** Iliad is another "expert" CDSS. It contains three modes of usage: Consultation, Simulation, and Simulation-Test. In *Consultation* mode, users enter real-life patient findings into the system. Iliad then analyzes these findings and compiles a list of possible diagnoses, with each diagnosis ranked in terms of its likelihood of correctness. A unique feature of Iliad is its handling of "gaps" in patient information. If the patient data appears incomplete, Iliad will suggest methods of completion and/or compromise, so that the clinician may continue working on a possible diagnosis. In *Simulation* mode, Iliad assumes the role of a complaining patient. It offers a typical real-life complaint and then demands input, testing, etc., from the clinician. The clinician's questions, responses, and diagnostic decisions are evaluated by Iliad, with feedback provided once analysis is complete. Finally, in *Simulation-Test* mode, Iliad runs a similar real-life patient simulation, except that feedback is not given to the clinician. Instead, Iliad silently evaluates his/her performance and then sends it to another user. Needless to say, because of its highly scholastic focus, Iliad is often used for educational purposes. In fact, studies have shown that it is very effective in training aspiring medical professionals for real-life practice [10].

  Unlike many other systems, which use knowledge-frame implementations, Iliad uses a framed version of the Bayes model for its analysis [11]. This makes it much easier for the system to recognize multiple diseases in a single patient (further information on Bayes classification can be found in Section 19.3.1.2). For diseases that are mutually dependent, a form of cluster analysis is included. This groups the diseases into independent categories, based not only on the disease type, but also on clinician-specified factors such as their specific point of infection. This is so that the diseases may be efficiently analyzed and a more effective Bayesian classifier may be devised.

The 1980s saw tremendous growth and development in the field of clinical decision support. Greater involvement from the Association of American Medical Colleges in clinical library practice provided the necessary funding and resources for developing functional computerized information systems. Such systems included everything from electronic health records to financial management systems. Furthermore, PDAs (personal digital assistants) aided the development of CDSS by giving them portability. Patient data and clinical decision-making software could now be carried in the clinician's pocket, allowing him/her to easily reach informed decisions without cutting into their time with the patient. Although PDAs were more akin to basic information systems than CDSS, they were major stepping-stones in the development of CDSS that would allow clinicians to make diagnostic and treatment decisions while remaining physically close to their patients.

19.2.2 CDSS Today

Today's CDSS have much broader and more flexible methods for making clinical decisions, using both clinician and machine knowledge to give a series of potential "suggestions," with the clinician deciding on the suggestion that is most appropriate to her specific needs [3].

- **VisualDx [12]:** This is a JAVA-based clinical decision support system that, as the name suggests, is often used as a visual aid in assisting healthcare providers with diagnosis. This is useful in instances where surface level diseases (such as those of the skin) are present, and doctors need visual representations of these diseases to aid with diagnosis. A unique feature of VisualDx is that, rather than being organized by a specific diagnosis, it is organized by symptoms and other visual clues. It uses a sophisticated matching process that visually matches images of the specific patient's abnormalities with pre-existing images within a built-in database of more than 6,000 illnesses. It then uses the results of these comparisons to recommend courses of treatment.

  VisualDX has significant limitations. In addition to a vast image database, the system contains a written summary of each image. Unfortunately, these summaries are relatively brief and are, therefore, prone to overgeneralization. For example, skin biopsies are often recommended for "sicker" patients. However, it is unclear what is actually meant by "sicker." This is especially problematic when we consider that skin biopsies are rarely performed unless standard skin therapy has proven ineffective. Nevertheless, VisualDx has been demonstrated to be quite useful when diagnosing surface-level illness. The system is operational to this day, with a significant update in 2010 enabling companionship with a similar product called UpToDate [3].

- **DXplain [13]:** This is a web-based diagnosis system developed in the late 1980s by the American Medical Association. A unique feature of this system is its simplicity: Clinicians enter patient information using nothing but their own medical vocabulary, and the system outputs a list of potential diagnoses from a knowledge base consisting of thousands of diseases (with up to ten different references each), along with the potential relevance of its choices. Therefore, it functions as a clinical decision support system for physicians with little computer experience.

  DXplain has been demonstrated to be both reliable and cost efficient, especially in academic environments [3]. For example, a 2010 study consisting of more than 500 different diagnostic cases was assigned to various Massachusetts General Medicine residents. They concluded that medical charges, Medicare Part A charges, and service costs significantly decreased when using DXplain for diagnostic recommendation [14]. DXplain has also been frequently demonstrated to give very accurate diagnoses. For example, in a 2012 study conducted by Lehigh University, the system was compared with four other CDSS. The conclusion drawn was that it was second only to Isabel (discussed below) in terms of accuracy [15].

- **Isabel [16]:** This is one of the most comprehensive CDSS available. Like DXplain, it is a web-based system designed with physician usability in mind. Originally, it focused mainly on pediatrics, but it was soon expanded to cover adult symptoms. Isabel contains two subsystems: a diagnostic checklist utility and a knowledge mobilizing utility. The diagnosis checklist tool enables physicians to enter patient demographics and clinical features into the system, which then returns a set of recommended diagnoses. The knowledge mobilizing utility may then be used to research additional information about the recommended diagnoses [3].

  Isabel has been demonstrated to give exceptionally accurate diagnoses of most patient cases. In the Lehigh University study, for example, it was shown to be the most accurate of the five systems tested. Other studies, such as a 2003 study conducted by the Imperial College School of Medicine, have also demonstrated this system to be very accurate [17]. Unfortunately, Isabel is a relatively new CDSS and, thus, more extensive testing must be performed in order to give a firm assessment of its overall reliability.

19.3 Various Types of CDSS

There are two main types of clinical decision support systems: **Knowledge-Based** and **Nonknowledge-Based.**

19.3.1 Knowledge-Based CDSS

Contemporary CDSS are rooted in early expert systems. These systems attempted to replicate the logic and reasoning of a human decision maker, reaching firm decisions based on existing knowledge. Knowledge-based CDSS rose out of the intuitive realization that medicine was a good field for applying such knowledge. A computer could (theoretically) mimic the thought processes of a real-life clinician and then give a finalized diagnosis based on the information at hand (Figure 19.1).

During the 1990s and 2000s, however, CDSS moved away from attempting to make rigorous clinical decisions in favor of offering a variety of possible diagnostic/treatment options and then allowing the clinician herself to make a finalized decision [7]. There are multiple reasons for this change in focus. These include an underlying fear of computers being inherently prone to errors, the realization that artificial intelligence still had a long way to go before it could successfully mimic the knowledge and reasoning skills of real-life clinicians, the infringement computerized decision making placed on physician/patient relations, etc. Thus, today's CDSS present a variety of diagnostic/treatment options to clinicians, allowing them to evaluate first-hand the patient's symptoms and personal testimonies while utilizing the systems as reference points for possible diagnoses.

Knowledge-based CDSS are those with a built-in reference table, containing inbred information about different diseases, treatments, etc. They use traditional AI methods (such as conditional logic) to reach decisions on courses of treatment. There are three main parts to a knowledge-based CDSS. They are the knowledge base, the inference engine, and the user communication method.

The **knowledge base** is essentially a compiled information set, with each piece of information structured in the form of IF-THEN rules. For example, IF a new order is placed for a slowly-changing blood test, AND IF the blood test was ordered within the past 48 hours, THEN we alert the

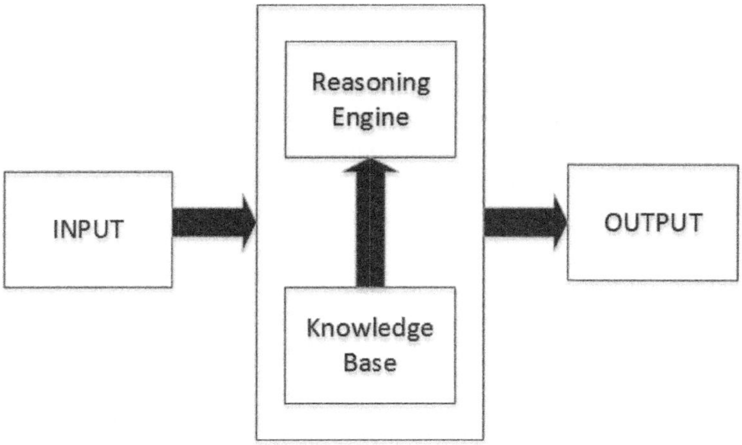

FIGURE 19.1: A general knowledge-based clinical decision support system.

physician to the possibility of duplicate test ordering. The knowledge base functions in conjunction with whichever algorithmic structure the system uses for its analysis. To put it simply, the user inputs patient information, and then the system searches through its knowledge base for matching diseases or treatment possibilities [2].

The **inference engine** applies a system of logic to the knowledge base, allowing it to "become smarter" by establishing new and/or updated knowledge. It contains the necessary formulae for combining the rules in the knowledge base with any available patient data, allowing the system to create patient-specific rules and conditions based on its knowledge of both the patient's medical history and the severity of his/her current condition. A particularly important aspect of the inference engine is its mutual exclusion from the knowledge base. Because CDSS development is very time consuming, reusability is key. Anybody should be allowed to construct a new CDSS through an existing inference engine. Unfortunately, most real-life systems are developed with a specific goal in mind (for example, diagnosing breast cancer). Thus, it is either difficult or impossible to use them beyond their intended purpose.

Finally, the **user communication method** is where the clinician herself inputs the patient's relevant data and then receives the corresponding results. In some CDSS, the patient data must be manually entered. Most of the time, however, patient data is provided through a computer-based record. The record is inputed either by the clinician or an external lab or pharmacy and is, thus, already electronically scaled. It is the clinician's job to properly manipulate the system to obtain the outcome she wishes. Diagnostic and treatment outcomes are generally represented as either recommendations or alerts. Occasionally, if an alert has been generated after an initial order was placed, automated emails and wireless notifications will be sent.

The usual format for a knowledge-based CDSS is that the clinician is asked to supply a certain amount of input, which is then processed through both the system's knowledge base and reasoning engine. It then outputs a series of possible diagnostic or treatment options for her.

19.3.1.1 Input

While there is substantial variance in the manner in which clinical information is entered into a CDSS, most systems require the user to choose keywords from his/her organization's word dictionary. The challenge clinicians typically face with this requirement is that different CDSS have different word vocabularies. The quality of output in a CDSS depends on how well its vocabulary matches the clinician's keywords. In general, however, items related to the patient's medical history and current symptoms are going to be the suggested input.

One potentially effective method of giving detailed input is to use an explicitly defined time model, in which the user specifies various time intervals and the events that occurred within them. Unfortunately, this complicates user input and would, thus, likely prove too cumbersome for the average clinician. A simpler solution would be to use an **implicit time model**, in which broad temporal information is part of the specified user input (for example, "history of recent exposure to strep") [7]. While this simplified approach has the disadvantage of temporal ambiguity (does "recent" mean "just last week" or "last year"?), it has proven to be a viable method of measuring time in a CDSS.

19.3.1.2 Inference Engine

The inference engine is the part of the CDSS that combines user input with all other necessary data to devise a final list of "decisions." To avoid confusion, this process is usually hidden from the user. There are many different methods of analyzing user input and devising results from it. One popular method is the utilization of production rules. These are logical IF-THEN statements that, when combined, form concrete solutions to problems. MYCIN is an example of a popular CDSS that uses production rules. However, the most popular method of probabilistic estimate in an inference engine is **Bayes' Rule**, which computes the conditional probabilities [7]. In mathematical terms, suppose we wish to compute the probability of event A given event B, (or $Pr(A|B)$). As long as we already have $Pr(B|A)$, along with "prior probabilities" ($Pr(A)$ and $Pr(B)$) at our disposal, we may use Bayes' Rule to compute $Pr(A|B)$ as follows:

$$Pr(A|B) = \frac{Pr(A) \cdot Pr(B|A)}{Pr(B)} \tag{19.1}$$

To give a practical example, suppose we wish to learn the likelihood of a patient having hepatitis given that she has jaundice. (i.e., $Pr(hepatitis|jaundice)$). To compute this probability, we begin by computing a more obvious probability: $Pr(jaundice|hepatitis)$. Intuitively, this could be solved by studying an established series of patients with hepatitis and then calculating the ratio of patients with jaundice to the total number of patients. We would then plug the resultant probability into Bayes' Rule, along with the general likelihoods of hepatitis and jaundice among the total patient population ("$Pr(hepatitis)$" and "$Pr(jaundice)$," respectively). We, thus, obtain the following:

$$Pr(hepatitis|jaundice) = \frac{Pr(hepatitis) \cdot Pr(jaundice|hepatitis)}{Pr(jaundice)} \tag{19.2}$$

The result is an estimate of the patient's likelihood for having hepatitis, given the presence of jaundice.

In medicine, there is the challenge of computing the likelihood of two disjoint yet potentially related events happening simultaneously in a patient [7]. For example, suppose we wish to compute the probability of a patient having both pneumonia and an abnormal chest radiograph:

$$Pr(pneumonia + abnormal\ CXR) \tag{19.3}$$

Intuitively, it would appear that the solution is as follows:

$$Pr(pneumonia + abnormal\ CXR) = Pr(pneumonia) \cdot Pr(abnormal\ CXR) \tag{19.4}$$

Unfortunately, this formula will not work since the probabilities for pneumonia and abnormal chest radiography are typically very small. Thus, we would obtain an absurdly small probability for both occurring simultaneously, even though we know patients with pneumonia typically have abnormal chest radiographies. Fortunately, we may modify the formula to give a more accurate prediction by multiplying the probability that a patient has pneumonia with the probability that she has an abnormal chest radiograph *given the presence of pneumonia*:

$$Pr(pneumonia + abnormal\,CXR) = Pr(pneumonia) \cdot Pr(abnormal\,CXR|pneumonia) \quad (19.5)$$

This will give us a much higher, and thus more accurate, probability estimate.

In general terms, we compute the probability of conditions "A" and "B" existing simultaneously in the following manner:

$$Pr(A+B) = Pr(A) \cdot Pr(B|A) \quad (19.6)$$

By slightly rearranging this equation, we obtain Bayes' Rule:

$$Pr(A|B) = \frac{Pr(A) \cdot Pr(B|A)}{Pr(B)} \quad (19.7)$$

A major roadblock when implementing Bayes' Rule is the possibility of a patient having multiple symptoms. Fortunately, this problem is slightly neutralized by the fact that most diseases are mutually exclusive of one another. With that said, a frame-based version of Bayes' Rule is used for taking all possible diseases into account. Illiad [11] is an example of a CDSS that successfully uses this mechanism. It uses a cluster-based framework that categorizes potential diagnoses by a common underlying thread (for example, chest pains). The logic used in these clusters is based not only on the dependencies of these possible diagnoses but also a user's understanding of how they would be categorized. For this very reason, Iliad uses Boolean statements [11]. Likewise, a Bayesian Network could be established through a series of Bayes' Rule implementations. This is essentially a graphical framework representing the cause-and-effect relationships of different events.

19.3.1.3 Knowledge Base

Naturally, for a CDSS to be successful, it must possess some form of medical knowledge. Furthermore, this knowledge must be implemented in whichever format the inference engine uses. Thus, a knowledge base must be created. The knowledge base contains all necessary medical information along with any rules or conditions necessary for analysis. For example, if the engine uses Bayes' Rule, medical knowledge must be encoded in such a manner that it allows for computation with this method of probabilistic estimates.

There are four forms of knowledge representation: logic, procedural, graph/network, and structured systems [18]. Logic is widely considered to be the most common form of knowledge representation. Medical knowledge is typically divided into two categories: declarative and procedural. **Declarative knowledge** consists of basic sentences and propositions stating hard facts, while **procedural knowledge** gives a more linear description of what actions or conclusions are feasible given the knowledge at hand. **Graph/network representation** is, as the name suggests, knowledge representation through the use of a graphical or network-based system (for example, DXPlain [13]), while **structured knowledge** is a categorized knowledge base.

Unfortunately, there is a crucial challenge in the implementation of knowledge bases that emphasize disease and treatment probability: many real-life probabilities in the clinical environment are unknown. While medical literature and consultation are certainly useful in terms of obtaining these probabilities, they often contain disparate numbers and estimates from one another, leaving the physician to guess the correct estimate. Furthermore, the probabilities of most diseases are dependent not only on specific symptoms but also on external factors such as the patient's geographic location and other demographical information. Lastly, knowledge bases must be regularly updated as new information becomes available. This is an ongoing issue with no clear solution, since many CDSS begin life as funded academic projects, for which maintenance must cease once funding has stopped.

19.3.1.4 Output

The output of a CDSS is generally in the form of a probabilistically ranked list of solutions. Generally, this list is in ASCII text format, but it may also be graphical. In some cases, factors other than probability are used in the ranking process. For example, in DXplain, diseases that are not necessarily likely but very risky when misdiagnosed are given special rank privileges. In fact, generally speaking, physicians are more interested in the least likely diagnoses than in the most likely ones, since less likely diagnoses are much easier to overlook.

19.3.2 Nonknowledge-Based CDSS

Nonknowledge-based CDSS differ from knowledge-based ones in that, rather than a user-defined knowledge base, they implement a form of artificial intelligence called *Machine Learning*. This a process by which a system, rather than consulting a precomposed encyclopedia, simply "learns" from past experiences and then implements these "lessons" into its knowledge base. There are two popular types of Nonknowledge-based CDSSs: Artificial Neural Networks and Genetic Algorithms [7].

19.3.2.1 Artificial Neural Networks

Artificial Neural Networks (ANN) simulate human thinking by evaluating and eventually learning from existing examples/occurrences [19]. An ANN consists of a series of nodes called "neurodes" (corresponding to the "neurons" in the human brain) and the weighted connections (corresponding to nerve synapses in the human brain) that unidirectionally transmit signals between them. An ANN contains three different components: input, output, and a hidden data processor. The input segment receives the data, while the output segment gives the finalized results. The data processing component, meanwhile, acts as an intermediary between the two. It processes the data and then sends the results to the output segment.

The structure of an ANN is very similar to that of a knowledge-based CDSS. However, unlike knowledge-based CDSS, ANNs do not have predefined knowledge bases. Rather, an ANN studies patterns in the patient data and then finds correlations between the patient's signs/symptoms and a possible diagnosis. Another significant difference is that knowledge-based CDSSs generally cover a much wider range of diseases than ANNs.

In order to function properly, ANNs must first be "trained." This is done by first inputing a large amount of clinical data into the neural network, analyzing it, and then hypothesizing the correct output. These educated guesses are then compared to the actual results, and the weights are adjusted accordingly, with the incorrect results being given more weight. We continue to iteratively run this process until a substantial number of correct predictions have been made.

The advantage of using ANN is that it eliminates the need for manually writing rules and seeking expert input. ANNs can also analyze and process incomplete data by inferring what the data should be, with the quality of analysis being consistently improved as more patient data is analyzed. Unfortunately, ANNs also have certain disadvantages. Due to their iterative nature, the training process is very time consuming. More importantly, the formulas/weights that result from this process are not easily read and interpreted. Therefore, with the system being unable to describe why it uses certain data the way it does, reliability is a major issue.

Nevertheless, ANNs have proven to be very successful in terms of predicting such diseases as oral cancer and myocardial infection. They have also been successfully used for the prediction of chronic diseases such as breast cancer recurrence [20] and have even shown promise in aiding the field of dentistry [21]. Thus, they are widely considered to be a viable method of clinical decision making.

19.3.2.2 Genetic Algorithms

The other key example of nonknowledge-based systems is the **Genetic Algorithm**. Genetic Algorithms are based on Charles Darwin's theories of natural selection and survival of the fittest. Just as species change in order to adapt to their environment, genetic algorithms regularly "reproduce" themselves in order to better adapt to the task at hand. As with Darwin's theory of "survival of the fittest," genetic algorithms generally begin by attempting to solve a problem through the use of randomly generated solutions [22]. The next step is to evaluate the quality (i.e., "fitness") of all the available solutions through the use of a "fitness function." The solutions are ranked by their fitness scores, with the more fit solutions having greater likelihood of "breeding" new solutions through the mutual exchange among themselves. These new solutions are evaluated similarly to their parent solutions, and the process iteratively repeats until an optimal solution is found.

Because of their more cumbersome nature, genetic algorithms have seen less use in clinical decision support than artificial neural networks. Nonetheless, they have been successfully used in fields such as chemotherapy administration and heart disease [23, 24].

19.4 Decision Support during Care Provider Order Entry

Care Provider Order Entry (CPOE) systems are decision support systems that allow clinicians to electronically input medical orders for whichever patients they are treating. Specifically, clinicians log in to a system and load their CPOE module and select the patient they are placing the order for. They write out the order and after successful review and modification, the order will be placed [25]. Here is an example of a typical care provider order entry form:

> While the CPOE's methodology depends on the clinician's specific domain, it is generally believed that allowing the physician to place an order and then providing feedback if the order is believed to be incorrect is the best way of handling care provider order entry. There are two reasons why this is preferred. One is that waiting on warning the physician of an inappropriate order until after it has been placed allows him/her to devise his/her own preferred course of action, discouraging overreliance on CDSS. The other reason is that a delay in warning the physician gives him/her the opportunity to correct any errors the system has detected. Whereas earlier warnings might underscore the errors and leave more room for mistakes.

In general, CPOE responsiveness depends on creating orders at the appropriate clinical level (i.e., the clinician's level of expertise and the user's specific condition). Unfortunately, because physicians and nurses generally have different ways of viewing these orders than the people carrying them out (pharmacists, radiologists, etc.), there tends to be confusion between the more general order of a physician and the corresponding technical terms for its content by whichever ancillary departments he/she consults. The accepted solution to this problem is for CPOE systems to avoid asking clinicians to perform tasks that fall outside their line of expertise. Pharmacists, for example, typically use pharmaceutical systems to fill and dispense whatever is specified in the CPOE system. If a higher level order is specified by the physician, the CPOE system could evaluate the pharmacy's own terminology and floor stock inventory and then determine the correct item to give the patient, giving the pharmacist more time to evaluate factors such as the order's clinical validity, safety, and efficiency [7].

Roles of Decision Support within CPOE—Decision support has several roles in CPOE [25]:

1. *Creating legible, complete, correct, rapidly actionable orders:* A CPOE system is able to avoid many of the traps/failings that often come with handwritten reports [26]. For example,

illegibility and incorrectness. Improved legibility is able to both reduce errors and reduce the amount of time clinical staff spends deciphering handwriting. Meanwhile, a "complete" order contains all necessary information to successfully place an order, while a "correct" order meets the requirements for safe and effective patient care. Needless to say, most CPOE systems are designed to ensure that both conditions are satisfied.

2. *Providing patient-specific clinical decision support:* A successful CPOE system should be able to generate decision support recommendations based on a patient's individual conditions. It should be able to generate a safety net for the clinician by merging patient-specific information (age, allergies, existing medications, etc.) with the general rules for proper practice. It should also improve patient care by promoting evidence-based clinical practice guidelines through factors such as order history or computer-based advice.

3. *Optimizing clinical care:* As the clinicians becomes accustomed to a CPOE system, they consider ways of customizing it so that their work becomes easier and more effective. Not only does this cater the system to the user's liking, but it could reduce the potential for violations such as inappropriate testing. For example, at Vanderbilt University, users of a system called WizOrder were encouraged to modify the program so that they could create Registry Orders where billing information would be more easily transferred. The challenge, in this case, comes from the need to improve the effectiveness of the system while maintaining usability. Thus, it is generally left up to the user to design a system that is able to successfully balance these two issues.

4. *Providing just-in-time focused education relevant to patient care:* Most CPOE systems provide useful educational prompts and links to more detailed description about their material, with the interface designed in a manner that encourages their use. These can be used in treatment summaries or through a corresponding web browser. Such links have the benefit of assisting the clinician with more complex orders.

Benefits and Challenges—The benefits of CPOE systems are that they can improve clinical productivity, provide solid educational support, and positively impact how patient care is given. They also make order entry much easier for both the clinician and the user, providing a computerized framework for placing orders. Thus, issues such as sloppy handwriting are nonexistent, while typos may be corrected through a built-in autocorrect feature. On the other hand, the manner in which error checking is handled may result in placing the orders containing unidentified errors. This could be especially dangerous if the order happens to be costly and critical to the patient's survival. If there is an error in it, then whatever money was spent on the order may get wasted. Worse yet, the patient's life may be in danger. Computerized order entry systems also have the disadvantage of relying on an Internet-based framework, meaning occasionally bad transmissions and server problems are inevitable.

19.5 Diagnostic Decision Support

Diagnostic Decision Support Systems are designed to "diagnose" diseases and conditions based on the parameters given as the input. In formal terms, diagnosis can be defined as "the process of determining by examination the nature and circumstances of a diseased condition [27]." What this means is that clinicians study the patient's life history before the illness has begun, how the illness came to be, and how it has affected the patient's current lifestyle [28]. Additionally, clinicians must ensure that the patient recognizes the seriousness of the disease and how to properly treat it.

Diagnostic Decision Support Systems attempt to replicate the process of diagnosis in a computerized format. The patient is asked a series of questions, and then a hypothetical diagnosis or set of possible diagnoses is output to him/her. The most user-centered systems give questionnaires inquiring about everything from the patient's family history to the patient's current health conditions. Upon completion, the patient is given a printout summarizing the conclusions drawn by the system and then suggesting possible courses of action. Similarly, there are certain medical websites sometimes offering diagnostic tools for assessing patients and recommending possible courses of treatment. A good example is Mayo Clinic's depression test [29]. It asks the patient to answer a series of questions relating to symptoms, family history, etc. (Figure 19.2) It then uses the answers to determine whether it would be a good idea to consult a professional psychiatrist for further examination.

SCORES

If you scored...	You may have...
54 & up	Severe depression
36 - 53	Moderate/severe depression
22 - 35	Mild to moderate depression
18 - 21	Borderline depression
10 - 17	Possible mild depression
0 - 9	No depression likely

This is not meant as a diagnosis tool.

FIGURE 19.2: The scoring criteria for Mayo Clinic's depression test. It explicitly states that it is not meant to be used as a diagnostic tool.

An organization known as the Foundation for Informed Medical Decision Making (FIMDM)[1] has worked to expand upon the traditional diagnostic decision support process by focusing primarily on treatment decisions that take into account the patient's personal preferences in terms of health outcomes. Specifically, they use video clips to depict the possible outcomes of each treatment, giving the patient an idea of what the experiences relating to these outcomes will be like and better preparing the patient for the clinical decision-making process. FIMDM provides tools for many diseases, ranging from breast cancer to coronary artery disease. Offline CD ROM-based software also exists for diagnostic decision support. Interestingly, in some instances, such software actually provides deeper and more detailed diagnostic information than what is available on the World Wide Web. For example, the American Medical Association has the "Family Medical Guide." This is a multilevel software package consisting of seven different modules:

1. A listing of possible diseases, disorders, and conditions.

2. A map of the human body.

3. A symptom check for the purposes of self-diagnosis and/or hypothesizing.

4. A description of the ideal body.

[1] http://www.informedmedicaldecisions.org/

5. A description of possible injuries and emergencies that require immediate attention.
6. Diagnostic imaging techniques.
7. Suggestions for how the patient's caregivers may properly care for him.

The program contains a large number of symptom flow charts, accessible through either pain-site diagrams or body system diagnosis. This is where the patient's personal inquiry comes into play: each chart contains a series of questions that require him/her to answer "Yes" or "No." Upon completion, the answers are tallied up, and a patient-specific recommendation is made based on the answers provided.

There is a considerable disagreement regarding how specific computer-generated medical advice should be provided. The common belief is that too much computerized advice will break patient/clinician relations, leading patients to self-diagnose without any formal evaluation. Fortunately, medical websites offering decision support usually give a list of options rather than a rigid diagnosis. They will usually assess patient symptoms and then devise a list of possible causes (with links for further reference), aiding him/her in deciding what condition they might have while leaving a reasonable amount of leeway to make a decision on their own. The Mayo Clinic website, for example, offers "Health Decision Guides" for a small number of diseases and conditions. These give basic information, such as the nature of the condition at hand, how it is diagnosed, and a detailed description of possible treatment options (including the pros and cons of each treatment). Each page is complemented by video clips that visually and verbally describe the condition. The purpose of such a page is not necessarily to provide the patient with a specific diagnosis but to give them more concrete background information so that they may come to a more informed conclusion with his/her clinician.

19.6 Human-Intensive Techniques

In general, there are two factors that must be considered when evaluating a clinician's ability to make a successful diagnostic or treatment-related decision: the extent of the clinician's medical knowledge and how well he/she is able to apply it to clinical problem solving [30]. Thus, when building a CDSS, one should account for the knowledge it will embody along with how it will be applied. Pragmatically, a system with little knowledge will be perceived as "dumb," while one with a limited number of knowledge-based applications will be perceived as exercising "poor judgment." Therefore, when designing a CDSS, we need a concrete methodology for implementing a knowledge base that is both extensive and reliable. This means that one will need to understand how to implement an appropriate amount of factual knowledge along with a reliable system of judgment that reaches the root of the problem and solves it, while discarding any irrelevant information.

In this section, we study a critical component of implementing a steady knowledge base, namely, the acquisition of knowledge through basic human interaction. We study how knowledge is acquired by analyzing real-life thought processes, as well as knowledge and beliefs, and then we use the results of this analysis to create a factual/judgmental knowledge base. This information is normally obtained by either physically interacting with real-life clinical "experts" or giving them direct access to a computer program that stores whatever information they can offer into its knowledge base.

There are quite a few reasons for why "expert" knowledge is valuable in clinical decision support [30]:

- **Knowledge preservation:** We wish to obtain private knowledge that would not otherwise be documented or recorded. This is so that, if the expert retires or passes away, the more esoteric but important aspects of his/her knowledge will remain within the CDSS.

- **Knowledge sharing:** Expert knowledge, once implemented into a CDSS, can be distributed among different platforms and used for external purposes such as training programs.
- **Forming a solid basis for decision aiding:** Expert knowledge may be used to create updated software that allows for better decision making.
- **Revealing the expert's underlying skills:** When an expert's knowledge is regularly used, her underlying skills and strategies are demonstrated, some of which could prove very useful in aiding decision making.

Of course, heavily emphasizing the concept of consulting "experts" for knowledge begs the question: What actually constitutes an "expert"? Furthermore, how do we distinguish an expert's knowledge and line of reasoning from those of an amateur or novice? While it is obvious that an expert will have extensive experience in her domain of expertise, equally important is her ability to build upon this knowledge and successfully adapt to changes in the environment, medical landscape, etc. In other words, a true "expert" understands the "how" rather than just the "what." This skill is, unfortunately, quite difficult to replicate with factual knowledge alone. Thus, a method must be developed that will allow a CDSS to learn and function in the exact same manner as a real-life expert.

One possible method for implementing these skills is **knowledge acquisition** (or KA). This is the process of identifying and utilizing knowledge from external sources, such as real-life experts and medical documentation, and then implementing it in such a manner that it may be evaluated and then validated by either the expert or the system itself. While biomedical literature often discusses the design of knowledge-based systems and evaluates their performance, "reproducible" methods of knowledge acquisition are usually documented elsewhere (despite being strongly correlated with the creation of a CDSS).

A knowledge base may include the relationships between potential findings and diagnoses (conceptual/factual knowledge), guidelines and algorithms for successful use of this knowledge (procedural knowledge), and a system of logic for applying these guidelines/algorithms within the underlying knowledge structure (strategic knowledge). These three knowledge branches combine to form a functional decision support system, with each form of knowledge being taken into account and then possibly expanded on.

It is possible for knowledge to be obtained through more than one expert, either through a consensus survey or by manually studying the opinions of several and then combining them into one knowledge base. Knowledge can be obtained from a variety of human experts and then translated into a form that was readable to a Decision Support System, either through the input of a human knowledge engineer or through a computer system known as a **knowledge authoring system**. This is a computer system that reads and interprets knowledge from multiple sources and then combines it into a form that is linguistically and semantically consistent. Once this is done, the scaled knowledge representation is implemented into the system as either the core knowledge base or an extension of the existing base.

19.7 Challenges of CDSS

Despite the promise CDSS holds, many physicians still choose not to use them. This is because, in spite of how much they have evolved over the last forty years, there remains many challenges in the field of clinical decision support. These correspond to factors such as machine adaptability (i.e., how capable the machine is of "learning" new medical knowledge while discarding outdated knowledge), clarity of treatment options, and how adept the machine is at making suggestions without interfering too much with patient/clinician interaction.

19.7.1 The Grand Challenges of CDSS

In 2008, a team of researchers at various medical schools compiled a list of what they considered to be the ten "Grand Challenges" of clinical decision support [31]. The ten challenges are split into three categories:

19.7.1.1 Need to Improve the Effectiveness of CDSS

Arguably the most important challenge in the field of clinical decision support is an ongoing need to improve the effectiveness of system interventions in patient/clinician matters. This means that CDSS should act as successful intermediaries between the clinician and the patient, offering diagnostic and/or treatment suggestions that are clear and useful without being intrusive. There are five mutually inclusive methods for improving these interventions.

1. Improve the human-computer interface: The human-computer interface should be as clear and intuitive as possible. An equally important need is for the interface to be designed in such a manner that clinical workflow is left uninterrupted. In their current form, CDSS tends to give alerts that are ignored by the clinician, due to a relatively poor human-computer interface. CDSS should be able to interact with the user by either unobtrusively pointing out the issues that the clinician has overlooked or adding significant pieces of knowledge to the general workflow or decision-making process, so that valid decisions may be made even if the clinician initially overlooked important details.

2. Summarize patient-level information: It might be humanly impossible to remember every major detail of a particularly complicated patient's data. However, in any case, clinicians need to be able to recall the most important facts and conclusions about the patient. Therefore, the CDSS must be able to intelligently give a quick summary of her clinical data and then create a brief synapse of the patient's medical history, current medical conditions, physiological patterns, and current treatments [31]. The patient data summarizer must also be able to summarize all the patient data in a manner that there exists a set of indicators that are able to give "at a glance" assessments of patient status. Additionally, automatic displaying of deeper and more specific clinical decision support should be possible with better data-driven derivation of a patient's condition as well as any related data available.

3. Prioritize and filter recommendations to the user: A CDSS should be able to give information that is useful specifically to the patient at hand. This information should be evaluated and prioritized based on factors such as expected mortality (or morbidity reduction), patient preference and lifestyle, cost, the general effectiveness of the treatment (if applicable), how much it would affect the patient's own comfort or external health, how much coverage is allowed by their insurance, genetics and health history, the clinician's own success history, etc. Problems typically arise from the clinician's own time restraints and the patient's limited ability to administer a large number of medications to himself or quickly make multiple difficult lifestyle changes. The biggest of these is the need to consider conflicting decision values, determining how to prioritize them and then rank them in the corresponding order, while ensuring the number of recommendations is still manageable by the clinician (i.e., reduce "alert fatigue").

4. Combine recommendations for patients with comorbidities: A major problem with today's clinical care guidelines for conditional and medicinal management is that most of them neglect the important issue of patients (especially the elderly) having multiple comorbidities and medications. In fact, the general lack of acknowledgment for existing comorbidities and issues is cited as a major reason for the underutilization of clinical guidelines by patients [31]. For example, a clinician may be seeking to treat a newly diagnosed diabetic patient but not recognize that the patient also has, for example, chronic obstructive pulmonary disease (COPD). Thus, the clinician's treatment suggestions for treating the patient's diabetes might significantly hinder treatment of this other condition. CDSS need to be able to take this important issue into account by weeding out the guidelines that are either redundant or intrusive of the patient's current treatment. One suggestion is for CDSS to combine the recommendations of two or more guidelines (each corresponding with both the condition at hand and any existing comorbidities) and present this combined suggestion to the clinician.

5. Use freetext information to drive clinical decision support: It is commonly believed that at least 50% of patient information is in the freetext portions of an electronic health record. This is the portion that allows the clinician to provide her own commentary on a patient's condition without the restraints of specialized questions. The information contained in freetext could prove very useful in giving more specific interventions and implementing existing patient information that would not otherwise be mentioned in the medical record.

19.7.1.2 Need to Create New CDSS Interventions

1. Prioritize CDS content development and implementation: Logically, the goal of decision support content should be to provide the most accurate and relevant information to the clinician without compromising financial cost too much. Unfortunately, successful implementation of this often takes many years. Prioritizing content implementation (i.e., interventions for improving patient safety, chronic disease management, preventive health interventions, etc.) must take various factors into account, such as the intervention's inherent value to the patient, the cost of healthcare, the reliability of the data, any difficulties that might arise in implementation, and the clinician's or patient's own views of the information's relevance [31]. While this system of data prioritizing might lead to disagreement in terms of how to properly implement future CDSS, it would significantly increase the use of the most valuable CDSS; greatly impacting the cost, safety, and quality of patient healthcare. It is very possible that, over time, this approach to prioritizing clinical decision support content may be superseded by a more refined approach.

2. Mine large clinical databases to create new CDSS: It goes without saying that there are many new patient guidelines and CDS interventions that are waiting to be developed and utilized. To establish these guidelines, we must be able to develop and test new algorithms and techniques that allow researchers to mine large data sets and expand the total knowledge base, while consequently improving CDS interventions. Similarly, a system that is able to search through scientific literature and then mine data from it to suggest potential clinical decision support guidelines would be quite useful. In other words, CDSS should be able to "learn" from large databases. Such a broad task creates quite a few challenges for the designer. In addition to the technical concerns that come with creating and implementing these algorithms, we must also address the many social and political issues associated with using such large databases. For example, as these resources cross institutional/organizational boundaries, we will need to be able to maintain patient privacy.

19.7.1.3 Disseminate Existing CDS Knowledge and Interventions

1. Disseminate best practices in CDS design, development, and implementation: Many healthcare organizations have been very successful with clinical decision support. Under scrutiny, these organizations tend to share common threads relating to issues such as design, communication, clinical practice style, and management [31]. Unfortunately, this information is usually not widely available to other organizations that are looking to adopt clinical decision support. Thus, we need to develop stronger methods for identifying and executing optimal CDS practices. A possible solution is to establish a measurement system for identifying the strength and feasibility of decision support practices. The CDS implementation process would be structured in a manner that allows information from successful users to be easily accessed and utilized by others. The establishment of methods to share successful CDS implementations and experiences would greatly benefit further research and development of CDSS.

2. Create an architecture for sharing executable CDS modules and services: The next step is to create an efficient means for sharing successful CDS modules. This could be done either remotely or through an installer. Either way, the central goal is for an electronic health record to be able to "subscribe" to these services while allowing healthcare organizations to implement their own interventions with little extra effort [31]. An important component of this challenge is to identify and standardize both the definitions and interfaces of the data required by the different CDS modules. Additionally, the architecture should have a broad enough encasing of clinical knowledge that many different inferences can be made through it. It should describe the general intervention device used (alert, order set, etc.) while still allowing for experimentation and competition. Such an implementation will help to overcome several of the barriers that come with implementing clinical decision support, as well as speed up the transition from research finding to widespread practice (a process that is estimated to take up to 17 years). Ideally, future research articles and consensus statements focused on CDSS should include a sharable CDS module in their standard format.

3. Create Internet-accessible clinical decision support repositories: The goal in this case is to create a number of Internet-accessible portals for high quality clinical decision support knowledge systems. These services should be easily downloaded, maintained, modified, installed, and used on any Certification Commission for Healthcare Information Technology (CCHIT) recognized electronic health record system [31]. Naturally, there needs to be a set of firm standards for accessibility of such a system, along with different trust levels and business models to maintain durability. The repositories should support local use of content in various healthcare organizations and also local customizations while being able to respond to system upgrades. Formalized knowledge management must be established and made available to users, so that diverse knowledge for various organizational stakeholders can be utilized. Similarly, we need to ensure that the system performs inference and guidance properly and that errors do not arise when new knowledge is implemented. This is crucial so that healthcare organizations and practitioners do not need to reinvent their own rules or interventions.

19.7.2 R.L. Engle's Critical and Non-Critical CDS Challenges

R.L. Engle, Jr., a professor at Cornell University, has extensively researched the problems that come with implementing CDSS and came up with a list of other factors that he believes contribute greatly to their lack of widespread use. He divides them into two separate categories: "Critical" and "Non-Critical" issues [32].

19.7.2.1 Non-Critical Issues

Some of the non-critical issues he describes include:

1. **The dubious reliability of computers:** Computers, like all technology, are known to occasionally falter. This, of course, poses a significant danger to clinicians attempting to use them for clinical decision support, since they could potentially fail at the most inopportune times.

2. **The overall complexity of computer systems:** Computers, let alone CDSS, usually have a learning curve. Unfortunately, many clinicians do not have the time to learn the underlying nuances of computer systems. Thus, CDSS are regarded as being inefficient and unnecessary to them.

3. **Fear of competition among clinicians regarding the effectiveness of their CDSS:** While a certain amount of competition among clinicians may be useful in continuing the progression of clinical decision support, too much of such competition could seriously hinder it and possibly result in bad relations among clinicians.

4. **The generally limited nature of these programs:** Most CDSS contain very limited knowledge bases, often specializing in one particular field of medicine. Thus, many clinicians will need to invest in several different systems (each with their own unique knowledge bases) so that they may obtain a broad range of clinical decision support options.

19.7.2.2 Critical Issues

One of the "critical" issues Engle describes with CDSS is the impossibility of developing a consistently adequate database and functional set of rules/conditions. Low accuracies in practical performance are unlikely to attract a typically busy clinician to the possibility of using a CDSS.

Another "critical" issue is the relative inaccessibility of CDSS. They are usually not implemented into large-scale information systems. While they have proven quite successful when used in limited domains (such as diagnosing a single illness), it is less clear how useful they are for broader problem domains. University of California–Berkeley professors Stuart Russell and Peter Norvig have suggested that this is largely because, unlike fields such as organic chemistry, the field of medicine lacks a general theoretical model and is consequentially fraught with massive uncertainty [33]. University of New Mexico professor George Luger and colleague William Stubblefield elaborate on this observation by suggesting five "deficiencies" in the technology behind expert systems that significantly hinder clinical decision making [34]. These deficiencies are as follows:

1. Shallow domain knowledge (i.e., a rather poor understanding of human physiology).
2. A lack of robustness and flexibility. Computer systems are unable to solve, or even recognize their inability to solve, a problem that lies outside their knowledge bases. This makes them incapable of devising effective strategies for solving problems outside their knowledge bases.
3. A marked inability to give detailed explanations of conditions and decisions.
4. Difficulties in verifying the validity of a decision.
5. An inability for such systems to learn from their own experience.

Another major shortcoming of CDSS, according to Engle, is their inability to properly work with specialized data. In order for CDSS to gain further acceptance within the medical community, they must be able to work with all kinds of data. The root of this problem can be divided into two broad categories: technical design issues and human-computer interaction [32].

19.7.3 Technical Design Issues

There are several problems that need to be taken into account in terms of the technical design.

19.7.3.1 Adding Structure to Medical Knowledge

In order to properly function, CDSS need a strong understanding of their underlying domains [7]. Bare facts do not suffice. Knowledge Representation is intended to provide CDSS with information that fleshes out the meaning behind these "facts" so that they are clear to the user. The knowledge representation scheme combines with basic domain-related facts to create the core knowledge base. Within the last 25 years, researchers have created various knowledge representation schemes, ranging from simple logic predicate lists to large network structures. The strength of a knowledge representation schema has a significant impact on both the types of problems being solved and the methodology for solving them.

19.7.3.2 Knowledge Representation Formats

In general, knowledge representation schemas fall into one of four categories [7]: logic, procedural, graph/network, or structured.

Logic-based knowledge representation was the first form of representation to gain significant mainstream appeal in the field of artificial intelligence. It is generally represented in terms of propositions, which are worldly declarations deemed to be either true or false. Once a series of propositions has been established, some of them may be combined to form sentences, which may in turn be represented by variables such as P or Q and then combined to form compound declarations such as "P and Q," "P or Q," etc. These statements must be utilized in their entirety. We cannot take a part of a statement and then use that alone to devise new declarations. Fortunately, there exists a form of logical representation that will allow us to split statements and create new declarations from these splits. This is called **First Order Logic** (or, in mathematical terms, "Predicate Calculus"). This relieves us of the limitations inherent to basic variable declarations by allowing us to have "variables within variables." This newfound sense of flexibility has proven successful in making logic-based knowledge a viable form of expert system development. In fact, the popular programming language PROLOG was designed specifically for logical research and programming.

Another form of knowledge representation is *Procedural Knowledge Representation*. This is based on the fact that logic-based representations are generally declarative, meaning they are made up of True/False statements and any questions presented are answered through standard logic inference [7]. For example, if we are diagnosing a disease like anemia associated with a value of "increased" for the Mean Cell Value (or MCV), we will need to look through all the relative logic predicates and then find those that have "increased" as a value, returning any that match what we are looking for. Procedural methods, on the other hand, give more detailed information about how the knowledge base may be used to answer a question. Rather than merely being a fact checker, it gives us a "process" to look for (i.e., "IF MCV is increased, THEN conclude pernicious anemia"). These procedural statements are provided in the form of "rules." Since MYCIN, rule-based systems have been the dominant form of expert system design within the medical industry, because of how detailed yet comprehensive they are.

Another form of knowledge representation is the *Network*. This is essentially a tree of "nodes" (representing facts, events, etc.) and the edges linking them. The flexibility of network systems has been particularly influential in the rise of Bayesian expert systems since the early 1990s. Even more significantly, the ability for networks to capture knowledge forms that would otherwise be difficult to map (like causual form) has made them viable forms of medical expert systems.

Finally, there is *Structured Representation*. This depicts knowledge in a nested, categorical manner. What makes structured representation a viable option is that it is humanly easy to read and modify. An example of a structured representation being used is in the Trial Bank Project. The Trial Bank project is a joint project between the *Annals of Internal Medicine* and *JAMA* to implement the designs and outcomes of randomized trials into structured knowledge bases. Its goal is to gradually transform text-based literature into a shared, machine-interpretable resource for evidence-adaptive CDSS [35].

19.7.3.3 Data Representation

There are many different methods of structurally representing the data [7]. Some are better suited for certain tasks than others.

The first structural data representation format to gain significant mainstream acceptance is **framing** [36]. Frames are data structures that encase the core concept that is being described along with information detailing how the concept is carried out. For example, the concept of "eating out" could be represented as:

Concept: Eating Out
Location: Restaurant
Actions: Ordering food (procedure), Paying (procedure)

Another popular form of data structuring is database management. In general, there are two types of databases that are found in the medical field: relational and object oriented. **Relational Databases** are structured much like Microsoft Excel spreadsheets. They consist of a series of "records," each containing a fixed number of fields. There is a designated "primary field" in the record structure, with the remaining fields directly related to it. The records are collected and then combined into a single table, with each row representing an individual record and each column representing the record's features. A major benefit of relational databases is their flexibility: Additional columns may be added, containing additional fields, deepening the information presented. Unfortunately, a column generally cannot hold anything more complex than a single feature. Thus, in instances where there is a need for a "record within a record," **Object-Oriented Database Management Systems (OODBMS)** are preferable. OODBMS's differ from relational systems in that they allow more complex data types to be stored in fields [37].

Structured query language (SQL) may be used to inquire about a database. Unfortunately, SQL does not allow the user to draw inferences from the data. While specific knowledge processing may not be available for databases, the ability to use higher level languages to analyze them is a major advantage.

19.7.3.4 Special Data Types

In the field of decision support, it is not enough to simply have a large medical domain. Specialized data types need to also be accounted for and addressed by the system. In addition to basic descriptions of the core features in patient diagnosis (current or past diseases, any tests performed, any drugs used, etc.), we need information about how they change and evolve over time [7]. To obtain this information, we may be required to study fields outside the core problem domain. For example, to understand the possible effects of a certain medication on a patient, we first need a basic understanding of human physiology. This is a major challenge for CDSS designers, since there exists no standardized format for depicting the research and development of a field such as physiology.

Handling dynamic knowledge bases has been a major challenge in the field of artificial intelligence since it was first devised. James F. Allen was the first person to offer a potential solution for handling such data. He suggested a format consisting of "time points" and "time intervals."[38] Unfortunately, this method is believed to be computationally infeasible when used to explain all possible cause-and-effect relationships [39]. Handling time-sensitive information requires not only a representation of instances and intervals but also a method of handling the time-sensitive concepts used by humans. Unfortunately, this is very difficult to represent through a computer. Basic concepts such as distinguishing between future and past events, recognizing different time dependencies (i.e., whether time is being measured by months, days, or years) and concurrency are mandatory for clinical decision support systems to be able to successfully determine prognoses, treatment outcomes, etc.

Ever since Allen's model was proposed, several efforts attempted to expand upon it and address these crucial issues. For example, Shahar and Musen, in 1992, proposed a model that also represents events as time intervals with beginnings and ends. However, these intervals also contained unique parameters indicating the types of events being represented with them, strengthening the causal relationships between them. Constantine F. Aliferis and his colleagues recognized that systems such as QMR, Iliad and MYCIN actually worked well in their respective domains despite lacking any sorts of temporal data models [40]. Furthermore, they argue that there exists no real evidence of implicit temporal models necessarily giving better results than explicit models. Thus, they suggested that explicit modeling is more useful for some activities (such as prognosis) than for others (such as diagnosis). Their overall conclusion is that systems relying on dynamic clinical data require explicit temporal methodologies, while those with relatively fixed knowledge bases and greater dependency on human input are able to perform well with implicit representations.

19.7.4 Reasoning

Because CDSSs were initially designed with "artificial intelligence" in mind, early medical expert systems usually focused on imitating the decision-making processes of real-life experts. That is ironic, given that most early CDSSs such as MYCIN and Pathfinder do not "reason" the way humans do. They have no significant comprehension of human anatomy/physiology, are unable to recognize temporal concepts and (most importantly) have no ability to learn/deduce new facts [7]. However, within their narrow range of knowledge, they have been demonstrated to successfully make decisions on par with a real human expert. Unfortunately, as their domain of knowledge is broadened, performance decreases. Particularly, the ability to make inferences from "first principles" and understand the effects time may have on disease processes are crucial to building robust systems with more human-like capabilities. Fortunately, many promising methods for enabling inferential/temporal reasoning within CDSSs exist. In addition to giving the system more human-like capabilities, they have also reduced the burden of large-scale calculations in networks and have helped in handling conflicting rules within the knowledge base.

19.7.4.1 Rule-Based and Early Bayesian Systems

As previously mentioned, the simplest form of reasoning used in medical diagnostic systems is propositional logic. Logic systems, by definition, apply a system of "locality" to their reasoning. This means that, if we have a statement "if a then b" and a is known to be true, then we conclude that b is true regardless of whatever else is known to be true. While locality may be useful in instances where every fact is either absolutely true or absolutely false, the field of medicine is much more complex than that. If we add the fact that "chest pain is present in esophageal reflux" to our knowledge base, then it is no longer implied that chest pain is necessarily caused by MI. Thus, locality no longer holds true within this knowledge base.

Russell and Norvig have presented three other reasons for the failure of logic-based systems in medical diagnosis. These are laziness, theoretical ignorance, and practical ignorance [33]. Laziness is demonstrated by the system designers not putting a satisfactory amount of effort into the model. Specifically, they may fail to establish a set of conditions that is deep enough to cover every possible rule without exception. Theoretical ignorance, meanwhile, is a realization that there is no uniform theory of medicine to assist with the development of a CDSS. Thus, clinicians may omit important details or conditions due to a lack of knowledge on their part. Lastly, practical ignorance is an acknowledgment that, for any particular patient, we rarely have access to all the necessary details about her even with complete knowledge of the applicable rules.

19.7.4.2 Causal Reasoning

Causal Reasoning is the use of more esoteric domain knowledge to assist with decision making. This is a popular form of reasoning, because real-life clinicians often resort to it when solving very challenging problems. University of Southern California professor Ramesh Patil has argued that causal reasoning has many benefits. Some of which include the ability to describe disease progression, the ability to analyze disease interaction, and the ability to understand certain disease mechanisms.

One of the first medical expert systems to utilize causal reasoning was CASNET [41]. This stored its knowledge as a network of pathophysiologic states, with each knowledge component organized hierarchically in terms of discovery time. For example, signs and symptoms were at the low end of the hierarchy, since they were among the first things to be noticed when diagnosing a disease. Connections between the hierarchy's nodes were typically represented as direct causal relationships, allowing the diseases at the highest level to represent finalized diagnoses. Reasoning is performed by running through a path in the hierarchical tree, from initial findings (i.e. patient signs and symptoms) to a final disease determination.

Two more examples of expert systems that use causal reasoning are the CHF Advisor [42] and ABEL [43] systems. The CHF Advisor uses a qualitative physiological model of its domain, with a "truth maintenance system" (TMS) securing interactions between the different parameters of the knowledge base. The TMS allows the program to determine the potential impact of changes in a variable within the model, so that they may be anticipated during diagnosis. ABEL, like CASNET, models its domain in a three-level hierarchical structure. The difference is that, in ABEL, the highest level of the hierarchy represents clinical states while the lowest level represents electrolyte stores and fluidic movement. One of the most important features of this system is its ability to determine and depict situations where a hypothesis is able to explain only a portion of a finding. This allows for greater flexibility in terms of clinical decision making, giving a less rigid representation of the cause-and-effect relationships between patient signs/symptoms and diseases.

While causal reasoning is a very effective form of reasoning, it has several disadvantages. First of all, it lacks mechanical knowledge of many important diseases, making general disease-tracking systems impossible to successfully implement (although causal knowledge may be implemented more trivially in systems with such broad domains). Another problem is the ambiguity in terms of how much detail is necessary for a "complete" system. For example, in CASNET, is three levels really enough for a robust expert system, or should there be more? Perhaps the most important problem, however, is a lack of expert-like "understanding." While causal reasoning-based expert systems may possess deep knowledge of their respective domains, they generally do not understand them the way a human clinician normally would. One final issue with causal networks is the matter of temporal relationships between findings.

19.7.4.3 Probabilistic Reasoning

Another popular form of reasoning is *Probabilistic Reasoning*. As Bayesian reasoning fell out of fashion during the 1970s, new reasoning systems known as "belief networks" began to develop. These were directed acyclic networks consisting of nodes containing both conditional and probabilistic data. These nodes had parent-child relationships (with the parent nodes "pointing" to their children). The effects the parent nodes had on their children were represented by conditional probability tables.

What made these networks popular was their ability to recognize the conditional distinctness of different findings—a task that was very difficult with Bayesian networks (particularly in large domains). This was accomplished through the use of causal relationships when designing the networks along with catch-all probability estimates (or "noise parameters"), allowing for a significant amount of leeway in terms of "correctness."

19.7.4.4 Case-Based Reasoning

Case-based systems can be described as follows: A "case" is a piece of knowledge suggesting an experience that teaches a lesson crucial to the reasoner's ability to reach his/her desired conclusion [7]. Case-based systems have two distinct components: The case itself and an index for retrieving it. Each individual case, meanwhile, has three components: The problem/situation description, the solution, and the outcome. The "problem/situation description" gives the situation and/or problem at hand. The "solution" describes the process of solving the problem. The result of a solution (success or failure) is the "outcome." Each case is accessed through the case index. To solve a problem in this fashion, we need to be able to match the current problem to a previous experience. Advocates of this approach to reasoning argue that this has the following advantages: an ability to solve more open-ended problems, an ability to solve them quickly and nonalgorithmically, and an ability to work with complex cases.

Unfortunately, case-based reasoning has several drawbacks. In larger knowledge bases, efficient indexing is a major concern. There is much debate regarding issues such as whether high or low level features should be factored into index construction and how to design a general framework for indexes. Nevertheless, case-based reasoning has proven to be very successful in CDSS construction and continues to be used in many CDSSs to this day.

19.7.5 Human–Computer Interaction

Perhaps the most important reason for the lack of widespread use of CDSS, according to Heathfield and Wyatt, is that most of them have not been designed to address the problems real-world clinicians normally face [44]. In general, they have been used for one of two purposes: limit the number of diagnostic hypotheses (which most real-life clinicians already excel at) or assist with diagnosis and treatment advice. While systems specializing in the latter have been very well received by the medical community, they are sparse compared to those that specialize in the former. Heathfield and Wyatt argue that the relatively limited number of systems designed for assisting with diagnosistic and treatment-related advice is a major reason for the lack of mainstream attention CDSS have received. The consensus is that a CDSS must account for the clinician's own work habits. It must be accessible during patient care, simple to learn, and easy to use. It can be noted that a stand-alone CDSS requiring a significant amount of input will not be used on a regular basis, due to their cumbersome nature. At the same time, the rather narrow focus of most systems suggests that they will be needed only on rare occasions, at which the simplest solution may be to forgo them altogether in favor of other decision support methods.

There are several other problems with CDSS. The primary one is the risk of there being too much focus put on computer-related technicalities (which language to use, what kind of hardware to use, etc.) at the expense of whichever problems the user is trying to solve. Another is that system designers may use the wrong models for solving problems and miscommunicate the design issues to their users. In addition, the broad and complex nature of clinical decision support makes it very vulnerable to issues such as funding, turnover, and changing organizational structures. Successful implementation of a CDSS requires that all these matters be addressed through specific organizational policies for the creation and utilization of knowledge-based tools.

Fortunately, measures have been taken to address these concerns. Problem Knowledge Couplers (PKCs), are designed with an interface that is simple enough for people outside of the medical industry to comprehend and use. While each coupler represents a single problem, in-house tutorials are included to guide the user in properly utilizing them. Unfortunately, the use of PKCs has not yet become widespread. The main reason why is because PKCs heavily invade a clinician's work environment, and it is unclear how useful they are for a large number of patients. For example, suppose the clinician has a coupler designed for headache diagnosis and management. Because most headaches are easily diagnosed and treated, the number of patients with headaches that would require a specialized computer system is very small. Many clinicians would, thus, seriously question whether such a system is worth the bother if it will only be used on rare occasions.

Perhaps the most effective method of addressing the criticisms lobbied at CDSS is the use of *Electronic Health Record Systems* (EHRSs) and *Computer-Based Physician Order Entry Systems* (CPOESs). EHRSs solve many of the issues pertaining to CDSS by providing a standardized user interface and data model for CDSS design. Access to external data (i.e., laboratory data, pharmaceutical data, etc.) is a standard feature in EHRSs and allows CDSS designers to focus more on data access and user interaction than data input. Alerts and reminder systems are included to reduce user-related errors and oversights. However, EHRS are still in their infant stages and will likely need more development time before reaching mainstream consciousness. As it stands, there exists no EHRS that are able to successfully handle the specific vocabulary and strong ontology required for automating complex guidelines. Until a firm set of standards for EHRSs is established, it is unlikely that support for such detailed knowledge will be implemented anytime soon. CPOESs, meanwhile, have proven very useful in hospital settings. Due to the wide range of legacy systems, implementing packaged EHRS software would be very difficult in such environments. While CPOESs may not have the sophisticated data integration of an "all-in-one" EHRS, they are functional within their limited range.

It is worth mentioning that user interface issues do not necessarily disappear with the use of electronic health record and care provider order entry systems. They simply shift focus. For example, a CPOES or EHRS designed for a drug interaction study during prescription allows this function to run in the background without the user needing to explicitly invoke or shut it down. However, without the ability to modify the parameters (for example, give a warning only when severe interactions are possible) or frequency of advice, clinicians may become hesitant to use the system. Similarly, when complex automated guidelines become feasible, system designers will need to be able to seamlessly provide information while quietly relegating the process into the background. In fact, it is very possible that the biggest challenge in terms of human-computer interaction is that many humans will not wish to take advice from a machine. At this stage, the only possible solution is to let the clinician specify a "threshold of intrusiveness" for the system that, once exceeded, will allow her to ignore it completely.

19.8 Legal and Ethical Issues

Given the sensitivity of information in the field of healthcare, it is quite natural that ethics and legality would be of great concern to both clinicians and CDSS designers. Ever since the birth of clinical decision support, numerous methods have been proposed to regulate what is and what is not allowed in this domain. These addressed issues ranging from the question of who should be allowed to use a "medical computer program" to the dangers present when physician autonomy has been violated. It has been accepted by the community that computers cannot supersede human decision makers. From an ethical standpoint, computers should not be used as a substitute for basic human decision making. Surprisingly, this viewpoint has been advocated at least as much by those who are in support of clinical decision support as it has by those who are against it, due in no small part to the fact that even those who use CDSSs must be wary of breaking individual patient relations.

19.8.1 Legal Issues

Legality is a crucial component of clinical decision support. In order for the field to prosper, there must be a grounded set of a standards for how and where it can be used. Unfortunately, there is quite a bit of ambiguity regarding how this issue should be handled in the field, because medicine and computers have legal standards that are very distinct from one another.

Liability: An important question in the field of clinical decision support is that of who should be held liable for the use, lack of use, or misuse of a computerized system to aid in clinical decision making. In the United States, service providers are legally held accountable for any injuries or fatalities sustained by their users, while other countries tend to have very different standards of accountability for injury or death. In any case, liability may be addressed in one of two ways: either through the **negligence standard** or the **strict liability standard**. These are general standards of liability in cases of injury or death. The difference between the two is that the negligence standard applies to services while the strict liability standard applies to goods or products. There is ongoing debate over whether CDSS are classified as services or goods, because they share characteristics of both. For example, a clinical diagnosis is clearly a service. However, a CDSS is a commercially manufactured item, which could just as easily classify it as a product. To further complicate things, the increasingly wide commercial availability of CDSS begs the question of what the patient's role was in a serious or fatal incident, while a clinician may be considered "negligent" if she accepts a faulty computer diagnosis or gives an errant diagnosis of her own. The clinician may also be held liable if she is believed to have violated basic reasonable person standards. Lastly, there is the question of whether a computer program classifies as an invention or a work of art. Both possibilities raise many legal questions of their own.

19.8.2 Regulation of Decision Support Software

When medical devices were regulated through the Federal Food, Drug, and Cosmetic Act of 1938, they were defined as "instruments, apparatus, and contrivances, including their components, parts, and accessories intended: (1) for use in diagnosis, cure, mitigation, treatment, or prevention of diseases in man or other animals; or (2) to affect the structure of any function of the body of man or other animals [45]." In 1976, congress devised the Medical Device Amendments, requiring that these devices were safe and effective before being sold. While, in 1990, a new regulation was established that emphasized postmarket surveillance rather than premarket approvals [46].

The FDA regards medical software as a device, falling under one of four categories:

1. **Educational and bibliographic software:** This is software intended for use in performing clerical functions such as data storage and accounting, or educational purposes. It is not used for professional medical practice and is, thus, usually not regulated.

2. **Software components:** This is software that is inherently present in medical devices, such as X-ray systems and ventilators. It is typically regulated.

3. **Software accessories:** These are typically attached to or used with physical devices. The corresponding functions include radiation treatment planning, offline study of EEG data and statistical analysis of pulse oximetry data. Because of their widespread professional use, they are actively regulated.

4. **Standalone software:** This is software that has no relation to external medical devices. CDSS fall under this category. There is continuous debate over whether standalone software should be regulated.

19.8.3 Ethical Issues

There are three major issues of ethical concern when it comes to CDSS [47]:

- **Care standards:** This implies that we must provide the best possible treatment without deviating from our personal range of care and avoid deceiving patients. The use of CDSS provides an additional layer of concerns: Do computers help or hinder our attempts at meeting these responsibilities? Do they give us any additional responsibilities? Most importantly, does the technology ultimately improve patient care? If the answer is "Yes," then we may safely say that we have met a crucial responsibility. On the other hand, if the answer is "No," then it is clear that we should not be using this technology.

  Unfortunately, the benefits of decision support (or lack thereof) are not always apparent. In some instances, it is not even possible to reach an overall consensus without experimenting on some kind of test subject at the risk of his/her own personal well-being. The idea of error avoidance is closely related to a general standard of care. Standards constantly evolve in health professions, because they cover the actions that are most successful in achieving specific goals. To fail to adhere to these standards is to increase error risk. Because errors and their consequences are generally regarded as harmful, the obligation to adhere to these standards is an ethical one.

Ethical standards are highly empirical in nature and are, thus, open to revision. New evidence forces frequent changes in these standards. And, to be sure, the precise content of any standard might be open to debate. The "reasonable person" standard, for example, involves truths that are often ambiguous and open to interpretation. This naturally results in major disagreement among otherwise fair and reasonable people. Similarly, a "community standard" sometimes fails to identify a proper distinction between error and success under the conditions with which it may be invoked. Therefore, it may sometimes be totally permissible to violate these standards if such action results in positive outcome and few negative consequences.

In terms of computer-assisted patient diagnosis, the issue is whether or not the use of CDSS increases the risk of error. While accurate diagnosis is usually linked to optimal treatment, this does not always happen. In some cases, patients may be properly treated despite a technically inaccurate diagnosis. While, in others, the patient may be improperly treated despite a technically correct diagnosis. Additionally, computers are capable of suggesting diagnoses that fall outside of traditional clinical contexts (such as in tests for blood-borne pathogens) [7]. In other words, a crucial ethical question we find ourselves asking is whether it is acceptable to use a CDSS in the midst of scientific ambiguity.

In cases such as these, we wish to progress technological development without risking patient treatment. One approach is to exercise "progressive caution." The idea behind this is that medical informatics is and always will be a work in progress, but users and society must ensure that we properly utilize the tools we are given in moving the field forward. We wish to ethically optimize the role of decision support while maintaining appropriate levels of scrutiny and skepticism of our current work in the field.

Ever since people first began addressing ethical issues in the field of medical informatics, it has been recognized that computers, in addition to aiding in the progression of medical science, contribute to changes in basic standards of patient care. These inevitable developments increase the likelihood that computer use will be required of clinicians. While this may seem intimidating to more cautious practitioners, it also opens the door for many exciting developments and opportunities in the field of medical practice.

- **Appropriate use/users:** Naturally, there are many ways in which a computerized decision support system might be misused. It may be used for purposes beyond that with which it was intended, or it may be used without sufficient enough training. There are many problems with decision support system misuse. First of all, a tool that is specially designed with a single purpose in mind is far less likely to work properly (if at all) when used for purposes beyond that with which it was intended. For example, one may very well perform a successful colectomy with a standard kitchen knife or slice a tomato with a scalpel. However, the likelihood of success is much greater when these tools are used for their intended purposes. Similarly, a medical computer system may be improperly used if, for example, it was designed for instructional purposes but used as an aid in clinical decision making instead. If the use of clinical decision support is to become more widespread, it is imperative that new tools and systems are properly documented and used by those who are well trained in their functionality.

  Identifying what constitutes qualification in the use of CDSS is crucial. If a novice uses such a system (especially one who is not a trained physician or nurse), she may rely too much on widely available resources such as online medical references, creating a risk for misinterpretation of the system's output. Meanwhile, if a medical professional uses a CDSS without proper training, she may improperly use the software or may not use it to its full capacity. These concerns may be addressed through a set of strict qualifications and training requirements for the users. Unfortunately, it is unclear what these qualifications should be and how much training should be required of potential users. Furthermore, there is the fear of CDSS being relied on too heavily by users. While computers have come a long way since clinical decision support was first devised in the 1970s, they are still incapable of trumping a human being in terms of cognitive functionality and interpretation. Thus, while such systems are useful in aiding decision making, they should not substitute human decision making.

- **Professional relationships:** Lastly, a major ethical issue in clinical decision support is in the field of professional relationships. Patients often place a massive amount of trust in medical professionals—sometimes too much. Meanwhile, many physicians put too little trust in patients and their judgment. This paradigm has led to the concept of "shared decision making," which is the idea that patients and caregivers should work together to make important clinical decisions. Evidence suggests that this is the most effective form of human-to-human decision making. If a computer is to be used in aiding these decisions, it must be evaluated in the exact same way.

  There are two important ethical problems that come into play here. The first is that the computer will create a barrier between the patient and the physician. Particularly, ambiguous diagnosis (especially when the stakes are high) is a major concern among both the patient and the physician. When a computer is relied on for decision making, we run the risk of committing the "computational fallacy"—the view that a computer-instigated decision is somehow more valid or accurate than a human decision. This is a potentially dangerous view not just because it undermines the physician's skills at decision making but also the patient's.

  Some of our concern may be alleviated by withholding information about the use of a CDSS from the patient. However, this raises the second important ethical question: Should patients be given this information in the first place? The answer depends on roughly two factors: The patient's general knowledge of medicine and medical statistics, and the clinician's general understanding of patient communication etiquette. In any case, it is inappropriate to use computerized output for the sake of outsmarting patients or forcing them to agree with a professional. On the other hand, as patients themselves gain further access to decision support software, they may use it to challenge the physician's viewpoints and attempt to self-diagnose. As CDSS evolve, this will become an even greater problem, because computers will play a larger role in shared decision making. Thus, overreliance on a computer's decision becomes a major risk, and the patient himself may constitute an inappropriate user.

19.9 Conclusion

Clinical Decision Support Systems provide a great opportunity for physicians to improve both the accuracy of medical diagnosis and the reliability of medical treatment. There are numerous support systems that are currently being used in clinical practice such as DXPlain and Iliad. Each system provides a unique opportunity for clinicians to indicate and diagnose diseases in whatever way he/she desires, allowing them to tailor the system to their personal preferences with regards to both potential diagnoses and interface. In addition to giving a more detailed account of the patient's condition than a single human clinician would be able to, it could potentially give legitimate treatment suggestions the clinician may not have even considered. A varied range of treatment suggestions sharing common symptoms may even indicate multiple health conditions within the patient.

However, while a computer-based decision system may certainly be helpful in clinical decision making, it is not a substitute for human interaction. Computerized systems, at this stage, are still incapable of accurately assessing the often complex symptoms that a patient typically experiences. These systems are also error prone and subject to problems such as poor reliability and misuse by inexperienced clinicians. Finally, they lack the sense of user friendliness that is mandatory for both a patient's assurance and a clinician's understanding of the situation.

Nevertheless, Clinical Decision Support Systems are a very promising option with regards to aiding physicians in diagnostic and treatment-related decisions. Because of their inherently progressive nature, they are expected to continue evolving and remedying the various challenges/obstacles plaguing them. Thus, in due time, they are expected to become an even more viable method of patient decision making than they are currently now.

Acknowledgments

This work was supported in part by National Science Foundation grant IIS-1231742 and the National Institutes of Health grant R21CA175974.

Bibliography

[1] L.T. Kohn, J. M. Corrigan, and M.S. Donaldson. *To Err Is Human: Building a Safer Health System.* National Academy Press, 2000.

[2] Amit X. Garg, Neill Adhikari, Heather McDonald, Rosas-Arellano M., P. J. Devereaux, Joseph Beyene, Justina Sam, and R. B. Haynes. Effects of computerized clinical decision support systems on practitioner performance and patient outcomes: A systematic review. *Journal of the American Medical Association*, 293(10):1223–1238, 2005.

[3] Mary Moore and Kimberly A. Loper. An introduction to clinical decision support systems. *Journal of Electronic Resources in Medical Libraries*, 8(4):348–366, 2011.

[4] R. A. Miller, M. B. First, and L.J. Soffer. The internist-1/quick medical reference project-status report. *Western Journal of Medicine*, 145(6):816–822, 1986.

[5] E. S. Berner, G. D. Webster, A. A. Shugerman, J. R. Jackson, J. Algina, A. L. Baker, E. V. Ball, G. C. Cobbs, V. W. Dennis, E. P. Frenkel, L. D. Hudson, E. L. Mancall, C. E. Rackley, and O. D. Taunton. Performance of four computer-based diagnostic systems. *New England Journal of Medicine*, 330(25):1792–1796, 1994.

[6] Edward Shortliffe. *Computer-Based Medical Consultations: MYCIN.* Elsevier, 2012.

[7] Eta S. Berner. *Clinical Decision Support Systems: Theory and Practice.* Springer, 2007.

[8] Thomas A. O'Callaghan, James Popple, and Eric McCreath. Shyster-MYCIN: a hybrid legal expert system. *Proceedings of the 9th International Conference on Artificial Intelligence and Law*, pages 103–104, 2003.

[9] Rebecca S. Crowley and Olga Medvedeva. An intelligent tutoring system for visual classification problem solving. *Artificial Intelligence in Medicine*, 36(1):85–117, 2006.

[10] Michael J. Lincoln, C. W. Turner, P. J. Haug, H. R. Warner, J. W. Williomson, O. Bouhaddou, Sylvia G. Jessen, Dean Sorenson, Robert C. Cundick, and Morgan Grant. Iliad training enhances medical students' diagnostic skills. *Journal of Medical Systems*, 15(1):93–110, 1991.

[11] Homer R. Warner, Peter Haug, Omar Bouhaddou, Michael Lincoln, Homer Jr. Warner, Dean Sorenson, John W. Williamson, and Chinli Fan. Iliad as an expert consultant to teach differential diagnosis. *Proceedings/the... Annual Symposium on Computer Application [sic] in Medical Care. Symposium on Computer Applications in Medical Care*, pages 371–376, 1988.

[12] Imad M. Tleyjeh, Hesham Nada, and Larry M. Baddour. VisualDX: Decision-support software for the diagnosis and management of dermatologic disorders. *Clinical Infectious Diseases*, 43(9):1177–1184, 2006.

[13] G. O. Barnett, J. J. Cimino, J. A. Hupp, and E. P. Hoffer. DXplain: An evolving diagnostic decision support system. *Journal of the American Medical Association*, 258(1):67–74, 1987.

[14] P. L. Elkin, M. Liebow, B. A. Bauer, S. Chaliki, J. Wahner-Roedler, D. Bundrick, Mark Lee, Steven Brown, David Froehling, Kent Bailey, Kathleen Famiglietti, Richard Kim, Ed Hoffer, Mitchell Feldman, and G. Barnet. The introduction of a diagnostic decision support system (DXplain) into the workflow of a teaching hospital service can decrease the cost of service for diagnostically challenging diagnostic related groups (DRGS). *International Journal of Medical Informatics*, 79(11):772–777, 2010.

[15] William F. Bond, L. M. Schwartz, K. R. Weaver, D. Levick, M. Giuliano, and M. L. Graber. Differential diagnosis generators: An evaluation of currently available computer programs. *Journal of General Internal Medicine*, 27(2):213–219, 2012.

[16] Mark L. Graber and Ashlei Mathew. Performance of a web-based clinical diagnosis support system for internists. *Journal of General Internal Medicine*, 23(1):37–40, 2008.

[17] P. Ramnarayan, A. Tomlinson, A. Rao, M. Coren, A. Winrow, and J. Britto. Isabel: A web-based differential diagnostic aid for paediatrics: Results from an initial performance evaluation. *Archives of Disease in Childhood*, 88(5):408–413, 2003.

[18] Guilan Kong, Dong-Ling Xu, and Jian-Bo Yang. Clinical decision support systems: A review on knowledge representation and inference under uncertainties. *International Journal Of Computational Intelligence Systems*, 1(2):159–167, 2008.

[19] B. Yegnanarayana. *Artificial Neural Networks*. PHI Learning Pvt. Ltd., 2009.

[20] J. M. Jerez-Aragones, J. A. Gomez-Ruiz, J. Munoz-Perez, and E. Alba-Conejo. A combined neural network and decision trees model for prognosis of breast cancer relapse. *Artificial Intelligence in Medicine*, 27(1):45–63, 2003.

[21] M. R. Brickley, J. P. Shepherd, and R. A. Armstrong. Neural networks: A new technique for development of decision support systems in dentistry. *Journal of Dentistry*, 26(4):305–309, 1998.

[22] David E Goldberg. *Genetic Algorithms*. Pearson Education India, 2006.

[23] Hyunjin Shin and Mia K. Markey. A machine learning perspective on the development of clinical decision support systems utilizing mass spectra of blood samples. *Journal of Biomedical Informatics*, 39(2):227–248, 2006.

[24] Latha Parthiban and R. Subramanian. Intelligent heart disease prediction system using canfis and genetic algorithm. *International Journal of Biological, Biomedical and Medical Sciences*, 3(3):157–160, 2008.

[25] Randolph A. Miller. The anatomy of decision support during inpatient care provider order entry (CPOE): Empirical observations from a decade of CPOE experience at Vanderbilt. *Journal Of Biomedical Informatics*, 38(6):469–485, 2005.

[26] K.E. Bizovi, B. E. Beckley, M. C. McDade, A. L. Adams, R. A. Lowe, A. D. Zechnich, and J. R. Hedges. The effect of computer assisted prescription writing on emergency department prescription errors. *Academic Emergency Medicine*, 9(11):1168–1175, 2002.

[27] S. B. Flexner and J. Stein. *The Random House College Dictionary, Revised Edition*. Random House, Inc., 1988.

[28] R. A. Miller. Why the standard view is standard: People, not machines, understand peoples' problems. *Journal of Medicine and Philosophy*, 15(6):581–591, 1990.

[29] Mayo Clinic. Mayo clinic depression test. http://www.mayoclinic.org/diseases-conditions/depression/basics/tests-diagnosis/con-20032977 Accessed: 2014-08-23.

[30] Robert A. Greenes. *Clinical Decision Support: The Road Ahead*. Academic Press, 2006.

[31] Dean F. Sittig, Adam Wright, Jerome A. Osheroff, Blackford Middleton, Jonathan M. Teich, Joan S. Ash, Emily Campbell, and David W. Bates. Grand challenges in clinical decision support. *Journal of Biomedical Informatics*, 41(2):387–392, 2008.

[32] R. L. Engle Jr. Attempts to use computers as diagnostic aids in medical decision making: A thirty-year experience. *Perspectives in Biology and Medicine*, 35(2):207–219, 1991.

[33] S. Russell and P. Norvig. *Artificial Intelligence: A Modern Approach*. Prentice-Hall, 2003.

[34] G. F. Luger and W.A. Stubblefield. *Artificial Intelligence and the Design of Expert Systems*. Benjamin/Cummings Publishing, 1989.

[35] Ida Sim. Clinical decision support systems for the practice of evidence-based medicine. *Journal of the American Medical Informatics Association*, 8(6):527–534, 2001.

[36] M. A. Minsky. A framework for representing knowledge. In *The Psychology of Computer Vision*, McGraw-Hill, 1975.

[37] F. Pinciroli, C. Combi, and G. Pozzi. Object oriented DBMS techniques for time oriented medical records. *Informatics for Health and Social Care*, 17(4):231–241, 1992.

[38] James F. Allen. Towards a general theory of action and time. *Artificial Intelligence*, 23(2):123–154, 1984.

[39] Y. Shahar and M.A. Musen. A temporal-abstraction system for patient monitoring. *Proceedings of the Annual Symposium on Computer Application in Medical Care*, page 121, 1992.

[40] C.F. Aliferis, G.F Cooper, R.A. Miller, B.G Buchanan, R. Bankowitz, and N. A. Guise. A temporal analysis of qmr. *Journal of the American Medical Informatics Association*, 3(1):79–91, 1996.

[41] S. M. Weiss, C. A. Kulikowski, S. Amarel, and A. Safir. A model-based method for computer-aided medical decision making. *Artificial Intelligence*, 11(1):145–172, 1978.

[42] W. Long. Medical diagnosis using a probabilistic causal network. *Applied Artificial Intelligence: An International Journal*, 3(2-3):367–383, 1989.

[43] R. Patil, P. Szolovitz, and W. Schwartz. Causual understanding of patient illness in medical diagnosis. *Seventh International Joint Conference for Artificial Intelligence*, 81:893–899, 1981.

[44] H. A. Heathfield and J. Wyatt. Philosophies for the design and development of clinical decision support systems. *Methods of Information in Medicine*, 32:1–8, 1993.

[45] Louis G. Iasilli. Federal food, drug, and cosmetic act. *St. John's Law Review*, 13(2):425–437, 2014.

[46] V.M. Brannigan. Software quality regulation under the safe medical devices act of 1990: Hospitals are now the canaries in the software mine. *Proceedings of the Annual Symposium on Computer Applications in Medical Care*, 1991:238–242.

[47] K. W. Goodman. *Ethics, Computing and Medicine: Informatics and the Transformation Of Health Care*. Cambridge University Press, 1997.

Chapter 20

Computer-Assisted Medical Image Analysis Systems

Shu Liao
Siemens Medical Solutions
Malvern, PA
shu.liao@siemens.com

Shipeng Yu
Siemens Medical Solutions
Malvern, PA
shipeng.yu@siemens.com

Matthias Wolf
Siemens Medical Solutions
Malvern, PA
mwolf@siemens.com

Gerardo Hermosillo
Siemens Medical Solutions
Malvern, PA
gerardo.hermosillovaladez@siemens.com

Yiqiang Zhan
Siemens Medical Solutions
Malvern, PA
yiqiang.zhan@siemens.com

Yoshihisa Shinagawa
Siemens Medical Solutions
Malvern, PA
yoshihisa.shinagawa@siemens.com

Zhigang Peng
Siemens Medical Solutions
Malvern, PA
zhigang.peng@siemens.com

Xiang Sean Zhou
Siemens Medical Solutions
Malvern, PA
xiang.zhou@siemens.com

Luca Bogoni
Siemens Medical Solutions
Malvern, PA
luca.bogoni@siemens.com

Marcos Salganicoff
Siemens Medical Solutions
Malvern, PA
marcos.salganicoff@siemens.com

20.1 Introduction

Medical imaging is the process to create images of human anatomies and structures for clinical studies. It plays an important role in modern healthcare as it provides high quality human anatomy images to aid disease monitoring, treatment planning, and prognosis. Its applications include, but are not limited to, early detection of cancer, image guided radiation therapy, and prediction of treatment outcome. One of the key challenges in the area of medical imaging is how to effectively extract useful features and information from the image so that insightful understanding of the human structures and organs imaged can be achieved. Nowadays, computer-aided diagnosis/detection (CAD) serves as a powerful analytic tools for medical image analysis. Specifically, advanced image processing techniques such as image enhancement, image segmentation, and image registration offer an efficient and effective way to interpret the human anatomy of interest.

The history of medical imaging can be dated back to 1895, when Wilhelm Conrad Roentgen discovered the X-ray, which can be used to measure the physical absorption ability of short wave electromagnetic waves of different human structures and project them on a 2D image. X-ray served as the basis bone imaging and angiography for screening of vascular malformation in early years. In 1950s, nuclear medicine began to play an important role in diagnostic imaging. One of the most famous imaging techniques in nuclear medicine today is the positron emission tomography (PET). The physical principle of PET is to emit positrons. When decaying, positrons combine with a local electron in the human body and generates two photons in opposite directions. By recording the arrival time of the two photons with the detector surrounding the patient, the metabolic information is obtained and structures with primary cancer can be easily detected.

Ultrasound is also one of the main modalities in medical imaging. Different from X-ray and PET, which are based on ionizing radiation, ultrasound only emits sound waves to the patient. The emitted sound waves pass through different tissues and organs of the patient and reflect back. The echo of the reflected sound waves is recorded and displayed as an image. As a noninvasive imaging technique, ultrasound is particularly useful for applications such as fetus imaging during pregnancy and breast imaging for early detection of cancer.

In 1970s, computed tomography (CT) imaging technique arose. An essential property of CT is that it first allowed multiple tomographic images (i.e., slices) to be obtained, which is different from the 2D projection technique in X-ray images. During the imaging of CT, the X-ray tube rotates around the patient and X-rays passed through the patient from different angles are received by detectors around the patient. Each image slice is reconstructed from multiple projections taken from different angles. CT offers the detailed 3D distribution of X-ray attenuation per volume unit.

The magnetic resonance image (MRI) technique also emerged in 1970s. During the imaging process, MRI scanners generate strong magnetic fields around the patient, and only protons in the human anatomy that are at the right value of the magnetic field resonate. The location of the single protons thus can be determined since the strength of the fields are known. MRI does not use ionizing radiation such as X-ray images and CT. Moreover, MRI normally has better soft tissue discrimination ability than CT. However, the image acquisition time for MRI is typically longer than CT.

Advances in medical technology in recent years have greatly increased information density for imaging studies. This may result from increased spatial resolution facilitating greater anatomical detail, increased contrast resolution allowing evaluation of more subtle structures than previously possible, increased temporal image acquisition rate, or digitization of image data. However, such technological advances, while potentially improving the diagnostic benefits of a study, may result in data overload while processing this information. This often manifests as increased total study time, defined as the combination of acquisition, processing and interpretation times. Even more critically, the vast increase in data may not always translate to improved diagnosis/treatment selection. This is why we are seeing a growing trend of applying advanced machine learning and pattern recognition techniques to medical image analysis.

In this chapter we discuss data analytics in CAD across various medical imaging areas, and describe a series of case studies that apply advanced data analytics in medical imaging applications. These are all examples that leverage clinically motivated image processing and machine learning techniques to extract key, actionable information from the vast amount of imaging data, in order to ensure an improvement in patient care (via more accurate/early diagnosis) and a simultaneous reduction in total study time for different clinical applications. We do not intend to cover the entire space of this fast-growing area, but just to illustrate the potential of data analytics to medical imaging applications.

This chapter is organized as follows: Section 20.2 summarizes the current CAD applications and their related technical contents, including diseases such as lung cancer, breast cancer, colon cancer, and pulmonary embolism. Section 20.3 describes a few case studies to highlight how analytics is used in specific medical imaging applications. Specifically, Section 20.3.1 provides an overview on deep learning techniques applied on automatic prostate MR segmentation task. Section 20.3.2 introduces existing techniques for automatic spine labeling. Section 20.3.3 provides an overview of existing automatic measurement techniques for knee diseases monitoring in clinical applications. Section 20.3.4 introduces existing techniques for PET image attenuation correction without CT images. Section 20.3.5 gives an overview of existing saliency detection methods on medical image analysis. Section 20.3.6 summarizes existing techniques for automatic PET-MR attenuation correction. Finally, Section 20.4 concludes the chapter and points out some future directions.

20.2 Computer-Aided Diagnosis/Detection of Diseases

Computer-aided diagnosis/detection (CAD) has become one of the major research subjects in medical imaging [17]. It is a procedure in radiology that supports radiologists in reading two-dimensional medical images such as X-ray and ultrasound, or volumetric data such as CT and MR scans. CAD tools in general refer to fully automated second reader tools designed to assist the radiologist in the detection of lesions. There is a growing consensus among clinical experts that the use of CAD tools can improve the performance of the radiologist. The proposed integration into the workflow of the radiologist is to use CAD as a second reader. The radiologist first performs an interpretation of the images as usual, while the CAD algorithms is running in the background or has already been precomputed. Structures identified by the CAD algorithm are then highlighted as regions of interest to the radiologist. The principal value of CAD tools is determined not by its stand-alone performance, but rather by carefully measuring the incremental value of CAD in normal clinical practice, such as the number of additional lesions detected using CAD. Secondly, CAD systems must not have a negative impact on patient management (for instance, false positives that cause the radiologist to recommend unnecessary biopsies and follow-ups).

Misinterpretations of lesions and failures to detect abnormalities are the 2 classes of errors in interpreting medical images. Many of the latter errors can be attributed to a phenomenon called "satisfaction-of-search," which occurs when a lesion is not detected because the detection of an initial lesion has satisfied the goal of the reader and reduced the detectability of a second lesion [5]. CAD systems can help to reduce the number of those errors.

From the machine learning and data mining perspective, analytical algorithms in CAD are aimed to either extracting key quantitative features summarizing vast volumes of data, or to enhancing the visualization of potentially malignant nodules, tumors, emboli, or lesions in medical images like CT scan, X-ray, MRI, etc. Most of these algorithms operate in a sequence of three stages:

1. **Candidate generation**: This stage identifies suspicious regions of interest (called candidates) from a medical image. This step is based on image processing algorithms, which try to search for regions in the image that look like the particular anomaly/lesion. While this step can detect most of the anomalies (around 90–100% sensitivity), the number of candidates is extremely high (on the order of 60–300 false positives/image).

2. **Feature extraction**: This step involves the computation of a set of descriptive morphological or texture features for each of the candidates using advanced image processing techniques.

3. **Classification**: This stage differentiates candidates that are true lesions from the rest of the candidates based on candidate feature vectors. The goal of the classifier is to reduce the number of false positives (to 2–5 false positives/series) without an appreciable decrease in the sensitivity.

Image quantification and enhanced visualization algorithms do not necessarily include a classifier, but they often use image processing and pattern recognition algorithms for candidate generation and feature extraction. CAD systems use all three stages described above and aid the radiologist by marking the location of likely anomalies on a medical image. The radiologist then makes a decision whether to conduct a biopsy or other follow-ups. In order to achieve efficient reader review, CAD systems demand as few false positives (2–5 false positives/patient, image) as possible while at the same time achieving high sensitivity ($> 80\%$).

The majority of the CAD systems are dealing with three organs – lung, breast, and colon – but other organs such as brain, liver, and skeletal and vascular systems are also subjected to CAD research. In the following we give an overview of some CAD approaches to different diseases, emphasizing the motivation, the specific challenges in diagnosis and detection, and some key points in the analytical solutions. For more detailed explanations and some other CAD applications, please refer to [17, 18, 3, 44].

20.2.1 Lung Cancer

Lung cancer is the most commonly diagnosed cancer worldwide, accounting for 1.2 million new cases annually. Lung cancer is an exceptionally deadly disease: 6 out of 10 people will die within one year of being diagnosed. The expected 5-year survival rate for all patients with a diagnosis of lung cancer is merely 15%, compared to 65% for colon, 89% for breast, and 99.9% for prostate cancer.

For lung cancer CAD systems are developed to identify suspicious regions called nodules (which are known to be precursors of cancer) in CT scans of the lung. Clinically, a solid nodule is defined as an area of increased opacity more than 5 mm in diameter, which completely obscures underlying vascular marking. Translating this definition into image features is the key challenge. While it is universally acknowledged that solid nodules can be precursors for lung cancer, recently there has been increased interest in detecting what are known as part-solid nodules (PSN) and ground-glass opacities (GGN). A GGN is defined as an area of a slight, homogeneous increase in density, which did not obscure underlying bronchial and vascular markings. GGNs are known to be extremely hard to detect.

One important factor when designing CAD systems for lung images is the relative difficulty in obtaining ground truth for lung cancer. Whereas, for example, in breast cancer virtually all suspicious lesions are routinely biopsied (providing definitive histological ground truth), a lung biopsy is a more risky procedure, with a 2% risk of serious complications (including death). It makes obtaining definitive lung cancer ground truth infeasible, particularly for patients being evaluated for early signs of lung cancer. So very often CAD systems are built using image annotations from multiple expert radiologists. See [11, 20] for more details on lung cancer CAD approaches and systems.

20.2.2 Breast Cancer

Breast cancer is the second most common form of cancer in women, after non-melanoma skin cancer. Breast cancer is the number one cause of cancer death in Hispanic women. It is the second most common cause of cancer death in white, black, Asian/Pacific Islander, and American Indian/Alaska Native women.

Breast cancer is an abnormal growth of the cell that normally lines the ducts and the lobules. X-ray Mammography, despite the ongoing controversy on its cost-effectiveness, is still widely used for breast cancer screening. CAD systems search for abnormal areas of density, mass, or calcification in a digitized mammographic image. These abnormal areas generally indicate the presence of cancer. The CAD system highlights these areas on the images, alerting the radiologist to the need for a further diagnostic imaging or a biopsy [41].

20.2.3 Colon Cancer

Colorectal cancer (CRC) is the third most common cancer in both men and women accounting for approximately 11% of all cancer deaths. Early detection of colon cancer is the key to reducing the 5-year survival rate. In particular, since it is known that in over 90% of cases the progression stage for colon cancer is from local (polyp adenomas) to advanced stages (colorectal cancer), it is critical that major efforts be devoted to screening of colon cancer and removal of lesions (polyps) when still in a early stage of the disease.

Colorectal polyps are small colonic findings that may develop into cancer at a later stage. Screening of patients and early detection of polyps via Optical Colonoscopy (OC) has proved to be efficient as the mortality rate from colon cancer is currently decreasing despite an aging population. CT Colonoscopy (CTC), also known as Virtual Colonoscopy (VC) is an increasingly popular alternative to standard OC. In VC, a volumetric CT scan of the distended colon is reviewed by the physician by looking at 2D slices and/or using a virtual fly-through in the computer-rendered colon, searching for polyps. Interest in VC is increasing due to better patient acceptance, lower morbidity, and the possibility of extra-colonic findings, with only a small penalty on sensitivity if the reader is a trained radiologist. CAD systems are able to exploit the full 3-D volume of the colon and use specific image processing and feature calculation algorithms to detect polyps [52, 2].

20.2.4 Pulmonary Embolism

Pulmonary Embolism (PE) is a sudden blockage in a pulmonary artery caused by an embolus that is formed in one part of the body and travels to the lungs in the bloodstream through the heart. PE is the third most common cause of death in the United States with at least 600,000 cases occurring annually. It causes death in about one-third of the cases, that is, approximately 200,000 deaths annually. Most of the patients who die do so within 30 to 60 minutes after symptoms start; many cases are seen in the emergency department.

Treatment with anti-clotting medications is highly effective, but sometimes can lead to subsequent hemorrhage and bleeding; therefore, the anti-clotting medications should be only given to those who really need. This demands a very high specificity in PE diagnosis. Unfortunately, PE is among the most difficult conditions to diagnose because its primary symptoms are vague, non-specific, and may have a variety of other causes, making it hard to separate out the critically ill patients who suffer from PE. A major clinical challenge, particularly in an emergency room scenario, is to quickly and correctly diagnose patients with PE and then send them on to treatment. A prompt and accurate diagnosis of PE is the key to survival. From the CAD perspective, PE detection is more challenging than lung nodule detection because of the vast network of pulmonary arteries in the lungs and the variable sizes they have, and the varying contrast depending on the quality of the acquisition. Advanced machine learning algorithms such as the multiple-instance learning have shown to achieve good performance in PE CAD [36].

20.3 Medical Imaging Case Studies

In this section we illustrate several case studies in medical image analysis, each of which leverages advanced data analytics for the specific application. They do not belong to the traditional CAD domain, but they provide important aspects of the modern computer-assisted medical imaging systems that rely on sophisticated machine learning algorithms. We will try to give an in-depth description of each case study, highlighting the motivation of the analytical solution, and describing the implementation in some detail. This is by no means a complete coverage of medical image analysis systems, but hopefully readers will gain insights from them and leverage these analytical solutions in their own applications.

20.3.1 Automatic Prostate T2 MRI Segmentation

Prostate cancer is the second leading cause of cancer death for American males. However, if the prostate cancer is detected and treated in its early stage, the survival rate of patients can be significantly increased. Image-guided radiation therapy (IGRT) is one of the major treatment methods

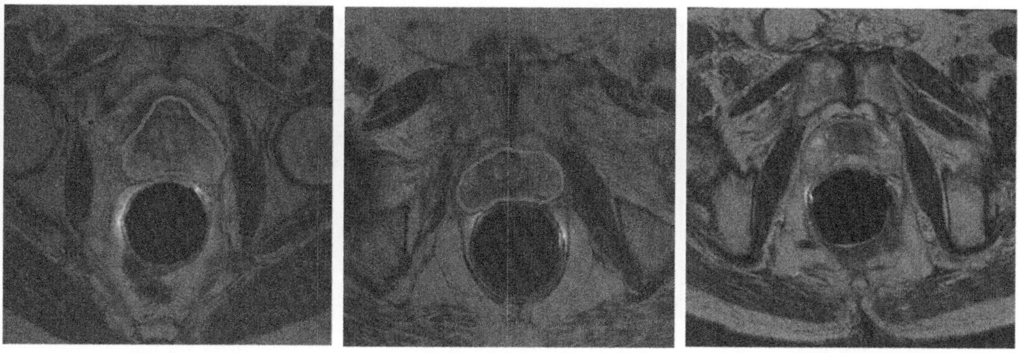

FIGURE 20.1 (See color insert.): Examples of the prostate T2 MR images obtained from three different patients, where the red contours are the segmentation groundtruth provided by an experienced radiation oncologist. Note that significant image appearance variations of the prostate can be observed across the three patients.

for prostate cancer [49]. An important step for IGRT is the accurate segmentation of prostate for treatment planning.

The T2 magnetic resonance image (MRI) is one of the most commonly used image modalities for prostate cancer treatment planning due to its superior soft tissue contrast between the prostate and its surrounding human anatomical structures. There are many novel methods proposed in the literature aim to tackle the prostate segmentation problem in T2 MR images. However, accurate segmentation of the prostate in T2 MR images still remains a challenging task. One of the main challenges is there are large image appearance variations across different patients for the prostate in T2 MR images, which is illustrated in Figure 20.1.

Therefore, how to extract discriminant and robust image features to represent the prostate T2 MR images is one of the key steps for the segmentation process. Hand-crafted features such as the Haar wavelet [38], histogram of oriented gradient (HOG) [16], local binary patterns (LBP) [42], and patch-based representation are widely used in medical image analysis in the literature for data representation. However, their representation power maybe limited to capture all the image appearance variations in prostate T2 MR images. Figures 20.2(b) and (c) show the color-coded difference maps obtained by using the Haar wavelet [38] and HOG [16] features, respectively as voxel signatures and comparing the reference voxel indicated in Figure 20.2(a) with all the other voxels in the image. It can be observed that the reference voxel is similar to many voxels belonging to other anatomical structures by using these two hand-crafted features, which significantly increases the risk of wrong segmentation.

Therefore, as illustrated in Figure 20.2, the common property of hand-crafted features such as Haar, HOG, and LBP is that the feature calculation kernels are fixed and predetermined regardless of the data at hand to study. Therefore, their flexibility and representation power may be varied across different datasets. Intuitively, the optimal features and data representation should be adapted to the patient data at hand. More specifically, the optimal features should also be "learned" from the patient dataset at hand, and this is the basic principle of deep learning [23, 34, 4], which aims to learn features from different abstract levels from the data at hand.

The history of deep learning can be dated back to the 1960s, where the first generation of neural network appeared. A typical neural network structure for the classification problem is illustrated in Figure 20.3.

In order to optimize the model parameters in the neural network, normally back-propagation algorithms [45] were used based on the labeled data. Moreover, in order to learn higher level abstrac-

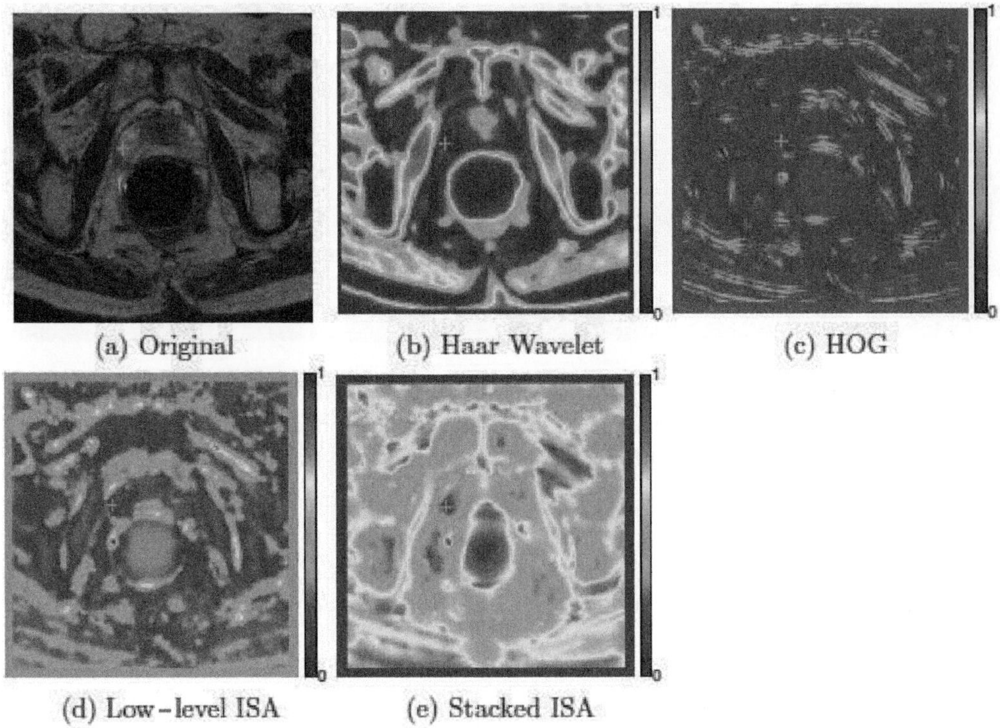

FIGURE 20.2 (See color insert.): (a) The original prostate image, where the green cross denotes the reference voxel. (b), (c), (d), and (e) are the color-coded difference maps obtained by comparing the feature representation between the reference voxel and all the other voxels by using the Haar wavelet [38] feature, HOG [16], low level ISA feature [34], and the stacked ISA feature [34], respectively.

tion information from the data, more layers are required in the neural network. Major drawbacks of back-propagation are: (1) It can be easily stuck at a local minimum; (2) it requires labeled data for optimization, which might be hard to obtain in clinical applications; and (3) it is computationally expensive, especially when more layers are added in the network (i.e., deep networks).

The fundamental breakthrough in learning deep networks occurred around 2006, when the idea was to learn the network in a greedy layerwise manner [4]. More specifically, it learns features one layer at a time with unsupervised learning methods, and features learned from the previous level are served as input for the next level. After training each layer, all the layers can be stacked together to form the deep architectures. Representative deep learning methods include the deep auto-encoder [24], stacked independent subspace analysis (ISA) [34], and deep convolutional neural network [35]. Figure 20.4 shows a typical example of training a deep auto-encoder with restricted Boltzmann machines (RBMs).

As an unsupervised and data specific feature learning framework, deep learning provides a feasible solution to learn the most informative features from the prostate T2 MR images to guide the segmentation. For instance, the stacked ISA [34] network can be adopted.

Figure 20.5 shows a basic ISA network, which takes the 3D image patch centered at each voxel in the prostate T2 MR training images as inputs. The simple units in the first layer aims to capture the squared nonlinear relationships between the patches, and the pooling units in the second layer aims to group and integrate the responses from the first layer to generate higher level abstraction information.

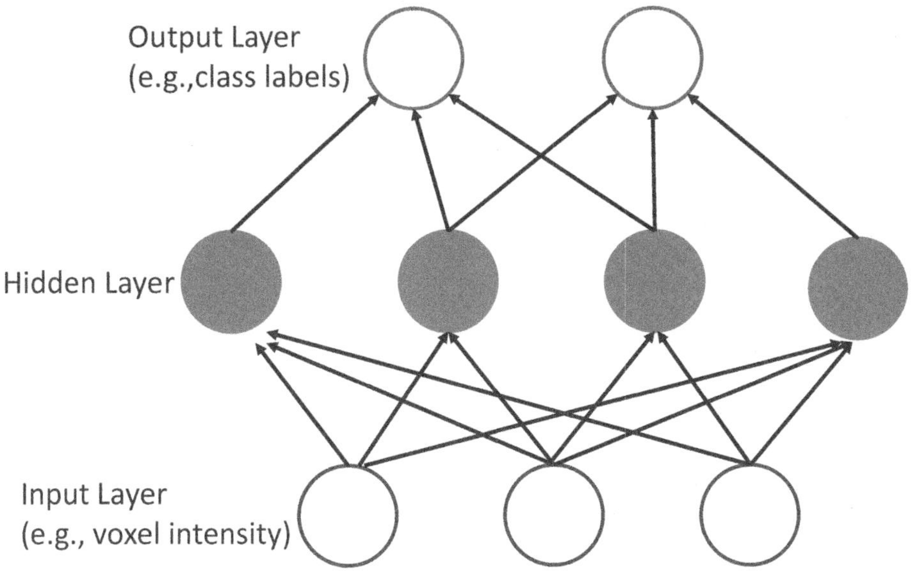

FIGURE 20.3: A typical example of a neural network, where the perceptrons in the hidden layer are learned to weight the features from the input layer in order to predict the correct class label in the output layer.

The basic ISA network can be mathematically formulated as followings: Given N input patches $\vec{x}_i$, it aims to estimate the parameter matrix $W \in R^{k\times d}$ associated with the first layer and the parameter matrix $V \in R^{m\times k}$ associated with the second layer by minimizing the following energy function:

$$\arg\min_{W,V} \sum_{i=1}^{N} \sum_{j=1}^{m} R_j(\vec{x}_i, W, V), \text{where } WW^T = I, \tag{20.1}$$

where $R_j(\vec{x}_i, W, V) = \sqrt{\sum_{l=1}^{k} V_{jl} (\sum_{p=1}^{d} W_{lp} \vec{x}_i^p)^2}$, and I is the identity matrix. d, k, and m denotes the dimension of $\vec{x}_i$, number of simple units, and the number of pooling units, respectively in the ISA network. Figure 20.6 shows typical simple unit structures learned by the basic ISA network from the prostate T2 MR images with $16 \times 16 \times 2$ dimensional patches.

In order to obtain higher level abstraction information, more layers are needed so that the deep ISA network is constructed. First, the low level ISA network is built as illustrated in Figure 20.5 for image patches with smaller sizes. Then, the trained low level ISA network is used as the basic building block to extract higher-level features from larger-image patches in a convolutional manner. The stacked ISA network architecture is illustrated in Figure 20.7.

As shown in Figure 20.2, features learned by the stacked ISA demonstrate superior discriminant and representation power for the prostate T2 MR images, where the reference voxel is only similar to its neighboring voxels with similar anatomical properties.

The learned features from the stacked ISA network can be integrated with any classifier or multiatlases-based segmentation methods to perform the segmentation task. For instance, it can be integrated with SVM [13], Adaboost [21], random forest [8], or sparse representation-based label propagation [37]. Figure 20.8 shows some typical segmentation results on prostate T2 MR images from three different patients by integrating the stacked ISA features with sparse representation-based label propagation [37].

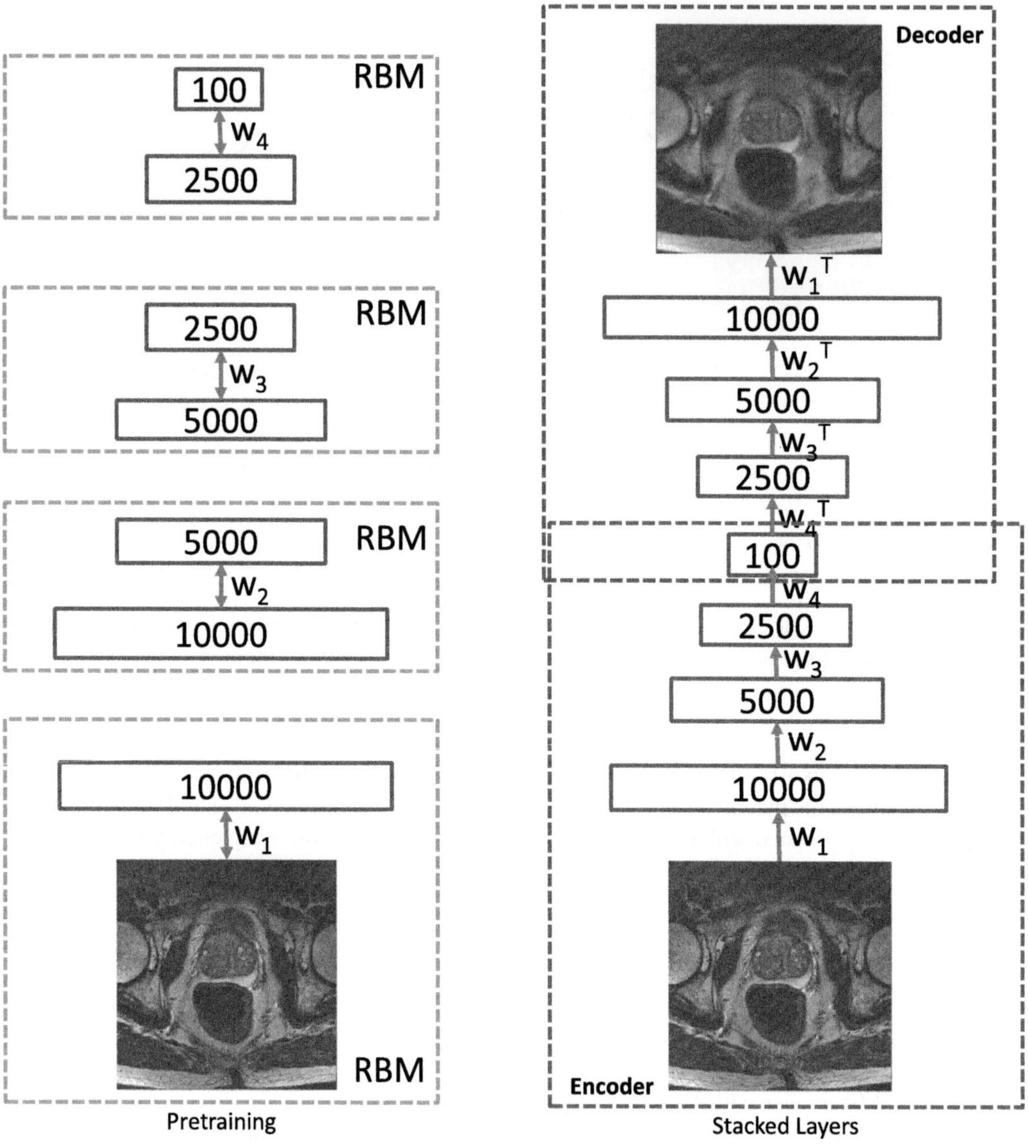

FIGURE 20.4: An example showing the construction of a deep auto-encoder with the restricted Boltzmann machines. In the pretraining process, each layer is independently trained, where the output of one RBM layer is served as the input for the next RBM layer. After the pretraining process, each trained layer is stacked together to form the deep auto-encoder architecture.

20.3.2 Robust Spine Labeling for Spine Imaging Planning

As one of the major organs in the human body, the spine relates to various neurological, orthopaedic, and oncological studies. Magnetic resonance imaging (MR) is often preferred for spine imaging due to the high contrast between soft tissues. However, MR imaging quality is highly dependent on the position and orientation of the slice group. For example, a high-resolution transversal slice group should be positioned in parallel to the intervertebral disc and centered at the junction of the spinal cord. In current MR workflow, high-res slice group positioning is performed manually in a 2D/3D scout scan. Compared to 2D scout, 3D scout a provides comprehensive anatomical context,

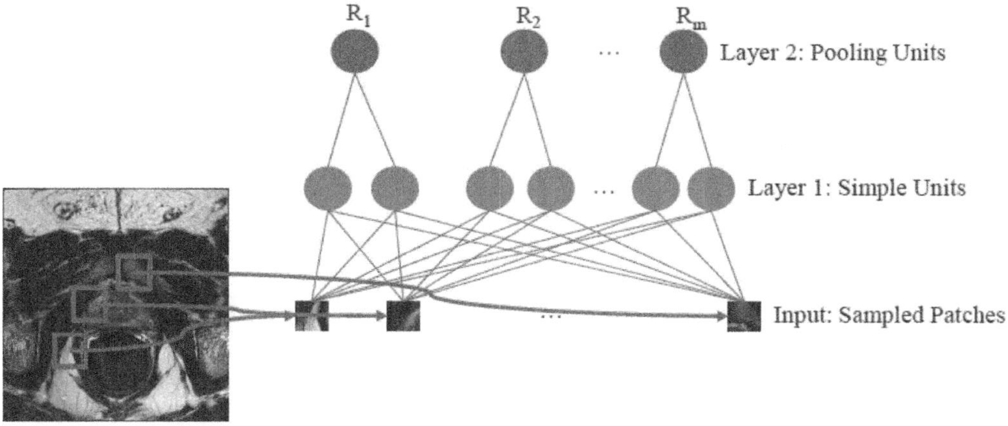

FIGURE 20.5: Illustration of a basic ISA network, where the network takes the image patches sampled from the prostate T2 MR training images as inputs. The basic ISA network contains two layers. In the first layer, it consists of simple units that aims to learn the squared nonlinear structures from the input patches. In the second layer, it consists of pooling units that aims to integrate the responses from the first layer.

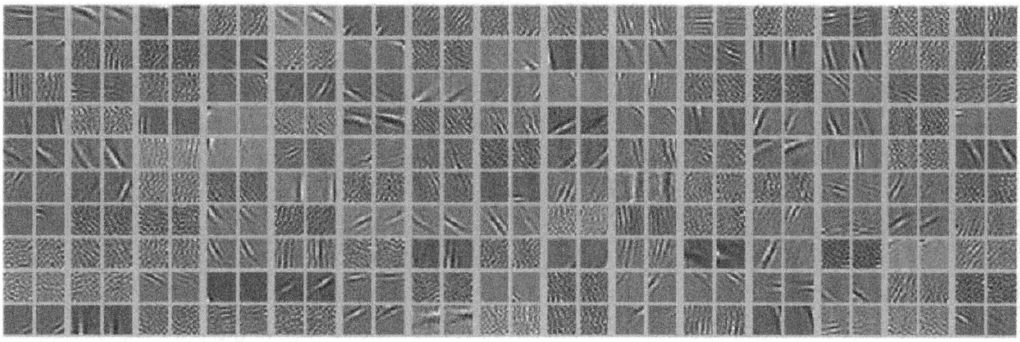

FIGURE 20.6: Typical structures learned from the prostate T2 MR images by the basic ISA network, with patch dimensions $16 \times 16 \times 2$.

which facilitates slice group positioning even in strong scoliotic cases. However, the manual positioning in 3D scout also takes more time due to cross-slice navigation. Therefore, automatic spine detection in 3D scout becomes very desirable to improve MR spine workflow.

Automatic spine detection work in MR can be traced back to the 1980s [12], where a heuristic algorithm is designed to detect lumbar discs in 2D MR slices. Alomari et al. [1] proposed a 2D lumbar vertebrae labeling system incorporating appearance and geometrical priors. However, more complicated spine geometry in 3D (especially for disease cases), and smaller/challenging appearance of cervical vertebrae, would make this approach limiting for 3D MR whole spine labeling. One of the first 3D whole spine detection methods was proposed by Schmidt et al. [47]. Local appearance cues learned by random trees are combined with nonlocal geometrical priors modeled by a parts-based graphical model. Another interesting method presented in [28] focuses on learning disc location in a nine-dimensional transformation space. Iterative marginal space learning is proposed to generate candidates comprising position, orientation, and scale, which are further pruned by an anatomical network. In general, state-of-the-art methods did achieve certain robustness by combin-

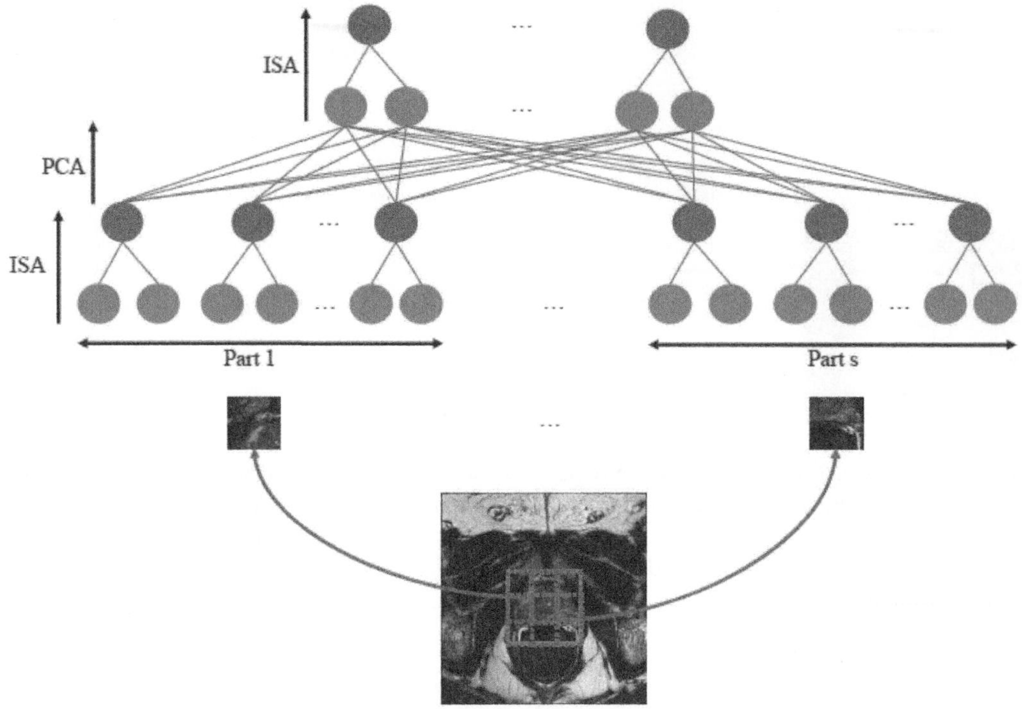

FIGURE 20.7: Illustration of the deep ISA network. The lower level ISA network is first pretrained with smaller image patches. Then, larger image patches are decomposed into *s* overlapping smaller image patches, and each smaller image patch is passed through the pretrained lower level ISA network to extract its own features. The responses from the *s* lower level ISA network are then passed through a PCA process to reduce the feature dimension and served as input to train the higher level ISA network.

ing low-level appearance and high-level geometry information. However, in the presence of severe imaging artifacts or spine diseases, which are more common in 3D MR scout scans, none of existing methods provides evidence of handling these cases robustly. (Note that spine detection algorithms for other imaging modalities [30] may not be borrowed to MR owing to the intrinsically different appearances.)

In fact, two unique characteristics of spine anatomies are mostly ignored in previous works. First, although the spine is composed of repetitive components (vertebrae and discs), these components have a different distinctiveness and reliability in terms of detection. Second, the spine is a nonrigid structure, where local articulations exist in-between vertebrae and discs. This articulation can be quite large in the presence of certain spine diseases. An effective geometry modeling should not consider vertebrae detections from scoliotic cases as errors just because of the abnormal geometry. Building upon these ideas, in this subsection, a spine detection method is proposed by exploiting these two characteristics. Instead of learning a general detector for vertebrae/discs or treating them as completely independent entities, we use a hierarchical strategy to learn "distinctiveness adaptive" detectors dedicated to anchor vertebrae, bundle vertebrae, and intervertebral discs, respectively. These detectors are fused with a local articulated model to propagate information from different detectors handling abnormal spine geometry. With the hallmarks of *hierarchical learning* and a *local articulated model*, this method becomes highly robust to severe imaging artifacts and spine diseases.

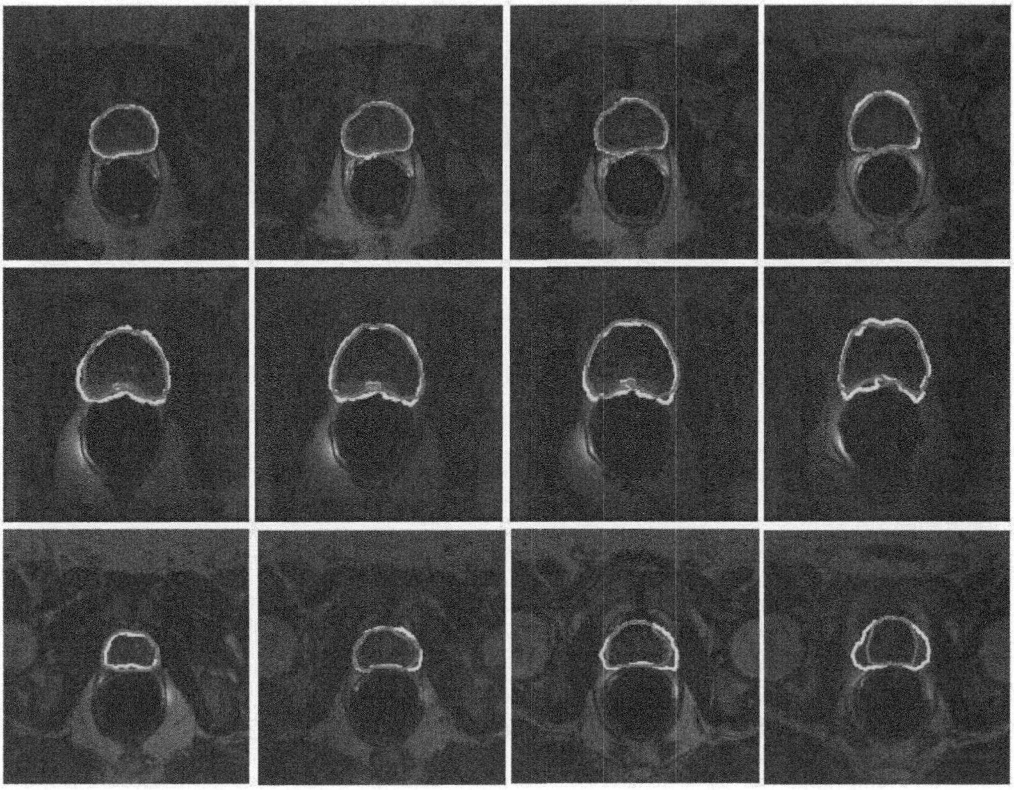

FIGURE 20.8: Typical segmentation results with the features learned from stacked ISA integrating with the sparse representation-based label propagation [37], where the yellow contours are the estimated prostate boundary, and the red contours are the segmentation groundtruths. Each row represents a different patient.

The human spine usually consists of 24 articulated vertebrae, which can be grouped as cervical (C_1-C_7), thoracic (T_1-T_{12}), and lumbar (L_1-L_5) sections. These 24 vertebrae plus the fused sacral vertebrae (S_1) are the targets of spine labeling in most clinical practices.

We define vertebrae and intervertebral discs as $V = \{v_i | i = 1 \cdots N\}$ and $D = \{d_i | i = 1 \cdots N-1\}$, where v_i is the *i-th* vertebra and d_i is the intervertebral disc between the *i-th* and *i+1-th* vertebra. Here, $v_i \in \mathbb{R}^3$ is the vertebra center and $d_i \in \mathbb{R}^9$ includes the center, orientation, and size of the disc. It is worth noting that i is not a simple index but bears anatomical definition. In this paper, without loss of generality, v_i is indexed in the order of vertebrae from head to feet, e.g., v_1, v_{24}, v_{25} represents C_1, L_5, and S_1, respectively.

Given an image I, a spine detection problem can be formulated as the maximization of a posterior probability with respect to V and D as:

$$(V^*, D^*) = arg \max_{V,D} P(V, D | I) \tag{20.2}$$

Certain vertebrae that appear either at the extremity of the entire vertebrae column, e.g., C_2, S_1, or at the transition regions of different vertebral sections, e.g., L_1, have much better distinguishable characteristics (Figure 20.9(a)). The identification of these vertebrae helps in the labeling of others, and are defined as "*anchor vertebrae*." The remaining vertebrae Figure 20.9(a) are grouped into a set of continuous "bundles" and hence defined as "*bundle vertebrae*." Vertebrae characteristics are differ-

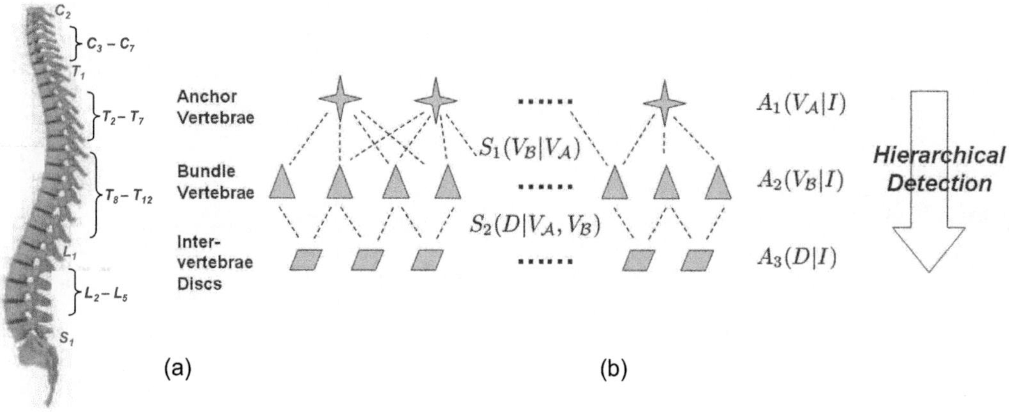

FIGURE 20.9: (a) Schematic explanation of anchor and bundle vertebrae. (b) Proposed spine detection framework.

ent across bundles but similar within a bundle, e.g., C_3-C_7 look similar but are very distinguishable from T_8–T_{12}.

Denoting $V_{\mathcal{A}}$ and $V_{\mathcal{B}}$ as anchor and bundle vertebrae, the posterior in Equation 20.2 can be rewritten and further expanded as:

$$P(V,D|I) = P(V_{\mathcal{A}},V_{\mathcal{B}},D|I) = P(V_{\mathcal{A}}|I) \cdot P(V_{\mathcal{B}}|V_{\mathcal{A}},I) \cdot P(D|V_{\mathcal{A}},V_{\mathcal{B}},I) \tag{20.3}$$

In this study, Gibbs distributions are used to model the probabilities. The logarithm Equation 20.3 can be then derived as Equation 20.4.

$$\begin{aligned} \log[P(V,D|I)] = \; & A_1(V_{\mathcal{A}}|I) && \Leftarrow P(V_{\mathcal{A}}|I) \\ & +A_2(V_{\mathcal{B}}|I) + S_1(V_{\mathcal{B}}|V_{\mathcal{A}}) && \Leftarrow P(V_{\mathcal{B}}|V_{\mathcal{A}},I) \\ & +A_3(D|I) + S_2(D|V_{\mathcal{A}},V_{\mathcal{B}}) && \Leftarrow P(D|V_{\mathcal{A}},V_{\mathcal{B}},I) \end{aligned} \tag{20.4}$$

Here, A_1, A_2, and A_3 relate to the appearance characteristics of anchor, bundle vertebrae, and intervertebral discs. S_1 and S_2 describe the spatial relations of anchor-bundle vertebrae and vertebrae-disc, respectively. It is worth noting that the posterior of anchor vertebrae solely depends on the appearance term, while those of bundle vertebrae and intervertebral discs depend on both appearance and spatial relations. This is in accordance to the intuition: While anchor vertebrae can be identified based on its distinctive appearance, bundle vertebrae and intervertebral discs have to be identified using both appearance characteristics and the spatial relations to anchor ones.

Figure 20.9(b) gives a schematic explanation of Equation 20.4. This framework consists of three layers of appearance models targeting to anchor, bundle vertebrae, and discs. The spatial relations across different anatomies "bridge" different layers (lines in Figure 20.9). Note that this framework is completely different from the two-level model of [1], which separates pixel- and object-level information. Instead, different layers of this framework target to anatomies with different appearance distinctiveness.

This framework was tested using 405 LSpine, CSpine, and WholeSpine scout scans with isotropic resolution 1.7 mm. (105 for training and 300 for testing). These datasets come from different clinical sites and were generated by different types of Siemens MR Scanners (Avanto 1.5T, Verio 3T, Skyra 3T, etc.). Quantitative evaluation is carried on 355 discs and 340 vertebrae from 15

WholeSpine scans. The average translation errors of discs and vertebrae are 1.91 mm and 3.07 mm. The average rotation error of discs is 2.33°.

20.3.3 Joint Space Measurement in the Knee

In this case study we show how data analytic approaches can help with quantification in medical imaging. One important quantification in Musculoskeletal Radiology (MSK) is Tibiofemoral joint space width (JSW) measurement. JSW is one of the measures for longitudinal studies on progression of knee osteoarthritis (OA), because JSW reduction can serve as a surrogate for the thinning of articular cartilage. Traditionally, this measurement is performed on weight-bearing radiographs [7]. However, the joint flexion and imaging parameters need to be carefully controlled by an experienced radiographer. Three-dimensional (3D) imaging modalities, such as MRI or CT, although not weight-bearing, records all anatomical information without occlusion. Therefore, the measurement of JSW in 3D carries some intrinsic advantages, and can be more reproducible. Examples are shown in Figure 20.10. The challenge, however, is that it is a very tedious task for the clinician to navigate to the correct 3D viewing-plane to perform the these measurements. In [54] the authors describe an approach using a data analytics-driven learning system to automatically detect landmarks and help to make this measurement more efficient.

The algorithm automatically navigates to the correct viewing-planes in a consistent manner, thus eliminating the need for manual manipulation of the 3D image volumes. The prototype algorithm first identifies a set of anatomical landmarks around the knee joint on the femur, tibia, and patella bones. A consistency check is performed to remove outliers based on a statistical spatial distribution model of these landmarks. Based on the remaining landmarks, the best viewing planes for measuring JSW are then calculated and presented to the user automatically (see Figure 20.11). More details can be found in Zhan et al. [54].

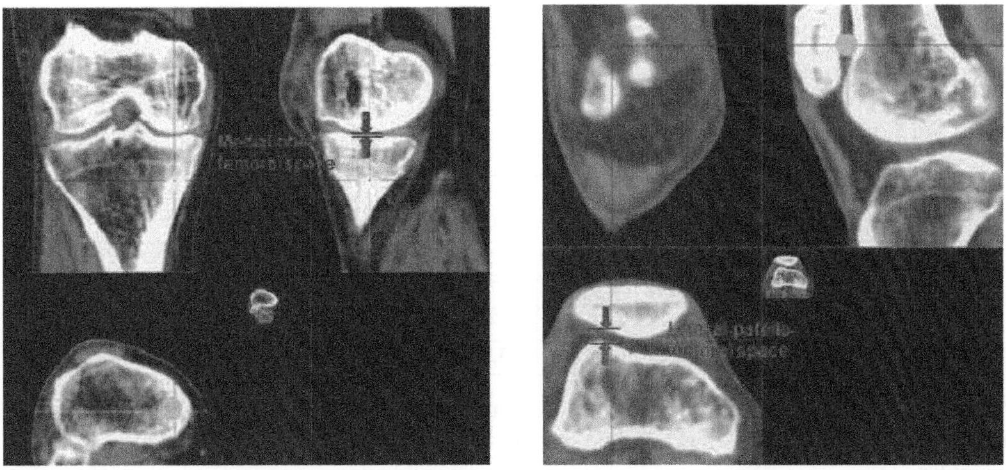

(a) (b)

FIGURE 20.10: Joint space width measurements in the knee. (a) "Medial-tibio-femoral space": widest distance between cortices of medial femoral condyle and opposing medial tibial condyle; (b) "Lateral-patello-femoral space": widest distance between cortices of lateral facets of patella and trochlea.

The prototype algorithm was evaluated using 30 randomly selected CT scans of the knee (mean age 51 yrs, range 12–76 yrs), all performed on 64-slice scanners, and reconstructed at 0.75–3mm slice thickness. One study was excluded due to metal artifacts. 29 remaining cases were reviewed by

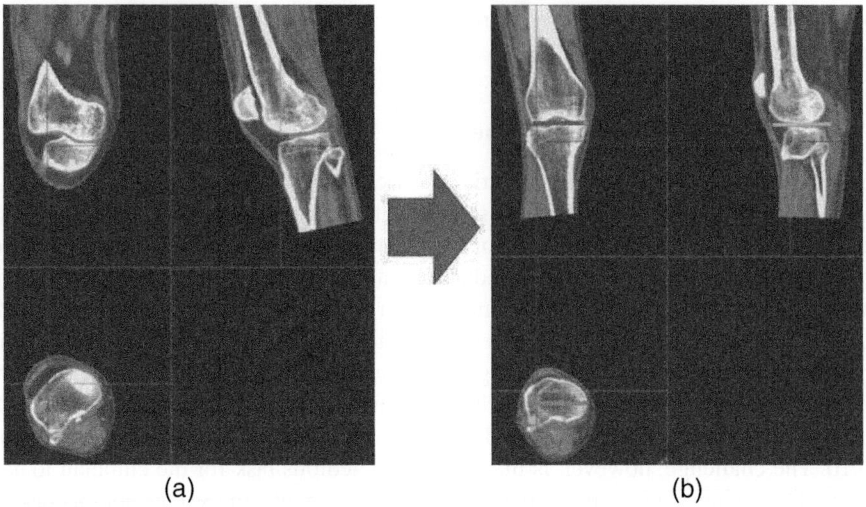

FIGURE 20.11: Computer auto-alignment of knee in CT. (a) original volume before alignment; (b) after alignment.

experienced musculoskeletal radiologist who measured joint space in the medial (Figure 20.10(a), lateral and patella-femoral (Figure 20.10(b) compartments of the knee using manual, conventional CT (CCT) views. The same measurements were then performed on computer auto-aligned CT (ACT) images obtained by the above prototype system which reorients the images for optimal display of the knee joint space. Differences in joint space measurements and time for evaluation were recorded.

The three measurements as well as the time spent on obtaining these measurements are summarized in Table 20.1.

TABLE 20.1: Evaluations of Computer Assisted (ACT) versus Manual (CCT) JSW Measurements

	CCT			ACT			*p*-value
	Mean	Range	SD	Mean	Range	SD	
MTF	3.2mm	1.1–8.2mm	1.4mm	3.2mm	1.1–7.9mm	1.5mm	0.06
LTF	4.5mm	1.5–7.9mm	1.6mm	4.7mm	1.5–11.1mm	2.3mm	0.3
LPF	3.2mm	1.4–5.8mm	0.9mm	3.3mm	1.5–6.8mm	1.3mm	0.2
Time	**47.6sec**	27–110sec	15sec	**33.8sec**	25–77sec	10sec	**<0.001**

Notes: Medial-tibio-femoral space (MTF), lateral-tibio-femoral space (LTF), and lateral-patella-femoral space (LPF). The difference in time spent is statically significant, while measurement results are similar.

All three measurements are relatively comparable between the manual (CCT) and automatic (ACT) approaches, with p-values ranging from 0.06 to 0.3. This is encouraging, considering that there are many variabilities affecting these measurements. The rotation angle of the volume is highly variable due to visual ambiguities of 2D views. For the manual approach, human cannot see or use all available 3D information at any given time point. Furthermore, for both approaches, the selection of measurement location and the drawing of measurement line are all performed manually, thus variable from user to user, and from time to time—even for the same user.

However, the time savings is statistically significant with a p-value less than 0.001. This example indicates that computer algorithms can potentially save radiologist's time in quantitative image anal-

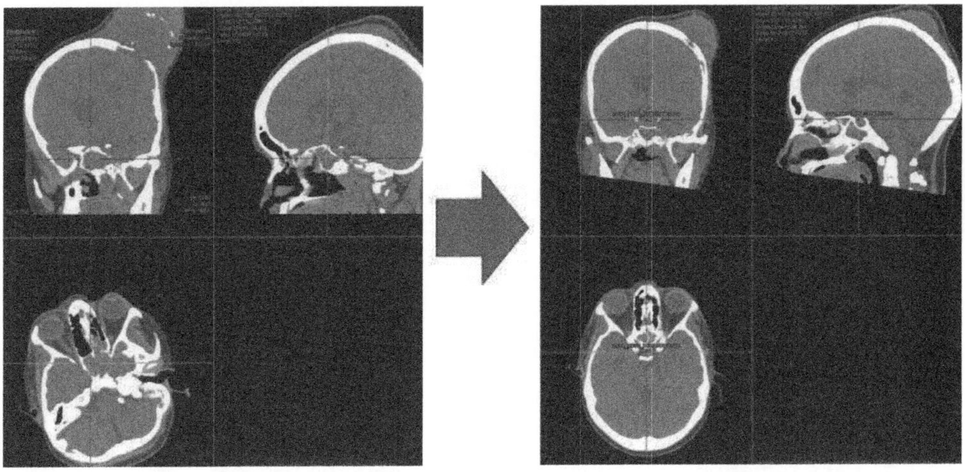

(a) (b)

FIGURE 20.12: Computer auto-alignment of brain in CT. (a) original volume before alignment; (b) after alignment.

ysis, and potentially lead to productivity improvements in reading. Additionally, presenting images in a canonical orientation may also aid in achieving improved consistency of reads, and improved comparison across time-points of acquisition.

The concept can be extended to other anatomies and for other measurements, and Figure 20.12 shows an example of automatically aligned CT head scan using the prototype algorithm. Even with a large, asymmetric pathology on top of the patient's head, the algorithm aligned the scan properly based on the anatomic mid-sagittal plane of the patient's brain.

20.3.4 Brain PET Attenuation Correction without CT

Dementia/epilepsy-related neuro-degenerative disorders are on the rise mainly due to increasing life expectancy. Currently, there are 35 million people worldwide that are affected by dementia, with 5 million new cases added every year. In the absence of new treatment breakthroughs, 80 million cases are predicted by 2040 [14]. Alzheimer's disease (AD), the most common form of dementia, is estimated to cause approximately 70% of all dementias [33]. Various causes of dementia pose a great diagnostic challenge for clinicians, especially for younger patients, and those with subtle signs of the disease. In recent years, ^{18}F-FDG PET imaging has become an effective tool in the clinician's arsenal for dementia patients and increasing their diagnostic confidence. Using the ^{18}F-FDG biomarker, PET images can pinpoint key areas of metabolic decline in the brain indicating dementia. Therefore, as treatments for dementia become available for clinical use, PET will play an important role in assessment and monitoring of future therapies [33]. The PET imaging workflow involves attenuation correction (AC) with CT to correct nonuniform absorption patterns within the body, which adds to the radiation dose exposure, especially for follow-up and monitoring applications. If one could do this step of attenuation correction without having to do a CT, this would be a huge benefit in preventing additional radiation exposure. This is the primary goal with focus towards Brain PET Imaging as outlined in Figure 20.13(a). Additionally, this could be useful for new bio-marker development and testing.

The essential goal of virtual attenuation correction is to recover the structural information. This task is very difficult in this study since PET only provides functional information and the correlation between the "structural" and "functional" information is usually weak. Therefore, we can "borrow"

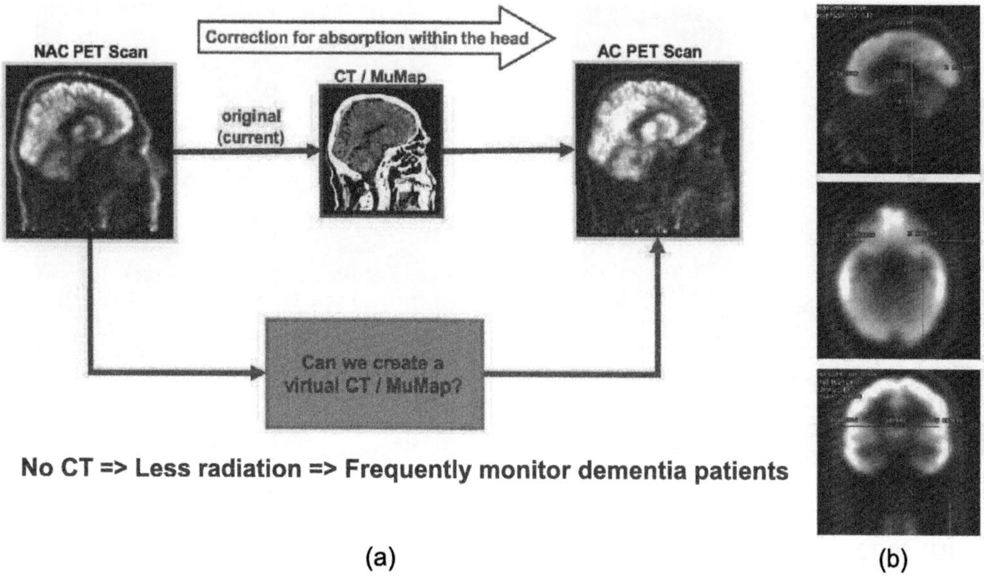

FIGURE 20.13: (a) Problem definition. (b) Representative landmarks defined in PET.

structural information from the nonattenuation corrected (NAC) PET-CT scan — namely a "model scan" — that has a pair of co-registered NAC PET (referred to as just PET hereafter) and CT images. More specifically, the current patient PET image is registered with the model PET image scan. The structural information can then be "borrowed" from the model scan by warping the model CT image scan to the patient space, using derived deformation fields.

The robustness and redundancy can be brought in with two additional steps. The first one incorporates a fusion step using multiple warped CT scans, which can effectively reduce bias to a single model (as shown in the multi-atlas segmentation framework [48]). As brain anatomies and function can vary significantly across patients, selecting the model scans closest to the current subject can be important for registration.

This problem can be alleviated through a model selection second step. Specifically, we can define, and learn from examples a set of distinctive anatomical landmarks in PET images. The spatial configurations (resistant to functional variations) can be employed to select the most similar models for a specific patient. This ensures not only more accurate registration, but more reliable structural information borrowed.

20.3.5 Saliency-Based Rotation Invariant Descriptor for Wrist Detection in Whole-Body CT images

Recent development of whole-body CT images with faster imaging speed has made it feasible in clinical workflow. It provides a comprehensive view of human anatomy. For example, in trauma cases, the radiologist can navigate through all bone structures of the body and evaluate the fracture risks. However, due to the large volume of whole-body scans, which is usually more than 500 slices and the arbitrary anatomical context of some structures, it is time consuming to manually navigate to the area wanted. Compared to other anatomies, wrist detection in whole-body CT is especially challenging, since (1) wrists and hands can be with arbitrary positions and orientations, especially when patients are in a coma or their upper limbs are injured, and (2) wrist and hands are often with highly diverse anatomical context, e.g., on the belly or beside the legs in some trauma cases;

the two hands could be crossed over each other that end up with different and complex anatomical context.

Efficiently detecting an anatomical structure (e.g., wrist, heart, liver, kidney) in medical images is an important component to build a fully automatic system. It leads to multiple applications such as semantic visual navigation, image retrieval, providing necessary initializations for the subsequent procedures, e.g., segmentation, measurements, and classification. There is a great amount of previous work on object detection. It has been proved to be effective and robust in many 2D scenarios. The general approach often uses Haar features to describe an image block and formulates it as a classification problem: whether an image block contains the target object or not [51]. However, extending this algorithm to anatomical structures detection in 3D images is not trivial due to the difficulty of effectively describing 3D features and the exponentially increased searching space with respect to the dimension of the space. Previous approaches working on 3D anatomical structures detection mainly are: classification-based approaches [56, 55] and regression-based approaches [15, 43]. A summary survey can be found in [29].

To improve upon the existing methods, we observed that a wrist has its own characteristic, i.e., a unique spatial configuration of salient bony landmarks. A healthy wrist always consists of eight bones forming the carpal bones, with the radius and the ulna on the arm, and metacarpal bones on the hand. Based on these observations, we can develop a saliency-based rotation invariant descriptor of the wrist bones and detect the wrist based on it. This detection algorithm starts from rotation invariant interest point detection and description. Specifically speaking, we use local extremes of difference of Gaussian (DoG) to extract interest points in images. For each interest point, a descriptor based on a pyramid of scale-distance 2D histograms is then constructed. It describes the spatial relations between neighboring interest points in a rotation-invariant fashion. It is worth noting that this descriptor is completely different from those well-known rotation-invariant features, for example, SIFT and SURF. Instead of describing local appearance features, this descriptor aims to provide a multi-scale view of spatial configurations among neighboring interest points. Both steps are guaranteed to be rotation invariant to handle the arbitrary rotated anatomical structures. This framework generates a list of "in-subject-distinctive" and "cross-subject-reproducible" interest points. The detection problem is then converted from detecting the anatomical structures in images directly to the interest point classification problem, whether or not it is the interest corresponding to the anatomy for which we are looking. Finally, a cascade of random forests [8] are learned to classify interest points to detect the point in which we are interested.

This detection system consists of three main steps: (1) Interest point detection, (2) construction of saliency-based rotation invariant descriptors, and (3) classification on interest points. The first two steps aim to extract a set of wrist candidates. These candidates should be distinctive in an image and repeatable through different subjects as well [50], i.e, we can easily distinguish an interest point from others in one subject and the feature for the same anatomical interest point should be consistent through different subjects. In the third step, a cascade set of random forests are applied to each candidate to determine whether it is the wrist. Compared to voxel-wise classification, the classification is only applied on candidates that form a much smaller hypothesis space.

20.3.6 PET MR

Positron Emission Tomography (PET) by directly imaging metabolic pathways and dynamic processes has become a valuable imaging technique for oncology, cardiology, and neurology [46]. However attenuation correction (AC) of raw PET data is essential for artifact-free quantitative evaluation and improved visual interpretation of PET images. AC is done by computing the attenuation integral along each line of response in the PET detector and correcting the measured counts.[1] The amount of attenuation is determined by the electron density and the thickness of the material.

In conventional stand-alone PET scanners attenuation is measured directly by acquiring a separate transmission image at the energy of the PET photons. However, with the advent of multimodal systems the combined PET with Computerized Tomography (PET/CT), AC can be done directly using the acquired CT transmission image [10]. This consists of a bi-linear transformation from the CT Hounsfield units to the respective linear attenuation coefficients.

Recently, combination of PET and Magnetic Resonance Imaging (MRI) [27] have been proposed as an alternative to the multi-modal PET/CT systems. However, MR is not capable of measuring transmission and attenuation directly since MR does not measure electron density of the material but mainly proton densities and tissue-relaxation properties. Therefore, MR-based attenuation correction techniques need to indirectly compute attenuation maps based on the MR image alone [6]. Two kinds of methods have been commonly proposed for MR-based attenuation correction (see Hofmann et al. [25] for a good review).

- **Segmentation-based approaches** This consists of segmenting an MR-image into different tissue classes (typically air, fat, soft tissue, and bone) and assigning a representative attenuation coefficient to each of these tissues [53, 32].

- **Atlas-based approaches** The second class of method consists of registering the MR image with an co-registered MR-CT atlas and then using the spatially registered CT for attenuation correction [31, 26].

A combination of local pattern recognition and atlas registration method was proposed by [26].

We can also develop a method to automatically predict the bone from the MR images [22]. While segmentation-based approaches work reasonably well for some tissues it has its own limitations. For example, air and compact bone do not produce any signal in the MR image but their attenuation coefficients are different. It is hard to distinguish bone from soft tissue based on the local MR intensities alone. Typically as a first-order approximation bone is treated as soft tissue. This can cause a large bias and lead to artifacts in PET in the massive cortical bones, specifically the femur, pelvis, spine, and skull. While atlas-based approaches can segment bones easily, any misregistration can result in a large bias and artifacts in the PET. The risk of introducing artifacts by erroneous segmentation of the bone is considered to be worse than constant and predictable underestimation. Hence, accurately segmenting bones from MR images is extremely useful for attenuation correction. In terms of attenuation correction, the most important bones can be considered to be the ones that cause the most attenuation, the ones which have a cortical structure that is either very dense or very thick. These bones would include the spine, pelvis, skull, and bones in the extremities like the femur. Therefore, one can develop a hybrid algorithm learning/registration-based algorithm for automatically predicting the bone attenuation map for PET-MR attenuation correction based on only MR image sequences. The bone attenuation map is the probability that a given voxel is a bone.

The algorithm is designed to combine both local and global information using two orthogonal paradigms as illustrated in Figure 20.14. The local information is predicted based on the observed MR image sequences and the global information is borrowed from a co-registered MR-CT atlas.

- **The learning-based local approach** We first use a binary classifier trained to discriminate bone from soft tissue to generate a bone probability map. The binary classifier is trained using a set of co-registered MR and CT images from the same patient. The classifier uses novel multi-image template features and a sparse logistic regression classifier to select only a sparse set of templates.

[1] Attenuating objects reduce the number of counts along a line of response. The measured number of counts I equals the unattenuated number of counts I_0 times the line integral of attenuation, $I = I_0 \exp(-\int(\mu(s)ds)$ where $\mu(s)$ is the electron density of the material at the energy of PET photons (511 keV) at the spatial location s. Sinograms must be corrected by attenuation correction factor, $ACF = \exp(-\int(\mu(s)ds)$.

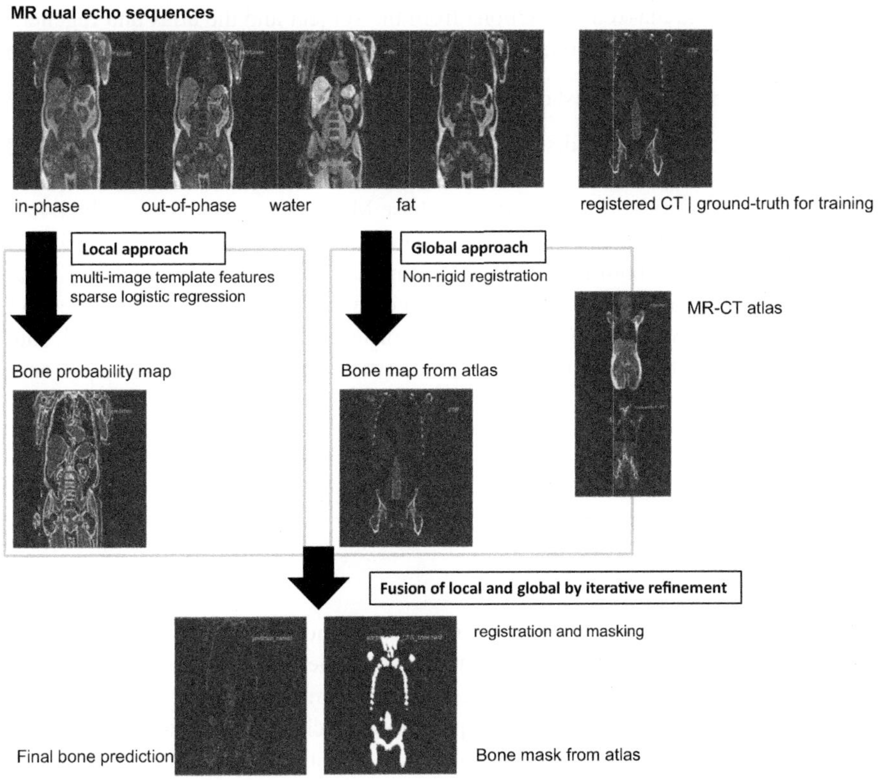

FIGURE 20.14: Overview of the approach. The proposed algorithm is designed to combine both local and global information using two orthogonal paradigms. The local information is predicted using a learning-based approach and the global information is borrowed from a co-registered MR-CT atlas.

- **The registration-based global approach** An orthogonal approach we use is to retrieve annotated bone maps of MR-CT exemplars by nonrigid registration. The registration applied to the CT image provides us the bone attenuation map.

For the learning-based method the location of the true positives is perfect but is has a lot of false positives. As we see later, the classifier cannot distinguish between bone and tissue boundaries since it does not use any global information. On the other hand, the registration-based method has very few false positives but the location of the true positives is not accurate due to errors in registration. The final algorithm combines both the local and global information by filtering the classifier response based on proximity with the retrieved bone map from the registration component. More specifically, we iterate the following steps:

1. We first register the subject MR image to the atlas MR and bring the atlas CT into the subject MR space.

2. A bone mask is generated by computing the distance map to bone locations in the atlas CT and considering only locations that are sufficiently close to the bone. The distance threshold is initially set to 10 mm.

3. The mask is then applied to the classifier prediction to eliminate some of the false positives. The same masking procedure is applied to the classifier prediction on the atlas image.

4. Now we register these masked predictions from the subject and the atlas and regenerate the atlas CT with the new deformation. This allows the registration to focus more on the bone.

5. We then reduce the distance threshold used to compute the mask.

The above steps are repeated until the distance parameter reaches a reasonably low value of 3 mm. At a steady state, the masked prediction and the masked atlas should match.

This method is designed to work with opposed phase MR imaging sequences, which is a technique used to characterize masses that contain both fat and water on a cellular level [19, 40]. This sequence is typically used in abdominal and pelvic imaging to diagnose adrenal and renal neoplasms, hepatic steatosis, and fat-containing tumors. Specifically, we use the MR dual-echo Dixon T1 image sequence that allows for inline computation of fat and water images. In total, four contrasts are available from this single acquisition (in-phase (standard T1), out-of-phase,[2] fat, and water contrast as shown in Figure 20.14).

20.4 Conclusions

In this chapter, we introduced medical imaging methods and motivated the demands and challenges for novel medical image analysis techniques. Machine learning techniques are widely used in the field of medical image analysis and have become key components in CAD systems. We have also briefly summarized medical image analysis applications such as CAD systems for different diseases, automatic clinical measurement on knee CT data, automatic spine labeling using hierarchical learning and local articulated models, automatic prostate T2 MRI segmentation with deep learning techniques for radiation therapy planning, PET-MR attenuation correction with a registration-based approach, PET attenuation correction without CT using a model-based approach, and wrist detection with saliency-based image descriptors.

In the past decade much research has been done. Many different CAD systems have been developed and CAD has been shown to be of clinical benefit. But CAD is not fully in widespread clinical use because either the number of false-positive findings is considered too high, the system is not fully accepted by readers, or poor integration into the radiologist's workflow hinders the use of CAD systems in daily clinical practice.

While today's CAD systems are mainly used in a second reader paradigm with the goal to reduce misses, tomorrow's CAD systems will have special skills and will be more specialized for screening applications and making the radiologist more efficient. CAD systems can be especially helpful for tasks where most of the reader's time is spent searching for lesions in 3D data requiring him or her to review many slices. CT Colonography (CTC or virtual colonoscopy) is such an example. Because of the complex shape of the human colon, the reader spends a lot of time visually tracing the colon and searching the entire colon wall for polyps. Mang et al. [39] describe a colon CAD system that addresses those challenges and substantially decreases reading time while maintaining an accurate detection of colorectal adenomas by shifting the radiologist's effort from "search" to "interpretation." In this system, the time-consuming task of searching colonic polyps is substituted by a CAD system that creates image galleries and provides tools and advanced renderings of potentially suspicious areas for quick review. Mang and coworkers show that average reading times of 20–25 minutes can be reduced to an average of about 3 minutes [39].

[2]When a voxel containing fat and water is imaged in phase, signal intensities are additive; when imaged out-of-phase, signals interfere with each other. Tissues that have equal fat and water lose signal intensity when in out-of-phase. Tissues that have equal fat and water lose signal intensity when in out-of-phase. Only tissues that have only fat or only water do not lose any signal intensity. Out-of-phase images have the characteristic India ink artifact, where voxels at the edge of the fat-water interface have intensity loss. They are also characterized by a decreased signal intensity within healthy bone marrow.

Instead of tracing the colon in 2D or a virtual flight through the colon in 3D, the reader only performs a quick scan through all the slices to (a) get an overall impression of the patient and (b) to not miss any large lesions that may have been missed by the CAD system. Potential colonic polyps are presented by a modified CAD system. This version of a CAD system differs from a conventional second reader CAD system by shifting the operating point on the ROC curve to increase sensitivity at the expense of also increasing the number of false positives. The operating point was set during the training of the system to be close to the saturation point of the sensitivity performance. To compensate for the additional time that is required to rule out those false positives, an advanced false-positive review tool was developed that consists of 2D and 3D rendered images of the potential lesion so that the interpretation can be performed in a faster and more efficient way. An example of the image gallery for a colonic polyp and a false positive are given in Figures 20.15 and 20.16, respectively.

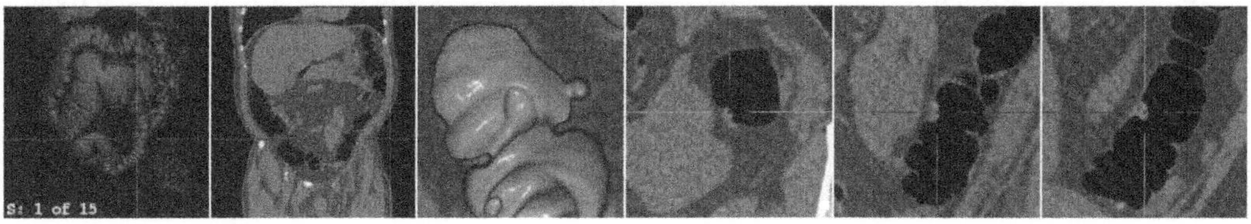

FIGURE 20.15: Image gallery of a potential lesion. From left to right: Global 3D overview of the location; coronal view of the location; 3D rendering of the colon wall showing the potential lesion; enlarged views in axial, coronal, and sagittal orientation.

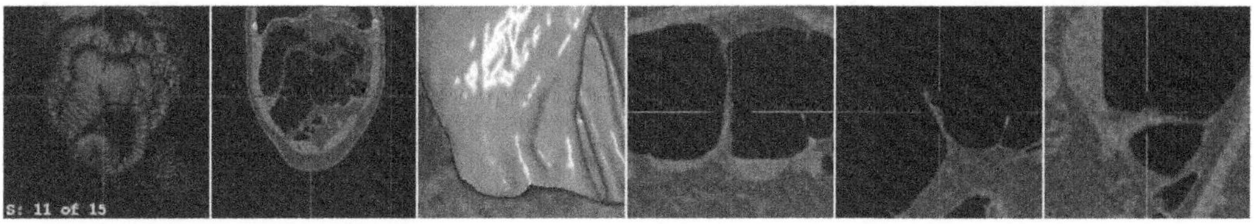

FIGURE 20.16 (See color insert.): Example of a false-positive finding. With the help of the additional images it can be easily identified as a fold.

If screening is to become available, CAD technology will become an important tool in helping readers by providing assistance in finding and measuring lesions. A CAD system to be considered suitable for a screening scenario should work with a high sensitivity while maintaining a low number of false positives. [9] introduces a CAD system for lung cancer screening that shows high nodule sensitivity with a low false-positive rate.

For the medical imaging case studies, we highlighted how advanced analytical methods can be leveraged for state-of-the-art medical image analysis. This is by no means a thorough review of this fast-growing field, and with new imaging techniques emerging and new analytical algorithms invented, we will see more exciting medical image applications in future. Data analytics, especially big data analytics and cloud-based data processing, will play an essential role in these future applications. The integration of medical images with clinical information, free text, and genomic analytics will also see more applications in the future.

Bibliography

[1] R. Alomari, J. Corso, and V. Chaudhary. Labeling of lumbar discs using both pixel- and object-level features with a two-level probabilistic model. *IEEE Transactions on Medical Imaging*, 30:1–10, 2011.

[2] J. C. Anderson and R. D. Shaw. Update on colon cancer screening: recent advances and observations in colorectal cancer screening. *Current Gastroenterology Reports*, 16(9):403, Sep 2014.

[3] U. Bagci, M. Bray, J. Caban, J. Yao, and D. J. Mollura. Computer-assisted detection of infectious lung diseases: a review. *Computerized Medical Imaging and Graphics*, 36(1):72–84, Jan 2012.

[4] Y. Bengio, P. Lamblin, D. Popovici, and H. Larochelle. Greedy layerwise training of deep networks. In *NIPS*, pages 153–160, 2006.

[5] Kevin S. Berbaum, Edmund A. Franken Jr., Donald D. Dorfman, Seyed A. Rooholamini, Mary H. Kathol, Thomas J. Barloon, Frank M. Behlke, Yutaka Sato, Charles H. Lu, George Y. El-Khoury, et al. Satisfaction of search in diagnostic radiology. *Investigative Radiology*, 25(2):133–140, 1990.

[6] T. Beyer, M. Weigert, H.H. Quick, U. Pietrzyk, F. Vogt, C. Palm, G. Antoch, S.P. Muller, and A. Bockisch. MR-based attenuation correction for torso-PET/MR imaging: pitfalls in mapping MR to CT data. *European Journal of Nuclear Medicine and Molecular Imaging*, 35(6):1142–1146, 2008.

[7] T.L. Boegård, O. Rudling, I.F. Petersson, and K. Jonsson. Joint space width of the tibiofemoral and of the patellofemoral joint in chronic knee pain with or without radiographic osteoarthritis: a 2-year follow-up. *Osteoarthritis Cartilage*, 11(5):370–376, 2003.

[8] Leo Breiman. Random forests. *Machine Learning*, 45(1):5–32, 2001.

[9] Matthew S. Brown, Pechin Lo, Jonathan G. Goldin, Eran Barnoy, GraceHyun J. Kim, Michael F. McNitt-Gray, and Denise R. Aberle. Toward clinically usable CAD for lung cancer screening with computed tomography. *European Radiology*, 24(11):2719–2728, 1–10, 2014.

[10] J.P.J. Carney, D.W. Townsend, V. Rappoport, and B. Bendriem. Method for transforming CT images for attenuation correction in PET/CT imaging. *Medical Physics*, 33:976, 2006.

[11] H. P. Chan, L. Hadjiiski, C. Zhou, and B. Sahiner. Computer-aided diagnosis of lung cancer and pulmonary embolism in computed tomography-a review. *Academic Radiology*, 15(5):535–555, May 2008.

[12] M. Chwialkowski, P. Shile, R. Peshock, D. Pfeifer, and R. Parkey. Automated detection and evaluation of lumbar discs in mr images. In *IEEE EMBS*, pages 571–572, 1989.

[13] C. Cortes and V. Vapnik. Support-vector networks. *Machine Learning*, 20:273–297, 1995.

[14] C.P. Ferri , M. Prince, and C. Brayne. Global prevalence of dementia: a delphi consensus study. *Lancet*, 366:2112–2117, 2005.

[15] Antonio Criminisi, Jamie Shotton, Duncan Robertson, and Ender Konukoglu. Regression forests for efficient anatomy detection and localization in CT studies. In *Medical Computer Vision. Recognition Techniques and Applications in Medical Imaging*, pages 106–117. Springer, 2011.

[16] N. Dalal and B. Triggs. histograms of oriented gradients for human detection. In *CVPR*, pages 886–893, 2005.

[17] Kunio Doi. Computer-aided diagnosis in medical imaging: Historical review, current status and future potential. *Computerized Medical Imaging and Graphics*, 31:2007.

[18] Leila H. Eadie, Paul Taylor, and Adam P. Gibson. Recommendations for research design and reporting in computer-assisted diagnosis to facilitate meta-analysis. *Journal of Biomedical Informatics*, 45(2):390–397, 2012.

[19] J.P. Earls and G.A. Krinsky. Abdominal and pelvic applications of opposed-phase MR imaging. *American Journal of Roentgenology*, 169(4):1071–1077, 1997.

[20] A. El-Baz, G. M. Beache, G. Gimel'farb, K. Suzuki, K. Okada, A. Elnakib, A. Soliman, and B. Abdollahi. Computer-aided diagnosis systems for lung cancer: challenges and methodologies. *International Journal of Biomedical Imaging*, 2013:942353, 2013.

[21] J. Friedman, T. Hastie, and R. Tibshirani. Additive logistic regression: a statistical view of boosting. *The Annals of Statistics*, 28:337–407, 2000.

[22] Gerardo Hermosillo, Vikas Raykar, and Xiang Zhou. Learning to locate cortical bone in MRI. *Lecture Notes in Computer Science*, 7588:168–175, 2012.

[23] G. Hinton, S. Osindero, and Y. Teh. A fast learning algorithm for deep belief nets. *Neural Computation*, 18(7):1527–1554, 2006.

[24] G. Hinton and R. Salakhutdinov. Reducing the dimensionality of data with neural networks. *Science*, 313(5786):504–507, 2006.

[25] M. Hofmann, B. Pichler, B. Scholkopf, and T. Beyer. Towards quantitative PET/MRI: a review of MR-based attenuation correction techniques. *European Journal of Nuclear Medicine and Molecular Imaging*, 36:93–104, 2009.

[26] M. Hofmann, F. Steinke, V. Scheel, G. Charpiat, J. Farquhar, P. Aschoff, M. Brady, B. Scholkopf, and B. J. Pichler. MRI-based attenuation correction for PET/MRI: a novel approach combining pattern recognition and atlas registration. *Journal of Nuclear Medicine*, 49:1875–1883, 2008.

[27] M.S. Judenhofer, H.F. Wehrl, D.F. Newport, C. Catana, S.B. Siegel, M. Becker, A. Thielscher, M. Kneilling, M.P. Lichy, M. Eichner, et al. Simultaneous PET-MRI: a new approach for functional and morphological imaging. *Nature Medicine*, 14(4):459–465, 2008.

[28] M. Kelm, S. Zhou, M. Shling, Y. Zheng, M. Wels, and D. Comaniciu. Detection of 3D spinal geometry using iterated marginal space learning. In *Medical Computer Vision*, 6533:96–105, 2010.

[29] S Kevin Zhou. Discriminative anatomy detection: classification vs. regression. *Pattern Recognition Letters*, 43:25–38, 2013.

[30] T. Klinder, J. Ostermann, M. Ehm, A. Franz, R. Kneser, and C. Lorenz. Automated model-based vertebra detection, identification, and segmentation in ct images. *Medical Image Analysis*, 13:471–482, 2009.

[31] E.R. Kops and H. Herzog. Alternative methods for attenuation correction for PET images in MR-PET scanners. In *IEE Nuclear Science Symposium Conference Record*, 6:4327–4330, 2007.

[32] E.R. Kops, P. Qin, M. Muller-Veggian, and H. Herzog. MRI based attenuation correction for brain PET images. *Advances in Medical Engineering*, 114:93–97, 2007.

[33] L. Mehta and S. Thomas. The role of pet in dementia diagnosis and treatment. *Applied Radiology*, 41:8–15, 2012.

[34] Q. Le, W. Zou, S. Yeung, and A. Ng. Learning hierarchical invariant spatio-temporal features for action recognition with independent subspace analysis. In *CVPR*, pages 3361–3368, 2011.

[35] Y. Lecun, L. Bottou, Y. Bengio, and P. Haffner. Gradient-based learning applied to document recognition. *Proceedings of the IEEE*, pages 2278–2324, 1998.

[36] J. Liang and J. Bi. Computer aided detection of pulmonary embolism with tobogganing and mutiple instance classification in CT pulmonary angiography. *Information Processing in Medical Imaging*, 20:630–641, 2007.

[37] S. Liao, Y. Gao, and D. Shen. Sparse patch based prostate segmentation in CT images. In *MICCAI*, pages 385–392, 2012.

[38] G. Mallat. A theory for multiresolution signal decomposition: the wavelet representation. *IEEE PAMI*, 11:674–693, 1989.

[39] Thomas Mang, Gerardo Hermosillo, Matthias Wolf, Luca Bogoni, Marcos Salganicoff, Vikas Raykar, Helmut Ringl, Michael Weber, Christina Mueller-Mang, and Anno Graser. Time-efficient CT colonography interpretation using an advanced image-gallery-based, computer-aided first-reader workflow for the detection of colorectal adenomas. *European Radiology*, 22(12):2768–2779, 2012.

[40] E.M. Merkle and R.C. Nelson. Dual gradient-echo in-phase and opposed-phase hepatic MR imaging: a useful tool for evaluating more than fatty infiltration or fatty sparing. *Radiographics*, 26(5):1409–1418, 2006.

[41] Robert M. Nishikawa. Current status and future directions of computer-aided diagnosis in mammography. *Computerized Medical Imaging and Graphics*, 31(4-5):224–235, 2007.

[42] T. Ojala, M. Pietikainen, and T. Maenpaa. Multiresolution gray-scale and rotation invariant texture classification with local binary patterns. *IEEE PAMI*, 24:971–987, 2002.

[43] Olivier Pauly, Ben Glocker, Antonio Criminisi, Diana Mateus, Axel Martinez Möller, Stephan Nekolla, and Nassir Navab. Fast multiple organ detection and localization in whole-body MR Dixon sequences. In *MICCAI 2011*, pages 239–247. Springer, 2011.

[44] R. Bharat Rao, Glenn Fung, Balaji Krishnapuram, Jinbo Bi, Murat Dundar, Vikas Raykar, Shipeng Yu, Sriram Krishnan, Xiang Zhou, Arun Krishnan, Marcos Salganicoff, Luca Bogoni, Matthias Wolf, and Jonathan Stoeckel. Mining medical images. In *Proceedings of the Third Workshop on Data Mining Case Studies and Practice Prize, Fifteenth Annual SIGKDD International Conference on Knowledge Discovery and Data Mining (KDD 2009)*, 2009.

[45] D. Rumelhart, G. Hinton, and R. Williams. Learning representations by back-propagating errors. *Nature*, 323:533–536, 1986.

[46] G.B. Saha. *Basics of PET Imaging: Physics, Chemistry, and Regulations*. Springer Verlag, 2010.

[47] S. Schmidt, J. Kappes, M. Bergtholdt, V. Pekar, S. Dries, D. Bystrov, and C. Schnrr. Spine detection and labeling using a parts-based graphical model. In *IPMI*, pages 122–133, 2007.

[48] S.K. Warfield, K.H. Zou, and W.M. Wells. Simultaneous truth and performance level estimation (staple): an algorithm for the validation of image segmentation. *IEEE TMI*, 23:903–921, 2004.

[49] M. Smitsmans, J. Wolthaus, X. Artignan, J. DeBois, D. Jaffray, J. Lebesque, and M. van Herk. Automatic localization of the prostate for online or offline image guided radiotherapy. *International Journal of Radiation Oncology, Biology, Physics*, 60:623–635, 2004.

[50] Tinne Tuytelaars and Krystian Mikolajczyk. Local invariant feature detectors: a survey. *Foundations and Trends® in Computer Graphics and Vision*, 3(3):177–280, 2008.

[51] Paul Viola and Michael Jones. Rapid object detection using a boosted cascade of simple features. In *CVPR 2001*, volume 1, pages I–511. IEEE, 2001.

[52] H. Yoshida and J. Nappi. Three-dimensional computer-aided diagnosis scheme for detection of colonic polyps. *IEEE Transactions on Medical Imaging*, 20(12):1261–1274, Dec 2001.

[53] H. Zaidi, M.L. Montandon, and S. Meikle. Strategies for attenuation compensation in neurological PET studies. *Neuroimage*, 34(2):518–541, 2007.

[54] Yiqiang Zhan, Maneesh Dewan, Martin Harder, Arun Krishnan, and Xiang Sean Zhou. Robust automatic knee MR slice positioning through redundant and hierarchical anatomy detection. *IEEE Transactions on Medical Imaging*, 30(12):2087–2100, 2011.

[55] Yiqiang Zhan, Xiang Sean Zhou, Zhigang Peng, and Arun Krishnan. Active scheduling of organ detection and segmentation in whole-body medical images. In *MICCAI 2008*, pages 313–321. Springer, 2008.

[56] Yefeng Zheng, Bogdan Georgescu, and Dorin Comaniciu. Marginal space learning for efficient detection of 2D/3D anatomical structures in medical images. In *IPMI*, pages 411–422. Springer, 2009.

Chapter 21

Mobile Imaging and Analytics for Biomedical Data

Stephan M. Jonas
Department of Medical Informatics
RWTH Aachen University
Aachen, Germany
SJonas@mi.rwth-aachen.de

Thomas M. Deserno
Department of Medical Informatics
RWTH Aachen University
Aachen, Germany
TDeserno@mi.rwth-aachen.de

21.1 Introduction

Biomedical imaging is an important tool in both medical practice and research. It is most important to monitor biological structures or processes that are not visible to the naked eye or cannot be assessed without damaging living tissue. It is used especially in medical diagnostics to evaluate the structure and functions of the human body, or the damage thereof. From the visualization of broken bones to the detection of aneurisms in the brain, no clinic can work without biomedical image data analytics.

Furthermore, only few breakthroughs in biomedical and pharmaceutical research would have been possible without the presence of biomedical imaging. Optical imaging techniques can nowadays be used to localize even individual organisms the size of a virus in living cells [32]. The development of new treatments or biomarkers depends on sophisticated imaging and image analytics techniques.

Since the first X-ray image in the late nineteenth century, numerous imaging modalities have been developed and are still being developed today. As there is no one-fits-all solution in biomedical imaging, a large variety of modalities with individual strengths and weaknesses have found their way into clinical research, diagnostics, treatment, and documentation. Biomedical imaging covers scales from the nano to macro and image data scales from kilo to terabyte for both functional and structural (morphological) imaging [46]. In addition, the introduction of computers and the switch to digital acquisition opened the door for many processing techniques. Even frontiers prior thought impossible, like the maximum resolution of optical imaging, have been solved with increasing computational power. Today, portable devices provide sufficient computational power for biomedical image processing and smart devices have been introduced in the operation theater Figure 21.1.

Digital images are composed of individual sample points that are aligned in a grid. In general, digital imaging consists of four different parts, each playing a key role in biomedical image data analytics:

- *Image formation* describes the process of creating a digital representation of a scene of the real world. In biomedical imaging, different imaging modalities capture the structure of an object like tissue or cells, or their functional aspects like metabolism. Also, different techniques for imaging the surface or a cross-section of an object can be used. Since biomedical imaging ranges from macro- (e.g., bones, limbs) to nano scale (cells, molecules), a wide range of different techniques exists and is used in common practice.

- *Image visualization* is the conversion and display of the digital representation into a viewable format, which is especially important for three-dimensional (3D) data. While visualization of two-dimensional (2D) images is usually straightforward and intuitive, visualization of volumetric data can be as simple as projecting a volume to partially visualizing structures or sections. Techniques known from other applications like CAD or computer games, which allow for fast display usually offer less flexibility and therefore, special visualization algorithms are often used in biomedical image analytics.

- *Image analysis* is used to transfer raw image data into more abstract forms that carry specific information usually hidden within the raw data. This process chains many steps, starting with basic preprocessing of an image to reduce noise or artifacts, to extracting significant object features from an image, combining multiple images (e.g., from different modalities), segmenting important objects like tumors or bone, and classifying the found features or segmented organs. One of the major problems in biomedical image analysis is the fact, that a direct access to data is often impossible due to *invivo* measurements. That means the validity of an image or a finding cannot be evaluated without destroying the sample. For example,

FIGURE 21.1: Biomedical imaging and image analytics has been changed from its beginning to today's mobile applications.

the presence of a tumor can be seen in an x-ray image, but the question whether the tumor is actually present or only an artifact can only be answered by performing a biopsy and thereby destroying tissue.

- *Image management* and communication is necessary especially in the clinical and research environments to store, re-locate, retrieve, send, and receive image data. Storage of patient data or data used in clinical trials is often of legal importance and therefore has to be performed properly. However, storing large amounts of data and finding information within the stored data poses a great challenge. Additionally, biomedical images are often acquired decentralized and with many modalities. Therefore, standards of communicating and consolidating imaging and patient data have to be employed.

Image mobility refers to application of portable computers such as smartphones or tablet computer to store, visualize, and process images with and without connections to servers, the Internet, or the cloud.

The remainder of this chapter introduces each of the four steps with particular focus on image mobility. The key concepts are explained and demonstrated using examples from everyday clinical routine or research. Section 21.2 will introduce the reader into the process of image formation. Key concepts of different imaging techniques that are common in biomedical imaging are explained and examples for different imaging modalities are given. Section 21.3 helps the reader to understand how acquired images are visualized with respect to their acquisition technique and a focus on visualization techniques of volumetric data. Section 21.4 details common steps in image analysis chains, from preprocessing to classification. Additional problems that occur in biomedical image analysis and their effect on evaluation of image analysis are discussed as well and possible solutions depicted. Section 21.5 deals with the setup of image communication networks in biomedical applications like hospitals and research centers. Management, archiving, and retrieval of images are discussed along with common standards for communication of medical image data. Within each section, a subsection on the application of all proposed techniques towards mobile devices is given.

21.2 Image Formation

Image formation is the process of transforming a "scene" of the physical world into a sparse, visual representation. Although any type of imaging results in an image, a 3D image is often called volume and a one-dimensional (1D) image is referred to as a signal or line.

The most common type of image formation is optical projection imaging, which is the process by which photo cameras capture a scene. Optical imaging uses visible and invisible light for the image formation process [8, 37]. Other common techniques used in biomedical image formation are nuclear imaging [23], where radioactive particles are applied to produce the image; radiography, which is based on high-energetic photons and used in plain radiography or computed tomography (CT); acoustic imaging, which is based on (e.g., reflected) sound waves (e.g., ultrasound) [24]; electrical image formation, where electrical potential differences are measured [48], such as in electrocardiography (ECG), electromyography (EMG), or electroencephalography (EEG); and magnetic resonance imaging (MRI) [26], where excitations due to magnetic fields are recorded. In this section, the basic principles behind these techniques are explained.

We distinguish two formation processes:

- *Projection imaging*: Projection of a three-dimensional scene onto a 2D plane along the imaging axis. Examples are common cameras or an x-ray.

- *Cross-sectional imaging*: Acquisition of samples along the imaging axis. Most prominent examples are MRI and CT, but also ultrasound and certain optical imaging techniques.

Imaging modalities can also be discriminated by the captured property:

- *Structural imaging* captures the physical appearance of the body, for example bones or tissue, as in an x-ray or histological images.

- *Functional imaging* modalities record a process, usually metabolic or fluid dynamics, for example, positron emission tomography (PET) or Doppler ultrasound.

In addition, imaging modalities are often distinguished by their effect on living tissue or cells:

- *Invasive imaging* destroys tissue or is in other ways damaging to the body. Examples are x-ray imaging or cryosectioning. The first can damage tissue if high dosage is applied, the second requires the sample to be frozen and sliced.

- *Noninvasive imaging,* in contrast, does not damage tissue or damage is not yet known. For instance, ultrasound and MRI are counted as noninvasive imaging techniques, since the only side effect that has been measured so far is a slight increase of tissue temperature.

Image data in general can be recorded either as 1D (a line), 2D (a plane), or 3D (a volume). The image space (definition range) is not continuous; therefore, an image is represented as sparse, individual samples (so-called pixels in 2D and voxels in 3D) with a distinct position in image space. The positions form a regular pattern or grid. Image resolution describes the number of samples an image sensor can capture. In contrast, spatial image resolution describes how large the part of the physical world is represented by an individual sample point.

Assuming a fixed aperture, the spatial resolution of a regular camera image depends on the number of pixels (among several other parameters) on the sensor. If an image of a melanoma is captured with a higher number of pixels but otherwise the same parameters as a comparison image, the spatial resolution is increased as each pixel represents a smaller part of the melanoma.

Additionally, a scene can be acquired multiple times over time, resulting in a video. This is

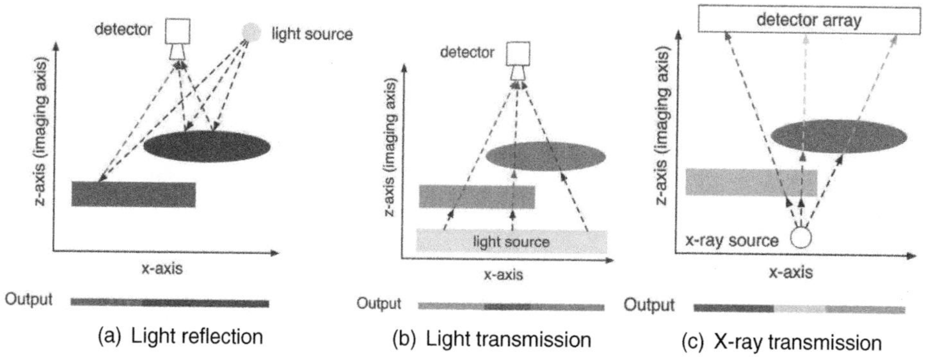

FIGURE 21.2: Different types of projection image formation with light reflection, light transmission (so-called back-illumination) and X-ray tranmission, and their output, shown for 1D data. Both, source and detector may be a formed as point or line sources.

usually marked by adding "+t" to the original image dimensionality (e.g., 2D+t is a video, 3D+t an animated volume).

While color technically adds one dimension to the acquired data (value range), it is usually not considered its own dimension. Instead, color is divided into channels (bands). An image with a single type of detector is a single-channel image. Colored images usually have separate red, green, and blue detectors or use color filters to acquire each color individually. This results in three color channels.

21.2.1 Projection Imaging

In projection imaging, a scene in 3D world space is projected along one axis to a 2D image space representation. The axis that is projected over is the optical axis, which is usually orthogonal to the imaging plane and would describe the depth information of the image. By integrating all information along the optical axis, the specific location is lost and the full 3D scene cannot be reproduced without additional information.

The most classical projection imaging technique is used in cameras to capture a scene on photosensitive film or a digital sensor. The image is formed by light emitted from one or several light sources and partially reflected from, or passing through, objects. The light is then captured on a sensor or film (Figure 21.2(a)). A limiting factor is the penetration depth and diffraction of light. This is especially important in many fields of medical imaging. For example, histological microscopy captures images of tissue on a microscopic slide. If one would simply shine light at a piece of tissue, it would only illuminate the top layer of the tissue, which would reflect parts of the light and absorb the remainder. Lower layers of the tissue would not be reached by light and therefore appear invisible in the image. Light would not pass through thick tissue. To create detailed images of tissue, it is therefore sliced into very thin layers and back-illuminated (Figure 21.2(b)). The light can pass through the tissue and be recorded on the other side. Thereby, a projection image with a very limited tissue depth is created.

X-ray imaging is very similar to optical projection imaging. Here, radiation instead of light is transmitted through an object or body and the projection is captured on the sensor (Figure 21.2(c)). Tissue and bones absorb X-rays based on their density (similar to light being absorbed by an object in back-illumination) and the resulting projection is a negative image of the density (less X-ray where higher density is present).

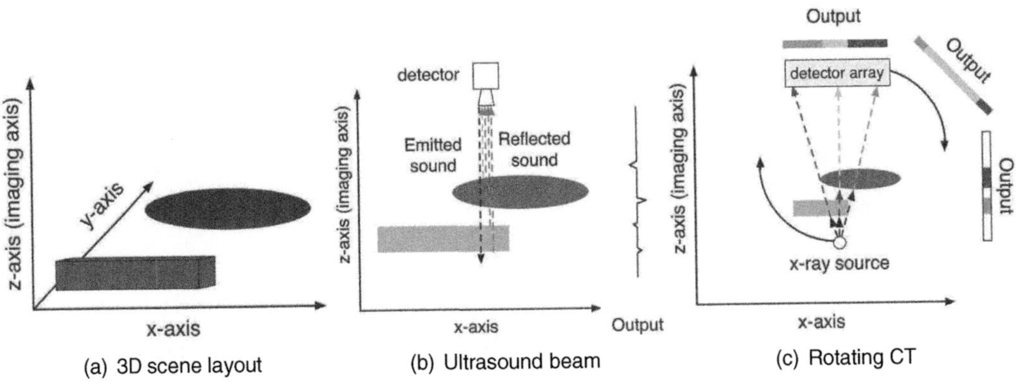

FIGURE 21.3: Different types of cross-sectional imaging formation techniques and their output.

21.2.2 Cross-Sectional Imaging

Cross sectional imaging describes imaging modalities that generate a depth representation of a part of the scene along the imaging axis (the axis going from the sensor into the scene, Figure 21.3). In some cases, acquisition results in a 1D line through the scene as in ultrasound. Other techniques like CT or MRI create a 2D slice in a single acquisition step. Commonly, these individual sections are combined to create a 2D image or 3D volume.

A prominent representative of cross-sectional imaging is ultrasound (sonography). Ultrasound measures depth by sending a sound impulse beyond the audible range into the scene. The sound is reflected at the interface between two materials, similar as light being reflected on the interface between air and water. By capturing the delay of the reflected sound, the depth of the interface can be calculated (Figure 21.2(b)). Earlier ultrasound systems used only one direction to measure the sound, resulting in a single line of the tissue (amplitude or A-mode).

By adding multiple sensors or a moveable scanning head to the imaging system, multiple A-scans with different directions can be acquired. Multiple line-scans acquired within a short time can be combined into a 1D+t, 2D, 3D, or even 3D+t representation. Recent systems are composed of a sensor array, which acquires a full 2D image at once. Here, a fan of rays is sent into the body, the depth information determines the image pixel position, and the intensity of the reflection is coded as the pixel's grayscale (brightness or B-mode).

A similar technique in optical imaging is called optical coherence tomography (OCT). OCT measures the delay in reflections of a near-infrared light beam sent into the tissue. A moveable mirror is used to create a 2D or 3D image by moving the optical path of the light beam. As described earlier, this technique has a more limited penetration depth (few millimeters in comparison to several centimeters in ultrasound) but higher spatial resolution, as the diameter of the light beam is slimmer than that of an ultrasonic wave.

More recent cross-sectional imaging techniques are CT and MRI. Both techniques acquire shifted 2D slices through the object, which are then recombined into a 3D volume. In case of CT, the slices are produced by rotating an X-ray tube and a detector around the object on the imaging plane and creating multiple 1D projections of the object from all directions (Figure 21.4(a)). These 1D acquisitions form a large system of linear equations that can be solved to estimate the density of the object at each position in space.

Since such a calculation is rather expensive, a different approach is commonly used. As the 1D projections represent the density along lines through the body, a back-projection is performed by accumulating the measured density for each of the projections. The density is accumulated at each

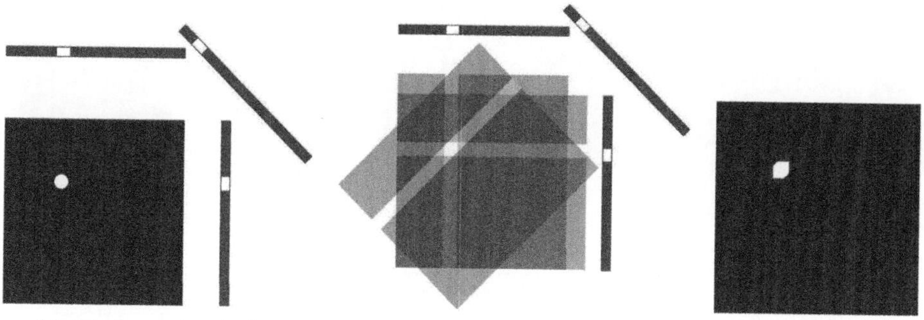

(a) 2D slice and projections (b) Superimposition (c) Filtered

FIGURE 21.4: CT image formation using back-projection technique. First, multiple projections through one slice are imaged, then these projections are back-projected and superimposed, and finally filtered.

position on the image (Figure 21.4(b)). As further improvement, the artifacts are reduced by filtering (Figure 21.4(c)).

CT is therefore not an intrinsic cross-sectional imaging modality but a computed one, thus the name. CT is especially useful when examining bones and tissue with high differences in density (Figure 21.5(a)). As soft tissue has a low density and absorbs only few X-rays, CT is not the best modality for imaging soft tissue.

MRI differs from CT in using the magnetic spin of hydrogen protons to generate a 3D volume representing the water density of the tissue and the chemical bounding of the molecules. Hence, MRI particularly highlights differences in soft tissue but does not have much sensitivity on bone, as hydrogen is not a major component of bony tissue. MRI creates a 2D image by first forming a strong magnetic field around the object and then applying radio frequency (RF) waves to orient the protons of the water molecules, synchronize their spin, and thereby exciting the hydrogen protons. On removal of the RF field, the atoms will return to an equilibrium state. The speed of this return to equilibrium (relaxation) is measured and results in an image. Three types of measurements are possible. The first (T1) is the measure of recovery from the longitudinal magnetization and accentuates fatty tissue (Figure 21.5(b)). The second (T2) is the measure of desynchronization of the spin and accentuates watery regions (Figure 21.5(c)). The third is called proton density weighted imaging and is a mixture of T1 and T2, mostly visualizing the number or protons in the probe. It enhances tissue with high number of rotating hydrogen atoms (Figure 21.5(d)).

A cross-sectional imaging technique, which does reconstruct the original object in 3D but destroys the object in the process, is cryosectioning. In this technique, an object (e.g., a body) is frozen and sliced down to a 1-micrometer thickness. Each slice is imaged using optical projection imaging (Figure 21.5(e)). By combining subsequent slices, a 3D volume is created.

21.2.3 Functional Imaging

Functional imaging methods assess functional rather than structural tissue properties. For example, so-called Doppler imaging captures displacement of an object along the imaging axis but not the actual structure of the object. By measuring the frequency shift (so-called Doppler shift) of an optical or ultrasonic beam that is sent into the object, the displacement of the object or the flow of a fluid can be estimated.

A simple example of the Doppler effect is a car driving towards you. Due to the car's speed that is superimposed to the speed of sound, the sound waves from the engine on front of the car are

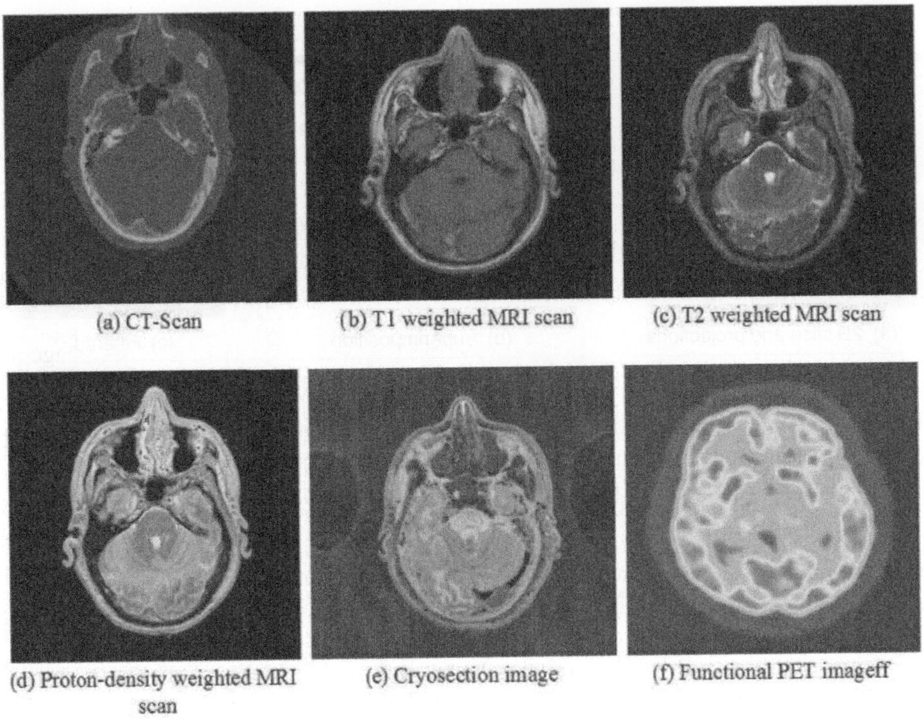

FIGURE 21.5 (See color insert.): Cross-sectional images of a male person taken with different imaging modalities [56].

compressed (higher frequency) while those at its back are stretched (lower frequency). Hence, when the car passes by, the sensed sound seems deeper.

Another functional imaging technique is positron emission tomography (PET). PET captures gamma rays that are emitted by a positron-emitting tracer. This tracer is usually a glucose analog that accumulates at positions in the body with high metabolism. This is very useful in cancer diagnostics and functional in brain imaging. In the latter, a person is given a task or displayed specific stimuli while brain PET is performed. The resulting image shows areas of high metabolism, which coincides with brain areas active during the task or processing of the stimuli (Figure 21.5(f)).

21.2.4 Mobile Imaging

In today's hospitals, image formation is done in special laboratories or departments. The reason for this is the size and prerequisites of many imaging machines (e.g., an MRI machine weighs multiple tons and requires specially shielded rooms). While many techniques will always require special equipment, the regular camera is one of the most used imaging modalities in hospitals. Here, mobile technology and smart devices, especially smartphones, allows new ways of easier imaging at the patient's bedside and possess the possibility to be made into a diagnostic tool that can be used by both professionals as well as lay people. Smartphones usually contain at least one high-resolution camera that can be used for image formation. However, careful consideration has to be taken when dealing with cameras in general, and with nonscientific cameras specifically.

Many parameters are usually reported on camera in public commercials, but not all of them are useful. Especially, pixel resolution can be misleading as the number of pixels itself is not a measure of quality. Quality is usually measured in signal-to-noise ratio (SNR). SNR is defined as the power of the signal by the power of noise.

$$SNR = \frac{P_{\text{signal}}}{P_{\text{noise}}} \tag{21.1}$$

Noise can be introduced in several steps of the image acquisition.

- Shot noise, which is dependent on the quality of the sensor and the discretization of different number of photons. This noise mostly occurs when only a few photons hit the sensor.
- Transfer noise, which is introduced by connectivity in the sensor. This is usually static for all images and can be reduced using background subtraction with an image acquired in complete darkness.

In case of a camera, the signal is the amount of light captured by the sensor. Since image noise is reduced, more photons are available. The most important parameter for the quality of an optical system is the amount of light accumulated on each pixel. This parameter is determined by the physical size of a pixel (or chip size in relation to number of pixels), as larger pixel acquires more light, and the diameter of the entry lens, which regulates the amount of light. The size of the entry lens is usually given in f-stop k (written as 1:k or f/k), the ratio of distance from sensor to entry lens to diameter of entry lens, the lower, the better. Most modern smartphones have similar optical parameters as regular consumer cameras, while being built at a far smaller scale. Table 21.1 shows camera models of the year 2013 from different vendors and their parameters.

TABLE 21.1: Comparison of Parameters of Different Smartphone Cameras

Camera	**f-stop**	**Sensor width x height (mm x mm)**	**Resolution (megapixel)**	**Physical pixel size (μm^2)**
iPhone 5s	f/2.2	4.54x3.42	8	≈ 1.9
Samsung Galaxy S4	f/2.2	4.54x3.42	13	≈ 1.2
Nokia Lumia 1020	f/2.2	8.80x6.60	41.3	≈ 1.4
Google Nexus 5	f/2.4	4.54x3.42	8	≈ 1.9

First integrations of these cameras into clinical routine and research have already shown manifold applications for mobile technology in medicine. One example is the usage of the smartphone camera to take pictures of test strips for automatic analysis [53]. Another example is the use of smartphone cameras to document necrotic skin lesions caused from the rare disease calciphylaxis in a multicenter clinical registry [18]. Here, special care must be taken when dealing with multiple different smartphones or lighting conditions due to different efficiencies in capturing colors. A color reference has to be used to calibrate the camera colors in a later step. To control illumination, zoom, and distance, the German company FotoFinder has developed an integrated lens system that is easily attached to and powered by an iPhone transforming it into a dermatoscope (Figure 21.6).

Beside the integrated camera, additional image formation methods can also be used on smart devices by either incorporating special sensors (like ultrasound or ECG) or by connecting them wired or wireless to more powerful imaging machines like micronuclear magnetic resonance (micro-NMR) for bedside diagnostic [30].

21.3 Data Visualization

The task of transforming an acquired image dataset into a perceptible form is called visualization. This is rather simple for most 2D methods like digital photographs, but can be more complex

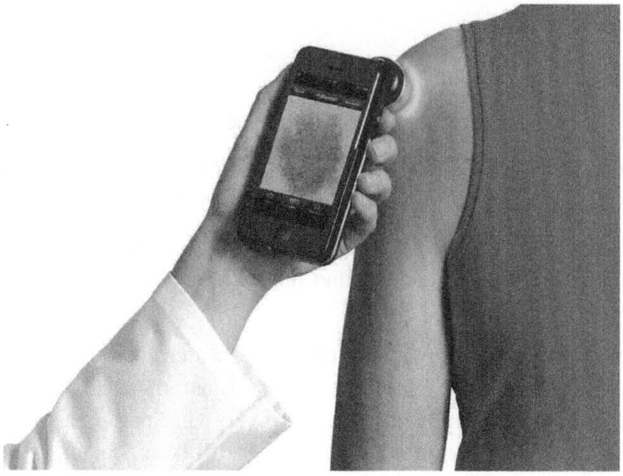

FIGURE 21.6: Special hardware for mobile medical imaging [54]. The app, however, only supports imaging, while computer-based image analysis is not part of the system.

for 3D volumes, in particular, if voxels are annotated with several features or monitored over time (3D+t). In general, all data is displayed by transforming it into a colored 2D representation. Hence, we need to consider the output devices as well as the definition and value ranges of the initial data.

21.3.1 Visualization Basics

The human eye is capable of detecting light between 390 and 700 nm wavelengths. Images that are recorded and displayed within this so-called visible spectrum show the data in "true color." But because many modalities like X-ray, ultraviolet, or infrared imaging capture wavelengths outside the visible spectrum, a modification of the recorded data has to be performed. The resulting image (e.g., a grayscale image for X-ray) is displayed in "false color." A special case of this is the so-called "pseudo color," which means that the color of an image has been artificed to enhance certain features. Here, a single channel image and a so-called color map are used to convert each value of the single channel into a corresponding color. As an example, the Doppler signal contains information on direction of movement for each position. This movement can be either positive (towards the detector), negative (away from the detector), or zero (no movement). To superimpose this information to morphologic image data (B mode), a different color scheme is applied (Doppler mode, compare Section 21.2.3). The zero level would be encoded in black, negative values in blue, and positive values in red. Larger absolute value of the signal results in brighter color (Figure 21.7).

21.3.2 Output Devices

All data is displayed on a computer screen, where colors are mixed from three basic channels: red, green, and blue (RGB). This results in a cubic color space (Figure 21.8(a)). Setting all three colors to the same value creates different shades of gray. Each color is usually scaled from 0 (dark) to 255 (bright). This equals a bit depth of 8, meaning that 8 bits in memory are allocated for each color channel yielding in total $256^3 \sim 16$ million possible values. Higher bit-depth color or gray values are also possible but rarely used, as they are not well supported by computer screens and file formats.

However, in some cases a higher contrast or distribution of color or gray values is needed, e.g., for diagnostics in radiology. Therefore, computer screens in diagnostic radiology support higher bit

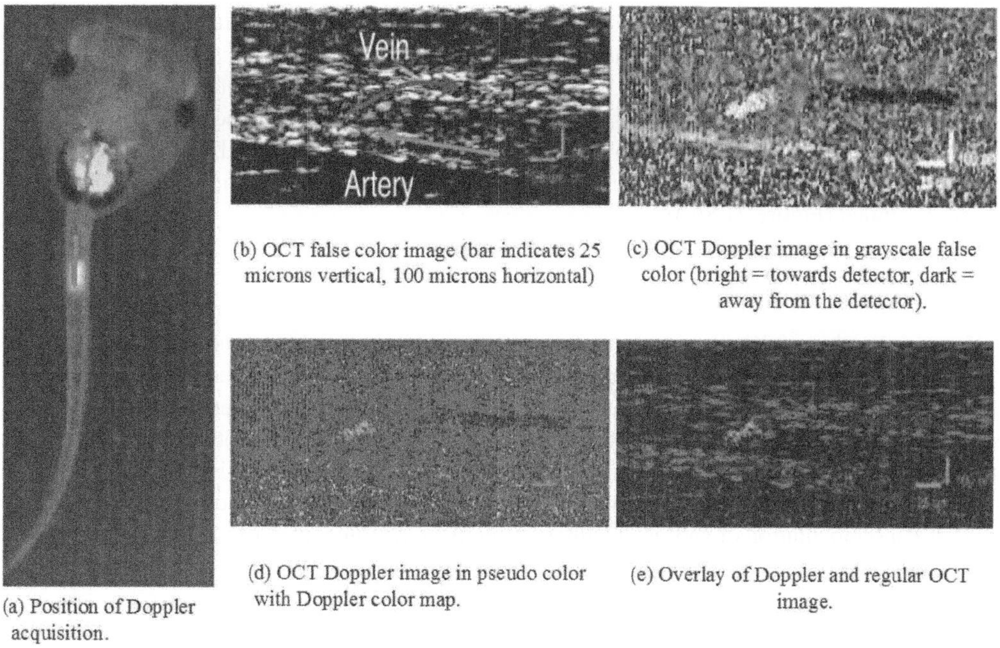
Vein
Artery
(a) Position of Doppler acquisition.
(b) OCT false color image (bar indicates 25 microns vertical, 100 microns horizontal)
(c) OCT Doppler image in grayscale false color (bright = towards detector, dark = away from the detector).
(d) OCT Doppler image in pseudo color with Doppler color map.
(e) Overlay of Doppler and regular OCT image.

FIGURE 21.7 (See color insert.): False and pseudo coloring applied in diagnostics OCT image data of frog embryo. [55].

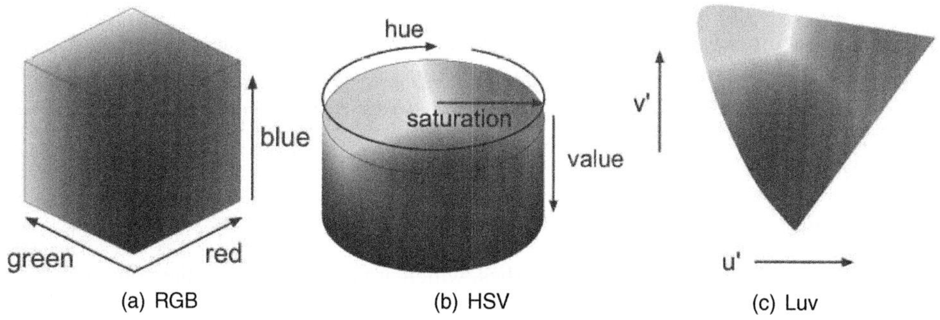

FIGURE 21.8 (See color insert.): Color spaces frequently used in biomedical imaging: red, green, blue (RGB); hue, saturation, value (HSV); and Luv, a colorspace with percepted uniformity (Wikipedia, modified).

depth (e.g., grayscale bit depth of 10), and have a better contrast (e.g., 1400:1 compared to 1000:1 regular) and brightness (e.g., 400 cd/m^2 brightness compared to 200 cd/m^2 regular) than regular computer screens [4].

Printers differ from screens in that the background color of a screen (no color turned on) is black, while the background color of a printout (paper) is white. Thus, higher values in color for screens result in brighter colors, while higher amounts of color from a printer result in darker colors. Therefore, printers usually use cyan, magenta, yellow, and black (CMYK) color space to compensate for the nonblack background. Black is used as a key ingredient when mixing the colors to minimize the fluid on the paper.

In image analysis, further color models are required, although human perception is also based on RGB-like receptors in the retina, human brain converts the measures to concepts such as hue, saturation, and value (HSV). Hue decodes the color, saturation the amount of color, and value the brightness (Figure 21.8(b)). Such color spaces are particularly useful for segmentation (e.g., stained cells in microscopy), since we want to end up with image parts corresponding to those that are observed by physicians. To cope with non-linearity in human perception, the Luv color space is frequently applied (Figure 21.8(c)).

21.3.3 2D Visualization

The visualization of 2D data is straightforward in many cases and consists of scaling the input data to the desired range (e.g., 0–255 for grayscale in regular and 0–1023 in radiology displays).

To combine multiple images from different sources, a technique called overlaying is often used. Here, one image is displayed in the background (usually in grayscale) and the other (usually colored) semitransparently on top (Figure 21.7(e)). Thereby, structural and functional images can be shown at the same time to highlight structures with high or low function. This technique is also often used to visualize a segmentation of an image with each segmented region encoded in a different color.

21.3.4 3D Visualization

For visualization of 3D data, a viewpoint (virtual camera) has to be chosen from which the 3D scene is observed. When moving or rotating a volume, in fact, the location of the viewpoint in relation to the volume is moved, not the volume itself.

Almost all 3D data in biomedical imaging is acquired as a stack of equidistant slices yielding cuboids rather than the full symmetric case cubes. While the same coloring techniques could be used, the coloring of a complete volume results in a cuboid of which only the outer layers are visible and all inner structures are hidden. Therefore, a mapping has to be available to assign each of the values of the 3D cuboid a transparency. In a simple case, a mapping could assign complete transparency to all tissue but bones. This would result in an image showing only the skeleton. Usually, tissue is mapped to be only semitransparent.

Two different approaches can be used to render 3D data:

1. *Volume rendering directly* visualizes 3D voxel-based data.
2. *Surface rendering* visualizes surface meshes, which are computed from the volume data.

Ray casting is one method of direct volume rendering and will be used as an example here. It is similar to the virtual camera placed in the scene capturing rays of light emitted by every voxel of the volume (Figure 21.9(a)). Since some parts of the volume represent transparent or semi-transparent matter, the rays of light are able to at least partially pass through voxels between them and the virtual camera. Since a forward calculation of all rays from all voxels would be very costly, a backward calculation is performed instead. The number of rays is given by the resolution of the target image; one ray per pixel is needed. Starting from the virtual camera, the rays are traversed toward the object. Each ray has an intensity or color value. If a ray travels through any (partly) opaque voxel, the color, weighted by the transparency, is accumulated onto the ray's value. This is performed until the ray reaches the end of the volume or until the value of the ray is too high to allow further accumulation. In other words, either there is nothing more to see, or the parts that have already traveled through would occlude the remaining object. Once this process has been completed for all rays, the entire output projection of the 3D volume has been calculated. Volume rendering is very common in medicine, as it allows the user not only to see the surfaces of structures such as organs and bones without segmentation, but also to give the physicians instantaneously an intuitive interpretation of surrounding tissue.

As direct volume rendering has the drawback of being computationally heavy, other solutions for faster rendering exist. One alternative method is surface rendering. Surface rendering is used in almost all modern 3D visualization tools outside of medicine. Surface rendering uses surface meshes consisting of many connected polygons (usually triangles) that approximate the actual surface of an object (Figure 21.9(b)). Each of the polygons itself is flat and the 3D shape is created by having many interconnected polygons with different angles to each other. Since this approach requires surface meshes, the 3D volume has to be segmented prior to display. The surface rendering approach thereby offsets parts of the complexity of rendering into the preprocessing of the visualized data.

To generate surface meshes from a volume, a method called marching cubes is used. Assuming an already segmented volume—a volume consisting of only true or false values depending whether the voxel at this location is part of the object or not—marching cubes selects a starting point within the volume to create an initial cube. Each cube spans between 8 points of the volume and is minimal in size. Now, more cubes are created that are neighboring the initial cube as long as at least one of the corner points is within the volume. All cubes that are either completely inside the object (all corners are part of the object), or completely outside of the object are not part of the surface. However, if the cube spans between voxel within and outside of the volume, a part of the surface has to be created at this point. In total 256 possible configurations of the corner points exist ($2^8 = 256$), which can be reduced to 15 different shapes due to rotation and mirroring of settings. A lookup table (LUT), an array that can be efficiently indexed, can be created for these 15 shapes using the binary configuration of the corner points. Based on these 15 shapes, the surface is constructed for each cube spanning between the inside and outside of the object. Improvements over this approach have been created that focus on smoother surfaces and other issues with this basic approach [38].

Once a mesh-based representation of the object or multiple objects has been created, rendering approaches that are less computationally expensive can be employed. The major advantage comes from the fact that the intersection of a line with a polygon can be calculated more efficiently than ray casting.

Adding lighting, reflections, and corresponding shadowing to the scene supports the visualization of 3D volumes. This is important, as volumes rendered without lighting may appear flat (Figure 21.9(c) and Figure 21.9(d)).

21.3.5 Mobile Visualization

Recently, visualization and display technology has been dominated by trends in mobile computing. For example, prior to the introduction of the first retina display with the iPhone 4 in 2010, almost all computer and smartphone displays had a pixel density of about 70–100 pixels per inch (ppi). Increase in resolution was mostly achieved through larger monitor screens. However, the introduction of the retina display increased the pixel density above 300 ppi, improving perceived contrast and also outperforming radiology displays in many other aspects (e.g., iPhone 4 brightness: 500 cd/m^2). Thereby, these new types of screens show great potential for radiologists [49].

Additionally, modern smartphones and tablet computers provide a high amount of processing power (e.g, 64-bit dual core, 1.3 GHz in iPhone 5s) that can be used for image visualization. Almost all 2D and surface-rendering visualization techniques can be employed in real time. Real time means that the result is delivered fast enough to make an impact on the current situation, or, in terms of visualization of data, so that no delay between action (e.g., zooming) and result (zoomed image) is perceived [40]. Usually, this requires 15 to 20 frames per second (fps).

Volume rending is computationally expensive, for example, a dataset of CT angiography can contain up to 6 GB of data in 512^3 pixels taken over time that have to be in memory during visualization. Therefore, most smart devices are not capable of performing volume rending natively. Remote visualization has been successfully implemented to display images, which have been rendered on a server, remotely on a tablet computer or smartphone. This so-called streaming is performed by sending video of a live view of an object from the server to the client (tablet computer or smart-

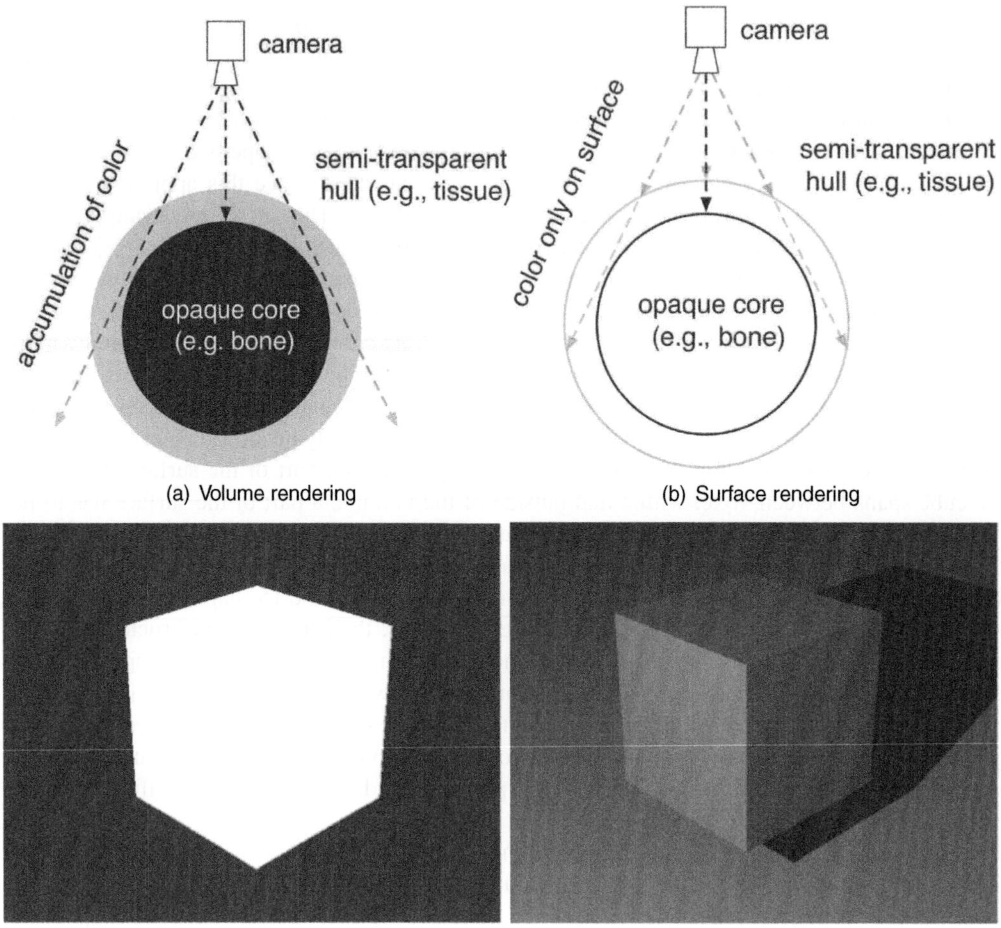

(a) Volume rendering (b) Surface rendering

(c) Without shadowing and lighting. (d) With drop shadow and lighting.

FIGURE 21.9: Comparison of volume (a) and surface rendering (b), where color is accumulated along each beam and only when crossing surfaces, respectively. Panels (c) and (d) depict 3D.

phone), for example, using H.264 video compression that is standard in mobile communication. On the other hand, the client captures touches, swipes, and other interactions of the user and sends these to the server to update the live view [25]. Streaming of video data has the benefit of allowing the user to use a mobile device while having the computational power of a workstation. The drawback of this approach is the needed bandwidth to stream images in real time from the server to the mobile device. For example, a video with 30 frames per second (fps) and a resolution of 1920 by 1080 pixels (FullHD/1080 p) requires about 1 Mb/sec bandwidth. This is not possible through most current wireless networks like 3G, which is limited between 350 and 2000 kilobits per second (kbit/s), depending on country and reception [58].

Important for distributed visualization on a range of different devices is calibration. This means that the same image is displayed in the exact same way on all devices, even if background illumination differs between these devices. For this, an application has been developed that allow users to calibrate their devices visually on their own [16]. In this application the user is guided through 8 steps, each showing a visual pattern. In each step, the user has to adjust a slider to change the visibility of the pattern. In the first step, a dark box is shown on black background and brightness has to be adjusted so that the dark box is barely visible. This allows adjusting for so-called clipping, which occurs if all values below a certain value are shown as black. In the second step, the same is performed for white with a bright box. In the next steps, a checker pattern of two different values is displayed. Perceived value is the average of the two values and has to be adjusted to match the surrounding color. This way, a curve of perceived and actual values can be calculated. Using this curve, all image intensities can be recalibrated using a color map or lookup table (compare Section 21.3.1).

One concern that is often raised when visualizing biomedical images on mobile devices is the appropriateness for diagnostics. For example, software that displays medical images might have to undergo investigation by the Food and Drug Administration (FDA) or other local legal authorities to be cleared for commercial marketing. Smartphones and tablet computers do not necessarily meet the requirements to undergo these studies. Therefore, the appropriateness and legitimacy of the device chosen for visualization should always be taken into account when considering the use of a mobile device for diagnostic or visualization of medical images.

21.4 Image Analysis

Image analysis is the task of extracting abstract information or semantics and knowledge from the raw pixels of image and signal data. This is the most challenging task in biomedical imaging as it supports researchers and clinicians in finding clues for disease or certain phenotypes (diagnostics), supports novices and experts in performing procedures (therapy) and follow-up to the outcome, and allows scientist to gain knowledge from imaging data.

With the growing number of digital imaging devices, automated knowledge extraction becomes more and more important. The new trend towards mobile and personalized health data additionally drives the need for automation. For example, many applications for the smartphone-based investigation of skin cancers do already exist but only a few are actually accurate [52] . Pulse frequency is determined accurately and contactless by any smartphone device simply filming the face and determining the very slight periodic changes in skin color, which are usually not observed by humans [44, 57].

Furthermore, personalized medicine offsets the classical doctor visits towards web-based services (e.g., WebMD). Therefore, mobile and cloud applications for the analysis of medical image data will take an important role in the future of biomedical data analytics.

A common biomedical image analysis task can be split up into several substeps:

1. *Preprocessing* to remove background noise or enhance the image
2. *Extraction* of features to be used in later steps
3. *Registration* of several images
4. *Segmentation* (localization and delineation) of regions of interest (ROIs)
5. *Classification* of the image or segmented parts and measurements

$\frac{1}{16}$	$\frac{2}{16}$	$\frac{1}{16}$
$\frac{2}{16}$	$\frac{4}{16}$	$\frac{2}{16}$
$\frac{1}{16}$	$\frac{2}{16}$	$\frac{1}{16}$

A	B	C
D	E	F
G	H	I

-1	0	+1
-2	0	+2
-1	0	+1

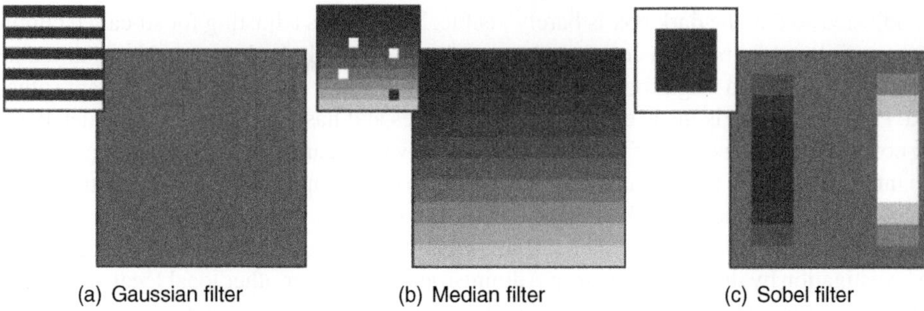

FIGURE 21.10: Spatial filters with template (top), original (icon on the left) and result (bottom).

21.4.1 Preprocessing and Filtering

Basically all images from biomedical imaging modalities and especially those from smartphone-cameras are noisy and contain artifacts. Therefore, preprocessing is required before the data can be used for analysis. Additional preprocessing can also help to prepare the image for certain analysis tasks, such as edge detection. Most of the preprocessing algorithms are low in computation time and memory requirements and hence suitable for mobile devices. Here, three common 2D filters will be discussed (Figure 21.10) [3]:

1. *Gaussian filter*: A Gaussian filter is commonly used to remove noise and recording artifacts from an image by blurring. The filter consists of a multidimensional Gaussian distribution that is convolved with the image. For convolution, the center value is replaced with the accumulated weighted values according to the mask. High frequency noise in the image is thereby reduced (Figure 21.10(a)).

2. *Median filter*: The media filter is also used to reduce noise. For this filter, a sliding window with a fixed size (here a 3x3 pixel) is moved across the image. The center point of the window is replaced by the median value within the window. For median computation, the image pixel values at current mask position (A to I) are sorted, and the center is replaced by the fifth value in the sorted row. This removes outliers in an otherwise smooth area while maintaining the value of the majority of the pixels (Figure 21.10(b)).

3. *Sobel filter*: The Sobel filter is used to enhance edges in the image. For this, an asymmetric filter is convolved with the image (Figure 21.10(c)). The mask that is visualized in Figure 21.10, is sensitive to vertical edges, in particular to vertical edges from black to white. Usually, this mask is turned by 90° and the signs are changed ending up with a set of eight different masks. All eight masks are applied individually and, for instance, the maximum is used as a replacement for the center pixel to obtain an edge map.

21.4.2 Feature Extraction

Features are simplified descriptors of an image or part of an image. Features are used to compare two images, or find similarities or shared objects between multiple images. Image features can be either global (describing the image as a whole) or local (describing a part of any size of the image).

A very basic global image feature is the image histogram (Figure 21.11). A histogram is a probability distribution of the pixel/voxel values in the image. For each possible value, the number of occurrences is counted in the image. This results in a very simplified representation as information on the intensity is maintained, but all spatial information is lost. Global features, such as the shape

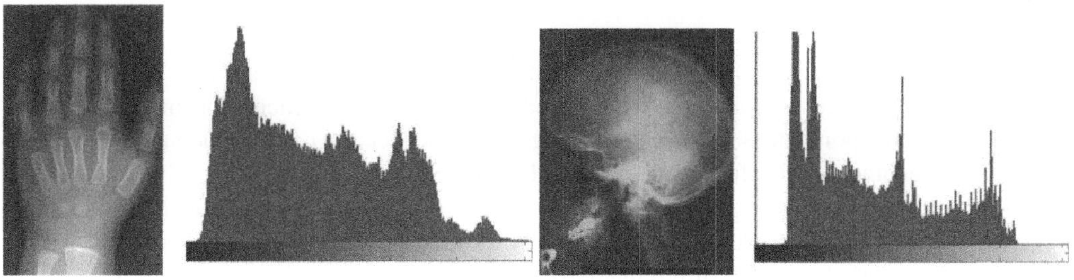

(a) Hand radiography (b) Skull radiography

FIGURE 21.11: Images and their histograms.

of the histogram, can be used, for instance, to distinguish between classes of images, e.g., hand and skull radiographs (Figure 21.11).

Local features describe only a part of the image at a certain spatial position. Most are created in two separate steps. The first one is feature detection, in which points of interest (POIs) are localized. The second step features description. For each of the detected points, a description of this position (possibly including some surrounding areas) is created. Since images can be acquired under different conditions like scale and rotation, certain invariance against these changes is needed for both detector and descriptor.

One feature detection method, which is inherently invariant against most changes in scale or rotation, is a simple corner detector. Corners are either the intersection of two edges in the image, or change in direction of a single edge. Since these definitions do not change whether the image is scaled, rotated or translated, corners are invariant against these changes. In contrast, a feature that would change with certain transforms are, for example, horizontal edges. While scaling and translation do not change the definition, a rotation does have an impact as horizontal edges are no longer horizontal after a 90 degree rotation. However, since straight lines or corners are very rare in biomedical imaging, more sophisticated features are required.

A robust feature detector is the scale invariant feature transform (SIFT), which consists of a detector and a descriptor [39]. Inherently, SIFT features are invariant against rotation, translation, and partially invariant to illumination. Additionally, scale invariance is achieved by systematically scaling the image to find POIs at different scales. The feature descriptors themselves are therefore not invariant to scale, but the method of detecting the positions for them is. To perform this, the image is filtered with a difference-of-Gaussian filter (essentially a band-pass filter, removing high and low frequencies) at different scales (so-called scale space, the scale is one dimension of this space). Local minima in the filtered and scaled images are then detected, which mark POIs for feature extraction. POIs along edges or with low contrast are not used. For feature description, the neighborhood around the detected POI is oriented based on the major orientation of the area. The neighborhood is then divided into a 4 by 4 grid with each grid cell containing 16 by 16 pixels. A histogram of the gradients (directionality) in each cell of the grid is calculated, and the result is stored as a feature vector. Gradients are only measured in eight directions. Therefore, the feature vector has a size of 8x4x4 = 128 values. Since orientation of the grid is aligned based on the major orientation of the region, the feature vector is created invariant to rotation. Invariance to lighting is achieved by not directly using the values of the image, but by using gradients, which are robust towards illumination changes up to a certain degree.

Many more improvements and novel techniques toward feature extraction have been developed [6, 45, 36, 1], but the key concepts are usually similar to the SIFT method.

21.4.3 Registration

The feature vector is used to find reference points in several images. As easy as it is for humans to identify that two images are captured from the same scene, it is as difficult for machine vision. Based on SIFT correspondences between two images, such a decision can be made automatically. Furthermore, a geometric transformation can be determined bringing the point of view of both images together. This process is called registration. Registration allows automatically comparing images form the same scene to determine the areas where changes have occurred over the time.

Registration is performed with different approaches [17]:

1. *Raw data-based* registration aligns two images based on the similarity in the image intensity or color using a correlation metric.

2. *Point-based* registration extracts landmarks or POIs in the image and creates a transformation matrix based on these.

3. *Edge-based* registration aligns the images based on edges. Such techniques are used, for instance, in fundus imaging.

4. *Object-based* registration is performed in high-level vision systems, where objects are identified first and registration is then based on shape or the center of gravity of these objects.

In all cases, one of the images is set as a reference image to which the other (follow-up) image is being registered. We further need to define the type of transform: translation, rotation, scaling, and other affine transforms; or nonrigid: elastic transforms that locally register parts of the image differently than other parts.

For raw data-based registration, the follow-up (moving) image is placed with a guessed transform (e.g., identity transform) on the reference (fixed) image and a correlation coefficient, mutual information, or other similarity measures [35] are calculated. This metric is improved iteratively by trying slight variations of the current transform. The variations are determined by an optimizer and for each iteration, a certain interpolation scheme is required to transform the follow-up image on the discrete grid [33, 34]. Finally, the best matching transform is chosen. Figure 21.12 depicts the general scheme of iterative image registration, which is composed of metric, optimizer, transform, and interpolator.

The point-based registration approaches are based on POIs, which have been extracted, for instance, using the SIFT algorithm. The POIs of the two images are matched pairwise and all strong matches are kept. A strong match is found if the most similar corresponding POI in the second image defines a point pair that is also found when switching reference and follow-up images. Based on these matches, the geometric transformation is determined.

Nonrigid registration elastically warps an image, usually enforcing exact superimposition of the point pairs. More frequent, a certain transform model is determined. Here, we can usually derive more equations from the point correspondences as required to determine the degrees of freedom (parameters) of the transform. For instance, a rigid transform in 3D is determined by three shift parameters along the orthogonal axes, and three rotational angels, which can be calculated from only two 3D point correspondences. A least-squares algorithm is applied to find the best match directly. Alternatively, the transformation matrix is calculated with random sample consensus (RANSAC). RANSAC chooses a subset of the matches and calculates a transformation matrix based on these. The matrix is then tested on the remaining matches and if enough samples agree, RANSAC terminates and returns the transformation matrix. This guarantees a robust result [22].

21.4.4 Segmentation

Segmentation is performed to distinguish regions in an image, for example foreground and background. It is therefore a labeling problem: All pixels or voxels in the image have to be associated

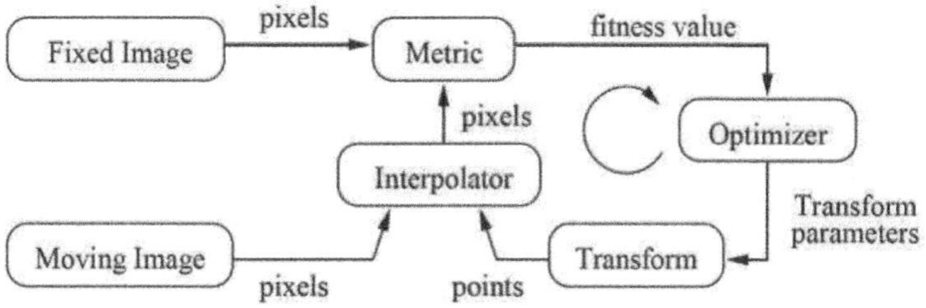

FIGURE 21.12: General scheme of iterative image registration. (Source: VTK Software Guide)

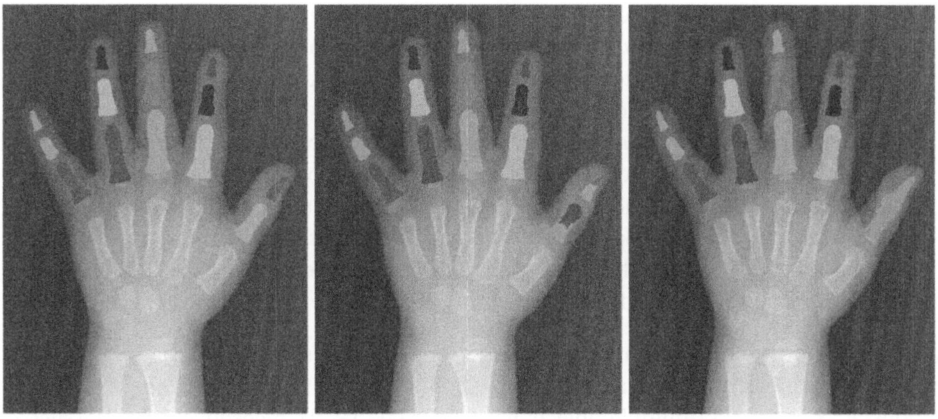

(a) Accurate segmentation of finger bones in a radiograph (b) Over segmentation in thumb bones (c) Under segmentation in thumb bones

FIGURE 21.13: Typical problems with segmentation.

with exactly one label each. Note that this labeling paradigm opposes the actual situation that in many imaging modalities, such as X-ray imaging or microscopy, each pixel or voxel is superimposed from several objects.

Segmentation can be performed on multiple abstraction levels and with or without manual interaction. Higher levels require more prior knowledge about the desired result:

1. *Pixel/voxel-based*: Segmentation uses the lowest level of abstraction. Simple thresholding, for example, differs foreground from background or between multiple objects (e.g., bone, tissue, and air in an X-ray or CT images). Automatic threshold determination is based on the Otsu algorithm. This method creates an image histogram and finds thresholds such that the quotient of interclass variances and intraclass variances is maximized [42].

2. *Edge-based*: Edges and boundaries of regions are closely related. For edge-based segmentation, first an edge-enhancing filter in combination with thresholding is used to detect edges. Canny edge detection applies a hysteresis function to result in a binary map of edge segments with one pixel thickness [11]. Objects completely framed by edges are then labeled as one region. However, edges are often discontinuous and have to be connected, e.g., using morphological operations. Another semiautomated method is called livewire, where the user clicks only some boundary points and based on gradient information, the computer finds the best connection in between. Since a cost map is calculated on initialization, the cheapest path is visualized instantaneously by a line following any user movement of the cursor (livewire) [20]. Based on an edge map of the image, the shape of an active contour is placed

and fitted to minimize an energy function that balances stiffness of the model and variation from the edge map.

3. *Region-based*: Region-based segmentation uses similarity in adjacent pixels or subregions. One approach here is statistical region merging, which first creates one region for each pixel (voxel). Neighbored regions are then merged iteratively until a certain threshold is reached (e.g., number of remaining regions preset by the user). Usually, the merging is performed based on statistical similarity (e.g., difference in average intensity or color) [41].

4. *Object-based*: High-level segmentation methods require prior knowledge about the object to segment. Examples are Hough transform, template matching, or active shape models [5, 14, 9]. In all cases, the shape of the object must be known a priori. The Hough transform can be used to estimate the position of any shape derived through mathematical formulation (e.g., line, circle). Each position on the image is transformed into the parameter space of any possible solution of the mathematical description and all pixels are accumulated. The set of parameters with highest accumulated representations in pixel space describes one possible segmentation result. In the second case, a template image containing a sample representation of the object is matched to the image computing its correlation on all positions. Finding the global maximum yields the position of best match. Active shape model segmentation uses a statistical model describing the shape and possible variance of the shape of an object. This requires a certain set of already segmented training data.

Segmentation often suffers from over- or undersegmentation (Figure 21.13). This means, that either too many regions are segmented (one object is labeled with more than one region) or too few regions are segmented (multiple objects have the same label), respectively. Both issues cannot be solved easily and require experience and knowledge by the user to choose the appropriate segmentation algorithm and parameters.

21.4.5 Classification

Classification of biomedical images can be used in multiple ways. Usually, the presence or absence of a certain type or property of an object is classified (e.g., cancerous or not), which yields a two-class or binary classification task. A more complex task is tumor staging, where the degree of a tumorous process is determined to select an appropriate therapy. Both tasks may be performed independently and consecutively. For example in screening mammography, images with suspicious regions must be detected. This process is called computer-aided detection (CADe), while the staging is called computer-aided diagnostics (CADx). The localization of a suspicious region is not per se part of classification; it is often combined into the process, as it is often part of the solution.

In general, classification is the problem of mapping objects with different content to multiple meaningful classes or labels. Prior knowledge about the properties of each class has to be formalized (e.g., seeking a bright object in front of a darker background when applying thresholding to classify each pixel as being either of both). All multiclass problems can be reduced to binary classification by building individual classifiers for each class against all other classes (one-vs.-all) or against each other class (one-vs.-one).

In the case of biomedical imaging, classes are often following normal distributions and are therefore overlapping. This means that an object might have similar or the same properties of class A, but might actually be of class B. The object will be classified falsely, which however, cannot be avoided. Therefore, a certain classification error is always possible and classification aims at optimizing towards the smallest classification error by choosing the best-suited features to describe the object properties. For example, if one would try to classify the gender of a person just by measuring the height, persons taller than a certain threshold are considered as males and smaller persons as fe-

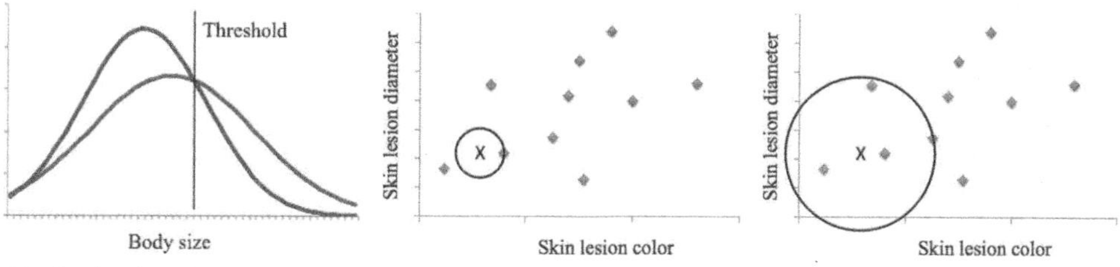

(a) Thresholding of gender based on the body size: female (upper curve) and male (lower curve).
(b) Nearest neighbor classification of melanoma and benign skin lesions.
(c) k-nearest neighbor classification of the same skin lesion as in (b).

FIGURE 21.14: Binary classification techniques.

males. This will, of course, result in many false classifications. While this error cannot be avoided, an optimal threshold exists that minimizes this error (Figure 21.14(a)).

Usually, more than one feature is evaluated for classification, yielding n-dimensional feature vectors. A basic classification technique is the so-called nearest neighbor (NN) classification [15]. A database of objects with known class labels must exist. If a new object has to be classified, the most similar object from the reference database is searched using a distance function that is calculated on the features (Figure 21.14(b)). The new object is classified with the same class, as its most similar counterpart in the database, its nearest neighbor. Since the NN approach is very sensitive towards outliers (single data points of class A within a group of class B that could distort the result), an extension to this approach exists called k-nearest neighbor (kNN). Instead of simply searching for the most similar object in the database, the k most similar objects are determined. The class is then decided by a majority vote between the k known classes (Figure 21.14(c)). Thereby, individual outliers are not influencing the classification result anymore.

Many other classification methods have been developed. Some are based on logical formulations (decision trees), others resembling the process by which the human brain performs classification tasks (artificial neural networks), or based on mathematical transformations (support vector machines) [19].

Once the image or the relevant ROIs have been classified, measures are extracted, which usually complete the image analysis chain.

21.4.6 Evaluation of Image Analysis

When analyzing biomedical data, one common problem is the definition of a so-called ground truth or gold standard. This means, that the true result of a classification or segmentation task is not obvious and the measurement of quality is therefore difficult. For example, when testing for cancer in screening mammography, the only way to know for sure whether cancer is actually present or not, is a biopsy of the breast. Even worse, the exact 2D outline of a (correctly) detected 3D mass that was projected to the 2D detector plane cannot be determined at all. Therefore, an evaluation dataset with a known presence or absence of the targeted condition has to be created to measure the accuracy of a test.

In the first example above, evaluation based on a ground truth would mean that a set of mammographies with accompanying data of tissue biopsies has to be collected. The outcome of the tissue biopsies (positive or negative for cancer) would be the ground truth. Other form of ground truth would be the exact location and extend of cancerous tissue. In general, when considering a known ground truth, sensitivity and specificity are suitable measures of accuracy of classification in biomedical tests. When using a test for a certain condition, four outcomes are possible:

- *True positive*: The test detects the condition and it is actually present.
- *False positive*: The test detects the condition, but it is actually not present.
- *True negative*: The test correctly detects the absence of the condition.
- *False negative*: The test detects the absence of the condition, while the condition is actually present.

The term "sensitivity" describes the rate of the correctly classified positive samples within samples with the condition (rate of true positives within the condition group). In other words: the percentage of sick people that were correctly identified. The specificity describes the opposite, the rate of correctly classified negative samples within the healthy group (rate of true negatives within the healthy group); or the percentage of healthy people, who were identified as such. In the best case, both rates are *1* (100% correctly classified both positive and negative). In the worst case, the assignment is random and sensitivity and specificity are both *0.5*. Sensitivity and specificity are both independent of the prevalence of the condition (probability of having the condition) and are therefore test specific.

In many other fields, error rate (number of falsely classified samples towards all samples) is used for the evaluation of a test. However, if the prevalence of a condition is very low (e.g., less than 1%), a small error rate (e.g., 1%) could already mean that the condition is never classified correctly. If the prevalence is much higher (50%), a test with low error rate (1%) is very sensitive and specific. Therefore, the error rate is not a suitable measure for biomedical test performance. Furthermore, the type of error (false positive, false negative) usually is of different relevance. For instance, a screening method needs to detect all true positives, while finding some false positives is tolerable. In contrast for differential diagnosis, a specific test must be developed, minimizing the false positive rate.

For example, we consider screening for the human immunodeficiency virus (HIV). Here, a simple and fast initial test with high sensitivity is performed (enzyme-linked immunosorbent assay, ELISA) to find all true positives and some false positives. The upside is that people marked negative by this test do not carry the disease with a very high chance. In a second round, the positively detected persons are screened with a secondary test (Western Blot), which is more complicated but has a high specificity. Thus, all persons with a possibility of having HIV are identified in the first step and this result is cleaned from false positives in the second step.

Referring back to the example on mammography and the shape of the mass, the "ground truth" is usually derived from a manual segmentation by an expert. However, even experts are usually inconsistent (intraobserver variability) and there is also a high interobserver variance between multiple experts. Therefore, manual references should not be termed ground truth.

Especially in segmentation, the lack of ground truth has been well addressed. One solution is the simultaneous truth and performance level estimation (STAPLE) algorithm [50]. In this iterative algorithm, a probabilistic estimation of the true "ground truth" is calculated based on the segmentation results of multiple experts or algorithms (observers). Each pixel or voxel is associated with a probability of it belonging to the foreground or background. In other words, each pixel or voxel is partially foreground and background at the same time, corresponding to its probability estimate. In a second step of the iteration, each observer (automatic or manual segmentation instance) is evaluated based on the currently estimated ground truth. Observers less agreeing with that estimate are considered less reliable and their segmentation is reduced in weight when updating the ground truth estimate. The iteration terminates when the ground truth estimation is stable.

This algorithm allows for a simultaneous calculation of a "true" ground truth and performance measure of each of the contributing segmentation results.

21.4.7 Mobile Image Analysis

One important aspect of mobile image analysis is the required computational power. Since most mobile devices cannot perform expensive calculations by themselves, one possibility is the offset of computation tasks to a server. Therefore, mobile image analysis can be distinguished into two different approaches:

- **Online analysis**: Here, the mobile device has to be connected to cloud services ("online"), or in general the Internet through wireless networks. Data required for the analysis task has to be transferred to another computer prior to analysis.
- **Offline analysis**: In this approach, no Internet connectivity is needed. All information used for the analysis is collected and the complete computation is also performed on the mobile device.

Both methods do have drawbacks: wireless networks are not as fast and reliable and computational power on mobile devices is highly limited. Therefore, a balanced approach towards mobile image analysis has to be implemented, which does not create delays due to computation or communication bottlenecks.

For example for the second approach, a mobile application for the diagnostics of preeclampsia has been developed [31]. In pregnancy, the preeclampsia disease majorly causes maternal and perinatal morbidity and mortality, especially in developing countries. Traditionally, the disease is diagnosed by a medical expert based on symptoms like hypertension and protein in urine, resulting in a substantial sensitivity but rather low specificity.

Recently, a novel test scheme has been developed [10]. For this test, urine of pregnant women, stained with Congo-red dye (which binds to a misfolded protein), is applied to a cellulose test sheet (which also binds to a misfolded protein). The sheet is then washed with specific solutions and the remaining amount of colored protein is an indicator for the presence or absence of preeclampsia. This test is easy to perform, but difficult to evaluate, as different intensities of the stained protein are difficult to compare.

A mobile image processing workflow has been designed, using the built-in camera of a smartphone (Figure 21.15). The camera captures an image of the test sheet before (Pix1) and after the washing (Pix2). The test sheet is standardized in size (aspect ratio) and localization of patients' samples (patient cells). Using edge detection and corner detection, the test sheet can be detected in the acquired image. First, the images are filtered with a Sobel filter to enhance edges, then thresholded to determine edges from background, and lastly, a Hough-line transform is applied to extract straight lines (compare Sections 21.4.1 and 21.4.2). Intersections in the four major lines (outlines of the sheet) are the corners. Using the positions of the corners, the two sheets can be extracted and registered by spanning both on a rectangle (compare Section 21.4.3). Based on the sheet standardization, the position of the patient cells can be determined and the urine dots segmented using a Hough circle transform (compare Section 21.4.4). With the known localization and extent of the patient samples, and with the registered images, a before and after analysis of the patients' urine samples can be achieved. The resulting retention ratio of the Congo-red dye can be displayed and mailed to a medical professional for classification. Classification of the resulting ratio into several stages of disease can be performed based on thresholding (compare Section 21.4.5). The mobile application is invariant towards lighting, viewpoint, and other user-related changes to reliably detect the test sheet and retention ratio. Furthermore, the application performs on outdated equipment and without additional resources such as an Internet connection or help of the user to be a useful tool when used by untrained personnel in austere settings. The user is guided through the acquisition process according to the acquisition protocol (Figure 21.16). All intermediate results of the image processing chain (sheet detection and extraction, patient cell and sample detection and segmentation) are presented to the user as a quality control.

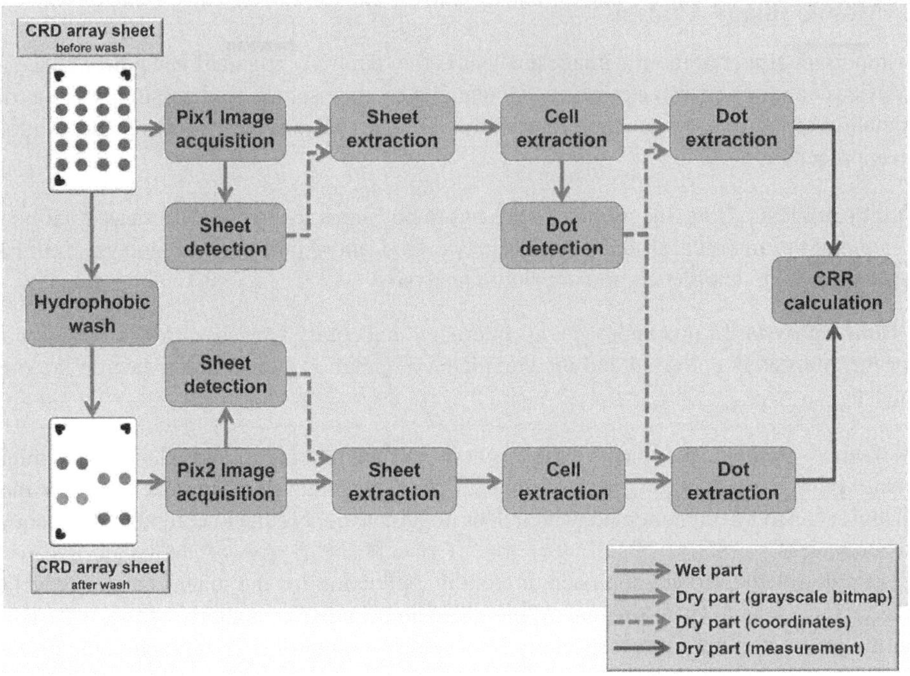

FIGURE 21.15: Display of the workflow in a mobile image processing application [31].

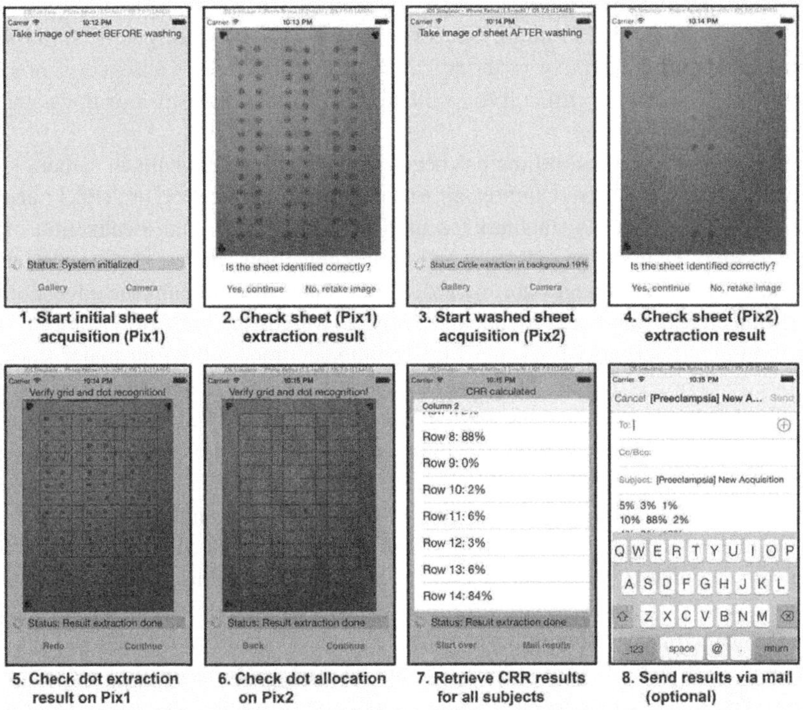

FIGURE 21.16: Application interface of mobile image processing application [31].

21.5 Image Management and Communication

Communication and management of biomedical images is important in clinical research and practice. Since imaging data is vital for the understanding of diseases and their progression, as well as diagnostics and treatment planning, images usually have to be stored for long periods of time and are communicated between many different agents. For example, X-ray images are acquired by a technician, sent to a physician for diagnostics and then stored in a central facility. With the rise of mobile devices in medicine, these devices also have to be integrated into existing workflows and communication protocols [13].

21.5.1 Standards for Communication

Since medical images are acquired in many different locations and by many different modalities (e.g., CT, MRI, ultrasound, ...) and are communicated to many other devices (e.g., printers, radiology workstations, image analysis systems, mobile devices, ...), a common communication standard is important. It is also very important to add patient and other metainformation (e.g., reports) into the file. Therefore, already in the 1980s, the National Electrical Manufacturers Association joined forces with the American College of Radiology to develop a first version of the digital imaging and communications in medicine (DICOM) standard, which is nowadays maintained by the DICOM standards committee. DICOM consists of two parts (in the beginning, there was a third part defining the communication protocol, which has been replaced by the common Internet TCP/IP protocol):

1. *DICOM Object Classes*: DICOM generically describes image properties, patient data, and metadata using a tag value concept. Each piece of information is addressed by its tag and, hence, can be placed on any position in the resulting data stream. This gives a high degree of freedom to developers and manufacturers. This concept allows storing multiple images within one DICOM file (e.g., a series of multiple CT slices or images from different modalities). DICOM also supports compression of image data, which is important for archiving.

2. *DICOM Service Classes*: A service describes the action that is intended with the data. They support storage and retrieval of image data as well as the organization of examinations. The basic DICOM services are:

   - Verify (check conformance of external network node)
   - Storage (actually two commands, "Store" for storage and "Move" to transfer)
   - Storage Commitment (confirm storage before deletion)
   - Query/Retrieve (search objects and initiate transfer with storage)
   - Modality Worklist Management (metadata to modality)
   - Modality Performed Procedure Step (confirm acquisition, may differ from requests)

Advanced services address the need to have images likewise ordered, displayed, and perceived by radiologists on different locations using different hard- and software. DICOM Softcopy Presentation States, for instance, standardize the same display on any hard-/software with respect to grayscale, color, contrast, rotation, and zoom. DICOM Structured Display define the screen layout by image boxes (e.g., axial, coronar, lateral views), while DICOM Hanging Protocols reproducible combine different images from the same examination (e.g., cranio-caudal (CC) and medio-lateral oblique (MLO) imaging directions from left and right breast in mammography).

Meanwhile, the International Organization for Standardization (ISO) has accepted DICOM as standard in medical imaging. It has been widely adopted by manufacturers and developers in the

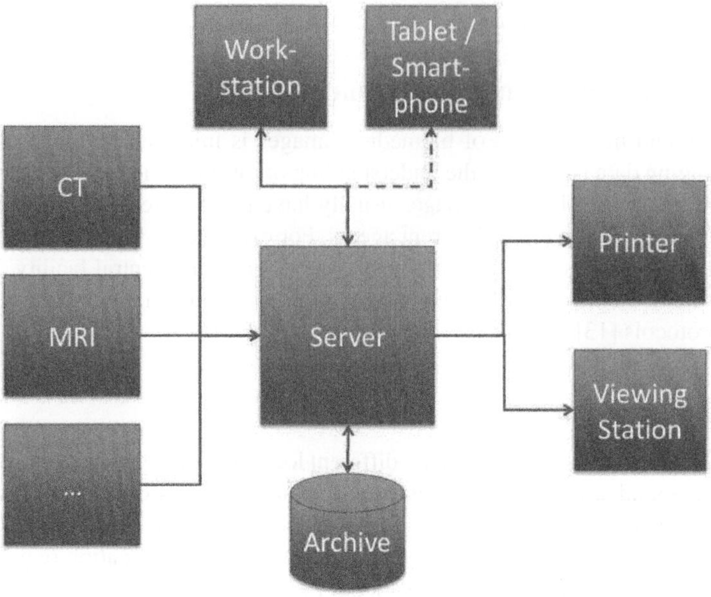

FIGURE 21.17: Example of a biomedical PACS composed of input (left), output, (right) and storage and communication (middle) component. The lines indicate data transfer according to the DICOM standard within a secured intranet (full line) or via the Internet (dashed line).

medical field. However, DICOM is not a standard for clinical workflows and communication with other nonimaging devices in hospitals (e.g., hospital information system, billing, ordering, etc.).

Also, due to the many degrees of freedom with the DICOM standard, the Integrating the Healthcare Enterprise (IHE) initiative was established in 1998 by a consortium of radiologists and information technologists aimed at standardizing the use of the DICOM standard. An IHE integration profile describes a clinical information need or workflow scenario and documents how to use established standards to accomplish it. A group of systems that implement the same integration profile address the need/scenario in a mutually compatible way, which is checked annually with so-called "connectathons" (interoperability showcases).

21.5.2 Archiving

Long-term storage of medical data is legally required in many countries and by many health organizations; medical image archiving is a central task of image management. Since medical images can easily be hundredths of megabytes in sizes for regular imaging modalities, up to terabytes for whole-slide imaging, and they have to be stored for periods of up to ten years, archiving has to be carefully considered [47]. The most important points are long-term readability, compression of the data to save storage space, and the inseparable association of images with patient data. Since the DICOM file format has been developed with long-term storage as one of the applications, it allows for all three: (i) storage with known standards to be used for years to come; (ii) compression of image data; and (iii) storage of patient data along with image data.

A system composed of units for image generation, storage, processing, and distribution, is called picture archiving and communication system (PACS). The PACS server persistently stores image and metadata that is retrieved and communicated to other PACS components (Figure 21.17).

With the rise of personalized health, health information might have to be stored during the lifetime of a person for 70 to 100 years. However, many so-called persistent memory media have a limited shelf life (e.g., optical discs like DVDs or CDs 10–25 years, magnetic tape up to 30 years, hard drives 3–5 years); so far, only one truly permanent storage solution exists (M-disc, up to 1000 years).[1] Therefore, PACS servers themselves are often mirrored onto secondary servers for backup reasons.

While archiving of medical information plays a vital role in personalized health, many security and privacy issues arise with long-term storage of personal health information. Most archiving servers are therefore separated from the Internet. This poses possible problems for the communication between these servers and mobile devices outside of the hospital network.

21.5.3 Retrieval

So far, image retrieval from any imaging archive is done by the alphanumeric metadata stored alone the image bitmaps. Contrarily, content-based image retrieval (CBIR) aims at managing images by pattern and retrieving images from an (PACS) archive by means of visual similarity. The saying "A picture is worth a thousand words" describes the inherent incompleteness of any natural language description of an image–a problem well known in the medical field, too [2].

A CBIR system is usually composed of four steps: (i) signature extraction is based on the image pattern and features such as color, texture, and shape; (ii) similarity computation quantifies the visual distance of two images or image patterns by means of their signatures; (iii) signature indexing structures the large number of signatures and images hosted in the archive to speed up the response time; and (iv) image retrieval that finally presents a corresponding set of retrieved images according to the most similar signatures.

The image retrieval in a medical applications (IRMA) framework has been used to derive several CBIR applications. If the image archive is annotated with ground truth, CBIR can even yield CADx applications. In Figure 21.18, for instance, the result of CBIR-based bone age estimation is presented to the user [21]. The query image and its extracted ROIs are shown at the topmost area of the interface. Their most similar counterparts retrieved from the archive are displayed below (scrollable) in decreasing similarity and with the validated bone age. Based on the reference ages and the similarity measures, the predicted age is calculated [29].

21.5.4 Mobile Image Management

Mobile devices like smartphones and tablet computers and also novel wearable technology are currently not well connected to PACS and hospital information systems. The problem of distributed information sources has to be solved for mobile communication [12] also. Furthermore, legal and regulatory concerns are still an issue and support of mobile devices is therefore limited [43]. Nonetheless, mobile devices will play a much larger role in diagnostics and treatment in the future and it is therefore important to keep the aspects of safety vs. mobility in mind when designing new communication and management options for biomedical images.

In 2010, for instance, scientists at Georgetown University Medical Center discovered how the Apple gadget can be used in an operation theatre: Surgeons are able to access real-time X-rays, CT scans, and laboratory reports with the new technology (Figure 21.19). The iPad also makes it possible for surgeons to have the data with them in both an operation theatre and throughout the rest of a hospital [51].

While portable devices such as smartphones allow for mobile acquisition of images, they still are mostly used to display information. In research and clinical trials, however, mobile apps have been developed to capture photographs of the patient and directly transfer the image data via wireless networks to the electronic case report form (eCRF) of that patient [28, 27].

Figure 21.20 exemplifies the OC-ToGo app. The study nurse logs into OpenClinica, an open

[1] http://www.mdisc.com/proving-ground/, http://www.archives.gov/records-mgmt/initiatives/temp-opmedia-faq.html

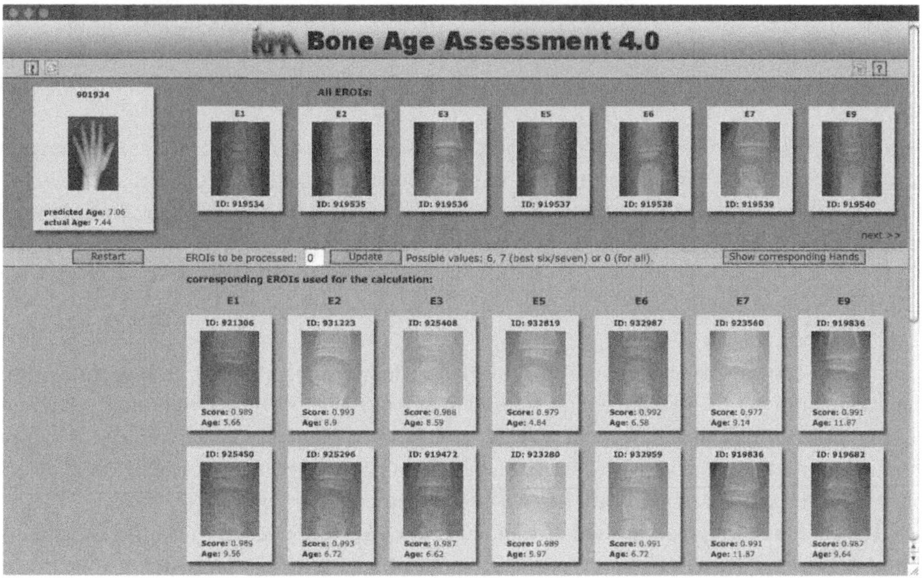

FIGURE 21.18: Result of a query to a CBIR system.

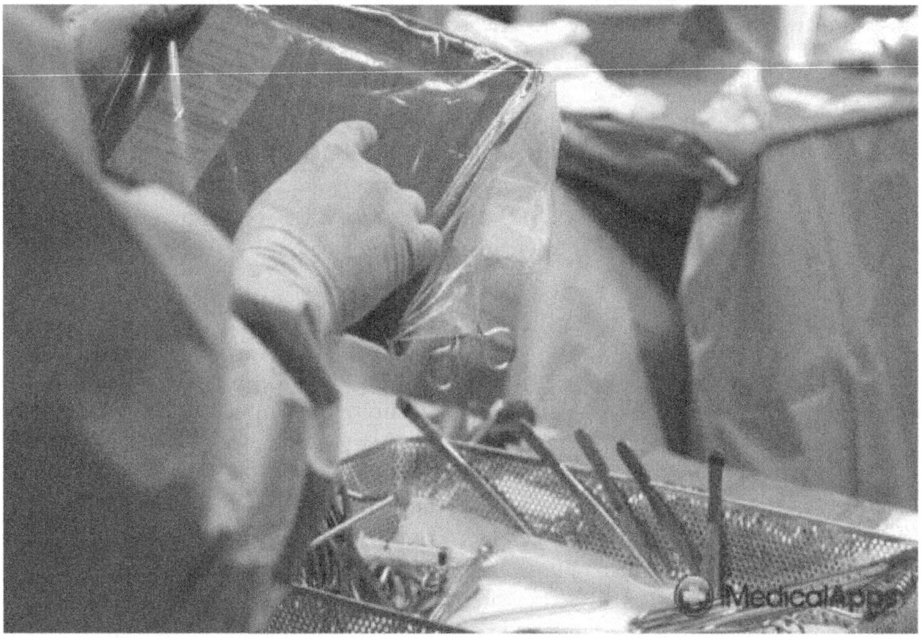

FIGURE 21.19: Use of the iPad in the surgical theatre.

source electronic data capture (EDC) system for clinical trials (1), selects study and patient accordingly (2), captures images until being satisfied (3), and transfer is started automatically (4) and confirmed, when ended (5). The image is secured on the server and not stored on the mobile device, which also is advantageous with respect to data security and data privacy issues.

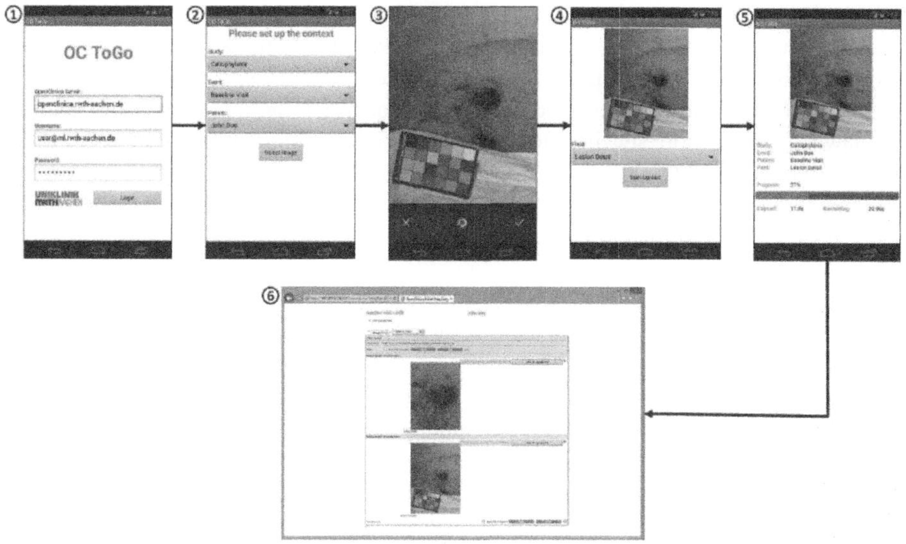

FIGURE 21.20: Workflow of the OC-ToGo App that allows users to capture events in clinical trials on a smartphone.

21.6 Summary and Future Directions

In this chapter, the core concepts of biomedical imaging and analysis in the mobile and stationary have been displayed. Specifically, the most important image formation modalities that are used in everyday clinical routine and research have been elaborated. The differences between the key formation techniques of projection and cross-sectional imaging and the different applications have been shown.

The importance of suitable image visualization for biomedical images with different dimensionality has been highlighted. A major focus was set on the implications for mobile devices with new display technology and limited bandwidth (e.g., 3G: 350–2000 kbit/s) and computational power (iPhone 4: 1 GHz, single core).

The same limitations also pose an impact on mobile and stationary image analysis of biomedical images. The image processing chain of preprocessing, filtering, feature extraction, registration, segmentation, classification, and measurement as well as the evaluation of medical image analysis have been shown.

In the last part, challenges in image management and communication for the clinical environment have been discussed. Here, the change towards mobile devices is expected to have a large impact.

In general, two key challenges of mobile devices in medicine and specifically in mobile imaging and analytics can be identified: performance and concordance with law. While capacity and computational power of mobile devices continuously increases, these devices are still far away from replacing conventional workstations. Especially limited processing power and memory (up to 3 GB in modern tablet computers, up to 128 GB in modern workstations) pose the largest problems. Algorithms solved in seconds on a workstation can still take minutes to hours on smartphones or tablet computers, which makes data analytics in real time impossible. The same yields for storage capacity (usually far less than 500 GB on smartphones and tablet computers, multiple terabytes on workstations). Another limiting factor that is often forgotten is the battery life of smart devices when used for heavy calculations. For example, smart wearables like Google Glass run out of battery life after about an hour of moderate usage. While all of this poses an additional burden to researchers in mobile biomedical imaging, the second limitation, concordance with law, is much more difficult for innovators. Privacy, especially in medicine, is a factor that is gaining more and more attention, as people and lawmakers get more sensitive to which information is shared with insurance companies and other third parties. Additionally, all software in medicine in contact with patients or patient-data—not limited to diagnostic support or patient data management—has to undergo clinical trials or at least be assessed by a regulatory instance to prove that the software is beneficial (or at least not harmful) for patients.

Future work will have to focus on integrating novel mobile devices, such as wearable technology and implantable devices both for patients and doctors. This "mobile revolution" will take place in the next ten years and will place sophisticated medical sensors in everybody's hands. The major challenge for biomedical image and data analysts will be the amount of data that will be collected by novel devices like miniaturized ECGs and implantable biosensors. Nowadays, doctors only see a fraction of the life of their patients, while the new devices will allow them to track their well-being on a daily basis. Since physicians will not have the capacity to monitor this huge amount of data captured with noisy devices, automatic methods for diagnostic support will have to be implemented. This will require a completely new class of methods for analyzing biomedical data. While today's analytical algorithms focus on detecting single events during a patient's visits, in the near future changes that carry out over days or even months can be detected.

On the other hand, doctors can soon access their patient's data everywhere on the planet, can discuss findings with experts thousands of miles away having all the information they might need at their fingertips. While this poses many potential improvements, a physician's time is one of the most limited resources in medicine. It is therefore important to create tools to aid physicians in their daily routine, supplying the needed information while avoiding information overload.

Integrating new devices into clinical workflow will pose an additional challenge towards cost effectiveness. Many recent developments in biomedicine and biotechnology that aimed for the improvement of clinical care had an adverse effect by increasing the complexity and costs of healthcare [7]. The new technology will therefore have to compensate by lowering costs and complexity, possibly by offsetting many expensive data capturing techniques to cheap, personal devices.

One huge advantage of mobile devices over the current infrastructure of healthcare is of course the mobility. While this will improve medical care in developed countries, it will have an even bigger impact on healthcare in developing countries. Mobile devices like smartphones put computational power, a large amount of sensors, and connectivity into the hands of millions of people that so far had only limited access to clinics and medical professionals. By extending smartphones with additional sensors for medical diagnostics, for the first time in history, medical care will be available for everybody. Simultaneously, a real-time status of global health will be available through social networks that will allow worldwide planning in disease prevention and intervention. It will be an exciting new age for biomedical imaging research and applications.

Bibliography

[1] A. Alahi, R. Ortiz, and P. Vandergheynst. Freak: Fast retina keypoint. In *Computer Vision and Pattern Recognition (CVPR), 2012 IEEE Conference on*, page 510-517. IEEE, 2012.

[2] Mostafa Analoui, D. Joseph Bronzino, and R. Donald Peterson. *Medical Imaging: Principles and Practices.* CRC Press, 2012.

[3] G. R. Arce. *Nonlinear Signal Processing: A Statistical Approach.* John Wiley & Sons, Jan. 2005.

[4] D. S. Atkinson. Display screen equipment: Standards and regulation. In J. Chen, W. Cranton, and M. Fihn, editors, *Handbook of Visual Display Technology*, pages 203–213. Springer Berlin Heidelberg, Jan. 2012.

[5] D. H. Ballard. Generalizing the hough transform to detect arbitrary shapes. *Pattern Recognition*, 13(2):111–122, 1981.

[6] H. Bay, A. Ess, T. Tuytelaars, and L. Van Gool. Speeded-up robust features (SURF). *Computer Vision and Image Understanding*, 110(3):346–359, June 2008.

[7] T. Bodenheimer. High and rising health care costs. Part 2: Technologic innovation. *Annals of Internal Medicine*, 142(11):932–937, June 2005.

[8] D. J. Brady. *Optical Imaging and Spectroscopy.* John Wiley & Sons, Apr. 2009.

[9] R. Brunelli. *Template Matching Techniques in Computer Vision: Theory and Practice.* Hoboken, NJ: Wiley; 2009.

[10] I. A. Buhimschi, U. A. Nayeri, G. Zhao, L. L. Shook, A. Pensalfini, E. F. Funai, I. M. Bernstein, C. G. Glabe, and C. S. Buhimschi. Protein misfolding, congophilia, oligomerization, and defective amyloid processing in preeclampsia. *Science Translational Medicine*, 6(245):245ra92, July 2014.

[11] J. Canny. A computational approach to edge detection. *IEEE Transactions on Pattern Analysis and Machine Intelligence*, PAMI-8(6):679–698, Nov. 1986.

[12] J. Choi, S. Yoo, H. Park, and J. Chun. MobileMed: A PDA-based mobile clinical information system. *IEEE Transactions on Information Technology in Biomedicine*, 10(3):627–635, July 2006.

[13] A. F. Choudhri and M. G. Radvany. Initial experience with a handheld device digital imaging and communications in medicine viewer: OsiriX mobile on the iPhone. *Journal of Digital Imaging*, 24(2):184–189, Apr. 2011.

[14] T. F. Cootes, C. J. Taylor, D. H. Cooper, and J. Graham. Active shape models-their training and application. *Computer Vision and Image Understanding*, 61(1):38–59, Jan. 1995.

[15] T. Cover and P. Hart. Nearest neighbor pattern classification. *IEEE Transactions on Information Theory*, 13(1):21–27, Jan. 1967.

[16] L. De Paepe, P. De Bock, O. Vanovermeire, and T. Kimpe. Performance evaluation of a visual display calibration algorithm for iPad. *SPIE Proceedings* Vol. 8319, Article 3: *Medical Imaging 2012: Advanced PACS-Based Imaging Informatics and Therapeutic Applications*, W.W. Boonn and B.J. Liu (Eds.), 831909–831909–7, 2012.

[17] T. M. Deserno. Fundamentals of biomedical image processing. In *Biomedical Image Processing*, pages 1–51. Springer, 2011.

[18] T. M. Deserno, I. Srndi, A. Jose, D. Haak, S. Jonas, P. Specht, and V. Brandenburg. Towards quantitative assessment of calciphylaxis. *SPIE Proceedings* Vol. 9035: *Medical Imaging 2014: Computer-Aided Diagnosis*, S. Aylward and L. Hadjiiski (Eds.), 2014.

[19] R. O. Duda, P. E. Hart, and D. G. Stork. *Pattern Classification.* John Wiley & Sons, 2012.

[20] A. X. Falco, J. K. Udupa, S. Samarasekera, S. Sharma, B. E. Hirsch, and R. d. A. Lotufo. User-steered image segmentation paradigms: Live wire and live lane. *Graphical Models and Image Processing*, 60(4):233–260, July 1998.

[21] B. Fischer, P. Welter, R. W. Gnther, and T. M. Deserno. Web-based bone age assessment by content-based image retrieval for case-based reasoning. *International Journal of Computer Assisted Radiology and Surgery*, 7(3):389–399, May 2012.

[22] M. A. Fischler and R. C. Bolles. Random sample consensus: A paradigm for model fitting with applications to image analysis and automated cartography. *Communications of ACM*, 24(6):381-395, June 1981.

[23] A. Giussani, C. Hoeschen. *Imaging in Nuclear Medicine*. Springer-Verlag Berlin, Germany, 2013.

[24] R. Gill. *The Physics and Technology of Diagnostic Ultrasound*. High Frequency Publishing.

[25] I. Gutenko, K. Petkov, C. Papadopoulos, X. Zhao, J. H. Park, A. Kaufman, and R. Cha. Remote volume rendering pipeline for mHealth applications. volume 9039, pages 903904–903904–7, 2014.

[26] E. M. Haacke, R. W. Brown, M. R. Thompson, and R. Venkatesan. *Magnetic Resonance Imaging: Physical Principles and Sequence Design*. 1999. New York: A John Wiley and Sons.

[27] D. Haak, J. Gehlen, S. Jonas, and T. M. Deserno. OC ToGo: bed site image integration into OpenClinica with mobile devices. SPIE Proceedings Vol. 9039: *Medical Imaging 2014: PACS and Imaging Informatics: Next Generation and Innovations*, M. Y. Law and T. S. Cook (Eds.), 2014.

[28] D. Haak, C. Samsel, J. Gehlen, S. Jonas, and T. M. Deserno. Simplifying electronic data capture in clinical trials: Workflow embedded image and biosignal file integration and analysis via web services. *Journal of Digital Imaging*, pages 1–10, May 2014.

[29] M. Harmsen, B. Fischer, H. Schramm, T. Seidl, and T. Deserno. Support vector machine classification based on correlation prototypes applied to bone age assessment. *IEEE Journal of Biomedical and Health Informatics*, 17(1):190–197, Jan. 2013.

[30] J. B. Haun, C. M. Castro, R. Wang, V. M. Peterson, B. S. Marinelli, H. Lee, and R. Weissleder. Micro-NMR for rapid molecular analysis of human tumor samples. *Science Translational Medicine*, 3(71):71ra1, 2011.

[31] S. M. Jonas, T. M. Deserno, C. S. Buhimschi, J. Makin, M. A. Choma, I. A. Buhimschi. Smartphone-based diagnostic of preeclampsia: an mHealth solution for the Congo red dot test in limited-resource settings. Lab Chip. *In review.*

[32] M. F. Juette, T. J. Gould, M. D. Lessard, M. J. Mlodzianoski, B. S. Nagpure, B. T. Bennett, S. T. Hess, and J. Bewersdorf. Three-dimensional sub-100 nm resolution fluorescence microscopy of thick samples. *Nature Methods*, 5(6):527–529, June 2008.

[33] T. Lehmann, C. Gonner, and K. Spitzer. Survey: interpolation methods in medical image processing. *IEEE Transactions on Medical Imaging*, 18(11):1049–1075, Nov. 1999.

[34] T. Lehmann, C. Gonner, and K. Spitzer. Addendum: B-spline interpolation in medical image processing. *IEEE Transactions on Medical Imaging*, 20(7):660–665, July 2001.

[35] T. Lehmann, A. Sovakar, W. Schmiti, and R. Repges. A comparison of similarity measures for digital subtraction radiography. *Computers in Biology and Medicine*, 27(2):151–167, Mar. 1997.

[36] S. Leutenegger, M. Chli, and R. Siegwart. BRISK: Binary robust invariant scalable keypoints. In *2011 IEEE International Conference on Computer Vision (ICCV)*, pages 2548–2555, Nov. 2011.

[37] R. Liang. Biomedical optical imaging technologies. *Biomedical Optical Imaging Technologies: Design and Applications, Biological and Medical Physics, Biomedical Engineering*. Springer-Verlag Berlin Heidelberg, 2013, 1, 2013.

[38] A. Lopes and K. Brodlie. Improving the robustness and accuracy of the marching cubes algorithm for isosurfacing. *IEEE Transactions on Visualization and Computer Graphics*, 9(1):16–29, Jan. 2003.

[39] D. G. Lowe. Distinctive image features from scale-invariant keypoints. *International Journal of Computer Vision*, 60(2):91–110, Nov. 2004.

[40] J. Martin. *Programming Real-Time Computer Systems*. Prentice-Hall International, 1965.

[41] R. Nock and F. Nielsen. Statistical region merging. *IEEE Transactions on Pattern Analysis and Machine Intelligence*, 26(11):1452–1458, Nov. 2004.

[42] N. Otsu. A threshold selection method from gray-level histograms. *Automatica*, 11(285-296):2327, 1975.

[43] S. G. Panughpath and A. Kalyanpur. Radiology and the mobile device: radiology in motion. *The Indian Journal of Radiology & Imaging*, 22(4):246–250, 2012.

[44] M.-Z. Poh, D. McDuff, and R. Picard. Advancements in noncontact, multiparameter physiological measurements using a webcam. *IEEE Transactions on Biomedical Engineering*, 58(1):7–11, Jan. 2011.

[45] E. Rublee, V. Rabaud, K. Konolige, and G. Bradski. ORB: an efficient alternative to SIFT or SURF. In *2011 IEEE International Conference on Computer Vision (ICCV)*, pages 2564–2571, Nov. 2011.

[46] I. Scholl, T. Aach, T. M. Deserno, and T. Kuhlen. Challenges of medical image processing. *Computer Science - Research and Development*, 26(1-2):5–13, Feb. 2011.

[47] R. E. Scott. e-records in health-preserving our future. *International Journal of Medical Informatics*, 76(56):427–431, May 2007.

[48] A. Nait-Ali (Ed.). *Advanced Biosignal Processing*. Springer 2009.

[49] R. Toomey. Handheld devices for radiologists: as good as monitors? *Imaging in Medicine*, 2(6):605–607, 2010.

[50] S. Warfield, K. Zou, and W. Wells. Simultaneous truth and performance level estimation (STAPLE): an algorithm for the validation of image segmentation. *IEEE Transactions on Medical Imaging*, 23(7):903–921, July 2004.

[51] F. M. Wodajo. The iPad in the hospital and operating room. *Journal of Surgical Radiology*, 2(1):19-23, 2011.

[52] J.A. Wolf, J.F. Moreau, O. Akilov et al. Diagnostic inaccuracy of smartphone applications for melanoma detection. *JAMA Dermatology*, 149(4):422–426, Apr. 2013.

[53] A. K. Yetisen, J. L. Martinez-Hurtado, A. Garcia-Melendrez, F. da Cruz Vasconcellos, and C. R. Lowe. A smartphone algorithm with inter-phone repeatability for the analysis of colorimetric tests. *Sensors and Actuators B: Chemical*, 196:156–160, June 2014.

[54] Source: FotoFinder, Germany

[55] Source: Engin Deniz, Yale University School of Medicine

[56] Source: Visible human project, Wikipedia

[57] `http://www.cardiio.com`

[58] `http://www.itu.int/osg/spu/imt-2000/technology.html`

Index

For Product Safety Concerns and Information please contact our EU representative GPSR@taylorandfrancis.com Taylor & Francis Verlag GmbH, Kaufingerstraße 24, 80331 München, Germany

Printed and bound by CPI Group (UK) Ltd, Croydon, CR0 4YY
08/05/2025
01864521-0001